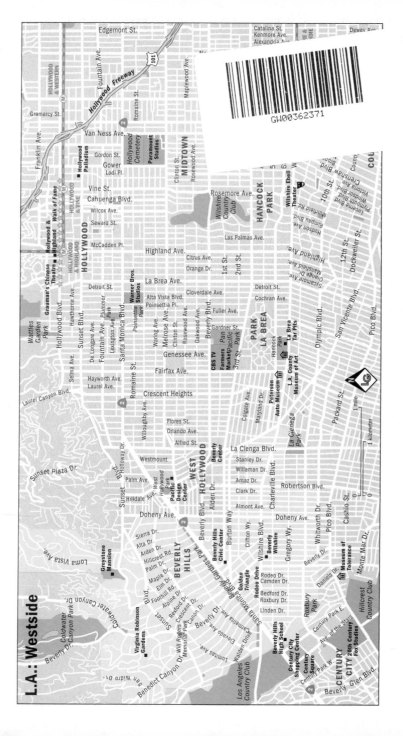

# L.A.: Westside

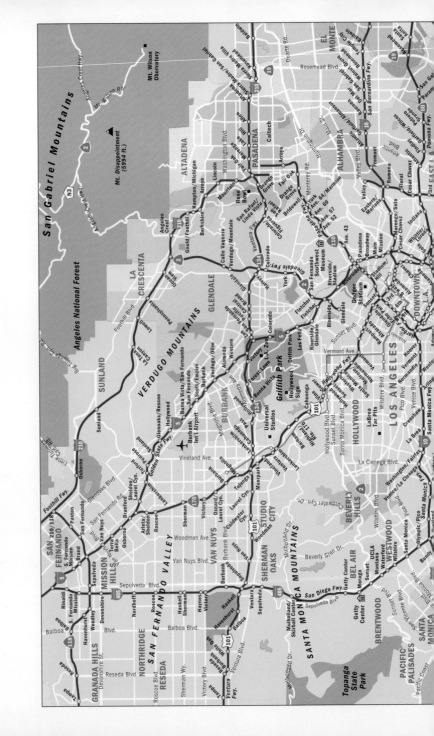

# Metropolitan
# Los Angeles

- ○ Metro Green Line
- ●—● Metro Blue Line
- ○—○ Metro Red Line

Pacific Ocean

0  2 miles
0  2 kilometers

L.A.: Santa Monica & Venice

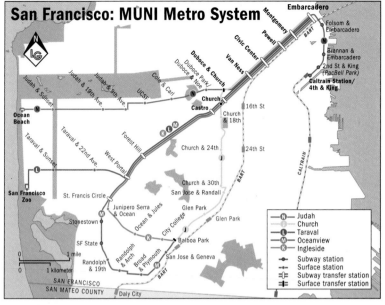

# San Francisco: MUNI Metro System

Embarcadero
Montgomery
Powell
Civic Center
Van Ness
Folsom & Embarcadero
Brannan & Embarcadero
2nd St & King (PacBell Park)
Caltrain Station/ 4th & King

Duboce & Church
Duboce Park/ Duboce & Noe
Cole & Carl
UCSF
Judah & 9th Ave.
Judah & 19th Ave.
Judah & Sunset

Church
Castro
16th St
Church & 18th

Ocean Beach

Taraval & Sunset
Taraval & 22nd Ave.
West Portal
Forest Hill

Church & 24th
24th St

San Francisco Zoo

St. Francis Circle
Church & 30th
San Jose & Randall

Junipero Serra & Ocean
Glen Park
Glen Park

Stonestown
Ocean & Jules
City College

SF State
Balboa Park

Randolph & Arch
Broad & Plymouth
San Jose & Geneva

Randolph & 19th

SAN FRANCISCO
SAN MATEO COUNTY
Daly City

0   1 mile
0   1 kilometer

Legend:
N — Judah
J — Church
L — Taraval
M — Oceanview
K — Ingleside

- Subway station
- Surface station
- Subway transfer station
- Surface transfer station

# San Francisco: BART System

N. Concord/Martinez
Pittsburg/ Bay Point
Concord

CONTRA COSTA COUNTY

Richmond
El Cerrito del Norte
Pleasant Hill
El Cerrito Plaza
Walnut Creek
Lafayette

MARIN COUNTY

North Berkeley
Berkeley
Ashby
Orinda
Rockridge

San Francisco Bay

Ft. Cronkhite

Embarcadero
Montgomery St.
Powell St.
Civic Center
West Oakland
MacArthur
19th St./Oakland
Oakland City Center/12th

Lake Merritt
Fruitvale

16th St./Mission
24th St./Mission

Coliseum/ Oakland Airport

SAN FRANCISCO

Glen Park
Balboa Park

Oakland International Airport

San Leandro

Daly City
Colma

Bay Fair

Castro Valley

Dublin/ Pleasanton

S. San Francisco
San Bruno

San Francisco Bay

Hayward

ALAMEDA COUNTY

South Hayward

San Francisco International Airport

Millbrae

SAN MATEO COUNTY

Union City

Fremont

Legend:
Richmond-Daly City
Pittsburg/Bay Point-Millbrae
Fremont-Daly City
Fremont-Richmond
Dublin/Pleasanton-SFO
SFO-Millbrae Shuttle
CalTrain

0   4 miles
0   4 kilometers

# San Francisco Transportation — San Francisco Bay

*Marina Park*

Crissy Field

TO GOLDEN GATE BRIDGE

Palace of Fine Arts and Exploratorium

Doyle Dr.

Marina Blvd.

**MARINA**

Bay St.

Franciso

Richardson Ave.

Chestnut St.

Lombard St.

Greenwich

**PRESIDIO**

Arguello Blvd.

West Pacific Ave.

Cherry St.

Maple St.

Spruce St.

Laurel St.

Walnut St.

Presidio Ave.

Baker

Broderick

**PACIFIC HEIGHTS**

Union St.

Green

Vallejo

Broadway

Pacific Ave.

Jackson St.

Washington

Octavia

Fillmore

Webster

Buchanan

Lafayet
Park

Alta
Park

**JAPAN-
TOWN**

California St.

Pine St.

Bush St.

Lyon

Divisadero St.

Pierce

Scott

Steiner St.

Laguna St.

Geary Expressway

8th Ave.

Arguello Blvd.

33

Geary Blvd.

University of
San Francisco

Masonic Ave.

Turk St.

Golden Gate Ave.

McAllister

Fulton St.

Grove St.

**WESTERN
ADDITION**

**ALAMO
SQUARE**

Cabrillo St.

Fulton St.

Grove St.

Hayes St.

Fell St.

Oak St.

Panhandle

Oak St.

Page St.

Haight St.

Waller St.

Duboce Ave.

Oak St.

13t

14th

*Golden Gate
Park*

**HAIGHT-
ASHBURY**

*Buena
Vista
Park*

Market St.

15th

16th

Miss
Dole

17th

9th Ave.

8th Ave.

7th Ave.

6th Ave.

5th Ave.

4th Ave.

3rd Ave.

2nd Ave.

Frederick St.

Clayton St.

Cole St.

Parnassus Ave.

Stanyan St.

Castro St.

Noe St.

Sanchez St.

Church St.

*Mission
Dolores
Park*

18th

19t

20t

Hil

22r

23

UCSF
Medical
Center

Clarendon Ave.

**CASTRO**

Diamond St.

Douglas St.

Liberty St.

Alvarado St.

*Twin
Peaks*

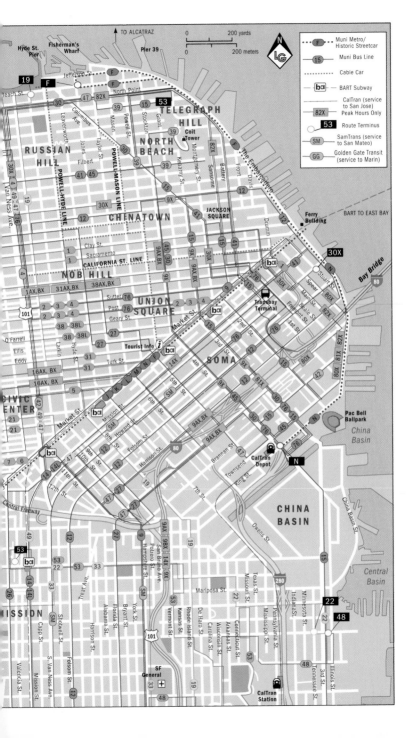

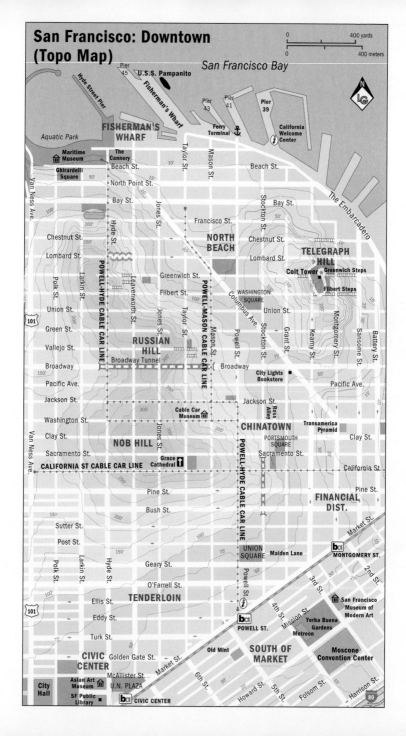

# San Francisco: Downtown (Topo Map)

San Francisco Bay

0 ——— 400 yards
0 ——— 400 meters

Pier 45
U.S.S. Pampanito
Fisherman's Wharf
Pier 43
Pier 41
Pier 39
Ferry Terminal
California Welcome Center

Hyde Street Pier

Aquatic Park

**FISHERMAN'S WHARF**

The Embarcadero

Maritime Museum
The Cannery
Beach St.
Beach St.

Ghirardelli Square
North Point St.
Bay St.
Bay St.
Stockton St.

Van Ness Ave.

Taylor St.
Mason St.

Francisco St.

**NORTH BEACH**

Chestnut St.
Chestnut St.

**TELEGRAPH HILL**

Lombard St.
Lombard St.

Coit Tower
Greenwich Steps

Greenwich St.
Filbert Steps

POWELL-HYDE CABLE CAR LINE
Leavenworth St.
Hyde St.
Larkin St.
Polk St.

Filbert St.
WASHINGTON SQUARE

POWELL-MASON CABLE CAR LINE
Columbus Ave.

Union St.
Union St.

Montgomery St.
Kearny St.
Grant St.
Sansome St.
Battery St.

Green St.

101

Jones St.
Taylor St.
Mason St.
Powell St.
Stockton St.

Vallejo St.

**RUSSIAN HILL**

Broadway Tunnel
Broadway
Broadway

City Lights Bookstore

Pacific Ave.
Pacific Ave.

Jackson St.
Jackson St.
Ross Alley

Cable Car Museum
Washington St.

**CHINATOWN**
Transamerica Pyramid

Clay St.
Clay St.

**NOB HILL**
Jones St.
PORTSMOUTH SQUARE

Sacramento St.
Sacramento St.

CALIFORNIA ST CABLE CAR LINE
Grace Cathedral
California St.

Pine St.
Pine St.

**FINANCIAL DIST.**

Bush St.

Sutter St.
POWELL-HYDE CABLE CAR LINE

Post St.

Market St.
MONTGOMERY ST.

Larkin St.
Hyde St.
Polk St.

Geary St.

UNION SQUARE
Maiden Lane

2nd St.

O'Farrell St.

Powell St.

**TENDERLOIN**

Ellis St.

3rd St.
4th St.
Mission St.

San Francisco Museum of Modern Art

101

Eddy St.
POWELL ST.

Yerba Buena Gardens
Metreon

Turk St.

Old Mint

**SOUTH OF MARKET**

Moscone Convention Center

**CIVIC CENTER**
Golden Gate St.

Market St.

McAllister St.

City Hall
Asian Art Museum
U.N. PLAZA

SF Public Library
CIVIC CENTER

6th St.
5th St.
Howard St.
Folsom St.
Harrison St.

80

## ■ THE RESOURCE FOR THE INDEPENDENT TRAVELER

"The guides are aimed not only at young budget travelers but at the indepedent traveler; a sort of streetwise cookbook for traveling alone."

—*The New York Times*

"Unbeatable; good sight-seeing advice; up-to-date info on restaurants, hotels, and inns; a commitment to money-saving travel; and a wry style that brightens nearly every page."

—*The Washington Post*

"Lighthearted and sophisticated, informative and fun to read. [Let's Go] helps the novice traveler navigate like a knowledgeable old hand."

—*Atlanta Journal-Constitution*

"A world-wise traveling companion—always ready with friendly advice and helpful hints, all sprinkled with a bit of wit."

—*The Philadelphia Inquirer*

## ■ THE BEST TRAVEL BARGAINS IN YOUR PRICE RANGE

"All the dirt, dirt cheap."

—*People*

"Anything you need to know about budget traveling is detailed in this book."

—*The Chicago Sun-Times*

"Let's Go follows the creed that you don't have to toss your life's savings to the wind to travel—unless you want to."

—*The Salt Lake Tribune*

## ■ REAL ADVICE FOR REAL EXPERIENCES

"The writers seem to have experienced every rooster-packed bus and lunar-surfaced mattress about which they write."

—*The New York Times*

"A guide should tell you what to expect from a destination. Here Let's Go shines."

—*The Chicago Tribune*

"Let's Go's] devoted updaters really walk the walk (and thumb the ride, and trek the trail). Learn how to fish, haggle, find work—anywhere."

—*Food & Wine*

# LET'S GO PUBLICATIONS

## TRAVEL GUIDES

Alaska 1st edition **NEW TITLE**
Australia 2004
Austria & Switzerland 2004
Brazil 1st edition **NEW TITLE**
Britain & Ireland 2004
California 2004
Central America 8th edition
Chile 1st edition
China 4th edition
Costa Rica 1st edition
Eastern Europe 2004
Egypt 2nd edition
Europe 2004
France 2004
Germany 2004
Greece 2004
Hawaii 2004
India & Nepal 8th edition
Ireland 2004
Israel 4th edition
Italy 2004
Japan 1st edition **NEW TITLE**
Mexico 20th edition
Middle East 4th edition
New Zealand 6th edition
Pacific Northwest 1st edition **NEW TITLE**
Peru, Ecuador & Bolivia 3rd edition
Puerto Rico 1st edition **NEW TITLE**
South Africa 5th edition
Southeast Asia 8th edition
Southwest USA 3rd edition
Spain & Portugal 2004
Thailand 1st edition
Turkey 5th edition
USA 2004
Western Europe 2004

## CITY GUIDES

Amsterdam 3rd edition
Barcelona 3rd edition
Boston 4th edition
London 2004
New York City 2004
Paris 2004
Rome 12th edition
San Francisco 4th edition
Washington, D.C. 13th edition

## MAP GUIDES

Amsterdam
Berlin
Boston
Chicago
Dublin
Florence
Hong Kong
London
Los Angeles
Madrid
New Orleans
New York City
Paris
Prague
Rome
San Francisco
Seattle
Sydney
Venice
Washington, D.C.

**COMING SOON:**
Road Trip USA

# CALIFORNIA

## 2004

**JENNIE LIN** EDITOR
**DAN SONG** ASSOCIATE EDITOR

RESEARCHER-WRITERS
**JAY GIERAK**
**KRISTIN MCCLOSKEY**
**AARON RUDENSTINE**
**ANDREW PRICE**

**BRIAN J. EMEOTT** MAP EDITOR
**JESSE REID ANDREWS** MANAGING EDITOR

MACMILLAN

# HELPING LET'S GO
If you want to share your discoveries, suggestions, or corrections, please drop us a line. We read every piece of correspondence, whether a postcard, a 10-page email, or a coconut. **Address mail to:**

**Let's Go: California**
**67 Mount Auburn Street**
**Cambridge, MA 02138**
**USA**

Visit Let's Go at **http://www.letsgo.com,** or send email to:

**feedback@letsgo.com**
**Subject: "Let's Go: California"**

In addition to the invaluable travel advice our readers share with us, many are kind enough to offer their services as researchers or editors. Unfortunately, our charter enables us to employ only currently enrolled Harvard students.

Published in Great Britain 2004 by Macmillan, an imprint of Pan Macmillan Ltd.
20 New Wharf Road, London N1 9RR
Basingstoke and Oxford
Associated companies throughout the world
www.panmacmillan.com

Maps by David Lindroth copyright © 2004 by St. Martin's Press.

Published in the United States of America by St. Martin's Press.

**Let's Go: California** Copyright © 2004 by Let's Go, Inc. All rights reserved. Printed in the United States of America. No part of this book may be used or reproduced in any manner whatsoever without written permission except in the case of brief quotations embodied in critical articles or reviews. Let's Go is available for purchase in bulk by institutions and authorized resellers. For information, address St. Martin's Press, 175 Fifth Avenue, New York, NY 10010, USA.

ISBN: 1 4050 3297 9
First edition
10 9 8 7 6 5 4 3 2 1

**Let's Go: California** is written by Let's Go Publications, 67 Mount Auburn Street, Cambridge, MA 02138, USA.

**Let's Go®** and the LG logo are trademarks of Let's Go, Inc.
Printed in the USA.

# ADVERTISING DISCLAIMER
All advertisements appearing in Let's Go publications are sold by an independent agency not affiliated with the editorial production of the guides. Advertisers are never given preferential treatment, and the guides are researched, written, and published independent of advertising. Advertisements do not imply endorsement of products or services by Let's Go, and Let's Go does not vouch for the accuracy of information provided in advertisements.

If you are interested in purchasing advertising space in a Let's Go publication, contact: Let's Go Advertising Sales, 67 Mount Auburn St., Cambridge, MA 02138, USA.

# HOW TO USE THIS BOOK

**BOOK ORGANIZATION.** The first three chapters of this book put you in a California state of mind. Chapter-by-chapter coverage of the Golden State begins in **San Francisco** and the **Bay Area,** then moves up Hwy. 1 into the **Far North,** south along the snowy **Sierra Nevada,** and down the **Central Valley** en route to the **Central Coast.** After that, the book hits **Los Angeles** and **Around LA,** skirts the ocean's edge to **San Diego,** cuts inland to the **Desert,** and culminates in Mexico's **Baja California.**

**PRICE RANGES & RANKINGS.** Our researchers list establishments in order of value and quality from best to worst. Our absolute favorites are denoted by the Let's Go thumbs-up (🖐). Since the best value does not always mean the cheapest price, we have incorporated a system of price ranges in the guide. The table below shows how prices fall within each bracket. See the Price Diversity chart on p. xi for descriptions of typical establishments within each price range. Symbols are based on the lowest cost for one person, excluding special discounts. Read listings carefully, as accommodations listed as ❶ may offer higher-range options as well. Los Angeles and San Francisco have accommodation and food price diversity charts to aid in planning. **All prices are in US dollars,** with the exception of Baja California, where prices may be quoted in US dollars or Mexican pesos.

| CALIFORNIA | ❶ | ❷ | ❸ | ❹ | ❺ |
|---|---|---|---|---|---|
| ACCOMMODATIONS | $1-17 | $18-34 | $35-54 | $55-79 | $80+ |
| FOOD | $1-6 | $7-11 | $12-16 | $17-22 | $23+ |

**PHONE AREA CODES & TELEPHONE NUMBERS.** The area code for each section is denoted by the ☎ icon at the top of that section's write-up. Phone numbers in text are preceded by a ☎, but do not include the area code, except in area-code crazy LA. To call a number in another area code, dial 1-(area code)-(phone number of establishment). The area codes 800, 888, and 877 indicate toll-free lines.

**GETTING AROUND.** Public transportation information is listed in its own section in major cities. In smaller locales, this information is collapsed into the "Orientation and Practical Information" section. Due to the sheer distances involved in travel within California, not to mention the state's car-centric culture, most travelers find that a car is essential for getting around. Essentials (p. 26) and the Practical Information section in each city have information on car rentals. The Desert chapter (p. 528) has important safety information for driving without getting burnt, stranded, or worse in the Southern California desert.

**SCHOLARLY ARTICLES.** Our experts survey famed writer John Steinbeck's California vision in *The Grapes of Wrath* (p. 331), equip you for great hiking in the Sierra Nevada (p. 230), and dish on the best Hollywood watering holes (p. 397).

**PLANNING YOUR ITINERARY.** The first chapter, **Discover California,** contains highlights of the state, including **Suggested Itineraries** (p. 5) that can help you plan your trip. The **Essentials** (p. 26) section has comprehensive hard information and tips on traveling, including creating a budget, making reservations, renting a car, renewing passports, and more. **Life and Times** (p. 8) has info on California's history, culture, and natural features that can help you make the most of your visit.

## A NOTE TO OUR READERS
The information for this book was gathered by *Let's Go* researchers from May through August of 2003. Each listing is based on one researcher's opinion, formed during his or her visit at a particular time. Those traveling at other times may have different experiences since prices, dates, hours, and conditions are always subject to change. You are urged to check the facts presented in this book beforehand to avoid inconvenience and surprises.

# Bevonshire Lodge

Special Promotions • Tour Arrangements
Prime Tourist Location • Free parking • Pool

Discounts available for three nights or more when
ad is presented. ISIC Student Discount available.

Daily Rates:

$50 to $70 + tax

Above rates are seasonal and may
vary during peak period

Near Farmers' Market • CBS Studios • Beverly Hills
Central to all major attractions and beaches

7575 Beverly Blvd.
Los Angeles, California, 90036-2728
United States of America

Phone: (323) 936-6154          Fax: (323) 934-6640

---

# Beverly Inn

Visit our website at
**www.beverlyinn.com**
for more info and reservations

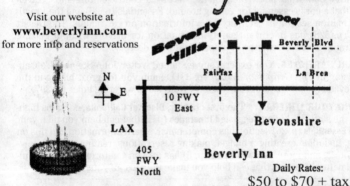

7701 Beverly Blvd.
Los Angeles, California, 90036-2113
United States of America

Phone: (323) 931-8108
Fax:     (323) 935-7103

Daily Rates:
$50 to $70 + tax
Above rates are seasonal and may vary during peak period
All newly renovated rooms
Multiple Night Discounts
Across from CBS Studios
Close to Shopping & Restaurants
Close to Universal Studios
Near Hollywood & Beverly Hills
ISIC Student Discount Available

# CONTENTS

**Bold** denotes a map

# RESEARCHER-WRITERS

**Jay Gierak**                    *So. Central Valley, Las Vegas, So. Cal.*

Jay showed us his love for the open road when he drove enthusiastically from Michigan to the Californian desert, relishing every inch of the highway. This desert gypsy crammed everything into the mail—t-shirts, sleazy Vegas brochures, and piles of colorful, amusing prose. A baseball player, free spirit, and WNBA power forward hopeful, Jay whistled all the way to California and didn't leave until a refreshing dose of quirky delight made its way into the book.

**Kristin McCloskey**            *North Coast, Bay Area, Central Coast*

Not even a fractured rib could delay Kristin—she plowed energetically through her route as if it were one of her crew races. When she wasn't researching, wine-tasting, and pitching four-person tents by herself, she was picnicking on the beach with the latest Harry Potter. While checking out a Central Coast eatery, she chatted up author Michael Cunningham as effortlessly as she punched out pragmatic, informative copy. She picked up a few dates, too.

**Aaron Rudenstine**                              *Greater LA Area*

A New York native and true city boy, Aaron charmed his way through LA, rubbing elbows with Farrah Fawcett, Bill Cosby's wife, and Jason Biggs, and "stumbling" into a Playboy model shoot. With his trusty press pass, this kid could sweet-talk his way into the Politburo. His hilarious exploits and on-the-money reporting of LA's quirks never failed to entertain us, but we still don't believe those stories of getting "hit on" by all those fine women (and men).

**Andrew Price**          *No. Central Valley, Sierra Nevada, Death Valley*

This *Let's Go: Germany* vet tried his hand at portraying his home state, and the results were so beautiful we had nothing left to do but admire them. A chain-smoking philosopher, Andy wandered alone through the forested mountains like a modern-day John Muir, clambering up arduous trails, whitewater-rafting in Yosemite, sleeping in his car in empty lots until the cops came, and surviving Death Valley even when his car didn't. Our mountain man was unstoppable.

**Caitlin Casey, Heather Jackie Thomason, Jordan Blair Woods**      *San Francisco, Bay Area*

**Lucas Laursen, Brendan J. Reed, Bryden Sweeney-Taylor**      *Nevada, Arizona, and more*

**Ben Davis**                                                                    *Oregon*

**Jon Stainsby**                                                      *Baja California*

**Michael B. Murphy**                        *editor, Let's Go: San Francisco 2004*

**Stephanie L. Smith** was a researcher-writer for *Let's Go: California 1997* and *New Zealand 1998*. She worked as a free-lancer for CitySearch Los Angeles and is now working in Hollywood as the features editor/writer for Channel One News online.

**Matt Heid** has researched for *Let's Go* in Alaska, the Yukon, Europe, and New Zealand. He is the author of *101 Hikes in Northern California* and *Camping & Backpacking the San Francisco Bay Area* (both available from Wilderness Press).

**Susan Shillinglaw, Ph.D.,** is the Director of the Center for Steinbeck Studies and a Professor of English at SJSU. She is the editor of the journal *Steinbeck Studies* (University of Idaho Press) and co-editor of *American and Americans and Selected Nonfiction*, and has also written many introductions to Steinbeck's classics.

# PRICE RANGES >> CALIFORNIA

Our researchers list establishments in order of value from best to worst; our favorites are denoted by the Let's Go thumbs-up (🖐). Since the best value is not always the cheapest price, we have incorporated a system of price ranges for quick reference. Our price ranges are based on a rough expectation of what you will spend. For **accommodations,** we base our price range off the cheapest price for which a single traveler can stay for one night. For **restaurants** and other dining establishments, we estimate the average amount that you will spend in that restaurant. The table below tells you what you will *typically* find in California at the corresponding price range; keep in mind that a particularly expensive ice cream stand may still only be marked a ❷, depending on what you will spend.

| ACCOMMODATIONS | RANGE | WHAT YOU'RE *LIKELY* TO FIND |
|---|---|---|
| ❶ | $1-17 | Camping; most dorm rooms, such as HI or other hostels or university dorm rooms. Expect bunk beds and a communal bath; you may have to provide or rent towels and sheets. |
| ❷ | $18-34 | Upper-end hostels, motels, or small hotels. You may have a private bathroom, or there may be a sink in your room and a shared bathroom. |
| ❸ | $35-54 | A small room with a private bath. Should have decent amenities, such as phone and TV. Breakfast often included in the price of the room. |
| ❹ | $55-79 | Similar to 3, but may have more amenities or be in a more touristed area. |
| ❺ | $80+ | Large hotels, popular B&B's, or upscale chains. If it's a 5 and it doesn't have the perks you want, you've paid too much. |

| FOOD | RANGE | WHAT YOU'RE *LIKELY* TO FIND |
|---|---|---|
| ❶ | $1-6 | Mostly street-corner stands, pizza places, or fast-food joints. Rarely ever a sit-down meal. |
| ❷ | $7-11 | Sandwiches, appetizers at a bar, or low-priced entrees. You may have the option of sitting down or getting take-out. |
| ❸ | $12-16 | Mid-priced entrees, possibly coming with a soup or salad. Tip'll bump you up a couple dollars, since you'll probably have a waiter or waitress. |
| ❹ | $17-22 | A somewhat fancy restaurant or a steakhouse. Either way, you'll have a special knife. Few restaurants in this range have a dress code, but some may look down on t-shirt and jeans. |
| ❺ | $23+ | Food with foreign names and a decent wine list. Slacks and dress shirts may be expected. Don't order PB&J. |

# ACKNOWLEDGMENTS

LET'S GO

**CAL 2004 THANKS:** Aaron, Andy, Jay, and Kristin. Sweet Cali love to our book-children. Jesse, who answered our calmly asked questions with manic girl-screeches. Brian, our earnest, effusive mapper who bore down on us with maps like a cheerful plague. Mike, crunch-master. Sarah for starting us off. Shelley, who made our storage closet a pod of gentle lovin', and Greg for shocking, unspeakable things.

**JENNIE THANKS:** Our seriously good-lookin' RWs. Dan, for his quick wit and sharp eye under the guise of slow speech and vacant stares. Together we wrote so... slowly. It was beautiful. Jesse, who grunts a lot and edits like nothing I've ever encountered. Charlie who "cut" himself and Greg who "electrocuted" himself, and both for teaching me many things I'll put to "use." Sarah, who always takes my side. I'll miss you. Our roommates for guacamole and shaving cream and Frances for rational thoughts. Vince for endless kindness, silly moments, and windy drives along PCH. Mom and Dad for worrying, Jocelyn for shacking me up, Jeff (p. 157) for being much cooler than I was at twelve. Or ever. Frame, for leaving emotional scars.

**DAN THANKS:** Our RWs for occasional misspellings, so that we had something to do. Jennie, for Skittles, writing good, Halo withdrawals, patience, having fun, asking me what I thought, and believing most of what I said. Sorry bout the peppers. Jesse—word. You and Jennie together were the best I've ever had. Now go take your Ritalin or I'll make you smell your feet. Ted Leo, NFG, and U2 for getting me through. Greg and Shelley for peace in the pod until Greg opened his mouth. PCH, Santa Monica, and LA for meaning something like home. Let's Go for this space. Special thanks to GZ, Chris, Amit, Steve, the Adams ladies, and Robin for knowing what I'm talking about but caring anyway. Love to Mom and Phil for their hope.

**BRIAN THANKS:** Jennie & Dan—simply put: the best. David S. who tries (and fails) to convince me that CA is better than Michigan. Let's Go: Flint in stores soon-take that OC! Petey for keeping it real in Mapland. Jason & Luke for putting this book to good use in LA.

**Editor**
Jennie Lin
**Associate Editor**
Dan Song
**Managing Editor**
Jesse Reid Andrews
**Map Editor**
Brian J. Emeott
**Typesetter**
Thomas Bechtold

**Publishing Director**
Julie A. Stephens
**Editor-in-Chief**
Jeffrey Dubner
**Production Manager**
Dusty Lewis
**Cartography Manager**
Nathaniel Brooks
**Design Manager**
Caleb Beyers
**Editorial Managers**
Lauren Bonner, Ariel Fox,
Matthew K. Hudson, Emma Nothmann,
Joanna Shawn Brigid O'Leary,
Sarah Robinson
**Financial Manager**
Suzanne Siu
**Marketing & Publicity Managers**
Megan Brumagim, Nitin Shah
**Personnel Manager**
Jesse Reid Andrews
**Researcher Manager**
Jennifer O'Brien
**Web Manager**
Jesse Tov
**Web Content Director**
Abigail Burger
**Production Associates**
Thomas Bechtold, Jeffrey Hoffman Yip
**IT Directors**
Travis Good, E. Peyton Sherwood
**Financial Assistant**
R. Kirkie Maswoswe
**Associate Web Manager**
Robert Dubbin
**Office Coordinators**
Abigail Burger, Angelina L. Fryer,
Liz Glynn
**Director of Advertising Sales**
Daniel Ramsey
**Senior Advertising Associates**
Sara Barnett, Daniella Boston
**Advertising Artwork Editor**
Julia Davidson, Sandy Liu
**President**
Abhishek Gupta
**General Manager**
Robert B. Rombauer
**Assistant General Manager**
Anne E. Chisholm

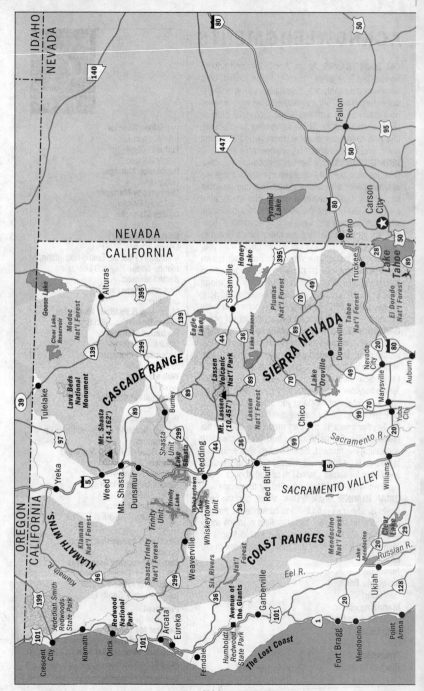

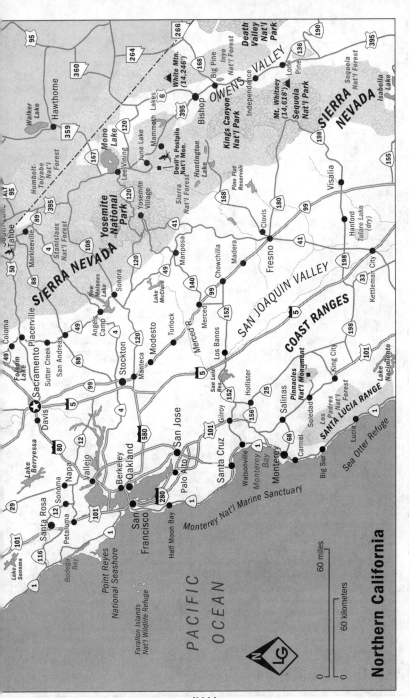

Northern California

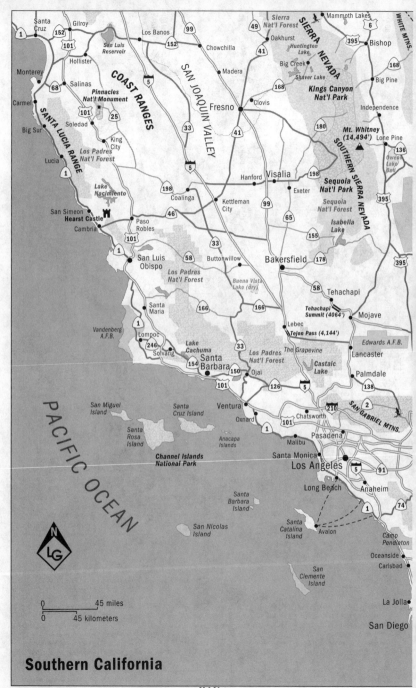

# Southern California

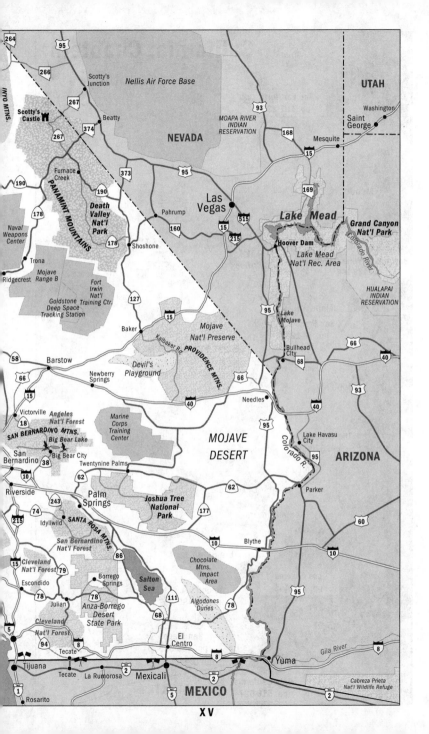

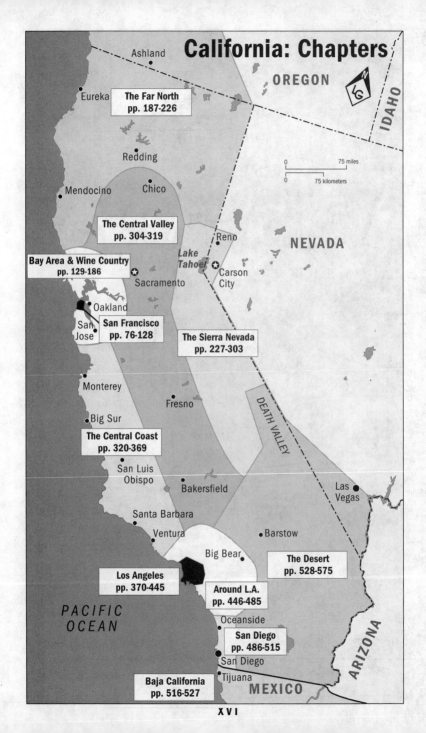

# California: Chapters

Ashland

OREGON

IDAHO

Eureka

**The Far North**
pp. 187-226

Redding

0 ___ 75 miles
0 ___ 75 kilometers

Mendocino

Chico

NEVADA

**The Central Valley**
pp. 304-319

Reno

Lake
Tahoe

**Bay Area & Wine Country**
pp. 129-186

Carson
City

Sacramento

Oakland

San
Jose

**San Francisco**
pp. 76-128

**The Sierra Nevada**
pp. 227-303

Monterey

Fresno

Big Sur

DEATH VALLEY

**The Central Coast**
pp. 320-369

San Luis
Obispo

Bakersfield

Las
Vegas

Santa Barbara

Ventura

Barstow

Big Bear

**The Desert**
pp. 528-575

**Los Angeles**
pp. 370-445

**Around L.A.**
pp. 446-485

PACIFIC
OCEAN

Oceanside

**San Diego**
pp. 486-515

ARIZONA

San Diego

**Baja California**
pp. 516-527

Tijuana

MEXICO

# DISCOVER CALIFORNIA

Experiencing California is like cruising down the length of its immortalized Highway 1. Crashing waves, sheer coastal bluffs, monumental redwoods, expansive ocean sunsets, and camera-clicking sightseers struck by it all converge on this asphalt horizon—exhilaration doesn't begin to describe the way it feels to be poised upon the very western edge of the country, with better times and wilder sights in the cliff-hugging turns ahead, and the past receding in your rearview mirror. This is a state that rejects the time-tested in favor of the unexplored, the busy, familiar path in favor of the road yet to be forged; this is where technology, pop culture, and the American dream go to be reborn.

Californians have always indicated, and many times dictated, national moods and trends. In the 1850s, frenzied gold miners sought mineral riches; in the 1960s, starry-eyed flower children sought peace. The 1990s were defined by Silicon Valley's dot-com techies striving at supercomputer speeds for the good life, and, as they have done for decades, starving would-be actors and botox-shooting beauty queens continue to flock here by the busload. Be it gold, free love, IPOs, or stardom, Californians dig deep for riches and imprint their forward-thinking, payoff-craving consciousness upon the world—and there's no better state to contain their insanity while fueling their dreams. From the stately snow-topped mountains to the scorched desert valleys, anticipation is always in the air. See for yourself—discover California in 2004.

---

### FACTS AND FIGURES

**Capital:** Sacramento.
**State Population:** 30,866,851.
**Length of Coastline per Resident:** 2¾ in.

**Length of Los Angeles Roadway per LA resident:** 114½ in.
**Length of San Andreas Fault:** 754 mi.

---

# WHEN TO GO

The myth of California as a haven of warmth and sunshine may hold true in Southern California, but it fails to incorporate the immense climatic diversity of the state's chilly mountains, cool northern regions, and searing interior desert. Morning and afternoon fog keeps the North and Central Coast at a temperate 50-70°F for most of the year, while coastal Southern California heats up year-round but rarely reaches an intolerable swelter. Along the coast, the summer tourist season runs from Memorial Day to Labor Day (May 31-Sept. 6 in 2004). Warm in summer (when campers flood the national parks) and mild in fall, the Sierra Nevada mountains are smothered in snow from November through March. The Mojave Desert of the state's southern interior scorches in the summer; like the mountain ski resorts of Tahoe, its main tourist season is the cooler period from September to March. For both the summer-loving coast and the winter-loving interior, accommodations are cheaper and less crowded in the off-season, but some sights might be closed.

DISCOVER

# THINGS TO DO

Bored? Scale a half-mile-high sheer granite cliff face overlooking a glaciated valley or engage in smoky, hypnotic séances for faux-Eastern cults in a celebrity-funded shrine. Try to revive the "Summer of Love" in the City by the Bay or, for kicks, spend a month in a 300 ft. high redwood tree with someone named Luna who has held Logging, Inc. at bay for three years. Crawl past the mirages that rise from expanses of shimmering sand dunes and frolic in the cool waters with otters, dolphins, and blonde, bronzed beach bums. Check out the **Highlights** box at the beginning of each chapter for more specific regional attractions; at every turn we'll show you where to start, but in the end it's up to you to define your adventure.

## ■ LET'S GO PICKS

**BEST HIPPIE-RUN HOSTEL: Point Reyes Hostel,** Marin County (p. 167). Three generations of iconoclasts run this hostel on the gorgeous Point Reyes National Seashore.

**BEST PLACE TO STRIKE IT RICH: Gold Country** (p. 227). We'll show you how. Then head to **Las Vegas,** NV (p. 544) to lose it all.

**BEST SUNSETS: Joshua Tree** (p. 529) and **Santa Barbara** (p. 358) provide more than some sand and a pretty ocean view.

**BEST SCENIC DRIVE: Marin Headlands,** Marin County (p. 159). Ghostly, misty drive west of the Golden Gate Bridge.

**BEST CHURROS: Disneyland,** Anaheim (p. 460). Mickey and friends dispense these strangely addictive fried treats.

**BEST CELEBRATION OF CHRISTOPHER MARLOWE'S WORK: The Oregon Shakespeare Festival,** Ashland, OR (p. 226). One guy could never have written all those plays.

# CITIES

San Francisco (p. 76) and Los Angeles (p. 370), California's primary urban centers, are separated by 419 mi. and a great environmental and cultural divide. They are at opposite poles of California's vast spectrum of climate, landscape, social and political orientation, and lifestyle. The state pits the sprawling LA Basin against the great San Francisco Bay, the land of sunshine against the city of fog, the home of freeway lovers against the haunt of ecofreaks, and the workplace of painfully hip media moguls against that of painfully otherwise dot-com execs. LA showcases Hollywood, the manufacturer of screen idols, while the Bay nurtures Berkeley, the breeding ground for iconoclasm. Most people tend to gravitate toward one city or the other, but love them or hate them, both are too flavorful not to be tried.

**SAN FRANCISCO.** San Francisco evokes images of antique cable cars trundling over hills, of pastel houses and earthy hippies, of the sweeping Golden Gate Bridge and ominous Alcatraz Island. More than just iconic, San Francisco is also wacky. It has inspired its residents to tread off the beaten path, from beatniks in **Haight-Ashbury** (p. 82) to Ansel Adams and Imogen Cunningham, whose works show at museums in **SoMa** (p. 112). The city's artistic innovation continues with experimental theater, dance, music, and exhibitions at **Fort Mason** (p. 103) and **Yerba Buena Center for the Arts** (p. 113). Even the graceful Victorian houses are given a zany (and very pretty) new life when painted all the colors of the rainbow in the **Castro** district (p. 99), a gay mecca. Vibrant Chicano and Asian-American communities assure an excellent array of delectable dining (p. 94) in the **Mission, Chinatown,** and **Japantown** districts. Park land, from the **Presidio** (p. 106) to **Golden Gate Park** (p. 108), blankets the city in green, providing dramatic vistas and outdoor lounge space.

**LOS ANGELES.** As the purveyor of much of the world's mass media, LA—where every waitress has a headshot and every parking valet a screenplay—holds a special place in the aspirations of many. Thousands head to Hollywood each year to "make it." Most never do, but vacationers can revel in the glitz and glamour that is Hollywood without sacrificing job security. Host to many a movie premiere, **Grauman's Chinese Theater** in Hollywood (p. 405) often sports celebrities, who strut and pose on the proverbial red carpet outside the theater. The stars still shine in the **Hollywood Walk of Fame** (p. 406), a sidewalk art display of industry greats, past and present. Unveiling ceremonies for recently added stars are a special treat. If you insist on knowing where to meet the stars and how to propel yourself into their world, check out our insider's scoop in tidbits such as: **So You Wanna Be In Pictures?** (p. 436) and **The Celebrity Tour** (p. 412). It ain't much, but it's a start, kiddo.

Once you're through with Hollywood, you can catch advanced screenings and get tickets for tapings of television shows in **Santa Monica** (p. 407) or work on that tan in the thriving beach communities at Santa Monica and **Venice** (see **Beach Culture**, p. 4). With its wealth of aspiring rock bands and comedy club kings, LA has some of the most happening, big-time **nightlife** (p. 439) on the planet. And if the unceasing traffic jams wipe the smile off your face, get Mickey or Minnie to surgically reattach it at **Disneyland** (p. 460). Don't miss the churros!

**SAN DIEGO.** The southernmost of California's major cities, San Diego is a quieter, more conservative alternative to Los Angeles. It hosts a wide selection of museums in **Balboa Park** (p. 499), two of the world's best zoological habitats in the **San Diego Zoo** (p. 499), and the **San Diego Wild Animal Park** (p. 513). San Diego's beaches are great for surfing (see **Surf**, p. 4) and support a laid-back waterfront culture (see **Beach Culture**, p. 4). The city is also a good base for a daytrip to the border town of **Tijuana**, Mexico, a poor man's tequila-infused Sodom and Gomorrah (p. 518).

**LAS VEGAS.** A 5hr. shot up I-15 from LA, Las Vegas (p. 544) is a gloriously overdone sin city, filled with grandiose casinos and schmaltzy entertainment spectaculars. Catch the **Cirque du Soleil** in action and gorge on **buffets** (p. 548) before hitting the Strip for an impassioned surge of **casino hopping** (p. 550). Near Las Vegas (p. 554), rugged **hiking terrain** surrounds **Hoover Dam** and jet-ski-happy **Lake Mead.**

# COASTLINES & TANLINES

The home of the Beach Boys and *Baywatch* offers a far wider range of coastal styles than those pop culture icons might suggest. Whether you want to careen along the coastal cliffs of the Pacific Coast Highway, bum with the beach bunnies on sparkling sand, search for the endless summer atop towering waves, or trudge across stunning, secluded shorelines, California is the place to do it.

**HIGHWAY 1.** Stretching the length of California, the legendary Pacific Coast Highway (Hwy. 1 or PCH) lays the foundation for a magnificent coastal tour (see **Suggested Itineraries**, p. 5). On the North Coast, Hwy. 1 winds along precarious cliffs between crashing surf and towering redwood trees (p. 187). Highlights of the northern route include a meditative stroll to the black sands of **Jones Beach** (p. 194) in the Sinkyone Wilderness or a picnic on the ▧**Mendocino Headlands** (p. 189). In the San Francisco Bay Area, Hwy. 1 passes **Point Reyes National Seashore** (p. 164), where you can stand high on the bluffs over a dramatic drop to the wild, whale-inhabited ocean. Crossing the San Andreas Fault, the highway cuts across the **Golden Gate Bridge** (p. 81) and through the city of San Francisco. Along the Central Coast, the highway skirts laid-back college towns and quirky **beach communities** (p. 320), and the precarious cliff-line crawl past forested **Big Sur** (p. 344), with a stop at **Pfeiffer Beach** (p. 347), offers unbeatable views. In Southern California, the PCH leads to hot surf spots and legendary beach bum haunts, but the most stunning stretch of shoreline is still a ferry ride away at **Catalina Island** (p. 451).

DISCOVER

**BEACH CULTURE.** Beach culture is the sense of lazy, lifelong summer vacation that pervades the California coast. It is a culture that seeps into one's willpower and drains it of anything unrelated to waves, boardwalks, piers, and ice cream parlors. The beach communities begin in earnest (and by "earnest" we mean casual lethargy) south of San Francisco, and dot the coast to the Mexican border.

On the Central Coast, beach communities crop up in the college towns that party between the redwood forests and the kelp forests. The waterfront in crunchy, liberal **Santa Cruz** (p. 322) has a crowded beach, a wharf under which sea lions bask, and the Boardwalk—a tacky whirligig of aging spin rides and colorful game booths straight out of the 50s. Farther south, **San Luis Obispo** (p. 351) lies near Pismo Beach, which is a more sedate sand-and-pier locale that can become a raging spring break party spot. Beneath the Spanish Revival architecture that dots its hills, ritzy **Santa Barbara** (p. 358) has stunning sunsets and raging nightlife.

The Southern California beach scene lacks the wacky students and New Age gurus of northern communities, and instead bows to the gods of sun and surf. In the LA area, carnivalesque **Venice Beach** (p. 409) features an eye-popping kaleidoscope of street vendors, sand sculptors, and chainsaw jugglers. Meanwhile, less manic **Santa Monica Beach** (p. 407) crowds with joggers and in-line skaters. Volleyball players spike balls and drinks on **Hermosa Beach** (p. 427), south of LA. Youthful crowds flock to surf shops at **Huntington Beach** (p. 465) in Orange County and to the noisy bars and grills of San Diego's **Mission Beach** and **Pacific Beach** (p. 503).

**SURF.** Every other town along the California coast claims the title "Surf City". Most of them are in Southern California, but the Central Coast has a few great spots as well. Santa Cruz sensation **Steamer's Lane** (p. 326) and the break next to the pier at **Pismo Beach** (p. 356) rage with wave-riders. North of LA, **Ventura** (p. 456) sleeps by some of the dreamiest waves on the coast. In Southern California, **Surfrider Beach** in Malibu (p. 410) is the best option near LA In Orange County, vets head for the mythical swells of **Huntington Beach** (p. 465), while beginners can test the waters at **San Clemente** (p. 468). The San Diego surf scene holds its own, particularly at **Oceanside** (p. 512), Tourmaline and Winandsea Beaches in **La Jolla** (p. 505), and beginner-friendly **Ocean Beach** on Point Loma (p. 503).

# WILDERNESS

California is an astoundingly diverse landscape of stately mountains, rugged coastlines, fertile valleys, and barren deserts. The vast granite peaks of the **Sierra Nevada** tower over a visually stunning landscape, while austere expanses created by dried lava flows and the snowy splendor of **Mount Shasta** (p. 214) inspire wonder in the **Cascade Range** of the Northern Interior. The North Coast and the Central Coast feature jagged coastlines and giant redwood trees, while the **Mojave Desert** of Southern California is a desolate landscape of rocks and sand dunes.

**HIKING.** On the hike to Tall Trees Grove in the North Coast's **Redwood National Park** (p. 201), the towering forest canopy blocks off the misty sunlight and the elements, leaving hikers in quiet, cathedral-like spaces. A trek through **Lassen Volcanic National Park** (p. 208) passes the steaming hydrothermal cauldron of Bumpass Hell and the bubbling waters of Cold Boiling Lake. In **Yosemite** (p. 251), the famed jewel of the Sierra, the narrow staircases of the Mist Trail climb through the dispersed sprays and alluvial rainbows of Vernal and Nevada Falls, while the heady bliss of gazing down from Half Dome justifies the harrowing ascent to the top. Not to be outdone by their celebrated neighbor, **Sequoia** and **Kings Canyon National Parks** (p. 270) have stunning and less crowded hikes along Eagle Lake Trail and the easy path through Zumwalt Meadows. Even farther into the Eastern Sierra, the **Whitney Portal Trail** (p. 302) ascends the highest mountain in the continental US, and a trek through the **Ancient Bristlecone Pine Forest** (p. 296) in the White Mountains will bring you face-to-face with the world's oldest living organisms. In the desert, a scramble along Skull Rock Interpretive Walk in **Joshua Tree** (p. 535) is a great way to try out bouldering while learning about flora and fauna in the Mojave.

**BIKING.** A bike tour of **Wine Country** (p. 174), the flat-fielded region north of San Francisco that produces some of the most celebrated wines in the world, is easy and pleasurable. In **Lake Tahoe**, bikers can take undemanding tours of the lake or go all out on its nearby winding roads (p. 242). When the snow melts, **Mammoth Lakes** (p. 303) morphs into a mountain bike park for those who scorn pavement. The most daring ride starts at 11,053 ft. and barrels down the rocky ski trails.

**SKIING.** While the attractions of coastal California get all the attention, the heights of the Sierras boast some of the best powder in North America. **Lake Tahoe** (p. 237) is one of the best places to ski in California. **Squaw Valley,** host of the 1962 Winter Olympics, and the aptly-named **Heavenly** are the top resorts. Many Southern Californians swoosh down **Mammoth Lakes** (p. 303) in the eastern Sierra rather than enduring a longer haul to Tahoe. **June Mountain** (p. 284), near Mammoth Lakes, is lesser known, but well loved by those who visit. Resorts in **Big Bear** (p. 472) lie within easy daytrip range from LA, but the skiing conditions are far inferior to those in the Sierra Nevada. Cross-country skiers find bliss amid the winter scenery of **Yosemite** (p. 251) and **Sequoia and Kings Canyon National Parks** (p. 270).

**WATERSPORTS AND FISHING.** The waters of **Lake Tahoe** (p. 237) are the ultimate playground for waterskiers, wakeboarders, and sailors. **Kayakers** can tour tranquil, mineral-rich **Mono Lake** (p. 281) or paddle out to the Pacific Ocean's otter-filled kelp forests near Santa Cruz (p. 322), Monterey (p. 334), or San Luis Obispo (p. 351). **Lake Mead** (p. 554), just across the border in Nevada, roars with motor boats and jet skis; the summer sailing at **Big Bear Lake** (p. 472) near LA proves a more sedate alternative. **June Lake** (p. 284) is a mountain fishing hot spot, while ocean fishermen harvest the teeming waters off San Diego (p. 508) and along the coast.

**ROCK CLIMBING. Joshua Tree** (p. 529) offers footholds for all levels of climbers; its most famed spots are Hidden Valley and Wonderland of Rocks. Experienced climbers tackle the famed granite faces of **Yosemite** (p. 251). Between LA and Palm Springs, climbers crank on Tahquitz and Suicide Rocks in rugged **Idyllwild** (p. 478). **Lake Tahoe** (p. 237) has very popular climbing sites of varying difficulty. The spectacular climb of Lover's Leap and the 90 ft. wall at Emerald Bay are two of the most popular spots. The River Gorge in **Owens Valley** (p. 293) and the Buttermilks in **Bishop** (p. 293) are lesser-known but thrilling climbs in the Eastern Sierra.

# SUGGESTED ITINERARIES

**THE BEST OF CALIFORNIA: A 3-WEEK EXPLORATION.** Start in **San Francisco** (p. 76) and spend 3 days getting a feel for Haight-Ashbury, Chinatown, and Alcatraz. Then head to **Tahoe** (p. 237) for 2 days on the lake—the hiking, biking, watersports, and skiing there are all sensational. Just across the border, test your luck in Nevada's casinos at **Reno** (p. 247). For relief, the breathtaking **Yosemite** (p. 251) is 4hr. away. Spend 3 days traversing its web of trails and bike paths, or admire the scenery from the valley floor. Head back to the coast for 3 days on the Monterey Bay in **Santa Cruz** (p. 322) and **Monterey** (p. 334), taking in both the Beach Boardwalk and the renowned Monterey Bay Aquarium and leaving time for **Carmel's** Point Lobos (p. 341) or a romp across the gorgeous UC-Santa Cruz campus. A day of camping in scenic **Big Sur** (p. 344) is a great way to experience the redwood forests. Move on to **Santa Barbara** (p. 358) for breathtaking beaches and an afternoon on State St. Next, wander **Los Angeles** (p. 370) for 3 days: see a movie at Grauman's Chinese Theater, get pierced at Venice Beach, and gawk at the Getty

DISCOVER

Museum. Don't miss the Happiest Place on Earth, **Disneyland** (p. 460), home to roller coasters, Mickey Mouse, and churros. Spend a day in **San Diego** (p. 486) to see the famous Zoo and the Wild Animal Park or hang out in Pacific Beach. Head to **Tijuana** (p. 518) in Mexico for a sketchy border town experience. Return to the States for a day in **Joshua Tree National Park** (p. 529) to climb boulders or see some of California's most beautiful sunrises and sunsets. Complete your journey with a day or two in **Las Vegas** (p. 544), where excess is an art form.

day at the Monterey Bay Aquarium and another in nearby **Carmel** (p. 341). A day's drive through **Big Sur** (p. 344) promises big views and bigger redwoods. Don't miss Hearst Castle (p. 349) on your day in **Cambria** and **San Simeon** (p. 347). A day in **San Luis Obispo** (p. 351) allows a stop at Pismo Beach (p. 356) or the Seven Sisters rock formations in **Morro Bay** (p. 357). **Santa Barbara** (p. 358) and its splendid mission are good for 2 days of beaches and shopping. From Santa Barbara, take a daytrip to **Channel Islands National Park** (p. 484) or **Ojai** (p. 367), before driving off into the sun.

THE BEST OF CALIFORNIA

GO COASTAL

**GO COASTAL: A 2-WEEK CRUISE.** This scenic drive takes you along Hwy. 1. Start off in **San Francisco** (p. 76) for 3 days in the foggy City by the Bay, spending time at Golden Gate Park, Chinatown, and Haight-Ashbury, and doin' time at Alcatraz. Head inland to **Wine Country** (p. 159) for 2 days of wine-tasting and bicycle rides. Travel south to **Santa Cruz** (p. 322) for 2 days of amusement at the beach Boardwalk, visiting UC Santa Cruz, and strolling the Pacific Garden Mall. Jaunt to **Monterey** (p. 334) for a

**PARK AVENUE: 2 WEEKS OF THE OUT-DOORS.** Hiking and camping are among the best ways to see California. Even those who don't like to rough it by tent-camping can find nearby hostels or motels and explore the parks on foot during the day. Start with 1 day on **Catalina Island** (p. 451), followed by 2 days in **Joshua Tree National Park** (p. 529) for great hikes and views, including some of the best desert sunsets in the West. In winter,

2 days are well-spent in **Death Valley National Park** (p. 535), when temperatures are bearable, desert wildflowers bloom in March and April. **Sequoia and Kings Canyon National Parks** (p. 270) are a good 2-day stop for hikes through the famous California sequoia trees. The most beautiful park in California is **Yosemite National Park** (p. 251), and a 3-day stopover allows enough time to hike up Yosemite Falls, ice skate at Curry Village, stargaze from Glacier Point, and (for the truly bold) brave Half Dome's 12hr. ascent. **Lassen Volcanic National Park** (p. 208) has excellent hikes and fewer tourists. Finish up at **Mount Shasta** (p. 214), where you can hike around the quiet peak and contemplate its mystical magnificence.

**MISSION ACCOMPLISHED: A 1-WEEK TRIP.** This drive through history follows **Father Junípero Serra's** 18th century foot trail, **El Camino Real,** which connects California's old missions. Start at **Mission Basilica San Diego de Alcalà** (p. 505) in the historic Old Town district, and then follow I-5 up the coast to the next stop, **Mission San Juan Capistrano** (p. 468), perhaps the most beautiful of the missions, set amongst the rolling hills of Orange County. A 2hr. drive north through LA brings you to the **San Fernando Mission** (p. 424), an amazing re-creation of the original 1797 structure, which has since burnt down. Drive up US 101 to Ventura, where the **Mission San Buenaventura** (p. 484) is still used as a parish church. From there, take US 101 north to discover the coastal serenity at **Mission Santa Barbara** (p. 327), precious Chumash footprints at **Mission Santa Ines** (p. 366), and the colorful Native American frescoes at **Mission San Miguel Archangel** (p. 357), and end at the gloriously restored mission in posh **Carmel** (p. 341).

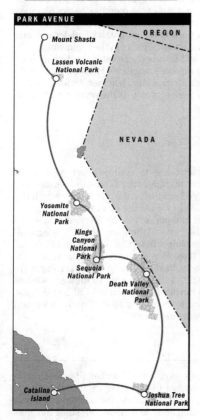

# LIFE & TIMES

With the largest population of any US state, California is the third-largest state in the nation, smaller only than Texas and Alaska, and bigger than Italy. Its border stretches over 800 miles from Oregon in the north to Mexico in the south. It is about 250 mi. between the Pacific Ocean on its western edge and Nevada and Arizona on its eastern border. This expanse is bursting with both urban and rural riches; California produces more agricultural products than any other US state, even while its population is over 91% urban and only 15% of its land is cultivated. California's huge population is saturated with ethnic variety. One-third of Mexican-Americans in the US live in California, Los Angeles has a sizable Japanese-American community, and San Francisco's Chinatown is the world's largest Chinese community outside of Asia. In California, the "minorities" are the majority.

For centuries, settlers have come to California in search of the elusive and the unattainable. Spanish conquistadors saw in it a utopian paradise, '49ers plumbed its depths furiously for the Mother Lode, and the naïve and beautiful still quest for stardom on its silver screen. Adventurers flock to the mountains and deserts, and stampedes of 2.2-child families overrun the national parks in their minivans, seeking peace among forests, granite cliffs, and lava beds. Dreamy-eyed, disenfranchised flower children converge wistfully on San Francisco's Haight Street, while laid-back tan-seekers chill out by the Santa Monica Pier. Whether it's for a dream, a mountain summit, a lost childhood, the perfect wave, or the perfect body, Californians are always reaching for something.

## LAND

Snow-dusted peaks, fertile valleys, scorching deserts, endless beaches—California truly has it all. The **Sierra Nevada** mountain range (p. 227) dominates much of the eastern third of the state with its jagged granite peaks and features both the ever-popular **Yosemite National Park** (p. 251) as well as the continental US's tallest mountain (**Mt. Whitney,** p. 302). Just west and parallel to the Sierras is the enormous San Joaquin or **Central Valley** (p. 304), one of the most productive agricultural regions in the world. The formidable **Mojave Desert** (p. 529) lies southeast of the Valley and the mountains, and those tenacious enough to withstand the heat will be rewarded with scattered diamonds: **Death Valley** (p. 535), **Las Vegas** (p. 544), and **Joshua Tree National Park** (p. 529). And, of course, to the very west of everything and running from border to border lies the famed California coast and Pacific Coast Highway, immortalized by countless movies and books, and several million of the most beautiful sunsets in history.

## FLORA & FAUNA

California's ecosystems vary with the state's geography. The plant life is extremely diverse, ranging from lush forests on the coast to flowering cacti in the Mojave Desert. California also supports many forms of animal life, including dangerously alluring creatures like rattlesnakes, mountain lions, and ninjas, but some travelers may be more beguiled by the large flippered animals that swim along the coast.

# PLANTS

**SIERRA NEVADA.** The trademark **giant sequoias** tower in small groves within national parks like Yosemite and Kings Canyon; they are the world's largest single organisms and are identifiable by their reddish-brown bark and enormous trunks. The trees can live for up to 3500 years—the small cones alone cling to the branches for almost 30 years. Few sequoias remain, and battles are constantly being fought between developers and environmentalists over the future of the trees. Also common to the area are **ponderosa** and **lodgepole pines,** which have medium-sized pine cones and golden, crackled bark. Broad-leafed trees such as **pacific dogwood** and **aspen,** with its milky-white bark, make for beautiful fall foliage. Wildflowers, like the punch-red **Indian paintbrush** and the yellow **monkeyflower,** flourish in the mountains during the warmer months.

**DESERT.** Cacti abound in this arid region, among them the brightly-flowering cholla, whose "teddy bear" variety looks deceptively soft and inviting. **Joshua trees** are widely recognizable by their twisted, intertwined branches and upward reaching fronds. They can be found throughout the desert, and are especially abundant in Joshua Tree National Park.

**PACIFIC COAST.** Relatives of the giant sequoias (and just as rare), **redwoods** are the tallest trees in the world. They too have reddish brown bark, which protects them and allows them to live for over 2000 years. Grape-sized pine cones and flat needles distinguish the trees. Farther south along the coast, the rushlike **Monterey cypress** and **pine** are found in coastal bluffs alongside the bright orange state flower, the **California poppy.**

**DANGEROUS PLANTS. Poison oak** is common at elevations below 5000 feet. The plant grows as a shrub or vine, with green, shiny, three-pronged leaves that turn red and drop in the fall. Berries are white or greenish-white. Contact with poison oak will cause an irritating red rash; if exposure is suspected, wash skin immediately with cold water and soap, and launder clothes several times before wearing again. You may want to include itch-relieving ointments in your first-aid kit (p. 38). Never burn poison oak; bad things will happen.

# ANIMALS

**SIERRA NEVADA. Marmots** are found high in the mountains; they are yellow-bellied 20 lb. ground squirrels who very easily become a nuisance when they chew through radiator hoses and camping gear in order to find a warm place to sleep. **Trout** swim in high mountain streams. **Deer** and other ground animals are common, and **grizzly** and **black bears** also roam the forest.

**DESERT.** Most desert animals are nocturnal, although during the day it isn't hard to spot **kangaroo rats** hopping across the sand or **roadrunners** (gray birds with fluffy heads and straight tails) racing away from wily **coyotes.**

**PACIFIC COAST.** Sea lions, otters, and whales swim along California's shore. The former tend to congregate, along with **seals,** near Monterey Bay and the Channel Islands, which are National Marine Sanctuaries. **Gray whales** (or at least their tails and spray) can be seen off the coast from December to March, as they move between the Arctic Sea and their breeding grounds in Mexico. The **California condor,** with a wingspan of nine feet and a life expectancy of up to 40 years, is one of the largest flying birds anywhere. Its existence was in question until the success of captive breeding attempts in the 1980s, and now almost fifty condors roam about California again, with the total condor population hovering around 200. Condor conservation efforts are spearheaded by environmental groups and zoos such as the ones in San Diego and Los Angeles.

**DANGEROUS ANIMALS.** Rattlesnakes, bears, and sharks are can be concerns in parts of California; for info on how to protect yourself, see **Snakes Will Bite You** (p. 44), **Bears Will Eat You** (p. 44) and **Sharks Will Chew On You** (p. 44). In addition, cougars, panthers, and coyotes have lost their homes to recent development, and some roam suburban areas at night and in the early morning. Attacks on people are few, but if walking at night, carry a stick and make noise.

# HISTORY

History? This is California—it just doesn't *do* history. Here, movie stars get face lifts and hippies rebel against tradition, plowing over the achievements and monuments of the past. Nevertheless, you can see the relics of Spanish colonialism in the missions and that telltale mark of Westernism—overreaching—in the failed ventures of ghost towns and gold rush monuments.

## EARLY YEARS AND EXPLORATION

Before California was California, it was Mexico. And before it was Mexico, or even New Spain, it was home to 100 Native American cultures, descendants of the original Paleo-Siberian immigrants, each with their own political system and language. Most tribes were peaceful and unaggressive and survived by hunting, fishing, and gathering. They lived without all but the most basic agricultural techniques before the arrival of the Europeans.

When the white men in big boats first came upon the region, it seemed to them a fantasy world, the stuff of dreams. Landing in Baja California in 1535, colonists under the leadership of infamous conquistador **Hernán Cortés** named the region after Queen Califia, the beautiful ruler of a mythical land full of gold and jewels in the Spanish romance *Las Sergas de Esplandian* (1510). In 1542, Spain made its first contact with the tribes of Upper California when explorer **Estévan Juan Rodríguez Cabrillo,** a Portuguese conquistador enlisted in the Spanish navy, sailed up the west coast of North America in a poorly provisioned ship manned by conscripts. His mission to find the mythical Strait of Anian failed, but the exploration party reached latitude 43° on what is now the Oregon coast.

Many more Spanish ships would follow, establishing a cultural presence that remains strong in everything from language to architecture to this day (for example, Stanford, a college often mistaken for the world's biggest Mexican restaurant). The Spanish began to settle the area en masse after 1769. Coastal cities like San Francisco (founded 1776) and Los Angeles (founded 1787) cropped up alongside Catholic **missions,** introduced by Father Junípero Serra to convert California's coastal Native Americans and serve as supply outposts for Spanish galleons.

## EARLY 19TH CENTURY

At the beginning of the 19th century, Spain's New World colonies rose in revolt against their parent country, and California accompanied them. In Mexico, radical priest **Miguel Hidalgo y Costilla** led the indigenous and mestizo populations in an 1810 uprising that developed into the Mexican Revolution. The revolutionaries continued even after the capture and execution of Hidalgo, gaining independence for a Mexican state that included California by 1822. With the mission system dissolved by 1833 and regulation from Mexico City ineffective, privileged Mexicans called **rancheros** dominated vast parcels of land, exerting de facto control over California. Staged "revolutionary" battles between ranchero-sponsored factions substituted for governmental checks on power.

# BEAR FLAG REPUBLIC

In the following years, a steady trickle of American settlers headed west to the mythical land fancifully described as "edenic" in national newspapers, eager to build their own little houses on the prairie. Capitalizing on imminent hostilities between the US and Mexico, which were battling for control of Texas, American settlers along the West coast joined US Captain John C. Fremont in the **Bear Flag Revolt** of 1846, proclaiming California's independence from Mexico. The Bear Flag Republic proved fleeting, as the US soon went to war with Mexico, acquiring California in the 1848 **Treaty of Guadalupe Hidalgo,** in which Mexico ceded half of its territory to the US, including California and most of what is now the Southwestern US for a paltry $15 million.

# THE GOLD RUSH

For the US, the timing was golden. Just as the Mexican cession became official, James Marshall discovered **gold** at Sutter's Mill near Sacramento (see **Coloma,** p. 235), and the Rush was on. The '49ers, a motley, half-million strong crew of fortune seekers with visions of nuggets and mother lodes dancing in their hairy heads, flooded the region beginning in 1849. Thousands of prospective prospectors sailed around South America's stormy Cape Horn, and those in wagon trains encountered savage winters and Native American attacks while crossing the Rockies and the Sierra Nevada. The most famous of the doomed settler trains was the **Donner Party,** forced by the fierce winter of 1846-47 into all-you-can-eat cannibalism at a snowbound outpost near what is now Donner Lake in the Sierra Nevada (see **This Party Bites!,** p. 245). By 1859 they had mined over 28 million ounces of gold, worth $10 billion at today's prices; their other accomplishments include razing redwood forests and annihilating native tribes who happened to be in the way. Five years later, the Rush petered out; graveyards and ghost towns have long marked its passing.

The massive influx of prospectors and settlers caused the non-native population to multiply six-fold within four years. Newly independent and economically booming, Gold Rush-era Californians quickly wrote their own constitution and inaugurated John C. Fremont as their first governor a full year before receiving the US Congress's 1850 grant of **statehood.** The completion of a transcontinental telegraph system in 1861 linked California with the East and put the ponies out to pasture. Industrialists, including Leland Stanford, Stanford University's founder, invested in the Central Pacific Railroad. Its tracks grew steadily eastward, largely thanks to the very cheap labor of imported, exploited Chinese. The golden spike linked the Central Pacific and Union Pacific Railroads in 1869 to form the **Transcontinental Railroad,** which made traveling cross-country to California a five-day venture, a far more attractive option for fortune-seekers than the month-long coach ride; plus, they could shoot buffalo from the train. In the 1870s and 80s, naturalist **John Muir** eloquently advocated conservation of wilderness in the Sierra Nevada Mountains, securing the preservation of Yosemite and Sequoia as national parks in 1890.

# EARLY 20TH CENTURY

The **great earthquake** of 1906 (7.7 on the Richter scale) destroyed much of San Francisco; city-wide fires from ruptured gas pipes and overturned stoves incinerated the all-wood houses and killed 452 people. Farther south, an unholy Eden of glitz and gasoline began to shimmer in the state's Southern reaches. In 1904, LA water bureau superintendent William Mulholland devised a plan to irrigate arid Los Angeles by constructing an aqueduct from the Owens Valley, 250 mi. northeast

LIFE & TIMES

of the city. The massive water redirection project fueled the exponential growth of LA and made possible the influx of movie studios and nubile young things dreaming of stardom, in the process transforming the once-lush Owens Valley into an alkali dust cloud. An extensive **streetcar system,** consisting of over 1150 mi. of track and connecting Los Angeles with four surrounding counties, reached its peak usage in the 1920s. To capitalize on the oil boom of the 1920s, Standard Oil, Firestone, and General Motors bought out and dismantled the streetcars and subways, ensuring the regency of the automobile on newly constructed freeways.

# GREAT DEPRESSION & WORLD WAR II

The Great Depression of the 1930s did not deal as harshly with California as with the rest of the country; its farm income sank to just half of pre-Depression levels while most other states fared worse. Thousands flocked here to escape the impoverished, cropless Dust Bowl of the Southern Plains. These **"Okies"** were perceived as a threat to native Californian workers, and at times local authorities aided farmers in blocking roads against them (as depicted in John Steinbeck's novel *The Grapes of Wrath;* see p. 17 and p. 331). Still, agriculture pressed forward; by 1939, oranges and other produce made California the leading agricultural state in the nation. The grape industry grew following the repeal of Prohibition, and by 1940, California supplied 90% of the nation's wine, table grapes, and raisins. Just across the border, Las Vegas boomed with casinos, hotels, glamour, and sin in the 40s, following its legalization of gambling and loosening of divorce laws a decade earlier.

Three months after the December 1941 Japanese bombing of Pearl Harbor, President Roosevelt authorized the US military to remove all persons of Japanese ancestry, both American and alien, from the West Coast and relocate them to **internment camps** in the continent's interior. Some historians believe that government and public support for Japanese-American internment was based on greed for their land and resources, as many of them owned sizable tracts of farmland in California. Now the internment camps are nothing but a few crumbled building foundations amid the interior wastelands, and a formative memory among California's Japanese-Americans (see **Tule Lake,** p. 225, and **Manzanar,** p. 301).

# RADICAL 60S & PSYCHEDELIC 70S

After the war production boom of the 1940s, construction projects such as the irrigation canals and freeways of Southern California promoted even swifter expansion. In 1964, California redefined the power center of America by overtaking New York as the nation's most populous state. During the early 1960s, the surf culture of Frankie and Annette, Gidget, and the Beach Boys created a carefree, sun-loving, convertible-cruisin' image of California that persists to this day. Later in the 1960s, the beach party ended and waves of political upheaval began to shake the college campuses of California. In Berkeley, clashes between students and police over civil rights spawned the **Free Speech Movement,** a precursor to future student activism and anti-war protests. Starting in 1965, César Chavez led California grape pickers on a five-year-long strike of California grapes that spread into a campaign for a nationwide grape boycott. In 1967, San Francisco's Haight-Ashbury district declared a **"Summer of Love,"** and young people voiced their disgust with the Establishment by, in Timothy Leary's words, "turning on, tuning in, and dropping out."

However, violence continually marred the flourishing liberal utopianism of the radical 1960s. The summer 1965 riots in **Watts,** Los Angeles, sparked by the arrest of a black man by a white policeman for drunk driving, left four dead and almost 1000 injured. Urban riots erupted throughout the nation in the latter half of the decade, forcing America to confront the severe urban conditions and racial tensions within. In the midst of mounting antiwar protests based at the University of California at Berkeley, the black empowerment coalition known as the **Black Panthers** challenged white California, **Charles Manson** and his cult won a gruesome celebrity through a series of ritual murders, and leftist golden child **Bobby Kennedy** was murdered in LA's storied Ambassador Hotel after winning the California primary of the 1968 presidential election. In the same period, conservative Southern California thrust right-wing powerhouse (and former actor) **Ronald Reagan** into the national political limelight, electing him governor.

In the 1970s, water and fuel shortages as well as the unbearable LA smog forced Californians to alter their ways of life, and attitudes all around lost their earlier sunniness. Governor Jerry "Moonbeam" Brown romanced singer Linda Ronstadt. The Symbionese Liberation Army, the most prominent of a few new revolutionary groups, kidnapped newspaper heiress **Patty Hearst** and temporarily converted her to their cause. The People's Temple of San Francisco gained international notoriety when its leader, **Jim Jones**, poisoned and killed over 1000 members in a mass-suicide service at his religious retreat in Guyana. Meanwhile, **Silicon Valley** in the south San Francisco Bay Area (first pioneered by Hewlett-Packard two decades earlier) began its reign as the capital of the computer world and the mecca for micro-chip enthusiasts across the country.

# THE 80S & 90S

In the 1980s, cellular phones the size of bricks jammed airways and BMWs jammed freeways. Illegal immigrants streamed across the border from Mexico in increasing numbers. A huge earthquake in 1989 leveled highways in the Bay Area and halted the World Series "Battle of the Bay" between the San Francisco Giants and the Oakland A's; two years later a massive fire in Oakland burned over 2000 homes. The most severe drought in California history, from 1987-1992, tested sectional tensions as Southern Californians continued to tap into depleted Northern California reservoirs.

The 1990s opened with a new wave of racial turmoil and unrest. The 1992 **Los Angeles Riots,** sparked by the acquittal of the four white police officers accused of beating Rodney King, revealed a new sphere of racial violence in which Latinos and Asians found themselves involved in the tensions between white and black America. The passage of **Proposition 187,** which denied all social services to illegal immigrants, renewed questions of ethnicity and tolerance. Most of the law was eventually struck down by the courts. Meanwhile, the **O.J. Simpson** trial and the media circus that broadcast it into homes across the country revealed the gaping racial divide between black and white perspectives on the effectiveness and objectivity of the American criminal justice system.

After the University of California system called a halt to all **affirmative action** programs, the general voting public passed **Proposition 209,** which outlawed affirmative action and quotas in state programs like public education and public employment. Before the proposition (strongly supported by then-governor Pete Wilson) was fully implemented, court injunction brought things to a screeching halt after a coalition of civil rights groups filed a complaint.

In the aftermath of all of this racial turmoil, Californians found a new way to cope: marijuana. Well, perhaps it is an old way, but the 90s brought about the most comprehensive fight for **marijuana legalization** the state had ever seen. **Proposition 215,** passed by voters in 1996, had allowed individual patients to grow and use marijuana for medical purposes only. However, the law came under a number of legal challenges, and has since been stripped down considerably.

The **dot-com boom** consisted of pimply 23-year-old techno-geeks converging on Silicon Valley (just out of San Francisco), forming companies containing some combination of "e," "net," and "tech" in their names, and having millions of dollars thrown at them by crazed venture capitalists still high from the fumes of their brand-new Lexus sport-utility vehicles. During the peak of the dot-com craze in the mid- and late 90s, everyone was riding high on the improvements in productivity and information dissemination that could (in theory) result from the Internet and new smaller, faster, cheaper computer processors. The NASDAQ stock index kept climbing and the money kept appearing magically, and it seemed for a while as though the dot-coms had ushered in a new era of steadily increasing prosperity. And, as usual, the new way of doing things was centered in the state that is all about redefining boundaries—California.

## TODAY

The dot-com bubble, which seemed indestructible for so long, finally burst when everyone suddenly realized that no one was actually making any money. Layoffs occurred en masse, and many companies went under altogether. The crazed optimism—in Alan Greenspan's words, the "irrational exuberance"—that defined the 90s is gone. That said, the strongest, most innovative high-tech corporations in the world remain in California, and the Silicon Valley is still a hotbed of innovation.

While the dot-com boom has come and gone, political turmoil remains omnipresent in California. The most recent controversial ballot initiative to be approved by the fickle California electorate is **Proposition 22** (passed in March, 2000)—dubbed the "gay marriage ban." Prop. 22 proclaims that only marriages between a man and a woman will be honored in the state. Gay rights activists bemoan the initiative's passage as the latest attempt by religious conservatives to deny homosexuals their fundamental civil liberties, while the authors of the proposition assert that it has allowed Californians to define marriage for themselves.

Los Angeles, as usual, endured public uproar over another **LAPD scandal.** Details first came to light in 1999, when it was revealed that officers of the Rampart Police Station—who patrolled an impoverished, mostly minority beat near downtown— were alleged to have been framing, beating, and even shooting innocent people since the mid-80s. The FBI and the US Justice Department joined the investigation into the rampant corruption. Dozens of LA's finest were implicated and relieved of duty, and more than 75 tainted convictions were overturned.

After the crippling energy crisis of 2000-01, politicians and energy companies are still reeling from the fallout. Governor Gray Davis (elected in 1998) is making headlines for his ineptitude during the crisis and for Republican attempts to recall his governorship. To the delight of Jay Leno and pundits everywhere, star **Arnold Schwarzenegger** entered the race for a shot at "terminating" the governor. Even in the middle of genuine political turmoil, a projected $8-billion budget deficit in 2004, and an unprecedented jump in the number of people leaving California in the rear view mirror, the Teflon State still manages to remain the center of attention.

## PEOPLE

California is like Disneyland's "It's a Small World" ride, but without the politically incorrect stereotypes and the haunting tune. There is now a nonwhite majority in California, with the Latino population accounting for a whopping 32 percent of the general population--and projected to rise to 50 percent by 2040. The population is also 12 percent Asian, 7.5 percent African-American, and 1 percent Native American. Minority populations are generally denser in urban areas, while outskirts and suburbs are proportionally more Caucasian. Many cities in California, particularly San Francisco and Los Angeles, house ethnic neighborhoods that retain the rich customs and cultures of their distant countries.

# CULTURE

## FOOD & DRINK

The 1980s saw the rise of **California Cuisine,** a new gourmet style revolutionized by Alice Waters at Chez Panisse in Berkeley. California Cuisine emphasizes fresh and natural ingredients with strong European, Asian, and Latin American influences. The more pretentious restaurants like Chez Panisse and Wolfgang Puck's Spago in Los Angeles, can be quite expensive. However, as always, deals can be found.

Apart from California Cuisine, the state's palate is (in)famous for its reverence of bizarre organic "edibles" like wheatgrass and alfalfa, especially in crunchy Northern California. Organic food junkies have been known to put such ingredients in sandwiches, burritos, and juices. Those who live dangerously can try similar experiments at home after a visit to any organic food store (and there are many) or to ▒**Trader Joe's** (☎ 800-SHOP-TJS/746-7857; www.traderjoes.com).

Also common are bean sprouts, tofu, and something called "pan-Asian fusion," which combines the style and ingredients of Chinese, Japanese, Thai, Cambodian, Vietnamese, Californian, and whatever else is in the kitchen cabinet. Food in the state retains a very strong Mexican influence. Particularly in Southern California, burritos and enchiladas rule the day at regional fast food places (excepting, of course, Taco Bell), inexpensive *taquerías*, and pricier, fancier restaurants.

## CUSTOMS & ETIQUETTE

### CIGS & BOOZE

California has the strictest smoking laws in the country. Smoking is banned in all public places, including transportation, bars, and restaurants. At the few accommodations, residences, and offices where smoking is allowed, it is a serious *faux pas* to blow smoke anywhere near somebody else's face. It's not unusual for militant bands of nonsmokers to accost (verbally or otherwise) smokers who disrespect their "space." Before reaching for those matches, be sure to ask those near you whether they mind if you light up.

While there is no questioning that California knows how to party, extreme public drunkenness is still not tolerated. Virtually all municipalities have laws in the books for drunk and disorderly conduct. Drunk driving is also a major no-no, and merely being in a car with an open container is illegal.

### IT'S ALL GOOD

Laid-back is the word in California. A strange phenomenon known as "California time" means that dinner at 6 only implies that food will be consumed sometime between 7 and midnight. It's not so important when something happens, but rather just that it does, eventually. In addition, the weekend for many begins at noon on Friday and ends at noon on Monday. Dress is generally very relaxed—during the day, shorts and sandals are acceptable for all but the most elite establishments. While you should still mind your pleases and thank-yous, manners and speech are also very laid-back.

## THE ARTS

Hollywood is usually considered California's greatest gift to the arts world. Long before the silver screen, however, Monet-trained artists painted the sands of Death Valley, and red-tiled missions were constructed overlooking the sea. As the curtain opened on the movie age, literary giants penned classic Depression-Era texts and singers crooned about the California girls. From Dorothea Lange to Blink-182, California exudes, accepts, and reshapes artistic expression, in every possible form.

# HISTORY

## ARCHITECTURE

Californian architecture has historically been connected to the conquistadors and their missionaries. In 1769 **Father Junípero Serra** built Mission San Diego de Alcala, the original Spanish outpost at the edge of the new world. The rancho adobe style with its Spanish tile and interior courtyard fell out of vogue during the Gold Rush years, but was revived with the construction of Stanford University and two-storied, open-balconied Spanish homes. Red-shingled bungalow homes with their bay windows were popularized in San Francisco. In the early 1900s, Californian eclectic architecture embraced a wide variety of styles, opening the double-doors for palatial fantasies like Hearst Castle, the **Julia Morgan** masterpiece. Writer **Nathanael West** best expressed the jumbled Californian technique when he noted satirically that LA's canyons were lined with "Mexican ranch houses, Samoan huts, Mediterranean villas, Egyptian and Japanese temples, Swiss chalets, Tudor cottages, and every possible combination of these styles." After World War II, Californian architecture became, for better or for worse, synonymous with tract housing, as the cities decentralized and the people fled to the suburbs. **Frank Lloyd Wright,** one of the most experimental architects of the 20th century, did his best to counteract the monotony, building his sleek geometric tributes to human existence.

## FINE ARTS

Fine art in California began as a pastime, with tourists pulling out brushes and pencils as they sat along the sea. **Guy Rose** was one of the first Californians to gain international fame as an artist—his impressionist stylings of eucalyptus trees and canyons furthered the popularity of painting out of doors. **Dorothea Lange's** 1930s photos of the working and living conditions of migrant workers helped convince the federal government to build public housing projects. Her 1936 photo *Migrant Mother* became a national symbol of the suffering caused by the Great Depression. One of America's most beloved artists, **Ansel Adams** did much of his best work between 1930-1960. His luminous, iconic photographs of California's landscapes and national parks helped his related efforts in conservation. **Edward Weston,** a transplanted Californian, was one of America's leading photographers between 1910-1940; his sensuous portraits are less immediately recognizable than Adams' but just as influential. In the mid-twentieth century, **Richard Diebenkorn** gave rise to the "abstract landscape"; his 1960s *Ocean Park* series of the Santa Monica seashore can be found in many California museums. **Robert Crumb's** dementedly insightful comics about the sex, drugs, and rock 'n' roll scene in San Francisco helped fuel the euphoric introspection of the late 60s counterculture; his cartoon histories of the blues redefined the comic genre. In the 1980s, **David Hockney** gained recognition for his brilliantly-hued, geometric, and pop-arty perspectives of Californian people and places.

## LITERATURE

California has been rooted in literary imagination since its beginnings—the name California was inspired by the fictional Queen Califia, a character in *Las Sergas de Esplandian* (1510), who reigned over a land of gems and biddies in a mythical 16th-century tropic. In later days, explorers and settlers praised this heralded paradise in verse and in legend, and with the gold rush the literary flow began in earnest. Vestiges of the early California that appeared in the writing of **Bret Harte** and

**Mark Twain** can still be seen in the relatively unspoiled hills and ghost towns of Gold Country. Even **Jack London,** Oakland's literary native son, spent time panning for gold and writing pastoral stories on the side. London's 1913 book *The Valley of the Moon* provides an evocative portrait of the Sonoma and San Joaquin Valleys before they were consumed by wineries and agribusiness. Poet **Robinson Jeffers** composed his paeans on the Big Sur coast of Monterey County, where novelist **Henry Miller** set up camp upon returning from Europe.

California's 20th-century urbanization gave its writers a new kind of fertile ground. **Raymond Chandler** and **Dashiell Hammett** depicted the wanderings of hard-boiled, world-weary detectives amid the seamy underbellies of Los Angeles and San Francisco. With *The Day of the Locust* (1939), **Nathanael West** probed the grotesque side of Hollywood, behind the makeup, shams, and illusions, portraying lives warped into empty savagery. **John Steinbeck** won the Nobel Prize in 1962 for his scrutiny of the Depression Era. In *The Grapes of Wrath* (1939), he depicted the hard life of Mid-westerners displaced to California by drought with heavy-handed symbolism and a sensitivity that earned him the Pulitzer. During the 1950s, **Jack Kerouac** and **Allen Ginsberg** combined candid autobiography with visionary rapture to become the gurus of the Beat Generation. They appropriated San Francisco's North Beach (along with New York's Greenwich Village) as a spiritual home to return to after the cross-country wanderings fictionalized in Kerouac's *On The Road* (1957). **Thomas Pynchon's** *The Crying of Lot 49* (1966) "went postal" with a paranoid sort of wandering that included potheads, technozoids, and a new slant on stamp collecting. **Armistead Maupin's** *Tales of the City* (1978) captured a wacky assortment of characters living on San Francisco's Barbary Lane. His *Vineland* (1990), an epic mess of pop culture and political conspiracy, romps through California, self-consciously name-dropping every town from Vacaville to Van Nuys. And for the children of the aforementioned potheads and technozoids, a kinder, gentler author by the name of **Beverly Cleary** penned the delightful *Ramona* series.

## MUSIC

California's musicians have often been socially engaged: **Jello Biafra** of the Dead Kennedys finished fourth in the 1979 San Francisco mayor's race, the late **Sonny Bono** was a Republican Congressman from Orange County, and **Frank Zappa** served in the Maryland State Legislature. Zappa was also Vaclav Havel's Minister of Culture in the Czech Republic until US Secretary of State **James Baker III** (or Baker's wife, a proponent of censorship in music) forced his resignation.

In Los Angeles, the squeaky-clean **Beach Boys** and **Jan and Dean** warbled harmonized odes to sun and fun in the 1960s, matching their British contemporaries in flair but with less appreciation for the sublime American blues tradition. The singer-songwriter movement of the 1970s **(Joni Mitchell, Jackson Browne, James Taylor)** eradicated the last traces of political advocacy from the lone-guitarist idiom it had inherited from American folk music. Audiences strained to hear as performers sang and gazed softly into their navels. Bands looking for renewed vigor found it in punk **(X)**, Mexican roots **(Los Lobos)**, or a combination of the two **(The Blasters).**

From the 1970s to the 1990s, the dissolute tried out several iterations of life in the fast lane. Hollywood produced **The Doors** and their lizard king **Jim Morrison,** the slickly countrified **Eagles,** and the triumphant sleaze of **Guns n' Roses.** The guitar gymnastics of Dutch import **Eddie Van Halen** were epoch-making for pop music technique in the early 1980s, while hair-metal **(Mötley Crüe, Quiet Riot)** and glam-metal **(Poison)** kept the fancy costumes but toned down rock's bluesiness to a limited number of loud, formulaic gestures.

Hippies established a nationally recognized San Francisco sound in the 1960s, as pot and LSD increased audience tolerance for long, indulgent jams grounded in Afro-Caribbean rhythm **(Santana),** blues **(Big Brother and the Holding Company,** who launched doomed vocalist **Janis Joplin** to stardom), or folk **(The Grateful Dead).** Baby boomers mustered great enthusiasm for the **Summer of Love** in 1967, as the groovy new sound enhanced the experience of copious sex and drugs. However, the notorious killing of an audience member by Hell's Angels at a 1969 Rolling Stones concert signaled that the "trip" was going bad.

The Bay Area also pulled to prominence several bands that were less dependent on psychedelic motifs. **Sly and the Family Stone's** breathtaking utopian vision of racial integration thumped with the help of slap-bass inventor Larry Graham, and **Creedence Clearwater Revival** of El Cerrito credibly impersonated bayou swamp rats. Meanwhile in suburbia, a sinister breed of short-haired, skateboarding boys pounded punk into shape in the 1980s until it became hard-core **(Dead Kennedys, Black Flag, The Minutemen, Suicidal Tendencies).**

## BOOB TUBE & THE SILVER SCREEN

**Hollywood** has no counterpart. Strictly a West Coast phenomenon, it evokes a bizarre mixture of disdain and jealousy from the New York entertainment world (from whose loins it sprang so long ago) as a glitzy, obnoxious, yet somehow glamorous and trendsetting proxy for legitimate art. "Tinseltown" exerts an increasingly influential hold over global pop culture.

The movie capital of the US had modest beginnings. Before 1910, independent New York filmmakers were continually harassed by a movie trust seeking to drive out competition. The independents moved west and set up shop in sunny Hollywood, then a sleepy sheep-raising town, from where a mere dash across the Mexican border could foil attempts to confiscate cameras and film. In addition, the filmmakers could take advantage of year-round sunny days to light shots (artificial lighting had not yet been perfected).

As the balance of movie power began to shift west, the Hollywood studios instituted the **"star system."** For the first time, actors themselves were advertised and used to attract adoring fans to movie after movie. One of the first film divas was Mary Pickford, also known as "America's Sweetheart." Charlie Chaplin, Buster Keaton, Douglas Fairbanks, and that lover of lovers, Rudolph Valentino, soon attained legendary status by virtue of their appearances on the silver screen.

The 1920s witnessed two major developments: sound and scandal. "Talkies," films with sound, were introduced with Al Jolson's *The Jazz Singer* in 1927. Scandals were ushered in when Fatty Arbuckle went on trial for the death of starlet Virginia Rappe. A suspicion that Hollywood was becoming a moral cesspool led to the appointment of Postmaster General Will Hays as "movie czar." His vilified Production Code Administration tightly regulated the content and presentation of sex and violence in films, but also prevented the establishment of a federal censorship system that was strongly advocated by the Catholic Church.

**Gone With the Wind** was the first large-scale Hollywood extravaganza, blazing the way for other studios to utilize exorbitant budgets, flamboyant costumes, and casts of thousands. A less extravagant but equally important film event occurred in 1941, when Orson Welles unveiled his masterpiece, **Citizen Kane,** a work whose innovations expanded contemporary ideas about film's potential. Then, in the 1950s, the Hollywood of the Cold War era bought into the pervasive **Red Scare.** Studios **blacklisted** actors, directors, and screenwriters with even the most vague connections to communist causes for fear of their potentially seditious influence in the national media. Many blacklisted actors and actresses weren't able to find work in Hollywood for years.

The increasing accessibility of **television** magnified the scope and impact of Hollywood's image industry. In the 1960s and 70s, shows like *The Brady Bunch* gave Americans a shared experience and collective memory of plotlines and theme songs. *Saved by the Bell* gave younger Americans a distorted vision of high school to aspire to, while *Full House* launched the careers of twin entertainment giants, Mary-Kate and Ashley Olsen. Competition from television studios shifted the focus of the film industry toward big-budget movies that couldn't be produced on the small-screen. *Jaws*, *Star Wars* and *E.T.* ushered in the summer blockbuster age.

## CURRENT SCENE

California is a magnet for innovative artistic talent; its studios and stages are full, and suburbia's garages spawn new bands daily. Digital television, the soaring popularity of DVDs, and worldwide movie openings allow California to continue to imprint its consciousness on the rest of the planet.

### ARCHITECTURE

The current postmodern focus is minimalist; the current king is **Frank Gehry**. Unique, unorthodox creations fight mass production with their twisting steel frames and angular plywood siding. The **Getty Center** and the **Walt Disney Concert Hall** are prime examples of this aesthetic. "California roadside vernacular" is about architecture imitating life, or at least, architecture imitating food. Hot-dog shaped hot dog stands and circular doughnut shops remain roadside staples.

### FINE ARTS

California's modern creations fuse different styles, textures, and mediums, with artists often dabbling in set design, photography, and the more traditional studio arts. Some museums and galleries, like **The Oakland Museum** and **The Pasadena Museum of California Art,** exclusively exhibit the work of California residents.

### LITERATURE

Fifth-generation Californian **Joan Didion's** essays examine the less-than-Golden State that writers blinded by Hollywood often neglect. Contemporary Americana owes one of its most pervasive catch-phrases to the lonely ennui of Palm Springs's resort culture, which spawned **Douglas Coupland's** *Generation X*. Suburban ennui has been the topic of many recent literary endeavors, as has cyberculture, explored by **Douglas Rushkoff** in works like *Ecstasy Club*. **Bruce Wagner's** *I'm Losing You* shows that Hollywood corruption never goes out of style.

### MUSIC

In the early nineties, the spokesmen of combative gangsta rap **(NWA, Dr. Dre, Eazy E, Ice Cube, Snoop Dogg)** spewed invective straight outta Compton at cops and East Coast rappers. **Eminem** got his start in the underground LA hip-hop scene. Rap and hard rock were fused into California's diverse milieu of the late 1980s with some leering **(Red Hot Chili Peppers)**, some grooving **(Fishbone)**, and some leftist ranting **(Rage Against the Machine)**. In the mid-90s, Los Angeles witnessed the emergence of New Swing, a white, middle-class revival of ethnic rhythms first tapped out during the zoot suit-clad Depression era.

To the north, Oakland's rappers **(Digital Underground, Too $hort, 2Pac)** built the loping Oaktown sound on Graham's hefty bass foundation. These days, newer artists like **Meat Beat Manifesto** bring electronic music into dance clubs all over the US. Ska music, from Jamaica via the UK, found its way to the Californian suburbs in a ska-revival revival, or **third wave;** in 1997, radio everywhere blared with Orange County's upbeat **No Doubt,** featuring pop princess Gwen Stefani, and the pseudo-punk "All-Stars" **Smash Mouth**. Despite the death of lead singer Bradley Nowell in 1996, wildly popular **Sublime** continues putting out their ska-punk-reggae in remix compilations and tours in the form of the **Long Beach Dub All-Stars**. Meanwhile, the pop punk genre finds its hero in the irreverent **Blink 182,** which crafts references to sodomy, masturbation, and bestiality into pure power chord goodness.

### FILM & TV

Throughout the 90s, movies with city-exploding, bullet-stopping, people-hurtling special effects became cash sinkholes as movie studios competed to put the biggest stars in the biggest spectacles. In this vein, *Titanic*, *The Matrix*, *Spiderman*, and George Lucas' lamentable *Star Wars* prequels have blown away movie audiences and box-office records. The mass-production of television became global; the adolescent fantasy show, *Baywatch*, captivated the entire world with its slow-motion shots of gorgeous models nearly bursting out of their red swimsuits. The epidemic of reality TV shows in the twenty-first century give normal Americans the chance to be as greedy and image-driven on national TV as their Hollywood idols. More recent shows like *Buffy the Vampire Slayer* and teeny-bopper movies like *Bring It On* have updated the popular idea of California as a superficial, plastic wasteland, fashioning the valley-girl anti-hero who struts about the moral wastes of LA with a tongue-in-cheek awareness of her own blonde vapidity.

# SPORTS

## BASEBALL

It's still called America's national pastime, and with five teams in the state, baseball excites passions and intrastate rivalries in California. The **San Francisco Giants** with single-season home run king Barry Bonds thrive in their brand-new PacBell Park, which features the occasional dinger hit into the Bay. Across the way, the **Oakland Athletics (A's)** pull off miracles on a minuscule payroll. The popular **Los Angeles Dodgers** tussle with the hated Giants for second place in the National League West, while the hapless **San Diego Padres** lounge in the cellar. Oh yeah—Walt Disney's magic still lives on in the form of the Rally Monkey and the Cinderella 2002 World Champion **Anaheim** (that'd be in Orange County) **Angels.**

## FOOTBALL

Even though fall doesn't really exist in California, the fall months still belong to Major League Baseball's more violent (and thus more popular) competitor, the National Football League (NFL). Watch the resurgent **San Francisco 49ers** try to revive the glory days of Montana to Rice and win back respect in the National Football Conference. Or go gangsta in the famed Black Hole with the bad-boy, blue-collar, precision-passing **Oakland Raiders**, who spent 1982-1995 in the LA desert vainly seeking greater profits before maverick owner Al Davis moved them back. LA has been devoid of professional football for nearly a decade, ever since the **Rams** fled for St. Louis around the same time that the Raid-uhs up and left for the Bay. Few Los Angelenos make the drive to San Diego to see the lowly **Chargers,** whose odds of having a winning season have improved somewhat under new head coach Marty Schottenheimer, although this hardly says much.

There are also two big rivalries in college football. The Division-I powerhouse **Stanford Cardinal** (the color, not the bird) annually thrash the UC Berkeley (commonly known as **Cal**) **Golden Bears** to great fanfare and sophomoric pranks the weekend before Thanksgiving in late November. Down south, the **UCLA Bruins** and the **University of Southern California (USC) Trojans** (and their thoroughly inebriated fans) duke it out for supremacy in the City of Angels each year in early November.

## BASKETBALL

The **Golden State Warriors,** who play in Oakland, tend to park their backsides on the doormat of the National Basketball Association (NBA). The Western conference powerhouse **Sacramento Kings** are still looking for that first championship ring, despite the best efforts of Chris Webber and his cowbell-clanging fans. Little love is lost between the young Kings and the star-studded **LA Lakers,** who have added All-Stars Gary Payton and Karl Malone to their stable of superstars—Shaquille O'Neal, Kobe Bryant, coach Phil Jackson and sixth man Jack Nicholson—in their quest to return to championship form. The Lakers' recent string of NBA championships (2000-2002), international brand appeal, and coterie of Hollywood stars at every Laker home game tend to make their "rivals," the ridiculously underachieving **LA Clippers,** look even worse than they normally do. Star Lisa Leslie and the **LA Sparks** have enjoyed success in the Women's National Basketball Association (WNBA) on par with their gold-garbed male counterparts, the Lakers.

## SPORTS WITH GOALIES

"Ice" and "indoors" are two unfamiliar words to most Californians, but hockey, if it does not thrive, at least survives in the state. The storybook sports year for Anaheim, whose Angels won the World Series for the first time, ended on a hollow note as the **Mighty Ducks** lost in the National Hockey League's Stanley Cup finals. The Ducks compete with their crosstown rivals, the **LA Kings.** In the Bay Area, the toothless **San Jose Sharks** skate nightly during the winter. Efforts to popularize soccer (non-American football) are still ongoing. The **San Jose Earthquakes** and **LA Galaxy** of Major League Soccer kick it to not-sold-out crowds all summer long.

# ADDITIONAL RESOURCES

## GENERAL HISTORY

*Americans and the California Dream,* Kevin Starr. A six-volume series of social, cultural, and political history by the State Librarian of California (Oxford University Press; 1996).

*Cadillac Desert: The American West and Its Disappearing Water,* Marc Reisner. A look back at how the West was won, one water project at a time (Penguin; 1993).

*Bottled Poetry: Napa Winemaking from Prohibition to the Modern Era,* James T. Lapsley. A detailed history of the region's growth as a grape-stomping paradise (University of California Press; 1996).

*Poet Be Like God: Jack Spicer and the San Francisco Renaissance,* Lewis Ellingham and Kevin Killian. An exploration of the literary world in the City by the Bay (Wesleyan University Press; 1998).

## FILM

### SAN FRANCISCO/BAY AREA

**The Maltese Falcon** (1941). Hard-boiled San Francisco detective Sam Spade (Humphrey Bogart) mixes with a cast of shady characters in pursuit of a golden, jewel-encrusted falcon statue—"the stuff that dreams are made of." Based on the novel by Dashiell Hammet.

**Vertigo** (1958). Alfred Hitchcock's complex tale about an altitude-averse San Francisco detective (Jimmy Stewart) and his encounter with a woman eerily troubled by the past. Features Mission Dolores and Mission San Juan Bautista in fantastic supporting roles.

**The Graduate** (1967). Young Dustin Hoffman has graduated from college into a meaningless, psychoerotic void set to the tunes of Simon and Garfunkel's acoustic caterwauling. Watch for the shot of the Bay Bridge and catch our hero driving the wrong way.

**Dirty Harry** (1971). Housewife heartthrob Clint Eastwood plays a dangerous San Francisco cop. In its 1983 sequel *Sudden Impact*, Harry impales his victim on the merry-go-round unicorn at the **Santa Cruz Beach Boardwalk** (see p. 326).

**The Rock** (1996). Alcatraz (see p. 116): only one man has ever broken out. Now five million lives depend on two men breaking in. Sean Connery and Nicolas Cage battle in California's most famous island prison (except for Disneyland's "It's a Small World" ride).

# THE CENTRAL VALLEY

☒ **The Grapes of Wrath** (1940). John Ford's gripping, naturalistic adaptation of Steinbeck's masterpiece about Depression-era sharecroppers. Many respected critics consider it better than the book. Henry Fonda's final monologue is for the ages.

**American Graffiti** (1973). Director George Lucas put himself on the Hollywood map with this humorous and lyrical rendering of four Modesto high school graduates' misadventures one summer night in 1962.

**Psycho** (1960). The Hitchcock classic, in which embezzler Janet Leigh has the misfortune to stay in a motel (on a highway between Fresno and Bakersfield) where the caretaker has dangerous, pathological cross-dressing tendencies.

# THE COAST

☒ **Citizen Kane** (1941). The ultimate classic, loosely based on the life of newspaper giant William Randolph Hearst, who nearly succeeded in purchasing and burning Orson Welles' masterpiece before it was ever shown. Although the film sets the mogul's Xanadu mansion in Florida, its real-world counterpart is **Hearst Castle** (see p. 349).

**The Birds** (1963). Birds begin attacking residents of **Bodega Bay** (p. 188) in this Alfred Hitchcock thriller.

# THE DESERT

**Bagdad Cafe** (1990). In this offbeat comedy by offbeat director Percy Aldon, a German housewife heeds the haunting siren of empty expanses. She dumps her husband in the Mojave and finds an unexpected new life at a small desert motel.

**Leaving Las Vegas** (1995). A tender romance starring Elisabeth Shue and Nicolas Cage set against a rich backdrop of alcoholism, depression, and prostitution.

**Zabriskie Point** (1970). Michelangelo Antonioni's counterculture protagonists get down and dirty at Death Valley Monument Zabriskie Point in this bizarre and revolutionary piece. Hang on for the trippy and mind-blowing climax.

# LOS ANGELES

☒ **Chinatown** (1974). Jack Nicholson sleuths through a creepy pastel Los Angeles. Robert Towne's script for this Roman Polanski thriller is one of the most studied screenplays in film schools. Hold your breath for the famous last line.

☒ **Pulp Fiction** (1993). Quentin Tarantino's ultra-cool, ultra-violent dive into four stories of San Fernando Valley lowlifes, Ezekiel-quoting assassins, washed up boxers and their lemonpie French girlfriends. Its hilariously profane dialogue, striking editing, and stylistic flair made it one of the most influential and quotable films of the nineties.

☒ **Swingers** (1996). LA's labyrinthine nightlife serves as backdrop for Mikey's mopey romanticism and Trent's dating escapades. Sadly enough, this comedy has defined the rules of dating and rebound dating for guys everywhere.

**Clueless** (1995). Alicia Silverstone stars in this like, meta-fluffy movie about the lives, fashions, and limited but somehow eloquent vocabulary of three high school Beverly Hills girls. The plot's similarities to Jane Austen's *Emma* flick this flick into legitimacy.

**Boyz 'N the Hood** (1991). A hard-hitting portrayal of life in the poverty-stricken neighborhoods of South Central LA. Director John Singleton's debut film.

LA Story (1991). Steve Martin's love song to the City of Angels. He even gets to roller blade in the Museum of Art! (See **Los Angeles County Museum of Art,** p. 415.)

**Speed** (1994). Police officer Keanu Reeves puts his sophisticated problem-solving skills to work in rescuing charming, girl-next-door turned bus driver Sandra Bullock and a vehicle full of passengers from a fiery death on the highways of LA.

**LA Confidential** (1997). *Chinatown* for the kids: a 1990s retro meta-*film noir* with a sprawling plotline, super-saturated colors, and rotary-sanded editing. Not the real thing, but neither is frozen yogurt.

## HOLLYWOOD

**Sunset Boulevard** (1950). Dark, satirical drama about a faded silent movie star in love with a cynical young screenwriter played by William Holden. Gloria Swanson, a former silent film queen herself, embodies a culture of self-absorbed decadence in her portrayal of the aging and vainglorious film star.

**The Player** (1991). Robert Altman's postmodern mirror trick of a motion picture. A menagerie of stars (playing themselves) and visual nods to every film ever made catalyze a cool dissection of morality in show biz.

**Rebel Without a Cause** (1955). Teen icon James Dean in the quintessential story of disaffected youth. Shot at Hollywood High. Catch the "remake" of this classic in the video for Paula Abdul's song *Rush, Rush,* with Keanu Reeves in the James Dean role.

# TRAVEL BOOKS

**Best Places to Kiss In Southern California** (Beginning Press; 1996), Caroline O'Connell, Megan Davenport, and Deborah Brada.

**A Climber's Guide to the High Sierra** (Random House; 1993), Steve Roper.

**Nature Writings** (Library of America; 1997), John Muir, ed. William Cronon.

**Wine Country Bike Rides** (Chronicle; 1997), Lena Emmery.

# SUGGESTED LISTENING

**Al Jolson,** "California, Here I Come" (1924).

**Bobby Troupe,** "Route 66", (1946). Also performed by Nat King Cole, The Rolling Stones, and Depeche Mode.

**Beach Boys,** "California Girls", *Summer Days (and Summer Nights!)* (1965).

**Mamas and the Papas,** "California Dreamin'", *California Dreamin'* (1966).

**Frank Zappa and the Mothers of Invention,** *Freak Out* (1966).

**Scott MacKenzie,** "San Francisco (Wear Some Flowers in Your Hair)", *San Francisco* (1967).

**Marvin Gaye (and the California Raisins),** "I Heard it Through the Grapevine", *In the Groove* (1968); originally performed by Gladys Knight and the Pips (1967).

**Grateful Dead,** *American Beauty* (1970).

**The Doors,** *LA Woman* (1971).

**Joni Mitchell,** "California", *Blue* (1971).

**Led Zeppelin,** "Going to California", *Led Zeppelin IV* (1971).

**Jackson Browne,** *Late for the Sky* (1974).

**Eagles,** "Hotel California", *Hotel California* (1976).

**Bob Seger,** "Hollywood Nights", *Stranger in Town* (1978).

**Jim Jacobs & Warren Casey,** *Grease, The Motion Picture Soundtrack* (1978).

**Dead Kennedys,** "California Über Alles", *Fresh Fruit for Rotting Vegetables* (1980).

**Missing Persons,** "Walking in LA", *Spring Session M* (1982).

**Guns 'n' Roses,** "Paradise City", *Appetite for Destruction* (1987).

**U2,** *The Joshua Tree* (1987).

**Tom Petty,** "Free Fallin'", *Full Moon Fever* (1989).

**Ice Cube,** "Once Upon a Time in the Projects", *AmeriKKKa's Most Wanted* (1990).

**Weezer,** "Surf Wax America", *Weezer* (1994).

**Green Day,** "Welcome to Paradise", *Dookie* (1994).

**No Doubt,** *Tragic Kingdom* (1995).

**Counting Crows,** "Long December", *Recovering the Satellites* (1996).

**Sublime,** "Doin' Time", *Sublime* (1996).

**2Pac and Dr. Dre,** "California Love", *All Eyez on Me* (1996).

**Blink-182,** *Dude Ranch* (1997).

**Shawn Mullins,** "Lullabye", *Soul's Core* (1998).

**Red Hot Chili Peppers,** *Californication* (1999).

**Rage Against the Machine,** *The Battle for Los Angeles* (1999).

**Aimee Mann,** "Red Vines", *Bachelor No. 2* (2000).

# HOLIDAYS & FESTIVALS

National holidays are always a reason to celebrate, and even if Californians don't work as hard as the rest of the country, they feel just as entitled to a day off. Holidays are accompanied by parades and the closing of businesses and mail service. Festivals are focused events celebrating an art form or a piece of cultural history.

| DATE IN 2004 | HOLIDAY | | DATE IN 2004 | HOLIDAY |
|---|---|---|---|---|
| January 1 | New Year's Day | | September 6 | Labor Day |
| January 19 | Martin Luther King, Jr. Day | | October 11 | Columbus Day |
| February 16 | Presidents' Day | | November 11 | Veterans' Day |
| May 31 | Memorial Day | | November 25 | Thanksgiving Day |
| July 4 | Independence Day | | December 25 | Christmas Day |

# CALIFORNIA'S FESTIVALS (2004)

| DATE | NAME & LOCATION | DESCRIPTION |
|---|---|---|
| Jan. 1 | ■ **Tournament of Roses Parade and Rose Bowl** (Pasadena) | Floats made entirely of roses parade down Colorado Ave. from 8-10am. The football champs of the Pac 10 and Big 10 conferences meet in the afternoon for the Rose Bowl. |
| late Feb. | **Chinese New Year Celebrations** (SF, LA) | Pageants, street fairs, fireworks and dragons usher in the Chinese New Year in these Chinese-American communities. |
| May 5 | **Cinco de Mayo** (everywhere) | Color, costumes, and mariachi bands celebrate Mexican pride throughout the state. |
| mid-June | **Playboy Jazz Festival** (LA) | Two days of entertainment by top-name jazz musicians of all varieties, from traditional to fusion. |
| June 23-24 | **Pride Day** (SF); **Gay Pride Weekend** (LA) | Art, politics, dances, and parades celebrate diversity. |
| July 4 | ■ **World Pillow Fighting Championships** (Kenwood) | Eager contenders straddle a metal pipe over a mud pit and beat each other to a muddy pulp with wet pillows. |
| mid-July | **National Nude Weekend** (Santa Cruz) | Enjoy bands (playing in the buff) or come paint the posing models (on canvas), at the Lupin Naturalist Club. |
| July 23-25 | **Gilroy Garlic Festival** (Gilroy) | Garlic-laced fried calamari, vendors, musicians come together to pay tribute to the stinky rose. Kissing optional. |
| late July | **North Beach Jazz Festival** | An assortment of musicians play at this free jazz festival. |
| 3rd week in Sept. | **Monterey Jazz Festival** | Big name blues musicians come to the Bay. |
| Oct. | **Folsom Street Fair** (SF) | Pride Day's raunchier, rowdier brother. Leather heaven. |
| Early Oct. | ■ **World Championship Grape Stomp** (Santa Rosa) | Wine-making on a massive scale in the Sonoma Valley, part of the summer-long Sonoma County Harvest Fair. |
| Nov. 1 | ■ **Dia de los Muertos** (SF) | Follow the drummers and dancing skeletons to the festive Mexican celebration of the dead. |
| Nov. | **Napa Valley Wine Festival** | Wine, music, and theater for the wine critic in everyone. |

LIFE & TIMES

# ESSENTIALS

## FACTS FOR THE TRAVELER

**ENTRANCE REQUIREMENTS**

**Passport** (p. 27). Required of citizens of all foreign countries except Canada.

**Visa** (p. 28). Visitors from most of Europe, Australia, and New Zealand can travel in the US for up to 90 days without a visa, although you may need to show a return plane ticket. Citizens of South Africa need a visa.

**Inoculations.** Up-to-date inoculations required of all travelers.

**Work Permit** (p. 28). Required of all foreigners planning to work in the US.

**Driving Permit** (p. 55). Required of those who plan to drive in the US.

## EMBASSIES AND CONSULATES

### US EMBASSIES AND CONSULATES ABROAD

Contact the nearest embassy or consulate to obtain information regarding visas and permits to the United States. Offices are only open limited hours, so call well before you depart. The US State Department provides contact information for US diplomatic missions at http://foia.state.gov/MMS/KOH/keyofficers.asp. Foreign embassies in the US are located in Washington, D.C., but there are consulates in the Southwest that can be helpful in an emergency. For a more extensive list of embassies and consulates in the US, consult www.embassy.org.

**AUSTRALIA. Embassy and Consulate:** Moonah Pl., Yarralumla **(Canberra),** ACT 2600 (☎02 6214 5600; fax 6214 5970; usembassy-australia.state.gov/consular). **Other Consulates:** MLC Centre, Level 59, 19-29 Martin Pl., **Sydney,** NSW 2000 (☎02 9373 9200; fax 9373 9184); 553 St. Kilda Rd., **Melbourne,** VIC 3004 (☎03 9526 5900; fax 9510 4646); 16 St. George's Terr., 13th fl., **Perth,** WA 6000 (☎08 9202 1224; fax 9231 9444).

**CANADA. Embassy and Consulate:** Consular Section, 490 Sussex Dr., **Ottawa,** P.O. Box 866, Station B, Ottowa, Ontario K1P 5T1(☎613-238-5335; fax 613-688-3081; www.usembassycanada.gov). **Other Consulates** (☎ 1-900-451-2778 or 1-888-840-0032; www.amcits.com): 615 Macleod Trail SE, Room 1000, **Calgary,** AB T2G 4T8 (☎403-266-8962; fax 264-6630); 1969 Upper Water St., Purdy's Wharf Tower II, suite 904, **Halifax,** NS B3J 3R7 (☎902-429-2480; fax 423-6861); 1155 St. Alexandre, **Montréal,** QC H3B 1Z1 (mailing address: P.O. Box 65, Postal Station Desjardins, Montréal, QC H5B 1G1; ☎514-398-9695; fax 981-5059); 2 Place Terrasse Dufferin, behind Château Frontenac, B.P. 939, **Québec City,** QC G1R 4T9 (☎418-692-2095; fax 692-4640); 360 University Ave., **Toronto,** ON M5G 1S4 (☎416-595-1700; fax 595-0051); 1075 W. Pender St., Mezzanine (mailing address: 1095 W. Pender St., 21st fl., Vancouver, BC V6E 2M6; ☎604-685-4311; fax 685-7175).

**IRELAND. Embassy and Consulate:** 42 Elgin Rd., Ballsbridge, **Dublin** 4 (☎01 66 88 777 or 66 87 122; fax 66 89 946; www.usembassy.ie).

**NEW ZEALAND. Embassy and Consulate:** 29 Fitzherbert Terr., Thorndon, **Wellington** (☎04 462 6000; fax 478 0490; usembassy.org.nz). **Other Consulate:** 23 Customs St., Citibank Building, 3rd fl., **Auckland** (☎09 303 2724; fax 366 0870).

**SOUTH AFRICA. Embassy and Consulate:** 877 Pretorius St., **Pretoria**, P.O. Box 9536, Pretoria 0001 (☎012 342 1048; fax 342 2244; usembassy.state.gov/pretoria). **Other Consulates:** Broadway Industries Center, Heerengracht, Foreshore, **Cape Town** (mailing address: P.O. Box 6773, Roggebaai, 8012; ☎021 342 1048; fax 342 2244); 303 West St., Old Mutual Building, 31st fl., **Durban** (☎031 304 4737; fax 301 0265); 1 River St., Killarney, **Johannesburg,** P.O. Box 1762, Houghton, 2041 (☎011 644 8000; fax 646 6916).

**UK. Embassy and Consulate:** 24 Grosvenor Sq., **London** W1A 1AE (☎020 7499 9000; fax 7495 5012; www.usembassy.org.uk). **Other Consulates**: Queen's House, 14 Queen St., **Belfast,** N. Ireland BT1 6EQ (☎028 9032 8239; fax 9024 8482); 3 Regent Terr., **Edinburgh,** Scotland EH7 5BW (☎0131 556 8315; fax 557 6023).

## CONSULAR SERVICES IN CALIFORNIA

**Australia,** 2049 Century Park East, 19th floor of the Century Plaza Towers between Olympic Blvd. and Santa Monica Blvd., **Los Angeles**, CA 90067 (☎310-229-4800); and 1 Bush St., #700, at Market St., **San Francisco**, CA 94104 (☎415-536-1970).

**Canada,** 550 S. Hope St., 9th fl., **LA**, CA 90071 (☎213-346-2700).

**Ireland,** 44 Montgomery St., #3830, **San Francisco**, CA 94104 (☎415-392-4214).

**New Zealand,** 12400 Wilshire Blvd., #1150, **LA**, CA 90025 (☎310-207-1605).

**South Africa,** 6300 Wilshire Blvd., #600, **LA**, CA 90048 (☎323-651-0902).

**UK,** 11766 Wilshire Blvd., #400, **LA**, CA 90025 (☎310-481-0031); 1 Sansome St., #850, at Market St., **San Francisco**, CA 94104 (☎415-617-1300).

# DOCUMENTS AND FORMALITIES

## PASSPORTS

**REQUIREMENTS.** All foreign visitors except Canadians need valid passports to enter the United States and to re-enter their own country. Canadians need to demonstrate proof of citizenship, such as a citizenship card or birth certificate. The US does not allow entrance if the holder's passport expires in under six months; returning home with an expired passport is often illegal, and may result in a fine.

**NEW PASSPORTS.** Citizens of Australia, Canada, Ireland, New Zealand, and the United Kingdom can apply for a passport at any post office, passport office, or court of law. Citizens of South Africa can apply for a passport at any Home Affairs office. All applications must be filed well in advance of the departure date, although most passport offices offer rush services for a very steep fee.

**PASSPORT MAINTENANCE.** Be sure to photocopy the page of your passport with your photo, as well as your visas, traveler's check serial numbers and any other important documents. Carry one set of copies in a safe place, apart from the originals, and leave another set at home. Consulates also recommend that you carry an expired passport or an official copy of your birth certificate in a part of your baggage separate from other documents. If you lose your passport, immediately notify the local police and the consulate of your home government. To expedite its replacement, it helps to have a photocopy. In some

ESSENTIALS

cases, a replacement may take weeks to process, and it may be valid only for a limited time. Any **visas** stamped in your old passport will be irretrievably lost. In an emergency, ask for **temporary traveling papers** that will permit you to re-enter your home country.

# VISAS, INVITATIONS, AND WORK PERMITS

**VISAS.** Citizens of South Africa and most other countries need a visa—a stamp, sticker, or insert in your passport specifying the purpose of your travel and the permitted duration of your stay—in addition to a valid passport for entrance to the US. See http://travel.state.gov/visa_services.html and www.unitedstatesvisas.gov for more information. To obtain a visa, contact a US embassy or consulate. Recent security measures have made the visa application process more rigorous and lengthy; apply well in advance of your travel date.

Canadian citizens do not need to obtain a visa for admission to the US. Citizens of Australia, New Zealand, and most European countries can waive US visas through the **Visa Waiver Program.** Visitors qualify if they are traveling only for business or pleasure (*not* work or study), are staying for fewer than **90 days,** have proof of intent to leave (e.g. a return plane ticket), possess an I-94W form, are traveling on particular air or sea carriers, and possess a machine-readable passport from their country of citizenship. Visit http://travel.state.gov/vwp for more info.

If you lose your I-94 form, you can replace it by filling out form I-102, although it's very unlikely that the form will be replaced within the time of your stay. The form is available at the nearest **Bureau of Citizenship and Immigration Services (BCIS)** office (www.bcis.gov), through the forms request line (☎800-870-3676), or online (www.bcis.gov/graphics/formsfee/forms/i-102.htm). **Visa extensions** are sometimes granted with a completed I-539 form; call the forms request line (☎800-870-3676) or get it online at www.immigration.gov/graphics/formsfee/forms/i-539.htm.

All travelers except Canadians who plan to stay more than 90 days also need to obtain a visa. Admission as a visitor does not include the right to work, which is authorized only by a **work permit.** Entering the US to study requires a special visa. For more information, see **Alternatives to Tourism,** p. 72.

# IDENTIFICATION

When you travel, always carry two or more forms of identification with you, including at least one photo ID; a passport combined with a driver's license or birth certificate is usually adequate. Never carry all your forms of ID together, and keep photocopies of them in your luggage and at home.

**TEACHER, STUDENT AND YOUTH IDENTIFICATION.** The **International Student Identity Card (ISIC),** the most widely accepted form of student ID, provides discounts on sights, accommodations, food, and transport; access to a 24hr. emergency helpline (in North America call ☎877-370-4742; elsewhere call US collect ☎+1-715-345-0505); and insurance benefits for US cardholders (see **Insurance,** p. 37). The ISIC is preferable to an institution-specific card (such as a university ID) because it is more likely to be recognized and honored abroad. Applicants must be degree-seeking students of a secondary or post-secondary school and must be at least 12 years of age. Because of the proliferation of fake ISICs, some services (particularly airlines) require additional proof of student identity, such as a school ID or a letter signed by your registrar and stamped with your school seal.

The **International Teacher Identity Card (ITIC)** offers teachers the same insurance coverage and similar but limited discounts. For travelers who are 25 years old or under but are not students, the **International Youth Travel Card (IYTC;** formerly the **GO 25** Card) offers many of the same benefits as the ISIC.

Each of the cards costs $22 or foreign currency equivalent. ISIC and ITIC cards are valid for 16 months; IYTC cards are valid for one year. Many student travel agencies (see p. 50) issue the cards, including STA Travel in Australia and New Zealand, Travel CUTS in Canada, USIT in the Republic of Ireland and Northern Ireland, SASTS in South Africa, Campus Travel and STA Travel in the UK, and Council Travel and STA Travel in the US. For more information, contact the **International Student Travel Confederation (ISTC),** Herengracht 479, 1017 BS Amsterdam, The Netherlands (☎+31 20 421 28 00; fax 421 28 10; www.istc.org).

## CUSTOMS

Upon entering the US, you must declare certain items from abroad and pay a duty on the value of those articles that exceeds the US customs allowance. Note that goods and gifts purchased at duty-free shops abroad are not exempt from duty or sales tax at your point of return and thus must be declared as well; "duty-free" merely means that you need not pay a tax in the country of purchase. Upon returning home, you must similarly declare all articles acquired abroad and pay a duty on the value of articles in excess of your home country's allowance.

# MONEY

## CURRENCY & EXCHANGE

The currency chart below is based on August 2003 exchange rates between local currency and Australian dollars (AUS$), Canadian dollars (CDN$), Irish pounds (IR£), New Zealand dollars (NZ$), South African Rand (ZAR), British pounds (UK£), US dollars (US$), and European Union euros (EUR€). Check the currency converter on financial websites such as www.bloomberg.com and www.xe.com, or a large newspaper for the latest exchange rates.

| DOLLAR ($) | | |
|---|---|---|
| AUS$1 = $0.66 | US$1 = AUS$1.53 |
| CDN$1 = $0.72 | US$1 = CDN$1.39 |
| IR£1 = $1.44 | US$1 = IR£0.70 |
| NZ$1 = $0.59 | US$1 = NZ$1.70 |
| ZAR1 = $0.14 | US$1 = ZAR7.40 |
| UK£1 = $1.60 | US$1 = UK£0.62 |
| EUR€1 = $1.13 | US$1 = EUR€0.89 |

As a general rule, it's cheaper to convert money in the US than at home. While currency exchange will probably be available in your arrival airport, it's wise to bring enough foreign currency to last for the first 24 to 72 hours of a trip.

When changing money abroad, try to go only to banks or other establishments that have at most a 5% margin between their buy and sell prices. Since you lose money with every transaction, **convert large sums** (unless the currency is depreciating rapidly), **but no more than you'll need.**

If you use traveler's checks or bills, carry some in small denominations (the equivalent of US$50 or less) for times when you are forced to exchange money at disadvantageous rates, but bring a range of denominations since charges may be levied per check cashed. Store your money in a variety of forms.

## TRAVELER'S CHECKS

Traveler's checks are one of the safest and least troublesome means of carrying funds. American Express and Visa are the most widely recognized brands; many banks and agencies sell them for a small commission. Check issuers provide refunds if the checks are lost or stolen, and many provide additional services, such as toll-free refund hotlines abroad, emergency message services, and stolen credit card assistance. Traveler's checks are readily accepted in the US. Ask about toll-free refund hotlines and the location of refund centers when purchasing checks, and always carry emergency cash.

**American Express:** Checks available with commission at select banks, at all AmEx offices, and online (www.americanexpress.com; US residents only). American Express cardholders can also purchase checks by phone (☎888-269-6669). AAA (see p. 57) offers commission-free checks to its members. Checks available in US, Australian, British, Canadian, Japanese, and European Union currencies. *Cheques for Two* can be signed by either of 2 people traveling together. For purchase locations or more information contact AmEx's service centers: In the US and Canada ☎800-221-7282; in the UK ☎0800 587 6023; in Australia ☎800 68 80 22; in New Zealand 0508 555 358; elsewhere US collect ☎+1 801-964-6665.

**Visa:** Checks available (generally with commission) at banks worldwide. For the location of the nearest office, call Visa's service centers: In the US ☎800-227-6811; in the UK ☎0800 51 58 84; elsewhere UK collect ☎+44 020 7937 8091. Checks available in US, British, Canadian, Japanese, and European Union currencies.

**Travelex/Thomas Cook:** In the US and Canada call ☎800-287-7362; in the UK call ☎0800 62 21 01; elsewhere call UK collect ☎+44 1733 31 89 50.

# CREDIT, DEBIT, AND ATM CARDS

Where they are accepted, credit cards often offer superior exchange rates—up to 5% better than the retail rate used by banks and other currency exchange establishments. Credit cards may also offer services such as insurance or emergency help, and are sometimes required to reserve hotel rooms or rental cars. **MasterCard** and **Visa** are the most welcomed; **American Express** cards work at some ATMs and at AmEx offices and major airports.

ATM cards are found throughout California. Depending on the system that your home bank uses, you can most likely access your personal bank account from abroad. ATMs get the same wholesale exchange rate as credit cards, but there is often a limit on the amount of money you can withdraw per day (around $500), and unfortunately computer networks sometimes fail. There is typically also a surcharge of $1-5 per withdrawal from ATMs not affiliated with your bank.

**Debit cards** are a relatively new form of purchasing power that are as convenient as credit cards but have a more immediate impact on your funds. A debit card can be used wherever its associated credit card company (usually MasterCard or Visa) is accepted, yet the money is withdrawn directly from the holder's checking account. Debit cards often also function as ATM cards and can be used to withdraw cash from associated banks and ATMs throughout California. Ask your local bank about obtaining one.

The two major international money networks are **Cirrus** (to locate ATMs call ☎800-424-7787 or www.mastercard.com) and **Visa/PLUS** (to locate ATMs call ☎800-843-7587 or www.visa.com). Most ATMs charge a transaction fee that is paid to the bank that owns the ATM.

# GETTING MONEY FROM HOME

If you run out of money while traveling, the easiest and cheapest solution is to have someone back home make a deposit to your credit card or debit (ATM) card. Failing that, consider **wiring money.** It is possible to arrange a **bank money transfer,** which means asking a bank back home to wire money to a bank in California. This is the cheapest way to transfer cash, but it's also the slowest, usually taking several days or more. Note that some banks may only release your funds in local currency, potentially sticking you with a poor exchange rate; inquire about this in advance. Money transfer services like **Western Union** are faster and more convenient than bank transfers—but also much pricier. Western Union has many locations worldwide. To find one, call or go online (US ☎ 800-325-6000, Canada ☎ 800-235-0000, UK ☎ 0800 83 38 33, Australia ☎ 800 501 500, New Zealand ☎ 800 27 0000, South Africa ☎ 0860 100031; www.westernunion.com). Money transfer services are also available at **American Express** and **Thomas Cook** offices (see p. 30).

ESSENTIALS

## COSTS

The cost of your trip will vary considerably, depending on where you go, how you travel, and where you stay. The most significant expense will probably be your round-trip (return) **airfare** to California (see **Getting to California: By Plane,** p. 49). Before you go, spend some time calculating a reasonable per-day **budget** that will meet your needs.

**STAYING ON A BUDGET.** To give you a general idea, a bare-bones day in California (camping or sleeping in hostels/guest houses, buying food at supermarkets) would cost about $30-35; a slightly more comfortable day (sleeping in hostels/guest houses and the occasional budget hotel, eating one meal a day at a restaurant, going out at night) would run $50-70; and for a luxurious day, the sky's the limit. Hostels usually cost $15-20 per day. Cheap motels will run you about $40, but prices rocket to $60 in season at coastal beach towns and ski resorts; the prices of campgrounds range from $5-20. Eating out will cost you $10-20 daily, but you can raid the supermarket for $5-10 per day. A rental car will set you back $35-55 per day; relying on public transportation will be considerably cheaper, but possibly more inconvenient and restrictive. Also, don't forget to factor in substantial emergency reserve funds when planning how much money you'll need.

**TIPS FOR SAVING MONEY.** Some simpler ways include searching out opportunities for free entertainment, splitting accommodation and food costs with other trustworthy fellow travelers, and buying food in supermarkets rather than eating out. Do your **laundry** in the sink (unless you're explicitly prohibited from doing so). With that said, don't go overboard with your budget obsession. Though staying within your budget is important, don't do so at the expense of your health or a worthwhile travel experience.

## TIPPING & BARGAINING

In the US, it is customary to tip waitstaff and cab drivers 15-20% (at your discretion). Tips are not usually included in restaurant bills, unless you are in a party of six or more. At the airport and in hotels, porters expect a tip of least $1 per bag to carry luggage. Except at flea markets, bargaining is generally frowned upon and fruitless in California.

## TAXES

Sales tax in California is similar to the European Value-Added Tax. The sales tax rate on normal consumer goods varies by county from 7.25% to 8.5%; there are additional federal taxes on tobacco products and alcoholic beverages. Most grocery items in California are not taxed; clothing items, however, are taxed. *Let's Go* does not usually include taxes in listed prices.

# SAFETY & SECURITY

> **EMERGENCY = 911.** For emergencies in the US, dial **911.** This number is toll-free from all phones, including coin phones. In a very few remote communities, 911 may not work. If it does not, dial 0 for the operator. In national parks, it is usually best to call the **park ranger station or warden**.

## PERSONAL SAFETY

**EXPLORING.** In California, crime is mostly concentrated in cities, but exercise caution no matter where you are. LA, East Palo Alto, Sacramento, and Fresno are the most dangerous cities in California, but that does not mean you cannot or should not visit them. Wherever possible, *Let's Go* warns of neighborhoods to be avoided when traveling alone or at night. Common sense and a little bit of planning will go a long way in helping you to avoid dangerous situations. Tourists are especially vulnerable to crime because they tend to carry large amounts of cash and are more easily disoriented than locals. Avoid unwanted attention by blending in as much as possible; the gawking camera-toter is a more obvious target for thieves than the low-profile traveler. Familiarize yourself with the area before setting out; if you must check a map on the street, duck into a cafe or shop. Always carry yourself with confidence. Be sure that someone at home knows your itinerary and never admit that you are traveling alone. At night, stick to busy, well-lit streets and avoid dark alleyways. If you feel uncomfortable, leave as quickly and directly as you can, but don't allow fear of the unknown to deter from you from traveling.

**SELF DEFENSE.** There is no sure-fire way to avoid all the threatening situations you might encounter while traveling, but a good self-defense course will give you concrete ways to react to unwanted advances. **Impact, Prepare, and Model Mugging** can refer you to local self-defense courses in the US (☎800-345-5425); visit the website www.impactsafety.org for a list of nearby chapters. Workshops (2-3hr.) start at $50; full courses (20hr.) run $350-500.

**DRIVING.** If you are using a **car,** learn local driving signals and wear a seatbelt. Seatbelts in cars and motorcycle helmets on motorcycles and mopeds are required by law in California. Children under 40 lbs. must ride in specially-designed carseats, available for a small fee from most car rental agencies. Study route maps before you hit the road, and if you plan on spending a lot of time on the road, spare parts may prove useful. If your car breaks down, wait for the police to assist you. For long drives in desolate areas, invest in a cellular phone and a roadside assistance program (see p. 57). If you are testing car and soul in the heat of the California desert, take special precautions for your drive. See the detailed explanation of **Driving in the Desert,** p. 424. Be sure to park your vehicle in a garage or well traveled area, and use a steering wheel locking device in larger cities. **Sleeping in your car** is one of the most dangerous (and often illegal) ways to get your rest.

*Let's Go* does not recommend **hitchhiking** under any circumstances, particularly for women—see **By Thumb,** p. 57, and **Women Travelers,** p. 57, for more info.

**TERRORISM.** In light of the September 11, 2001 terrorist attacks, there is an elevated threat of further terrorist activities in the United States. Terrorists often target landmarks popular with tourists; however, the threat of an attack is generally not specific or great enough to warrant avoiding certain places or modes of transportation. Stay current with the daily news and watch for alerts from federal, state, and local law enforcement officials. Allow extra time for airport security and remember that sharp objects in carry-on luggage will be confiscated. For more information on the terror threat to the US, visit www.terrorismanswers.com. The box on **travel advisories** below lists offices and webpages that can provide updated information on your home country's government's advisories about travel.

**TRAVEL ADVISORIES.** The following government offices provide travel information and advisories by telephone, by fax, or via the web:

**Australian Department of Foreign Affairs and Trade:** In Australia ☎ 1300 555135; from elsewhere 61 2 6261 1555; faxback service 02 6261 3111; www.dfat.gov.au.

**Canadian Department of Foreign Affairs and International Trade (DFAIT):** In Canada and the US call ☎ 800-267-8376, elsewhere call +1 613-944-4000; www.dfait-maeci.gc.ca. Call for their free booklet, *Bon Voyage...But.*

**New Zealand Ministry of Foreign Affairs:** ☎ 04 439 8000; fax 04 439 8532; www.mft.govt.nz/travel/index.html.

**United Kingdom Foreign and Commonwealth Office:** ☎ 087 0606 0290; fax 7008 0155; www.fco.gov.uk.

**US Department of State:** ☎ 202-647-5225; faxback service 202-647-3000; http://travel.state.gov. For *A Safe Trip Abroad*, call 202-512-1800.

# FINANCIAL SECURITY

**PROTECTING YOUR VALUABLES.** There are a few steps you can take to minimize the financial risk associated with traveling. First, **bring as little with you as possible.** Second, secure your belongings either in your pack or in a hostel or train station locker with combination **padlocks.** Third, **carry as little cash as possible.** Keep your traveler's checks and ATM/credit cards in a **money belt,** along with your passport and ID cards. Fourth, **keep a small cash reserve separate from your primary stash.** This should be about $50 sewn into or stored in the depths of your pack, along with your traveler's check numbers and important photocopies.

**CON ARTISTS & PICKPOCKETS.** In large cities, **con artists** often work in groups, and children are among the most effective. Beware of certain classics: sob stories that require money, rolls of bills "found" on the street, mustard spilled (or saliva spit) onto your shoulder to distract you while they snatch your bag. **Never let your passport out of your sight,** especially near the Mexican border. Don't let your bags out of sight; never trust a new "friend" who offers to guard your bags. Beware of **pickpockets** in city crowds, especially on public transportation. Also, be alert in public telephone booths. If you must say your calling card number, do so very quietly; if you punch it in, make sure no one can look over your shoulder.

**ACCOMMODATIONS & TRANSPORTATION.** Never leave your belongings unattended; crime occurs in even the most secure-looking hostel or hotel. Bring your own **padlock** for hostel lockers, and don't ever store valuables in any locker.

Be particularly careful on **buses** and **trains;** horror stories abound about determined thieves who wait for travelers to fall asleep. Carry your backpack in front of you where you can see it. When traveling with others, sleep in alternate shifts. When alone, use good judgement in selecting a train compartment: never stay in an empty one, and use a lock to secure your pack to the luggage rack. Try to sleep on top bunks with your luggage stored above you (if not in bed with you), and keep important documents and other valuables on your person. If traveling by **car,** don't leave valuables (such as radios or luggage) in it while you are away.

## DRUGS & ALCOHOL

In California, as in the rest of the US, the drinking age is a strictly enforced 21. **Never drink and drive**—you risk your own life and those of others, and getting caught results in imprisonment and fines. It is illegal to have an open container of alcohol inside a car at any time, even if you are not drinking it. Possession of controlled substances are always illegal. If you carry prescription drugs, it is vital to have a copy of the prescriptions, especially near the Mexican border. Cigarette purchasers must be at least 18 years old with photo ID.

## HEALTH

Common sense is the simplest prescription for good health while you travel. The US has an excellent health-care system and travelers can usually be treated easily for injuries and health problems. Travelers complain most often about their gut and their feet, so take precautionary measures: drink lots of fluids to prevent dehydration and constipation, and wear sturdy, broken-in shoes and clean socks.

## BEFORE YOU GO

In your **passport,** write the names of any people you wish to be contacted in case of a medical emergency, and list any allergies or medical conditions. Matching a prescription to an American equivalent is not always easy, safe, or possible, so carry up-to-date, legible prescriptions or a statement from your doctor stating the medication's trade name, manufacturer, chemical name, and dosage. While traveling, be sure to keep all medication with you in your carry-on luggage. For tips on packing a basic **first-aid kit** and other health essentials, see p. 38.

### IMMUNIZATIONS & MEDICAL PRECAUTIONS

Travelers over two years old should make sure that the following vaccines are up to date: MMR (measles, mumps, and rubella); DTaP or Td (diptheria, tetanus, and pertussis); OPV (for polio); HbCV (for haemophilus influenza B); HBV (for hepatitis B); and Varicella (for chickenpox). For recommendations on immunizations and prophylaxis, consult the CDC (see below) in the US or the equivalent in your home country, and check with a doctor for guidance.

Those with medical conditions (such as diabetes, allergies to antibiotics, epilepsy, or heart conditions) may want to obtain a **Medic Alert** membership (first year $35, annually thereafter $20), which includes among its benefits a stainless steel ID tag engraved with personal medical info and a 24hr. collect-call number. Contact the Medic Alert Foundation, 2323 Colorado Ave, Turlock, CA 95382, USA (☎ 888-633-4298, outside US ☎ 209-668-3333; www.medicalert.org).

### USEFUL ORGANIZATIONS & PUBLICATIONS

The US **Centers for Disease Control and Prevention (CDC;** ☎ 877-FYI-TRIP/394-8747; fax 888-232-3299; www.cdc.gov/travel) maintains an international travelers' hotline and an informative website. The CDC's comprehensive booklet *Health Information for International Travel,* an annual rundown of disease, immunization, and general health advice, is free to view online or $29 to purchase via the Public Health Foundation (☎ 877-252-1200). Consult the appropriate government agency of your home country for consular information sheets on health, entry requirements, and other issues for various countries (see the listings in the box on **Travel Advisories,** p. 33). For quick information on health and other travel warnings, call the **Overseas Citizens Services** (M-F 8am-8pm call ☎ 202-647-5225 or 888-407-4747; after-hours 202-647-4000), or contact a passport agency, embassy, or consulate abroad. US citizens can send a self-addressed, stamped envelope to the Overseas Citizens Services, Bureau of Consular Affairs, Room 4811, US Department of State, Washington, D.C. 20520-4818. For information on medical evacuation services and travel insurance firms, see the US government's website (http://travel.state.gov/medical.html) or that of the **British Foreign and Commonwealth Office** (www.fco.gov.uk).

For detailed information on travel health, including a country-by-country overview of diseases (and a list of travel clinics in the USA), try the **International Travel Health Guide,** by Stuart Rose, MD ($25; www.travmed.com). For general health info, contact the **American Red Cross** (☎202-303-4498; www.redcross.org).

# ONCE IN CALIFORNIA

## MEDICAL ASSISTANCE ON THE ROAD
In case of medical emergency, dial ☎911 from any phone and an operator will dispatch paramedics, a fire brigade, or the police as needed. Emergency medical care is also readily available in California at any emergency room on a walk-in basis. If you do not have insurance, you will have to pay for emergency and other medical care (see **Insurance,** p. 37). **Non-emergency care** is available at any hospital or doctor for a fee. Appointments are required for non-emergency medical services.

## ENVIRONMENTAL HAZARDS
**Heat exhaustion and dehydration:** Heat exhaustion leads to nausea, excessive thirst, headaches, and dizziness. Avoid it by drinking plenty of fluids, eating salty foods (e.g. crackers), and abstaining from dehydrating beverages (e.g. alcohol and caffeinated beverages). Continuous heat stress can eventually lead to heatstroke, characterized by a rising temperature, severe headache, delirium and cessation of sweating. Cool victims with wet towels and seek medical attention. Heat exhaustion is a significant concern in the California desert and can cause problems even in temperate locations.

**Sunburn:** It's all about having fun in the warm California sun. But with pleasure comes potential for pain—spending just 15 minutes in the bright sun can result in burns, and the sunburn-prone often burn even on cloudy days. Apply sunscreen liberally. If you get sunburned, drink more fluids than usual and apply an aloe-based lotion. Severe sunburns can lead to sun poisoning, a condition that affects the entire body, causing fever, chills, nausea, and vomiting. Sun poisoning should always be treated by a doctor.

**Hypothermia and frostbite:** A rapid drop in body temperature is the clearest sign of overexposure to cold. Victims may also shiver, feel exhausted, have poor coordination or slurred speech, hallucinate, or suffer amnesia. *Do not let hypothermia victims fall asleep.* To avoid hypothermia, keep dry, wear layers, and stay out of the wind. When the temperature is below freezing, watch out for frostbite. If skin turns white or blue, waxy, and cold, do not rub the area. Drink warm beverages, stay dry, and slowly warm the area with dry fabric or steady body contact until a doctor can be found.

**Earthquakes:** Running the length of California, the San Andreas and other faults occasionally shake, rattle, and roll everything in sight. While most temblors are harmless, stronger ones do strike in the state every few years. When you feel shaking, simply move away from any objects that could possibly fall on you; if indoors, duck underneath a desk or stand inside a doorway. In a car, pull over and wait for the quake to subside.

**High altitude:** Allow your body a couple of days to adjust to less oxygen at higher elevations. Altitude sickness/acute mountain sickness (AMS) is characterized by headaches, loss of appetite, fatigue, dizziness, and confusion. Those suffering from AMS should stop ascending in all cases and seriously consider descending in altitude. Note that the effects of alcohol are more potent and UV rays stronger at high elevations.

ESSENTIALS

## INSECT-BORNE DISEASES

Many diseases are transmitted by insects, mainly mosquitoes, fleas, ticks, and lice. While hiking and camping, particularly in wet and forested areas, wear long pants and long sleeves, tuck your pants into your socks, and use a mosquito net. Use insect repellents such as DEET and soak or spray your gear with permethrin (licensed in the US for use on clothing).

**Lyme disease:** A bacterial infection carried by ticks and marked by a circular bull's-eye rash of 2 in. or more. Ticks live on bushes and trees, and are especially common in rural, forested regions of the Pacific coast. Other symptoms include fever, headache, fatigue, and aches and pains. Antibiotics are effective if administered early. Untreated, Lyme can cause problems in joints, the heart, and the nervous system. If you find a tick attached to your skin, grasp the head with tweezers as close to your skin as possible and apply slow, steady traction. Removing a tick within 24 hours greatly reduces the risk of infection. Do not try to remove ticks by burning them or coating them with nail polish remover or petroleum jelly.

## FOOD- & WATER-BORNE DISEASES

Prevention is the best cure: be sure that your food is properly cooked and the water you drink is clean. Virtually all tap water in California is chemically treated to be safe for drinking. Always wash your hands before eating.

**Traveler's diarrhea:** Results from drinking untreated water or eating uncooked foods. Symptoms include nausea, bloating, and urgency. Try quick-energy, non-sugary foods with protein and carbohydrates to keep your strength up. Over-the-counter anti-diarrheals (e.g. Imodium) may help. The most dangerous side effect is dehydration; drink 8 oz. of water with ½ teaspoon of sugar or honey and a pinch of salt, uncaffeinated soft drinks, or eat salted crackers. If you develop a fever or your symptoms don't go away after 5 days, consult a doctor. For children with diarrhea, consult a doctor immediately.

**Dysentery:** Results from a serious intestinal infection caused by certain bacteria. The most common type is bacillary dysentery, also called shigellosis. Symptoms include bloody diarrhea (sometimes mixed with mucus), fever, and abdominal pain and tenderness. Bacillary dysentery generally only lasts a week, but it is highly contagious. Amoebic dysentery, which develops more slowly, is a more serious disease and may cause long-term damage if left untreated. A stool test can determine which kind you have; seek medical help immediately. Bacillary dysentery can be treated with the drugs norfloxacin or ciprofloxacin (commonly known as Cipro). If you are traveling in high-risk (especially rural) regions, consider obtaining a prescription before you leave home.

**Giardiasis:** Transmitted through parasites (microbes, tapeworms, etc.) and acquired by drinking or cooking with untreated water from streams or lakes. Symptoms include stomach cramps, bloating, fatigue, weight loss, flatulence, nausea, and diarrhea.

## OTHER INFECTIOUS DISEASES

**Rabies:** Transmitted through the saliva of infected animals; fatal if untreated. By the time symptoms (thirst, malaise, fever, headache and muscle spasms) appear, the disease is in its terminal stage. If you are bitten, wash the wound thoroughly, seek immediate medical care, and try to have the animal located. A rabies vaccine, which consists of 3 shots given over a 28-day period, is available but is only semi-effective.

**Hepatitis B:** A viral infection of the liver transmitted via bodily fluids or needle-sharing. Symptoms, which may not surface until years after infection, include jaundice, loss of appetite, fever, and joint pain. A 3-shot vaccination sequence is recommended for health-care workers, sexually active travelers, and anyone planning to seek medical treatment abroad; it must begin 6 mo. before traveling.

**Hepatitis C:** Like Hepatitis B, but the mode of transmission differs. IV drug users, those with occupational exposure to blood, hemodialysis patients, and blood transfusion recipients are at the highest risk, but the disease can also be spread through sexual contact or sharing items like razors and toothbrushes that may have traces of blood.

## AIDS, HIV, & STDS

For detailed information on **Acquired Immune Deficiency Syndrome (AIDS)** in the US, call the **US Centers for Disease Control's** 24hr. hotline at ☎ 800-342-2437, or contact the **Joint United Nations Programme on HIV/AIDS (UNAIDS),** 20, ave. Appia, CH-1211 Geneva 27, Switzerland (☎ +41 22 791 3666; fax 22 791 4187; www.unaids.org).

The Council on International Educational Exchange's pamphlet *Travel Safe: AIDS and International Travel* is posted online at www.ciee.org/Isp/safety/travelsafe.htm, along with links to other online and phone resources. According to US law, HIV positive persons are not permitted to enter the US. HIV testing, however, is conducted only for those who are planning to immigrate permanently. Travelers from areas with particularly high concentrations of HIV positive persons or those with AIDS may be required to provide more info when applying.

**Sexually transmitted diseases** (STDs) such as gonorrhea, chlamydia, genital warts, syphilis, and herpes are easier to catch than HIV and can be just as serious. **Hepatitis B and C** can also be transmitted sexually (see p. 36). Though condoms may protect you from some STDs, oral or even tactile contact can lead to transmission. If you think you may have contracted an STD, see a doctor immediately.

# INSURANCE

Travel insurance generally covers four basic areas: medical/health problems, property loss, trip cancellation/interruption, and emergency evacuation. Although your regular insurance policies may well extend to travel-related accidents, you may consider purchasing travel insurance if the cost of potential trip cancellation/interruption or emergency medical evacuation is greater than your current insurance can absorb. Prices for travel insurance purchased separately generally run about $40 per week for full coverage.

**Medical insurance** (especially university policies) often covers costs incurred abroad; check with your provider. **US Medicare** does not cover foreign travel, with the exception of travel to Canada and Mexico. **Canadians** are protected by their home province's health insurance plan for up to 90 days after leaving Canada; check with the provincial Ministry of Health or Health Plan Headquarters for details. **Homeowners' insurance** often covers theft during travel, as well as loss of travel documents (passport, plane ticket, railpass, etc.) up to $500.

**ISIC** and **ITIC** (see p. 28) provide basic insurance benefits, including $100 per day of in-hospital sickness for up to 60 days, $3000 of accident-related medical reimbursement, and $25,000 for emergency medical transport. Cardholders have access to a toll-free 24hr. helpline (run by the insurance provider **TravelGuard**) for medical, legal, and financial emergencies (US and Canada ☎ 877-370-4742). **American Express** (US ☎ 800-528-4800) grants some cardholders automatic car rental insurance (collision and theft, but not liability) and ground travel accident coverage of $100,000 on flight purchases made with the card.

**INSURANCE PROVIDERS. STA** (see p. 50) offers a range of plans that can supplement your basic coverage. Other private insurance providers in the US and Canada include: **Access America** (☎ 866-807-3982; www.accessamerica.com); **Berkeley Group** (☎ 800-797-4514; www.berkely.com); **GlobalCare Insurance Services Inc.** (☎ 800-821-2488; www.globalcare-cocco.com); and **Travel Assistance International** (☎ 800-821-2828; www.travelassistance.com). Providers in the **UK** include **Columbus Direct** (☎ 020 7375 0011; www.columbusdirect.co.uk). In **Australia,** try **AFTA** (☎ 02 9264 3299; www.afta.com.au).

# PACKING

**Pack lightly:** Lay out only what you absolutely need, then take half the clothes and twice the money. If you plan to hike often, also see **Camping & the Outdoors,** p. 43.

**LUGGAGE.** If you plan to cover most of your itinerary by foot, a sturdy **frame backpack** is unbeatable. (For the basics on buying a pack, see p. 45.) Toting a **suitcase** or **trunk** is fine if you plan to live in one or two cities and explore from there, but not a great idea if you plan to move around frequently. In addition to your main piece of luggage, a **daypack** (a small backpack or courier bag) is useful.

**CLOTHING.** For travel in Northern California, pack layers of clothing—mornings and evenings tend to be cold year-round while days can vary drastically. A sweater and light jacket or windbreaker may be necessary even in mid-summer. From late fall to early spring, be sure to bring a rain jacket (Gore-Tex® is both waterproof and breathable) or umbrella and a mid-weight jacket or heavy sweater. Because Southern California is consistently warm and dry, you might be able to get away without much of the rain and cold gear, but be prepared for the occasional fluke cold front. Although heavy jackets are unnecessary on the coast or in the desert, pack heavy-duty gear for a trek into the snow-capped Sierra Nevadas or Cascades. Wherever you go, **sturdy shoes** and **thick socks** can save your feet. **Flip-flops** or waterproof sandals are crucial for grubby hostel showers. You may also want to add one outfit beyond the jeans and t-shirt uniform, and maybe a nicer pair of shoes. Remember that if you plan to visit any religious or cultural sites, you'll need something besides tank tops and shorts to be respectful.

**CONVERTERS & ADAPTERS.** In the US, electricity is 120 volts AC. **International travelers** using 220/240V electrical appliances should buy an **adapter** (which changes the shape of the plug) and a **converter** (which changes the voltage; $20). Don't make the mistake of using only an adapter (unless appliance instructions explicitly state otherwise). For more info, visit http://kropla.com/electric.htm.

**CELLULAR PHONES.** A cell phone can literally be a lifesaver on the road; it is highly recommended that travelers carry one, especially when traveling alone. Major cellular providers in California include Verizon (www.verizonwireless.com), Sprint (www.sprintpcs.com), and AT&T (www.attws.com).

**FIRST-AID KIT.** For a basic first-aid kit, pack: bandages, pain reliever, antibiotic cream, a thermometer, a Swiss Army knife, tweezers, moleskin, decongestant, motion-sickness remedy, diarrhea or upset-stomach medication (Pepto Bismol or Imodium), an antihistamine, sunscreen, insect repellent, and burn ointment.

**FILM.** Buying film and developing it in California is fairly affordable and very easy (it costs about $10 for a roll of 24 color exposures). Less serious photographers may want to bring a **disposable camera** or two rather than an expensive permanent one. Despite disclaimers, airport security X-rays *can* fog film, so buy a lead-lined pouch at a camera store or ask security to hand-inspect it. Always pack film in your carry-on luggage, since higher-intensity X-rays are used on checked luggage.

**OTHER USEFUL ITEMS.** For safety purposes, you should bring a **money belt** and small **padlock.** Basic **outdoors equipment** (water bottle, compass, waterproof matches, pocketknife, sunglasses, sunscreen, hat) may also prove useful. **Quick repairs** of torn garments can be done on the road with a needle and thread; also consider bringing electrical tape for patching tears. To do laundry by hand, bring detergent, a small rubber ball to stop up the sink, and string for a makeshift clothes line. **Other things** you might forget are: an umbrella, sealable plastic bags (for damp clothes, soap, food, shampoo, and other spillables), an alarm clock; safety pins, a flashlight, earplugs, garbage bags, and a small calculator.

# New Central Hotel & Hostel

250-bed hostel open all year
bunks and large doubles with regular mattresses
4 beds per room, private rooms
smoking and nonsmoking rooms

**$20***

☐ Shared Accomodations
☐ Double Rooms
☐ Private Rooms
☐ Free linen, kitchen
☐ Weekly Rates

*per night (depending on bed and season)
travelers' check, VISA, MasterCard accepted
passport and travel documents requested
no membership required

1412 Market Street
San Francisco, CA 94102
Phone: (415) 703-9988
Fax: (415) 703-9986
E-mail: Newcentralhotel@aol.com

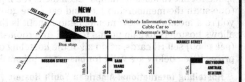

ESSENTIALS

**IMPORTANT DOCUMENTS.** Don't forget your passport, traveler's checks, ATM and/or credit cards, adequate ID, and photocopies of all of the aforementioned in case these documents are lost or stolen (see p. 28). Also check that you have any of the following that might apply: a hosteling membership card (see p. 40), driver's license (see p. 28), travel insurance forms, and/or rail or bus pass (see p. 53).

# ACCOMMODATIONS

## HOSTELS

Hostels are generally laid out dorm-style, often with large single-sex rooms and bunk beds, although a few also offer private rooms. They sometimes have kitchens and utensils, equipment rentals, storage areas, transportation to airports, breakfast, and laundry facilities. There can be drawbacks: some hostels close during certain daytime "lockout" hours, have a curfew, don't accept reservations, impose a maximum stay, or, less frequently, require that you do chores. In California, a dorm bed in a hostel will average around $15-25 per night. Many hostels require proof of foreign citizenship or international travel (such as an airline ticket).

 **A HOSTELER'S BILL OF RIGHTS.** There are certain standard features that we do not include in our hostel listings. Unless we state otherwise, you can expect that every hostel has no lockout, no curfew, a kitchen, free hot showers, some system of secure luggage storage, and no key deposit.

**BOOKING HOSTELS ONLINE** One of the cheapest and easiest ways to ensure a bed for a night is by reserving online. Our website features the **Hostelworld** booking engine; access it at **www.letsgo.com/resources/accommodations.** Hostelworld offers bargain accommodations everywhere from Argentina to Zimbabwe with no added commission.

**ESSENTIALS**

## HOSTELLING INTERNATIONAL

Joining a youth hostel association in your own country (listed below) automatically grants you membership privileges in **Hostelling International (HI),** a federation of national hosteling associations. HI hostels are scattered throughout California, and may accept reservations for a nominal fee via the **International Booking Network** (☎202-783-6161; www.hostelbooking.com). Two comprehensive hostelling websites are HI's umbrella organization's web page (www.iyhf.org), which lists contact info for national associations, and www.hostels.com/us.ca.html, which has hostels in California and other resources.

Most HI hostels also honor **guest memberships**—you'll get a blank card with space for six validation stamps. Each night you'll pay a nonmember supplement (one-sixth the membership fee) and earn one guest stamp; get six stamps, and you're a member. A new membership benefit is the Free Nites program, which allows hostelers to gain points toward free rooms. Most student travel agencies (see p. 50) sell HI cards, as do all of the hosteling organizations listed below. All prices listed below are valid for **one-year memberships** unless otherwise noted.

**Hostelling International-American Youth Hostels (HI-AYH),** 8401 Colesville Road, Suite 600, Silver Spring, MD, 20910 (☎301-495-1240; fax 495-6697; www.hiayh.org). US$28, over 55 US$18, under 18 free.

The HISTORICAL
# HOTEL STILLWELL
In the heart of the New Downtown

- 250 rooms, all with tub, shower, phone, color TV, air conditioning and maid service
- On-site coffee shop, Indian restaurant, Mexican restaurant and cocktail lounge.
- 5 minute walk to the Dodger, Staple and Convention Centers, MOCA, Disney Hall, and the Music Center.
- Convienient access to Universal Studios, Hollywood Mann's Chinese Theatre, Disneyland, L.A. night life and beaches
- Ample parking

Single Room $49 and up
Double Room $59 and up

L.A. Convention Center

838 South Grand Avenue • Los Angeles, California 90017
Tel: (213) 627-1151 • Fax: (213) 622-8940
For Reservations call Toll Free 1-800-553-4774
email: hstillwell@aol.com • www.stillwell-l.a.com

**Australian Youth Hostels Association (AYHA),** 11 Rawson Pl., Sydney, NSW 2000 (☎02 9281 9444; fax 9281 9311; www.yha.org.au). AUS$52, under 18 AUS$16.

**Hostelling International-Canada (HI-C),** 205 Catherine St. #400, Ottawa, ON K2P 1C3 (☎613-237-7884; fax 237-7868; www.hihostels.ca). CDN$35, under 18 free.

**An Óige (Irish Youth Hostel Association),** 61 Mountjoy St., Dublin 7 (☎830 4555; fax 830 5808; www.irelandyha.org). €25, under 18 €10.50.

**Youth Hostels Association of New Zealand (YHANZ),** P.O. Box 436, 166 Moorhouse Ave., Level 1, Moorhouse City, Christchurch (☎03 379 9970; fax 365 4476; www.yha.org.nz). NZ$40, under 18 free.

**Hostels Association of South Africa,** 3rd fl. 73 St. George's House, Cape Town 8001 (☎021 424 2511; fax 424 4119; www.hisa.org.za). R79, under 18 R40.

**Scottish Youth Hostels Association (SYHA),** 7 Glebe Crescent, Stirling FK8 2JA (☎ 870 1 55 32 55; fax 871 3308 562; www.syha.org.uk). UK£6, under 18 £2.50.

**Youth Hostels Association (England and Wales),** Trevelyon House, Dimple Rd., Matlock, Derbyshire DE4 3YH, UK (☎01629 5962600; fax 01629 592702; www.yha.org.uk). UK£13.50, under 18 UK£6.75.

ESSENTIALS

## HI-AYH COUNCIL OFFICES IN CALIFORNIA

**Golden Gate Council,** 425 Divisadero St. #307, San Francisco 94117 (☎415-863-1444, travel center 415-701-1320; hiayh@norcalhostels.org).

**Central California Council,** P.O. Box 2538, Monterey 93942 (☎209-383-0686; hiayh-ccc@aol.com).

**Los Angeles Council,** 1434 2nd St., Santa Monica 90401 (☎310-393-6263, travel center 310-393-3413; hiayhla@aol.com).

The Two Best-Kept Secrets in Hollywood

∞ THE HIDDEN HOSTELS ∞

Tucked away in the "Wilshire Miracle Mile" and Beverly Hills • Two charming and personally managed hideaways • Quietly famous for their high standards and low, reasonable rates • Now you know the secret too!

WILSHIRE-ORANGE HOTEL

6060 W. 8th St., Los Angeles, CA 90036
(323) 931-9533 PH
(310) 550-0374 FAX

One block south of Wilshire Blvd., one half-block east of Fairfax • Located in a quiet residential community • La Brea tar pits, LA County Museum, Farmer's Market, restaurants, buses, and Beverly Hills within walking distance • All rooms have color TV and refrigerators • Street parking • Please call in advance, reservations highly recommended • Rates from $45 (shared bath with one other room), private bath from $54 single/double occupancy, $10 each additional person

HOTEL DEL FLORES

409 N. Crescent Drive/P.O. Box 5708, Beverly Hills, CA 90210
(310) 274-5115 PH
(310) 550-0374 FAX

Splendid location, three blocks east of Rodeo Drive • 24-hour switchboard with phones in each room • Color TV • Refrigerators and microwave available • Central to buses, restuarants, and shopping • Area where stars—past, present, and future—live, dine, and play • Pay and free street parking can be negotiated • Rates from $55 (shared bath), private bath from $65, $10 each additional person

**San Diego Council,** 437 J St., #315 San Diego 92101 (☎619-338-9981; hiayhsd1@aol.com).

# OTHER TYPES OF ACCOMMODATIONS

## HOTELS

Hotel singles in California generally cost about $35-75 per night, and doubles are $50-100. You'll typically have a private bathroom and shower with hot water, though some cheaper places may offer only shared restrooms. Not all hotels take reservations, and few accept traveler's checks in a foreign currency.

## BED & BREAKFASTS (B&BS)

Cozy alternatives to impersonal hotels, B&Bs (private homes with rooms for travelers) range from decent to sublime. Rooms in B&Bs generally cost $50-70 for a single and $70-90 for a double in California, but on holidays or in expensive locations (such as Napa Valley), prices can soar to over $300. For more info on B&Bs, see **Bed & Breakfast Inns Online,** P.O. Box 829, Madison, TN 37116 (☎615-868-1946; www.bbonline.com), **InnFinder,** 6200 Gisholt Dr. #105, Madison, WI 53713 (☎608-285-6600; fax 285-6601; www.innfinder.com), or **InnSite** (www.innsite.com).

## UNIVERSITY DORMS

Many **colleges and universities** open their residence halls to travelers when school is not in session; UC Berkeley, for example, offers summer visitor housing on a per night basis. Getting a room may require some phone calls and advanced planning, but rates tend to be low, and many offer free local calls and Internet access.

# International House at the 2nd Floor

*"Hostelling Host to the Beach Areas!!"*

## 2 Great Locations

| PACIFIC BEACH | MISSION BEACH |
|---|---|
| 4501 Cass St. | 3204 Mission Blvd. |
| (at Garnet) | (at Ventura) |
| Tel: 858-274-4325 | Tel: 858-539-0043 |
| San Diego, CA | San Diego, CA |

*You want surf - We've got it!*
*You want non-stop partying - We have it!*
*You want prime location - We're at it!*
*You want to save money -*
*YEAH! $14 - $21 pp / night*

Email: the2ndfloorpb@aol.com • Fax: 858-483-5831
www.sandog.com/atthebeach/secondfloor.htm

# CAMPING & THE OUTDOORS

With proper equipment, camping is an inexpensive and relatively safe way to experience California's huge assortment of national parks and other scenic areas. California presents a variety of camping opportunities; few naturally spectacular areas in the world are as accessible to the traveler. An excellent resource for the adventure traveler is the **Great Outdoor Recreation Pages** (www.gorp.com).

## USEFUL PUBLICATIONS & RESOURCES

A variety of publishing companies offer hiking guidebooks to meet the educational needs of novice or expert. For information about camping, hiking and biking, write or call the publishers listed below to receive a free catalog.

**Family Campers and RVers/National Campers and Hikers Association, Inc.,** 4804 Transit Rd., Bldg. #2, Depew, NY 14043 (☎/fax 716-668-6242; www.fcrv.org). Membership fee ($25) includes their publication *Camping Today.*

**Sierra Club Books,** 85 Second St., 2nd fl., San Francisco, CA 94105 (☎415-977-5500; www.sierraclub.org/books). Publishes resource books on hiking, camping, and women traveling in the outdoors, as well as an array of California-specific hiking books.

**The Mountaineers Books,** 1001 SW Klickitat Way, #201, Seattle, WA 98134 (☎206-223-6303; fax 223-6306; www.mountaineersbooks.org). Over 400 titles on hiking, biking, mountaineering, natural history, and conservation.

**Wilderness Press,** 1200 Fifth St., Berkeley, CA 94710 (☎800-443-7227 or 510-558-1666; fax 558-1696; www.wildernesspress.com). Over 100 hiking guides and maps, including dozens for California.

**Woodall Publications Corporation,** 2575 Vista Del Mar Dr., Ventura, CA 93001 (☎800-323-9076 or 805-667-4100; www.woodalls.com). Woodall publishes the annually updated *Woodall's Campground Directory* ($22).

## NATIONAL PARKS

California has no less than eight national parks, and they contain some of the most spectacular and varied scenery found in the country. The state's most popular park is **Yosemite** (see p. 251), with extensive trails, jagged peaks, formidable rock faces, and awe-inspiring waterfalls. Beyond Yosemite, there are the enormous drive-through trees of **Sequoia** and **Kings Canyon** (see p. 270), the rock-climbing Mecca of **Joshua Tree** (see p. 529), the scorched desert beauty of **Death Valley,** and enough to make even the most weathered adventurer go wild, and the most frazzled city-dweller go still. (See **Suggested Itineraries: Park Avenue,** p. 6.)

The **National Park Service,** Fort Mason, Bldg. 201, San Francisco, CA 94111 (☎888-GO-PARKS/467-2757; www.nps.gov) provides info on the parks. The NPS sells an annual pass that grants admission to all national parks in the United States for $50 per year. Without a pass, most parks charge admission fees upon entering.

## WILDERNESS SAFETY

### THE GREAT OUTDOORS

**Stay warm, stay dry, and stay hydrated.** The vast majority of life-threatening wilderness situations can be avoided by following that simple advice. Prepare yourself for an emergency, however, by always packing rain gear, a hat and mittens, a first-aid kit, a reflector, a whistle, high energy food, and extra water for any hike. Dress in wool or warm layers of synthetic materials designed for the outdoors; never rely on cotton for warmth, as it is useless when wet.

Check **weather forecasts** and pay attention to the skies when hiking. Whenever possible, let someone know when and where you are going hiking, either a friend, your hostel, a park ranger, or a local hiking organization. Do not attempt a hike beyond your ability—you may be endangering your life. See **Health,** p. 34, for information about outdoor ailments and basic medical concerns.

## RATTLESNAKES WILL BITE YOU

Only 18% of snakes in California are venomous snakes (all rattlesnakes). The other 82% are only misunderstood. Rattlesnakes have broad, triangular heads and a rattle on the end of their tail, and are typically found in dry areas below 6000 feet, but have been known to range as high as 8000 feet. Exercise common sense by watching where you step, sit, reach, and tromp. Wear long pants and thick boots when exploring the outdoors. If you encounter a snake, stand still until it slithers away. If the snake is backed into a corner, stay still for a while and then back away slowly, stepping gently. Unless it is surprised and bites reflexively, a rattlesnake will coil defensively and shake its rattle before it strikes. If bitten, get to a medical facility as quickly as possible.

## BEARS WILL EAT YOU

If you are hiking in an area that might be frequented by bears, ask local rangers for information on bear behavior before entering any park or wilderness area, and obey posted warnings. No matter how irresistibly cute a bear appears, don't be fooled—they're powerful and unpredictable animals that are not intimidated by humans. If you're close enough for a bear to be observing you, you're too close. If you surprise the bear, speak in low, soothing tones (think Barry White) and back away slowly. Do not run, as tempting as it may be—the bear may identify you as prey and give chase. If you will be traveling extensively in bear-infested areas, consider taking **pepper spray.** If the bear attacks, spray at its face and eyes. Without pepper spray, different strategies should be used with different bear species. Black bears (black coloration, tall ears, no shoulder hump) are carrion eaters—if you play dead, you are giving them a free meal. The best course of action is to make noise and fight back—resistance will usually deter a black bear. If you're standing toe to toe with a grizzly bear (blonde-brown to black fur, distinct shoulder hump in profile, visible claws), a predator, fighting back will get you killed. Play dead—drop to the ground and shield your face and chest with your arms.

Don't leave food or other scented items (trash, toiletries, the clothes that you cooked in) near your tent Putting these objects into canisters is now mandatory in some national parks in California, including Yosemite. **Bear-bagging,** hanging edibles and other scented objects from a tree out of paws' reach, is the best way to keep your toothpaste from becoming a condiment. Bears are also attracted to **perfume,** so cologne, scented soap, deodorant, and hairspray should stay at home.

For more information, consult *How to Stay Alive in the Woods*, by Bradford Angier (Macmillan Press, $8).

## SHARKS WILL CHEW ON YOU

You are far, far more likely to suffer an injury from a bee sting or a toilet bowl than from a shark attack. Nevertheless, there are generally one or two unprovoked shark attacks per year along the California coast. Sharks hang out near steep dropoffs around sandbars and in prime feeding grounds, often marked by birds diving for fish. Sharks are most active at twilight or in darkness; they are attracted to erratic movements and bright colors. To avoid sharks, do not be mistaken for a seal or a fish. Don't wear shiny jewelry, which simulates the sheen of fish scales, and don't enter the water if you're bleeding (unless you're bleeding because you've been half-eaten by a bear, in which case you might as well).

# CAMPING & HIKING EQUIPMENT

## WHAT TO BUY...

Good camping equipment is both sturdy and light. Camping equipment is generally more expensive in Australia, New Zealand, and the UK than in North America. Also see **Going Hiking? Outdoor Equipment Tips From a Hiking Expert,** p. 230.

**Sleeping Bag:** Most sleeping bags are rated by season ("summer" means 30-40°F at night; "four-season" or "winter" often means below 0°F). They are made either of **down** (warmer and lighter, but miserable when wet) or of **synthetic** material (heavier, more durable, and warmer when wet). Prices range $80-210 for a summer synthetic to $250-300 for a good down winter bag. **Sleeping bag pads** include foam pads ($10-20), air mattresses ($15-50), and Therm-A-Rest self-inflating pads ($45-80).

**Tent:** The best tents are free-standing (with their own frames and suspension systems), set up quickly, and only require staking in high winds. Low-profile dome tents are the best all-around. Good 2-person tents start at $90, 4-person at $300. Seal the seams of your tent with waterproofer, and make sure it has a rain fly. Other tent accessories include a **battery-operated lantern,** a **plastic groundcloth,** and a **nylon tarp.**

**Backpack: Internal-frame packs** mold better to your back, keep a lower center of gravity, and flex adequately to allow you to hike difficult trails. **External-frame packs** are more comfortable for long hikes over even terrain, as they keep weight higher and distribute it more evenly. Make sure your pack has a strong, padded hip-belt to transfer weight to your legs. Any serious backpacking requires a pack of at least 4000 in.$^3$ (16,000cc), plus 500 in.$^3$ for sleeping bags in internal-frame packs. Sturdy backpacks cost anywhere from $125-420—this is one area in which it doesn't pay to economize. Fill up a pack with something heavy and walk around the store with it to get a sense of how it distributes weight before buying it. Either buy a **waterproof backpack cover,** or store all of your belongings in plastic bags inside your pack.

**Boots:** Be sure to wear hiking boots with good **ankle support.** They should fit snugly and comfortably over 1-2 pairs of wool socks and thin liner socks. Break in boots over several weeks before traveling in order to spare yourself painful and debilitating blisters.

**Other Necessities: Synthetic** layers, like those made of polypropylene, and a **pile jacket** will keep you warm even when wet. A **"space blanket"** helps to retain body heat and doubles as a groundcloth ($5-15). Bring a **plastic water bottle. Water-purification tablets** are useful for when you can't boil water. Although most campgrounds have campfire sites, it pays to bring a small **metal grate** or **grill.** For those places that forbid fires or the gathering of firewood, you'll need a **camp stove** (the classic Coleman starts at $40) and a propane-filled **fuel bottle** to operate it. Also don't forget a **first-aid kit, pocketknife, insect repellent, calamine lotion,** and **waterproof matches** or a **lighter.**

## ...AND WHERE TO BUY IT

The mail-order/online companies listed below offer lower prices than many retail stores, but a visit to a local camping or outdoors store will give you a good sense of the look and weight of certain items.

**Campmor,** 28 Parkway, P.O. Box 700, Upper Saddle River, NJ 07458 (☎888-226-7667, elsewhere US ☎201-825-8300; www.campmor.com).

**Discount Camping,** 880 Main North Rd., Pooraka, South Australia 5095, Australia (☎08 8262 3399; fax 8260 6240; www.discountcamping.com.au).

**Eastern Mountain Sports (EMS),** 1 Vose Farm Rd., Peterborough, NH 03458 (☎888-463-6367 or 603-924-7231; www.ems.com).

**L.L. Bean,** Freeport, ME 04033 (US and Canada ☎800-441-5713, UK 0800 891 297, other countries 207-552-3028; www.llbean.com).

ESSENTIALS

**Recreational Equipment, Inc. (REI),** Sumner, WA 98352 (US and Canada ☎800-426-4840, other countries 253-891-2500; www.rei.com).

**YHA Adventure Shop,** 19 High St., Middlesex, TW18 4QY, UK (☎1784 458625; fax 1784 464573; www.yhaadventure.com). Britain's largest outdoor equipment suppliers.

## CAMPERS & RVS

Renting an RV will always be more expensive than tenting or hostelling, but it's cheaper than staying in hotels and renting a car (see **Rental Cars,** p. 54), and the convenience of bringing along your own bedroom, bathroom, and kitchen makes it an attractive option. Rates vary widely by region, season, and type of RV. It always pays to contact several companies to compare vehicles and prices. **El Monte RVs** (☎800-337-2214; www.elmonterv.com) has nine locations in California.

## ORGANIZED ADVENTURE TRIPS

**Organized adventure tours** offer another way of exploring the wild. Tourism bureaus can often suggest outfitters; other good sources of info are specialty camping and outdoor stores and organizations like **REI** and **EMS** (see above).

**Specialty Travel Index,** 305 San Anselmo Ave., Ste. 309, San Anselmo, CA 94960 (☎888-624-4030 or 415-455-1643; fax 415-455-1648; www.specialtytravel.com). Worldwide tours.

**AmeriCan Adventures & Roadrunner,** P.O. Box 189, Rockaway, NJ 07866 (☎800-221-0596; in the UK +44 (0)1295 256 777; fax 973-903-8551; www.americanadventures.com). Organizes group adventure camping and hostelling trips (with transportation and camping costs included).

# KEEPING IN TOUCH

## BY MAIL

### DOMESTIC RATES

First-class letters sent and received within the US take 1-3 days and cost $0.37; **Priority Mail** packages up to 1 lb. generally take 2 days and cost $3.85, up to 5 lb. $7.70. **All days specified denote business days.** For more details, see www.usps.gov.

### SENDING MAIL FROM CALIFORNIA

**Airmail** is the best way to send mail home from the US. **Aerogrammes,** one form of airmail, are printed sheets that fold into envelopes and are available at post offices. Write "*par avion*" or "air mail" on the front. Most post offices will charge exorbitant fees or simply refuse to send aerogrammes with enclosures. **Surface mail** is by far the cheapest and slowest way to send mail. It takes one to three months to cross the Atlantic and two to four to cross the Pacific—good for items such as souvenirs or other articles you've acquired along the way that are weighing down your pack. For all the countries below save Canada, postcards and aerogrammes cost 70¢, and letters up to 1 oz. cost 80¢. Allow 5-7 days for regular airmail home. These are standard rates for packages from the US to:

**Australia:** Packages up to 1 lb. $14.50, up to 5 lb. $32.75.

**Canada:** Postcards/aerogrammes 50¢. Letters up to 1 oz. cost 60¢. Packages up to 1 lb. $13.25, up to 5 lb. $16.75.

# GREEN TORTOISE ADVENTURE TRAVEL

**Unique camping treks in comfortable converted sleeper coaches**

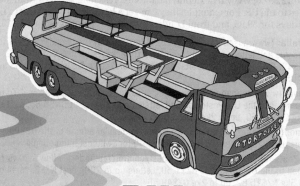

▲ **BAJA** ▲
▲ **LA RUTA MAYA** ▲
▲ **COPPER CANYON** ▲
▲ **GUATEMALA** ▲
▲ **BELIZE** ▲
▲ **HONDURAS** ▲
▲ **NICARAGUA** ▲
▲ **COSTA RICA** ▲

**GREEN TORTOISE ADVENTURE TRAVEL**
**GOOD PEOPLE, GREAT FOOD, REAL TIMES**

**494 BROADWAY, SAN FRANCISCO, CA. 94133**
**USA & CANADA: 800-TORTOISE**
**S.F. BAY AREA & WORLDWIDE: 415-956-7500**

**VISIT OUR WEB SITE: www.greentortoise.com**

**Ireland:** Up to 1 lb. $14, up to 5 lb. $22.75.

**New Zealand:** Up to 1 lb. $12.50, up to 5 lb. $28.75.

**The UK:** Up to 1 lb. $16, up to 5 lb. $32.

## SENDING MAIL TO CALIFORNIA

**Mark envelopes "air mail" or "*par avion*,"** or your letter or postcard will never arrive. In addition to the standard postage system whose rates are listed below, **Federal Express** (☎ 800-247-4747; in Australia 13 26 10; in New Zealand 0800 73 33 39; in the UK 0800 12 38 00; www.fedex.com) handles express mail services from most home countries to the US. For example, they can get a letter from New York to Los Angeles in 2 days for $9.95, and from London to New York in 2 days for UK£25.80.

**Australia:** (www.auspost.com.au/pac). Allow 4-6 days for regular airmail to the US. Postcards and letters up to 20g cost AUS$1; packages up to 0.5kg AUS$12, up to 2kg AUS$42. **EMS** (not the US sportswear chain store) can get a letter to the US in 2-5 days for AUS$33.

**Canada:** (www.canadapost.ca/personal/rates/us/default-e.asp). Allow 4-7days for regular airmail to the US. Postcards and letters up to 30g cost CDN$0.65; packages up to 0.5kg CDN$5.60, up to 2kg CDN$15.95.

**Ireland:** (www.letterpost.ie). Allow 5-6 days for regular airmail to the US. Postcards and letters up to 25g cost IR£0.57. Add IR£3.40 for Swiftpost International.

**New Zealand:** (www.nzpost.co.nz/nzpost/control/ratefinder). Allow 7 days for regular airmail to the US. Postcards NZ$1.50. Letters up to 200g cost NZ$2; small parcels up to 0.5kg NZ$15.82, up to 2kg NZ$49.56.

**UK:** Allow 4 days for airmail to the US. Letters up to 20g cost UK£0.68; packages up to 0.5kg UK£4.77, up to 2kg UK£17.89. **UK Swiftair** (www.consignia-online.com) delivers letters a day faster for UK£3.30 more.

## RECEIVING MAIL

Mail can be sent via **General Delivery** to almost any city or town with a post office. Address letters to:

Marilyn MONROE

General Delivery

Truckee, CA 96161

USA

The mail will go to a special desk in the central post office, unless you specify a post office by street address or postal code. It's best to use the largest post office, since mail may be sent there regardless of what is written on the envelope. It is usually safer and quicker to send mail express or registered. When picking up your mail, bring a form of photo ID, preferably a passport.

## BY TELEPHONE

## CALLING HOME FROM CALIFORNIA

A **calling card** is probably your cheapest bet. Calls are billed collect or to your account. **To call home with a calling card,** contact the operator for your service provider in the United States by dialing the given toll-free access number.

You can often also make **direct international calls** from pay phones, but if you aren't using a calling card, you may need to drop coins as quickly as your words. Where available, prepaid phone cards (see below) and occasionally major credit cards can be used for direct international calls, but they are still less cost-effective.

Don't be left out...

# Get your travel on.
## The International Student Identity Card

$22 is all it takes to save hundreds.

Accepted worldwide for awesome discounts!

The International Student Identity Card (ISIC) is a great way to take advantage of discounts and benefits such as airfare, accommodations, transportation, attractions, theme parks, hotels, theaters, car rentals and more!

visit www.ISICus.com to find out about discounts and the benefits of carrying your ISIC.

Call or visit STA Travel online to find the nearest issuing office and purchase your card today:

www.ISICus.com          (800) 474.8214

# enough already...
# Get a room.

## Book your next hotel with the people who know what you want.

» hostels
» budget hotels
» hip hotels
» airport transfers
» city tours
» adventure packages
» and more!

**(800) 777.0112**
**www.statravel.com/hotels**

## STA TRAVEL

**WE'VE BEEN THERE.**

Exciting things are happening at www.statravel.com

## CALLING WITHIN CALIFORNIA

The simplest way to call within the country is to use a coin-operated pay phone. You can also buy prepaid phone cards, which carry a certain amount of phone time. Phone rates typically tend to be highest during the morning and work hours (9am-5pm), lower in the evening, and lowest on Sunday and late at night.

*Let's Go* has recently partnered with ekit.com to provide a calling card that offers a number of services, including email and voice messaging. Before purchasing any calling card, always be sure to compare rates with other cards, and to make sure it serves your needs (a local phonecard is generally better for local calls, for instance). For more information, visit www.letsgo.ekit.com.

## TIME DIFFERENCES

California is 8 hours behind Greenwich Mean Time (GMT). The entire state observes daylight savings time, so clocks are set forward one hour in the spring and backward one hour in the fall.

| 4AM | 7AM | NOON | 2PM | 7PM | 9PM |
|------|------|------|------|------|------|
| Vancouver | Toronto | London | Istanbul | Beijing | Sydney |
| Seattle | New York | (GMT) | Jerusalem | Hong Kong | Canberra |
| San Francisco | Philadelphia | Lisbon | Cairo | Manila | Melbourne |
| Los Angeles | Boston | Dublin | Riyadh | Singapore | |

# BY EMAIL AND INTERNET

Though in some places it's possible to forge a remote link with your home server, in most cases this is a much slower (and thus more expensive) option than taking advantage of free **web-based email accounts** (e.g., www.hotmail.com and www.yahoo.com). Travelers with laptops can call an Internet service provider via a **modem.** Long-distance phone cards specifically intended for such calls can defray normally high phone charges; check with your long-distance phone provider to see if it offers this option. Most California cities have public libraries with free Internet terminals. Establishments offering **Internet access** are listed in the **Practical Information** sections of those cities. Additional cybercafes throughout the Golden State can be found at www.cyberiacafe.net/cyberia/guide/ccafe.htm.

# GETTING TO CALIFORNIA

## BY PLANE

When it comes to airfare, a little effort can save you a bundle. If your plans are flexible enough to deal with the restrictions, courier fares are the cheapest. Tickets bought from consolidators and standby seating are also good deals, but last-minute specials, airfare wars, and charter flights often beat these fares. The key is to hunt around, to be flexible, and to ask persistently about discounts. Students, seniors, and those under 26 should never pay full price for a ticket.

## AIRFARES

Airfares to California remain steady throughout the year, save for a peak in prices during the summer; national holidays are also expensive. It is cheapest to travel midweek (M-Th morning), as round-trip prices are often bumped up $40-50 on the weekend. Traveling with an "open return" ticket or arriving in and departing from different cities ("open-jaw") can be pricier than round-trip flights. Patching one-way flights together is the most expensive way to travel. Flights from or to major cities such as San Francisco, Los Angeles, and San Diego will tend to be cheaper.

ESSENTIALS

ESSENTIALS

If California is only one stop on a more extensive globe-hop, consider a **Round-the-World (RTW)** ticket. Tickets usually include at least five stops and are valid for about a year; prices range $1200-5000. Try World Perks at **Northwest Airlines/KLM** (☎800-447-4747; www.nwa.com) or **Star Alliance** (www.staralliance.com), a consortium of 22 airlines including **United Airlines** (☎800-241-6522; www.united.com).

The chart below shows sample round-trip fares between various destinations and either of the two major airport hubs in California—San Francisco (SFO) or Los Angeles (LAX), with LAX typically being the cheaper of the two. Be forewarned that airline prices change frequently; these are just estimates.

| ROUND-TRIP BETWEEN CALIFORNIA AND: | PRICE (IN US$) |
|---|---|
| Any North American destination | $200-650 |
| UK and Ireland | $350-1100 |
| Sydney, Australia | $900-1200 |
| Auckland, New Zealand | $850-1200 |
| Cape Town or Johannesburg | $950-1400 |

# BUDGET & STUDENT TRAVEL AGENCIES

While knowledgeable agents specializing in flights to California can make your life easy and help you save, they may not spend the time to find you the lowest possible fare—they get paid on commission. Travelers holding **ISIC and IYTC cards** (see p. 28) qualify for big discounts from student travel agencies. Most flights from budget agencies are on major airlines, but in peak season some may sell seats on less reliable chartered aircraft.

**USIT,** 19-21 Aston Quay, Dublin 2 (☎01 602 1600; www.usitworld.com). Ireland's leading student/budget travel agency has 22 offices throughout Northern Ireland and the Republic of Ireland. Offers programs to work in North America.

**CTS Travel,** 30 Rathbone Pl., London W1T 1GQ, UK (☎020 7290 0630; www.ctstravel.co.uk). A British student travel agency with offices in 39 countries including the US: Empire State Building, 350 Fifth Ave., Suite 7813, New York, NY 10118 (☎877-287-6665; www.ctstravelusa.com).

**STA Travel,** 7890 S. Hardy Dr., Ste. 110, Tempe AZ 85284 (24hr. reservations and info ☎800-781-4040; www.sta-travel.com). A student and youth travel organization with over 150 offices worldwide (check their website for a listing of all their offices), including US offices in Boston, Chicago, LA, New York, San Francisco, Seattle, and Washington, D.C. Ticket booking, travel insurance, railpasses, and more. In the UK, walk-in office 11 Goodge St., **London** W1T 2PF (☎020 7436 7779). In New Zealand, Shop 2B, 182 Queen St., **Auckland** (☎09 309 0458). In Australia, 366 Lygon St., **Carlton** Vic 3053 (☎03 9349 4344).

**Travel CUTS (Canadian Universities Travel Services Limited),** 187 College St., **Toronto,** ON M5T 1P7 (☎416-979-2406; fax 979-8167; www.travelcuts.com). Offices across Canada and the United States in Seattle, San Francisco, Los Angeles, New York and elsewhere. Also in the UK, 295-A Regent St., **London** W1B 2H9 (☎0207 255 2191).

# COMMERCIAL AIRLINES

The commercial airlines' lowest regular offer is the **APEX** (Advance Purchase Excursion) fare, which provides confirmed reservations and allows "open-jaw" tickets. Generally, reservations must be made seven to 21 days ahead of departure, with seven- to 14-day minimum-stay and up to 90-day maximum-stay restrictions. These fares carry hefty cancellation and change penalties (fees rise in summer). Book peak-season APEX fares early; by May you will have a hard time getting your desired departure date. Use **Microsoft Expedia** (www.expedia.com) or **Travelocity** (www.travelocity.com) to get an idea of the lowest published fares, then use the resources outlined here to try and beat those fares.

## STANDBY FLIGHTS

Traveling standby requires considerable flexibility in arrival and departure dates. Companies dealing in standby flights sell vouchers rather than tickets, along with the promise to get to your destination (or near your destination) within a certain window of time (typically 1-5 days). You call in before your specific window of time to hear your flight options and the probability that you will be able to board each flight. You can then decide which flights you want to try to make, show up at the appropriate airport at the appropriate time, present your voucher, and board if space is available. Vouchers can usually be bought for both one-way and round-trip travel. You may receive a monetary refund only if every available flight within your date range is full; if you opt not to take an available (but perhaps less convenient) flight, you can only get credit toward future travel. Carefully read agreements with any company offering standby flights as tricky fine print can leave you in a lurch. To check on a company's service record in the US, call the Better Business Bureau (☎212-533-6200). It is difficult to receive refunds, and clients' vouchers will not be honored when an airline fails to receive payment in time.

## TICKET CONSOLIDATORS

Ticket consolidators, or "bucket shops," buy unsold tickets in bulk from commercial airlines and sell them at discounted rates. The best place to look is in the Sunday travel section of any major newspaper (such as *The New York Times*), where many bucket shops place tiny ads. Call quickly, as availability is typically extremely limited. Not all bucket shops are reliable, so insist on a receipt that gives full details of restrictions, refunds, and tickets, and pay by credit card (in spite of the 2-5% fee) so you can stop payment if you never receive your tickets. For more info, see www.travel-library.com/air-travel/consolidators.html.

### TRAVELING FROM THE US & CANADA

**Travel Avenue** (☎800-333-3335; www.travelavenue.com) searches for best available published fares and then uses several consolidators to attempt to beat that fare. Other consolidators worth trying are **Interworld** (☎305-443-4929; fax 443-0351); **Pennsylvania Travel** (☎800-331-0947); **Rebel** (☎800-227-3235; www.rebeltours.com); and **Travac** (☎800-872-8800; fax 212-714-9063; www.travac.com). Other consolidators on the web include the **Internet Travel Network** (www.itn.com); **Travel Information Services** (www.tiss.com); **TravelHUB** (www.travelhub.com); and **The Travel Site** (www.thetravelsite.com). Keep in mind that these are just suggestions to get you started; *Let's Go* does not endorse any of these agencies. As always, be cautious, and research companies before you hand over your credit card number.

## CHARTER FLIGHTS

Charters are flights a tour operator contracts with an airline to fly extra loads of passengers during peak season. Charter flights fly less frequently than major airlines, make refunds particularly difficult, and are almost always fully booked. Schedules and itineraries may also change or be cancelled at the last moment (as late as 48 hours before the trip, and without a full refund), and check-in, boarding, and baggage claim are often much slower. However, they can also be cheaper.

**Discount clubs** and **fare brokers** offer members savings on last-minute charter and tour deals. Study contracts closely; you don't want to end up with an unwanted overnight layover. **Travelers Advantage,** Trumbull, CT, USA (☎877-259-2691; www.travelersadvantage.com; a US$60 annual fee includes discounts and cheap flight directories), can provide more information.

---

 **FLIGHT PLANNING ON THE INTERNET.**
Many airline sites offer special last-minute deals on the Web. Other sites do the legwork and compile the deals for you—try www.bestfares.com, www.flights.com, www.lowestfare.com, www.onetravel.com, and www.travelzoo.com.

■ **StudentUniverse** (www.studentuniverse.com), **STA** (www.sta-travel.com), and **Orbitz.com** provide quotes on student tickets, while **Expedia** (www.expedia.com) and **Travelocity** (www.travelocity.com) offer full travel prices. **Priceline** (www.priceline.com) allows you to specify a price, and obligates you to buy any ticket that meets or beats it; be prepared for antisocial hours and odd routes. **Skyauction** (www.skyauction.com) allows you to bid on both last-minute and advance-purchase tickets.

An indispensable resource on the Internet is the *Air Traveler's Handbook* (www.cs.cmu.edu/afs/cs/user/mkant/Public/Travel/airfare.html), a comprehensive listing of links to everything you need to know before you board a plane.

---

# GETTING AROUND CALIFORNIA

## BY PLANE

It is possible to fly between the Bay Area and Southern California for surprisingly little—in fact, flying is often cheaper than traveling by train or bus. **Southwest Airlines** (☎800-I-FLY-SWA/435-9792; www.southwest.com) frequently offers $39 or $49 one-way deals between Oakland or San Jose and Los Angeles or San Diego. **United Airlines** (☎800-241-6522; www.united.com) also frequently offers deals between the Bay Area and the Southland. Intrastate flights can also be caught from Orange County and Sacramento.

## BY TRAIN

Locomotion is still one of the least expensive (and most pleasant) ways to tour the US and Canada, but discounted air travel may be cheaper, and much faster, than train travel. As with airlines, you can save money by purchasing your tickets as far in advance as possible, so plan ahead and make reservations early. It is essential to travel light on trains; not all stations will check your baggage.

### AMTRAK

Amtrak (☎800-872-7245; www.amtrak.com) is the only provider of intercity passenger train service in California. Most cities have Amtrak offices which directly sell tickets, but tickets must be bought through an agent in some small towns. The web page lists up-to-date schedules, fares, arrival and departure info, and allows you to make reservations. **Discounts** on full rail fares are given to: senior citizens (15% off), Student Advantage cardholders (15% off; call ☎800-962-6872 to purchase the $20 card), travelers with disabilities (15% off), ages 2-15 accompanied by a paying adult (50% off), children under 2 (free), and current members of the US armed forces, active-duty veterans, and their dependents (25% off; www.veteransadvantage.com). "Rail SALE" offers online discounts of up to 90%. Amtrak also offers some **special packages**—check the website or call for more information.

ESSENTIALS

# BY BUS

Buses generally offer the most frequent and complete service between cities and towns in California. Often a bus is the only way to reach smaller, remote towns for those without a car. In rural areas and across open spaces, however, bus lines tend to be sparse. *Russell's Official National Motor Coach Guide* ($16 per issue including postage) is an invaluable tool for constructing an itinerary. Updated each month, *Russell's Guide* has schedules of every bus route (including Greyhound) between any two towns in the United States and Canada. *Russell's Guide* also publishes two semiannual supplements which are free when ordered with the main issue: a directory of bus lines and stations, and a series of route maps (both $9 if ordered separately). To order any of the above, write **Russell's Guides, Inc.,** P.O. Box 178, Cedar Rapids, IA 52406 (☎319-364-6138; fax 362-8808).

## GREYHOUND

Greyhound (☎800-231-2222; www.greyhound.com) is the only bus service that operates throughout the entire state. Reserve with a credit card over the phone at least 10 days in advance, and the ticket can be mailed anywhere in the US. Reservations are available only up to 24hr. in advance or at the bus terminal. Schedule information is available at any Greyhound terminal or agency and on the website.

**Advance purchase fares:** Reserving space far ahead of time ensures a lower fare, but expect smaller discounts between June 5 and Sept. 15. Fares are often lower for 14-day, 7-day, or 3-day advance purchases. For 3-day advance purchase M-Th, 2 people ride for the price of 1 ticket. Call for up-to-date pricing or consult the web site.

**Discounts on full fares:** Senior citizens with a Greyhound Senior Club Card (10% off); children ages 2-11 (50% off); Student Advantage card holders (up to 15% off); disabled travelers and an attendant (two tickets for the price of one); active and retired US military personnel and National Guard Reserves (10% off with valid ID); Veterans Administration affiliates (25% off with VA form 3068). With a ticket purchased 3 or more days in advance during the spring and summer months, a friend can travel along for free (with some exceptions).

**Ameripass:** ☎800-454-7277. Allows adults unlimited travel through the US. 7-day pass $229; 10-day pass $279; 15-day pass $349; 30-day pass $459; 45-day pass $519; 60-day pass $625. Student discounts available. Children's passes half-price. Before purchasing an Ameripass, total up the separate bus fares between towns to make sure that the pass is more economical or at least worth the flexibility it provides.

**International Ameripass:** For travelers from outside North America. ☎800-454-7277 for info. 7-day pass $219; 10-day pass $269; 15-day pass $329; 30-day pass $439; 45-day pass $489; 60-day pass $599. International Ameripasses are not available at the terminal; they can be purchased in foreign countries at Greyhound-affiliated agencies; telephone numbers are listed on the website. Passes can also be ordered at the website, or purchased by calling ☎800-229-9424 in the US.

## GREEN TORTOISE

Green Tortoise, 494 Broadway, San Francisco, CA 94133 (☎800-867-8647; www.greentortoise.com), offers a slow-paced, whimsical alternative to straightforward transportation. Green Tortoise's communal "hostels on wheels"—diesel buses remodeled for living and eating on the road—offer aptly named **Adventure Tours.** All tours depart from and return to San Francisco; travelers are responsible for getting to San Francisco themselves. Prices include transportation from San Francisco to the destination, sleeping space on the bus, tours of the regions

ESSENTIALS

through which you pass, and the cost of food for the communally prepared meals. Green Tortoise offers trips to Yosemite National Park (3 days June-Oct., $180; 2 days Apr.-Sept., $135) and Death Valley National Park (3 days, $200), as well as other tours in the continental US. Prepare for an earthy trip; buses have no toilets or showers and little privacy. Reserve one to two months in advance. Deposits ($50 for California trips) are generally required; however, many trips have space available at departure. Reservations can be made over the phone or online.

## ADVENTUREBUS

Run by **AdventurePlanet**, 34560 Ave. B, Yucaipa, CA 92399 (☎888-737-5263, outside the US 001-208-726-8410; www.adventurebus.com), AdventureBus runs fun-packed tours through cities, towns, and national parks in California and the Western US. Transportation in "extremely unconventional" buses driven by knowledge-able guides provides fun and like-minded company. $450 for the Grand Canyon Super Loop; nine- to 16-day trips run from $700.

## CONTIKI

For those who want someone else to do the itinerary planning for them, Contiki Travel (☎1-888-CONTIKI/266-8454; www.contiki.com) runs comprehensive bus tours starting at $575 for six days. Tours include accommodations, transportation, and some meals.

# BY CAR

## ▨ AMERICAN AUTOMOBILE ASSOCIATION (AAA)

AAA is the high priest of California's vehicular religion. To join the automobile club, call 800-JOIN-AAA/564-6222 or go to www.aaa.com. AAA offers free trip-planning services, maps, and guidebooks, and 24hr. emergency road service any-where in the US (☎800-AAA-HELP/222-4357). Also included are free towing and commission-free American Express Traveler's Cheques from over 1000 offices across the country, as well as discounts on Hertz car rental (5-20%), Amtrak tick-ets (10%), and various motel chains and theme parks. AAA has reciprocal agree-ments with the auto associations of many other countries, which often provide you with full benefits while in the US. Check with your auto association for details. Membership in the California branch costs $64 to join and $44 per year, plus $21 for each additional family member. Costs at other AAA branches vary slightly.

## RENTING

**Car rental agencies** fall into two categories: national companies with hundreds of branches, and local agencies that serve only one city or region. National chains usually allow you to pick up a car in one city and drop it off in another. There is usually a minimum rental period and a hefty drop-off charge of several hundred dollars). The drawbacks of car rentals include steep prices (a com-pact car rents for $25-45 per day) and high minimum ages for rentals (usually 25). But in a state that glorifies cruisin' the freeway, rental cars can be your ticket to freedom and control over your itinerary. Most branches rent to cus-tomers ages 21 to 24 with an additional fee, but policies and prices vary from agency to agency. **Alamo** (☎800-327-9633; www.alamo.com) rents to customers ages 21 to 24 with a major credit card for an additional $20 per day. **Enterprise** (☎800-736-8222; www.enterprise.com) rents to customers ages 21 to 24 with a variable surcharge. **Dollar** (☎800-800-4000; www.dollar.com) and **Thrifty** (☎800-367-2277; www.thrifty.com) locations do likewise for varying surcharges. **Rent-A-Wreck** (☎800-944-7501; www.rent-a-wreck.com) specializes in supplying vehi-cles that are past their prime for lower-than-average prices; a bare-bones compact less than eight years old rents for around $20 to $25. There may be an additional charge for a **collision and damage waiver (CDW)**, which usually comes to about $12 to 15 per day. Major credit cards (including MasterCard and American Express) will sometimes cover the CDW if you use their card to rent a car; call your credit card company for specifics.

Because it is mandatory for all drivers in the US, make sure with your rental agency that you are covered by **insurance.** Be sure to ask whether the price includes insurance against theft and collision. Some credit cards cover standard insurance. If you rent, lease, or borrow a car, and you are not from the US or Canada, you will need a **green card,** or **International Insurance Certificate,** to certify that you have liability insurance and that it applies abroad. Green cards can be obtained at car rental agencies, car dealerships, some travel agents, and some border crossings. If you are driving a conventional rental vehicle on an **unpaved road,** you are almost never covered by insurance.

**AUTO TRANSPORT COMPANIES.** These services match drivers with car owners who need cars moved from one city to another. Would-be travelers give the company their desired destination and the company finds a car that needs to go there. Expenses include gas, tolls, and your own living expenses. Some companies insure their cars; with others, your security deposit covers any breakdowns or damage. You must be over 21, have a valid license, and agree to drive about 400 mi. per day on a fairly direct route. Popular transport companies include: **Auto Driveaway Co.,** 310 S. Michigan Ave., Chicago, IL 60604-4298 (☎800-346-2277; www.autodriveaway.com). **Across America Driveaway,** 936 Hermosa Ave., Hermosa Beach, CA 90254 (☎800-677-6686; www.schultz-international.com).

## INTERNATIONAL DRIVING PERMIT

If you do not have a license issued by a US state or Canadian province or territory, you might want an International Driving Permit (IDP). While the US allows you to drive with a foreign license for up to a year, the IDP may facilitate things with police if your license is not in English. You must carry your home license with your IDP at all times. You must be 18 to obtain an IDP, which is valid for a year, and must be issued in the country in which your license originates.

## CAR INSURANCE

Collision insurance is required by state law in California. Most credit cards cover standard insurance. If you rent, lease, or borrow a car, you will need a **green card** or **International Insurance Certificate** to certify that you have liability insurance and that it applies abroad. Green cards can be obtained at car rental agencies, car dealers (for those leasing cars), some travel agents, and some border crossings.

## ON THE ROAD

Tune up the car before you leave, make sure the tires are in good condition and are properly inflated, and obtain comprehensive, dependable maps. **Rand McNally's Road Atlas,** covering all of the US and Canada, is one of the best (available at bookstores and gas stations, $11; California state map $5). If staying in major California cities for an extended period of time, you may want to invest in a Thomas Guide ($30) for the county or counties in which you are staying. A **compass** and a **car manual** can also be very useful. Always carry a **spare tire** and **jack, jumper cables, extra oil, flares,** a **flashlight,** and **blankets** (in case you break down at night or in winter). If you don't know how to **change a tire,** learn before heading out, especially if you are planning to travel in deserted areas. Blowouts on dirt roads are exceedingly common. If you do

E S S E N T I A L S

have a breakdown, **stay with your car;** if you wander off, there's less likelihood trackers will find you. Those traveling long, isolated stretches of road may want to consider purchasing a **cell phone** in case of a breakdown.

When traveling in the summer or in the desert, bring lots of **water** (a suggested 5 liters of water per person per day) for drinking and for the radiator. Refer to **Desert Survival** (see p. 528) for essential desert driving tips. The California Department of Transportation also has a road conditions hotline at ☎ 800-427-7623.

When driving, buckle up—seat belts are required by law in California. The speed limit in California varies depending on the road (some rural freeways have speed limits as high as 75mph, while residential areas are generally under 35mph). Heed speed limits at all times; not only does it save gas, but most local police and highway patrolmen make frequent use of radar and airplanes to catch speed demons, for whom fines range from $100-$150. Gas in California costs around $2.00 per gallon, but prices vary widely depending on geographical area and the whims of OPEC. Drivers should take necessary precautions against carjacking, a frequent crime in the state. Carjackers, who are usually armed, approach victims in their vehicles and force them to turn over their cars. **Sleeping in a car or van** parked in the city is both illegal and extremely dangerous. Don't do it.

**HOW TO NAVIGATE THE INTERSTATES.** A number of major interstates and highways criss-cross California. Travelers moving north-south have the choice of three major routes. If you're looking for speed, hop on **Interstate 5,** which runs north-south from Oregon through Sacramento, the San Joaquin Valley, Los Angeles, and San Diego on its way to the Mexican border. I-5 is the most direct and fastest route from LA to San Francisco (6-8hr.), but it's also painfully boring, affording at best a numbing view of Central Valley farms, flatlands and pungent cow pastures. Parallel to I-5, **US 101** winds closer to the coast, through Eureka, Santa Rosa, San Francisco, San Luis Obispo, and Santa Barbara, ending in LA With a travel time of eight to 10 hours from San Francisco to LA, it's slower than I-5, but a considerably more scenic and pleasant drive. The third option is ◪**Highway 1,** the Pacific Coast Highway (PCH), which hugs the California coast. PCH is very slow, contorted, and often traffic-congested, but the scenery is some of the most spectacular in the world, particularly on the breathtaking, cliff-hanging turns of Big Sur (see p. 344). California's east-west routes are more simple. I-80 heads east from San Francisco to Sacramento and climbs through the Sierra Nevada to North Lake Tahoe and Reno. Further south, I-10 moves east from LA to Palm Springs and Joshua Tree, intersecting near San Bernadino with I-15, which cruises northeast to Las Vegas.

# BY TWO WHEELS

## BY BICYCLE

Safe and secure cycling requires a quality helmet and lock. A good helmet costs about $40—much cheaper than critical head surgery. U-shaped **Kryptonite** or **Citadel** locks ($30-60) carry insurance against theft for one or two years if your bike is registered with the police. **Bike Nashbar,** P.O. Box 1455, Crab Orchard, WV 25827 (☎800-627-4227), will beat any nationally advertised in-stock price by 5¢, and ships anywhere in the US or Canada. Their techline (☎800-888-2710; open M-F 8am-6pm EST) fields questions about repairs and maintenance. The following books are useful: *Best Bike Rides in Northern California,* by Kim Grob (Globe Pequot; $13); and *Mountain Bike! Southern California: A Guide to Classic Trails,* by David Story (Menasha Ridge; $16).

For more info on bike trips, contact **Adventure Cycling Association,** P.O. Box 8308, Missoula, MT 59807 (☎800-755-2453; www.adv-cycling.org). It's a national, nonprofit organization that researches and maps long distance routes and organizes bike tours (75-day Great Divide Expedition $2800, 6-9 day trip $650-800). Annual membership is $30 and includes access to maps and routes and a subscription to *Adventure Cyclist* magazine.

## BY MOTORCYCLE

The wind-in-your-face thrill, burly leather, and muscled roar of a motorcycle free of windows or upholstery has built up quite a cult following, but motorcycling is the most dangerous of roadtop activities. Of course, safety should be your primary concern. Helmets are required by law in California; wear the best one you can find. Those considering a long journey should contact the **American Motorcyclist Association,** 13515 Yarmouth Dr., Pickering, OH 43147 (☎800-262-5646; www.ama-cycle.org), the lynchpin of US biker culture. A full membership ($39 per year) includes a subscription to the extremely informative *American Motorcyclist* magazine, discounts on insurance, rentals, and hotels, and a bad-ass patch for your riding jacket. And of course, slide a copy of Robert Pirsig's *Zen and the Art of Motorcycle Maintenance* (1974) into the back pocket of your jeans.

## BY THUMB

*Let's Go* urges you to consider the great risks and disadvantages of **hitchhiking** before thumbing it. Hitching means entrusting your life to a randomly selected person who happens to stop beside you on the road. While this may be comparatively safe in some areas of Europe and Australia, it is generally *not* so in the US or Canada. We strongly urge you to find other means of transportation and to avoid situations where hitching is the only option.

# SPECIFIC CONCERNS

## WOMEN TRAVELERS

Women exploring on their own inevitably face some additional safety concerns, but it's easy to be adventurous without taking undue risks. If you are concerned, consider staying in hostels which offer single rooms that lock from the inside or in religious organizations with rooms for women only. Stick to centrally located accommodations and avoid solitary late-night treks or metro rides.

Always carry extra money for a phone call, bus, or taxi. **Hitchhiking** is never safe for lone women, or even for two women traveling together. When on overnight or long train rides, if there is no women-only compartment, choose one occupied by women or couples. Look as if you know where you're going and approach older women or couples for directions if you're lost or uncomfortable. Generally, the less you look like a tourist, the better off you'll be. Dress conservatively, especially in rural areas. Wearing a **wedding band** may help prevent unwanted overtures.

Your best answer to verbal harassment is no answer at all; feigning deafness, sitting motionless, and staring straight ahead at nothing in particular will do a world of good that negative reactions usually don't achieve. The extremely persistent can sometimes be dissuaded by a firm, loud, and very public "Go away!" Don't hesitate to seek out a police officer or a passerby if you are being harassed. Memorize the emergency numbers (☎911) in places you visit, and consider carrying a keychain whistle. A self-defense course will prepare you for a potential attack and raise your level of awareness of your surroundings (see **Self Defense,** p. 32).

For general information, contact the **National Organization for Women (NOW),** 733 15th St. NW, 2nd Floor, Washington, D.C. 20005 (☎202-628-8669; www.now.org), which has branches across the US that can refer women travelers to rape crisis centers and counseling services.

# TRAVELING ALONE

As a lone traveler, try not to stand out as a tourist, look confident, and be especially careful in deserted or very crowded areas. If questioned, never admit that you are traveling alone. Maintain regular contact with someone at home who knows your itinerary. For more tips, pick up *Traveling Solo* by Eleanor Berman (Globe Pequot Press, $18) or subscribe to **Connecting: Solo Travel Network,** 689 Park Road, Unit 6, Gibsons, BC V0N 1V7, Canada (☎604-886-9099; www.cstn.org; membership $35).

# OLDER TRAVELERS

Senior citizens are eligible for a wide range of discounts on transportation, museums, movies, theaters, concerts, restaurants, and accommodations. If you don't see a senior citizen price listed, ask, and you may be delightfully surprised. The books *No Problem! Worldwise Tips for Mature Adventurers,* by Janice Kenyon (Orca Book Publishers; $16) and *Unbelievably Good Deals and Great Adventures That You Absolutely Can't Get Unless You're Over 50,* by Joan Rattner Heilman (NTC/Contemporary Publishing; $15) are both excellent resources. For more information, contact one of the following organizations:

**Elderhostel,** 11 Ave. de Lafayette, Boston, MA 02111 (☎877-426-8056; www.elderhostel.org). Organizes 1- to 4-week educational adventures for those 55+.

**The Mature Traveler,** P.O. Box 1543, Wildomar, CA 92595 (☎909-461-9598; www.thematuretraveler.com). Monthly newsletter with deals, discounts, tips, and travel packages for the senior traveler. Subscription $30.

**Walking the World,** P.O. Box 1186, Fort Collins, CO 80522 (☎800-340-9255; www.walkingtheworld.com), runs walking-focused trips for travelers 50+. Trips run to destinations ranging from California to Iceland.

# BISEXUAL, GAY & LESBIAN TRAVELERS

Although California is regarded as a progressive state, prejudice against gays and lesbians is still present. Homophobia may be a problem for the openly gay or lesbian traveler, particularly in rural areas. Many cities, however, have large and active queer communities. San Francisco, of course, is the birthplace of the Gay Pride Parade and the Rainbow Flag, an international icon of BGLT pride, while Los Angeles and San Diego's Hillcrest boast lively gay communities and a significant BGLT center. Even outside the major cities, smaller outposts of gay culture still exist. Palm Springs, known as an elderly resort community, increasingly caters to a younger, homosexual clientele. Guerneville, in the Russian River Valley north of San Francisco, is a small town known for its exceptionally high percentage of homosexuals. *Let's Go* includes local gay and lesbian info lines and community centers when available. Below are additional resources. **Out and About** (www.planetout.com) also offers a newsletter addressing travel concerns.

**International Lesbian and Gay Association (ILGA),** 81 rue Marché-au-Charbon, B-1000 Brussels, Belgium (☎+32 2 502 2471; www.ilga.org). Provides political information, such as homosexuality laws of individual countries.

**Giovanni's Room,** 1145 Pine St., Philadelphia, PA 19107 (☎215-923-2960; www.queerbooks.com). An international lesbian/feminist and gay bookstore with mail-order service (carries many of the publications listed below).

**Gay's the Word,** 66 Marchmont St., London WC1N 1AB, UK (☎+44 20 7278 7654; www.gaystheword.co.uk). The largest gay and lesbian bookshop in the UK, with both fiction and non-fiction titles. Mail-order service available.

> **FURTHER READING: BISEXUAL, GAY & LESBIAN**
> *Spartacus International Gay Guide 2001-2002.* Bruno Gmunder Verlag ($33).
> *Damron Men's Guide, Damron Road Atlas, Damron's Accommodations,* and *The Women's Traveller.* Damron Travel Guides ($14-19). For more info, call ☎800-462-6654 or visit www.damron.com
> *Ferrari Guides' Gay Travel A to Z, Ferrari Guides' Men's Travel in Your Pocket,* and *Ferrari Guides' Inn Places.* Ferrari Publications ($16-20). Purchase the guides online at www.ferrariguides.com.
> *The Gay Vacation Guide: The Best Trips and How to Plan Them,* Mark Chesnut. Kensington Publishing Corporation (US$15).
> *Gayellow Pages USA/Canada,* Frances Green. Gayellow pages ($16). Visit Gayellow pages online at www.gayellowpages.com.

# TRAVELERS WITH DISABILITIES

Federal law dictates that all public buildings should be handicapped-accessible, and recent laws governing building codes make disabled access more the norm than the exception. US Customs requires a certificate of immunization against rabies for **guide dogs** entering the country.

In the US, Amtrak and major airlines will accommodate disabled passengers if notified at least 72 hours in advance. Hearing-impaired travelers may contact Amtrak using teletype printers (☎800-523-6590 or 800-654-5988). Greyhound buses will provide free travel for a companion; if you are alone, call Greyhound (☎800-752-4841) at least 48 hours, but no more than one week, before you leave, and they will assist you. For information on transportation availability in individual US cities, contact the local chapter of the Easter Seals Society.

If you plan to visit a national park run by the National Park Service, obtain a free **Golden Access Passport,** which is available at all park entrances and from federal offices whose functions relate to land, forests, or wildlife. The Passport entitles disabled travelers and their families to free park admission and provides a 50% discount on all campsite and parking fees. For further reading, check out *Resource Directory for the Disabled,* by Richard Neil Shrout (Facts on File; $45).

## USEFUL ORGANIZATIONS

**Mobility International USA (MIUSA),** P.O. Box 10767, Eugene, OR 97440 (voice and TDD ☎541-343-1284; www.miusa.org). Sells *A World of Options: A Guide to International Educational Exchange, Community Service, and Travel for Persons with Disabilities* ($35), and provides other useful travel info.

**Society for Accessible Travel & Hospitality (SATH),** 347 Fifth Ave., #610, New York, NY 10016 (☎212-447-7284; www.sath.org). An advocacy group that publishes free online travel information and the travel magazine *OPEN WORLD* ($18, free for members). Annual membership $45, students and seniors $30.

ESSENTIALS

ESSENTIALS

## TOUR AGENCIES

**Directions Unlimited,** 123 Green Ln., Bedford Hills, NY 10507 (☎800-533-5343). Books individual and group vacations for the physically disabled; not an info service.

**The Guided Tour Inc.,** 7900 Old York Rd., #114B, Elkins Park, PA 19027 (☎800-783-5841; www.guidedtour.com). Organizes travel programs for persons with developmental and physical challenges in California and elsewhere in the United States.

# MINORITY TRAVELERS

California is a multicultural state, but not always harmoniously so. Although "minority" groups are now the majority in California, anti-immigrant feeling persists in many areas, especially toward Mexican immigrants. Racial tensions between blacks and whites have been known to flare up in the inner cities, particularly in historically riot-prone Los Angeles. Racial and ethnic minorities sometimes face both blatant and (more often) subtle discrimination and/or harassment. Verbal harassment is now less common than unfair pricing, false info on accommodations, or inexcusably slow or unfriendly service at restaurants. Report individuals to a supervisor and establishments to the **Better Business Bureau** for the region (www.bbb.org, or call the operator for local listings); contact the police in extreme situations. *Let's Go* always welcomes reader input regarding discriminating establishments. Be aware that racial tensions do exist even in large, ostensibly progressive areas, and try to avoid confrontations.

In towns along the US-Mexican border, the **Border Patrol** for the US Immigration and Naturalization Service (INS) remains on a constant lookout for Mexican nationals who have crossed the border illegally. In border towns, they may pull over anyone who looks suspicious, search their vehicles for smuggled goods or people, and ask for identification. The INS also runs checkpoints along the interstates south of Los Angeles to catch illegal immigrants. All cars must stop at these points, and the INS workers may search vehicles that arouse suspicion.

# DIETARY CONCERNS

**Vegetarians** should have a food fest in veggie-noshing, soy milk-guzzling California. *Let's Go* often indicates vegetarian options in restaurant listings; other places to look for vegetarian and vegan cuisine are local health food stores, as well as large natural food chains such as ▓**Trader Joe's** and **Wild Oats.** Vegan options are more difficult to find in smaller towns and inland; be prepared to make your own meals. The **North American Vegetarian Society,** P.O. Box 72, Dolgeville, NY 13329 (☎518-568-7970; www.navs-online.org), publishes info about vegetarian travel, including *Vegetarian Journal's Guide to Natural Food Restaurants in the US and Canada* ($12). You might also try the Vegetarian Resource Group's website (www.vrg.org/travel) or Jed Civic's *The Vegetarian Traveler: Where to Stay If You're Vegetarian, Vegan, Environmentally Sensitive* (Larson Publishing; $16).

Travelers who keep kosher should contact synagogues in larger cities for information on kosher restaurants. Your own synagogue or college Hillel should have access to lists of Jewish institutions across the nation. You may also consult the kosher restaurant database at www.shamash.org/kosher. A good resource is the *Jewish Travel Guide*, edited by Michael Zaidner (Vallentine Mitchell; $17). If you are strict in your observance, you may have to prepare your own food on the road.

# OTHER RESOURCES

Listed below are publishers, periodicals, and websites that can serve as jumping off points for your own research.

# USEFUL PUBLICATIONS

Most of California's big coastal cities offer countless news and entertainment periodicals. In San Francisco, try the *Chronicle*, *SF Weekly*, and the *Bay Guardian*. In LA, pick up copies of the *Times* and *LA Weekly*. In San Diego, the *Union-Tribune* provides news and the *Reader* has the nightlife scoop.

**ESSENTIALS**

# TRAVEL PUBLISHERS

**Hunter Publishing,** 470 W. Broadway, fl. 2, South Boston, MA 02127 (☎617-269-0700; www.hunterpublishing.com). Has an extensive catalog of travel guides and diving and adventure travel books.

**Rand McNally,** P.O. Box 7600, Chicago, IL 60680, (☎847-329-8100; www.randmcnally.com), publishes road atlases.

# WORLD WIDE WEB

Almost every aspect of budget travel is accessible via the web. At the keyboard, you can make a hostel reservation, get advice on travel hotspots from fellow travelers, or find out how much your flight will cost. Listed here are budget travel sites to start off your surfing; other relevant web sites are listed throughout the book.

Our website, www.letsgo.com, now includes introductory chapters from all our guides and a wealth of information on a monthly featured destination. As always, our website also has info about our books, a travel forum buzzing with stories and tips, and additional links that will help you make the most of a trip to California.

# THE ART OF BUDGET TRAVEL

**How to See the World:** www.artoftravel.com. A compendium of great travel tips, from cheap flights to self defense to interacting with local culture.

**Rec. Travel Library:** www.travel-library.com. A fantastic set of links for general information and personal travelogues.

# INFORMATION ON CALIFORNIA

## GENERAL

**California Division of Tourism:** www.gocalif.ca.gov. The glossy tourist brochures in e-form, as well as useful maps and regional guides.

**Official California Government Page:** www.ca.gov. Lists state government services and contact information.

**Maps and Driving Directions:** www.mapquest.com. Offers thorough street-level maps of the entire country.

## THE OUTDOORS

**National Park Service:** www.nps.gov. A wealth of information on the US National Park system, including maps and reservation information.

**California State Parks Official Site:** www.cal-parks.ca.gov. Maps and reservation info.

**California Surf Reports:** www.surfrider.org/cal5.htm. A fairly thorough and frequently updated description of surf conditions up and down the California coast.

**The Ski Report:** www.skicentral.com/rpt-california.html. Describes ski conditions at major slopes in California.

## LOS ANGELES

**LA Times:** www.latimes.com. Full content of the daily newspaper, with free registration.

**LA Transit Info:** www.ladottransit.com. Subway and bus maps, as well as fare info.

## SAN FRANCISCO

**San Francisco Chronicle:** www.sfgate.com/chronicle. The city's largest daily.

**San Francisco Transit:** www.ci.sf.ca.us/muni/index.htm. Map, schedule, and fare info.

# ALTERNATIVES TO TOURISM

In 1961, about 1.7 million people in the world were traveling internationally each year. In 2002, nearly 700 million trips were made; this number is projected to reach a billion by 2010. The dramatic surge in tourism has created an interdependence between many destinations and the tourists they host, and California is no exception. The amount spent by only ten international visitors in California has the same impact on the state's economy as if it had exported one car, and the tourist industry is now California's third-largest employer.

*Let's Go* strives to improve the traveler-destination interchange by imparting the philosophy of **sustainable travel**. The majority of travelers respect and care about the communities and environments they explore, but even conscientious tourists can inadvertently damage natural wonders and cultural enclaves. The growth of the 'ignorant tourist' stereotype—the tourist who tramples endangered flowers to get a close-up of a bear, or the tourist who mistakes a shrine for a toilet—is dismaying; we believe the idea of sustainable travel is among the most important travel tips we can give.

Two rising trends in sustainable travel are ecotourism and community-based tourism. **Ecotourism** focuses on the conservation of natural habitats and on methods of expanding the economy without exploitation or overdevelopment. **Community-based tourism** aims to channel tourist dollars into the local economy by emphasizing tours and cultural programs that are run by community members and often benefit disadvantaged groups.

**Volunteering** is another great way to become involved in natural habitats and local communities while traveling, whether you make it the main component of your trip or simply lend a hand for a day—when you serve a community, you engage with it. In California, you can patrol the harbors and coasts, work on trails, teach English to immigrants, or place yourself behind one of a thousand advocacy issues. Later in this section, we recommend organizations that can help you search for a worthy opportunity suited to your interests.

There are many other ways you can integrate yourself with the communities you visit. Studying at a college or language program is one option. Another is working. Many travelers structure and fund their trips by the work they do along the way—either odd jobs as they go, or full-time stints in cities where they plan to stay for some time. Both long-term and short-term employment opportunities abound in California's major cities, though eligibility for many of these opportunities may depend upon having a California (or US) driver's license or the ability to communicate fluently in English. Restaurants and other service industry businesses frequently have openings as well for travelers who will be cooling their heels in the area for a couple of months before jetting out again.

For those who seek more active involvement, Earthwatch International, Operation Crossroads Africa, and Habitat for Humanity offer fulfilling volunteer opportunities all over the world. For more on volunteering, studying, and working in California and beyond, consult Let's Go's alternatives to tourism website, **www.beyondtourism.com**.

# A NEW PHILOSOPHY OF TRAVEL

We at *Let's Go* have watched the growth of the 'ignorant tourist' stereotype with dismay, knowing that the majority of travelers care passionately about the state of the communities and environments they explore—but also knowing that even conscientious tourists can inadvertently damage natural wonders, rich cultures, and impoverished communities. We believe the philosophy of **sustainable travel** is among the most important travel tips we could impart to our readers, to help guide fellow backpackers and on-the-road philanthropists. By staying aware of the needs and troubles of local communities, today's travelers can be a powerful force in preserving and restoring this fragile world.

Working against the negative consequences of irresponsible tourism is much simpler than it might seem; it is often self-awareness, rather than self-sacrifice, that makes the biggest difference. Simply by trying to spend responsibly and conserve local resources, all travelers can positively impact the places they visit. Let's Go has partnered with **BEST** (**Business Enterprises for Sustainable Travel,** an affiliate of the Conference Board; see www.sustainabletravel.org), which recognizes businesses that operate based on the principles of sustainable travel. Below, they provide advice on how ordinary visitors can practice this philosophy in their daily travels, no matter where they are.

 ## TIPS FOR CIVIC TRAVEL: HOW TO MAKE A DIFFERENCE

Travel by train when feasible. Rail travel requires only half the energy per passenger mile that planes do. On average, each of the 40,000 daily domestic air flights releases more than 1700 pounds of greenhouse gas emissions.

Use public mass transportation whenever possible; outside of cities, take advantage of group taxis or vans. Bicycles are an attractive way of seeing a community first-hand. And enjoy walking—purchase good maps of your destination and ask about on-foot touring opportunities.

When renting a car, ask whether fuel-efficient vehicles are available. Honda and Toyota produce cars that use hybrid engines powered by electricity and gasoline, thus reducing emissions of carbon dioxide. Ford Motor Company plans to introduce a hybrid fuel model by the end of 2004.

Reduce, reuse, recycle—use electronic tickets, recycle papers and bottles wherever possible, and avoid using containers made of styrofoam. Refillable water bottles and rechargable batteries both efficiently conserve expendable resources.

Be thoughtful in your purchases. Take care not to buy souvenir objects made from trees in old-growth or endangered forests, such as teak, or items made from endangered species, like ivory or tortoise jewelry. Ask whether products are made from renewable resources.

Buy from local enterprises, such as casual street vendors. In developing countries and low-income neighborhoods, many people depend on the "informal economy" to make a living.

Be on-the-road-philanthropists. If you are inspired by the natural environment of a destination or enriched by its culture, join in preserving their integrity by making a charitable contribution to a local organization.

Spread the word. Upon your return home, tell friends and colleagues about places to visit that will benefit greatly from their tourist dollars, and reward sustainable enterprises by recommending their services. Travelers can not only introduce friends to particular vendors but also to local causes and charities that they might choose to support when they travel.

# VOLUNTEERING

Though the US is considered wealthy by most objective standards, there is no shortage of issues, nor of organizations that work to resolve those issues. California offers countless volunteering experiences in its huge expanses of wilderness and coast, in its urban centers, and in its communities of spirited people who support a truly phenomenal number of causes. Combined with the thrill of travel, engaging with one's surroundings as a volunteer can be a heady experience.

Most people who volunteer in the US do so on a short-term basis, at organizations that make use of drop-in or once-a-week volunteers. These opportunities can be found in virtually every city and town and are referenced in this section. The best way to find groups that fit your interests and schedule is to take initiative; check with local volunteer centers, call organizations you admire, and follow up on the database links we provide. A few, more intensive volunteer services may charge you a fee to participate. These costs can be surprisingly hefty (although they frequently cover airfare and most, if not all, living expenses). Most people choose to go through a parent organization that takes care of logistical details and often provides a supportive group environment.

Before handing your money over to any program, make sure you know exactly what you're getting into. It's a good idea to get the names of **previous participants** and ask them about their experience. Whoever you talk to, the **questions** below are a good place to start:

Will you be the only person in the program? If not, what are the other participants like? How old are they? How much will you interact with them?

Is room and board included? If so, what is the arrangement? Will you be expected to share a room? A bathroom? What are the meals like?

Is transportation included? Are there any additional expenses?

How much free time will you have? Will you be able to travel around the region?

What kind of safety network is set up? Will you still be covered by your home insurance? Does the program have an emergency plan?

# CONSERVATION AND WILDLIFE

Conservation is huge in California. People conserve everything from plastic to trees to big, big redwood trees to water to land to gas; practically only in California will you find people poking along in battery-powered zero emissions vehicles. Protecting wildlife and endangered species, battling air and water pollution, and preserving resources and habitats are a way of life in parts of California, though perhaps you wouldn't know it to look at LA. Opportunities for getting involved in conservation and wildlife protection are countless; to start, the **California Council for Wildlife Rehabilitators** lists wildlife rehabilitation centers by region at www.ccwr.org, the **California Coastkeeper Alliance** links to its regional branches of coast protection programs at www.cacoastkeeper.org, the **Trail Center** lists outdoor volunteer opportunities at www.trailcenter.org/links/links-vol.htm, and **California State Parks** at www.parks.ca.gov is useful for locating the nearest state park.

**Pacific Crest Trail,** 5325 Elkhorn Blvd., PMB #256, Sacramento, CA, 95842 (☎916-349-2109; www.pcta.org). Volunteers can help maintain and monitor trails, or work as trail cooks. One-time efforts always appreciated. Visit website for the nearest trail crew.

**Orange County Coastkeeper,** 441 Old Newport Blvd., Suite 103, Newport Beach, CA 92663 (☎949-723-5424; www.coastkeeper.org). Maintains a kelp reforestation program, conducts beach debris surveys, and monitors the harbor.

**Wildlife Rescue,** 4000 Middlefield Rd., Building V, Palo Alto, CA 94303 (☎650-494-7417; www.wildliferescue.ws). Runs a rescue hotline and an animal rehabilitation shelter. Opportunities for advocacy and educational speaking also exist.

**Heritage Resource Management Department of US Forest Service,** P.O. Box 31315, Tucson, AZ 85751-1315 (☎800-281-9176 or 520-722-2716; www.passportintime.com). The Passport in Time program needs volunteers for archaeological surveys and the recording of oral histories within the parks.

**Earthwatch,** 3 Clocktower Pl., Suite 100, Box 75, Maynard, MA 01754 (☎800-776-0188 or 978-461-0081; www.earthwatch.org). Arranges 1- to 3-week programs in the United States and around the world to promote conservation of natural resources. Fees vary based on program location and duration; costs average $1700 plus airfare.

# THE ARTS

The arts are inseparable from Californian identity. High culture, low culture, weird culture—all of it is integral to the vibrancy of life in California. The best and most personal way to become involved is simply to pick up the phone and call your favorite opera, theater, museum, orchestra, arts festival, or venue and ask how you can help. Contacting the **California Arts Council** (www.cac.ca.gov) is another great way to support the arts in a state that thrives on artistic sensitivity.

**Los Angeles Philharmonic Orchestra,** 151 South Grand Ave., Los Angeles, CA 90012 (☎323-850-2165; www.laphil.org). Take part in fundraising, music education, or the support of music in schools. Volunteers can also work with the Hollywood Bowl.

**The J. Paul Getty Museum,** Visitor Services Dept., Volunteer Program, 1200 Getty Center Dr., Los Angeles, CA 90049 (☎310-440-7303; www.getty.edu). Volunteers greet visitors, answer questions, work in offices, and help out with special events. Must be 18+.

**The New Conservatory Theatre Center (NCTC),** 25 Van Ness Ave., San Francisco, CA 94102 (☎415-861-4914; www.nctcsf.org). Provides entertaining and educational programs for youths, along with a wide array of performances for the entire San Francisco community. The NTCTC is always looking for new volunteers, from costume designers to ushers to administrative workers.

**The Institute for Unpopular Culture (IFUC),** P.O. Box 1523, 1850 Union St., suite 4, San Francisco, CA 94123 (☎212-925-6951; www.ifuc.org). IFUC seeks to aid artists whose work may not have mass appeal. The Institute sponsors gallery shows, short films, and increased interaction between dot-commers (the money) and artists (the talent), reviving the patron system of old. Volunteers are needed throughout the year to assist with research and administrative work.

# URBAN ISSUES

In the urban centers of California, as in most cities, there is a large discrepancy between high-income and low-income families. Organizations that try to bridge this gap focus on literacy, domestic abuse, housing, health, and food. The huge number of immigrants in California's cities also generates a profusion of organizations that deal with language barriers, refugees, and concerns specific to individual ethnic and religious groups. For extensive networks of opportunities available in California's three largest cities, check out **The Volunteer Center of San Francisco** (☎415-982-8999; www.vcsf.org), **Volunteer San Diego** (☎858-636-4131; www.volunteersandiego.org), and **LA Works** (☎323-224-6510; www.la-volunteer.org).

**America's Literacy Directory** (☎800-228-8813; www.literacydirectory.org/volunteer.asp). A service of the National Institute for Literacy, this online directory allows you to search for volunteer opportunities with more than 5000 literacy programs in the US.

**California Literacy,** 133 N. Altadena Dr., Suite 410, Pasadena, CA 91107 (☎800-894-READ/7323; www.caliteracy.org/volunteering.html). Tutor adults, work with those who have reading disabilities, or teach English as a Second Language (ESL) classes.

**Center for the Asian Pacific Family,** 543 North Fairfax Ave., Room 108, Los Angeles, CA, 90036 (☎323-653-4045; www.apanet.org/members/cpaf.html). For those in search of a long-term volunteering experience, CAPF, which works with domestic violence and sexual assault, runs several programs that require a one-year commitment: three shelters; childcare, child development, and tutoring programs for abused children; women's advocate programs; and a 24hr. crisis hotline.

**The Shelter Network,** 1450 Chapin Ave., 2nd Floor, Burlingame, CA 94010 (☎650-685-5880; www.shelternetwork.org). Offers housing for homeless families and individuals. Some volunteer responsibilities at the Shelter Network (painting the shelters, gardening, cleaning) are one-time tasks, and others (tutoring, office support) require a three-month commitment–but of course all volunteers are welcome.

**US Department of Housing and Urban Development,** 451 7th St. SW, Washington, DC 20410 (☎202-708-1112; www.hud.gov). Maintains listings of local homeless assistance programs, shelters, food banks, hospitals, and advocacy groups in every state (www.hud.gov/homeless/hmlsagen.cfm). **The National Coalition for the Homeless** boasts a similar directory online (www.nationalhomeless.org/local/local.html).

**Homeless Veteran Program,** a division of the **Department of Veterans Affairs** (800-827-1000; www.va.gov/homeless/). Provides outreach to homeless veterans living on the streets and in shelters, offering psychiatric care and information on health care and housing assistance. The website lists program coordinators by state. AmeriCorps opportunities available.

# YOUTH AND ELDERLY

The birthplace of teenage angst, the US constantly struggles to understand and connect with its youth, often with an alarmed concern for the future. In California, big sibling programs abound with volunteering opportunities, as do summer camps, day cares, children's museums, tutoring programs, and programs for disadvantaged, disabled, or abused children. Perhaps a less-often recognized population is the elderly, though there are many programs that cater to seniors as well. **California Department of Aging** (www.aging.state.ca.us) is a helpful place to start.

**Big Brothers Big Sisters of America,** 230 N. 13th St., Philadelphia, PA 19107 (☎215-567-7000; www.bbbsa.org). Celebrating its 100th anniversary in 2004, Big Brothers Big Sisters provides mentorship, friendship, and support to hundreds of thousands of American kids. Paired Bigs and Littles work on homework together, visit museums, participate in community service, and just hang out.

**Meals on Wheels Association of America,** 1414 Prince St., Alexandria, VA 22314 (☎703-548-5558; www.mowaa.org). Visit the website for a list of over 300 communities in California serviced by Meals on Wheels. Buy, prepare, and deliver meals to the elderly and the needy. Public awareness and research projects are also available.

## ADVOCACY

The organizations listed below are but a sampling of the causes that spark rallies, demonstrations, and organizing in California. Each Californian, it seems, has a cause, whether it is for equality of race, religion, sex, or sexual preference, HIV/AIDS outreach, a political issue, a particular species of tree or bird, or whether it is for something as obscure as the recognition of fruitarians.

**Ecolutions,** 10271 West Pico Blvd., Los Angeles, CA 90064 (☎310-203-0683). An environmental education organization, Ecolutions employs its creative volunteers in web and graphic design, administration, children's outreach, and one-time events.

**Equality California,** 2370 Market St., San Francisco, CA 94114 (☎415-581-0005; www.eqca.org). Works on lesbian, gay, bisexual, and transgender legislation, as well as LGBT pride. Volunteer tasks might range from the administrative to rallies and outreach.

**Marriage Equality California,** P.O. Box 8, Venice, CA 90294 (☎877-356-4125; www.marriageequalityca.org). With chapters throughout California, MECA works to end discrimination toward gay and lesbian marriages. They are always looking for people to get involved in parades, town hall meetings, rallies, and domestic partner registrations.

**American Lung Association** (☎800-586-4872/LUNG-USA; www.lungusa.org). Works on anti-smoking campaigns, tobacco prevention in schools, and advocacy in public policies that pertain to lung health.

# STUDYING IN CALIFORNIA

Study programs range from basic language and culture courses to college-level classes, often for credit. In order to choose a program that best fits your needs, you will want to research all you can before making your decision—determine costs and duration, as well as what kind of students participate in the program and what sort of accommodations are provided. In programs that have large groups of students, especially ones who speak the same foreign language, there is a trade-off. The comfort level may be higher, but non-native speakers will not have the same opportunity to better their English by practicing with native Californians, nor will those already proficient in English develop as close ties with the local community. For accommodations, dorm life provides a better opportunity to mingle with fellow students, but there is a lower chance of experiencing the local scene. If you live with a family, there is a potential to build lifelong friendships with locals and to experience day-to-day life in more depth, but conditions can vary greatly from family to family.

If you wish to genuinely experience college the way that many American college students remember it, all you need is a case of the cheapest available beer and a friend to help you cheer on the local football team. Of course, popular cliche often snorts at the idea of education in California, where skaters and starlets worship the sun (or the mirror) rather than Shakespeare. But many outstanding American institutions of higher learning are located in California, including Stanford, Caltech, and the superb, three-tiered state university system. The public university system consists of the University of California (www.ucop.edu/pathways), California State University (www.calstate.edu), and the community college system. Community or junior colleges are smaller, do not have graduate schools, and usually serve students who cannot attend

ALTERNATIVES TO TOURISM

school full-time, or who plan to eventually transfer to a four-year school after two years. Unfortunately, public state schools charge non-Californians significantly higher tuition and are extremely popular with residents, who receive priority consideration in admissions.

Advanced non-native English speakers seeking to studying in California can consider a visiting student program lasting either a semester or a full academic year, or the more complicated option of enrolling full-time. The best method by far is to contact colleges and universities in your home country to research any exchange programs between American colleges and schools in your country.

## VISAS AND WORK PERMITS

An important reminder: all non-US travelers planning a stay of more than 90 days (180 days for Canadians) need to obtain a visa. **The Center for International Business and Travel (CIBT),** 23201 New Mexico Ave. NW #210, Washington, D.C. 20016 (☎800-925-2428; www.cibt.com), or 6300 Wilshire Blvd., #1520, Los Angeles, CA 90048 (☎323-658-5100), secures "pleasure tourist" or B-2 visas to and from all possible countries for a variable service charge (six-month visa around $45). If you lose your I-94 form, you can replace it at the nearest **Immigration and Naturalization Service (INS)** office (☎800-375-5283; www.ins.usdoj.gov), though it's unlikely that the form will be replaced within the time of your stay. Visa extensions are sometimes attainable with an I-539 form; call the forms request line (☎800-870-3676).

Foreign students who wish to study in the US must apply for a student permit from the US government. There are two non-immigrant visa categories for persons wishing to study in the United States. The "F" visa is for **academic studies,** while the "M" visa is for **nonacademic or vocational studies.** An applicant coming to the US to study **must be accepted for a full course of study** by an educational institution approved by the INS. The institution will send the applicant **Form I-20A-B,** a Certificate of Eligibility for Non-Immigrant **(F-1)** Student Status for Academic and Language Students. A nonacademic or vocational institution will send the student **Form I-20M-N,** a Certificate of Eligibility for Non-Immigrant **(M-1)** Student Status for Vocational Students. F-1 student visa applicants must also prove they have enough **readily available funds** to meet expenses for the first year of study, and that adequate funds will be available for each subsequent year of study. M-1 student visa applicants must demonstrate that sufficient funds are immediately available to pay all tuition and living costs for the entire period of intended stay.

Although visa applicants may apply at any US consular office abroad, it is usually easiest to qualify in their country of permanent residence. Applications must be accompanied by a nonrefundable $45 **application fee** and include: the completed and signed application, **Form OF-156,** freely available at US consulate offices; a **passport** valid for travel to the United States and with a validity date at least six months beyond the applicant's intended period of stay in the United States; one **photograph,** showing full face, without head covering, against a light background; **Form I-20A-B** ("F" applicants) or **Form I-20M-N** ("M" applicants), obtained from the appropriate educational institution; finally, evidence of sufficient **funds.**

If English is not your native language, you will probably be required to take the Test of English as a Foreign Language (TOEFL), which is administered in many countries and is often required for application to many American universities. The international students office at the institution you will be attending can give you the specifics. Contact **TOEFL/EST Publications,** P.O. Box 6151, Princeton, NJ 08541 (☎609-771-7100; www.toefl.org). The Educational Testing Service, the organization that administers the TOEFL, has a California branch at 2371 Systron Drive, Concord, CA 94518 (☎925-808-2000).

# LANGUAGE SCHOOLS

Unlike American universities, language schools often are independently run international or local organizations or divisions of foreign universities that rarely offer college credit. Language schools are a good alternative to university study if you desire a deeper focus on the language, a slightly less rigorous courseload, or a less expensive but still effective education. These programs are also good for younger high school students who might not feel comfortable with older students in a university program. There is a mulititude of language schools located in California's major cities; many of them often will cater to specific ethnicities or nationalities. Some good programs include:

**Eurocentres,** 101 N. Union St. Suite 300, Alexandria, VA 22314, USA (☎703-684-1494; www.eurocentres.com) or in Europe, Head Office, Seestr. 247, CH-8038 Zurich, Switzerland (☎+41 1 485 50 40; fax 481 61 24). Language programs for beginning to advanced students with homestays in California.

**Language Studies International,** 2015 Center St., Berkeley, CA 94704 (☎510-841-4695; www.lsi.edu) or 1706 5th Ave., San Diego, CA 92101 (☎619-234-2881). Intensive language programs in Berkeley and San Diego for students of all levels. Living options include dorms, homestays, and hotels.

**Osako Sangyo University Los Angeles (OSULA) Education Center,** 3921 Laurel Canyon Blvd., Los Angeles, CA 91604 (☎818-509-1484; www.osula.com). Offers intensive and general English classes in a residential college setting in the suburbs of LA.

**Monterey Institute of International Studies,** 460 Pierce Street, Monterey, CA 93940 (☎831-647-4100; www.miis.edu). The language center runs the eight-week Intensive ESL Program and the more general English for Academic Preparation Program, which offers courses on three levels of study. Located in the beautiful coastal city of Monterey.

**INTRAX English Institute,** 2226 Bush St., San Francisco, CA 94115 (☎415-434-1221; www.intraxinc.com). ESL programs taught in San Francisco and San Diego. Offers courses focused on easing international students into the American college system. INTRAX also operates a Work/Travel service that helps international university students find jobs in the US during their summer vacations, and several Homestay programs in San Francisco, Los Angeles, and San Diego for international youth, ages 13-22.

# FILM SCHOOLS

Hollywood is the cinematic capital of the universe—there is no better place to gain behind-the-scenes experience than in the studio backlots of Studio City and Burbank. To this end, there are numerous film schools and colleges with high-caliber film programs in the Los Angeles area, many of which run shorter summer and semester programs. Some good options to check out:

**New York Film Academy,** 100 E. 17th St., New York, NY 10003 (☎818-733-2600; www.nyfa.com). The Los Angeles location allows would-be actors, filmmakers, and screenwriters the chance to hone their skills on studio sets. Program lengths vary from four weeks to one year, with classes in acting, screenwriting, digital imaging, filmmaking, and 3D animation. Program costs range from $3000 to $22,500.

**University of Southern California School of Cinema-Television,** Summer Production Workshop, 850 W. 34th St., Los Angeles, CA 90089-2211 (☎213-740-1742; www.usc.edu/schools/cntv/programs/spw). Boasting a luminous alumni list that includes Jedi boy George Lucas, screenwriter John Milius (*Apocalypse Now),* and producer Laura Ziskin (*Spider-Man),* the world-renowned film school offers summer workshops with classes in writing, digital imaging, directing and producing. University housing is available, as are classes for students who have already logged some hours (or years) in the industry.

**American Film Institute,** 2021 N. Western Avenue, Los Angeles, CA 90027 (☎323-856-7600; www.afi.com). Committed to "advancing and preserving the art of the moving image," the LA branch of the Institute offers seminars and workshops on topics varying from digital TV editing, notably the "Directing Workshop for Women" which was established in 1974. Some programs are free, but housing and meals are not provided. The annual AFI Fest, in the fall, lasts for over a week and has numerous screenings and receptions, featuring established and up-and-coming directors.

**The Los Angeles Film School,** 6363 Sunset Blvd., Suite 400, Los Angeles, CA 90028 (☎323-860-0789; www.lafilm.com). Located in Hollywood, the LA Film School trains students aspiring to careers in many different areas of filmmaking, including directing, screenwriting, production design, and cinematography. Six-week digital camera-based workshops, an eight-month feature development program, and a full-year immersion program are offered. Tuition and equipment costs range from $6500 for a basic six-week course to $26,500 for international students in the full-year program.

**Cinema Make-up School,** 3780 Wilshire Blvd., Suite 300, Los Angeles, CA 90010 (☎213-368-1234; cinemamakeup.com). Numerous courses offered in different styles of make-up from film and television to fashion to beauty and salon. Tuition does not include lab fees or make-up equipment costs. Total costs range from $8250 for Film & Television to $10,000 for the Master Make-up course, which is a general introduction to make-up in various mascara-dependent industries.

# WORKING

As with volunteering, work opportunities tend to fall into two categories. Some travelers want long-term jobs that allow them to get to know another part of the world as a member of the community, while other travelers seek out short-term jobs to finance the next leg of their travels.

# LONG-TERM WORK

If you're planning on spending a substantial amount of time (more than three months) working in California, search for a job well in advance. International placement agencies are often the easiest way to find employment in the US, especially for service industry jobs. **Internships,** usually for college students, are a good way to segue into working abroad, although the paycheck is scanty (if it exists at all). However, many swear the experience and the opportunity to

## WORK PERMIT INFORMATION

All foreign visitors are required to have a **visa** if they are planning a stay of over 90 days (180 days for Canadians) or if they intend to work or study in the US. Travelers must also have proof of intent to leave (like a return plane ticket or an I-94 card). An additional **work permit** (or **"green card"**) is required of all foreigners planning to work in the US. Speaking broadly, there are two types of work permits. Employment-Based Visas are generally issued to skilled or highly educated workers who already have jobs in the States. Temporary Worker Visas have fixed time limits and very specific job classifications. There are limits on the number of work permits given out, so even if you qualify, you may not get one. Your employer must obtain this document, usually by demonstrating that you have skills that locals lack. Friends in the US can sometimes help expedite work permits or arrange work-for-accommodations exchanges.

**To obtain visas and work permits,** contact a US embassy or consulate. Check http://travel.state.gov/links.html for US listings. Visa extensions are sometimes attainable with a completed I-539 form; call the Bureau of Citizenship and Immigration Service's (BCIS) form request line (800-870-3676) or get it online: http://www.immigration.gov/graphics/formsfee/forms/i-539.htm. For more info, see http://travel.state.gov/visa_services.html and www.unitedstates.gov.

Recent security measures have made the visa application process more rigorous and therefore lengthy. **Apply well in advance of your travel date.** The process may seem complex, but it's critical that you go through the proper channels—the alternative is potential deportation.

observe new business practices and gain new knowledge is well worth it. Be wary of advertisements or companies that claim the ability to get you a job abroad for a fee—the listings are sometimes outdated, and often available online or in newspapers. If using such an organization, make sure it's reputable. Some good ones include:

**Council Exchanges,** 52 Poland St., London W1F 7AB, UK (☎44 020 7478 2000; US ☎888-268-6245; www.councilexchanges.org), charges a US$300-475 fee for arranging short-term work authorizations (generally valid for 3-6 months) and provides extensive information on different job and internship opportunities in California and the US.

**Alliances Abroad,** 702 W. Ave., Austin, TX 78701 (☎888-622-7623; www.alliancesabroad.com) runs a Seasonal Work in the USA program on the H2-B work visa that runs up to 10 months, or a Work & Travel in the USA program on the J-1 visa that arranges employment for students on their summer vacations.

**Camp Counselors USA,** Green Dragon House, 64-70 High Street, Croydon CRO 9XN UK (☎020 8668 9051; www.workexperienceusa.com) places people aged 18-30 as counselors in summer camps in the US. Also has a work experience placement program.

**Association for International Practical Training (AIPT),** 10400 Little Patuxent Pkwy. Suite 250, Columbia, MD 21044-3519, USA (☎410-997-2200; www.aipt.org). The AIPT Experience USA program welcomes students from outside the US during their summer vacations, whether in Dec. or June. For up to four months, the student will work or train at his or her place of employment while having the freedom to explore the city or country. The organization sponsors a student's J-1 visa application and matches him or her with an American employer. US$50 application fee. For internship opportunities in technical fields, **IAESTE** (www.iaeste.org) provides 8- to 12-week programs for college students who have completed 2 years of technical study. US$25 application fee.

## AU PAIR WORK

Au pairs are typically women, aged 18-27, who work as live-in nannies, caring for children and doing light housework in foreign countries in exchange for room, board, and a small spending allowance or stipend. Most au pairs speak favorably of their experience. Drawbacks, however, often include long hours of constantly being on duty and the somewhat mediocre pay. In California, weekly salaries typically fall slightly below $150, with about 45 hours of work expected. Much of the au pair experience really does depend on the family you're placed with. The agencies below are good starting points for looking for employment as an au pair.

**Accord Cultural Exchange,** 750 La Playa, San Francisco, CA 94121, USA (☎415-386-6203; www.cognitext.com/accord).

**Au Pair Homestay,** World Learning, Inc., 1015 15th St. NW, Suite 750, Washington, DC 20005, USA (☎800-287-2477; fax 202-408-5397).

**Au Pair in America,** River Plaza, 9 West Broad Street, Stamford, CT 06902 (☎800-928-7247; www.aupairinamerica.com).

**Childcare International, Ltd.,** Trafalgar House, Grenville Pl., London NW7 3SA (☎+44 020 8906 3116; fax 8906-3461; www.childint.co.uk).

**InterExchange,** 161 Sixth Ave., New York, NY 10013, USA (☎212-924-0446; fax 924-0575; www.interexchange.org).

## SHORT-TERM WORK

Traveling for long periods of time can get expensive; therefore, many travelers try their hand at odd jobs for a few weeks at a time to make some extra cash to carry them through another month or two of touring around. A common way to make some extra cash in California is picking fruit. Those who try agricultural labor should be prepared for a difficult, character-building experience. Go to the local Farm Labor Office for more information. Most agriculture in California is concentrated in the San Joaquin Valley, although regional farms abound up and down the coast as well. The high season for harvest is May to October. Another popular option is to work several hours a day at a hostel in exchange for free or discounted room and/or board. Most often, these short-term jobs are found by word of mouth, or simply by talking to the owner of a hostel or restaurant. Many places, especially due to the high turnover in the tourism industry, are always eager for help, even if only temporary. Jobs (helping as a mover, working in cafes) can usually be found in bigger cities, like Los Angeles and San Francisco. For something a bit more glamorous, head to Hollywood, where day-jobs as movie extras abound. *Let's Go* tries to list temporary jobs like these whenever possible; look in the practical information sections of larger cities. The organizations listed below offer short-term jobs in popular destinations.

**Willing Workers on Organic Farms (WWOOF),** P.O. Box 2675, Lewes, UK BN7 1RB (www.phdcc.com/sites/wwoof; $20), allows you to receive room and board at organic farms in California (and other parts of the world) in exchange for help on the farm.

**Concession Services Corporation at Yosemite National Park,** P.O. Box 578, Yosemite National Park, CA 95389 (☎209-372-1236), hires part-time and permanent staff to work in the park.

**Bill's Home Hostel,** 1040 Cielo Lane, Nipomo, CA 93444-9039 (bdennen@slonet.org), allows travelers free room and board in exchange for two hours of work.

**ALTERNATIVES TO TOURISM**

**Cenex Central Casting,** 220 Flower St., Burbank, CA 91506 (☎818-562-2755) is LA's largest and most reputable casting service that will place extras on movie sets. $20 cash for "photo fee." Travelers who have a sponsor not eligible to work.

---

### FOR FURTHER READING ON ALTERNATIVES TO TOURISM

*Alternatives to the Peace Corps: A Directory of Third World and US Volunteer Opportunities,* by Joan Powell. Food First Books, 2000 (US$10).

*How to Live Your Dream of Volunteering Overseas,* by Collins, DeZerega, and Heckscher. Penguin Books, 2002 (US$17).

*International Directory of Voluntary Work,* by Whetter and Pybus. Peterson's Guides and Vacation Work, 2000 (US$16).

*International Jobs,* by Kocher and Segal. Perseus Books, 1999 (US$18).

*Overseas Summer Jobs 2003,* by Collier and Woodworth. Peterson's Guides and Vacation Work, 2002 (US$18).

*Work Abroad: The Complete Guide to Finding a Job Overseas,* by Hubbs, Griffith, and Nolting. Transitions Abroad Publishing, 2000 ($16).

*Work Your Way Around the World,* by Susan Griffith. Worldview Publishing Services, 2001 (US$18).

*Invest Yourself: The Catalogue of Volunteer Opportunities*, published by the Commission on Voluntary Service and Action (☎718-638-8487).

---

Find (Our Student Airfares are cheap, flexible & exclusive) great Student Airfares everywhere at StudentUniverse.com and Get lost.

 StudentUniverse.com

Student Airfares everywhere

# SAN FRANCISCO

If California is a state of mind, San Francisco is euphoria. Welcome to the city that will take you to new highs, leaving your mind spinning, your tastebuds tingling, and your calves aching. Though it's smaller than most "big" cities, the City by the Bay more than compensates for its size with personality that simply won't quit. The dazzling views, daunting hills, one-of-a-kind neighborhoods, and laid-back, friendly people create a kind of charisma not to be found anywhere else. The city packs an incredible amount of vitality into its 47 square miles of thriving art communities, bustling shops, and some of the country's hippest nightclubs and bars.

By Californian standards, San Francisco is steeped in history—but it's a history of eccentrics and troublemakers that resonates more strongly today in street culture than in museums and galleries. The lineage of free spirits and outlaws dates back to the 19th century, to the smugglers and pirates of the Barbary Coast and the 49ers who flocked here during the madness of the California Gold Rush. As the last stop in America's voracious westward expansion, San Francisco has always attracted artists, dreamers, and outsiders. With the 1950s came the Beats—brilliant young writers who captured the rhythms of be-bop jazz in their poetry of discontent. The late 60s ushered in the most famous of San Fran's rabblerousers—hippies and flower children, who spiced up one generation and freaked out another by making love, not war.

## HIGHLIGHTS OF SAN FRANCISCO

**GOLDEN GATE BRIDGE.** Yeah, yeah, we know. It's totally cliché, so cliché that it's on two out of three SF postcards. Well, don't hate it because it's beautiful—grab a windbreaker and see for yourself just what all the (justified) fuss is about (p. 106).

**A GIANTS GAME AT PACIFIC BELL PARK.** Not only do you get to cheer on the Giants (and maybe see a right-field homer make a splash), but the bleacher seats come with fabulous views of the game, the city, and the Bay (p. 123).

**MISSION MURALS.** This urban street art brilliantly combines artistic excellence, technical perfection, and community politics. Standouts include Balmy Alley and a three-building tribute to guitar god Carlos Santana (p. 115).

**ALCATRAZ.** High-concept Bruckheimer flicks aside, "The Rock" is the coolest attraction in the Bay. First a military detention hall and then the original high security civilian prison, this prison has enough ghost stories to keep you up for days (p. 116).

**CASTRO STREET ON FRIDAY AND SATURDAY NIGHTS.** Before they duck into bars or head to SoMa for the clubs, San Francisco's pretty gay boys and girls stroll Castro St. Don't come expecting a freak show—this is high-class and happy (p. 126).

The tradition of free spirit and subversion persists. Anti-establishment politics have become establishment here as rallies and movements continue to fill the streets and newspapers. The queer community became undeniably visible in the 70s as one of the city's most vocal and powerful groups. In addition, Mexican, Central American, and Asian immigrants have made San Francisco one of the most racially diverse cities in the United States. And then, in a wave of mid-90s, computer-crazed prosperity, young computer workers ditched the bland suburbs of Silicon Valley for the cooler breezes of San Francisco, and upstart Internet companies infiltrated the forgotten spaces of lower-rent neighborhoods. For a while, the Frisco fight was old-timers and hippies vs. dot-commers, but when the Clinton-era national surplus went the way of the dodo, high-end yuppification collapsed, leaving neighborhoods to reassess their futures. San Fran is changing with the times but some things stay the same: the Bay will always be foggy, the hills steep, and the tourists always the only ones wearing shorts. For more coverage, see ▨*Let's Go: San Francisco 2004.*

# THE LOCAL LEGEND

## ▨ INTERCITY
# TRANSPORTATION

### OH WILLIE!

**BY PLANE.** Busy **San Francisco International Airport** (**SFO**; general info ☎650-821-8211) is 15 mi. south of downtown by US 101. Plan your transportation from the airport by calling the SFO Travelers Aid (☎650-821-2735; open daily 9am-9pm) or TravInfo (☎817-1717), or by accessing the ground transport section of www.flysfo.com, which includes links to the web pages of all public transportation services as well as a driving route planner. **Information booths,** located on the arrival levels of all terminals and in the international departures terminal, offer detailed fare and schedule info. **Travelers' Aid Society** booths can be found on the departure levels of all terminals. (Both open daily 10am-9pm.)

San Mateo County Transit (**SamTrans;** Bay Area ☎800-660-4287, outside the Bay Area 650-817-1717; www.samtrans.com) runs two buses between SFO (from the lower level, in front of Swissair) and downtown San Francisco. Express bus KX reaches the Transbay Terminal downtown with a few stops along Mission St. and allows only one small carryon bag per passenger (35min.; 5:30am-12:50am; adults $3, seniors at off-peak times and children under 17 $1.25). Bus #292 makes frequent stops on Mission St. and allows any amount of luggage (1hr.; 4:30am-12:45am; adults $2.20, children under 17 $1.50, seniors at off-peak times 50¢).

Another option is to take a SamTrans bus to the **Bay Area Rapid Transit (BART)** system, which runs through the city and other Bay Area destinations. Three BART stops in San Francisco connect to the **San Francisco Municipal Railway (MUNI),** San Francisco's public transportation system. SamTrans bus BX runs from the airport to the Colma BART station just south of the city (20min.; every 20-30min. M-F 5:45am-11:30pm, Sa-Su 6:30am-11:30pm; adults $1.10, under 17 75¢, seniors 50¢).

Many van services leave from the airport and for $10-15 per person will take you directly to your lodging. Door-to-door commercial shuttles are the most convenient way of getting downtown from SFO ($10-14). Most shuttles circulate at the airport around the lower level central island outside the baggage claim and do not require reservations. For a complete list of companies, ask at the SFO Info Booth.

Popularly known as "Da Mayor," Willie L. Brown, Jr., is currently serving his second term in office as executive of San Francisco.

How did he make it through the debates of two campaigns? In September 1999, he explained, "I just keep making shit up...I use a little bit of ebonics...and then come to the punch line."

Brown continues the tradition of liberal politics established by his predecessors George Moscone and Dianne Feinstein. While issues such as the MUNI public transportation system, homelessness, and a number of alleged scandals have continued to plague Brown's leadership, he has successfully delivered on his commitments to civil rights, the environment, and community safety.

He also keeps the press and gossip-mongers happy with a sharp wit, a flair for showmanship, and a quick temper that has led him to such gaffes as calling 49ers quarterback Elvis Grbac an "embarrassment to humankind" (a comment for which he later apologized).

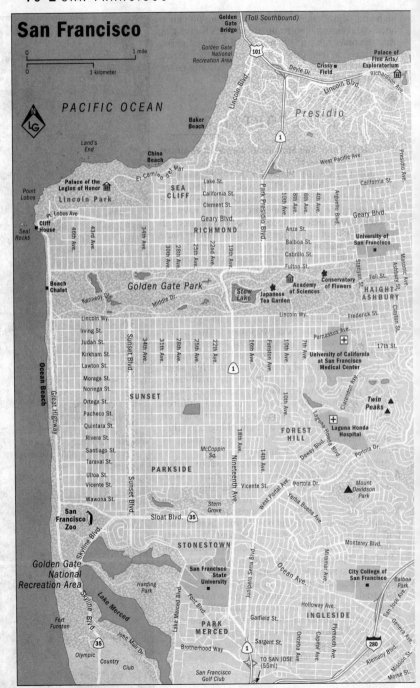

# San Francisco

Golden Gate Bridge (Toll Southbound)

Golden Gate National Recreation Area

PACIFIC OCEAN

Land's End

Point Lobos

Seal Rocks

Cliff House

Beach Chalet

Ocean Beach

Great Highway

San Francisco Zoo

Golden Gate National Recreation Area

Fort Funston

Olympic Country Club

Baker Beach

China Beach

El Camino del Mar

Palace of the Legion of Honor

Lincoln Park

Pt. Lobos Ave.

SEA CLIFF

Lake St.
California St.
Clement St.
Geary Blvd.

RICHMOND

46th Ave.
43rd Ave.
34th Ave.
30th Ave.
28th Ave.
25th Ave.
22nd Ave.
19th Ave.

Golden Gate Park

Kennedy Dr.

Middle Dr.

Stow Lake

Japanese Tea Garden

Academy of Sciences

Conservatory of Flowers

Lincoln Wy.
Irving St.
Judah St.
Kirkham St.
Lawton St.
Moraga St.
Noriega St.
Ortega St.
Pacheco St.
Quintara St.
Rivera St.
Santiago St.
Taraval St.
Ulloa St.
Vicente St.
Wawona St.

Sunset Blvd.
34th Ave.
31st Ave.
28th Ave.
25th Ave.
22nd Ave.

SUNSET

16th Ave.
Funston Ave.

Lincoln Wy.

18th Ave.

Nineteenth Ave.

McCoppin Sq.

PARKSIDE

Stern Grove

Sloat Blvd.

Skyline Blvd.

Lake Merced

John Muir Dr.

Harding Park

Lake Merced Blvd.

Font Blvd.

San Francisco State University

STONESTOWN

Junipero Serra Blvd.

PARK MERCED

Brotherhood Way

Garfield St.
Sargent St.

TO SAN JOSE (55mi)

San Francisco Golf Club

Lincoln Blvd.

Presidio

Doyle Dr.

Crissy Field

Palace of Fine Arts/ Exploratorium

Richardson Ave.

Lincoln Blvd.

West Pacific Ave.

California St.

Geary Blvd.

Park Presidio Blvd.

10th Ave.
8th Ave.
6th Ave.
4th Ave.

Arguello Blvd.

Anza St.
Balboa St.
Cabrillo St.
Fulton St.

University of San Francisco

Masonic Ave.
Ashbury St.

Fell St.

Stanyan St.

HAIGHT ASHBURY

Clayton St.

Frederick St.

Parnassus Ave.

17th St.

University of California at San Francisco Medical Center

10th Ave.

7th Ave.

Clarendon Ave.

Twin Peaks

FOREST HILL

Laguna Honda Hospital

Laguna Honda Blvd.

Dewey Blvd.

14th Ave.

Vicente St.

West Portal Ave.

Portola Dr.

Yerba Buena Ave.

Mount Davidson Park

Monterey Blvd.

Miramar Ave.

Ocean Ave.

Holloway Ave.

INGLESIDE

Ortaba Ave.

Capitol Ave.

Plymouth Ave.

City College of San Francisco

San Jose Ave.

Balboa Park

Geneva Ave.

Alemany Blvd.

Mission St.

Morse St.

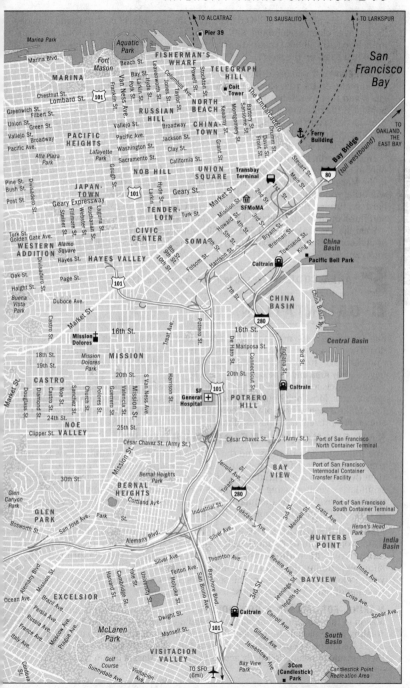

**Taxis** to downtown from SFO depart from the lower level central island outside the baggage claim area (about $30). Check free area guides for coupons. Any San Francisco taxi will take you to the airport, but it's better to call for pick-up than to try to hail a cab on the street.

**BY FREEWAY.** If you are driving into San Francisco **from the south,** approach the city directly on **US 101, I-280,** or **Route 1.** I-280 crosses US 101 in South San Francisco and then continues through eastern Potrero Hill to end just southeast of SoMa. US 101 runs along the border of Potrero Hill and the Mission, then bears left through SoMa and becomes **Van Ness Avenue.** Hwy. 1 turns into **19th Avenue** around San Francisco State University and runs through Sunset, Golden Gate Park, Richmond, and the Presidio.

**From the north,** US 101 and Hwy. 1 lead over the **Golden Gate Bridge** (southbound-only toll $3). Hwy. 1 turns into **19th Avenue,** while US 101 turns into **Lombard Street** in the Marina. From there you have two options. Taking a right on **Divisadero Street** will bring you to the Haight and then the Castro. Alternatively, continuing on Lombard St., turning right on Van Ness Ave., and following it between Pacific Heights and Russian and Nob Hills will bring you to **Market Street** near the Civic Center.

**From the east,** take **I-5** to **I-580** to **I-80,** which runs across the **Bay Bridge** (westbound-only toll $2) into SoMa and then connects with US 101 just before it runs into Van Ness Ave.

 **AREA CODE.** The area code in San Francisco is **415.**

# ✴ ORIENTATION

San Francisco is 403 mi. north of Los Angeles and 390 mi. south of the Oregon border. The city proper lies at the northern tip of the peninsula separating the San Francisco Bay from the Pacific Ocean. (For info on other cities surrounding the bay, see **Bay Area and Wine Country,** p. 129.)

San Francisco's diverse neighborhoods are loosely organized along a few central arteries. Most neighborhoods are compact enough to explore comfortably on foot. Make a mental note of the steep hills in each district—a two-block detour can sometimes prevent a strenuous climb.

## SAN FRANCISCO NEIGHBORHOODS

The following descriptions and the listings of sights and restaurants will move roughly southwest from the tourist-laden western section of downtown, and then over to the residential sections in the east. If you find that neighborhood boundaries get confusing, don't stress—San Francisco, like any living, breathing city, doesn't follow the imaginary boundaries that books like this one need to rely on. That said, a good map is a must.

**FISHERMAN'S WHARF & THE PIERS.** The eastern portion of San Francisco's waterfront is one of its most visited—and most reviled—tourist destinations. Aside from the while-you-wait caricature artists, "olde-fashioned fudge shoppes," penny-flattening machines, and novelty t-shirts, the only natives you're likely to find here are the sea lions. **Piers 39** through **45** provide access to some of San Francisco's most iconic attractions.

**MARINA, FORT MASON & COW HOLLOW.** The residential Marina, between Fort Mason to the east and the expansive Presidio to the west, is home to more young, wealthy professionals (and failed dot-commers) than any other part of San Francisco. Neighboring Fort Mason provides a cultural counterbalance to the area with theaters and museums. Directly across the lengthy Marina Green near the Presidio stands the breathtaking **Palace of Fine Arts** and the fun-for-kids-of-all-ages **Exploratorium** (see p. 102). On the southern border of the Marina, bustling Chestnut and Lombard St. are packed with motels, eateries, and trendy bars. A few blocks south, the neighborhood of Cow Hollow houses herds of San Francisco's elite.

**NORTH BEACH.** On Columbus Ave. at Broadway, shops shift from selling ginseng and roast duck to proffering provolone and biscotti. The legendary Italian community of North Beach, also the birthplace of the **Beat movement,** lies north of Chinatown. In the early 1950s, a group of poets and writers including Jack Kerouac, Allen Ginsberg, Maynard Krebs, and Lawrence Ferlinghetti came to North Beach to write, drink, and raise hell. They lashed out at the conformity of postwar America, embraced Eastern religions and be-bop jazz, and lit a fuse that would eventually set off the counterculture explosion of the late 1960s. Since then, North Beach has experienced a major nightlife surge. Finely clad peninsula- and city-dwellers flock to the zillions of Italian restaurants around Columbus Ave. and stay for the cozy bars and hot live acts around Broadway and Kearny St.

**CHINATOWN.** The largest **Chinese** community outside of Asia, with over 100,000 people Chinatown is also the most densely populated of San Francisco's neighborhoods. Chinese laborers began coming to San Francisco in the mid-19th century as refugees from the Opium Wars and were put to work constructing the railroads of the West. In the 1880s, white Californians secured a law against further Chinese immigration to prevent the so-called "Yellow Peril." Stranded in San Francisco, Chinese-Americans banded together to protect themselves in this small section of downtown. To this day, Chinatown remains mostly Chinese, although it has attracted visitors since the 1850s, when sailors used to stagger down from Barbary Coast saloons looking for women, alcohol, and opium.

**NOB HILL AND RUSSIAN HILL.** In the late 19th century, Nob Hill attracted the West's great railroad magnates and robber barons. Today, their showy mansions make it one of the nation's most prestigious addresses. Russian Hill, to the north, is named after Russian sailors who died during an expedition in the early 1800s and were buried on the southeast crest.

**UNION SQUARE.** Union's big scene is retail. It is home to **chic shops,** ritzy hotels, and prestigious **art galleries.** The area is also home to the heart of San Francisco's **theater district.** Enticements for the budget traveler also abound: affordable accommodations, nighttime fun, and—of course—window shopping.

**GOLDEN GATE BRIDGE AND THE PRESIDIO.** The great span of the Golden Gate Bridge reaches across the San Francisco Bay from Marin County to the Presidio. Originally the northernmost Spanish military garrison in California, the Presidio served first the Mexican and then the American army until the 1990s. Most of the buildings have been converted for civilian use, but the Presidio can still feel rather deserted. Its miles of **paths** and **hills,** however, are wide open to the public and worth a visit. **Crissy Field,** in particular, is a newly restored and beautiful shoreline park that serves sunbathers, ballplayers, and nature lovers.

**LINCOLN PARK.** Lincoln Park's great chunk of green is positioned perfectly for snapping a shot of the Golden Gate Bridge and the Bay. Rugged terrain for hiking and biking meet high culture at the **California Palace of the Legion of Honor.** The **Sutro Baths** offer a Californian version of ancient ruins.

**GOLDEN GATE PARK.** Golden Gate Park covers 1017 lush acres. Beginning in the 1870s, the city undertook decades of work to transform the desert-like region into a vibrant green patch of loveliness. Today, nine lakes, a herd of bison, two windmills, and a science center are a few of the attractions.

**FINANCIAL DISTRICT AND EMBARCADERO.** Although much of modern-day Bay Area business may be conducted online, the city still has its share of pressed suits and corner offices. Corporate worker bees swarm the Financial District, where towering banks blot out the cheerful sun. A surprising number of parks and architectural standouts add character to the area.

**CIVIC CENTER.** There's no mistaking the colossal Civic Center, with its mammoth classical buildings arranged around two vast plazas. Home to the opera, symphony, and most of San Francisco's major theater, the district is grandest at night, when beautifully lit flags and fountains flank bumper-to-bumper limousine traffic.

**HAYES VALLEY.** To the west of the Civic Center, recently gentrified **Hayes Valley** is small, glitzy, and increasingly upscale. Currently home to young artists and designers, the neighborhood has not always boasted such a swinging scene. Destruction caused by the 1989 earthquake led to a drastic makeover, and the rough-and-tumble district has become San Francisco's latest beauty queen.

**TENDERLOIN.** The indistinctly defined region known as the Tenderloin is economic light years away from its neighbors, Union Square and Civic Center. Sporadic attempts at urban renewal have done a (small) bit to improve the poverty of the quarter and its residents. Nevertheless, **avoid walking here alone**, especially in the rectangle bordered by Ellis St., Van Ness Ave., Leavenworth St., and Golden Gate Ave., or at night after visiting one of its nighttime hot spots.

**SOUTH OF MARKET AREA (SOMA).** The most visited, culturally rich part of SoMa lies north of Folsom St., between 2nd and 4th St. These blocks are filled with the concrete and glass expanses of **Yerba Buena Gardens,** Sony Metreon, and the Moscone Convention Center. The **San Francisco Museum of Modern Art (SFMoMA)** presides over the cultural milieu. Several blocks south, between **Pacific Bell Park** (home of the San Francisco **Giants;** see p. 123) and the freeway, tiny but vibrant South Park is surrounded by old and new eateries as well as the "cyberspace gulch" of upstart Internet and design companies. The stretch from 7th to 12th St. along Folsom St. as you head toward the Mission is known for being hip, with trendy cafes, inexpensive restaurants, myriad legendary clubs, and several establishments dedicated to the wearing and selling of leather.

**PACIFIC HEIGHTS.** Climbing up Fillmore St. from Japantown brings you straight into Pacific Heights, just southwest of the Marina and Cow Hollow. Stunning views of both the city and the Bay, the legendary **Fillmore Street jazz scene,** and elegantly restored **Victorian homes** all put Pacific Heights on the map.

**JAPANTOWN (NIHONMACHI).** After it was destroyed by the 1906 earthquake, **Japanese** immigrants moved into the area now called Japantown, a mile west of downtown. For a time, its closely packed homes and shops constituted one of the largest Japanese enclaves outside Japan. Few returned after the community was broken apart by internment during WWII, but the name stuck.

**HAIGHT-ASHBURY.** East of Golden Gate Park and smack dab in the center of the city, the Haight has aged with uneven grace since its hippie heyday. Once a haven for conscientious objectors to the Vietnam War, "Hashbury" embraced drug use and Eastern philosophies during anti-war protests and marches. The hippie voyage reached its apogee in 1967's "Summer of Love," when Janis Joplin, the Grateful Dead, and Jefferson Airplane all made music and love here within a few blocks of one another. Today the counterculture hangs out with the over-the-counter tourist culture, especially in Upper Haight. The Lower Haight still clings to the good ol' days despite the latest additions of Internet cafes and smoothie joints.

**CASTRO.** Scout's honor, *this* is where the boys are. Much of San Francisco's **gay** community (mostly male along with a smaller number of young lesbians) makes the Castro home. Cruisy bars and cafes are everywhere, same-sex public displays of affection raise nary an eyebrow, and tank tops and chiseled abs are *de rigueur.* Aside from being fabulous, the Castro is also pretty.

**MISSION.** Founded by Spanish settlers in 1776, the Mission is home to some of the city's oldest structures, as well as some of the hottest young people and places around. Colorful **murals** celebrate the prominent **Latino** presence that has long defined the Mission. The area grows increasingly diverse and gentrified along Valencia St. Politically, the Mission is the city's most radical pocket, marked by left-wing bookstores, active labor associations, and bohemian bars and cafes filled. The area is also home to a cohesive lesbian community and gay male presence.

**RICHMOND.** Beneath its fog and blank facade of stuccoed buildings, the Richmond is a riot of immigrant history and student life. This mainly residential area is home to Irish-, Russian-, and Chinese-Americans. East of Park Presidio Blvd., the **Inner Richmond,** festooned with cut-price grocery stores and excellent ethnic cuisine, is known as **"New Chinatown."** The **Outer Richmond** holds a handful of Russian delis, an abundance of Irish pubs, and an imposing orthodox church.

**ALCATRAZ AND ANGEL ISLAND.** Although the one on Alcatraz is by far the better known, both Alcatraz and Angel Island once housed prisons. Because of its location in the middle of the Bay, Alcatraz was thought to be inescapable and was used to house the nation's hardest criminals. Angel Island was used in the late 19th century as a detention center for Chinese immigrants and then as a WWII POW camp. Today, its shores and trails are surprisingly perfect for picnicking and hiking.

# ▐ LOCAL TRANSPORTATION

**BY PUBLIC TRANSPORTATION.** San Francisco's main public transportation systems are the **MUNI Metro subway** and **bus system,** which operate throughout the city, and **BART,** which provides wider coverage of the Bay Area and speedy but limited service in San Francisco. Each system is described below and has its own infrastructure, but are all overseen by the **Metropolitan Transportation Commission** (☎510-464-7700; www.transitinfo.org), which provides transit information for the nine-county San Francisco Bay Area.

A decent public transit system makes San Francisco something of an anomaly in a state full of auto-philes; the Bay Area is the easiest place on the West Coast to explore without a car. The system (particularly the Metro system) may be slower and less developed than its counterparts on the East Coast, but the city is so walkable that most find a combination of foot and vehicle perfect for getting around.

Most transportation within the city falls under the authority of the **San Francisco Municipal Railway** (MUNI; pronounced MEW-nee; ☎673-6864; www.sfmuni.com)—something of a misnomer since the system includes **buses** (electric trolley and diesel), **cable cars** (the only ones in the world still operating), a **subway,** and **streetcars.** The MUNI Metro system, whose cars alternate between subway (below ground) and surface-rail (above ground) transportation at various points in the city, offers more limited but speedier service than the MUNI bus system. Downtown, all six Metro lines (F, J, N, L, M, and K) travel underground along the central artery of **Market Street.** With the exception of the F line, they all travel underground from the **Embarcadero Station** to at least the **Church Street Station.** The **F** line runs antique streetcars along Market St., from the **Embarcadero** to the **Castro Street Station,** and as of this year connects to Fisherman's Wharf via the Northern Waterfront/Embarcadero. As they travel "outbound" (away from the Ferry Terminal and the Embarcadero), they all stop at the **Embarcadero, Powell, Civic Center, Van Ness,** and **Church Street stations;** if you're just traveling along this short downtown stretch, it doesn't matter which car you catch. If you're heading any farther, however, take care to snag the appropriate car before the lines split off from one another. The **J** and **N** emerge from the tunnel at **Church Street,** while the **K, L,** and **M** routes continue underground past **Castro Street** and emerge above ground at the **West Portal Station.**

   **Single-ride fares** on MUNI buses, streetcars, and the subway cost $1.25 (seniors and ages 5-17 35¢, under 4 free); if you need one, ask for a **free transfer** (valid for 2 additional rides including BART rides within a 90min. period). Single-ride fares on the cable cars are pricier (adults $3, seniors and disabled $2, under 6 free; before 7am and after 9pm $1), with no transfers. **MUNI passports,** sold at the Powell St. Visitors Center and at some accommodations, are valid on all MUNI vehicles including cable cars (1-day $9, 3-day $15, 7-day $20). The **Weekly Pass** is cheaper ($12) but must be purchased for a single work week and requires an additional $1 to ride the cable cars. The **Monthly FastPass** (adults $45; seniors, disabled, and ages 5-17 $10) includes in-town BART trips (from Embarcadero to Balboa Park) and cable cars.

   MUNIs are an emblem of San Francisco. Declared a national historic landmark in 1964, the colorful cable cars are about image, not practicality. They are noisy, slow (9½ mph), expensive (see **Fares,** above), and usually crammed, making them an unreliable method of getting around. You won't be the first person to think of taking one to Fisherman's Wharf. Still, there is something charming about these relics, and you'll probably want to try them, especially if you have a MUNI passport. To avoid the mobs, get up early and climb the hills with the sunrise. All lines run daily from 6am to 1:30am. There are three lines from which you can choose: Powell-Mason (PM), California Street (C), and Powell-Hyde (PH).

   **Golden Gate Ferry** (☎ 923-2000; www.goldengateferry.org) sails across the Bay to Marin County from the **Ferry Building** at the foot of Market St., east of Pier 1. Ferries serve **Larkspur** (M-F 20 trips per day, first ferry leaves SF 6:35am, last ferry leaves Larkspur 8:15pm; adults $3.25, seniors $1.60, ages 6-12 $2.45; Sa-Su and holidays 5 trips per day, first ferry leaves SF 10:40am, last ferry leaves Larkspur 5:40pm; $5.30) and **Sausalito** (M-F 9 trips per day, first ferry leaves SF 7:40am, last ferry leaves Sausalito 7:20pm; adults $5.60, seniors $2.80, ages 6-12 $4.20, under 5 free; Sa-Su 6 trips per day, first ferry leaves SF 11:30am, last ferry leaves Sausalito 6:10pm; $5.30; increased service May-Sept.). Both lines are wheelchair-accessible. Transfers are free between bus routes and ferries.

   The **Blue and Gold Fleet** (☎ 705-8200, tickets ☎ 705-5555; www.blueandgold-fleet.com) runs to Alcatraz (14 trips per day; $9.25 round-trip, seniors $7.50, ages 5-11 $6; audio tour $4, for children $2; AmEx/D/MC/V) and Angel Island (M-F 4 per day, Sa-Su 3 per day; $12 round-trip, ages 6-12 $6.50, under 6 free) and between SF and Tiburon, Vallejo, Alameda, and Oakland. The Blue and Gold also offers an Island Hop to Alcatraz and Angel Island. (Sept.-June daily, May-June M and Th-Su; adults $36.75, seniors $34, ages 5-11 $22, under 5 free; includes audio tour on Alcatraz and Tram-Tour on Angel Island). The **Harbor Bay Ferry** (☎ 510-769-5500; www.harborbay-ferry.com) goes between SF and Alameda. The **Red and White Ferry** (☎ 673-2900; www.redandwhite.com) runs between SF and Point Richmond; the **Baylink Ferry** (☎ 877-643-3779; www.baylinkferry.com) services SF to Vallejo with a bus to Sacramento. All ferries leave the **Ferry Building** near the Embarcadero.

**BY REGIONAL PUBLIC TRANSPORTATION.** All regional buses operate from the **Transbay Terminal,** 425 Mission St., at 1st St. An information center on the second floor has maps and free phone lines for bus information. (☎ 495-1569. Open daily 4:30am-12:30am.) **Golden Gate Transit** provides regional fixed-route bus service in San Francisco, Marin, and Sonoma Counties. Limited service is also available between Central Marin and Western Contra Costa Counties. (☎ 923-2000;

www.goldengatetransit.org. M-F 6am-10pm, Sa-Su reduced service; $1.50-6.30 depending on distance; discounts for seniors, disabled, and youth.) **Alameda County (AC) Transit** operates bus service to and in Oakland and Berkeley. (☎800-448-9790; www.actransit.org; $1.35-2.75 (transbay fares); discounts for seniors, disabled, and youth.) **San Mateo Transit (SamTrans)** serves the peninsula with hundreds of trips along the Bayshore corridor between Palo Alto and downtown San Francisco. Additional frequent SF service is provided along El Camino Real and Mission St. Hundreds of other daily trips serve SFO, Daly City, Hayward, and 20 other cities in the county. (☎800-660-4287 or 650-817-1717; www.samtrans.com. Most routes daily 6am-6pm; $1-3, discounts for seniors and youth.)

Connections to neighboring cities are well-coordinated and speedy via **BART,** with five lines connecting San Francisco with the **East Bay** (see p. 129), including Oakland, Berkeley, Concord, and Fremont. All stations provide free maps and schedules and all stops are wheelchair-accessible. (☎989-2278; www.bart.org. Service M-F 4am-midnight, Sa 6am-midnight, Su 8am-midnight; times at individual stops may vary. Fare within San Francisco $1.10, to the East Bay up to $4.70.)

**Caltrain** (Bay Area ☎800-660-4287, elsewhere 510-817-1717; www.caltrain.com) leaves from the **Caltrain Depot** at 4th and King St. in SoMa (M-F 5am-midnight, Sa 7am-midnight, Su 8am-10pm), and runs to Palo Alto ($4.50, seniors and under 12 $2.25) and San Jose ($6, seniors and under 12 $3), making many stops along the way. Fares are calculated on the basis of zones and monthly passes are available. Be sure to check ahead as service is somewhat unreliable due to construction.

**BY BIKE.** Though even the hardiest bike couriers have been spotted walking their bikes, San Francisco is a great city to traverse by bike or in-line skates despite the steep, punishing hills. Check out our color topographical map of downtown (in the middle of this book) to plan a flatter route. Most modes of public transportation in the Bay Area accommodate bicycles. When riding on roads also used by cable cars and trains, beware of getting your tires stuck in the grooves.

The Department of Parking and Traffic runs the **SF Bicycle Program** (☎585-2453), which organizes numbered **bike routes** around the city. Rectangular **signs** showing a silhouetted bike and the Golden Gate Bridge mark the routes. Even numbers on the signs refer to north-south routes, with the numbers increasing from east to west; odd numbers refer to east-west routes, with the numbers increasing from north to south; three-digit numbers refer to connector routes; and green signs are local routes, while signs with a red Golden Gate Bridge icon indicate crosstown routes. These bike paths may run separate from motor vehicle traffic, alongside traffic in the street in a marked bike lane, or with traffic on a street with a wide-curb lane. The SFBP hotline has info on bike lockers, MUNI racks, and safety resources. The non-profit **SF Bicycle Coalition** (☎431-2453; www.sfbike.org) promotes bike use, advocates for transit improvement, and gets members bike shop discounts and other goodies.

Safe and secure cycling requires a quality **helmet** (required by state law) and **lock.** A good helmet costs about $40—much cheaper than critical head surgery. Most rental shops have helmets for very reasonable daily and weekly rates. U-shaped **Kryptonite** or **Citadel** locks ($30-60) carry **insurance** against theft for one or two years if your bike is registered with the police.

**BY TAXI.** Taxis are not as easy to hail on the street in San Francisco as they are in many American cities, so it's often a good idea to call a cab in advance. **San Francisco Yellow Cab** (☎626-2345), **National Cab Company** (☎648-4444), and **Town Taxi** (☎546-1616) are a few of the local taxi companies.

**BY CAR.** A car is not necessary for getting around the area and may be more trouble than it's worth, unless you would like the convenience of your own wheels on a daytrip. Contending with the treacherous **hills** is the first task; if

# Downtown San Francisco

**◆ ACCOMMODATIONS**
Millennium, 48
Patisserie Café, 61
Adelaide Hostel & Hotel, 33
Pat's Café, 3
Ansonia Abby Hotel, 31
Rico's, 5
Central YMCA of San Francisco, 46
Sushigroove, 10
The Embassy Hotel, 42
Zarzuela, 7
Fort Mason Hostel, 1
Golden Gate Hotel, 27
**♫ NIGHTLIFE/MUSIC**
Green Tortoise Hostel, 15
111 Minna, 41
Hostel at Union Square, 38
The Bigfoot Lodge, 24
Interclub Globe Hostel, 63
Café Trieste, 13
New Central Hotel & Hostel, 56
The EndUp, 58
Pacific Tradewinds Hostel, 26
Hotel Utah Saloon, 59
Phoenix Hotel, 43
The Stud, 65
The San Remo Hotel, 4
Velvet Lounge, 16
SoMa Inn, 57
Vesuvio Café, 18

**★ ENTERTAINMENT**
Biscuits & Blues, 34
Blue Lamp, 35
Curran Theatre, 36
Exit Theater, 44
Geary Theater, 37
Golden Gate Theater, 47
Herbst Theatre, 50
Louise M. Davies
Symphony Hall, 52
The Lumière, 25
The Orpheum, 54
Saloon, 14
San Francisco Ballet, 51
War Memorial Opera House, 51

**■ SHOPPING**
American Rag, 29
City Lights Bookstore, 17
Imperial Tea Court, 12
Lyle Tuttle's Tattoo Art Studio, 6
Mr. S. Leather, 60
San Francisco Shopping Center, 45

**♦ FOOD**
Ananda Fuara, 53
Basil, 62
The Butler and the Chef Cafe, 55
Café Bastille, 28
Café Bean, 30
Café Bosse, 64
Café Venue, 39
Chef Jia, 31
The Crêpe House, 23
Dottie's True Blue Café, 32
Gelato Classico, 8
Golden Gate Bakery, 19
House of Nanking, 20
Kay Cheung's, 22
Lalitai Thai Restaurant
and Bar, 49
L'Osteria del Forno, 11
Mario's Bohemian
Cigar Store Café, 9
McCormick, 2
Mela Tandoori, 40

you've arrived in a standard (manual) transmission vehicle, you'll need to develop a fast clutch foot, since all hills have stop signs at the crests. If you're renting, get an automatic transmission. Make sure to stop for cable cars because they won't stop for you. **Seat belts** in cars and **helmets** on motorcycles and mopeds are required by law.

**Parking** in San Francisco is rare and expensive even where legal, and a network of zealous traffic cops doles out copious tickets despite local protests against the city's rigorous regulations. The many broken parking meters indicate an irate citizenry, but the time limit still applies to such spaces, and you may be ticketed up to three times for a single offense. Whatever you do, don't block a sidewalk disabled-access ramp—the ticket is a whopping $250. You can stow your car all day in residential Richmond or Sunset—just make certain you heed signs indicating weekly street-cleaning times. To park near a popular area, your best bet may be a **parking garage.** Below is a list of car rental agencies.

 **City,** 1748 Folsom St. (☎877-861-1312), between Duboce and 14th St. Compacts from $29-35 per day, $160-170 per week. Small fee for unlimited mileage. Must be 21; $8 per day surcharge for drivers under 25. Open M-F 7:30am-6pm, Sa 9am-4pm. Additional location: 1433 Bush St. (☎866-359-1331), between Van Ness Ave. and Polk St.

**Budget,** 321 Mason St. (☎800-527-0700), in Union Sq. Compacts from $30 per day. Must be 21; $20 surcharge per day for drivers under 25. Open M-F 6am-9pm, Sa 6:30am-7pm, Su 6:30am-9pm.

**Thrifty,** 520 Mason St. (☎415-788-8111), at Post St. Compacts from $27 per day. Unlimited mileage. Must be 21; under 25 $25 per day surcharge. Open daily 7am-7pm.

> **! PREVENT RUNAWAYS.** The street signs admonishing you to "Prevent Runaways" refer not to wayward youth but to cars poorly parked on hills. When parking facing uphill, turn front wheels away from the curb, and leave the car in first gear if driving a standard transmission. If your car starts to roll, it will stop (you hope) when the tires hit the curb. When facing downhill, turn the wheels toward the curb and leave the car in reverse. *Always* set the emergency brake.

# ⓘ PRACTICAL INFORMATION

## TOURIST & FINANCIAL SERVICES

**Visitor Information: Visitor Information Center** (☎391-2000; 24hr. info recordings 391-2001; www.sfvisitor.org), in Hallidie Plaza, at Powell St. Open M-F 9am-5:30pm, Sa-Su 9am-3pm; phones open M-F 8:30am-5pm.

**Consulates: Australia,** 1 Bush St. #700, at Market St. (☎536-1970). **Ireland,** 44 Montgomery St. (☎392-4214), at Sutter St. **UK,** 1 Sansome St. #850, at Market St. (☎617-1300).

**Currency Exchange:** Available at the airport and most banks. **American Express,** 455 Market St. (☎536-2600; www.americanexpress.com). Open M-F 8:30am-5pm, Sa 9am-3:30pm. **Bank of America Foreign Currency Services,** 1 Powell St. (☎953-5102), at Eddy St., near Market St. Open M-F 9am-6pm, Sa 9am-2pm. **Foreign Exchange Ltd.,** 429 Stockton St. (☎677-5100), near Sutter St. Open M-F 9am-5:30pm; Apr.-Sept. Sa 9:15-4:45pm. **Thomas Cook,** 75 Geary St. (☎362-3452; www.us.thomascook.com). Open M-F 9am-5pm, Sa 10am-4pm.

# LOCAL SERVICES

**San Francisco Public Library** (www.sfpl.lib.ca.us). **Main Branch,** 100 Larkin St. (☎415-557-4400), between Grove and Fulton St. Open M 10am-6pm, Tu-Th 9am-8pm, F noon-6pm, Sa noon-5pm, Su noon-5pm. Other branches in the **Mission,** 300 Bartlett St. (☎355-2800), at 24th St.; in **Chinatown,** 1135 Powell St. (☎335-2888), near Jackson St.; and in **North Beach,** 2000 Mason St. (☎274-0270), at Columbus St.

**Ticket Agencies: Tickets.com** (☎478-2277 or ☎800-225-2277). Open daily 8am-6pm. **TIX Bay Area** (☎433-7827; www.theatrebayarea.org), in a kiosk in Union Sq. on the corner of Geary and Powell St. Offers tickets for almost all shows and concerts in the city as well as information about city tours and MUNI passes. on Stockton St. between Post and Geary St. Half-price tickets often available on day of show and on Sa. Open Tu-Th 11am-6pm, F-Sa 11am-7pm, Su 11am-3pm.

**Road Conditions: CalTrans,** ☎800-427-7623 within California; ☎916-445-7623 elsewhere. **TravInfo,** ☎817-1717.

**National Weather Service,** ☎650-364-7974.

**Laundromats: Self-Service Laundromat,** 600 Bush St. near Stockton St. in **Union Sq.** Wash $1.75; dry 25¢ per 10min. Open daily 7am-10pm, last load 9pm. **Doo Wash,** 817 Columbus Ave. (☎885-1222), near Lombard St. in **North Beach.** Video games, pool table, and TV. Wash $1.50, dry $1. Open daily 7am-11pm; last load 9:30pm.

**Television: ABC** (Channel 7, KGO); **CBS** (Channel 5, KPIX); **Fox** (Channel 2, KTVU); **NBC** (4, KRON); **PBS** (9, KQED); **WB** (20, KBWB).

**National Public Radio:** KQED 88.5 FM; KAWL 91.7 FM.

# EMERGENCY & COMMUNICATIONS

**Police:** ☎553-0123. **Fire:** ☎558-3200. **Poison:** ☎800-876-4766.

**24hr. Crisis Lines: AIDS Hotline,** ☎415-863-2437. **Crisis Line for the Handicapped,** ☎800-426-4263. **Drug Crisis Line,** ☎415-362-3400. **Rape Crisis Center,** ☎415-647-7273. **Suicide Prevention,** ☎415-781-0500.

**Hospitals: Central Public Health Center,** 470 27th St. (☎415-271-4263), at Telegraph Ave. in Oakland. Make appointments far in advance. Open M-F 8-11:30am and 1-4pm. **Haight-Ashbury Free Medical Clinic,** 558 Clayton St. (☎415-487-5632), at Haight St. Appointments only. Open M-Th 9am-9pm, F 1-5pm. **Lyon-Martin Women's Clinic,** 1748 Market St. #201 (☎415-565-7667), at Octavia St. Open for drop-ins Th 1-3pm. Clinic hours: M-Tu and Th-F 8:30am-5pm, W 8:30am-7:30pm.

**Internet Access:** Most **public library** locations. **The Blue Danube,** 306 Clement St. (☎415-221-9041), at 4th Ave. Internet access $3 per 20min., $5 per 40min., $7 per hr. Open daily 7am-9:30pm. **Chat Cafe,** 498 Sanchez St. (☎415-626-4700), at 18th St. Free with purchase ($2.50 per hr.). Open M-F 6:30am-7:30pm, Sa 8am-7:30pm, Su 8am-6:30pm. **The Crêpe House,** 1755 Polk St. (☎415-441-2421), at Washington St. DSL Internet access $10 per hr. Open Su-Th 7:30am-9:30pm, F-Sa 7:30am-10:30pm.

**Post Offices:** 24hr. automated service, connects to local post offices: ☎800-275-8777. **Bernal Heights Station,** 45 29th St., at Mission St. Open M-F 8:30am-5pm. **Postal Code:** 94110. **Chinatown Station,** 867 Stockton St., at Clay St. Open M-F 9am-5:30pm, Sa 9am-4:30pm. **Postal Code:** 94108. **Civic Center: Federal Building Station,** 450 Golden Gate Ave., at Larkin St. Open M-F 8:30am-5pm. **Postal Code:** 94102. **Geary Station,** 5654 Geary Blvd., at 21st Ave. Open M-F 9am-5:30pm, Sa 9am-4:30pm. **Postal Code:** 94121. **Haight-Ashbury: Clayton St. Station,** 554 Clayton St., at Haight St. Open M-F 9am-5:30pm, Sa 9am-4pm. Postal Code: 94117.

## PUBLICATIONS

The largest Bay Area **daily** is the *San Francisco Chronicle* (50¢), run by executive editor Phil Bronstein, Sharon Stone's husband, and owned by the Hearst Corporation. the *San Francisco Examiner*, the paper actually founded by the yellow journalist William Randolph Hearst himself, has lunchtime and evening editions. The two papers share a Sunday edition ($1.50). The pink *Datebook* section of the Sunday edition is also a worthwhile entertainment resource. Free publications flood San Francisco cafes, visitors centers, and sidewalk boxes, including the progressive *SF Bay Guardian* (www.sfbg.com; Wednesdays) and it's major competitor *SF Weekly* (www.sfweekly.com). Harder to find, but worth the effort, are two special-interest rags: *Poetry Flash*, which has info on literary happenings in the Bay Area and beyond, available at discerning bookstores, and *Bay Area Music (BAM)*, available at the livelier eateries in town. The *Bay Area Reporter* appears every Thursday and has articles on gay pride as well as an entertainment section.

Various tourist-targeting, coupon-filled free glossies are in sidewalk boxes in the heavily trafficked Fisherman's Wharf and Union Square areas, as well as at visitors centers. Among these are the *Bay City Guide*, *San Francisco Guide*, and *San Francisco Quick Guide*.

# ⌂ ACCOMMODATIONS

For those who don't mind sharing a room with strangers, San Francisco's better **hostels** (below) are homier, cheaper, and safer than most budget **hotels** (p. 92). Book in advance if at all possible, but since many don't take reservations for summer, you might have to just show up or call early (well before noon) on your day of arrival. Travelers with cars should also consider the **Marin Headlands Hostel**, a beautiful spot just minutes from the city across the Golden Gate Bridge (see p. 106). Some hostels ask for a foreign passport as identification; US citizens are usually welcome but sometimes must prove they are not local residents.

## ACCOMMODATIONS BY PRICE

| UNDER $17 (❶) | | UNDER $79 (❹) | |
|---|---|---|---|
| New Central Hotel and Hostel (92) | CC | 🏠 The San Remo Hotel (92) | RH |
| SoMa Inn (92) | SoMa | 🏠 Ansonia Abby Hotel (92) | US |
| San Fran Int'l Guesthouse (92) | MI | The Embassy Hotel (93) | CC |
|  |  | Metro Hotel (94) | HA |
| **UNDER $34 (❷)** | | San Francisco Zen Center (92) | HA |
| 🏠 Fort Mason Hostel (91) | FM | Hayes Valley Inn (93) | HV |
| 🏠 Green Tortoise Hostel (91) | NB | 🏠 The Red Victorian B&B and Art (92) | HA |
| Pacific Tradewinds Hostel (91) | CH |  |  |
| 🏠 Adelaide Hostel (91) | US | **$80+ (❺)** | |
| Hostel at Union Square (HI-AYH) (91) | US | Golden Gate Hotel (94) | US |
| Central YMCA of San Francisco (91) | TE | 🏠 Phoenix Hotel (93) | TE |
| Interclub Globe Hostel (92) | SoMa | 🏠 The Parker House (93) | CA |
| Easy Goin' Guesthouse (91) | MI | Inn on Castro (93) | CA |
|  |  | Noe's Nest (93) | NV |
|  |  | The Seal Rock Inn (93) | RI |

**CA** castro **CC** civic center **CH** chinatown **FM** fort mason **HV** hayes valley
**HA** haight-ashbury **MI** mission **NB** north beach **NV** noe valley
**RH** russian hlll **RI** richmond **SoMa** south of market **TE** tenderloin **US** union square

# HOSTELS

■ **Adelaide Hostel & Hotel,** 5 Isadora Duncan (☎359-1915 or 800-359-1915; fax 359-1940; www.adelaidehostel.com; info@adelaidehostel.com), at the end of a little alley off Taylor St. between Geary and Post St. in **Union Square.** Warm hosts, sizable common areas, and reasonable prices make this quiet 18-room oasis the perfect hotel in which to meet a bloke from Australia or a lass from Ireland. Steep stairs let you flex your buff Frisco calves. All rooms have large windows, TV (some with free 300-channel satellite), and wash basin. Small, shared hallway bathrooms. Hostel offers shuttle to SFO each morning ($8). 24hr. reception. Check-out noon. Reserve online or by phone at least 10 days in advance. Dorms $24; singles and doubles from $65. ❷

■ **Fort Mason Hostel (HI-AYH),** Bldg. #240 (☎771-7277; sfhostel@norcalhostels.org), at the corner of Bay and Franklin St. past the administrative buildings, in **Fort Mason.** Beautiful surroundings give this 160-bed hostel a campground feel. Not a place for partiers—strictly enforced quiet hours and other rules such as no smoking or alcohol. Movies, walking tours, kitchen, dining room, bike storage. Huge, clean kitchen, and cute cafe with vegetarian dinner ($3). Usually booked weeks in advance, but a few beds are reserved for walk-ins. Minor chores expected. Lockers, laundry (wash $1, dry $1), and parking. Reception 24hr. Check-in 2:30pm. Check-out 11am. No curfew, but lights out at midnight. IBN reservations available. Dorms $24.50. ❷

■ **Green Tortoise Hostel,** 494 Broadway (☎834-1000; www.greentortoise.com), off Columbus Ave. at Kearny St. in **North Beach.** A brothel, ballroom, and apartment flat preceded this super-mellow and friendly pad. Get to know fellow travelers and crash a keg party or special event in the Fior D'Italia ballroom. Free sauna. Free Internet access. Breakfast and kitchen access included. Storage lockers $1 per day; smaller free lockers under every bed. Laundry (wash $1.25, dry 75¢). Key deposit $20. 10-day max. stay. Reception 24hr. Check-in noon. Check-out 11am. Reservations recommended; call at noon on arrival day for walk-in availability. 4-, 6-, and 8-bed dorms $19-22; private rooms $48-56. No credit cards. ❷

**Hostel at Union Square (HI-AYH),** 312 Mason St. (☎788-5604; www.norcalhostels.org), between Geary and O'Farrell St. in **Union Square.** TV, Internet access ($1 per 10min.), and weekly events like free walking tours, ballgame outings, and nightly movie. $5 deposit for locker, iron, board game, or key. 21-night max. stay. Reception 24hr. Quiet hours midnight-7am. IBN reservations available. Reserve by phone with credit card or show up around 8am. Tidy and unadorned dorm-style triples and quads $22; non-members $25. Private rooms $60; nonmembers $66. Under 13 half-price with parent. ❷

**Pacific Tradewinds Hostel,** 680 Sacramento St. (☎433-7970; fax 291-8801; www.hostels.com/pt), at Kearny St. in **Chinatown.** Tradewinds' friendly staff and sardine-can intimacy serve as a sanctuary for solo travelers. Linens, laundry, free DSL, no lockout. 2-week max. stay. Reception 8am-midnight. Reservations recommended. Dorms $16-24; double beds $16-22 per person. ❷

**Central YMCA of San Francisco,** 220 Golden Gate Ave. (☎345-6700; fax 885-5439; www.centralymcasf.org), at Leavenworth St. east of Hyde St. in the **Tenderloin.** Opened in 1910, the Tenderloin Y houses 3 floors of hotel space—106 simple rooms, all with TVs, and some with private baths. Energize in the elegant and affordable cafe with complimentary continental breakfast for the free fitness facility's yoga workshops and cardio-kickboxing. Pool, towels, lockers, laundry, mail facilities, and cheap parking. Key and remote deposit $20. Dorms $25; singles $40-50; doubles $50-60; triples $65-78. ❷

**Easy Goin' Travel and California Dreamin' Guesthouse,** 3145-47 Mission St. (☎552-8452; www.easygo.com), at Precita Ave **in Mission.** Super-friendly staff and excellent amenities more than make up for the slightly removed new location of this independent

SAN FRANCISCO

SAN FRANCISCO

hostel. In-room TVs, kitchen, free coffee, TV lounge, laundry, Internet, bike rental, basic cable, pay phone, and travel services. $20 security and key deposit. 2-night min. Check-in noon. Check-out 11am. Reservations recommended. Dorm beds $18-19; private rooms $40-43. Additional location: Harrison and 7th. Check-in and booking through the Mission St. location; shuttle to Harrison and 7th St. provided. ❷

**Interclub Globe Hostel,** 10 Hallam Pl. (☎431-0540), off Folsom St. between 7th and 8th St. in **SoMa.** Former incarnations include a flophouse, bathhouse, leather bar, drug den, and hospice. An aquarium allows to you sleep with the fishes. 24hr. Internet access. Happening common room has pool table, TV, microwave, and fridge. All rooms have private bath. Refundable key deposit $10, safe deposit $10. Check-out noon. Passport required. Spare 5- to 8-bed dorms $19, 3 nights $45; private single or double $50; off-season rates lower. No credit cards or personal checks. **Passport required.** ❷

**SoMa Inn,** 1082 Folsom St. (☎863-7522; fax 558-8562), between 6th and 7th St. Clean, no-frills rooms on an industrial block of Folsom St. Shared hall bath. Kitchen and Internet. Reception 24hr. Refundable key deposit $5. 8-bed dorms $17; singles $28; doubles $36; triples $66; quads $88. Weekly $99.50/$160/$180/$330/$440. ❶

**San Francisco Zen Center,** 300 Page St. (☎863-3136; www.sfzc.org), near Laguna St. in the **Lower Haight.** If rigorous soul searching is not for you, but meditative peace of mind sounds appealing, stay at the Zen Center as a guest. Breakfast included. Single and double rooms $66-105. Weekly and monthly rates. ❹

**New Central Hotel and Hostel,** 1412 Market St. (☎703-9988), between Van Ness Ave. and Polk St. This conventional no-frills hostel is dim and austere but clean. Lockers, TV room, kitchens, laundry, and free linens. Proof of travel required. 24hr. reception. Check-in anytime. Check-out 11am. Dorms $17 per night, $105 per week. Private room with shared bath $40, with private bath $52. ❶

**San Francisco International Guesthouse,** 2976 23rd St. (☎641-1411), at Harrison St., in the **Mission.** No sign; look for the blue Victorian near the corner. Hardwood floors and wall tapestries. Free coffee and foreign magazines. TV area, 2 kitchens (smoking and non-smoking), guest phones, and free Internet. 5-night min. stay. Getting in can be as difficult as escaping Alcatraz; the Guesthouse does not take reservations, is almost always full, and caters primarily to international visitors. All you can do is try calling. Dorm beds $15; private doubles $30. Passport with international stamps "required." ❶

# HOTELS

▨ **Ansonia Abby Hotel,** 711 Post St. (☎673-2670 or ☎800-221-6470; fax 673-9217), between Jones and Leavenworth St. in **Union Square.** Keep this gloriously affordable secret to yourself. Overnight storage and safety deposit, TV and fridge in every room, and access to DSL-equipped computer lab. Free breakfast daily 7-8:30am, dinner M-Sa. Laundry facilities. Check-out 11am. Singles $56-66; doubles $66, with bath $79. Cheap weekly rates (from $211) available Sept.-Apr. for Bay Area summer students. ❹

▨ **The San Remo Hotel,** 2237 Mason St. (☎776-8688; www.sanremohotel.com), between Chestnut and Francisco St. in **Russian Hill.** Built in 1906, this hotel has rooms that are small but elegantly furnished with antique armoires, bedposts, lamps, and complimentary (if random) backscratchers. The sparkling shared bathrooms with brass pull-chain toilets harken back to the end of the 19th century. The hotel's penthouse offers a private garden, bathroom, and windowed rooftop room with an amazing view of the city. Friendly staff. Free modem connections. Laundry room (wash $1.50, dry $1). Check-in 2pm. Check-out 11am. Reservations required. Singles $55-85; doubles $65-95; triples $95. Penthouse $155 per night; reserve 6-9 months in advance. ❹

▨ **The Red Victorian Bed, Breakfast, and Art,** 1665 Haight St. (☎864-1978; www.red-vic.com) west of Belvedere St. in the **Upper Haight.** The "Summer of Love" lives on in this B&B and gallery of meditative art. Striving to create peace through tourism, guests come together at breakfast to meditate and chat. All 18 rooms are individually decorated with themes like sunshine, redwoods, playground, and butterflies. Even the hall bathrooms have their own motifs. Breakfast included. Reception 9am-9pm. Check-in 3-9pm or by appointment. Check-out 11am. Reservations required. Rooms from $79-200 with discounts for stays longer than 3 days. ❹

**The Parker House,** 520 Church St. (☎621-3222 or 888-520-7275; www.parkerguesthouse.com), near 17th St. in **Castro.** Serene and stylish. Regularly voted best LGB B&B in the city. A beautiful parlor, with dark wood paneling, grand piano, and flowers galore. Every room has cable and modem ports, but best of all, there are heavenly down comforters and a spa and steam room downstairs. Breakfast included in a sunny porch-room overlooking rose gardens. Parking $15 per day. 2-night min. stay on weekends, 4-night min. stay some holiday weekends. Check-in 3pm. Check-out noon. Reservations recommended. Rooms with shared bath from $119, with private bath from $139. ❺

**Phoenix Hotel,** 601 Eddy St. (☎776-1380 or 800-248-9466; www.thephoenixhotel.com), at Larkin St. Hip rooms decorated in a funky beach-resort-meets-safari style and a gorgeous blue-and-white-tiled swimming pool make this throwback to the 50s an oasis in the urban **Tenderloin.** Free access to the popular Bambuddha Lounge next door. All rooms equipped with xylophones. Parking included. Doubles start at a pricey $139, but may go as low as $89-109 on a slow night. ❺

**Inn On Castro,** 321 Castro St. (☎861-0321; www.innoncastro2.com), near Market St. in **Castro.** Brightly refurbished Victorian exterior complements the cozy living room—the perfect place to enjoy a good book, the Inn's popular full breakfast, or a swig of complimentary brandy. Common kitchen opens onto deck with beautiful, sweeping view of the East Bay, while the immaculately clean dining area and comfy common lounge are reminiscent of a compulsive friend's apartment. Gay-owned and -operated, but straight-friendly. Parking $15 per day. Reception 7:30am-10:30pm. Singles $100-165; doubles $115-185; patio suite $185; neighborhood apartments $135-250. ❺

**Hayes Valley Inn,** 417 Gough St. (☎431-9131 or 800-930-7999; www.hayesvalleyinn.com), just north of Hayes St. in **Hayes Valley.** European charm means small, clean rooms and shared baths. Although you will get to know your neighbor, the rooms are well maintained and all have cable TV, phone, and private sink. Some smoking and pet-friendly rooms. Continental breakfast. Check-in 3pm. Check-out 11am. Reservations recommended for summer and holidays. In summer singles $58; doubles $68-79; queens $78-89; queen turret $88-99. In winter singles $42/$48-56/$54-61/$58-66. ❹

**Noe's Nest,** 3973 23rd St. (☎821-0751; www.noesnest.com), between Noe and Sanchez St. in **Noe Valley.** Feels like a home with all the family memorabilia around. The 7 rooms—all with private bath, phone, cable TV, VCR, and modem ports—are individually themed. Huge breakfast served in the proprietor's kitchen or on the front patio or back garden. Hot tub. Laundry service available. 2-night min. stay on weekends. Flexible check-in and check-out. Reservations required. Singles and doubles $119-179. ❺

**The Seal Rock Inn,** 545 Point Lobos Ave. (☎752-8000; www.sealrockinn.com), at 48th Ave. opposite the Sutro Baths in the **Richmond.** Though the area is remote, it's a quiet, attractive place to escape city chaos. Pastel houses with well-kept gardens run right to the beach. Seal Rock's big, clean rooms are a great deal, especially for families. Pool and patio area. Free parking. Check-in 1pm. Check-out 11am. Singles $120-140; doubles $130-150; $10 per additional person, $5 per child. Reduced rates Sept.-May. ❺

**The Embassy Hotel,** 610 Polk St. (☎673-1404 or 888-814-6835; www.embassyhotelsf.com), at Turk St. A rare find in **Civic Center**—respectable, affordable, and not too far into unpleasant territory. Rooms are neat, if spartan. Adjoining bar, TV, Internet access, telephones, and free parking. Continental breakfast included. Singles $59-79; doubles $69-89. Higher summer rates. ❹

**Metro Hotel,** 319 Divisadero St. (☎861-5364), between Oak and Page St. in the **Lower Haight.** Slightly removed from the hubbub lies this charming retreat with a sunny backyard garden. Private baths in all rooms. 28-day max. stay. Reception 7:30am-midnight. Check-out noon. Reserve well in advance. Singles $66; doubles $77; triples $120. ❹

**Golden Gate Hotel,** 775 Bush St. (☎392-3702 or ☎800-835-1118; fax 392-6202; www.goldengatehotel.com), between Mason and Powell St. in **Union Square.** The amicable owners and their cat, Captain Nemo, invoke a warm, homey feel in this antique gem of a hotel. Wicker chairs, floral bedspreads, antiques, and big bay windows. German, French, and Spanish spoken. Continental breakfast and afternoon tea (4-7pm) included. Garage parking $15 per day. Doubles with sink $85, with bath $115. ❺

# ◖ FOOD

Strolling and sampling the food in each neighborhood is an excellent way to get a taste for the city's diversity. For the most up-to-date listings of restaurants, try the *Examiner* and the *SF Bay Guardian.* The glossy *Bay Area Vegetarian* can also suggest places to graze.

## FISHERMAN'S WHARF

Pier 39 and Fisherman's Wharf overflow with opportunities to refuel, but because this is tourist central, most eateries charge fairly expensive rates for average food, though you may feel compelled to try some clam chowder and sourdough bread.

▧ **Pat's Café,** 2330 Taylor St. (☎776-8735), between Chestnut and Francisco St. One of a string of breakfast joints, Pat's stands out from the crowd, not just because of its bright yellow building, but also for its huge, delicious, home-cooked meals. Burgers, sandwiches, and big breakfasts ($4-7). Open daily 7:30am-2pm. No credit cards. ❶

**McCormick and Kuleto's,** 900 North Point St. (☎929-1730), in Ghirardelli Sq. Can't leave the wharf without trying crabcakes or clam chowder, but skeptical about the vendors on the piers? This stylish seafood restaurant offers a comprehensive menu and a spectacular view of Aquatic Park. Most entrees $10-25, brick-oven pizzas $7.50-10.50. Open daily 11:30am-11pm. ❸

## MARINA, FORT MASON & COW HOLLOW

The **Marina Safeway,** 15 Marina Blvd., between Laguna and Buchanan St., is legendary as a spot to pick up more than just groceries. (☎563-4946. Open 24hr.) For purists and puritans, there is a **Real Food Company,** 3060 Fillmore St., on the corner of Filbert St. (☎567-6900. Open daily 8am-9pm.)

▧ **Marina Submarine,** 2299 Union St. (☎921-3990), at Steiner St. in Cow Hollow. Often a long (but worthwhile) wait for superlative subs that satisfy in several sizes ($4-7). Open M-F 10am-6:30pm, Sa 11am-4:30pm, Su 11am-3:30pm. No credit cards. ❷

▧ **Home Plate,** 2774 Lombard St. (☎922-4663), off Pierce St. in the Marina. Hard-to-beat, hearty breakfast, brunch, and lunch (most items under $8). Friendly service and scones with homemade strawberry-apple jam with every meal. Open daily 7am-4pm. ❶

▧ **La Canasta,** 3006 Buchanan St. (☎474-2627), near Union St. in Cow Hollow. Hard-working cooks at this tiny kitchen give you their best tacos, burritos, and ensaladas. The Mexican food is fresh and cooked in healthy oils. Soups fashioned on the spot. All food is take-out only. Almost everything on the menu under $5. Open daily 11am-10pm. ❶

**Pizza Orgasmica,** 3157 Fillmore St. (☎931-5300), at Greenwich St. in Cow Hollow. With pizzas suggestively named "menage a trois" and "doggie style," it's hard not to get excited. Prices can get fairly steep (pies $10-23) so don't miss the all-you-can-eat special (11am-4pm; $5.50). Open Su-W 11am-midnight, Th 11am-2:30am, F-Sa 11am-2:30am. ❷

# FOOD BY TYPE

**AMERICAN& DINERS**
Café Bosse (98) SoMa ❶
🍴 Home Plate (94) MA ❷
🍴 Pat's Café (94) FW ❶
🍴 Welcome Home (99) CA ❷

**BREAKFAST**
🍴 Café Bean (97) US ❶
Kate's Kitchen (100) LH ❷

**BRUNCH**
🍴 Dottie's True Blue Café (97) US ❶
🍴 Squat and Gobble (100) UH ❷

**CALIFORNIA CUISINE**
🍴 Cafe Venue (98) FDE ❸
🍴 Home (99) CA ❸

**CHINESE**
🍴 Chef Jia (97) CH ❶
🍴 Golden Gate Bakery (97) CH ❶
🍴 House of Nanking (96) CH ❷
Kay Cheung's Restaurant (97) CH ❶
Lee Hou Restaurant (100) RI ❶
Taiwan Restaurant (101) RI ❷

**DESSERT**
Bombay Ice Creamery (100) MI ❶

**ETHIOPIAN**
Cafe Ethiopia (100) MI ❶

**FRENCH AND CREPERIES**
The Butler and the Chef (98) SoMa ❶
Café Bastille (98) FDE ❹
The Crêpe House (97) NH ❶
Patisserie Café (98) SoMa ❷
Sophie's Crepes (99) JT ❶

**GROCERY STORES**
Marina Safeway (94) MA
Real Food Company (94) MA

**INDIAN AND PAKISTANI**
Mela Tandoori (97) US ❷

**ITALIAN**
🍴 Café Abo (100) MI ❶
Gelato Classico (96) NB ❶
🍴 L'Osteria del Forno (96) NB ❷
🍴 Mario's Bohemian Cigar Café (96) NB ❷

**JAPANESE**
Sushigroove (97) RH ❷
Mifune (99) JT ❶
🍴 Isobune (99) JT ❷

**MEDITERRANEAN**
🍴 La Mediterranée (99) CA, PH ❷

**MEXICAN**
🍴 La Canasta (94) MA ❶
🍴 Rico's (97) RH ❶
Taquería El Farolito (100) MI ❶

**MIDDLE EASTERN**
Blue Front Café (100) UH ❷

**PIZZA**
Marcello's (100) CA ❶
🍴 Pizza Orgasmica (95) MA ❷
🍴 Pizza Inferno (99) PH ❷

**SANDWICHES**
🍴 Marina Submarine (94) MA ❷

**SEAFOOD**
McCormick and Kuleto's (94) FW ❸

**SPANISH**
🍴 Zarzuela (97) RH ❸

**THAI**
Basil (99) SoMa ❷
🍴 Lalitai Thai Restaurant (98) CC ❸
Nirvana (99) CA ❷

**VEGAN**
Millennium (98) CC ❸

**VEGETARIAN**
🍴 Ananda Fuara (98) CC ❷

**VIETNAMESE**
Le Soleil (100) RI ❶

SAN FRANCISCO

**CA** castro **CC** civic center **CH** chinatown **FDE** financial district & the embarcadero **FW** fisherman's wharf **LH** lower haight-ashbury **MA** marina, fort mason, & cow hollow **MI** mission **NB** north beach **NH** nob hill **JT** japantown **PH** pacific heights **RH** russian hlll **RI** richmond **SoMa** south of market **UH** upper haight-ashbury **US** union square

## NORTH BEACH

In North Beach, California cuisine merges with the taste of Little Italy and tourist-aimed restaurants brim, offering unique, *delicioso* tastes that blend old and new.

▨ **L'Osteria del Forno,** 519 Columbus Ave. (☎982-1124), between Green and Union St. Acclaimed Italian roasted and cold foods, plus homemade breads. Terrific thin-crust pizzas (slices $2.50-3.75, whole pizzas $10-17) and foccacia sandwiches ($5-6.50) abound. Salads and antipasti ($4.50-8.50) and entrees ($7-15). Open Su-M and W-Th 11:30am-10pm, F-Sa 11:30am-10:30pm. No credit cards. ❷

▨ **Mario's Bohemian Cigar Store Café,** 566 Columbus Ave. (☎362-0536), at Union St. on the corner of Washington Sq. The Beats frequented this laid-back cafe; these days, locals drop by to have coffee ($1-4) and drinks (wine $4, beer $3). A great place to hang out and grab some first-rate grub (hot focaccia sandwiches $4.25-8; pizza $7-9; pasta $8.25). Open Su-Th 10am-11pm, F-Sa 10am-midnight. ❷

**Gelato Classico,** 576 Union St. (☎391-6667), near Stockton St. Ice cream can't compete with this smooth, creamy gelato. Try sweet spumoni or classic tiramisu, or coppimista. Small $2.75; medium $3.50; large $4.25. Open daily noon-10pm. No credit cards. ❶

## CHINATOWN

San Fran's Chinese cuisine is widely held to be unsurpassed outside of Asia. Chinatown is filled with cheap restaurants; in fact, their multitude and outward similarity may make a choice nearly impossible. Finding vegetarian or vegan food is harder than it might seem; many vegetable dishes use oyster sauce or broth, and rice dishes sometimes include egg. Chinatown's dim sum is not to be missed; the area is home to many spectacular bakeries, teahouses, and specialty restaurants.

---

**GIMME SUM DIM SUM** Dim sum ("little bits of the heart") are the foods traditionally eaten at a Cantonese or Southern Chinese *yum cha* ("tea lunch"). This heavenly dining experience involves many small dishes eaten in the morning or early afternoon, typically on Sundays, in mass quantities. Waiters and waitresses push carts laden with all sorts of Chinese "finger foods" (from dumplings and buns to chicken feet). When they stop at your table, point to whatever looks good (or use the handy mini-menu below). The waiter will stamp a card to charge you by the dish.

**Cha Siu Bao.** Steamed BBQ pork buns.

**Haar Gao.** Steamed shrimp dumplings.

**Dan Taat.** Tiny tart shells filled with sweet egg custard.

**Siu Mai.** Shrimp and pork in a fancy dumpling "basket."

**Walteep.** The classic steamed pork dumplings.

**Jiaozi.** The classic: steamed pork dumplings.

**Dou Sha Bao.** Steamed buns filled with sweet red bean paste.

**Loh Bak Goh.** Mashed turnip patty. Don't knock it until you've tried it.

**Fun Gwor.** Chicken and mushroom dumplings.

**Yuebing.** Flaky frosted pastry with bean paste filling.

---

▨ **House of Nanking,** 919 Kearny St. (☎421-1429), near Columbus Ave. Big, high-quality portions offset a low-key setting and a low-key check in this famous Chinatown institution. Many entrees under $8. Some regulars trust their server to select their meal. Open M-F 11am-10pm, Sa noon-10pm, Su noon-9:30pm. ❷

■ **Golden Gate Bakery,** 1029 Grant Ave. (☎781-2627). This tiny bakery's moon cakes, noodle puffs, and vanilla cream buns (all $.75-1.50) draw long lines of tourists and locals. Open daily 8am-8pm. No credit cards. ❶

■ **Chef Jia,** 925 Kearny St. (☎398-1626), at Pacific St. Lots of good, cheap food in a small, informal space. Yummy lunch specials (all under $5) served 11:30am-4pm (try the spicy string beans with yams) and evening rice plate specials from 4-10pm (all $4.80). Entrees $6-7. Open daily 11:30am-10pm. No credit cards. ❶

**Kay Cheung's Restaurant,** 615 Jackson St. (☎989-6838), at Kearny St. Patrons line up on weekends to sample some of the best dumplings Chinatown has to offer. The shrimp dumplings are a must-eat. Tasty seafood entrees straight from the tank ($4-7.50). Dim sum ($2.15 per plate) served 9am-2pm. Open daily 9:30am-9pm. ❶

## NOB HILL & RUSSIAN HILL

■ **Rico's,** 943 Columbus Ave. (☎928-5404), between Taylor and Lombard St. An unpretentious cafeteria-style restaurant. Choose from over a dozen enormous specialty burritos ($3.50-6), sandwiches ($5.50), and quesadillas ($7). Open daily 10am-10pm. ❶

**Zarzuela,** 2000 Hyde St. (☎346-0800), at Union St. Authentic Spanish homestyle cooking and a festively upscale setting make *chorizo al vino* ($4-7) the highlight of the evening. Entrees $8-14. Open Tu-Th 5:30-10pm, F-Sa 5:30-10:30pm. ❸

**The Crêpe House,** 1755 Polk St. (☎441-2421), at Washington St. in Nob Hill. Eggplant, chicken pesto, and nutella all find $5-7 lodging in this rustic coffeehouse-style establishment. Good selection of salads ($6-8) and sandwiches ($6.25) High-speed Internet access available ($10 per hr.). Open Su-Th 7:30am-9:30pm, F-Sa 7:30am-10:30pm. No credit cards. ❶

**Sushigroove,** 1916 Hyde St. (☎440-1905), between Union and Green St. Without a full kitchen, this chic, inexpensive sushi-*sake* joint (most sushi and *maki* $3-7) serves up a lot of rolls (many vegetarian) but nothing that has seen the inside of an oven. Valet parking ($10). Open Su-Th 6-10pm, F-Sa 6-10:30pm. ❷

## UNION SQUARE

While not as ubiquitous as in nearby Chinatown or North Beach, satisfying, inexpensive food does exist in the primarily high-end Union Square, provided you're willing to move away from the main shopping thoroughfares to the quieter side streets.

■ **Dottie's True Blue Café,** 522 Jones St. (☎885-2767), between Geary and O'Farrell St. The French toast tastes so rich since Dottie makes it with her fluffy homemade bread. Hearty portions, quirky variations like chicken-apple sausage, ceramic turtle salt shakers, and the grilled eggplant with goat-cheese sandwich ($6) often keep a line waiting outside. Open M and Th-Su 7:30am-3pm. ❶

■ **Café Bean,** 800 Sutter St. (☎923-9539). All-day breakfasts like steaming eggs and toast ($4) and Dutch pancakes ($4) or hearty lunch fare like huge barbecue turkey sandwiches ($6.50) make Café Bean attractive to tourists, business people, and wayward hipsters. Internet access $3 per 20min. Open M-Sa 6am-7pm, Su 6am-5pm. ❶

**Mela Tandoori,** 417 O'Farrell St. (☎447-4041), between Jones and Taylor St. A clay oven infuses barbecue meats with a delicious sweet spiciness. Mood lighting, an indoor fountain, and naan-a-plenty transform chicken tandoori ($9) into an affordably romantic sample of the Indian subcontinent. Extensive vegetarian options ($5.95). Open M-Sa 11:30am-2:30pm and 5:30-10:30pm, Su 1-9:30pm. ❷

## FINANCIAL DISTRICT & EMBARCADERO

In the Financial District, corner cafes vend authentic Mediterranean grub at rock-bottom prices. Pedestrian side streets, nestled between banks, are packed with pavement bistros. Sit-down restaurants serve *haute cuisine* with liberal portions of ambience, though you may need an MBA to afford more than an appetizer.

SAN FRANCISCO

▓ **Cafe Venue,** 721 Market St. (☎546-1144), between 3rd and 4th St. Oh, to be a decadent San Franciscan, washing down roasted eggplant on sourdough ($4.50) with a wheatgrass "shot" ($1) to energize for an afternoon of Union Square shopping. The people-watching patio juxtaposes Market Street's bustle, and a similarly diverse menu offers pasta ($6), smoothies ($3), and even spirits in a conspicuously affordable venue. Open M-F 7am-7pm, Sa 8am-5:30pm, Su 11am-5:30pm. No credit cards. ❸

**Café Bastille,** 22 Belden Pl. (☎986-5673), between Pine and Bush St., and Kearny and Montgomery St. In this strip of pricey pavement cafes, Bastille stands out for its quality food and carefree atmosphere. The menu is filled with light French offerings like crepes ($12.50), steak with wild mushroom pudding ($18.50), mussels and *frites* ($13), and a heavenly chocolate almond dessert crepe ($5). Open daily 11:30am-10pm. ❹

## CIVIC CENTER

San Francisco's home to opera, musicals, and movies has fewer restaurants than would be expected. The Opera Plaza, Van Ness Ave., and McAllister St. have a sprinkling of appetizing eateries hidden among fast-food chains. Nearby Hayes Valley has some popular pre-opera offerings as well.

▓ **Ananda Fuara,** 1298 Market St. (☎621-1994), at Larkin St. If you can handle the sky blue interior, this vegetarian cafe with vegan tendencies offers creative combinations of super-fresh ingredients. The most popular dish and house specialty is the "neatloaf" (topped with mashed potatoes and gravy; $10.25). Open M-Tu and Th-Sa 8am-8pm, W 8am-3pm, occasional Su brunch; call for dates. No credit cards. ❷

▓ **Lalitai Thai Restaurant and Bar,** 96 McAllister St. (☎552-5744), at Leavenworth St. Mood-lighting, an elaborate water-lily mural, and a touch of plastic foliage give this elegant Thai restaurant an Alice-In-Wonderland, feasting-with-the-frogs feel. Daily and weekly lunch specials $7.25. Most dinner entrees $11, with veggie options. Reservations recommended. Open M-F 11am-10pm, Sa 11:30am-10pm. ❸

**Millennium,** 580 Geary St. in Savoy Hotel (☎345-3400), at Larkin St. Though the award-winning menu is vegan, Millennium is an entirely tie-dye-free area and the first restaurant in the US to feature an all-organic wine list. Feast on gourmet cuisine in a romantic, soft-jazz setting. Entrees, like the Szechuan Eggplant Crêpe, range from $13-19 and gather global influences. Reservations recommended. Open daily 5-9pm. ❸

## SOUTH OF MARKET AREA (SOMA)

Hidden amid the industrial hum of SoMa are some of the city's best restaurants. For doing it yourself, try **Rainbow Grocery,** 1745 Folsom St., at 13th St., a worker-owned grocery cooperative. (☎863-0620. Open daily 9am-9pm.)

**Patisserie Café,** 1155 Folsom St. (☎703-0557; www.patisseriecafe.com; for cooking classes write chefmohamed@yahoo.com), between 7th and 8th St. A place where you can get a cheap breakfast (coffee and croissant $3), a reasonable lunch (fancy sandwich and dessert $9), or a decadent dinner (appetizers around $6, entrees $9-12) while pondering the artistically experimental decor. Open M-F 8am-5pm. ❷

**Cafe Bosse,** 1599 Howard St. (☎864-2446), at 12th St. Bright, shiny, and quick, Bosse provides restaurant-quality meals with cafeteria-style decor. Burgers, breakfast omelettes, and lunch specials (all about $6-7). Try the Philly cheesesteak. Lots of veggie and salad options, too. Open M-F 7am-4pm. ❶

**The Butler and the Chef Cafe,** 155A South Park Ave. (☎896-2075; www.thebutlerandthechef.com), between Bryant, Brannan, 2nd, and 3rd St. Pierre serves breakfast crepes ($3-7), delicious *croque-monsieur* or baguette sandwiches (from $6), and a huge assortment of wine ($4) in a stellar reproduction of a Parisian street cafe, complete with a mini-gallery displaying local photographers. Open M 7:30am-6pm, Tu-Sa 7:30am-9:30pm. ❶

**Basil,** 1175 Folsom St. (☎552-8999; www.basilthai.com), near 8th St. Somberly sophisticated ambiance sets the mood for delectably classy Thai with a dash of spice for upwardly mobile youth. Curries and entrees "from the grill" or "from the wok" include "drunken tofu" and piquant "mussels inferno" (all $9-12). Open M-F 11:30am-2:45pm and 5-10pm, Sa-Su 5-10:30pm. ❷

## PACIFIC HEIGHTS

▨ **Pizza Inferno,** 1800 Fillmore St. (☎775-1800), at Sutter St. The multicolor paint job and wild interior make this pizza parlor trendier than you might expect. Lunch specials include a slice of pizza, large salad, and soda ($6). Happy Hour M-F 4-6:30pm and 10-11pm with 2-for-1 pizzas and pitchers of beer for $11. Open daily 11:30am-11pm. ❷

▨ **La Méditerranée,** 2210 Fillmore St. (☎921-2956), between Sacramento and Clay St. Another location at 288 Noe St. (☎431-7210), at 16th and Market St. in the Castro. Narrow, colorful, and bustling, La Méditerranée feels like a street in southern Europe. Lunch specials (served until 5pm, about $6.50) and entrees ($7-9) are light and Mediterranean-inspired with a home-cooked taste. Filled phyllo dough ($7.50-9) and quiche of the day ($7) are both must-tries. Open Su-Th 11am-10pm, F-Sa 11am-11pm. ❷

## JAPANTOWN

▨ **Isobune,** 1737 Post St. (☎563-1030), in the Kintetsu Bldg., upper level. Swipe sushi as it sails by your moat-side seat in America's first sushi boat restaurant. Color-coded plates correspond to prices ($1.50-3.75). Sake $3. Open daily 11:30am-10pm. ❷

**Mifune,** 1737 Post St. (☎922-0337), in the Kintetsu Bldg., upper level. Excellent and much-loved noodle restaurant. Choices include *udon* (heavy flour noodles) or *soba* (slender buckwheat noodles). Hot noodles from $4.50; cold noodles from $5.25. *Sake* from $2.80. Open Su-F 11am-9:30pm, Sa 11am-10pm. ❶

**Sophie's Crepes,** 1581 Webster St. (☎929-7732), in the Kinokuniya Bldg., upper level. Walk through the **Japan Center** (p. 99) and virtually every group of teens is munching on delicious crepes. Made from the owner's secret crepe mixture and stuffed with fruits, Nutella, or gelato, take-out crepes are as big a hit in Japantown as they are in Japan. Savory crepes $2.95-4.95; sweet crepes $2.45-5.70; gelato $3-4; sundaes $4-5. Open Su and Tu-Th 11am-9pm, F-Sa 11am-10pm. No credit cards. ❶

## CASTRO

Slightly posh diners and cafes dominate the Castro's culinary offerings, where little is as cheap as in the nearby Mission. But quality munchies cheaper than Streisand tickets do exist. Head away from Castro St. along Market St. toward Noe and Sanchez St. Or shop at **Harvest,** 2285 Market St., a "ranch market" with organic food and outdoor benches. (☎626-0805. Open daily 8:30am-11pm.)

▨ **Welcome Home,** 464 Castro St. (☎626-3600), near the Castro Theatre. If grandma were a drag queen, this would be her kitchen. Dinners $7-10. W all-you-can-eat spaghetti and salad $9. Open daily 8am-4pm. No credit cards. ❷

▨ **Home,** 2100 Market St. (☎503-0333), at 14th and Church St. Red-hued living room, patio fireplace, and one hot family bring unpretentious sophistication to this housewarming. Entrees $8-13. Early-bird special includes three-course dinner with a glass of wine (Su-Th 5-6pm $12)."Flip-Flop" cocktail party 2-6pm, and dinner 5:30-10pm. Backyard bar open daily 5pm for $5 cocktails. Open M-Th 5:30-10pm, F-Sa 5:30-11pm, and Su brunch 10:30am-3pm ($11). ❸

▨ **Nirvana,** 544 Castro St. (☎861-2226), between 18th and 19th St. A gorgeous waitstaff, heavenly Thai entrees ($7-12), a plethora of vegetarian options (sauteed, satayed vegetables in Buddha's Garden $11), and specialty drinks like the nirvana coloda ($7-8) all help you reach apotheosis in a simple, swanky setting. Open M-Th 4:30-10pm, F 2-10:30pm, Sa 11:30am-10:30pm, Su noon-10pm. ❷

SAN FRANCISCO

**Marcello's,** 420 Castro St. (☎863-3900). No-frills joint serves locally adored pizza with a list of toppings as long as your...leg. Slices $2-3; whole pizzas $10-23. Beer $2. Open Su-Th 11am-1am, F-Sa 11am-2am. No credit cards. ❶

## MISSION

The Mission is famous for its delicious Mexican specialties, but the area is also home to other excellent cuisines.

▨ **Café Abo,** 3369 Mission St. (☎821-6275), near 30th St., directly across from the Safeway. A bizarre fusion of art gallery, island resort, political activism and Yoda paraphernalia, Café Abo has some of the best sandwiches ($8-9) and mouth-watering miniature pizzas ($5-6) in the city. Loosely Italian-inspired and organic whenever possible. Open M-F 7:30am-4pm and 6pm-10pm, Sa 8am-4pm. No credit cards. ❷

▨ **Taquería El Farolito,** 2779 Mission St. (☎824-7877), at 24th St. The spot for cheap and authentic Mexican food—chow down as Latin beats blast through this fast-food joint. After any kind of evening activity in the Mission, El Farolito is a great late-night fix. Tacos $1.75. Open Su-Th 10am-3am, F-Sa 10am-4am. No credit cards. ❶

**Bombay Ice Creamery,** 548 Valencia St. (☎431-1103), at 16th St. It's not just the ice cream, but also the food that merits a visit to Bombay. The mango *kulfi* ($2.50) is to die for (get it with rose water and sweet rice noodles). The *bhel* (a puffed rice dish; $3.50) and the *dhai puris* ($3.50) are both delicious. Open Tu-Su 11am-8pm. ❶

**Cafe Ethiopia,** 878 Valencia St. (☎285-2728), just north of 20th St. Large portions of Ethiopian food characterize this pleasant cafe. Be sure to try honey wine ($3.75). Ample vegetarian options. Everything on menu $4-8. Open M and W-Su 11:30am-9:30pm. ❶

## HAIGHT-ASHBURY

▨ **Squat and Gobble,** 1428 Haight St. (☎864-8484; www.squatandgobble.com), between Ashbury St. and Masonic Ave. This popular, light-filled cafe offers enormous omelettes ($5-7) and equally colossal crepes ($4-7). Lots of salads, sandwiches, and vegetarian options, too. Additional locations: 237 Fillmore St. in the **Lower Haight** and 3600 16th St. in the **Castro.** Open 8am-10pm daily. ❷

**Blue Front Café,** 1430 Haight St. (☎252-5917), between Ashbury St. and Masonic Ave. This Genie-marked joint is a great place to fill your tummy with starchy goodness. Large portions, flowing conversation, and general wackiness. Down a beer or ginseng chai (both around $2.50), to go with your sizeable wrap ($6) or Middle Eastern meal ($5-8.50). 10% student discount. Open Su-Th 7:30am-10pm, F-Sa 7:30am-11pm. ❷

**Kate's Kitchen,** 471 Haight St. (☎626-3984), near Fillmore St. Start your day off right with one of the best breakfasts in the neighborhood (served all day). It's often packed, so sign up on a waiting list outside. Try the "French Toast Orgy," with fruit, yogurt, granola, and honey ($5.25) or anything else on the extraordinarily economical menu ($4-8). Open M 9am-2:45pm, Tu-F 8am-2:45pm, Sa-Su 8:30am-3:45pm. No credit cards. ❷

## RICHMOND

Some locals claim that Chinese restaurants in the Richmond are better than those in Chinatown. Clement St., between 2nd and 12th Ave., has the widest variety.

**Lee Hou Restaurant,** 332 Clement St. (☎668-8070), at 5th Ave. Some of the best dim sum New Chinatown has to offer. Service is basic, but come for the food. 13 pieces of dim sum $8. Lunch $4-10. Open Su-Th 8am-1am, F-Sa 8am-2am. ❷

**Le Soleil,** 133 Clement St. (☎668-4848), between 2nd and 3rd Ave. Serves Vietnamese food at prices so low they rival Chinatown's best. Huge vegetarian selection and nothing on the menu cracks $8. Lunch and dinner menus available. Entrees average $5-7; imported beers $3.50 per glass. Open Su-Th 11am-10pm, F-Sa 11am-10:30pm. ❶

**Taiwan Restaurant,** 445 Clement St. (☎387-1789), at 6th Ave. Watch the cooks fold your dumplings in the window of this yummy, cheap, veggie-friendly spot which serves Northern Chinese cuisine and some mean dim sum. Lines out the door on weekends. Lunch $3.50; dinner $5-8. Open M-F 11am-9:30pm, Sa-Su 10:30am-10:30pm.❷

# ◎ SIGHTS

## FISHERMAN'S WHARF & THE PIERS

Fisherman's Wharf is home to eight blocks of touristy carnivalesque aquatic spectacle. Sifting through the while-you-wait caricature artists, "olde-fashioned fudge shoppes," penny-flattening machines, and novelty t-shirts, patrons can catch amazing glimpses of sea lions, Alcatraz, and a rich naval tradition. Piers 39 through 45 provide access to San Fran's most famous attractions. Perhaps the best way to appreciate the wharf is to wake up at 4am, put on a warm sweater, and go down to experience the loading and outfitting of small ships, the animated conversation, the blanket of morning mist, and the incredible view. The western edge, near Municipal Pier, is quieter than the main Wharf piers.

**PIER 39.** Self-titled "San Francisco's Number One Attraction," Pier 39 is a shamelessly commercial collection of 110 speciality shops, restaurants, vendors, and entertainment. Even the world-famous sea lions—found by the eastern tip of the pier—seem to enact a tourist-directed performance of splashing and snorting. The **California Welcome Center,** located at the top of the Marina Plaza stairs, features an Internet cafe, snacks, info, and occasional discounts for attractions in the city and beyond. For a whirlwind city-tour, experience **The Great San Francisco Adventure** at **Pier 39 Cinemax.** In huge-screen format, you can fly over the Golden Gate Bridge, feel a 3.0 scale earthquake, race down Lombard St., watch a 49ers game, and dive to the ocean depths—in only 30 minutes! If that leaves you feeling giddy, head to the end of the pier to unwind with live street performances at **Center Stage** or a jaunt on the **Venetian Carousel.** *(☎981-7437. Shops, attractions, and fast food open Su-Th 10am-9pm, F-Sa 10am-10pm; restaurants open Su-Th 11:30am-10pm, F-Sa 11:30am-11pm. Cinemax: ☎956-3456. Shows every 45min. First show 10am. Adults $7.50, seniors $6, children $4.50. California Welcome Center and Internet Cafe: ☎956-3493. Open Su-Th 9am-9pm, F-Sa 9am-10pm.)*

**PIER 45.** Still used by fishermen in the early morning, Pier 45 is also home to the **USS Pampanito** (SS-383). In retirement after sinking six enemy ships during its Pacific patrols, this World War II *Balao*-class fleet submarine now serves as a National Historic Park museum. *(☎775-1943. Open June-Sept. M-Th 9am-6pm, F-Su 9am-8pm; Oct.-May M-Tu and Th-Su 9am-8pm, W 9am-6pm. Adults $7, seniors $5, ages 6-12 $4, under 6 free.)*

**GHIRARDELLI SQUARE.** Chocolate-lovers' heaven, Ghirardelli Square, houses a mall in what used to be a chocolate factory. Don't worry, you don't need a Willy Wonka golden ticket to sample the savory sweets; visit the **Ghirardelli Chocolate Manufactory,** with its vast selection of chocolatey goodies, or the **Ghirardelli Chocolate Shop and Caffe,** with drinks, frozen yogurt, and a smaller selection of chocolates. Both hand out ☒free samples of chocolate at the door, but on tourist-heavy days, the Caffe is often less crowded. The **soda fountain,** an old-fashioned ice-cream parlor, serves huge sundaes ($6.25) smothered with its world-famous hot fudge sauce. *(Mall: 900 North Point St. ☎775-5500. Stores open M-Sa 10am-9pm, Su 10am-6pm. Ghirardelli Chocolate Manufactory: ☎771-4903. Open Su-Th 10am-11pm, F-Sa 10am-midnight. Soda fountain: Open Su-Th 10am-11pm, F-Sa 10am-midnight. Chocolate Shop and Caffe: ☎474-1414. Open M-Th 8:30am-9pm, F 8:30am-10pm, Sa 9pm-10pm, Su 9am-9pm.)*

**HYDE STREET PIER.** Along with the curving Municipal Pier, Hyde Street Pier encloses an area of the Bay known as the Aquatic Park. Sittin' on the dock of the Bay, you can watch the daring locals swim laps in frigid 50°F water. If you feel like joining, the **South End Rowing Club** and the **Dolphin Club** are open to the public on alternate days for $6.50 where you can thaw out in their saunas. Hyde Street Pier is also part of the National Historic Park, offering guided tours of the vessels, schooners, and ferryboats as well as a boat-building class to satisfy your nautical needs. *(On Hyde St. ☎561-7100. Open 9:30am-5:30pm. Adults $5, under 16 free. Guided Pier Walks offered 4 times daily; call for times. Dolphin Club: 502 Jefferson St. ☎441-9329. Open in summer W 11am-6pm; in winter 10am-5pm. South End Rowing Club: 500 Jefferson St. ☎929-9656. Open in summer Tu, Th, and Sa 11am-6pm; in winter 10am-5pm. Boating Class: ☎929-0202.)*

**THE CANNERY.** Built in 1907 as the del Monte canning factory, once the largest peach cannery in the world, **The Cannery** has been converted into a marketplace-style plaza. Its maze of shady terraces and European-inspired garden courtyards offers respite from wharfside hubbub and ballyhoo. Three levels of balconies, bridges, and walkways house some charming restaurants, shops, and entertainment. *(2801 Leavenworth St. www.thecannery.com.)*

## MARINA

Pastel stucco houses with lavish gardens, stunning views of Marin, and a high quotient of young beautiful socialites characterize the residential Marina. You would never know that the area was one of the worst struck by the 1989 earthquake in which massive fires destroyed several buildings. The main attractions stretch along the waterfront across the northern edge of the city.

■ **EXPLORATORIUM.** *Scientific American* called this "the best science museum in the world," and *Let's Go* calls it a mad scientist's dream. Displays include interactive tornadoes, computer planet-managing, and giant bubble-makers poised to take over the universe. Don't miss demonstrations like the cow's eye dissection or the changing special exhibitions. Within the Exploratorium dwells the **Tactile Dome,** a pitch-dark maze of tunnels, slides, nooks, and crannies designed to help refine your sense of touch. Claustrophobes beware. *(3601 Lyon St. ☎563-7337 or 561-0360; www.exploratorium.edu. Open Tu-Su 10am-5pm. Adults $12; students, seniors, disabled, and youth 9-17 $9.50; children 4-8 $8.00, under 3 free. Free 1st W of each month. Tactile Dome: reservations ☎561-0362; reservations@exploratorium.edu. $15 (includes general admission). Credit card required for reservation; book at least one day in advance.)*

■ **WAVE ORGAN.** Past the Golden Gate Yacht Club at the end of a long jetty rests one of San Francisco's best hidden treasures: the Wave Organ, an acoustic environmental sculpture made up of 25 pipes jutting out of the ocean that create musical sounds as waves crash against it. Conceived by Peter Richards, the project was completed in 1986. George Gonzalez, a sculptor and stone mason, designed the seating area around the pipes using granite and marble pieces from a decimated cemetery. All sorts of carvings can be discerned if you look closely. The music itself is quite subtle, like listening to a sea shell, and is best heard at high tide. If you take the time, tones from the organ will begin to harmonize with the clinking boat masts, fog horns, and seagulls, synthesizing a sublime oceanic symphony.

■ **PALACE OF FINE ARTS.** With its open-air dome and curving colonnades, The Palace of Fine Arts is one of the best picnic spots in the city. It was reconstructed from remnants of the 1915 Panama-Pacific Exposition, which had been built to commemorate the opening of the Panama Canal and exemplify San Francisco's recovery from the 1906 earthquake. Shakespearean plays are performed here during the summer and the nighttime illumination is glorious. The **Palace of Fine Arts Theater,** located directly behind the rotunda, hosts dance and theater performances and film festivals. *(On Baker St., between Jefferson and Bay St. next to the Exploratorium. Open daily 6am-9pm. Free. Theater ☎569-6504; www.palaceoffinearts.com. Call for times and ticket prices.)*

# FORT MASON

Fort Mason Center is home to the original headquarters of the 1906 earthquake relief site. Its initial purpose, quite singular in scope, contrasts now with the diverse cultural museums and resources that inhabit the Fort. From theater and craft to Italian and African-American art, the innovative and impressive array of attractions in Fort Mason remains relatively unknown to both travelers and locals. Fort Mason Center is a quiet waterfront counterpart to the tourist blitz of nearby Fisherman's Wharf. On the first Wednesday of every month, all museums are free and open until 7pm. The grounds are also home to a popular hostel and the headquarters of the **Golden Gate National Recreation Area (GGNRA).** While not as spectacular as some other lands under the GGNRA's aegis, these manicured greens are a swell spot for strolling. *(The eastern portion of Fort Mason near Gashouse Cove. ☎ 441-3400, ext. 3; www.fortmason.org.)*

**MUSEUM OF CRAFT AND FOLK ART.** The tiny but culturally rich MOCFA houses a fascinating collection of crafts and functional art (vessels, clothing, furniture, and jewelry) from past and present, near and far. The museum showcases everything from 19th-century Chinese children's hats to war-time commentary made through light bulbs. Second floor is not wheelchair-accessible. *(Bldg. A., 1st fl. ☎ 775-0991; www.mocfa.org. Open Tu-F and Su 11am-5pm, Sa 10am-5pm. Adults $4, students and seniors $3, under 18 free. Free Sa 10am-noon and 1st W of each month 11am-7pm.)*

**AFRICAN-AMERICAN HISTORICAL AND CULTURAL SOCIETY MUSEUM.** The African-American Historical and Cultural Society Museum displays artifacts and artwork as well as modern works of African and African-American artists. The museum also has a permanent collection by local artists. *(Bldg. C, #165. ☎ 441-0640. Open W-Su noon-5pm. Adults $3, seniors and children over 12 $1, under 12 free. 1st W of each month free.)*

**MUSEO ITALO AMERICANO.** The only museum in the country dedicated solely to Italian and Italian-American art, Museo Italo Americano is home to a small collection by artists from several centuries and offers a selection of cultural programs, such as language classes and lectures. *(Bldg. C, #100. ☎ 673-2200; www.museoitaloamericano.org. Open W-Su noon-5pm. Adults $3, students and seniors $2, under 12 free.)*

# NORTH BEACH

North Beach is worth visiting both during the daytime and during its neon-lit evenings. Over the years, the old Italian community has made way for beatniks, hippies, and even you, without compromising its Old-World feel.

**WASHINGTON SQUARE.** Washington Sq., bordered by Union, Filbert, Stockton, and Powell St., is North Beach's *piazza*, a pretty, not-quite-square, tree-lined lawn. The statue in Washington Sq. is of Benjamin Franklin. The wedding site of Marilyn Monroe and Joe DiMaggio, the park fills every morning with practitioners of *tai chi*. By noon, sunbathers, picnickers, and bocce-ball players take over. At 666 Filbert St., the **St. Peter and St. Paul Catholic Church** beckons tired sightseers to take refuge in its dark, wooden nave. Turn-of-the-century San Francisco philanthropist and party-girl Lillie Hitchcock Coit donated the **Volunteer Firemen Memorial** in the middle of the square after being rescued from a fire as a young girl.

**TELEGRAPH HILL.** Overlooking Washington Park and North Beach, Telegraph Hill was originally the site of a semaphore that signaled the arrival of ships in Gold Rush days. Today, tourists hike up the hill to visit **Coit Tower,** which stands 210 ft. high and commands a spectacular view of the city and the Bay. During the Depression, the government's Works Progress Administration employed artists to paint the colorful and surprisingly subversive murals on the dome's inside. *(MUNI bus #39 goes all the way to Coit tower. If driving, follow Lombard St. to the top,* *where there is free 30min. parking M and F 9am-5pm, Tu-Th and Sa-Su 8am-5pm. Tower:* ☎ *362-0808. Open daily 10am-7pm.* **Elevator fare:** *Adults $3.75, over 64 $2.50, ages 6-12 $1.50, under 6 free. Free guided tours of murals Th 10:15am, Sa 11am.)*

**SAN FRANCISCO ART INSTITUTE.** The oldest art school west of the Mississippi, the San Francisco Art Institute is lodged in a converted mission and has produced a number of American greats including Mark Rothko, Ansel Adams, Dorothea Lange, and James Weeks, to name a few. Student projects hang throughout the school, and given the place's history, you never know whom you might discover. As you enter, to the left is the **Diego Rivera Gallery,** one wall of which is covered by a huge 1931 Rivera mural. The gallery hosts weekly student exhibits with receptions every other Tuesday. Farther down the lefthand hallway are the **Walter and McBean Galleries,** which show professional exhibits. Outside these galleries and across the airy modern "quadrangle," **Pete's Cafe** serves up cheap burgers and sandwiches ($4.50), making for a nice picnic spot with fantastic views of the bay. *(800 Chestnut St., between Leavenworth and Jones St.* ☎ *771-7020 or 800-345-7324; www.sfai.edu. Receptions Tu 5-7pm.)*

**CITY LIGHTS BOOKSTORE.** Drawn by low rents and cheap bars, the Beat writers came to national attention when Lawrence Ferlinghetti's City Lights Bookstore, opened in 1953, published Allen Ginsberg's *Howl.* Banned in 1956 and then subjected to an extended trial at the end of which a judge found the poem "not obscene," the book and its publisher vaulted the Beats into literary infamy. City Lights has expanded since its Beat days and now stocks widely fiction and poetry, but it remains committed to publishing young poets and writers under its own imprint. Black and white signs beckon visitors to sit down, turn off their "sell-phones," and flip through the books. Index card boxes in the back stairwell hold postings for jobs, housing, and rides, and writers without permanent addresses can have their mail held in the store. See also **Shopping: Books,** p. 117. *(2261 Columbus Ave.* ☎ *362-8193. Open daily 10am-midnight.)*

# CHINATOWN

Locals of all backgrounds bargain in Chinatown's markets and feast in its affordable eateries. A distinct mix of Chinese and American culture has emerged over time. American politics have blended with Chinese perspectives, while food and desserts have adapted to American cooking styles and tourist tastes.

■ **WAVERLY PLACE.** Find this little alley (between Sacramento and Washington St. and between Stockton St. and Grant Ave.) and you'll want to spend all day gazing at the incredible architecture. The fire escapes are painted in pinks and greens and held together by railings made of intricate Chinese patterns. Tourists can also visit **Tien Hou Temple,** 125 Waverly Place, the oldest Chinese temple in the US.

**GRANT AVENUE.** The oldest street in San Francisco is a sea of Chinese banners, signs, and architecture today. During the day, Grant Ave. and nearby streets are brimming with tourists who stop at every block to buy health balls and chirping boxes and pretend not to notice the Chinese porn mags lining some shop windows. At Bush St. and Grant Ave. stands the ornate, dragon-crested **Gateway to Chinatown,** a gift from Taiwan in 1970. "Everything in the world is in just proportion," say the Chinese characters above the gate. Most of the picturesque pagodas punctuating the blocks were designed around or after 1900, not as authentic replicas of Chinese architecture, but as temptations for Western tourists. While Grant Ave. is the center of many Chinatown activities, to get a true taste of the neighborhood you must venture off into the alleys and side streets.

**ROSS ALLEY.** Ross Alley was once lined with brothels and gambling houses; today, it has the cramped look of old Chinatown. The narrow street has stood in for the Orient in such films as *Big Trouble in Little China, Karate Kid II,* and

*Indiana Jones and the Temple of Doom.* Squeeze into a tiny doorway to watch fortune cookies being shaped by hand at the ◪**Golden Gate Cookie Company.** All cookies that don't come out according to the baker's high standards are put in big tins for free taste-testing. *(56 Ross Alley. ☎ 781-3956. Bag of cookies $3, with "funny," "sexy," or "lucky" fortunes $5. Open daily 10am-8pm.)*

**CHINESE CULTURAL CENTER.** A stone bridge leads from the park at Portsmouth Sq. to the other side of Kearny St., where the Chinese Cultural Center hosts two small galleries of Chinese-American art and offers classes. The center also sponsors two **walking tours** of Chinatown. *(750 Kearny St., on the 3rd fl. of the Holiday Inn. ☎ 986-1822; www.c-c-c.org. Open Tu-Sa 10am-4pm. Heritage Walk Sa and Su 2pm. $15, under 18 $8.)*

## NOB HILL & RUSSIAN HILL

In a fairly expensive, mostly residential area, the main attractions here are the views and a few noteworthy sights. You'll find more activity as the area merges into Union Sq. and the Tenderloin.

**THE CROOKEDEST STREET IN THE WORLD.** The famous curves of **Lombard Street** seem to grace half of San Francisco's postcards, and rightfully so. The flowerbeds along the curves are beautifully manicured and the eight curves themselves—installed in the 1920s so that horse-drawn carriages could negotiate the extremely steep hill—are uniquely San Francisco. From the top of Lombard St., pedestrians and passengers alike enjoy a fantastic view of the city and harbor. The view north along Hyde St.—Fisherman's Wharf and lonely Alcatraz floating in the bay—isn't too shabby either. *(Between Hyde and Leavenworth St., running down Russian Hill.)*

**GRACE CATHEDRAL AND HUNTINGTON PARK.** The largest Gothic edifice west of the Mississippi, **Grace Cathedral** is Nob Hill's stained glass-studded crown. A labyrinthine entryway helps clear the minds of entering devotees. The main doors that beckon visitors in are replicas cast from Lorenzo Ghiberti's Doors on Paradise in Florence's famed Duomo Cathedral. Inside, modern murals mix San Franciscan and national historical events with saintly scenes. The altar of the AIDS Interfaith Memorial Chapel celebrates the church's "inclusive community of love" with a lustrously intricate Keith Haring triptych. Outside, this all-accepting behemoth of Christian modernity looks onto the neatly manicured turf and trees of **Huntington Park,** equipped with a park and playground. *(1100 California St., between Jones and Taylor St. ☎ 749-6300; www.gracecathedral.org. Open Su-F 7am-6pm, Sa 8am-6pm. Services: Su 7:30, 8:15, 11am, 3, and 6pm; M-F 7:30, 9am, 12:10, and 5:15pm; Sa 9, 11am, and 3pm. Tour guides available M-F 1-3pm, Sa 11:30am-1:30pm, Su 1:30-2pm. Suggested donation $3.)*

**CABLE CAR POWERHOUSE AND MUSEUM.** After the journey up Nob Hill, you'll understand what inspired the development of the vehicles celebrated at this museum. More an educational breather than a destination in its own right, the modest building is the working center of San Francisco's cable car system. Look down on 57,300 ft. of cable whizzing by, or view displays to learn more about the cars, some of which date back to 1873. *(1201 Mason St., at Washington St. ☎ 474-1887. Open Apr.-Oct. daily 10am-6pm; Nov.-Mar. 10am-5pm. Free.)*

## UNION SQUARE

The three-block radius around Union Square houses prestigious art galleries, the heart of San Francisco's theater district, upscale hotels, several multi-floor shopping centers, and just about every imaginable boutique. There's plenty of European retail therapy around, most spectacularly at the nine-story **San Fran-**

cisco **Shopping Centre** on Market St. at 5th St., where six curving escalators propel you past hundreds of ways to splurge. On the fringes of Union Square, the homeless languish on the sidewalks.

**GALLERIES.** The **Martin Lawrence Gallery** is a two-story space that houses America's largest collection of work by painter Marc Chagall, as well as a number of pieces by Keith Haring, Andy Warhol, and Pablo Picasso. The gallery would feel like a very intimate modern art museum were it not for the $2 million price tags on some works. *(366 Geary St., between Powell and Mason St. ☎956-0345. Open M-Th 9am-8pm, F-Sa 9am-10pm, Su 10am-7pm.)* **Hang** is a sleek, urban gallery, housed in a cozy chrome warehouse in which the works *hang* from the exposed beams in the ceiling. The Hang Annex, located directly across the street tends to display monthly solo shows while the original Hang changes its art every few days. Both galleries specialize in rental of works "by emerging artists for emerging collectors." *(56 Sutter St., between Powell and Mason St. ☎434-4264; www.hangart.com. Open M-Sa 10am-6pm, Su noon-5pm.)* If you're more partial to classical photography, the newly opened **sf black & white gallery** transforms a spare urban space into a backdrop for its collection of simple and elegant black and white images of San Francisco. Photographs go for as low as $30. The owners are in the process of transforming the back room into a chic bar called "The Darkroom" where patrons will be served over an extended lightboard topped with slides. *(619 Post St., at Taylor St. ☎929-9424. Open daily 9am-9pm.)* **The Academy of Art College** has galleries that showcase student work on a bi-weekly basis. *(10 Bush St., between Kearny St. and Grant Ave. ☎274-8680. Additional locations: 625 Sutter St. ☎274-2229 and 79 New Montgomery St. ☎274-2292. Locations open daily 9am-5pm but if students are milling around, it may be possible to get in later.)*

# GOLDEN GATE BRIDGE & THE PRESIDIO

## GOLDEN GATE BRIDGE

When Captain John Fremont coined the term "Golden Gate" in 1846, he meant to name the harbor entrance to the San Francisco Bay after the mythical Golden Horn port of Constantinople. In 1937, however, the colorful name became permanently associated with Joseph Strauss's copper-hued engineering masterpiece—the Golden Gate Bridge. Built for only $35 million, the bridge stretches across 1¼ mi. of ocean, its towers looming 65 stories above the Bay. It can sway up to 27 ft. in each direction during high winds. On sunny days, hundreds of people take the 30min. walk across the bridge. The views from the bridge are amazing, especially from the Vista Point in Marin County just after the bridge. To see the bridge itself, it's best to get a bit farther away. Fort Point and Fort Baker in the Presidio, Land's End in Lincoln Park, Mt. Livermore on Angel Island, and Hawk Hill off Conzelman Rd. in the Marin Headlands all offer spectacular views of the Golden Gate on clear days.

## PRESIDIO

When Spanish settlers forged their way up the San Francisco peninsula from Baja California in 1769, they established *presidios*, or military outposts, along the way. San Francisco's Presidio, the northernmost point of Spanish territory in North America, was dedicated in 1776. The settlement stayed in Spanish hands for only 45 years before the deed was passed to Mexico when it won its independence from Spain. In 1848, the United States took over the Presidio as part of the Treaty of Guadalupe Hidalgo that ended the Mexican-American War. Gold fever stimulated expansion of the outpost and, eventually, the Presidio gained particular importance during WWII after the attack on Pearl Harbor. Crissy Field's Intelligence School and the Letterman Army Hospital became leaders in their respective fields during the war.

SAN FRANCISCO

Today, the Presidio is part of the **Golden Gate National Recreation Area (GGNRA)**, run by the National Park Service in conjunction with the Presidio Trust, which is raising funds to make the park self-sufficient by 2013 and coordinating the ongoing renovation and modernization of roads, buildings, and trails in the park.

**MAIN POST.** The once-grand barracks that make up Main Post are now a semi-historic playground for the San Francisco Film Society and any other non-profit agency willing to fork over funds for a lease. Remnants of the original Spanish settlement are on view in the Officer's Club, one of the many historic buildings that surround the 1776 Parade Ground. The William Penn Mott, Jr. Visitors Center offers free maps, glossy viewbooks, and pocket walking tour guides that explain the park's present and past. *(102 Montgomery St. ☎ 561-4323; www.nps.gov/psrf. Open daily 9am-5pm.)*

**SAN FRANCISCO NATIONAL CEMETERY.** This 28-acre cemetery, which houses the graves of over 30,000 soldiers and their families, was the first national cemetery on the West Coast. The 450 soldiers of the all-black Buffalo Soldier regiments of the US Army as well as Pauline Cushman Fryer, the Union's most famous female spy, rest here. Maps and registers are available inside the entrance gate. *(Just off of Lincoln Blvd. in the center of the Presidio. P.O. Box 29012, Presidio of San Francisco. ☎ 650-589-7737.)*

**FORT POINT.** Fort Point, under the Golden Gate Bridge in the northernmost corner of the park, used to be called "the Gibraltar of the West." During the Civil War, Fort Point was the West Coast's main defense post against the Confederate Army, housing a garrison of men and nearly 200 guns and cannons. Today, the cavernous fort is open to the public and boasts historical recreations such as cannon-loading demonstrations by volunteers in Civil War uniforms, free guided and audio tours, and exhibits. The top tier of the four-story building is windy but the view is worth the climb. *(☎ 556-1693; www.nps.gov/fopo. MUNI buses #28 and 29 stop at the Golden Gate Bridge, where dirt paths and paved roads lead to the fort. Cars take Lincoln Ave. to Long Ave. to Marine Dr.; limited parking. Open daily 10am-5pm, though schedule may vary due to ongoing "seismic upgrading." Wheelchair-accessible.)*

# LINCOLN PARK

At the northwest end of San Francisco, Lincoln Park has spectacular views of the Pacific and the Golden Gate Bridge. The bulky patch of meandering paths and historical sights is a fabulous place for an afternoon hike or summertime picnic.

**CLIFF HOUSE.** At the northern tip of Ocean Beach, Lincoln Park begins not with greenery and mountainous paths but with a monument of San Francisco's earlier days. The precarious Cliff House, built in 1909, is the third of that name to occupy this spot—the previous two burned down. It has slowly deteriorated due to decades of neglect, and plans are in the works to restore the complex to its original glory. The Golden Gate National Recreation Area Visitors Center, housed within the Cliff House, distributes information on Lincoln Park, Ocean Beach, and the entire GGNRA. Don't feed the coin-operated binoculars that look out over Seal Rocks—instead, head inside for a free look through the GGNRA telescope. *(☎ 556-8642. Open daily 10am-5pm.)* Along with overpriced restaurants, the Cliff House hosts the **Musée Mécanique,** an arcade devoted to games of yesteryear. *(☎ 386-1170. Open daily 10am-8pm; in winter M-F 11am-7pm, Sa-Su 10am-8pm. Entrance free, but most games 25¢.)* Next to the Musée Mécanique, overlooking the cliffs and the Pacific, rests the **Camera Obscura.** The building has a periscope-like mirrored lens on its roof; as the lens turns in circles, light from outside is bounced down into the "dark room" and onto a concave viewing plate, showing the ocean vistas and nearby Seal Rocks, all at 700% magnification. *(☎ 750-0415. Open daily 11am-sunset, weather permitting—you can't see anything in fog. $2. Closed for renovations until summer 2004.)*

**SUTRO BATHS AND SUTRO HEIGHTS PARK.** Adolph Sutro's 1896 bathhouse, known as the Sutro Baths, lies in ruins just north of Cliff House. Up the hill from the intersection of Point Lobos and 48th Ave., and to the east of the Cliff House and the Baths, is spectacular Sutro Heights Park. Sadly underused, the park offers unparalleled views of the city and surrounding watery expanses. A lion-guarded gate recalls the day when the hill was the sight of Adolph's grand private estate.

**CALIFORNIA PALACE OF THE LEGION OF HONOR.** In the middle of Lincoln Park, between the golf course and the **Land's End** wilderness, sits a magnificent enclave of European proportions and aspirations. The California Palace of the Legion of Honor was built in 1924 after one of San Francisco's leading ladies, Mrs. Alma Spreckels, fell in love with the temporary "French Pavilion" built on Golden Gate Park for the Panama International Exhibition. The pavilion was a replica of the *Palais de la Legion d'Honneur* on Paris' Left Bank, and Spreckels was determined to build one of equal stature. A copy of Rodin's *Thinker* beckons visitors into the grand courtyard, where a little glass pyramid recalls another Paris treasure, the Louvre. A thorough catalogue of great masters, from Rubens to Dalí (including the largest collection of Rodin sculptures outside Paris) hangs inside. Other draws include a pneumatically operated 4500-pipe organ, played in free weekly recitals *(Sa-Su 4pm)*, and a gilded ceiling from a 15th-century *palacio* in Toledo, Spain. Free tours given on Sa in a different language (either French, Spanish, or Italian) each week. Just outside the Palace, a **Holocaust Memorial** offers a sobering reminder of one of history's darkest moments. The memorial depicts the Holocaust as a mass of emaciated victims with a single, hopeful survivor looking out through a barbed-wire fence to the beauty of the Pacific. (☎ 863-3330; www.legionofhonor.org. Open Su and Tu-Sa 9:30am-5pm. Adults $8, seniors $6, under 17 $5, under 12 free. $2 discount with MUNI transfer; Tu free. Wheelchair-accessible. Holocaust Memorial free to public.)

# GOLDEN GATE PARK

In-line skaters, neo-flower children, and sunbathers meet in this lush garden-within-the-city, which spreads 3½ mi. from the Haight to the Ocean, and separates residential Richmond and Sunset districts with 1½ mi. of greenery, north to

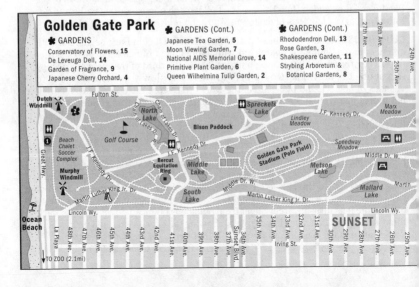

**Golden Gate Park**

❀ **GARDENS**
Conservatory of Flowers, **15**
De Leveuga Dell, **14**
Garden of Fragrance, **9**
Japanese Cherry Orchard, **4**

❀ GARDENS (Cont.)
Japanese Tea Garden, **5**
Moon Viewing Garden, **7**
National AIDS Memorial Grove, **14**
Primitive Plant Garden, **6**
Queen Wilhelmina Tulip Garden, **2**

❀ GARDENS (Cont.)
Rhododendron Dell, **13**
Rose Garden, **3**
Shakespeare Garden, **11**
Strybing Arboretum &
Botanical Gardens, **8**

south. It is bounded by Fulton St. to the north, Stanyan St. to the east, Lincoln Way to the south, and Ocean Beach to the west, except for a strip called the Panhandle, which juts east between Fell and Oak St. into the Haight. Originally the "carriage entrance," it contains the oldest trees in the park. The heavily trafficked section of Hwy. 1 running through the park is called Park Presidio By-Pass Dr. going north and Cross-Over Dr. going south.

Inside, the park is laid out in a sprawling design. Open green meadows, groves of shrubs, and myriad little gardens patch together the larger developed areas, namely the museum complex in the eastern third of the park, Stow Lake, the Stadium, the golf course, and soccer fields near the western edge. Don't rush through the park—San Franciscans bask in it all weekend long. Intriguing museums and cultural events pick up where the lush flora and fauna finally leave off, and athletic opportunities abound. On Sundays, traffic is banned from park roads, and bicycles and in-line skates come out in full force.

**GARDENS & SIGHTS.** Despite its sandy past, the soil of Golden Gate Park is rich enough today to support a wealth of flowers, particularly in spring and summer. The **Conservatory of Flowers** is scheduled to reopen after renovations soon after summer 2003, but the nearby Conservatory Valley, much like the Kew Gardens in London, seems afflicted with obsessive-compulsive disorder—not a bloom is out of place in this unbelievable display of botanic symmetry. Across JFK Dr. from the Conservatory, just south of **Lily Pond,** the **National AIDS Memorial Grove** rests among the fragile, flowering dogwoods and giant redwoods of **De Laveaga Dell.** The grove is a site for remembrance and renewal, at once somber and rejuvenating. (☎750-8340. Tours Th 9:30am-12:30pm and by special arrangement starting at the Main Portal of the Grove, near the corner of Middle Dr. East and Bowling Green Dr. Free.)

The **Strybing Arboretum and Botanical Gardens** is home to 7500 varieties of plants, including collections from Chile, New Zealand, and the tropical, high-altitude New World Cloud Forests. Pretend to munch on faux-prehistoric dinosaur-salad at the **Primitive Plant Garden** near the Friends Gate in the northern part of the Arboretum. On the eastern side, near the **Strybing Store** and **Russel Library of Horticulture,** is the **Garden of Fragrance,** designed especially for the visually impaired—all labels are in Braille and the plants are chosen specifically for their textures and scents. On the western

SAN FRANCISCO

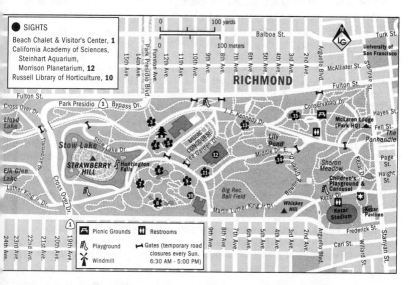

● SIGHTS

Beach Chalet & Visitor's Center, **1**
California Academy of Sciences,
  Steinhart Aquarium,
  Morrison Planetarium, **12**
Russell Library of Horticulture, **10**

🏕 Picnic Grounds    🚻 Restrooms
🎠 Playground    ⊢ Gates (temporary road
🌀 Windmill        closures every Sun.
                 6:30 AM - 5:00 PM)

side is the grand and spacious **Moon Viewing Garden,** perfect for celestial happenings and werewolf sightings. *(On Lincoln Way at 9th Ave. ☎ 661-1316; www.strybing.org. Open M-F 8am-4:30pm, Sa-Su 10am-5pm. Free guided tours from Strybing Store M-F 1:30pm, Sa-Su 10:30am and 1:30pm; from North Entrance Su, W, F 2pm.)*

Near the **Music Concourse** off of South Dr., the **Shakespeare Garden,** filled with crab-apples and red brick, contains almost every flower and plant ever mentioned by the Bard. Plaques with the relevant quotations are hung on the back wall, and there's a map to help you find your favorite hyacinths and rue. *(Open daily dawn-dusk; in winter Su and Tu-Sa dawn-dusk. Free.)* The **Rhododendron Dell,** between the Academy of Sciences and John F. Kennedy Dr., honors park designer John McLaren with a splendid profusion of his favorite flower. The 850 varieties bloom the first weeks of spring. Ring-like **Stow Lake** sits in the middle of the park. Cross one of two stone bridges and wreak fruit-filled havoc on the big, green island of **Strawberry Hill.**

**SPRECKELS LAKE AND AROUND.** Brimming Spreckels Lake, on JFK Dr., is populated by crowds of turtles that pile onto a big rock to sun themselves. The multi-national collection of gardens and museums in Golden Gate Park would not be complete without something distinctly American…like a herd of bison. A dozen shaggy beasts loll about a spacious paddock just west of Spreckels. In the northwest of the park, the Dutch Windmill has done its last good turn in the cheery Queen Wilhelmina Tulip Garden, which bursts forth color from 10,000 bulbs in March. Rounding out the days of yore is the Children's Playground with its carousel (circa 1912), accompanied by a $50,000 Gebruder band organ. *Let's Go* recommends riding the ◼ostrich or the ◼purple dragon. *(Open June-Sept. daily 10am-5pm; Oct.-May Tu-W and F-Su 9am-4pm. Adults $1, ages 6-12 25¢.)*

**BEACH CHALET.** The Beach Chalet, a Spanish-Colonial-style villa built in 1925, sits on the western edge of the park on the Great Hwy., south of Fulton St. During the Great Depression, the WPA enlisted the French-born artist Lucien Labaudt to design frescoes for the chalet's walls—the elaborate paintings of 1930s San Francisco were completed just in time for WWII, when the building was used as an army outpost. The walls were restored for the chalet's reopening in 1996, and the building now serves as the official **Visitors Center** for Golden Gate Park. *(☎ 751-2766. Open daily 9am-7pm)*

**JAPANESE TEA GARDEN.** The **Japanese Cherry Orchard** blooms intoxicatingly the first week in April at Lincoln Way and South Dr., near the elegant Japanese Tea Garden, created for the 1894 Mid-Winter Exposition. The oldest Japanese garden in the US, the Tea Garden is a serene collection of wooden buildings, small pools, graceful footbridges, carefully pruned trees, and lush plants. *(☎ 752-4227. Open in summer daily 8:30am-6pm; in winter 8:30am-5pm. Adults $3.50, seniors and ages 6-12 $1.25. Free for all in summer 8:30-9:30am and 5-6pm and in winter 8:30-9:30am and 4-5pm.)*

## MUSEUMS

◼**CALIFORNIA ACADEMY OF SCIENCES.** The Academy of Sciences, east of Stow Lake, near 9th Ave., houses several smaller museums specializing in different fields of science. **The Steinhart Aquarium,** with over 600 aquatic species, is livelier than the natural history exhibits. *(Shark feedings M-W and F-Su 10:30am, 12:30, 2:30, and 4:30pm. Open ocean fish feedings 1:30pm. Penguin feeding daily 11:30am and 4pm.)* The **Morrison Planetarium** recreates the heavens above with impressive sky shows. *(Sky shows M-F 2pm, with additional summer showings. Adults $2.50; students, seniors, and ages 6-17 $1.25.)* The rest of the Academy is considered the **Natural History Museum.** In the Space and Earth Hall, you can learn how the earth rotates and see a piece of moonrock. The Earthquake room explains all about those quakes famous around the Bay Area, and the Earthquake Theater lets visitors experience a little rock 'n' roll in person. More zaniness lurks down the corridor, where the Far Side of Science gallery pays tribute to Gary Larsen. (☎ 750-7145; www.calacademy.org. Open June-Aug. daily 9am-6pm; Sept.-May 10am-5pm. Adults $8.50; students, seniors, and ages 12-17 $5.50; ages 4-11 $2. Extended hours (open until 8:45pm) and free entrance 1st W of each month. $2.50 discount for bicycle riders; indoor bike parking available. Discounts also available with MUNI pass or transfer.)

## FINANCIAL DISTRICT & EMBARCADERO

Although much of modern-day Bay Area business may be conducted online, the city still has its share of pressed suits and corner offices. Hidden parks and a handful of sights provide subtle distraction from the overwhelming banking biz. The leading lady of the city's skyline, the **Transamerica Pyramid**, is, according to New Age sources, directly centered on the telluric currents of the Golden Dragon Ley line between Easter Island and Stonehenge. Planned as an architect's joke and co-opted by one of the leading architectural firms in the country, the building earned disdain from purists and reverence from city planners after the fact. Unless you're an employee, tight security means there is no chance of a top-floor view, although the lobby is currently undergoing renovation to modernize a virtual viewing lounge in the Washington St. entrance so you can peer down on the masses from ground-level. (600 Montgomery St., between. Clay and Washington St.) At the foot of Market St., **Justin Herman Plaza** and its formidable 1971 Vaillancourt Fountain, made of precast aggregate concrete, invite total visitor immersion. Bands and rallyists often rent out the area during lunch. Dubbed "a famous city's most famous landmark" by Herb Caen, the 660 ft. waterfront **Ferry Building**, at the foot of Market St., has lost a bit of grandeur over the years, as bigger and better buildings develop along the Embarcadero and steal the spotlight. A. Page Brown designed the elegant port with repeated archways and Corinthian columns to recall Roman aqueducts.

## CIVIC CENTER

Most of San Francisco's theater scene dominates the beautiful, majestic Civic Center. The palatial **San Francisco City Hall**, modeled after Rome's St. Peter's Basilica, is the centerpiece of the largest US gathering of Beaux Arts architecture. (1 Dr. Carlton B. Goodlett Pl., at Van Ness Ave. ☎ 554-4000. Open M-F 8am-8pm, Sa-Su noon-4pm.) Overlooking the Civic Center, the **State Building's** grandeur is comparable to City Hall's in both structure and function. Home to the state Supreme Court, it also features a small but interesting art collection in the lobby at the Golden Gate Ave. entrance and an exhibition room near the McAllister St. entrance. (350 McAllister St., between Polk and Larkin St.) The **United Nations Plaza** is sometimes host to the city's **farmer's market** and, most other days, to a general assembly of pigeons. (In summer, the farmer's market pops up on Polk St. Su and W. 5:30am-5:30pm.)

The seating in the glass-and-brass **Louise M. Davies Symphony Hall** was designed to give most audience members a close-up view of performers. Visually, the building is a smashing success, as is the **San Francisco Symphony.** See p. 120 for more info. (201 Van Ness Ave. ☎ 552-8000; tickets ☎ 431-5400. Open M-F 10am-6pm, Sa noon-6pm.) The well-regarded **San Francisco Opera Company** (see p. 120) and the **San Francisco Ballet** (see p. 120) perform at the recently renovated **War Memorial Opera House**. (301 Van Ness Ave., between Grove and McAllister St.)

## HAYES VALLEY

Artists of all types, from architects to fashion and interior designers, have begun to open studios on and around Hayes St. As if a natural extension of the artist community, cafes have sprung up, providing the essential social and caffeine

**FROM THE ROAD**

## REIMAGINING A CITY

I loved the idea of San Francisco before I ever stepped foot on its soil. This city had fostered some of the greatest social movements in America, always refusing to conform. I especially wanted to explore Haight-Ashbury, where, in my opinion, the last generation of great social rebels had settled. I didn't expect a reenactment of 1967's Summer of Love, but I wasn't prepared for what I found.

The Haight is primarily a shopping area now. It has dozens of eateries, boutiques, and tourist traps. A big mural of Janis, Jimi, and Jerry is a rare reminder of the area's history, but it has been updated to include Tupac. I knew it would be different but I was confused. Where was the energy that had inspired the music, art, and political devotion of the sixties?

As I wandered around, I began to figure it out. The energy was there, but it was different now. It was more subtle, more underground, but still palpable if you looked in the right places. A community of backpackers dwells in the far reaches of Upper Haight, Amoeba Music hosts free concerts, and the community has banded together to keep chains like McDonald's and Starbucks out. The people still do things their own way and don't care what anyone has to say about it. Though it's no longer a hotbed of unrest, the spirited independence of the Haight endures.

-Caitlin Casey, 2004

reprieves. Then enter the young trendsetters, and *voilà:* you have yourself a thriving new chic neighborhood. For the most part, the popularity and success of the area has been due to the community's talented artists, both of the culinary and visual sort. Success has also brought higher prices—starving artists are few and far between. An established contemporary art stronghold, the Bucheon Gallery dazzles the art world with new exhibits every five weeks. The gallery also helps young artists—locals and foreigners alike—find exposure in the who-do-you-know art world. Receptions are open to the public. *(540 Hayes St., near Octavia St.* ☎ *863-2891; www.bucheon.com. Open Tu-Sa 11am-6pm, Su noon-5pm. Free.)*

# TENDERLOIN

**Do not walk alone here, as the area can be dangerous, especially at night.** Witness the scene more safely by day, and also check out the vibrant cultural offerings. The **509 Cultural Center/Luggage Store Gallery** (☎ 255-5971) presents performing arts events, exhibitions, and arts education initiatives at the 509 Cultural Center, 509 Ellis St., and the Luggage Store, 1007 Market St., near 6th St. Started by a group of artists and residents in the late 80s, the group strives to draw on the neighborhood's rich diversity to gain a sense of community. Annual festivals include the "In The Street" theater festival in June. The **Art Institute of California** hosts occasional student shows in its lobby. The place is great for a brief viewing, but don't expect to find a multitude of works—it cannot hold more than fifteen paintings. *(1170 Market St. at UN Plaza, near 8th St.* ☎ *865-0198. Open M-Th 8am-8pm, F 8am-5pm, Sa 10am-4pm.)*

# SOUTH OF MARKET AREA (SOMA)

To the uninitiated, South of Market may appear a bleak stretch of industrial wasteland, but the area is actually home to a good bit of excitement. This is where the leather and Levi's community began to congregate in the 1940s and 50s. From there, a wild and wonderful nightlife scene emerged. The leather and whips still crack in some bars and clubs and come out full force at the Folsom Street Fair (see p. 127), but now the area is also home to a wide variety of hip nightlife and vibrant daytime art venues.

■ **SAN FRANCISCO MUSEUM OF MODERN ART (SFMOMA).** Fascinating for its architecture as well as for the art it contains, this black and gray marble-trimmed museum houses five spacious floors of art, with emphasis on design, photography, and audiovisuals. Its contemporary European and American collections are impressive—SFMOMA has the most 20th-century art this side of New York, including impressive collections of Warhol, Johns, Rauschenberg, and Stella. (*151 3rd St., between Mission and Howard St. ☎ 357-4000; www.sfmoma.org. Open Sept. 3-May 24 M-Tu and F-Su 11am-5:45pm, Th 11am-8:45pm; May 25-Sept. 2 M-Tu and F-Su 10am-6pm, Th 10am-9pm. Adults $10, over 62 $7, students with valid ID $6, under 13 free. Th 6-9pm half-price. Free 1st Tu of each month. Four free gallery tours per day.*)

**YERBA BUENA CENTER FOR THE ARTS.** The center runs an excellent theater and gallery space that emphasizes performance, film, viewer involvement, and local multicultural work—essentially anything that can be considered "adventurous art." It is surrounded by the **Yerba Buena Rooftop Gardens,** an oasis of foliage and gurgling fountains in a predominantly concrete neighborhood. (*701 Mission St., at 3rd St. ☎ 978-2787; www.yerbabuenaarts.org. Open Su and Tu-Sa 11am-6pm. Adults $6, free 1st Tu of month; seniors and students $3, free every Th. Free tours with admission Th 5pm and Sa 4pm.*)

**ZEUM.** Within the gardens but a sight unto itself, this completely interactive "art and technology center" is aimed primarily at children and teens. Beside studios for arts and crafts, claymation, and karaoke, Zeum has a music performance space and an ice skating and bowling center. The best draw is the **carousel,** built in 1906 and reopened after a 25-year hiatus. (*221 4th St., at Howard St. ☎ 777-2800; www.zeum.org. Open in summer Tu-Su 11am-5pm, off-season W-Su 11am-5pm. Adults $7, students and seniors $6, ages 4-18 $5, under 4 free. Carousel: open daily 11am-6pm. $2 for 2 rides.*)

# PACIFIC HEIGHTS

Along Union and Sacramento St., Pacific Heights has the greatest number of **Victorian buildings** in the city. The Heights sustained serious damage in the 1989 earthquake—Victorian restoration has become a full-fledged enterprise here. Pierce and Clay St., in particular, have an abundance of grand homes. The Public Library offers free tours of Pacific Heights mansions during the summer.

Churchgoers and architecture buffs alike will appreciate **St. Dominic's** towering altar that is carved in the shape of Jesus and the 12 apostles. With its imposing gray stone and Gothic-style architecture, St. Dominic's is a must-see. (*2390 Bush St., at Steiner St. Open M-Sa 6:30am-5:30pm, Su 7:30am-9pm. Mass M-F 6:30, 8am, and 5:30pm; Sa 8am and 5:30pm; Su 7:30, 9:30, 11:30am, 1:30, 5:30, and 9pm candlelight service.*) If you have any breath left after the steep climb up to the **Alta Plaza,** the views will snatch it away. Gaze downhill for a panoramic view of downtown San Fran and Twin Peaks, or uphill along Pierce Street to catch a spectacular glimpse of the Bay. Sunbathe on the grassy slopes or swing like a carefree kid in the playground; this is a great place to spend a mellow afternoon or pack a picnic.

# JAPANTOWN

Walking all the way through Japantown takes just minutes and is the only way to go. Stores hawk Pokémon paraphernalia and karaoke bars warble J-pop along Post St. around the Japan Center. The five-tiered **Peace Pagoda,** a gift to the community from the Japanese government, once sat amid cherry trees and a reflecting pool. It is currently in the midst of a slow restoration process to convert its bleak paved lot into the inviting centerpiece of the Japan Center. A brighter example of Japanese architecture is the **Soto Zen Mission Sokoji Buddhist Temple,** where some meditation services are open to the public. (*1691 Laguna St., at Sutter St. ☎ 346-7540. Public Zazen services Su 8am. Arrive 15min. early.*)

# HAIGHT-ASHBURY

All around Haight and Ashbury St., vestiges of the 60s exist in semi-harmony with chain stores and boutiques. Music and clothing top the list of legal merchandise. Inexpensive bars and ethnic restaurants, action-packed street life,

SAN FRANCISCO

SAN FRANCISCO

anarchist literature, and shops selling pipes for, um, tobacco also contribute to groovy browsing possibilities. While the Upper Haight tends to attract a younger tourist crowd, the Lower Haight is the stomping ground for longtime locals, though visitors are always welcome. Feel the love yet?

The former homes of several countercultural legends continue to attract visitors, even though new residents inhabit the cribs. From the corner of Haight and Ashbury St., walk up Ashbury St. to #710, just south of Waller St., to check out the house occupied by the **Grateful Dead** when they were still the Warlocks. Look across the street for the **Hell's Angels'** house. If you walk back to Haight St., go right three blocks and make a left on Lyon St. to check out **Janis Joplin's** old abode, 122 Lyon St., between Page and Oak St. Cross the Panhandle, continue three blocks to Fulton St., turn right, and wander seven blocks toward the park to see where the Manson "family" planned murder and mayhem at the **Charles Manson** mansion, 2400 Fulton St., at Willard St. The **San Francisco Public Library** sponsors a free walking tour focused on the area's pre-hippie incarnation as a Victorian-era resort. (☎557-4266. Tours leave Su 11am from the Park Branch Library at 1833 Page St., near Cole St.)

## LSD: FROM THE MAN TO THE PEOPLE

In 1938, in Basel, Switzerland, Albert Hoffman synthesized a compound called lysergic acid diethylamide (LSD). The new wonder drug was said to cure psychosis and alcoholism. In the early 50s, the CIA adopted LSD for **Operation MK-ULTRA**, a series of Cold War mind control experiments. By the end of the 60s, the drug had been tested on 1500 military personnel in a series of ethically shady operations. Writers Ken Kesey, Allen Ginsberg, and the Grateful Dead's Robert Hunter were first exposed to acid as subjects in government experiments. The CIA soon abandoned the unpredictable hallucinogen, but its effects had been discovered by bohemian proto-hippies in the Haight. Amateur chemists began producing the compound, and prominent intellectuals like Timothy Leary and Aldous Huxley advocated its use as a means of expanding consciousness. In October 1966, the drug was made illegal in California, and Kesey's Merry Pranksters hosted their first public **Acid Test**, immortalized in Tom Wolfe's journalistic novel *The Electric Kool-Aid Acid Test*. Once a secret weapon of the military-industrial complex and a potential panacea of the mental health industry, acid became an ingredient in much of the youth culture of the time, juicing up anti-war rallies and love-ins across the Bay and the country.

**PARKS.** Several parks dot the Haight. You may see police lurking in the bushes, as the parks are rumored to be popular places to buy marijuana. Buena Vista Park, which runs along Haight St. between Central and Baker St. and continues south, resembles a dense jungle. The lush and exotic fauna provides a private/public haven for those who want to do their own thing. An unofficial crash pad and community center for San Francisco skaters, Buena Vista is supposedly safer than Alamo Square, which lies northeast of the Haight at Hayes and Steiner St. Across Alamo Square's gentle grassy slope, a string of beautiful and brightly colored Victorian homes known as the Painted Ladies—a subject of thousands of postcards—glow against the backdrop of the metropolitan skyline.

# CASTRO

Rainbow flags hoisted high, out and proud lesbian, gay, bisexual, and transgender (LGBT) folk find comfort and fun on the streets of the Castro. The concept, as well as the reality, of an all-queer neighborhood draws queer tourists and their friends from around the world, pushing the already absolutely fabulous Castro scene over the top. Those out and about are the main attraction on the picture-perfect streets, where seeing and being seen is practically a full-time occupation. Stores throughout the area cater to gay mecca pilgrims with everything from rainbow flags and pride-wear to the latest in LGBT books, dance music, and trinkets of the more unmentionable variety. Also see **Gay & Lesbian Nightlife**, p. 126, or **From the Road: Rainbow Delirium**, p. xxx, for more on San Francisco's LGBT culture. Trevor Hailey, a resident since 1972, is consistently recognized as one of San Fran's top tour leaders. Her 4hr. walking tour covers Castro life and history from the Gold Rush to the present. (*☎550-8110; trvrhailey@aol.com. Tours Tu-Sa 10am. $40; lunch included. Reservations required.*) The steeply sloped areas to the south and west of Castro Village tend to be residential and the vibrantly painted old **Victorians**, of which Collingwood and Noe St. have their fair share, are worth visiting. For architecture without the walk, look for the faux-baroque **Castro Theatre** at 429 Castro St.

# MISSION

The Mission is slowly outgrowing its reputation as one of the most underappreciated neighborhoods in the city. Beyond the fabulous food and kickin' nightlife, the Mission is home to a vibrant community of painters and writers struggling to keep themselves and their messages heard in the face of dot-commers and rising rents. The sights in the area require some effort to find, but the rewards are plenty.

**MISIÓN DE LOS DOLORES (MISSION DOLORES).** Established over two centuries ago and located in the old heart of San Francisco, the Mission Dolores is thought to be the city's oldest building. Founded in 1776 by Father Junípero Serra, it was originally named in honor of St. Francis of Assisi. Later, due to its proximity to the Laguna de Nuestra Señora de los Dolores (Lagoon of Our Lady of Sorrows), the mission became universally known as Misión de los Dolores. Bougainvillea, poppies, and birds-of-paradise bloom in its cemetery, which was featured in Alfred Hitchcock's 1958 film *Vertigo*. (*3321 16th St., at 16th and Dolores St. ☎621-8203. Open May-Oct. daily 9am-4:30pm; Nov.-Apr. 9am-4pm. Adults $3; ages 5-12 $2. Mass: in English M-F 7:30, 9am; Sa 7:30, 9am, 5pm; Su 8, 10am. In Spanish Su noon.*)

**MISSION MURALS.** A walk east or west along 24th St., weaving in and out of the side streets, reveals the Mission's magnificent murals. Simply walking up and down Mission St. will yield a taste as well, but the concentration is decidedly on 24th. Continuing the long Mexican mural tradition made famous by Diego Rivera and José Orozco, the Mission murals have been a source of pride for Chicano artists, schoolchildren, and community members since the 1980s. Standouts include the more political murals of Balmy Alley off 24th St. between Harrison and Folsom St., a three-building tribute to guitar god Carlos Santana at 22nd St. and Van Ness Ave., the face of St. Peter's Church at 24th and Florida St., and the urban living center on 19th St. between Valencia and Guerrero St.

**OTHER SIGHTS. La Galeria la Raza** celebrates local Chicano and Latino artists with exhibitions and parties. Attached to the gallery is **Studio 24**, a space where Chicano and Latino artists sell artwork, crafts, and jewelry. (*2857 24th St., between Bryant and Florida St. ☎826-8009; www.galeriadelaraza.org. Usually open W-Sa noon-6pm. Call to confirm. Free. Store: Open Tu-Sa noon-6pm.*) **16th St.** is perhaps the most pulsing, pluralistic, personality-filled boulevard in all of San Francisco; people-watching possibilities make it a sight unto itself. **Mission Dolores Park**, which stretches from 18th to 20th St. between Church and Dolores St., is prime hang-out turf for residents of the Mission, the Castro, and Noe Valleys. **Osento**, 955 Valencia St., between 20th and 21st St., is a Japanese-style bathhouse for ladies, with wet and dry saunas, a jacuzzi, an outdoor dipping

SAN FRANCISCO

pool, sundecks, and a meditation room. (*282-6333. Open daily 1pm-1am. Last admission at midnight. 14+. $10-20, senior discount, over 70 free. One hour massage $60-80. No credit cards.)*

## ALCATRAZ

*The Blue and Gold Fleet (* 705-8200, tickets 705-5555; www.blueandgoldfleet.com) runs to Alcatraz (14 per day; $9.25 round-trip, seniors $7.50, ages 5-11 $6; audio tour $4 extra). Ticket lines can be painfully long. Reserve at least a day and preferably a week in advance, especially in summer.*

Mention Alcatraz and most people think of hardened criminals and daring escapes. In its 29 years as a maximum-security federal penitentiary, Alcatraz did encounter a menacing cast of characters: Al "Scarface" Capone, George "Machine Gun" Kelly, and Robert "The Birdman" Stroud, among others. There were 14 separate escape attempts—some desperate, defiant bolts for freedom, others carefully calculated and innovative. On the Rock, the award-winning cell-house audio tour takes you back to the infamous days of Alcatraz. Listen to the screaming gulls and booming foghorn and watch the palm trees blowing in the wind outside. From the dining-room window, view the glittering hubbub of San Francisco life and experience some of the isolation that plagued the prison's inmates. But there's more to the history of Alcatraz than gangsters and their antics. A **Park Ranger guided tour** can take you around the island and through its 200 years of occupation: from a hunting and fishing ground for Native Americans, to a Civil War defensive outpost, to a military prison, a federal prison, and finally a birthplace of the movement for Native American civil rights. Now part of the **Golden Gate National Recreation Area,** Alcatraz is home to diverse plants and birdlife. The Agave Trail footpath lets you explore these habitats (open Sept.-Jan.). For general orientation, the dockside theater gives a 13min. video of the Rock's history and resources. Next door is the bookstore, offering videos, audiotapes, books, and gifts to round out the Alcatraz experience. Check the website for occasional book-signings by former prisoners, guards, and residents.

## ANGEL ISLAND

*The Blue and Gold Fleet (* 705-8200, tickets 705-5555; www.blueandgoldfleet.com) runs to Angel Island (M-F 2 per day, Sa-Su 3 per day; $10.50 round-trip, ages 6-12 $5.50, under 6 free).*

Picturesque **Angel Island State Park** sits in the middle of San Francisco Bay. A 20min. ferry ride from San Francisco or Marin brings you to rolling hills, biking and hiking trails, and sprawling picnic grounds. The island is a heavenly escape from the bustle of the city, except for those sunny weekends when all of San Francisco shows up. In addition to great views, the island harbors some rich history. For over 2,000 years, Coastal tribes native to Marin County paddled here to hunt and fish. Spaniard Juan Manuel de Ayala "discovered" the island and gave his name to the sheltered cove he established as a harbor. The Mexicans used Angel Island to rear cattle until 1859, when it was taken over by the US Army. The forts left by the Army have housed a Civil War encampment, a Spanish-American War quarantine station, a missile site, and an immigration station. From 1910 to 1940, Angel Island served as a holding site for immigrants, mostly Chinese. During WWII, the station was used as a POW camp.

Public grills dot the lawn in front of the **Visitor Center** at Ayala Cove. On weekends and summer weekdays, this area fills up with families; but if the screeching of small children is precisely what you're trying to escape, serenity is only a hike away. Just behind the picnic grounds, the Visitor Center has exhibits and free 20min. orientation videos about the history and activities of the island. Adjacent to the center, the **Park Ranger Station** offers tours of the Immigration Station, Camp Reynolds, and Fort McDowell. For a leisurely island circuit, the one-hour **Tram Tour** hits all major historic sites and provides some decent views. With a bit of legwork, the bike and hike trails allow some escape from the masses and reward with stunning panoramas. **Bikes** can be brought on the ferry or rented near the docks at Ayala Cove. Bikers are allowed only on the perimeter road and the steeper fire road. The perimeter road balances exhausting uphills with exhilarating downhills. Hikers can choose several trails to the 781 ft. summit of Mt. Livermore. If the exertion leaves you famished, a **dock-side cafe** serves coffee, soft drinks, alcohol, snacks ($3-4), sandwiches, and ice cream ($2-3). Maps at the gift shop are available for $1.

If a daytrip isn't enough, you can **camp** at one of the nine eco-friendly hike-in sites. All sites have running water, pit toilets, BBQ, table, and food-lockers. No wood fires allowed; bring charcoal or a stove.

# ⌐| SHOPPING

## BOOKS

San Francisco has bookstores to fit every niche market and bibliophilic bent. The highest concentration of small, local stores can be found on **Haight Street** and in the **Mission.** Used bookstores are also abundant along Irving St. in the **Sunset** district and around Columbus Ave. and Broadway in **North Beach.** (For more booksellers across the Bay, see **Berkeley: Shopping,** p. 138.)

■ **City Lights Bookstore,** 261 Columbus Ave. (☎362-8193), near Broadway in **North Beach.** This Beat generation landmark, famous for promoting banned books in the 1950s and 60s, has a wide selection of fiction, poetry, art, and, of course, Beat literature. Founder and owner Lawrence Ferlinghetti remains committed to publishing and publicizing the work of new authors. Open daily 10am-midnight. See **Sights,** p. 104.

■ **A Different Light Bookstore,** 489 Castro St. (☎431-0891), near 18th St. in the **Castro.** All queer, all the time, with more-than-plentiful special interest subdivisions, including poetry, travel, and of course, transsexual Asian firefighters. Also the ultimate resource for free Bay Area mags, a popular community bulletin board, and free monthly readings by notable queer authors. Open daily 10am-10pm.

**Green Apple Music and Books,** 506 Clement St. (☎382-2272), at 6th Ave. in **Richmond.** Green Apple's popularity gives it a chaotic marketplace feel—no quiet, comfy-armchair perusing here. The main store covers everything from cooking to transportation; find fiction and a small but significant DVD and used CD section in the **Annex,** 2 doors down at 520 Clement St. Open M-Th and Su 10am-10:30pm, F-Sa 10am-11:30pm. Annex closes 15 min. earlier.

**Needles and Pens,** 482 14th St. (☎255-1534), near Guerrero St. in the **Mission.** Selling 'zines of all sorts, Needles and Pens is a unique and high-caliber bookstore. If you've never heard of a "'zine," stop by for an important education. A small selection of handmade clothes as well. 'Zines $1-5. Open Su and Th-Sa noon-7pm. No credit cards.

**Phoenix Books and Music,** 3850 24th St. (☎821-3477; www.dogearedbooks.com), at Vicksburg St. between Church and Sanchez St. in **Noe Valley.** New, remainder, and used books and CDs. Extensive fiction and children's sections, great bargains on hardcovers (most $4-15), and a friendly and knowledgeable staff. Sister stores: **Red Hill Books,** 401 Cortland St. (☎648-5331) and **Dog Eared Books,** 900 Valencia St. (☎282-1901). All open M-Sa 10am-10pm, Su 10am-8pm.

## MUSIC

■ **Amoeba Music,** 1855 Haight St. (☎831-1200; www.amoebamusic.com), between Shrader and Stanyan St. in the **Upper Haight.** *Rolling Stone* dubbed this the best record store in the world. The Haight St. Amoeba stocks an amazing selection of used CDs, plus a parade of vintage concert posters. The store doubles as a venue for free concerts by some big names and a weekly in-house DJ series (see **Entertainment,** p. 120). Open M-Sa 10:30am-10pm, Su 11am-9pm.

**Aquarius Records,** 1055 Valencia St. (☎647-2272), at 21st St. in the **Mission.** Tiny store known worldwide for obscure selection of all genres of music and a staff to guide you when you don't know where to start: Japanese Rock or 60s psychedelics? Its real specialties are drum & bass, indie, and imports from all over the globe. New and used. Great vinyl section, too. Open M-W 10am-9pm, Th-Su 10am-10pm.

**Open Mind Music,** 342 Divisadero St. (☎621-2244; www.openmindmusic.com), at Page St. in the **Lower Haight.** Insane quantities of new and used vinyl and collectibles: dance, down tempo, new hip-hop, experimental, lounge, and, yes, even Zeppelin. Listening stations to sample before you buy. Open M-Sa 11am-9pm, Su noon-8pm.

## CLOTHES

■ **Departures From the Past,** 2028 Fillmore St. (☎885-3377), at Pine St., in **Pacific Heights.** Extraordinary collection of genuine vintage clothing for men and women. Particularly impressive range of lingerie (if secondhand lingerie doesn't make you itch). Tons of wacky accessories including but not limited to: costume jewelry, sunglasses, hats, gloves, and bow ties. Open M-Sa 11am-7pm, Su noon-6pm.

**Manifesto,** 514 Octavia St. (☎431-4778), just north of Hayes St. in **Hayes Valley.** Local designer makes 1950s-inspired clothes for men and women. The retro-looking dresses and shirts are well cut, reasonably priced ($65-150), and more flattering than many of their authentic cousins. Open Su noon-5pm, Tu-F 11am-7pm, Sa 11am-6pm.

**American Rag,** 1305 Van Ness Ave. (☎474-5214), at Fern St. in **Pacific Heights.** A California vintage clothing institution. Shopaholics will adore big-name retro styles up front while bargain-hunters will be tempted by plentiful racks of vintage in the back. Even thrift prices aren't great (most pants, skirts, and jeans $30-45) but the selection is staggering. Open M-Sa 10am-9pm, Su 10am-7pm.

**Buffalo Exchange,** 1555 Haight St. (☎431-7737), between Clayton and Ashbury St. in the **Upper Haight.** One of those rare thrift stores that actually allows you to be thrifty and get high-quality clothes, shoes, and accessories. Almost everything under $20. Additional locations: 1800 Polk St. (☎346-5726) in **Nob Hill** and 2585 Telegraph Ave. (☎510-644-9202) in **Berkeley**. Open Su-Th 11am-7pm, F-Sa 11am-8pm.

## TATTOOS & PIERCINGS

California law states that **you must be 18 years old** to get a tattoo. Generally, minors need an adult present for piercing.

**Lyle Tuttle's Tattoo Art Studio,** 841 Columbus Ave. (☎775-4991), in **North Beach.** Lyle Tuttle opened his modern, clean tattoo studio in the 1960s, permanently decorating the skins of Janis Joplin, Joan Baez, and Cher. While the eminently professional Tuttle, age 71, himself covered in tattoos from head to foot, no longer tattoos behind the bar, his proteges continue the tradition, amidst a small but impressive collection of tattoo memorabilia—consider it an added bonus if you drop by when someone's under the needle behind the bar. Tattoos start at $60. Open daily noon-9pm. No credit cards.

**Mom's Body Shop,** 1408 Haight St. (☎864-6667), in the **Upper Haight.** This family-run establishment takes great pride in its craftsmanship, proclaiming tattoos just "like Mom's apple pie." Piercings from $10. Tattoos $120 per hr., min. $60. Appointments or walk-ins welcome. Open daily in summer noon-9pm; in winter noon-8pm

# EROTICA

■ **Good Vibrations,** 1210 Valencia St. (☎974-8980; www.goodvibes.com), at 23rd St. in the **Mission.** The well-known erotica cooperative for enthusiastic do-it-yourselfers (see their "Make Your Own Dildo" kit). The woman-owned and -operated sex store is so tasteful, you could almost take your parents there. Try out "Tester" bottles of lube or observe the progression from wooden cranks to C-cell batteries in a small but informative display of vibrator evolution dating back to 1910. Excellent collection of instructional books $15-100+. 18+ to enter. Open Su-W noon-7pm, Th-Sa 11am-8pm. Additional locations: 1620 Polk St. (☎345-0400), at Sacramento St. in **Pacific Heights** and 2504 San Pablo Ave. (☎510-841-8987) in **Berkeley.**

**Mr. S. Leather,** 310 7th St. (☎863-7764 or ☎800-746-7677; www.mr-s-leather.com), between Folsom and Harrison St. in **SoMa.** Selections range from $2 cock-rings to 500 types of dildos to a $2900 flying sleep sack/bondage suit. A huge variety of men's leather clothes and a helpful staff have made Mr. S a shopping mecca for the leather community for the last decade. Sister store **Madame S.,** 321 7th., across the street, specializes in leather and latex "hâute fetish couture." (☎863-9447; www.madame-s.com). Mr. S. open daily 11am-7pm. Madame S. open Su and W-Sa noon-7pm.

# MISCELLANEOUS

■ **Imperial Tea Court,** 1411 Powell St. (☎788-6080 or 800-567-5898; www.imperial-teas.com), at Broadway in **Chinatown.** This oasis of serenity is a must for tea lovers. Exotic scents waft about this little shop's soothing earthen tones and singing rainbow finches. Open M and W-Sa 11am-6:30pm.

**Does Your Father Know?,** 548 Castro St. (☎241-9865), between 18th and 19th St. in the **Castro.** Your dad told you not to waste your money on touristy trinkets. Now you can show him you didn't listen *and* you're queer! DYFK is stocked with Castro's finest kitschy, trivial junk, from Judy Garland figurines to glow-in-the-dark vibrators and boxes of penis pasta. Open M-Th 9:30am-10pm, F-Sa 9:30am-11pm, Su 10am-9pm.

**Under One Roof,** 549 Castro St. (☎503-2300; www.underoneroof.org), between 18th and 19th St. in the **Castro.** More sophisticated than your average kitsch shop, Under One Roof donates 100% of the profit from every sale—be it an AbFab magnet, scented bath oil, or a Pride holiday ornament—to organizations working to fight AIDS. Sign-up and orientation are simple for those looking to join the all-volunteer staff that has helped raise over $9 million to date. Open M-Sa 10am-8pm, Su 11am-7pm.

# MALLS

**San Francisco Shopping Centre** (☎495-5656), on Market St. at 5th St., near **Union Square.** Lobbying for an uptown feel, the high-end retailers lacking Union representation have formed a coalition around 6 curving escalators (the only ones in the world), giving shoppers 9 stories of collective bargaining. Open M-Sa 9:30am-8pm, Su 11am-6pm.

**Stonestown Galleria,** 19th Ave. and Winston Dr. (☎759-2623; www.shopstonestown.com), between **Stern Grove** and the SF State University campus. This 2-story shopping mall caters more to spendthrift sophisticates than to students. 250 mall favorites and a grease-laden food court will satisfy mainstream shopping spree needs. Open M-Sa 10am-9pm, Su 11am-6pm. Hours of stores and restaurants may vary.

# ⚑ ENTERTAINMENT

## LIVE MUSIC

The live music scene in San Fran is a vibrant mix of class and brass, funk and punk, hippies and hip-hop, and everything in between. Wailing guitars and scratchy voices still fill the halls of San Francisco's most famous rock clubs, where several stars in the classic rock pantheon got their starts. If you're in a mellow mood, low-profile, funked-up soul seems to draw today's pimped-out booty shakers, while the San Francisco Symphony, with Michael Tilson Thomas as music director, reaches world-class status.

The distinction between bars, clubs, and live music venues is hazy. Most bars occasionally have bands, and small venues have rock and hip-hop shows. Start looking for the latest live music listings in *SF Weekly* and *The Guardian*. Hardcore audiophiles might also snag a copy of *BAM*. *The List* is an online calendar of rock gigs all over Northern California (http://jon.luini.com/thelist.txt).

## CLASSICAL

**Louise M. Davies Symphony Hall,** 201 Van Ness Ave. (☎431-5400), near the **Civic Center,** houses the **San Francisco Symphony** in an impressive if controversial structure. The cheapest seats are on the center terrace, directly above the orchestra—the acoustics are slightly off, but you get an excellent (and rare) head-on view of the conductor (and the rest of the audience). Prices vary with performance. Open M-F 9am-5pm.

**War Memorial Opera House,** 301 Van Ness Ave. Open for tickets 2hr. before each show. Box office, 199 Grove St. Open M-Sa 10am-6pm. **San Francisco Opera** (☎864-3330; www.sfopera.com). Tickets start at $23. Standing-room-only tickets ($10, cash only) available from 10am on day of performance.

**San Francisco Ballet** (☎865-2000; www.sfballet.org) shares the War Memorial Opera House with the San Francisco Opera (p. 120). Tickets start at $30; available online or by phone M-Sa noon-6pm. Discounted standing-room-only tickets at the Opera House 2hr. before performances.

**Herbst Theatre,** 401 Van Ness Ave. (☎392-4400), near the **Civic Center,** provides a plush setting for a year-round schedule of classical soloists, quartets, and smaller symphonies, plus occasional lectures by renowned authors, artists, and other intellectuals. Box office open M-F 9:30am-5pm, Sa 10am-4pm.

## ROCK & HIP-HOP

▨ **Café du Nord,** 2170 Market St. (☎861-5016), between Church and Sanchez St. in **Castro.** Takes you back in time to a red velvet club with speakeasy ambience. Excellent live music nightly—from pop and groove to garage rock. Local favorites include vintage jazz, blues, and R&B. Special weekly events include the popular M Night Hoot, a showcase of local singing and songwriting talent. Happy Hour daily until 7:30pm with swank $2.50 martinis, Manhattans, and cosmos. Cover $5-10 after 8:30pm. 21+. Open Su-Tu 6pm-2am, W-Sa 4pm-2am.

▨ **Justice League,** 628 Divisadero St. (☎440-0409, info 289-2038), at Hayes St. in the **Lower Haight.** Live hip-hop is hard to find in San Fran, but the Justice League fights ever onward for a good beat. Excellent variety of artists. M 10pm Club Dred, reggae and dub. W 10pm Bang Bang, soul night. 21+. Cover $5-25, usually $10-14. Usually open daily 9pm-2am. Tickets at www.ticketweb.com, **Red Top Clothing,** 1472 Haight (☎552-6494), and **Open Mind Music** (☎621-2244), at Divisadero and Page St.

▨ **Bottom of the Hill,** 1233 17th St. (☎626-4455; 24hr. info 621-4455; www.bottomofthe-hill.com), between Missouri and Texas St., in **Potrero Hill.** Intimate rock club with tiny stage is the best place to see up-and-comers before they move to bigger venues. Most Su afternoons feature local bands and all-you-can-eat barbecue for $5-10. 21+. Cover $5-10. Open M-Th 8:30pm-2am, F 3pm-2am, Sa 8:30pm-2am, Su hours vary.

▨ **Amoeba Music,** 1855 Haight St. (☎831-1200; www.amoebamusic.com), just east of Stanyan St., in **Upper Haight.** Free concerts in the store—you stand in the aisles. Some fairly well-known acts. Weekly DJ series. Open M-Sa 10:30am-10pm, Su 11am-9pm.

## JAZZ & BLUES

**Biscuits & Blues,** 401 Mason St. (☎292-2583; www.biscuitsandbluessf.com), at Geary St., in **Union Square.** "Dedicated to the preservation of hot biscuits and cool blues," this basement joint will make you feel downright Southern, with fried chicken, sweet potato pie, okra like mama used to make, and live, kickin' blues every night. Entrees $10-12 (smoked turkey and chicken jambalaya with rice and sauce piquante is a must have!). Drinks $3-7. All ages. Tickets $15. Open M-F 5pm-11:30pm, Sa-Su 5pm-1am.

**Saloon,** 1232 Grant Ave. (☎989-7666), between Columbus Ave. and Vallejo St., in **North Beach.** The oldest bar in San Francisco (est. in 1861) still looks like, well, a saloon. Live bands nightly M-F 9:30pm-1:30am, Sa-Su 4-8pm and 9:30pm-1:30am. Cover F-Sa $3-5; 1-drink min. other nights. Open daily noon-2am. No credit cards.

**Blue Lamp,** 561 Geary St. (☎885-1464; www.bluelamp.com), at Taylor St., in **Union Sq.** Local bands (including the owners) perform nightly at 9:30pm at this friendly and comfortable venue. Rock usually dominates the weekends, while weekdays see a lot of folk jams. Su nights boast one of the city's longest running open blues jams, and M nights feature an acoustic open mic for undiscovered performers. Drinks average $4. 21+. Cover usually $5-6 on weekends. Open daily 3pm-2am. No credit cards.

**Boom Boom Room,** 1601 Fillmore St. (☎673-8000; www.boomboomblues.com), at Geary St., near **Japantown.** Once owned by John Lee Hooker, Boom Boom is known as the city's home to "blues and boogie, funk and bumpin' jazz" and features live music 7 nights a week, often with big-name acts. This place is leading the revival of the 50s Fillmore Jazz scene with style. Cover varies by act. Open daily 4pm-2am.

# DANCE

▨ **Alonzo King's Lines Contemporary Ballet** (☎863-3360; www.linesballet.org), in **Hayes Valley.** Dancers combine elegant classical moves with athletic flair to the music of great living jazz and world music composers. Springtime shows are performed at the Yerba Buena Center for the Arts. Tickets $15-25.

▨ **Oberlin Dance Company,** 3153 17th St. (☎863-9834; www.odctheater.org), between South Van Ness and Fulsom St. in the **Mission.** Mainly dance, but occasional theater space with gallery attached. Tickets $10-20 dollars, but occasional 2-for-1 and "pay what you can" nights. $1 parking across the street. Box office open W-Sa 2-5pm.

**Dancer's Group,** 3252A 19th St. (☎920-9181; www.dancersgroup.org), at Shotwell St. in the **Mission.** Promotes cultural dance and original works. Open M-F 10am-4pm.

# LIVE THEATER

Downtown, **Mason Street** and **Geary Street** constitute **"Theater Row,"** the city's prime place for theatrical entertainment. **Fort** Mason, near Fisherman's Wharf, is also a popular area. For the latest on shows, check local listings in free mags and the newspaper. TIX Bay Area, in a kiosk in Union Sq. on the corner of Geary and Powell St., offers tickets for almost all shows and concerts and information about city tours and MUNI passes. Assure yourself a seat in advance, or try for cash-only, half-price tickets the day of. (☎433-7827; www.theaterbayarea.org. Open Tu-Th 11am-6pm, F-Sa 11am-7pm.)

**Magic Theatre,** Bldg. D, 3rd fl. (☎441-8822; www.magictheatre.org), in **Fort Mason** (use Fort Mason Center entrance). Sam Shepard served as playwright-in-residence here from 1975 to 1985. Today, the theater stages both international and American premieres. W-

SAN FRANCISCO

Th $22-32, F-Su $27-37. Senior and student rush tickets, available 30min. before the show $10. Shows at 8 or 8:30pm. Su matinees 2 or 2:30pm $15, reduced cost previews ($17). Call for exact times. Box office open Tu-Sa noon-5pm.

**Geary Theater,** 415 Geary St. (☎749-2228; www.act-sfbay.org), at Mason St., in **Union Square.** Home to the renowned American Conservatory Theater, the jewel in SF's theatrical crown. The elegant theater is a show-stealer in its own right. Tickets $11-61 (cheaper for previews and on weekdays). Half-price student, teacher, and senior tickets available 2hr. before showtime. Box office open Su and Tu-Sa noon-6pm.

**Theatre Rhinoceros,** 2926 16th St. (box office ☎861-5079; www.therhino.org), at South Van Ness Ave., in the **Mission.** The oldest queer theater in the world, the Rhino has been an innovator in the arts community since 1977. The theater emphasizes playwriting by and for the gay, lesbian, bisexual, transgender community. Tickets $10-30. Discounts for students, seniors, disabled, and groups of 10+. Box office open Su and Tu-Sa 1-6pm. No wheelchair access.

**The Orpheum,** 1192 Market St., at Hyde St. near the **Civic Center.** Box Office (☎512-7770), 6th St. at Market St. This famous San Francisco landmark hosts the big Broadway shows. Two sister theaters in the area host smaller shows: **Golden Gate Theatre,** 1 Taylor St., and **Curran Theatre,** 445 Geary St. Individual show times and prices vary.

**848 Community Space,** 848 Divisadero St. (☎922-2385; www.848.com), between Fulton and McAllister St., near the **Upper Haight.** Basically a glorified living room, the 848 is a community space that tries to do a little of everything. Comedy troupes, one-act plays, and music dominate the calendar but everything from night-long tribal rituals to live erotica readings have taken place here. Check the website for listings. M yoga ($12); Tu night contact improv classes ($8) and jams ($3). Shows free-$15. No credit cards.

**Exit Theater,** 156 Eddy St. (☎931-1094, box office 673-5944; www.theexit.org), between Mason and Taylor streets in the **Tenderloin.** Also at 277 Taylor St. between Eddy and Ellis St. 2 locations and 3 venues produce independent and experimental theater for a youthful, urban audience. Special events like Classic Absurdity Theater Festival in February; sassy DIVAfest, 2 weeks in May devoted to "theater of a female persuasion"; and the big daddy of national indie theater, the San Fran Fringe Festival, showcasing 250 performances over 12 days in Sept. Tickets $12-20, $8 and under for San Fran Fringe. No credit cards.

# MOVIES

For a complete listing of features and locations, check the weekly papers or call **MovieFone** (☎777-FILM/3456). Keep in mind that San Francisco movie theaters, even the massive AMC-1000, have nowhere near enough parking.

◪ **Castro Theatre,** 429 Castro St. (☎621-6350, automated 621-6120; www.thecastrotheatre.com), near Market St. in the **Castro.** This landmark 1922 movie palace has live organ music before evening showings. Eclectic films, festivals, and double features. Far from silent—bawdy crowds turn many a movie into *The Rocky Horror Picture Show.* Highlights include the Sing-along Sound of Music, for those who believe Julie Andrews would be better with chest hair. Adults $8, seniors and under 12 $5. Matinees W and Sa-Su $5. Box office opens 1hr. before 1st show. No credit cards.

◪ **Roxie,** 3117 16th St. (☎863-1087; www.roxie.com), off Valencia St. in the **Mission.** This trendy movie house shows sharp indie films and fashionably foolish retro classics, plus a late-night series of truly disturbing European gore flicks. Try to walk with a companion at night. Adults $8, seniors and under 13 $4. Bargain matinees: 1st show W and Sa-Su $5, seniors and kids free. Discount pass (good for 5 shows) $22. No credit cards.

**The Lumière,** 1572 California St. (showtimes ☎267-4983, box office 885-3201; www.landmarktheatres.com), between Larkin and Polk St. in **Nob Hill.** Indie, foreign, and art films. Adults $9; seniors, children, and 1st show each day $5.75 (before 6pm).

## SPECTATOR SPORTS

The **San Francisco Giants** (☎467-8000 or 800-734-4268; www.sfgiants.com) play baseball at the newly opened **Pacific Bell Park** in SoMa, near the water off Townsend St. The Giants' season is April through October. Most games sell out before the season even starts, except for 500 seats reserved for day-of-game sale. (Tickets $10-42. Tours of the park $10.) The five-time Super Bowl champion **49ers** (☎468-2249; www.49ers.com) still play at San Francisco's old-time field—the notoriously windy **Candlestick Park** (☎467-1994). Now officially called **3COM Park,** the stadium is 8 mi. south of the city with its own exit off US 101. MUNI bus #29 will also take you right there. Football pre-season starts in early August. The main season runs from September through the last Sunday in January.

# 🎭 NIGHTLIFE

Nightlife in San Francisco is as varied as the city's personal ads. Everyone from "shy first-timer" to "bearded strap daddy" to "pre-op transsexual top" can find a place to go on a Saturday (or Tuesday) night. The spots listed below are divided into coffeehouses, bars, and clubs, but these lines get pretty blurred after dark. Every other bar calls itself a cafe, every second cafe is a club, and half the clubs in town declare themselves lounges. Don't fret—there are 10,000 night spots in the city, and you're sure to find something that suits your fancy. If the spots listed below don't inspire you, check out the nightlife listings in *SF Weekly,* the *Guardian,* and *Metropolitan.* **Unless otherwise noted, all clubs are 21+ only.** San Francisco is not a particularly friendly city to underagers.

## COFFEEHOUSES

🏠 **Vesuvio Café,** 255 Columbus Ave. (☎362-3370), next to Jack Kerouac Alley, in **North Beach.** Jack and his friends started their day by howling like Dharma Bums over pints at Vesuvio and then café-crawled their way up Columbus Ave. The wooden, tiled, and stained-glass bar with an upstairs balcony remains a great place to drink. Draught beers $4.25, bottled beers $3.50, pitchers $9-12. Happy Hour M-Th 3-7pm: drinks $1 off, pitchers and bottles of wine $3 off. Open daily 6am-2am. No credit cards.

🏠 **Caffè Trieste,** 601 Vallejo St. (☎392-6739), at Grant Ave. Though every bar in **North Beach** claims to be a Beat haunt, this is the genuine article. While Vesuvio's is where the gang got trashed, Trieste remained their more mellow living room. The leftovers still hang out in the front. It hasn't changed much since then—a few new photos of famous patrons, but the jukebox still plays opera, and it's still the cornerstone of North Beach's remaining Italian community. Live Italian pop and opera concerts every Sa 1:45-6pm (since 1973) alone are worth a stop here. Espresso drinks $1.50-3.25; bottles of beer $2-3; glasses of wine $2.25-3.75. Open M-Sa 10am-6pm. No credit cards.

**Spike's,** 4117 19th St. (☎626-5573; www.spikescoffee.com), between Castro and Collingwood St., in **Castro.** Candy, sweets, and dog-friendly treats at this juice and coffee joint merit walking with Fido away from the center of Castro Village. Neighborly Spike's place is also one of the few cafes with seating. Open daily 6:30am-8pm.

**The Horseshoe Café,** 566 Haight St. (☎626-8852), between Steiner and Fillmore St., in the **Lower Haight.** Big-screen TV, movie, and music video projections in the back. DSL Internet access and plenty of space to read, write, or ruminate over chai iced tea ($2.25), coffee ($1.25), or cookies (50¢). Open daily 6am-midnight. No credit cards.

## BARS & PUBS

🏠 **Hotel Utah Saloon,** 500 4th St. (☎546-6300; www.thehotelutahsaloon.com), at Bryant St., in **SoMa.** Excellent and unpretentious saloon—with an original Belgian Bar from 1908—and one of the friendliest crowds around. More than your average bar food,

SAN FRANCISCO

## ROM THE ROAD

### RAINBOW DELIRIUM

No city could live up to the queer utopian visions that many harbor for San Francisco. Nevertheless, it does offer nightlife options that could overwhelm even the most seasoned gay partier. Some general guidelines: the Castro is a safe place to begin, especially for bars. **Bar on Castro, SF Badlands,** and **The Pilsner Inn** tend to attract younger crowds. **Moby Dick** and **Twin Peaks** will lead you to the neighborhood stalwarts.

If you're looking to dance all night, you'll inevitably wind up in SoMa). **The EndUp** is a popular after-hours hotspot. Similarly, SoMa may be the place to go for leather and Levis.

Queer women may want to explore **SoMa** and the **Mission.** **The Lexington** is an SF classic. **Wild Side West** in Bernal Heights claims to be the oldest lesbian bar in SF.

If you're under 21, you're basically out of luck. Some SF cafes, though, can be just as stimulating as the 21+ scene. One rare club option is **Club Faith,** 715 Harrison St., at 3rd St. in SoMa, whose cover may be a bit high, but at east they let you in for the progressive house and hip-hop. ☎ 905-4100; www.club-faithsf.com. 18+. Cover $12. Open Th 9:30pm-2:30am.)

-Michael Murphy, 2004

including build your own burgers (from $7). Downstairs stage hosts live rock or country music nightly and one of the best open mics in the city on M (shows begin 8:30-9pm). Beer $3.75. 21+. Show cover $3-7. Open M-F 11:30am-2am, Sa-Su 6pm-2am.

🏳 **Place Pigalle,** 520 Hayes St. (☎552-2671), between Octavia and Laguna St. in **Hayes Valley.** After a long day at work, the designers, boutique owners, and artists of Hayes St. relax on vintage velvet sofas at this big, dark, airy bar. Weekend nights the wine flows freely, the music blares, and crowds of 20- and 30-somethings with bohemian sensibilities pack the place beyond capacity. Occasional DJs and a rotating art exhibit liven up the back room. Happy Hour daily 4-7pm (beer, house wines $2.75). Open daily 4pm-2am.

🏳 **The Bigfoot Lodge,** 1750 Polk St. (☎440-2355), between Clay and Washington St. in **Nob Hill.** Campy bear heads, a gigantic Big Foot, and bartenders uniformed as scouts keep up more of an image than does the easy-going crowd in this log cabin retreat. Beer $3.50-4.50, cocktails around $5. Happy Hour daily from opening until 8pm. Open M-F 3pm-2am, Sa-Su noon-2am.

🏳 **111 Minna,** 111 Minna St. (☎974-1719; www.111minnagallery.com), at 2nd St. in **SoMa.** "Art and Leisure" at this funky up-and-comer's gallery by day, hipster groove-spot by night. Cocktails and beer $3-10. Open M-Tu noon-10pm, W noon-11pm, Th-F noon-2am, Sa 10pm-2am, Su 9pm-2am. Cover $5-15 for bands and progressive house DJs.

**Hush Hush,** 496 14th St. (☎241-9944), at Guerrero St., in the **Mission.** You'll feel oh so hip when you find Hush Hush, since this hot spot is too cool to need a sign; look for the blue awning with 496 in white. Large leather booths, pool, and local DJs spinning almost every night have everyone whispering about this place. MC Battle 1st Tu of every month. Smile Su with Rock DJs. Open daily 6pm-2am. No credit cards.

## CLUBS

🏳 **Velvet Lounge,** 443 Broadway (☎788-0228), between Kearny and Montgomery St., in **North Beach.** Decked-out 20- and 30-somethings pack this club and thump along to top 40, hip-hop, and house. F occasional live cover bands. No sneakers or athletic wear. Cover usually $10. Open W-Sa 9pm-2am.

**Nickie's BBQ,** 460 Haight St. (☎621-6508; www.nickies.com), east of Fillmore St. in the **Lower Haight.** After many incarnations (including a brothel where Nickie worked), this venue has evolved into one of the chillest, friendliest small clubs in the city. Live DJ M-Sa. Grateful Dead M, world music T, reggae W, and an eclectic mix of funk, hip-hop, and dance music Th-Sa. Cover $5. Open daily 9pm-2am. No credit cards.

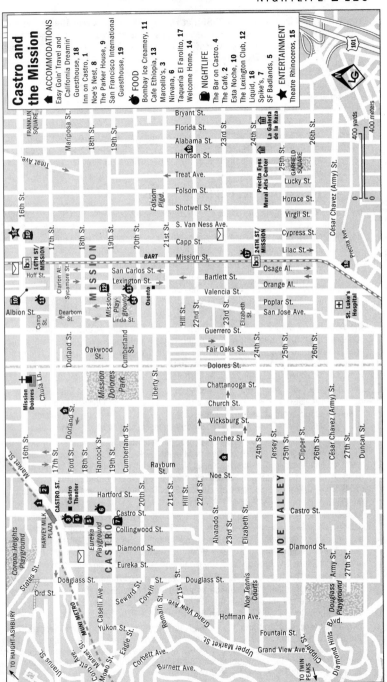

## Castro and the Mission

### ▲ ACCOMMODATIONS
Easy Goin' Travel and California Dreamin' Guesthouse, **18**
Inn on Castro, **1**
Noe's Nest, **8**
The Parker House, **9**
San Francisco International Guesthouse, **19**

### ♦ FOOD
Bombay Ice Creamery, **11**
Cafe Ethiopia, **13**
Marcello's, **3**
Nirvana, **6**
Taqueria El Farolito, **17**
Welcome Home, **14**

### ■ NIGHTLIFE
The Bar on Castro, **4**
The Café, **2**
Esta Noche, **10**
The Lexington Club, **12**
Liquid, **16**
Spike's, **7**
SF Badlands, **5**

### ★ ENTERTAINMENT
Theatre Rhinoceros, **15**

**The Top,** 424 Haight St. (☎864-7386), at Fillmore St., in the **Lower Haight.** Host to some of the finest house DJs in SF. A definite must for turntable loyalists. Su House and M Hip Hop are huge. House on W and F, too. Drum and Bass Tu and Sa. Happy Hour until 10pm. 21+. Cover $5 after 10pm. Open daily 7pm-2am. No credit cards.

**Liquid,** 2925 16th St. (☎431-8889), at South Van Ness Ave, in the **Mission.** Nightly mix usually includes trip-hop and hip-hop, but mainly house. Young but mellow crowd fills the small space. Meet a cutie and practice those long-forgotten back seat skills; all of Liquid's couches are car seats. 21+. Cover $4-5. Open daily 9pm-3am. No credit cards.

**El Rio,** 3158 Mission St. (282-3325), between César Chavez and Valencia St. In **Mission.** A classy, mixed club with stylish lighting and decor, large outdoor patio, and well-groomed bartenders. Salsa Su, including a dance lesson and patio barbecue. F 5-7pm free oysters on the half-shell. Drinks $4-10. Occasional cover $5-8. Open M-Th 5pm-2am, F-Su 3pm-2am. No credit cards.

# GAY & LESBIAN NIGHTLIFE

▓ **The Bar on Castro,** 456 Castro St. (☎626-7220), between Market and 18th St. A refreshingly urbane **Castro** staple with dark plush couches perfect for eyeing the stylish young crowd, scoping the techno-raging dance floor, or watching Queer as Folk on Su. Happy Hour M-F 3-8pm (beer $2.25). Su beer $1.75. Open M-F 4pm-2am, Sa-Su noon-2am. No credit cards.

▓ **SF Badlands,** 4121 18th St. (☎626-9320), near Castro St. in **Castro.** Strutting past the sea of boys at the bar, the Castro's prettiest faces and bodies cruise a futuristic blue-and-chrome dance floor, where Madonna, George Michael, and Destiny's Child—all in enthralling teleprojection—make San Fran Badlands just as amazing as its heart-stealing Dupont Circle twin. Cover F-Sa $2. Open daily 2pm-2am. No credit cards.

**The Café,** 2367 Market St. (☎861-3846), between 17th and 18th St., in **Castro.** The Café is chill in the afternoon with pool and pinball, but come evening, it morphs into speaker-pumping, house- and pop-remix bliss, when the dance floor, balcony, and patio crowds rotate in a constant game of see-and-be-seen. Repeat *Guardian* awards for best gay bar. No cover. Open M-F 2pm-2am, Sa-Su 12:30pm-2am. No credit cards.

**The Lexington Club,** 3464 19th St. (☎863-2052), at Lexington St., in the **Mission.** The only bar in San Francisco that is all lesbian, all the time. Jukebox plays all the grrly favorites. Though there's not much room for dancing, bar-goers sometimes spill out into the streets. Tarot Tu with Jessica. Happy Hour M-F 3-7pm. Open daily 3pm-2am. No credit cards.

**The Stud,** 399 9th St. (☎252-7883), at Harrison St. in **SoMa.** This legendary bar and club (a 35-year-old stallion) recreates itself every night of the week—go Tu for the wild and wacky midnight drag and transgender shows known as "Trannyshack," Th for Reform School boy-cruising party, F for ladies' night, Sa for Sugar's free delicious eye-candy. Crowd is mostly gay. Cover $5-9. Open M, W, F, and Su 5pm-2am, Tu 5pm-3am, Th and Sa 5pm-4am. No credit cards.

**The EndUp,** 401 6th St. (☎357-0827; www.theendup.com), at Harrison St. in **SoMa.** San Francisco institution—complete with outdoor garden and patio—where everyone eventually ends up. DJs spin progressive house for the mostly straight KitKat Th, the pretty-boy Fag F, and the blissful hetero-homo mix during popular all-day Sa-Su parties. Sa morning "Otherwhirled" party 4am. Infamous Su 'T' Dance (27 years strong) 6pm-4am. Cover $5-15. Open Th 10:30pm-4am, F 10pm-4am, Sa 6am-noon and 10pm-4am and Su 6am-4am. No credit cards.

**Esta Noche,** 3079 16th St. (☎861-5757), at Valencia St. Where the **Mission** meets the Castro. The city's premier gay Latino bar hosts regular drag shows. The bar is quite popular and space is tight on weekends. Domestic bottles and drafts $2.25. Happy Hour daily 4-9pm. Cover F-Su $5-10. Open Su-Th 1pm-2am, F-Sa 1pm-2am. No credit cards.

**Wild Side West,** 424 Cortland Ave. (☎647-3099), at Wool St., in **Bernal Heights.** The oldest lesbian bar in SF is a neighborhood favorite for women and men alike. There's pool, a cool jukebox, cheap beer ($2.50-3.50), and a friendly atmosphere. The hidden highlight is a junkyard jungle with benches, fountains, and scrap-art statues in back. Open daily 1pm-2am. No credit cards.

# ■ SEASONAL EVENTS

An astounding array of seasonal events go up in San Francisco no matter what time of year you visit. The summer is especially full, and events like Pride, which can draw crowds of more than 700,000 (as big as than the population of the city!) make finding a hotel room or parking space difficult. Events below are listed chronologically. The Visitors Center (☎391-2001) has a recording of current events.

## SPRING

**San Francisco International Film Festival** (☎561-5000; www.sffs.org), Apr.-May, Kabuki and Castro Theaters. The oldest film festival in North America, showing more than 100 international films of all genres over 2 weeks, most $9.

**Cinco de Mayo** (☎256-3005), during the weekend nearest May 5. The Mission explodes with colorful costumes and mariachi bands to celebrate Mexican Independence.

**Examiner Bay to Breakers** (☎359-2800; www.baytobreakers.com), on the 3rd Su in May starting at the Embarcadero at 8am. The largest foot race in the US, with up to 100,000 participants, covers 7½ mi. in inimitable San Francisco style. Runners win not only on their times but on their costumes as well. Special centipede category.

**Carnaval** (☎920-0125; www.carnavalSF.com), Memorial Day weekend. San Francisco's take on Mardi Gras, featuring Latino, jazz, and samba Caribbean music and more.

## SUMMER

**San Francisco International Gay and Lesbian Film Festival** (☎703-8650; www.frameline.org), during the 11 days leading up to Pride Day (June 26-27 in 2004), at the Roxie (at 16th and Valencia St.) and Castro Theatre (at Castro and Market St.). California's 2nd-largest film festival and the world's largest lesbian and gay media event. Tickets go fast. $6-15.

▓ **Pride Day** (☎864-3733; www.sfpride.org), on the last Su in June (June 27 in 2004). The High Holy Day of the queer calendar. Officially it's called Lesbian, Gay, Bisexual, Transgender Pride Day, with a **parade** and events downtown starting at 10:30am. Pink Saturday, the night before, brings a sea of bodies to the Castro.

**North Beach Jazz Festival** (☎771-2061; www.nbjazzfest.org), the last week of July or beginning of Aug. at venues from Washington Sq. Park to Telegraph Hill. Every Sa afternoon June-Sept. at the Cannery free jazz performances. Free-$15.

**Nihonmachi Street Fair** (☎771-9861), in early Aug. in Japantown. Lion dancers, *taiko* drummers, and karaoke wars.

## FALL

▓ **San Francisco Fringe Festival** (☎931-1094; www.sffringe.org), starting the 1st Th after Labor Day (Sept. 9 in 2004), at several theaters downtown. Experimental theater at its finest, with 62 international companies presenting short shows, all less than $8.

▓ **Ghirardelli Square Chocolate Festival** (☎775-5500; www.ghirardellisq.com), in early Sept., in Ghirardelli Sq. Welcome to chocolate heaven. All kinds of chocolate goodies to be sampled, with proceeds going to Project Open Hand.

▓ **Día de los Muertos** (Day of the Dead; ☎821-1155), Mission. Follow the drummers and dancing skeletons to the festive Mexican celebration of the dead (Nov. 2). The party starts in the evening at the Mission Cultural Center, on Mission at 25th St.

**Vivas Las Americas!** (☎705-5500; www.pier39.com), in mid-Sept. at Pier 39. Music and dance performances celebrating Hispanic heritage.

**Folsom Street Fair** (☎861-3247; www.folsomstreetfair.com), on the last Su in Sept. (Sept. 26 in 2004), on Folsom St. between 7th and 11th St. Pride Day's raunchier, rowdier brother. The Hole in the Wall gang lets it all hang out in leather and chains.

## WINTER

■ **Chinese New Year Celebration** (☎ 982-3000) and **Parade** (☎ 391-9680; www.chineseparade.com), during the month of Feb., in Chinatown. North America's largest Chinese community celebrates the Year of the Sheep in San Francisco's largest festival. Flower Fair, Miss Chinatown USA Pageant, a Coronation Ball, and a Community Street Fair are among the festivities. Watch the Parade (starting around 5:30pm) from Market and 2nd St. to Columbus Ave. Don't miss the Chinese New Year Treasure Hunt (www.sftreasurehunt.com). Free.

**Messiah** (☎ 864-4000), in Dec., Symphony Hall. Some say San Franciscans can't keep their mouths shut. At the **Sing-It-Yourself-Messiah** (☎ 564-8086), also at Symphony Hall, they don't have to. $30-70.

**San Francisco Independent Film Festival** (☎ 820-3907) in Jan. or Feb. The best of Bay Area indie films at various locations.

**Dr. Martin Luther King Jr.'s Birthday Celebration** (☎ 510-268-3777; contact Jackie Keys-Guidry), Jan. 19-21, in Yerba Buena Gardens. Includes a candlelight vigil and "Making the Dream Real" march and rally on Jan. 21 to honor the great civil rights leader.

# BAY AREA & WINE COUNTRY

Beyond the docks of San Francisco are a number of dynamic complements to the City by the Bay: Berkeley's cafes, Oakland's blues, Wine Country's vineyards, and Silicon Valley's now precarious tech industry. The bay and the surrounding mountains and rivers give shape to a sprawl that would otherwise be as disorienting as that of Los Angeles.

## HIGHLIGHTS OF THE BAY AREA

**TAKE DOWN THE MAN.** In the East Bay, **Berkeley** still pulses with vigorous political ferment, visible on the campus of UC Berkeley (p. 135), on Telegraph Avenue (p. 135), and on the shelves of its bookstores (p. 138).

**COASTLINE DRIVES.** North of San Francisco, the **Marin Coast** (p. 159) has breathtaking drives and seaside views. South of San Francisco, the Pacific Coast Highway glides by the lush farm lands and deserted beaches of **San Mateo County** (p. 155).

**WINES AND BIKES.** North of San Francisco and inland, tourists rush to the famous wineries of the **Napa Valley** (p. 168); the vineyards in the **Russian River Valley** (p. 181) are more peaceful. Napa is an ideal place for a road bike tour, while **Mount Tamalpais** (p. 166) in Marin is great for mountain biking.

# EAST BAY

Longer and older than its Golden Gate neighbor, the **Bay Bridge** carries the weight of San Francisco traffic east to **Oakland,** where freeways fan out in all directions. The urbanized port of Oakland sprawls north into **Berkeley,** an assertively post-hippie college town. The two towns have long shared an interest in activism, reflected in wonderfully progressive and effective city government and policies. Berkeley, bookish and bizarre as ever, offers outstanding boutiques and cafes, while its sister city Oakland echoes with the sounds of progressive blues and jazz.

## BERKELEY       ☎ 510

Famous as an intellectual center and a haven for iconoclasts, Berkeley continues to live up to its reputation. Although the peak of its political activism occurred in the 1960s and 70s—when students attended more protests than classes—**UC Berkeley** continues to cultivate consciousness and an intellectual atmosphere. The vitality of the population infuses the streets, which are strewn with hip cafes and top-notch bookstores, all slightly psychedelic. **Telegraph Avenue,** with its street-corner soothsayers, hirsute hippies, and itinerant musicians, remains one of this town's main draws. Travelers looking to soak up all that Berkeley has to offer should also venture to the north and south of the UC Berkeley campus.

# ☞ TRANSPORTATION

Freeway congestion can make driving in the Bay Area frustrating, especially during rush hours. Drivers fortunate enough to reach Berkeley despite the traffic will face congestion, numerous one-way streets, vexing concrete planters, and an earnest quest for a parking spot—the city's holy grail. If you're driving from San Fran, cross the Bay Bridge on **I-80** and take one of the four Berkeley exits. The **University Ave. Exit** leads most directly to UC Berkeley and downtown. Reasonably priced public lots (most are $10-15 per day) let you ditch your car and explore on foot.

**Public Transportation: Berkeley TRiP,** 2033 Center St. (☎644-POOL/7665), provides commuter-oriented information on public transportation, biking, carpooling, Segways, and other alternative rides. They also sell extended-use transit passes and maps. Open Tu-F noon-5:30pm. Satellite office at 2543 Channing Way, open M-F 9am-2pm. **Bay Area Rapid Transit** or **BART** (☎465-2278; www.bart.gov) has 3 Berkeley stops. The Downtown Berkeley station, 2160 Shattuck Ave., at Center St., is close to the western edge of campus, while the North Berkeley station, at Delaware and Sacramento St., lies 4 blocks north of University Ave. To get to Southern Berkeley, take the BART to the Ashby stop at the corner of Ashby and Adeline St. (20-30min. to downtown SF, $2.65). **Alameda County (AC) Transit city buses** #15, 43, and 51 run from the Berkeley BART station to downtown Oakland on Martin Luther King, Jr. Way, Telegraph Ave., and Broadway, respectively (adults $1.50; seniors, disabled, and ages 5-12 75¢; under 5 free; 1hr. transfers 25¢).

**Ride Share: Berkeley Ride Board,** 1st level of the student store in the Student Union. **KALX Radio, 90.7 FM** (☎642-5259), broadcasts a daily list of those needing or giving rides at 10am and 10pm. Call to put your request on the air for free.

**Taxis: A1 Yellow Cab** (☎644-2552) and **Berkeley Yellow Cab** (☎548-2561). 24hr.

**Car Rental: Budget,** 600 Gilman St. (☎800-763-2999), at 2nd St. Car prices vary each day. Unlimited mileage. Call for current prices. Must be 21; under 25 surcharge $20 per day. Open M-F 7am-6pm, Sa 7am-4pm, Su 9am-4pm.

# ⊁ ☷ ORIENTATION & PRACTICAL INFORMATION

Just across the Bay Bridge, northeast of San Francisco and just north of Oakland, resides the not-so-little Berkeley community famous for acting up and speaking out. The **Marina** rests on the western side of Berkeley while **Tilden Regional Park** climbs the sharp grades to the east. Undergraduates from **UC Berkeley** tend to do their thing on the campus's south side, while graduate students stick to the north. **Downtown Berkeley,** around the **BART station** at Shattuck Ave. and Center St., is where you'll find banks, public libraries, restaurants, and shops, while Addison St. is fast becoming the area's theater district. The magnetic heart of town, **Telegraph Avenue** runs south from the Student Union and is lined with bookstores, cafes, palm readers, and panhandlers. North of campus around Shattuck Ave., between Virginia and Rose St., the **Gourmet Ghetto** has some of California's finest dining. Farther afield, **4th Street,** near the waterfront (take MUNI bus #51 bus west), and **Solano Avenue** to the northwest (take MUNI bus #15 north) are home to yummy eats and shops. The intersection at **College** and **Ashby Avenue** (take MUNI bus #51 south) also offers delectable dining. Quality cafes, music stores, and specialty shops grace the **Rockridge** district on the border between Berkeley and Oakland.

**Visitor Information: Berkeley Convention and Visitor Bureau,** 2015 Center St. (☎549-8710), at Milvia St. Helpful maps, friendly service, up-to-date practical information, accommodation resources, tons of brochures. Open M-F 9am-5pm. **UC Berkeley Visi-**

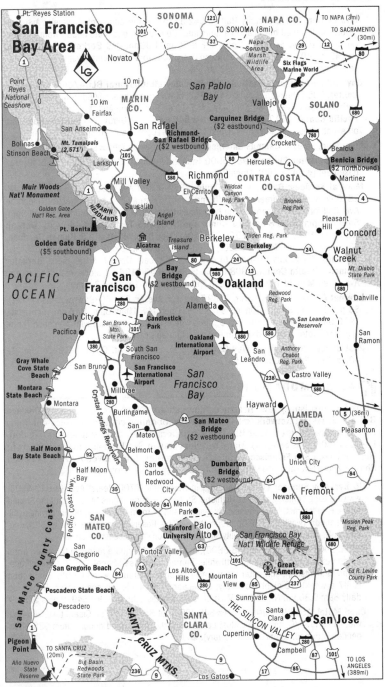

San Francisco
Bay Area

Point Reyes National Seashore

Pt. Reyes Station

SONOMA CO.

NAPA CO.

TO NAPA (3mi)

TO SACRAMENTO (30mi)

TO SONOMA (8mi)

Novato

Napa-Sonoma Marsh Wildlife Area

Six Flags Marine World

San Pablo Bay

Vallejo

SOLANO CO.

MARIN CO.

Fairfax

San Anselmo

San Rafael

Carquinez Bridge ($2 eastbound)

Richmond-San Rafael Bridge ($2 westbound)

Crockett

Benicia

Benicia Bridge ($2 northbound)

Bolinas
Stinson Beach

Mt. Tamalpais (2,571)

Larkspur

Hercules

Martinez

Muir Woods Nat'l Monument

Mill Valley

Richmond

CONTRA COSTA CO.

El Cerrito

Wildcat Canyon Reg. Park

Briones Reg. Park

Golden Gate Nat'l Rec. Area

Sausalito

Albany

Pleasant Hill

Concord

Pt. Bonita

MARIN HEADLANDS

Angel Island

Berkeley

Tilden Reg. Park

Golden Gate Bridge ($5 southbound)

Alcatraz

Treasure Island

UC Berkeley

24

Walnut Creek

PACIFIC OCEAN

San Francisco

Bay Bridge ($2 westbound)

Oakland

980

13

Mt. Diablo State Park

Daly City

Alameda

Redwood Reg. Park

Danville

Candlestick Park

San Bruno Mtn. State Park

Oakland International Airport

San Leandro Reservoir

San Ramon

Pacifica

South San Francisco

San Leandro

Anthony Chabot Reg. Park

Gray Whale Cove State Beach

San Bruno

San Francisco International Airport

San Francisco Bay

Castro Valley

Montara State Beach

Millbrae

Hayward

ALAMEDA CO.

TO 5 (36mi)

Montara

Burlingame

San Mateo Bridge ($2 westbound)

Pleasanton

Half Moon Bay State Beach

San Mateo

238

Belmont

Half Moon Bay

San Carlos

Dumbarton Bridge ($2 westbound)

Union City

Crystal Springs Reservoirs

Redwood City

Newark

Fremont

Woodside

Menlo Park

SAN MATEO CO.

Stanford University

Palo Alto

Mission Peak Reg. Park

San Gregorio

Portola Valley

San Francisco Bay Nat'l Wildlife Refuge

Great America

Ed R. Levine County Park

San Gregorio Beach

Los Altos Hills

Mountain View

Pescadero State Beach

Pacific Coast Hwy.

SANTA CLARA CO.

Sunnyvale

Santa Clara

San Jose

Pescadero

San Mateo County Coast

Cupertino

THE SILICON VALLEY

Pigeon Point

Año Nuevo State Reserve

TO SANTA CRUZ (20mi)

SANTA CRUZ MTNS.

Big Basin Redwoods State Park

Campbell

Los Gatos

TO LOS ANGELES (389mi)

0    10 mi

0    10 km

**tors Center,** 101 University Hall (☎642-5215), at the corner of University Ave. and Oxford St. Detailed maps and campus info. Guided campus tours depart from the center M-Sa 10am, Su 1pm. Open M-F 8:30am-4:30pm. **UC Berkeley Switchboard** (☎642-6000) can direct you to info on everything from community events to drug counseling. Open M-F 8am-5pm.

**Gay and Lesbian Organizations: UC Berkeley Multicultural BLGA/Queer Resource Center,** 305 Eshleman Hall (☎642-6942; http://queer.berkeley.edu), at Bancroft Way and Telegraph Ave. Open Sept.-May M-F 10am-9pm; June-Aug. by appointment only. **Pacific Center,** 2712 Telegraph Ave. (☎548-8283), at Derby St. Counseling and info on events, housing, and clubs. Open M-F 10am-10pm, Sa noon-3pm, Su 6-9pm.

**Emergency:** ☎911. **Campus Emergency** from campus phones ☎9-911, or 642-3333.

**Police: Berkeley Police** ☎981-5900 (non-emergency). **Campus Police,** Sproul Hall basement (☎642-6760). Open 24hr.

**Medical Services: Berkeley Free Clinic,** 2339 Durant Ave. (☎800-625-4642 or 548-2570; www.berkeleyfreeclinic.org/home.html), at Dana St. 2 blocks west of Telegraph Ave. Call for hours of service; the best times to talk to a real person are M-F 3am-9pm, Sa 8am-5pm, Su 5-8pm. **STD Clinic and HIV/AIDS Testing:** ☎644-0425. **Dental:** ☎548-2745. **Counseling:** ☎548-2744. **Berkeley Dept. of Health & Human Services,** 830 University Ave. (☎981-5350), at 6th St. Medical help on a sliding payment scale. Specialty clinics vary from day to day, so call ahead. Open M-F 8am-5pm. **Berkeley Women's Health Center,** 2908 Ellsworth St. (☎843-6194), 1 block west of Telegraph Ave. Open M and F 8am-noon and 1-5pm, Tu-Th 9am-1pm and 2-6pm.

**Internet Access: UC Computer,** 2569 Telegraph Ave. (☎649-6089; www.transbay.net). $3 per 15min., $5 per 30min., $7 per hr. Open M-F 10am-6pm. **Berkeley Espresso,** 1900 Shattuck Ave. (☎848-9576). Free wireless Internet access with purchase (bring your own laptop). Open daily 6am-11pm. No credit cards.

**Post Office:** 2000 Allston Way (☎649-3155), at Milvia St. Open M-F 9am-5pm, Sa 10am-2pm. **Postal Code:** 94704.

# ACCOMMODATIONS

There are surprisingly few cheap accommodations in Berkeley. The **Berkeley-Oakland Bed and Breakfast Network** (☎547-6380; www.bbonline.com/ca/berkeley-oakland) coordinates some great East Bay B&Bs with a range of rates (singles $50-150; doubles $60-150; twins $85-150). Many travelers stay in San Fran and make daytrips to Berkeley (**see San Francisco,** p. 90). No-frills motels line University Ave. between Shattuck and Sacramento streets, while ritzier joints are downtown.

**UC Berkeley Summer Visitor Housing,** in Stern Hall, 2700 Hearst Ave. (☎642-4108; www.housing.berkeley.edu), at Highland St. College dorm rooms; great location. Shared baths. Free Internet, local phone calls, games, and TV room. Meals and photocopying available. Laundry (wash $1.35). Open June to mid-Aug. Reservations online. Singles $53; doubles $68; 7th night free. Availability limited by season due to construction. ❸

**YMCA,** 2001 Allston Way (☎848-6800), at Milvia St. Adequate rooms in the co-ed hotel portion of this YMCA make it worthwhile. Shared bath. Use of pool and fitness facilities. Communal kitchen, computer room, and TV lounge. All rooms wired for DSL connection ($5-7 a week). 10-night max. stay; applications available for longer stays. Reception daily 8am-9:30pm. No curfew. Must be 18+. Singles $39; doubles $49; triples $59. ❸

**Capri Motel,** 1512 University Ave. (☎845-7090), at Sacramento St. Clean, tasteful rooms with cable TV, A/C, and fridge. Must be 18+ with ID. Singles and doubles from $85 (independently owned, so prices tend to vary). ❺

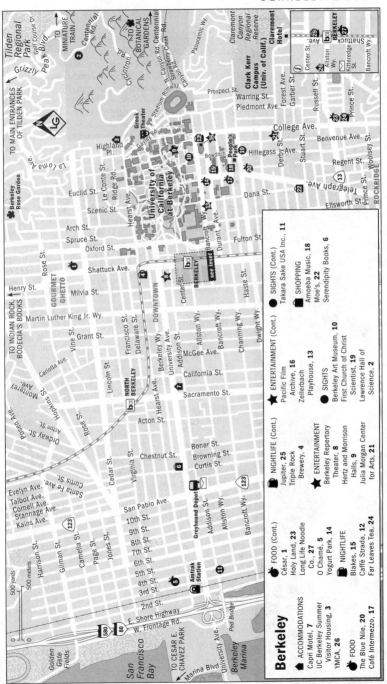

### Berkeley

**▲ ACCOMMODATIONS**
Capri Motel, 7
UC Berkeley Summer
Visitor Housing, 3
YMCA, 26

**♦ FOOD**
The Blue Nile, 20
Café Intermezzo, 17
César, 1
Holy Land, 23
Long Life Noodle
Co., 27
O Chamé, 5
Yogurt Park, 14

**♦ NIGHTLIFE**
Blakes, 15
Caffè Strada, 12
Far Leaves Tea, 24
Jupiter, 25
Triple Rock
Brewery, 4

**★ ENTERTAINMENT**
Berkeley Repertory
Theater, 8
Hertz and Morrison
Halls, 9
Julia Morgan Center
for Arts, 21
Pacific Film
Archive, 16
Zellerbach
Playhouse, 13

**● SIGHTS**
Berkeley Art Museum, 10
First Church of Christ
Scientist, 19
Lawrence Hall of
Science, 2
Takara Sake USA Inc., 11

**■ SHOPPING**
Amoeba Music, 18
Moe's, 22
Serendipity Books, 6

## ROM THE ROAD

### HE SOUL OF BERKELEY

Having spent one summer in Berkeley, I was familiar with the communal spirit that infuses its air. But it wasn't until I came as a writer that I found just how open and giving Berkeley residents really are.

On my first day in the city I stopped ritually at one of the best bookstores in town. I was purchasing a tiny but expensive art book by one of my favorite drawers, Yoshitoma Nara, when the cashier said to me "Fortunately, art books are not one of my vices." I asked him what, in that case, his vices were. "Oh, tequila. And pot, but I grow my own, so that doesn't cost me." I told him I was new to town. He chuckled, handing me my book, and told me to come back in a few days.

Two days later, I stopped in the store out of curiosity. The same guy was there, and when we made eye contact I announced that I was going to browse the fourth floor. A few minutes later, the cashier appeared and asked, "Are you the person who said she was new to town?" I nodded my head, yes, and he extended a cookie and an envelope marked "Welcome!" containing a smokable item. Cherry pie has been pushed aside, and Berkeley is raising the standards for community.

-Heather Thomason, 2004

## ◘ FOOD

Berkeley's **Gourmet Ghetto,** at Shattuck Ave. and Cedar St., is the famous birthplace of California Cuisine. When chef Alice Waters opened *Chez Panisse* in 1971, she introduced the nation to the joys of goat cheese and polenta. Since Berkeley has to feed thousands of starving students, the area is also home to pizza joints and hamburger stands, although the ghetto mentality makes menu items a bit more interesting. The north end of **Telegraph Avenue** caters to student appetites and wallets with late night offerings along **Durant Avenue.** If you'd rather talk to a cow than eat one, you're in luck because Berkeley does greens like nowhere else. **Solano Avenue,** to the north, is great for Asian cuisine, while **4th Street** is home to more upscale (but cheaper than Gourmet Ghetto) eats. If you've got access to a kitchen or just like fresh veggies, **farmer's markets,** run by the Ecology Center (☎548-3333), sprout up Saturdays at Center St. and Martin Luther King, Jr. Way (10am-2pm) and Tuesdays at Derby St. and MLK Way (summer 2-7pm; off-season 2-6pm).

◪ **Café Intermezzo,** 2442 Telegraph Ave. (☎849-4592), at Haste St. This veggie-lover's paradise serves heaping salads with homemade dressing, huge sandwiches on freshly baked bread, and tasty soups, all at delicious prices. Salad and sandwich combo $5.50. Sandwiches $5. Salads $3.50-7. Open daily 10am-10pm. No credit cards. ❶

◪ **César,** 1515 Shattuck Ave. (☎883-0222), just south of Vine St. A great place for wining and dining, with savory tapas ($3-12), *bocadillos* (a small sandwich on french bread, $5-7), desserts ($4-5), and an impressive list of spirits. Open, airy, European feel. Open daily noon-midnight; kitchen closes Su-Th 11pm, F-Sa 11:30pm. ❷

◪ **Yogurt Park,** 2433 Durant Ave. (☎549-2198, for daily list of yogurt flavors 549-0570), just west of Telegraph Ave. An icon of Berkeley gastronomic life. Yogurt $1.75-2.20; additional toppings 65¢. Huge portions. Open daily 10am-midnight. No credit cards. ❶

**Holy Land,** 2965 College Ave. (☎665-1672), just south of Ashby Ave. Fantastic Falafel $5; Schuperlative Schwarmma $5.75. Pitas $5-6. Lunches $8, dinner after 4pm $15-20. Open M-F and Su 11am-9pm. ❷

**O Chamé,** 1830 4th St. (☎841-8783), between Virginia and Hearst St. Innovative Japanese fusion cooking. Become one with a bowl of *soba* or *udon* noodles and get tipsy while sipping *sake* ($5). Appetizers $5-12 (try the white corn and green onion pancake). Entrees and soups $10-20. Open for lunch M-Sa 11:30am-3pm; dinner 5:30-9:30pm. ❸

**The Blue Nile,** 2525 Telegraph Ave. (☎540-6777), between Blake and Dwight St. Wait-resses in traditional gowns serve huge portions of Ethiopian food in a lavish setting. Eat *injera* bread with your fingers while sipping *mes* (honey wine $2). Variety of vegetarian dishes (lentils abound). Open Su and Tu-Sa 5-10pm. Reservations recommended. ❸

**Long Life Noodle Co. and Jook Joint,** 2261 Shattuck St. (☎548-8083), at Kittredge St. You name the noodle, they've got it: Japanese, Chinese, Korean, Thai, Vietnamese noo-dles, *udon*, ramen, egg, and *soba*. Wok-tossed dishes, soups, and noodles $6-9. Mango Martini $5. Open Su-Th 11:30am-9:30pm, F-Sa 11:30am-10:30pm. ❷

# 🔎 SIGHTS & SEASONAL EVENTS

## TELEGRAPH AVENUE

You haven't really visited Berkeley until you've strolled the first five or so blocks of **Telegraph Avenue,** which runs south from Sproul Plaza as far as down-town Oakland. The action is close to the university, where Telegraph Ave. is lined with a motley assortment of cafes, bookstores, and used clothing and record stores. Businesses come and go at the whim of the marketplace, but the scene—a rowdy jumble of 60s and 90s counterculture—persists. Vendors push tie-dye, Tarot readings, and jewelry; the disenfranchised hustle for change; and characters looking like Old Testament prophets carry on hyper-dimensional conversations, transmitting knowledge and meditations accrued from years of Berkeley experience.

Berkeley's active presses, which can be found in corner boxes and at cafes, are invaluable for an up-to-date list of happenings around town, including the latest goings-on in San Francisco. Look in bookstores and bins for the free weekly *East Bay Express* (www.eastbayexpress.com), filled with theater, film, and concert listings. If you can find a recent edition of *Resource*, the guide given to new Berkeley students, grab it (try the Visitors Center at 101 University Hall). The *Daily Californian* (www.dailycal.org), which publishes on Tues-days and Fridays in the summer and daily during the academic year, carries uni-versity news and features.

**FIRST CHURCH OF CHRIST SCIENTIST.** Built in 1910, architect Bernard May-beck's masterpiece is a conglomeration of Gothic, Renaissance, Classical, Japa-nese, Mediterranean, and industrial styles. *(2526 Dwight St., at Bowditch St. ☎845-7199. Open during services W 8pm, Su 11am; tours at noon on the 1st Su of each month.)*

**▨TAKARA SAKE USA INC.** Learn the history and science of *sake* making (through a museum and video) and sample 15 different types. The knowledgeable hosts won't laugh in your face when you wobble out the door, another victim of Japan's merciless firewater. *(708 Addison St., just west of 4th St. Take #51 bus to 4th St. and walk down to Addison St. ☎540-8250; www.takarasake.com. Open daily noon-6pm. Free.)*

## UC BERKELEY

In 1868, the private College of California and the public Agricultural, Mining, and Mechanical Arts College united as the **University of California.** The stunning 178-acre university was the first of the nine University of California campuses, so by seniority it has sole right to the nickname "Cal." With over 30,000 students and 1350 full pro-fessors, the University is especially active when classes are in session, from late August to mid-May. If you'd like to sit in on some classes, track down a course cata-log and schedule at the campus bookstore or online (www.berkeley.edu). The cam-pus is bound on the south by Bancroft Way, on the west by Oxford St., on the north by Hearst Ave., and on the east by **Tilden Park.** Remodeling often occurs during aca-demic downtime, so watch for closings. Maps of campus are posted everywhere; the **Visitors Center** (p. 130) hands out campus maps (10¢) and offers free tours.

BAY AREA

**█BERKELEY ART MUSEUM.** BAM is most respected for its collection of 20th-century American and Asian art, in particular the Hofmann Collection. Rotating exhibits showcase experimental work. Also associated with **The Pacific Film Archive.** *(2626 Bancroft Way, at College Ave. ☎642-0808; www.bampfa.berkeley.edu. Open Su and W-Sa 11am-7pm. Adults $8; students, seniors, disabled, and ages 12-17 $5. Free first Th of each month.)*

**SPROUL PLAZA.** In October 1964, students protested the arrest of one of their own who had been distributing civil rights pamphlets, galvanizing a series of confrontations that lasted several years. Mario Savio, a student and member of the widely influential Free Speech Movement, addressed a crowd from the steps of the plaza, arguing for students' rights to free expression and assembly. Savio was eventually jailed and expelled, but in 1997 the plaza steps were named in his honor. A popular social (and activist) hangout during the school year.

**SATHER TOWER. Sather Tower,** better known as the **Campanile** (roughly Italian for "bell tower") and a 1914 monument to Berkeley benefactor Jane Krom Sather, is the third-tallest free-standing clocktower in the world (at 307 ft.). For a great view, ride to its observation level (M-F 10am-4pm, $2; tip-top is not wheelchair-accessible). A 61-bell **carillon** plays during the school year weekdays at 7:10am, noon, and 6pm, and gives a 45min. concert on Sundays at 2pm.

**LAWRENCE HALL OF SCIENCE.** High atop the eucalyptus-covered hills east of the main campus is one of the finest science museums in the Bay Area. Ever-changing exhibits stress hands-on science activities catering to children but fun for all ages. The courtyard offers a life-sized model whale, a stunning view of the bay, and stargazing workshops on clear Saturday evenings. Visit the Planetarium for its "Constellations Tonight" show and be sure to check out the outdoor "Forces That Shape The Bay" exhibit. *(On Centennial Dr. Take bus #8 or 65 from the Berkeley BART station and keep your transfer for $2 off admission. Once there, use the University shuttle (50¢; ☎642-5149), or brace yourself for the steep walk. ☎642-5132; www.lawrencehallofscience.org. Open daily 10am-5pm. Adults $8; students, seniors, and ages 5-18 $6; ages 3-4 $4.)*

**OTHER UC BERKELEY SIGHTS.** In the northeastern part of Main campus, the impressive marble Hearst Greek Theatre, built in 1903, is modeled after a classical amphitheater in Epidavros, Greece. It is used for university ceremonies and concerts. The Grateful Dead used to play here annually. *(☎642-4864.)* Though the bulk of the impressive collection is rarely, if ever, on display, the **Phoebe Hearst Museum of Anthropology** is a pleasant, quick stop for displays and exhibits from California, ancient Egypt, and pre-Colombian Peru. *(103 Kroeber Hall, at the corner of Bancroft Way and College Ave. ☎643-7648; http://hearstmuseum.berkeley.edu. Open Tu-F 10am-4:30pm, Sa-Su noon-4:30pm. $2, seniors $1, ages 16 and under 50¢.)* The UC Museum of Paleontology has a complete Tyrannosaurus rex skeleton. *(Wallace Atrium, 1011 Valley of Life Sciences Building. ☎642-1821; www.ucmp.berkeley.edu. Open M 8am-9pm, Sa-Su 1-5pm. Free.)* The **Botanical Gardens** contain over 13,000 varieties of plant life from around the world, including a huge number of rare and endangered plants. Agatha Christie supposedly came here to examine a rare poisonous plant whose deadly powers she later put to use in a mystery novel. If at the Gardens, also visit the Stephen Mather Redwood Grove across the street. *(200 Centennial Dr., in Strawberry Canyon, midway between the UC Stadium and Lawrence Hall of Science. ☎643-2755; www.mip.berkeley.edu/garden. Labor Day-Memorial Day open daily 9am-5pm except Christmas and the 1st Tu of each month; Memorial Day-Labor Day open daily 9am-7pm. $3, seniors $2, ages 3-18 $1; Th free.)*

**WITH WHAT ARMY?** On the night of February 4, 1974, **Patty Hearst,** heiress to the William Randolph Hearst newspaper empire, was abducted from her Berkeley flat by three members of the radical leftist **Symbionese Liberation Army.** She was allegedly coerced and brainwashed under humiliating conditions of confinement. She then began making public statements through tape recordings, condemning the capitalist "crimes" of her parents. The Symbionese Liberation Army extorted $2,000,000 from the Hearst family in the form of a food giveaway to the poor. They also got Patty Hearst to join in at least two robberies, of a San Francisco bank and an LA store. The Symbionese Liberation Army never had more than eleven or twelve members, six of whom—including the leader, Donald DeFreeze—were killed in a police shootout and house fire in Los Angeles on May 17, 1974. Hearst remained at large with her captors/confederates, criss-crossing the country. On Sept. 18, 1975, she was captured in San Francisco by the FBI. Hearst was tried and convicted in March 1976 for bank robbery and felonious use of firearms. Sentenced to seven years, she spent three in prison and was released in February 1979.

## PARKS & RECREATION

Berkeley's parks provide respite from the craziness of campus life. North of campus, the ◪**Berkeley Rose Garden,** built by the Works Projects Administration in the Depression era, spills from one terrace to another in a vast semicircular amphitheater. The roses are pruned in January in preparation for Mother's Day (May 9, 2004), when the garden is at its glorious peak. (Open May-Sept. dawn-dusk.) Berkeley's biggest confrontation between the People and the Man was not fought over Freedom of Speech or the war in Vietnam, but over a muddy vacant lot between Dwight and Haste St. In April 1969, students, hippies, and radicals christened the patch of university-owned land **People's Park,** tearing up pavement and laying down sod to establish, in the words of the *Berkeley Barb,* "a cultural, political freak out and rap center for the Western world." When the university moved to evict squatters and build a parking garage on the site, resistance stiffened. Governor Ronald Reagan sent in 2000 troops, and the conflict ended with helicopters dropping tear gas on students in Sproul Plaza, one bystander shot dead by police, and a 17-day National Guard occupation. The park's grassy existence represents a small victory over the establishment. At the north end of Shattuck Ave., the basalt face of **Indian Rock** challenges thrill-junkies with short but demanding climbs. For the vertically challenged, side steps lead to an impressive view of the Headlands. (Open daily dawn-dusk.)

In the pine and eucalyptus forests east of the city lies the beautiful anchor of the East Bay park system, **Tilden Regional Park,** east of the city. Hiking, biking, running, and riding trails criss-cross the park and provide impressive views of the Bay Area. The **ridgeline trail** makes for an especially spectacular bike ride. For those looking to frolic without getting sweaty, a 19th-century **carousel** inside the park is a fun option. By car or bicycle, take Spruce St. to Grizzly Peak Blvd. to Canon Ave. AC Transit buses #7 and 8 run from the Berkeley BART station to the entrance at Grizzly Peak Blvd. and Golf Course Dr. (☎635-0135. Open daily dawn-dusk.) Also inside the park, Lake Anza's small, sandy beach is a popular swimming spot during the hottest summer days, though not the place to go for a quiet, romantic dip, as **Lake Anza** tends to be brat central. (☎843-2137. Open in summer 11am-6pm. $3, seniors and children $2.) At the north end of the park, the **Environmental Education Center** offers exhibits and naturalist-led programs. (☎525-2233. Open Su and Tu-Sa 10am-5pm. Free.) **Grizzly Peak** and **Inspiration Point** provide breathtaking panoramas of the entire Bay Area. **Wildcat Canyon** is a less developed park than Tilden, with gorgeous hiking through grassy meadows and densely wooded canyons. (Adjacent to Tilden Park. Open daily dawn-dusk.)

BAY AREA

## RECENT NEWS

### BATTLE OF THE BULB

The artists and outlaws of an East Bay area known as the Albany Bulb have attracted a passionate following in the past four years. Vagrants living in the area have created an open-air gallery, studio, and home out of a trash-dump abandoned in the 1980s.

When the area became recognized as part of the Golden Gate Fields State Park in 1999, officials evicted the large homeless population living there. However, many artists continue to squat there in innovative lodgings, such as huts woven from fennel. Their work—including clay and styrofoam carvings, wooden sculptures, and rusting junk metal—reflect what one artist describes as a "visual ecological history of the post-industrial debris, gradually decaying."

Recent plans to redevelop the area into a park and soccer fields have sparked fierce debate. The artists and their followers want the Bulb to remain one of the few unregulated areas left in the Bay Area. In the summer of 2002, however, the council voted that the Bulb should be off-limits to most of the artists because of their works' often sexually explicit content. The final deciding vote on the new park plan will be taken in December 2003.

*Follow the debate on www.albanyletitbe.com.*

## ▣ SHOPPING

Telegraph Ave. is an excellent source for books, music, and secondhand clothing, along with homemade tie-dye, jewelry, and pipes. If you are willing to walk or drive a few miles off Telegraph, you will be rewarded with some of Berkeley's best bookstores and sex shops. Chain stores seem misplaced in this happy land of independent and locally-supported stores. The undisputed champion of the buy-sell-trade music scene is ◪**Amoeba Music,** 2455 Telegraph Ave., near Haste St. Go crazy in the warehouse-sized store with its tons of new and used CDs, including a popular collection of music and mutterings by Telegraph Ave.'s least coherent residents. (☎549-1125; www.amoebamusic.com. Open M-Sa 10:30am-10pm, Su 11am-9pm.)

From a bibliophilic standpoint, Berkeley's book trade is the 8th wonder of the world. Leave yourself more time to browse than you think you'll need. Telegraph Ave. is home to some good book nooks, including ◪**Moe's,** 2746 Telegraph Ave., between Dwight and Haste St., which was featured in *The Graduate* and has four well-arranged floors worth of secondhand knowledge as well as new books at a 10% discount. "More Moe's" has art and antiquarian books on the 4th floor. (☎849-2087; www.moesbooks.com. Open daily 10am-11pm.) Just down the street is **Shambhala,** 2482 Telegraph Ave., at Dwight St., the incense-foggy place to go for tarot cards, a hazy conversation, and a few books on the Kaballah, Tibetan Buddhism, and the Zohar. (☎848-8443. Open daily 11am-8pm.) An inspiring prose paradise beckons on University and Shattuck Ave. The dusty collection at ◪**Serendipity Books,** 1201 University Ave., has earned Baywide respect. (☎841-7455. Open M-Sa 9am-5pm.)

## ♫ ENTERTAINMENT

### ON CAMPUS

**Zellerbach Playhouse,** near the corner of Bancroft Way and Dana St. Shared by professional dance and theater companies and student ensembles alike, Zellerbach is a community favorite. Summertime shows usually musicals and romantic comedies. Tickets during the academic year $6-12; summer shows $5-10, students and seniors $3-6.

**CAL Performances,** in Zellerbach Hall (☎642-9988; www.calperformances.berkeley.edu). Info and tickets for concerts, plays, and movies. Open M-F 10am-5:30pm, Sa 10am-2pm.

**Hertz and Morrison Halls** (☎642-0527), on campus between Bowditch St. and College Ave. The Berkeley music department hosts noon concerts, including (but certainly not limited to) the African Music Ensemble, the Berkeley Contemporary Chamber Players, the Javanese Gamelan, and the 1991 Grammy-nominated University Chamber Chorus.

## OFF CAMPUS

🖾 **Pacific Film Archive,** 2575 Bancroft Way (☎642-1124; www.bampfa.berkeley.edu/pfa), near Bowditch St. With a new facility and a huge collection of archived foreign and independent films, the PFA is a great place to catch any number of underground, experimental, and hard-to-find flicks. Tickets $5. Ticket office open M-F 11am-5pm.

**Berkeley Repertory Theater,** 2025 Addison St. (☎845-4700). The best-known and arguably the finest theater in the area, with an eclectic repertoire of classics and unknowns. Half-price tickets may be available Tu-Th on the day of the show—line up at the box office at noon. Box office open Su and Tu-Sa noon-7pm.

**Julia Morgan Center for Arts,** 2640 College Ave. (☎845-8542; tickets 925-798-1300; www.juliamorgan.org), at Derby St., shares space with a preschool and yoga center in a beautiful building that was once a church. Noted for its graceful mix of materials, this building was Morgan's first commission. The theater hosts diverse performances including the **Berkeley Opera.** Open M-Sa 10am-6pm, Su noon-5pm.

## 🔋 NIGHTLIFE

Because Berkeley is so close to SF proper, when hard-core clubbers need to bump and grind, they just take the bridge. What Berkeley does offer is an unrivaled array of casual brewpubs and brainy cafes. Crowded at almost any hour of the night or day, they serve as surrogate libraries, living rooms, and lecture theaters; espresso drinks and microbrews loosen the tongues of an already talkative city. Many bars have some great live music offerings as well.

🖾 **Jupiter,** 2181 Shattuck Ave. (☎843-8277), near the BART station. Stained glass, church pews, and elaborate Gothic paneling you'll only see if the place is empty—but it won't be. Terrific pizza (9 in. pie $8). Live music in the spacious beer garden (Tu-Sa; in winter Su and W-Sa). Th Night "Beat Down" offers trance and hip-hop, accompanied by psychedelic projections on a massive brick wall. Su nights catch indie shorts projections. No cover. Open M-Th 11:30am-1am, F 11:30am-2am, Sa noon-2am, Su noon-midnight.

🖾 **Far Leaves Tea,** 2979 College Ave. (☎665-9409; www.farleaves.com), just south of Ashby Ave. Meditative tea shop offering a vast selection of teas (with emphasis on traditional Chinese and Taiwanese green and oolong blends). Teas range from $1.25-6. Brew your own while you sit on floor pillows, breathe, and sip with a book, a friend, or your own reflections. Also offers Chinese tea ceremony classes. Open daily 11am-9pm.

**Caffè Strada,** 2300 College Ave. (☎843-5282), at Bancroft Way. The glittering jewel of the caffeine-fueled intellectual scene. Go to be seen, discuss philosophy, or just enjoy the beautiful terrace. Small latte $1.95. Most drinks under $2.50. Try the *Strada Bianca,* white hot chocolate ($1.90). Open daily 6:30am-midnight. No credit cards

**Blakes,** 2367 Telegraph Ave. (☎848-0886), at Durant Ave. A jam-packed and unabashed meat market, but at least the cuts are premium. The pint-sized upstairs has a loud sports bar feel, while the middle floor is mellow with more seating. In the basement, kick it to the loud beats of local bands. Some shows 18+. Beverages from $2.50. Appetizers $2-5. Meals $4-8. Happy Hour daily 4-7pm. Drink specials 9pm-midnight. Cover $3-7. Open M-F 11:30am-2am, Sa noon-2am, Su noon-1am.

**Triple Rock Brewery,** 1920 Shattuck Ave. (☎843-2739; www.triplerock.com), north of Berkeley Way. Boisterous and friendly, the Rock was the first of Berkeley's many brewpubs. Long and ever-changing menu of ales, stouts, and porters (made 2-3 times a

week, through their hands-on 7-barrel process). Award-winning Red Rock Ale $3.25.
Open Su-W 11:30am-midnight, Th-Sa 11:30am-1am (later, if busy). Rooftop garden
closes at 9pm, kitchen closes Su-W 10:30pm, Th-Sa midnight.

# OAKLAND                                                          ☎510

Led by mayor and one-time US presidential hopeful Jerry Brown, the city of Oakland launched a public relations campaign to promote the lower prices and
warmer weather across the bay. Indeed, newcomers to the Bay Area too easily forget that Oakland, with 400,000 people, 81 languages, and considerable land mass,
is a thriving city in its own right. Although historically less economically blessed,
Oakland has maintained a commercial center and some beautiful residential
neighborhoods. Travelers often fail to incorporate Oakland into their perspective
of the Bay Area, even though an afternoon downtown, a gourmet dinner in Rockridge, and a legendary live music scene are just a short car or BART ride away.

## ◰ TRANSPORTATION

Drivers can take **I-80** from San Francisco across the Bay Bridge to **I-580** and
connect with Oakland **I-980 South,** which has downtown exits at 12th St. and
19th St. Get traffic updates from **TravInfo** (☎817-1717).

> **Buses: Greyhound,** 2103 San Pablo Ave. (station info ☎834-3213, schedules and
> reservations 800-231-2222). **Buses** depart daily to: **LA** (adults $45, round-trip $82;
> 8hr.); **Sacramento** ($13/$21; 1½hr.); **Santa Cruz** ($12/$22; 2½hr.). Seniors and
> children receive discounted tickets; call for rates. **As always, be careful at night.**
>
> **Public Transportation: Bay Area Rapid Transit (BART:** ☎465-2278; www.bart.gov) is
> the most convenient way to travel from San Francisco to and within Oakland. BART
> runs from downtown San Francisco to Oakland's stations at **Lake Merritt** (Dublin/
> Pleasanton or Fremont trains), **12th Street** (Richmond or Pittsburg/Bay Point trains),
> **19th Street** (Richmond or Pittsburg/Bay Point trains), **Rockridge** (Pittsburg/Bay
> Point trains), and **Coliseum** (Dublin/Pleasanton or Fremont trains). **Alameda County
> (AC) Transit** (☎817-1717, ext. 1111; www.actransit.org). Adults $1.35; seniors,
> disabled, and ages 5-12 65¢; under 5 free. 1hr. transfers 25¢. **Transbay** routes to
> San Francisco (adults $2.75; seniors, disabled, and ages 5-12 $1.35). All AC buses
> are wheelchair-accessible and equipped with bike racks. **Ferries: Alameda/Oakland
> Ferry** (☎522-3300; www.eastbayferry.com). Purchase tickets on board. Ferries run
> between Oakland, Alameda, the SF Ferry Building, and Pier 41/Fisherman's Wharf.
> Adults $5, round-trip $10; seniors and disabled $3, $6; children 5-12 $2.25, $4.50;
> under 5 free. Free AC and MUNI transfers; MUNI transfers must be validated on ferry.
>
> **Taxis: A1 Yellow Cab** (☎843-1111). 24hr.

## ◼◪ ORIENTATION & PRACTICAL INFORMATION

The scarcity of noteworthy sights and cheap and safe accommodations make
Oakland a better daytrip than vacation destination. Oakland's main artery is
**Broadway,** which runs northeast under the Nimitz Fwy. (I-880) at 5th St., and
separates **Old Oakland** (to the west) from **Chinatown** (to the east). The **city center**
is at 13th St. and Broadway, but the greater downtown area occupies all of **Lake
Merritt,** including Lakeside Park on the north side and the Lake Merritt Channel
on the south side. North-south addresses are numbered to match the east-west
cross streets; for example, 1355 Broadway is between 13th and 14th St. To get
to **Jack London Sq.** and the waterfront from the 12th St. BART stop, just head
down Broadway away from the hills. North of downtown, past some of Oakland's poorest areas, are a few Berkeley-esque neighborhoods with boutiques,

BAY AREA

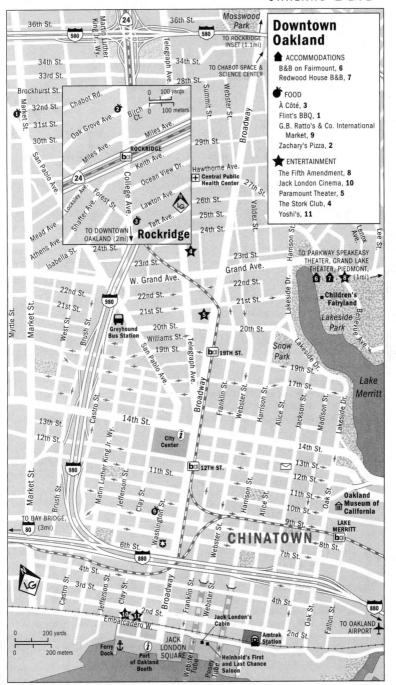

36th St.

Mosswood Park

**Downtown Oakland**

🏠 ACCOMMODATIONS
B&B on Fairmount, **6**
Redwood House B&B, **7**

🍎 FOOD
À Côté, **3**
Flint's BBQ, **1**
G.B. Ratto's & Co. International Market, **9**
Zachary's Pizza, **2**

⭐ ENTERTAINMENT
The Fifth Amendment, **8**
Jack London Cinema, **10**
Paramount Theater, **5**
The Stork Club, **4**
Yoshi's, **11**

TO ROCKRIDGE INSET (1.1mi)

TO CHABOT SPACE & SCIENCE CENTER

34th St.
33rd St.
Brockhurst St.
32nd St.
31st St.
30th St.
28th St.

Chabot Rd.
Birch Ct.
Oak Grove Ave.
Miles Ave.
Miles Ave.

0    100 yards
0    100 meters

Summit St.
Webster St.
Broadway

29th St.

ROCKRIDGE
Keith Ave.
Ocean View Dr.
Lawton Ave.
Taft Ave.

Hawthorne Ave.
Central Public Health Center

College Ave.
Forest St.
Shafter Ave.
Locksley Ave.

26th St.
25th St.

24th St.
**Rockridge**

TO DOWNTOWN OAKLAND (2mi)

Mead Ave.
Athens Ave.
Isabella St.

Valdez St.

27th St.

23rd St.
W. Grand Ave.
22nd St.
21st St.

Grand Ave.
22nd St.
21st St.
20th St.

TO PARKWAY SPEAKEASY THEATER, GRAND LAKE THEATER, PIEDMONT, (1mi)
**6  7  8**

Children's Fairyland

Lakeside Park

Lee St.
Lenox Ave.
Bellevue Ave.
Lakeside Dr.
Harrison St.

Myrtle St.
Market St.
22nd St.
21st St.
West St.
Brush St.

Greyhound Bus Station

20th St.
Williams St.
19th St.

**19TH ST.**

Snow Park

Lake Merritt

San Pablo Ave.
Telegraph Ave.

Franklin St.
Webster St.
Harrison St.
Alice St.
Jackson St.
Madison St.

19th St.
17th St.

13th St.
12th St.

14th St.

City Center ℹ

11th St.

Martin Luther King Jr. Wy.
Jefferson St.
Clay St.
Castro St.

Broadway

**12TH ST.**

14th St.
13th St.
12th St.
11th St.
10th St.
9th St.

Oakland Museum of California

LAKE MERRITT

Oak St.

TO BAY BRIDGE, (3mi)

Washington St.

**9**

6th St.

**CHINATOWN**

8th St.
7th St.

4th St.
3rd St.

Jefferson St.
Clay St.
Castro St.
Brush St.
Market St.

Franklin St.
Webster St.

4th St.
2nd St.

Fallon St.

TO OAKLAND AIRPORT

0    200 yards
0    200 meters

Embarcadero W.

**10  11**

Ferry Dock
Port of Oakland Booth ℹ

JACK LONDON SQUARE

Jack London's Cabin

Webster Tube
Posey Tube

Heinhold's First and Last Chance Saloon

Amtrak Station
2nd St.

grocers, and restaurants. **Rockridge** (take Broadway north off 580), with its well-kept lawns, lies toward Berkeley and is accessible from downtown Oakland by BART or AC Transit bus #51.

**Visitor Information: Oakland Visitors Information Bureau,** 475 14th St., Suite 120 (☎839-9000), between Broadway and Clay St. Free maps of the city and brochures. Open M-F 8:30am-5pm. **Port of Oakland Information Booths** (24hr. info ☎814-6000; www.jacklondonsquare.com), on Broadway in Jack London Sq. under the Barnes & Noble bookstore. Info focuses on waterfront sights. Also at Oakland International Airport. Open daily 9am-4pm.

**Police:** 455 7th St. (☎238-3481).

**Medical Services: Highland Hospital,** 1411 E. 31st St. (☎437-4800), at Beaumont Ave. 24hr. emergency care.

**Pharmacy: Leo's Day and Night Pharmacy,** 1776 19th St. (☎839-7900), at Broadway. Open M-F 9am-6:30pm.

**Post Office:** Main Office, 1675 7th St. at Peralta St. Open M 6:30am-midnight, Tu-Th 8:30am-midnight, F 8:30am-11pm. **Postal Code:** 94615

## ■ ACCOMMODATIONS

Although Oakland is full of motels, few downtown are as safe, clean, or economical as those in San Francisco and Berkeley. Motels clustered along W. MacArthur Blvd. near the MacArthur BART station are around $45 per night for a room with private bath. Ask to see the room before checking in. Commercial inns and hotels (cleaner and safer, but bland), are also clustered around Broadway at Jack London Sq. Try one of the beautiful and affordable B&Bs sprouting up in the northern part of the city. For more information, contact the **Berkeley-Oakland Bed and Breakfast Network** (www.bbonline.com/ca/berkeley-oakland).

**A B&B on Fairmount,** 640 Fairmount Ave. (☎653-7726; www.bbonline.com/ca/fairmount), in Piedmont. Beautiful Victorian home with 3 airy rooms, all with private bath. Tea served in living room with views of the sunset over the hills; huge, homestyle breakfast, made with ingredients from vegetable garden in back, served in the sunny conservatory. 2-night min. stay. 2-week max. stay. Check-in after 3pm. Check-out 11am. Singles from $85; doubles from $95. Every consecutive 7th night is free. No credit cards. ❺

**Redwood House B&B,** 4244 39th Ave. (☎530-6840; tyler_don@yahoo.com), east of Piedmont. Ornate Victorian house brimming with antiques. Lush house plants, tufted silks, marble surfaces, and stained glass detail around every corner. Master suite with jacuzzi is a steal at $121; smaller but equally luxurious rooms $100. No credit cards. ❺

## ■ FOOD

All-American staples like burger joints, breakfast diners, and barbecue shacks dominate in Oakland. More gourmet cafes, mostly open for breakfast and lunch, have sprung up on Washington and Clay St. between 7th and 12th St. Oakland's **Chinatown,** west of Broadway around 9th St., features a host of dim sum restaurants, Vietnamese and Cambodian cuisine, and Asian markets. Every Friday from 8am to 2pm, the **Old Oakland farmer's market** (☎745-7100) takes over 9th St. between Broadway and Clay St., offering fresh fruits, vegetables, and some of the best baked goods in the Golden State. A similar **market** takes over a corner of Jack London Sq. on Broadway, near the waterfront. (☎800-949-3276. Su 10am-2pm.)

**Zachary's Pizza,** 5801 College Ave. (☎655-6385), at Oak Grove Ave. Loyal fans claim Zach's makes the best pizza in the Bay, zealots say west of Chicago, extremists insist it's the best in the world. *Let's Go* won't go that far, but Zach's makes a pretty good pie. Slices under $3. Open Su-Th 11am-10pm, F-Sa 11am-10:30pm. No credit cards. ❶

**Flint's BBQ,** 3114 San Pablo Ave. (☎652-9605), south of 32nd St. No side dishes, no appetizers...hell, no tables or chairs. A serious BBQ joint offering heaping take-out only portions of pork or beef ribs, beef links, and chicken ($9-10). Sandwiches $7.50. *Not* a vegetarian option. Open daily 11am-11pm. No credit cards. ❷

**G.B. Ratto's & Co. International Market,** 821 Washington St. (☎832-6503), is a 104 year-old Oakland institution with more ingredients than ready-to-eats, except for the excellent sandwich counter ($3.50-6.75). Open M-F 9am-6pm, Sa 9:30am-5pm. ❶

**À Côté,** 5478 College Ave. (☎655-6469). Critics rave about the French-inspired menu and velvet decor. Entrees $7-14. Open Tu 5:30-10pm, W 5:30-11pm, Th 11:30am-2pm and 5:30-11pm, F-Sa 11:30am-2pm and 5:30pm-midnight, Su 11:30am-2pm. ❸

# ◉ SIGHTS

Haunted by Gertrude Stein's withering observation that "there is no there there," Oakland's tourist literature wages a war of attrition against its former resident, assuring visitors that City Square is "always there for you" and "there is shopping there." Free walking tours of the city (reservations recommended; ☎238-3234; www.oaklandnet.com) highlight the *thereness* of downtown's best sights, including Roslyn Mazzilli's sculpture in City Square's upper plaza, defiantly entitled "There!" For a slightly militant view of the city, take the **Black Panther Legacy Tour.** Former Party chief-of-staff David Hillard guides visitors through a first-hand account of the events, locations, and personalities that defined the Party. (☎986-0660; www.blackpanthertours.com. Reservations required for Sa tours. $20.)

**OAKLAND MUSEUM OF CALIFORNIA.** The three garden-topped levels of Bauhaus-inspired poured concrete at the Oakland Museum of California showcase the collections of three established area museums, brought together in 1969 to reflect the collective artistic, historical, and environmental legacy of Oakland and California. The **Cowell Hall of History** documents the cultural and political forces that shaped centuries of California dreaming. **The Hall of California Ecology** on the first floor recreates the state's eight biotic zones and the **Gallery of California Art** includes photography by Ansel Adams, paintings by Richard Diebenkorn, and myriad modern masterpieces. *(1000 Oak St., on the southwestern side of the lake. From the Lake Merritt BART station, walk 1 block north on Oak St. toward the hills. ☎238-2200 or 888-625-6873; www.museumca.org. Open Su noon-5pm, W-Sa 10am-5pm, 1st F of each month until 9pm. Adults $6; seniors, students, and 6-18 $4; under 6 free. 2nd Su of each month free.)*

**LAKE MERRITT.** Lake Merritt was dammed off from the San Francisco Bay in 1869 and now provides a place for sailing, biking, and jogging—not to mention political protest. Activity revolves around **Lakeside Park,** which has the nation's oldest urban bird sanctuary. The **Lake Merritt Boating Center** rents boats, and leads lake tours. *(Park: ☎238-7275. Parking $2. Lake: ☎238-2196. $10 deposit for boat rentals. Rentals 50% off for seniors and disabled. Open June-Sept. M-F 9am-6pm, Sa-Su 10am-6pm; Oct. daily 10:30am-5pm, Nov.-Feb. M-F 10:30am-3:30pm, Sa-Su 10:30am-4pm; Mar.-May M-F 10:30am-4pm, Sa-Su 10:30am-5pm. Boating Center: 568 Bellevue Ave. ☎238-2196; www.oaklandnet.com/parks/programs/boating.asp. Lake tours Sa-Su. Adults $1.50, children and seniors 75¢.)*

**JACK LONDON SQUARE.** An eight-block commercial district named for Oakland's native son, author of *White Fang* and *The Call of the Wild*, is a nice first stop on the way to other Oakland outings. **Jack London's Cabin,** near Webster St., was the author's home during his 1890s prospecting days. Next to the cabin, the small wooden **Heinold's First and Last Chance Saloon** has barely changed since London's

BAY AREA

days, except, presumably, for the addition of the London-themed mural. The same gaslight still burns, the sunken floor and bar from 1906 have never been fixed, and 120-odd years of knickknacks continue to pile up on the walls. *(Cabin: Along the waterfront. Take Broadway south. Event info ☎814-6000. Saloon: 56 Jack London Sq., at the foot of Webster St. ☎839-6761; www.firstandlastchance.com. Open M noon-10pm, Tu-Th noon-midnight, F-Sa noon-2am, Su 11am-10pm. $4 pints, $4 cocktails. No credit cards.)*

**CHABOT SPACE AND SCIENCE CENTER.** This incredible 3-year-old complex offers stargazing both indoors at the **Planetarium** and outdoors with high-powered telescopes, daily screenings in the **Tien MegaDome Theater,** and interactive exhibits in various science and computer labs. *(Space and Science Center: 10000 Skyline Blvd, at Skyline Blvd., in Joaquin Miller Park in the Oakland Hills. ☎336-7300; www.chabotspace.org. Open Sept. 2-June 18 Tu-Su 10am-3pm; June 17-Sept. 1 Su noon-5pm, Tu-Th 10am-5pm, F-Sa 10am-7:30pm. $11; students, seniors, and ages 4-12 $8; under 3 free. Planetarium and Tien MegaDome Theater: Open same hours as Science Center plus F-Sa 7:30-9pm. $6 for each; students, seniors, and ages 4-12 $5; under 3 free. Double and triple venue prices also available.)*

# 🎵 📷 ENTERTAINMENT & NIGHTLIFE

## LIVE MUSIC

The **live music scene** is one of the best reasons to make the Oakland trip in the first place. Whether it's West Coast blues, Oaktown hip-hop, or progressive jazz, Oakland's music venues are unsurpassed. Because many artists lack institutional representation, check posters and local papers for shows. *Urban View*, the free Wednesday weekly, and the daily *Oakland Tribune* (50¢, Su $1.25) are good resources and are available in boxes throughout the city. **Koncepts Cultural Gallery** is an organization that hosts groundbreaking progressive jazz sessions. (☎451-5231; www.oaklandculturalarts.org) The **Paramount Theater,** 2025 Broadway, at 21st St., hosts national music acts like Nina Simone and George Benson. *(☎465-6400; www.paramounttheater.com. Films: $5-7. Music: Box office open Tu-F noon-6pm, Sa noon-5pm, and 2hr. before performances. Tours: ☎893-2300. $1. 1st and 3rd Sa each month 10am. Guided tours begin at Box Office entrance on 21st St. and last 2hr.)*

**⊠ The Fifth Amendment,** 3255 Lakeshore Ave. (☎832-3242), at Lake Park Ave. Not the most famous, but one of the best. Jazz and blues musicians take the stage in this downtown club, where there's never a cover or drink minimum and the crowd is serious about its music. 21+. Shows Su and Th-Sa, usually at 9pm. Open M and W-Su 4pm-2am.

**Yoshi's,** 510 Embarcadero W. (☎238-9200; www.yoshis.com), in Jack London Sq. Yoshi's is an upscale institution, bringing together world-class sushi and world-class jazz. Big names command big cover prices; tickets sometimes sell out but are often available at the door. 1-drink minimum. Cover usually $20-25. Local musician nights (usually M) $8-10. Family discount Su matinee: adult (with child) $10, child $5. Seniors and students with valid ID can get half-price tickets for selected shows. Shows M-Sa 8, 10pm; Su 2, 8pm. Box office open daily 10:30am-11pm.

**The Stork Club,** 2330 Telegraph Ave. (☎444-6174). Laid-back country western bar by day, rock party by night. Kitschy Christmas decor year-round. 21+. Indie rock, punk, and underground Tu-Sa around 9pm, Open mic Su 9pm with "Girl George." No cover but 2-drink min. 21+. Cover from $5. Open Su and Tu-Sa 4pm-2am. No credit cards.

## CINEMA & FINE ARTS

The **Paramount Theater,** 2025 Broadway (☎465-6400), at 21st St., is an exquisite Art Deco movie palace. The Paramount shares its stage with the **Oakland East Bay Symphony** and the **Oakland Ballet.** The Symphony performs five Friday concerts yearly, with open rehearsals the preceding Thursday afternoon. The Symphony also sponsors free noon concerts. The ballet performs several programs, including an unconventional *Nutcracker Sweetie*. (Symphony ☎444-0801; www.oebs.org. Ballet ☎893-2300; www.oaklandballet.org. Symphony tickets $15-55. Ballet tickets $8-45. Box office open Tu-F noon-6pm, Sa noon-5pm, and 2hr. before shows.)

Another groovy place to see a movie is the **Parkway Speakeasy Theater,** 1834 Park Blvd., a theater with lounge seating where you can order pizza ($3 per slice), pasta, sandwiches, and wine or beer by the pitcher ($8) or pint ($4) right at your seat. Keep an eye open for special Thrillville features. (☎834-1506; www.picturepubpizza.com. Tickets $5. 21+ enforced. Rocky Horror Picture Show F midnight ($5). 17+. Weekend matinees $3, all ages.) The classic **Grand Lake Theater** features Wurlitzer organ music before F and Sa evening shows and all the latest, hottest movies. (☎452-3446; www.rrfilms.com. Adults $8.50; children, seniors, and matinee $5.) Also, there's the more mainstream **Jack London Cinema,** on Washington St. at Embarcadero. (☎452-3446; www.rrfilms.com. $8.75, seniors and matinees $5.75.)

### SPORTS & SEASONAL EVENTS

Baseball's **Oakland Athletics (A's)** and football's **Oakland Raiders** both play in the **Oakland Coliseum** (☎569-2121) at the intersection of the I-880 (Nimitz Fwy.) and Hegenberger Rd. The Coliseum has its own BART station. The NBA's **Golden State Warriors** play basketball in the **Coliseum Arena,** adjacent to the Oakland Coliseum. (Box office open M-F 10am-6pm, Sa 10am-4pm.)

**California Canoe & Kayak,** 409 Water St. in Jack London Sq., rents paddling equipment, offers classes, and plans adventure trips. (☎893-7833 or 800-366-9804; www.calkayak.com. Open M-Th 10am-6pm, F-Sa 10am-7pm, Su 10am-5pm. Boat rentals daily 10am-5pm; last boat leaves 4pm. $15-25 per hr., $50-60 per day.)

🔲**Midnight Mass,** 3010 Geary Blvd., at the Bridge Theatre, presents a series of summer midnight Sa screenings of campy classic films. (☎267-4893; www.peacheschrist.com). Lake Merritt's Lakeside Park hosts several festivals over the summer. In June, the **Festival at the Lake** (☎286-1061) takes over Oakland with a long weekend of international foods, crafts, and nonstop music. On Father's Day Sunday (June 13 in 2004), **Juneteenth** (☎238-7765) commemorates the anniversary of the Emancipation Proclamation and black history and culture with parades, soul food, blues, and R&B. The park also has **free Shakespeare performances** in summer. (☎415-422-2222 or 800-978-7529; www.sfshakes.org.)

# SOUTH BAY

The San Francisco peninsula extends southward into what was once a valley of fruit orchards and is now the breeding ground of America's electronics industry. From the enormous Mexican restaurant of Stanford University to San Jose and beyond, the entire area known as the Silicon Valley is as clean as its offices and as sterile as its dot-commers.

# PALO ALTO ☎ 650

Dominated by the beautiful 8000-acre Stanford University campus, well-manicured Palo Alto looks like "Collegeland" at a Disney theme park. Stanford's perfectly groomed grounds, sparkling lake, and Spanish mission-style buildings have a manufactured quality that suits the university's speedy rise to international acclaim. The city that Stanford calls home is equally manicured, with a neat downtown strip of restaurants, bookstores, and boutiques. Its nightlife caters to students and suburbanites, while weekday Happy Hours help singles wind down.

BAY AREA

# ⌐ TRANSPORTATION

Palo Alto is 35 mi. southeast of San Francisco, near the southern shore of the bay. Take **US 101** to the University Ave. Exit or take the Embarcadero Rd. Exit directly to the Stanford campus. Alternatively, motorists from San Francisco can split off onto **I-280 (Junípero Serra Highway)** for a longer but more scenic route. From I-280, exit at Sand Hill Rd. and follow it to the northwest corner of Stanford University.

The **Palo Alto Transit Center,** on University Ave., serves local and regional buses and trains. (☎323-6105. Open M-F 5am-12:30pm.) A train-only depot lies on California Ave., 1¼ mi. south of the transit center. (☎326-3392. Open M-F 5:30am-12:30pm.) The transit center connects to points north via **San Mateo County buses** and to Stanford via the free **Marguerite Shuttle.**

**Trains: CalTrain,** 95 University Ave. (☎800-660-4287), at Alma St. Street-side stop at Stanford Stadium on Embarcadero Rd. To **San Francisco** ($4.50) and **San Jose** ($3). Half-price for seniors and disabled. Operates M-F 5am-midnight, departing 10min. and 40min. past the hour (service on weekends is suspended pending construction).

**Buses: SamTrans** (☎800-660-4287). To downtown **San Francisco** ($3.50, under 17 $1.50) and **San Francisco International Airport** ($1.25). To reach Palo Alto from SF, take **SamTrans** express bus KX from the Transbay Terminal in San Francisco to the Stanford Shopping Center. Operates daily 6am-10pm departing every 30min. on the hour.

**Public Transportation: Santa Clara Valley Transportation Authority** (☎408-321-2300 or 800-894-9908). Local and county-wide transit. $1.25, ages 5-17 70¢, seniors and disabled 40¢. Day pass $3, ages 5-17 $1.75, seniors and disabled $1. Express buses $2. The **Marguerite** Shuttle (☎723-9362) provides free service around Stanford University, stopping at red-and-white shuttle stop signs, including the Palo Alto Caltrain. Operates M-F 6am-8pm. The city of Palo Alto provides a free **crosstown shuttle,** operating M-F 7am-6pm, and an **Embarcadero shuttle** (☎329-2520; www.city.palo-alto.ca.us/shuttle) operating M-F 6-9am, Sa-Su 11:45am-1:45pm and 3-6pm.

**Taxis: Yellow Cab** (☎321-1234 or 800-595-1222). 24hr. $2.50 per mi.

**Car Rental: Budget,** 4230 El Camino Real (☎424-0684, reservations 800-527-0700; www.budget.com). From $40 per day. Unlimited mileage. Must be at least 21 with credit card. Under 25 surcharge $20 per day. Open M-Sa 7am-6pm, Su 9am-5pm.

**Bike Rental: Campus Bike Shop,** 551 Salvatierra Ln. (☎723-9300), across from Stanford Law School. A bike allows you to take advantage of Palo Alto's flat boulevards and rolling hills. $15 per day, $20 overnight, helmets $3 (under 18 free). Major credit card or $150-300 cash deposit. Open M-F 9am-5pm, Sa 9am-3pm.

# ■✱❷ ORIENTATION & PRACTICAL INFORMATION

The pristine lawns of residential Palo Alto are not easily distinguished from the manicured campus of Stanford University. Despite its name, **University Avenue,** the main thoroughfare off US 101, belongs much more to the town than to the college. Cars coming off US 101 onto University Ave. pass very briefly through **East Palo Alto,** a community incorporated in 1983 after Palo Alto and Menlo Park had already annexed most of their revenue-producing districts. East Palo Alto once had one of the highest violent crime rates in the nation. The town has cleaned up its act and grown safer in recent years, but you'll find that the contrast with the immaculate tree-lined lawns of Palo Alto is still striking.

**Stanford University** spreads out from the west end of University Ave. Abutting University Ave. and running northwest-southeast through town is **El Camino Real** (part of Rte. 82). From there, University Ave. turns into Palm Dr., which accesses the heart of Stanford's campus, the **Main Quad.**

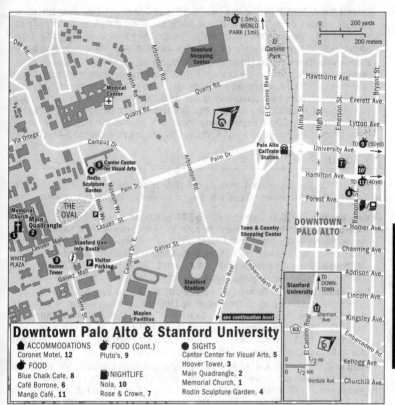

## Downtown Palo Alto & Stanford University

**ACCOMMODATIONS**
Coronet Motel, **12**

**FOOD**
Blue Chalk Cafe, **8**
Café Borrone, **6**
Mango Café, **11**

**FOOD (Cont.)**
Pluto's, **9**

**NIGHTLIFE**
Nola, **10**
Rose & Crown, **7**

**SIGHTS**
Cantor Center for Visual Arts, **5**
Hoover Tower, **3**
Main Quadrangle, **2**
Memorial Church, **1**
Rodin Sculpture Garden, **4**

**Visitor Information: Palo Alto Chamber of Commerce,** 122 Hamilton Ave. (☎324-3121), between Hude and Alta St. Open M-F 9am-5pm. **Stanford University Information Booth** (☎723-2560), across from Hoover Tower in Memorial Auditorium. Visitors can obtain parking passes, maps, and information about the university. Free student-led 1hr. **tours** depart daily 11am and 3:15pm. Open daily 8am-5pm.

**Police:** 275 Forest Ave. (☎329-2406, after hours 329-2413).

**Internet Access: Palo Alto Main Library,** 1213 Newell Rd. (☎329-2436). Open M-F 10am-9pm, Sa 10am-6pm, Su 1-5pm. **Downtown Branch,** 270 Forest Ave. (☎329-2641). Open Tu-F 11am-6pm. Free.

**Post Office: Main Office,** 2085 E. Bayshore Rd. (☎800-275-8777). Open M-F 8am-5pm. **Postal Code:** 94303. **Hamilton Station,** 380 Hamilton Ave. (☎323-2650). **Postal Code:** 94301.

## ACCOMMODATIONS

Motels are plentiful along **El Camino Real,** but rates can be steep. Generally, rooms are cheaper farther away from Stanford. More reasonably priced accommodations may be found farther north toward Redwood City. Many Palo Alto motels cater to business travelers and are actually busier on weekdays than on weekends.

**Coronet Motel,** 2455 El Camino Real (☎326-1081), at California St. Clean, spacious rooms with big windows, cable TV, pool, telephone, private baths, and kitchenette. Under new management and cheap considering its proximity to Stanford. Check-out 11am. Singles $55; doubles $60. $5 charge per person for parties that exceed two people. Weekly rates available. ❹

**Hidden Villa Ranch Hostel (HI-AYH),** 26870 Moody Rd. (☎949-8648), about 10 mi. southwest of Palo Alto in the Los Altos Hills. The first hostel on the Pacific Coast (opened in 1937); functions as a working ranch and farm in a wilderness preserve. Recent renovations have completely rebuilt dorms and extended living, kitchen, and dining rooms. Heated cabins and 35 beds. Dorm, family, and private rooms. Reception 8am-noon and 4-9:30pm. Reservations required for weekends and groups. Open Sept.-May. Dorms $15, non-members $18, children $7.50; private cabins $30-42. ❶

# 🍴 FOOD

Dining in Palo Alto is centered around posh restaurants downtown around University and California avenues. Those watching wallets should stay on University Ave.

🍴**Café Borrone,** 1010 El Camino Real (☎327-0830), adjacent to Kepler's Books in Menlo Park. Bustling, brasserie-style cafe spills out onto a large patio. Borrone serves freshly baked bread, sinful gateaux ($2-4), coffee drinks, Italian sodas, wine ($5-6 per glass), and beers ($3.75 per pint). Check the chalkboard for daily specials or choose from a wide range of delicious salads ($4-9), sandwiches ($5-10), and quiches ($6). Open M-Th 8am-11pm, F-Sa 8am-midnight, Su 8am-5pm. ❷

**Blue Chalk Cafe,** 630 Ramona St. (☎326-1020). Started by a Stanford Business School student for a project, this elegant restaurant became an instant hit with both students and silicon-professionals. California Cuisine includes shrimp and crab cakes ($9.25), grilled salmon and steaks ($19), and penne pasta with veggie Thai green curry ($15). Happy Hour M-F 3-7pm. Open for lunch M-F 11am-2:30pm and dinner M-Sa 5-10pm. Bar open M-Sa 11am-1:30am. ❸

**Pluto's,** 482 University Ave. (☎853-1556). Out-of-this-world cafeteria-style restaurant. Design your own salad from heaps of fresh fixings ($5) or choose from grilled meats and veggies to fill a sandwich ($5-6). Open M-Th 11am-10pm, F 11am-11pm, Sa 11:30am-11pm, Su 11:30am-10pm. ❶

**Mango Café,** 435 Hamilton Ave. (☎325-3229), 1 block east of University Ave. Reggae music and Caribbean cuisine. Seriously spicy Jamaican "jerked joints" ($6) and tropical smoothies ($3.50). Veggie options. Entrees range from $8-12, lunch specials from $5-10. Delicious bread pudding $3. Open M-Sa 11:30am-2:30pm and 6-10pm. ❷

# 👁 SIGHTS

## STANFORD UNIVERSITY

Undoubtedly Palo Alto's main tourist attraction, the secular, co-educational **Stanford University** was founded in 1885 by Jane and Leland Stanford to honor their son who died of typhoid. The Stanfords loved Spanish colonial mission architecture and collaborated with **Frederick Law Olmsted,** designer of New York City's Central Park, to create a red-tiled campus of uncompromising beauty. The school has produced such eminent conservatives as Chief Justice William Rehnquist, and the campus has been called "a hotbed of social rest."

**MAIN QUADRANGLE.** The oldest part of campus is the site of most undergraduate classes. The walkways are dotted with diamond-shaped, gold-numbered stone tiles that mark the locations of time capsules put together by each year's graduating class. *(Serra St., between Lasuen and Lomita Mall. Free tours at 11:15am and 3:15pm depart from Information Booth in Memorial Auditorium.)*

**MEMORIAL CHURCH.** Memorial Church is a non-denominational gold shrine with stained glass windows and glittering mosaic walls like those of an Eastern Orthodox church. *(Just south of the Main Quad, at Escondido Mall and Duena.* ☎ *723-3469; http://religiouslife.stanford.edu/memorial_church. Open M-F 8am-5pm. Free tours F 2pm.)*

**HOOVER TOWER.** The tower's observation deck has views of campus, the East Bay, and San Francisco. *(East of the Main Quad, near Serra St.* ☎ *723-2053. Open daily 10am-4:30pm. Closed during finals and academic breaks. Adults $2, seniors and under 13 $1.)*

**IRIS & B. GERALD CANTOR CENTER FOR VISUAL ARTS.** The Visual Arts Center displays its eclectic collection of painting and sculpture for free. *(328 Lomita Dr., at Museum Way off Palm Dr.* ☎ *723-4177. Open W and F-Su 11am-5pm, Th 11am-8pm.)*

**RODIN SCULPTURE GARDEN.** The extensive garden contains a stunning bronze cast of *Gates of Hell,* among other larger figures. It's an ideal spot to enjoy a picnic lunch. *(At Museum Way and Lomita Dr.* ☎ *723-4177. Free tours Sa-Su 2pm.)*

## SHOPPING

**Bell's Bookstore,** 536 Emerson St. (☎323-7822). Family-run since 1935, Bell's is a favorite among locals and Stanfordites. It's packed floor-to-ceiling with old, new, and rare books arranged by subject. Selection includes a large range of hardback and out-of-print texts. Open M-Th 9:30am-5:30pm, F 9:30am-9pm, Sa 9:30am-5pm.

**Stanford Shopping Center** (☎617-8585 or ☎800-772-9332; www.stanfordshop.com), between campus and El Camino Real. High-street designer clothes, department stores, speciality food shops, and restaurants line tree-shaded avenues. Its patio cafes are perfect for people-watching. Open M-F 10am-9pm, Sa 10am-7pm, Su 11am-6pm.

## ENTERTAINMENT

The Stanford-run *Palo Alto Daily* and local *Palo Alto Weekly* both contain listings of what's going on all over town. The free *Metro* and *Palo Alto Daily News,* available in downtown sidewalk boxes, also publish the local lowdown.

**Dinkelspiel Auditorium** (☎723-2448), at El Camino Real and Embarcadero. Called "the Dink" by locals, the auditorium holds classical concerts and other events through the Tressider Union ticket office (☎725-2787). Open M-F 10am-5pm, Sa noon-4pm.

**Stanford Theater,** 221 University Ave. (☎324-3700). Dedicated to Hollywood's "Golden Age." Devotes exhibition seasons to directors and stars, such as Billy Wilder and Cary Grant. The Wurlitzer organ plays before and after the 7:30pm show and accompanies silent films every W. Double features $6, seniors $4, under 18 $3.

**The Lively Arts at Stanford** (☎723-2551; http://livelyarts.stanford.edu), brings semi-big name concerts to Frost Amphitheater and Memorial Auditorium, usually at discount prices. The Memorial also hosts movies on Su in term-time. Adults $3, students $2.

## NIGHTLIFE

Palo Alto may not host the wild nightlife found in San Francisco, but it still has a few bars and hot spots that are great for sitting back and having a few beers. The upscale aspirations of Palo Alto force visitors to throw out a few extra, but welcome visitors, Stanford students, and Silicon Valley professionals alike.

**Nola,** 535 Ramona St. (☎328-2722). There is a fiesta everyday in this vibrant, super-popular bar. Colorful strings of lights and patio windows open onto a cool, courtyard dining area. Late-night menu offers quesadillas ($7-9), crab cakes ($7), and gumbo ($7) to accompany your cocktails ($6-7). Open daily 5:30pm-2am.

**Rose & Crown,** 547 Emerson St. (☎327-7673). This low-key pub with an Ace jukebox is good for throwing darts or quietly nursing a Guinness. British bar menu includes fish and chips ($7-9), bangers and mash ($9), and ploughman's lunch ($7). Happy Hour M-F 4-6pm. 16 oz. draft beer $3. Weekly entertainment includes Su Jazz night (7:30pm) and M comedy showcase (9pm). Organize a team for Tu Quiz Night on general knowledge, sports, entertainment, and famous faces. Open M-F 11:30am-1:30am, Sa noon-1:30am, Su 1pm-1:30am.

# SAN JOSE ☎408

Founded in 1777 in a bucolic valley of fruit and walnut orchards, San Jose was California's first civilian settlement. The area's primary business was agriculture until the middle of the 20th century, when the technology sector began to develop. In 1939, the first computer company, Hewlett-Packard, had modest beginnings here—in Dave Packard's garage. By the early 1970s, many of San Jose's orchards had been replaced by offices, and the moniker "Silicon Valley" began to take hold.

For several decades, San Jose has been the country's foremost center of technological innovation, with its residents boasting the second-highest average disposable incomes of any US city. Because of shifting economic conditions in recent years, however, San Jose residents have broadened their one-track focus on the high-tech to include other industries. Museums, restaurants, hotels, and vineyards have all sprouted up around the city as part of an effort to expand San Jose beyond the world of microchips and barefoot office techies.

## ▄ TRANSPORTATION

**Airport: San Jose International,** 1661 Airport Blvd. (☎277-5366). Turn right onto Airport Blvd. from Coleman Ave. off I-880, or Guadalupe Pkwy. off US 101. Also accessible by **Valley Transit Authority (VTA)** light-rail. Free shuttles connect the terminals.

**Trains: Amtrak,** 65 Cahill St. (☎287-7462 or 800-USA-RAIL/872-7245), to **LA** (11hr., $51-78, depending on day/time) and **San Francisco** (1hr., $10-14). **CalTrain,** 65 Cahill St. (☎291-5651 or 800-660-4287), at W. San Fernando Blvd., to **San Francisco** with stops at peninsula cities (1½hr.; every hr. M-F 5am-10pm, Sa 6:30am-10pm, Su 7:30am-10pm; $5.25).

**Buses: Greyhound,** 70 S. Almaden Blvd. (☎295-4151 or 800-231-2222), at Santa Clara St. To **LA** (7hr., $40) and **San Francisco** (1¼hr., $5). Luggage lockers for ticketed passengers ($2 per 6hr.). Open daily 5am-midnight. The station has security guards.

**Public Transportation: Santa Clara Valley Transportation Agency (VTA),** 2 N. First St. (☎321-2300), offers modern buses and a light-rail system. ($1.40, day pass $4; ages 5-17 85¢/$2.50; seniors and disabled 45¢/$1.25. Exact change.) **Bay Area Rapid Transit** or **BART** (☎510-441-2278) bus #180 serves the Fremont station from 1st and San Carlos St. in downtown San Jose ($2). To **San Francisco** (45-55min., $4.05-4.45).

## ▄ ORIENTATION

San Jose lies at the southern end of the San Francisco Bay, about 50 mi. from San Francisco (via US 101 or I-280) and 40 mi. from Oakland (via I-880). I-280 is renowned for its roadside scenery along the stretch called Junípero Serra Fwy. and is often less congested than Hwy. 101. (For info on reaching San Jose from San Francisco using public transit, see **CalTrain,** p. 150.)

San Jose is centered around the convention-hosting malls and plazas near the intersection of east-west **San Carlos Street** and north-south **Market Street.** Bars, restaurants, and clubs crowd around 1st St. in the so-called **SoFA District.** The **Transit Mall,** the center of San Jose's bus and trolley system, runs north-south along 1st

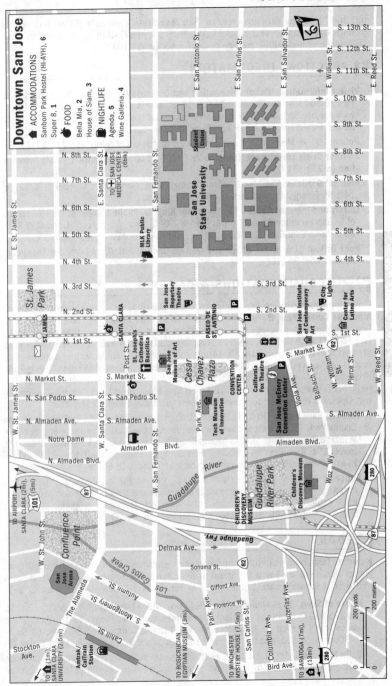

Downtown San Jose

ACCOMMODATIONS
Sanborn Park Hostel (HI-AYH), 6
Super 8, 1

FOOD
Bella Mia, 2
House of Siam, 3

NIGHTLIFE
Agenda, 5
Wine Galleria, 4

and 2nd St. in the downtown area. **San Jose State University (SJSU)** has grassy grounds that span several blocks between S. 4th and S. 10th St. Founded in 1857, SJSU is the oldest public college in California. (☎924-1000.)

# ⁊ PRACTICAL INFORMATION

**Visitor Information: Visitor Information and Business Center,** 150 W. San Carlos St. (☎726-5673 or 888-SAN-JOSE/726-5673, events line 295-2265; fax 977-0901; www.sanjose.org), at Market and San Carlos St. in the San Jose McEnerny Convention Center. Free maps. Open M-F 9am-5pm, Sa 11am-5pm.

**Police:** 201 W. Mission St. (non-emergency dispatch ☎277-8900, info 277-2211).

**24-Hour Crisis Lines: Rape Crisis** (☎287-3000). **Suicide Prevention/Crisis Intervention** (☎279-3312).

**Medical Services: San Jose Medical Center,** 675 E. Santa Clara St. (☎998-3212), at 14th St. Emergency room (☎977-4444) open 24hr.

**Library and Internet Access: Martin Luther King, Jr. Public Library,** at the intersection of E. San Fernando St. and 4th St. (☎808-2000; www.sjlibrary.org). Open M-W 8am-8pm, Th-Sa 9am-6pm, Su 1-5pm, with expanded hours during the school year.

**Post Office:** 105 N. 1st St. (☎292-0487). Open M-F 8:30am-5pm, Sa 7am-noon. **Postal Code:** 95113.

# ⋔⋔ ACCOMMODATIONS & CAMPING

County parks with campgrounds surround the city, as do chain motels. **Mount Madonna County Park ❶,** on Pole Line Rd. off Hecker Pass Hwy., has 117 sites in a beautiful setting, available by reservation or on a first-come, first-camp basis. (☎842-2341 or 842-6761, reservations 355-2201. Sites $15; RVs $25.) The area around **Saratoga ❶,** on Rte. 85, 14 mi. southwest of San Jose, has a number of campsites, as well as miles of horse and hiking trails in **Sanborn-Skyline County Park.** From Rte. 17 South, take Rte. 9 to Big Basin Way and turn left onto Sanborn Rd. (☎867-9959, reservations 355-2201. Open late Mar. to mid-Oct. for walk-in camping. Open for day use year-round from 8am to sunset. Sites $8; RVs $25.)

**Sanborn Park Hostel (HI-AYH),** 15808 Sanborn Rd. (☎741-0166), in Sanborn-Skyline County Park, 20 mi. west of downtown San Jose. Those looking for peace and quiet are in luck; redwoods surround this beautiful facility. Clean rooms and 39 beds. Linen 50¢, towels 25¢. Reception 5-10:30pm. Check-out 9am. 11pm curfew. Dorms $12, US non-HI-AYH members $14, foreign non-members $15, under 18 $6. ❶

**Super 8,** 1860 The Alameda (☎293-9361). Convenient, comfortable, albeit rather expensive, this Super 8 is close to many attractions and 1 mi. from the San Jose airport. Pool, cable TV, free parking, continental breakfast, restaurant on premises. Singles $75-77; doubles $85. 10% discount for seniors and AAA. ❹

# ◖ FOOD

Familiar fast-food franchises and pizzerias surround SJSU. More international cheap eats lie along **South 1st Street** or near **San Pedro Square,** at St. John and San Pedro St. A **farmer's market** takes place at San Pedro Sq. (May-Dec. F 10am-2pm.)

**House of Siam,** 55 S. Market St. (☎279-5668), with a bigger branch at 151 S. 2nd St. (☎295-3397). Features excellent Thai entrees (some meatless) $8-15. Beware the spice level! Market St. location open M-F 11am-2:30pm and 5-9:30pm, Sa-Su 5-9:30pm. S. 2nd St. location open M-F 11am-3pm and 5-10pm, Sa-Su noon-10pm. ❸

**Bella Mia,** 58 S. 1st St. (☎280-1993). This eatery serves up regional Italian-American cuisine (entrees $13-26) in an inviting atmosphere. The lasagna ($15) and chicken foresta ($15) are especially popular. Full bar; drinks start at $5. Also holds special dinner nights like Murder Mystery and Comedy Cocktail; ask the host for tickets. Open M-F 11:30am-3pm and 5-9:30pm, Sa 5-9:30pm, Su 11am-3pm (brunch) and 5-9pm. ❹

##  SIGHTS

Although geographically contained within the Santa Clara Valley and politically bounded by Santa Clara County, the San Jose area lacks a recognizable, vital center. In fact, many of the corporate headquarters of high-tech giants like Intel and Hewlett-Packard are actually in Mountain View and Sunnyvale, farther up north on the peninsula toward San Francisco. These companies are wary of visitors, and tourists will only see anonymous, low-profile buildings of mirrored glass. In San Jose proper, a few well-funded museums are the only real diversions.

**TECH MUSEUM OF INNOVATION.** This is the most tourist-savvy attraction in San Jose. Underwritten by high-tech firms, the Tech features hands-on, cutting-edge science exhibits and an IMAX theater, all in a sleek geometric environment. *(201 S. Market St. ☎ 795-6224. Exhibits open daily 10am-5pm; Oct.-Mar. closed on Mondays. $9, seniors $8, ages 3-12 $7. Combination tickets for exhibits and one IMAX film $16/15/13.)*

**WINCHESTER MYSTERY HOUSE.** This odd Victorian house is little more than that, but for those with a penchant for the unusual, the (space) ship has landed. Sarah Winchester was the eccentric, if not simply crazy, heir to the Winchester rifle fortune. After the death of her daughter and husband, she was convinced by an occultist that the spirits of all the men ever killed by her family's guns would seek vengeance if construction on her home ever ceased. Work on the mansion continued 24hr. a day for over 38 years. A 160-room maze of doors, windows, and stairs elaborately designed to "confuse the spirits" is the end result. *(525 S. Winchester Blvd. Near the intersection of I-880 and I-280, west of town. ☎ 247-2101. Open mid-Oct. to Aug. daily 9am-7pm; Sept.to mid-Oct. Su-Th 9am-5pm, F-Sa 9am-7pm. $18, over 65 $15, ages 6-12 $12, under 6 free.)*

**ROSICRUCIAN EGYPTIAN MUSEUM.** Rising out of the suburbs like the work of a mad pharaoh, this grand structure houses over 3000 ancient Egyptian artifacts, including a walk-in tomb and spooky animal mummies. This collection, the largest exhibit of Egyptian artifacts in the western US, belongs to the ancient and mystical Rosicrucian Order, whose past members (and searchers of a higher wisdom) include Amenhotep IV, Pythagoras, Sir Francis Bacon, Rene Descartes, Benjamin Franklin, and Isaac Newton. Join a free tour by the friendly staff. *(1342 Naglee Ave. at Park Ave. ☎ 947-3635; www.rosicrucian.org. Open Tu-F 10am-5pm, Sa-Su 11am-6pm. $9, students and seniors $7, ages 5-10 $5, under 5 free. Under 15 must be accompanied by an adult.)*

**THE SAN JOSE MUSEUM OF ART.** Neighbor to the Tech, this modern museum not only features contemporary art but is itself progressive in design and mission; admission is free to encourage public awareness of 20th- and 21st-century art, and the museum offers a wide range of exhibits, lectures, programs, and hands-on events for families. *(110 S. Market St. ☎ 294-2787. Open Tu-Th 11am-5pm, F 11am-10pm, Sa-Su 11am-5pm. Free.)*

**OTHER MUSEUMS. The Children's Discovery Museum,** across from the light-rail station, is filled with hands-on, science-based toys. *(180 Woz Way. ☎ 298-5437; www.cdm.org. Open Tu-Sa 10am-5pm, Su noon-5pm. $6, seniors $5.)* Nearby stand the **San Jose Institute of Contemporary Art** *(451 S. 1st St.; ☎ 283-8155; open Tu-Sa noon-5pm)* and the **Center for Latino Arts** *(510 S. 1st St.; ☎ 998-2783; open W-Sa noon-5pm).*

## NIGHTLIFE

The brightest nightspots are in the strip of downtown known as the SoFA District, along 1st St., which runs north-south. **Bars are 21+.**

BAY AREA

**Wine Galleria,** 377 S. 1st St. (☎298-1386). Located between Café Matisse and d.p. Fong Galleries to form a triumvirate of "Art for the Senses." Sample wines by the glass ($5-12) or bottle ($12-600; $12-40 is average) as you browse through blown glass sculptures or cuddle on comfy leather sofas. Galleria open Tu-Sa 5pm-midnight. Café Matisse open M-Th 7:30am-midnight, F 7:30am-2am, Sa 8am-2am, Su 9am-midnight. d.p. Fong open Tu-Sa 1-6pm or by appointment.

**Agenda,** 399 S. 1st St. (☎287-3991; www.agendalounge.com). Eat a tasty dish of New American cuisine ($15-27) and then head to the outdoor patio to hear the hottest acid jazz in town for free (non-diners pay $10 cover). It gets crowded, so plan on eating earlier to get great tables (show starts at 7:30pm). Upstairs lounge serves 25 microbrews. Open Tu-Sa 5:30pm-2am. Kitchen closes at 10pm.

## ♪ ◐ ENTERTAINMENT, SEASONAL EVENTS & SPORTS

For information on entertainment and events, look for the weekly *Metro*, available for free on downtown street corners. **City Lights,** 529 S. 2nd St. (☎295-4200; www.cltc.org), at William St., offers unique, cutting-edge theater in an intimate and flexible seating space. Local actors put on a variety of performances—classics, adaptations, and some original work. **Camera Cinemas** (☎998-3300) shows art-house, classic, and foreign flicks, and hosts film festivals at three locations: **Camera 1,** 366 S. 1st St., **Camera 3,** at S. 2nd and San Carlos St., and **Towne 3,** 1433 The Alameda (☎287-1433). The **cafe ❶** at Camera 3 offers sandwiches like "Tokyo Decadence" (teriyaki-marinated chicken, mozzarella, and veggies on toast, $6) and "Deja Vu" (vegan, $5.25). Sandwiches come with blue tortilla chips and salsa. (Open daily 11am-11pm.) The **Student Union and Concert Hall,** 1 Washington Sq. (☎924-1120), at SJSU, hosts concerts and other performances. Concert hall performances are free on Thursdays during the school year.

Topping the list of annual highlights is the May **Blues Festival** (☎924-6262), the biggest, baddest concert in Northern California. On the last weekend in September, the **San Pedro Square Brew-Ha-Ha** fills the downtown area with microbrew sampling, stand-up comedy, and fun for all. (☎279-1775.)

The NHL **San Jose Sharks** (☎287-7070) play at the San Jose Arena while the MLS **San Jose Earthquakes** (☎260-6300) let loose at Spartan Stadium, on 7th St. off I-280.

# NEAR SAN JOSE

## SANTA CLARA                    ☎408

A suburb of a suburb, the town of Santa Clara lies off US 101 at the De La Cruz Exit, between San Jose to the southeast and the mammoth **Paramount's Great America** theme park to the north. Great America, off US 101 at Great America Pkwy., is a forest of roller coasters, log rides, and other fiendish contraptions designed to spin you, flip you, soak you, drop you, and generally separate you from your stomach. If you come on a weekday, you'll beat some of the crowds. (☎988-1776. Open June-Aug. Su-F 10am-9pm, Sa 10am-10pm; Sept.-Oct. and Mar.-May Sa 10am-10pm, Su 10am-9pm. $46, seniors and disabled $40, children ages 3-6 or under 48 inches $34. Parking $10.) Alternately, get wet at the area's best collection of waterslides, Paramount's **Raging Waters,** located off US 101 at the Tully Rd. Exit. It's great on a hot day, but don't expect to be the only one seeking a soaking. (☎654-5450. Open June-Aug. daily 10am-6pm; May and Sept. Sa-Su 10am-6pm. $26, seniors $16, under 42 inches $19. After 3pm $20, under 42 inches $16.)

**Mission Santa Clara,** 500 El Camino Real, was the first California mission to honor a woman—Clare of Assisi—as its patron saint. The mission was established on the Guadalupe River in 1777, moving to its present site in 1825. Summer masses are held in the mission's beautiful church, complete with a functional organ. (Mass M-F noon, Su 10am.) **Santa Clara University,** which is built around the mission, was established in 1851, making it California's oldest institution of higher learning. Subsequent restorations have refitted the structures to match the beauty and bliss of the surrounding rose gardens and 200-year-old olive trees. Get a free parking pass from the university security guard as you drive in.

# SAN MATEO COUNTY                    ☎ 650

The bluffs of the San Mateo County Coast obscure the hectic urban pace of the city to the north. Most of the energy here is generated by the coastal winds and waves. The **Pacific Coast Highway (PCH)** maneuvers its way along a rocky shoreline past colorful beach vistas, generations-old ranches, and the small communities of Pacifica, Half Moon Bay, and Pescadero. The forests of La Honda and the suburban sprawl of Burlingame rest inland. Although it's possible to drive quickly down the coast from San Francisco to Santa Cruz, haste is waste—especially if you drive off a cliff.

## ■*▐ ORIENTATION & PRACTICAL INFORMATION

On this stretch of the Pacific coast, it's good to have a car. Stunning ocean views off **Highway 1** compete with the road for drivers' attentions. Hwy. 1 winds along the San Mateo County Coast from San Francisco to **Big Basin Redwoods State Park.** This expanse of shore is scattered with isolated, sandy beaches, most of which are too cold for swimming. Keep your eyes peeled for the unmarked, stunning, crowdless beaches along the coast. If traveling by foot, you'll have a tougher time. SamTrans services the area only somewhat successfully (see below). Bus route maps are available at CalTrain and BART stations. The shore from Pacifica to Half Moon Bay is serviced by buses #1C, 1L, and 90H.

**Public transportation: San Mateo County Transit (SamTrans),** 945 California Dr. (☎508-6455 or 800-660-4287; www.samtrans.com). Bus #17 and 294 service Half Moon Bay on a limited basis. #17 runs along the coast from El Granada to Half Moon Bay from 6am-5:30pm. #294 runs from Hillsdale to Linda Mar Park-and-Ride; San Mateo to Pacifica M-F from 5:30am-7:30pm, Sa-Su only from Linda Mar to Half Moon Bay. Bus route maps are available at CalTrain and BART stations; call for specific schedules. Adults $1.25, seniors and disabled 60¢, ages 5-17 75¢, under 5 free. Monthly pass $40, seniors and disabled $18, ages 5-17 $22.

**Bike Rental: The Bike Works,** 20 Stone Pine Ctr. (☎726-6708), off Main St. Friendly staff will set you up with a mountain bike ($7 per hr., $35 per day; helmet included). Open M-F 10am-6pm, Sa 10am-5pm, Su 11am-4pm.

**Visitor Information: Half Moon Bay Coastside Chamber of Commerce and Visitors Bureau,** 520 Kelly Ave. (☎726-8380; www.halfmoonbaychamber.org). An amiable staff, lots of brochures, and local bus service maps sit in a Victorian house just east of Hwy. 1. Open M-F 9am-4pm.

**San Mateo County Convention and Visitors Bureau,** Seabreeze Plaza, 111 Anza Blvd., #410 (☎800-288-4748). Get off Rte. 101 at the Broadway exit, follow signs to Airport Blvd., take a left, and follow road around to Anza Blvd. Turn left; it's the mirrored building on your right, across the street from the Embassy Hotel. Near SFO, this sleek office offers info on the Central Coast and San Francisco area, including brochures and helpful maps. Open M-F 8:30am-5pm.

**San Mateo County Parks and Recreation Department,** James V. Fitzgerald Marine Life Reserve, P.O. Box 451, Moss Beach (☎728-3584), off Hwy. 1, 7 mi. north of Half Moon Bay. Open daily dawn-dusk.

**Police: Half Moon Bay:** 537 Kelly Ave. (☎726-8288). **San Mateo General Information:** ☎522-7710.

**Internet Access: Half Moon Bay Library,** 620 Correas St. (☎726-2316), off Main St. Free Internet. Open M-W 10am-8pm, Th 1-8pm, F 10am-6pm, Sa 10am-5pm, Su 1-5pm.

**Post Office: Half Moon Bay:** 500 Stone Pine Rd., at Main St. Open M-F 8:30am-5pm, Sa 8:30am-noon. **San Mateo:** 1630 S. Delaware St. Open M-F 8:30am-5pm, Sa 8:30am-12:30pm. **Postal Code:** 94402 (San Mateo), 94019 (Half Moon Bay).

# ACCOMMODATIONS & CAMPING

**San Benito House,** 356 Main St. (☎726-3425). Your money will be well spent on one of San Benito House's 12 airy, pristine rooms, each impeccably decorated with antique furnishings. Most rooms have private baths with claw-footed bathtubs. Communal access to gleaming hall showers and sauna. Continental breakfast included; guests receive 10% off dinner Su and Th-Sa in the acclaimed restaurant downstairs. Bar open daily 4pm-around midnight. Check-in after 3pm. Check-out 11am. Reservations recommended. Rooms $75, with private bath $125, with living room suite $160. ❹

**HI-AYH Pigeon Point Lighthouse Hostel,** on Hwy. 1 (☎879-0633), 6 mi. south of Pescadero. 4 houses, each with a homey common room and equipped kitchen. 53 beds. Chores required. Check-in 4:30pm. Check-out 10am. Lockout 10am-4:30pm. Curfew 11pm. Reservations recommended. Phone reservations 5:30-10pm. Wheelchair-accessible. Dorms $15, non-members $18; extra $15 for 2-person rooms. ❶

**Costanoa,** 2001 Rossi Rd. (☎879-1100, reservations ☎262-7848; www.costanoa.com), on the east side of Rte 1, 25 mi. south of Half Moon Bay, between Pigeon Pt. and Año Nuevo. The Ritz Carlton of roughing it. All accommodations include access to dry sauna and showers with heated floors. Campsites $30-40; canvas cabins (includes heated mattress) $95-130; lodges $205-240. ❸

**Francis Beach Campground,** 95 Kelly Ave. (☎726-8820), on Francis Beach. 57 campsites with firepits and picnic tables. Clean bathrooms. June 1-Sept. 30 7-night max. stay; off-season 15-night max. stay. Check-out noon. Wheelchair-accessible. No reservations. Tent and RV sites $13; seniors $10. Hiker and biker sites $1 per person; 1-night max. stay. Day use of beach $2; seniors $1. Hot showers 25¢ per 2min. ❶

**HI-AYH Point Montara Lighthouse Hostel** (☎728-7177), on Lighthouse Point, at Hwy. 1 and 16th St., 25 mi. south of San Francisco and 4 mi. north of Half Moon Bay. SamTrans #294 stops 1 block north, though bus drivers will often drop you off at the lighthouse if you ask. Revel in this isolated 45-bed facility with 2 kitchens and serene surroundings. Ask for a room with a view of the coast. Laundry ($2 per load). Reception 7:30-10am and 4:30-9:30pm. Lockout 10am-4:30pm. Curfew 11pm. Make reservations well in advance for weekends, groups, and private rooms. Wheelchair-accessible. Members $17, non-members $20, children $12; $15 extra for private rooms. ❶

# FOOD

Despite the area's remote feel, a surprising number of restaurants cater to hungry travelers. Those looking for late-night snacks or planning to picnic can find a 24hr. **Safeway,** 70 N. Cabrillo Hwy. (☎726-1143), at the junction of Hwy. 1 and 92.

**3-Zero,** 8850 Hwy. 1 (☎728-1411, www.3-zero.com), at the Half Moon Bay Airport. Watch planes take off, while you stay grounded with your huge and hearty home style breakfast ($4-8). Menu and owner come equipped with wit and charm. Also serves "launch" (lunch; $5.50-8). Visit website for discounts. Open daily 7am-3pm. ❷

**Moon Juice,** Stone Pine Ctr. (☎712-1635), off Main St. Turn right off Rte. 92, head south on Main St., and Stone Pine Ctr. is on your left. Under new family management, this little juice and smoothie store will brighten your morning. Come for lunch, dinner, or snacks. Be sure to get a dose of wheatgrass for a moon-like glow. Juices $1.50-6. ❷

**The Flying Fish Grill** (☎712-1125), at Main St. and Rte. 92, by Tom and Pete's Market. This small roadside cafe serves inexpensive, local seafood. Famous fish tacos $3-4.35. Other oceanic offerings $7-14. Take-out available. Open Tu-Su 11:30am-8:30pm. ❷

**Half Moon Bay Brewing Co.,** 390 Capistrano Rd. (☎728-2739; www.hmbbrewingco.com), at the edge of Pillar Point Harbor in Princeton, half a mile from Mavericks. One of Half Moon Bay's singles hot spots. Fresh seafood $14-20; pub grub $8.50-13; and micro-brewed beers (pints $4.25). Ocean-view seating. Live music and dancing Su 4-8pm. Open Su-Th around 9:30pm, F-Sa around 10pm, bar stays open 1hr. later. ❷

**Jeffrey's,** 42 South B St. (☎348-8698). Somewhere between a dive and a nice family restaurant comes this hearty independent hamburger joint. Try an avocado burger ($5.50) or another pleasantly cheap menu item ($4-7). Open daily 11am-9pm. ❶

**Taqueria La Cumre,** 28 North B St. (☎344-8989). This restaurant, which also has a San Francisco branch, has won the "best burrito" award in every major Bay Area magazine. Filling and tasty Mexican meals for under $8.50. Be prepared for long lines at lunchtime. Open Su-Th 11am-9pm, F-Sa 11am-10pm. ❷

## 👁 🔼 SIGHTS & OUTDOOR ACTIVITIES

Wide, sandy, and fairly deserted **state beaches** dot the coast along Hwy. 1 (Cabrillo Hwy.) in San Mateo County. Each state beach charges $2, a fare which covers admission to *all* state parks for the entire day. All beaches have parking lots and restrooms and are open daily 8am-sunset. Keep your eyes peeled for unmarked beaches along the coast; they're often breathtaking, crowdless spots with free parking. The water is too chilly for most swimmers and surfers never venture out without full-body wetsuits. Rip currents and undertows are frequent, so be careful if you choose to brave the cold. The creeks near these beaches are often contaminated—signs will be posted at entrances to warn you, but simply staying out of them is generally a good idea.

**GRAY WHALE COVE BEACH.** This stunning beach, shielded by high bluffs from the highway above, used to be one of the more popular *private* nude beaches in the Bay Area. Now legendary as the first "clothing-optional" *state* beach, Gray Whale Cove offers some of the most gorgeous and not quite so gorgeous views on the coast. *(12 mi. south of San Francisco, in Devil's Slide—the curvy, cliffy stretch of Hwy. 1 a few mi. south of Pacifica. You'll know it by the large parking lot on your left; it's the only one in the Slide—the beach is across the street. Take SamTrans bus #1L. Open daily 8am-sunset. $2.)*

**HALF MOON BAY STATE BEACH.** Lining the coast next to town, **Half Moon Bay State Beach** is actually composed of several smaller beaches. The **Coastal Trail,** a paved path perfect for joggers, bikers, and dogwalkers, runs 3 mi. along all four beaches and then continues north. At the end of Kelly Ave., **Francis Beach** lies closest to town and is the southernmost of the four. Although it's the least scenic of the bunch, it is the only one with a campsite (**Francis Beach State Campground,** p. 156), a guard station that operates year-round, and wheelchair-accessibility. To the north of Francis, the wider and prettier **Venice Beach** is down a flight of stairs at the end of a dirt road leading from Venice Blvd. off Hwy. 1. **Dunes Beach** and **Roosevelt Beach** are down a short but steep trail at the end of Young Ave. off Hwy. 1. Strong tides and undertows make swimming dangerous at the beaches, but they also create great waves and winds for board- and windsurfing. Windsurfers have to go a ways out to sea to catch the strong gusts because the half-moon shape of the bay protects the shores, making for wonderful picnicking and sunbathing options. *(On the coast right next to the town of Half Moon Bay. Francis Beach ☎726-8820.)*

**DOWNTOWN HALF MOON BAY.** The **Community United Methodist Church,** built in 1872, stands as a well-kept example of the city's registered landmarks. The **Half Moon Bay Jail,** just two houses north of the church, was built in 1911 and used as an incarceration facility for the entire county. Today, the austere building houses artifacts from Half Moon Bay's Spanishtown. **Johnston House,** at the south end of Main St., built in 1853 by 49er James Johnston, is the earliest American home still standing along the San Mateo County coastline, as well as one of the few examples of "New England" salt box architecture on the West Coast. *(Church: at the corner of Johnston and Miramontes St. ☎726-4621. Jail: 505 Johnston St. ☎726-7084; www.spanish-townhs.org. Open Su and Sa 1-4pm. Johnston House: Drive to south end of Main St., make a left on Higgins Canyon Rd. ☎726-0329; www.johnstonhousehmb.org.)*

**SAN GREGORIO & POMPONIO STATE BEACHES.** These two beaches are dramatically set below **the most scenic stretch of Hwy. 1**. Of all of the beaches in the area, they are arguably the most picturesque—and often the most deserted. Walk to the southern end of San Gregorio to find little caves in the shore rocks. Between San Gregorio and Pomponio State Beaches, there allegedly rests a gorgeous, less frequented beach at the unmarked turnout at Marker 27.35 along Hwy. 1. It's difficult to find without aid; keep an eye out for mysteriously vacant cars parked along the highway. *(San Gregorio: 8 mi. south of Half Moon Bay. Pomponio: 10 mi. south of Half Moon Bay. Both open daily 8am-sunset. $2.)*

**PEBBLE BEACH & PIGEON POINT.** Though threatening signs attempt to discourage them from doing so, kids tend to pocket handfuls of tiny, smooth pebbles from **Pebble Beach.** Law-abiding parents have been known, however, to mail the stolen stones back to the Half Moon Bay Visitors Center. A paved and level trail heads south from the parking lot along the bluffs; reaching the tidal pools below for exploration requires a bit of a climb down. **Pigeon Point,** 4 mi. south of Pebble Beach, takes its name from a hapless schooner that crashed into the rocky shore on its inaugural voyage in 1853. The point turns heads with its tidepools, 30 ft. plumes of surf, and 115 ft. operating lighthouse (the tallest on the West Coast) which houses 1008 glass prisms. *(Pebble Beach: 19 mi. south of Half Moon Bay, 2 mi. south of Pescadero Rd. Open 8am-sunset. $2. Pigeon Point: 23 mi. south of Half Moon Bay, 6 mi. south of Pescadero Rd. Lighthouse and Point info ☎879-2120. Hostel: ☎879-0633.)*

**AÑO NUEVO STATE RESERVE.** This wildlife reserve has several hiking trails that offer views of Año Nuevo Island, the site of an abandoned lighthouse now taken over by birds, seals, and sea lions. Free hiking permits are available at the ranger station by the entrance and at the **Visitors Center** (though seal-viewing permits are only issued up until 3:30pm). The Visitors Center also features real-time videos displaying the animal adventures on the island. From mid-December to late March, the reserve is the mating place of the 15 ft., 4500 lb. **elephant seal.** Thousands of fat seals crowd the shore and like frat boys looking to score, the males fight each other for dominance over a herd of females. Before mid-August, you can still see the last of the "molters" and the young who have yet to find their sea legs. Don't get too close—if they don't get you, the cops might; law requires staying 25 ft. away at all times. *(50 mi. south of San Francisco, 25 mi. south of Half Moon Bay, and 20 mi. north of Santa Cruz. Park information ☎879-0227. No pets. Open daily 8am-sunset. Visitors Center open daily 8:30am-3:30pm. Parking $2; seniors $1.)*

**HILLER AVIATION MUSEUM.** This impressively packed museum features flying machines from past and present, as well as imaginative renditions of future models. *(601 Skyway Rd. From San Francisco take US 101 south to Holly St./Redwood Shores Pkwy. exit. Go east onto Redwood Shores Pkwy., right onto Airport Rd., and right onto Skyway Rd. ☎654-0200. Open daily 10am-5pm. Adults $8, seniors and ages 8-17 $5, under 8 free.)*

**COYOTE POINT RECREATION AREA & MUSEUM.** For the animal enthusiast, the recreation area features a small but impressive array of live animals in natural habitats, including an aviary and an aquarium. The park also offers great waterside views of the planes flying into SFO. *(1651 Coyote Point Dr. From San Francisco, take US*

*101 to Poplar Ave. Exit just south of the airport. Follow signs into Coyote Point Recreation Area and Museum. Recreation Area: ☎573-2592. Open in summer 8am-8pm; in winter 8am-5:30pm. Park admission $4 per car. Museum: ☎ 342-7755. Open Su noon-5pm, Tu-Sa 10am-5pm. $3, seniors and ages 13-17 $2, ages 4-12 $1, under 12 free.)*

**PARKS AND TRAILS. Memorial County Park** offers 65 mi. of redwood trails, open to hiking, horseback riding, and some to bicycling, stretching through three parks. The **Heritage Grove** spans 12 sq. mi. and has the oldest and largest redwood trees in the Santa Cruz mountains. Among the many redwood parks, **Butano State Park** also stands out for its sweeping views of the Pacific Ocean. Its 3200 acres offers 20 mi. of hiking and mountain biking trails off Pescadero Rd., 9 mi east of Hwy. 1. For those who prefer concrete but still want scenic settings, the **Sawyer Camp Trail** is popular among the local bicyclist, inline skater, jogger, and hiker set. It stretches 10 mi. along the Crystal Springs reservoir. *(Memorial: Pescadero Rd. Go east from Hwy. 1 to Cloverdale. ☎879-0212. Visitor Center open May-Sept. daily 10am-4pm. Heritage: Pescadero Rd. to Alpine, make a right. Butano: 5 mi. south of Pescadero. From the north, take Pescadero Rd. east from Hwy. 1 to Cloverdale. From the south, take Gazos Creek from Hwy. 1 to Cloverdale. ☎879-2040. Sawyer: 1801 Crystal Springs Rd. ☎589-4294. Open M-F. Prior to arrival, visitors with disabilities who need assistance should contact ☎800-777-0369; www.parks.ca.gov.)*

**FILOLI ESTATE.** If "old money" is your bag, check out this rare example of an early 1900s country estate, including a pristine Gregorian Revival House and a magnificent 16-acre garden. *(On Canada Road. From San Fran, take I-280 South to Edgewood Rd. West, turn right on Canada Rd. ☎364-8300; www.filoli.org. House and Garden tours Tu-Sa 10am-2:30pm. Closed Oct.-Feb. Adults $10, children 7-12 $1, under 7 free, students $5.)*

**BURLINGAME MUSEUM OF PEZ MEMORABILIA.** Admission to the largest public display of Pez Candy dispensers in the world is (thankfully) free. Enjoy the smaller (bite-sized) things in life at this once-in-a-lifetime stop. *(214 California Dr., between Burlingame and Howard Ave. Get off US 101 at Broadway Ave., head west, and turn left on California Dr. Also accessible by CalTrain; get off at the Burlingame Station. ☎347-2301; www.burlingamepezmuseum.com. Open Tu-Sa 10am-6pm.)*

**LA HONDA.** A winding cross-peninsular trip down Rte. 84 will bring you to the little logging town in the redwoods where author Ken Kesey lived with his merry pranksters in the 1960s, before it got too small and they took off across the US in a psychedelic bus. The shady, scenic drive makes this detour worthwhile, even if you aren't familiar with Kesey's gang, but *Let's Go* recommends reading a copy of Tom Wolfe's █*The Electric Kool-Aid Acid Test* before making the journey.

# NORTH BAY & WINE COUNTRY

## MARIN COUNTY                    ☎415

Just across the Golden Gate Bridge, the jacuzzi of the bay—Marin (muh-RIN) County—bubbles over with enthusiastic (some might say dogmatic) residents who help the area strike a nice balance between upscale chic and counterculture nostalgia. If the new VW Beetle were sold nowhere but here, Volkswagen still might reap a tidy profit. Marin is strikingly beautiful, politically liberal, and visibly wealthy. The locals might seem a bit smug, but protective scowls give way to pleasant smiles when visitors appreciate the land and care for it as their own. The cathedral stillness of ancient redwoods, sweet smell of eucalyptus (though not a native species), brilliant wildflowers, high bluffs, and crashing surf along Hwy. 1 are ample justification for civic pride and earnest preservation concerns.

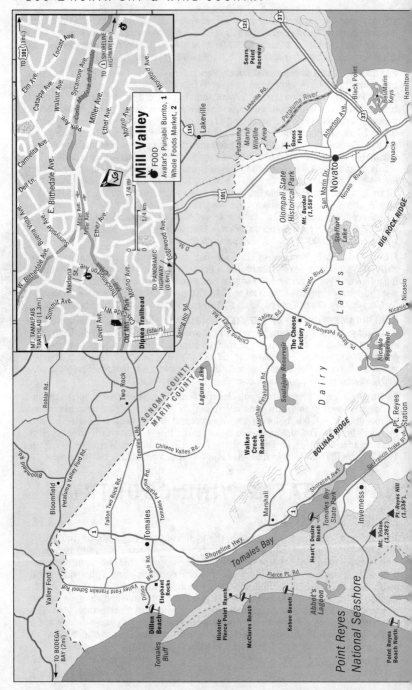

## Mill Valley

● FOOD
Avatar's Punjabi Burrito, **1**
Whole Foods Market, **2**

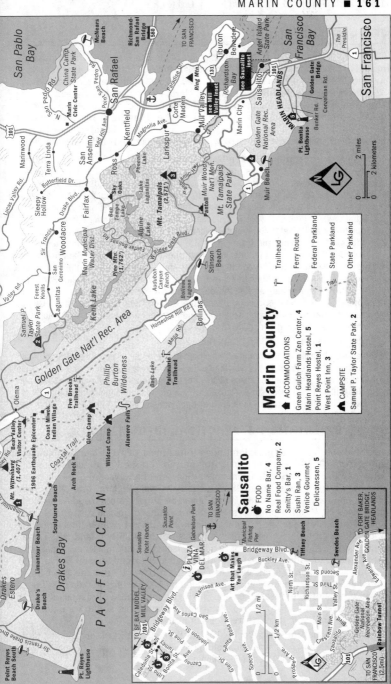

**Marin County**

▲ ACCOMMODATIONS
Green Gulch Farm Zen Center, **4**
Marin Headlands Hostel, **5**
Point Reyes Hostel, **1**
West Point Inn, **3**

▲ CAMPSITE
Samuel P. Taylor State Park, **2**

**Sausalito**

● FOOD
No Name Bar, **4**
Real Food Company, **2**
Smitty's Bar, **1**
Sushi Ran, **3**
Venice Gourmet Delicatessen, **5**

# ☞ TRANSPORTATION

The Marin peninsula lies at the northern end of the San Francisco Bay and is connected to the city by **US 101** via the **Golden Gate Bridge.** US 101 extends north inland to Santa Rosa and Sonoma County, while **Hwy. 1** winds north along the Pacific coast. The **Richmond-San Rafael Bridge** connects Marin to the East Bay via **I-580. Gas** is scarce and expensive in West Marin, so fill up in town before you head out for the coast. If you start running low in West Marin, head toward Point Reyes Station where you'll find one of few gas stations in the area. Drivers should exercise caution in West Marin, where roads are narrow, sinuous, and perched on the edges of cliffs.

**Public Transportation: Golden Gate Transit** (☎ 455-2000, in SF 923-2000; www.goldengate.org; phones operated M-F 7am-7pm, Sa-Su 8am-6pm), provides bus service between San Francisco and Marin County via the Golden Gate Bridge, as well as local service in Marin. Within Marin County, bus #63 runs on the weekends from Marin City through Sausalito, Mount Tamalpais State Park, and Stinson Beach (adults $4.75, under 18 $3.65, seniors and disabled $2.40, under 6 free). Bus #65 goes from San Rafael to Samuel P. Taylor Park and Point Reyes Station on weekends (adults $3.30, seniors and disabled $1.65, under 6 free). **West Marin Stagecoach** (☎ 526-3239; www.marin-stagecoach.org; phones operated daily 8am-5pm) now provides **weekday service** connecting West Marin communities to the rest of the county. Stops include: Muir Beach, Pt. Reyes Station, Samuel P. Taylor Park, and Stinson Beach. Anyone can flag the bus to pull over or drop off between scheduled stops, provided there is a safe place. Free Golden Gate Transit transfers. Call or check the website for specific schedules and more detailed routes. $1.50 each way; seniors, disabled, and under 18 75¢.

**Taxis: Belaire Cab Co.** (☎ 388-1234). Open 24hr.

**Bike Rental: Cycle Analysis,** out of a hitch-up in the empty, grassy lot at 4th and Main St. off Hwy. 1 in **Point Reyes Station** (☎ 663-9164; www.cyclepointreyes.com). Cycle Analysis rents unsuspended bikes ($30), front-suspension mountain bikes ($35), and child trailers ($25-30). Helmets included. Also provides emergency repairs and offer advice for self-guided tours. Open M-Th by appointment, F-Su 10am-5pm.

# ✷ ☎ ORIENTATION & PRACTICAL INFORMATION

National seashore and park land constitutes most of West Marin. **Highway 1** splits from US 101 north of Sausalito and runs up the Pacific coast through Muir Beach, Stinson Beach, Olema, Inverness, and Pt. Reyes. About 4 mi. north of where Hwy. 1 splits from US 101, the **Panoramic Highway** branches off of Hwy. 1 and winds its way up to **Mount Tamalpais** and the Muir Woods. The **Marin Headlands** sit 10 mi. from downtown San Francisco, just across the Golden Gate Bridge. Beaches and coastal wonders line Hwy. 1, which runs along the Marin coast from Marin City and continues north. Slightly inland, Mt. Tamalpais is about 15 mi. northwest of San Francisco; the state park encompasses a large area just inside the coast from Muir Beach to around Stinson Beach. Muir Woods stands about 5 mi. west of US 101 on Hwy. 1. And the **Point Reyes National Seashore,** a near-island surrounded by 100 mi. of isolated coastline, is a wilderness of pine forests, chaparral ridges, and grassy flatlands, about 15 mi. northwest of San Francisco. **Point Reyes Station** sits about 2 mi. north of Olema and about 20 mi. northwest of San Francisco.

**Visitor Information: Marin County Visitors Bureau,** 1013 Larkspur Landing Circle (☎ 499-5000; www.visitmarin.org), off the Sir Francis Drake Blvd. Exit from US 101, near the ferry terminal. Open M-F 9am-5pm.

**Park Visitor Information:**

**Marin Headlands Visitors Center,** Bldg. 948, Fort Barry (☎331-1540), at Bunker and Field Rd. Talk to the helpful staff about hiking and biking in the park and pick up maps, trail advice, and permits for free campsites. The center is also a museum and a store with artifacts. Open daily 9:30am-4:30pm. Wheelchair accessible.

**Point Reyes National Seashore Headquarters** (also referred to as **Bear Valley Visitor Center;** ☎464-5100; www.nps.gov/pore), on Bear Valley Rd., a half-mile west of Olema. Rangers distribute camping permits, maps, and sage advice on trails, tides, and weather conditions, and lead guided hikes. The headquarters house excellent exhibits on the cultural and natural history of Pt. Reyes. Open M-F 9am-5pm, Sa-Su and holidays 8am-5pm.

**Pan Toll Ranger's Station,** 801 Panoramic Hwy. (☎388-2070), in Mt. Tamalpais State Park, about 2½ mi. inland from Stinson Beach. Operates Mt. Tam's campgrounds and trails. Rangers offer suggestions and explain restrictions on the trails. Bus #63 stops on the weekends (about 8 times daily) at the Ranger's Station.

**Muir Woods National Monument Visitors Center** (☎388-2596; www.nps.gov/muwo), near the entrance to Muir Woods. Muir Woods trail map $1 (free download on website). Great selection of hiking, biking, and driving maps of Marin and Mt. Tam. Open daily 9am-6pm.

**Library: Stinson Beach Library,** 3521 Shoreline Hwy. (☎868-0252). Free Internet Open M 10am-1pm, Tu 1-5pm and 6-9pm, F 10am-1pm and 2-6pm, Sa 10am-1pm.

**Police:** ☎258-4610 in San Anselmo. **Marin County Sheriff:** ☎479-2311.

**Medical Services: Marin General Hospital and Community Clinic,** 250 Bon Air Rd. (☎925-7000, clinic ☎461-7400), in **Greenbrae,** off the US 101 San Anselmo exit. 24hr. emergency care. Clinic open for appointment only M and Th 8am-7pm, W 9am-7pm, Tu and F 8am-5pm.

**Post Office:** In **Stinson Beach:** 15 Calle Del Mar, at Shoreline Hwy. Open M-F 8:30am-5pm. **Postal Code:** 94970.

# ▛ ACCOMMODATIONS

▩ **West Point Inn** (info ☎388-9955, reservations ☎646-0702), on Mt. Tamalpais, 2 mi. up Stage Rd. Park at the Pan Toll Ranger Station ($4) and hike or bike up. Not the lap of luxury, but one hell of an experience. This turn-of-the-century inn was built in 1904 and hasn't changed much since. Propane-generated heat, light, and refrigeration. No other electricity around. 35-person capacity. 7 private rooms. 5 private cabins. Well-equipped shared kitchen. $30, under 18 $15, under 5 free. Bring your own linens, sleeping bags, food, and flashlight, but not your pets. Reservations required. Sa vacancies are rare. Closed Su and M nights. Call for handicap arrangements. If you want to visit, but not for the night, West Point offers a pancake breakfast on the 3rd Su of the month May-Oct. 9am-1pm. Adults $6, children $5. ❹

**Green Gulch Farm Zen Center,** 1601 Shoreline Hwy. (☎383-3134; www.sfzc.org). If your hostel just isn't enlightened enough, Green Gulch's guest student program allows serious students of Zen to stay at the center for $15 per night for a minimum of 3 days and up to 6 weeks. Singles $75-90; doubles $125-140. ❹

**Marin Headlands Hostel (HI-AYH),** Bldg. 941 on Rosenstock (☎331-2777 or 800-909-4776; www.headlandshostel.homestead.com), up the hill from the Visitors Center and next to the Headlands Center for the Arts. Two spacious and immaculate Victorian houses, with 100 beds, a game room, kitchens, and common rooms. Internet 10¢ per min. Linen $1; towels 50¢. Laundry $1.50. Key deposit $10. 15 nights per yr. max. stay. Check-in 3:30-10:30pm. Check-out 10am. Lockout 10am-3:30pm. Reservations recommended 2 months in advance for private rooms and weekends. Dorms $18, under 17 (with parent) $9. Private rooms for 2 or more people $54. ❷

## ⚑ CAMPING

**The Headlands** (☎331-1540; www.nps.gov/goga/camping/index.htm) offers 3 small walk-in campgrounds with 11 primitive campsites for individual backpackers and small groups. Bring your own water and camp stove. No fires allowed. No pets either. Showers and kitchen ($2 each) at Headlands Hostel (p. 163). Free outdoor cold showers at Rodeo Beach. 3-day max. stay per site; 9-day max. stay per year. Reserve up to 90 days in advance. For all campgrounds, individual sites are free with a permit that can be obtained at the Headlands Visitors Center (p. 163). ❶

**Kirby Cove** (☎ 800-365-2267), off Conzelman Rd. west of the Golden Gate Bridge, in the Marin Headlands. Accessible by car, it consists of 4 campsites in a grove of cypress and eucalyptus trees on the shore, with fire rings and pit toilets. Kirby Cove is designed for larger groups. Bring your own water. No pets. 3-day max. stay; 1 weekend reservation per group per year. Open Apr.-Nov. Sites $25. ❷

**Point Reyes National Seashore** (☎663-8054; www.nps.gov/pore; open for reservations M-F 9am-2pm, walk-in 9am-5pm) has walk-in and boat-in camping only. Two camps are coastal and 2 are inland—some have exquisite ocean views. Charcoal grills, non-potable running water, and pit toilets. 4-night max. stay. Reservations recommended. Sites for 1-6 people $12. Boat-in camping at Tomales Bay; call or check web page for info. Pick up permits at Point Reyes National Seashore Headquarters (p. 164). ❶

**Samuel P. Taylor State Park,** P.O. Box 251 (☎488-9897; www.parks.ca.gov; Reserve America 800-444-7275; www.park-net.com), on Sir Francis Drake Blvd., 15 mi. west of San Rafael in **Lagunitas.** A family campground in a lush setting beneath stately, second-growth redwoods. Often crowded on weekends. Sites are shady, though not always quiet. Running water, flush toilets, and free hot showers. Day-use parking $4. 7-night max. stay. Check-out noon. Reservations recommended. Sites $15, seniors $13. Hike/bike sites 2-night max. stay and no reservations. $2 per person. ❶

## ◨ FOOD

Marinites take their fruit juices, tofu, and non-fat double-shot cappuccinos very seriously. Restaurateurs know this and raise both alfalfa sprouts and prices. You can always stock up for the ferry ride home in Sausalito with the organic produce from **Real Food Company,** 200 Caledonia St. (☎332-9640. Open daily 9am-9pm.) In Mill Valley on the outskirts of town, **Whole Foods,** 414 Miller Ave., specializes in organic groceries. (☎381-1200. Open daily 8am-8pm.)

### SAUSALITO

**Venice Gourmet Delicatessen,** 625 Bridgeway (☎332-3544; www.venicegourmet.com). Serves sharable sandwiches ($6) and side dishes ($3-5) in a Mediterranean-style marketplace with water-side seating. Open daily in summer 9am-7pm; in winter 9am-6pm. ❷

**Sushi Ran,** 107 Caledonia St. (☎332-3620; www.sushiran.com), is a local favorite. It offers upscale Asian fare, including *sake* bar and vegetarian *maki*. California roll $6.50. Open for lunch M-F 11:30am-2:30pm; dinner M-Sa 5:30-11pm, Su 5:30-10:30pm. ❺

### ELSEWHERE IN MARIN COUNTY

▩ **Avatar's Punjabi Burrito,** 15 Madrona St. (☎381-8293), in Mill Valley. Take chickpeas, rice, chutney, yogurt, and spice. Add tofu and veggies or other things nice. Wrap in yummy Indian bread, and you have a delicious meal for $5.50-8.50. Rice plates and mango lassi also available. Open M-Sa 11am-8pm. ❷

**Bubba's Diner,** 566 San Anselmo Ave. (☎459-6862), in San Anselmo. A local favorite that serves all the essentials with daily specials. "Bubbas famous oyster sandwich" $13. Open M and W-F 9am-2pm and 5:30-9pm, Sa-Su 8am-2:30pm and 5:30-9:30pm. ❸

**Comforts,** 335 San Anselmo Ave (☎454-9840), in San Anselmo. Delivers upscale deli counter delectables like pasta, chili, and salads at $3.50 per half-pound in addition to made-to-order hot and cold sandwiches ($6.50). Open M-F 6:30am-7:30pm, Sa 7:30am-7:30pm, Su 8:30am-3pm. ❷

## 🔆 🔥 SIGHTS AND OUTDOOR ACTIVITIES

Marin's proximity to San Francisco makes it a popular daytrip destination. Virtually everything worth seeing or doing in Marin is outdoors. An efficient visitor can hop from park to park and enjoy several short hikes along the coast and through the redwood forests in the same day, topping it off with a pleasant dinner in one of the small cities. Those without cars, however, may find it easier to use one of the two well-situated hostels as a base for hiking or biking explorations.

### SAUSALITO
Originally a fishing center full of bars and bordellos, the city at Marin's extreme southeastern tip has long since traded its sea-dog days for retail boutiques and overpriced seafood restaurants. The palm trees and 14 ft. elephant statues of Plaza de Vina del Mar Park look out over a wonderful view of San Francisco Bay, making for a sunny, self-consciously Mediterraneanesque excursion. The sheer number and variety of quality art galleries in the small town make it worth checking out, regardless of the touristy feel.

Half a mile north of the town center is the **Bay Model and Marinship Museum,** 2100 Bridgeway, a massive working model of San Francisco Bay. Built in the 1950s to test proposals to dam the bay, the water-filled model recreates tides and currents in great detail. (☎332-1851. Open Tu-Sa 9am-4pm. Free.)

### MARIN HEADLANDS
The fog-shrouded hills just west of the Golden Gate Bridge constitute the Marin Headlands. These windswept ridges, precipitous cliffs, and hidden sandy beaches offer superb hiking and biking minutes from downtown. For instant gratification, drive up to any of the look-out spots and pose for your own postcard-perfect shot of the Golden Gate Bridge and the city skyline, or take a short walk out to Point Bonita. If you intend to do more serious hiking or biking, choose one of the coastal trails that provide easy access to dark sand beaches and dramatic cliffs of basalt greenstone. Either way, bring a jacket in case of sudden wind, rain, or fog.

**POINT BONITA.** One of the best short hikes is to the lighthouse at Point Bonita, a prime spot for seeing sunbathing California sea lions in summer and migrating gray whales in the cooler months. The cute little lighthouse at the end of the point really doesn't seem up to the job of guarding the whole San Francisco Bay, but has done so valiantly since 1855; in fact, its original glass lens is still in operation. At the end of a narrow, knife-like ridge lined with purple wildflowers, the lighthouse is reached by a short tunnel through the rock and a miniature suspension bridge. Even when the lighthouse is closed, the short walk (1 mi. from the Visitors Center, a half-mile from the nearest parking) provides gorgeous views on sunny days. *(Lighthouse: 1 mi. from Visitors Center, ½ mi. from nearest parking. Open M and Sa-Su 12:30-3:30pm. Guided walks M and Sa-Su 12:30pm. Free. No dogs or bikes through tunnel.)*

**BIG GUNS.** Formerly a military installation charged with defending the San Francisco harbor, the Headlands are dotted with machine gun nests, missile sites, and soldiers' quarters dating from the Spanish-American War to the 1950s. **Battery Spencer,** on Conzelman Rd. immediately west of US 101, offers one of the best views of the city skyline and the Golden Gate Bridge, especially around sunset on

## THE LOCAL LEGEND

### BURNING GREASE

People have been riding bikes "off-road" for as long as they have been riding bikes. But mountain biking (the extreme, knee-shattering sport) was born in Marin County in the early 70s, when a group of hotshot road racers headed out to Mt. Tamalpais's rocky fire roads.

Gary Fisher, Charlie Kelly, Joe Breeze, and others rode 30s bikes with fat balloon tires and coaster brakes that handled the rough terrain better than their fancy road bikes. Eventually, someone made the fateful claim, "I'm fastest."

In October 1976, the first **Repack race** was held on northern Mt. Tamalpais, down a steep, winding 2 mi. course with a 1300 ft. drop. By the course's end, all the grease in the bike's coasters had vaporized, and the racers finished trailing a plume of smoke. After each race, the brakes needed to be re-packed with grease (hence the race's name).

Enthusiasts came together yearly at Repack, trading ideas to improve the sport and their equipment. Fisher added derailleur gears and Breeze built the first modern frame. In 1979, Fisher, Kelly, and Tom Ritchey collaborated to create MountainBikes, the first exclusively off-road bike company.

the (rare) clear day. Farther into the park is the **NIKE Missile Site** on Field Rd. *(Battery Spencer on Conzelman Rd. just west of US 101. NIKE Missile Site on Field Rd., at Fort Berry and Fort Cronkite. ☎331-1453. Open W-F and 1st Su of the month 12:30-3:30pm.)*

**OTHER ACTIVITIES.** The 1 mi. walk from the Visitors Center down to sheltered **Rodeo Beach,** a favorite of cormorants and pelicans, is easy and pleasant. For more ambitious hiking or biking, a good map is a must. Pick one up at the **Visitors Center** at Bunker and Field Rd. (up to $1.50). The **Wolf Ridge** and **Tennessee Valley** trails are perennial favorites; ask rangers for other suggestions and camping info. Bring a jacket for the sudden descent of rain, wind, or fog.

## MOUNT TAMALPAIS & MUIR WOODS

Between the upscale towns of East Marin and the rocky bluffs of West Marin rests beautiful **Mount Tamalpais State Park** (tam-ull-PIE-us). The park has miles of hilly, challenging trails on and around 2571 ft. Mount Tamalpais, the original "mountain" in "mountain bike." The bubbling waterfall on **Cataract Trail** and the **Gardner Lookout** on Mount Tam's east peak are worthy destinations. Visit the **Pan Toll Ranger's Station,** on Panoramic Hwy., for trail suggestions and biking restrictions. Although this is the home of the mountain bike, cyclists that go off designated trails and fire roads risk incurring the wrath of eco-happy Marin hikers. On weekends and holidays, bus #63 stops at the ranger station between the Golden Gate Bridge and Stinson Beach. (☎388-2070. Free. Parking up to $2.)

At the center of the state park is **Muir Woods National Monument,** a 560-acre stand of old coastal redwoods 5 mi. west of US 101 on Hwy. 1. (Open 8am-dusk.) Spared from logging by the steep sides of Redwood Canyon, these massive, centuries-old redwoods are shrouded in silence. The level, paved trails along the canyon floor are lined with wooden fences, but a hike up the canyon's sides will soon take you away from the tourists and face-to-face with wildlife. (☎388-2595. Open 9am-6pm. $2.) Avoid the fee by hiking in 2 mi. from the Pan Toll Ranger Station.

## MARIN COAST

**Highway 1** reaches the Pacific at Muir Beach and then twists its way up the rugged coast. It's all beautiful, but the stretch between Muir and Stinson Beaches is the most breathtaking, especially when driving south on the sheer-drop-to-the-ocean side of the highway. If you're riding a bike, don't expect the white-knuckled drivers of passing cars to allow you much elbow room.

**BEACHES.** Sheltered **Muir Beach** is scenic and popular with families. The crowds thin out significantly after a 5min. climb on the shore rocks to the left. Six miles to the north, **Stinson Beach** attracts a younger, rowdier, better-looking surfer crowd, although cold and windy conditions often leave them languishing on dry land. The Bard visits Stinson Beach from July to October during **Shakespeare at Stinson.** Between Muir and Stinson Beaches lies the nude **Red Rocks Beach,** a secluded spot reached by a steep hike down from a parking area 1 mi. south of Stinson Beach. *(Muir Beach open dawn-9pm. Stinson Beach open dawn-dusk. ☎868-1115; www.shakespeareat-stinson.org. Bus #63 runs from Sausalito to Stinson Beach on weekends and holidays.)*

**ZEN CENTER.** Just inland from Muir Beach is the **Green Gulch Farm Zen Center,** a Buddhist community, retreat, and organic farm. Visitors are free to explore the tranquil grounds and gardens and on Sunday mornings the public is welcome at meditation (9:25am) followed by a lecture on Zen Buddhism (10:15am) and tea. Would-be Zen masters are asked to wear dark, loose-fitting clothing for *zazen* meditation. *(1601 Shoreline Hwy. ☎383-3134; www.sfzc.org. Su parking $5, free when 3+ people carpool.)*

**BOLINAS.** Continuing a few miles northwest from Stinson Beach along Hwy. 1, you'll find the **Audubon Canyon Ranch.** Dedicated to preserving the surrounding lands as well as other areas in Marin and Sonoma counties, the ranch provides educational programs and conducts several research projects. Come watch great blue herons and great egrets nest, or go for a hike on the 8 mi. of trails. Immediately past the lagoon is the unmarked turn-off for the village of Bolinas—a tiny colony of hippies, artists, and writers. Many of the tiny art galleries and eateries that dot the town have no set hours, and watching three generations of hippies walk side-by-side down the street emphasizes the village's strong atemporal vibe. Eccentric Bolinas residents have included authors Richard Brautigan *(Trout Fishing in America)* and Jim Carroll *(The Basketball Diaries).* To graze while you gaze, try Northern California cuisine at **Coast Cafe,** open for breakfast, lunch, and dinner, but don't tell them we sent you. For years, locals have hoped to discourage tourist traffic by tearing down any and all signs marking the Bolinas-Olema road. Press coverage of the "sign war" won the people of Bolinas exactly the publicity they wanted to avoid, but for now, at least, the town remains unspoiled in ways that Sausalito is not—and they intend to keep it that way, so don't expect to feel welcomed. But who needs signs anyway? Driving north from Stinson Beach, the Bolinas-Olema road is the first left after coming around the lagoon; turn there and follow the road to the end. From Olema, take Hwy. 1, and hang a right after (or on) Horseshoe Hill Rd. before the lagoon.*(Driving north from Stinson Beach, the Bolinas-Olema road is the first left after coming around the lagoon; turn and follow the road to the end. From Olema, take Hwy. 1, and hang a right after (or on) Horseshoe Hill Rd. before the lagoon.Audubon: Across from the Bolina Lagoon. ☎868-9244; www.egret.org. Open mid-Mar. to mid-July Sa-Su 10am-4pm, Tu-F 2-4pm by appointment. Coast Cafe: 46 Wharf Rd. ☎868-2298.)*

## POINT REYES

A near-island surrounded by nearly 100 mi. of isolated coastline, the **Point Reyes National Seashore** is a wilderness of pine forests, chaparral ridges, and grassy flatlands. Five million years ago, this outcropping was a suburb of Los Angeles, but it hitched a ride on the submerged Pacific Plate and has been creeping northward along the San Andreas Fault ever since. In summer, colorful **wildflowers** attract crowds of gawking tourists, but with hundreds of miles of amazing trails, it's quite possible to gawk alone. Hwy. 1 provides direct access to the park from the north or south; Sir Francis Drake Blvd. comes west from US 101 at San Rafael.

The park headquarters are at the **Point Reyes National Seashore Headquarters,** just west of Olema. There, rangers distribute camping permits and can suggest trails, drives, beaches, and picnic areas. *(☎464-5100; www.nps.gov/pore. Open M-F 9am-5pm, Sa-Su 8am-5pm.)* The **Earthquake Trail** is a three-quarters of a mile walk along the infamous San Andreas Fault Line that starts right at Bear Valley. Lovely **Limantour**

BAY AREA

**Beach** sits at the end of Limantour Rd., 8 mi. west of the Visitors Center, which runs a free shuttle bus to the beach in summer. The ◙**Point Reyes Hostel** is at the bottom of a steep valley, 2 mi. from the end of Limantour Rd. The dramatic landscape around the hostel is still scarred by a major forest fire that torched the region in 1995. Both Limantour and Point Reyes Beaches have high, grassy dunes and long stretches of sand, but strong ocean currents along the point make swimming very dangerous. Swimming is safest at **Hearts Desire Beach,** north of the Visitors Center on sheltered **Tomales Bay.** To reach the dramatic **Point Reyes Lighthouse** at the very tip of the point, follow Sir Francis Drake Blvd. to its end (20 mi. from the Visitors Center) and head right along the stairway to Sea Lion Overlook. From December until February, migrating gray whales can be spotted from the overlook. (Lighthouse Visitors Center ☎669-1534. Open Th-M 10am-4:30pm.)

## SAN RAFAEL

San Rafael is the largest city in Marin County, but it holds little to interest the budget traveler. If you do stop here on your way to or from Northern California, the main strip for eating and shopping lies along **4th Street.**

If you have a car, you might picnic at **China Camp State Park,** an expanse of grassy meadows east of the city. It's named for the ramshackle remains of a Chinese fishing village that once housed thousands of laborers who were forced from the city. (Open daily 8am-8pm; Visitors Center open daily 10am-5pm. Parking $3.) Six miles north of San Rafael is an exit for Lucas Valley Rd., where Jedi master George Lucas toils away at **Skywalker Ranch,** crafting the next installment of the Star Wars saga. There's no point in stopping for a sneak preview—Lucas's home and studios are fiercely guarded by Imperial stormtroopers.

## ◙ NIGHTLIFE

If you really wanted to party, you'd head back to the city, but Marin County does offer a number of low-key live music venues and easygoing watering holes. San Rafael probably has the most action, with many more bars than are listed here.

**New George's,** 842 4th St. (☎457-1515; www.newgeorges.com), in San Rafael, under a movie-style marquee at Cijos St., is the frequent winner of the "best live music and nightlife in Marin" award. The daytime cafe becomes a jumping club by night. Live music Tu-Sa at 9pm. Latin music Su nights. Cover charge varies. Open daily 2pm-2am.

**Smitty's Bar,** 214 Caledonia St. (☎332-2637), in Sausalito. Has resisted upward mobility to remain a rough around the edges favorite of Sausalito's "boat people." Shuffleboard, pool, 3 TVs, and a wall of bowling trophies to admire. Domestic pints $2.75, schooners $3.75, pitchers $7. Open daily 10am-2am.

**No Name Bar,** 757 Bridgeway (☎332-1392), in Sausalito. Once a haunt of the Beats, the bar with no name now serves a mixed crowd of tourists and locals. Heated patio out back. Live blues or jazz music most nights—the biggest draw is Dixieland Jazz every Su afternoon (no cover). Rudimentary sandwich menu 11am-4pm. Open 10am-2am.

# NAPA VALLEY ☎707

Napa catapulted American wine into the big leagues in 1976, when a bottle of red from Napa's **Stag's Leap Vineyards** beat a bottle of critically acclaimed (and unfailingly French) Château Lafitte-Rothschild in a blind taste test in Paris. While not the oldest, and not necessarily the best, Napa Valley is certainly the best-known of America's wine-growing regions. Its golden hills, natural hot springs, and sunlight inspired Gold Rush millionaires to build luxury spas for vacationers in the 1850s. Indeed, it wasn't until the 1960s, when the now big-name wineries like Mondavi first opened, that the region was able to assert itself not as a spa retreat, but as

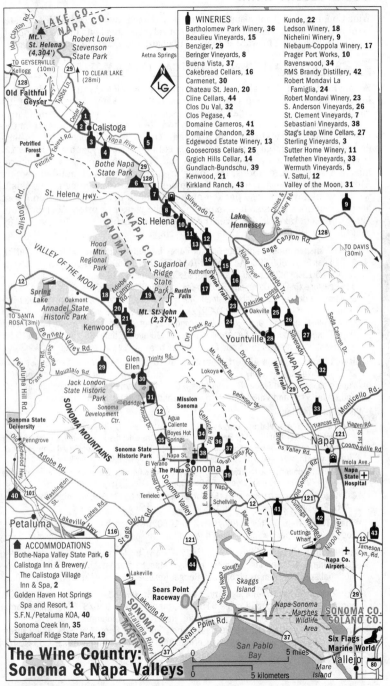

**WINERIES**

Bartholomew Park Winery, **36**
Beaulieu Vineyards, **15**
Benziger, **29**
Beringer Vineyards, **8**
Buena Vista, **37**
Cakebread Cellars, **16**
Carmenet, **30**
Chateau St. Jean, **20**
Cline Cellars, **44**
Clos Du Val, **32**
Clos Pegase, **4**
Domaine Carneros, **41**
Domaine Chandon, **28**
Edgewood Estate Winery, **13**
Goosecross Cellars, **25**
Grgich Hills Cellar, **14**
Gundlach-Bundschu, **39**
Kenwood, **21**
Kirkland Ranch, **43**

Kunde, **22**
Ledson Winery, **18**
Nichelini Winery, **9**
Niebaum-Coppola Winery, **17**
Prager Port Works, **10**
Ravenswood, **34**
RMS Brandy Distillery, **42**
Robert Mondavi La
  Famiglia, **24**
Robert Mondavi Winery, **23**
S. Anderson Vineyards, **26**
St. Clement Vineyards, **7**
Sebastiani Vineyards, **38**
Stag's Leap Wine Cellars, **27**
Sterling Vineyards, **3**
Sutter Home Winery, **11**
Trefethen Vineyards, **33**
Wermuth Vineyards, **5**
V. Sattui, **12**
Valley of the Moon, **31**

**ACCOMMODATIONS**

Bothe-Napa Valley State Park, **6**
Calistoga Inn & Brewery/
  The Calistoga Village
  Inn & Spa, **2**
Golden Haven Hot Springs
  Spa and Resort, **1**
S.F.N./Petaluma KOA, **40**
Sonoma Creek Inn, **35**
Sugarloaf Ridge State Park, **19**

**The Wine Country:
Sonoma & Napa Valleys**

Wine Country. Now firmly established as such, Napa draws a mostly older, well-to-do crowd, but in the midst of the tasting carnival there are plenty of young, budget-minded folks looking forward to their fill of chardonnay and their share of class.

## ■ ▶ ORIENTATION & PRACTICAL INFORMATION

Scenic **Route 29 (Saint Helena Highway)** runs north from **Napa** through Napa Valley and the well-groomed villages of **Yountville** and **Saint Helena** (where it's called Main St.) to **Calistoga's** soothing spas. The relatively short distances between wineries can take unpleasantly long to cover on weekends when the roads crawl with visitors. The **Silverado Trail,** parallel to Rte. 29, is less crowded, but watch out for cyclists. Napa is 14 mi. east of Sonoma on **Route 12.** If you're planning a weekend trip from San Francisco, avoid Saturday mornings and Sunday afternoons; the roads are packed with like-minded people. Although harvest season in early September is the most exciting time to visit, winter weekdays are less packed and offer more personal attention. Most accommodations are also less expensive in the winter or offer specials. From San Francisco, take US 101 over the Golden Gate Bridge, then follow Rte. 37 east to catch Rte. 29, which runs north to Napa.

**Public Transportation: Napa City Bus,** or **Valley Intercity Neighborhood Express (VINE),** 1151 Pearl St. (☎800-696-6443 or 255-7631, TDD 226-9722), covers Vallejo (M-F 5:20am-8pm, Sa 6:15am-5:30pm, Su 11am-6pm; $1.50, students $1.10, seniors and disabled 75¢) and Calistoga (M-F 5:20am-8pm, Sa 6am-6:40pm, Su 9:30am-4:30pm; $2, students $1.45, seniors and disabled $1; free transfers). The nearest Greyhound station is in Vallejo, 1500 Lemon St. (☎643-7661 or 800-231-2222). A bus runs to Napa and Calistoga, but it's very slow—almost 3hr. from Vallejo to Calistoga—and does not stop near wineries. To: Napa (at the Napa State Hospital, 2100 Napa-Vallejo Hwy.; 12:30 and 5:25pm; $8.25 one-way, $15.25 round-trip) and Calistoga (5:25 and 8pm; $11.25 one-way, $21.25 round-trip).

**Airport Service: Evans Airport Transport,** 4075 Solano Ave. (☎255-1559 or 944-2025), in Napa, runs daily shuttles from the **San Francisco** and **Oakland** airports via Vallejo to downtown Napa. Reservations required. To **Napa** ($29 one-way, children 12 and under $15) and **Vallejo** ($24 one-way, children 12 and under $15).

**Visitor Information:**

**Napa Conference & Visitors Bureau,** 1310 Town Ctr. (☎226-7459; www.napavalley.com/nvcvb.html). Very friendly staff. Free maps and info. Also sells the *Napa Valley Guidebook* ($6) with more comprehensive listings and fold-out maps. Ask about any specials during your visit (they come in daily) and pick up coupons from local businesses. Open daily 9am-5pm.

**St. Helena Chamber of Commerce,** 1010A Main St. (☎963-4456), across from Taylor's Refresher (see p. 172). Eager to help. Open M-F 10am-5pm.

**Calistoga Chamber of Commerce,** 1458 Lincoln Ave. (☎942-6333; www.calistogafun.com). Open M-F 10am-5pm, Sa 10am-4pm, Su 11am-3pm.

**Winery Tours: Napa Valley Holidays** (☎255-1050; www.napavalleyholidays.com). Afternoon tours $75 per person, $85 with round-trip transportation from San Francisco.

**Car Rental: Budget,** 407 Soscol Ave. (☎224-7846), in Napa. Cars $40 per day; under 25 surcharge $20 per day. Unlimited mileage. Must be at least 21 with credit card. Promotional specials often available; call Budget Reservation Center at ☎800-537-0700.

**Bike Rental:** ◨ **St. Helena Cyclery,** 1156 Main St. (☎963-7736). Hybrid bikes $7 per hr., $30 per day; road bikes $15/$50; tandem bikes $20/$70. All bikes come with maps, helmet, lock, and picnic bag. Reservations recommended for road and tandem bikes. Open M-Sa 9:30am-5:30pm, Su 10am-5pm. **Getaway Adventures** (☎800-499-BIKE/2453, Calistoga office 942-0332, Petaluma office 763-3040; www.getawayadventures.com), behind the gas station at the corner of Rte. 29 and

Lincoln Ave., in Calistoga. $9 per hr., $20 per half-day, $28 per day. 2hr. minimum. Also leads bike tours in Napa Valley. Open M-Th 9:30am-5:30pm, F-Su 9:30am-6pm; open fewer hours in off-season, usually M and Th-Su 9:30am-5pm.

**Police:** In **Napa,** 1539 1st St. (☎253-4451). In **Calistoga,** 1235 Washington St. (☎942-2810).

**Hospital: Queen of the Valley,** 1000 Trancas St. (☎252-4411), in Napa.

**Post Office:** 1627 Trancas St. (☎255-0360), in Napa. Open M-F 8:30am-5pm. **Postal Code:** 94558.

# ACCOMMODATIONS & CAMPING

Rooms in Napa Valley can go quickly despite high prices; reserving ahead is best. Though Napa is close to the Bay Area and has the advantages of a city, smaller towns will prove more wallet-friendly. Calistoga is a good first choice; the quaint town is a short drive from many wineries and is close to Old Faithful Geyser, Petrified Forest, and Bothe-Napa State Park. It is also home to natural hot-spring spas. The least expensive alternative, as always, is camping, but be prepared for the intense heat which might drive you back to the air-conditioned civilization.

**Golden Haven Hot Springs Spa and Resort,** 1713 Lake St. (☎942-6793; www.goldenhaven.com), a few blocks from Lincoln Ave. in Calistoga. More of a nice motel than a resort. Large, well-decorated standard-issue rooms with TVs and phones. Rooms with king beds, kitchenettes, jacuzzis, and saunas also available. Mineral swimming pool and hot tub access. No children under 16. Weekends 2-night min. stay, holiday weekends 3-night min stay. Queen $79, with private sauna $145; king $95, with private kitchenette $135, with private jacuzzi $185. Nov.-Mar. M-Th $69/$115/$75/$109/$145. ❺

**Calistoga Inn and Brewery,** 1250 Lincoln Ave. (☎942-4101; www.calistogainn.com), at the corner of Rte. 29 in Calistoga. 18 clean, simple, country inn double- and queen-sized rooms. Microbrewery and restaurant downstairs; the walk home from the pub is just a short stumble upstairs. Shared bathrooms. Restaurant and bar open 11:30am-11pm. Rooms Su-Th $75, F-Sa and holidays $100. ❹

**The Calistoga Village Inn & Spa,** 1880 Lincoln Ave. (☎942-0991), has clean, basic rooms with cable TV, phones, and private bath. Rooms with jacuzzi available. Heated mineral pools and hot tub, on-site spa, and restaurant. Doubles $79; queen $89, with sitting area $109, with kitchenette and hot tub $159; king with sitting area and Roman tub $139; 2 bedrooms $119. Nov.-Mar. M-Th rates are $10-20 less. 10% discount on spa treatments for guests. Ask about special packages for lodging, spa, and meals. ❹

**Bothe-Napa Valley State Park,** 3801 Rte. 29 (☎942-4575, reservations 800-444-7275), north of St. Helena. The fifty quiet sites near Ritchey Creek Canyon often fill to the max. Fairly rustic, though there are toilets, fire pits, and picnic tables at each site. Pool $2, under 17 free. Check-in 2pm. Picnic area day use $4. Hot showers 25¢ per 4min. Park open daily 8am-dusk. $16, seniors $10. ❶

# FOOD

Eating in Wine Country ain't cheap, but the food is usually worth it. Picnics are an inexpensive and romantic option—supplies can be bought at the numerous delis or Safeway stores in the area. Most wineries have shaded picnic grounds, often with excellent views, but most require patronage to use. The **Napa farmer's market,** at Pearl and West St., offers a sampling of the valley's non-alcoholic produce. (☎252-7142. Open daily 7:30am-noon.)

**ɔRINK TO YOUR MIND**

I have definitely consumed my
air share of fermented grape bever-
ɪges in my lifetime, and I even went
ɔ a wine-tasting party with a
"reputed expert" once, but as I wandered into the wineries around
Sonoma Valley, I slowly realized how
ittle I knew.

It wasn't that I was ridiculed or
gnored. To the contrary, the staff was
varm and receptive to all of my ques-
ions, no matter how basic they were.
Nonetheless, my ignorance of the
anguage of winemaking made me
eel a bit uncomfortable.

In the beginning, I would look
ɔver the tasting menu and choose
he wine with the most awards or
he highest price. Sometimes I
vould simply ask the server to
choose. They were happy to oblige
especially when I mentioned cost
ɪs a criterion), but I wanted to feel
nore instrumental in the process.
"he approach wasn't wrong, just
veak. As I asked more questions,
asted more wines, and read more
nfo, I began to feel like I knew a
ɔit more about wine and what I
vas doing. The whole process
ɔecame much less intimidating.

I discovered that a few hundred vine types exist in the world,
ɔut that most Californian wines
ɪre made from about a dozen
najor ones, known as varietals.
"hough soil, climate, and the
nand of the winemaker all play
mportant roles in creating a
vine's flavor, certain characteris-
ics of each varietal always come
through in a wine. By law, at

**Taylor's Refresher,** 933 Main St. (☎963-3486), on
Rte. 29 across from the Merryvale Winery, in St. Helena. A roadside stand dishing up big burgers ($4.50-
7) and truly phenomenal milkshakes ($4.60) since
1949. Outdoor seating only. Beer and wine served.
Open daily 11am-9pm. ❷

**First Squeeze Cafe & Juice Bar,** 1126 First St.
(☎224-6762), in Napa, offers sandwiches, soups,
salads, and smoothies. Try their most popular plate,
huevos rancheros ($8), or grab a fresh fruit smoothie
($4). Also serves beer and wine. Breakfast every day
until 2pm. Free downtown delivery. Open M-F 7am-
3pm, Sa-Su 8am-3pm. ❷

**Calistoga Natural Foods and Juice Bar,** 1426 Lincoln
St. (☎942-5822), in Calistoga. One of a few natural
foods stores in the area. Organic juices ($3-5),
smoothies ($4.50), sandwiches ($4-6.25), and vegetarian specialties like the Cherry Wrapture ($6.50) and
Yummus Hummus wrap ($6.50). Organic groceries
also sold. Open M-Sa 9am-6pm. ❷

**Armadellos,** 1304 Main St. (☎963-8082), in St. Helena. Tasty, vegetarian-friendly Cali-Mexican dishes
(mostly $6-13), served in a spicy atmosphere. Beer
and wine available. Open Su-Th 11am-9pm, F-Sa
11am-10pm. ❷

# 🔳 WINERIES

There are more than 250 wineries in Napa County,
nearly two-thirds of which line Rte. 29 and the Silverado Trail in Napa Valley, home of Wine Country's heavyweights. Nationally recognized
vineyards include Inglenook, Fetzer, and Mondavi.
Some wineries have free tastings and some have
free tours; all have large selections of bottled wine
available for purchase at prices cheaper than in
stores. Many wineries offer further reduced rates
to visitors who purchase a tasting or become a
club member. Style and atmosphere, from architecture down to visitor hospitality, vary from
estate to estate; experiencing the larger touristy
operations coupled with the smaller-name vineyards adds to the fun. No matter their marketing
approach, the wineries listed below (from south to
north) do card for underage drinkers; visitors must
be 21+ to taste or purchase alcohol.

A good way to begin your Napa Valley experience
is with a tour such as the ones offered at **Domaine
Carneros** or **Beringer,** or a free tastings class, like the
one on Saturday mornings at **Goosecross Cellars,** 1119
State Ln. (☎944-1986; open daily 11am-4pm), in
Yountville. Many a well-educated lush has begun a
successful career by going to wine school.

**Kirkland Ranch,** 1 Kirkland Ranch Rd. (☎254-9100), south of Napa off Rte. 29. Reminiscent of a ranch house, this family-operated winery has windows overlooking the production facilities. True to its Country Western style, the winery's walls are adorned with family pictures of cattle-herding cowboys. Tours by appointment. Tastings $5. US military personnel and veterans receive 30% off wine purchases.

**Domaine Carneros,** 1240 Duhig Rd. (☎257-0101), off Rte. 121 between Napa and Sonoma. Picturesque estate with an elegant terrace modeled after a French *château*. "Be prepared to feel like royalty" is their slogan. Owned by Champagne Taittinger and known for its sparkling wines. The free tour and film (daily every hr. 10:15am-4pm) is a great way to kick off a day of wine tasting. No tastings here, but wines by the glass $5-10 with complimentary *hors d'oeuvres*. Open daily 10am-5:30pm.

## YOUNTVILLE & SURROUNDS

**Clos Du Val Wine Company, Ltd.,** 5330 Silverado Trail (☎259-2225; www.closduval.com), north of Oak Knoll Rd., in Yountville. Small, stylish grounds attract lots of tourists. Tastings $5; price applicable towards wine purchase. Free tours by appointment. Open daily 10am-4:30pm.

**Domaine Chandon,** 1 California Dr. (☎944-2280 or 800-934-3975; www.chandon.com), in Yountville. Owned by Moët Chandon (the French makers of Dom Perignon), the winery produces 4-5 million bottles of sparkling wine annually. The sleek Visitors Center and manicured gardens evoke a Zen-like meditative spirit. French restaurant on site. 3 tastes for $9, by the glass $4.50-12. Open daily 10am-6pm.

**Stag's Leap Wine Cellars,** 5766 Silverado Trail (☎944-2020; www.cask23.com). "The tiny vineyard that beat Europe's best," reads the souvenir glass that comes with the portfolio or flights ($30) tasting. Call in advance to arrange a free 1hr. tour that includes a complimentary tasting. Open daily 10am-4pm.

## OAKVILLE

**Niebaum-Coppola Estate Winery,** 1991 St. Helena Hwy. (☎968-1100). Famed film director Francis Ford Coppola and his wife bought the historic 1880 Inglenook Chateau and Niebaum vineyards in 1975. Restoring the estate to production capacity, Coppola also added a family history museum upstairs; it includes memorabilia from his films such as the desk from *The Godfather* and his Oscar and Golden Globe statues (free access). $8.50 fee includes 4 tastes and commemorative glass. Regular tours ($20) given daily at 10:30am, 12:30, and 2:30pm; vineyard tours ($20) at 11am daily; Rubicon tours ($45) by reservation Su, Th, and Sa at 1pm. Open daily 10am-5pm.

made from a specific varietal in order to list that varietal on the label. Each varietal (and its wines) has specific, distinguishing attributes. For example, the white grape Chardonnay produces rich, crisp, complex wines. Most are dry and full-bodied with medium acidity, and smell faintly like apples, melons, or figs. Cabernet Sauvignon, a red grape, can make a velvety wine. Sometimes hints of cedar, black currants, or stewed fruit are discernible. Once I knew what to expect, it became fun to compare the variations of scents and flavors between different varietals.

After grasping the concept of varietals and memorizing their typical characteristics, I learned how soil and climate subtly affect flavor. Vineyards fall into distinct geographical regions, called appellations. Topography, climate, and soil define each area and impart characteristics to the grapes grown under these conditions. For a winemaker to include an appellation on the label, 85% of the wine must come from that area. Trying to detect differences in similar wines from various appellations became a game.

The most important bit of information I learned, however, was the differences in bottle sizes. Buying anything larger than a Jeroboam (3 liters or 4 glasses) left me far too drunk to taste what I was drinking anyway. The 15 liter Nebuchadnezzar would have to wait for larger crowds. To really compare wines and develop a critical palate, I had to restrict my tasting. It's worth it though, for at my next wine tasting party I'll be the "reputed expert." *Salud!*

-Eliza Dick, 2003

**Robert Mondavi Winery,** 7801 Rte. 29 (☎963-9611 or 800-766-3284; www.robertmondaviwinery.com), 8 mi. north of Napa. Massive and touristy, with a beautiful mission-style visitors complex, 2 tasting rooms selling by the glass ($7), and the atmosphere of a luxury summer resort. Offers a variety of tours. The Vineyard and Winery tour takes place daily every hr. 10am-4pm. Reserve 1hr. in advance. Tour $10; includes 3 tastes and *hors d'oeuvres.* The other 6 tours are each given one day per week at 10am or 11am, some seasonally, and cost $30-95 per person. Open daily 9am-5pm.

## ST. HELENA & CALISTOGA

**Edgewood Estate Winery,** 401 St. Helena Hwy. (☎963-7293), in St. Helena. Don't let the lack of cars and crowds outside deter you; a warm, attentive staff and five tastes for $4 can be found within this small, pretty lodge. Garden patio seating perfect for savoring wines by the glass. Open daily 11am-5:30pm.

**V. Sattui,** 1111 White Ln. (☎963-7774 or 800-799-2337; www.vsattui.com), at Rte. 29, in St. Helena. One of the few wineries in the valley that only sells at its winery. The family-owned operation has a gourmet cheese counter, meat shop, and bakery. Picnic area for customers. Free tastings. Open daily Mar.-Oct. 9am-6pm; Nov.-Feb. 9am-5pm.

**Beringer Vineyards,** 2000 Main St. (☎963-7115; www.beringer.com), off Rte. 29, in St. Helena. Huge Gothic Revival estate mobbed with tourists. Historic tours of Rhine House mansion and grounds every 30min.; includes tasting (10am-5pm; $5, under 21 free). To taste Beringer's better wines, try the reserve room on the 2nd floor of the Rhine House mansion (samples cost 10% of the wine's price, about $2-10, and will be credited towards wine purchase). Open daily 10am-5pm.

## 👁 ⚠ SIGHTS & OUTDOOR ACTIVITIES

Napa's gentle terrain makes for an excellent bike tour. The area is fairly flat, although small bike lanes, speeding cars, and blistering heat can make routes more challenging, especially after a few samples of wine. The 26 mi. **Silverado Trail** has a wider bike path than Rte. 29. ◪**St. Helena Cyclery,** 1156 Main St., rents bikes (see **Practical Information,** p. 170).

The annual **Napa Valley Wine Festival,** in which around fifty vintners raise money for public education through dinners, tours, and rare vintage auctions, takes place in early November. Every weekend in February and March, the **Mustard Festival** (☎259-9029; www.mustardfestival.org) lines up different musical or theatrical presentations. **Napa Valley Fairgrounds** (☎942-5111) hosts a weekend fair in August, with wine tasting, music, juggling, rides, and a rodeo. In the summer, there are free afternoon concerts at **Music-in-the-Park,** downtown at the riverfront. Contact **Napa Parks and Recreation Office** (☎257-9529) for more info.

**CALISTOGA.** Calistoga is known as the "Hot Springs of the West." Sam Brannan, who first developed the area, meant to make the hot springs the "Saratoga of California," but he misspoke and promised instead to make them "The Calistoga of Saratina." Luckily, history has a soft spot for millionaires; Brannan's dream has come true and Calistoga is now a center for luxurious yet small-scale spas and resorts. His former cottage houses the **Sharpsteen Museum,** 1311 Washington St., which traces the town's development in exhibits designed by a Disney animator. *(Open daily 11am-4pm; in winter noon-4pm. Free.)*

Calistoga's luxuriant mud baths, massages, and mineral showers will feel even more welcome after a hard day of wine-tasting. Be sure to hydrate beforehand; alcohol-thinned blood and intense heat do not mix. A basic package consisting of a mud bath, mineral bath, eucalyptus steam, blanket wrap and 25min. massage costs around $80. Salt scrubs and facials are each about $50. The **Calistoga Village Inn & Spa** gives friendly service. *(☎942-0991. Mud bath treatment $45; 25min. massage $45; 25min. facial $49; ultimate 3hr. package of mud bath treat-*

*ment, salt scrub, 55min. massage, and mini facial $185.)* For a less pretentious spa, try **Golden Haven.** *(☎942-6793. Mud bath treatment $65, 30min. massage $45, 30min. facial $45.)*

Cooler water is at **Lake Berryessa** (☎966-2111), 20 mi. north of Napa off Hwy. 128, where swimming, sailing, and sunbathing are popular along its 169 mi. shoreline.

**OLD FAITHFUL GEYSER OF CALIFORNIA.** This steamy wonder should not be confused with its more famous namesake in Wyoming. The geyser regularly jets boiling water 60 ft. into the air; although it "erupts" about every 40min., weather conditions affect its cycle. The ticket vendor will tell you the estimated time of the next spurt. *(1299 Tubbs Ln. off Hwy. 128., 2 mi. outside Calistoga. ☎942-6463. Open daily 9am-6pm; in winter 9am-5pm. $6, seniors $5, ages 6-12 $2, disabled free.)*

**MARINE WORLD.** This 160-acre Vallejo attraction is an enormous zoo-oceanarium-theme park. It has animal shows and special attractions like the Lorikeet Aviary, the Butterfly Walk, and the Shark Experience. The park was recently purchased by Six Flags. *(Off Rte. 37, 10 mi. south of Napa. ☎643-6722. Vallejo is accessible from San Francisco by BART (☎510-465-2278) and the Blue and Gold fleet (☎415-705-5444). Open Mar.-Aug. Su-Th 10am-8pm, F-Sa 10am-9pm; Sept.-Oct. Su and F-Sa 10am-6pm. $34, seniors $25, ages 4-12 or under 48 inches $17. Parking $6.)*

**OTHER SIGHTS. The Petrified Forest,** 4100 Petrified Forest Rd., west of Calistoga, was formed over three million years ago when molten lava from a volcano eruption 7 mi. northeast of Mt. St. Helen covered a forested valley and preserved the trees. The quarter-mile trail is wheelchair-accessible. *(☎942-6667. Open daily 10am-6pm; winter 10am-5pm. Free.)* Experience an authentic Venetian gondola ride on Napa River with **Gondola Servizio Napa,** 540 Main St., inside Hatt Market. *(☎257-8495. 30min. private ride $55 per couple; $10 each additional person.)* **Napa Valley Wine Train,** 1275 McKinstry St., offers dining and drinking on board in the style of the early 1900s, traveling from Napa to St. Helena and back. *(☎253-2111 or 800-427-4124; www.winetrain.com. Train ride 3hr. M-F 11am and 6pm; Sa-Su 8:30am, 12:10, 5:30pm. Ticket and meal plans $35-90. Advance reservations and payments required.)*

# SONOMA VALLEY ☎707

Sprawling Sonoma Valley is a quieter alternative to Napa, but home to bigger wineries than the Russian River Valley. Many wineries are on winding side roads rather than a freeway strip, creating a more intimate wine-tasting experience. Sonoma Plaza is surrounded by art galleries, novelty shops, clothing stores, and Italian restaurants. Petaluma, west of the Sonoma Valley, has more budget-friendly lodgings than the expensive wine country.

## ▮ TRANSPORTATION

From San Francisco, take **US 101 North** over the Golden Gate Bridge, then follow Rte. 37 E to Rte. 116 N, which turns into Rte. 121 N and crosses Rte. 12 N to Sonoma. Alternatively, follow US 101 N to Petaluma and cross over to Sonoma by Rte. 116. Driving time from San Francisco is about 1-1½hr.

**Route 12** traverses the length of Sonoma Valley, from **Sonoma** through **Glen Ellen** to **Kenwood** in the north. The center of downtown Sonoma is **Sonoma Plaza,** which contains City Hall and the Visitors Center. **Broadway** dead ends at Napa St. in front of City Hall. Numbered streets run north-south. **Petaluma** lies to the west and is connected to Sonoma by **Route 116,** which becomes **Lakeville Street** in Petaluma.

**Buses: Sonoma County Transit** (☎576-7433 or 800-345-7433; www.sctransit.com) serves the entire county. Bus #30 runs from **Sonoma** to **Santa Rosa** (daily every 1½hr. 6am-4pm; $2.05, students $1.70, seniors and disabled $1, under 6 free); buses #44 and #48 go to **Petaluma** (M-F; $1.75, students $1.45, seniors and disabled 85¢). A

**SummerPass** allows unlimited summer rides for those under 18 ($20) and can be bought at the Safeway on Mendocino Ave. Within Sonoma, **county buses** stop when flagged down at bus stops (M-Su 8am-4:25pm; 95¢, students 75¢, seniors and disabled 45¢). **Golden Gate Transit** (☎541-2000 from Sonoma County or 415-923-2000 from San Francisco, TDD 257-4554) runs buses frequently between **San Francisco** and **Santa Rosa. Volunteer Wheels** (☎800-992-1006) offers door-to-door service for people with disabilities. Call for reservations. Open daily 8am-5pm.

**Bike Rental: Sonoma Valley Cyclery,** 20093 Broadway (☎935-3377), in Sonoma. Bikes $6 per hr., $25 per day; includes helmet. Open M-Sa 10am-6pm, Su 10am-4pm.

## 🛈 PRACTICAL INFORMATION

**Visitor Information: Sonoma Valley Visitors Bureau,** 453 E. 1st St. (☎996-1090; www.sonomavalley.com), in Sonoma Plaza. Maps $2. Open June-Oct. daily 9am-7pm; Nov.-May 9am-5pm. **Petaluma Visitors Program,** 800 Baywood Dr. (☎769-0429), at Lakeville St. Open May-Oct. M-F 9am-5:30pm, Sa-Su 10am-6pm; shorter weekend hours in the off-season. The free visitor's guide has listings of restaurants and activities.

**Road Conditions:** ☎817-1717.

**Police:** ☎778-4372 in Petaluma, ☎996-3602 in Sonoma.

**Hospital: Petaluma Valley,** 400 N. McDowell Blvd. (☎781-1111).

**Post Office: Sonoma,** 617 Broadway (☎996-9311), at Patten St. Open M-F 8:30am-5pm. **Petaluma,** 120 4th St. (☎769-5352). Open M-F 8:30am-5pm, Sa 10am-2pm. **Postal Code:** 95476 (Sonoma), 94952 (Petaluma).

## 🏠🏕 ACCOMMODATIONS & CAMPING

Pickings are pretty slim for lodging; rooms are scarce even on weekdays and generally start at $85. Less expensive motels cluster along **US 101** in Santa Rosa and Petaluma. Campers with cars should try the **Russian River Valley** (see p. 181).

**Redwood Inn,** 1670 Santa Rosa Ave. (☎545-0474), in Santa Rosa. A decent drive from Sonoma. Clean, comfortable rooms and suites with kitchenettes, cable TV, phones, and bath. Singles $55; doubles $65. $5 less in winter. AARP and AAA discounts. ❹

**Sonoma Creek Inn,** 239 Boyes Blvd. (☎939-9463 or 888-712-1289), west off Hwy. 12, in Sonoma. Just 10min. from the Sonoma Plaza, restaurants, and wineries. Colorful rooms with kitchenette, cable TV, phone, and full bath. Rooms $89-159. ❺

**Sugarloaf Ridge State Park,** 2605 Adobe Canyon Rd. (☎833-5712), off Rte. 12, north of Kenwood in the Mayacamas mountains. Arranged around a central meadow with flush toilets and running water (but no showers) are 49 sites with tables and fire rings. In summer and fall, take advantage of the sky-watching at Ferguson Observatory inside the park; see www.rfo.org for details. Reserve sites through ReserveAmerica (☎800-444-7275; www.reserveamerica.com). Sites $15, seniors $10; day use $4. No credit cards at the park, but ReserveAmerica accepts MC/V. ❶

**San Francisco North/Petaluma KOA,** 20 Rainsville Rd. (☎763-1492 or 800-992-2267; www.petalumakoa.com), in Petaluma off the Penngrove Exit. Suburban camp with 300 sites plus a recreation hall with activities, petting zoo, pool, store, laundry facilities, and jacuzzi. Many families. Hot showers. Check-in 1pm. Check-out 11am. 1-week max. tent stay. Reservations recommended. 2-person tent sites $31-35; each additional adult $5, child $3. RVs $38-41. Cabins (sleep 4; no linens) $55-60. ❸

# 🔲 FOOD

Fresh produce is seasonally available directly from area farms or at roadside stands and farmer's markets. *Farm Trails* maps are free at the Sonoma Valley Visitors Bureau. Those in the area toward the end of the summer should ask about the ambrosial **crane melon**, a tasty hybrid of fruits grown only on the Crane Farm north of Petaluma. The **Sonoma Market**, 520 W. Napa St., in the Sonoma Valley Center, is an old-fashioned grocery store with deli sandwiches ($5-7) and very fresh produce. (☎996-0563. Open daily 6am-9pm.) The **Fruit Basket**, 18474 Sonoma Hwy., sells inexpensive fruit. (☎996-7433. Open daily 7am-7pm. No credit cards.) All things generic can be found at **Safeway**, 477 W. Napa St. (☎996-0633. Open 24hr.)

🔲 **Sonoma Cheese Factory,** 2 Spain St. (☎996-1931 or 800-535-2855; www.sonoma-jack.com), in Sonoma. Forget the wine for now—take a toothpick and skewer the free cheese samples. You can even watch the cheese-making process in the back room. Sandwiches ($4.50-5.50). Open daily 8:30am-5:30pm. ❷

**Maya,** 101 E. Napa St. (☎935-3500), at the corner of 1st St. E in Sonoma's Historic Town Square. Brings Yucatan spirit to Sonoma. The festive decor, mouth-watering food, and extensive wine and tequila menu are truly impressive. Entrees $10-20. Occasional live music in summer. Open daily 11am-11pm. ❸

**Basque Boulangerie Cafe,** 460 First St. E., (☎935-7687), in Sonoma Plaza. This little cafe is always packed; when you fight your way to the counter, you'll see why. Below the wall of freshly baked French breads is a counter filled with tarts, mini-gateaus, and pastries ($2-20). Delicious sandwiches $5.50 for lunch. With 24hr. advance notice they'll even arrange a box lunch ($10.50) for vineyard picnicking. Open daily 7am-6pm. ❸

**Murphy's Irish Pub,** 464 First St. E. (☎935-0660; www.sonomapub.com), tucked in an alleyway off Sonoma Plaza. A sign here reads, "God created whiskey to keep the Irish from ruling the world." Ponder the geopolitical ramifications over a grilled chicken sandwich ($7.50), fish 'n' chips ($6.25), or other popular pub grub. Extensive beer list. Live music on the outdoor patio almost every night (8pm). Open daily 11am-11pm. ❷

**Meritage Restaurant,** 522 Broadway (☎938-9430), in Sonoma. This bistro serves up the best breakfast in town ($6-10) and a mouth-watering weekend brunch (around $10). Try homemade gelato and unusual sorbet flavors. Lunch specials $8-9. The Oyster Bar is a favorite. Pastas and entrees $13-24. Open M and W-F 11am-9:30pm, Sa-Su 10am-9:30pm. Brunch served Sa-Su 10am-3pm. ❹

**The Vasquez House,** 414 First St. E. (☎938-0510), in El Paseo de Sonoma. Inconspicuously tucked behind touristy shops, this historic house hides a library and a minuscule tea room serving coffee, tea, and lemonade (75¢), along with freshly baked "indulgences" ($1). Open Su and W-Sa 1:30-4:30pm. No credit cards. ❶

# 🔲 WINERIES

Sonoma Valley's wineries, near Sonoma and Kenwood, are less touristy but just as elegant as Napa's. As an added bonus, there are more complimentary tastings of current vintages. Take a close look at the *Let's Go* map or bring an extra one along (they're all over the place and free), as there are few winery signs to guide you.

## IN & AROUND SONOMA

🔲 **Gundlach-Bundschu,** 2000 Denmark St. (☎938-5277; www.gunbun.com), off 8th St. E. Established in 1858, this is the 2nd oldest winery in Sonoma and the oldest family-owned, family-run winery in the country. Fragrant wines and a setting of pronounced loveliness. In the summer it hosts outdoor events like the Mozart series. Free wine storage cave tours Sa-Su at noon, 1, 2, and 3pm. Free tastings daily 11am-4:30pm.

**Buena Vista,** 18000 Old Winery Rd. (☎938-1266; www.buenavistawinery.com). Take E. Napa St. from Sonoma Plaza and turn left on Old Winery Rd. The oldest premium winery in the valley. Famous stone buildings are preserved just as Mr. Haraszthy built them in 1857 when he founded the California wine industry. Theater shows July-Sept. Historical presentation and guided tour daily at 2pm. All other tours are self-guided. Tastings ($5, including glass) daily 10am-5pm.

**Ravenswood,** 18701 Gehricke Rd. (☎938-1960 or 888-669-4679; www.ravenswood-wine.com), north of Sonoma. "Unwimpy" wines from a surprisingly light-hearted group that says "wine should also be fun." Price of tastings ($4) applicable to wine purchase and well worth it. Tours by appointment daily at 10:30am. Open daily 10am-4:30pm.

## GLEN ELLEN

🍇 **Benziger,** 1833 London Ranch Rd. (☎935-4046 or 888-490-2379; www.benziger.com). This winery is known for its big, buttery, rich, and accessible wines. Tourists flock here for the acclaimed 45min. tram ride tour ($10, under 21 $5) through the vineyards, which runs in the summer M-F every hour 11:30am-3:30pm and Sa-Su every half-hour 11:30am-3:30pm. Self-guided tours lead from the parking lot through the vineyards and peacock aviary. Tastings of current vintage free, limited $5, reserves $10. With tram tour, free reserve tasting and 20% discount on purchases. Open daily 10am-5pm.

## KENWOOD

**Kunde,** 10155 Sonoma Hwy. (☎833-5501; www.kunde.com), near Kenwood. The cave tours at Kunde offer respite from the sun. Known for its Chardonnays. Free tastings and cave tours hourly Su and F-Sa 11am-3pm, Tu-Th 11am. Open daily 10:30am-4:30pm.

**Ledson Winery and Vineyards,** 7335 Sonoma Hwy. (☎833-2330; www.ledson.com). A relatively new vineyard, known as a Merlot estate, that does not market its wines. Hosts free music concerts every summer weekend noon-4pm. BBQ meal $12. Home to many benefits and shows throughout the year. Tastings ($5) daily 10am-5pm.

**Kenwood,** 9592 Sonoma Hwy. (☎833-5891; www.kenwoodvineyards.com). One of a few wineries using organic grapes. Known for its Jack London Wolfe wine (they buy the grapes from the author's estate). Free tastings of current vintage, private reserves $5. Free 15min. tours daily 11:30am and 2:30pm. Open daily 10am-4:30pm.

## 👁 SIGHTS & SEASONAL EVENTS

**SONOMA STATE HISTORIC PARK.** Within the park, an adobe church stands on the site of the **Mission San Francisco-Solano,** the northernmost and last of the 21 Franciscan missions. It marks the end of the El Camino Real, or the "Royal Road." Built in 1826 by Padre Jose Altimira, the mission has a fragment of the original California Republic flag, the rest of which was burned in the 1906 post-San Francisco earthquake fires. *(E. Spain and 1st St., in the northeast corner of town. ☎938-1519. Open daily 10am-5pm. $2, children under 17 free. Includes admission to Vallejo's Home, Sonoma Barracks, Petaluma Adobe, Bale Grist Mill, and Benicia Capital Historic State Park.)*

**GENERAL VALLEJO'S HOME.** The site is often referred to by its Latin name, *Lachryma Montis,* meaning "Tears of the Mountain." This "Yankee" home of the famed Mexican leader, who also was mayor of Sonoma and a California senator, is open for tours of the museum, pond, pavilions, and gardens. The grounds are graced with a serene picnic area designed in part by Vallejo and his wife. *(Located on W. Spain St. at Third St. ☎938-1519. Open daily 10am-5pm. $2, under 17 free.)*

**JACK LONDON STATE PARK.** Around the turn of the 20th century, hard-drinking and hard-living Jack London, author of *The Call of the Wild* and *White Fang,* bought 1400 acres here, determined to create his dream home. London's hopes were frustrated when the estate's main building, the Wolf House, was destroyed by arsonists in 1913. London died three years after the fire and is buried in the park, his grave marked by a volcanic boulder intended for the construction of his house. The nearby **House of Happy Walls,** built by London's widow in fond remembrance of him, is now a two-story museum devoted to the writer. The park's scenic half-mile **Beauty Ranch Trail** passes the lake, winery ruins, and quaint cottages. There are many longer trails that provide a greater challenge. Take **Lake Trail** (1 mi.) from the parking lot to the lake. There, follow **Mountain Trail** (½ mi.) to a lovely vista point. Continue on Mountain Trail all the way to the Park Summit (2½ mi.) or circle around Woodcutter's Meadow on the **Fallen Bridge Trail** (1¼ mi.) to return. *(Take Hwy. 12 4 mi. north from Sonoma to Arnold Ln. and follow signs.* ☎*938-5216. Park open daily 9:30am-7pm; in winter 9:30am-5pm. Museum open daily 10am-5pm.)* **Sonoma Cattle and Napa Valley Trail Rides** also amble through the fragrant forests. *(*☎*996-8566. 2hr. ride $55.)*

**SEASONAL EVENTS. Sonoma Plaza** hosts festivals and fairs nearly every summer weekend. **Kenwood** heats up **July 4** for the Kenwood Footrace, a tough 7½ mi. course through hills and vineyards. A chili cookoff and the **World Pillow Fighting Championships** continue the party. At the Championships, eager contenders hover over a mud pit and beat each other with wet pillows. (See **No Work, All Play,** p. 179)

# SANTA ROSA   ☎ 707

Famed horticulturist Luther Burbank once said of Santa Rosa (pop. 140,000), "I firmly believe, from what I have seen, that this is the chosen spot of all the earth, as far as nature is concerned." But whatever natural beauty Luther admired gave way long ago to the concerns of developers, who cast tract housing here and shopping malls there, effectively hiding Santa Rosa's ecological superiority to Sonoma County under a veil of suburban torpor. Now most people stop in Santa Rosa for a quick bite on their way between the Bay Area and Wine Country.

■*✷***🔎 ORIENTATION & PRACTICAL INFORMATION.** Santa Rosa is at the intersection of **US 101** and **Route 12,** 57 mi. north of downtown San Francisco. **Cleveland Avenue** marks the city's western edge. The town center is occupied by a mall that interrupts A, 2nd, 3rd, 4th, and 5th St. **Mendocino Avenue** and **4th Street** define the bustling yet spotless downtown area. The **Railroad Square** area,

## NO WORK, ALL PLAY
### KENWOOD PILLOWFIGHTS

From opposite sides of a creek two competitors slide along an aluminum pole to the center of a mud pit. A referee, waist-deep in mud, hands a wet, muddy pillow to each contender. Two more refs seated in lawn chairs at each end of the pole squirt water from their hoses into the pit to dilute the thick mud. Both contenders straddle the pole...

The fights at the Kenwood World Pillow Fighting Championships are an odd union of jousting and mud wrestling. The rules are simple—the first contender to knock his opponent off the pole twice moves on to the next round—but the competition is fierce. A local radio station provides amusing commentary to the cheering crowd, which suns itself happily downs foamy beer, and gnaws on giant drumsticks.

The festivities also include body painting, rock climbing, ring tossing, and a cushy kiddie pillow-fighting ring for future champions. The church across the street starts off the day with a pancake breakfast, and the championship finals end the day at 4:30pm. Though only locals can enter the tourney, watching the fights is just as entertaining, and much drier. Fun for all ages, the annual Kenwood World Pillow Fighting Championships are a must for travelers in Wine Country on **July 4th.**

*On Warm Springs Rd. off Hwy. 12 in Sonoma, close to Sonoma Plaza. $5 all-day entrance fee. Free parking along the street. Contact Sonoma Valley Visitor's Bureau (*☎*707-996-1090; see p. 179) for more info.*

bounded by **4th, 5th,** and **Wilson Streets,** houses Santa Rosa's trendiest shops and most charming cafes. The neighborhoods surrounding the heart of the city are not the safest; **exercise caution after dark.**

**Greyhound,** 435 Santa Rosa Ave., 4 blocks from 2nd St., runs **buses** to San Francisco. (☎545-6495 or 800-231-2222. 4 per day; $15 one-way, $28.50 round-trip.) **City Bus** (☎543-3333) covers the main streets of Santa Rosa ($1, students K-12 75¢, seniors and disabled 50¢, under 5 free). Carry exact change and get a schedule at the Visitors Bureau. **Rincon Cyclery,** 4927 Sonoma Hwy., at Rte. 12, rents mountain and road bikes, hybrids, and tandems. (☎800-965-2453. Free maps. $7 per hr., $25 for the first day, $20 per additional day, $100 per week. 2hr. min. rental. Open M-F 10am-6pm, Sa-Su 10am-5pm.) The **Greater Santa Rosa Convention and Visitor Bureau,** 9 4th St. at Wilson St. in the old North-West train depot, sells maps and brochures. (☎577-8674 or 800-404-7673; www.visitsantarosa.com. Open M-Th and Sa 9am-6pm, F 9am-7pm, Su 10am-6pm.) The **Sonoma County Wine and Visitors Center,** 5000 Roberts Lake Rd., east of US 101 in Rohnert Park, sells maps of area wineries and a tasting directory. (☎586-3795. Open daily 9am-5pm.) Other local services include: **police** (☎543-3600); **Santa Rosa Memorial Hospital,** 1165 Montgomery Dr. (☎546-3210); and the **post office,** 730 2nd St., between D and E St. (☎528-2209; open M-F 8am-6pm, Sa 8am-2pm). **Postal Code:** 95402.

**⌂ ACCOMMODATIONS.** Santa Rosa offers basic roadside motels in addition to a few swanky downtown lodgings. **The Redwood Inn ❹,** 1670 Santa Rosa Ave., offers limited local calls and cable TV in impeccably clean rooms. Breakfast snacks, coffee, and kitchenette are in each room. (☎545-0474. Singles $50-60; doubles $60-85. Winter rates $5 less. 10% AAA discount.) **The Country Inn ❹,** 2363 Santa Rosa Ave., has tidy rooms with cable TV, phones, refrigerators and coffee. There is also an outdoor pool. (☎546-4711. Singles M-F $49, Sa-Su $69; doubles $59, Sa-Su $79. Winter $5 less. 10% discount for seniors.) The historic **Hotel La Rose ❺,** 308 Wilson St., across from the Visitors Center, is located in Railroad Square, which adds to its charm and price. Rooms come with cable TV, phones, a European breakfast, welcome gift baskets, and access to a rooftop jacuzzi. Check-in after 3pm; check-out by noon. (☎579-3200 or 800-527-6738; www.hotellarose.com. Rooms from $199 in summer; $129 in winter. AAA and AARP members 10% off and Saver's Club and Quest Card holders 50% off, depending on availability.) **Motel 6 ❸,** 6145 Commerce Blvd. (☎585-8888 or 800-466-8356; www.motel6.com), just minutes south of Santa Rosa. From Hwy. 101 S, take the Rohnert Park Expressway Exit, turn right off the ramp onto Expressway, and then make a left at the first light. Motel 6 offers the standard clean rooms with HBO and outdoor pool. (Rooms Su-Th $44, F-Sa $50).

**❐ FOOD.** Fresh produce can be found at the weekly **farmer's market** at 4th and B. St. (W 5-8:30pm). **Organic Groceries,** 2481 Guerneville Rd., near Fulton St., has every organic food you've ever heard of, in bulk. (☎528-3663. Open M-F 9am-8pm, Sa-Su 10am-7pm.) **The Rose Pub & Restaurant ❸,** 2074 Armory Dr., serves classic, old-world Irish dishes like Kerry Pie ($9) and seafood options like black tiger shrimp ($14). A puffed pastry filled with potatoes, carrots, mushrooms, and peas in a curry sauce ($9) will delight vegetarians. (☎546-7673; www.therosepubandrestaurant.biz. Pub open Tu-Th 3-midnight, F-Sa 3pm-2am; kitchen open Tu-Th 4-9pm, F-Sa 4-10pm.) **Mixx ❹,** 135 Fourth St., has modern American dishes infused with Mediterranean, Asian, and Southwestern spices. (☎573-1344. Lunch $9-16. Dinner $16-28. Open M-Sa 11:30am-2pm and 5:30-9pm. Make reservations on weekends.)

**◉♫ SIGHTS & ENTERTAINMENT.** The **Luther Burbank Home & Gardens,** at Santa Rosa and Sonoma Ave., is a great place to stop and smell the chamomile. At the age of 26, the horticulturist Burbank fled to California from Massachusetts to carry out his extensive plant-breeding experiments, with the aim of improving the quality of plants and increasing the world's food supply. He created over 800 new varieties of plants, some of which are exhibited. (☎524-5445. Gardens open 8am-dusk. Free. House open Apr.-Oct. Su and Tu-Sa 10am-3:30pm. Free. Tour every 30min. until 3pm. $4, seniors and ages 12-18 $3, under 12 free.)

**Luther Burbank Center for the Arts,** 50 Mark West Springs Rd., is the new state-of-the-art home for big-name music concerts as well as lesser-known talent. The 2003 summer season hosted artists like James Brown, LeAnne Rimes, Olivia Newton-John, and the Rev. Al Green. (☎546-3600; www.lbc.net. Box office open M-Sa noon-6pm.) The **Redwood Empire Ice Arena,** 1667 W. Steele Ln., is decorated with original stained glass artwork inspired by characters such as Snoopy from the famed Peanuts comics strip. (☎546-7147. $5.50, under 11 $4.50; skate rental $2.) Next door, **Snoopy's Gallery** continues the ice rink's artistic theme. Good grief! Every souvenir imaginable is sold here. (Open daily 10am-6pm.) Haven't had enough? The **Charles M. Schulz Museum,** One Snoopy Pl. (☎579-4452; www.charlesmschulzmuseum.org) celebrates the legacy of Mr. Schulz and the Peanuts gang.

If you are biking or driving, Sonoma County's backroads offer scenery that surpasses even that on Rte. 12. **Bennett Valley Road,** between Kenwood and Santa Rosa, **Petaluma Hill Road,** between Petaluma and Santa Rosa Ave., and **Grange/ Crane Canyon Road,** connecting the two, provide beautiful views of the countryside. If you are biking, be alert; the surroundings can distract you from the blind turns, hills, and drivers. Conversely, drivers along these routes should watch for bikers.

Annual events include the **Dixieland Jazz Festival** (☎539-3494; www.sonomacountydixiejazz.org), with non-stop music and dancing in August. **The Green Music Festival** at Sonoma State University, 1801 East Cotati Ave. in Rohnert Park, is a celebration of music, art, and ideas. Events are scheduled throughout July and August. (☎546-8742. M-F between 9am-6pm. Tickets $8-48.) The **Sonoma County Fair** is a two-week extravaganza from late July to early August. In the first weekend of October, Santa Rosa celebrates local food, wine, and artists at the **October Harvest Fair.** There are over 500 wines represented. ($5 admission. An additional $6 buys a wine glass and two tastes.) Also in the fall, the ◼**World Championship Grape Stomp Contest** offers much more than fragrant, sticky feet. Live jazz and bluegrass music, horse rides, and a petting zoo draw locals and tourists alike. (Sonoma County Fairgrounds ☎545-4203; www.sonomacountyfair.org.)

# RUSSIAN RIVER VALLEY ☎707

The Russian River Valley is a well-kept secret. Though many of its wineries have been operating nearly as long as their counterparts to the southeast, they are neither as well-known nor as crowded. Along with small, intimate vineyards, the area is home to beautiful coastline, second-growth redwoods, and a scenic river. In quiet Sebastopol, hippies and farmers coexist peacefully, biding their time until the next great social reckoning or marijuana raid. Unpretentious Guerneville is a small, gay-friendly community that plays host to those who want the Great Outdoors without having to sacrifice nightlife. Farther north and east, Healdsburg is a town of beauty and bucks, as well as a good base for winery exploration.

## ◼◼ ORIENTATION & PRACTICAL INFORMATION

The **Russian River** winds through western Sonoma County before reaching the Pacific Ocean at Jenner. The river flows south, roughly following **US 101** until **Healdsburg,** where it veers west. A number of small towns line this western stretch of river, including **Guerneville, Monte Rio,** and **Forestville.** This area is quite compact by California standards; none of the towns are more than a

TO POINT ARENA (20mi), MENDOCINO (40mi)

SKYLINE RIDGE

WALTERS RIDGE

Lake Sonoma Wildlife Management Area

Cloverdale

TO UKIAH (30mi)

Big Mtn.

Centennial Mtn.

Lake Sonoma

Asti

Salt Point State Park

Plantation

Gualala River

Seaview Rd.

Stewart Point - Skaggs Springs Rd.

Rockpile Rd.

Lake Sonoma Rec. Area

River Rd.

101

**WINERIES**
Belvedere, 11
Chateau Souverain, 2
Clos du Bois, 3
Davis Bynum Winery, 17
Field Stone Winery, 9
Hop Kiln Winery, 13
Joseph Swan Vineyards, 19
J Wine Company, 14
J.W. Morris Winery, 8
Kendall Jackson Cellars, 21

Korbel Champagne Cellars, 12 (inset)
Limerick Lane Cellars, 15
Martinelli Vineyards, 20
Michel-Schlumberger, 1
Porter Creek Winery, 16
Rabbit Ridge Vineyards, 10
Roshambo Winery, 6
Simi Winery, 5
Topolos at Russian River, 18
Trentadue Winery, 4
William Wheeler Winery, 7

Oak Mtn.

Las Lomas

Bufano Peace Statue

Fort Ross State Historic Park

Fort Ross Rd.

Meyers Grade Rd.

1

Big Oat Mtn.

Canyon Rd.

Bradford Mtn.

128

Geyserville

Dry Creek Rd.

Wine Creek Rd.

2
3

Lytton

4

5

Austin Creek State Rec. Area

Queens Pk.

Armstrong Redwoods State Reserve

Mill Creek Rd.

Healdsburg

7
8

9

Black Mtn.

Cazadero

Cazadero Hwy.

Old Cazadero Rd.

Pole Mtn.

10
6

11

Wild Hog Hill

Sweetwater Springs Rd.

Westside Rd.

Jenner

Goat Rock

116

Guerneville

River Rd.

Rio Nido

12

101

PACIFIC OCEAN

Bridgehaven

1

Red Hill

Ocean View

Duncans Mills

**see inset**

Monte Rio

Hacienda

Russian River

13

15

Limerick Ln.

14

Windsor

Sonoma Coast State Beaches

Serano Del Mar

Carmet

SHEEP RIDGE

Sugarloaf

Salmon Creek

Bohemian Hwy.

Camp Meeker

Rio Dell

**Burke's Canoes**

Shiloh Reg. Park

17

16

East Side Rd.

Redwood Hwy.

Shiloh Rd.

Mark West Springs Rd.

Bodega Marine Life Refuge

Bodega Bay

Bodega Harbor

Occidental

Forestville

Graton Rd.

Graton

18

19

Laguna Rd.

Sonoma Co. Airport

River Rd.

21

Bodega Head

Doran Reg. Park

Bodega

Freestone

Molino

Ragle Ranch Reg. Park

Occidental Rd.

Guerneville Rd.

20

Fulton Rd.

Fulton

TO SONOMA (25mi), THE VALLEY OF THE MOON

Valley Ford Cutoff

Valley Ford Rd.

Sebastopol

12

Santa Rosa

12

Spring Lake

Bennett Valley Rd.

Dillon Beach

Tomales Bluff

Elephant Rocks

Fallon

Dillon Beach Rd.

Valley Ford

Knowles Corner

Todd Rd.

Bloomfield Rd.

Bloomfield

116

Stony Pt. Rd.

Petaluma Hill Rd.

Point Reyes Nat'l Seashore

Tule Elk Reserve

Tomales Bay

Tomales

SONOMA CO. MARIN CO.

Fallon Two Rock Rd.

Cunningham

Two Rock

101

Rohnert Park

Cotati

Crane Cyn. Rd.

Crane Creek Reg. Park

Tomales Petaluma Rd.

Petaluma Valley Ford Rd.

Sonoma State University

Penngrove

Pressley Rd.

Bodega Rd.

Stony Pt. Rd.

Sonoma Mtn.

Petaluma

**Petaluma Adobe State Historic Park**

Chileno Valley Rd.

D St.

Frates Rd.

Adobe Rd.

TO SONOMA (10mi)

116

Lakeville Hwy.

Petaluma River

Stage Gulch Rd.

TO NOVATO (10mi), SAN FRANCISCO (30mi)

## Russian River Communities

summer only crossing

Duncan Mills Museum

Monte Cristo

Duncan Mills

116

Moscow Rd.

Villa Grande

Northwood

Monte Rio

Cazadero Hwy.

Guernewood Park

Montesano

Vacation Beach

Ped. Bridge

El Bonita

Guerneville

River Rd.

Rolands

Rio Nido

May's Canyon Rd.

12

Odd Fellows Park

Bohemian Grove (private)

116

## Sonoma County

40min. drive apart. **Sebastopol,** not a river town itself, claims kinship to those towns because of its location on **Route 116,** "the road to the Russian River." To reach Sebastopol, travel west on **Route 12** from Santa Rosa.

**Buses: Golden Gate Transit** (in Sonoma ☎541-2000, in San Francisco 415-923-2000) connects the Russian River area and the Bay Area. Free maps at visitors centers. Bus #78 heads north from Freemont Dr. between Mission and Howard to **Sebastopol** (2hr.; 4:17, 4:55, 5:19pm; $6.30). Morning buses to Santa Rosa available. **Sonoma County Transit** (☎576-7433 or 800-345-7433) has a county-wide route (#20) from Santa Rosa to the Russian River area. Leaves from 2nd St. and B St. (M-F 10 per day, 5am-8pm; Sa-Su 3 per day, 10:30am-6:45pm; to Sebastopol $1.50, to Guerneville $2.)

**Bike Rental: Bicycle Factory,** 195 N. Main St. (☎829-1880), Sebastopol. Mountain bikes $8 per hr., $24 per day (with helmet, lock, and water bottle). Open M-F 10am-6:30pm, Sa 10am-5pm, Su 10am-4pm.

**Visitor Information: Sebastopol Area Chamber of Commerce,** 265 S. Main St. (☎823-3032). Open M-F 9am-5pm. **Healdsburg Chamber of Commerce,** 217 Healdsburg Ave. (☎433-6935). Open M-F 9am-5pm, Sa-Su 10am-2pm. **Guerneville Chamber of Commerce and Visitors Bureau,** 16209 1st St. (24hr. info line ☎869-9000). Open Su-W 9:30am-7pm, Th-Sa 9:30am-8pm.

**Post Office: Sebastopol,** 290 S. Main St. (☎823-2729). Open M-F 8:30am-5pm. **Healdsburg,** 409 Fosscreek Circle (☎433-9276). Open M-F 8:30am-5pm. **Postal Code:** 95472 (Sebastopol), 95448 (Healdsburg).

## ACCOMMODATIONS & CAMPING

The Russian River Valley's least expensive option is camping, for the tourist industry on the Russian River caters to a well-heeled, elegant, B&B-patronizing crowd. Nonetheless, there are a couple of indoor options that won't break the bank.

**Johnson's Beach Resort** (☎869-2022), on 1st St. in the center of Guerneville. The family-run, family-oriented resort is a throwback to younger, more innocent days: burgers, hot dogs, and beers are all the same price ($1.50), and the speakers play Sinatra. Boat rentals (canoes and kayaks $7 per hr., $20 per day; paddle boats $7 per hr.; inner-tubes $3 per day) are the cheapest on the river. The campground looks like a parking lot, but the friendly atmosphere more than makes up for it. Free river access. Recreation and laundry room. The **Russian River Jazz Festival** is held here. Reservations available for cabin rentals of 1 week or more; everything else, including camping, is first come, first served. Open May 15-Oct. 15. Sites $12, each additional person $2; RVs $20-25; well-worn cabins with fridge and TV $50-60. No credit cards. ❶

**The Willows,** 15905 River Rd. (☎869-2824 or 200-953-2828), in Guerneville. Directly on the Russian River. Staying here is more like camping in someone's backyard than in the woods. Many amenities, like free canoes and kayaks, outdoor jacuzzi and sauna, and use of a semi-outdoor kitchen, are all included. The atmosphere caters to a diverse crowd and welcomes all except pets. The scene may get a little wild at times. May-Sept. sites $20 per person. Rooms $69-139; $60-119 in winter. ❷

**River Village Resort & Spa,** 14880 River Rd. (☎869-8139 or 800-529-3376; www.rivervillageresort.com), in Guerneville. Across the street from the Russian River. Pool and spa treatment. Rooms are delightfully decorated with hand-crafted furniture and art. Pets allowed in some cottages. Offers many concierge services. Reservations advised for weekends and holidays; minimum stay may be required. Rooms $90-195. ❺

## ◗ FOOD

The health-conscious Russian River Valley sprouts good and good-for-you restaurants. The entire area is overflowing with food fit for the gods.

▨ **Willow Wood Cafe Market,** 9020 Graton Rd. (☎823-0233), off Rte. 116 in Graton. This out-of-the-way cafe and country market is more than worth the detour. Food so fresh, you'd think they harvest for each individual order. Try the roast pork tenderloin sandwich ($9.75) for lunch or the polenta with goat cheese ($8.75) for dinner. Chai ($2.75) comes in big ceramic bowls. Open M-Th 8am-9pm, F-Sa 8am-9:30pm, Su 9am-3pm. ❷

▨ **Screamin' Mimi's,** 6902 Sebastopol Ave. (☎823-5902), Sebastopol. The best ice cream and sorbet around ($2-3.75). This colorful shop makes rich delights such as its signature Mimi's Mud (espresso, fudge, and Oreo). They also have a full line of coffees and teas. Open June-Sept. daily 11am-11pm; Oct.-May Su-Th 11am-9:30pm, F-Sa 11am-11pm. ❶

**Sparks,** 16248 Main St. (☎869-8206), Guerneville. Serves organic vegetarian and vegan fare. Unique plates like oyster, mushroom, and vegetable kebabs drizzled in savory Brazilian sauce ($12), and seasonal beverages like hibiscus and mint cooler sweetened with chicory syrup ($1.50) or sangria ($4.50). Menu changes often. Cooking classes M-W ($65). Open Su and Sa 10am-3pm and 5:30-9pm, Th-F 5:30-9pm. ❸

**Raymond's Bakery,** 5400 Cazadero Hwy. (☎632-5335; www.raymonds-bakery.com), Guerneville. Take Rte. 116 west and turn right onto Cazadero Hwy. Owned by a friendly young couple, Raymond's Bakery is quickly becoming one of Guerneville's local favorites. Tucked 12 mi. back in the redwoods, the bakery produces freshly baked breads ($2.50-3.50 loaf), homemade cookies (75¢), and pastries ($2.75-5.25) that will make it worth the trip. The onion rolls and fresh focaccia sandwiches ($4.50) are especially popular. Open M and Th-Su 8am-6pm. ❶

**East-West Cafe,** 128 N. Main St. (☎829-2822), Sebastopol. Mediterranean platters make this the best local vegetarian-friendly restaurant. Weekday breakfast specials $7-8. Free-range chicken or tofu fajitas $8. Drinks include Thai iced tea, ginger honey lemonade, wine, and beer. Open M-F 7:30am-9pm, Sa 8am-9pm, Su 8am-8pm. ❷

## ◉ ⚂ SIGHTS & ACTIVITIES

Russian River Valley **wineries** are typically smaller, more remote, and less crowded than those in Napa and Sonoma. The *Wine Country Map of the Russian River Wine Road,* free at every visitors center in Wine Country, has an excellent map and lists every winery in the area, complete with hours, services, and products. Some *Let's Go* favorites follow. Traveling a few miles northwest along Rte. 116 from Sebastopol brings visitors to **Forestville,** the site of **Topolos at Russian River Vineyards,** 5700 Rte. 116 (Gravenstein Hwy.), known best for their Zinfandels and efforts toward an all-organic vineyard. (☎887-1575 or 800-867-6567. Restaurant open Su and W-Sa 11:30am-2:30pm and 5:30-9:30pm; tasting room open daily 11am-5:30pm.) Just outside Guerneville, the **Korbel Champagne Cellars,** 13250 River Rd., bubble with popular free tours, which cover the cellars, brewery, rose gardens, and tasting room. Korbel is also home to the biggest bottle of champagne in the world (350 lbs.) and a **deli ❶** that offers gourmet sandwiches for $6. (☎824-7000. Tours daily 10am-3:30 pm. Tastings daily 9am-4:30pm; in winter 9am-4pm.) The unpretentious **Hop Kiln Winery,** 6050 Westside Rd., in Healdsburg, is a historic landmark. Visitors are welcome to complimentary wine, olive oil, and chutney tastings. (☎433-6491. Open daily 10am-5pm for tasting. Grounds close 5:15pm.) Those with an interest in art will like **Roshambo Winery,** 3000 Westside Rd., 3 mi. south of Healdsburg. It has a gallery and overlooks miles of vines framed by rolling, gold-green mountains. (☎888-535-WINE/9463. Open Su-M and W-Sa 10:30am-4:30pm. Gallery openings 4-8pm as announced.) Fountains abound at the more intimate **Trentadue Winery,** 19170 Geyserville Ave., 1 mi. south of Geyserville. Tourists can watch wine-making in action (though tours depend on available personnel) or picnic under a canopy of grape leaves, clematis, and potato lions. (☎433-3104. Tasting room open daily 11am-4:30pm.) Also in Geyserville, the award-winning **Château Souverain,** 400 Souverain Rd. (turn left at the Independence Ln. Exit off US 101), offers wine-tasting to the country club elite. An elegant **cafe ❹** looks out on the winery and its magnificent expanse of vineyards. (Winery ☎433-8281, retail 433-8100, cafe 433-8197. Tastings daily 10am-5pm. Cafe open M-Th 11:30am-2:30pm and F-Su 5:30-8pm.)

**Burke's Canoe Trips** rents canoes for the 10 mi. river trip to Guerneville. The fee includes a ride back; Burke's runs two buses every 30min. to shuttle people. (☎887-1222. Canoes $42 per day. Call ahead for return service to your car. Open May-Oct. M-F 9:30am-6pm, Sa-Su 9am-6pm. No credit cards.) **Russian River Kayaks,** 2030 Rte. 116, has a private landing right on the river. (☎865-2141. Kayaks or bikes $5 per hr., $15 per 4hr., $25 per day. Open M-Sa 8am-5:30pm, Su 10am-4pm. Later returns can be arranged.) Just 10min. north of Guerneville, enjoy the shaded beauty of the redwoods in the **Armstrong Woods State Park** (☎869-2015). Hiking, biking, and horseback riding opportunities abound. The 1 mi. **Pioneer Trail** starts at the Visitors Center parking lot and skirts Fife Creek. For a challenging trek, take the **East Ridge Trail** (6¾ mi.), which climbs 1600 ft.

## 📷 NIGHTLIFE

Guerneville is *the* night spot in the Russian River Valley. It is predominantly a gay scene, although no one is made to feel unwelcome. 🅢**Stumptown Brewery,** 15145 River Rd., 1 mi. east of Guerneville, is a funky venue with unique in-house brews ($4-7) and live music. An outdoor patio looks out over the Russian River. (☎869-0705. Open daily noon-2am. Cash only.) The **Rainbow Cattle Co.,** 16220 Main St., with its posters of men in thongs and stickers stating "Hate Stops Here," proudly welcomes everyone. (☎869-0206. Open daily 6am-2am.)

Sebastopol's **Apple Blossom Festival,** in late April, has entertainment, crafts, and food. The **Sebastopol Music Festival** (☎800-648-9922) also occurs at this time. There are free concerts each Sunday from 2-4pm, June through August, on the plaza in Healdsburg. The **19th Festival of Art and Wine** (☎824-8717), in Duncan Mills, occurs in late June. The **Russian River Valley Winegrowers Grape to Glass Weekend** (☎522-8726), in mid-August, is the big event of the season, when over 30 wineries offer free tours and tastings. **The Russian River Jazz Festival** is a major event at Johnson's Beach Resort, blasting trombone, trumpet, and piano melodies down the river the weekend after Labor Day. (☎869-3940. Tickets from $26.)

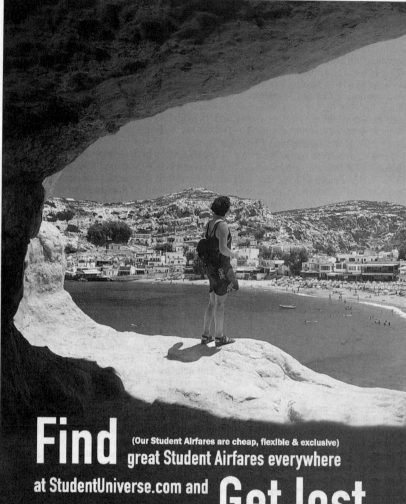

**Find** (Our Student Airfares are cheap, flexible & exclusive)
great Student Airfares everywhere
at StudentUniverse.com and **Get lost.**

 StudentUniverse.com

Student Airfares everywhere

# THE FAR NORTH

California's vast, oft-forgotten Far North offers a peaceful escape from the crowding and congestion that typifies California life. Small, friendly towns dot the countryside, and the wilderness of the coasts and mountains is among the most remote in the state. The Far North stretches from Mendocino County north along the coast to the Oregon border and east into the rich, densely forested Cascades. Along the way, this region offers plenty of activities for the small-town enthusiast, the nature-lover, and the outdoor adventurer.

## HIGHLIGHTS OF THE FAR NORTH

**REDWOODS AND COASTLINE.** The North Coast features sky-scraping trees and breathtaking coastal views; some of the best of these are in **Redwood National and State Parks** (p. 201), the **Lost Coast** (p. 193), and the **Avenue of the Giants** (p. 192).

**MOUNTAINS.** The stunning, sacred **Mount Shasta** (p. 214) attracts bikers, hikers, and climbers, while **Lassen Volcanic National Park** (p. 208) offers spectacular camping.

**CAVERNS.** Amid dry grasses, sagebrush, and rock formations, **Lava Beds National Monument** (p. 222) is rife with fascinating caves.

**OREGON SHAKESPEARE FESTIVAL.** The Bard's greatest hits reign again in **Ashland, Oregon** (p. 226) at this renowned annual series of Elizabethan dramatic performances.

# THE NORTH COAST

Wind-swept and larger than life, the North Coast is a hidden jewel of California's natural wonders. Redwoods, golden prairies, and undiscovered black sand beaches will make the traveler marvel; the North Coast's untouched wilderness and isolation are simply stunning.

The North Coast begins in the San Francisco Bay Area and continues to the Oregon border. Roadtrips on the North Coast can follow one of two scenic highways. **Highway 1** offers coastal views along the shores of Marin, Sonoma, and Mendocino Counties. An hour north of Fort Bragg, Hwy. 1 turns sharply inland and travels away from the coast, merging with **US 101** for the journey north. South of this juncture, US 101 meanders through the heart of California's wine country on its way to sleepy farmlands and pine forests curtained in fog.

Both highways skip a stretch of coastline known as the **Lost Coast** (see p. 193), which contains some of the most rugged scenery in the state. Lost Coast marijuana farmers are (in)famous for cultivating what smokers consider to be some of the kindest bud in the world. US 101 brings travelers to the Avenue of the Giants, home of the redwoods that make the region famous. North of Eureka and Arcata, US 101 winds back to the coast where more redwoods tower peacefully, protected within the long strips of Redwood National and State Parks (see p. 201).

# HIGHWAY 1

Easy driving it is not, but Highway 1 (the Pacific Coast Highway, or PCH) is one of the world's most breathtaking stretches of road. North of San Francisco, the famous highway snakes along cragged cliffs between pounding surf and monolithic redwoods. The quaint coastal hamlets spaced along PCH offer opportunities to recover from the heart-stopping journey. Be prepared, however, for slow trail-

**FAR NORTH**

ers on the road and sky-high prices. The least expensive options are outdoors: camping, hiking, and picnicking. The coast is also home to some of the loveliest inns and B&Bs around, which may persuade travelers to splurge after a week in the wilderness. For more on Hwy. 1, see **Central Coast,** p. 320, and **Bay Area,** p. 129.

**BODEGA.** Heading north, the highway leaves the Bay Area via San Rafael, nearing the breathtaking Point Reyes National Seashore (see **Marin,** p. 159). Hwy. 1 takes a brief inland turn before meeting the ocean again at surf haven **Bodega Bay.** On the Sonoma coast west of Bodega Bay, the **Bodega Head Loop** is a short coastal hike with pristine beach and ocean views. To reach the 1½ mi. trail from the town, turn left on E. Shore Rd. Turn west on Bay Flat Rd. and continue around the bay past Spud Point Marina to Bedge Head parking, the trailhead's location. The small town of Bodega Bay displays its seafaring roots in the incredibly fresh salmon and crab at oceanside restaurants. The **Visitors Center,** 850 Coast Hwy. 1, has info on the North Coast. (☎707-875-3866. Open M-Th 10am-6pm, F-Sa noon-8pm, Su 11am-7pm.) Both the towns of Bodega Bay and Bodega, 1½ mi. away, were featured in Alfred Hitchcock's 1963 film *The Birds*. See pictures at the Visitors Center.

**Sonoma Coast State Beach** begins just north of Bodega Bay off Hwy. 1. The 5000 acres of land offer 16 mi. of beach, spectacular views, and places to picnic, hike, and camp. However, unpredictable currents make these beaches dangerous (see **Sleeper Waves,** p. 196). The most popular coastal campgrounds are **Bodega Dunes ❶** (hot showers, sites $16) and **Wright's Beach ❷** (sites $20). Call ReserveAmerica for reservations at ☎800-444-7275. If the campsites are full, the clean rooms with TV and private bath at **Bodega Harbor Inn ❹,** off Hwy. 1 in Bodega Bay, are your cheapest bet. (☎875-3594; www.bodegaharborinn.com. Rooms $60-82.)

**FARTHER NORTH.** Heading up, Hwy. 1 hits **Jenner** at the mouth of the Russian River. Jenner's **Goat Rock Beach,** with its astounding waves and coast, is the site of a famous harbor seal rookery. Twelve miles up the coast from Jenner is **Fort Ross State Historic Park** (☎707-847-3437; entrance fee $4), a lonely walled fort clinging to the ocean bluffs and marking the eastern limit of former imperial Russia. Russians migrated here from Alaskan outposts to hunt otters and find farmland, but left in 1841, after decimating the otters population and losing vast sums of money. **John Sutter,** of mill and creek fame, bought the fort for a song, primarily to get the redwood threshing table inside. The Fort now houses a small museum and bookstore, and features the only reconstructed Russian buildings in the continental US. (Museum open daily 10am-4:30pm.) **Reef Campground and Day Use Area ❶,** 2 mi. south of the Fort, offers 21 primitive campsites with fire rings and picnic tables. (first-come, first-served. Water spigots. Flush toilets. Dogs allowed. Open Apr.-Nov. Sites $10; day use $4.) **Salt Point State Park ❶,** north of Fort Ross, 20 mi. from Jenner, comprises 6000 acres, including 6 mi. of rugged coast. There are 109 sites with firepits and picnic tables. (☎707-847-3221, reservations through **ReserveAmerica** 800-444-7275. No showers. Dogs allowed. Drinking water and toilets. Open for day use sunrise-sunset. Sites $12, walk-ins $10; day use $4, hike/bike $2.)

Farther north on Hwy. 1 in Mendocino County, the fog-shrouded **lighthouse** and **museum** of **Point Arena** deserve a stop. The 115 ft. lighthouse is vintage 1906, built after the San Francisco earthquake demolished the 1870 original. (☎707-882-2777. Open daily May-Sept. 10am-4:30pm; Oct.-Apr. 11am-3:30pm. Entrance fee $5. Guided tours included.) Nearby **Manchester State Beach ❶** has 46 tent sites and hike/bike sites. (☎707-937-5804. Flush toilets. Sites $9, seniors $7; day use $5.)

**BOONVILLE.** Twenty-seven miles to the east over Mountain View Rd. is Boonville, where perhaps the only attraction is the few old-timers who are "white-oakin" (working hard) to keep the rapidly fading local language of Boontling (basi-

cally a complex slang) alive. Get some "bahl gorms" (good food) and a "horn of
zeese" (coffee; under $1) at **Boont Berry Farm ❷**, 13981 Rte. 128, which is known for
its BBQ tofu on brown rice ($6.50 per lb.) and $5.75 avocado, chicken, and cheese
sandwiches. (☎707-895-3576. Open M-Sa 10am-6pm, Su noon-6pm.)

# MENDOCINO                                             ☎707

Teetering on bluffs over the ocean, isolated Mendocino (pop. 1107) is a charming
coastal community of art galleries, craft shops, bakeries, and B&Bs. The town's
weathered shingles, white picket fences, and clustered homes seem out of place
on the West Coast; maybe that's why Mendocino was able to masquerade for years
as the fictional Maine village of Cabot Cove in the TV series *Murder, She Wrote*.

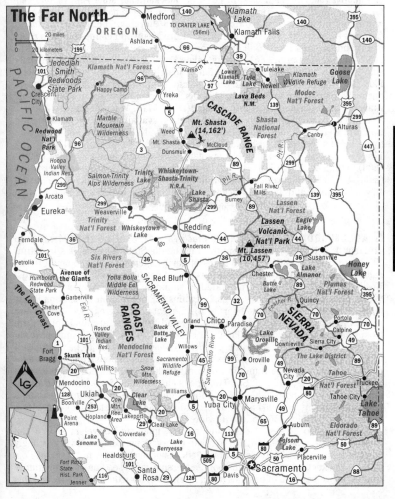

**⚡ 7 ORIENTATION AND PRACTICAL INFORMATION.** Mendocino sits on
**Highway 1,** right on the Pacific Coast, 30 mi. west of US 101 and 12 mi. south of Fort
Bragg. Although driving is the easiest way to reach Mendocino, once there, the
tiny town is best explored on foot. Mendocino, like all northern coast areas, can be
very chilly, even in summer. Travelers should prepare for 40-70°F temperatures.

The nearest **bus** station is two hours away in Ukiah. Greyhound runs two
buses per day to Ft. Bragg. **Mendocino Stage** provides a shuttle service along the
north Mendocino coast and runs buses between Ft. Bragg and Ukiah. (☎964-
0167. 2 per day, $10.) **Mendocino Transit Authority,** 241 Plant Rd., makes one
round-trip daily between Santa Rosa, Ukiah, Willits, Fort Bragg, and Mendocino.
(☎800-696-4682. One-way $16, round-trip $26.50.)For **visitor information,** head to
the **Fort Bragg-Mendocino Coast Chamber of Commerce,** 332 N. Main St., in Fort
Bragg. (☎961-6300 or 800-726-2780. Open daily 9am-5pm.) For **park-related general information,** call ☎937-5804 or go to the **MacKerricher State Park Visitors Center,** 2½ mi. north of Fort Bragg. (☎964-8898. Open in summer daily 11am-3pm; in
winter Sa-Su 11am-3pm.) **Catcha Canoe and Bicycles, Too!,** at Hwy. 1 and
Comptche-Ukiah Rd., specializes in hand-crafted redwood canoes but also rents
quality bikes and kayaks. Call ahead for tide info. (☎937-0273 or 800-320-BIKE/
2453. Canoes $18 per hr., $54 per day; bikes $10/$30; kayaks $12/$36. Open daily
9am-5pm.) **Lost Coast Kayaking** gives fantastic guided tours of Van Damme State
Park. (☎937-2434. 2hr.; $45. Daily 9, 11:30am, 2pm. Reservations are necessary
but walk-ins may get lucky. Open May-Oct.) For clean clothes, head to **Colombi
Laundromat,** 647 Oak St., in Fort Bragg. (☎964-5773. Wash $1.75, dry 25¢ per
8½min. Open daily 7am-11pm.) **Internet access** is available at the **Regional Branch
Library of Mendocino,** 499 Laurel St., at the corner of N. Whipple St. and Laurel St.,
three blocks east of Main St. in Fort Bragg. (Open Tu-W 11am-7:45pm, Th-F
11am-5:45pm, Sa 10am-4:45pm.) Emergency services include the **police** (☎961-
0200), with a station in Fort Bragg, the **sheriff** (☎963-4086), and a **rape crisis line**
(☎964-4357). **Mendocino Coast District Hospital** is located at 700 River Dr. (☎961-
1234), Ft. Bragg, and the **post office** is at 10500 Ford St., two blocks west of Main
St. (☎937-5282; open M-F 7:30am-4:30pm). **Postal Code:** 95460.

**📍 ACCOMMODATIONS. Jug Handle Creek Farm ❶,** 5 mi. north of Mendocino
off Hwy. 1, across the street from the Jug Handle State Reserve, is a beautiful
133-year-old house sitting on 40 acres of gardens, campsites, and small rustic
cabins. One hour of chores (or $5) is required per night. (☎964-4630. 30 beds.
No linen. Reservations recommended in summer, walk-ins welcome. Dorms
$20, students $14, children $9; sites $9; cabins $28 per person.) **Nicholson House
Inn ❺,** 951 Ukiah St., is in the heart of town, right next to great restaurants and
just a block from the ocean. Phones, TV, and breakfast are available in the
Hospitality Living Room. (☎937-0934 or 800-962-0934. 2-night min. stay on
weekends, 3-night min. stay on holidays. All reservations are to be paid in full
in advance. Rooms $90-174. $5 less in winter.) Less expensive and less eye-
pleasing options can be found in Fort Bragg. The most budget-friendly option
is **Colombi Motel ❸,** 647 Oak St., five blocks east of Main St. It has clean single
and double units with cable TV, a phone, and private bath; some units also
have a full kitchen. (☎964-5773. Motel office inside market. Check-out 11am.
Singles $45; doubles $55. $5 less in winter.)

There are also scores of campsites nearby; interested travelers should call
ReserveAmerica (☎800-444-7275) to make reservations, which are very strongly
advised in summer. **MacKerricher State Park campground ❶,** 2½ mi. north of Fort
Bragg, has excellent views of tidepool life, passing seals, sea lions, and migratory
whales, as well as 9mi. of beaches and a murky lake for trout fishing. Around this

lake is **Lake Cleone trail** (1 mi.)—a short, easy hike that features thick cypress trees and a pretty marsh. Access the trail from Cleone Camp or Surfwood Camp. (☎937-5804. Showers, bathrooms, and drinkable water. Sites $16; day use free. Reservations necessary in summer.) Woods and fog shelter 30 sites at **Russian Gulch State Park campground ❶**, 8 mi. south of Fort Bragg on Hwy. 1. Campers have access to a beach, redwoods, hiking trails, and a 35 ft. waterfall. The **Falls Loop trail** (7 mi.) leads from the campground to a scattering of old-growth redwoods and rock-pounding falls. (☎937-5804. Showers and flush toilets. No hookups. Open Apr.-Oct. Sites $15. Discounts for seniors. Hike/bike $2; day use $4.)

🄲 **FOOD.** All of Mendocino's breads are freshly baked, all vegetables locally grown, all wheat unmilled, and almost all prices inflated. Picnicking on the Mendocino Headlands is the cheapest option and should be preceded by a trip to **Mendosa's Market,** 10501 Lansing St., the closest thing in Mendocino to a real supermarket. It's pricey for a supermarket, of course, but most items are fresh and delicious. (☎937-5879. Open daily 8am-9pm.) Restaurants in Mendocino often close unusually early. **Tote Fête ❶**, 10450 Lansing St., has delicious tote-out food. An asiago, pesto, and artichoke heart sandwich ($4.75) hits the spot. The bakery in the back has a flower garden and a small fountain. (☎937-3383. Open M-Sa 10:30am-7pm, Su 10:30am-4pm. Bakery open daily 7:30am-4pm.) **Lu's Kitchen ❷**, 45013 Ukiah St. west of Lansing St., is a local favorite. It serves leafy vegetarian cuisine in an informal, outdoor atmosphere. (☎937-4939. Prices range $5-10. Open daily 11:30am-5:30pm. Closed Jan.-Mar. and on very rainy days.) **Mendocino Cookie Co. ❶**, 303 N. Main St. across from the Visitor's Center in Fort Bragg, offers a caffeine fix and sugar high all at once with a potent super-large latte ($3) and sweet white chocolate chip and macadamia cookies ($1.10), along with freshly baked muffins, scones, and croissants. Get a buy-one-get-one-free cookie coupon at the Visitor's Center. (☎937-4843. Open daily 6:30am-5:30pm. Cookies half price after 5pm.) **Cafe Beaujolais ❺**, 961 Ukiah St. at the corner of Evergreen, has a garden that welcomes wandering. To enjoy the fresh goods from their on-site, brick-oven bakery, wake up early—they run out quickly. (☎937-5614. Dinner $19-25. Bakery open daily 11am-4pm and 5:45-9pm. Garden open daily 11am-4pm. Closed in Dec.) **Albion Inn ❺**, 3790 N. Hwy. 1, south of Mendocino, has a spectacular ocean view and award-winning food. The menu changes periodically, but always count on roasted garlic caesar salad ($8), lime & ginger prawns ($24), and grilled Pacific king salmon ($23) to satisfy taste buds. (☎937-1919 or 800-479-7944. Reservations suggested. Open M-F 5:30-9pm, Sa-Su 5-9pm.)

🄶🄹 **SIGHTS AND ENTERTAINMENT.** Mendocino's greatest natural feature lies 900 ft. to its west, where the earth comes to a halt and falls off into the Pacific, forming the impressive coastline of the ▣**Mendocino Headlands.** The windy quarter-mile stretch of land that separates the town from the rocky shore remains an undeveloped meadow of tall grass and wildflowers, despite its obvious value as a site for even more multi-million dollar vacation homes.

In **Fort Bragg,** the California Western Railroad, also called the **Skunk Train,** at Hwy. 1 and Laurel St., offers a jolly, child-friendly diversion through its Redwood Route, and has since 1885. A steam engine, diesel locomotive, and vintage motor-car take turns running between Fort Bragg and Northspur. (☎964-6371 or 800-777-5865; www.skunktrain.com. 3hr. round-trip; departs Fort Bragg daily at 10am and 2:15 pm. $35, children 5-11 $17, under 5 free. Reservations recommended.)

Poor drainage, thin soil, and ocean winds have created an unusual bonsai garden 3 mi. south of town at the **Pygmy Forest** in **Van Damme State Park ❶** (camping $16; day-use $4). The Pygmy Forest, off Hwy. 1 past the park (after turning left,

FAR NORTH

drive 3½ mi. to a parking lot and look for a sign), is open for free to hikers. The **ecological staircase** at **Jug Handle State Park** is a terrace of five different ecosystems formed by a combination of erosion and tectonic uplift, with each ecosystem roughly 100,000 years older than the one below it.

An abundance of hot springs in the Mendocino area proves once and for all that the region is a natural paradise. **Orr Hot Springs,** 13201 Orr Springs Rd., is just east of Mendocino, off Comptche Ukiah Rd. Those wishing to simmer their stress away should take the North State St. Exit off US 101. Sauna, steam room, and gardens make the world disappear at this clothing-optional resort. (☎462-6277. Day-use $20. 18+. Open daily 10am-10pm.) In July, enjoy the Mendocino Music Festival, a two-week melee of classical music, opera, and cultural dance. Tickets for some events go quickly. (☎937-2044; www.mendocinomusic.com. Tickets $15-40.)

# AVENUE OF THE GIANTS                                              ☎707

About 10 mi. north of Garberville off US 101 in the **Humboldt Redwoods State Park,** the Avenue of the Giants winds its way through 31 mi. inhabited by the world's largest living organisms above ground level. Hiking, swimming, fishing, biking, and rafting opportunities abound in this rugged area.

🛈 **PRACTICAL INFORMATION. Greyhound** (☎923-3388 or 800-231-2222) runs **buses**—two north and two south daily—out of Garberville to Eureka ($14), Portland ($59), and San Francisco ($34). Meet the bus behind the Six Rivers National Bank, 432 Church St., one block east of Redwood Dr.

The **Humboldt Redwoods State Park Visitors Center,** just south of Weott on the Avenue, has a very knowledgeable staff that can highlight the Avenue's groves, facilities, trails, and bike routes while providing safety tips on camping. The center also has hands-on displays for kids about area wildlife. (☎946-2263. Open Apr.-Oct. daily 9am-5pm; Oct.-Apr. Su and Th-Sa 10am-3pm.) The **Garberville-Redway Chamber of Commerce,** 773 Redway Dr., Jacob Garber Square, offers information on local events and attractions. (☎800-923-2613. Open M-F 10am-5pm.) The **post office** is at 368 Sprowl Creek Rd. (☎923-2652. Open M-F 8:30am-5pm.) **Postal Code:** 95542.

🏠🏕 **ACCOMMODATIONS & CAMPING.** In Myers Flat, the bed and breakfast **Myers Inn ❺** has ten clean, homey bedrooms and offers boating and fishing tours. Hot breakfast included. (☎943-3259 or 800-500-6464; www.myersinn.com. Rooms $125-150. AAA discount.) The **Brass Rail Inn ❹,** 3188 Redwood Dr., Redway, has been a brothel, dinner house, and teahouse in past incarnations, but is now a perfectly respectable motel. (☎923-3931. Singles $50-55; doubles $50-72.) **The Redway Inn Motel ❹,** 3223 Redwood Dr., has bright, clean rooms with cable TV. (☎923-2660. Singles $50; doubles $55.) Farther north on the Avenue, the **Madrona Inn ❹,** 2907 Ave. of the Giants, in Phillipsville, has pink cottages, some with kitchens and two bedrooms. (☎943-1708. Cottages $55-100. Additional person $5. Pets $5.)

To sleep directly among the giants, camping is the best bet. In **Humboldt Redwood State Park,** camping options are plentiful. Each developed campsite offers coin showers, flush toilets, and fire rings. (☎946-2409. Sites $15.) The most remote site, wildlife-filled **Albee Creek ❶,** on Mattole Rd. 5 mi. west of US 101, near Rockefeller Forest, has access to biking and hiking trails and is open year-round. (Sites $15.) **Hidden Springs ❶,** near Myers Flat, is situated on a hillside in a mixed forest and has 154 semi-secluded sites with hot showers. Few hiking trails start directly at the campsite, but the South Fork of Eel River is a short hike away. (Open mid-May through mid-Oct. Sites $15.) Conveniently located next to the Visitors Center, **Burlington ❶** offers fully developed campsites, but is near the drone of the nearby freeway. RV hookups. (Open mid-May to Sept. Sites $15. Day use $4. Hike/bike $2) **Richardson Grove State Park ❶** (☎247-3318), off US 101 8 mi. south of Garberville, has sites ($15) with toilets and showers. Call ReserveAmerica (☎800-444-7275) for reservations at any of the above. For overnight campouts, **Grasshopper Trail Camp ❶** is near the summit of Grasshopper Peak. (Primitive sites with pit toilets. $1 per person. Register in advance at headquarters.)

▢ **FOOD.** Nearby Garberville offers a number of civilized eating options. **Sentry Market**, on Redwood Dr., is the largest supermarket for miles. (☎923-2279. Open daily 7am-10pm.) Locals highly recommend **Calico's Cafe ❷**, on Redwood Dr. next to Sherwood Forest Motel, for its homemade pastas, salads, and burgers as well. Try the garlicky fettucine gorgonzola ($9) made from scratch. (☎923-2253. Open M-Th 8am-9pm, F-Sa 8am-10pm, Su 11am-9pm.) **Nacho Mama's ❷**, at Redwood Dr. and Sprowl Creek Rd., is an organic Mexican fast-food stand with healthy burritos, dolphin-free albacore tacos, and refreshing soy wildberry or peach frosties. (☎923-4060. Entrees $3-9. Open M-Sa 11am-7pm.) For a 100% all-ranch burger ($5-8), stop by the **Chimney Tree Coffee Shop ❷**, 1111 Avenue of the Giants, just south of Phillipsville. There is also a hokey "hobbit" trail and a burnt-out, hollow "Chimney" redwood for the kids. (☎923-2265. Open daily 10:30am-7pm.)

▣▢ **SIGHTS & SEASONAL ACTIVITIES.** Scattered throughout the area are several tourist traps, such as **Eternal Tree House** and the **Drive-Thru Tree** ($1.50), along with plenty of Bigfoot merchandise. Young children will be entertained by a train ride through the redwoods ($3). Indispensable maps for longer trails are available at the Visitors Center ($1) or at any of the campsites (see p. 192).

There are a number of short day hikes. Half a mile north of Miranda, the **Stephens Grove Trail** is an easy three-quarter mile walk, passing the remnants of the old Stephens Grove campsite that was wiped out by a flood in 1964. Farther north, south of the Visitors Center, the half mile **Kent-Mather** loop trail begins at the **Garden Club of America Grove** and wanders through redwood sorrel and lady ferns; look for ospreys near the river. At **Founder's Grove**, the half-mile loop features the 1300 to 1500-year-old **Founder's Tree**, and the former tallest tree in Humboldt Redwoods State Park, the fallen 350 ft. **Dyerville Giant**, whose massive, three-story rootball looks like a mythic entanglement of evil.

Uncrowded trails wind through **Rockefeller Forest** in the park's northern section, which contains the largest grove of continuous old-growth redwoods in the world. The **Grasshopper Peak Trail**, a strenuous 14 mi. round-trip hike, starts at the Big Tree parking lot 4 mi. west of the Avenue on Mattole Rd. This is a hilly, all-day backcountry hike and will take you 3379 ft. high to a gorgeous panoramic view.

With its sizable population of artists, Garberville's **art festivals** are a big draw. **Jazz on the Lake** and the **Summer Arts Fair** begin in late June, followed by the popular **Shakespeare at Benbow Lake** in late July. Early August brings a marathon of jamming' on the banks of the Eel River with **Reggae on the River,** a wild three-day festival. For more info on these annual events, call ☎800-923-2613 or the Chamber of Commerce (see **Practical Information,** p. 192).

# LOST COAST ☎707

The Lost Coast can elude even the most observant visitor. When Hwy. 1 was built, the rugged coastline between Usal and Ferndale had to be bypassed and the highway moved inland; hence, this part of the coast was "lost" to modernization, leaving the jagged mountains, rocky shores, and black sand beaches comparatively undeveloped. Bring a map and 4WD because many roads are

**FAR NORTH**

unpaved, steep, and poorly marked; it can be easy to get, well, lost. Be careful when exploring—you don't want to wander into someone's **marijuana farm.** Leave Humboldt County's marijuana farmers' cabins and crops alone. Be especially careful around harvest time, usually October and November.

---

# ELK MACHISMO

Easy to spot thanks to their massive size and signature cream-colored rumps, Roosevelt elk have rebounded from near extinction to populate the prairies of Sinkyone Wilderness State Park and Redwood National and State Parks. In the fall, male elks (bulls) put their game to the test in rivalries to control an entire group of females, known as a "harem." A challenger bull approaches an already spoken-for harem and bugles, urinates, and kicks up turf in a show of desire. If the bull-in-residence answers the challenge, some poor cream-rump could end up losing an antler. However, one of the bulls usually backs down before things escalate to an antler clash, as should visitors who make the mistake of getting too close.

---

## SINKYONE WILDERNESS STATE PARK

To get to Sinkyone from the south, it is possible take Hwy. 1 north to the narrow, sometimes treacherous Usal Rd., where Hwy. 1 starts to turn inland toward Leggett. But before you attempt to traverse this backcountry road, call ahead to the ranger's office (☎986-7711) to make sure it's passable. The ranger-recommended route to Sinkyone is to take US 101 to Redway and follow the signs to **Shelter Cove** along Briceland-Thorn Rd. Ten miles down is the Four Corners intersection. To the left is Usal Rd., which eventually leads south to Usal Beach along a drive that makes Hwy. 1 seem like child's play (4WD required). To the right is Chemise Mountain Rd., which leads back to Shelter Cove. Allow 2hr. to travel the winding wooded route with occasional vistas of the rugged Lost Coast.

On the other side of the intersection, Briceland-Thorn Rd. becomes **Bear Harbor Rd.,** another treacherous drive—a road so narrow it only fits one car at a time—crafted for the fearless or insane. As you pull around the numerous blind hairpin turns, don't be bashful about announcing your presence with a firm honk. The mountain road passes by **Jones Beach, Needle Rock,** and the **Needle Rock Visitors Center,** which offers maps ($1), camping permits, and firewood. (☎986-7711. Visitors Center opening hours vary, but closing is always 5pm. Pit toilets; no water. 14-night max. stay. Sites $12. First-come, first-camp. Fills in summer.) The road eventually leads to **Bear Harbor,** growing increasingly difficult toward the end. The dedicated, however, will find their reward in the rustic beauty of the three neighboring campgrounds: **Orchard, Railroad,** and **Bear Harbor.** Surrounded by lush ferns, black sand, and transplanted eucalyptus trees, the sites are a half a mile's hike from the road. Be prepared to share your space with the **Roosevelt elk** (see **Elk Machismo,** above). The blocked-off road to **Jones Beach** is just 2 mi. down Bear Harbor Rd.

One of the more popular Lost Coast beaches, **Usal Beach ❶** has a self-registration kiosk and camping areas (unmarked sites $12, trail camps $2). About 300 ft. farther up the dirt road is a short bridge and turn-off leading to a parking area and some windy beachside sites (no drinking water). The southern trailhead of the difficult **Lost Coast Trail** begins at Usal and leads 52 mi. up the coast to **Mattole River.** However, most people hike the Lost Coast north to south so that the wind is with them. Many also only travel from the **Mattole Campgound** to **Black Sands Beach,** near Shelter Cove, because that 25 mi. stretch hugs the coast. Again, trail maps are essential and are available at state parks or the Needle Rock Visitors Center.

# KING RANGE NATIONAL CONSERVATION AREA

■ **ORIENTATION.** Stretching 24 mi. along the coast between Shelter Cove and Petrolia, the **King Range National Conservation Area** provides some of the best primitive camping in California, with clean creeks, beaches, and an abandoned lighthouse. It also contains one of North America's most unstable mountain ranges, which sits on a fault line between three different tectonic plates. Intense earthquakes push the ocean floor upward an average of 10 ft. every 1000 years. In 1992, a single earthquake raised King Range almost 4 ft. in a matter of minutes. 4WD vehicles are necessary to traverse many of the roads. **King Peak Road** travels through dense forest in the central part of the conservation area and leads to **Lightning, Saddle Mountain,** and **Horse Mountain Creek** trailheads and the **Horse Mountain** and **Tolkan** campsites. 4WD vehicles are required and no motor homes or trailers are permitted north of Horse Mountain Campground. **Chemise Mountain Road** meanders through Douglas fir and leads to Roosevelt elk at the **Hidden Valley** trailhead (where the southern **Lost Coast Trail** begins), the **Nadelos and Wailaki campsites,** and **Sinkyone Wilderness State Park.** Use low gears on downgrades, watch for oncoming traffic on one-lane stretches, and allow faster cars behind you to pass.

■ **CAMPING.** Camping permits are required at all campgrounds for commercial outfitters but not for individuals or families. Fire permits are required for everyone and can be purchased at the **King Range Bureau of Land Management (BLM)** office, on Shelter Cove Rd., 7 mi. from Shelter Cove. (☎ 986-5400; www.ca.blm.gov/arcata. Open M-Sa 10am-5pm.) Permits may also be obtained at many local general

The Lost Coast

FAR NORTH

stores, such as the nearby one in Petrolia. **Tolkan ❶** is windy, secluded, and on a steep ridge. (13 sites, picnic tables, pit toilets, fire rings, no water. No RVs. Sites $8.) **Wailaki Campground ❶** is slightly closer to civilization and more developed. (Toilets, fire pits, and picnic tables. Sites $8.) **Horse Mountain Camp ❶**, which is not located by the trailhead, is the most remote developed campground. Its 9 sites are windy and cool, but lack water. (Sites $8.) **A.W. Campground ❶**, between Honeydew and Mattole on Mattole Rd., is managed by Humboldt County and sits on the Mattole River. (Flush toilets, showers. Sites $12). **Mattole Beach Campground ❶**, at the northern part of King Range, is at the end of Lighthouse Rd., 45min. north of Honeydew off Mattole Rd. (Pit toilets, no drinking water. Sites $5. Day use free.)

🔲🗾 **SIGHTS & HIKES.** The windy, flat beach in King Range is framed by steep grass-covered mountains and rolling dunes. Here campers can enjoy the **Mattole River Estuary,** a nursery for young salmon and a home to egrets and brown pelicans, or take off on the challenging **Lost Coast Trail** (25 mi. one-way to Shelter Cove, allow three days). Although it is possible to hike the trail one-way and then backtrack to your vehicle, most campers use the **shuttle service** (see **Shelter Cove,** p. 197). The trek is long but rewarding with ever-changing vistas of mountains and coastline, as well as views of sea lions, shore birds, and black-tailed deer. All drinking and bathing water is supplied by the fresh water streams that run through the area. The ridge trails have no water, so if you plan a side hike, come prepared. You may also see a black bear, especially if your camp is not clean. **Bear canisters** are required on all King Range land and can be rented at the BLM office ($15). Always be on the lookout for poison oak, ticks, and rattlesnakes. A portion of the trail is impassable during high tide; it is necessary to check **tide tables.** Do this at the King Range BLM, or buy them in Garberville or Petrolia. It's a good idea to stop by the BLM office or call ahead to let them know your plans.

**SLEEPER WAVES.** Sleeper waves are overpowering waves that crash ashore and then forcefully pull back whatever or whomever they happen upon. Many beaches have posted warnings about such dangerous currents, and it is safest to simply stay out of treacherous waters. However, if a sleeper wave yanks you into the surf, do not swim toward shore. Doing so will only tire you out in a futile battle against the current. Instead, swim parallel to the beach until you're out of the wave's clutches.

The northern 25 mi. portion of Lost Coast trail ends in Shelter Cove at **Black Sands Beach,** which is open to beachcombing only at low tide. Do not attempt a swim here; dangerous **riptides** will pull you into the deep blue sea. From Black Sands Beach, those who want to see the seaside beauty without hiking the entire Lost Coast Trail can hike north to Big Flat (8½ mi.). This stretch is all beach hiking and impassable during high tide, but remains a favorite with hard-core surfers seeking killer waves and camping enthusiasts enjoying the large coastal terrace. From Big Flat, a great inland day hike is **Rattlesnake Ridge Trail,** which leads to the fern-shrouded canyon of Big Flat Creek (4 mi. one-way to Bear Hollow Camp).

Hikes abound in King Range. Three miles into the Lost Coast Trail, from Mattole, lies the **Punta Gorda Lighthouse.** It was first lit in 1917 and was known as the Alcatraz of lighthouses because of its remote location and reputation for being the assignment with which to punish deviant keepers. Allow half a day for the journey there and back, as most of the trail is slow-going sand hiking. **King Peak Trail** climbs 4087 ft. to reach a panoramic view of endless forested peaks and more than 100 mi. of Pacific coastline. The hike is a moderate, steady climb from Lightning trailhead (2 mi. one-way) or a very gradual ascent from Saddle Mountain trailhead (5 mi. one-way). There is a spring near the top at Maple Camp for water.

## SHELTER COVE

The tamest part of the wild Lost Coast, Shelter Cove was once a trading post. Native Americans bartered with each other on Point Delgada and settlers built a shipping port for fishing and wood products. Shelter Cove is still home to a tiny community of fishermen and now welcomes vacationers as well. Tourists can view sea lions perched on coastal rocks at **Sea Lion Rock,** along lower Pacific Dr., or inspect tidepools and an historic lighthouse at **Mal Coombs Park,** next to **Mario's Marina,** 533 Machi Rd. (☎986-1401), where the only open-daily restaurant and the site for chartering and launching boats are located. Pick up news and advice at the **Shelter Cove Deli ❷,** 492 Machi Rd., the only place in town where you can get fish 'n' chips ($6.75), Shelter Cove souvenirs, a tide table, and aspirin all at once. The closest thing in town to an information booth, the deli also provides details on over 100 campsites next to the marina and runs shuttle services that take hikers from Black Sands Beach parking lot to the trailhead at Mattole Beach. (☎986-7474. Shuttles to be arranged. $125 per vehicle. Tent sites $16, RVs with full hookups $27. Open M-F 7am-8pm, Sa-Su 6am-8pm.) With bath and TV, the rooms at the **Shelter Cove Beachcomber Inn ❹,** 412 Machi Rd., are the best deals on this stretch of coast. Some have kitchens and fireplaces. (☎986-7551 or 800-718-4789. Singles from $55.) For an unobstructed ocean view and pet friendliness, stay at **Shelter Cove Motor Inn ❺,** 205 Wave Dr. All rooms have a small kitchenette and an ocean view. (☎986-7521 or 888-570-9676; www.sheltercove-motorinn.com. One queen bed $88; family units $120 in the summer, $75-105 in the winter. 10% discount for AOPA, AARP and AAA members.) The pricier **Oceanfront Inn and Lighthouse ❻,** 10 Seal Ct., also has seaside rooms. All have private beach access and a private deck overlooking the ocean. (☎986-7002. Rooms with kitchen available. One queen bed $125; the private lighthouse suite for two $175.) The **Cove Restaurant ❸** is on the inn's first floor. (☎986-1197. Lunch $7-13, dinner $9-18. Open daily 11:30am-9pm.)

## FERNDALE

The northernmost Lost Coast town of **Ferndale** (pop. 1320) exemplifies small-town perfection. The amphitheater-like **cemeteries** near **Russ Park** on Ocean Ave. give a sense of the town's history and provide a breathtaking view of the Victorian town with its grazing dairy cattle. The accommodations here are mainly exorbitantly priced B&Bs, but if you have been saving for a splurge, this is the place.

One option is California's oldest B&B, the **Shaw House ❺,** 703 Main St. Founded in 1860, the Carpenter Gothic Revival-style home offers 7 rooms, a sit-down hot breakfast, and afternoon tea. (☎786-9958; www.shawhouse.com. Check-in between 4-6pm. Check-out 11am. Rooms in summer $85-165; in winter $75-165.) ▓**Village Baking and Catering ❶,** 472 Main St., is worth a stop off the highway. Try the incredible Special Turkey Sandwich with homemade artichoke relish ($4.25), sip coffee drinks ($1-2.25), or delight in gooey sticky buns for under $2. (☎786-9440. Open M-Sa 7am-3pm, Su 7am-1:30pm.)

One of Ferndale's oddest features, the annual Arcata Kinetic Sculpture Race (see **Sights,** p. 201), ends at the studio of the event's founder, **Hobart Galleries,** 393 Main St., at Brown St.

F A R  N O R T H

# EUREKA

☎707

Eureka (pop. 27,218) was born out of the demands of mid-19th-century gold prospectors, who wanted a more convenient alternative to the tedious overland route from Sacramento. The Humboldt Bay provided such a route, and Eureka was thus founded. The decline of the region's gold mining and lumber businesses has led Eureka to shift its effort from its previous reliance on natural resources to fishing and tourism. The town may not be as appealing as some of its more inviting neighbors, but Old Town Eureka is regaining some of its historic attraction. Next to the harbor are quaint shops, restaurants, and art galleries in old Victorian-style buildings. Don't judge Eureka only by driving through on Hwy. 101. The city's perimeter may reek of fish matter, but the center of Eureka has a pleasant, old-town charm.

**⚡🖫 ORIENTATION & PRACTICAL INFORMATION.** Eureka straddles **US 101,** 7 mi. south of Arcata and 280 mi. north of San Francisco. To the south, US 101 is referred to as Broadway. In town, US 101 is called 4th St. (heading south) and 5th St. (heading north).

**Greyhound buses** depart twice a day for San Francisco ($33-35) from 1603 4th St. at Q St. (☎442-0370 or 800-231-2222. Open M-F 9am-2pm, 3:30-5:45pm, and 8-10pm.) The **Humboldt Transit Authority,** 133 V St., runs regional buses between Scotia and Trinidad ($1.40-2) via Arcata. Most buses pick up passengers along 5th St. or Broadway. (☎443-0826. Open M-F 8am-noon and 1-4:30pm.) The **Eureka/Humboldt Visitors Bureau,** 1034 2nd St., will answer specific questions. (☎443-5097 or 800-809-5908, out-of-state 800-346-3482. Open M-F 9am-5pm.)

Eureka's **Chamber of Commerce,** 2112 Broadway, has information and brochures. Ask about any discounts that may be offered in town. (☎442-3738 or 800-356-6381. Open M-F 8:30am-5pm, Sa-Su 10am-4pm.) An **ATM** is at the **Bank of America,** near the corner of E and 4th St. and at the **Eureka Co-op** on 5th St., at L. St. **Summer Street Laundromat** is at 111 Summer St. (☎443-7463. Wash $2.75-4.00, dry 25¢ per 7min. Open daily 7am-9pm.) Eureka has **police** (☎441-4044) and **fire departments** (☎441-4054). The **Eureka General Hospital** is at 2200 Harrison Ave. (☎445-5111 ext. 4699). The **post offices** are located at 337 W. Clark St., near Broadway St. (☎442-1768; open M-F 8:30am-5pm and Sa noon-3pm) and 514 H St. at 5th St. (☎442-1828; open M-F 8:30am-5pm). **Postal Code:** 95501.

**🛏🛖 ACCOMMODATIONS & CAMPING.** Travelers will find many budget motels off US 101, but most are unappealing; be selective. Walking around alone at night, especially along Broadway, is not recommended. Old Town Eureka is more suitable for evening dinners and strolls. For an indulgent night, head to **🏠Cafe Waterfront ❺,** in Old Town at First and F St. The restaurant owns two plush Victorian rooms with a kitchen and breakfast nook to share. It feels like a private harbor-view apartment. (☎444-1301. Breakfast included. Rooms in summer $125-175; winter $100-150.) **Motel 6 ❸,** 1934 Broadway, lies south of town off US 101 and offers satellite TV. (☎445-9631. Singles $44; doubles $46. Additional person $3. Rates may vary in July and Aug.) Pricey but dependable, the **Red Lion Hotel ❺,** on US 101 at the northern edge of town, has immaculate rooms. (☎445-0844. Rooms $104-114. $10-15 discounts for AAA members.) Most of the area's camping is closer to Arcata than Eureka. **Big Lagoon County Park ❶,** 20 mi. north of Eureka on US 101, is a favorite. The park has 32 sites with flush toilets, drinking water, and a big lagoon for swimming, canoeing, and kayaking. (☎445-7652. No hookups. Sites $12. Day-use $2; arrive early to beat the rush.)

❒ **FOOD. Eureka Co-op,** 1036 5th St. at L St., sells bulk grains, organic produce, and deli foods. (☎443-6027. Open M-Sa 7am-9pm, Su 8am-9pm.) There are also two **farmer's markets** that run in the summer and fall. (Old Town Gazebo June-Oct. Tu 10am-1pm; Henderson Center July-Oct. Th 10am-1pm.) **Ramone's Bakery and Cafe ❶,** 209 E St., between 2nd and 3rd St., specializes in homemade truffles, fresh-baked pies, and the ever-popular "Chocolate Sin," a chocolate and liqueur torte. Sandwiches ($4), soups ($3), and salads ($4) are also available. (☎445-2923. Open M-Sa 7am-6pm, Su 7am-4pm.) Across the street, experience a taste of Italian tradition at **Gabriel's ❹,** 216 E St. Stuff yourself with pastas ($13-18), pizzas, and calzones ($11-13), but save room for homemade desserts ($5-7) like cannoli and spumoni. (☎445-0100. Entrees $15-25. Open M-F 11:30am-2:30pm and 5-9pm, Sa 5-10pm.) **Saffire Rose Cafe ❷,** 525 2nd St., is located in the historic Vance Hotel. Dine inside an old-fashioned brass elevator and listen to live jazz at night. Grilled panini sandwiches ($6-9) and salads ($6-10) are offered for both lunch and dinner, and there is a dinner buffet special on weekend nights. (☎441-0805. Call for jazz details. Open daily 9am for coffee, breads, and pastries, Su-Th 11am-9pm, F-Sa 11am-midnight.) **Cafe Marina ❸,** 601 Startare Dr., is off US 101 at the Samoa Bridge Exit (Rte. 255). From there, take the Woodley Island Exit north of town. Outdoor dining on the marina is the perfect way to enjoy their fresh seafood, like the spicy blackened snapper. The polished bar is a night spot for local fishermen. (☎443-2233. Sandwiches $6-13. Entrees $10-16. Open in summer daily 7am-10pm; off-season daily 7am-9pm.)

◪ **VICTORIANS, ART & DUNES.** Eureka is very proud of its bevy of restored **Victorian homes,** a few of which are worth driving past. Self-guided tour maps are available at the Chamber of Commerce. Some of the more handsome houses are now expensive B&Bs. If you drive by, don't miss the much-photographed, dramatically stark **Carson Mansion,** which belonged to a prominent logger in the 1850s. **Art galleries,** Eureka's main claim to fame, cluster downtown. Check out **First Street Gallery,** 422 1st St. (☎443-6363), **The Ink People Gallery,** 411 12th St. (☎442-8413), and the **Morris Graves Museum of Art,** 636 F St. (☎442-0278) for their interesting collections. Ask the Chamber of Commerce about current exhibits. The **dunes recreation area,** in Samoa off Rte. 255 (past the cookhouse and left at Samoa Bridge, on the north end by the jetty), was once a thriving dune ecosystem. Now, this peninsula offers beach access and dune hiking.

# ARCATA                                                    ☎707

Arcata (ar-KAY-ta; pop. 16,500) is like a transplanted slice of Berkeley in the remote northern corner of California. At the intersection of US 101 and Rte. 299, Arcata typifies the laid-back existence that characterizes the North Coast. Check out the town's many murals, Victorian homes, and characters living "alternative" lifestyles. Arcata's neighbor, Humboldt State University, focuses on forestry and marine biology (Earth First! was founded here). All over Humboldt County, students get baked in the sun—and on the county's number-one cash crop.

◪ **PRACTICAL INFORMATION. Arcata Chamber of Commerce,** 1635 Heindon Rd., has visitor information. (☎822-3619. Open daily 9am-5pm.) An **ATM** is at **US Bank,** 953 G St. Just like in college, the most convenient **laundromat** is M.O.M.'s, 5000 Valley West Blvd. (☎822-1181. Open daily 7:30am-9:30pm.) **Adventure's Edge,** 650 10th St., rents outdoor equipment. (☎822-4673. Tents $20 for the first 3 days, $3 per additional day. Sleeping bags $14/$2. Sea kayaks $30 same-day return, $35 per 24hr. Cross-country ski packages $18 per 3 days. Open M-Sa

9am-6pm, Su 11am-5pm.) Other services include **Mad River Hospital,** 3800 Janes Rd. (☎822-3621), and the **post office,** 799 H St. (☎822-3570; open M-F 8:30am-5pm). **Postal Code:** 95521.

**☎☎ ACCOMMODATIONS & CAMPING.** Arcata has many budget motels off US 101 at the Giuntoli Exit. One of these is **Motel 6 ❸,** 4755 Valley West Blvd. It is clean and quiet, and offers cable TV, pool, and A/C. (☎822-7061. Singles $40; 2nd adult $6 extra, additional adults $3 extra; kids under 17 free. AARP discount.) Find classier, pricier digs at the historic **Hotel Arcata ❹,** 708 9th St., in the town's center. (☎826-0217 or 800-344-1221. Su-Th singles $75; doubles $120. F-Sa $80/$145.)

Popular **Clam Beach County Park ❶,** on US 101, 7½ mi. north of Arcata, has dunes and a huge beach with seasonal clam digging; call ahead. (☎445-7651. Campsites with water and pit toilets $8, entrance fee for hikers and cyclists $3.) **Patrick's Point State Park ❶,** 15 mi. north of Arcata, is an excellent spot for **watching whales** and seals. The 124 sites offer terrific ocean views, lush vegetation, and treasure-hunting in the beach's tidepools. (☎677-3570. Showers and flush toilets. No dumpsite. $12 per vehicle; no hookups. Day use $2 per car. Reservations strongly recommended; call ReserveAmerica, ☎800-444-7275.)

**☎☎ FOOD & ENTERTAINMENT. Golden Harvest Cafe ❷,** 1062 G St., a popular breakfast venue, has menu options for vegetarians and vegans. (☎822-8962. All dishes $4-10. Open M-F 6:30am-3pm, Sa-Su 7:30am-3pm.) **Crosswinds ❷,** 860 10th St., in a beautifully restored Victorian home, offers a number of breakfast and lunch variations in large portions. Vegan substitutes are available for all meat used in the Mexican, Italian, and Californian specialties, which cost $5-13. (☎826-2133. Open Su and Tu-Sa 7:30am-2pm.) The **Arcata Co-op ❷,** on 8th St. at I St., is a standard supermarket except for the unusual amounts of tofu, ginseng cola, and soy milk lining its shelves. (☎822-5947. Open daily 6am-10pm.) **Folie Douce ❹,** 1551 G St., is a chic, tucked-away venue for dinner and drinks with a seasonal menu. (☎822-1042. Appetizers $8-9. Wood-fire oven pizzas $9-12. Entrees $16-27. Kitchen open Tu-Th 5:30-9pm, F-Sa 5:30-10pm; bar stays open late.) A **farmer's market,** offering tie-dyed dresses, candles, and the usual fresh produce, livens up the Arcata Plaza on Saturdays from April to November (9am-1pm). Several local bands playing at full volume make the affair a weekly party.

As a college town, Arcata maintains its share of bars, most of which are on 9th St. in the town square. **Humboldt Brewery,** 856 10th St. at I St., is a popular local microbrewery with a collection of sports memorabilia lining the walls. Unusual beers like the Red Nectar Ale go well with a game of pool. (☎826-2739. Open M-Tu 4pm-midnight, W-Sa noon-midnight.) **Jambalaya Restaurant and Saloon ❹,** 915 H St., at 9th and H St., is a great place to hang with locals, eat a filling meal ($13-23), and listen to occasional live jazz and blues. (☎822-4766. Open Su and Tu-Sa 5pm-late.)

**☎☎ SIGHTS & SEASONAL EVENTS.** Experience Arcata by taking a short **walking tour** around the **Arcata Plaza,** in the center of town near the intersection of 8th and H St. The plaza hosts folk music on the weekends and an annual **Summer Solstice Festival** on the weekend nearest the summer solstice. The Natural History Museum (13th and G St.) is a brief walk from the plaza and home to an impressive collection of whale skulls. Nearby **Redwood Park,** at 14th and Union St., contains lots of nooks for picnicking among the giants. Behind the park lies **Arcata Community Forest,** which has picnic spaces, meadows, redwoods, and hiking trails (free), and does not allow camping. A former "sanitary" landfill, the 75-acre **Arcata Marsh and Wildlife Sanctuary** lies at the foot of I

St., across from Samoa Blvd. Visitors can take a tour to see how this saltwater marsh/converted sewer system works with treated waste, or wander the trails around the lake. Take **Sanctuary Trail** (2 mi.; 1hr.) on the northern edge of Humboldt Bay for great bird watching opportunities. (☎826-2359. Tours Sa 8:30am and 2pm; meet at info center. Open daily 9am-5pm.)

The 32-year-old **Kinetic Sculpture Race,** held annually over Memorial Day weekend, is Humboldt County's oddest festival. A few dozen insane and/or intoxicated adventurers attempt to pilot unwieldy homemade vehicles on a grueling three-day, 38 mi. trek from Arcata to Ferndale over road, sand, and water. Vehicles from previous competitions are on display at a museum in Ferndale (see p. 197).

# REDWOOD NATIONAL & STATE PARKS ☎707

With ferns that grow to the height of humans and redwood trees the size of skyscrapers, Redwood National and State Parks will leave an impression. The redwoods in the parks are the last remaining stretch of the old growth forest that used to blanket two million acres of Northern California and Oregon. Wildlife runs free here, with black bears and mountain lions roaming the backwoods and Roosevelt elk grazing in the meadows. While a short tour of the big sights and the drive-through trees certainly give visitors ample photo opportunities, a more memorable experience of the redwoods may require heading down a trail into the quiet of the forest, where you can see the trees as they have stood for thousands of years.

## AT A GLANCE

**AREA:** 112,613 acres.

**CLIMATE:** Cool and foggy.

**FEATURES:** Redwoods, Fern Canyon, Battery Point Lighthouse.

**HIGHLIGHTS:** Whale-watching off the Coastal Trail, hiking to the Tall Trees Grove.

**GATEWAYS:** Orick (p. 206), Klamath (p. 206).

**CAMPING:** Developed and undeveloped sites. (See p. 203.)

**FEES & RESERVATIONS:** Entrance free. $2 per day for Jedediah Smith, Del Norte Coast, and Prairie Creek Redwoods. $2 per day per car for daytime parking.

FAR NORTH

## ✈ ORIENTATION

Redwood National and State Parks is an umbrella term for four contiguous redwood parks. The parks span 40 mi. of coast and two counties, with information centers and unique attractions throughout. **Redwood National Park** is the southernmost of four; the others, from south to north, are **Prairie Creek Redwoods State Park, Del Norte Coast Redwoods State Park,** and **Jedediah Smith Redwoods State Park.** The tiny town of **Orick** is close to the southern limit of the parks. Just south of town is an extremely helpful ranger station. **Crescent City,** with park headquarters and a few basic services, is at the far northern end of the park region.

## ⊏ TRANSPORTATION

**Orick** and **Klamath** border the national forest to the south and north. **US 101** traverses most of the parks. The slower but more scenic **Newton Drury Parkway** runs parallel to US 101 for 31 mi. from Klamath to Prairie Creek (watch for bikers).

## 🛈 PRACTICAL INFORMATION

**Entrance Fees:** Charges are particular to each park, and often differ depending on whether you are camping, parking, or just hiking. Usually there is no charge to enter, and $2 per car for day-use of parking and picnic areas. South of Orick are free off-highway areas; ask at visitors centers for locations.

**Buses: Greyhound,** 500 E. Harding St., Crescent City (☎464-2807). Greyhound runs two buses daily, one in the morning and one in the evening, to **San Francisco** and **Portland**. Station is only open when buses are scheduled to arrive. Bus fare approximately $60. Call for exact rates and departure times.

**Auto Repairs: AAA Emergency Road Service** (☎800-222-4357). 24hr.

**Visitor Information:**

**Thomas A. Luchi Visitors Center** (☎464-6101, ext. 5265), on US 101, 0.5 mi. south of Orick. Shows an informative video on redwoods. Several different kinds of maps available. Info on trails and campsites doled out by enthusiastic and helpful rangers. Open daily 9am-5pm.

**Redwood National Park Headquarters and Information Center,** 1111 2nd St. (☎464-6101, ext. 5064), Crescent City. Headquarters of the entire national park, although ranger stations are just as well-informed. Open daily 9am-5pm. Closed Su in winter.

**Prairie Creek Information Center** (☎464-6101, ext. 5301), on the Newton Drury Scenic Pkwy. in Prairie Creek Redwood State Park Campground. Open in summer M-Th 9am-5pm, F-Su 9am-6pm, though hours may vary depending on available staff; in winter daily 10am-5pm.

**Crescent City-Del Norte County Chamber of Commerce,** 1001 Front St. (☎464-3174), Crescent City. Free coffee, brochures, and coupons. Very knowledgeable and friendly staff to assist you with your travel plans. Open M-Sa 9am-7pm.

**Hiouchi Ranger Station** (☎464-6101, ext. 5067), on US 199 across from Jedediah Smith Redwoods Park. Open June-Sept. daily 9am-5pm.

**Six Rivers National Forest Station** (☎457-3131), on US 199 in Gasquet, has info about recreation opportunities in the Smith River National Recreation area and nearby campgrounds Panther Flat, Grassy Flat, and Big Flat. Open summer M-Sa 8am-4:30pm; winter M-F 8am-4:30pm.

**Jedediah Smith State Park Information Center** (☎464-6101, ext. 5113), on US 199 across from the Hiouchi Ranger Station in the campground. Open Su and W-Sa 10am-2pm.

---

**REDWOOD CHAINSAW MASSACRE** Rising up hundreds of feet above the ground, the lofty trees in Redwood National Park have towered in lush profusion for 150 million years. Native Americans called them "the eternal spirit" because of their 2000-year life span, ability to adapt to climatic changes, and resistance to insects, fire, and even lightning. The redwoods were indeed almost invincible—until the era of logging. With money on their minds (1 tree builds 22 houses) and saws in their hands, loggers cleared 96% of the virgin coast redwoods in one century. Despite the economic boom that the logging industry brought to the area's small towns, conservationists fought back to maintain the forest ecology. Concerned citizens began buying redwood plots from loggers in the 1920s, and in 1968 the Redwood National Park was formed by the federal government, preserving these silent giants for the next few hundred generations. Present-day activists insist that the Pacific Lumber Co., which still harvests the trees outside of national park areas, must stop their programs entirely. In order to get their point across, Earth First! volunteers stage "tree sits," sometimes spending months in tents suspended from the trees, 180 ft. up.

---

**ATM: Bank of America,** 240 H St. at 2nd St. in Crescent City.

**Laundromat:** 101 Laundromat and Dry Cleaners, 503 L. St. (☎464-9230). Wash $1.75, dry 25¢ per 8½min.

**Road Conditions:** ☎800-GAS-ROAD/427-7623.

**24-Hour Rape Crisis Line:** ☎465-3013.

**Medical Assistance: Sutter Coast Hospital,** 800 E. Washington Blvd., Crescent City (☎464-8511).

**Internet Access: Humboldt County Library, Arcata Branch,** 500 7th St., Arcata (☎822-5954), has free Internet access. Open Tu 2-5pm, W 1-8pm, Th-Sa 10am-5pm.

**Post Office: Crescent City:** 751 2nd St. (☎464-2151). Open M-F 8:30am-5pm, Sa noon-2pm. **Orick:** 121147 US 101 (☎488-3611). Open M-F 8:30am-noon and 1-5pm. **Klamath:** 141 Klamath Blvd. (☎482-2381). Open M-F 8am-4:30pm. **Postal Code:** 95531 (Crescent City), 95555 (Orick), 95548 (Klamath).

# ▐ ACCOMMODATIONS

**Ravenwood Motel,** 151 Klamath Blvd. (☎866-520-9875), off US 101. Clean rooms with a modern decor. Conveniently located next to a market, cafe, and laundromat. Doubles $58; family units with full kitchen $100. ❸

**Camp Marigold,** 16101 US 101 (☎482-3585 or 800-621-8513), 3 mi. north of Klamath Bridge. Stay in a log cabin with full kitchen and cable TV. RV hookups available. 1-bed studios $48; doubles $78; 6-person lodge $195. ❸

**Historic Requa Inn,** 451 Requa Rd. (☎482-1425 or 866-800-8777), west off US 101. This bed and breakfast with lace-curtained windows and a Victorian-styled parlor has a glorious view overlooking the picturesque Klamath River. Offers evening dining. Rooms $79-120. Reservations recommended June-Sept. ❺

**Redwood Youth Hostel (HI-AYH),** 14480 US 101 (☎482-8265), at Wilson Creek Rd. 7 mi. north of Klamath. This 30-bed hostel is run by a friendly young family. Chores and rules (no shoes inside) keep the house immaculate. Kitchen and 2 ocean-view sundecks. No sleeping bags allowed, so bring your own sleepsack or rent linen ($1). Check-in 5-9pm. Check-out 10am. Lockout 11am-5pm; day storage available. Curfew 11pm. Reservations recommended in summer. Dorms $16, under 17 $7. Pay in advance. ❶

**Patrick Creek Lodge & Historic Inn,** 13950 Hwy. 199 (☎457-3323; www.patrick-creeklodge.com), in Gasquest, northeast of Hiouchi. Established in 1926, this lodge is a home-away-from-home for travelers. Fish along the famous Smith River, hike or kayak by day, and enjoy a toasty fire and "creative cuisine" at the lodge by night. Singles $47; doubles $80-90; 2-bedroom suites $100; cabin for 2 $130, for 4 $170, each additional person $20. Credit card required for reservations and check-in. ❸

# ▐ CAMPING

Redwood National Park offers several backcountry campsites; all are free and accessible only by hiking from roads or parking lots. **Nickel Creek Campground,** at the end of Enderts Beach Rd. outside Crescent City, has ocean access and toilets, but no showers or water. **Flint Ridge** is off the end of Redwood National and State Parks Coastal Dr., and has neither water nor showers, but toilets are available. There are also **State Park campsites ❶,** which are easily accessible and have all the amenities except electricity. Call ReserveAmerica (☎800-444-7275) for reservations, which are necessary in summer (sites usually $15). North of Crescent City on US 199 is **Jedediah Smith Redwoods State Park ❶.** Amenities include picnic tables, grills, water, restrooms, and showers. Campfire programs and nature walks also offered during the summer. (Campsites are $15, $4 for day use, and $1 for hikers/bikers without vehicles at designated campsites.)

FAR NORTH

The **Del Norte Coast Redwoods State Park** offers magnificent ocean views and inland camping at **Mill Creek Campground,** right off US 101. Camping in **Prairie Creek Redwoods State Park** is possible at Elk Prairie, where elk munch away and ignore tourists as long as the cameras stay at a distance (see **Elk Machismo,** p. 194). Camping is also possible at Gold Bluffs Beach, where the sound of the rolling Pacific will calm the soul. Smith River National Recreation Area at **Six Rivers National Forest** (☎457-3131) has several campgrounds. **Big Flat Campground ❶,** for those seeking serious isolation, is 14 mi. up South Fork Rd. off US 199 ($8; no hookups). Situated directly on the Smith River, **Panther Flat ❶,** on US 199, 25min. north of Crescent City, has water, showers, and a day-use picnic area. (Sites $15; in winter $10.)

## ☕ FOOD

There are more picnic tables than restaurants in the area, so the best option for food is probably the supermarket. **Orick Market** has reasonably priced groceries. (☎488-3225. Open M-Sa 8am-7pm, Su 9am-6pm.) In Crescent City, head to the 24hr. **Safeway,** 475 M St. (☎465-3353), on US 101 between 2nd and 5th St.

If your travel plans don't include cooking, the **Palm Cafe ❷,** on US 101, is one of the few places to eat in Orick. Locals and visiting hikers and bikers eat in mom-and-pop environs. The homemade fruit, coconut, and chocolate pies ($2.25) are delicious. (☎488-3381. Open daily 5am-8pm.) **Glen's Bakery and Restaurant ❶,** at 3rd and G St., opened in 1947 and has always been a family affair. The multitude of dedicated regulars love the huge pancakes ($4) and sandwiches ($4-6.50). Breakfast served all day. (☎464-2914. Open Tu-Sa 5am-6:30pm.)

## 🥾 HIKING

In the parks, all plants and animals are protected—even feathers dropped by birds of prey are off-limits. **California fishing licenses** (one-day licenses $30) are required for fresh and saltwater fishing off any natural formation, but fishing is free from any man-made structure (check out Battery Point in Crescent City). There are minimum-weight and maximum-catch requirements specific to both. Call the Fish and Game Department (☎445-6493) to obtain a permit.

The redwoods are best experienced on foot. The National Park Service and the California Department of Parks and Recreation conduct many ranger-led activities for all ages in the summer (see **Visitor Information,** p. 202, or call the Redwood Information Center at ☎464-6101). Hikers should take particular care to wear protective clothing—**ticks** (see **Insect-Borne Diseases,** p. 36) and **poison oak** (see **Dangerous Plants,** p. 9) thrive in these dark places. **Roosevelt elk** roam the woods and are interesting to watch but dangerous to approach, as encroachers on their territory are promptly circled and trampled (see **Elk Machismo,** p. 194). Also look out for the **black bears** and **mountain lions** that inhabit the park. Before setting out, get advice and trail maps at the Visitors Center.

### ORICK AREA
The Orick Area covers the southernmost section of Redwood National and State Parks. The **Visitors Center** lies on US 101, just 1 mi. south of Orick and half a mile south of the Shoreline Deli (the Greyhound bus stop). A popular sight is the **Tall Trees Grove,** accessible by car to those with permits (free from the Visitors Center) when the road is open. Allow at least three to four hours for the trip. From the trailhead at the end of Tall Trees Access Rd., off Bald Hills Rd. from US 101 north of Orick, it's a 1¼ mi. hike down (about 30min.) to some of the tallest trees

FAR NORTH

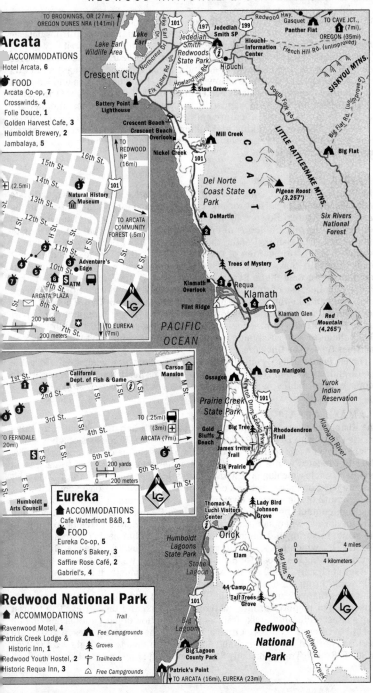

## Arcata

**ACCOMMODATIONS**
Hotel Arcata, **6**

**FOOD**
Arcata Co-op, **7**
Crosswinds, **4**
Folie Douce, **1**
Golden Harvest Cafe, **3**
Humboldt Brewery, **2**
Jambalaya, **5**

## Eureka

**ACCOMMODATIONS**
Cafe Waterfront B&B, **1**

**FOOD**
Eureka Co-op, **5**
Ramone's Bakery, **3**
Saffire Rose Café, **2**
Gabriel's, **4**

## Redwood National Park

**ACCOMMODATIONS**

Ravenwood Motel, **4**
Patrick Creek Lodge &
Historic Inn, **1**
Redwood Youth Hostel, **2**
Historic Requa Inn, **3**

⎯⎯ Trail
▲ Fee Campgrounds
🌲 Groves
⌐ Trailheads
△ Free Campgrounds

in the world. The return hike up is steep—allow an hour. If the road is closed, hardy souls can see these giants by hiking the 16 mi. round-trip from **Dolason Prairie Trail** to **Emerald Ridge Trail,** which connects with **Tall Trees Trail.**

**Orick** (pop. 650) is a somewhat desolate town overrun with souvenir stores selling burl sculptures (over-crafted and expensive wood carvings) and cows (which outnumber the people). However, it also has a post office and a market for campfire groceries. **Patrick's Point State Park ❶,** 18 mi. south of Orick along US 101, offers one of the most spectacular views along the coast, and merits a day or two for campers and nature enthusiasts heading north to the redwoods (sites $15; day-use $4; hiking and biking $2). During **whale-watching** season (Nov.-Dec. and Mar.-May), observe the migration of gray whales from the towering cliffs of the point.

## PRAIRIE CREEK AREA

The Prairie Creek Area, equipped with a **ranger station, visitors center,** and **state park campgrounds,** is perfect for hikers, who can explore 70 mi. of trails in the park's 14,000 acres. Be sure to pick up a trail map ($1) at the ranger station before heading out; the loops of criss-crossing trails can confuse. Starting at the Prairie Creek Visitors Center, the **James Irvine Trail** (4½ mi. one-way) snakes through a prehistoric garden of towering old-growth redwoods. Winding past small waterfalls that trickle down 50 ft. fern-covered walls, the trail ends at **Fern Canyon** on **Gold Bluffs Beach. Rhododendron** (7¾ mi. one-way) is another choice pick because of its beautiful blossoms and many possibilities; if you get tired, you can take the convenient switchback, **South Fork Trail.** The less ambitious can elk-watch on the meadow in front of the ranger station or cruise part of the **Foothill Trail** (¾ mi. one-way) to the 1500-year-old, 306 ft. high **Big Tree.** This behemoth is a satisfying alternative for those who don't want to trek to **Tall Trees Grove** (see **Orick Area,** above).

The **Elk Prairie Trail** (1½ mi. one-way), built for the visually impaired, skirts the prairie and loops around to join the nature trail. The **Revelation Trail** is accessible to people with disabilities, and is frequented every now and then by stray elk.

## KLAMATH AREA

The Klamath Area to the north consists of a thin stretch of parkland connecting Prairie Creek with Del Norte State Park. The town itself consists of a few stores stretched over 4 mi., so the main attraction here is the spectacular coastline. The **Klamath Overlook,** where Requa Rd. meets the steep **Coastal Trail** (8 mi.), is an excellent **whale-watching** site with a fantastic view (provided the fog doesn't obscure it), though the overlook can be crowded by North Coast standards.

The mouth of the **Klamath River** is a popular commercial fishing spot (permit required; contact the Redwood Visitors Info Center, ☎464-6101, ext. 5064) in fall and spring, when salmon spawn, and in winter, when steelhead trout do the same. In spring and summer, sea lions and harbor seals congregate along Coastal Dr., which passes by the remains of the **Douglas Memorial Bridge** and continues along the ocean for 8 mi. of incredible views. Kitsch meets high-tech at **Trees of Mystery,** 15500 US 101 N., just north of Klamath. It is a three-quarter-mile walk through a maze of curiously shaped trees and elaborate chainsaw sculptures that talk and play music. There is also a small, free Native American museum that displays ornate costumes, baskets, and tapestries. The tourist trap's latest addition, the **Sky Trail,** is a multi-million dollar gondola snaking up the hill to offer an exclusive bird's eye view of the towering trees. A 200 ft. tall Paul Bunyan and his blue ox Babe mark the entrance to the sight. (☎ 482-2251 or 800-638-3389. Trail open daily 8am-6:30pm; gift shop and museum open 8am-

7:30pm. $15, seniors $12, children $8. Parties of 5 or more get a 20% discount, as do those who pick up a discount card at the Crescent City Chamber of Commerce, ☎800-343-8300.)

## CRESCENT CITY AREA

An outstanding location from which to explore the parks, Crescent City calls itself the city "where the redwoods meet the sea." The **Battery Point Lighthouse** is on a causeway jutting out from Front St.; turn left onto A St. at the top of Front St. It houses a museum open only during low tide. (☎464-3089. Open Apr.-Sept. W-Su 10am-4pm, tide permitting. $2, children 50¢.) From June through August, the national park offers **tidepool walks,** which leave from the Enderts Beach parking lot. (Turn-off 4 mi. south of Crescent City; call ☎464-6101, ext. 5064 for schedules.) The trailhead is at the **Crescent Beach Overlook** on Enderts Beach Rd., just off US 101. A scenic drive from Crescent City along **Pebble Beach Drive** to **Point Saint George** snakes past coastline that looks transplanted from New England; craggy cliffs, lush prairies, and an old lighthouse add to the atmosphere.

Annual highlights include the **World Championship Crab Races,** featuring races and crab feasts on the 3rd Sunday in February. The Sea Cruise, a parade of over 500 classic cars, happens over three days on the 1st or 2nd weekend in October. Call the Crescent City/Del Norte County Chamber of Commerce (☎800-343-8300) for information regarding any of these events.

## HIOUCHI AREA

This inland region, known for its rugged beauty, sits in the northern part of the park region along US 199 and contains some excellent hiking trails, most of which are in **Jedediah Smith Redwoods State Park.** Several trails lie off Howland Hill Rd., a dirt road easily accessible from both US 101 and US 199. From US 199, turn onto South Fork Rd. in Hiouchi and right onto Douglas Park Rd., which then turns into Howland Hill Rd. From Crescent City, go south on US 101, turn left onto Elk Valley Rd., and right onto Howland Hill Rd. Drive through **Stout Grove,** which some say makes the **Avenue of the Giants** pale in comparison. From here one can also take the wheelchair-accessible **Stout Grove Trail** (½ mi.) and admire the ancient redwoods up close. The trailhead is near the eastern end of Howland Hill Rd., and the paved section is just past the trail. The **Mill Creek Trail** is a moderate 4 mi. hike with excellent swimming, accessible from the Mill Creek Bridge on Howland Hill Rd., and from the footbridge in the Jedediah Smith campground during summer. The more strenuous **Boy Scout Trail** off Howland Hill Rd. splits after 3 mi.; the right-hand path goes to the monstrous Boy Scout Tree, and the left ends at Fern Falls. Two miles west of Jedediah State Park on US 199 lies the Simpson-Reed Grove, a circular trail through an old stand of redwoods.

The untapped beauty of **Six Rivers National Forest** (☎457-3131) is directly east of Hiouchi. The Smith River, the state's last major undammed river, rushes through rocky gorges on its way from the mountains to the coast. This area offers the best salmon, trout, and steelhead fishing around, and excellent camping awaits on the riverbanks. There are also numerous hiking trails throughout the forest.

# NORTHERN INTERIOR

Vast golden plains, rock-strewn hills, and swift rivers all lie in the relatively unpopulated and unfrequented Northern Interior. The Cascade Mountains interrupt the expanse of farmland to the southeast with quiet peaks, lush wilderness, and the two enormous glaciated mountains of Mt. Shasta and Mt. Lassen. Past and present volcanic activity has left behind a surreal landscape of lava beds, cratered mountains, lakes, waterfalls, caves, and recovering forest areas. The forests and peaks of the Sierra Nevada and Gold Country, a sprinkling of small towns steeped in the history of the Gold Rush, begin south of this beautiful, sweeping landscape.

## LASSEN VOLCANIC NATIONAL PARK ☎530

Lassen Volcanic National Park, the most geothermically active area in the Cascade Range, is one link in a chain of seismic and volcanic sites around the Pacific Rim intimidatingly dubbed the "Ring of Fire." Mt. Lassen's most recent large-scale activity occurred in 1914, when tremors, lava streams, black dust, and a series of enormous eruptions ravaged the area. The geological ruckus climaxed a year later when Mt. Lassen spewed a cloud of smoke and ash seven miles into the sky. The area was established as a national park in 1916 shortly thereafter. Even now, the eruption is discernible in Lassen's unearthly pools of boiling water, barren stretches of moonscape, occasional sulphur stench, and young, revitalized forests.

### AT A GLANCE

**AREA:** 106,372 acres.

**CLIMATE:** Fairly cold in the summer (sometimes with near-freezing temperatures at night), Lassen gets snowed-in during the winter, and most of the roads are blocked off.

**HIGHLIGHTS:** Witness Bumpass Hell, smell Sulphur Works, take in the view from Panorama Point.

**FEATURES:** Cold Boiling Lake, Mt. Lassen, the Devastated Area.

**GATEWAYS:** Redding (p. 213), Red Bluff.

**CAMPING:** Camping 7- to 14-day max. stay, Backcountry 14-day max. stay.

**FEES & RESERVATIONS:** $10 entrance fee for vehicles, $5 for walk-ins and cyclists, is valid for 7 days. $25 annual fee. Free wilderness permit is required for backcountry camping.



### ORIENTATION

Lassen National Park is located squarely in the middle of Lassen National Forest, about 50 mi. east of Redding (via Rte. 44) and Red Bluff (via Rte. 36). Rte. 89 winds through the major attractions on the west side of the park, and can be followed all the way through the park once the snow melts (usually by late June). The park's eastern side is less developed. The **Pacific Crest Trail** (see **From Crest to Crest: the Trail of the West,** p. 235) passes right through the center of the park, intersecting with Warner Valley in the south.

### TRANSPORTATION

The park can be easily reached from **Redding** via Rte. 44 (see p. 213) and Red Bluff via Rte. 36. **Route 89** winds through the park and connects to Rte. 44 at the northern entrance of the park and Rte. 36 at the southern entrance. From **Chester** (71 mi. east of Red Bluff on Rte. 36), two dirt roads enter the park from the southeast, one leading north to Juniper Lake and the other northwest to Warner Valley.

## 🔢 PRACTICAL INFORMATION

**Information Stations:** There are two information stations in Lassen, offering wilderness permits, publications, and information about the entire park: the Loomis Museum, at Manzanita Lake near the north entrance (☎595-4444, ext. 5180; open June 27-Sept. 1 daily 9am-5pm; closed Sept. 21-May 30; open the rest of the year F-Su 9am-5pm), and the helpful Park Headquarters, in Mineral (☎595-4444; open daily 8am-4:30pm).

**Fees & Reservations:** Park entrance fee $10 per vehicle, $5 per bike or walk-in, valid for 7 days. Annual passes $25. Backcountry camping requires a free wilderness permit.

**WHEN TO GO.** Lassen is one of the least visited national parks and is fairly quiet until July, when the summer tourists show up. The park is open year-round; rangers ski to work when the roads close. Those visiting Lassen in the winter should have previous outdoors experience.

## 🏠 🏕 ACCOMMODATIONS & CAMPING

### INSIDE THE PARK

Due to the danger of rock slides and lava flows, few permanent structures exist in the park. The only indoor lodging in Lassen is the upscale and charming **Drakesbad Guest Ranch ❾**, in Warner Valley in the park's southern end. This 110-year-old guest ranch isn't cheap, but it comes with three meals a day and scenic, secluded surroundings. Take Rte. 36 to Chester, turn right at the firehouse, and follow the signs. (☎529-1512, ext. 120; www.drakesbad.com. Open June-Oct. Singles and doubles from $121 per person; bungalows from $139 per person. Reservations necessary.) Fortunately, **camping** in the park is beautiful and abundant. Unfortunately, temperatures approach near-freezing at night, even in August. Check the snow situation before leaving; campgrounds often remain closed well into the summer. All sites are on a first-come, first-camp basis; register on site. **Backcountry camping ❶** is limited to 14 days per year with a free wilderness permit. Fires are prohibited, as is the use of all soaps (even biodegradable ones) in the lakes. Portable propane or gas stoves are allowed. Stop by the park headquarters for info on safety, ecological rules, and a list of restricted areas. Geothermically active sites such as Bumpass Hell and Devil's Kitchen are closed to backcountry camping.

🏕 **Summit Lake North,** 6700 ft., 17½ mi. south of the Manzanita Lake entrance. Summit Lake's deep blue water glitters through the pine trees surrounding 46 popular sites. Summit Lake North and its cousin on the other side are usually the first to fill up. Drinking water and flush toilets. 7-day max. stay. Open July-Sept. Sites $16. ❶

🏕 **Summit Lake South,** 6700 ft., just around the lake from the Summit North campground. All 48 sites have the same views as North Summit. Many trails begin here. Drinking water. No showers or flush toilets. 7-day max. stay. Open July-Sept. Sites $14. ❶

**Manzanita Lake,** 5900 ft., just inside the park border, near the northwest entrance. Most of the 179 sites have some privacy, but are better geared toward family camping than quiet solitude. Pay phone, concession services, motorless boating, drinking water, flush toilets, laundry, showers, dump station, and gas. 14-day max. stay. Open early June-late Oct. Sites $16; late Sept.-late Oct. $10. ❶

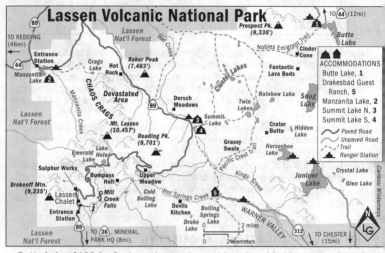

Lassen Volcanic National Park

ACCOMMODATIONS
Butte Lake, **1**
Drakesbad Guest
  Ranch, **5**
Manzanita Lake, **2**
Summit Lake N, **3**
Summit Lake S, **4**

〜〜 Paved Road
〜〜 Unpaved Road
〜〜 Trail
▲ Ranger Station

**Butte Lake,** 6100 ft., 6 mi. south on a dirt road from Rte. 44, 17 mi. east of Old Station. Less crowded than Manzanita and the Summit campsites. The 46 sites double to 101 sites during late summer once all the snow melts. On Bathtub Lake, promising the warmest swimming in the park. Flush toilets and piped water. Boating and fishing access. Open late May-late Sept. Sites $14. ❶

## OUTSIDE THE PARK

The nearest indoor accommodations to the northern entrance of the park are 12 mi. north in **Old Station.** There are also a handful of motels in **Mineral** near the southern entrance. Less costly motels are in **Redding,** 50 mi. west on Rte. 44 (see p. 213); **Red Bluff,** 50 mi. west on Rte. 36; and **Chester,** southeast on Rte. 36. **Lassen National Forest,** which surrounds the park, has several developed campgrounds. Six of them line Rte. 89 for the first 10 mi. north of the park. Campgrounds are generally open May through October. **Big Pine ❶,** 4500 ft., is the closest. (Piped water, vault toilets. 19 sites. $10.) **Bridge ❶,** 4000 ft., and **Cave ❶,** 4300 ft., both have drinking water and trailer-only sites for $11, though tents may be used if you don't mind bumpy ground. Several campgrounds also lie east of Mineral on Rte. 36 in the Almanor Ranger District (☎258-2141). A number of campgrounds dot the southwestern shore of **Eagle Lake,** in the eastern part of Lassen National Forest. **Christie, Merrill,** and **Aspen Grove** have piped water and are in the Eagle Lake Ranger District. (☎257-4188. Sites $13-15.) **McCarthy Point ❹,** once an active fire lookout, has since been converted into a guest cabin. Accommodations include a kitchen and a bedroom accommodating up to six. (☎258-2141. Su-Th $40, F-Sa $60. Security deposit $200. Reserve at least two weeks ahead.)

## ❖ FOOD

The budget Lassen meal consists of groceries bought in an outlying town. For prepared meals, try the **Lassen Chalet ❶,** a cafeteria-style restaurant and gift shop just inside the southwest entrance. Their large burgers ($4-6) are filling but only available until 5pm. (☎595-3376. Open daily 9am-6pm; late May-late June and Sept. to mid-Oct. 9am-4pm.) For a wider selection, try the **Mineral Lodge Cafe ❶,** 1 mi. east of Park Headquarters on Rte. 36, which serves huge breakfasts, burgers, and sandwiches for around $6. (☎595-4422. Open M-Th 8am-3pm and 5-8pm, F-Su 8am-8pm.) Across the street is a small grocery store, the **Gas Mart and Deli.** (☎595-3222. Open M-Sa 8am-6:30pm, Su 8am-5pm.) At the park's north end, the **Manzanita Camper Service Store,** at the Manzanita Lake Campground, has a small selection of pricey groceries, a snack bar, fishing licenses, gasoline, guides, and maps. It also launches lakeworthy boats. (☎335-7557. Store open daily 8am-8pm; late May-late June and Sept. to mid-Oct. 9am-5pm. Snack bar closes 1hr. before store.)

## 🎯 🔼 SIGHTS & HIKES

Lassen is very car-friendly: roadside sights are clearly numbered for tourists, and most are accessible from Rte. 89, depending on snow conditions. Check with Park Headquarters before heading out at all times of the year. Drivers can pick up the *Lassen Road Guide,* a booklet keyed to roadside markers ($6), at any park entrance ranger station. A comfortable drive through the park (including a few stops) should take two hours, but allow a full day to accommodate short hikes.

**FROM THE LOOMIS MUSEUM VISITORS CENTER.** There are a few easy, relaxing walks in the area surrounding the Loomis Museum Visitors Center at Rte. 89's north entry into the park. The hike to **Crags Lake** starts 500 yd. from the Visitors Center and runs 1¾ mi. one-way, climbing 700 ft. (2-4hr. round-trip). The walk winds through dense forest, emerging above a huge rocky basin and the warm lake. Other shorter, easier hikes hook around Lily Pond (1 mi. interpretive hike) and Reflection Lake (¾ mi.), both across the street from the Visitors Center. The 1½ mi. loop trail around Manzanita Lake makes for a relaxing stroll.

**ALONG ROUTE 89.** Many of the park's most popular sights are conveniently located just off Rte. 89. If the road has opened for the summer, this can be done by car as well as foot. If not, grab a pair of snowshoes. Coming from the south, the first sight (or smell, rather) is **Sulphur Works,** where the earth hisses its grievances and a short boardwalk runs above some of Lassen's active sulphur vents. Although the guard rails may prevent you from getting burned, if the wind changes direction, you're likely to get a face full of rotten-egg mist. The boardwalk is wheelchair accessible. About 4½ mi. farther along Rte. 89 is **Emerald Lake.** When partially thawed by the sun, it shimmers bright green with icy cold, 300 ft.-deep waters around a snowy center. Swimming is fine for fish but too cold (40°F) for the warm-blooded. No fishing is allowed.

The 1½ mi. hike to **Bumpass Hell,** the largest group of hot springs west of Yellowstone, wanders through the park's largest hydrothermal area. Volcanic heat six miles below makes its presence known by boiling this huge cauldron of water and mud at the surface. The man who discovered Bumpass Hell lost his leg to the stew; to avoid any danger to your own life and limb, stay on the trail. Snowbound **Cold Boiling Lake** is 1¾ mi. further on up the same trail. The lake water always appears to boil or simmer due to its placement above a flatulent fissure, despite the year-round snow. For easier access, start from King's Creek.

**Mount Lassen** is the world's largest plug-dome volcano—a volcano with lava flow so viscous and slow that it solidifies as it emerges and plugs the volcano vent. From the parking area, a little over 1 mi. from Bumpass Hell, a steep, 2½ mi., 4-5hr. trek off Rte. 89 will lead to the 10,457 ft. summit. Even if it's sunny and 90°F, take along extra clothes (especially a windbreaker) for the gusty peak, as well as sunblock and lots of water. Solid shoes are important, too; 18 in. of snow can clog the upper 2 mi. of trail even in summer. Guidebook available at trailhead (50¢). Those opting out of the hike can still get excellent views of Reading Peak, Mt. Harkness, and Lake Almanor at **Panorama Point,** a pull-off 1 mi. from the Mt. Lassen trailhead.

About 5 mi. from Mt. Lassen is the **King's Creek Picnic Area,** near a wildflower meadow. From here, trails loop back toward more southerly destinations on Rte. 89, heading to Cold Boiling Lake (¾ mi.) and Bumpass Hell (4 mi.), or to Crumbaugh Lake (1¼ mi.), all the way to Southwest Campground (5¼ mi.). A little farther north on Rte. 89, at mile marker 32, is the trailhead to King's Creek Falls, Summit Lakes, and Drakesbad. The trail to **King's Creek Falls** follows the idyllic, cascading King's Creek 1½ mi. to the rushing falls. **Summit Lake** can be reached on foot from King's Creek or from Rte. 89, 5 mi. farther on, if it's open. **Dersch Meadow,** north of the summit, is a good place to spot grazing deer and circling birds of prey.

A little over 3 mi. from Summit Lake, a short trail leads to what is left of **Devastated Area,** the forested zone that was annihilated by debris spewed out of Mt. Lassen in 1915. Conifers have reclaimed the land here, and as the forest nears maturity, it is becoming difficult to see any traces of the destruction. In a decade or so, the forest will look virtually as it did before the eruption. **Hot Rock** sits 2 mi. farther along Rte. 89. The 300-ton boulder was once a part of Mt. Lassen, but was swept down by a massive lava flow to its current location. Though it never melted from the lava, the rock got so hot that it boiled the mud around it for months.

Heading up to the north end of the park, check out **Chaos Crags and Jumbles,** 6 mi. from Hot Rock, a broken, messy field of rock that avalanched down several volcanic domes and now looks like the landscape of another planet. The final stop, at the northernmost end of Rte. 89, is the **Loomis Museum** (p. 209), which showcases an extensive collection of photographs of the 1914 blast.

**OVERNIGHT HIKES.** A network of trails explores much of the wilder eastern portion of the park, rising and dipping through coniferous forests, hidden lakes, and the occasional lava bed. Of the 150 mi. of trails (including a stretch of the Pacific Crest Trail), the **Manzanita Creek Trail,** near Manzanita Lake campground, and the **Horseshoe Lake** area, east of Summit Lake, are the driest throughout the summer. Both trails make enjoyable overnight trips. Manzanita Creek Trail parallels a lovely creek through rolling woodlands that bear scant resemblance to the boiling cauldrons to the south. To the east, the Horseshoe Lake area is rich in ice-cold lakes and deer-filled pine forests. A number of scenic loops can also start from the Summit Lake North campground. The 10 mi. loop to Lower Twin Lake and the Cluster Lakes features, unsuprisingly, many beautiful lakes. The 11½ mi. loop around Grassy Swale to Lower Twin Lake is greener and less crowded. Wilderness permits are required for backcountry camping.

By mid-summer, the shallow waters of Lake Manzanita and Lake Summit can warm to swimming temperatures. Bathtub Lake in the northeast corner of the park is traditionally the warmest of all. Several lakes in the park have native **rainbow trout,** and Hat Creek is stocked with trout. A state license is required to go **fishing,** and some areas may have additional rules—Manzanita, for example, has "catch and release" and barbless hook policies.

# NEAR LASSEN

Lassen is near three less-traveled and less-developed wilderness areas. If you're not driving a 4WD vehicle, ask about the road conditions on the wilderness areas at Park Headquarters. Pick up a free **wilderness permit** from the US

Forest Service. A topographic map of the area ($4), available at ranger stations, is invaluable for finding trails and trying to figure out what the heck you're staring at. All wilderness areas have a no-trace policy, so everything packed in must be packed out.

## CARIBOU WILDERNESS

Caribou Wilderness, a gently graded plateau, borders the park to the east. For the easiest access, take Rte. 44 or 36 to Hwy. A-21 for 14 mi., then take Silver Lake Rd. to the **Caribou Lake Trailhead.** Its many quiet, clean lakes support water lilies and wildflowers in early summer and treat hikers to solitude. The more desolate **Cone Lake Trailhead** can be reached by taking Forest Service Road (F.S.) 10, off Rte. 44 north of County Hwy. A-21. For the ultimate in isolated beauty, make the trek to the **Hay Meadows Trailhead.** Head north on F.S. 10 from Rte. 36 (near Chester), then turn left after 14 mi. F.S. 10 can be rough; a 4WD vehicle is necessary.

## THOUSAND LAKES WILDERNESS

Thousand Lakes Wilderness (and all the trout in those lakes) can be accessed from F.S. 16 off Rte. 89, 4 mi. north of the park's northern entrance. Seven miles from Rte. 89, the road forks; F.S. 16 continues to the right to **Magee Trailhead,** a strenuous trail that leads to Magee Peak, 8594 ft., and deserted Magee Lake. Insect repellent is a must. The left fork, **Tamarack Trailhead,** is easier and travels to Lake Eiler via Eiler Butte. Going north, take F.S. 33 N25 and turn left just after Wilcox Rd. When the road forks, turn left onto F.S. 33 N23Y. This 7 mi. stretch of road requires 4WD. **Subway Cave** is part of the Thousand Lakes wilderness but can be easily accessed by car—it's off Rte. 89, just past the Rte. 44 split. The 1300 foot-long lava tubes were created when lava flowing in a trench began to harden on top. The lava below kept flowing through the trench, leaving large hollow tunnels. The cave is pitch-black and cool with uneven footing, so bring a friend, a sweater, sturdy shoes, and a lantern or strong flashlight with extra batteries.

## ISHI WILDERNESS

The spectacular Ishi Wilderness, named for the last survivor of a Yahi Yana tribe, comprises rugged terrain at a lower altitude, making it friendly to off-season exploration. Take Rte. 36 from Red Bluff 20 mi. to Payne's Creek Rd. Then take a right on Plum Creek Rd., and another right on Ponderosa Way. This rough road skirts the eastern edge of the wilderness, where most trailheads lie. Ishi is a series of river canyons with dense islands of Ponderosa pine and sparse, sun-scorched grasslands in the south; it's sweltering in the summer. **Mill Creek Trailhead** runs along the 1000 ft. canyon, where gentle waters await swimmers. Keep an eye out for red-tailed hawks and golden eagles. The Tehana Deer Herd, the largest migratory herd in California, spends its winters in Ishi (not so fast, Elmer—hunting isn't allowed). The **Deer Creek Trail** is another scenic hike, with a trailhead at the southern end of the Ishi Wilderness on Ponderosa Way.

# REDDING                                                        ☎ 530

At first glace, Redding may seem little more than city planning gone awry. Virtually unwalkable, riven with freeways, and dispersed without a central downtown, it isn't the most charming of California's cities. Redding's position, however, at the crossroads of I-5 and Rte. 44 and 299, as well as its quantity of hotels and restaurants, makes it a convenient, if not essential, supply stop for Shasta Lake, Lassen Volcanic National Park, and Trinity Wilderness to the west.

FAR NORTH

**⚁ PRACTICAL INFORMATION.** Redding is on I-5, 160 mi. north of Sacramento and 100 mi. south of Yreka. Shasta Lake is 16 mi. north of Redding on I-5, and Mt. Shasta is 60 mi. north. There is an unstaffed **Amtrak train** station at 1620 Yuba St. (☎800-USA-RAIL/872-7245). Buy a ticket on the train or directly through Amtrak. Trains depart to: Sacramento (4hr., 1 per day, $26); San Francisco (6hr., 1 per day, $40); Portland (12-13hr., 1 per day, $77). **Greyhound buses,** 1321 Butte St. (☎241-2531 or 800-231-2222), at Pine St., depart from the 24hr. station to: Sacramento (4hr., 6 per day, $23); San Francisco (5-8hr., 6 per day, $35); Portland (8-10hr., 5 per day, $54). **Enterprise,** 357 Cypress St., rents compact **cars** for $40 per day with 100 mi. included and 18¢ per additional mile. Renters must be 21+ with a major credit card. (☎223-0700. Under-25 surcharge $10 per day. Open M-F 7:30am-6pm, Sa 9am-noon.) Get informed at the **Visitors Bureau,** 777 Auditorium Dr., off Rte. 299 at the Convention Center Exit. (☎225-4100 or 800-874-7562; www.visitredding.com. Open M-F 8am-6pm, Sa-Su 10am-5pm.) Call the **Shasta Lake Ranger District,** 14225 Holiday Rd., for local conditions or camping info. (☎275-1589. Open M-Sa 8:30am-5pm, Su 8am-4:30pm.) Other services include: **police,** 1313 California St. (☎225-4200); **Redding Medical Center,** 1100 Butte St. (☎244-5400), at East St.; and the **post office,** 2323 Churn Creek Rd. (☎223-7523; open M-F 8:30am-5:30pm, Sa 9am-3pm). **Postal Code:** 96049.

**⚃⚄ ACCOMMODATIONS & FOOD.** The Visitors Bureau has free vacation planners with a variety of coupons for area and state accommodations. Standard, inexpensive rooms can be found at the **Hilltop Lodge ❸,** 2240 Hilltop Dr. The rooms are a little scuffed but clean and comfortable, and all have phone, cable TV, A/C, and access to an outdoor pool. (☎221-5432. Singles and doubles $39 on weekdays, $49 on weekends.) **Oak Bottom campground ❶,** 1200 ft., on Rte. 299, 13 mi. west of Redding on beautiful Whiskeytown Lake, has beaches and swimming areas. The camp has 100 sites with solar-powered showers but no hookups. (Reservations ☎800-365-2267, dispatch 241-6584, campground headquarters 359-2344. May-Sept. waterfront tents $18, interior $16; Oct.-Apr. all sites $8. RVs $14.) There are numerous campgrounds on **Shasta Lake ❶,** 1100 ft. (Take the Gilman Rd. Exit on I-5. Sites $6-26.) ⚑**Buz's Crab ❷,** 2159 East St., next to Safeway, has a huge selection of the best seafood in the area at fantastic prices; accordingly, it's packed with locals. Fish (and oysters and calamari) and chips ($3-8), hot crab sandwiches ($6.25), seafood wraps ($6), and crabcake burgers ($7.50) are all delicious. (☎243-2120; www.buzscrab.com. Open daily 11am-9pm.)

# MOUNT SHASTA ☎530

Visible from 200 mi. away, Mount Shasta rises dramatically out of completely flat plains to a frosted, 14,161 ft. peak. Shasta attracts nature buffs, thrill-seekers, mineral-bath pilgrims, and extreme sports enthusiasts, all entranced by the striking vista. In 1873, one Shasta worshipper described the mountain as "lonely as God, white as a winter moon." The description stuck, and is now engraved on the Mt. Shasta plaque in the base city of Mt. Shasta (pop. 3806).

Shasta Indians believed that a great spirit dwelled within the volcano, and modern-day spiritualists are drawn to the mountain by its mystical energy. In 1987, thousands of New Age believers gathered here to witness the great clerical event of Harmonic Convergence, which climaxed when a resident turned on her TV set and saw an angel displayed on the screen. Spiritual significance aside, climbers come to tackle the slopes and Bay-area yuppies flock to relax in the fragrant mountain air. The town of Mount Shasta is moderately tourist-oriented in a New Age sort of way; it has vegetarian restaurants, spiritual bookstores, outdoor equipment shops, and a friendly, pervasive serenity.

## ⬛ 🔢 ORIENTATION & PRACTICAL INFORMATION

The town of Mt. Shasta is 60 mi. north of Redding on **Interstate 5**, 50 mi. west of Lassen Volcanic National Park, and 275 mi. north of San Francisco. The town can be used as a base for daytrips to Lava Beds, Lassen, Burney Falls, and the Shasta Recreation Area. Everitt Memorial Hwy. leads to the Mt. Shasta trailheads.

**Trains: Amtrak's** closest station is the unattended one in Dunsmuir (9 mi. south on I-5), 5750 Sacramento Ave. (☎800-872-7245). Prices range greatly depending on demand, so call ahead. Trains depart to: **Portland, OR** (10½hr., 1 per day, $38-82); **Redding** (2hr., 1 per day, $9-18); **San Francisco** (8½hr., 1 per day, $29-62).

**Buses: Greyhound** (☎800-231-2222) has a flag stop in the parking lot at 4th St. and Mt. Shasta Blvd. To **San Francisco** ($52-56) and **Redding** ($15). Cash only.

**Public Transportation: Siskiyou Stage** (☎800-247-8243) offers minibus transit between Weed, Mt. Shasta (next to the Black Bear Diner in the Mt. Shasta Shopping Center), and Dunsmuir. Operates M-F; call for times. $2-5.

**Visitor Information: Mount Shasta Visitors Center,** 300 Pine St. (☎800-397-1519). Open M-Th 9am-5:30pm, F-Sa 9am-6pm, Su 9am-4pm. **Shasta-Trinity National Forest Service,** 204 W. Alma St. (☎926-4511), across the tracks from the intersection of Alma St. and Mt. Shasta Blvd., has loads of info on outdoor activities in and around Mt. Shasta. Find out which campgrounds and trails are open, and grab maps, brochures, or fire and wilderness permits. Mountain climbers and hikers must sign the trail register outside. Open M-Sa 8am-4:30pm, Su 9am-3pm. **Shasta Lake Info Center** (☎275-1589) is 10 mi. north of Redding at the Mountaingate Wonderland Blvd. Exit off I-5.

**ATM: Bank of America,** 100 Chestnut St. (☎926-8950 or 800-521-2632). Open M-Th 10am-4pm, F 10am-5pm.

**Equipment Rental: House of Ski and Board,** 316 Chestnut St. (☎926-2359; www.hosab.com), 1 block behind Mt. Shasta Blvd. Rents, sells, and services skiing, climbing, and snowboarding equipment at reasonable rates. Boots, bindings, and skis $10 per day, $18 for 3 days. Snowboard and boots $17 per day, $32 for 3 days. Snowshoes $8 per day. Open M-F 9am-6pm, Sa 8am-6pm, Su 10am-5pm. A **cycle shop** is in the same building and rents mountain bikes. $22 half-day, $26 full-day, $75 for a week. **5th Season,** 300 N. Mt. Shasta Blvd. (☎926-3606), rents camping gear, outdoor equipment, skis, and bikes. Sleeping bag with pad $18 for 3 days; $6 each additional day. 2-person tent $40 for 3 days. Ski rental $40 for 3 days. Bike rentals $36-48 per day. Also offers mountain-climbing and alpine touring equipment. Open spring-fall M-F 9am-6pm, Sa 8am-6pm, Su 10am-5pm; in winter daily 8am-6pm.

**Weather, Climbing, and Skiing Conditions: 24hr. Weather** ☎842-4438. **Climbing Conditions** ☎926-9613. **Ski Report** ☎926-8686.

**Library and Internet Access: Mount Shasta Library,** 515 E. Alma St. (☎926-2031). Internet access free for 1hr. Open M and W 1-6pm, Tu noon-6pm, Th and Sa 1-5pm.

**Laundromat: Launderland,** in Mt. Shasta Shopping Center off Lake St. Wash $1.50, dry 25¢ per 8 min. Open M-Sa 7am-9pm, Su 8am-9pm.

**Police:** 303 N. Mt. Shasta Blvd. at Lake St. (☎926-7540).

**Crisis Lines:** Notify the sheriff (☎841-2900 or 800-404-2911) of missing climbers.

**Hospital: Mercy Medical Center,** 914 Pine St. (☎926-6111).

**Post Office:** 301 S. Mt. Shasta Blvd. (☎926-1343). Open M-F 8:30am-5pm. **Postal Code:** 96067.

FAR NORTH

**Mount Shasta Area**

FAR NORTH

## ACCOMMODATIONS

For those tired of camping or on the run, S. Mt. Shasta Blvd., south of McCloud Ave., is lined with large motels that promise convenience. There are also a few, more local accommodations that provide a more personal experience.

**Alpenrose Cottage Guest House,** 204 E. Hinckley St. (☎926-6724; www.hostels.com/alpenrose), near the KOA driveway, offers roses, wind chimes, a sundeck view of Mt. Shasta, two docile household pets, and the unshakeable feeling that you're visiting your grandma. Joyful owner Betty Brown is friendly and helpful. Wood-burning stove, open kitchen, TV room, and library. Hummingbird viewing in summer. Free laundry. With 4 beds available, it's best to reserve a room in advance, especially in summer. $35 per person, $30 for multiple-night stay; $60 per couple. No credit cards. ❸

**Finlandia Motel,** 1612 S. Mt. Shasta Blvd. (☎926-5596). A clean, 2-level motel presumably of Finnish design. Deluxe rooms have vaulted ceilings, bathtubs, and access to a spa and sauna, while economy rooms are more like standard motel rooms. Some rooms have mountain views. Economy singles from $60, with kitchen $65; doubles from $75. Deluxe rooms from $67. Non-summer months about $10 cheaper. ❹

## CAMPING

The US Forest Service (☎926-4511) runs a few area campgrounds. The campgrounds closest to town, however, are primarily commercial. Pick up a campground map from the Visitors Center. No-fee campgrounds require a campfire permit, available at the Forest Service station.

**Lake Siskiyou Campground** (☎926-2618 or 888-926-2618; www.lake-sis.com), 3 mi. southwest of town. Exit I-

5 via Lake St., follow Hatchery Ln. ¼ mi., then go south on Old Stage Rd. and W.A. Barr Rd. This family-oriented site provides a not-quite-roughing-it-yet experience, complete with paved roads and video arcade. Beach access and rental paddleboats, motorboats, and canoes. Coin-operated laundry, flush toilets, hot showers. Reserve in advance. Tent sites $18; RV sites with full hookup and TV $25. ❷

**McBride Springs Campground,** 5000 ft., 5 mi. east of Mt. Shasta off Everitt Memorial Hwy. This compact and secluded campground has 9 drive-up sites with views, water, and hiking access. Well-maintained outhouses. 7-night max. stay. Sites $10. ❶

**Panther Meadow,** 7500 ft., sits on Mt. Shasta 8 mi. down the road from McBride Springs, and offers astounding views. High elevation means it is cold at night, even during the summer. 10 walk-in sites with pit toilets; no water. 3-night max. stay. Free. ❶

**Castle Crags State Park** (☎ 235-2684 or 800-444-7275), 2000 ft., 15 mi. south of Mt. Shasta on I-5 (take the Castella Exit). A large, clean, low elevation campground. The 67 tent and RV sites are spacious, though some are a bit too close to the interstate for comfort. Rock climbing on the crags, swimming, fishing, and hiking opportunities. Facilities include water, flush toilets, hot showers, and an information center. Sites $12. ❶

## ⚡ FOOD

Shasta has many grocery stores, the largest of which is **Ray's Food Place,** 160 Morgan Way, in the Mt. Shasta Shopping Center off Lake St. near I-5. (☎ 926-3390. Open daily 7am-11pm.) In the summer, **produce stands** across the street provide cheaper, fresher fruits and veggies. **Mount Shasta Supermarket,** at the corner of Chestnut and E. Alma St., is a pricier specialty store. (☎ 926-2212. Open M-Sa 8am-7pm, Su 8am-6pm.) **Berryvale Natural Foods,** 305 S. Mt. Shasta Blvd., caters to the health-conscious with organic produce, soy products, great microbrews, and enough tie-dye to make you dizzy. (☎ 926-1576. Open M-Sa 8:30am-7:30pm, Su 10am-6pm.)

🔯 **Laurie's Mountain View Cafe,** 401 N. Shasta Blvd. (☎ 926-4998). This tiny cafe, covered with Deadhead and Native American decorations, has a sunny patio, freshly baked goods, original sandwich creations (salmon, pesto, and cheese $7), and smoothies. Microbrews and imported beers available. Fish and chips (F) and BBQ (Sa) with occasional live music in summer. Open June-Oct. Su-Th 7am-4pm, F-Sa 7am-8pm; Nov.-May daily 7am-4pm. No credit cards. ❷

**Lily's,** 1013 S. Mt. Shasta Blvd. (☎ 926-3372). Don't let the white picket fence fool you; hiding in this little house is perhaps the most extensive and creative menu in town. Meals fairly priced considering the quality, the preparation, and the huge windows. For breakfast, both vegetarian eggs benedict ($8) and non-veggie Benedict Arnold ($9) are enticing, as is the "Chicken Rosie," with raspberries, hazelnut liqueur, and cream ($16), or the ribeye steak ($17). Open daily in summer 7am-10pm; in winter 8am-9pm. ❹

**Black Bear Diner,** 401 W. Lake St. (☎ 926-4669; www.blackbeardiner.com). This busy, small chain draws crowds of folksy locals, hikers, and hippies hungering for the huge portions, friendly service, and Black Bear merchandise. Hungry Bear's Breakfast is 3 eggs, sausage, hash browns, 2 biscuits, and a slab of ham ($8). Dinners are heaping plates of comfort food ($8-11). Vegetarian options. Open daily 5:30am-11:30pm. ❷

## 👁 🏔 SIGHTS & OUTDOOR ACTIVITIES

The mountain attracts people climbing to new heights by foot, pickaxe, or spiritual magnetism, yet anyone can enjoy Mt. Shasta without breaking a sweat if their cars do the work. The **Everitt Memorial Highway** provides excellent views of the mountain as it winds 14 mi. from the town of Mt. Shasta to the Ski Bowl

**FAR NORTH**

trailhead. Parking is available at Bunny Flats and at the end of the road. Once the snow melts (usually around mid-July), one can drive past Bunny Flats to the Panther Meadow campground, the highest car-accessible point. A number of **day hikes** begin in this area, including the steep 2 mi. hike to Grey Butte and another 2 mi. hike through Red Butte to Squaw Meadows from the Old Ski Bowl (three-quarters of a mile from Panther Meadow). The **Horse Camp Trail,** at Horse Camp, is another interesting 2 mi. hike that begins at Bunny Flat and affords great views of Avalanche Gulch and the Red Banks. Because these "trails" are often unlabeled and ill-defined, it's a good idea to plan your route with a map from the Ranger Station before setting out.

**FISH, ROCKS, AND BOOKS.** The **Mount Shasta State Fish Hatchery,** half a mile west of I-5, monitors the production of nearly 10 million baby trout every year. The dense mass of swimming trout in the hatchery troughs is truly a spectacle. Visitors can buy fish food and toss it in to cause total pandemonium. Just don't jump in, no matter what the fish say. Guided tours are provided. *(3 Old State Rd. ☎926-5508. Closed Jan. and Feb. Open daily 7am-dusk. Free.)* Next door, the **Sisson Museum** has a small-town shotgun approach to its exhibits; learn about everything from the history of cameras and WWII guns to domestic life in the gold-rush era. *(☎926-5508. Open Apr.-Oct. M-Sa 10am-4pm, Su 1-4pm. Free.)* For a more literary experience, stop by the **Village Books Bookstore.** A bulletin board out front posts the latest New Age activities. The store boasts a surprisingly impressive selection of magazines, bestsellers, literature, plenty of material on Yoga and spirituality, and a small cafe. *(320 N. Mt. Shasta Blvd. ☎926-1678 or 800-344-0436. Open M-Sa 9:30am-9pm, Su 11am-5pm.)*

**MOUNT SHASTA SKI PARK.** Downhill skiers and snowboarders can tackle the intermediate-level ski trails of **Mount Shasta Ski Park,** while cross-country skiers can try the ski park's **Nordic Center** or go for challenging backcountry skiing (maps and info from Ranger service; see **Visitor Information,** p. 215). In summer, **mountain bikers** rage down the snow-free ski trails. Logging roads in the national forests make excellent backcountry biking trails. Climbers of all skill levels love the park's outdoor wall. *(Ski Park: 10 mi. east of I-5. ☎926-8600 or 800-754-7427; www.ski-park.com. Hours vary by season. Opens for the summer on June 26th; opening date in winter depends on snow. Lift tickets $33, ages 8-12 and over 64 $17, under 8 $7. Tu adults $26. Night skiing W-Sa 4-10pm $20/$13/$3. Ski rental packages from $21. Nordic Center: trail pass and rental $22/$18/$9. Biking: $12/$4/$8, rentals $20 for 6hr. Climbing: 2 climbs $5, 3hr. $12.)*

## CLIMBING MOUNT SHASTA

At 14,162 ft., Mt. Shasta is not an easy climb, and requires mountaineering skills even on its easiest route. Weather conditions are notoriously unpredictable. 17 routes lead to the Shasta summit, each with its own challenges and rewards.

All climbers must stop at the US Forest Service (see p. 215) for weather updates, climbing conditions, safety registration, a free wilderness permit, a summit pass for climbs over 10,000 ft. ($15), and the mandatory human waste pack-out system. All adventurers should stop by for up-to-date maps and info before venturing into the wilderness. Mt. Shasta rangers are particularly knowledgeable, friendly, and helpful, whether you're going for a jump in a lake, an afternoon hike, or an all-out trip to the summit. Parking is free at trailheads, though this is subject to change.

**AVALANCHE GULCH.** The most popular and accessible route to the summit starts at Bunny Flat on the mountain's southwest side, off Everitt Memorial Hwy. A short, steep trail leads to Horse Camp, where hikers will find the historic **Sierra Club Cabin ❶,** which is occupied in the summer by a caretaker. This is a good place to set up base camp for the necessary early morning ascent. *(First-come, first-served. No accommodations in the cabin itself. $5 fee to tent near the* *cabin; $3 for a bivy sack.)* Alternately, **first-night camping ❶** is permitted on the Bunny Flat parking lot or anywhere in the surrounding area, as long as you have a wilderness permit (see p. 215). While the climb can be done in one day, most first-time climbers choose to spend the night at **Helen Lake** (10,443 ft.). Though Avalanche Gulch is not a technical climb, it does require crampons, a helmet, and an ice axe, even in summer.

**OTHER CLIMBS.** Some significantly more difficult technical climbs also start at Bunny Flat, as well as at North Gate, Brewer Creek, and Clear Creek. Since Mt. Shasta City is at a mere 3,500 ft., acclimating to Shasta's extreme elevations probably necessitates some mini-climbs before attempting to summit.

## BEYOND MOUNT SHASTA

**CASTLE CRAGS STATE PARK.** Castle Crags is an awe-inspiring piece of wilderness of trails, rivers, and lakes. When viewed from I-5, the dramatic spires resemble castle fortifications; the crags are easily accessible and provide stunning views. Twenty-eight miles of well-maintained hiking trails span the area. To see Mt. Shasta in its glory, try the strenuous 2.7 mi. **Castle Crags Trail,** accessible from the Vista Point parking area. The first three quarters of the hike are steep in parts but walkable; however, bouldering and trailblazing is required to reach Castle Dome, 2250 ft. higher than the trailhead. Water supplies can be replenished at Indian Spring. Buy a topographical map of the area from the ranger station ($1). The **Pacific Crest Trail** (see **From Crest to Crest: the Trail of the West,** p. 235) runs for 19 mi. through the wilderness, curving around serene alpine lakes. Access the trail at the south fork of Sacramento Rd. Maps and permits are available at the Forest Service. Be cautious: much of the stone here is dangerous and unstable. Nearby **Cantara Loop** has good rock faces for beginners, and **Pluto Caves** has fun lava tubes--underground tunnels formed by lava flow. There is also an outdoor climbing wall at the **Mt. Shasta Ski Park** (see p. 218). For more climbing info, call **5th Season** (see p. 215) or the **US Forest Service** (see p. 215). Camping is free in the area of the Shasta-Trinity National Forest surrounding Castle Crags, and the state park runs a full service campground. Abutting the wilderness area is **Castle Lake,** which offers beautiful hiking trails as well as fishing, swimming, and camping, though camping is restricted within 200 ft. of the lake. *(Off I-5, 15 mi. south of Shasta. ☎ 235-2684.)*

**STEWART MINERAL SPRINGS.** Brought to this popular spiritual destination on the brink of death, Mr. Stewart attributed his subsequent recovery to the water's healing energy. Spiritual properties aside, the secluded saunas and hot tubs make for a soothing, relaxing soak. *(4617 Stewart Springs Rd., in Weed. ☎ 938-2222; www.stewartmineralsprings.com. Open Su-W 10am-6pm, Th-Sa 10am-10pm. Oct.-Apr. daily 10am-6pm. Baths $20. Tent and RV sites $15. Motel rooms $45, with kitchen $49-79; cabins $59-89.)*

**MCCLOUD RIVER AREA.** Somewhat out of the way, the McCloud area features 13 mi. of rivers and storybook waterfalls, all easily accessed by foot. Many places are perfect for swimming, boating, hiking, and camping. The area is growing in popularity, but many trails and facilities are still unmarked. Forest Service rangers have helpful maps with detailed directions. *(10 mi. east of the town of Mt. Shasta on I-5.)*

**OTHER SIGHTS AND ACTIVITIES.** The **Squaw Valley Creek Trail** is an enjoyable, gentle 5 mi. trail south of McCloud. Unique vegetation and a thick carpet of moss line the creek, which connects pristine waterfalls and pools suitable for fishing and swimming. *(Trailhead 9 mi. south of McCloud; follow the signs to Squaw Valley Creek Rd.)* An easy 30min. and 50min. hike up the river from Fowlers leads to the breathtaking **Falls of the McCloud River.** From Fowlers Campground, walk toward the river for the trailheads to the lower, middle or upper falls. *(6 mi. east of McCloud. On Rte. 89, follow signs to Fowlers Campground. One can park just outside the actual campground to avoid paying.)* **Fowlers Camp,** 3600 ft., is the only overnight site in the area and has toilets, picnic units, water and handicap facilities. *(First-come, first-camp. Sites $12.)*

### AREA LAKES

Around Mt. Shasta are alpine lakes great for secluded swimming and fishing, including **Deadfall Lake, Castle Lake, Toad Lake,** and **Heart Lake.** Stop by the ranger station for detailed info on these spots. **Lake Siskyou** is the most popular and accessible, albeit somewhat crowded. Beach use is $1 and boats can be rented.

**LAKE SHASTA.** Thirty minutes south of Mt. Shasta on I-5 (15min. north of Redding), Lake Shasta is the largest reservoir in California. All sorts of watercraft explore its sapphire blue surface; campgrounds and picnic areas pepper the 450 mi. of coast. The beachless lake is best enjoyed by simply jumping in the water. Completed in 1945, the **Shasta Dam,** at the southern end of the lake, is three times taller than Niagara Falls, and is the second-largest dam in the US after the Grand Coulee in Washington; views from the dam are spectacular. Visit the **Dam Visitor Center,** in Dam Park. *(☎ 275-4463. Open daily M-F 8am-4:30pm, Sa-Su 8:30am-5pm.)*

**WHISKEYTOWN UNIT.** Eight miles west of Redding is the popular beaches, marinas, campsites, and hiking trails of **Whiskeytown Lake and Recreation Center,** easily accessible from Rte. 299. It's not quite Coney Island, but in peak summer season the lake bustles with boats. The recreation area boasts many well-maintained **campgrounds ❶**, save for the RV sites which may consist of a crowded parking lot with minimal shade. *(Entry into the area is $5 per vehicle per day, $10 for a week.)*

The **Whiskeytown Unit Visitors Center,** at Rte. 299 and Kennedy Memorial Dr., south of the lake, has day use permits. Reserve campsites through Biospherics *(☎ 800-365-2267; http://reservations.nps.gov).* The **Oak Bottom Campground,** off Rte. 299, has 22 RV sites and 100 developed tent sites near a beach, picnic area, snack bar, and marina, as well as drinking water and flush toilets; unfortunately, the RV sites lack hookups. *(Sites May 15-Sept. 15 $16, lakeside $18; Sept. 16-May 14 $8.)* Nearby **Oak Bottom Marina** rents ski boats, sailboats, patio boats, and canoes. *(☎ 359-2269. Open M-Th 7am-8pm, F-Su 7am-9pm. Canoes $21 for 3hr.; sailboats $42 for 3hr.)* If the crowds cramp your style, you can pick up back-country camping and hiking permits at **Park Headquarters,** which provides info on a number of first-come, first-served primitive **campsites ❶**. *(☎ 246-1225. 14-day max. stay. Camping permits $10. Open daily spring-fall 9am-6pm; in winter 10am-4pm. All sites $10 per night; in winter $5.)*

# YREKA                                                              ☎ 530

Yrekan rebels taught us this lesson in December 1941: to get the attention of chi-chi southern California and the space cadets of Oregon, take to the streets with shotguns, barricade the roads, set up a provisional government, and declare your independence as the Great State of Jefferson. Three days after this little "rebellion," the situation was shelved in the wake of a certain bombing at Pearl Harbor. Alas! Yreka's 15 minutes came and went as the capital of Jefferson: a "state that never was and never will be, but that has lived in men's minds for a hundred years." The dream continues to live on for some—you can't miss the barn just south of Yreka on I-5 with "State of Jefferson" proudly painted on its sloped roof.

Now, Yreka (why-REE-ka; pop. 7500) is a good ol' American town—strip malls, motels, and cheap lube jobs. Yreka makes a good stop on the way to the wealth of outdoor activities in the area, but it is hardly a destination in and of itself.

## ▣ ⓘ ORIENTATION & PRACTICAL INFORMATION.

Yreka is conveniently stationed on I-5, 20 mi. south of the Oregon border, 40 mi. north of the town of Mt. Shasta, and 260 mi. north of Sacramento. Greyhound (☎842-3145; open daily 8am-5pm) **buses** roll to: **Redding** (2hr., 3 per day, $21-23); **Mt. Shasta** (50min., 1 per day, $10-11); **Portland** (8-9hr., 2 per day, $65); and **San Francisco** (9-10hr., 3 per day, $57). **Enterprise**, 1275 S. Main St., rents compact cars for $32 a day with 100 free mi. and 20¢ for each additional mi. (☎841-0525. Must be 21 with a major credit card. Under 25 surcharge $10 per day. Open M-F 8am-5pm, Sa 9am-noon.) The **Chamber of Commerce**, 117 W. Miner St., dishes out both information and tasty ice cream. (☎842-1649; www.yrekachamber.com. Open M-Sa 9am-5pm, Su 10am-4pm; winter M-F 9am-5pm.) Other services include: **Klamath National Forest Headquarters** and **Clouds National Forest Ranger,** 1312 Fairlane Rd. (☎842-6131; open M-F 8am-4:30pm); the **hospital,** 444 Bruce St. (☎842-4121); and the **post office,** 401 S. Broadway at Center St. (☎842-9372. Open M-F 8:30am-5pm). **Postal Code:** 96097.

## ⓕ ACCOMMODATIONS.

The southern end of Main St. is the most promising for high-value accommodations. **The Klamath Motor Lodge ❸,** 1111 S. Main St., is a friendly spot with large, immaculate rooms, phones, microwaves, popcorn, cable TV, A/C, fridge, and a grassy picnic area with a grill and pool. (☎842-2751 or 800-551-7255. Singles from $52, doubles $64; in winter $48/$59.) **The Miner's Inn ❹,** 122 E. Miner St., right off I-5, is a step above the standard motor lodge. Spacious, spotless rooms have cable TV, phone, and coffee, while several suites are two bedroom apartments with kitchens. The grounds include two heated pools. (☎842-4355. Singles and doubles $74-84, suites with kitchen $105; in winter $3-5 less.)

## ⓒ FOOD.

Yreka fare ranges from truck-stop convenience to New Age soul-enriching nutrients to tourist taverns. At Main and W. Minor St. are two 24hr. family restaurants with standard Denny's-style fare. Additionally, **Nature's Kitchen ❷,** 412 S. Main St., is decorated with faux vines, fresh flowers, candles, and a mishmash of Christian and Hindu iconography, but it's all charming and the waitstaff is bright and friendly. Try a Monterey Jack and avocado sandwich with a sesame-and-garlic seasoned salad or a bowl of soup for only $6. An organic bakery and espresso bar are also part of this establishment. (☎842-1136. Open M-Sa 8am-

# FROM THE ROAD

## AFRAID OF THE DARK?

My echoed laugh returned to me in the damp 42°F chill. "What the hell am I doing here?" I asked myself, about a thousand feet inside Valentine Cave. Man has sent himself into space and has gone to the depths of the ocean—but at this moment, in this cave, there seemed nothing more absurd and contradictory to self-preservation than putting oneself into this exact situation: subterranean burial, deep within a lava tube. This thought alternated with flashlight paranoia. I'd take four steps forward then stare at the lantern's beam. Is it getting weaker? Yes, it's getting weaker. No, it isn't. Am I talking to myself? Take four steps. Repeat.

My heart had barely settled when I nervously started into Golden Dome. Just past the twilight zone, I squinted, shook my head, and shone my flashlight on the area that had caught my eye. A man was seated near me, at the edge of my light, 400 ft. into the cave. What was he doing here, alone, in the dark? I didn't care to ask, and started back, quietly so as not to disturb his silent meditation. But then I wondered: maybe he's hurt, or even dead? I walked back, and called out, "Hello?" No answer. "HELLO?" I advanced, an impending sense of heroism only faintly overcoming an impending sense of doom. But wait, the head...is separate from the torso. Disbelief passed into humiliation as it quickly became obvious the "man" was a pile of rocks. Strange things you see down here, alone...

-Carleton Goold

3pm.) Another local favorite, **Poor George's Family Restaurant ❶**, 108 Oberlin St., just west of Main St., is what Denny's wishes it could be. Amid a juke box, paintings of bald eagles, and other Americana, seniors and skaters alike munch on burgers (around $6), sandwiches ($4-6), salads ($3-6), and steak and eggs ($8). Breakfast ($4-9) is served all day. (Open M-F 6am-7:45pm, Sa-Su 7am-1:45pm.)

# LAVA BEDS NATIONAL MONUMENT ☎530

At first glance, Lava Beds National Monument appears to be a stark sea of sagebrush, arid grasses, and craggy rocks. But beneath this 72 sq. mi. expanse lies a complex web of more than 400 lava-formed caves and otherworldly tunnels. Cool, quiet, and often eerie tubes are the product of lava flows from the Mammoth crater around 30,000 years ago, and range from 18 in. crawl spaces to 80 ft. cathedrals. As the outer layer of a flow contacts the colder ground or air around it, it hardens and creates a sheet that insulates the molten lava inside. The hot, fluid lava continues to flow away, leaving hollow conduits under the earth after the lava flow ceases.

In spring and fall, nearby Tule Lake Refuge provides a stopover for migratory birds, some of which come from as far away as Siberia. The fall migration is particularly spectacular, when a million ducks and half a million geese literally darken the sky. In winter, this is the best place in the contiguous US to see a bald eagle.

For people, however, Lava Beds and the Tule Lake Refuge appear to be a challenging destination, due mostly to their remoteness and harsh climate: expect blistering heat and little water in the monument. Local accommodations are sparse, and those seeking less desolate motels should plan on making the drive to Mt. Shasta (see p. 214) or Klamath Falls, OR (see p. 225).

## ✳ 🛈 ORIENTATION & PRACTICAL INFORMATION

Although cold weather can pervade the high desert climate at any time of the year, summer weather tends to be arid, with hot days and cool nights. It takes a day to really appreciate the park, and you'll need a car not only to access the park but also to explore its northern areas. The nearest spot to catch a bus, rent a car, or find a hospital is across the Oregon border in **Klamath Falls** (p. 225), 50 mi. north of Lava Beds. **Redding** (p. 213) and **Medford**, OR also offer these services but are a few hours away. There is no public transportation to the area. Tulelake **police** is located at 24th St. and C St. (☎800-404-2911 or 667-5284).

Lava Beds is southwest of the blink-and-you'll-miss-it town of Tulelake (pop. 1000) and northeast of Mt. Shasta. The **Visitors Center** is in the southeast corner of the park. There are two northern entrances near Tulelake. The **southeast entrance** (25 mi. south of town) is closest to the Visitors Center. The two **east entrances** are closer to Klamath Basin Wildlife Refuge and the Oregon border. The **north entrance** is on Rte. 139. The road to the **northeast entrance** splits from Rte. 139 about 8 mi. southeast of Tulelake, and winds through the wilder northern areas of the monument for 25 mi. to the Visitors Center. Visitors coming from the south on I-5 must take a circuitous route, following US 97 North, then Rte. 161 East to S. Hill Rd. For cheap gas, hop over the Oregon border on Rte. 139 North to Merrill.

**Lava Beds Visitors Center**, in the park's southeastern corner, near a cluster of accessible caves, has exhibits on Modoc culture and gives daily tours. Summer presentations on the lava tubes, wildflowers, and the Modoc tribe are held at the nearby outdoor theater. The well-informed staff lends flashlights to explorers (free; return them by 5:30pm, in winter by 4:30pm) and sells hardhats for $3.25. **Bring plenty of water and food**—there are no concessions at the monument. (☎667-2282; www.nps.gov/labe. Open May 26-Sept. 1 daily 8am-6pm; Sept. 2-May 25 8am-5pm. Center tours daily 10am and 2pm. Outside tours daily 9pm. $5 per vehicle.)

## ACCOMMODATIONS, CAMPING & FOOD

There are a few roadside motels in Tulelake. Each is fairly isolated, set between agricultural fields and Rte. 139. The best of the bunch is the **Ellis Motel ❸**, 2238 Rte. 139, 1 mi. north of Tulelake, which sits alone behind a manicured lawn with only a row of large shady trees between it and the highway. There are 11 small, simple rooms, some with kitchens. (☎667-5242. Singles from $35; doubles from $45.)

The only developed campground in Lava Beds is **Indian Well ❶**, opposite the Visitors Center, featuring picnic tables, firepits, and a fantastic view of the stars. You can now bypass the hellish walk across the jagged volcanic rocks to this long-used Indian camp by driving right up to the sites. Drinking water and flush toilets are available May-October. (☎667-2282. 43 sites. No reservations accepted. $10.) The monument has two **wilderness areas** separated by the main north-south road for backcountry **camping ❶**. A wilderness permit is not required. Cooking is limited to stoves, and camps must be at least 1 mi. from trailheads, roads, and parking areas, and 150 ft. from cave entrances. **Modoc National Forest** borders the monument and offers free off-road **camping ❶**. Nearby **Medicine Camp** and **Hemlock campgrounds ❶** have water, flush toilets, and opportunities to fish, swim and boat (sites $7). More info is available at the **Modoc Doublehead Ranger Station,** 1 mi. south of Tulelake on Rte. 139., near a set of metal silos. (☎667-2246. Open M-F 8:30am-4:30pm.)

**Jock's,** at Modoc and Main St., is a decently sized but slightly overpriced grocery store. (☎667-2612. Open M-Sa 7am-8pm, Su 9am-6pm.) **Captain Jack's Stronghold Restaurant ❷**, 5 mi. south of Tulelake, 1 mi. south of the turn-off to Lava Beds, serves homemade soups and breads, and has a sizable salad bar. The diverse menu, prime location, and welcoming floral decorations attract locals and tourists. (☎664-5566. Breakfast and lunch $6-8. Dinner $8-13. Open Feb.-Nov. Tu-W 7am-8pm, Th-Sa 7am-9pm, Su 9am-8pm.)

## SIGHTS & OUTDOOR ACTIVITIES

**SPELUNKING.** The lava beds, (mostly) linear lava tubes, offer novice cavers relatively easy expeditions into the underground. But "easy" is not to say that the caves aren't pitch black, perfectly silent, and generally spooky; though never more than a few hundred feet below the surface, the caves can give a sense of isolation and, at times, fear, that few other experiences provide. Hardhats, on sale at the Visitors Center (see p. 222) for $3.25, or other helmets, are essential unless you're under 12 inches tall: the unusually sharp ceilings have an uncanny affinity for human heads. Another necessary cave-going accessory is a sweatshirt or jacket; the sun-swept desert can be scorching, but the caves below are cool and damp. Cave tours, leaving from the Visitors Center (mid-June to Sept. 1 daily 2pm), explain the fascinating phenomena associated with the caves. Solo exploring is not recommended but is allowed; bring steely nerves and *at least* two flashlights. Inquire at the Visitors Center for guidelines and information.

Of the over 400 caves in the park, nearly three dozen can be explored by the public. (All caves are technically public, but under the Cave Protection Act, only a few can have their location disclosed. Feel free to wander around for the other 400 or so if you know what you're doing.) The **Mushpot Cave,** in the middle of the Visitors Center's parking lot, has a short, well-lit trail to acquaint visitors with cave formations. South of the Visitors Center is perhaps the best and most surreal of the area's "public" caves, **Valentine Cave,** with unnaturally smooth walls and a frozen waterfall. Townsend Bats stream back to the **Skull Ice Cave,** 3½ mi. north, every February. On an equally eerie note, this cave with 80 ft. high ceilings is where a rancher found two human skeletons chilling alongside wagonloads of bighorn sheep skulls. The ice covering the cave floor undoubtedly attracted the animals. The 2¼ mi. **Cave Loop Road,** which starts and finishes at the Visitors Center, passes by 20 caves, but gives little guidance beyond the entrance stairways. Parking is available at each entrance. **Sentinel Cave** has crisscrossing tunnels, skylights, and two entrances for added fun and confusion. **Golden Dome** is structurally unremarkable, save for the lavacicles on the yellow hydrophobic bacteria-encrusted ceiling. The most complex of the public tunnels is the **Catacombs Cave.** Visitors will crawl a good deal of the over 1 mi. of interconnected passageways. Bring a technical map, available at the Visitors Center ($4.50), and allow 4-6hr.

**HIKING.** Trails of varying difficulty wander through the park. Hikers should keep in mind that the area is essentially a desert, with little shade and extreme heat. The **Whitney-Butte Trail** goes through rocky brush to the black Callahan Lava Flow, a 3.5 mi. (one-way) route from the trailhead at Merrill Cave. The **Mammoth Crater** is more a sight than hike, but offers all the benefits of a huge volcanic crater with none of the annoying molten rock and exploding cinder. For an overnight hike, the Lyons Trails traverses 10 mi. from Skull Cave to Hospital Rock over the rocky, hot plain in the park's eastern reaches. Consult a ranger before you go.

Four miles north of the Visitors Center is **Schonkin Butte.** The steep three-quarter mile ascent takes about 30min. and leads to a fire lookout that gives a broad view of the landscape rising up to the massive white face of Mt. Shasta. Close to Lava Bed's northern entrance is **Captain Jack's Stronghold,** a natural lava fortress where Modoc warriors and US troops battled during the Modoc War. Go only if your imagination is strong: few traces of the struggle remain. **Petroglyph Point,** just outside the northern entrance, is a cliff wall of a former island covered with a large collection of native rock carvings. Native Americans had to paddle across a lake to the cliff, where they engraved mountain- and human-like images. A few carvings from before 1950, such as Japanese characters engraved by prisoners of the internment camps, are also historic. Sadly, the ugly barbed wire fence guarding the walls prevents further efforts to leave inscrutable messages for posterity.

# BEYOND LAVA BEDS

The first wildlife refuge in the US, **Klamath Basin National Wildlife Refuge** teems with waterfowl. **Tule Lake** and **Lower Klamath National Wildlife Refuges** are the most accessible from Lava Beds. The drive from Tulelake to Lava Beds runs through the Tule Lake refuge, which is visible from Rte. 161 just north of Tulelake. Over a million birds migrate through the refuge each year, including bald eagles and pelicans; the best time to see the eagles is winter. **Lower Klamath and Tule Lake Wildlife Refuge Visitors Center and Headquarters,** on Hill Rd., 4 mi. south of Rte. 161 and 18 mi. north of Lava Beds Visitors Center, has a small **museum** with a high-quality slide show and many a stuffed bird or beast. A canoe route starting from the museum is open July-September, and has two marked miles of "trails" for quiet and up-close observation. (☎ 667-2231. Open M-F 8am-

4:30pm, Sa-Su 10am-4pm.) Car tours are available in the Tule Lake and Lower Klamath Refuges. The "Tule Lake tour" is best. A 10 mi. trail open to hiking, biking, and cross-country skiing meanders through the Klamath Marsh Refuge. The still waters and low mountains make perfect photographic backdrops for images of the active wildlife in these fragile wetlands.

The **Tule Lake** internment camp is a relic of a dark side of American history. More than 18,000 Japanese-Americans were held here by the US government during WWII. The camp is in Newell, 4 mi. north of Petroglyph Point. Not much remains except a plaque, a couple of ruined buildings, and old fence-lines.

## CRATER LAKE & KLAMATH FALLS ☎541

The deepest lake in the US, the seventh deepest in the world, and one of the most beautiful anywhere, Crater Lake is one of Oregon's signature attractions. Formed about 7700 years ago in an eruption of Mt. Mazama, it began as a deep caldera and gradually filled itself with many centuries' worth of melted snow. The circular lake plunges from its shores to a depth of 1936 ft. Though it remains iceless in the winter, its banks, which loom as high as 2000 ft. above the 6176 ft. lake surface, are snow-covered most of the year. **Crater Lake National Park** averages over 44 ft. of yearly snow; snowbound roads an keep the northern entrance closed into July. Before July, enter the park from the south. The park entrance fee is $10 for cars, $5 for hikers and cyclists. The **Amtrak** Spring St. depot (☎884-2822; open daily 7:30-11am and 8:30-10pm) is in Klamath Falls, on the east end of Main St.; turn right onto Spring St. and immediately left onto Oak St. One train per day runs to Portland ($36-60). **Greyhound,** 3817 US 97 N (☎882-4616; open M-F 8am-1am, Sa 6-9am and midnight-12:45am), rolls one per day to Bend (3hr., $20), Eugene (10hr., $40), and Redding, CA (4hr., $30). The **Chamber of Commerce,** 507 Main St. (☎884-0666 or 800-445-6728; www.klamath.org; open M-F 8am-5pm), has visitors information. Get free **backcountry camping** permits at the **William G. Steel Center,** 1 mi. from the south entrance of the park. (☎594-2211, ext. 402. Open daily 9am-5pm.) **Crater Lake National Park Visitors Center** is on the lake shore at Rim Village. (☎594-3100. Open June-Sept. daily 8:30am-6pm.) The **post office** is at 317 S. 7th St. in Klamath. (☎800-275-8777. Open M-F 7:30am-5:30pm, Sa 9am-noon.) **Postal Code:** 97604.

From the Visitors Center at the rim to the **Sinnott Memorial Overlook,** it is an easy 300 ft. walk to the park's most panoramic and accessible view. High above the lake, **Rim Drive,** which does not open entirely until mid-July, is a 33 mi. loop around the rim of the caldera. Trails to **Watchman Peak** (¾ mi. one-way, 1hr.), on the west side of the lake, are the most spectacular. The strenuous 2½ mi. hike up **Mt. Scott,** the park's highest peak (almost 9000 ft.), begins near the lake's eastern edge. The steep **Cleetwood Cove Trail** (2¼ mi. round-trip, 2hr.) leaves from the north edge of the lake and is the only route down to the water. It is also the home of **Wizard Island,** a cinder cone rising 760 ft. above the lake, and **Phantom Ship Rock,** a rock formation. Picnics, fishing, and swimming are allowed, but surface temperatures reach a maximum of only 50°F. Park rangers lead free tours daily in the summer and periodically in the winter, when they don their snowshoes.

An easy base for forays into Crater Lake, Klamath Falls has several affordable hotels. The **Townhouse Motel ❶,** 5323 6th St., 3 mi. south of Main St., offers clean, comfy rooms. (☎882-0924. Cable TV, A/C, no phones. Singles $30; doubles $35.) **Mazama Campground ❶,** near the park's south entrance off Rte. 62, is swarmed by tents and RVs from mid-June until October. (☎594-2255. Showers 75¢ per 4min. Wheelchair accessible. No reservations. Sites $15; RVs $17, electric hookup $19.) Where's **Waldo's Mongolian Grill and Tavern ❸?** It's at 610 Main St. and ready to grill your choice of veggies, meats, and sauces. (☎884-6863. Medium bowl $8.50. All-you-can-eat $10. Open M-Th 11am-11:30pm, F-Sa 11am-1am.)

## RECENT NEWS

### WHO'S THE SUCKER?

Farmers in the dusty Klamath Basin have counted on dependable irrigation from the Klamath River since 1905. But for several years before the summer of 2001, the Klamath Basin worked up a huge precipitation debt, receiving only about half of its 11 in. average. Environmentalists alerted the federal government. Citing possible extinction of suckerish and coho salmon populations if water levels declined any further, the US Bureau of Reclamation shut down irrigation water to 1400 farmers downstream in Southern Oregon and Northern California.

Over the course of the chaotic summer, farmers forcibly opened headgates four times, and armed federal agents had to be called in. Snowpack and slightly improved rainfall ensured water releases in 2002. To some extent, though, the damage was already done; younger farmers in Tule Lake have already left for wetter pastures. Fueling the flames was a pronouncement by the National Academy of Sciences finding that the science behind the conclusion that lowered water would kill the fish was "baseless." Complicating matters further, saving water for the fish deprived waterfowl of it and bald eagles in the Lower Klamath Basin. No solution seems readily available—some turn to the Bible, while others feel the government should buy out farmers. In any case, tension is building, as the drought, though lessened, is by no means over, and signs attesting to the frustration of the farmers remain:

## ASHLAND ☎ 541

Set near the California border, the intimate town of Ashland is the unlikely but intriguing stage for the world-renowned **Oregon Shakespeare Festival**, P.O. Box 158, Ashland, OR 97520 (☎ 482-4331; www.osfashland.org). From mid-February to October, drama devotees can choose among 11 Shakespearean and newer works performed in Ashland's three elegant theaters: the outdoor **Elizabethan Stage**, the **Angus Bowmer Theater**, and the intimate **Black Swan**. Ticket purchases are recommended six months in advance; mail-order and phone ticket sales begin in January. (In spring and fall $22-39; in summer $29-52. $5 fee per order for phone, fax, or mail orders.) At 9:30am, the **box office**, 15 S. Pioneer St., releases unsold tickets for the day's performances and sells 20 standing room tickets for sold-out shows on the Elizabethan Stage ($11). Half-price rush tickets are sometimes available 1hr. before performances. **Backstage tours** provide a wonderful glimpse of the festival from behind the curtain. (Tu-Sa 10am. $10, ages 6-17 $7.50, under 6 not admitted.)

Ashland is in the foothills of the Siskiyou and Cascade Ranges, 285 mi. south of Portland and 15 mi. north of the California border, near the junction of I-5, Rte. 99, and Rte. 66. Greyhound (☎ 482-8803) runs from the BP Station, 2073 Rte. 99 N, at the north end of town, and sends three per day to Portland (8hr., $43); Sacramento (7hr., $45); and San Francisco (11hr., $49). **Visitor info: Chamber of Commerce**, 110 E. Main St. (☎ 482-3486). **Ashland District Ranger Station**, 645 Washington St., off Rte. 66 by Exit 14 on I-5, provides info on hiking, biking, and the Pacific Crest Trail. (☎ 482-3333. Open M-F 8am-4:30pm.) The **post office** is located at 120 N. 1st St., at Lithia Way. (Open M-F 9am-5pm.) **Postal Code:** 97520.

In winter, Ashland is a budget paradise; in summer, hotel and B&B rates double, while the hostel pads prices a little. Only rogues and knaves arrive without reserving in advance. **Ashland Hostel ❷**, 150 N. Main St., is well-kept and cheery with an air of elegance. (☎ 482-9217. Laundry and kitchen. Check-in 5-10pm. Lockout 10am-5pm. Curfew midnight. Dorms $20; private rooms $50. Cash or traveler's checks only.) The incredible food selection on N. and E. Main St. has earned the plaza a culinary reputation independent of the festival. **Morning Glory ❷**, 1149 Siskiyou Blvd., deserves a medal for "most pleasant dining environment," earned both inside by the fireplace and bookcases, and outside by the rose-entwined wooden porticos. (☎ 488-8636. Sandwiches around $9. Open daily 7am-2pm.)

# THE SIERRA NEVADA

The Sierra Nevada is California's backbone. It marks the 450 mi. line where two gigantic tectonic plates, the Pacific and North American, collided four hundred million years ago. Stretching from stifling Death Valley to just below the Oregon border, the range is a living record of the tireless work of the elements—a product of Mt. Lassen's volcanic activity hundreds of millions of years ago and granite-smoothing glaciation a mere few thousand years ago. It also nurtures some of the most breathtaking scenery in the country, including Lake Tahoe's crystalline waters, Mono Lake's giant tufa formations, Sequoia National Park's redwoods, and the roiling rivers of Yosemite, but the entire range is worthy of homage and scrutiny, and millions of visitors eagerly undertake the pilgrimage every year.

Temperatures in the Sierra Nevada are as diverse as the terrain. Even during the generally warm summer, overnight lows can dip into the 20s (check local weather reports). Normally, only US 50 and I-80 are open during the snow season. Exact dates of road closures vary from year to year; check with a ranger station for road conditions, even through June. In summer, protection from exposure to ultraviolet rays at high elevations is necessary; always bring sunscreen and a hat. For additional outdoors advice, see **Essentials: Camping and the Outdoors**, p. 43.

## HIGHLIGHTS OF THE SIERRA NEVADA

**LAKE TAHOE.** Tahoe hosts world-class **skiing** (p. 244) and some of the state's best **watersports, biking, hiking** (p. 243), and **rock climbing** (p. 244).

**YOSEMITE.** Join the herd of tourists at Yosemite National Park, where you can hike **Half Dome** (p. 261), watch climbers squeezing up **El Capitan** (p. 260), or retreat to the beautiful **backcountry** (p. 265) to enjoy the park in peace.

**SEQUOIA & KINGS CANYON.** Sequoia and Kings Canyon National Parks feature incredible views from **Moro Rock** (p. 276), great backcountry hiking and camping in **Zumwalt Meadow** (p. 278), and the **deepest canyon in the United States** (p. 557).

**OWENS VALLEY.** Stand among the **oldest living things on Earth** (p. 296) and slide down the **largest land-locked sand dunes in the world** (p. 296).

**CLIMB EVERY MOUNTAIN.** Inyo National Forest offers the **tallest mountain in the contiguous US** (p. 302), as well as the remnants of one of the country's most romantic periods (p. 301) and one of its most shameful (p. 301).

# GOLD COUNTRY

In 1848, California was a rural backwater of only 15,000 people. That year, sawmill operator James Marshall wrote in his diary: "This day some kind of mettle...found in the tailrace...looks like goald." Rumors began spreading of untold riches buried in the hills, but media skepticism muted the excitement until President James K. Polk, in December 1848, declared the rumors to be true. By the end of the next year, some 90,000 miners from around the world had headed for California and its Mother Lode, a 120 mi. expanse of gold-rich seams. "Gold fever" brought on a stampede of over half a million prospecting men and families over the next decade. Many of the first prospectors found the rumors to be accurate and made fortunes mining easily-accessed surface gold. These stores were rapidly depleted, however, and few subsequent prospectors struck it rich. Miners, sustained by dreams of instant wealth, worked long and hard, but most could barely squeeze sustenance out of their fiercely guarded claims. Many miners died of malnutrition. Mark Twain described the diet as "Beans and dishwater for breakfast, dishwater and beans for dinner. And both articles warmed over for supper." In Coloma, during one miner's funeral, a mourner spotted "color" (gold) in the open grave. In the ensuing gold frenzy, the coffin was quickly removed, and everyone in attendance, including the preacher, took to the ground with shovels. Five years after the big discovery, the panning gold was gone, and miners could survive only by digging deeper and deeper into the rock. All but a few mines were abandoned by the 1870s, along with most of the towns around them.

Today, while gold remains buried deep in them thar hills, the towns of Gold Country have slowed down and lazily mine tourist purses instead. Strung along the appropriately-named Rte. 49 and the beautiful Sierra foothills, "Gold Rush Towns" are relaxed and dotted with the relics of the Gold Rush era. Prepare for stomach-dropping roads and jaw-dropping views when traveling Rte. 49; travelers without an off-road vehicle should be wary of straying too far from the highway. Traffic from the coast connects with Rte. 49 via I-80 through Sacramento, which serves as an apt starting point for a Gold Country tour. If you tire of Gold Country lore, vineyard touring, river rafting, and spelunking are popular in the area. Most of Gold Country is about 2hr. from Sacramento and 3hr. from San Francisco.

# SONORA ☎ 209

A band of roaming prospectors from Sonora, Mexico, were the first to stumble upon gold in the canyons around present-day Sonora in 1848. The settlers named their small mining encampment after their homeland and created a famously wild Mexican frontier town. The thousands of white 49ers who later flooded the area wouldn't stand for Mexicans mining their diggings, and they began enforcing a steep foreigner mining tax, driving out the original miners in a few short years. Things settled down as gold became scarce and tourists became plentiful, and today gold panning is for weekends—the hordes of straw-hatted, modern-day prospectors are probably antiquing.

■■ **ORIENTATION & PRACTICAL INFORMATION.** The drive to Sonora takes about 2½hr. from **Sacramento** (100 mi.), and 4hr. from **San Francisco** (130 mi.). Sonora's layout is complicated by the fact that two highways enter the town from three directions. **Washington Street** runs north-south through town and becomes Rte. 49 N at the north end. At the south end, it branches, and the east fork becomes Rte. 108. In the middle of town, Washington St. intersects with **Stockton Street**, which becomes Rte. 49 South.

The **Visitors Bureau,** 542 W. Stockton Rd., gives out local informational publications and free maps of the county. (☎533-4420 or 800-446-1333; www.thegreatunfenced.com. Open M-F 9am-7pm, Sa 10am-6pm, Su 10am-5pm.) Other services include: **police,** 100 S. Green St. (☎532-8143); **Tuolomne General Hospital,** 101 Hospital Rd. (☎533-7100; 24hr. emergency care); and the **post office,** 781 S. Washington St. (☎536-2728. Open M-F 8:30am-5pm, Sa 10am-2pm). **Postal Code:** 95370.

■□ **ACCOMMODATIONS & FOOD.** Built in 1896, the Spanish-style **Sonora Days Inn ❹,** 160 S. Washington St., stands apart from most standard chain motels in its age and authenticity. Spacious rooms all have A/C and cable TV, and most have fridges and microwaves. Rooms in the inn are large, with floral wallpaper and colonial furniture. The hotel also houses a rooftop pool, steakhouse, and saloon. (☎532-2400 or 800-329-9466. Doubles $70 and up; lower in winter.) Cheaper accommodations that are only slightly less convenient lie on Rte. 108 east of Sonora. **Camping** is abundant in the Stanislaus National Forest (see p. 266), 15 mi.

east of Sonora on Rte. 108. The Miwok Ranger District is closest to town, but has few developed campgrounds. **Fraser Flat ❶**, 4800 ft., 25 mi. east on Rte. 108 to the Spring Gap turnoff, then 3 mi. north on Rd. 4N01, has 38 sites near the South Fork of the Stanislaus River. (Piped water, vault toilets. Open May-Sept. Sites $12. $5 for an extra vehicle.) **Dispersed camping** is free and does not require a permit in most of the forest, though campfire permits are often required.

**Nanna's Cafe ❷**, 362 S. Stewart St., is a cut above most casual eateries. This popular, subtly elegant cafe/deli serves up wood-fired pizzas and delicious sandwiches for $7-13. The large tri-tip sandwich is perfectly seasoned with caramelized onions and hot mustard. The arbor outside provides a charming setting. (☎533-3289. Open M-Th 7am-8pm, F 7am-9pm, Sa 8am-9pm, Su 11am-5pm.) **Banny's Cafe ❸**, 83 S. Stewart St., a block east of Washington St., has eclectic lunches ($6-11) and dinners ($11-15) that fuse Mediterranean, Southwestern, and Asian flavors. Entrees like the grilled eggplant ($8) and the andouille sausage sandwich ($7) are welcome variants to local cuisine. (☎533-4709. Open M-Sa 11am-9pm, Su 11am-8pm.)

**◨ ◪ SIGHTS & ACTIVITIES. Columbia State Historic Park** is a preserved 1850s mining town. Take Rte. 49 North from Sonora to Parrot's Ferry Rd. and look for signs to the park. Once the "Gem of the Southern Mines" and rich in placer gold (loose gold found in rivers), Columbia supported 5000 people and 150 businesses, putting over $1 billion into the local economy. The only transportation option in the park is horse and buggy for around $5. (☎532-0150. Information office at 11255 Jackson St. open daily 8am-4:30pm. Free.) Just 10min. south of Sonora in Jamestown, **Railtown 1897 State Historic Park** is remarkable as a restored and operating 19th-century railroad roundhouse. Heading south on Rte. 49 to Jamestown, the park is 1 mi. south on 5th St. The park's trains have been featured in dozens of films and television shows. Tours and weekend train rides are offered. (☎984-4936. Open daily 9:30am-4:30pm. Train rides on the hour Apr.-Oct. 11am-3pm. $6, under 12 $3.) Visit the Stanislaus National Forest (see p. 266) for fine hiking, fishing, mountain biking, and rafting opportunities. Gear up at the **Sierra Nevada Adventure Co.**, 173 S. Washington St. (☎532-5621. Kayaks and canoes from $45 per day.)

# CALAVERAS COUNTY ☎209

Unsuspecting Calaveras turned out to be literally sitting on a gold mine—the most bountiful, southernmost part of the "Mother Lode"—when the big rush hit. Over 550,000 lb. of gold were extracted from the county's earth during its heyday. A journalist from Missouri named Samuel Clemens, a hapless miner but a gifted spinner of yarns later known as **Mark Twain,** allegedly based "The Celebrated Jumping Frog of Calaveras County" on a tale he heard in Angels Camp Tavern. This short story single-handedly put both the county and the writer on the map, and Calaveras has capitalized upon it since 1928 by holding annual **frog-jumping contests** in conjunction with the county fair in the third week of May. (www.frogtown.com. 4-day fair $11-13 per day.)

A drive along scenic **Route 49** is a great way to glimpse Calaveras County. Pint-sized **San Andreas,** at the juncture of Rte. 26 and 49, is the county's hub and most densely populated area. The **Calaveras County Information Center,** in downtown Angels Camp, is a great historical resource, and the place to go for frog-related apparel. (☎736-0049 or 800-225-3764; www.visitcalaveras.org. Open M-F 9am-6pm, Sa 11am-6pm, Su 11am-4pm.) Just south of Angels Camp on Rte. 49 is **Tuttletown,** Mark Twain's one-time home, but now little more than a historic marker.

**OUTDOORS.** Calaveras County encompasses dramatically varied landscape, from the rolling foothills of the Sierra in the west to 8000 ft. peaks in Stanislaus National Forest (see p. 266) in the east. Excellent outdoor recreation is available in the For-

# Outdoor Equipment Tips from a Wilderness Expert.

Affordable, exhilarating fun, a hike through the world's wild natural beauty offers a travel experience unlike any other. Before heading out, consider the following equipment tips:

**THE BASICS.** A map of the area and a simple compass are critical for not getting lost. A knife and sunscreen should always be brought along. Carry at least one liter of water (two liters is preferable) and drink regularly to avoid cramps and dehydration.

**FOOTWEAR.** Your feet are the single most important component of your total hike experience. Appreciate them. Care for them. Appropriate hiking footwear provides stability and support for your feet and ankles while protecting them from the abuses of the environment. Mid-weight hiking boots are a good all-around choice, but appropriate footwear may range from running shoes to heavyweight boots depending on the hiking environment and support desired. Note that stability over uneven ground is enhanced by a stiffer sole and higher ankle collar—good for travel along rugged trails and for hikers with weak ankles.

**PACK.** The best packs will have a padded waist belt that allows you to carry pack weight on your hips and lower body rather than shoulders. When trying on packs, loosen the shoulder straps, position the waist belt so that the top of your hips (the bony iliac crest) is in the middle of the belt, and then tighten the shoulder straps. Ideally, the straps will attach to the pack slightly above (and off) the shoulders, preventing the pack weight from being borne by the easily fatigued muscles of your shoulders and back. For day-hikes, a pack with a capacity of 1000-2000 cubic inches (16-32L) is recommended.

**CLOTHING.** Go synthetic. Cotton clothing absorbs a lot of moisture and dries slowly, leaving a wet layer next to your skin which conducts heat away from your body roughly 20 times faster than dry clothing. This greatly increases the risk for hypothermia, especially in cool, windy conditions. Blue jeans are th worst. Nylon and polyester are the most com mon synthetic materials, absorb little mois ture, and dry extremely fast.

**RAIN GEAR.** Waterproof/non-breathable rai gear is generally the best way to go. While i does not breathe and traps your sweat next t your body while you hike (sticky, sticky), it i cheap—you should be able to find a jacket fo $25-50. Waterproof/breathable raingear i impervious to liquid water, but allows wate vapor (sweat) generated by the body to pas through to the outside and thus keeps yo more comfortable. Gore-Tex is still considere the best waterproof/breathable barrier, bu there are a variety of similar products whic perform admirably.

**SURVIVAL.** Always be prepared for the unex pected night out. Carrying waterproo matches, a head lamp/flashlight, extra clothe and extra food will keep you warm and con fortable during the night. A whistle is a powe ful distress signal and can save your life if yo become immobilized. Bring a basic first ai kit—at a minimum this should include an ove the-counter painkiller (aspirin, ibuprofen); long, 2-4 in. wide elastic bandage for wrappin sprained ankles, knees, and other joints; an the basics for treating a bleeding wound: ant biotic ointment, sterile gauze, small bandage medical tape, and large band-aids.

**OTHER TIPS.** Always purify water taken fro backcountry sources. Filters and purifiers ar expensive, bulky, and time-consuming to use Iodine is cheap, easy, and compact. Hikin time can be estimated using the followin guidelines: A reasonably fit individual ca expect to travel 2-3 mi. (3-5km) per hour ove level ground and descents, 1-2 mi. (2-3km) pe hour on gradual climbs, and only about 1 mil (1.6km)—or 750-1000 feet (200-300m) of eleva tion—per hour on the steepest ascents.

Matt Heid was a Researcher-Writer for *Let's Go: Alaska and Western Canada 1993, Europe 1995*, and *New Zealand 1998*. He is the author of *101 Hikes in Northern California* and *Camping and Backpacking the San Francisco Bay Area* (Wilderness Press).

est, as well as in **Calaveras Big Trees State Park,** just inside Stanislaus National Forest on Rte. 4, about 35min. from Angels Camp. (*795-3840, reservations 795-2334. Day use $4.*) Featuring two timeless groves of Giant Sequoia, the world's oldest and biggest living organisms, and over 6000 acres of forest, stream, and lake along the Sierra's western slope, the park showcases world-class natural spectacles. There are three primary trails. **North Grove** (1 mi.), from the Visitors Center parking lot, is a gentle stroll to the first redwoods discovered by European settlers. The slightly more difficult, half-mile long **Grove Overlook Trail** looks down on the North Grove from the surrounding hills. About 10 times as many trees (over 1000) can be found at the end of the more challenging, and hence quieter 3½ mi. **South Grove Trail.** Just after Beaver Creek Bridge along South Grove Trail is the trailhead to **Bradley Grove** (2½ mi.), which provides a chance to see young sequoias, about 30 years old, planted by the former caretaker of the South Grove. **Fishing** is permitted in the Stanislaus River and the stocked Beaver Creek with a license (available at local gas stations), though there are some catching restrictions. **Camp** at **North Grove ❶,** right inside the park entrance, or **Oak Hollow ❶,** 4 mi. up, with piped water, flush toilets, and showers. (Sites $15, seniors $13.) In winter, family-friendly skiing at **Bear Mountain** is the major draw. The mountain features 1900 vertical feet and 67 runs, including a half-pipe and terrain park. (*753-2301; www.bearvalley.com. Day passes $43, ages 13-23 $36, ages 8-12 $15, ages 65-74 $10, under 7 and over 74 free.*)

**CAVERNS.** Most who flocked to Calaveras County throughout its history of settlement were interested in what lay underground. Today, many still head underground, but for different reasons. A labyrinthine limestone cave network snakes below ground, offering visitors an exciting chance to glimpse the Calaveras underworld. Three caverns have been developed for visitors. To get to the most popular cavern from Angel's Camp, travel 10min. east on Rte. 4 to Parrott's Ferry Rd., then turn right and continue 1 mi. to Moaning Cavern Rd. **Moaning Cavern,** 5350 Moaning Cave Rd., is a vast vertical cave. The remains of unlucky prehistoric people have been found at the bottom. The central chamber is 160 ft. below the surface and is large enough to hold the Statue of Liberty. Visitors can walk the 234 steps down, and the more adventurous (over 18 or over 12 with parental consent) can rappel their way down. Reservation-only 3hr. adventure tours start where the rappeling trip ends, venturing into the cavern's dark passages. (*736-2708. Open daily 9am-6pm; in winter M-F 10am-5pm, Sa-Su 9am-5pm. Stairs $12, ages 3-13 $6; rappel $45; adventure trip $99.*) **Mercer Cavern,** off Rte. 4 on Sheep Rd. in Murphys, is filled with elaborate multi-colored crystalline formations. All tours are 45min. and descend by walkway into six ten-million year old chambers. (*728-2101. Open Su-Th 9am-5pm, F-Sa 9am-6pm; in winter daily 10am-4:30pm. Tours $10, ages 5-12 $6.*) During the Gold Rush, **California Caverns,** at Cave City, 9 mi. from San Andreas off Mountain Ranch Rd., served as a naturally air-conditioned bar and dance floor, and a shot of whiskey could be purchased for a pinch of gold dust. The caverns sobered up on Sundays for church services, and one stalagmite served as an altar. Hour-long walking tours are available as well as a few different rugged spelunking trips that explore cramped tunnels, waist-high mud, and underground lakes. (*736-2708. Open daily 10am-5pm. 1hr. walking tour $11, ages 3-13 $5.50; 2hr. expeditions $99, ages 8-16 $65.*)

**WINERIES.** Winemaking is as old as gold prospecting in the county. Most of the area's nine flourishing vineyards are located on Rte. 49, just north of San Andreas, and on Rte. 4, near Murphys. The largest vineyard in the county, **Stevenot Winery,** on Sheep Ranch Rd., off Main St. in Murphys, has won hundreds of awards for its bold creations. (*728-0638. Main tasting room open daily 10am-5pm. 2nd tasting room at 451 Main St., in Murphys, open daily 10:30am-5:30pm.*) **Ironstone Vineyards,** on Six Mile Rd., 1½ mi. south of Main St., is another large vineyard, producing 250,000 cases a

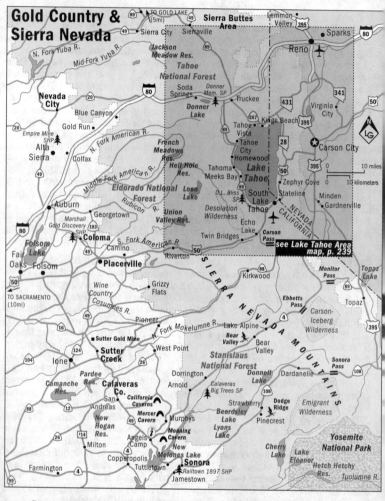

year. Spacious and new visitor facilities include a museum, tasting room, demonstration kitchen, gallery, and deli. (☎728-1251. *Free 45min. tours daily 11:30am, 1:30, 3:30pm. Sa additional tour 2:30pm. Tasting room open daily 11am-5pm.*)

## SUTTER CREEK                                                    ☎ 209

Sitting in the heart of Gold Country, Sutter Creek markets itself more as an alternative to the Wine Country of Napa and Sonoma than as a Gold Rush throwback, resulting in a more affluent tourist set than those found in many other Rte. 49 towns. This former mining encampment, named after the pioneering prospector John Sutter, was one of the Gold Rush's few success stories. Its bounty made fortunes for mine owners like Leland Stanford, who used his earnings to start a railroad business, become governor, and establish a university. Today, Rte. 49 turns into a short and quaint Main St. lined with shops and beautiful Victorian houses.

Sutter Creek is 67 mi. east from Sacramento via Rte. 50 to Rte. 49, and 90 mi. west of South Lake Tahoe. In town, Rte. 49 becomes Main St., where the majority of historical sights and commercial activity can be found. **Amador Rapid Transit System** (☎223-2877) sends two **buses** per day to and from Sacramento to Rancho Murieta, where another bus goes to Sutter Creek for $1. Visitor information can be found at the **Sutter Creek Visitors Center,** at the end of Eureka St., in Knight's Foundry. (☎267-1344. Open M-F 9:30am-4pm, Sa 10am-3pm.) Other services in Sutter Creek include the **police** (☎267-5646) and the **post office,** 3 Gopher Flat Rd., near Main St. (☎267-0128. Open M-F 8:30am-5pm.) **Postal Code: 95685.**

There are well over a dozen B&Bs within walking distance of town, including charming **Grey Gables ❺,** 161 Hanford St. (☎267-1039; www.greygables.com), and elegant **The Foxes ❻,** 77 Main St. (☎267-5882). The typical bed and breakfast decor and amenities apply, for around $120-250 per night. Somewhat lower priced rooms can be found at the **Sutter Creek Inn ❺,** 75 Main St., a domestic, well-decorated Greek Revival house on a relaxing yard, claiming to be California's first B&B. (☎267-5606; www.suttercreekinn.com. Doubles with bath from $82.)

Food in town is not cheap, with a number of restaurants specializing in fine dining and expensive wines. **The Back Roads Coffeehouse ❶,** 74 Main St., serves light lunch fare, freshly baked pastries and bagels, and caffeine-based drinks. (☎267-0440. Open Tu-F 7am-3pm, Sa-Su 7am-4pm). The **Sutter Diner ❷,** 291 Hanford St., smokes its beef brisket for over 10hr. Ask for daily BBQ offerings—they aren't on the menu. Most dishes cost $7-10. (☎267-1551. Open M 7am-2pm, W-Su 7am-8pm.)

Most sights in town are on Main St. Still in operation, **Knight's Foundry,** at the end of Eureka St., built and serviced hard rock mining equipment. It operates on water power, just as it did in 1873. (☎267-0201. Call for a tour.) **Sutter Gold Mine,** 1 mi. north of town on Rte. 49, takes you into an abandoned hard rock gold mine. On the deep mine exploration, you can see a modern gold mine in action. (☎866 762-2837. Open daily 8am-6pm; in winter 9am-5pm. 1hr. family tours $10, 3½hr. deep mine exploration $99 by reservation only.) Before Napa and Sonoma became California's wine country, the Sierra foothills were the state's biggest producer. Prohibition hit the region hard, however, and the area's 40 **vineyards** have only recently begun to prosper again. **Sutter Ridge,** 14110 Ridge Rd., 1 mi. south on Rte. 49 and 2½ mi. east on Ridge Rd., is a 170-acre vineyard run by a 4th-generation wine-making family. (☎267-1316. Open F-

# THE HIDDEN DEAL

## A HUT OF ONE'S OWN

Renting one of the Forest Service's three huts is an exceptional deal for groups. These structures range from small shacks to large mountain chalets, and are found in the heart of Eldorado National Forest.

**Robbs Hut** was built in 1938, and served as a forest service fire lookout until 1976. It provides a great base for cross-country skiing in the winter and mountain biking in the summer, and sleeps up to six people comfortably. There is no access to water or utilities, but the hut does have an outdoor barbecue and outdoor toilet.

The **Van Vleck Bunkhouse** sits on the edge of a glorious 40-acre meadow. The last remnant of a cattle ranch, the bunkhouse provides a great view of the Crystal Range and easy access to hiking, bird watching, fishing, mountain biking, and horseback riding. Water, propane lights, and a wood stove sweeten the deal for six lucky campers.

The **Loon Lake Chalet,** overlooking the Loon Lake Reservoir, can accommodate up to 20 people in its second-story warming room and third-story loft. The chalet is heated and has a small kitchen, gas fireplace and vault toilets.

All three huts provide a change of pace for those sick of pitching tents and waking up to the roar of nearby RV engines. (Info ☎644-2349, reservations 877-444-6777. Robbs Hut $45. Van Vleck Bunkhouse $55. Loon Lake Chalet $65.)

Su 11am-4:30pm.) **Argonaut Winery,** 13825 Willow Creek Rd., 11 mi. from town, northwest via Rte. 49 and south via Willow Creek Rd., is a small vineyard with weekend tastings. (☎245-5567. Open Sa-Su 10am-5:30pm.)

# PLACERVILLE                                                      ☎530

In its Gold Rush prime, Placerville (pop. 9301) was the third-largest town in California. Although its past is preserved in a restored, historic downtown full of eateries and antique shops, Placerville remains relaxed and unfazed, without the over-hype typical of many Gold Country towns.

**▄ ⁊ ORIENTATION & PRACTICAL INFORMATION.** About one-third of the way from Sacramento to Lake Tahoe on US 50, Placerville is strategically positioned to ensnare campers, boaters, and skiers. Most streets, like **Main Street,** run parallel to US 50 to the south. **Route 49** also bisects the town, running north to Auburn (10 mi.), and south toward Calaveras County.

**Greyhound** (☎800-231-2222) **bus** service makes drop-offs and pick-ups at 222 Main St. at Pacific St., going to Reno (6hr., 1 per day, $20) and Sacramento (1½hr., 2 per day, $12). At **Enterprise,** 583 Placerville St., cars are $33 per day, 100 mi. included, or $43 per day with unlimited mileage. (☎621-0866. Under-25 surcharge $10 per day.) The **Chamber of Commerce,** 542 Main St., has maps and info. (☎621-5885. Open M-F 9am-5pm.) Other services are the **police,** 730 Main St. (☎642-5210; www.hangtowncops.org), and the **post office,** 3045 Sacramento St., south of US 50. (☎642-5280. Open M-F 8:30am-5pm, Sa 8:30am-noon.) **Postal Code:** 95667.

**▛▟ ACCOMMODATIONS & FOOD.** One of the best deals in this consistently overpriced town is the **National 9 Inn ❹,** 1500 Broadway, which has spotless new rooms and comfortable queen beds. (☎622-3884. Singles $49; doubles $55-75.) **Camping** is plentiful in the Eldorado National Forest, east of town. **Sand Flat ❶,** 3800 ft., has 29 sites and is on Rte. 50, 28 mi. east of town. (Vault toilets, water. First-come, first-camp. Sites $12.) **Dispersed camping** is free and does not require a permit, although campfire permits are required for wood fires and stoves.

For a *Dukes of Hazzard* experience, saunter into ▧**Poor Red's ❸,** on El Dorado's Main St., 5 mi. south of Placerville on Rte. 49. The split-level bar and small dining room of this BBQ place are always packed. Their famous two-glass "Golden Cadillac" (responsible for 3% of American consumption of galliano) is only $6. (☎622-2901. Sandwiches around $6. Entrees $9-17. Open M-Sa 5pm-11pm, Su 2-11pm.) The historic **Cozmic Cafe and Bar ❶,** 594 Main St., dates from 1859. It may look unexceptional, but walk through to the back to check out the seating in a 150 ft. walk-in mine shaft. (☎642-8481. Sandwiches $5-6. Fresh fruit smoothies $3.50-5. Espresso $1.50-2.50. Th movie night, F open mic, Sa live band. All start around 7pm. Open M-W 7am-3pm, Th 7am-8pm, F-Sa 7am-11pm, Su 8am-3pm.) **Sweetie Pies ❷,** 577 Main St., is known for its huge cinnamon buns, full espresso bar, light lunches (sandwiches $6), and popular breakfast menu ($4-7). Homemade pie by the slice ($3.25) is delicious. Eat on the charming front patio. (☎642-0128. Open M-W 6:30am-4pm, Th-Su 7am-9pm.) Alternatively, forage for fresh food at the **farmer's market** in the Ivy House parking lot. (Open Th 5-8pm, Sa 8am-noon.)

**◪ ⚒ SIGHTS & OUTDOOR ACTIVITIES.** Placerville was once known as "Hangtown, USA" because of its reputation for handing out speedy justice at the end of a rope. Now the **Historic Hangman's Tree,** 305 Main St., is a friendly neighborhood bar with a life-size replica of a hanged man (George) outside, and a ghost (Willy) inside. The old-fashioned bar keeps old-fashioned hours. (☎622-3878. Open M-Sa 6am-10pm, Su 6am-5pm.)

SIERRA NEVADA

The hills around Placerville are filled with fruit and good cheer. By bike and car, travelers can tour the apple orchards and wineries off US 50 in the area known as **Apple Hill.** The fall is particularly busy with public events, concerts, and plenty of apple-picking. **Larsen Apple Barn** (☎644-1415) has 12 varieties of apples and a large picnic area in which to enjoy them. A complete listing and map of orchards is available from the Chamber of Commerce (see p. 234) and at many orchards. Locals claim that **Denver Dan's,** 4354 Bumblebee Ln. (☎644-6881), has the best prices, while **Kid's,** 3245 N. Canyon Rd. (☎622-0184), bakes the best apple pie in the area. Most orchards are open only Sept.-Dec., but **Boa Vista Orchards,** 2952 Carson Rd. (☎622-5522), is open year-round, selling fresh pears, cherries, and other fruits from a huge open barn. For free wine tasting, try **Lava Cap Winery,** 2221 Fruitridge Rd. (☎621-0175. Open daily 11am-5pm.) Also visit **Madroña Vineyards,** 2560 High Hill Rd. (☎644-5948), or the sophisticated **Boeger Winery,** 1709 Carson Rd. (☎622-8094. Open daily 10am-5pm.) Those visiting in June should not miss **Brewfest,** when hordes of forty-something locals pony up $20 for a small tasting glass and wander to over 30 downtown businesses for free beer. Streets close to traffic and there's a band on every block. (☎672-3436. Usually in late June.)

There are at least 16 maintained trails between Hwy. 50 and 88 in the **Eldorado National Forest.** About 50 mi. east of town, the relatively difficult **Bryan Meadows Trail** passes 3 mi. through lodgepole pine to meet the Pacific Crest Trail. From the same trailhead, follow the **Sayles Canyon Trail** (4½ mi.) to a mountain meadow. To get to the trailhead, take Rte. 50 east 48 mi. to Sierra-at-Tahoe Rd., continue 2 mi. to Bryan Rd., turn right, and go another 2½ mi. The **Information Center,** 3070 Camino Heights Dr., in Camino, 9 mi. east of Placerville on Rte. 50, dispenses info and permits. (☎644-6048. Open daily 8am-5pm; in winter M and Th-Su 8am-5pm.)

# FROM CREST TO CREST: THE TRAIL OF THE WEST

As the longest hiking route in America, the **Pacific Crest Trail (PCT)** snakes, swerves, and scales up 2650 mountainous miles from Mexico to Canada, passing through all sorts of climates along the way, from deserts to sub-Arctic regions. True to its name, the PCT always keeps to the crest; the trail maintains an average elevation of over 5000 ft. It dishes out quality as well as quantity, passing through some of the most pristine wilderness on the west coast while topping out at the summit of **Mount Whitney** (14,494 ft.), the highest peak in the contiguous United States. Although the PCT was begun in 1968, the trailblazing task was so immense that it was not officially completed until 1993. No matter how much of the trail you choose to bite off, proper supplies and conditioning are vital. The **Pacific Crest Trail Association** (☎916-349-2109 or 888-728-7245; www.pcta.org) gives tips on how to prepare for the journey. Contact them at 5325 Elkhorn Blvd., Box 256, Sacramento, CA 95842.

SIERRA NEVADA

## COLOMA ☎530

The 1848 Gold Rush began in Coloma at John Sutter's water-powered lumber mill, operated by James Marshall. Today the tiny town (pop. 175) is overshadowed by its Gold Rush history and the adjacent American River. The town revolves around the **James Marshall Gold Discovery State Historic Park.** Near the site where Marshall struck gold is a replica of the original mill. (☎622-3470. Open daily 8am-dusk. Day use $4 per car, seniors $3; walk-ins $2, under 16 free. Display your pass in your car or be ticketed.) Picnic grounds across the street surround the **Gold Discovery Museum,** 310 Back St., which presents the events of the Gold Rush through dioramas, artifacts and film. (☎622-3470. Open daily 10am-4:30pm.) **Camping** can be found 2 mi. downstream at **Camp Lotus ❷,** 700 ft., on Basie Rd. off Lotus Rd. The sites are large and shady, and sit on the banks of the American River. (☎622-8672. Water, flush toilets, free hot showers, nearby store, and sand volleyball courts. Check in from 2pm; check out at noon. Sites Su-Th $18, F-Sa $24.)

The real reason to come to Coloma is to experience the natural attractions. The **American River's** class III currents, among the most accessible rapids in the West, attract thousands of rafters and kayakers every weekend. Farther north along Rte. 49, the river flows into **Folsom Lake** and a deep gorge perfect for hiking and swimming. Many of the **rafting** outfitters in the county offer tours in the waters surrounding Coloma. Contact **Zephyr Whitewater** (☎800-359-9790), **Motherlode River Trips** (☎800-427-2387), **Oars Inc.** (☎800-346-6277), or **Whitewater Connection** (☎800-336-7238)—all float river-worthy boats. (Half-day $69-79, full-day $89-109.)

## NEVADA CITY                                              ☎530

New Age meets ages past in Nevada City, a quaint town in the Sierra foothills full of rustic hippies. Although the tourist board seems hellbent on creating the illusion of yesteryear, the eccentricity of the residents belies the mining town image.

Many buildings in the town are of historical interest, including the dozens of **Victorian homes,** the **National Hotel** (claiming to be the nation's oldest in continual operation), and the historic 1860 **Firehouse.** A museum in the firehouse has exhibits on pioneer life, mining, the Nisenan and Maidu Indians, and the once-large Chinese population. (Open daily 11am-4pm; in winter M-Tu and Th-Su 10am-3pm. Free.) A walking tour map is available from the **Chamber of Commerce** at the end of Commercial St., near the Shell station and bank. (☎265-2692 or 800-655-6569. Open M-F 9am-5pm, Sa 11am-4pm.) Most historical buildings in Nevada City have been transformed into cappuccino bars, New Age bookstores, and vegetarian eateries.

The ▨**Outside Inn ❹**, 575 E. Broad St., is a redesigned 40s-era motel catering to energetic adventurers. The rooms all have tasteful outdoors themes, and some sit on a peaceful creek. (☎265-2233. A/C, library with maps and recreational info, patio, grill, swimming pool, and Internet in every room. Rooms from $65, with kitchenette from $85.) US Forest Service and California Parks Department operate **campgrounds** east of town on Rte. 20. **Scotts Flat ❷** has wooded RV and tent camping near a popular lake. (☎265-5302. Water, flush toilets, hot showers. Sites $14-23.) To get a little further from the crowds, free sites are available at **Bowman Lake,** 16 mi. north on Rte. 20. 4WD recommended. Nevada City's health-conscious congregate at **Earth Song ❸,** 135 Argall St., a natural foods market and cafe where vegetarians stock up on soy burgers, Welsh and Cornish cuisine, and organic produce. Delicious, largely organic entrees run $7-18. (☎265-9392. Market open daily 8am-9pm. Cafe open daily 11am-3pm and 5-8pm.) Another popular hangout is **Cafe Mekka ❷,** 237 Commercial St. The interior looks like a set designer's studio. Browse among the children's books, modern art, and chaises over an artichoke heart, pesto, and brie sandwich ($7), or sip coffee with the evening crowd. (☎478-1517. Open M 8am-7pm, Tu-Th 8am-10pm, F-Sa 8am-12am, Su 8am-11pm.)

History awaits you at the **Empire Mine State Historic Park,** on Empire St. Exit off Rte. 20 west of town. Peering down the cool, dark mine shaft, you may wonder if you'd go 12,400 ft. down for a chance at the big money—5.8 million ounces of gold were extracted from the mine during its 106 years of production. The estate and woods make peaceful hikes, but beware of poison oak, rattlesnakes, and mountain lions. Tours are offered on summer weekends. (☎273-8522; www.empiremine.org. Open daily May-Aug. 9am-6pm; Sept.-Apr. 10am-5pm. $2, under 17 free.)

The Nevada City area has trails for hikers of every ability. The **Nevada City Ranger Station,** 631 Coyote St., of the Tahoe National Forest, provides information on recreation and camping. (☎265-4531. Open M-F 8am-5pm, Sa 8am-4:30pm.) Take the **Loch Leven Trail** (3½ mi.) to the Loch Leven chain of granite-bed glacial lakes. The trailhead is just east of the Big Bend Visitors Center, at the Big Bend Exit off I-80 east from Nevada City. **Bridgeport State Park,** in Penn Valley off Rte. 20, features a number of hikes including an easy 1¼ mi. one over the largest covered bridge in the West and around the river canyon. The **Yuba River,** which has been immortalized countless times in song, boasts many swimming holes, many of which just sit under or around the covered bridge; explore more remote ones for prime skinny dipping opportunities by hiking the Independence Trail. Whitewater rafting and kayaking are great ways to experience the rugged beauty of the area. **Wolf Creek Wilderness,** 595 E. Main St. (☎477-2722), in Grass Valley, rents kayaks year-round and runs multiple kayaking trips and clinics. They also rent snowshoes and cross-country skis. In the winter, snowshoe tours and avalanche clinics are held here.

## SIERRA BUTTES AREA                                              ☎530

A craggy ridge of volcanic peaks north of Donner Pass, the **Sierra Buttes** are the highlight of the **Lakes Basin Recreation Area,** a stretch of wilderness spanning Plumas and Tahoe National Forests. The snow-capped **Sierra Buttes** themselves rise dramatically farther up Gold Lake Rd., amid the surrounding small alpine lakes and densely forested hills. For trail access, take the Sardine Lake turn-off 1 mi. north of Rte. 49, bear right past Sardine Lake, and continue 1½ mi. past Packer Lake. 4WD is recommended. The mountains and over 40 glacial lakes in the area are among the least traveled outdoors destinations in the state. Hiking trails lead through the small but beautiful range, while the fishing and boating in the lakes are good and quiet. The area is 6 mi. north of Sierra City. Five miles east of Sierra City, on the corner of Rte. 49 and Gold Lake Hwy., lies **Bassetts Station,** an all-purpose establishment that has offered **lodging ❹,** dining, gas, and supplies for over 125 years. Stop in for info. (☎862-1297. 3 rooms $70-75. Open daily 7am-9pm.)

The Gold Lake Hwy. leads to **Sardine Lake,** 1 mi. from Rte. 49 past Bassetts Station. A number of self-register campsites sit on this small, shallow lake. Five miles farther on Gold Lake Hwy. is **Gold Lake** itself. The adjacent **Gold Lake Pack Station** offers guided horseback rides around the area, usually 9am-4pm; call for schedules. (☎283-2014. $28-98 per person depending on the length of the ride.) The turn-off for Frasier Falls is 6 mi. from the Bassetts Station, across from the first lake turn-off. The roads can be rough. Follow signs for 4 mi. to the Frasier Falls parking lot. The falls are then a 30min. walk. There are six **campgrounds** along the route from the Bassetts turn-off to Frasier Falls. Most have toilets but no water or showers, and all are first-come, first-camp. Sites range free-$16. Gold Lake and Snag Lake are especially beautiful campgrounds. For those in the mood for cushier digs, the **Gold Lake Lodge ❺** has rustic cabins, includes a great breakfast and dinner, and provides easy access to many hiking trails. (2-night min. stay. Cabins from $95.)

# LAKE TAHOE                                              ☎530/775

Outdoor fanatics from across the globe are attracted to Tahoe's natural beauty, and the burgeoning entertainment and hotel industries eagerly support their excursions. After roads were cut into the forested mountain terrain during the Gold Rush, new money started to arrive; by the turn of the century, the lake had become a haven for San Francisco's rich and famous. Now, everyone can enjoy Tahoe's pure blue waters, tall pines, and high-rise casinos silhouetted by the glow of the setting sun. In a town without an off-season, visitors can revel in an array of activities from keno to kayaking. An outdoor adventurer's dream in any season, Tahoe has miles of biking, hiking, and skiing trails, long stretches of golden beaches, lakes stocked with fish, and any watersport imaginable.

**SIERRA NEVADA**

The area code for Lake Tahoe is **530** unless otherwise specified. The Nevada side is **775**.

# ◧ TRANSPORTATION

**Trains: Amtrak** (☎800-USA-RAIL/872-7245). Runs trains between Chicago and San Francisco that stop at the Truckee Depot in downtown Truckee. One west-bound train daily to **Sacramento** (4½hr., $22-40) and **Oakland/San Francisco** (6½hr., $45-93), and one east-bound train to **Reno** (1hr., $10-21).

**Buses: Greyhound** (☎800-231-2222). At the Truckee Depot, get buses to **Sacramento** (3hr.), **San Francisco** (5½hr., 5 per day, $37-39), and **Reno** (1hr., 3 per day, $10-12).

**Public Transit:**

**Tahoe Casino Express** (☎775-785-2424, 800-446-6128). Provides shuttle service between the Reno airport and South Shore Tahoe casinos. (Daily 6:15am-12:30am; $19, round-trip $34, children under 12 free.)

**Tahoe Area Regional Transport** or **TART** (☎550-1212 or 800-736-6365; www.laketahoetransit.com). Connects the western and northern shores from Incline Village through Tahoe City to Meeks Bay, where it joins with South Lake Tahoe (STAGE) buses in the summer. Stops daily every hour or half hour 6:30am-6pm, depending on the route. Buses also run to Truckee and Squaw Valley and back 5 times per day (7:30am-4:45pm). $1.25, day pass $3. Exact fare required.

**South Tahoe Area Ground Express** or **STAGE** (☎542-6077). Operates in both NV and CA on the South Shore. It runs several routes between the Stateline, NV casinos and the Hwy. 89/50 intersection. (6:40am-12:40pm. $1.25, day pass $2, 10-ride pass $10.) Casinos operate complimentary shuttle services along Hwy. 50 to California ski resorts and motels.

**Bus Plus** (☎542-6077) runs door-to-door service within city limits (24hr., $3) and within El Dorado County (7am-7pm, $5). Summer buses connect STAGE and North Shore's TART at Emerald Bay.

**Car Rental:** Many have branches in Nevada casinos. **Avis** (☎775-588-3361) in Caesars Tahoe, Stateline, NV. **Enterprise** (☎775-586-1077) in the Horizon lobby, Stateline, NV. **Hertz** (☎775-586-0041) in Harvey's, Stateline, NV.

# ◢ ORIENTATION

In the northern Sierra on the California-Nevada border, Lake Tahoe is a 3hr. drive from San Francisco. The lake rests about 100 mi. northeast of Sacramento (via **Highway 50**) and 35 mi. southwest of Reno (via **Highway 395** and **431**). Coming from the south, **Highway 395** runs 20 mi. east of the lake. Lake Tahoe is divided into two main regions, **North Shore** and **South Shore.** The North Shore includes **Tahoe City** in California and Incline Village in Nevada, while the South Shore includes **South Lake Tahoe** in California and Stateline in Nevada. Proclaimed "The Most Beautiful Drive in America," Hwy. 50 combines with Hwy. 28 and 89 to form a 75 mi. asphalt ring around the lake; the entire winding loop takes nearly 3hr. to complete by car.

Tahoe City centers around the intersection of **Highways 89 and 28.** Hwy. 89 is called **West Lake Boulevard** and heads south to the beaches and parks of the west shore, and Hwy. 28, the main commercial drag, is known as **North Lake Boulevard** in central Tahoe City. **Highway 50 (Lake Tahoe Boulevard)** is the main drag of South Lake Tahoe and Stateline, NV. At the western end of South Lake, Hwy. 89 heads up the lake's shore. The major cross streets in South Lake are **Ski Run Boulevard, Wildwood Avenue,** and **Park Avenue.**

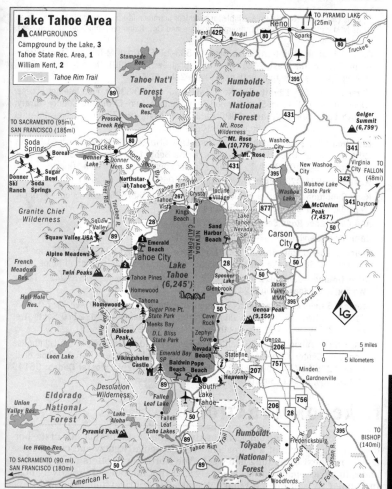

**Lake Tahoe Area**

▲ CAMPGROUNDS

Campground by the Lake, **3**
Tahoe State Rec. Area, **1**
William Kent, **2**

〰〰 Tahoe Rim Trail

SIERRA NEVADA

# ❷ PRACTICAL INFORMATION

## Visitor Information:

**North Lake Tahoe North Visitors Bureau,** 380 North Lake Blvd. (☎583-3494; www.mytahoevaca-tion.com). A helpful office with tons of info on the area. Open M-F 9am-5pm, Sa-Su 9am-4pm.

**Lake Tahoe Visitors Authority,** 1156 Ski Run Blvd. (☎544-5050 or 800 288-2463; www.virtu-altahoe.com), in South Lake. An information clearinghouse for the entire lake with a particular focus on the South Shore. Open M-F 8:30am-5pm.

**Tahoe-Douglas Chamber of Commerce and Visitors Center,** 195 Hwy. 50 (☎775-588-4591; www.tahoechamber.org), in Stateline, NV. Open daily May-Oct. 9am-6pm, Nov.-Apr. 9am-5pm.

**Taylor Creek Visitors Center** (USFS; ☎543-2674; www.fs.fed.us/r5/ltbmu), 3 mi. north of South Lake Tahoe on Hwy. 89. A good resource for planning outdoor excursions, with detailed maps of the area. Issues permits for the Desolation Wilderness. Camping fee $5 per person per night, $10 per person for 2 or more nights, $20 for.1-year pass. Under 12 free. Reservations (☎644-6048, $5) are available for overnight permits mid-June through Labor Day. Open daily Memorial Day weekend through mid-June and Oct. 8am-4pm, mid-June through Sept. 8am-5:30pm.

**Bank: US Bank,** 705 North Lake Blvd. (☎583-2346). Open M-Th 9am-5pm, F 9am-6pm. **Bank of the West,** 2161 Lake Tahoe Blvd. (☎531-3390). Open M-Th 9am-5pm, F 9am-6pm, Sa 9am-1pm. Both banks have **24hr. ATM.**

**Library: Tahoe City Library,** 740 North Lake Blvd. (☎583-3382). Free Internet access. Open Tu and Th-F 10am-5pm, W noon-7pm, Sa noon-4pm. **El Dorado County Library: South Lake Tahoe Branch,** 1000 Rufus Allen Blvd. (☎573-3185). Free Internet access. Open Tu-W 10am-8pm, Th-Sa 10am-5pm.

**Laundromat: Big Tree Cleaners,** 531 North Lake Blvd. (☎583-2802). Wash $1.50, dry 25¢ per 10min. Open daily 7am-10pm. **Uncle Bob's Laundromat,** 2180 Lake Tahoe Blvd. (☎542-1910). Wash $1.25, dry 25¢ per 8min. Open daily 7am-10pm.

**Weather:** ☎541-0200, enter category number 5050.

**Road Conditions:** California ☎800-427-7623 or 546-LAKE/5253 ext. 43 outside of CA; Nevada, ☎877-687-6237 or 775-793-1313.

**AAA Emergency Road Service:** ☎800-222-4357.

**24hr. Road Service:** ☎587-6000 or 800-937-4757.

**Police: Placer County Sheriff,** 2501 North Lake Blvd. (☎581-6330), east of Tahoe City on Hwy. 28. **South Lake Police,** 1352 Johnson Blvd. (☎542-6100), off Al Tahoe Blvd.

**Crisis Hotlines: General,** ☎800-992-5757. **Gamblers Anonymous,** ☎573-2423. **Tahoe Women's Services,** ☎546-3241.

**Medical Services: Incline Village Community Hospital,** 880 Alder Ave. (☎775-833-4100), off Hwy. 28 in Incline Village. **Barton Memorial Hospital,** 2170 South Ave. (☎541-3420), at 3rd St. and South Ave. off Lake Tahoe Blvd.

**Post Office: Tahoe City,** 950 North Lake Blvd. (☎800-275-8777). In the Lighthouse Shopping Center. Open M-F 8:30am-5pm. **South Lake Tahoe,** 1046 Al Tahoe Blvd. (☎800-275-8777). Open M-F 8:30am-5pm, Sa noon-2pm. **Postal Codes:** 96145 (Tahoe City), 96151 (South Lake).

# ∩ ACCOMMODATIONS

On the South Shore, the blocks along Hwy. 50 on the California side of the border support the bulk of the area's motels. Particularly glitzy and cheap, these motels run next to nothing mid-week. The North Shore offers more polished and refined accommodations along Hwy. 28, but the rates are relatively high. In Tahoe City and Incline Village, the especially pricey lodgings tend to be booked solid, well in advance for weekends and holidays. Fall and spring are the most economical times of the year to visit Tahoe. Look for discount coupons in newspapers. Whatever your budget, the nearby campgrounds are great options in warmer months.

■ **Firelite Lodge,** 7035 North Lake Blvd. (☎800-934-7222 or 546-7222), in Tahoe Vista 8 mi. east of **Tahoe City.** Sleek, modern quarters with microwaves, refrigerators, coffee makers, patios overlooking the pool, and spas. Guest laundry service. Open daily 8am-11pm. Singles in summer and winter from $59; in spring and fall from $49. ❸

■ **Tahoe Valley Lodge,** 2214 Lake Tahoe Blvd. (☎800-669-7544 or 541-0353; www.tahoevalleylodge.com), in **South Lake.** These immaculate, luxurious rooms take the mountain motif to an extreme with rough-hewn logs and mile-high comforters. All rooms have queen-sized beds, cable TV, and coffeemakers; many have microwaves, refrigerators, and in-room spas. Reception 24hr. Singles $95; doubles $125. ❺

**Royal Inn,** 3520 Lake Tahoe Blvd. (☎544-1177), in **South Lake.** Clean rooms and cable TV. Heated pool and laundry facilities. Singles Su-Th $28-35; doubles $39-49. Rates inflate greatly on weekends and holidays. Mention *Let's Go* for a possible discount. ❷

**Tahoe City Inn,** 790 North Lake Blvd. (☎581-3333 or 800-800-8246; www.tahoecity-inn.com), in downtown **Tahoe City.** Standard rooms include queen beds, coffeemakers, mini-fridges, and cable TV. Deluxe rooms sport kitchenettes, jacuzzis, and access to an extensive video library. Su-Th $85-160, F-Sa $105-160; late Apr. to mid-June and late Sept.-late Nov. Su-Th $59-140, F-Sa $79-140. ❹

**Doug's Mellow Mountain Retreat,** 3787 Forest Ave. (☎544-8065). From the north, turn left onto Wildwood Rd. west of downtown **Stateline,** then left on Forest Ave. A woodsy house in a residential neighborhood. Doug supplies a modern kitchen, BBQ, and fireplace. Internet access $5 per hr. No curfew. Flexible check-in and check-out. Dorms $15; private rooms $25. Discounts for stays over a week. ❶

**Tamarack Lodge,** 2311 North Lake Blvd. (☎583-3350 or 888-824-6323), 3 mi. north of **Tahoe City,** across from Lake Forest Beach. Clean, friendly lodge in the woods. Outdoor BBQ and fireplace, phones, and cable TV. Some rooms come with kitchenettes and some cabins with full kitchens. Rooms from $54; from $44 in low season. Cabins (sleeping 4) $125; $105 in low season. ❸

# ⚑ CAMPING

The Taylor Creek Visitors Center provides up-to-date information on camping (see **Tourist and Information Services,** p. 239). Campgrounds ring the entire lake, but **Route 89** is inundated with sites between Tahoe City and South Lake Tahoe. Sites can be booked on weekends in July and August, so it pays to reserve in advance; call the **California State Parks Reservation Center** (☎800-444-7275) for California State Parks or the **National Recreation Reservation System** (☎877-444-6777; www.reserveusa.com) for California Land Management. Backcountry camping is allowed in designated wilderness areas with a permit from the Forest Service (see **Practical Information,** p. 239). The listings below run from north to south.

**Tahoe State Recreation Area** (☎583-3074), on the eastern edge of Tahoe City off Hwy. 28. A thin strip of land along the lake with a long pier. 39 sites with water, flush toilets, and showers (50¢). Open May-Nov. Sites $15; $4 per additional vehicle. ❶

**William Kent** (☎583-3642), on Hwy. 89, 2 mi. south of Tahoe City, with 95 shady sites, is one of the most popular campgrounds on the west shore. Beach access, clean flush toilets, and water. Open June-Sept. 6. Sites $16; $5 per additional vehicle. ❷

**D.L. Bliss** (☎525-7277), 11 mi. south of Homewood off Hwy. 89. One of the most scenic campgrounds on the lake. Access to Lester Beach and the trailheads for Rubicon and Lighthouse Trails. 168 sites with grills, water, flush toilets, and showers. Open late May to Sept. Sites $15-19; $5 per additional vehicle. ❷

**General Creek** (☎525-7982), in Sugar Pine Point State Park 1 mi. south of Tahoma, off Hwy. 89. This popular campground has 175 sites, tennis courts, bike and cross-country ski trails, a nature center, historic mansion, and lakeside dock. Water, BBQ pits, and flush toilets. Showers 50¢. Open year-round. Sites $15; $4 per additional vehicle. ❷

**Eagle Point** (☎541-3030), in Emerald Bay State Park 12 mi. north of South Lake Tahoe off Hwy. 89. Above Emerald Bay, 100 sites boast spectacular views. Grills, water, flush toilets, and showers. Open late May to Sept. Sites $15; $5 per additional vehicles. ❷

**Fallen Leaf** (☎544-0426), 2 mi. north of South Lake Tahoe off Hwy. 89. 206 shady sites beside Fallen Leaf Lake with access to Baldwin and Pope Beaches; a good option for those looking to mix the action of South Lake Tahoe with the call of the wild. Water, flush toilets, but no showers. Open late May-Sept. $18. ❷

SIERRA NEVADA

**Campground by the Lake** (☎542-6096), at Hwy. 50 and Rufus Allen Blvd. in South Lake Tahoe. 170 city-run sites on 35 acres across from beach and picnic areas. Free casino shuttle, showers, and flush toilets. Open Apr. 1-Oct. 31. Sites $21; RV hookups $29. ❷

# ◘ FOOD

In the south, casinos offer perpetually low-priced buffets, but grilles and burger joints dot the shores, promising reasonable prices, similarly large portions, and better food. If you want to forage, try **Safeway**, 850 North Lake Blvd. (☎583-2772; open daily Sept.-June 6am-10pm; July-Aug. 6am-1am), or 1020 Johnson Blvd., at Lake Tahoe Blvd. and Johnson Blvd. in South Lake (☎542-7740; open 24hr.).

**Jakes on the Lake** (☎583-0188), in Boatworks Shopping Mall in **Tahoe City.** A taste of the South Seas in a relaxed wood-paneled dining room. Hawaiian-inspired creations dominate the menu alongside options like the New Rack of Lamb ($22). Open M-F 11:30am-2:30pm and 5:30-9:30pm, Sa-Su 11:30am-2:30pm and 5-9:30pm. ❹

**Sprouts Natural Foods Cafe,** 3123 Harrison Ave. (☎541-6969), at the intersection of Lake Tahoe Blvd. and Alameda Ave. in **South Lake.** Satisfying natural foods in unnaturally large portions. Try the breakfast burrito with avocados ($5), a tasty smoothie ($3-3.75), or a shot of wheat grass ($2). Open daily 8am-10pm. ❶

**The Red Hut Cafe,** 2723 Lake Tahoe Blvd. (☎541-9024), in **South Lake.** Another location at 22 Kingsbury Grade (☎588-7488). A Tahoe original since 1959, the friendly staff dishes out homestyle cooking like waffles piled with fruit and whipped cream ($5.75) and avocado burgers ($6.50). Open daily 6am-2pm. No credit cards. ❶

**Syd's,** 550 North Lake Blvd. (☎583-2666), in the center of **Tahoe City.** Serves coffee ($2-3), smoothies ($3.75), and sandwiches like Hummus Humongous ($4.50) and The Gobbler ($5) on different breads. Open daily 6:30am-5pm; July-Aug. 6am-7pm. ❶

**Sancho's,** 7019 North Lake Blvd. (☎546-7744), in Tahoe Vista 8 mi. east of **Tahoe City.** This little hole-in-the-wall is a local favorite. Tacos ($1.50), burritos ($4.50), and tostadas ($3.75), with filling choices like carne asada, carnitas, and chorizo. Try the terrific Tostada ceviche with shrimp and mahi-mahi ($4.50). Open daily 11am-9pm. ❶

**Lakeside Beach Grill,** 4081 Lakeshore Blvd. (☎544-4050), on the water between Park and Stateline Ave., near **South Lake.** Right on the beach. Tasty menu complements spectacular views. Try inventive entrees ($7-11) like the calamari burger in a relaxed setting. Open daily June-Sept. 11am-7pm. ❷

# ◪ OUTDOOR ACTIVITIES

## SUMMER ACTIVITIES

### BEACHES

Many beaches dot Lake Tahoe, providing the perfect setting for a day of sunning and people-watching. Parking generally costs $3-7; bargain hunters should leave cars in turn-outs on the main road and walk to the beaches.

**NORTH SHORE. Sand Harbor Beach,** 2 mi. south of Incline Village on Hwy. 28, has gorgeous granite boulders and clear waters that attract swimmers, sunners, snorkelers, and boaters to its marina. The parking lot ($5) often fills by late morning. **Tahoe City Commons Beach,** in the heart of Tahoe City off North Lake Blvd., has a playground, sandy beach, and pristine lake waters great for swimming.

**SOUTH SHORE. Baldwin Beach,** on the South Shore, and neighboring **Pope Beach,** near the southernmost point of the lake off Hwy. 89, are popular, shaded expanses of shoreline. Find a parking spot on the highway and avoid the fee. Quiet spots on both beaches can be found on their edges. **Nevada Beach,** on the east shore, 3 mi. north of South Lake Tahoe off Hwy. 50, is close to the casinos but offers a sandy sanctuary from the jangling slot machines. Recently renovated **Zephyr Cove Beach,** 5 mi. north of South Lake Tahoe, hosts a youthful crowd keen on beer and bikinis.

**WEST SHORE.** The West Shore offers **Meeks Bay,** 10 mi. south of Tahoe City, a family-oriented beach with picnic tables, volleyball courts, BBQ pits, campsites, and a store. **D.L. Bliss State Park,** 17 mi. south of Tahoe City on Hwy. 89, is home to **Lester** and **Calawee Cove Beaches** on striking Rubicon Bay. It's also the trailhead for the Rubicon Trail, which leads to the Vikingsholm mansion. Parking here ($5) is limited; check the Visitors Center at the entrance or park on the road and walk in.

## HIKING

Hiking is a great way to explore the Tahoe Basin. Visitors centers and ranger stations provide detailed info and maps for all types of hikes. Backcountry users must obtain a wilderness permit (see **Practical Information,** p. 239) for any hike into Desolation Wilderness; 700 hikers are allowed in this area on any given day. Due to erratic weather conditions in the Sierra, hikers should always bring a jacket as well as drinking water. Ask where the snow has melted—it's not usually all gone until July. **Alpenglow Sports,** 415 North Lake Blvd., in Tahoe City, offers a wide array of outdoor gear. (☎583-6917. Open M-F 10am-6pm, Sa-Su 9am-6pm.)

After decades of work, the 165 mi. **Tahoe Rim Trail** has been completed. The route encircles the lake, following the ridge tops of the Tahoe Basin. The trail welcomes hikers, equestrians, and, in most areas, **mountain bikers.** Camping is allowed on most parts of the trail, but backcountry permits are required in Desolation Wilderness. Hiking is moderate to difficult. On the western shore, the route is part of the Pacific Crest Trail. There are eight trailheads around the lake, so consult a ranger station for a trail suited to your interests. Popular trailheads include **Spooner Summit,** at the junction of Hwy. 50 and 28, and **Tahoe City,** on Fairway Dr. off Hwy. 89.

**NORTH SHORE.** At 10,778 ft., **Mount Rose,** in Mt. Rose Wilderness, is one of the tallest mountains in the region as well as one of the best climbs. The panoramic view from the summit includes views of the lake, Reno, and the surrounding Sierras. The 6 mi. (12 mi. round-trip) trek starts out as an easy dirt road hike but ascends switchbacks for the last few miles. Take Hwy. 431 N from Incline Village to the trailhead. The **Granite Chief Wilderness,** west of Squaw Valley, is a spectacular destination; its rugged trails and mountain streams wind through secluded forests in 5000 ft. valleys up to the summits of 9000 ft. peaks. The **Alpine Meadows Trailhead,** at the end of Alpine Meadows Rd. off Hwy. 89 between Truckee and Tahoe City, and the **Pacific Crest Trailhead,** at the end of Barker Pass Rd. (Blackwood Canyon Rd.), provide convenient access into the wilderness.

**SOUTH SHORE.** The southern region of the basin offers many moderate to strenuous hiking trails. The picturesque **Emerald Bay,** on Hwy. 89 between South Lake Tahoe and Tahoe City, is best explored on foot. This crystal-clear lake area embraces Tahoe's only island, Fannette, and dramatic waterfalls make the area a mini-paradise. ◪**Emerald Bay State Park,** which abuts Desolation Wilderness, offers hiking and biking trails of varying difficulty, as well as camping. One of the best hikes in Tahoe is **Rubicon Trail,** which wraps 6 mi. around the beach and granite cliffs. There are trailheads at D.L. Bliss Park and Vikingsholm. The challenging **Eagle Falls Trail** heads into the heat of Desolation Wilderness and offers spectacular views of the High Sierra. The trail starts from the Eagle Lake parking lot and ascends into Desolation Wilderness. Permits are required for this hike.

The nature trails around the Taylor Creek Visitors Center, 3 mi. north of South Lake Tahoe on Hwy. 89, are more leisurely. The **Lake of the Sky Trail** (half-mile round-trip) is dotted with informative signs. The centerpiece of the Visitors Center is the **River Profile Chamber,** which shows a cross-section of a Tahoe creek. The chamber is accessed by Rainbow Trail (half-mile round-trip).

**Lower** and **Upper Echo Lakes,** off Hwy. 50 south of Tahoe, are much smaller, wilder versions of Tahoe; granite tablets and pine trees tower over the lakes, stretching for miles of pristine backcountry. **Echo Chalet,** 2 mi. west of Hwy. 50 on the near shore of Lower Echo, operates **boat** service across the lake. (☎659-7207. Runs M-Th 8am-6pm, F-Su 8am-7pm in high season. $7 one-way; pets $3.) From the drop-off point, a well-maintained path (part of the Pacific Crest Trail) skirts the north shore of the lakes to the Upper Echo boat landing and into Desolation Wilderness. Day hiking wilderness permits are available at the chalet; mandatory overnight permits are issued at the forest service (see **Practical Information,** p. 239). Another 2 mi. along Hwy. 50, just before Twin Bridges, is the **Horsetail Falls** trailhead. These impressive falls, dropping toward the Pacific, are accessed by a short (1¼ mi.) but tough hike through the slippery canyon. Inexperienced hikers should beware—each year, Forest Service helicopters rescue a few sight-seekers.

### ROCK CLIMBING
**Alpenglow Sports,** 415 North Lake Blvd., in Tahoe City, provides rock and ice climbing literature and lots of know-how. (☎583-6917. Open M-F 10am-6pm, Sa-Su 9am-6pm. Shoe rental $8 per day.) Pleasant climbs abound in Lake Tahoe, but safety precautions and equipment are a must. The inexperienced can try bouldering in **D.L. Bliss State Park.** Popular climbing spots dot the South Shore, including the celebrated **Ninety-Foot Wall** at Emerald Bay, **Twin Crags** at Tahoe City, and **Big Chief** near Squaw Valley. **Lover's Leap,** in South Lake Tahoe, is an incredible, albeit crowded, route spanning two giant cliffs. East of South Lake Tahoe off Hwy. 50, **Phantom Spires** has amazing views, while **Pie Shop** offers serious exposure.

## WINTER ACTIVITIES

### DOWNHILL SKIING
With world-class alpine slopes, 15 ski resorts, knee-deep powder, and California sun, Tahoe is a skier's mecca. Visitors centers provide info, maps, free publications like *Ski Tahoe* and *Sunny Day.* Daily ski info updates are online at www.visitortips.com/tig/skitahoe. All the major resorts offer lessons and rent equipment. Look for multi-day packages that offer significant discounts over single-day rates. Lifts at most resorts operate daily 9am-4pm; arrive early for the best skiing and shortest lines. Prices do not include ski rental, which generally costs $20-30 for a full day. Numerous smaller ski resorts offer cheaper tickets and shorter lines. **Granlibakken** (☎583-4242 or 800-543-3221) is the oldest ski resort at Lake Tahoe and sports the cheapest lift tickets ($18); **Homewood Mountain Resort** (☎525-2992) has top-notch tree skiing, great views of the lake, and 1260 acres. Skiing conditions range from bikini to frostbite, and snow (artificial or otherwise) covers the slopes into early summer. Low-season skiing may not compete with winter powder, but it's cheaper. Rates listed below are for peak season.

▨ **Squaw Valley** (☎583-6985 or 888-SNOW-321/766-9321; www.squaw.com), 5 mi. north of Tahoe City off Hwy. 89. The site of the 1960 Olympic Winter Games, and with good reason: the groomed bowls make for some of the West's best skiing. Squaw boasts 4000 acres of terrain across 6 Sierra peaks. The 33 ski lifts, including the 110-passenger cable car and high speed gondola, access high-elevation runs for all levels. Open late Nov.-May. Full-day lift ticket $58; half-day $42, seniors and ages 13-15 $29, under 12 $15, over 76 free. Night skiing mid-Dec. to mid-Apr. daily 4-9pm; $20.

**Heavenly** (☎775-586-7000), on Ski Run Blvd. off South Lake Tahoe Blvd. The largest and most popular resort in the area, with over 4800 skiable acres, 29 lifts, and 84 trails. Its vertical drop is 3500 ft., Tahoe's biggest. Few shoots or ridges. Its lifts and slopes straddle the California-Nevada border and offer dizzying views of both states. Full-day lift ticket $57, ages 13-18 $47, seniors and ages 6-12 $29.

**Mt. Rose** (☎800-754-7673 or 775-849-0704), 11 mi. from Incline Village on Rte. 431. A local favorite. Long season, short lines, and advanced focus. Full-day lift ticket $48, ages 13-17 $38, seniors $28, ages 6-12 $12, over 70 (mid-week) and under 6 free; half-day $38, ages 13-17 $33. Tu 2-for-1, W students $19, Th women $19.

**Alpine Meadows** (☎583-4232 or 800-441-4423), on Hwy. 89, 3 mi. north of Tahoe City. Family vacation spot and local hangout. Over 2000 skiable acres. Not as commercial as Squaw, with long expert bowls and good powder skiing. Full-day lift ticket $56, ages 13-18 $42, ages 65-69 $30, ages 7-12 $10, over 70 $8, under 6 $6.

**Northstar-at-Tahoe** (☎562-1010; www.skinorthstar.com), on Hwy. 267 13 mi. north of Tahoe City. Family-oriented ski area emphasizes beginning and intermediate trails. 200 new acres on Lookout Mountain cater to advanced skiers, and its 2420 total acres are the most on the North Shore. Full-day lift ticket $57, ages 13-22 $44, under 13 $19.

## CROSS-COUNTRY SKIING AND SNOWSHOEING

One of the best ways to enjoy the solitude of Tahoe's pristine snow-covered forests is to cross-country ski across the thick braid of trails around the lake. **Porters,** 501 North Lake Blvd., in Tahoe City, rents cross-country skis for $10-15. (☎583-2314. Open daily Oct.-Apr. 8am-6pm; May-Sept. 9am-6pm.) The region also boasts renowned cross-country ski resorts. **Spooner Lake,** at the junction of Hwy. 50 and 28, offers 57 mi. of machine-groomed trails and incredible views. (☎775-749-5349. $19, children $3.) **Tahoe X-C,** 2 mi. northeast of down-

# ON THE MENU

## THIS PARTY BITES!

It's hard to pass through Truckee without seeing memorials to the Donner Party. Their tragic story began in April 1846, when a group of Midwesterners (led by George Donner) set off for what they'd heard were Edenic lands in California. The ill-fated party took a "shortcut" in Wyoming advocated by explorer Lansford Hastings, who had never actually seen the shortcut. They hacked through the wilderness, losing cattle and abandoning wagons. When they eventually rejoined the main trail, they were three weeks behind.

By late October they reached Truckee Meadows (present-day Reno) but were exhausted, demoralized, harassed by Paiute Indians, and out of food. When they reached Truckee (now Donner) Lake around Nov. 4, snow was on the ground. The party made three unsuccessful attempts to cross the pass over the Sierras and was finally forced to settle around the lake. The thaw they hoped for never came, and, trapped by 22 ft. of snow, many resorted to cannibalism before they were finally rescued in April 1847. Only 47 of the initial 89 people survived. After national news of the horrific incidents emerged, migration to California fell off for several years until the torrent of the Gold Rush washed out all memories of that winter. An Annual Donner Party Hike (☎587-2757) reenacts the fateful journey every October (meal not included).

town Tahoe City on Dollar Hill off Hwy. 28, maintains 40 mi. of trails for all abilities winding through North Shore forests. (☎583-5475. $18; mid-week $13; children $6.) Snowshoeing is easier to pick up. Follow hiking or cross-country trails, or trudge off into the woods. Equipment rentals are available at sporting goods stores for about $15 per day. Check local ranger stations for ranger-guided winter snowshoe hikes.

# ☒ NIGHTLIFE

In Tahoe City, the nightlife is centered around the pub scene. In South Lake Tahoe, however, it's about late-night gambling in the casinos, which are busy 24/7. To get in, you must be 21 and have a government-issued form of picture ID.

**Pierce Street Annex,** 850 North Lake Blvd., in the Lighthouse Shopping Center in Tahoe City. The most popular bar in town; crowded nightly. All sustenance comes in liquid form. Free pool on Su, DJ W-Sa, locals night Th. (☎583-5800. Open daily 2pm-2am.)

**Caesar's Palace,** 55 Hwy. 50 (☎888-829-7630 or 775-588-3515). Roman theme pervades the casino/restaurant/club complex. The popular **Club Nero** (☎775-586-2000) is a hot spot for dancing and drinking, with $1 drinks on M, Latino night on Tu, wet t-shirt contests and free admission for ladies on W, ladies night with free admission and well drinks until midnight Th-Sa, and $1 drafts on Su. Cover $5-25. Open daily 9pm.

**The Brewery,** 3542 Lake Tahoe Blvd. (☎544-BREW/2739). Stop in and try one of the 7 microbrews on tap. The sassy Bad Ass Ale packs a fruity punch, and pizzas (starting at $10) come crammed with as many toppings as you want. Laid-back atmosphere makes this spot a favorite for locals. Open Su-Th 11am-10pm, F-Sa 11am-2am.

# NEAR LAKE TAHOE ☎530

The area surrounding Lake Tahoe is a rare find in the High Sierra: pristine mountains near major urban outposts, offering the best of both worlds. Innumerable outdoor recreation opportunities reel in visitors by the score; after the sun goes down, they head to beachside barbecues, the dimly lit yuppie bars of Tahoe City, or the gambling of South Lake Tahoe and Reno, just across the Nevada border.

A former wagon staging ground for settlers turned posh mountain retreat for Silicon Valley socialites, **Truckee** (pop. 13,864) lies just off I-80 in the Sierra Nevada, 200 mi. northeast of San Francisco, 35 mi. west of Reno, and 12 mi. north of Lake Tahoe. The saloons are now salons and the wagons of choice are Mercedes-Benz and BMW, but today as in the late 1800s, tourism to Lake Tahoe is Truckee's lifeblood. A few miles west, encircled by gray granite cliffs, is **Donner Lake,** where the hapless Donner party famously self-destructed (see **This Party Bites!,** p. 245).

Just west of Truckee, **Donner Memorial State Park** is the local playground, with hiking and biking trails, picnic areas, and access to scenic Donner Lake. The **climbing** at **Donner Summit** is world-renowned. Along Old Hwy. near Donner Pass, there are over 400 routes ranging from easy scrambles to climbs rated up to 5.13. Popular climbs include ascents up **School Rock** (beginner) or the precarious **Snow Shed** (advanced). The hiking, mountain biking, and rock climbing in the surrounding mountains of the **Tahoe National Forest** are exemplary. No wilderness permits are required for day use or camping, but free campfire permits are required in undeveloped sites for both fires and stoves during the summer season. (US Forest Service Truckee Ranger District ☎587-3558; www.r5.fs.fed.us/tahoe/tkrd. Open June-Aug. M-Sa 8am-5pm; Sept.-May M-F 8am-4:30pm.) Several hikes depart from the Donner Summit Trailhead, 8 mi. west of town on I-80 near the Castle Peak Area/Boreal Ridge Rd. Exit (follow the signs). The **Summit Lake Trail** follows the PCT north for 2 mi. through beautiful forest passing through an I-80 underpass, then branches off to tranquil, trout-filled Summit Lake. The **Pacific Crest Trail** climbs from the Donner Summit Trailhead to the summit of Mt. Judah (6 mi. one-way). The trail passes through a gauntlet of huge granite boulders.

In the winter, local resorts open for all sorts of snowplay. **Royal Gorge,** off I-80 at the Soda Springs/Norden exit, 10 mi. west of Truckee along Donner Pass Rd. (Old Hwy. 40) is the nation's premier cross-country ski resort, its 90 trails covering over 200 mi. of beginner and expert terrain. (☎800-500-3871 or 426-3871. Midweek $21.50, weekend $26, kids $12/$14.) **Tahoe Donner,** near the Donner State Park exit on I-80, boasts terrific snow and lighted trails for night skiing. (☎587-9484. $17, kids $9.) **Soda Springs,** 2 mi. from the Soda Springs/Norden exit off I-80, 10 mi. west of Truckee, specializes in tubing and sledding in addition to skiing and snowboarding. (☎426-1010. Day pass for all runs $23, ages 8-17 $10, under 7 and over 70 free.)

**Boreal** (☎426-3663), directly off I-80, 10 mi. west of Truckee, opens its mostly beginner and intermediate slopes earlier than many resorts and saves skiers the drive to Tahoe. (Nine lifts and 41 trails. Night skiing. Full-day lift ticket $34, ages 5-12 $10, over 60 $18, over 70 and under 5 free. Call about midweek discounts.) **Sugar Bowl,** off I-80 at Soda Springs/Norden exit, then 3 mi. east on Donner Pass Rd. (Old Hwy. 40) is home to the first chairlift in California and first gondola in the country, which along with 10 others provides access to 1500 acres of varied terrain. (☎426-9000. Lift tickets $35 midweek, $54 weekend, $35 half-day weekend; kids $13.)

# RENO                                                         ☎775

With decadent casinos only a die's throw away from snowcapped mountains, Reno embodies both the capitalist frenzy and the natural splendor of the West. The hub of northern Nevada's tourist cluster, including nearby Lake Tahoe, the "biggest little city in the world" compresses the gambling, entertainment, and dining experience of Las Vegas into a few city blocks. Built as much around the allure of a quick buck as a quick break-up, the city rose to prominence as a celebrity destination where getting a divorce was easier than making a hard eight on the craps table. Reno continues to be the Sierra's answer to Las Vegas, attracting risk-takers who crave the rush of hitting it big without the theme-park distractions.

## ⊏ TRANSPORTATION

**Flights: Reno-Tahoe International Airport,** 2001 E. Plumb Ln. (☎328-6499 or 888-766-4685), off Hwy. 395 at Terminal Way, 3 mi. southeast of downtown. Most major hotels have free shuttles for guests; otherwise, take Citifare bus #13 (daily 6:15am-1:30am). Taxis from downtown to airport $10-12.

**Trains: Amtrak,** 135 E. Commercial Row (☎329-8638 or 800-872-7245). Ticket office open daily 8:30am-5pm. Purchase tickets at least 30min. early. 1 train per day heads to **Sacramento** (5hr., $65), continuing to **San Francisco** (via Emeryville; 7½hr., $71).

**Buses: Greyhound,** 155 Stevenson St. (☎322-2970 or 800-231-2222), between W. 1st and W. 2nd St. Open 24hr. To: **Las Vegas** (1 per day, 10hr., $72 one-way express); **San Francisco** (12 per day, 5-6hr., $30-32 one-way).

**Public Transportation: Reno Citifare** (☎348-7433) serves the Reno-Sparks area. Main terminal between Plaza St. and E. 4th on Center St. Major routes operate 24hr. $1.50, ages 6-18 $1.25, seniors and disabled 75¢. **Sierra Spirit** (☎348-RIDE/7433) circles downtown Reno, hitting stops along Sierra and Center St. between 9th and Liberty St. every 10min. Runs Su-W 10am-8pm, Th-Sa 10am-midnight. 50¢.

SIERRA NEVADA

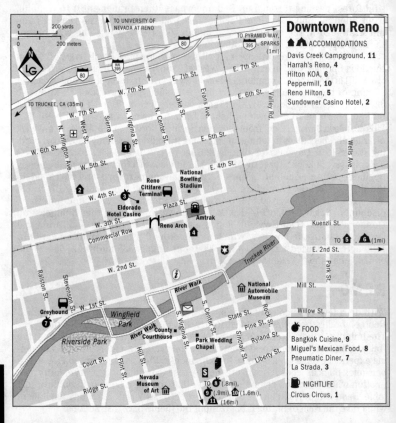

**Downtown Reno**

**🏠⚑ ACCOMMODATIONS**

Davis Creek Campground, **11**
Harrah's Reno, **4**
Hilton KOA, **6**
Peppermill, **10**
Reno Hilton, **5**
Sundowner Casino Hotel, **2**

**🍴 FOOD**
Bangkok Cuisine, **9**
Miguel's Mexican Food, **8**
Pneumatic Diner, **7**
La Strada, **3**

**🍸 NIGHTLIFE**
Circus Circus, **1**

**Taxis: Whittlesea Checker Taxi,** ☎322-2222. **Reno-Sparks Cab,** ☎333-3333.

**Car Rental: Alamo** (☎323-7940 or 888-426-3296), **Avis** (☎785-2727 or 800-831-2847), and **Budget** (☎800-527-7000 or 800-527-0700) are all in the airport. Outside the airport are **Enterprise,** 809 W. 4th St. (☎328-1671 or 800-736-8222), and **Rent-A-Wreck,** 295 Gentry Way (☎322-7787 or 877-880-5603).

## ◤ ORIENTATION

Fifteen miles from the California border and a 445 mi. desert sprint north from Las Vegas, Reno sits at the intersection of **I-80,** which stretches between Chicago and San Francisco, and **Highway 395,** which runs along the eastern slope of the Sierra Nevada from Southern California to Washington.

Many of the major casinos are "downtown" between West and Center St. and 2nd and 6th St. The neon-lit streets of downtown Reno are heavily patrolled, but **avoid straying too far east of the city center at night.** Virginia St., indisputably Reno's main drag, runs south of the Truckee River, where cheaper accommodations, outlying casinos, and countless strip malls can be found. The #1 bus services Virginia St. from downtown Reno to Meadowood Mall. Sparks, along

I-80 a few miles to the northeast, boasts several casinos that cater primarily to locals. The *Reno/Tahoe Visitor Planner*, available at information kiosks throughout the city, contains a local map and is a helpful city guide. The legal drinking and gambling age is 21.

## 🔊 PRACTICAL INFORMATION

**Visitor Information: Reno-Sparks Convention and Visitors Authority,** 1 E. 1st St. (☎800-FOR-RENO/367-7366; www.renolaketahoe.com), on the 2nd fl. of the Cal-Neva Building. Open M-F 8am-5pm.

**ATMs:** Reno thrives on fast money; ATMs abound. Small fee for out-of-state withdrawals.

**Library and Internet Access: Washoe County Library Downtown Reno Branch,** 301 S. Center St. (☎327-8300), between Ryland and Liberty St. Free Internet access. Open M 10am-8pm, Tu-Th 10am-6pm, F and Su 10am-5pm.

**Marriage:** Men and women over 18 (and those 16-17 with a parental OK) can pick up a marriage license at the **Washoe County Recorder's Office,** 75 Court St. (☎328-3275), for $55—all you need is a partner and an ID. Open daily 8am-midnight, including holidays. Numerous chapels in Reno are eager to help you tie the knot.

**Divorce:** To obtain a divorce permit, you must be a resident of NV for at least 6 weeks and pay a $265 fee. Call ☎329-4101 (M-F 9am-4pm) to arrange a lawyer referral.

**Laundromat: LaunderLand Coin-op Laundry,** 680 E. 2nd St. (☎329-3733), at 2nd and Wells St. Wash $1.75, dry free. Open daily 7am-10:30pm; last load 9:30pm.

**Emergency:** ☎911. **Police:** 455 E. 2nd St. (☎334-2121 or 334-COPS/2677).

**24hr. Crisis Lines: General Counseling and Rape Crisis,** ☎800-992-5757. **Compulsive Gamblers Hotline,** ☎800-522-4700.

**Medical Services: St. Mary's Hospital,** 235 W. 6th St. (☎770-3000, emergency ☎770-3188), between West St. and Arlington Ave. 24hr.

**Post Office:** 50 S. Virginia St. (☎786-5936), at the corner of Mill and Virginia St. Open M-F 8:30am-5pm. **Postal Code:** 89501.

## 🔒 ACCOMMODATIONS

While weekend prices at casino resorts are usually on the high side, weekday rates and off-season discounts offer great accommodations deals. Prices fluctuate, so call ahead. Though some motels have low rates, the prices may reflect a lack of wholesomeness in a few; heterosexual prostitution is legal in most of Nevada (though not in Reno itself). The rates below don't include Reno's **12% hotel tax.**

**Harrah's Reno,** 219 N. Center St. (☎800-427-7247 or 786-5700), between E. 2nd St. and Commercial Row. A Reno staple, Harrah's provides luxurious rooms in a central location. Two towers house 964 rooms, seven restaurants, a pool, and a health club. The 65,000 sq. ft. casino attracts large crowds with Reno's highest table limits, while Sammy's Showroom and the Plaza host top performers. Free valet parking. Singles and doubles M-Th start at $49; F-Su $89. ❸

**Reno Hilton,** 2500 E. 2nd St. (☎800 648-5080 or 789-2000), off Hwy. 395 at the Glendale Exit. Boasting more than 2000 elegant rooms, a 9000-seat outdoor amphitheater, a driving range, a 50-lane bowling center, a health club and spa, and a shopping mall, this is Reno's biggest, most extravagant hotel/casino. Press your luck in the 115,000 sq. ft. casino, or for something even more stomach-churning (depending on how you wager), check out the Ultimate Rush reverse bungee. Rooms $35-149. ❸

**Sundowner,** 450 N. Arlington Ave. (☎800-648-5490 or 786-7050), between W. 4th and W. 5th St. This working man's casino represents the meat and potatoes of Reno's gambling industry. No frills, but rooms are standard and clean. Pool, hot tub, and jacuzzi on premises. Rates are among the lowest. Rooms Su-Th start at $26, F $50, Sa $70. ❷

**Peppermill,** 2707 S. Virginia St. (☎800-648-6992 or 826-2121), between Carano Ln. and Brinkby Ave. Just south of downtown, the Peppermill grew from a small coffee shop to the sprawling hotel and casino it is today in a quarter of a century. Each of the 1100 rooms is adorned with mirrors and marble. Work on your tan at the grandiose Waterfall Pool and Spa. Home to 7 restaurants and 12 themed bars; crams all Reno has to offer within its walls. Rates Su-Th $59 (as low as $39 in off-season), F-Sa $119. ❸

## CAMPING

To escape the jangling slot machines, drive to the woodland campsites of **Davis Creek Park ❶,** 18 mi. south on Hwy. 395 to Hwy. 429. (☎721-4901. Volleyball courts and trout-packed Ophir Creek Lake. Showers and toilets on site. Sites $15, each additional car $5; pets $1.) Adventurous campers hike the challenging Ophir Trail (6 mi. one-way), which ascends over 4000 ft. to meet the Tahoe Rim Trail. Closer to the action is the **Hilton KOA ❷,** 2500 E. 2nd St. (☎888-562-5698, 789-2147), next to the Reno Hilton. There's no grass in sight, but campers have access to the Hilton's pool, tennis courts, and fitness center. (Hookups $27-38.)

## FOOD

The cost of eating out in Reno is low, but the food quality doesn't have to be. Casinos offer a wide range of all-you-can-eat buffets and next-to-free breakfasts, but you can escape the clutches of these giants to find inexpensive eateries outside.

**Pneumatic Diner,** 501 W. 1st St. (☎786-8888 ext. 106), at the corner of Ralston and W. 1st St. in the Truckee River Lodge. This funky diner blends Italian, Mexican, French, and Middle Eastern food with all-natural ingredients. Beverage concoctions (try Snoopy; $1.50-4), breakfast ($1.50-6.50), sandwiches (try the ratatouille baguette; $5.50), and other delights ($4-7.50). Open M-F 11am-11pm, Sa 9am-11pm, Su 7am-11pm. ❷

**Bangkok Cuisine,** 55 Mt. Rose St. (☎322-0299), at S. Virginia and Mt. Rose. The savory Thai food and elegant setting create a welcome haven from Reno's ubiquitous steaks and burritos. All sorts of soups ($4-7), noodles ($8-12), fried rices ($8-12), curries ($8-10), and specialties (stuffed Thai omelette; $8). Open M-Sa 11am-10pm. ❷

**La Strada,** 345 N. Virginia St. (☎348-9297), in the Eldorado Hotel. Serves award-winning Italian cuisine in the heart of the Eldorado. Pastas made fresh daily $10-20. Beef and fish entrees $13-24. Enjoy elegance on a budget. Open daily 5pm-10pm. ❸

**Miguel's Mexican Food,** 1415 S. Virginia St. (☎322-2722). Miguel's is a Reno classic, praised by locals and critics alike. A substantial lunch menu ($6-9) offers delicious fare in generous servings. Don't miss the outstanding guacamole ($7) and *sopapillas* (3 for $1). Dinner entrees $5-14. Open Su noon-8pm; Tu-Th 11am-9pm; F-Sa 11am-10pm. ❷

## NIGHTLIFE

Reno is like a giant adult amusement park, its casinos the main attractions. Prudently, casinos offer free gaming lessons. The most popular games and minimum bets vary between establishments, but slots are ubiquitous. Drinks are usually free if you're gambling; beware alcohol's inhibition-loosening effects.

Almost all casinos offer live nighttime entertainment, but most shows are not worth the steep admission prices. **Harrah's**, 219 N. Center St. (☎786-3232), is an exception, carrying on a dying tradition with its **Night on the Town** in Sammy's Showroom. At **Circus Circus**, 500 N. Sierra St. (☎329-0711), a small circus on the midway above the casino floor performs "big top" shows approximately every half-hour (M-Th 11:30am-11:30pm; F-Su 11:15am-11:45pm). For more entertainment listings and info on casino happenings, check out the free *This Week* or *Best Bets* magazines. *The Reno News & Review*, published every Thursday, provides an alternative look at weekly happenings and events off the beaten casino path.

## 🎵 🖼 ENTERTAINMENT & SEASONAL EVENTS

There's far more to Reno culture than its nightlife. The newly reopened **Nevada Museum of Art,** 160 W. Liberty St., is housed in an architectural delight that was inspired by Black Rock Desert. The museum has galleries and a sculpture plaza but also hosts visiting shows by the likes of Diego Rivera, Edward Hopper, and Dennis Oppenheim. (☎329-3333. Open Su, Tu-W, F-Sa 11am-6pm, Th 11am-8pm. Admission $7, students and seniors $5, ages 6-12 $1, ages 5 and under free.) Cultural events heat up in the summer; the popular **Artown** festival (☎322-1538; www.renoisartown.com), is held every July for the entire month. The event features dance, jazz, painting, and theater, and almost everything is free. August roars in with the chrome-covered, hot-rod splendor of **Hot August Nights** (☎356-1956; www.hotaugustnights.com), a celebration of classic cars and rock 'n' roll.

For the more athletically inclined, the annual **Reno Rodeo** (☎329-3877; www.renorodeo.com), one of the richest in the West, gallops in for eight days in late June. In September, the **Great Reno Balloon Race** (☎826-1181), in Rancho San Rafael Park, and the **National Championship Air Races** (☎972-6663; www.air-race.org), at Reno/Stead Airport, draw an international group of contestants who take to the sky as spectators look on. If you prefer more old-fashioned modes of transportation, nearby Virginia City hosts **Camel Races** (☎847-0311) during the weekend after Labor Day, in which both camels and ostriches scoot about town.

# NATIONAL PARKS & FORESTS

Far from the urban centers and the industry of coastal California, the central Sierra cultivates wilderness in its unbridled majesty. Clear streams flow through endless forest while high Sierra peaks remain untouched. This rugged wilderness is the legacy of a long-standing conservation movement pioneered by John Muir in the late 19th century (see **The Naturalist,** p. 265). The two main park areas in the Sierra Nevada are Yosemite National Park (near Stanislaus National Forest and Mono Lake) and Sequoia and Kings Canyon National Parks (framed by the Sierra National Forest to the north and Sequoia National Forest to the south). National parks attract adventure-hungry tourists from around the world; solitude awaits among the less-heralded treasures of more remote areas.

## YOSEMITE NATIONAL PARK ☎209

In 1868, a young Scotsman named John Muir arrived by boat in San Francisco and asked for directions to "any place that is wild." Anxious to run this crazy youngster out of town, Bay Area folk directed him east to the heralded lands of Yosemite. The wonders that Muir beheld there sated his lust for wandering and spawned a lifetime dedicated to conservationism. His efforts won Yosemite its national park status in 1890. Sequoia and Kings Canyon earned the same distinction that year.

# Sierra Nevada: National Parks and Forests

Stanislaus National Forest
Lake Eleanor
Groveland
120
TO SONORA (26mi)
Coulterville
49
Big Oak Flat Entrance
Hetch Hetchy Reservoir
Tuolumne Meadows
Tioga Pass Entrance
120

TO LAKE TAHOE (80mi)
207
Bodie State Historical Park
359
Hoover Wilderness
395
167
Lee Vining
Mono Lake
MONO LAKE TUFA STATE RESERVE
Humbolt-Toiyabe National Forest

**Yosemite National Park**
Yosemite Village
Glacier Pt.
140
El Portal
Wawona
Mariposa Grove
Mariposa
TO MERCED (30mi)
49
41
Eastman Lake
Oakhurst

June Mountain Ski Resort
158
Ansel Adams Wilderness
June Lake
Crestview
203
Mammoth Lakes
Mono Craters
Inyo National Forest
Benton
120
6
264
Devils Postpile Nat'l Monument
Mammoth Mountain
Crowley Lake
Sierra National Forest

NEVADA
CALIFORNIA

Bass Lake
Mammoth Pool Res.
Mono Hot Springs
Lake Edison
Mono Pass Trail
395
Pacific Crest Trail
145
Big Creek
Huntington Lake
41
Millerton Lake
168
Shaver Lake
Florence Lake
WHITE MOUNTAINS
Ancient Bristlecone Pine Forest
Fresno-Yosemite Int'l Airport
Clovis
Dinkey Creek
Courtright Res.
Sierra National Forest
Wishon Res.
John Muir Wilderness
South Lake
168
Bishop
Inyo National Forest
168
Fresno
180
Pine Flat Reservoir
Big Pine
Sanger
180
**Kings Canyon National Park**
Inyo Nat'l Forest
Tinemaha Res.
395
OWENS VALLEY
INYO MOUNTAINS
EUREKA VALLEY
Death Valley Rd.
Orange Cove
Hume Lake
Grant Grove
201
63
245
198
180
Badger
Cedar Grove
KINGS CANYON
CALIFORNIA BIGHORN SHEEP ZOOLOGICAL AREA
SALINE VALLEY
99
38
Crystal Cave
Wuksachi Village
General Sherman Tree
Independence
Visalia
Woodlake
Mineral King
**Sequoia National Park**
Manzanar Nat'l Hist. Site
216
Lemon Cove
Three Rivers
198
Exeter
Mt. Whitney (14,494')
Highest point in Continental U.S.
Lone Pine
Tulare
137
65
**Death Valley National Park**
Porterville
Lake Success
136
190
Springville
PANAMINT MOUNTAINS
190
Sequoia National Forest
142
TULE RIVER INDIAN RESERVATION
Golden Trout Wilderness
Owens Lake (dry)
65
Ducor
Inyo National Forest
Kern River
190
Olancha
COSO RANGE
22
Delano
California Hot Springs
TO LAS VEGAS (150mi)
155
Panamint Springs
190
Woody
Sequoia National Forest
395
Naval Weapons Center
178
TO BAKERSFIELD (10mi)
155
Wofford Heights
Kernville
Pacific Crest Trail
TO LOS ANGELES (125mi)
Ballarat Ghost Town
65

0    25 miles
0    25 kilometers

Host to its own full-service hospital, kennel, daycare center, Lions and Rotary Clubs, eight religious congregations, a golf shop, one of the grandest hotels in California, and more informative programs than PBS, Yosemite and its more than four million yearly visitors have given rise to a small city in the middle of one of the most awesomely wild regions in America. With only 6% of the park (roughly the size of Rhode Island) developed and paved for visitors, most of Yosemite remains undisturbed and untamed. Despite the endless rows of tents, RVs, and SUVs that clog the paved 6%, Yosemite Valley, at the bustling, awe-inspiring heart of the park, still lives up to its old name: "The Incomparable Valley."

## AT A GLANCE

**AREA:** 1189 sq. mi.

**CLIMATE:** Temperate forest.

**FEATURES:** Tuolumne (tah-WALL-um-ee) Meadows, Mariposa Grove, Hetch Hetchy Reservoir, Yosemite Valley.

**HIGHLIGHTS:** Hike to Glacier Point, photograph Bridalveil Falls, whitewater raft on the Merced River.

**GATEWAYS:** Mariposa, Sonora (p. 228), Mammoth Lakes (p. 291), Oakhurst, and Merced (p. 315).

**CAMPING:** Reservations necessary to get a spot. 7-night max. stay in the Valley and Wawona, 14-night max. stay elsewhere. Permits needed for camping in the high country within the Park.

**FEES & RESERVATIONS:** Necessary-pass $10 per hiker, biker, or bus ride; $20 per car. Good for one week. Annual pass $40. National park passes also accepted here.

## ■ ORIENTATION

In all, Yosemite covers 1189 sq. mi. of mountainous terrain, most of which is completely rugged and wild and some of which is quite developed. The center of activity in the park, **Yosemite Valley** hosts the park's most enduring and photographed monuments, including **El Capitan, Half Dome,** and **Yosemite Falls.** The immense valley and all its granite monoliths were carved out by glaciers over thousands of years. **Yosemite Village,** the Valley's service, shopping, and information center, feels more like Disneyland than a national park. Facing the sheer southern wall of the valley and incomparable 360-degree views, **Glacier Point** brims all summer with tourists and their cars. **Tuolumne Meadows,** in the park's northeastern corner, is a beautiful rock-strewn alpine meadow surrounded by snow-capped peaks and swift streams. **Mariposa Grove** is a forest of giant sequoia trees at the park's southern end. Wawona, just north of Mariposa Grove, is a historic, upscale development that features museums, the luxurious Wawona hotel, and a golf course. The vast majority of the park, however, is wild. (7-day pass $10 per hiker, biker, or bus rider; $20 per car. Annual pass $40. National park passes accepted.)

## ■ TRANSPORTATION

Yosemite lies 200 mi. east of San Francisco (a 3½hr. drive) and 320 mi. northeast of LA (a 6-9hr. drive, depending on the season). It can be reached via Rte. 140 from Merced, Rte. 41 from Fresno, or Rte. 120 from Manteca or from Lee Vining.

**BY BUS OR TRAIN.** Yosemite runs public **buses** that connect the park with Fresno, Merced, and Mariposa. **Yosemite VIA** runs buses from the Merced bus station at 16th and N St. to Yosemite. (☎ 384-1315 or 800-VIA-LINE/842-5463. 4 trips per day; $10 one-way.) Buses also make stops in Cathy's Valley, Mariposa,

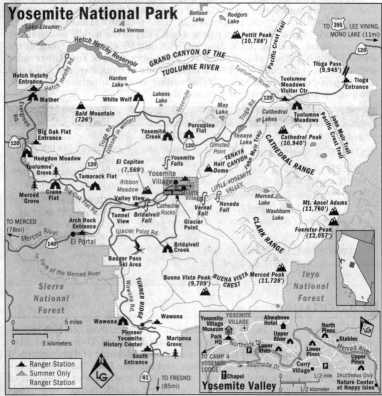

**Yosemite National Park**

Ranger Station
Summer Only Ranger Station

0    5 miles
0    5 kilometers

**Yosemite Valley**

Midpines, and El Portal. VIA meets Amtrak trains from San Francisco arriving at the Merced train station. Tickets can be purchased from the driver. (☎384-1315. Buses run M-F 8am-5pm. Fares include Yosemite entry.) **Yosemite Gray Line (YGL)** runs buses to and from **Fresno Yosemite International Airport (FYI)**, Fresno hotels, and Yosemite Valley ($20). A service called **YARTS** (☎877-989-2787 or 388-9589) provides four daily trips to Yosemite from Merced, making stops similar to VIA along the way, and sends one bus a day along Rte. 120 and Rte. 395, hitting Mammoth and June Lakes, Lee Vining, and Tuolumne Meadows. (Buses depart Merced bus station 7, 8:45, 10:30am, 5:25pm. $20 round-trip from Merced, Mammoth and June Lakes, Lee Vining, Tuolumne Meadows; other fares less. Fares include Yosemite entry.) **Amtrak** runs a **bus** from Merced to Yosemite (4 per day; $22) and **trains** (☎800-USA-RAIL/872-7245) to Merced from **San Francisco** (3½hr.; 5 per day; $22-29) and **LA** (5½hr.; 4 per day; $28-51). The trains connect with the waiting YGL bus.

The energetic guides of **Incredible Adventures,** 350 Townshend St. #423, San Francisco 94107, lead excellent hiking and sightseeing trips to great Yosemite spots, catering to young, spirited backpackers. (☎415-642-7378 or 800-777-8464; www.incadventures.com. 3-day/3-night trips depart from San Francisco June-Oct. W and Su; $190 including meals, entrance fee, equipment, transportation, and tax. 2-day trips $150. Daytrips run throughout the year; $95 with free hotel or hostel pick-up.) **Green Tortoise** sends its "hostels on wheels" from San Francisco on two- (Apr.-Sept.) and three-day (June-Oct.) tours of Yosemite (for details, see p. 53).

The best bargain in Yosemite is the **free shuttle bus,** which runs in Yosemite Valley, and, in summer, between Wawona and Mariposa Grove and Tioga Pass and Tenaya Lake. Comfortable but often crowded, the buses have knowledgeable drivers and wide viewing windows. (Every 10-20min.; daily 7am-10pm.) **Hikers' buses** run daily to Glacier Point and to Tuolumne Meadows/Lee Vining. (☎372-1240; www.yosemiteparktours.com. Late June to Sept. 6; $20.50 round-trip.) To get to the shuttle, drive into the Valley and park near Curry and Yosemite Villages.

The closest airport to Yosemite is Fresno Yosemite International, 4995 E. Clinton Way (☎559-621-4500), which is international only in that it has some flights coming in from Mexico. Most flights are from western US cities like LA, San Francisco, and Las Vegas. Five national rental car agencies serve the airport and VIA runs buses from the terminal to the park.

**BY CAR.** As is usually true in the US, driving is the most convenient way to enter the park, though traffic and parking hassles can rival those of rush-hour LA on summer weekends. Be sure to fill the tank before heading out, as there is no gas in Yosemite Valley except for emergency gas at the Village Garage ($15 for 5 gallons). There are overpriced 24hr. gas stations at Crane Flat, Tuolumne Meadows, and Wawona. Within the Valley, there is really no reason to drive since the shuttle system is free and very convenient. Those intending to visit the high country in spring and fall should arm cars with snow tires (sometimes required even in summer). Of the five major approaches to the park, **Route 120** to the Big Oak Flat entrance is the curviest. A less nauseating alternative is Rte. 41 from Fresno into the valley, featuring the famous **Inspiration Point** from which white man reputedly first beheld the valley. The eastern entrance, **Tioga Pass,** is closed during snow season, with snow often lasting until July, but makes for a spectacular summer drive. (For info on winter driving, see **Wintertime in Yosemite,** p. 264.)

**BY BICYCLE.** Cycling into the park is permitted from any of the entry points and will land you a half-off admission price. Cycling is a great way to see Yosemite Valley; many sights are within 2 mi. of the valley center and easily viewed from the 12 mi. of paved, flat bike paths in the Valley. One popular bike trail is the wide paved road from the valley campgrounds to Mirror Lake (6 mi. round-trip), which is closed to motorized vehicles. Yosemite's bike paths are ideal for leisurely rides and circumventing automobile traffic; serious cyclists should not expect a workout. Off-road mountain biking is not permitted in the park, but all paved roads are open to cyclists. See **Outdoor Activities** (p. 260) for more information on bike trails.

# ◼ PRACTICAL INFORMATION

**General Park Information** (☎372-0200; general info www.nps.gov/yose, visitor info www.yosemite.org). Info on weather, accommodations, and activities. All visitors centers have free maps and copies of *Yosemite Guide* and *Yosemite Today*. **All hours listed are valid late May-Sept. unless otherwise noted.**

**Camp Reservations:** ☎800-436-7275; www.reservations.nps.gov.

**Yosemite Valley Visitors Center** (☎372-0299), in Yosemite Village. Sign language interpreter in summer. Books, maps, exhibits, and the *Spirit of Yosemite* orientation film every half-hour. Open daily 8am-6pm; winter 9am-5pm.

SIERRA NEVADA

**WHEN TO GO.** Yosemite's moderate climate makes it a comfortable destination year-round. Less snow means more tourists, however, and Yosemite Valley is generally overrun from June to Sept. Those seeking a quiet visit to this national wonder should consider going during the colder winter months.

**Wilderness Center,** P.O. Box 545, Yosemite National Park 95389 (☎372-0745; www.nps.gov/yose/wilderness), in Yosemite Village. Wilderness permit reservations up to 24 weeks in advance (☎372-0740; $5 per person per reservation; M-F 8:30am-4:30pm), or first-come, first-served (free). 40% of backcountry quota is held for first-come, first-camp. The center's staff cannot plan your trips but has tons of info. Bear canisters, maps, and guidebooks for sale. Open daily 7:30am-6pm; in winter 8am-5pm.

**Tuolumne Meadows Visitors Center** (☎372-0263), on Tioga Pass Rd. 55 mi. east of Yosemite Village. The high-country headquarters, with visitor services. Open in summer daily 9am-7pm; in spring and fall 9am-5pm; closed in winter. **Wilderness Center,** off Tioga Rd. on the road to Tuolumne Lodge, issues permits. Open daily 8am-5pm.

**Big Oak Flat Info Station** (☎379-1899), on Rte. 120 W. in Crane Flat. Open daily 8am-5pm. Wilderness permits available daily 8am-4:30pm.

**Wawona Info Station** (☎375-9531), on Rte. 41, 6 mi. from the southern entrance near Mariposa Grove, on the Wawona Hotel grounds. Large selection of books. Open daily 8am-4:30pm. Wilderness permits issued.

## LOCAL SERVICES

**Auto Repairs: Village Garage** (☎372-8320), in the center of the village. Open daily 8am-noon and 1-5pm. Cars towed 24hr. Emergency gasoline available. AAA and National Auto Club accepted.

**Bike Rental: Yosemite Lodge** (☎372-1208) and **Curry Village** (☎372-8319) for $5.50 per hr., $21 per day. Wheelchairs also available at both shops for $5 per hr., $20 per day. Driver's license or credit card required as security deposit. Both open daily 9am-6pm, weather permitting; open on a limited basis after Sept. 6.

**Equipment Rental: Yosemite Mountaineering School** (☎372-8344 or 372-8436), on Rte. 120 at Tuolumne Meadows. Sleeping bags $10.50 per day, backpacks $8.50 per day; 3rd day half-price. Climbing shoes rented to YMS students only. Driver's license or credit card required for deposit. Rock climbing classes daily. Open daily 8:30am-noon and 1-5pm. For info on ski and snowshoe rental, see **Wintertime in Yosemite,** p. 264.

**24-Hour ATM: Bank of America,** in Yosemite Village. The bank also has a check-cashing service. Open daily 8am-4pm. There are also ATMs in Village Store, Yosemite Lodge, Curry Village market, Wawona store, and El Portal.

**Gas Stations:** There is no gas in Yosemite Valley. Tank up in **Crane Flat** (open daily 8am-8pm), **El Portal, Wawona** (9am-6pm), or **Tuolumne Meadows** (8:30am-5pm) before driving into the High Sierra where prices rise with the elevation. All 24hr. Credit card.

**Laundromat:** Laundry facilities open at **Housekeeping Camp.** Wash $1.25, dry 25¢ per 10min. Open daily 7am-10pm. In winter, laundry facilities available at **Camp 6,** across the street from the Village Store. Open daily 7am-10pm.

**Swimming Pools:** At Yosemite Lodge, Wawona Hotel, and Curry Village. $2 per day; free for guests of Ahwahnee Hotel, Yosemite Lodge, and Curry Village. All open 10am-5pm.

**Showers: Housekeeping Camp** ($2, children $1.50). Includes towel and soap. Open daily 24hr. **Curry Village** (free for guests). Open 24hr. Also at **Tuolumne Meadows** and **White Wolf Lodges** ($2). Open daily noon-3:30pm.

**Weather and Road Conditions:** ☎372-0200. 24hr.

## EMERGENCY & COMMUNICATIONS

**Medical Services: Yosemite Medical Clinic** (☎372-4637), two blocks from the eastern end of Yosemite Village. 24hr. emergency room. Walk-in urgent care and appointments M-Sa 8am-5pm. **Dental services** (☎372-4200) available next to the Medical Clinic.

**Internet Access: Yosemite Bug Hostel** (☎966-6666), on Rte. 140, 30 mi. west of Yosemite in Midpines (see p. 259). Internet access $1 for 10min.

**Post Office: Yosemite Village,** next to the Visitors Center. Open M-F 8:30am-5pm, Sa 10am-noon. Lobby open 24hr. **Curry Village,** near the registration office. Open May 31-Sept. 6 M-F 2:30-4pm. **Yosemite Lodge,** open M-Th 11:30am-2:45pm, F 11:30am-4:30pm. **Wawona,** open M-F 9am-5pm, Sa 9am-1pm. **Tuolumne Meadows,** open M-F 9am-5pm, Sa 9am-1pm. **Postal Code:** 95389.

## 📷 CAMPING

One of the first views of Yosemite a visitor gets during the summer may be of the endless "tent cities" in the Valley. Don't expect to get a spot without reservations, which have to be made well in advance for summer visits. (☎800-436-7275, TDD 888-530-9796, outside the US 301-722-1257; http://reservations.nps.gov. Reservations available by phone or website daily 7am-7pm, Pacific time, or mail NPRS, P.O. Box 1600, Cumberland, MD 21502. Reservations available up to 5 months in advance on the 15th of every month. Spots in the Valley usually fill up within a few days of becoming available.) Cancellation lotteries are held at the campground reservations office in Curry Village (daily 8am and 3pm) but the odds are against you. Camp 4, in the Valley, is first-come, first-served, but people line up for spots in the mornings. Camping is plentiful and usually easily available in the surrounding national forests; these are good alternatives if you can't get a spot in Yosemite. During the summer, there is a seven-night maximum stay for those in the Valley or at Wawona and a 14-night maximum stay for campers outside the Valley (except Wawona). All drive-in campsites provide picnic tables, firepits or grills, a cleared tent space, parking, and a food storage area. Natural stream water (serving Tamarack Flat, Yosemite Creek, and Porcupine Flat) must be boiled, filtered, or treated to prevent giardia (an intestinal disease; see **Food- and Water-borne diseases,** p. 36). Iodine water treatments can be bought at any supply store. Backcountry camping is prohibited in the Valley but encouraged outside of it (see **Backcountry,** p. 265). Toilet facilities are everywhere, but only vault toilets are available at Tamarack Flat, Yosemite Creek, and Porcupine Flat. RVs are prohibited in Tamarack, Yosemite Creek, and walk-in sites. Dump stations are available in the Valley (year-round) and in Wawona and Tuolumne Meadows (summer only). Only the Upper Pines and Camp 4, in the Valley, Wawona, and Hodgdon Meadow campgrounds are open year-round; the rest are open in summer, usually from June to Sept.

### IN YOSEMITE VALLEY

All drive-in campsites require reservations, which should be made as far in advance as possible, up to five months prior to camping on the 15th. **All Valley campgrounds fill completely every summer night.**

**Camp 4,** 4000 ft., at the western end of the Valley, past Yosemite Lodge. 150 yd. from the parking lot. 35 walk-in sites fill up before 9am most mornings. Caters to seasoned climbers swapping stories of exploits on vertical rock faces. Be prepared to meet new friends, since every site is filled with 6 randomly assembled people. Water, flush toilets, and tables. First-come, first-camp. Limited parking. $5 per person. ❶

SIERRA NEVADA

■ NATIONAL PARKS & FORESTS

**Lower Pines,** 4000 ft., in Yosemite Valley's busy eastern end. Commercial, crowded, and plagued by car traffic. No serene nights under the stars here. Next to **North Pines** campsite (4000 ft.; open Apr.-Sept.; 81 sites) and the **Upper Pines** campsite (4000 ft.; 238 sites). Water, toilets, tables, and showers. Sites $18. All require reservations. ❷

## BEYOND YOSEMITE VALLEY

Outside the Valley, campsite quality vastly improves.

▨ **Hodgdon Meadow,** 4900 ft., on Rte. 120 near Big Oak Flat Entrance, 25 mi. from the Valley. Warm enough for winter camping. 105 thickly wooded sites provide some seclusion even when the campground is full. Water, toilets, and tables. Sites May-Sept. $18; Oct.-Apr. $12 and first-come, first-camp. ❷

**Tuolumne Meadows,** 8600 ft., on Rte. 120, 55 mi. east of the Valley. Drive into the sprawling campground or escape the RVs in the 25 sites saved for walk-in hikers. Ranger programs every night. Pets allowed in western section only. 152 sites require advance reservations, 152 saved for same-day reservations. Open July-Sept., depending on snow. Drive-in sites $18; backpacker sites $3 per person. ❶

**Wawona,** 4000 ft., off Rte. 41, 1 mi. outside Wawona, 27 mi. from Yosemite Valley. 93 open, unshaded sites near the South Fork of the Merced River. Water, flush toilets, and tables. Pets allowed. May-Sept. sites $18 and reservations required; Oct.-Apr. sites $12 and first-come, first-camp. ❷

**Tamarack Flat,** 6300 ft., 23 mi. northeast of the Valley. Take Rte. 120 east on Tioga Rd. and follow the rough road for 3 mi. (only if your car can take it; not recommended for RVs and trailers). 52 rustic drive-in sites. Fewer amenities, but campers can enjoy peace and quiet. First-come, first-camp. Open June-Sept. Sites $8. ❶

**Bridalveil Creek,** 7200 ft., 25 mi. south of the Valley on Glacier Point Rd. Peaceful, beautiful grounds convenient for serious backpackers aiming for Glacier, Dewey, and Taft Points. A 2 mi. walk to beautiful McGurk Meadow. 110 sites. First-come, first-camp. Open July to early Sept. Sites $12. ❶

**Porcupine Flat,** 8100 ft., 15 mi. from Tuolumne Meadows off Tioga Rd. RV sites in the front section. 52 first-come, first-camp sites. Open late July to Sept. Sites $8. ❶

**White Wolf,** 8000 ft., off Rte. 120 east, 31 mi. from the Valley. Lots of boulders to lounge upon. Open late July to early Sept., depending on snow. 74 sites $12. ❶

**Crane Flat,** 6200 ft., centrally located on Big Oak Flat Rd. near the Tioga Pass turnoff. Surrounded by meadows and boulders. 166 well-spaced and peaceful sites tend to fill up later than other area sites, due to Crane Flat's distance from popular trails. Open June-Sept. Reservations required. Sites $18. ❷

## ⌂ ACCOMMODATIONS

### INSIDE THE PARK

When American Transcendentalist Ralph Waldo Emerson visited Yosemite in 1884, the park's accommodations were so simple that he was awakened in the morning by the clucking of a hen climbing over his bed. These days, Yosemite's accommodations have become much more comfortable, but at times you may feel as if you need to be Emerson himself to get a room in the valley. Spring and summer rates are high (suites at the luxurious Ahwahnee Hotel start at $357) and space is tight. Reservations are necessary and can be made up to one year in advance by calling ☎ 559-252-4848. Rates fluctuate, but tend to be higher on weekends and during the summer (those given below are for summer weekends). Check-in is usually around 11am. **All park lodgings provide access to dining and laundry facilities, showers, and supplies.**

**Curry Village** (☎ 252-4848), 2 mi. southeast of Yosemite Village. Less packed than Yosemite Village. 628 accommodations, featuring a pool (open 11am-5pm), nightly shows at the amphitheater, snack stands, cafeteria, and an ice rink (Nov.-Feb.). Rangers tell stories about Yosemite's history nearly every night. Standard motel room $112; cabin with bath $92, without bath $77; canvas tent cabin $60. ❹

**Housekeeping Camp** (☎ 372-8338). A quarter mile west of Curry Village, this army barracks-style camp feels slightly less developed. Canvas-capped concrete "camping shelters" hold up to 4 people (6 with cots) and include 2 bunk beds, a double bed, a picnic table, a firepit with grill, lights, and outlets for $64. Showers and laundry available as well as camping equipment rental. ❶

**Tuolumne Meadows Lodge** (☎ 372-8413), on Tioga Pass Rd., in the park's northeastern corner. In the high country, these rustic cabins are set off from the street and are more tranquil than the Village. Popular for its convenient backcountry access. Canvas-sided cabins, wood stoves, no electricity. Cabins $67; additional adult $9, child $4. ❹

**White Wolf Lodge** (☎ 372-8416), on Tioga Pass Rd. in the park's western area. Far from Yosemite Village's bustle and adjacent to a beautiful meadow. Open late June to early Sept. Cabins with bath $84; tent cabin doubles $63; each additional person $9. ❹

**Yosemite Lodge** (☎ 372-1274), west of Yosemite Village and directly across from Yosemite Falls. Feels like a family motel, but lodge rooms are spacious with private patios and A/C. Right next to pool and bike rental. Lodge rooms $146; standard rooms $110; each additional person $11. ❺

## OUTSIDE THE PARK

Lodging in the park may be convenient, but it's also expensive and hard to get, especially during the summer months. For the same price as a canvas cabin in the valley, you can find high-quality hotel accommodations in scenic and, ironically, more pristine areas. For more info on gateway towns and accommodations, access the **Yosemite Area Traveler Information (YATI)** web site (www.yosemite.com). YATI has computer terminals at the Yosemite Valley Visitors Center (see p. 255), the Greater Merced Chamber of Commerce (see p. 315), the Yosemite Sierra Visitors Bureau (see p. 255), and the Tuolumne County Visitors Bureau (see p. 256).

**Yosemite Bug Hostel** on Rte. 140 in Midpines (☎ 966-6666; www.yosemitebug.com), 25 mi. west of Yosemite. Look carefully for the sign. A woodsy, spirited resort spot. International backpacking crowd lounges in hammocks. Beer on tap, full guest kitchen, library with games, cafe with exceptional food, and a swimming hole with a waterfall. Occasional live music outdoors. Discounts on public transportation to park ($10 round-trip, 3-day pass $20). Internet access $1 per 10min. Dorms $16; tent sites $17; family and private rooms with shared bath $40-70; private rooms with bath $55-115. ❷

**Evergreen Lodge,** 33160 Evergreen Rd. (☎ 379-2606; www.evergreenlodge.com), 7 mi. off Rte. 120, 1 mi. before park entrance. Over 80 years old and advertised almost exclusively through word-of-mouth, this lodge near the quieter Hetch Hetchy region is secluded and cozy. The spacious cabins have porches, an outdoor patio and grill, and an on-site restaurant, bar, deli, and market. Standard cabins $79; family cabins $99; large family cabins $104. $10 extra during the busy season. ❹

**Yosemite View Lodge** on Rte. 140 (☎ 379-2681 or 800-321-5261; www.yosemite-motels.com), 2 mi. east of El Portal just outside the park. Descend from the mountains and kick back in luxury. Huge hotel squats on the banks of the Merced River. 3 pools, 6 jacuzzis (2 right on the banks of the Merced), high-vaulted wood ceilings, kitchenettes in every elegant room. Rooms $139-209. $50 less in off-season. ❺

## ⌐ FOOD

The **Village Store** (open June-Sept. daily 8am-10pm; Oct.-May 8am-9pm) is your best bet for groceries, with a huge selection and only moderately inflated prices. Smaller, pricier stores are in the Yosemite Lodge (daily June-Sept. 8am-10pm; Oct.-May 8am-9pm), at Wawona (open daily 8am-8pm), Crane Flat (open daily 8am-8pm), El Portal (open daily 8am-8pm), and Tuolumne Meadows (open 9am-6pm). Consider buying all of your cooking supplies, marshmallows, and batteries in Merced or Fresno en route to the park.

### IN YOSEMITE VALLEY
Yosemite's center of commerce is crammed at lunchtime. It may be more pleasant to make like a forest animal and carry your meal away to eat in seclusion.

    **Mountain Room Restaurant** (☎372-9033), in Yosemite Lodge. Outstanding views of Yosemite Falls from nearly every seat in the restaurant make this ideal for a post-hike meal. Filling portions of hearty American fare $17-28. Open daily 5:30-9pm. ❺

    **Ahwahnee Dining Room** (☎372-1489). Linen tablecloths, 34 ft. high ceilings, chandeliers, and strict dress codes make this stately National Historic Landmark a dining option if you've just made a killing on the stock market. Elegant and expensive American cuisine $30-50. Open M-F 7-10:30am, 11:30am-3pm, and 5:30-9:15pm; Su brunch 7am-3pm. Bar open 11am-11pm. Reservations recommended. ❺

    **Degnan's Delicatessen** (☎372-8454), in Yosemite Village. Inside a convenience store and adjacent to an ice cream parlor and pizza place. Huge sandwiches and small veggie sandwiches $5.75. Now offering coffee-shop fare as well. Open daily 7am-7pm. ❷

### BEYOND YOSEMITE VALLEY
Other restaurants in the park are generally in the hotels. Check Yosemite's publications for lunchtime bargains. The moderately upscale Tuolumne Meadows and White Wolf Lodges both offer American-style dishes. Tuolumne Meadows also has a small grill with lower priced but still filling food. Wawona has an expensive restaurant in its hotel and a snack shop in the golf store. Glacier Point also has a snack shop. Call ☎372-1000 for current dining information. Cheaper, often better dining opportunities can be found just outside of the park. The **Yosemite View Restaurant** ❸, on Rte. 140 at the Yosemite View Lodge in El Portal, offers fine dining in a gleaming building with a high wooden ceiling, stone fireplace, and lots of tourists. It's a better deal than the Ahwahnee but the atmosphere can't compare. Fuel up at its breakfast buffet for $10. (☎379-9307. Entrees $13-24. Open daily 7-11am and 6-10pm.) Seven miles down the road, the **Cedar Lodge Restaurant** ❸, on Rte. 140 in El Portal, serves somewhat overpriced food until late at night. (☎379-2316. Entrees $9-19. Open daily 7am-10pm; lounge serves until 1:30 am.)

## ⚡ OUTDOOR ACTIVITIES

**BY CAR OR BICYCLE.** Although the view is better if you get out of the car, you can see a large portion of Yosemite from the bucket seat. The **Yosemite Road Guide** ($3.50; at every visitors center) is keyed to roadside markers and outlines a superb tour of the park; you might as well have a ranger riding shotgun. Spectacular panoramas and beautiful glades are omnipresent along **Route 120 (Tioga Pass Road)** from Crane Flat to Tuolumne Meadows. This stretch of road is the highest highway strip in the country; as it winds down from Tioga Pass through the park's eastern exit, it plunges a mile down to reach the lunar landscape of Mono Lake. The drive west from the pass brings you past **Tuolumne Meadows** with its colorful grasses and rippling creeks to shimmering Tenaya Lake. No less incredible are the views afforded by the southern approach to Yosemite, **Route 41.** Most recognizable is the Wawona Tunnel turnout (also known as **Inspiration Point**), the view from which many visitors will recognize as the subject of many Ansel Adams photographs. From the point, **Yosemite Valley** unfurls its famed, humbling beauty. **El Capitan,** a gigantic granite monolith (7569 ft.), looms over awestruck crowds. If you stop and look closely (with binoculars if possible), you will see what appear to be specks of dust moving on the mountain face. They are actually world-class climbers inching toward fame, and at night their flashlights shine from impromptu hammocks hung from the granite. Nearby, **Three Brothers** (three adjacent granite peaks) and misty **Bridalveil Falls** are captured by hundreds of snapshots every day. A drive into the heart of the Valley leads to the staggering **Yosemite Falls** (the highest falls in North America at 2425 ft.), **Sentinel Rock,** and mighty **Half Dome.**

The view from **Glacier Point,** off Glacier Point Rd. from Rte. 41, conveys the epic scale of the Valley. This gripping overlook, 3214 ft. above the valley floor, can stun even the most wilderness-weary traveler. Half Dome curves majestically from the Valley's south side and water seems to tumble down Nevade Falls in slow motion. When the moon is full, this is an extraordinary (and very popular) place to visit. Arrive at sunset and watch the fiery colors fade over the valley as the stars appear, the clouds shimmer in silver, and the moon starts to cross the horizon.

To marvel at specimens of the Sierra Nevada's most famous flora, take the short hiking trail through the giant sequoias of **Mariposa Grove,** 35mi. south of the Valley near the southern entrance. This self-guided walk begins off Mariposa Grove Rd. at the Fallen Monarch, a massive trunk lying on its side, and continues to both the 209-foot-tall, 2700-year-old Grizzly Giant and the fallen Wawona Tunnel Tree. Ancient Athens was at its height when many of these trees were saplings.

## SUMMERTIME IN YOSEMITE

**DAY HIKING IN THE VALLEY.** For the full Yosemite experience, visitors must travel the outer trails on foot. World-class hiking abounds for anyone willing to lace up a **pair of boots.** Daytrip trails are well populated—at nearly any point in the day, you may find yourself stuck behind groups of other tourists on trails. Hiking just after sunrise is the best and sometimes the only way to beat the crowds. But even then, trails like Half Dome are already busy. A colorful trail map of short day hikes from the Valley with difficulty ratings and average hiking times is available at the Visitors Center (50¢; see **Yosemite Valley Visitors Center,** p. 255). The **Mirror Lake Loop** is a level 3 mi. walk past Mirror Lake (half a mile), up Tenaya Creek, and back. **Bridalveil Falls,** another Ansel Adams favorite, is an easy quarter-mile stroll from the nearby shuttle bus stop, and its cool spray is as close to a shower as many Yosemite campers will get. The **Lower Yosemite Falls Trail** is a favorite of all ages and starts just opposite the Yosemite Lodge. On moonlit nights, mysterious moonbows (the moon's answer to the rainbow) can sometimes be spotted off the water. Both the Lower Yosemite and Bridalveil Falls trails are wheelchair accessible. **Upper Yosemite Falls Trail,** a back-breaking 3½ mi. trek to the windy summit, climbs 2700 ft. but rewards the intrepid hiker with an overview of the vertiginous 2425 ft. drop. Those with energy to spare can trudge on to **Yosemite Point** or **Eagle Peak,** where views of the valley below rival those from more-heralded Glacier Point. The trail begins with an extremely steep, unshaded ascent. Leaving the marked trail is not a wise idea—a sign warns, "If you go over the waterfall, you will die."

From the Happy Isles trailhead at the eastern end of the Upper Pines campground, the **John Muir Trail** leads 211 mi. to Mt. Whitney, but most visitors prefer to take the slightly less strenuous 1½ mi. **Mist Trail** along the Merced River and past the base of **Vernal Falls** to the top of **Nevada Falls.** This is perhaps the most popular day-use trail in the park, and with good reason—views of the falls from the trails are outstanding, and the cool drops from the nearby water-pounded rocks are more than welcome during the hot summer months. Grab a shuttle from the Visitors Center. From Nevada Falls, the trail continues to the base of **Half Dome,** Yosemite's most recognizable monument and a powerful testament to the power of glaciation. Dedicated hikers trek to the top and enjoy the breathtaking vista of the Valley. The hike is 17 mi. round-trip, rises a total of 4800 vertical ft., and takes a full day to complete (6-12hr.). Don't attempt this hike unless you are in top shape and have done strenuous hikes before. If you want to make it a two-day excursion, **camping ❶** is available at Little Yosemite Valley with a wilderness permit. The final 800 ft. of the walk is a steep climb up the east side of the famous rock face. Equipped with cables, this precarious final challenge is well worth the thrill of sitting on top of the world. Enthusiasts of all ages and origins share high-fives with adrenaline-silly strangers and cheer each other on toward the end.

Although you'll have to share your achievement with the multitudes who opt to drive, the steep 5 mi. hike to **Glacier Point** will earn you the satisfaction of knowing you've worked for the staggering views. The 3200 ft. ascent is grueling, making the presence of a snack bar at the top welcome as well as absurd. You can find the trailhead on Southside Dr., 1 mi. southwest of the village. The wildflower-laden **Pohono Trail** starts from Glacier Point, crosses Sentinel Creek (spectacular **Sentinel Falls,** the park's second-largest cascade, lies to the north), and parallels the south rim of the Valley on its way to **Taft Point, Dewey Point,** and other secluded lookouts. A concession bus leaves from the valley in the morning for the **Four Mile Trail** (4¾ mi.) and the **Panorama Trail** (8 mi.), both of which also start at Glacier Point.

**DAY HIKING OUTSIDE THE VALLEY.** Tioga Rd. slices through the park, making its way into windswept high country otherwise inaccessible to day hikers. From the west, the lush **White Wolf** trails depart from the campground, lie generally flat, and head to fishing and swimming at **Harden** (3 mi. northwest) and **Lukens Lakes** (1 mi. east, uphill). The 4 mi. hike down to **North Dome,** providing great views of Yosemite Valley and Half Dome, isn't too difficult, but the hike back up is more strenuous. The trailhead is 5 mi. past where Tioga Rd. crosses Yosemite Creek. At a turn-off about 8 mi. from the creek crossing, the hike to **Mt. Hoffmann** (10,850 ft.) is a moderate 3 mi. to the top of the geographic center of the park. Along the way, you'll pass gorgeous **May Lake.** Halfway between the turn-off for Mt. Hoffmann and Tenaya Lake is the pullout for **Olmstead Point,** a must-see vista of Tenaya Canyon, stretching out to Yosemite Valley with views of the backside of Half Dome. Two miles farther east is **Tenaya Lake,** a large, clear alpine lake popular with swimmers.

**Tuolumne Meadows** (8600 ft.), a park village in the real high country at the eastern end of Tioga Rd., is the second most popular area in the park after Yosemite Valley. A huge number of greatly rewarding day hikes weave through the region. The 3½ mi., 1000 ft. ascent to **Cathedral Lakes** is moderately difficult and will take you to a swimming spot with an incredible view of the unmistakable Cathedral Peak. **Elizabeth Lake** is an easier 2 mi. haul to another outstanding glacier-carved mountain lake, situated at the base of Unicorn Peak. The Visitors Center has info on the many hiking opportunities in the region. Visitors should venture onto unfamiliar trails; scarcely a hike exists in Yosemite that doesn't give hikers jaw-dropping views and quiet moments of harmony. For a taste of "real" rock climbing without the requisite equipment and training, Yosemite day hikers and climbers clamber up **Lembert Dome** above Tuol-

SIERRA NEVADA

umne Meadows. This gentle (by rock climbing standards), solid granite incline is riddled with foot- and hand-holds. The 1½ mi. hike to the dome begins 200 yards east of the Dog Lake parking area.

For views rivaling those of the Valley without the hordes of tourists, head to the much less visited **Hetch Hetchy Reservoir.** John Muir spent many of his later years in an ultimately futile fight to prevent Hetch Hetchy Valley (which was acknowledged to be as stunning as Yosemite Valley) from being turned into a big water trough for San Francisco. Take Rte. 120 west to the Big Oak Flat Entrance, turn right (1 mi.) on Evergreen Rd., and continue for 16 mi. Park by the O'Shaughnessy Dam. The area boasts several idyllic day hikes, but back-country access can be even more stunning. Permits are available one day before or on the day of the hike at the Hetch Hetchy entrance, or make advance reservations for $5 per person (☎372-0740). The **Wapama Falls** trail (2½ mi.) is a fairly easy hike with spectacular views at every turn. The trail continues to **Rancheria** (an additional 4 mi.), a popular place to camp. **Bring bear canisters—the bears here are particularly aggressive.**

**OTHER ACTIVITIES.** The world's best **climbers** come to Yosemite to test themselves at angles past vertical. If you've got the courage, you can join the stellar rock climbers by taking a lesson with the hard-core **Yosemite Mountaineering School** (see p. 256). Classes range from covering the basics to teaching alpine ascents and lead climbing; most are 7 hours long. Reservations are useful and require advance payment, although drop-ins are accepted. (☎372-8344. In Curry Village open daily 8:30am-noon and 1-5pm; in Tuolumne Meadows daily 9am-5pm. Classes in Curry Village begin at 8:30am; 3-6 people $70, individual courses $170. Intermediate lessons on weekends and alternating weekdays $80-90.)

Guided **horseback rides** start at $51 for a 2hr. ride. All-day rides are $94. There are stables at: Yosemite Valley (☎372-8348; open Apr.-Sept. daily 7:30am-5pm); Wawona (☎375-6502; open early summer daily 7:30am-5pm); and Tuolumne Meadows. (☎372-8427. Open June-Sept. daily 7:30am-5pm.)

**Fishing** is allowed from April through November in any of Yosemite's lakes, streams, or rivers, but any park ranger will tell you that your prospects are notoriously bad. Anglers undaunted by the dismal odds may obtain a fishing license from grocery or sporting goods stores in Yosemite Valley, Wawona, Tuolumne, or White Wolf. (Non-resident 10-day license $30, under 16 free. There are also 2 free fishing days per season. Consult the *Fishing in Yosemite National Park* handout for specific guidelines.) Tackle is available at the **Village Sport Shop.** (☎372-1286. Open daily 8:30am-6pm.) Those frustrated with Yosemite's so-called fishing can **bird-watch** instead; the Visitors Center gives out field checklists.

**Rafting** is permitted on the Merced River (10am-4pm) from June to July or when deemed safe, but no motorized crafts are allowed. Rafts can be rented at the Curry Village Recreation Center. For organized rafting trips, **All Outdoors,** 1250 Pine St. #103, Walnut Creek 94596 (☎925-932-8993 or 800-247-2387) leads trips on the north fork of Stanislaus River (leave from Calaveras Big Trees State Park), the Merced River (Mt. View Store, Midpines), the Kaweah River (Kaweah General Store), and Goodwin Canyon (Stanislaus River Park, Sonora). Most full-day trips cost $119 during the week and $144 on weekends. **Swimming** is allowed throughout the park except where signs to the contrary are posted. Those who prefer their water chlorinated can swim in the public pools at Curry Village, Yosemite Lodge, and Wawona. (Open daily 10am-6pm. $2 for non-guests.)

**ORGANIZED ACTIVITIES. Open-air tram tours** (☎372-1240) leave from Curry Village, Ahwahnee Hotel, Yosemite Lodge, and the Village Store. Tickets are available at lodging facilities and the Village Store tour desk. The basic 2hr. **Valley Floor Tour**

points out Half Dome, El Capitan, Bridalveil Falls, and Happy Isles. (Departs daily 10am-3pm on the hour and at 6pm. $20.50, seniors $18.50, ages 5-12 $15.50.) The 4hr. **Glacier Point Tour** climbs 3200 ft. to the point for a view of the valley 7300 ft. below. (Departs daily June-Oct. 8:30, 10am, and 1:30pm from Yosemite Lodge. $29.50, ages 5-12 $16.50). The **Moonlight Tour,** on nights with a full (or nearly full) moon, offers unique nighttime views of the valley (2hr., $20.50).

Park rangers lead a variety of informative hikes and other activities for visitors of all ages. Daily **junior ranger** (ages 7-10) and **senior ranger** (ages 11-13) activities allow children to hike, raft, and explore aquatic and terrestrial life. (Free with the purchase of a cute coloring handbook. Reservations required in advance through the Yosemite Valley Visitors Center, see p. 255.) Rangers also guide a number of free walks. **Discover Yosemite Family Programs** address a variety of historical and geological topics. (3hr.; daily 9am; most wheelchair accessible.) Rangers also lead strenuous, 4-8hr. **Destination Hikes** into the high country from Tuolumne Meadows. Other free, park-sponsored adventures include 2hr. **photographic walks,** which are lessons/adventures led by professional photographers. (Hikes leave Tu, Th, Sa-Su at 9am. Sign up and meet at the Ansel Adams Gallery; see p.266). **Sunrise photo walks** leave most mornings from the Yosemite Lodge tour desk at 6:30am (free). The **Glacier Point Sunset Photo Shoot** is offered Saturday nights from June to September. Bring lots of film; this is an incredible spot, especially at sunset. Late in the day, the Valley's dusky hues become a photographer's dream. The workshop with a professional photographer is free, but the scenic tram ride up to the point is not. (Departs 1hr. before the meeting time and returns 4hr. later; $20.50.) However, you can always drive and meet the group at the Glacier Point Amphitheater.

## WINTERTIME IN YOSEMITE

In Yosemite's quietest season, the cold dramatically transforms the landscape as the waterfalls freeze over and snow masks the meadows. The Sierras are known for heavy winter snowfall; Yosemite is no exception. Unlike most of the mountain range, though, Yosemite Valley remains accessible year-round. **Route 140** from Merced, a designated all-weather entrance, is usually open and clear. Although Tioga Pass and Glacier Point Rd. invariably close at the first sign of snowfall, **Route 41** from the south and **Route 120** from the west typically remain traversable. Verify road conditions before traveling (☎372-0200) and carry chains. Many valley facilities remain open even during the harshest winters. Camping is generally permitted in Lower Pines, Camp 4, Hodgdon Meadow, and Wawona; most indoor accommodations offer big reductions (with the notable exception of the Ahwahnee). Park tours move "indoors" to heated buses; even the Merced and Fresno buses (see **Transportation,** p. 253) operate, road conditions permitting. Although Yosemite may lose some of its celebrity appeal in the winter, the crowds clear out and the visitor's experience is guaranteed to be more personal and serene.

Several well-marked trails for **cross-country skiing** and **snowshoeing** cut into the backcountry of the valley's South Rim at Badger Pass and Crane Flat. Rangers host several snowshoe walks from mid-December through March, but the hushed winter forests are perhaps best explored without guidance. Snowshoes and cross-country skis can be rented from the **Yosemite Mountaineering School** (see p. 256). **Badger Pass Rental Shop** (see below) also rents winter equipment and downhill skis. Backcountry skiers can stay at Ostrander Ski Hut, 9 mi. south of Badger Pass, or Glacier Point Hut, at the end of Glacier Point Rd. Both provide heated accommodations and meals and require reservations. Guided cross-country skiing trips (☎327-8444) with meals and accommodations at the huts are also available.

The state's oldest ski resort, **Badger Pass Ski Area,** on Glacier Point Rd. south of Yosemite Valley, is the only downhill ski area in the park. The resort's powder may not rival Lake Tahoe's (see p. 244), but its family-fun atmosphere fosters learning and various lessons and package deals are available. Free shuttles connect Badger Pass with Yosemite Valley. (☎372-8430. Lifts open 9am-4:30pm. Group ski lessons $22 per 2hr., private lessons from $44. Rental packages $18 per day, under 12 $13. One-day lift tickets M-F $22, under 12 $13; Sa-Su $28/$13.)

**Ice skating** at Curry Village is a beautiful (if cold) experience, with Half Dome towering above a groomed outdoor rink encircled by snow-covered pines. (☎372-8319. Open in winter M-F noon-9:30pm, Sa-Su 8:30am-9:30pm. $5; skate rental $2.) **Sledding** and **tobogganing** are permitted at Crane Flat, off Rte. 120.

---

**THE NATURALIST** When **John Muir** was 29, a piece of metal struck his eye in the industrial shop where he worked as an inventor. The accident left Muir blind, and the month that he struggled with his condition became a time of profound personal epiphany. Muir's blindness left him with an expanded sense of vision; he vowed that if he ever recovered his sight, he would use it to observe nature's beauty. And recover it he did. In subsequent years, Muir later claimed, "I wandered afoot and alone" with no concern as "to which one of the world's wildernesses I first should [come upon]." In 1868, Muir's travels led to Yosemite, and he formed a life-long bond to the Valley. Partly because of his advocacy, Congress created Yosemite National Park in 1890. Years later, Muir's writing caught the eye of President Theodore Roosevelt, who visited the naturalist in Yosemite. Often called the "Father of our National Park System," Muir was one of the nation's first and most influential conservationists.

---

## BEYOND YOSEMITE VALLEY: THE BACKCOUNTRY

Most folks moseying through Yosemite never leave the Valley, but a wilder, more isolated Yosemite awaits those who do. The Wilderness Center in Yosemite Valley offers maps and personalized assistance for such adventurers. (For advice on keeping yourself and the wilderness intact, see **Wilderness Safety,** p. 43.) Topographical maps (most around $8) and hiking guides are especially helpful in navigating Yosemite's nether regions. Equipment can be rented or purchased at the Mountaineering School at Tuolumne Meadows (see p.256) or at the Mountain Shop at Curry Village, but backpacking stores in major cities are less expensive.

Backcountry camping is prohibited in the Valley (those caught face a $60 fine and park eviction), but is generally permitted along the high country trails with a free wilderness permit (see p. 256); each trailhead has a limited number of permits. The five wildly popular **High Sierra Camps** (situated between 5¾ and 10 mi. from each other) allow multi-day hikers to take a break from backcountry camping and sleep on mattresses, eat real food, and take showers. Request a lottery application by calling ☎559-252-4848, but do so far in advance. There is a 40% quota held on 24hr. notice at the Yosemite Valley Visitors Center, the Wawona Ranger Station, and Big Oak Flat Station (see **Visitor Information,** p. 255). Popular trails like Little Yosemite Valley, Clouds Rest, and Half Dome fill quickly. (Permits free; reservations $5. Call ☎372-0740 or write Wilderness Permits, P.O. Box 545, Yosemite National Park 95389.) In the high country, many hikers stay at undeveloped mountain campgrounds, which offer a few bear lockers. Hikers can also store food in hanging bear bags (see **Bears Will Eat You,** p.44) or in rented plastic canisters from the Yosemite Valley Sports Shop ($5 per day). **Canisters** are highly recommended and mandatory in some areas—bear-bagging is considered more of a delay tactic.

With over 800 mi. of trails, backcountry hiking opportunities are virtually limitless. Many of the most popular trails start from Happy Isles Nature Center in the Valley and Tuolumne Meadows. Heading off from the Nature Center is the extraordinary 211 mi. **John Muir Trail,** which connects with the **Pacific Crest Trail** at Tuolumne Meadows and then heads south to Kings Canyon and Sequoia National Park and the highest peak in the lower 48 states, Mt. Whitney (elev. 14,494 ft.). Making a go at any portion of this trail, including the 27 mi. journey to Tuolumne Meadows from the Valley, makes for an unforgettable experience. Traversing the entire trail takes anywhere from three weeks to a few months.

## 👁 🎧 SIGHTS & ENTERTAINMENT

Rangers lead different, usually free activities, from nature walks to historical presentations to star-gazing, every day at nearly every park village. Check *Yosemite Today* or local bulletin boards and ranger stations for schedules and information.

The **Ansel Adams Gallery,** next to the Visitors Center, is a gift shop and activity center featuring work by famous wilderness photographers and artists including, of course, the man himself. Sign up for a fine-print viewing to see the precious stuff—you'll most likely be shown around with a group of people, but occasionally the staff will give private showings. The gallery offers free camera walks three times a week at 9am from the village. (☎372-4413; www.anseladams.com. Open daily 9am-6pm; in winter 9am-5pm.) The **Art Activity Center,** in Yosemite Village next to the store, takes pride in its artist-in-residence program and offers an art instruction class. Classes offer different types of art, from watercolor to sketching to acrylic. (☎372-1442. Open daily 9:30am-4:30pm. Class offered daily 10am-2pm. Advance signup recommended. Supplies are not included, but are for sale.)

Just behind the gallery, Native American cultural events take place in the **Miwok-Paiute Village,** a collection of Native American sweatlodges, roundhouses, *umachas* (homes), placards describing indigenous fauna, and a diorama that recycles hokey narration when you press the red button. The large *Hangie* (roundhouse) is a humbling piece of construction still serving as a cultural center for local Miwok and Paiute Indians (village open dusk to dawn). Further information can be garnered at the **Yosemite Village Museum,** next to the Visitors Center. Inside is a reconstruction of Ahwahnee village life, Indian craft demonstrations, and a display of the park's enormous art collection, including watertight woven baskets and amazing headdresses. (Open daily 9am-4:30pm.) Pick up the guide at the Visitors Center and tour the resting places of Native Americans and whites who played important roles in the park's formation at the **Yosemite Cemetery,** across from the museum.

In 1903, John Muir gave President Theodore Roosevelt a now-famous tour of Yosemite. Thespian Lee Stetson has assumed Muir's role, leading 1hr. hikes along the same route (free). Stetson also presents one-man shows such as **The Spirit of John Muir, Conversation with a Tramp,** and **Wild Stories with John Muir.** Stetson has recently begun a new show reenacting the encounter between Muir and Roosevelt entitled **The Tramp and the Roughrider.** There are six different theatrical presentations, changing from year to year. (Shows play 3 times per week at 8pm, usually M, W, F. $7.50, children $3.25.)

## STANISLAUS NATIONAL FOREST  ☎ 209

Occupied first by the Miwok Indians and then overrun with gold prospectors over a century ago, Stanislaus has since quieted down, somewhat overshadowed by its celebrity southeastern neighbor, Yosemite. The park's varied landscape, from golden hills and raging rapids to crystalline alpine lakes and dense forests, remains relatively pristine. The 900,000 acres of central Sierra forest, including nearly 200,000 acres of untrammeled wilderness, teems with trails and recreational opportunities. The park is organized into four ranger districts: Calaveras, Groveland, Miwok, and Summit. It also encompasses parts of the Carson-Iceberg, Emigrant, and Mokelumne federal wilderness areas.

Maps, brochures, permits, and advice can be found at **Park Headquarters,** 19777 Greenly Rd., across from the county library in Sonora. (☎ 532-3671. Open M-F 8am-4:30pm.) Permits are required for overnight trips into the wilderness areas and for building campfires outside of developed campsites. Dispersed camping (camping outside of developed campgrounds) is permitted throughout most of Stanislaus and requires no permit or fee. The exception is recreation areas like Pinecrest and Alpine Lake and wilderness areas, which require permits. One or two campsites in each district accept reservations, but the vast majority are first-come, first-camp.

**SUMMIT DISTRICT.** Encompassing large sections of the Emigrant Wilderness, the family-friendly Pinecrest Recreation Area, a number of glacial lakes, and sub-alpine meadows, the Summit Ranger District serves as both an entry point into the backcountry and a venue for less remote fishing, camping, biking, and nordic skiing. The **ranger station,** 1 Pinecrest Lake Rd., off Rte. 108 at Pinecrest Lake, has info on all the camping and recreational activities in the area. (☎ 965-3434. Open daily 8am-5pm; in winter M-Sa 8am-4:30pm.) The district hosts 25 campgrounds, most at 6000-7000 ft. elevations. Campsites abound to the east along Rte. 108 (free-$17). **Cascade Creek ❶,** 6000 ft., 11 mi. from Pinecrest, and **Niagara Creek ❶,** 6600 ft., 17 mi. from Pinecrest on Eagle Meadow Rd., both have beautiful, forested sites (14 and 10 sites respectively, $6) with fire rings and vault toilets, but no running water. **Pinecrest ❷,** the largest campsite in the district, is right next to the Pinecrest Recreation Area, offering swimming, fishing, boating, and hiking. The 200 campsites have drinking water and flush toilets and require a reservation. (Reservations ☎ 877-444-6777, TDD 877-833-6777. Open May-Oct. Sites $19.) The only free campground is **Beardsley Dam ❶,** 3400 ft., on the Beardsley Reservoir, 7½ mi. off Rte. 108 on Beardsley Rd., with 26 sites. **Herring Creek ❶,** 7350 ft., with seven sites, and **Herring Reservoir ❷,** 7350 ft., with 42 sites, both on Herring Creek Rd. off Rte. 108, only request a donation, however, so pick your price. All sites are open May-Oct.

**Pinecrest Lake,** about 30 mi. east of Sonora on Rte. 108, is popular with families. The alpine lake, set amid granite mountains and pine trees, serves as a small resort area, offering a swimming area, fishing pier (and rainbow trout stocking), picnic sites, and a 4 mi. hiking trail around the lake. **Boat rentals** are available at the marina. (☎ 965-3333. Kayaks $7 per hr.; paddleboats $10 per hr.; motorboats $30 per 2hr.; party boats $175 per half-day.) Every June, the lake hosts a **fishing celebration** (☎ 532-3671) that includes a fishing and casting contest and a free lunch (yes, there is such a thing, but it's hot dogs, not fish).

**Route 108** is a 60 mi. drive northeast through the forest, starting in Sonora and ending at the Sonora Pass on the border of the Toiyabe National Forest. The drive itself is quite scenic and rich in history. Pick up an audio cassette tour at the ranger station to play in your car as you make the trip. There are also many day hikes to chose from in the area, all between 1 and 4 mi. long and ranging in difficulty from quite easy to moderate. A few of them, such as the **Trail of the Gargoyles** (3 mi.), which is lined with twisted geological formations, and the **Trail of the Ancient Dwarfs** (2½ mi.), which follows a line of natural bonsai trees, can be supplemented with guides from the ranger station that point out items of geological and botanical interest. Many backcountry hikes into the Emigrant and Carson-Iceberg Wildernesses start along Rte. 108; obtain a wilderness permit, topographical maps, and more information at the ranger station. For stunning views of the **Stanislaus River** and its dammed reservoir, take Rte. 108 18 mi. east of Pinecrest to **Donnell Vista.** The popular and excellent **Gooseberry-Crabtree Trail** is a 15 mi. gravel and dirt road **mountain biking** loop that makes a difficult 2000 ft. ascent but rewards the tenacious biker with awesome vistas.

**CARSON-ICEBERG WILDERNESS.** Occupying the northeast corner of the park and bordered to the north by Rte. 108, to the south by Rte. 4, and to the east by Rte. 395, Carson-Iceberg is 160,000 acres of volcanic peaks, granite canyons, sinuous

**SIERRA NEVADA**

creeks, and pure solitude. While the high elevations, steep terrain, and scarce lakes eliminate this region from most itineraries, adventurous travelers are rewarded with the unspoiled wilderness terrain all to themselves. What lakes the area does have are heavily visited, especially **Sword Lake** and **Lost Lake.** Major trailheads are Wheat's Meadow and County Line in the Summit Ranger District and Silver Valley and Stanislaus Meadow in the Calaveras Ranger District. Stanislaus Peak and Sonora Peak are accessible from the Pacific Crest Trail (for more info, see **From Crest to Crest: the Trail of the West,** p. 235), and give persevering climbers a humbling panorama of the Sierra. The Pacific Coast Trail includes a 5 mi. roundtrip cross-country scramble from **Saint Mary's Pass,** 1 mi. before **Sonora Pass** on Rte. 108. It has a great view of the Central Valley, but the 3000 ft. climb is tiring. All mechanized vehicles (including bicycles) are prohibited in the wilderness.

**CALAVERAS DISTRICT.** In the northwest corner of the forest, the Calaveras Ranger District is blessed with some quieter lakes, high-elevation hikes, the best rock climbing around, and the raging North Fork Stanislaus River. The **ranger station,** 5341 Rte. 4, at Hathaway Pines, contains the Dardanelles, a series of volcanic by-products. (☎ 795-1381. Open M-F 8am-5pm, Sa 8:30am-2pm; in winter M-F 8am-4:30pm, Sa 9am-1pm.) **Wa Ku Luu Hep Yoo Campground ❶,** on Boardscrossing-Sourgrass Rd. off Rte. 4 in Dorrington, is shady and cool and has water, flush toilets, and hot showers at its 49 sites as well as commercial rafting opportunities. The camp is on the site of an ancient Miwok village and features a number of preserved artifacts. (Open June-Oct. Sites $13.) Daredevil **rock climbing** and more bouldering opportunities abound here. Box Canyon offers 70-100 ft. technical climbs (rated moderately at 5.5-5.9). Park half a mile east of the Bear Valley junction with Rte. 4. More challenging climbs can be found at Spicer Road Crags and Spicer Terraces, both along Spicer Reservoir Rd. Guided expeditions are available through **Mountain Adventure Seminars** (☎ 753-6556 or 800-36-CLIMB/25462).

**GROVELAND DISTRICT.** Covering the area south of Sonora and west of Yosemite, Groveland District is best known for its lakeside recreation and its run of the Tuolumne Wild and Scenic River. The **Ranger Station,** 24545 Rte. 120, is 9 mi. west of Groveland. (☎ 962-7825. Open daily 8am-5:30pm; in winter 8am-4:30pm; Apr.-May Su-F 8am-5:30pm.) **The Pines ❶,** 3200 ft., 9 mi. west of Groveland on Rte. 120, is the closest campground to the entrance. The 12 sites have piped water and vault toilets. (Open year-round. Sites $10.) **Cherry Lake Campground ❶,** 4700 ft., 20 mi. down Cherry Lake Rd. off Rte. 4, has 46 sites, water, and access to boating and fishing on Cherry Lake. (Open Apr.-Oct. Sites $12.) **Cherry Valley,** a bit scarred from a fire, is half a mile north of Cherry Lake, just west of Yosemite. The stark glacier-carved canyon has space for hikers. A bridge crossing the South Fork Tuolumne on Rte. 120 marks the site of the popular swimming **Rainbow Pool,** a resort that burned down in the 1950s. Short hikes criss-cross the area but the only extended hikes are in the mountainous Emigrant Wilderness, an area marked by alpine meadows and rocky hills. A trailhead at **Eagle Meadow** leads down to Coopers Meadow and **Three Chimneys,** a brick-red volcanic formation.

# SIERRA NATIONAL FOREST ☎ 559

Spanning the foothills of the San Joaquin Valley to the sheer walls of the High Sierras, the 1.3 million acres of the Sierra National Forest are characterized by steep gorges, glacial lakes, and endless conifers. Nearly half of the forest is federally designated wilderness that offers sweet solitude, while the region's crowded rivers and lakes serve as recreational centers, primarily for fishing enthusiasts. Information on popular activities and the 60 campgrounds in the

SIERRA NEVADA

forest can be obtained at the **Sierra National Forest Supervisor's Office,** 1600 Toll-house Rd., off Rte. 168 just outside the gateway town of Clovis. (☎297-0706. Open M-F 8am-4:30pm.)

A **backcountry permit** is required for overnight stays in all of the designated wilderness areas (Ansel Adams, Dinkey Lakes, John Muir, Kaiser, and Monarch), which constitute 46% of the forest. Obtain permits for the Ansel Wilderness by writing the Mariposa/Minarets Ranger District and permits for the John Muir and Kaiser Wilderness areas by writing the Pineridge/Kings River District (for addresses, see below). Trailhead quotas are in effect from May 1 to November 1. Forty percent of the permits are offered daily first-come, first-served, but these quotas fill quickly. It is also possible to write away for an advance reservation. ($5 per person. Mail requests should be sent 20 days in advance.)

**NORTHWESTERN MARIPOSA DISTRICT.** Information on the northwestern Mariposa District can be obtained by calling or writing the **Mariposa/Minarets Ranger District Office,** 57003 Rd. 225, North Fork, P.O. Box 10 93643. (☎877-2218. Open M-F 8am-4:30pm.) In summer, parched San Joaquin Valley residents crowd **Bass Lake,** taking advantage of fishing, boating, and waterskiing opportunities. The lake's marinas bustle with activity in the summer and the lake is well-stocked with salmon, catfish, trout, crappie, bluegill, and bass. To join the water fun, rent equipment from **Miller's Landing,** 37976 Rd. 222. (☎642-3633; www.millerslanding.com. Canoes $5 per hr., jet-skis $85 per hr., patio boats $180 per 5hr.) **Lupine** and **Cedar Bluff Campgrounds ❷** are right on the lake and stay open year-round for strong-willed ice fishers or wintertime Yosemite patrons. Between the two, there are 113 sites, all with flush toilets and water. (Sites $16.) Some of the best **hikes** in the Sierra are also nearby. Off Sky Ranch Rd. from Rte. 41, **Nelder Grove** is a large tract of pine, fir, incense cedar, and 106 seldom-visited giant sequoias. The grove also contains a campground once used for thousands of years by the Southern Sierra Miwok Indians. Another trail winds to the **Bull Buck Tree,** a 246 ft. giant that is even more impressive without the crowds of gaping tourists common in other parts of the Sierra. The more challenging **Willow Creek Trail** passes both Angel Falls and the aptly named **Devil's Slide Waterfall** en route to McLeod Flat Rd.; the meandering **Mono Trail** is another option. Take Rte. 41 to the Bass Lake turn-off and follow Rd. 222 about 4 mi. to the parking lot at the trailhead.

**KINGS RIVER DISTRICT.** The far reaches of the Kings River District rise to 13,000 ft. at the Sierra Crest. Most of the region's activity centers around the Dinkey Creek area and the Pine Flat Reservoir. The **Kings River Trail,** beginning at the end of Garnet Dike Rd. on the north side of Kings River, is the most popular in the area, winding through the tranquil wilderness. The 269 ft. **Boole Tree,** at the end of Converse Basin Rd., 5 mi. past Grant Grove off Rte. 180, is the largest giant sequoia outside of the national parks system. Four free **camping** sites, located along Kings River, are open during the summer. **Whitewater rafting** on the Kings River is popular, especially in spring when melting snow raises the water levels. **Kings River Expeditions** offers a variety of guided trips; get a group together to reduce costs. (☎233-4889. Open M-F 8am-5pm.) Trail bikes and 4WD vehicles raise dust on five off-highway routes that provide access to camping and fishing.

**PINERIDGE DISTRICT.** Easily accessible from Rte. 168, the Pineridge District is the forest's most popular region due to its wealth of opportunities for swimming, boating, biking, rafting, fishing, hiking, and camping. **Camp Edison ❷** is a centrally located private campground that has its own marina, convenience store, trout farm, and lake access. (☎841-3134. 252 well-spaced sites with electric hookup, flush toilets, showers, tables, and fire pits. Sites from $22.) The **Pineridge/Kings River Ranger District Office**, 29688 Auberry Rd. in Prather, is one of the forest's busiest centers. The office gives weekly ranger talks and guided hikes followed by marshmallow roasts—call for details. (☎855-5360. Open daily 8am-4:30pm.)

**HUNTINGTON LAKE.** Just one reservoir in the Big Creek Hydroelectric system developed by Southern California Edison, Huntington Lake, 21 mi. farther east along Rte. 168, is known for its excellent boating and summertime regattas, windsurfing, waterskiing, and fishing. The lake's two marinas turn blue and white with sailboats in the summer. The best hiking from the lake ventures into the Kaiser and Dinkey Lakes Wilderness Areas. Seven **campgrounds ❶** cluster around the lake ($16); register at the **Eastwood Visitor Center** at the junction of Rte. 168 and Kaiser Pass Rd. Past Kaiser Pass, the road becomes narrow and slightly treacherous—honk your horn on the sharp turns to announce your presence. The terrain at the end of this road is definitively High Sierra—alpine lakes, green crowds of conifers, craggy summits, and crisp mountain air. Mountain bikers can speed down dozens of trails from the leisurely Tamarack Trail to the 66 mi. Dusy/Ershin Rd.

# SEQUOIA & KINGS CANYON
# NATIONAL PARKS                                     ☎ 559

Protected from deforestation nearly as soon as it was discovered by European Americans, Sequoia National Park, which was expanded in the 1940s to include Kings Canyon to the north, is the nation's second oldest national park, after Yellowstone. Though they cover only a small portion of the parks, the most popular attractions are the groves of giant sequoia, the earth's most massive living things. The largest specimen of giant sequoia, the General Sherman tree, weighs over 2.7 million pounds and has a base circumference of over 100 feet. In that same small grove stand four of the world's five largest trees, each about as old as Western civilization. The parks themselves stretch north-south along the middle elevations of the Sierra Nevada, through an abundance of meadows and braided creeks. In addition to the sequoias, the parks contain the 6000 ft. Kern Canyon and Kings Canyon, the deepest in North America, carved out by the deep blue rapids and falls of Kings Creek. Most of these sights can be reached by car or by short walking expeditions, but the majority of the parks' lands are completely undeveloped, its gorges and wild rivers attracting serious hikers and backpackers to its 800 miles of backcountry trails.

| **AT A GLANCE** | |
|---|---|
| **AREA:** 864,411 acres. | **GATEWAYS:** Fresno (p. 316), Visalia, Three Rivers. |
| **CLIMATE:** Temperate redwood forests. | |
| **FEATURES:** General Sherman Tree, Moro Rock, Grizzly Falls. | **CAMPING:** Some campgrounds take reservations. |
| **HIGHLIGHTS:** Drive through Tunnel Log, spelunk in the Crystal Cave, hike through Redwood Mountain Grove. | **FEES & RESERVATIONS:** Entrance fee for 7 days for those on foot, bike, or motorcycle $5. $10 7-day entrance fee per vehicle. Annual pass $20. |

SIERRA NEVADA

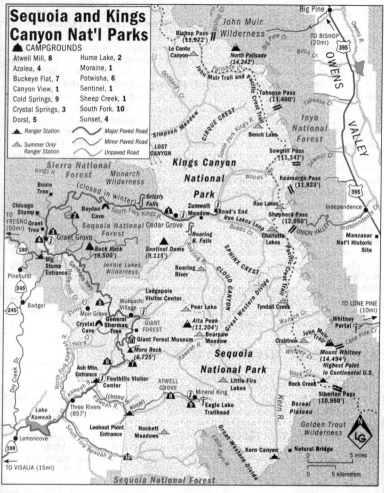

**Sequoia and Kings Canyon Nat'l Parks**

▲ CAMPGROUNDS

| | |
|---|---|
| Atwell Mill, **8** | Hume Lake, **2** |
| Azalea, **4** | Moraine, **1** |
| Buckeye Flat, **7** | Potwisha, **6** |
| Canyon View, **1** | Sentinel, **1** |
| Cold Springs, **9** | Sheep Creek, **1** |
| Crystal Springs, **3** | South Fork, **10** |
| Dorst, **5** | Sunset, **4** |

▲ Ranger Station     Major Paved Road
▲ Summer Only Ranger Station    Minor Paved Road
     Unpaved Road

## ORIENTATION

The parks' most popular sights are concentrated in four areas: **Giant Forest** and **Mineral King** in Sequoia, and **Grant Grove** and **Cedar Grove** in Kings Canyon. Pristine backcountry comprises the eastern two-thirds of Sequoia and the northern two-thirds of Kings Canyon. Seasonal changes are dramatic in this part of the Sierra. Anything beyond the frontcountry of Generals Highway is accessible only during the summer, as snow lasts throughout the year on some peaks. Dogwood, aspen, and oak display brilliant colors in the fall. Snow season is from November to March, and, although trails are open year round, they may have snow as late as mid-June. Spring here is unpredictable, bringing late storms, low fog, and runoff flooding as well as falling rock.

SIERRA NEVADA

By car, the two parks can only be accessed from the west. From **Fresno**, Rte. 180 runs east 60 mi. to Kings Canyon's **Grant Grove** entrance and terminates 30 mi. later in **Cedar Grove** at the mouth of the Canyon itself. Rte. 180 is typically closed from late October to late April due to the threat of winter storms and falling rocks, and one can only get as far as the Hume Lake turn-off. From **Visalia**, Rte. 198 winds its way past Lake Kaweah to Sequoia's Ash Mountain entrance, where it becomes the **Generals Highway,** named for its route between the General Grant and General Sherman trees. An especially serpentine and sometimes unpredictable speedway, Rte. 198 climbs through 2000 vertical feet of hairpin turns. Drivers should exercise special caution and switching into a low gear on downhill grades is recommended. The drive from Ash Mountain through Sequoia's Giant Forest to Grant Grove takes about 2hr. The road is usually open from mid-May to October, permitting entrance deeper into the forest. During the winter, entry points to Grant Grove and Giant Forest, and the Generals Highway connecting the two, are kept open except when the weather makes for hazardous conditions. Tire chains may be required. The **Mineral King** turn-off branches from Rte. 198 just before the main entrance into the park. This drive is accented by high-country panoramas, but drivers should beware of looking away from the road—the five unpaved miles and endless switchbacks make it difficult to steer straight. No gas is officially sold in the park, so be sure to fill up before entering. In a pinch, Hume Lake and Kings Canyon Lodge, in Sequoia National Forest (see p. 279), northwest of the park, sell gas at a premium. The only park access from the east is by trail; enter either park from the **John Muir Wilderness** and **Inyo National Forest,** both accessible from spur roads off US 395. One of the most popular trails begins in Onion Valley and enters the park over Kearsarge Pass. Hikers venturing in from the east should secure backcountry permits in advance.

## 🛈 PRACTICAL INFORMATION

Camping supplies, amenities, gas, and groceries in the parks are no-frills but expensive. The **San Joaquin Valley** (see p. 304), **Three Rivers** (8 mi. southwest on Rte. 198), and **Visalia** (25 mi. southwest on Rte. 198) offer a better selection of supplies.

> **WHEN TO GO.** Just like other areas of the Sierra Nevada, the parks are overrun with tourists in the summer. Nonetheless, this is the best time for hikes and water activities, since winter and spring weather are unreliable and can quite frigid. The roads are often smothered with more than 15 ft. of snow in the winter, making tire chains a necessity.

### SEQUOIA

**Visitor Information: Foothills Visitors Center** (☎565-3341), at the park headquarters. Open daily 8am-5pm; in winter 8am-4:30pm. **Lodgepole Visitors Center** (☎565-4436), on Generals Hwy. 4 mi. east of Giant Forest. Open daily May-Sept. 8am-6pm; Oct.-Apr. 9am-4:30pm. Wilderness permits available 7am-4pm in summer; self-register in winter. **Mineral King Ranger Station** (☎565-3764), 1 mi. before the end of Mineral King Rd. The headquarters for the remote Mineral King region offer maps, hiking info, books, first aid, and wilderness permits. Open May-Sept. daily 7am-4:30pm.

**Gas:** The nearest reasonable option is in Three Rivers, Hume Lake, or Kings Canyon Lodge, a 15min. drive from Grant Grove in Kings Canyon. Prices are exorbitant.

**Auto Repair: AAA Emergency Road Service** (☎800-400-4222).

**Markets: Lodgepole's** market is well stocked with food and outdoor supplies at reasonable prices. (Open daily Oct.-Apr. 9am-4:30pm; May 9am-6pm; June-Sept. 8am-8pm.) Two stores in Three Rivers, **Village Market** (open M-Sa 8am-8pm, Su 9am-6pm) and **Three Rivers Market** (open daily 7:30am-8pm), offer better selections on food and gear. **Silver City Resort** (☎ 561-3223) in Mineral King carries some supplies. Fresno and Visalia are larger Central Valley cities near the parks, both with abundant supplies.

**Showers:** Opposite the Lodgepole Visitors Center. $2. Open daily May-Sept. 8am-1pm and 3-7:45pm; Oct.-Apr. 9am-1pm and 3-5:45pm.

**Laundromat:** In the Lodgepole Market Center. Wash $1.25; dry 50¢ per 10min. Open daily Oct.-Apr. 9am-4:30pm; May 9am-6pm; June-Sept. 8am-8pm. Last load half an hour before closing.

**Medical Services: Kaweah Delta Hospital** (☎ 624-2000), off Rte. 198, in Visalia.

**Post Office:** At Lodgepole. Open M-F 8:30am-1pm and 1:30-4pm. 24hr. stamp machine in lobby. General delivery mail to: Sequoia National Park, CA. **Postal Code:** 93262.

# KINGS CANYON

**Visitor Information:** In addition to providing info, the following Visitors Centers sell self-guided tours. Different crowd-pleasing tours include Congress Trail, Mineral King, General Grant Tree and Trail, and the Zumwalt Meadow Trail. Walks, talks, and slide shows at Grant and Cedar Groves take place daily during the summer and on winter weekends.

**Grant Grove Visitors Center** (☎ 565-4307), Grant Grove Village, 2 mi. east of the Big Stump entrance by Rte. 180. Books, maps, local wilderness permits and exhibits. Nightly campfire programs and daily hikes. Open daily 8am-5pm; in winter 8am-4:30pm.

**Cedar Grove Ranger Station** (☎ 565-3793), 30 mi. farther down Rte. 180 by Kings River. Near trailheads into Kings Canyon high country, half a mile south of Cedar Grove Village. Books, maps, and first aid. Open mid-June to Sept. 6 daily 9am-5pm; in fall Su and Sa 9am-5pm.

**Road's End Kiosk** (info ☎ 565-3791), 6 mi. east of Cedar Grove Village. Issues wilderness permits and sells maps and bear canisters. Open daily 7:30am-3pm; in winter, self-register.

**Gas:** The nearest options are both along Rte. 180: **Hume Lake Christian Camp** (☎ 335-2000), 10 mi. east of Grant Grove, and **Kings Canyon Lodge** (☎ 335-2405), 13 mi. east of Grant Grove. More reasonable prices can be found down at Three Rivers, south of the park on Rte. 198. Only emergency gas is available at Grant Grove Market.

**Auto Repair:** Attendants at Grant Grove (☎ 335-5500) can handle minor repairs and lockouts. For major repairs or service outside the Grant Grove area, call **Michael's** (☎ 638-4101), in Reedley. **AAA Emergency Road Service** (☎ 800-400-4222).

**ATM:** At Grant Grove Market and Cedar Grove Market. $2 surcharge.

**Markets: Grant Grove Market, Cedar Grove Market,** and the **Hume Lake General Store** carry a limited selection of camping basics and groceries. Grant Grove Market open daily 8am-9pm. Cedar Grove Market open daily 7am-9pm. Hume Lake General Store open Su-F 8am-7pm, Sa 8am-10pm.

**Showers: Cedar Grove Village,** $3 per person, towel $1. Open daily 8am-7pm. **Grant Grove Village,** $3 per person, towel $1. Open daily 11am-4pm.

**Laundromat:** Cedar Grove Village. Wash $1; dry 25¢ per 15min. Open daily 8am-7pm.

**Medical Services: Fresno Community Hospital** (☎ 459-6000), at Fresno and R St.

**Post Office: Grant Grove Village** (☎ 335-2499), near the Visitors Center. Hours vary widely, but generally M-F 9am-3:30pm; Sa 9am-12:30pm. A stamp machine and mailbox are next to the Visitors Center. General delivery to: Kings Canyon National Park, CA. **Hume Lake,** at the Hume Lake Christian Camp. Open June-Oct. M-F 9am-4:30pm, Sa 9:30am-2pm. **Postal Code:** 93633 (Grant Grove), 93628 (Hume Lake).

SIERRA NEVADA

## ⚠ CAMPING

Although campgrounds fill quickly, a few spots should still be available on most non-holiday weekends. Only **Lodgepole** in Sequoia fills regularly, partly because of its proximity to Giant Forest Village and partly because it's one of only two campgrounds in either park that accepts summer reservations (the other is **Dorst**). Both Lodgepole and Dorst prefer it when campers reserve ahead, even if unreserved sites are available. (☎ 800-365-2267; http://reservations.nps.gov. Both campgrounds open 4am-4pm.) Most campgrounds are open from mid-May to October, with a 14-night maximum stay during the summer and one month total per year. There are no RV hookups in the parks, but dump stations are available at Potwisha, Lodgepole, Dorst, and Princess. Contact a ranger station for more info. **Backcountry camping** is free with the requisite permit (see **Practical Information,** p. 272). Black bears, though usually not aggressive toward humans, are common in both parks. In developed campsites, all odorous, edible items should be locked away in bear boxes provided at the site. Backcountry campers can rent a bear canister at visitors centers. For more information, see **Bears Will Eat You,** p. 44.

### SEQUOIA

▨ **Buckeye Flat,** 2800 ft., past park headquarters, a few mi. from the Ash Mountain entrance on Rte. 198. All 28 sites are spacious and lie in a grove of low, shady buckeye trees and stark rock outcroppings. Great views of the mountains above; great swimming in the sparkling water below. Closed to RVs. Flush toilets, drinking water. Sites $18. ❷

**Potishwa,** 2100 ft., is a full-service campground nearby with 42 well-spaced sites where RVs are welcome. No RV hookups, but dump stations available. Good swimming across the street. Flush toilets, drinking water. Sites $18. ❷

**Atwell Mill,** 6650 ft., **and Cold Springs,** 7500 ft., 20 mi. along Mineral King Rd. in the Mineral King area. Two secluded sites a mile apart. Pit toilets, piped water, and picnic tables for the 61 tent sites overlooking a stream. Steep, winding roads and a ban on trailers keep the RVs away. Store, restaurant, showers, and phones are 2-3 mi. away in Silver City. Marmots have been causing trouble; check ranger postings to see if the area is secure. Open May 31-Oct. Sites $12. ❶

**South Fork,** 3600 ft., on South Fork Rd., 13 mi. from Rte. 198. Ten sites near the ranger station, a river, and some backcountry roads. Vault toilets, no drinking water. Not recommended for trailers or RVs. Sites $12. ❶

**Dorst,** 6800 ft., 12 mi. north of Giant Forest and 8 mi. north of Lodgepole. Huge campground of over 200 sites convenient to Sequoia attractions. The wide paved road and woodchip paths wind through gentle hills, a small stream, and enormous pines. Because of its choice location, be sure to reserve a spot (☎ 800-365-2267). Dump station and pay phone. Closed in winter. Sites $20. ❷

### KINGS CANYON

▨ **Sunset, Azalea,** and **Crystal Springs,** 6500 ft., are within a stone's throw of Grant Grove Village (and all its services) but remain quiet. Sunset (200 sites) features gentle wooded hills and brilliant views of the San Joaquin Valley but is often closed unless other sites start to overflow. Azalea (113 sites), open year-round (free in winter), is well-forested and often calm but packed with RVs during busy weekends. Crystal Springs (62 sites) is the smallest and most remote. Like Sunset, it is also frequently closed. All offer flush toilets, water, and privacy. Azalea has a dump station. Sites $18. ❶

**Sheep Creek, Sentinel, Canyon View,** and **Moraine,** 4600 ft., on Rte. 180 at Kings River near Cedar Grove, 32 mi. east of Grant Grove. Store, food, laundry, and showers nearby. Within a few mi. of Road's End and Kings Canyon trailheads. All are well-forested and near Kings Creek. Sheep Creek (111 sites) has more secluded tent sites in the back of the campground. Sentinel's 82 sites are flatter and near the Cedar Grove Amphitheater. Moraine, with its canyon vistas, serves primarily as overflow and opens only on the busiest weekends. All have flush toilets, water, and dump stations. Access roads and campgrounds usually closed Oct.-May. Canyon View accepts reservations from groups. Sites $18. ❶

## █ OTHER ACCOMMODATIONS

For those who just want a roof over their heads, motels with all the creature comforts can be found in the outlying towns. Within the parks, the lodges are the cheapest option. When traveling in a group, look for hotels with suites or cabins, which usually work out to be significantly less per person than doubles. The **Kings Canyon Park Service** (☎335-5500; P.O. Box 909, Kings Canyon National Park 93633) is in charge of accommodations and reservations in the park. **Grant Grove Lodge and John Muir Lodge ❸** (☎335-5500; www.sequoia-kingscanyon.com), in Grant Grove Village, has wooden structures with canvas tops, no electricity, and communal baths (from $45), rustic wooden cabins with or without electricity ($55 or $60), and cabins with private bath and electricity (from $100). The cheapest accommodations hover at higher rates at the **Cedar Grove Lodge ❺** in Cedar Grove Village. (☎565-0100, reservations 335-5500. Rooms $99; $110 with a kitchenette and patio.)

Outside the park, small spots can be a better value but are still pricey. Motels and lodges abound in **Three Rivers,** 6 mi. west of the park on Rte. 198. **Visalia,** 30 mi. southwest of the park on Rte. 198, is home to standard motels and a few finds.

▧ **The Sierra Lodge,** 43175 Sierra Dr./Rte. 198 (☎561-3681) in Three Rivers. This funky pastel motel sits just outside the parks with spacious rooms, high ceilings, valley and river views, a large pool, BBQ, refrigerators, coffeemakers, kitchenettes, fireplaces, and balconies. The 5 suites are huge and feel more like condos. Rooms from $49; $39 in the winter. Suite with kitchen and fireplace $100-160. ❸

**The Sequoia Motel,** 43000 Sierra Dr./Rte.198 (☎561-4453; www.sequoiamotel.com), in Three Rivers. This newly remodeled motel has 11 rooms and 4 very domestic cabins with fireplaces. Pool, picnic area, and extensive garden. Even the smallest of the rooms has a patio and private bath. Rooms from $66; 6-person cabins $110-165. ❹

**Ben Maddox House,** 610 N. Encinia St. (☎800-401-9800), in Visalia. A stately four-room ground-level bed & breakfast built from sequoia trees in 1876. Sits on a well-groomed lot with palm trees. The amenities include 14-foot ceilings, a pool, patio, spa, full breakfast, and in-room Internet connections. Singles $85-95; doubles $90-110. ❺

## ◪ FOOD

Believe it or not, the majority of visitors to the parks do not camp and usually rely on the plain, expensive fare provided courtesy of the US Department of the Interior. If you have a small camp stove, some BBQ briquettes (available at park markets), or don't mind a cold meal, you can stock up on provisions at a park market (see **Practical Information,** p. 272) or in Three Rivers. **Village Market** in Three Rivers may help you produce an affordable meal if you're cooking for a group. (☎561-4441. Open M-Sa 8am-8pm, Su 9am-6pm.)

**Grant Grove Restaurant** (☎ 335-5500), in Grant Grove Village, across from the visitors center. Coffee shop atmosphere. Good portions of standard American fare: pancakes with eggs, club sandwiches, steaks, and pastas. Breakfast $4-8. Lunch $6-8. Dinner $10-18. Open daily 7am-9pm. Pizza available 10:30am-10:30pm. ❸

**Serrano's Mexican Restaurant,** 40869 Sierra Dr. (☎ 561-7283), in Three Rivers. This colorful, painted cocina serves up delicious and authentic Mexican food in healthy portions. Free chips and salsa fresca warm up taste buds for large dinner plates ($8-10). The lunch special is your choice of two items for $5. Open daily 9am-10pm. ❷

**Anne Lang's Emporium,** 41651 Sierra Dr. (☎ 561-4937), in Three Rivers. The lingering scents of potpourri and coffee permeate the air in this friendly deli that overflows with potted plants and country atmosphere. Terraces overlook the Kaweah River. Large sandwiches ($5) come with potato salad and fruit. Salads $3-6. Open M-F 9:30am-5:30pm, Sa-Su 10am-5pm. ❶

## 👁 🏔 SIGHTS & ACTIVITIES

### SEQUOIA

**Giant Forest** is the center of activity in Sequoia and hosts the largest specimens of giant sequoia trees, including the most massive of them all, General Sherman. John Muir named the grove during his extensive explorations of the area and recounted his epiphanous experiences to the American public in his plea for conservation, *My First Summer in the Sierra*. Branching off eastward from the Giant Forest Museum on Generals Hwy., a 3 mi. dead-end road leads to Moro Rock, Crescent Meadow, and **Tunnel Log** (2¾ mi. from the village). This giant sequoia fell in 1937 and was hollowed out so cars could drive through it.

**GENERAL SHERMAN TREE.** The tallest of the park's marvels, this towering pine was discovered in 1879 and named by a Civil War veteran after William Tecumseh Sherman, the stone-faced Union general who led a famous campaign to decimate the South's war-making capabilities and accidentally burned Atlanta to the ground in the process. Standing 275 ft. tall, measuring 102 ft. around its base, weighing over 1385 tons, and estimated to be around 2500 years old, the world's largest living thing looms regally over the forest. Many sequoias in the forest are over 3000 years old; their extensive root systems, fire-resistant bark, and insect-repelling juices make them the ultimate survivors. The 2 mi. **Congress Trail,** the park's most popular trail, boomerangs around General Sherman and other trees named for US political big shots, and passes through the heart of the grove. The three-quarter-mile **Big Trees Trail** is a short, wheelchair-accessible loop lined with informative panels. It starts at the Giant Forest Museum, which is easy to find with the trail guides available at all park visitors centers. (See **Practical Information,** p. 272.)

**MORO ROCK.** The granite monoliths and meadows of the Giant Forest area are perhaps more impressive than the trees that made it famous. If you've ever wanted to feel like a daredevil rock climber without the peril, the 400-step granite staircase leading up Moro Rock will oblige—and if the arduous climb up the stairs doesn't leave you breathless, the stunning 360-degree view of the southern Sierra will. The Great Western Divide lies to the east and foothills recline into the San Joaquin Valley to the south and the west.

**CRESCENT MEADOW.** At the end of Crescent Meadow Rd., beyond the parking lot, rests this fabulous bed of flora, which Muir called "the gem of the Sierra." Its emerald grasses are dotted with the colors of rubies and amethysts; wildflowers gleam beneath the cedars and sequoia that line the drive. The Park Service requests that you stay on marked trails, but if there are too many talkative tourists, you can take the short hike to **Tharp's Log,** a hollowed-out sequoia that housed the first Anglo settler in the area. For ultimate serenity, venture out from the meadow along the High Sierra trail to Mt. Whitney, 71 mi. to the east.

**CRYSTAL CAVE TOURS.** Crystal Cave Rd. branches off Rte. 198 a few miles south of the Giant Forest Museum and winds 6 mi. to Crystal Cave. Discovered by two trail construction workers fishing on their day off in 1918, this is one of the few caves on Sequoia's western side that are open to the public. Reached by a half-mile hike from the road, the cave is lined with smooth limestone stalagmites and stalactites, moistened by a dark underground stream, and inhabited by hordes of Mexican free-tailed bats. Tours last 45min. and proceed along lighted walkways, stopping often to note interesting features. Marble Hall, the cave's largest chamber, is 141 ft. long and over 40 ft. high. The temperature inside is a constant 50°F, so wear warm clothing. (☎565-3159. *Tickets must be purchased 1½hr. in advance at the Lodgepole or Foothills Visitors Centers. Tours given May 31-Sept. 6 daily every 30min. 11am-4pm; less frequently the rest of the year. $9, seniors $7, children $5, under 6 free.)*

# HOW DO I GET A TREE NAMED AFTER ME?

Until the 1920s, it was as simple as waving a paintbrush, a hammer, and a nail, and declaring "MY TREE!" Pioneers, visitors, and tough guys would post makeshift plaques on random trees and proclaim ownership, or at least namesakehood. This may account for the abundance of trees named after Civil War generals, all of which were Union generals until The Daughters of the Confederacy feistily tacked up the names of two enduring Southern heroes.

In 1933, Dr. Morton W. Fraser, a long-time fan of the forest, was buried beneath a tree in Giant Forest, now named Burial Tree and etched with a small tombstone. Another two-tree combo grew in such a way that a swampy cesspool of scum water collected between them. Rumor has it that a ranger once found a couple of black bears kicking back in this pool on a hot summer day and subsequently called the tree Bear's Bathtub.

**OTHER ACTIVITIES.** For those craving the underground scene, **Boyden Cavern** lies on Rte. 180, 10 mi. west of Cedar Groves, in Kings Canyon itself. (☎866-762-2837. *45min. tours run Apr.-Nov. every hr. 11am-4pm; tours June-Sept. 10am and 5pm. $9, ages 3-13 $4.50, under 3 free. National park entrance fee required. No reservations necessary.)* Whitewater rafters can ride the bucking rivers with **Kaweah White Water Adventures,** on Rte. 198 in Three Rivers. May and June are the best months for high water. (☎561-1000 or 800-229-8658. *Class 3 rapids, half-day $80 per person; classes IV and V, full-day $130 per person.)* Visitors interested in renting horses can contact the stables at Grant Grove (☎335-9292), Cedar Grove (☎565-3464), or Horse Corral (☎565-3404). All offer guided rides. *(Open mid-May to mid-June daily 8am-6pm. $25 per hr., $100 per day).* Bicycles, off-road vehicles, and snowmobiles are not permitted on hiking trails or in the backcountry, but Forest Service roads in the area make good bike trails.

# KINGS CANYON

**GRANT GROVE.** The most developed portion of Kings Canyon is Grant Grove, named for its commanding attraction, the General Grant Tree. The 3500-year-old general, the third largest sequoia in the world, is famed for its archetypal sequoia shape. It has been designated the "Nation's Christmas Tree" and serves as the only

SIERRA NEVADA

living shrine to the American war dead. The **Grant Tree Trail,** just past the Sunset campground, consists of a paved half-mile loop and a glance at the mammoth sequoia. The trail is the best way to see the famous dead trees, **Fallen Monarch** and **Centennial Stump.** The huge Fallen Monarch (a felled sequoia) once housed a saloon and a stable, and has been lying on the forest ground undecayed for an unimaginably long time. The 24 ft. wide Centennial Stump stubbornly resisted nine days of hacking. When it arrived at the 1876 Centennial Exposition in Philadelphia, Easterners refused to display it, dismissing it as "another California hoax."

Some awe-inspiring views of the Sierras can be had from the Kings Canyon area; this is what they mean by "purple mountains' majesty" in "America the Beautiful." The most easily accessible views are at **Panoramic Point,** at the end of a steep 2¼ mi. road that leaves from behind the Visitors Center. If the road is closed, use the 2 mi. North Boundary Trail (1 mi. west of Grant Grove Village) to access Pan Point. Tremendous views also exist from **Buena Vista Peak,** a 1 mi. hike from Generals Hwy., 7 mi. south of Grant Grove, and **Big Baldy,** a moderately difficult 2 mi. hike from the trailhead 8 mi. south of the grove. **Park Ridge Trail** is one of the most scenic and well-marked treks in the park. The 1½ mi. round-trip hike along the **Dead Giant Loop** borders national park and national forest lands, and provides interpretive information on the differences between the two. Just north of the park entrance on Rte. 180 lies the **Big Stump Basin Trail,** a 1 mi. self-guided walk through an 1890s-era logging camp that laid the area's sequoias to waste.

**CEDAR GROVE.** The most incredible sights in Kings Canyon lie in the canyon itself, 30 mi. east of Grant Grove on Rte. 180. The combined efforts of ancient glaciers and the South Fork Kings River over countless millennia have cleaved a groove here deeper than even the Grand Canyon. Sheer rock walls and fertile hills rise up around the turbulent blue-green river that tumbles down below, all contributing to a dramatically scenic (and miraculously secluded) area.

Once within the grove, you can explore the Kings River's banks and marvel at the depth of the canyon (8200 ft. in some spots). **Zumwalt Meadows,** accessible via an easy 1½ mi. trail loop, has a rocky site from which bears and mule deer may be seen foraging in the flora below. A guide is available at the trailhead. **Roaring River Falls** and **Mist Falls** are at their best in late spring and early summer, when the streams that feed them are swift and swollen. The Roaring River Falls plunge into a large rocky basin before flowing out to the river and are easily reached by road. Look for signs just beyond Cedar Grove Village. Mist Falls requires a relaxed 4hr. hike. The breathtaking **Grizzly Falls,** located 7 mi. west of Cedar Grove, is a leisurely 50 yd. walk from the highway.

**Road's End** is a naturally U-shaped glacial valley at the eastern end of Rte. 180 with parking for those entering the backcountry. The most popular backcountry foray from Road's End is **Rae Lakes Loop,** which traverses an all-star list of the Sierra's best: glaciated canyons, gentle meadows, violent rapids, and inspiring lakes. Along the five-day trail are two backcountry ranger stations, open only during the summer, and campgrounds at 7 mi. intervals. Trails into the High Sierra (including the **Pacific Crest Trail**) also depart from here. Obtain permits at the **Road's End Kiosk** (see **Practical Information,** p. 273).

## ◙ BACKCOUNTRY HIKES

In the backcountry, visitors should be wary of bears, which are adorable, fuzzy, and very dangerous (see **Bears Will Eat You,** p. 44). **Group tours** led by the park's pack stations (☎ 563-3445) provide safety in numbers. The fashionable guide to backcountry safety, *Backcountry Basics,* is available at the Visitors Center ($10).

After being dwarfed by an army of redwoods named after dead American politicos, conquering a trail or two is a good way to bolster the ego. Near Giant Forest, **Little Baldy Trail** starts at Little Baldy Saddle, 9 mi. north of General Sherman on the Generals Hwy., and climbs 1¾ mi. with a 700 ft. vertical ascent to a rocky summit. The more challenging **Garfield Trail** climbs 4½ mi. to the Garfield sequoia grove from South Fork Campground. The 4½ mi. **Moro Rock Trail** leads from the rock to Roosevelt Tree and Triple Tree (three trees grown together). It winds by Tunnel Log and ends in the Hazelwood area.

**Redwood Mountain Grove,** the world's largest grove of redwood trees, lies near Quail Flat, 6 mi. south of Grant Grove and 4 mi. north of Giant Forest Village. A 10 mi. trail makes two shorter loops through the grove along Redwood Creek, a tributary of the Kaweah River's North Fork where azaleas bloom in May and June. The trail features small waterfalls, young sequoias, and Tunnel Tree. **Mist Falls** heads out from Road's End on 5 mi. of relatively flat hiking to a grand waterfall. The trail can be followed another 3 mi. to Paradise Valley. The long and strenuous **Don Cecil** and **Hotel Creek Trails,** which begin within walking distance of the village, head toward Cedar Grove and the awesome canyon, making for full-day hikes.

The extensive system of backwoods trails presents even more spectacular views. The 7 mi. round-trip **Marble Falls Trail** begins by the Potwisha campground and twists through hills to a 2000 ft. peak at the foot of **Marble Falls.** For those who want the easy payoff, the top of Marble Falls can also be accessed from a much shorter trail off Cave Rd. Ask for directions to Admiration Point at a ranger station. The moderately strenuous hike from the Lodgepole Visitors Center to the glistening **Twin Lakes** (13½ mi. round-trip) reminds visitors that some of the beauty of the park can be found in little things as well; flowers, brooks, and chipmunks abound in picturesque Cahoon Meadow. A few trails lead deep into the park, connecting with the Pacific Crest Trail and crossing into Inyo National Forest. Ask a ranger about the High Sierra Trail and the Woods Creek Trail.

The Mineral King area was acquired by the park system in 1978 after lawsuits prevented the Walt Disney Corporation from building a ski resort on the site. Some of the best scenery in the park awaits those willing to brave the winding drive with blind corners and steep drop-offs. The valley is 7500 ft. deep with steep trails leading up to mountain lakes and meadows. A booming mining area in the 1800s, the region now offers magnificent day and backcountry hiking and climbing. The walk to **Aspen Flat** from Mineral King Pack Station is an easy, rewarding day hike, flanked by soda springs and wildflowers. Perhaps the most astounding view of the region is the sink hole of Eagle Creek, where it completely disappears underground—no one knows where the water ends up. The moderately difficult **Eagle Lake Trail** (6¾ mi. round-trip), which starts 1 mi. down the road from the ranger station, brings you to this impressive work of nature. Listen for furry marmots and pikas along the trail—they'll whistle if you startle them.

# SEQUOIA NATIONAL FOREST ☎ 559

The Sequoia National Forest is on the southern end of the majestic Sierra Nevada range, which peters out in the Mojave Desert 60 mi. south of the park. It is bounded on the north by the Kings River, on the west by the San Joaquin Valley, on the east by the Owens Valley, and on the south by Telephone Ridge. The Kern River slices through its southeast region. The forest is best known for its 38 groves of towering giant sequoia trees and the Hume Lake Dam, the first multiple arch concrete dam built in the US.

The **Forest Headquarters,** 900 W. Grand Ave., on Rte. 65 in Porterville, has detailed maps of the forest ($7) featuring the national forest's six designated wilderness areas. There is a park fee to enter the forest from the north since you have to come through Kings Canyon National Park. (☎784-1500. Open M-Sa 8am-4:30pm.) Backcountry excursions to the **Golden Trout Wilderness** require wilderness permits, available at any district ranger's office. The **Hume Lake Ranger District Office**, 35860 E. Kings Canyon Rd., on Rte. 180 in Dunlap, 32 mi. east of Fresno near the forest entrance, provides camping info. (☎338-2251. Open May 31-Sept. 6 M-Sa 8am-4:30pm; Sept. 7-May 30 M-F 8am-4:30pm.)

**Camping** in the forest is abundant, quiet, and sometimes free. In the Hume Lake District, **Big Meadow ❶** (7600 ft.), on Big Meadow Rd. 13 mi. southeast of Grant Grove from Generals Hwy., has 25 sites for tents and trailers at no charge, though there's no water available. More popular sites in the area include **Stony Creek ❶** and **Upper Stony Creek ❶** (6400 ft.), both 14 mi. southeast of Grant Grove on Generals Hwy. Both can be reserved in advance, though many sites are first-come, first-served. (☎877-444-6777. Stony Creek sites $16, Upper Stony Creek $12.) As the name implies, **Quaking Aspen ❶** (7000 ft.), in the Tule River/Hot Springs District, is surrounded by beautiful quaking aspen. It lies next to a small meadow and a few of the sites are very secluded. (Water, toilets, hiking, and fishing. Sites $14.)

**Hiking** in the district is quiet. There is a strenuous 40 mi. stretch of the **Pacific Crest National Scenic Trail** that passes through the forest on its 2600 mi. journey between Canada and Mexico (see **From Crest to Crest: The Trail of the West**, p. 235). The **Trail of 100 Giants** is a more relaxing, interpretive 35min. walk in the southern section of the forest. The trail is evenly paved, and you can still see many giant sequoias, making it perfect for wheelchairs and strollers. The moderately strenuous 2 mi. **Sherman Pass Trail** starts from the Sherman Pass parking lot on Sherman Pass Rd. and climbs to the mountain's peak for a view of the surrounding forest, recently devastated by fire. The lower elevation 2¼ mi. **Packsaddle Cave Trail** (trailhead is 16 mi. north of Kernville on State Mtn. 99) takes you to its namesake, the Packsaddle Cave. These trails are "OHV," meaning that hikers share the road with off-road vehicles and horses. One hundred and fifty miles of **backcountry hiking** can be found in the Golden Trout Wilderness, accessible on Rte. 190 and Rte. 395, and Monarch Wilderness, accessible on Rte. 180. These areas are remote and unforgiving; expeditions require serious preparation.

**Outdoor Adventures** runs two-day **whitewater rafting trips** on the Lower Kern for about $300 per person, day and half-day trips on the Upper Kern for $100-150, and serious three-day trips on the Class V rapids of the North Fork Kern for $750-800. (☎800-323-4234; www.kernrafting.com.) **Whitewater Voyages** gives kayaking instruction and also has Kern, Kings River, and Tuolumne River rafting trips. (☎800-488-7238; www.whitewatervoyages.com. 2-4 day kayaking courses $250-500; rafting $100-200 per day.)

The northern section of Sequoia National Forest surrounds **Kings Canyon Highway,** the road connecting to Kings Canyon National Park's Grant Grove area. The **Hume Lake District** contains the awesome remnants of what used to be the largest grove in the world before the logging industry came.

# EASTERN SIERRA

Unlike the western side of the Sierra, which descends leisurely into the Central Valley foothills, the eastern side's jagged heights drop off precipitously, drawing a dramatic silhouette against the skies. The eastern Sierras rise abruptly from the Owens Valley floor, creating a striking topography, the result of lifting and faulting that shaped the Sierra ridge 10 million years ago and gave rise to an unparalleled outdoor scene. Die-hard fishermen are drawn to the June Lake area, downhill enthusiasts flock to the incomparable snow and mountain biking trails of Mammoth Lakes, and outdoorsmen in search of the Wild West wander the high-elevation trails of Lone Pine. And for those interested only in staying still and soaking in the stunning mountain scenery, the eastern Sierra will still oblige.

# LEE VINING & MONO LAKE ☎760

As the snow thaws in June, Rte. 120 in the stunning Tioga Pass opens to motorists, making the town of Lee Vining (pop. 315) a great eastern gateway to Yosemite or a quiet getaway destination itself. The town's focus is the vigilant preservation of nearby natural marvel Mono Lake. Sitting at the western flank of the Great Basin desert, home to similarly saline lakes like Pyramid and The Great Salt Lake, Mono Lake is sustained by freshwater inflows from surrounding mountains. Without any natural outlet, evaporation is the sole equilibrating force in the lake, but since salts and minerals are left behind as the lake dries, salinity has built up to two to three times that of ocean levels. This process of drainage by evaporation has been going on for nearly a million years, making Mono Lake one of the oldest in the Western Hemisphere. The lake's mythological appearance is marked by tufa, spires of calcium carbonate which form when calcium-rich springs well up in the carbonate-filled salt water. These spires reach nearly 15 ft. above the water in places.

Today, Mono supports not only its own delicate and unique ecosystem, but also the water needs of greater metropolitan LA. Although Mono Lake's water has always been too salty to use, its freshwater inflows are extremely pure. LA's rapid growth, lack of freshwater supplies, and political might resulted in these inflows being completely diverted in 1941. By 1982, the lake's levels had dropped 50 ft., its volume had halved, and its salinity had doubled. Delicate tufa were exposed, riparian forests withered, local trout populations were devastated, and the Californian shore's gulls and brine shrimp faced tough prospects for survival. Various parts of the ecological fabric in the area quickly began to fray. In the past 20 years, however, locals and lake-lovers have rejoiced to see the lake rise 15 ft. as the combined efforts of Congress, the US Forest Service, the Audobon Society, and the Mono Lake Committee succeeded in reducing the flow south by half.

The small town of Lee Vining happily serves as host to Yosemite adventurers and Mono Lake visitors alike. Although quite small (the town only stretches about 4 city blocks), its Visitors Center has a wealth of information about outdoor activities in the area and its restaurants and accommodations take care of the basics, sometimes with admirable success.

## ✦ ⁊ ORIENTATION & PRACTICAL INFORMATION

Lee Vining provides stunning access to Yosemite via **Inyo National Forest,** and the best access to Mono Lake and Bodie. Lee Vining is 70 mi. north of Bishop on US 395 and 10 mi. west of the Tioga Pass entrance to Yosemite. Bodie is 28 mi. northwest of Lee Vining off US 395. Addresses in Lee Vining consist only of P.O. Box numbers, so general directions or cross-streets are provided instead.

▨ **Mono Lake Committee and Lee Vining Chamber of Commerce** (☎647-6595; www.monolake.org, lodging, dining, and local services www.leevining.com), in the orange and blue clay building at Main and 3rd St., Lee Vining. Like a friendly eco-gift shop, with its exhibits, posters, books, and extensive lake and preservation info. Walking and canoe tours (see **Sights and Activities,** p. 283). Open daily late June-Sept. 6 9am-10pm; Sept. 7-late June 9am-5pm.

**Mono Basin National Forest Scenic Area Visitors Center** (☎873-2408; www.fs.fed.us/r5/inyo), Inyo National Forest, off US 395 a half-mile north of Lee Vining. This new angular structure resembles a modern-day cathedral or *Architectural Digest* centerfold. Houses a record of the community's care for the basin. Interpretive tours, an informative film, patio talks, and info on Mono County's wilderness areas. Topographical maps ($6-20) and free wilderness permits. Open M-F 9am-5:30pm; in winter Su and F-Sa 9am-4pm. Summer tours of the tufa towers daily at 10am, 1pm, 6pm. $3, under 18 free.

**Kayak Rental: Caldera Kayaks** (☎935-4942; www.calderakayak.com), at Crowly Lake Marina, Mammoth Lakes. Kayaks $25 per half-day, $35 per day. Double kayaks $5 more. Natural history kayak tour of Mono Lake ($65 per day).

**ATMs:** In the Mobile station on the southern end of town, in the Chevron station on the northern end of town, and in the Lee Vining Market near Main and 4th St.

**Laundromat: Mono Vista RV Park** (☎647-6401), at the north end of the town. Wash $1.25; dry 50¢. Showers $2 per 5min. Open 9am-6pm.

**Weather:** ☎935-7663.

**Internet Access:** At the Chamber of Commerce. $2 per 15min.

**Post Office** (☎647-6371), in the big brown building on 4th St., Lee Vining. Open M-F 9am-2pm and 3-5pm. **Postal Code:** 93541.

# ACCOMMODATIONS

When Tioga Pass is open (early June-Sept.), Lee Vining is an ideal stop on the way from Reno or Death Valley to Yosemite, making hotel vacancies scarce on Friday afternoons and holidays. Lodgings are easier to arrange for weekdays, but camping and picnics are always cheaper alternatives to motels and restaurants. Many hotels and campgrounds are closed in winter; call ahead. Most cheap options are on **Main Street** or 10 mi. south of town on the 14 mi. **June Lake Loop** (see p. 284).

**El Mono Motel** (☎647-6310), at Main and 3rd St., offers a charming slice of modern California: fake Spanish name, white stucco exterior, espresso bar, and art nouveau posters in the lobby. The rooms are small but beautifully decorated with a personal, stylish flair and have cable TV but no phone. Pets allowed. Open Apr.-Oct. Singles and doubles with shared bath $49. 4-person rooms $82. ❸

**Tioga Lodge** (☎647-6423 or 888-647-6423), 2 mi. north of Lee Vining on the western shore of Mono Lake. Each cabin-like room in this complex of blonde wood is beautifully decorated with a turn-of-the-century Sierra theme. All rooms have excellent views of the lake. Idyllic small meadow has a swing, gazebo, and creek. Singles $97; doubles $107. Rooms from $58 before Tioga Pass opens. ❺

**Gateway Motel** (☎647-6467 or 800-282-3929; www.yosemitegatewaymotel.com), in the center of town on the lake side. Each of 18 standard rooms has a spectacular view of Mono Lake below; several have balconies. Phone, cable TV, coffee, and spa. Rooms from $89; in winter $49. ❺

# CAMPING

None of the area's campgrounds take reservations but sites are ubiquitous; a pre-noon arrival time will all but guarantee a spot. An afternoon arrival probably will, too. Most sites are clustered west of Lee Vining toward Yosemite along Rte. 120.

**Inyo National Forest Campgrounds,** close to town. Many campgrounds are on Rte. 120 heading into town. **Lundy** and **Lower Lee Vining** are the best locations for travelers headed for Mono Lake. No water. Open May-Oct. Sites $7. ❶ The **June Lake Loop** area south on US 395 has 6 sites (see **Camping**, p. 286). Most sites $15; **Bloody Canyon Trailhead** free. First-come, first-camp. ❶

**Ellery Lake,** 9500 ft., on Tioga Pass Rd. at Rte. 120 across from Tioga Pass Resort. 12 first-come, first-camp sites near a brook with fishing and swimming in the nearby lake. Running water, chemical toilets. Sites $13. ●

# ◘ FOOD

For a town that consists of a Main St. and little more, Lee Vining has a pleasant range of options for food. **Lee Vining Market,** on US 395 at the southern end of town, is the closest thing to a grocery store. (☎ 647-1010. Open daily 7am-10pm.) **Tioga Gas Mart,** at the intersection of Rte. 120 and Rte. 395, is not your average gas station. It offers fancy coffees, chai, pizza, deli, grilled food, groceries, a gourmet food selection, and 93-octane gas. The grassy picnic area overlooks Mono Lake. (☎ 647-1088. Open daily 7am-10pm. Gas 24hr.)

**Nicely's** (☎ 647-6477), on Rte. 395 3 stores north of the Visitors Center, has hot sandwiches ($5-7), burgers ($5-7), and monster salads ($7-9). A local favorite with the ambience of a diner. The large maroon interior is often packed. Open daily 6am-9pm; in winter M-Tu and Th-Su 6am-9pm. ❷

**Mono Cone** (☎ 647-6606), on Rte. 395 at the northern end of town. This hamburger stand is a local institution whose opening signals the beginning of summer. The prices are small, the portions are large, and the seating is outdoors. Their corn dogs ($2), floats ($3), and frosty cones ($1.50) are the best in town. Open daily 11am-9pm. ●

# ◉ ⋏ SIGHTS & ACTIVITIES

**BODIE.** One of the most well-preserved ghost towns in the US, Bodie became known as "the most lawless, wildest, and toughest mining camp the far West has ever known," according to State Park pamphlets. It looks pretty tame now. Named after Waterman S. Body, who discovered gold here in 1859, the town had its heyday from 1877 to 1881, when it was home to 10,000 people, 65 saloons, 750 million modern-day dollars in gold and silver, numerous opium dens, and, in its most treacherous times, up to one homicide per day. "Goodbye, God, I'm going to Bodie!" wrote one little girl in her diary, coining a phrase that captured the town's rough-and-tumble character. The toughest town in the West survived until 1932, when the infamous Bodie Bill, a 2½-year-old child, incinerated 90% of the town with one match. The remaining ten percent, however, is now ghost town: absolutely genuine and brimming with a haunting romantic appeal. (*Off US 395 32 mi. north of Lee Vining, then 13 mi. east on Hwy. 270. Open daily May 31-Sept. 6 8am-7pm; Sept. 7-May 30 8am-4pm. Entrance $2. Self-guide booklet $1.*) The small **Bodie Museum** displays some Wild West stories and artifacts. (*Open summer only daily 9am-6pm. For more info, call Bodie State Historic Park at ☎ 647-6445 or write P.O. Box 515, Bridgeport, CA 93517.*)

**MONO LAKE.** In 1984, Congress set aside 57,000 acres of land surrounding Mono Lake and named it the **Mono Basin National Forest Scenic Area** (☎ 873-2408). To get there, take US 395 S to Rte. 120, then go 4 mi. east and take the Mono Lake South Tufa turn-off 1 mi. south to Tufa Grove. For a $3 fee (Golden Eagle, Golden Age, and Golden Access passes accepted), travelers may investigate the **South Tufa Formations,** an area with the greatest concentration of these dramatic calcium carbonate spires that pierce the smooth, icy blue surface of this inland sea. Free summer tours led by knowledgeable naturalists depart from the South Tufa parking lot daily at 10am, 1, and 6pm. Five miles north of Lee Vining on US 395 and 1 mi. east on Cemetery Rd. is **Mono Lake**

**SIERRA NEVADA**

**County Park,** a public playground with a wheelchair-accessible boardwalk trail to a smaller tufa grove, as well as to bathrooms, picnic tables, and swings. Rangers lead a number of free hikes throughout the summer, including bird-watching excursions, a hike to Panum Volcano, and stargazing trips. Inquire at the Visitors Center (☎873-2408) about schedules.

The Mono Lake Committee offers **canoe tours** of the lake that include a crash course in conservation and Mono's natural history. (☎647-6595. 1hr. tours depart from South Tufa at Mono Lake mid-June to early Sept. Sa-Su 8, 9:30, 11am; bird-watching is better on earlier tours. Arrive 30min. early for lifejacket fitting and photos of placid lakewater reflections. Tours $17, ages 4-12 $7. Reservations required.) Caldera Kayaks offers full-day **kayak tours and rentals** (see p. 282).

In this arid basin, the summer temperatures at high noon inspire tourists to seek shade. The 20min. slide show presentation at the Mono Lake Committee is beautifully done, informative, rabble-rousing, and free. **The US Forest Service Scenic Area Visitors Center** shows a film that requires less thought. ($3; includes 20min. film, exhibits, and access to South Tufa area.) The **Mono Basin Historical Society Museum** in Guss Hess Park, Lee Vining, is a great way to get informed about the Basin's rich past. In the old Mono Lake schoolhouse, this museum has the standard balance of Gold Rush trinkets and Native American artifacts. (☎647-6461. Admission $1.)

**HIKING.** The unique terrain of this geological gallery—from the flat, alien landscape around Mono Lake to the mountainous forests along Rte. 120—makes it a great place for hikers of all levels. Easier trails include a quarter-mile boardwalk to tufa and the lake, **Old Marina Area Trail,** 1 mi. north of Lee Vining on Rte. 395, the 1 mi. **Lee Vining Creek Trail,** which begins behind the Mono Basin Visitors Center, and the **Panum Crater Trail,** 5 mi. south on US 395 near the South Tufa turn-off, leading to a volcanic dome. Those undaunted by the prospect of a punishing trek should head 10 mi. east of US 395 on Rte. 120, where an exceptionally steep trail leads 1 mi. to the glistening **Gardisky Lake.** Another peaceful but tough hike starts at **Lundy Lake,** off US 395, 7 mi. north of Lee Vining, and leads to **Crystal Lake** and the remains of an old mining town. The well-maintained hike gains 2000 ft. in its 3 mi. ascent and offers little shade. Bring plenty of sunscreen and bug spray. Other moderate-to-difficult trails also depart from Lundy Lake, including the 5½ mi. trail though **Lundy Canyon** to 20 Lakes Basin and the 3½ mi. trail up out of Lundy Canyon to **Lakes Canyon.**

# JUNE LAKE LOOP                                                   ☎760

While there certainly is dramatic and expansive wilderness around June Lake, the townsfolk in this glacier-carved valley off Rte. 395 have their focus squarely set on the smaller lakes and mountains forming the June Lake Loop enclave. This means that hiking, rock climbing, mountain biking, and the like tend to take a backseat to swimming and fishing in the summer and skiing in the winter. From the last Saturday in April to the end of October, the four beautiful lakes traced by the loop become altars for the cult of fishing. Locals and thousands of visitors flock to the town's marinas on quests for the elusive monster trout, trophies to mount back home, or just something for the frying pan. In the winter, the family-friendly June Mountain and the slopes around the loop make for excellent skiing and snowsports, with smaller crowds and lower fees than at Mammoth.

## ■ ⍰ ORIENTATION & PRACTICAL INFORMATION

Just off US 395, 7 mi. south of Lee Vining, the 14 mi. June Lake Loop winds by Grant, Silver, Gull, and June lakes before rejoining US 395. In June Lake Town, Boulder Dr. is also referred to as Main St. before it becomes Loop Rd. Addresses in the June Lake Loop consist only of P.O. Box numbers; general directions or cross streets are provided instead.

**Buses: CREST** (☎800-922-1930) buses from **Carson City, Nevada** to June Lake firehouse Tu and Th-F. Fare $13. Greyhound makes stops in Carson City from around the country. Reserve CREST tickets in advance.

**Boat Rental: June Lake Marina** (☎648-7726) has 6-horsepower (half-day $39, full-day $44) and 15-horsepower ($49/$54) motorboats. Open daily 6am-7pm. **Gull Lake Marina** (☎648-7539) has motorboats (half-day $37, full-day $48), large pontoon boats ($90/$150), and paddleboats ($10 per hr.). Open daily 6am-7pm.

**Visitor Information: June Lake Chamber of Commerce** (☎648-7584; www.junelake-chamber.com) offers tourist info. Open M-F 8am-5pm. Another info kiosk at the south entrance. **June Lake Properties** (☎648-7705) makes reservations.

**Laundromat: Carson Peak Laundromat,** across from the Fern Creek Lodge. Wash $2, dry 25¢ per 8min. Open 8am-9pm.

**Frontier Pack Train** (☎648-7701). Guided horseback trips including overnight packing trips. $25 per hr., half-day $55, full-day $85.

**Weather:** 24hr. snow report (☎873-3213 or 888-JUNE-MTN/586-3686).

**Emergency: 24hr. Sheriff** (☎932-7549).**Forest Service** (☎647-6525).

**Post Office:** on Boulder Dr. (☎648-7483), across from Trout Town Joe Cafe. Open M-F 9am-2pm and 3-5pm. **Postal Code:** 93529.

## ▚ ACCOMMODATIONS

True to its resort town nature, there are plenty of places to stay in the June Lake area. Many of them are very pleasant but only a few are affordable. Still, prices are significantly lower than in Mammoth Lakes and the many cabins, condos, and suites available mean cheap and comfortable lodging for larger groups and families. **A 12% bed tax applies to all indoor accommodations in Mono County.**

▨ **Fern Creek Lodge,** on Rte. 158 (☎648-7722 or 800-621-9146; www.ferncreek-lodge.com), 13 mi. from Lee Vining, 2 mi. past June Lake Town. Apartment units and cabins, some small and rustic, some nearly full-sized houses. All have fully-equipped kitchens and cable TV. 2-person cabin $60-65; 14-person cabin $230 and up. ❸

**Boulder Lodge,** on Boulder Dr. (☎648-7533; www.boulderlodge.com), near the beginning of June Lake. Spacious, clean rooms with cable TV and private bath. Perks include a pool table, small arcade, sauna, recreation facilities, and large indoor pool. Most lake-view rooms have patios with great views of June Lake. Doubles from $68; suites from $98. Prices about 15% higher in the summer. ❹

**Reverse Creek Lodge,** on Loop Rd. (☎648-7535 or 800-762-6440; www.reversecreek-lodge.com), has chalets, big log cabins, and small cabins, all with private bath, kitchen, cable TV, and a patio with a grill. A-frame chalets (for up to 6 people) are larger, include 2 full baths, gas fireplaces, and grills, and look out on nearby Carson Peak. Recently remodeled small cabins $65; 2-bedroom cabins $85-120; chalets $125-140. ❹

**June Lake Motel,** on Boulder Dr. (☎648-7547, reservations only 800-648-6835; www.junelakemotel.com), is a fisherman's dream. Near town, the large facility rents multi-unit cabins, condos, motel rooms with and without kitchens, and full houses. Besides a jacuzzi, sauna, BBQs, and cable TV, it offers a fish-cleaning station, fish freezing, fish rags, and free ice. Motel rooms from $62; 4-person rooms with kitchen from $92; cabins $92-135; well-equipped lake-view condominiums from $145. ❹

**June Lake Villager Motel,** on Boulder Dr. (☎648-7712 or 800-655-6545; www.junelakevillager.com.) Though lacking great views, these motel rooms, kitchenette rooms, suites, and cabins are charming and have exceptionally low mid-week rates in winter. Fish-cleaning station, ice, VCRs, coffeemakers, relaxing patio with grill. In winter there's firewood for rooms with fireplaces and an indoor jacuzzi. Singles from $55, with kitchen $70; cabins $120. In winter singles from $50, with kitchen $65; cabins $95. ❺

## ⛏ CAMPING

Camping is a more affordable option than motels in the June Lake Loop and can get you just as close to the area's lakes. There are six Inyo National Forest campgrounds, as well as a few privately operated sites. Most campsites are open only during fishing season (last Saturday in April to Oct. 31).

**Grant Lake Resort** (☎648-7964), 7600 ft., off Rte. 158 toward Lee Vining, in the most remote part of the June Lake Loop. Tackle shop, marina, and boat rental (half-day $30, full-day $40). Each site has water, hookup, and firepit. Most sites offer shade and many overlook the big and somewhat less crowded Grant Lake, which has good fishing. Reservations recommended in the summer. Send a check for camping fee to P.O. Box 627, June Lake, CA 93529. Open late Apr. to Oct. Tent sites $15, seniors $12. ❶

**Oh! Ridge Pine Cliff Resort** (☎648-7558), 7600 ft., by the June Lake shore. Private RV site and campground not affiliated with the National Forest Service campground. The resort has a general store, gas, propane, laundry (8am-8pm), basketball court, and showers. Every site has a fire ring. Open mid-Apr. to Oct. On-site trailer rentals $160-400 weekly, full RV hookup $20, water and electric hookup $16, tent sites $12. ❶

**Oh! Ridge Campground,** 7600 ft., is right next door to the Resort and has access to a swimming beach and flush toilets. The campground is rarely filled, RVs are few, and sites are large. Quieter and more spacious than most. Open Apr.-Nov. Sites $15. ❶

**June Lake Campground,** 7600 ft., next to the marina. On a busy lake near shops and a restaurant, this densely vegetated campground feels like it's set aside from the main rush of campers and RVs, despite being just lakeside of Main St. 28 sites, 6 for walk-in tent campers only. Water and flush toilets. Showers at marina. Sites $15. ❶

**Silver Lake Campground,** 7200 ft., a National Forest site. Right on the lake, considerably far from June Lake Town and near a number of trailheads. The grassy campsites don't have much shade but do have elbow room. 63 sites with flush toilets and water. Good fishing access. Open late Apr. to Oct. Sites $15. ❶

## 🍴 FOOD

The **June Lake General Store** is a supermarket, hardware store, liquor store, and deli in one. (Open daily 8am-7pm.) Options outside of the June Lake Loop are the smaller market at **Fern Creek Lodge** (☎648-7722; open daily 8am-9pm; in winter hours are slightly shorter) and the **Silver Lake Resort Store** (open daily 7am-9pm).

**Tiger Bar** (☎648-7551; www.thetigerbarcafe.com), at Knoll Ave. and Rte. 158. Good Mexican fare for lunch and standard American food for dinner, all reasonably priced. The quirky decor in this popular and loud restaurant and bar features black-and-white photos of the area. Pool table, TV, and pinball machine. Huge Tostada Grande $8.25. Burgers with fresh fries or chips $7-8. Full breakfasts $4-7. American-style dinners $9-15. Open daily 8am-close; kitchen open until 10pm. ❷

**Trout Town Joe,** 2750 Boulder Dr. (☎648-1155), across from the post office. A stylish and comfy coffeehouse popular with locals, TTJ is a perfect place for a creative salad or sandwich ($4-7) or a cup of coffee ($1.25-3). Open daily 7am-3pm. ❷

**Eagle's Landing Restaurant,** at the Double Eagle Resort (☎648-7897), 2 mi. outside of June Lake, is *the* place to go to treat yourself. This beautiful new lodge building has gorgeous mountain views from every table. You can grab a drink at the **Eagle's Nest Saloon** and watch a game on their 42 in. plasma screen TV. The house specialty is rotisserie chicken basted in lemon-herb garlic and barbecue sauce ($16). Logger-type breakfasts $6-11. Burgers $7. Entrees $14-26. Open daily 7am-8:30pm. ❸

## 🔘 🔺 SIGHTS & ACTIVITIES

In the summer months, all minds in June Lake are on one thing—**fishing.** The June Lake Loop (State Rte. 158) traces the outer edge of four bountiful lakes: **June Lake** (☎648-7726), closest to the South June Lake Junction with Rte. 395; **Gull Lake** (☎648-7539); **Silver Lake** (☎648-7525); and the expansive **Grant Lake** (☎648-7964) to the north. There are also a number of fishable streams in the Loop like Rush and Alger Creeks, as well as lakes accessible only by foot or horse. Each of the four main lakes sells California fishing licenses (required for anyone over 16) and has its own tackle shop and a marina that rents motorboats ($40-50 per day), so even the unprepared can join in the fun. The lakes are stocked twice a month with rainbow, brook, and German brown trout. Although all the lakes yield big fish every day, many serious anglers prefer Gull and Grant Lakes. June Lake is a popular spot for sunbathing, swimming, and recreational boating. Quieter **Walker Lake** and **Parker Lake** are accessible by short day hikes from trailheads just north of Grant Lake. **Rush Creek, Agnew Lake,** and **Gem Lake** can all be accessed from the **Rush Creek Trail,** which starts across from the Silver Lake campground (2¼ mi. to Agnew Lake; 3 mi. to Gem Lake).

There are a few moderate **day hikes,** most leading to trout-filled lakes, and some excellent backcountry trails into the Ansel Adams Wilderness where one can connect to the John Muir Trail. Across from the June Lake firehouse, the trail to **Yost Lake** is a moderate 5 mi. hike through the aspen and fir forest of the June Mountain Ski Area. The separate **Yost Creek Trail,** departing about 1 mi. south of Silver Lake, will take you to Yost Lake or Fern Lake, which are both beautiful and quiet. About a mile into the hike, the trail forks near a waterfall; the right branch leads a steep 1½ mi. to Fern Lake, while the left trail is a moderate 2½ mi. hike to Yost Lake. Much of the backcountry can be explored on **horseback.** Contact the **Frontier Pack Train** (see **Orientation and Practical Information,** p. 285) for more information.

Increasingly popular but still much less crowded than Mammoth Mountain, **June Mountain Ski Resort** caters to the snowboarding crowd, dedicating nearly half the mountain to "enhanced terrain" parks of half-pipes, rails, and jumps perfect for catching huge air. Excellent powder, tremendous views, and short lines (if any) make this an attractive alternative to the larger, more well-known resort to the south. Accordingly, it's also less expensive to ski here. (☎648-7733. Day pass $47, ages 19-23 $42, ages 13-18 $37, seniors and under 13 $27.)

# MAMMOTH LAKES ☎760

Home to one of the most popular ski resorts in the United States, the town of Mammoth Lakes (pop. 5305) has developed into a giant year-round playground. The snowfall averages over 350 inches a year, creating 3500 acres of skiable ter-

SIERRA NEVADA

rain. High altitudes mean that snow lasts as late as July some years, cutting the off-season down to four months. And as soon as the snow melts, mountain bikers invade the town by thousands to take on Mammoth Mountain, skateboarders come to test their skills in some of the stiffest competitions in the country, and fisherfolk come to the magma-warmed creeks to catch some hot fish. Beyond all the hair-raising adventure, Mammoth Lakes also supports a significant cultural scene marked by concerts and festivals, and a small but very lively nightlife.

# ▐ TRANSPORTATION

**Bus: CREST** (☎800-922-1930) runs buses Tu and Th-F at 1:45pm from **Carson City,** arriving in **Mammoth Lakes** around 4:40pm. Fare $15.

**Airport: Reno/Tahoe International** (☎775-328-6400). Served daily by major carriers. Mammoth Shuttle provides bus connections to town (see below).

**Public Transit:**

**Inyo-Mono Dial-A-Ride** (☎872-1901; www.countyofinyo.org) provides service to **Bishop, Bridgeport, Lee Vining, June Lake,** and **Crowley Lake** from McDonald's at Mammoth Lakes and K-Mart at Bishop. M, W, Sa; fare depends upon location.

**Mammoth Shuttle Service** (☎934-3030) provides on-call service for intercity travel M-Th 8am-midnight, F-Sa 8am-2am.

**Mammoth Area Shuttle** or **MAS** (☎934-3030) offers a red line shuttle to town and the main ski lodge. During ski season, shuttles connect to chairlifts daily every 15min. 7am-midnight. Free. In summer, a shuttle daily every 20min. 7:30pm-5:30pm goes from main lodge to **Reds Meadow, Devils Post Pile,** and 8 other stops in the forest. To enter these areas 7am-7pm, the shuttle is required. Last run out of Reds Meadow 8pm. Day pass $7, good for duration of trip if camping.

**Sierra Express** (☎924-8294) is a door-to-door shuttle service that runs 7am-2am. Rates fluctuate.

**Car Rental: U-SAVE,** 49 Laurel Mt. Rd., (☎934-4999 or 800-207-2681). 4WD vehicles from $56 per day with 150 mi. included, $372 per week with 1050 mi. included; 25¢ per additional mi. Compacts from $42 per day, $252 per week. Single day rates 10% higher. Rentals available at the **Chevron** (☎934-8111) next to the post office. Cars $40-90 per day, 150 mi. included; 25¢ per additional mi.

**Auto Repairs: AAA Emergency Road Service** ☎800-400-4222.

# ✳ ▐ ORIENTATION & PRACTICAL INFORMATION

Mammoth Lakes is off US 395, 160 mi. south of Reno, 325 mi. north of LA, and 40 mi. southeast of the eastern entrance to Yosemite. Rte. 203 runs through the town as **Main Street** and then veers off to the right as **Minaret Road,** which turns into Lake Mary Rd. as it heads to the area's lakes. In winter, the normally desolate US 395, which runs directly below the brooding heights of the Eastern Sierra, is packed with weekend skiers from LA making the 6hr. journey up to the slopes.

**Equipment Rental: Footloose Sports Shop,** 3043 Main St. (☎934-2400), rents ski and snowboard packages from $25 per day; mountain bikes from $24. Ski tuning, boot fitting, and trail info. Open Su-W 7am-8pm, Th-Sa 7am-9pm. In summer open daily 8am-8pm. **Rick's Sport Center,** 3241 Main St. (☎934-3416). Daily fishing rod rental $10. 10-day non-resident license $30, yearly pass $83. Package fishing deal (waders, booties, fins, and float tube) $30 per day. Fly-fishing lessons available for $110 per half-day. Open daily 6am-8pm; off-season 7am-7pm.

**Visitor Information: Inyo National Forest Visitors Center and Chamber of Commerce** (☎924-5500; www.visitmammoth.com), on Rte. 203 west of US 395, north of town. Offers area info, discounts on accommodations and food, *Mammoth Times* (50¢), free video, exhibits, and walks. Accommodation reservations. Open daily 8am-5pm.

**Bank: Bank of America,** 3069 Main St. (☎934-6830). Open M-Th 9am-5pm, F 9am-6pm, Sa 9am-1pm. **24hr. ATM.**

**Laundromat: Mammoth Lakes Laundromat** (☎934-8207), on Laurel Mountain Rd., 1 block off Main St. Wash $1.50, dry 25¢ per 7½min. Friendly staff. Open daily 8:30am-6:30pm. Last wash 1½hr. before closing.

**Weather:** ☎934-7669.

**Ski Conditions: Mammoth Mountain Snow Conditions** (☎934-6166). **Mammoth Mountain Ski Area** (☎934-2571). **June Mountain Ski Area** (☎648-7733).

**Medical Services: Mammoth Hospital,** 85 Sierra Park Rd. (☎934-3311). Offers 24hr. emergency care.

**Post Office:** 3330 Main St. Open M-F 8:30am-5pm. **Postal Code:** 93546.

# ACCOMMODATIONS

As with most ski resorts, lodging is much more expensive in the winter. Condo rentals are a comfortable choice for groups of three or more and start at $100 per night. **Mammoth Reservation Bureau** (☎800-462-5571; www.mammothvacations.com) can make rental arrangements. For lone travelers, dorm-style motels are the cheapest option. Reservations are highly recommended for winter stays. **A 12% bed tax applies to all indoor accommodations in Mono County.**

**Davison St. Guest House,** 19 Davison Rd. (☎924-2188), off Main St. Under new, enthusiastic management, this homey lodge is one of the best values in town. Dorm rooms are small but the house has a full kitchen, outdoor BBQ, huge common room with comfy couches, TV/VCR, and stereo. Dorms $25; private rooms $60-75. ❷

**Holiday Haus,** 3905 Main St. (☎934-2414). Spacious, clean, and very pleasant rooms and cabins, some with fireplaces and kitchens. Centrally located with spa on site. Owned by friendly locals, this is a great deal. Summer M-Th doubles from $45; in winter from $50. Suite for up to 6 with kitchen from $70 in winter. ❹

**Swiss Chalet,** 3776 Viewpoint Rd. (☎934-2403 or 800-937-9477), just off Main St. Twenty-one hilltop motel rooms with vaulted wood ceilings and stunning mountain views. Cable TV, refrigerator, ski rack, and coffee are in the immaculate rooms and hand-painted wooden signs hang outside each door. Sundeck, jacuzzi, and sauna make for easy relaxation after a day on the slopes. Rooms $65-85; in winter $70-120. ❺

# CAMPING

There are nearly 20 Inyo Forest public **campgrounds** ❶ (sites $13-16) in the area, sprinkled around Mammoth Lakes, Mammoth Village, Convict Lake, Red's Meadow, Agnew Meadow, and June Lake. All sites have piped water and most are near fishing and hiking. Interested parties should contact the **Mammoth Ranger District** (☎924-5500) for info. Reservations can be made at nearby Sherwin Creek for New and Old Shady Rest (☎877-444-6777; www.reserveusa.com).

**Twin Lakes,** 8600 ft., a half-mile off Lake Mary Rd., about 2 mi. outside town. In a pine forest, the 95 lush sites are a minute's walk from fishing and swimming at Twin Lakes. General store nearby with essentials and showers. Perfect view of Twin Falls rushing into the southern end of Upper Twin Lake. Piped water and flush toilets. 7-night max. stay. Open June-Oct. Sites $14. Showers $2. ❶

SIERRA NEVADA

**Lake Mary,** 8900 ft., on Lake Mary Loop Rd. Camping can't get much better than these 48 sites: clear mountain lake water, trout practically jumping into your boat, relaxing beaches, and a general store for when you tire of roughin' it. 14-night max. stay. Open June to mid-Sept. Sites $14. ❶

**New Shady Rest,** 7800 ft., on Rte. 203 across from McDonald's. A great option if you want to pitch your tent at one of the 94 sites that are a short walk from the heart of town. The golden arches can be seen through the trees and the sounds of traffic are omnipresent, reminiscent of a backyard camp-out. 14-night max. stay. Sites $15. ❶

## FOOD & NIGHTLIFE

Mammoth Lakes abounds with delis, cafes, and pizza joints to feed the high-adrenaline, low-funds crowd, but adventurous palates need not dispair. Plenty of restaurants have more creative menus than the omnipresent fast food franchises, though such culinary creativity may come with prices as high as the neighboring peaks.

**Schat's Bakery and Cafe,** 3305 Main St. (☎934-6055, Vermeer Deli 934-4203). Arguably the best bakery in town, with cappuccino ($2.75) and 1 lb. loafs of succulent sourdough ($3). Inside the bakery, the **Vermeer Deli** ❷ is perfect for picnic assembly with famously fresh sandwiches like the albacore tuna with sundried tomatoes ($7.50). Bakery open Su-Th 5:30am-6pm; F-Sa 5:30am-8pm. Deli open daily 10am-2pm. ❶

**Whiskey Creek** (☎934-2555), at Lake Mary Rd. and Minaret St. This modern, upscale restaurant serves up meaty and exploratory American cuisine in an atmosphere of dimly lit sophistication (entrees $18-23). The large bar area is a nightlife hub with a DJ on W and live music F-Sa. Microbrews $3. Happy Hour M-F 5-7pm with $1 drafts. Bar open daily 5pm-1:30am; kitchen open daily 5:30-10pm. ❺

**Nick-n-Willies Pizza & Subs,** 76 Old Mammoth Rd. (☎934-2012). The best pizza in town; the huge sub sandwiches aren't bad either. Wide variety of toppings include chipotle, sun dried tomatoes, feta cheese, and pesto. Cheese slice $3, small pizza $11. Hot Pizzawich or Hot Thai Chicken subs $6-7. Open daily 11:30am-9pm. ❶

**Base Camp Cafe,** on Main St. (☎934-3900), across from the post office. Excellent and inexpensive meals in a joint plastered with skate company stickers. Breakfast can be had for as little as $2. Sandwiches ($4-6) include mouth-watering turkey breast with cranberries on a French loaf. Brown bag lunches available as early as 7:30am ($8; call ahead). Open M-W 7:30am-3pm, Th-F and Su 7:30am-8pm, Sa 7:30am-9pm. ❷

## SIGHTS

There's plenty to see in Mammoth Lakes, much of which is accessible by the **MAS shuttle service** (see p. 288). This mandatory shuttle (runs daily 7am-7pm) was introduced to keep the area from being completely trampled and runs from the Mammoth Mountain Gondola Building to the Devil's Postpile monument, Agnew Meadows, and numerous trailheads and **campgrounds** ❶ (sites $12-14). The shuttle system makes the Gondola Building the hub for many outdoor activities in the area. Day passes and camping passes are $7.

**DEVIL'S POSTPILE NATIONAL MONUMENT AND RAINBOW FALLS.** The Devil's Postpile is a sheer basalt wall 60 ft. high, made of eerily uniform hexagonal columns that formed less than 100,000 years ago when the basalt lava that oozed through Mammoth Pass cooled and contracted. A glacier then plowed through the area, carving away a chunk of the solidified basalt and exposing this cross-section view. A pleasant 2 mi. walk from the Devil's Postpile Monument, the middle fork of the San Joaquin River drops 101 ft. into a glistening green canyon pool at Rainbow Falls. Although Postpile and Rainbow Falls are the most popular attractions, the park has more to offer; take a stroll around Sotcher Lake, steep yourself in Fisher Creek Hot Springs, or hike part of the John Muir Trail to fully appreciate the marvels on display. To really get to know Postpile, camp at one of the six area **campgrounds ❶** (7600-8400 ft.; sites $14), all of which have piped water. *(From US 395, the Devil's Postpile/Rainbow Falls trailhead can be reached by a 15 mi. drive past Minaret Summit on Rte. 203. Driving in is prohibited, however; take the shuttle bus. Guided ranger walks daily 11am. For campers, shuttle passes valid for the duration of the trip; mention this when purchasing.)*

**FUN WITH VOLCANOES.** The **Inyo Craters** are huge conical volcanic blast holes in the ground filled with bright green water. Only 500 years old, they're proof of the area's shaky underground history. The quarter-mile jaunt to the craters can be reached from Mammoth Scenic Loop Rd., a gently winding thoroughfare that leads to sights between Rte. 203 and US 395. A 10 mi. **mountain biking** loop explores the craters up close. **Obsidian Dome,** 14 mi. north of Mammoth Junction and one mile west of US 395 on Glass Flow Rd. (follow the sign to Lava Flow), is a vast blob of solid volcanic glass that was formed by the quick chilling of lava 1000 years ago.

# ◪ OUTDOOR ACTIVITIES

Mammoth is like a Mountain Dew commercial come to life—extreme activities abound, from climbing to dogsledding. **Mammoth Mountain High Adventure** gets people up high. The stately climbing wall stands like a modern-day shrine to extreme sports, beckoning both the inexperienced and the professional. (☎924-5683. Open daily 10am-6pm. $6 per climb, $13 per hr., $22 per day; discount for groups of 3 or more.) The **Map and Compass Course** has more of an outdoor sleuth/guerrilla warfare approach to freedom. ($15 round-trip for 2hr. course; includes compass rental, map, and intro lesson.) Swing, tightrope walk, and rappel to freedom in the **High Ropes Course.** (4hr.; Th-Sa 1pm, Su 10am. $43, group rate $40 per person.)

Visitors can ride the **Mammoth Mountain Gondola** for a view miles above the rest. (☎934-2571. Open daily 8am-4pm. $16 round-trip, children $8; day pass for gondola and trail use $25. Chair ride $10 round-trip, children $5.) Exit the gondola at the top for a mountain biking extravaganza of more than 80 mi. of twisted trails in **Mammoth Mountain Bike Park,** where the ride starts at 11,053 ft. and heads straight down on rocky ski trails. (☎934-0706. Helmets required. Open 9am-6pm. Day pass $29, children $15. Unlimited day pass and bike rental $62/$31.) In case you somehow exhaust your options for recreation, a bus also runs daily to **Yosemite National Park** (see **Transportation,** p.288) from the mountain lodge.

## HIKING

Day hikes in the area are clustered around the Mammoth Lakes Basin and Reds Meadow. A quick half-mile hike from the Twin Lakes turn-off on Lake Mary Rd. culminates in spectacular views of Owens Valley and Crowley Lake from the **Panorama Dome.** Lake Mamie has a picturesque picnic area and many short hikes leading out to Lake George, where exposed granite sheets attract climbers. For short but stunning hikes through wildflowers and amazing scenery, trek the **Crystal Lake Trail** (2½ mi.) or the **Barrett Lake Trail,** both of which leave from the Lake George entrance parking lot. **Horseshoe Lake** is a popular swimming spot and also the trailhead for the impressive Mammoth Pass Trail. The fork in the trail leads to **McLeod Lake** on the left or **Red's Meadow** on the right. In Agnew Meadows (take the shuttle), moderate trails lead to the tranquil **Shadow** (3½ mi.) and **Ediza** (6½ mi.) lakes from the campground. Also departing from Agnew Meadows is a very challenging day hike or a less strained overnighter, the trail to **Thousand Island Lake** (10 mi.). **Mammoth Sporting Goods** (☎934-3239) and **Sandy's Ski & Sport** (☎934-7518) can equip more experienced hikers with gear and info on more challenging climbs.

## FISHING

Not one of the over 100 lakes near town (60 are within a 5 mi. radius) actually goes by the name of Mammoth Lake. The area's largest, most beautiful lake, the 1 mi. long **Lake Mary,** is popular for boating, sailing, and fishing. Anglers converge on the Mammoth area each summer to test their skills on some of the best **trout lakes** in the country. Permits are required for anyone over 16 (the visitors center has info on other regulations) and can be expensive for non-residents. Fanatics will find the frequent fishing derbies well worth the price of entry, but less competitive types might prefer to try their luck at the area's serene and well-stocked backcountry waters. Manmade reservoir **Crowley Lake** in Owens Valley, 12 mi. south of town, is a fishing mecca, yielding over 80 tons of rainbow trout each summer and attracting a city's worth of people on opening day. (☎935-4301. Motorboat rental $55 per day; parking included. Parking without rental $6 per day. **Campsites** ❷ with full hookup $25.) Just south of town on Rte. 395, **Convict Lake** is deep and home to some monster trout, but its clear water and windy surroundings can make catching one a challenge. (☎934-3800. Fishing boats $15 per hour, $65 per day. **Campsites** ❶ are $13.) **Owens River,** south on Rte. 395 to Benton Crossing Rd. and then 3 mi. to a bridge and a dirt road that follows the river, is a great spot for fly fishing.

The trout-filled **Hot Creek Geothermal Area,** 5 mi. south of town off US 395 at Hot Creek Rd., also allows catch-and-release fishing. The waters here are warmed by the liquid magma sending up steam from miles below the creek bed following a toasty volcanic blast. Hungry trout bathe in these warm waters year-round. Several trails lead to the springs, but be careful—a close look may result in a severe burn. Tours of the hot springs and trout hatchery are given (open daily 8am-4pm).

## SKIING AND WINTER RECREATION

With 150 downhill runs, 28 lifts, and miles of nordic trails, Mammoth is one of the country's premier winter resorts. The season extends from November to June; in a good year, downhill skiing can last through July. Visiting during a slow time (avoiding weekends and major holidays) keeps costs lower. Rent skis in town (see **Equipment Rental,** p. 288); resort-run shops usually charge 10-20% more. Mammoth Mountain lift tickets can be purchased at the **Main Lodge,** at the base of the mountain on Minaret Rd. Group ski lessons are available for all levels ($54, beginners $35) every day. A special first-timers package includes rentals, day pass, and a lesson for $78. (☎934-2571. Open daily 7:30am-3pm. Experienced day pass $45, teens $35, children and seniors $22. Beginner day pass $25 for all ages.) A free **shuttle bus (MAS)** transports skiers between lifts, town, and the Main Lodge (see p. 288). The US Forest Service provides info and tips on the area's cross-country trails.

Mammoth has miles of trails and open areas for **snowmobiles.** The **Mammoth Lake Snowmobile Association** maps out open and restricted areas. Visitors over 16 years old with a driver's license can rent snowmobiles at **Center Street Polaris DJ Snowmobile.** (☎934-4020. Open M-Sa 8am-4:30pm. One-rider $85 per 2hr., $167 per 4hr.; two-rider $115/$245.) Mammoth has lately pioneered **bobsledding;** although runs are slow enough for non-Olympians, they can be exhilarating, especially at night. **Bobsledz,** on Minaret Rd. halfway to the lodge, can hook you up. (☎934-7533. Open daily 10am-4pm; in summer 4:30-7:30pm.)

**June Mountain Ski Area,** at US 395 N and Rte. 158 W, 20 mi. north of Mammoth Lakes, has less stellar skiing and correspondingly shorter lines than Mammoth. (☎648-7733. Lift tickets $45, ages 19-23 $40, ages 13-18 $35, children and seniors $25. Lift tickets are available in the Tram Haus next to the parking lot.)

## ◖ SEASONAL EVENTS

Almost every weekend in every season Mammoth is host to some wild festival, from triathlons to skateboarding contests, from dogsledding to canoe races—it's like a year-round summer camp. The **Mammoth Festival of Beers and Bluesapalooza** chugs truckloads of over 40 microbrews and piles of BBQ dishes to the sounds of some of the country's best blues in early August. (☎934-0606. Unlimited beer and 4 food coupons $36; music only $28.) The **Mammoth Lakes Jazz Jubilee,** in mid-July, is a local favorite. (☎934-2478. Day entry $30, 3 day pass $60.) The **Mammoth Motorcross Race** (☎934-0642), in late June, is one of the area's most popular athletic competitions, and the **National Mountain Biking Championships** (☎934-0651), in early September, attracts nearly 50,000 people. Winter festivities include some cross-country ski races, a **Snowshow Play Day** (☎934-7566) in February, a **Winterfestival** (☎934-6643) in March, and a **marathon** (☎934-2442) in late March.

# BISHOP & OWENS VALLEY ☎760

Situated in the northern end of Owens Valley minutes from world-class hiking, climbing, horseback riding, and fishing, Bishop is the place for visitors to stop and recharge en route to the surrounding rivers, mountains, and desert valleys. The largest city in the Eastern Sierras, this resort town has many of the things missing from the rest of the region, such as international cuisine, bookstores, and coffeehouses, as well as some things that are better off missed, like casinos and strip-malls. Opportunities to fish in the clear lakes of Bishop Creek Canyon, boulder in the Buttermilks, or enjoy the seasonal festivals make the town worth visiting. Owens Valley is wedged between the Sierras and the towering White Mountains, making it "the deepest valley on Earth." In the early 20th century, Owens Valley's freshwater streams provided water for the budding city of LA, leading to the water scandal that the movie *Chinatown* (1974) grossly fictionalized.

## ◖ ◖ ORIENTATION AND PRACTICAL INFORMATION

Bishop is located on Rte. 395 in the northern end of Owens Valley. Lone Pine, at the base of Mt. Whitney, is 60 mi. south. Via the Tioga Pass, the town is 140 mi. from Yosemite. Death Valley is 165 mi. to the southeast, LA is 270 mi. south, and Reno is 205 mi. north via Rte. 395.

**Bus:** Greyhound has canceled service to the Eastern Sierra, but you can take it to Carson City, where **CREST** (☎800-922-1930) runs Tu and Th-F at 2pm, arriving in Bishop at 6:30pm. One-way fare $20.

**Public Transportation: Dial-A-Ride** (☎872-1901 or 800-922-1930). Runs fixed route around town (50¢); will travel up to 1 mi. off-route for an additional 75¢. Call ahead for flexible stops M-Th 8am-5pm, F-Sa 8am-midnight (last call 11:30pm). Door-to-door buses also serve the area (includes trailheads; rates based on distance traveled). Shuttles run twice daily (7am and 5:30pm) to **Mammoth** ($5.50) and **Crowley Lake** ($3).

**Visitor Information:**

**Bishop Area Chamber of Commerce and Visitors Bureau,** 690 N. Main St. (☎888 395-3952 or 873-8405; www.bishopvisitor.com), at City Park. Area maps and info. Get a free copy of *Bishop, California Vacation Planner* for up-to-date listings of special events. Open mid-Apr. to mid-Oct. M-F 9am-5pm, Sa-Su 10am-4pm; mid-Oct. to mid-Apr. M-F 9am-4:30pm, Sa-Su 10am-4pm.

**White Mountain Ranger Station,** 798 N. Main St. (☎873-2500; www.fs.fed.us/r5/inyo). Campground and trail info for all of Inyo National Forest. Weather report and message board. Reserve wilderness permits up to 6 months ahead; must be picked up by 10am on day of. Walk-in permits for all trails. Open daily mid-May to mid-Sept. 8am-5pm; mid-Sept. to mid-May M-F 8am-4:30pm.

**Bank: Washington Mutual,** 400 N. Main St. (☎873-5031). **24hr. ATM.** Open M-F 9am-6pm, Sa 9am-1pm.

**Laundromat: Sierra Suds,** 163 Academy St. (☎873-8338). Wash $1.25, dry 25¢ per 10min. Open daily 7am-9pm. Last wash 8pm.

**AAA Emergency Road Service:** ☎800-400-4222. Call ☎872-8241 for local branch.

**Road Conditions: Caltrans,** ☎800-427-7623.

**Fishing Licenses:** Available at **Culver's Sporting Goods,** 156 S. Main St. (☎872-8361). For non-residents, 10-day license $30.70, annual $82.45. Open Apr.-Oct. M-Th 6am-8pm, F-Sa 8am-9pm; Nov.-Feb. daily 7am-5pm; Mar. daily 7am-6pm.

**Emergency:** ☎911.

**Police: Bishop Police Department,** 207 W. Line St. (☎873-5866).

**Hospital: Northern Inyo Hospital,** 150 Pioneer Ln. (☎873-5811), off W. Line St. 24hr. emergency care.

**Library and Internet Access: Inyo County Free Library,** 210 Academy St. (☎873-5115). 30min. free. Open M-Th 10am-8pm, F 10am-6pm, Sa 10am-1pm.

**Post Office:** 595 W. Line St. (☎873-3526 or 800-275-8777). Open M-F 7:30am-4pm, Sa 9am-1pm. **Postal Code:** 93514.

# ▟ ACCOMMODATIONS

Hotels are plentiful in Bishop but cheap hotels are not. Thrifty travelers are better off camping. Those traveling in groups, especially those looking to fish, may find a cabin is the best option. Try the **Cardinal Village Resort ❺,** at the North Fork of Bishop Creek Canyon (☎873-4789; www.cardinalvillageresort.com), or **Bishop Creek Lodge ❺,** 2100 S. Lake Rd. (☎873-4484; www.bishopcreekresorts.com), at the south fork of Bishop Creek Canyon. (2- to 3-night min. stay, $90-275.)

**El Rancho Motel,** 274 Lagoon St. (☎872-9251 or 888-872-9251). 2 blocks west of Main St. A quintessential motel; drive right up to your door. 16 rooms with TV, A/C, coffeemakers, and refrigerators. Reception 7:30am-11:30pm. Kitchen $8 extra. Singles $40-55; doubles $45-67. Extra occupant $5. Prices lowest Nov. to mid-Apr. ❸

**Bardini House,** 515 Sierra St. (☎873-8036, 872-4413, or 872-1348). A small house in a residential neighborhood. Kitchen, grill, and back patio for guest use. 10-night max stay. Reservation required. Dorm-style beds $10. ❶

**Chalfant House,** 213 Academy St. (☎800 641-2996 or 872-1790). This homey B&B is worth the extra bucks for the hardwood floors, patchwork quilts, and wood stove in the parlor. Breakfast and refreshments. Check-in 3-7pm. Singles and doubles from $80. ❹

**Bishop Village Motel,** 286 W. Elm St. (☎872-8155 or 888-668-5546). Caters to fishermen and other outdoorsfolk with a grilling area and fish-freezing facilities. Quiet, comfortable rooms one block from Main St. Heated pool. Rooms have refrigerators and cable TV; some have kitchens. Economy rooms $39-49; suites $69-79. ❸

# ▞ CAMPING

Most campgrounds around Bishop are well-kept and easily accessible. Sites host a consistent flow of campers throughout the summer but are especially crowded during the Mule Days celebration over Memorial Day weekend and the Tri-County Fair over Labor Day weekend (book a year in advance).

There are over 30 **Inyo National Forest** campgrounds in the Bishop Ranger District (most open May-Oct.). The closest campgrounds to town are private, however, and can be found on or near Rte. 395 just north and south of Bishop. **Millpond ❶**, 4500 ft., 6 mi. north of Bishop on Saw Mill Rd., has 70 cool, shady spots near Millpond County Park and McGee Creek. (☎ 873-5342. Open Mar.-Oct. Sites $16 and up.) Southwest of town on Rte. 168 are many USFS campgrounds. The wheelchair- accessible **Four Jeffrey ❶**, 8100 ft., boasts 100 open sites on a hillside above the south fork of Bishop Creek. (Open late Apr. to Oct. Sites $14, extra vehicle $5.) For wilder camping, **North Lake ❶**, 9500 ft., and **Sabrina Lake ❶**, 9000 ft., both have stunning scenery, trail access to the John Muir Wilderness, and fishing, of course. These chilly sites feature vault toilets, water, and lots of nature. (North open mid-June to Sept.; Sabrina mid-May to Sept. 7-day limit. Sites $14, extra vehicle $5.) **Pleasant Valley ❶**, 4100ft., 6½ mi. north of town off of Hwy. 395, is home to 200 sites for year-round camping near the Happy and Sad Boulders and Owens River Gorge. Water and toilets. (14-day limit. Sites $10.) Nearby, on the west side of Hwy. 395, free camping can be found 5 mi. west on Round Valley Rd. (off Saw Mill Rd.) at **Horton Creek ❶**, 5000 ft. Fifty-three unshaded sites have vault toilets, but no drinking water. (14-day limit. Open May-Oct.)

Some of the best camping can be found north of town, between Bishop and Mammoth Lakes, on Rte. 395. **Rock Creek ❶**, 7000-10,000 ft., has ten campgrounds with over 300 sites scattered about the canyon, nearly all of which are secluded and shady. Excellent fishing, mountain biking, climbing, and hiking abound. Most sites have piped water and flush toilets. (Open May-Oct. Sites $15-16.)

## 🗋 FOOD

Stock up on groceries at **Manor Market,** 3100 W. Line St., which is locally owned and offers natural foods (☎ 873-4296. Open M-Sa 6am-9pm, Su 6am-8pm), or **Vons,** 1190 N. Main St. (☎ 872-9811; open 24hr.).

**Taqueria Las Palmas,** 136 E. Line St. (☎ 873-4337). This authentic taqueria is popular with locals and climbing bums. The friendly waitstaff dishes out specialty flautas buffalo burritos ($9) and a full range of Mexican beers. Open daily 11am-9pm. ❷

**Western Kitchen,** 930 N. Main St. (☎ 872-3246). Along with classic American fare, this western kitchen also serves eastern dishes. Try an omelette ($5-7) or steak ($7-9), or choose from an extensive list of Thai specials ($7.50-$9.50). Open daily 6am-9pm. ❷

**Erik Schat's Bakery,** 763 N. Main St. (☎ 873-7156). Breads and pastries ($3-5) are baked daily and served with coffee. The hearty salads, soups, and sandwiches ($3.50-7) like the Mule Kick are especially rejuvenating after a day in the hills. Try the sheepherder's bread. Open May-Oct. M-Th and Sa 6am-6:30pm, F 6am-10pm, Su 6am-8pm; Nov.-Apr. M-Th and Sa 6:30am-6:30pm, F 6am-10pm, Su 6:30am-7pm. ❶

**Kava Coffeehouse,** 206 N. Main St. (☎ 872-1010). Scarf healthy eats like Kava Quiche ($5). Coffee and fresh smoothies ($4). Local artists' wares grace the cabinets. Chess night Tu (5-8pm). Open M-F 6:30am-8:30pm, Sa 7am-8:30pm, Su 7am-3:30pm. ❶

## 🔼 OUTDOOR ACTIVITIES

### EAST OF BISHOP

The mountains forming the Owens Valley are a backpacker's Eden. In the eastern half of Inyo National Forest, which is split by Hwy. 395, the yellow sands of **White Mountains** rise to heights that rival the Sierras but without the fanfare. To escape the crowds gallivanting on the western slopes of the valley, head east; you'll see more cows than people. If it's elevation you want, tackle the tough 7½ mi. slog to the top of White Mountain Peak (14,246 ft.), the third-tallest mountain in California. The hike gains 2500 ft. on the way to the summit from the locked Bancroft Gate at the White Mountain Research Station. Park your car at the station on White Mountain Rd., 26 mi. from Hwy. 168 and 38 mi. from Big Pine. Unlike Mt. Whitney, a day-use permit is not necessary, but you can get nearly as high.

Scattered across the face of the White Mountains are California's **bristlecone pines,** the oldest living organisms on the planet. Gnarled, twisted, and warped into fantastic shapes, the trees may grow only one inch in height every 100 years. The preservative qualities of the cold, dry altitudes (the trees grow at extreme elevations of up to 12,000 ft.) have allowed the "Methuselah" specimen in the Schulman Group to survive for 4700 years (to prevent vandalism, visitors are not told which one it is). To reach the **Ancient Bristlecone Pine Forest** (☎873-2500 or 873-2573), follow Hwy. 168 off Hwy. 395 at Big Pine for 12 mi. Turn left at the sign. The 11 mi. paved road climbs to **Schulman Grove,** at nearly 10,000 ft. Before the grove, 8 mi. down the road, you'll come to **Sierra View Overlook;** on a clear day you can see the great wall of the Sierras, including parts of Yosemite and Mt. Whitney. Two short **hikes** head out from Schulman. The moderately strenuous 4½ mi. Methuselah Walk and easy 1 mi. Discovery Trail lead through the hills and past these astonishing trees. The drive to the even-higher Patriarch Grove, home of some of the most astonishing trees, is a beautiful but unpaved 12 mi. from Schulman.

A number of valleys are tucked beneath eastern slopes of the White and Inyos, including Fish Lake Valley, Deep Springs Valley (home of **Deep Springs College**), part of Death Valley, and the uninhabited ▓**Eureka Valley,** the valley directly northwest of Death Valley. Its magnificent and haunting sand dunes create one of the region's most surreal landscapes. If the sand is cool, flip off your shoes, climb to the top of the dunes, and roll down. The friction between the sand you disturb and the grains beneath it causes a deep resonation that sounds like a bizarre hum. Native Americans called it "the singing of the sands." Death Valley Rd., off Hwy. 168 east of Big Pine, passes through Eureka Valley on its way to Scotty's Castle. The paved and gravel Death Valley Rd. runs 37 mi. southwest from the intersection with Hwy. 168 before turning off near Eureka Valley Rd., a 10 mi. gravel and dirt track that cuts across the valley floor to the dunes. 4WD is preferable, especially if there's snow or if the road is washed out; see **Desert Survival,** p. 528.

## WEST OF BISHOP

A lot of fun can be had near Bishop in Big Pine and Bishop Creek Canyons, to the south and west, and in Buttermilk Country and Rock Creek, to the west and northwest. Wilderness permits are required year-round for overnight trips in the **John Muir Wilderness,** which includes most of the Eastern Sierra from Mt. Whitney to Mammoth. All trailheads within the Wilderness have usage quotas, but 40% of permits are available on a walk-in basis (☎873-2483; $5 fee to reserve). Head south on Hwy. 395 to Big Pine, then west on Crocker St. for 10 mi. to reach the mouth of **Big Pine Canyon,** which was cut into the thick groves of Jeffery Pines by Big Pine Creek. This area is home to the southernmost glaciers in the US, remnants from the last Ice Age that shaped the landscape. The largest of these glaciers is **Palisade Glacier,** 2 mi. in length and many hundred feet thick. The **North Fork Trail** (or **Big Pine Lakes Trail**) is a popular route for hikers, as well as rock and ice climbers looking to access the glacier or Palisades, the rock pinnacles above it. The trail passes First, Second, and Third Lakes as well as the stone cabin of Hollywood legend Lon Chaney before reaching the foot of Palisade Glacier. It's an 18 mi. round-trip hike with a 4500 ft. elevation gain to the base of the glacier. The summit of North Palisade (14,242 ft.), one of the tallest peaks in the Sierras, is another 2000 ft. higher. **Fishing** enthusiasts favor Big Pine's obscure **South Fork Trail,** which leads to lakes full of trout. The route becomes sketchy above Willow Lake (4 mi. from trailhead).

Six miles north of Big Pine and 7 mi. south of Bishop on Hwy. 395 are **Keough's Hot Springs.** The springs have been exploited as a full-fledged business venture, complete with a pool, lifeguards, and snack bar. (☎872-6911. $7.) At night, however, the water that was diverted into the pool continues down the hill and makes for terrific hot tubbing in the creek. To reach these healing waters, turn onto Keough Hot Springs Rd. and after a half-mile, make a right turn down to the creek.

Follow Line St. (Hwy. 168) west of Bishop to the lakes and campgrounds of **Bishop Creek Canyon.** Within the canyon walls, 15 mi. down the highway, the road splits. Turning left at the fork will take you to **South Lake** (9700ft., 9 mi.), while continuing straight will take you to **Lake Sabrina** (9125ft., 5 mi.). Both mountain reservoirs are stunning, teem with fish, and offer trailhead access into the Sierras. The official angling season spans from late April to late Oct. Contact the Chamber of Commerce (☎873-8405) for general fishing and tournament info. From South Lake, hikers can pick up the **Bishop Pass Trail,** which connects with trails leading to Green, Treasure, and Chocolate Lakes, as well as mountain meadows that fill with wildflowers come spring. More adventurous hikers can forge deeper into the wilderness along the trail and tackle some of the nearby 13,000 ft. peaks, including **Mount Goode** (13,085 ft.).From the fork, Hwy. 168 continues west 4 mi. to **Sabrina Basin,** which offers secluded hiking and fishing opportunities. On the southern side of the road **Cardinal Pinnacle** offers a number of multi-pitch routes on superb granite. Lake Sabrina is the trailhead for routes up to pristine alpine lakes including Blue, Hungry Packer, and Midnight Lakes. **North Lake** can be accessed by a single-lane dirt road heading north just before Lake Sabrina. From the campground here, the **Paiute Pass Trail** follows the north fork of Bishop Creek up to Paiute Pass (11,423 ft.), where it joins the **John Muir Trail.**

Nearly 8 mi. up Hwy. 168, the Buttermilk Rd. turnoff leads to some world-famous boulders in **Buttermilk Country.** Named for the dairy farms that once refreshed stagecoach parties passing the region, the area is marked by giant granite boulders great for climbing and mountain biking. About 4 mi. down the road, you'll come to the **Peabody Boulders,** the most celebrated of the outcroppings.

The forests and mountains along **Rock Creek Canyon** are frequented year-round. Hair-raising precipices, plunging canyons, and alpine wildflowers mesmerize photographers and casual onlookers alike. Take Hwy. 395 24 mi. north of Bishop, turn west on Rock Creek Rd., and continue up Rock Creek Canyon as far as you can go: in the summer, Mosquito Flat (10 mi.), and in the winter, the locked gate. **Little Lakes Valley** cradles a necklace of trout-filled lakes in the shadow of 13,000 ft. peaks. The **Little Lakes Trail** sets out from Mosquito Flat and climbs gradually to explore the upper valley's lakes and meadows. **Mono Pass Trail,** which branches off from the Little Lakes trail about a quarter of a mile from the trailhead, leads to beautiful **Ruby Lake** and its staggering sheer granite walls. It continues to Mono Pass (12,040 ft.) and connects with the John Muir Trail. Rock Creek also boasts some great mountain biking on the **Lower Rock Creek Trail,** which starts at Tom's Place. There are numerous **campgrounds ❶** on the way to Mosquito Flat (see above) and plenty of day-parking at

SIERRA NEVADA

each of the three trailheads. In winter, the evergreen forests and lake basins of this "range of light" (as Muir described the Eastern Sierra) make for spectacular **cross-country skiing.**

## 🎵 ENTERTAINMENT

There might not be a hopping bar scene in Bishop, but hog-riders and other wild spirits manage to find excitement at the few watering holes that line Main St. (Hwy. 395). **Rusty's,** 112 N. Main St (☎873-9066; open daily 8am-2am), is among the most popular (and darkest). Although activity and excitement seem to permeate everyday life in Bishop, several annual events add more spice to the metropolis. Haul your ass to town during Memorial Day weekend for the largest mule event in the world, **Mule Days** (☎872-4263; www.muledays.org). View 110 mule sporting events, 30,000 mule-obsessed fans, 700 mules, and the famous Mule Days Parade, which is long enough to be listed in the Guinness Book of World Records. The **Hotrods, Hippies & Polyester 50s-70s Dance** (☎873-3588) grooves every February, and the **Air Show** usually flies by on Fourth of July weekend. The City Park (behind the Visitors Center) has hosted **evening concerts** in the gazebo for 40 consecutive summers. (June-Aug. M 8-9pm. Free.) Food, games, and fun characterize the massive **Tri-County Fair** (☎873-3588) over Labor Day weekend, which features rodeos, homemade salsa, beer and wine contests, and a demolition derby.

# LONE PINE                                     ☎760

Flanked to the west by the looming High Sierra and the otherworldly Alabama Hills, to the south by the unrivaled Mt. Whitney, and to the east by Death Valley, it's no wonder that Lone Pine (pop. 2016) has attracted the attention of Hollywood's location scouts. *Roy Rogers, The Lone Ranger, Gladiator,* and (regrettably) *Gone in 60 Seconds* are a few examples of the over 300 TV shows and films shot in this striking landscape. The dramatic contours of Lone Pine's scenery certainly stir up the awe, excitement, and twinge of fear that evoked by the mythic Western frontier depicted by Hollywood and American history books. Still, Lone Pine remains unsuffocated by its celebrity associations; the town is as much about Mt. Whitney as it is the movies. Hikers, mountaineers, anglers, mountain bikers, rock climbers, and artists all flock to this legendary American wilderness for the serious outdoor experience.

## ✳🛈 ORIENTATION & PRACTICAL INFORMATION

Straddling US 395, Lone Pine is the first Sierra town northeast on Rte. 136 from Death Valley. Independence, the Inyo county seat, is 15 mi. north, while Bishop is 60 mi. north. LA is 4hr. away, 212 mi. south along US 395, and southwest along Rte. 14. Yosemite is a 5-6hr., 210 mi. drive north on US 395. Upon reaching Lone Pine, US 395 becomes Main St.; Washington St. is one block west.

> **Buses:** Since Greyhound canceled service to the Eastern Sierra, getting to Lone Pine by bus is rather difficult. You can take Greyhound or Amtrak to Carson City, where **CREST** (☎800-922-1930) departs on Rte. 395 Tu and Th-F at 1:45pm and arrives in Bishop, 60 mi. north of Lone Pine, at 6:30pm. A separate, non-connecting bus passes through Bishop on its way to Lone Pine on M, W, F. Contact CREST to figure out the best way to match up buses.

**Airport: Inyokern Airport (IYK);** (☎377-5844), in Inyokern, 70 mi. south on Rte. 395. Daily service to and from Los Angeles International Airport by United Airlines (☎377-5000; www.ual.com). $200-300 round-trip.

**Car Rental: Lindsey Automotive,** 361 S. Washington St. (☎876-4789). Rates from $60 per day. 150 mi. included. Must be at least 21 with credit card. Open M-F 8am-5pm. After-hours service available for a charge. **Avis** (☎446-5556) has an office at the Inyokern Airport.

**Auto Repairs: Don's Garage,** 1506 S. Main St. (☎876-4600). Open M-F 8am-5pm, Sa 9am-3pm.

**AAA Emergency Road Service:** ☎872-8241.

**Visitor Information:**

**Interagency Visitors Center** (☎876-6222), at US 395 and Rte. 136, about 1 mi. south of town. Joint venture between a number of agencies, including the Forest Service and University of California. Excellent maps and guidebooks, plus small exhibits. Informative handouts on hiking in the area. Open daily 8am-4:50pm.

**Chamber of Commerce,** 120 S. Main St. (☎876-4444 or 877-253-8981; www.lonepinechamber.com), in Lone Pine. Same services as the Visitors Center. Cheerful, knowledgeable employees. Open M-F 7:30am-5pm, Sa 9am-1pm.

**Mount Whitney/Inyo National Forest Ranger Station,** 640 S. Main St. (☎876-6200; www.fs.fed.us/r5/inyo), in Lone Pine. Programs on regional wildlife and history. Topographical and trail maps for backcountry camping. Gives out free **wilderness permits,** which are required for overnight backcountry trips. All trails within the Ansel Adams, John Muir, Hoover, and Golden Trout Wildernesses have overnight usage quotas (usually 10-30 people). Reserve permits ($5) up to 6 months in advance for the quota season, May 1-Nov. 1; self-register in the winter. 40% of trail quotas are saved for walk-ins during the quota season. Mt. Whitney has 60 overnight and 130 day-use **Mt. Whitney permits,** all of which must be reserved in advance (no walk-ins). All permit applications must be submitted in Feb. (the earlier in the month, the better). Contact the ranger station or visit the website for an application, which must be mailed or faxed in. Some spots are usually left over, and can be reserved beginning in May. Station open daily 8am-6pm. If you're not climbing Mt. Whitney, **Wilderness Reservations** can be phoned in daily 10am-4pm at ☎760-873-2483.

**Laundromat: Coin-Op Laundromat,** 105 W. Post St., just off Main St. Wash $1.25, dry 25¢ per 12min. Open daily 7am-9pm. Change machines.

**Showers: Kirk's Barber Shop,** 114 N. Main St. (☎876-5700; $4) or on the mountain at the **Whitney Portal Store** ($3).

**Police: Inyo County Sheriff,** Lone Pine Substation, 210 N. Washington St. (☎876-5606). County Headquarters (☎878-0383).

**Hospital: Southern Inyo,** 501 E. Locust St. (☎876-5501).

**Library and Internet Access: Lone Pine Public Library** (☎876-5031), on S. Washington St. Open M-Tu and Th-F 9am-noon and 1-5pm, W 6-9pm, Sa 10am-1pm. 30 min. Internet limit if there's a line.

**Post Office:** 121 Bush St. (☎876-5681), between Jackson and Main St. Open M-F 9am-5pm. **Postal Code:** 93545.

# ACCOMMODATIONS

Many clean but high-priced motels are available here. Weekdays are cheapest, but rates fluctuate widely depending on demand; make reservations or arrive early.

**Historical Dow Hotel,** 310 S. Main St. (☎876-5521, reservations 800-824-9317; www.dowvillamotel.com). Built during Lone Pine's Hollywood heyday to house pouty movie stars, the welcoming lobby of this old hotel has several couches, a TV, a tea and coffee bar, and a fireplace. Pool and jacuzzi open 24hr. Convenient location.

SIERRA NEVADA

Doubles with shared bath from $40, with private bath from $50. ❸ Next to the more upscale **Dow Villa Motel,** which has newer rooms, more amenities, and great mountain views. Rooms (some sleeping up to 6 people) $75-115. ❺

**Alabama Hills Comfort Inn,** 1920 S. Main St. (☎876-8700; www.comfortinn.com), 1 mi. south of Lone Pine. Named for the frequently filmed hills nearby, this motel with interior corridors is becoming a Comfort Inn. Rooms here are a cut above standard, and all have fridge, microwave, and cable TV. Heated pool. Singles Apr.-Oct. from $59; Nov.-Feb. $49. $10 extra for double, patio, or balcony. AAA discount 10%. ❹

**De La Cour Ranch** (☎876-0022), 2½ mi. past Lubken Canyon Rd. on Horseshow Meadow Rd., off Whitney Portal Rd. outside of Lone Pine in the foothills. Secluded, spacious cabin with a bedroom and living room, full kitchen, and bathroom. Futon and loft sleep 4 inside, 2 tent bungalows sleep another 4. Feels like home. Cabin $150, weekly $750. Reserve in advance. ❺

## ⛏ CAMPING

Camping is cheap, scenic, and conveniently located. As with motels in the area, make reservations or arrive early.

▨ **Whitney Portal Campground** (Mt. Whitney ranger ☎876-6200, reservations 800-444-6777), 8000 ft., on Whitney Portal Rd., 13 mi. west of town. Surrounding evergreens, a rushing stream, and phenomenal views make this an exceptional campground. Campground hosts Nicki and Jim are happy to chat. Served by the **Whitney Portal Store,** which carries light food, guidebooks, and outerwear. (Open May-Oct. daily during sunlight hours.) Pay phone and a small **restaurant ❷.** 7-night max. stay. Some sites are reserved for first-come, first-camp. Open June-Oct. Sites $14; group sites $30. ❶

**Diaz Lake Campground** (☎876-5656), 3700 ft., on US 395, 2 mi. south of Lone Pine. 200 quiet, tree-lined sites overlooking Diaz Lake. Watersports fanatics will love the sites on the lake's far shore; the shoreline facilitates smooth watercraft launches. Grills, flush toilets, and showers. 15-day max. stay. Open year-round. Sites $10. ❶

**Portagee Joe,** 3800 ft., half a mile from Lone Pine on Whitney Portal Rd., within walking distance of town. Tree-lined camping by a small stream. 15 sites. Water and vault toilets. 14-day max. stay. Sites $10. Walk-in sites $6. ❶

**Lone Pine Campground** (reservations ☎877-444-6777), 6000 ft. Take Whitney Portal Rd. from Lone Pine for about 7 mi. 43 immaculate sites in close proximity to numerous trailheads, stellar views of the soaring granite faces, and soft gravel to pitch a tent on. Water and vault toilets. 14-day max. stay. Open April-Nov. Sites $12, seniors $6. ❶

## ◨ FOOD

Lone Pine has a smattering of diners, cafes, and a few fancier restaurants. Grab groceries in town at **Joseph's Bi-Rite Market,** 119 S. Main St., which also has a hearty, if heavy, hot deli. (☎876-4378. Open daily 8am-9pm.) This may not be the place for international cuisine, but reasonably priced homey meals are abundant.

**High Sierra Cafe,** 446 Main St. (☎876-5796). Down-to-earth food and prices. The BBQ beef sandwich ($5.50) is a great post-climb treat. A favorite of the locals, it's the only restaurant open daily 24hr. Its entire menu is fair game at all hours. ❷

**Mt. Whitney Restaurant,** 227 S. Main St. (☎876-5751). Decorated with memorabilia and photos from Westerns, this diner serves classic American grub for $6-14. The large breakfasts (around $6) provide good fuel for a day's hike. Open 6:30am-9:30pm.

**Seasons Restaurant** (☎876-8927), on the corner of Rte. 395 and Whitney Portal Rd. The most upscale restaurant in town, serving continental cuisine ($10-25) including some excellent seafood entrees. There are precious few vegetarian options but a great selection of Californian and imported wines, as well as microbrews. Open daily 5-10pm; in winter open M-Sa 5-10pm. ❹

## 🅖 SIGHTS

Lone Pine is surrounded by strange, beautiful scenery, from the deserts in the east to the rolling foothills and striking mountains in the west. All of the Sierra's tallest peaks are here, including the famous Mount Whitney (elevation 14,494 ft.).

Well before Whitney Portal, along Whitney Portal Rd., is **Movie Road,** which winds 12 miles through the famous **Alabama Hills.** A bouldered dreamscape of golden-brown granite formations, the hills were the stage set for fictionalized Hollywood cowboy 'n' Indian tales like the 1920s *How the West Was Won*, television shoot-'em-ups like *Bonanza* and *Rawhide*, and, more recently, countless SUV commercials. Recent flicks include *Maverick, Star Trek: Generations*, and *Gladiator*. In all, over 300 feature films and shows were shot here. The Chamber of Commerce dispenses a **movie location map** that will help you find where any film was shot. Lone Piners celebrate the Hills' glamorous career with the annual **Lone Pine Film Festival** (☎876-9103; $25 for all screenings and a tour of the hills) every Columbus Day weekend, when only films shot in the region are screened.

The **Eastern California Museum,** 155 N. Grant St., off Market St. in Independence, has a collection featuring local Paiute and Shoshone handicrafts, preserved equipment used by locals to construct the Los Angeles aqueduct, and a display on the Manzanar internment camp. Just behind the museum is a recreation of a small 1880s pioneer village, Little Pine. (☎878-0258. Open Su-M and W-Sa 10am-4pm. Donation appreciated.)

On US 395, between Lone Pine and Independence, lies the **Manzanar National Historic Site,** symbol and relic of one of the most shameful chapters in American history. Previously known as a "relocation" camp, it was the first of 10 internment centers that the US established after Japan's 1941 attack on Pearl Harbor to contain Japanese Americans, whom the government saw as potential enemy sympathizers. From 1942 to 1945, 10,000 people were brought here to the dusty, bare Owens Valley floor with whatever they could manage to carry in two suitcases. Conspicuously ignored by the government and America's collective memory, the camp is reduced to a few building foundations and some barbed wire. On the last Saturday of every April, an annual pilgrimage of former internees is held at the camp's cemetery. The day of remembrance and education is open to the public.

Once a big lake used to transport bullion from the nearby gold mines, **Owens Dry Lake,** 5 mi. south of town on Rte. 395, is now a big and colorful dry lakebed rich with minerals. In a familiar story from the 1920s, freshwater streams that fed the lake were diverted to the LA aqueduct, leaving the 75 sq. mi. area to dry up under the sun. The pretty green and pinkish hues at the lake bottom are the results of algae and bacteria. The dry salts exposed when the water disappeared have caused a serious dust problem in the area; in fact, the Environmental Protection Agency has deemed the area around Owens Lake the dustiest in the US.

One of the best-preserved ghost towns in the state, **Cerro Gordo** (☎876-1860), or "Fat Hill," once produced nearly 10,000 lb. of silver a day, all of it bound for LA, where it accounted for one-third of all business transactions in the Port of LA in the late 1800s. After the silver was exhausted, zinc briefly revived the mines in the early 1900s. Today, the town's remains are private property. Nonetheless, they are open to the public, featuring old time hotels, offices, a brothel, mining structures, and a museum. Cerro Gordo is 8 mi. down a dirt road from Keeler, off Rte. 270 south of Lone Pine. Call ahead if you want to visit.

## HIKING

Climbing Mt. Whitney requires significant preparation, both in terms of physical endurance and logistics. Unlike other Inyo trails, the main Mt. Whitney trail requires a permit for both overnight trips *and* day hikes. During the off-season there is no limit to the number of permits issued, but between May 15 and Nov. 1 there are daily quotas. Throughout the month of February, lottery applications (☎873-2483; www.fs.fed.us/r5/inyo) are accepted for both day and overnight permits for the quota season. In this lottery, overnight hikers have about a 60% chance of getting a spot, while day hikers have about a 90% chance, though these odds are highly dependent on dates and group size. A small number of permits for the quota season go unissued every year and can be reserved beginning in May.

As one of the most popular trails in the nation, the **Mount Whitney Trail** to the highest point in the lower 48 states is full of both experienced and amateur adventurers looking for bragging rights. The trailhead for **Mount Whitney** is at 8365 ft. and ascends over 6000 ft. to the 14,491 ft. summit. Hikers should be wary of the effects of altitude, hiking slowly and allotting extra time in their itinerary. But most importantly, spend some time hiking at higher altitudes; altitude sickness is a miserable affliction. Many campers spend a few days in the area before attempting higher climbs. Also remember that this is bear country. Ingenious bears rip apart backpacks and BMWs alike to get at anything odorous (see **Bears Will Eat You,** p. 44). Rent a bear-proof food container at one of the ranger stations ($5 per trip). The 11 mi. trek to the top of Mt. Whitney usually takes two to three days, though the very fit and acclimated can summit and return in one long day. While more of a strenuous hike than a mountain climb, this non-technical route is feasible only in late spring and summer when there is no ice. Temperatures can dip below freezing on the mountain at any time of year, so only attempt the journey with proper equipment and outerwear. For rock climbers, Mt. Whitney's **East Face** is a year-round technical challenge. A backcountry route to the Mt. Whitney summit, the **Cottonwood Lakes Trail** (10,000 ft. at the trailhead) continues over 40 mi. between the forests that abut the John Muir Wilderness and Sequoia National Park, passing some of the most incredible nature spots in the country along the way. Follow Whitney Portal Rd. for 4 mi. from Lone Pine and take Horseshoe Meadow Rd. 20 mi. to the trailhead. The trail is on the quota system from June to September 15.

Many moderate **day hikes** explore the Eastern Sierra out of the Whitney Portal. The hour-long hike along **Horseshoe Meadow Trail** to **Golden Trout Wilderness** passes several dozen high mountain lakes that reflect the Inyo Mountains. **Horseshoe Meadow** has walk-in **camping** ❶ (sites $6) and equestrian facilities ($12 per horse). The **Meysan Lake Trail** is a tough 4¾ mi. haul from Whitney Portal to an exquisite high-altitude lake and a number of rock climbing opportunities. Consider buying a topographical map, as the trail can be difficult to follow at times. The **Whitney Portal Trail** offers a more challenging 6hr. hike from the Lone Pine campground to Whitney Portal campground. The trail follows Lone Pine Creek to densely forested higher altitudes and offers incredible views of Mt. Whitney and the Owens Valley.

If you've got bulletproof muscles and high-octane willpower, you may want to line up for some of the toughest footraces in the world. On the first Saturday in May, Lone Pine stages the high-elevation **Wild Wild West Marathon,** considered the 7th most difficult marathon in North America. Interested athletes can enter by contacting the **Chamber of Commerce** (see p. 299). For those of you yawning, there is the 135 mi. Badwater (Death Valley) to Mt. Whitney **Ultramarathon** (☎ 510-528-3263; www.badwaterultra.com; see p. 542) in sweltering late July. This invitation-only odyssey usually takes two to three days for the world's top endurance athletes to complete. The unimaginably tough winners tend to finish in just over a full day of pain, sucking down a liquid diet of Red Bull and lactic acid. You're unlikely to ever find a more intense athletic event anywhere.

SIERRA NEVADA

# THE CENTRAL VALLEY

California's Central Valley minds its own agribusiness. Lifestyles here revolve around agriculture and colleges. Although the Central Valley has recently become home to many Bay Area commuters, it still seems far removed from the spotlight that scrutinizes its kooky neighbors, those cities to the west. One of the most fertile and productive regions in the world, the San Joaquin Valley stretches from the Tehachapi Range south of Bakersfield to just north of Stockton, where it becomes known as the Sacramento Valley. From there, the Valley continues northward past Chico, before it is engulfed by the Cascades. The land is flat, the air is oven-hot, and the endless fields and rows of fruit trees dominate the landscape along the razor-straight slashes of I-5 and Rte. 99. No other region in the state seems so irreconcilable with the glitz of California that captures popular imagination.

## SACRAMENTO          ☎916

Sacramento (area pop. 1.9 million) is the indistinct capital of a highly distinctive state. In 1848, Swiss emigré John Sutter, fleeing debtor's prison back home, purchased 48,000 dusty acres from the Miwok tribe for a few trinkets. His trading fort became the central pavilion for the influx of gold miners to the Valley in the 1850s. Over the next century, mansions and suburban bungalows gradually changed the landscape, paving the way for future residents Ronald Reagan and the Brady Bunch. Sacramento balances the nonstop bustle of San Francisco to the west with the tranquility of the mountains to the east, remaining as slow-paced as any small town (especially in summer, when temperatures can soar to 115 degrees). But don't let the city's daytime friendliness fool you; **exercise caution at night downtown.**

## ▐ TRANSPORTATION

**Airport: Sacramento International** (☎929-5411; http://airports.co.sacramento.ca.us), 12 mi. north on I-5. 2 terminals host 12 airlines serving hundreds of destinations worldwide. Cabs are expensive ($22-25 to downtown); vans are cheaper ($9-10); call **Super-Shuttle** for pick-up (☎800-258-3826). **Yolo Bus** (☎530-666-2877) runs public buses downtown. (Every hr. 5am-10pm, $1.25.)

**Trains: Amtrak,** 401 I St. (☎800-USA-RAIL/872-7245), at 5th St. To: **San Francisco** (2hr., 5 per day, $19); **Reno** (3hr., 7 per day, $20); **LA** (8-14hr., 4 per day, $42); and **Seattle** (8½-20hr., 1 per day, $59-110). Station open daily 5am-midnight. **Be careful around the station at night.**

**Buses: Greyhound,** 715 L St. (☎800-229-9424), between 7th and 8th St. To: **San Francisco** (2-3hr., 20 per day, $13-14); **Reno** (3hr., 12 per day, $21-23); **Seattle** (16-20hr., 8 per day, $69); **LA** (7-9hr., 10 per day, $42-45). Lockers available. Open 24hr. **Be careful around the station at night.**

**Public Transit: Sacramento Regional Transit Bus and Light Rail,** 1400 29th St. (☎321-2877; www.sacrt.com). Bus operates 5am-10pm, light rail 4am-midnight. Fare in city center 50¢. Outer destinations $1.50 (free transfer); seniors, disabled, and ages 5-12 75¢. Day passes $3.50.

**Taxis: Yellow Cab** (☎444-2222 or 800-464-0777). Open 24hr.

**Car Rental: Enterprise,** 2700 Arden Way (☎486-9900). Cars from $34 per day, and as low as $20 per day on weekends. Must be 21 with major credit card. Open M-F 7:30am-6pm, Sa 9am-1pm.

# Worry Free Travel is Just a Click Away

Trip Cancellation
International Medical Insurance
Emergency Evacuation
All Nationalities

Personalize your travel insurance needs
with our online Policy Picker®

USA / Canada:  1 800 234 1862
International: +1 703 299 6001

w.Letsgo.WorldTravelCenter.com    Travel Insurance Experts

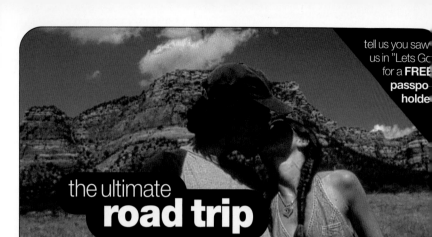

tell us you saw
us in "Lets Go
for a **FREE**
passpo
holde

the ultimate
**road trip**

**don't trip out planning your big road trip.**
put contiki in the driver's seat with hassle-free vacations
designed for 18 to 35 year olds. make new friends, enjoy
your free time and explore the sights in a convenient
vacation that gives you more bang for your buck... **from
only $70/day** including accommodations, sightseeing,
many meals and transportation. with contiki leading the
way, you can leave the road map at home!

> **7 days eastern discovery**
new york, washington d.c., us naval academy, kennedy space center

> **10 days canada & the rockies**
vancouver, calgary, banff national park

> **13 days wild western**
san francisco, grand canyon, las vegas, yosemite national park

*prices subject to change, land only.

for more info on our trips...
**see** your travel agent
**call** 1-888-CONTIKI
**visit** www.contiki.com

**contiki**
**VACATIONS** for **18-35** year olds

CST# 1001728-20

> **europe** > **australia** > **new zealand** > **america** > **canada**

## Sacramento

**ACCOMMODATIONS**
Courtyard by Marriott, **12**
Sacramento Hostel
(HI-AYH), **2**
Vagabond Inn Midtown, **9**

**FOOD**
33rd St. Bistro, **6**
Cafe Bernardo, **8**

**FOOD (Cont.)**
The Fox and Goose, **10**
Maalouf's, **1**
Rubicon Brewing Company, **7**

**NIGHTLIFE**
Faces, **5**
Old Ironsides, **11**
Torch Club, **3**
True Love Coffeehouse, **4**

Sacramento Light Rail

**Bike Rental: American River Bike Shop,** 9203 Folsom Blvd. (☎363-2671). Other locations at 256 Florin Rd. and 2645 Macaroni Ave. Bikes $4 per hr., $20 per day. Grab a friend for a tandem ride ($6 per hr., $30 per day) around the American River. Open M-F 9am-7pm, Sa 9am-6pm, Su 10am-5pm.

## ORIENTATION & PRACTICAL INFORMATION

Sacramento is at the center of the **Sacramento Valley.** Five major highways converge on the capital of California: **I-5** and **Route 99** run north-south with I-5 to the west, **I-80** runs east-west between San Francisco and Reno, and **US 50** and **Route 16** bring traffic westward from Gold Country. Numbered streets run north-south and lettered streets run east-west in a grid. The street number on a lettered street corresponds to the number of the cross street (2000 K St. is near the corner of 20th St.). The capitol building, parks, and endless cafes and restaurants occupy the **downtown area** around 10th St. and Capitol Ave.

**Visitor Information: Sacramento Convention and Visitor Bureau,** 1303 J St., #600 (☎264-4740; www.sacramentocvb.org). Congenial. Open M-Sa 8am-5pm.

**Police:** 5770 Freeport Blvd. (☎264-5471; www.sacpd.org), at I St.

**CENTRAL VALLEY**

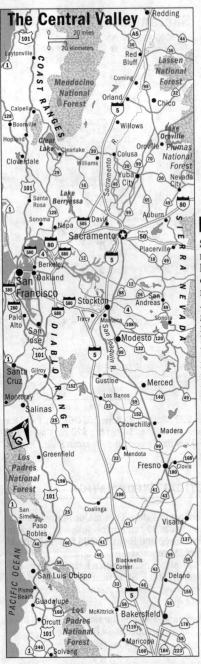

**The Central Valley**

CENTRAL VALLEY

**Medical Services: UC Davis Medical Center,** 2315 Stockton Blvd. (☎734-2011), at Broadway.

**Crisis Hotline: Suicide Prevention and Crisis Response** (☎368-3111). Open 24hr.

**Library and Internet Access: Sacramento Library,** 828 I St. (☎264-2700), between 8th and 9th St. Free **Internet access** 1hr. per person per day. Open M and F 10am-6pm, Tu-Th 10am-9pm, Sa 10am-5pm, Su noon-5pm.

**Post Office:** 801 I St. (☎556-3415). Open M-F 8am-5pm. **Postal Code:** 95814.

## 🛏 ACCOMMODATIONS

Sacramento has many hotels, motels, and B&Bs, but waves of lawyers, businesspeople, and politicians can flood accommodations, making it hard to find a room. Advance reservations are always a good idea. **West Capitol Avenue** has many cheap hotels, but they might be on the seedy side, so investigate before making plans. Within Sacramento proper, **16th Street** is home to many hotels and motels. Rates fluctuate seasonally, but standard chain hotel and motel rooms usually go for $50-150 per night. **Camping** is most popular with RVers, but tent sites are usually available, even in the metropolitan area. **KOA Sacramento ❷** is centrally located. Take I-80 west of downtown and exit at West Capitol Ave. (☎371-6771, reservations 800-562-2747. Campsites $27; RV sites with full hookup $37; cabins $46.)

**🏠 Sacramento Hostel (HI-AYH),** 900 H St. (☎443-9691, reservations 800-909-4776 ext. 40), at 9th St. This pastel Victorian mansion, built in 1885, looks more like an elegant B&B than a hostel with its high sloping ceilings, grand mahogany staircase, and stained-glass atrium. Huge modern kitchen, 3 large living rooms, library, TV/VCR, and an extensive selection of video rentals ($1). Dorm-style rooms are spacious and immaculate. Guests are given 1 brief chore in the morning. Laundry. Check-in 7:30-9:30am and 5-10pm. Check-out 9:30am. Hostel closed 10am-5pm. Doors lock at 11pm, so speak to the receptionist before going out. Dorms $16-18 for HI-AYH members, $19-21 for nonmembers. Family, couple, and single rooms available. Group rates. ❷

**Courtyard by Marriott,** 4422 Y St. (☎455-6800), at the UC Davis Medical Center. A full-fledged hotel at a relatively low price. Grounds have exercise room, pool, whirlpool, laundry, restaurant, cocktail lounge, and coffee shop. Rooms include cable TV, irons, hairdryers, and high-speed Internet connections. Doubles from $74, but reserve ahead to get the cheapest rates. ❺

**Vagabond Inn Midtown,** 1319 30th St. (☎454-4400; www.vagabondinn.com), between M and N St. A clean, well-maintained chain motel with many comfortable rooms and below-market rates, though its outside may be a little scuffed. Rooms have cable TV, phone, and free newspapers. Doubles from $50; online rates as low as $42. ❸

## ◪ FOOD

Food in Sacramento is plentiful and good, thanks to a hip midtown, varied immigrant populations, and a dose of Californian culinary inventiveness. Many eateries are concentrated on **J Street** or **Capitol Avenue** between 19th and 29th St. The stretch of Fair Oaks Blvd. between Howe and Fulton is also home to great restaurants of all price ranges. Old Sacramento is filled with gimmicky restaurants that tend to be on the more expensive side.

▨**The Fox and Goose,** 1001 R St. (☎443-8825), at 10th St. Situated in a huge glass factory with colored windows, built in 1913 and renovated in the 1970s, the Fox and Goose has fostered a unique atmosphere blending authentic English public house atmosphere and American alternative culture. Great brunch and night spot; filling meals served three times a day. Serves everything from a proper pot of tea to European beer ($3), bangers ($5), pasties ($6), and fish 'n' chips ($6). Open mic nights and live music Th-Sa. Open M-F 7am-2pm and 5:30pm-midnight, Sa-Su 8am-2am. ❶

**33rd St. Bistro,** 3301 Folsom Blvd. (☎455-2233), at 33rd. St. Opened by two classically trained chef brothers who weren't afraid to experiment. Mixes flavors of the Pacific Northwest, American South, Mediterranean, and Caribbean seamlessly and successfully. Popular and busy, this wood and slate bistro has gained a wide local following for its carefully designed dishes as well as its reasonable prices. Entrees $9-17. Desserts $4-5. Open Su-Th 8am-10pm, F-Sa 8am-11pm. ❸

**Cafe Bernardo,** 2726 Capitol Ave. (☎443-1189; www.cafebernardo.com), at 28th St. This bright cafe with outdoor seating serves up light, fresh, and delicious fare cafeteria-style to a yuppie crowd. Outdoor seating. Delectable sandwiches ($6-8), salads ($2-7), and soups ($2-4). Open Su-Th 7am-10pm, F-Sa 7am-11pm. ❷

**Maalouf's Taste of Lebanon,** 1433 Fulton Ave. (☎972-8768), east of downtown. Mixing Middle Eastern and Mediterranean influences, Lebanese food is bold and flavorful. With its kebab and schwarma sandwiches ($3-5) and appetizer favorites like kibbe and falafel ($2-4), this place is no exception. Frequented by the local Lebanese community. Open M-Sa 11am-9:30pm. ❶

**Rubicon Brewing Company,** 2004 Capitol Ave. (☎448-7032), at 20th St. Cool, laid-back microbrewery with decent, standard pub food. Patrons can watch the brewing process from the dining area, and the results are worth trying (pint $3). Sandwiches $5-8; Rubicon wings $6.25 for a dozen. Su brunch. Open M-F 11am-11:30pm, F 11am-12:30am, Sa 8:30am-12:30am, Su 8:30am-10pm; kitchen closes earlier. ❶

## 👁 🏔 SIGHTS & OUTDOOR ACTIVITIES

Sacramento has traditionally been more of a pit stop on the way to the lakes and mountains in the east, but people are realizing there are plenty of reasons to stay. Debates about the budget, recalling Gov. Gray Davis, and water shortages rage daily in the elegant **State Capitol**, at 10th St. and Capitol Ave. (☎324-0333. 1hr. tours depart daily every hr. 9am-4pm. Free tickets distributed in Room B27 on a first-come, first-serve basis.) Colonnades of towering palm trees and grassy lawns make **Capitol Park** a shaded oasis in the middle of downtown's busy bureaucracy. The **State Historic Park Governor's Mansion,** at 16th and H St., was built in 1877, serving as the residence of California's governor and his family until then-governor Ronald Reagan opted to rent his own pad. (☎324-0539. Open daily 10am-4pm. Hourly tours $2, under 16 free.)

**Old Sacramento** attracts nearly five million visitors annually and has been refurbished to resemble its late 19th-century appearance. But the cobblestone streets and wooden sidewalks primarily house gift shops and restaurants, and the horse-drawn carriages are not enough to mask the roaring freeway. Attractions include a restored riverboat, California's first theater, a military museum, and Tunel 21, the restaurant owned by the Sacramento Kings' center Vlade Divac. The world-renowned 100,000 sq. ft. ☒**California State Railroad Museum,** at 2nd and I St., exhibits 23 historic locomotives, half of which you can walk through. (☎323-9280. Open daily 10am-5pm. $4, under 17 free. 1hr. train rides from the Train Depot in Old Sacramento Apr.-Sept. weekends; $6, ages 6-12 $3, under 6 free.)

The **Crocker Art Museum,** 216 O St., between 2nd and 3rd St., is relatively small but packs a punch with permanent works by Brueghel, Rembrandt, and Jacques-Louis David, and large rotating exhibits downstairs. What makes the Crocker stand apart, however, is its superb collection of contemporary Californian art, including pieces by local burnout artist Robert Arneson. (☎264-5423. Open Su, Tu-W, and F-Sa 10am-5pm, Th 10am-9pm. $6, seniors $4, ages 7-17 $3, under 7 free. Tours available; book a week in advance.) Chimps, hippos, giraffes, lions, white tigers, and an albino alligator are among the nearly 400 critters bumming around at the **Sacramento Zoo,** William Land Park at Parkland Dr. and Sutterville Rd. off I-5 at the Sutterville Exit. The zoo sits in a beautiful eucalyptus-filled park and emphasizes protection of endangered species and the careful recreation of natural habitats. (☎264-5885; www.saczoo.com. Open daily Sept.-May 10am-4pm; June-Aug. 9am-4pm. $7, weekends and holidays $6; ages 3-12 $4.25/$3.75; under 3 free.)

The rushing waters of the American River flow near Sacramento, and its gurgling calls out to adventuresome **river rafters.** Rent rafts at **American River Raft Rentals,** 11257 S. Bridge St., in Rancho Cordova, 14 mi. east of downtown on US 50. Exit on Sunrise Blvd. and take it north 1½ mi. to the American River. (☎635-6400. Open daily 9am-6pm; rentals available until 1pm. 4-person raft $38; kayak $27. $2 launch fee, $3.50 per person for return shuttle.)

The **American River Recreation Trail and Parkway,** spanning over 30 mi. from Discovery Park to Folsom Lake, is a nature preserve where you can still glimpse the downtown skyline. Five million people a year visit to cycle, jog, swim, fish, hike, and ride horses. You can enter the trail in Old Sacramento or at designated entrance points along the river. **Folsom Lake State Recreation Area,** 25 mi. east of town on I-80 (take Douglas Blvd.), hosts a giant, 11,000-acre reservoir that offers swimming, boating, fishing, and wake-boarding, and surrounds the hills with over 100 mi. of trails. (☎988-0205. Open daily 6am-10pm. $2-6 per vehicle.)

# ENTERTAINMENT

Sacramento bustles with free afternoon concerts and cheap food in summer. The Friday edition of the *Sacramento Bee* contains a supplement called *Ticket*, which gives a rundown of events, restaurants, and night spots. For weekend music and activities, check the free weeklies, such as *Sacramento News and Review* and *Inside the City*. The free *Alive and Kicking* has schedules and information about music and arts throughout the city. **Bass tickets**, 1409 28th St. Suite 206 (☎453-2730; www.tickets.com), is the largest ticket vendor in the area; call them for event times, locations, and prices.

Aside from the ubiquitous multiplexes, Sacramento has a good number of art and **film** theaters. The unique **Crest Theater**, at 10th and K St., was built in 1913 as a vaudevillian stage and is now a theater screening an impressive parade of independent films. Inside are three cinemas with palatial stairways, gilded ceilings, crystal chandeliers, and decadent paisley carpet. It is also a popular local venue for live indie rock and other big-name performances (contact Bass for tickets). (☎442-5189. $8.50, children, seniors, and matinee shows $5.) Since 1942, the **Sacramento Theatre Company**, 1419 H St. (☎443-6722), has been staging classic and contemporary plays. Seven productions, often lesser-known critical hits, go up each year from September to May (tickets $18-36).

If you're visiting Sacramento in the spring, catch a **Sacramento Kings** basketball game and scream alongside the Kings fans, reputed to be the loudest in the NBA. The Kings play at the Arco Arena, 1 Sports Pkwy. (☎928-6900. To order single-game tickets by phone, call ☎649-8497, 530-528-8497, or 209-485-8497.)

**Friday Night Concert Series** (☎442-2500), at Cesar Chávez Park, 10th St. and I St. Live bands, food stands, and beer gardens. In summer every F 5-9pm. Free.

**Dixieland Jazz Jubilee** (☎372-5277). Over 100 bands play every Memorial Day weekend in Old Sac in late May, attracting over 100,000 listeners. Free.

**International Street Fair,** on 11th St. between J and L St. A celebration of Sacramento's multi-ethnicity. Food, vendors, kids' activities, and performances. Mid-July 5-9pm.

**Shakespeare Lite** (☎442-8575), St. Rose of Lima Park, 7th St. and K St. Comedic abridged versions of the Bard's work. Pack a picnic. June to mid-July Th noon-1pm.

**California State Fair** (☎263-3000; www.bigfun.org). This agriculturally inclined fair doesn't skimp on spinning rides, fairway food, or bungee jumping. Mid-Aug. to early Sept. Tickets $7, seniors $5, children $4.50.

# NIGHTLIFE

Capital-dwellers slither about in their natural habitat of brass and mahogany bars and coffeehouses. Sacramento's midtown entertainment parlors, on the other hand, afford a view of city residents who are odder-looking and more frequently body-pierced than their fellow citizens in the government. The **Fox and Goose** (see p. 307) is a splendid nightlife option. For the more energetic, there are clubs scattered around Sacramento's periphery.

**True Love Coffeehouse,** 2406 J St. (☎492-9002), at 24th St. A cozy, quirky hangout thriving on the pulse of Sacramento alternative culture, especially the music scene. A small stage is given over to all sorts of unusual and compelling entertainment, from movie screenings to waffle night to documentary films and, of course, live music. Check out the large, shaded patio out back. Usually no cover, but some performances $6-7. Open Su-Th 5pm-midnight, F-Sa 5pm-2am.

**Old Ironsides** (☎443-9751), at 10th and S St. The first bar in Sacramento to get its liquor license after Prohibition, Old Ironsides is split into two rooms, one for grooving and one for boozing; both are filled with laid-back and interesting locals. Check out the Lipstick DJ night on Tu or the open mic night on Wed. Open M-F 11am-1:30am, Sa-Su 6pm-1:30am. Live music on Th, F, Sa with a $5-10 cover.

**Torch Club,** 904 15th St. (☎443-2797; www.thetorchclub.com), at I St. The ultimate blues and bluegrass venue in town with an atmosphere to prove it. Blues legends rambling through town and the local upstarts attract hardcore soul music enthusiasts. Deep wailing and foot-stomping exuberance gives these tunes a redemptive, releasing vitality. Live bands play every night. 21+. Cover varies, often free. Open daily 10am-2am.

**Faces,** 2000 K St. (☎448-7798), at 20th St. *The* mid-town gay club scene. High-stylin' with 5 huge areas (dance, video, social bar, microbrew bar, and patio). Su afternoon BBQ 5:30pm. Occasional amateur stripteases Th nights (and every night, if you pound enough Heineken). 21+. Open daily 4pm-1:45am.

# DAVIS                                                                                                ☎530

Eleven miles west of Sacramento on I-80, residents of Davis (pop. 66,299) fancy themselves to be living in the model eco-conscious town—and their self-image is certainly substantiated. Not only is Davis a leader in recycling, its streets also sport energy-saving traffic signals and as many bikes as residents—more per capita than any other US city. The character of the city is largely shaped by the students of the University of California at Davis (UCD), and town activity is centered around the campus and adjacent downtown. On Wednesday nights in the summer, locals flock to **Davis Farmer's Market,** in Central Park at 4th and C St., to partake in fresh produce, restaurant food stands, picnics, live world-music, and fusion bands. (☎756-1965. Open May-Oct. W 4:30-8:30pm, Sa 8am-noon; Nov.-Apr. W 2-6pm.)

**▶ PRACTICAL INFORMATION.** Amtrak, 840 2nd St. (☎800-USA-RAIL/872-7245), provides **train** service to **Sacramento** (16 per day, $5.50) and **San Francisco** (11 per day, $17). **Unitrans** (☎752-2877) connects downtown and the UCD campus (75¢). **Yolo Bus** (☎371-2877) serves Davis and Sacramento ($1.25; seniors, disabled, and ages 5-12 50¢). Get info at the **Visitors Bureau,** 130 G St. (☎297-1900; www.davisvisitor.com; open M-F 8:30am-4:30pm) or the **UC Davis Information Center,** in the Memorial Union on campus (☎752-2222, campus events 752-2813; open May-Aug. M-F 10am-4pm; Sept.-Apr. 8am-7pm). The **Yolo County Library, Davis Branch,** 315 14th St., provides 1hr. of free **Internet access** per person per day. (☎757-5591. Open M 1-9pm, Tu-Th 10am-9pm, F-Sa 10am-5:30pm, Su 1-5pm.) The **post office,** 2020 5th St. (☎800-275-8777), is open M-F 7am-5:30pm, Sa 9am-4pm. **Postal Code:** 95616.

**▶☐ ACCOMMODATIONS AND FOOD.** Motels in Davis do not come cheap, and during university events rooms are scarce. **University Park Inn ❹,** 1111 Richards Blvd., off I-80 at the Richards Blvd. Exit, is six blocks from campus, and four from downtown. It has 40 spotless rooms with cable TV and a pool. (☎756-0910. Doubles with queen bed $75, with king bed $85. AAA discount. Continental breakfast.)

A true college town, Davis is peppered with ethnic restaurants and quirky cafes. The downtown area between E and G St. south of 3rd St. is always a sure bet for a slice of pizza, a vegetarian smorgasbord, or a cup of joe. To stock a picnic basket, check out the **Davis Food Co-op,** 620 G St., which has a colossal selection of organic produce, bulk and fresh deli foods, and 15min. of free

Internet access. (☎758-2667. Open daily 8am-10pm.) The **Crepe Bistro ❷**, 234 E St., practically a Davis legend, is right in the middle of downtown, and staffed by longtime, oft-tattooed Davis residents. Besides being a great place to relax outside over substantial crepes ($3-7), the bistro also serves a mean breakfast omelet ($4-8) that has risen to local fame. (☎753-2575. Open M-F 10:30am-10pm, Sa-Su 9:30am-10pm.) **Redrum Burger ❷** (formerly Murder Burger), 720 Olive Dr., looks like a 50s diner on crystal meth. They serve massive hamburgers ($3), and for the true carnivores, a full one-pound burger ($9). For an agricultural alternative, try the ostrich burger ($5), and top off your meal with a super-thick milkshake ($2.50) that complements burgers of any kind. (☎756-2142. Open Su-Th 10am-10pm, F-Sa 10am-11pm.)

## ◩◪◫ ACTIVITIES, NIGHTLIFE & ENTERTAINMENT.

Of the UC schools, the **University of California at Davis** is the largest in square miles and also tops the list in agriculture and viticulture (vine cultivation). For a personal experience with all things green, head to the **UCD Arboretum** on Putah Creek, featuring trees and plants of Mediterranean climate from around the world. (☎752-4880. Open 24hr.)

At night, students party on the huge dance floor of **The Graduate**, 805 Russell Blvd., in the University Mall. The Friday night specials, 7-for-1 drinks at 10pm that work their way down to 2-for-1, make Friday night the night to go. The Graduate can be hit-or-miss; beware line-dancing nights. (☎758-4723. Open daily 10:30am-2am.) For the more sophisticated, the spot of choice is **Sophia's Thai Bar**, 129 E St., a tiny bar with tropical decor, aquariums, and occasional live music. (☎758-4333. Open Su-W 5pm-12am, Th-Sa 5pm-2am.) South of 3rd St., G St. also houses many bars that get especially lively during the school year and early summer.

Davis is marked by more than 40mi. of bike trails and rocks. For trail maps and ratings, stop by the Chamber of Commerce or a bike shop in town. Try **Ken's Bike and Ski**, 650 G St., for rentals. (☎758-3223. Open M-F 8am-10pm, Sa 9am-7pm, Su 12-5pm. Street bikes $10 per day or $6 for 4hr.; mountain bikes $28/$14.) For some practice before hitting the rocks outside, check out the **Rocknasium**, 720 Olive Dr. Ste. Z, in a warehouse just past Redrum Burger (see above), which offers climbing for all levels. The 70 routes include a bouldering cave and extensive lead climbing. (☎757-2902. Open M-F 11am-11pm, Sa 10am-9pm, Su 10am-6pm. $12, students $10; equipment rental $8/$6.)

# THE HIDDEN DEAL

## THE HOTDOGGER

The hot dog—that institution of American barbecue and baseball stadium culture—is sometimes taken for granted. It's prepared carelessly, supplemented inadequately with mere packets of ketchup, and even—gasp—microwaved. At The Hotdogger, though, hot dog preparation is elevated to an art form. This tiny, hole-in-the-wall joint with just enough indoor seating for four people focuses all its energies on this one hallowed food, and Davis locals have been taking advantage of the savory results for years.

Stop by and let the charismatic staff and exuberant owner teach you about the true American hot dog. A wide variety will greet you: hot dogs, hotlinks, sausages, eight varieties of mustard, endless condiments, and a few special combinations like the infamous Gut Bomb (Louisiana hot link, hot peppers, onions, salsa, chili, and cheddar cheese; $4.50). The standard Dog Deal is a classic hot dog, a bag of chips, and a soda for $2. There is plenty of outdoor seating where most patrons enjoy their franks. Whatever you're in the mood for, The Hotdogger raises the bar intimidatingly high for any backyard chef without raising the price.

*129 E St. ☎530-753-6291. Open M-F 11am-6:30pm, Sa 11am-4pm. Also has a stand at the Farmer's Market on W nights in the summer.*

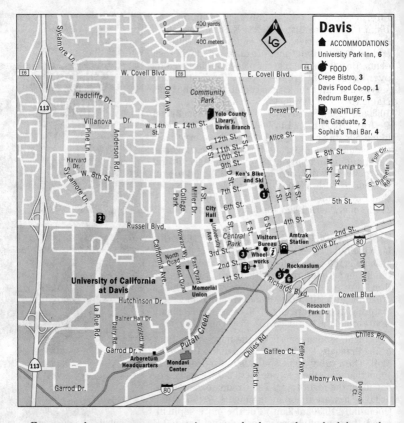

For some less strenuous entertainment, check out the schedule at the recently-finished **Mondavi Center for the Arts,** Mrak Hall Dr. at Old Davis Rd. Built for UCD by wine tycoon Robert Mondavi, this striking new sandstone performance center draws heavyweights such as Joshua Redman, Ladysmith Black Mambazo, and Salman Rushdie, and is easily at the center of cultural enrichment in Davis. (☎ 754-ARTS/2787; www.mondaviarts.org. Box Office at One Shields Ave. Open M-F 10am-6pm, Sa noon-6pm. Tickets $20-50.)

# CHICO                                                                    ☎ 530

Chico (pop. 55,437) is an idyllic, small town full of young intellectuals, families, and carefree college kids on beach cruisers. As the home of the Sierra Nevada Brewing Company, this place knows how to please visitors, not only with its numerous bike trails and swimming holes in the incomparable Bidwell Park, and its hip and lively downtown, but also with its ubiquitous cheap beer. The abundance of this sweet nectar, combined with the area's natural beauty and small-town atmosphere, recently earned it a spot as one of the "Top 10 places to retire in the US," and Cal State Chico is perennially one of Playboy's "Top 10 Party Schools." But Chico is more than just lotus-eating; it has an active cultural scene rife with music and theater.

CENTRAL VALLEY

**▎ PRACTICAL INFORMATION**. The **Amtrak train** station (☎800-USA-RAIL/872-7245) is just a platform on Orange St., at W. 5th St. Trains go to Sacramento (2hr., 4 per day, $19) and San Francisco (5½hr., 3 per day, $30). **Greyhound,** 450 Orange St. (☎343-8266), at the Amtrak station, sends **buses** to: Red Bluff (1hr., 4 per day, $9-10); Sacramento (2½hr., 3 per day, $14-15); and San Francisco (5-6hr., 3 per day, $30-32). The **Chamber of Commerce,** 300 Salem St., at 3rd St., has wall-to-wall tourist brochures and a friendly staff. (☎891-5559 or 800-852-8570; www.chicochamber.com. Open M-F 9am-5pm, Sa 10am-3pm.) Other services include **police,** 1460 Humboldt Rd. (☎895-4912), and **Enloe Hospital,** 1531 W. 5th St. (☎895-9111), at Esplanade St. The **post office** is at 550 Vallombrosa Ave. (☎343-2068. Open M-F 8:30am-5:30pm, Sa 9:30am-12:30pm.) **Postal Code:** 95926.

**▎▎▎ ACCOMMODATIONS, CAMPING & CHEAP BEER**. As a big college town, Chico has plenty of inexpensive hotels and motel rooms to offer, many for as low as $40 a night. **Town House Motel ❸,** 2231 The Esplanade, is a clean and quiet remodeled motel close to downtown. Standard rooms have cable TV and A/C. (☎343-1621. Singles from $40; doubles from $45.) **Thunderbird Lodge ❸,** 715 Main St., downtown, is a no-frills motel with large, clean rooms and brown shag carpet. (☎343-7911. Singles $45-55; doubles $55-65.) The closest place to get beer is at **Chevron,** 110 W. 9th St., at Main St. (☎891-8055. Open 24hr.)

For camping, pick up a useful camping brochure at the Chamber of Commerce. The camping closest to Chico is at the **Woodson Bridge State Park campground**. Take Rte. 99 North for 12 mi., make a left on South Ave. and drive about 3 mi. There are over 35 sites with water and toilets. (☎800-444-7275. Self-register. Sites $18.) Numerous campgrounds also lie a little farther afield at **Lake Oroville,** 30 mi. from Chico on Rte. 99 S (9 mi. from Oroville Dam Exit), which offers fishing, swimming, boating, and a 35 mi. bike trail. **Bidwell Canyon ❷** is very close to the water and used mostly by RVs. (☎534-2409. Full hookup $20, with no tent discount.) **Loafer Creek ❶** is more forested and less crowded than Bidwell, with a beach and swimming area. (☎538-2219. Sites $14.) Camping is abundant in the Lassen and Plumas National Forests, both a short distance east of Chico. Lassen has many campgrounds on Rte. 32, about 35 mi. north of Chico, near Lake Almanor.

**▎▎ FOOD & CHEAP BEER**. It is hard not to find great-tasting, ridiculously inexpensive food and drink in Chico, given the unrelenting demand for it placed by the college population. Declared a "legend" by *Chico News and Review,* **Burger Hut ❶,** with locations at 933 Nord Ave. and 2451 Forest Ave., makes the best burger in town for as cheap as it gets. The "Student Special," a flame-kissed burger that you pile with toppings yourself, with fries and soda, is a steal at $3.70. (☎891-1418; www.burgerhut.net. Open M-Sa 10am-9pm, Su 11am-9pm.) **Madison Bear Garden ❷,** 316 2nd St., at Salem St., is marked by its spicy atmosphere and party potential. An enormous outdoor patio and cheap beer garden, dance floors, pool tables, and a horse and buggy hung from the ceiling make this a hot spot for hundreds of rowdy revelers. (☎891-1639. Burgers, salads, and sandwiches $5-7. Pint of beer $1 Sa 9pm-1am. Open Su-M 11am-midnight, Tu-Sa 11am-1:30am. Kitchen closes at 10pm.) Beer also flows at the sedate and classy **Sierra Nevada Brewing Co. ❸,** 1075 E. 20th St., home of the brand's brewery, a tap room, and grill. Tours of the brass-and-mahogany brewery are a great way to pay your respects to the brew gods. Some may come to try the butternut squash ravioli, the artichoke crusted halibut, or the vegetarian options, but no one can deny the 11 different Sierra Nevada brews on tap for

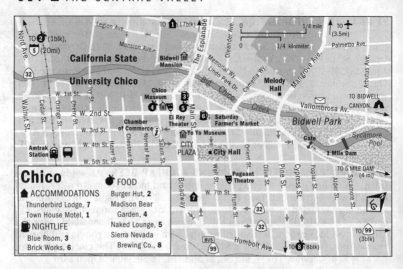

$2.50 a pint. Lunch ($6-10) and top-notch dinner ($8-21) are served at the pub. (☎345-2739. Tours Su-F 2:30pm, Sa noon-3pm. Live music a few nights per month at 7:30pm, $10-20. Pub open Su and Tu-Th 11am-9pm, F-Sa 11am-10pm.) For couches and caffeine, head to the artsy, relaxed **Naked Lounge ❶**, 118 W. 2nd St., where the coffee is fair trade and highest-grade, and the music is free jazz. (☎895-0676. Double espresso $2. Open daily 6:30am-midnight.)

**⬛⬛⬛ SIGHTS, ENTERTAINMENT & CHEAP BEER.** Most of the residents of Chico would agree that the two best things to do in Chico are to frolic in its awesome playground, Bidwell Park, during the day, and to indulge in the youthful revelry of this party-school town after dark. With over 3600 acres, **Bidwell Park** (☎895-4972) is one of the nation's largest municipal parks and undoubtedly Chico's most cherished attraction; throngs flock to its trails, parks, golf course, and swimming holes on balmy summer days. The park is easily accessed by car from Vallombrosa Ave., Mangrove Ave., or 4th S.t, and is divided into upper and lower sections. The upper part is largely undisturbed canyonland, while the lower part is more developed and friendly to jogging, biking, playing baseball, and sunning. In the upper part, **North Rim Trail,** on Wildwood Ave. upon entering the park, explores the hardy, rugged terrain. **Bear Hole,** the first of many swimming holes here, is often overrun by college kids. Further north, the trails get rougher but the swimming holes get better (and less crowded). In the lower section of the park, **One-Mile Recreation,** near downtown by 4th St., is a great spot for picnicking, playing frisbee, or loafing around while drinking cheap beer. There is also an amazing public swimming pool built into the river. The **Chico Creek Nature Center,** 1968 E. 8th St., is a museum and interpretive center for the park, exploring and preserving its natural life. (☎891-4671. Open Su and Tu-Sa 11am-4pm. Free talks, exhibits, and nature walks.)

Besides Bidwell Park, there are a number of worthwhile sights and cultural experiences; pick up a copy of the downtown walking tour guide at the Visitors Center. The highlights of the tour include: a stroll around **Cal State Chico's** campus, at W. 2nd St. and Normal Ave.; a swing over to the **National YoYo Museum,** home of the world's largest yo-yo (256 lb.), inside Bird in Hand at Broadway and

W. 3rd St. (☎893-1414; open M-Sa 10am-6pm, Su 11am-4pm; National YoYo Contest in early Oct.; free); and a tour through the historic **mansion**, 525 The Esplanade, of John Bidwell, the influential founder of Chico. (☎895-6144. Tours on the hour Su and Sa 10am-4pm, W-F noon-4pm. $2, under 16 free.) Entertainment options in town include two excellent independent movie theaters: **Pageant Theater**, 351 E. 6th St. (☎343-0663; www.pageantchico.com), with sofas in the front row; and **El Rey Theater**, 230 W. 2nd St., a restored single-screen Vaudevillian theater nearly 100 years old (☎342-2727; tickets $8, students with ID $6). The **Blue Room**, 139 W. 1st St., shows bold, often unconventional plays to an appreciative audience and occasionally hosts traveling productions. (☎895-3749. Tickets $12, students with ID $10, Th $6. Box office open W-Sa noon-5pm.) For **live music** of the rock, rap, and indie pop variety, as well as Top 40 dancing, try **Brick Works**, 191 E. 2nd St. (☎895-7700; www.thebrickworks.com. Tickets $5-20.) The **Concert in the Park Series** hosts free musical and theatrical performances in Downtown Park Plaza, at 5th and Main St. (☎345-6500. May-Sept. F 7-8pm.) For the music of poetry, check out the **Shakespeare in the Park** performances. (☎891-1382. Varied schedule throughout summer.)

# MERCED  ☎209

The wide streets of downtown Merced (pop. 63,893) project an order and openness shared by the entire town. The good-natured atmosphere makes Merced one of the best places to stop before heading for Yosemite's northern entrance.

■■ ⁊ **ORIENTATION & PRACTICAL INFORMATION.** Situated on Rte. 99 at the midpoint between Sacramento and Fresno, Merced maintains a small-town image along its quaint Main St., while the area north of Bear Creek hosts standard suburban mall and restaurant chains. Self-titled the "Gateway to Yosemite," Merced has excellent public transportation into the park. The regional **YARTS** provides bus trips directly to Yosemite. Call ahead to ask about the varying schedules. (☎877-989-2787; www.yosemite.com/yarts. $20 round-trip, seniors and kids under 16 $14. Kids under 16 free with purchase of adult ticket. Fare includes park admission.) Greyhound, 710 W. 16th St. (☎722-2121 or 800-231-2222), runs **buses** to San Francisco (every 3hr., $26) and LA (every 2hr., $29). Amtrak **trains**, 324 W. 24th St., run to LA and Reno, among other destinations. (☎800-USA-RAIL/872-7245. Open daily 7:15am-8:45pm.) Public transportation within Merced, simply called **The Bus** (☎384-3111 or 800-345-3111), may be flagged down at any street corner along designated routes. (Runs M-F 7am-6pm, Sa 9am-5pm. Single fare $1, all-day pass $3 within the city limits, $4 otherwise.) The **Merced Chamber of Commerce** and the **California Welcome Center**, 690 W. 16th St., have information on travel, activities, and Yosemite road conditions, as well as maps and brochures detailing local restaurants, accommodations, and transportation options. (Chamber of Commerce ☎384-7092. Open M-F 8:30am-5pm. Welcome Center ☎384-2791. Open daily 8am-5pm.) Other services include: **police**, 611 W. 22nd St. (☎385-6912); **Mercy Hospital and Health Services**, 2740 M St. (☎384-6444; open 24hr.); and the **post office**, 2334 M St. (☎723-3741; open M-F 8am-5:30pm). **Postal Code:** 95340.

⁊⁊ **ACCOMMODATIONS & FOOD.** The friendly hosts of the eight-bed **Merced Home Hostel ❷** pick up guests from the bus and train stations between 5pm and 9pm. Visitors must call in advance; without reservations, the address is not disclosed. (☎725-0407. Bunks $18; private rooms $39.) Over half a dozen budget-friendly motels lie along the appropriately-named Motel Dr., two exits south of downtown Merced on Rte. 99, where chain motels like the refurbished

**Days Inn ❹** (☎ 722-2726; singles $69; doubles $79) and the more inexpensive **Sierra Lodge ❺**, 951 Motel Dr. (☎ 722-3926; singles $45; doubles $55), can be found.

While fast-food joints are abundant, especially along Olive Ave., cheap home-grown eats can also be found. **Mandarin Shogun ❷**, 1204 W. Olive Ave., has a pleasant all-you-can-eat buffet (lunch $6, dinner $8; seniors 10% discount) with a variety of entree and dessert choices. (☎ 722-6313, delivery 722-1881. Lunch daily 11am-2:30pm, dinner Su-Th 5-9:30pm, F-Sa 5-10pm.) In the heart of downtown Merced, **The Cinema Cafe ❸**, 661 W. Main St., alternates traditional diner breakfast fare in the summer with more elaborate dinner cuisine that includes fresh fish ($13) and lamb ($11). (☎ 722-2811. Breakfast and lunch around $6. Open M-F 6am-2pm, Sa-Su 6am-1pm; also open in the summer for dinner F-Sa 5-9pm.) All over Merced you will run across another meal option—small, hole-in-the-wall Mexican food joints like **La Nita's ❷**, 1327 W. 18th St., which serves tasty Mexican dishes and margaritas. (☎ 723-2291. Entrees $6-10. Open Tu-Sa 9am-9:30pm, Su 8am-9:30pm.)

**◧ SIGHTS.** Though Merced functions primarily as a rest stop and portal to the Yosemite's wilderness, three small attractions are tucked away in the Merced area. The old **Courthouse**, 21st and N St., is the oldest building in Merced and houses a museum with free tours. Volunteer residents lead the tours, sometimes adding colorful, personal anecdotes. (☎ 722-6291. Open W-Su 1-4pm.) **Applegate Park** and its **Zoo**, 1045 W 25th St., provide a shady spot to escape the Valley heat. The zoo houses rescued animals native to California, including mountain lions, bobcats, foxes, the occasional one-eyed animal, and an American black bear named Sissy. (☎ 385-6840. $1.25, ages 3-10 75¢, over 60 50¢, under 3 free. Open daily 10am-5pm; winter 10am-4pm.) To the northwest of Merced is the **Castle Airport** and **Air Museum**, 5050 Santa Fe Dr., in Atwater. Aviation buffs and history enthusiasts can wander among the restored aircraft and small collection of Air Force memorabilia. (☎ 723-2178. Open M and W-Su 9am-5pm, Tu 10am-5pm; closed in November. $7, seniors and teens $5, children under 7 free.)

# FRESNO ☎ 559

Fresno (pop. 430,000) struggles to balance its agricultural past with its ever-growing urban population. Truly an asphalt jungle, Fresno is dusty, hot, and in many places crime-ridden. However, some interesting attractions, decent digs, and cheap eats are available for travelers headed for the mountains.

**◪ PRACTICAL INFORMATION.** Greyhound, 1033 Broadway Ave. (☎ 268-1829), runs **buses** to San Francisco six times a day (M-Th $25, F-Su $27) and LA six or more times daily ($24). Amtrak **trains**, 2650 E. Tulare St. Bldg. B, also run to San Francisco and LA, and are slightly more expensive. (☎ 800-872-7245/USA-RAIL. Open daily 7:15am-8:45pm.) Local transportation is provided by **Fresno Area Express (FAX)**, 2223 G St. (☎ 498-1122). For schedules and routes, visit the transportation offices at the Manchester Shopping Center, Shields and Blackstone Ave. The **Fresno Chamber of Commerce**, 2331 Fresno St. (☎ 495-4800; www.fresnochamber.com; open M 9am-5pm, Tu-Th 8am-5pm, F 8am-4:30pm), and the **Convention and Visitor Bureau**, 848 M St. in the Water Tower (☎ 233-0836; open M-F 8am-5pm) have info on accommodations, food, and attractions. The main **post office** is located at 1900 E St. (☎ 497-7566. Open M-F 8:30am-5:30pm.) **Postal Code:** 93721.

**◪◧ ACCOMMODATIONS & FOOD.** Chain motels line the highways that run through Fresno. The most inexpensive accommodations can be found off Rte. 99, with rooms averaging $40, but the area around Motel Dr. requires **extra cau-**

**tion.** Accommodations near Shaw Ave., the major east-west thoroughfare, may be a safer (though more expensive) alternative. The **Red Roof Inn ❸**, 5021 N. Barcus Ave., is a good choice with large, clean rooms. (☎276-1910 or 800-733-7663. Pool, cable TV, A/C, pets allowed. Singles with queen bed from $45.) **Piccadilly Inn ❺**, 2305 W. Shaw Ave., is a high-end place where you get what you pay for: workers in suits and quiet, spacious, well-maintained rooms. A pool, spa, cable TV, A/C, restaurant, and banquet rooms all add to the luxury. (☎226-3850. Singles start at $95.)

The trendy Tower District, on E. Olive Ave. between N. Palm Ave. and N. Blackstone Ave., is Fresno's best bet for good eats, as well as the gathering place of the young, the trendy, and the artsy. The **Daily Planet ❸**, 1121 N. Wishon Ave., masters contemporary American flavor in a dining room with an art deco flair. Though the diners are often an over-30 crowd, the bar attracts a wider range of ages. (☎266-4259. *Prix fix* dinners $10-17.) **Cafe Revue ❶**, 620 E. Olive Ave., is the place to see and be seen. A friendly staff serves up coffeehouse favorites in a chic cafe and patio area, and poetry books grace the tables. (☎449-1844. Drinks and pastries $1-4. Open M-Th 7am-11pm, F 7am-midnight, Sa 8am-midnight, Sun 8am-11pm.) At **Livingstone's Bar ❸**, 831 Fern St., an eclectic cast of characters enjoys good eating and good company. (☎485-5198. Dinner $10-20. Late-night Happy Hour W 10pm-midnight, drinks $2. Open daily 11am-2am, Su brunch 10am.)

🔲 **SIGHTS.** If you have time for only one thing in Fresno, stop by the **Baldasare Forestiere Underground Gardens,** on Shaw Ave., one block east of Rte. 99. Forestiere, one of the most famous settlers of Fresno, migrated to Fresno from Sicily around the turn of the century to farm. But when he found hardpan instead of fertile topsoil, he moved underground, gardens and all, to escape the heat. His descendants now lead tours through the tunnels of his 40-room, dirt-walled house. (☎271-0734. Summer tours W-Sun at 10am, noon, and 2pm; fall-spring Sa-Su at noon and 2pm. $8, seniors $7, teens $6.) Fresno also offers the **Fresno Metropolitan Museum of Art,** 1515 Van Ness Ave. Collections include Ansel Adams photography and the largest institutional collection of puzzles in the US. (☎441-1444. Open Su, Tu-W, F-Sa 11am-5pm, Th 11am-8pm. $7, students and seniors $4, ages 3-12 $3. Th nights $1.) **Roeding Park** and **Chaffee Zoological Gardens,** on Olive Ave. one block east of Rte. 99, are

## IN RECENT NEWS

### BUILDING A FUTURE

A couple of years ago, downtown Fresno was not a place you felt safe in at night, nor a place you'd want to visit during the day. When the suits went home after work, the area cleared out. Weekend entertainment was found in the surrounding wilderness and in nearby cities; Fresno locals wouldn't dream of returning to their city for play. The city was built up by leapfrog development and the creation of shopping centers, and as tract housing spread outward, Fresno's downtown became neglected and outdated.

Slowly, things are changing. With the recent completion of a 12,500 seat, $46 million Triple A ballpark, Fresno is attempting to revitalize a downtown that had, of late, fallen into disrepair. Also, the city government has mandated that governmental agencies seeking relocation move downtown. Moreover, they have begun work on a $120 million courthouse, a $200 million medical center, and a $50 million office tower. Eventually, they hope that these buildings will draw business back into the downtown area, making it a safe, vibrant cultural and culinary center for locals and tourists alike. Until then, come for a Grizzlies game at the stadium, and enjoy the intimate and economical attraction of minor league baseball. Soon there will be stores for pre-gaming, and bars and clubs for seeking solace after the ninth inning.

great for picnics or entertaining children. The zoo is fairly standard, but gives camel rides when weather permits. (☎498-2671; www.chaffeezoo.org. Park entrance $1. Zoo entrance $6, seniors $4, ages 2-12 $4. Open Mar.-Oct. 9am-5pm; Nov.-Feb. 10am-4pm.) Baseball enthusiasts or families seeking competitive sports entertainment at minor league prices can visit the recently-completed, $46 million Grizzlies Stadium, 1800 Tulare St., where the **Fresno Grizzlies** play AAA-ball. (☎442-1994, tickets 442-1047; www.fresnogrizzlies.com.)

# BAKERSFIELD                                      ☎661

Virtually every West Coast chain store that has opened in the past twenty years has a home in Bakersfield (pop. 230,771). Although convenient for the scores of long-haul truckers looking for a place to rest on the road to Fresno, Bakersfield is more of a pit stop than a tourist locale. While Bakersfield is one of the fastest growing cities in California, there's still not much for tourists besides cheap motels and commercial outlets.

**⚐ PRACTICAL INFORMATION.** The **Greater Bakersfield Chamber of Commerce** is located at 1725 Eye St., at the intersection with 18th St. (☎327-4421. Open M 9am-5pm, Tu-F 8am-5pm.) Bakersfield is serviced by **Golden Empire Transit (GET)**, a reliable public transportation system. (☎869-2438; www.getbus.org. Single fare 75¢; one day pass $1.75; monthly pass $25.) Greyhound, 1820 18th St. (☎327-5617), runs frequent **buses** to San Francisco ($38), Fresno ($13), and LA ($17). Other services include: **police,** 1601 Truxtun Ave. (☎326-7111); **Bakersfield Memorial Hospital,** 420 34th St., at Union Ave. (☎327-1792; open 24hr.); and the **post office,** 1730 18th St. (☎861-4346). **Postal Code:** 93302.

**🛏🍴 ACCOMMODATIONS & FOOD.** Bakersfield's reputation as a good overnight stop is well earned, as it teems with inexpensive hotels. Clean, safe chain motels cluster at the Olive St. exit off Hwy. 99 North and wage price wars that keep things cheap. For a non-chain option, try the **California Inn ❸,** 3400 Chester Ln., behind Carl's Jr. at Real Rd., which offers a pool, spa, and sauna, as well as mini-fridges, microwaves, TV, laundry, and free internet access. (☎328-1100. Singles $45.) Or try the local chain motel, **E-Z 8 Motels ❸,** 5200 Olive Tree Ct., with TV, mini-fridge, pool, laundry, and spa. (☎392-1511. Singles $34; doubles $47.)

For a cultural twist on typical Central Valley fare, head to **Wool Growers Restaurant ❹,** 620 E. 19th St., an eatery featuring French Basque food. Try the lamb chops ($18) or garlic chicken ($14) in heaping portions. (☎327-9584. Open M-Sa 11:30am-2pm and 6-9:30pm.) **Jake's Tex-Mex Cafe ❷,** 1710 Oak St., is also a local favorite for its Texas-style barbeque, with a kiss from the Golden State. The tri-tip beef ($8) and Jake's famous chocolate cake ($2) are unbeatable. (☎322-6380. Open M-Sa 11am-8:30pm.) For a sweeter taste of Bakersfield tradition, explore the hugely popular **Dewar's ❶,** 1120 Eye St. The candy shop and old-fashioned soda fountain have been open since 1909, and all their treats are an art perfected. Ice cream and floats $1-5. (☎322-0933. Open Su-Th 10am-9pm, F-Sa 10am-10pm.)

**◪ SIGHTS.** Do-si-do over to **Buck Owens' Crystal Palace,** 2800 Buck Owens Blvd., a sort of Hard Rock Cafe for country music with a restaurant, theater, and museum. Live music and dancing on W-Sa nights is popular with locals and tourists alike. (☎328-7560. Entrees $7-27. Open daily 11am-midnight. Dinner M-Sa 5pm-midnight, Su brunch 9:30am-2pm. $6-10 cover.) The 16-acre **Kern County Museum** complex, 3801 Chester Ave., has over 50 structures dedicated to Kern County's history and culture. Buildings focus on local themes, including agriculture, community development, and native cultures. The new interactive petroleum exhibit traces the history of oil and its influence on Bakersfield. (☎852-5000; www.kcmuseum.org. Open M-Sa 10am-5pm, Su noon-5pm. Ticket office closes daily at 3pm. $6, seniors and students $5, children $4.)

CENTRAL VALLEY

# THE CENTRAL COAST

The 400 mi. stretch of coastline between LA and San Francisco embodies all that is purely Californian: rolling surf, a seaside highway built for cruising, dramatic bluffs topped by weathered pines, self-actualizing New Age adherents, and always a hint of the offbeat. This is the solitary magnificence that inspired John Steinbeck's novels and Jack Kerouac's musings. Among the smog-free skies, sweeping shorelines, and dense forests, inland farming communities and old seafaring towns beckon enticingly. The landmarks along the way—Hearst Castle, the Monterey Bay Aquarium, Carmel, the historic missions—are well worth visiting, but the real point of the Central Coast is the journey itself.

---

## HIGHLIGHTS OF THE CENTRAL COAST

**SANTA CRUZ.** Santa Cruz (p. 322) unites New Age crazies, surfers, and trippy students with fog-drenched forests, a bustling downtown, and a tacky beachside milieu.

**MONTEREY BAY AQUARIUM.** The elaborate displays at the immense aquarium (p. 339) create habitats for delicate sunfish, luxuriant kelp forests, and critters of the deep.

**BIG SUR.** The quiet forests and roaring coastline of Big Sur (p. 344) continue to inspire mystics and weirdos.

**HEARST CASTLE.** At San Simeon, media mogul William Randolph Hearst's hilltop mansion (p. 349) fabulously commemorates its builder's wealth.

**SANTA BARBARA.** Built in a graceful Spanish style, the hilly city of Santa Barbara (p. 361) is full of carefree living, crazy nightlife, and stunning coastal environs.

---

# PACIFIC COAST HIGHWAY

The apotheosis of Californian roads, the **Pacific Coast Highway** (known to Angelenos as **PCH,** to other Californians as **Highway 1,** and on maps as **Route 1**), stretches along much of the state's coastline. Begun in 1920, PCH required $10 million and 17 years to complete. From San Francisco, the highway runs along the craggy shorelines of San Mateo County to loopy Santa Cruz and sedate Monterey. South of Monterey, the highway follows the 90 mi. strip of thinly inhabited coast known as **Big Sur** (p. 344). Climbing in and out of Big Sur's mountains, Hwy. 1 inches to the edge of jutting cliffs that hang precipitously over the surf. William Randolph Hearst's **San Simeon** (p. 347) anchors the southern end of Big Sur. Between **San Luis Obispo** (p. 351) and genteel **Santa Barbara** (p. 358), the route winds past vineyards, fields of wildflowers, and miles of beaches. From Santa Barbara to lazy, surf-crazed Ventura, the highway curves and finally skirts the coastal communities of LA. The **Bay Area** (p. 129), **North Coast** (p. 187), and **Los Angeles** (p. 370) sections touch more upon the PCH.

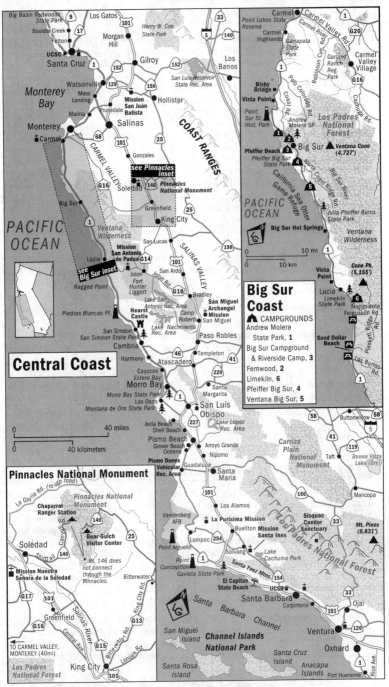

Big Sur Redwoods State Park · 9 · Los Gatos
Boulder Creek · 17
Felton · 101 · Morgan Hill · Henry W. Coe State Park · 33 · 140 · 5
UCSC
Santa Cruz · 1 · Gilroy · 152 · Los Banos
Watsonville · 152
Moss Landing · 129 · Mission San Juan Batista · 156 · Hollister · San Luis Reservoir State Rec. Area
Monterey Bay
Marina · Prunedale · COAST RANGES
Monterey · 68 · Salinas · 101 · 25
Carmel · Gonzales · 198
CARMEL VALLEY
Big Sur · G16 · Soledad · 146 · Pinnacles National Monument
see Pinnacles inset
Greenfield
King City · 25

PACIFIC OCEAN

Ventana Wilderness

San Lucas · SALINAS VALLEY
Lucia · Mission San Antonio de Padua · G14
Jolon · San Ardo
see Big Sur inset
Fort Hunter Liggett · G18 · Bradley
Ragged Point · Jolon Rd. · Lake San Antonio Rec. Area · Camp Roberts · San Miguel Archangel Mission · San Miguel
Piedras Blancas Pt. · Lake Nacimiento Rec. Area · Paso Robles
San Simeon · Hearst Castle
San Simeon State Park
Cambria · Harmony · 46 · Templeton · 41 · 229

**Central Coast**

Cayucos
Estero Bay · Santa Margarita
Morro Bay · Morro Bay State Park · 1
Los Osos · 58
Montana de Oro State Park · San Luis Obispo
0 · 40 miles · 227 · Lake Lopez Rec. Area
0 · 40 kilometers · Avila Beach · Shell Beach
Pismo Beach · Arroyo Grande
Grover Beach · Nipomo
Oceano
Pismo Dunes Vehicular Rec. Area · Guadalupe · Santa Maria
101

Carmel · Carmel Valley Rd. · 1
Point Lobos State Reserve · Carmel River · G20
Carmel Highlands · Robinson Cyn. Rd. · Garland Ranch Reg. Park · Carmel Valley Village
Garrapata State Park · Palo Colorado Rd. · G16
Bixby Bridge · Coast Rd. · Los Padres National Forest
Vista Point
Point Sur St. Hist. Park · Andrew Molera SP · Big Sur · Ventana Cone (4,727')
Pfeiffer Beach · Pfeiffer Big Sur State Park · North Coast Ridge Rd.
Big Sur River · Big Sur Ridge Rd.
California Sea Otter Game Refuge · Julia Pfeiffer Burns State Park
PACIFIC OCEAN · Ventana Wilderness
Big Sur Hot Springs
0 · 10 mi
0 · 10 km
Vista Point · Cone Pk. (5,155')
Lucia · Limekiln State Park · Nacimiento Fergusson Rd.
Sand Dollar Beach · Plaskett Ridge Rd. · Los Burros Rd.

**Big Sur Coast**
▲ CAMPGROUNDS
Andrew Molera State Park, **1**
Big Sur Campground & Riverside Camp, **3**
Fernwood, **2**
Limekiln, **6**
Pfeiffer Big Sur, **4**
Ventana Big Sur, **5**

Buttonwillow · 58 · 5
Carrizo Plain National Monument · 41 · 119 · Taft · Buena Vista Lake (Dry) · Maricopa

166 · Sisquoc Condor Sanctuary · 33 · Mt. Pinos (8,831')
Los Alamos
Vandenberg AFB · La Purisima Mission
Buellton · Mission Santa Ines · Los Padres National Forest
Lompoc · 254 · Solvang · Lake Cachuma Park
Point Arguello · Point Conception · 1 · Gaviota State Park · Santa Ynez Mtns. · 154 · UCSB
El Capitan State Beach · Santa Barbara · 33 · Ojai
Santa Barbara Channel · Carpinteria · 101
San Miguel Island · Channel Islands National Park · Ventura · 126
Santa Rosa Island · Santa Cruz Island · Oxnard · 1
Anacapa Islands · Port Hueneme · Rice Ave.

**Pinnacles National Monument**
La Gloria Rd. (rough road)
Pinnacles National Monument
Chaparral Ranger Station · Canon Rd. · 146
Soledad · Bear Gulch Visitor Center · 25
Shirttail · 146 · Rt. 146 does not connect through the Pinnacles.
Mission Nuestra Señora de la Soledad · Bitterwater
G17 · 101
Greenfield · King City Rd. · G13
TO CARMEL VALLEY, MONTEREY (40mi) · G16 · Central Ave. · Bitterwater Rd. · Lonoak Rd. · G15
Salinas River · Los Padres National Forest · King City · 101

# SANTA CRUZ                                              ☎831

One of the few places where the 1960s catchphrase "do your own thing" still applies, Santa Cruz (pop. 56,000) simultaneously embraces sculpted surfers, aging hippies, free-thinking students, and same-sex couples. The atmosphere here is fun-loving but far from hedonistic, intellectual but nowhere near stuffy. This small city has both Northern California cool and Southern California fun, whether you find it gobbling cotton candy on the boardwalk or sipping wheatgrass at poetry readings.

Along the beach, tourism and surf culture reign supreme. Nearby Pacific Ave. teems with independent bookstores, cool bars, trendy cafes, and pricey boutiques. On the inland side of Mission St., the University of California at Santa Cruz (UCSC) sprawls luxuriously across miles of rolling forests and grasslands filled with prime biking routes and wild students. Restaurants offer avocado sandwiches and industrial coffee, while merchants hawk UCSC paraphernalia alongside fliers for courses. Be careful about visiting on Saturday or Sunday, since the town's population virtually doubles on summer weekends, clogging area highways as daytrippers make their way to and from the Bay Area.

## ▌ TRANSPORTATION

**Buses: Greyhound,** 425 Front St. (☎423-1800 or 800-231-2222). To: **LA** (6 per day; $42 one-way, $82 round-trip); **San Francisco** (5 per day, $11); **San Jose** (M-Th 5 per day, $6). Open daily 8:30-11:30am and 1-6:45pm as well as during late bus arrivals and departures.

**Trains: Amtrak** (☎800-872-7245). The closest train station is in **San Jose**, which can be reached by Greyhound bus.

**Public Transportation: Santa Cruz Metropolitan Transit District (SCMTD),** 920 Pacific Ave. (☎425-8600, TDD 425-8993; www.scmtd.com; open M-F 8am-4pm), in the Pacific Garden Mall. The free *Headways* has route info. $1, seniors and disabled 40¢, under 46 inches free; day pass $3/$1.10/free. Buses run daily 6am-11pm.

**Taxis: Yellow Cab** (☎423-1234). Initial fee $2.25, each additional mi. $2. Open 24hr.

**Bike Rental: The Bike Shop of Santa Cruz,** 1325 Mission St. (☎454-0909). Mountain or round-the-town bikes $10 per hr., $40 per day. 2hr. min. rental. HI members receive $5 off rentals and 10% off parts or accessories. Open daily 9am-6pm. **Family Cycling Center,** 912 41st Ave. (☎475-3883). Kid trailers $15 per day, beach cruisers $20, standard mountain bikes $30, super-lites $50. Open M-Sa 10am-6pm, Su 10am-5pm.

## ✳ ❼ ORIENTATION & PRACTICAL INFORMATION

Santa Cruz is on the northern tip of Monterey Bay, 65 mi. south of San Francisco. Through west Santa Cruz, Hwy. 1 becomes **Mission Street.** The **University of California at Santa Cruz (UCSC)** blankets the hills inland from Mission St. Southeast of Mission St. lies the waterfront and the downtown. Down by the ocean, **Beach Street** runs roughly east-west. The narrow **San Lorenzo River** runs north-south, dividing the Boardwalk scene from quiet, affluent residences. **Pacific Avenue** is the main street downtown. Along with **Cedar Street,** Pacific Ave. carves out a nightlife niche accessible from the beach motels. Resident-traffic-only zones, one-way streets, and dead-ends can make Santa Cruz highly frustrating to navigate by car. It's cheapest to park at a motel or in free 2hr. public lots off Pacific Ave.

**Santa Cruz County Conference and Visitor Council,** 1211 Ocean St. (☎425-1234 or 800-833-3494; www.santacruzca.org). Extremely helpful staff. Publishes the free *Santa Cruz County Traveler's Guide* with helpful information and discounts. Cyclists should pick up the extensive "bike adventure kit." Open M-Sa 9am-5pm, Su 10am-4pm.

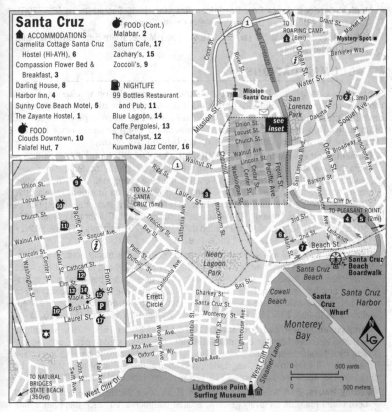

**Santa Cruz**

♠ ACCOMMODATIONS
Carmelita Cottage Santa Cruz
  Hostel (HI-AYH), **6**
Compassion Flower Bed &
  Breakfast, **3**
Darling House, **8**
Harbor Inn, **4**
Sunny Cove Beach Motel, **5**
The Zayante Hostel, **1**

🍴 FOOD
Clouds Downtown, **10**
Falafel Hut, **7**

🍴 FOOD (Cont.)
Malabar, **2**
Saturn Cafe, **17**
Zachary's, **15**
Zoccoli's, **9**

🍸 NIGHTLIFE
99 Bottles Restaurant
  and Pub, **11**
Blue Lagoon, **14**
Caffe Pergolesi, **13**
The Catalyst, **12**
Kuumbwa Jazz Center, **16**

**Downtown Info Center,** 1126 Pacific Ave. (☎459-9486). Open daily noon-6pm. An information **kiosk** sits in front of the Cowell's Beach boardwalk. (☎421-9552). Open July 1-Sept. 6 daily 10am-5pm.

**California Parks and Recreation Department,** 600 Ocean St. (☎429-2850), across from the Holiday Inn. Info on camping and beach facilities in Santa Cruz; for reservations, call ReserveAmerica (☎800-444-7275). Open M-F 8am-5pm.

**Library:** 224 Church St. (☎420-5730). Free **Internet access** available in 1hr. sessions, but expect a wait. Open M-Th 10am-9pm, F 10am-6pm, Sa 10am-5pm, Su 1-5pm.

**Bi-Gay-Lesbian Organizations: Lesbian, Gay, Bisexual, and Transgender Community Center,** 1328 Commerce Ln. (☎425-5422; www.diversitycenter.org), north of Pacific Garden Mall. Publishes *Manifesto* and distributes the *Lavender Reader,* a quarterly journal. Helpful staff supplies info about events and outings. Open daily; hours vary.

**Laundry: Ultramat,** 501 Laurel St. (☎426-9274). Wash $2, dry 25¢ per 7min. Morning wash special (9:30-11:30am) $1. Open daily 7am-midnight.

**Weather Conditions:** ☎656-1725. Operated by the Bay Area National Weather Service out of Monterey. Automated weather report 24hr.

**Police:** 155 Center St. (☎471-1131). Open 24hr.

**Crisis Lines: Women's Crisis Line** (☎685-3737). Open 24hr. **Suicide Prevention Service** (☎458-5300). Open 24hr.

CENTRAL COAST

**Medical Services: Santa Cruz Dominican Hospital,** 1555 Soquel Dr. (☎462-7700). Take bus #71 on Soquel Dr. from the Metro Center. Open 24hr.

**Post Office:** 850 Front St. (☎426-8184). Open M-F 8:30am-5pm, Sa 9am-4pm. **Postal Code:** 95060.

# ACCOMMODATIONS

Santa Cruz gets jam-packed during the summer, especially on weekends. Room rates skyrocket and availability plummets. Surprisingly, the nicer motels tend to have the more reasonable summer weekend rates, but more expensive rates at other times. Reservations are always recommended. Shop around—price fluctuation can be outrageous. Camping may be the best budget option.

**Carmelita Cottage Santa Cruz Hostel (HI-AYH),** 321 Main St. (☎423-8304), 4 blocks from the Greyhound stop and 2 blocks from the beach. Centrally located but in a quiet neighborhood, this 40-bed Victorian hostel is run by a young staff. Kitchen, common room, and storage lockers available. Chores requested. Linen provided. Towels 50¢. Overnight parking free, day permits $1.25. July-Aug. 3-night max. stay. Reception 8-10am and 5-10pm. Lockout 10am-5pm. Strict curfew 11pm. Call for reservations, but no refunds after 48hr. prior to reservation date. Dorms $20, members $17, ages 12-17 $15, ages 4-11 $10, ages 3 and under free. ❷

**Harbor Inn,** 645 7th Ave. (☎479-9731), near the harbor a few blocks north of Eaton St. A beautiful 19-room hotel well off the main drag. Summer weekend rates are likely to be lower than other motels' absurd prices. Rooms have queen-sized beds, cable TV, microwaves, and fridges. In late June, you can pick plums from the trees out back. Check-in 2-7pm; call to arrange late check-in. Check-out 11am. Reservations recommended. Rooms Su-Th from $75-115, F-Sa from $75-175; off-season $65-105/$75-115. ❺

**Compassion Flower Bed & Breakfast,** 216 Laurel St. (☎466-0420). Beautifully restored Victorian home in downtown. Gourmet breakfast, garden patio, and jacuzzi. Run by a female couple and their children who take extra care to be environmentally friendly. Will cater to vegan, vegetarian, and special diets. 2-night min. stay may be required for some rooms. Rooms $115-175. $15 per additional person. ❺

**Darling House,** 314 West Cliff Dr. (☎458-1958; www.darlinghouse.com). A 1910 ocean-front mansion on lovely gardens. Shared bathrooms, but each room has a sink and hardwood interiors. Continental breakfast. Sa stays usually require 2-night min. Rooms from $95-260 depending on view. Check with Visitors Center for discounts. ❺

**Sunny Cove Beach Motel,** 1610 E. Cliff Dr. (☎475-1741), near Schwan Lagoon. Far from downtown, but pleasant, well-kept suites have kitchens and cable TV. Outdoor pool. Market and beach 1 block away. Pets allowed. Rooms Su-Th $60-100, F-Sa $80-130. Weekly rates available. ❹

**The Zayante Hostel,** on East Zayante Rd. (☎335-4265), across the street from the market, near Felton. A former hippie and folk-rock nightclub. Outdoor cabins have beds underneath makeshift skylights, with leafy vines creeping through the walls. Plan on meeting a variety of characters, some traveling and some lingering indefinitely. Linens provided, but it's not a bad idea to bring your own. Dorms $16. Cash only. ❷

# CAMPING

Reservations for state campgrounds can be made through ReserveAmerica (☎800-444-7275) and should be made early. Sites below are listed geographically, moving north toward Santa Cruz and then past Santa Cruz into the mountains. New Brighton State Beach and Big Basin Redwoods State Park, two of the more scenic spots, are both accessible by public transportation. As with any other kind of lodging in Santa Cruz, campgrounds fill up quick and early.

■ **Big Basin Redwoods State Park,** 21600 Big Basin Way (☎338-8860), in Boulder Creek, 23 mi. northwest of Santa Cruz. Go north on Rte. 9 to Rte. 236 through Boulder Creek. Although removed from the city, Big Basin offers the best camping in the region. 80 mi. of cool, breezy trails, including the 2-day, 30 mi. **Skyline-to-the-Sea Trail** (trailhead parking $5). To reserve one of the 145 campsites with showers, call ReserveAmerica (☎800-444-7275, for tent cabins 800-874-8368). $5 non-refundable reservation fee. Reservations for all options required well in advance during the summer. Sites $16; day use (sunrise-sunset) $5 per car. Backcountry sites including parking $5. ❶

**Sunset State Beach,** 201 Sunset Beach Rd. (☎763-7063), in Watsonville, on Hwy. 1, 16 mi. south of Santa Cruz. Take the San Andreas Rd. Exit and turn right onto Sunset Beach Rd. Wind through eucalyptus-lined roads and end up by a stunning beach. Reservations highly recommended in summer. Food lockers, picnic tables, and coin showers. 90 sites with fire rings $16; day use (6am-sunset) $5; hike or bike $2. ❶

**Manresa Uplands State Beach Park,** 205 Manresa Rd. (☎761-1795), in La Selva Beach, 13 mi. south of Santa Cruz. Take Hwy. 1 and exit at San Andreas Rd. Veer right and follow San Andreas Rd. for 4 mi., then turn right on Sand Dollar Rd. 64 walk-in, tent-only sites $16; day use (6am-10pm) $5 per car, seniors $4. ❶

## ☐ FOOD

Santa Cruz offers an astounding number of budget eateries. The healthful restaurant community goes out of its way to embrace vegans—**tofu** can be substituted for just about anything. Fresh local produce sells at the **farmer's market** (W 2:30-6:30pm) at Lincoln and Cedar St. downtown.

■ **Zoccoli's,** 1534 Pacific Ave. (☎423-1711). This phenomenal deli makes sandwiches for $4-5. Daily pasta specials ($6.75) come with salad, garlic bread, cheese, and salami. Only the freshest ingredients. Open M-Sa 10am-6pm, Su 11am-5pm. ❷

■ **Malabar,** 1116 Soquel Ave. (☎423-7906), at Seabright Ave. Healthy, vegetarian Sri Lankan cuisine. Incredible flatbread served by candlelight with ghee and garlic ($2.50). Hefty entrees are reasonably priced ($5-9). Open M-Th 11am-2:30pm and 5:30-9pm, F 11am-2:30pm and 5:30-10pm, Sa 5:30-10pm. No credit cards. ❷

**Zachary's,** 819 Pacific Ave. (☎427-0646). With savory potatoes, freshly baked bread, and enormous omelettes, laid-back and earthy Zachary's will give you reason to laze about at the beach for the rest of the day. Basic breakfast (2 eggs, oatmeal-molasses toast, and hash browns) for under $5. Beware of the crowds; eat at the counter to avoid the wait. Open Su and Tu-Sa 7am-2:30pm. ❶

**Saturn Cafe,** 145 Laurel St. (☎429-8505, downtown lunch delivery 429-9069), at Pacific Ave. At this planetary-punk themed restaurant, the hard-working waitstaff does its best to keep your table clean and your coffee fresh. Excellent vegetarian meals. Veggie breakfast plates like tofu scramble with fakin' bacon or veggie sausage and pancakes (can be made vegan) $6. Open Su-Th 11:30am-3pm, F-Sa 11:30am-4pm. ❷

**Falafel Hut,** 309 Beach St. (☎423-0567), across the street from the Boardwalk. A good place for a quick late-night snack, it serves a variety of Middle Eastern and American dishes. The Lebanese owners pride themselves on their falafel sandwiches ($4.25), but the chicken ($5) is hard to beat. Open daily 11am-11pm. ❶

**Clouds Downtown,** 110 Church St. (☎429-2000). Modern and friendly atmosphere. Fresh American cuisine with a Pacific Rim influence. Attracts a more mature, affluent crowd, or at least those with dates to impress. Salads $5-12. Entrees $13-22. Open M-Th 10am-11pm, F-Sa 11am-11pm, Su 11am-10pm. F-Sa bar open until 2am. ❹

## 👁 SIGHTS

**SANTA CRUZ BEACH BOARDWALK.** Santa Cruz has a great beach, but the water is frigid. Many casual beachgoers catch their thrills on the Boardwalk, a three-block strip of over 25 amusement park rides, guess-your-weight booths, shooting galleries, and corn-dog vendors. It's a gloriously tacky throwback to 50s-era beach culture, providing a loud, lively diversion that seems to attract every sun-drenched family, couple, and roving pack of teenagers in California. Highly recommended is the **Giant Dipper,** a 1924 wooden roller coaster, where Dirty Harry met his enemy in 1983's *Sudden Impact*. If stomach-turning rides don't sound appealing, there's always Buccaneer Bay Miniature Golf or the video games inside Neptune's Kingdom. While the Boardwalk is relatively safe, be cautious of the surrounding community at night. *(Boardwalk open daily May 31-Sept. 6, plus many off-season weekends and holidays. $30 per 60 tickets, with most rides 4 or 5 tickets; all-day pass $25 per person. Some height restrictions. Miniature golf $4.)*

**UNIVERSITY OF CALIFORNIA AT SANTA CRUZ (UCSC).** Five miles northwest of downtown sprawls this 2000-acre campus, accessible by bus (#10, 12, 16, 19, or 91), car, or bicycle (for those who brave the uphill climb). 1960s governor Ronald Reagan's plan to make UCSC a "riot-proof campus" (free of a central point where radicals could inflame a crowd) had a beneficial side effect: the university's decentralized and forested layout. Although the campus appears tranquil, spread out over spectacular rolling hills and redwood groves, Santa Cruz is famous (or infamous) for its leftist politics and conspicuous drug culture. Once the "safety school" of the UC system, UCSC now turns away scores of aspiring Banana Slugs (the school's mascot). Student-led tours of the campus are available by reservation only. If driving, make sure you have a parking permit on weekdays (available at the kiosk inside the main campus entrance, the police station, or the parking office; $4). Trails behind the campus are perfect for day hikes. The UCSC **Arboretum,** one of the finest in the state, grows some of the world's rarest flowers. Also impressive is the UCSC **Farm & Garden,** where students of the Center for Agroecology and Sustainable Food Systems are hard at work growing acres of vegetables, plants and flowers. The UCSC **Seymour Marine Discovery Center,** at Long Marine Laboratory, is another fascinating spot for nature lovers. Located on the bluffs overlooking Monterey Bay, the center exhibits current scientific research for the public to observe and touch. *(For UCSC campus tours call ☎ 429-2231 M-F 8am-5pm. Arboretum open daily 9am-5pm. Free. Seymour Marine Discovery Center, 100 Shaffer Rd. ☎ 459-3799. Adults $5; students, seniors, and children ages 6-16 $3. 1st Tu of every month free.)*

**SURFER STATUE & SANTA CRUZ SURFING MUSEUM.** The bronze Surfer Statue, just southwest of the lighthouse on W. Cliff Dr. near Steamer's Ln., is a monument "dedicated to all surfers, past, present, and future." This inspirational figure, erected in 1992, is often graced with a *lei*. Inside the lighthouse itself is a small surfing museum, which opened in 1986. The main room displays vintage artifacts, photos, and videos, concentrating on the personal stories of local surfers from the 1920s to the present. *(☎ 429-3429. Open Su-M and W-Sa noon-4pm. Free.)*

**SANTA CRUZ WHARF.** Jutting off Beach St. is the longest car-accessible pier on the West Coast. Seafood restaurants and souvenir shops will try to distract you from the expansive views of the ocean. Munch on candy from local favorite **Marini's** (☎ 423-7258) while watching sea lions hang out on rafters beneath the end of the pier. *(Parking $1 per hr., under 30min. free. Disabled patrons free.)*

**MISIÓN DE EXALTACIÓN DE LA SANTA CRUZ.** This peaceful adobe church and fragrant garden offer contemplative quiet. *(126 High St. Turn north on Emmet St. off Mission St. ☎ 426-5686. Open Su 10am-2pm, Tu-Sa 10am-4pm. Donation requested.)*

## 🎫 🎿 BEACHES & ACTIVITIES

The **Santa Cruz Beach** (officially named Cowell Beach) is broad, reasonably clean, and packed with volleyball players. If you're seeking solitude, you'll have to venture farther afield. Away from the main drag, beach access points line Hwy. 1. Railroad tracks, farmlands, and dune vegetation make several of these access points somewhat difficult to reach, but the beaches are correspondingly less crowded. Maps of these beaches are listed in the *Santa Cruz Traveler's Guide*, available at the Visitors Center (see **Practical Information,** p. 322). Many of the sites listed under **Camping** (see p. 324) let out onto pristine and unfrequented beaches. Folks who want to **bare everything** can head north on Hwy. 1 to the **Red, White, and Blue Beach,** down Scaroni Rd. Look for a piece of wood painted in patriotic colors that marks the elusive turn-off to the beach. Sunbathers must be 18 or accompanied by a parent. ($10, after 3pm $15. Beach open Feb.-Oct. daily 10am-6pm.) For a free all-over tan, try the **Bonny Doon Beach,** off Hwy. 1 at Bonny Doon Rd., 11 mi. north of Santa Cruz. Magnificent cliffs and rocks surround this windy and deserted spot.

The best vantage points for **watching surfers** are along W. Cliff Dr. To learn more about the activity, stop in at **Steamer's Lane,** the deep water off the point where surfers have flocked since Hawaiian "Duke" Kahanamoku kick-started California's surf culture here 100 years ago. Surfers also gather at the more remote "Hook" along **Pleasure Point,** north of Santa Cruz in Live Oak. For surfing lessons, contact the **Richard Schmidt Surf School,** 236 San Jose Ave., or ask around for him at the beach. Schmidt is much respected by the locals, who say that he can get anyone surfing. (☎ 423-0928; www.richardschmidt.com. 1hr. private lesson $65, 2hr. group lesson $70. Lessons include equipment.)

Around the point at the end of W. Cliff Dr. is **Natural Bridges State Beach.** Only one natural bridge remains standing, but the park offers a pristine beach, awe-inspiring tidepools, and tours during **monarch butterfly** season (Oct.-Mar.). In November and December, thousands of the stunning butterflies swarm along the beach and cover the nearby groves with their orange hues. (☎ 423-4609. Open daily 8am-dusk. Parking $3, seniors $2, disabled $1.)

**Outdoor sports** enthusiasts will find ample activities in Santa Cruz. Parasailing and other pricey pastimes are popular on the wharf. **Kayak Connection,** 413 Lake Ave., offers tours of the Elkhorn Slough (9:30am or 1:30pm; $40) and the Santa Cruz Harbor ($40-45), and rents ocean-going **kayaks** at decent rates. (☎ 479-1121. Paddle, life jacket, brief instruction, and wetsuit included with rentals. Open M-F 10am-5pm, Sa-Su 9am-6pm. Open-deck single $33 per day, closed-deck single $37.) Beware of cheaper rental agencies that don't include instruction sessions; closed-deck ocean kayaking can be dangerous. You must provide ACA certification for a closed-deck kayak unless you go to **Elkhorn Slough,** a beautiful estuary where it is safe for unexperienced kayakers to use a closed-deck kayak. This incredible spot has an amazing array of wildlife.

You can try **rock climbing** on 13,000 sq. ft. of artificial terrain at **Pacific Edge,** 104 Bronson St. #12. The gym also includes a weight room, a sauna, and showers. (☎ 454-9254. Open M 4-10pm, Tu 8am-10pm, W and F 11am-10pm, Sa 10am-9pm, Su 10am-7pm. Day pass for experienced climbers $14, ages 11 and under $7. Basic safety classes for beginners offered Th 7-9pm, Sa-Su 10:30am-12:30pm and 3:30-5:30pm. $31.50, ages 11 and under $16.)

## 🎵 🎬 ENTERTAINMENT & NIGHTLIFE

Underage kids and those asking for spare change gather downtown, especially along Pacific Ave. Nevertheless, this strip is also home to a host of bustling coffee shops and a few laid-back bars. There are comprehensive weekly events listings in the free local publications *Good Times* and *Metro Santa Cruz*, and also in *Spotlight* in Friday's *Sentinel* (all available at cafes and bookstores). The Boardwalk bandstand offers free summertime Friday concerts, usually by oldies bands, around 6:30 and 8:30pm. The Santa Cruz Parks and Recreation Department (see **Practical Information,** p. 323) publishes info in the free *Summer Activity Guide*.

■ **Caffe Pergolesi,** 418A Cedar St. (☎426-1775). Chill coffeehouse/bar with small rooms and a roomy patio for reading, writing, or socializing. Four types of hot chocolate. $3 pints daily 7-9pm. Cheap coffee M-F 1-3pm. Desserts like cookies and pies $1.50-3.50. Open M-Th 6:30am-11:30pm, F-Sa 7:30am-midnight, Su 7:30am-11:30pm.

■ **99 Bottles Restaurant and Pub,** 110 Walnut Ave. (☎459-9999). This modest but lively bar in the heart of downtown offers standard bar meals (burgers $7) and 99 different types of beer. Happy Hour (beers $3, pitchers $8.75) M and F 4-6pm, Tu-W 4-6pm and 10pm-1:30am, Th ("Thirsty Thursdays") 4pm-1:30am. Open M-Th 11:30am-1:30am, F-Sa 11:30am-2am, Su 11:30am-midnight. Kitchen closes at 10pm.

**Kuumbwa Jazz Center,** 320 Cedar St. (☎427-2227; www.kuumbwajazz.org). Known throughout the region for great jazz and innovative off-night programs. Those under 21 are welcome in this small and low-key setting. Coffees, sodas, beer, and wine. The big names play here on M; locals have their turn on F. Tickets ($12-23) sold through **Logos Books and Music,** 1117 Pacific Ave. (☎427-5100; open Su-Th 10am-10pm, F-Sa 10am-11pm), as well as at www.ticketweb.com. M shows 7 and 9pm; F 8pm.

**Blue Lagoon,** 923 Pacific Ave. (☎423-7117). Mega-popular gay-straight club has won all kinds of local press awards from "best bartender" to "best place you can't take your parents." Bar in front, 3 pool tables in back, and dancing people everywhere. Happy Hour with $3 drinks daily 6-9pm. Su Bloody Marys $3. Stronger-than-the-bouncer drinks $3-4. Cover $2-5. Open daily 4pm-1:30am.

**The Catalyst,** 1011 Pacific Ave. (☎423-1338). The town's primary music/dance venue draws national, college, and local bands. Pool and darts upstairs, deli and bar downstairs. Sandwiches $4-8. Cover and age restrictions vary widely with show ($5-30; as young as 16+). Adjacent bar area strictly 21+. Shows W-Sa. Open M-Sa 9am-2am, Su 9am-5pm. Food served Su-Tu 9am-3pm, W-Sa 9am-10pm.

## 🎪 SEASONAL EVENTS

**Whale-watching season,** Dec.-Mar. Boats depart from the Santa Cruz Municipal Wharf. Trips $5-30. Some guarantee sightings. For more info, contact the Santa Cruz Visitors Info Center (☎425-1234).

**Migration Festival** (☎423-4609), at the Natural Bridges State Park. In early Feb., celebrate the journeys of the migrating elephant seals, salmon, shorebirds, whales, and monarch butterflies that pass through the Central Coast. Music, crafts, and booths.

**Santa Cruz Blues Festival** (☎479-9814; www.santacruzbluesfestival.com). 2 days in late May. Big-name blues musicians. $30, children under 12 $20.

**Lesbian, Gay, Bisexual, Transgender Pride Day** (☎761-9652), 1st Su in June. Now in its 25th year. Parade and music.

**Surf City Classic** (☎420-5273; santacruzwharf.com), late June. More than 150 classic surf vehicles roll into the beautiful Santa Cruz Municipal Wharf. These so-called "woodies" generate a fine fuss. 50s- and 60s-themed music and food add to the fun.

**Musical Saw Festival,** at Roaring Camp Railroads, Felton (☎335-4484), late June. Musicians and listeners are invited to workshops for jam and open mic sessions featuring performances of musical saws and folk instruments from around the world.

**Shakespeare Santa Cruz,** at UCSC (☎459-2159), mid-July to Sept. Nationally acclaimed, innovative outdoor festival. All-show passes available.

**Santa Cruz Hot and Cool Jazz Fest** (☎888-474-7407), 3 days in mid-July. Jazz artists from the West play in 4 venues along the beach. Boardwalk concerts are free, concerts at Coconut Grove and Seaside Bowl $15-25 each.

**Cabrillo Music Festival** (☎426-6966), first 2 weeks in Aug. Held downtown in the Civic Auditorium, the festival brings contemporary and classical music to the Central Coast. Purchase tickets ($15-35) in advance for good seats.

# NEAR SANTA CRUZ  ☎831

Santa Cruz is surrounded by gently sloping hills with delightful hiking; the paths are only mildly strenuous and the scenery is magnificent. To the north, **Big Basin Redwoods State Park,** the very first (and perhaps best) of the California state parks, offers trails that tenderfoots can enjoy. South of Big Basin, the gorgeous **Henry Cowell Redwoods State Park** (see p. 324) has trails suitable for daytrips. Bikers revel among the second-growth redwoods at **Nisene Marks State Park.** Heading south from Santa Cruz on Hwy. 1, take the Seacliff Beach Exit, cross over the highway, and turn right on Soquel Ave. The park will be on your left. **Ano Nuevo State Reserve,** on New Years Creek Rd., in Pescadero, is home to enormous seals that can be viewed on a 3 mi. (round-trip) trek across uneven and sandy terrain. The Visitors Center also offers Naturalist-led tours. (☎879-2025. Open 8am-sunset.)

The **Roaring Camp Railroads,** on Graham Hill Rd., runs an old steam-powered passenger train on a spectacular route from Felton through the redwoods to Bear Mountain and holds seasonal historic celebrations. (☎335-4484. Round-trip $15, ages 3-13 $10.) To reach Felton, take Rte. 9, which passes through Henry Cowell Redwoods State Park. In Felton, take Graham Hill Rd. southeast and bear south to Roaring Camp as indicated by road signs.

Santa Cruz county is home to "renegade" **wineries.** Calling the area "the anti-Napa," local wine-makers follow their experimental instincts to create award-winning, successful concoctions such as "sulphiteless" and "ginseng" wine. Pick up a map at the Visitors Center or contact the **Santa Cruz Mountains Winegrowers Association** (☎479-9463; www.scmwa.com) for more info.

# SALINAS & SALINAS VALLEY  ☎831

The heart of John Steinbeck Country beats in Salinas, an agricultural town 90 mi. south of San Francisco and 25 mi. inland from Monterey. Steinbeck, the first of two American authors to win both the Pulitzer and Nobel Prizes, lived here until he was 17, and his ashes are buried here today. Salinas is where Steinbeck set *East of Eden* and *The Red Pony*, and appears to a lesser extent in many of his other works. Aside from real-life echoes of Steinbeck's writing and a highly acclaimed rodeo, Salinas also offers travelers pieces of Great Depression and World War II culture. For most, though, the town is simply a brief diversion while driving along US 101 or Rte. 68 to Monterey.

South of Salinas, US 101 heads for faraway San Luis Obispo, running through the wide, green Salinas Valley, where the towns of Gonzales, Soledad, Greenfield, and King City (all 10-15 miles apart) serve mainly as farming communities and truck stops. Framed by the rolling San Lucia mountain range, acre upon acre of lettuce, artichokes, broccoli, cauliflower, carrots, grapes, and chili peppers thrive here in the self-proclaimed "salad bowl of the world." Driving down US 101, beware of the speed trap around King City, where wily highway patrolmen dwell. For a more intimate, scenic route, take smaller roads like Rte. 146.

## ⌷ PRACTICAL INFORMATION

**Trains: Amtrak,** 11 Station Pl. (☎422-7458 or 800-827-7245), in Salinas. Offers bus/train combo and train-only service. To: **LA** (bus/train $46-69; train only $54-94) and **San Francisco** (bus/train $16-24). Waiting room open Tu-Sa 11am-8pm.

**Buses: Greyhound,** 19 W. Gabilan St. (☎424-4418 or 800-231-2222), in Salinas, 1 block from the MST Center. Several buses per day to: **LA** ($38.39); **San Francisco** ($17.50); **Santa Cruz** ($10.25). Open daily 5am-midnight.

**Public Transportation: Monterey-Salinas Transit** or **MST,** 110 Salinas St. (☎424-7695), at Central Ave. in Salinas. Fare per zone $1.75; seniors, ages 5-18, and handicapped 85¢. One-zone day pass $3.50/$1.75. Multiple-zone day pass $7/$3.50. Same-zone transfers free up to 2hr. Bus #20 or 21 will take you to Monterey. (See listing for MST in **Monterey: Practical Information,** p. 335.)

**Visitor Information: Salinas Valley Chamber of Commerce,** 119 E. Alisal St. (☎424-7611), in Salinas, has city maps ($2) and plenty of info on the Salinas Valley and Monterey Peninsula. Open M 9:30am-5pm, Tu-F 8:30am-5pm. At the **King City Chamber of Commerce and Agriculture,** 203 Broadway (☎385-3814), staff members are available to answer questions but are short on brochures (maybe because the region is short on tourist activities). Open M-F 10am-noon and 1-4pm.

**Road Conditions:** ☎800-427-7623. Available 24hr.

**Police:** Salinas (☎758-7321); King City (☎385-8311).

**Medical Services: Salinas Valley Memorial Hospital,** 450 E. Romie Ln. (☎757-4333), in Salinas.

**Post Office: Salinas,** 100 W. Alisal St. (☎770-7142). Open M-F 8:30am-5pm. For General Delivery, use the post office at 1011 Post Dr. **King City,** 123 S. 3rd St., at Bassett St. Open M-F 8:30am-4:30pm. **Postal Code:** 93901 (Salinas), 93930 (King City).

## ⌂ ACCOMMODATIONS

Generally, the further south from Salinas accommodations are, the lower their prices will be. Salinas has several expensive hotels, but standard chain motels cluster at the E. Market St. Exit off US 101.

▨ **Traveler's Hotel,** 16½ East Gabilan St. (☎758-1198), is the best moderately-priced option in Salinas. Recently renovated hotel with cable TV, mini-fridge, coffee maker, and private bath. Coin-operated laundry. No off-street parking. Singles $45-66; doubles $55-77. 10% discounts for AARP and AAA members, seniors, and military. ❹

**El Dorado Motel,** 1351 N. Main St. (☎449-2442 or 800-523-6506), near the California Rodeo. Clean rooms with cable TV and private baths. Laundry facilities on site. Apr.-Sept. singles $45-65; doubles $77-85. Oct.-Mar. singles $45; doubles $55. ❹

**Greenfield Inn,** 22 4th St. (☎674-5995), in Greenfield. Small rooms with TV and bath $35; additional people $5 each. One loft available for $50. ❸

CENTRAL COAST

## California and *The Grapes of Wrath*

*he Grapes of Wrath* is, for many, Steinbeck's quintessential California fiction,
the book that brings together his compassion for social outcasts, his vision of
place, and his awareness of the unreal-
d possibilities inherent in westward migration. It
a book that owes as much to its journalistic roots
to its mythic underpinning—an exiled people in
ght to the promised land. "You know he was a
ssionary," said Toby Street, a Stanford friend of
inbeck's. "He was trying to expose, not from the
ndpoint of interfering with lives of people, but
re from the standpoint of exposition. He was
ays trying to show you what a time, what a bad
e we were having."

n the summer of 1936, George West, editorial
ge editor of the liberal San Francisco *News*,
ed Steinbeck to cover the migrant situation in
lifornia. As reporter and witness, Steinbeck
veled first to Hoovervilles—makeshift road-
e settlements—in Kern County and then
red Arvin Camp, a new migrant camp near
kersfield that was depicted in John Ford's
ssic 1940 film adaptation of the novel and still
ses migrant workers today. Arvin Camp was
second of a projected fifteen federally funded
ups to be established in California to alleviate
sing problems for Southwest migrants pour-
in from the Dust Bowl regions. While at Arvin,
inbeck gathered material by reading manager
n Collins' detailed reports of the migrants'
es and speaking to destitute Oklahomans. In
ober 1936, the *News* published his series of
articles, titled "The Harvest Gypsies." Each
cle was accompanied by Dorothea Lange's
tos of the migrants' desperate lives. Both the
tos and Steinbeck's lucid exposés compelled
ders to participate in the actuality of migrant
erty; his prose nudged readers on a visual
r of dilapidated shacks and leaking tents. By
ember 1936, Steinbeck knew that his next
book" would be the migrants' story.

he *Grapes of Wrath* touched a national (and
rnational) chord. Over 45,900 copies were
t to bookstores before it was even published
April 14, 1939, and it sold 83,361 copies in its
month, a record for Viking Press. California
er Frank Taylor wrote in *Forum* in Novem-
1939, "Californians are wrathy over *The
pes of Wrath*...Though the book is fiction,

many readers accept it as fact." Accepting the
book purely as an historical document was the
initial reaction of many readers both in California
and in Oklahoma. In Steinbeck's home state,
impassioned charges were leveled against many
of the novel's points and implications. The book
treated California's Associated Farmers—one of
the most virulent organizations in American history—with well-deserved contempt; it implied
that large landowners lured thousands of
migrants to the state in order to keep wages low
with overabundant cheap labor. It suggested that
police were in league with the powerful elite in
hounding the migrants. And it depicted an
unthinkable level of human poverty, misery,
homelessness, and hunger.

Those initial objections suggest much about
the California quality of *The Grapes of Wrath*.
The book is concerned with contours of power
and how those who wield control—whether
banks, tractors, landowners, or angry mobs—
strip freedom from those they control. In California, the powerless have long been migrants: Chinese, Japanese, Filipino, Mexican, and "Okie."
*The Grapes of Wrath* also presents a probing
assessment of what it means to own ownership
of land and water rights in this state. California
has a long history of rapacious dealings in land—
and this book is very much about the use and
misuse of California's vast resources: land, water,
produce. The Californian dream and its dark
underside are evident; Steinbeck balances prosperity and plenty against failure, waste, and
shame, deconstructing the mythic Western sagas
of gunslingers, horse thieves, and the likes of
Billy the Kid. The rugged loner is exchanged for
the embrace of the family, and the real story of
western expansion is told.

It was and is a definitive American book—a
book about movement, the dream of a new home
and land, and the resilience of realigned families.
Steinbeck's most famous and controversial novel
is a text so thoroughly engrained in the American
social conscience that even now it speaks eloquently of poverty, exile, and self-determination.
Steinbeck reported in a 1938 interview, "These
people have that same vitality that the original
Americans who came here had; and they know
just what they want." These Okies were, for
Steinbeck, the state's newest pioneers.

san Shillinglaw, Ph.D., is the Director of the Center for Steinbeck Studies and a Professor of English at
J. She is the editor of the journal Steinbeck Studies (University of Idaho Press) and co-editor of American
d Americans and Selected Nonfiction, and has also written many introductions to Steinbeck's classics.

## ⛺ CAMPING

There is no camping at **Pinnacles National Monument** (p. 333), but east of the monument is **Pinnacles Campground Inc. ❶**, a privately owned campground with 78 tent sites (6-person max.), 15 group sites ($6), 36 RV sites, a pool, flush toilets, and hot showers. All sites are first-come, first-camp. (☎389-4462. 4-night max. stay. $7 per person. Electrical hookups $4 extra.)

There are five other campgrounds on the east side of Pinnacles: **Bolado Park ❶**, 27 mi. north of the park (☎628-3421; $7.50 per vehicle, $12 per RV); **Hollister Hills State Vehicular Recreation Area ❶**, 35 mi. north (☎637-3874; $6 per vehicle); **Mission Farm RV Park ❷**, 40 mi. north (☎623-4456; $28 per RV); **KOA Campground ❷**, 50 mi. north (☎623-4263; $20 per tentsite or RV, $30 for full hookup); and **Fremont Peak State Park ❶**, 52 mi. north (☎623-4255; $3 per vehicle). Be warned—there is no road access from the east side of the park to the west side (the drive is 70 mi. around to the other side), although it is possible to hike through. Camps to the west are: **Paraiso Hot Springs ❸**, 25 mi. west of the park (☎678-2882; $40 per person); **Arroyo Seco ❶**, 45 mi. west (☎678-2882; $16 per site); **Salinas Valley Fairgrounds ❶**, in King City (☎385-3243; trailers and RVs only; $15 per night for partial hook-up, $20 for full hook-up); **San Lorenzo Regional Park ❶**, in King City ($16 per tent site, $19 per RVs, $21 for full hookup); and **Cuidad del Rey Motel and Trailer Park ❷**, 2 mi. south of King City (☎385-4828; $25 per RV site).

## 🍴 FOOD

Spurn the freeway's fast food joints. Those visiting Old Salinas by the Steinbeck Center can stop by the popular **First Awakenings ❷**, 171 Main St., for gourmet apple cinnamon pancakes ($6) or one of many egg dishes—crepes, omelettes, frittatas, or the "your way" option for $4.50-7.25. (☎784-1125. Open daily 7am-2pm.) A more traditional greasy-spoon diner would be **Sang's Cafe ❷**, 131 Main St., right next to the Steinbeck Center. (☎424-6012. Large home-style breakfasts $4.25-9. Open Tu-Sa 6:30am-2:30pm.) The more upscale **Monterey Coast Restaurant and Brewery ❸**, 165 Main St., serves tasty American fare with a few sophisticated entrees like pork chops with red wine, apples, and potatoes ($20) and artichoke, sun-dried tomato, and goat cheese pizza ($11). They also make their own brews and host live jazz at lunch on Sundays. (☎758-2337. Open Su-Th 11am-11pm, F-Sa 11am-midnight.) **Hullaballoo ❹**, 228 S. Main St., is more expensive ($9-25) but has more options and very large portions. They also have a cafe in the Steinbeck Center. (☎775-4738. Open M-Th 11am-3pm and 4-9pm, F 11am-3pm and 4-10pm, Sa 4-10pm, Su 4-9pm.)

## 👁🗨 STEINBECK SIGHTS & SEASONAL EVENTS

The town of Salinas salivates over Nobel and Pulitzer Prize winner and hometown author, John Steinbeck. The enormous **National Steinbeck Center**, 1 Main St. (☎796-3833; www.steinbeck.org), hosts 37,000 sq. ft. of movies to watch, games to play, and stories to hear. Of course, it all evokes Steinbeck's inspiration: the Salinas Valley. One does not have to be a Steinbeck lover or even have read any of his well-known works to appreciate the interactive and provocative trip into

Steinbeck's world of American small-town culture. The Center is usually teeming with schoolchildren who love the Center's hands-on multimedia approach. Those desiring a more relaxing atmosphere will find it in the art gallery, whose works depict the Salinas area. The Center is constructing a 6500 sq. ft. exhibit called "Valley of the World" to celebrate Salinas's other claim to fame: its agricultural riches. (Open daily 10am-5pm. Adults $11; teachers, military, seniors (over 62), students with ID, and ages 13-17 $8; ages 6-12 $7; ages 5 and under free.) The nearby **gravesite** at 758 Abbot St. and **Steinbeck House,** 132 Central St., are less dazzling but more intimate ways to enter Steinbeck's world.

Salinas's biggest non-literary tourist pull is the **California Rodeo Salinas,** on N. Main St. at Laurel Dr. The rodeo is the fourth-largest in the world, attracting bull wrestlers and riders from across the West in the third week of July. Though the rodeo lasts only four days, related events like cowboy poetry readings take place from May to July. (P.O. Box 1648, Salinas, CA. 93902. ☎ 800-549-4989; www.carodeo.com. $11-18, season tickets $60-72.)

# PINNACLES NATIONAL MONUMENT
☎ 831

Towering dramatically over the dense, dry brushwood east of Soledad, Pinnacles National Monument comprises the spectacular remnants of an ancient volcano. Set aside as a national monument in 1908, it preserves the erratic, unique spires and crags that millions of years of weathering carved from prehistoric lava flows. Thirty miles of hiking trails wind through the park's low chaparral, boulder-strewn caves, and pinnacles of rock, many of which make for great challenges for experienced climbers. The Monument also offers opportunities for caving (flashlights are required on cave trails). **Bench Trail** is an easy two-mile path with access to park facilities from Pinnacles Campground, Inc., along Chalone Creek. At the end of Bench Trail are links to **Bear Gulch** and **Old Pinnacles. Bear Gulch** (1 mi.) is a moderate, shaded walk at the bottom of a valley connecting the Bear Gulch Visitors Center and Chalone Creek. **Old Pinnacles** is also a shaded walk along canyon bottom but is slightly easier and longer (2¼ mi.). Both trails will lead toward cave-exploring options: **Bear Gulch Cave Trail** and **Balconies Cave Trail,** respectively. The **High Peaks Trail** runs a strenuous 5½ mi. across the park between the east and west entrances, offering amazing views of the surrounding rock formations. A magnificent array of **wildflowers** blooms in the spring, and the park offers excellent **birdwatching** all year long. Pinnacles has a wide range of wildlife, including mountain lions, bobcats, coyotes, rattlesnakes, golden eagles, and peregrine falcons. Since Pinnacles is far from city lights and has very few clouds, the **night sky** over the monument puts on quite a show. Taking Rte. 25 to Rte. 146, the park headquarters are at the eastern entrance, but maps, water, and restrooms are also available at a station on the west side off Rte. 146 from US 101. (Headquarters ☎ 389-4485. Open daily 7:30am-9pm. Park entrance $5.)

The **Mission Nuestra Señora de la Soledad (Our Lady of Solitude),** 36641 Fort Romie Rd., in Soledad off Arroyo Seco, was built in 1791. Floods destroyed the building, but it was restored in 1955 and now has a small museum. An annual fiesta is held the last Sunday in October and an annual barbecue takes place on the last Sunday in June. (☎ 678-2586. Open Su-M and W-Sa 10am-4pm.)

Between Salinas and Monterey, 4 mi. off Hwy. 68 on River Rd., is the home of many movie-star animals. At **Wild Things,** 400 River Rd., visitors can see how animals are housed, nurtured, and trained for film and television. (☎ 455-1901; www.wildthingsinc.com. Tours daily 1pm. Adults $10, ages 14 and under $8. Private tours $15/$10.)

# MONTEREY

☎831

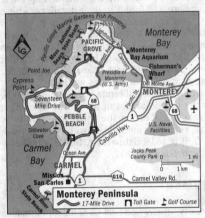

Monterey (pop. 33,000) makes good on its public claim to have preserved more of its heritage than any other Californian city. Although luxury hotels and tourist shops abound and the *Cannery Row* of Steinbeck fame has all but vanished, a number of important sites bear witness to the city's colorful past. The "Path of History," marked by little yellow medallions embedded in the sidewalks, passes by such landmarks as Colton Hall, the site of the California Constitutional Convention in 1849, and the Robert Louis Stevenson House, where the author found shelter in 1879. Most of this heritage owes its preservation to Monterey's other distinguishing feature: abundant wealth. Multi-million-dollar homes and golf courses line the rocky shoreline, and droves of luxury cars cruise the pristine city streets, cutting a sharp contrast with Monterey's gritty industrial past.

## ⎔ TRANSPORTATION

Motorists approach Monterey from **US 101** via Rte. 68 west through Salinas or from coastal **Highway 1.** Monterey is relatively isolated, but prodigious summer traffic jams and one-way signs abound, and complicated traffic signals don't help. Frustrated visitors can park for free in the Del Monte Shopping Center and explore by foot and shuttle instead. Monterey's primary attractions are within striking distance from **Alvarado Street.** Another great way to see the peninsula is **bicycling,** but exercise caution on the narrow, twisting roads and the often windy coast. Pay lots ($5-8 per day) and free 1-2hr. street parking are also available.

**Airport: Monterey Airport** (☎648-7000; www.montereyairport.com). From Hwy. 1, take Rte. 68 1½ mi. east and exit onto Olmsted Rd. Small airport with intrastate and national service. Rental car agencies: **Avis** (☎800-331-1212), **Budget** (☎800-527-0770), **Hertz** (☎654-3131), and **National** (☎227-7368).

**Buses:** Greyhound (☎373-4735 or 800-231-2222) departs from 1042 Del Monte Ave. To: **San Francisco** (4-8hr.; 3 per day; M-Th $17.50, $35 round-trip; F-Su $19/$37.50); **Santa Barbara** (7hr.; 3 per day; M-Th $35, $68 round-trip; F-Su $37.50/$73); and **Santa Cruz** (1hr.; 3 per day; M-Th $11, $22 round-trip; F-Su $12.50/$24).

**Public Transportation: Monterey-Salinas Transit** or **MST,** 1 Ryan Ranch Rd. (☎899-2555, TDD 393-8111. MST phone lines open M-F 7:45am-5:15pm, Sa 10am-2:30pm.) The free *Rider's Guide,* available on buses, at motels, and at the Visitors Center, contains route info. MST serves the region from Watsonville in the north (where it connects to SCMTD; see **Santa Cruz,** p. 322) to Carmel in the south, as well as inland to Salinas. Many buses stop at the **Transit Plaza** downtown, where Munras, Tyler, Pearl, Alvarado, and Polk St. converge. MST has 4 zones, each encompassing 1 or 2 towns. Fare per zone $1.75; seniors, ages 5-18, and disabled 85¢. Same-zone transfers free up to 2hr. Exact change required. Between May 31 and Sept. 6, MST offers 2 extra services: the **Waterfront Area Visitors Express (WAVE)** goes to Monterey sights from the Del

Monte Shopping Center for free and **Bus #22** runs twice daily May-Oct. between Monterey and Big Sur ($3.50; seniors, ages 5-18, and disabled $1.75).

**Taxi: Yellow Cab** (☎646-1234). Initial charge $2; each additional mi. $2.

**Bike Rental: Bay Bikes,** 640 Wave St. (☎646-9090), on Cannery Row directly on the waterfront bike path, **Recreation Trail.** There is also a smaller, usually less crowded location on the bike path near **Fisherman's Wharf.** Bikes $10 per first 2hr., $4 each additional hr.; $22 per day. Includes lock and helmet. Will deliver and retrieve bikes for day rentals. Open daily 9am-7pm.

# ✱🔋 ORIENTATION & PRACTICAL INFORMATION

The Monterey Peninsula, 116 mi. south of San Francisco, consists of **Monterey,** the largely residential **Pacific Grove,** and **Pebble Beach,** an exclusive nest of mansions and golf courses. **Alvarado Street** runs north-south through Old Monterey and hosts most local nightlife. Parallel to it is **Pacific Street,** a main thoroughfare. At its northern end stand luxury hotels and the giant DoubleTree Conference Center; beyond the plaza lies a big parking lot, the marina, and Fisherman's Wharf. Perpendicular to Alvarado St., **Del Monte Avenue** runs northeast to the coast; on the other side, **Lighthouse Avenue** leads northwest through Pacific Grove, where it turns into **Central Avenue** and veers back to Lighthouse Ave., ending at Point Piños Lighthouse.

**Visitor Information: Monterey Peninsula Visitor and Convention Bureau,** 150 Olivier St. (☎657-6400, 649-1770, or 888-221-1010; www.montereyinfo.org). Free pamphlets and *Walkabout Map.* The 120-page *Visitor's Guide* ($6) is chock-full of info. Open M-Sa 10am-6pm, Su 10am-5pm. There is also a smaller **Visitors Center,** 401 Camino El Estero (☎649-1770). Open May-Sept. M-F 10am-6pm, Sa-Su 10am-5pm; Oct.-Apr. daily 10am-5pm.

**Library and Internet Access: Monterey Public Library,** 625 Pacific St. (☎646-3930), diagonally across from City Hall. Pleasant courtyard. 2hr. free parking. Open M-W 10am-9pm, Th-F 10am-6pm, Sa 10am-5pm, Su 1-5pm.

**Laundromat: Wash n' Dry,** 619 Lighthouse Ave. Wash $1.50, dry 25¢ per 10min. Self-service. Change machine. Soap 50¢. Open 24hr.

**Road Conditions:** ☎800-427-7623.

**Police:** 351 Madison St. (☎646-3830), at Pacific St.

**Crisis Lines: Rape Crisis** (☎375-4357). 24hr. **Suicide Prevention** (☎649-8008). 24hr.

**Post Office:** 565 Hartnell St. (☎372-4003). Open M-F 8:30am-5:00pm, Sa 10am-2pm. **Postal Code:** 93940.

# 🔋 ACCOMMODATIONS

Inexpensive hotels line **Lighthouse Avenue** in Pacific Grove (bus #2, partly covered by #1), and on the 2000 block of **Fremont Street** in Monterey (bus #9 or 10). Others cluster along **Munras Avenue** between downtown Monterey and Hwy. 1. The cheapest hotels in the area are in the less appealing towns of Seaside and Marina, just north of Monterey. Prices fluctuate widely depending on the day and local events.

**Monterey Carpenter's Hall Hostel (HI-AYH),** 778 Hawthorne St. (☎649-0375), 1 block west of Lighthouse Ave. This 45-bed hostel is fairly new and perfectly located. Although it lacks the quaint, homey feel of other California hostels, it boasts clean, modern facilities and a comfy living room with a piano, library, and games. Free make-your-own pancake breakfast with tea, hot chocolate, and coffee every morning. Limited shower time: visitors get 2 tokens per day, each good for 3min. of hot water. Towels 50¢. No sleeping bags; linens provided. Free parking lot. Lockout 11am-5pm. Curfew 11pm. Small chore requested. Reservations essential June-Sept. Dorms $22, non-members $25, ages 7-17 $17, under 6 $12.65; private rooms (for up to 4) start at $59.40 for 2. ❷

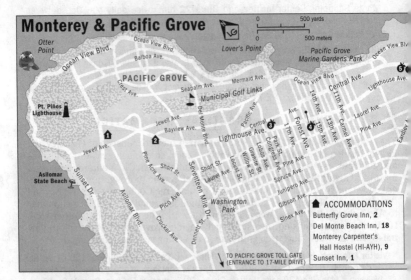

**Del Monte Beach Inn,** 1110 Del Monte Blvd. (☎649-4410), near downtown and across from the beach. Cute, Victorian-style inn with pleasant rooms, each with TV. Near a fairly loud road. Continental breakfast and tea in sunny main room. Hall phone. Check-in 2-8pm. Reservations recommended. Rooms with shared bath Su-Th $55-66, F-Sa from $77; rooms with private bath and one with kitchenette $88-99. ❹

**Butterfly Grove Inn,** 1073 Lighthouse Ave. (☎373-4921). 28 rooms with TV, phones, and private bath. Continental breakfast and pool. Ocean views, full kitchens, fireplaces, and jacuzzi available. Summer rates $99-179; winter rates from $69. ❺

**Sunset Inn,** 133 Asilomar Blvd. (☎375-3936), in Pacific Grove. Located in a quiet neighborhood less than 1 mi. from the ocean. Rooms have cable TV, phones, and private bath. Some have a fireplace and jacuzzi. Continental breakfast included. Prices can vary widely, so reserve ahead. Walk-ins may receive lower prices. Rooms Apr.-Sept. Su-Th from $119, F-Sa from $149; Oct.-Mar. $59/$79. ❺

## ☕ CAMPING

In expensive Monterey, camping is an excellent option for the budget traveler. Call the **Monterey Parks** line (☎755-4895 or 888-588-2267) for camping info and ReserveAmerica (☎800-444-7275) for reservations.

**Veterans Memorial Park Campground** (☎646-3865), in Via Del Rey, 1½ mi. from downtown. Take bus #3. From Rte. 68, turn left onto Skyline Dr. From downtown, go south on Pacific St., turn right on Jefferson St., and follow the signs. Located on a hill with a view of the bay. Playground, barbecue pits, and hot showers, but no hookups. 40 first-come, first-camp sites available; arrive before 3pm in summer and on weekends. 3-night max. stay. Walk-in sites $5; with vehicle $20. ❷

**Laguna Seca Recreational Area** (☎758-3604 or 888-588-2267), on Rte. 68 near the racetrack, 10 mi. east of Monterey. This hilly, oak-strewn camp overlooks valleys and the Laguna Seca Raceway (see p. 339). Of the 175 sites, 99 have hookups. If nobody is on duty, pitch your tent and rangers will come by and collect. Gun range, restrooms, BBQ pits, tables, and hot showers. Reservations accepted. Sites $20; hookups $25. ❷

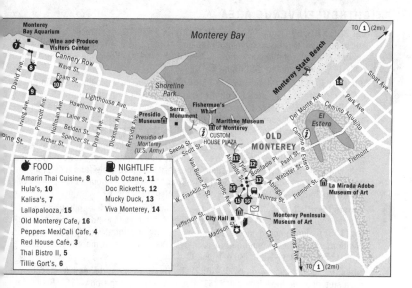

**FOOD**

Amarin Thai Cuisine, **8**
Hula's, **10**
Kalisa's, **7**
Lallapalooza, **15**
Old Monterey Cafe, **16**
Peppers MexiCali Cafe, **4**
Red House Cafe, **3**
Thai Bistro II, **5**
Tillie Gort's, **6**

**NIGHTLIFE**

Club Octane, **11**
Doc Rickett's, **12**
Mucky Duck, **13**
Viva Monterey, **14**

 **FOOD**

Once a hot spot for the canned sardine industry (hence the name Cannery Row),
Monterey Bay now yields crab, red snapper, and salmon. Seafood is bountiful but
often expensive—early-bird specials (usually 4-6:30pm) are easy on the wallet.
**Fisherman's Wharf** has smoked salmon sandwiches ($7) and free chowder samples.
Seafood spurners, take heed; artichokes and strawberries also abound. Get free
samples of fruit, cheese, and seafood at the **Old Monterey Market Place,** on Alvarado
St. (☎655-2607. Open Tu 4-8pm.) **Whole Foods,** 800 Del Monte Ctr. (☎333-1600), off
Munras Ave., is a grocery store conveniently located at the Del Monte Shopping
Center; pick up picnic supplies before catching the WAVE or a bus to town.

### CANNERY ROW & DOWNTOWN

**Kalisa's,** 851 Cannery Row, across from the Monterey Aquarium. This simple yellow
structure was the basis for La Ida Cafe in Steinbeck's *Cannery Row.* Hearty, healthy,
inexpensive sandwiches and salads ($4-7.25). The homemade ice cream ($2.50-4.50)
will also please the palate. Open M-Sa 8:30am-8pm, Su 8:30am-7pm. ❷

**Old Monterey Cafe,** 489 Alvarado St. (☎646-1021), serves breakfast anytime ($4-10).
Old Monterey banana pancakes $5.50; cinnamon raisin swirl french toast $6; burgers
and sandwiches $5-7; Athenian Greek salad $9.50. Open daily 7am-2:30pm. ❷

**Amarin Thai Cuisine,** 807 Cannery Row (☎373-8811), near the aquarium in a complex
of touristy shops. Fresh and unique California-style Thai food. Many vegetarian dishes
such as tofu with vegetables and chili pepper sauce ($13). Lunch $6-11, dinner $10-
13. Open M and W-Sa 11:30am-3:30pm and 5:30-9:30pm, Su noon-3:30pm. ❸

**Lallapalooza,** 474 Alvarado St. (☎645-9036). This American dinner house and martini
bar serves up portions that are a bit pricey but immense ($8.25-22). Excellent service
and trendy, olive-themed decor. Many simply sample the slew of specialty martinis ($6-
9). Open M-Th 4pm-midnight, F-Sa 4pm-12:45am, Su 4-11pm. ❹

CENTRAL COAST

## LIGHTHOUSE AVENUE AREA

🍴 **Thai Bistro II,** 159 Central Ave. (☎372-8700), in Pacific Grove. Graced with a flower-encircled patio, this bistro offers both top-quality Thai cuisine and a comfortable atmosphere. Mixed vegetable curry and tofu $8. Lunch combos ($6) come with soup. Open daily 11:30am-3pm and 5-9:30pm. ❷

🍴 **Tillie Gort's,** 111 Central Ave. (☎373-0335). This vegetarian mecca has been in the biz for over 30 years. Large portions of fresh dishes like Mexican fiesta salad ($8.25), eggplant francese ($7.75), or spinach ravioli ($8.25), and sweet treats like berry cheesecake or chocolate vegan cake ($4.50) will please even the most devout carnivore. Beer and wine also served. Open daily 8am-10pm; Nov.-May M-F 11am-10pm. ❷

**Red House Cafe,** 662 Lighthouse Ave. (☎643-1060). Simple American favorites with a gourmet European flair. Only the freshest ingredients from local growers are used. Patience is not only a virtue, but usually a necessity, to get a table (and a carefully prepared meal). Small dinner plates $8-11. Daily entree specials about $17. Open Su and Tu-W 8am-3pm, Th-Sa 8am-3pm and 5-8pm. No credit cards. ❸

**Peppers MexiCali Cafe,** 170 Forest Ave. (☎373-6892), between Lighthouse Ave. and Central Ave. Serves fresh-Mex fare like snapper Yucatan ($11) and chicken caribe fajitas ($10) for lunch and dinner in a fun, lively setting decorated with "pepper" art. Reservations strongly recommended in evenings. Beer, wine, and margaritas available. Open M-Sa 11:30am-10pm, Su 4-10pm. ❸

**Hula's,** 622 Lighthouse Ave (☎655-4852). Try Hawaii-inspired dishes like macadamia encrusted ono and fresh island fisti ($13) or have a wrap or rice bowl ($8). Beer, wine, and sake available. Open Tu-Sa 11:30am-2:30pm and 5:30-10pm. ❸

## 🅖 SIGHTS

■**MONTEREY BAY AQUARIUM.** The biggest of Monterey's attractions, this extraordinarily impressive aquarium benefits from and encourages the city's committed interest in marine ecology. Gaze through the **world's largest window** at an enormous marine habitat containing green sea turtles, giant ocean sunfish, large sharks, and impressive yellow- and blue-fin tuna. Don't miss the new, provocative exhibit connecting the shape, movement, and beauty of jellyfish to various art forms. Get a glance at the **sea otters** during feeding time, a view of the **shorebird aviary** and living kelp forest housed in a two-story-tall glass case, and a chance to wet hands in the petting pool of damp bay denizens (stingrays included). Be patient; the lines for tickets, admission, viewing, and food can be unbelievable. Pick up tickets the day before and save 20-40min. *(886 Cannery Row. ☎648-4888 or 800-756-3737; www.montereybayaquarium.org. Open daily June to early Sept. and holidays 9:30am-6pm; early Sept. to late May 10am-6pm. $18; students, seniors, and ages 13-17 $16 with ID; disabled and ages 3-12 $9. Audio tour in English, German, French, Japanese, or Spanish $3.)*

**CANNERY ROW.** Lying along the waterfront south of the aquarium, this was once a dilapidated street crammed with languishing sardine-packing plants. The ¾ mi. row has been converted into a different commercial venture of tourist-packed mini-malls, bars, and a pint-sized carnival complex. All that remains of the earthiness and gruff camaraderie celebrated by John Steinbeck in *Cannery Row* and *Sweet Thursday* are a few building facades: 835 Cannery Row was the Wing Chong Market, the bright yellow building next door is where *Sweet Thursday* took place, and Doc Rickett's lab, 800 Cannery Row, is now owned by a private men's club. Take a peek at the **Great Cannery Row Mural;** local artists have covered 400 ft. of a construction-site barrier on the 700 block with depictions of 1930s Monterey. The 2nd floor "Taste of Monterey" **Wine and Visitors Center** offers a taste of the county's booming wine industry with well-priced bottles and winery maps. The wide variety of regional wine, plus the knowledgeable staff and inspiring view of the bay, makes it a good starting place for tasting tours. (700 Cannery Row. ☎888-646-5446. 6 tastings $5; fee can go towards wine purchases. Open daily 11am-6pm.)

**MARITIME MUSEUM OF MONTEREY.** Ship models, photos, navigation tools, logs, and other paraphernalia illustrate the history of Monterey, as does the free 14-minute film. The museum's centerpiece is the original Fresnel lens of Point Sur Lighthouse. The entire lens is a two-story structure of gear-works and cut glass that was later replaced by the electric lighthouse. (5 Custom House Plaza, across from Fisherman's Wharf in downtown Monterey. ☎373-2469. Open Su and Tu-Sa 11am-5pm. $5; seniors, ages 13-17, military, and disabled $2.50; under 12 free with an adult.)

**OTTER POINT.** Catch a glimpse of otters in the wild from this spot, as well as several others nearby. Touching an otter is illegal, and "harassing" one in Monterey Bay may lead to a $10,000 fine. (In Pacific Grove, 2½ mi. south from the Coast Guard Pier.)

**PATH OF HISTORY WALKING TOUR.** Monterey's early days spawned a unique architectural trend that combined Southern details like wraparound porches with Mexican adobe features like 3 ft. thick walls and exterior staircases. The **Path of History,** marked by yellow sidewalk medallions, snakes through Monterey State Historic Park in downtown, passing numerous historic buildings including the *Royal Presidio Chapel,* built in 1794, and the *Larkin House,* home to the US consul to Mexico during the 1840s. Walking the path unguided or with the paper brochure costs nothing, but a tour led by the state park rangers is worth the extra money. (Tours leave daily from Maritime Museum at 10:30am and Cooper Museum Store at 2pm. ☎649-7118. Houses open daily 10am-5pm; in winter 10am-4pm. Tours $5.)

**OTHER SIGHTS.** The **Monterey Peninsula Museum of Art** has two locations. The Civic Center branch holds changing shows, mostly of California artists. (559 Pacific St. ☎372-5477. Open Su 1-4pm, W-Sa 11am-5pm. $5, students and military $2.50, under 12 free.) **La Mirada,** off Fremont across from Lake El Estero, has exhibits on Californian history and collections of regional Asian and Pacific Rim art. (720 Via Mirada. ☎372-3689. Open Su 1-4pm, W-Sa 11am-5pm. $5, students and military $2.50, under 12 free.)

## 🔘 SEASONAL EVENTS

**Laguna Seca Raceway** (☎800-327-7322; www.laguna-seca.com), on Rte. 68 east of Monterey. Late May to early Oct. (office open M-F 8am-5pm). The raceway hosts the Monterey Sports Car Grand Prix (late July), Historic Automobile Races (late Aug.), and the Monterey Grand Prix Indy Car World Series (early Oct.).

**AT&T National Pro-Am Golf Tournament** (☎649-1533 or 800-541-9091; www.attpb-golf.com), at Pebble Beach. Feb. 2-8, 2004. Celebrity and PGA tour match-ups.

**Monterey Bay Blues Festival** (☎394-2652; www.montereyblues.com). Brings big-name blues musicians to the Bay in late June.

**Monterey Bay's Theatrefest** (☎622-0700; www.pacrep.org), between the Customs House and the Pacific House at the head of Fisherman's Wharf. Late June to early Aug. Free afternoon theater Sa-Su 11am-5pm. Evening shows $15, students and seniors $8.

**Annual Winemaker's Celebration** (☎375-9400; www.montereywines.org). Over 25 Monterey County wineries release new vintages and special wines in early Aug. Also features educational exhibits on topics like grapevine pruning and cork display, live music, and a silent auction.

**Monterey County Fair** (☎372-5863; www.montereycountyfair.com), at Monterey County Fairgrounds, in mid-Aug. Livestock exhibitions, live music, amusement park, and food.

**Monterey Jazz Festival** (☎373-3366; www.montereyjazzfestival.org). Mid-Sept. The longest-running jazz festival in the world. Miles Davis and Dizzy Gillespie played here.

## ⚑ OUTDOOR ACTIVITIES

Several companies on Fisherman's Wharf offer critter-spotting boat trips around Monterey Bay. The best time to go is during gray whale migration season (Nov.-Mar.), but the trips are hit-or-miss year-round. The lucky spot dolphins frolicking in the current. The unlucky see millions of gallons of water. **Chris's Fishing Trips,** 48 Fisherman's Wharf, offers daily whale watching tours and fishing boat charters. (☎375-5951. Open daily 4am-5pm. 2-3hr. whale watching tours May-Nov. 11am and 2pm. $25, under 13 $20. 2hr. gray whale migration tours Dec.-Apr. $18, under 13 $12. Boat charters for tuna, salmon, rock cod, halibut, and sea bass also available.)

The local swells may not be the stuff of legends, but they provide a good (and cold) testing ground for enthusiastic water-goers. **On The Beach Surf Shop,** 693 Lighthouse Ave., rents surfboards, boogie boards, and wetsuits just a few steps from the water. (☎646-9283. Surfboard rentals $10 per half-day, $20 per day; boogie boards $5/$10; wetsuits $6/$12. Open M-Th 10am-7pm, F-Sa 9am-8pm, Su 10am-6pm.) Sea kayaking above kelp forests and among floating otters can be a heady experience. **Monterey Bay Kayaks,** 693 Del Monte Ave., also provides rentals and tours. (☎373-5357 or 800-649-5357. Call for lesson information. Rentals $30 per person. Includes gear, wetsuit, and instruction. 3hr. beach tours given by biologist $55. Open daily 9am-6pm; in summer Su-Th 9am-6pm, F-Sa 9am-8pm.)

There are several designated bike paths in the area. The best is the Monterey Peninsula Recreation Trail, which follows the coast for approximately 20 mi. from Castroville to Asilomar St. in Pacific Grove. Bikers can then continue through Pacific Grove to Pebble Beach along famous 17 Mile Drive (see p. 341). The Recreation Trail shares the road with cars after Lover's Point, 2½ mi. from Fisherman's Wharf, and gets quite windy. However, those biking, running, or in-line skating will do so beside spectacular views of pristine coastline, cyprus trees, and marine life.

## ◖ NIGHTLIFE

Monterey knows how to cut loose at night, but some areas of the peninsula quiet down early. The main action is downtown along Alvarado St.; there are also a few Lighthouse Ave. bars. Those under 21 have few options. Covers tend to be low.

▨ **Mucky Duck British Pub,** 479 Alvarado St. (☎655-3031). Empty front window booths might fool you, but many patrons are in the back beer garden, listening to music, having a smoke, or staying warm around a coal-burning fire. Monterey locals have voted the Pub's beer the city's best for 6 years in a row. Come early to avoid waits. Live music and karaoke M-F from 5, 6, or 8pm; DJ Sa-Su from 9pm. Quiz night Tu 8pm—win cash prizes. Parking lot in back. Open daily 11:30am-2am.

▨ **Club Octane,** 321-D Alvarado St. (☎646-9244), on the 2nd floor at Del Monte Ave. Strobe lights and heavy smoke machines throb like teenage hormones. 2 bars and dance floors with different DJs. Pool tables and a smoking deck. Male and female burlesque M 9:45pm. No hats, tennis shoes, or beach flip-flops. Parking structure adjacent. Cover Su-M $7, F-Sa $5, W-Th free. Open M and W-Su 8pm-1:30am.

**Viva Monterey,** 414 Alvarado St. (☎646-1415). An intense crowd lives it up amid creative wall art. Liquid creations like "Swedish Passion" start at $5. 3 black-lit pool tables. No cover for live music (usually alternative rock). On Th nights, professionals and amateurs alike pound out beats at the "Circle of Rhythm" jam session. Open Su-M and W-Sa 7:30pm-2am, Tu 3:30pm-2am. Shows M-Sa 9:30pm.

**Doc Rickett's,** 180 East Franklin St. (☎649-4241). Named after Ed Ricketts, the marine biologist who inspired Steinbeck's doctor characters. Comedy and dancing F-Sa, sushi grill ($5-25) every night, and live entertainment M-W. No cover. Open M-Sa 5pm-2am.

# NEAR MONTEREY                              ☎831

Monterey's neighbors to the west and north have more dramatic coastlines and more impressive surf than the beaches of Monterey itself. Around the northern end of the peninsula, the beach runs uninterrupted for nearly 4 mi., first as **Pacific Grove Municipal Beach,** then as **Asilomar State Beach.** Bus #2 stops within four blocks of the ocean in Pacific Grove. The numerous tidepools along the rocky shore are intriguing places to explore.

**SUNSET DRIVE.** West of Monterey in Pacific Grove, Sunset Dr. provides a free, 6 mi. scenic alternative to 17 Mile Drive (see below). Appropriately, Sunset Dr. is the best place in the area to watch the sun go down. People arrive a full two hours before sunset in order to secure front row seats along the road, also known as Ocean Blvd. At the western tip of the peninsula stands **Point Piños Lighthouse,** the oldest continuously running Pacific Coast lighthouse, which now houses exhibits on Coast Guard history. (☎648-3116. Open Su and Th-Sa 1-4pm. Free.)

**PACIFIC GROVE.** Pacific Grove took root as a Methodist enclave over 100 years ago, and many of the Victorian houses are still in excellent condition. This unpretentious town (which falls eerily quiet at night) has a beautiful coastline, numerous lunch counters, and lots of antique and artsy home furnishing stores. Browse second-hand clothing, book, and music stores along Lighthouse Ave., or outlet-shop-'til-you-drop at the **American Tin Cannery,** on Ocean View Blvd. near New Monterey. Thousands of **monarch butterflies** winter in Pacific Grove from October to March. Look, but don't touch; bothering the butterflies is a $1000 offense. The **Pacific Grove Museum of Natural History,** at Forest and Central Ave. one block north of Lighthouse Ave., has exhibits on monarchs and other local wildlife. The stuffed birds and whale rooms are top-notch. (☎648-5716. Open Su and Tu-Sa 10am-5pm. Free.)

**17 MILE DRIVE.** The famous 17 Mile Drive meanders along the coast from Pacific Grove through **Pebble Beach** and the forests around Carmel. Once owned by Del Monte Foods, Pebble Beach has become the playground of the fabulously well-to-do. Its enormous, manicured golf courses creep up almost to the shore's edge, in bizarre contrast to the dramatically jagged cliffs and turbulent surf. The drive is rolling, looping, and often spectacular, although plagued by slow-driving tourists and a hefty $7.50 entrance fee. To drive in and out as you please in one day, present your receipt to the guard and have him or her record your license plate number. Save money by biking it (bicyclists and pedestrians are allowed in for free) or drive along Sunset Dr. instead (see above). Along 17 Mile Drive, make sure to stop at **Fanshell Overlook** to see massive harbor seals and their pups rest up on the pure white shore, and at the **Lone Cypress,** an old, gnarled tree growing on a rock promontory, valiantly resisting the onslaught of determined, jostling photographers. The image of this tree, prevalent in Northern California, is now the official logo of the Pebble Beach community.

# CARMEL                                     ☎831

Moneyed Californians migrate to Carmel (pop. 4400; officially Carmel-by-the-Sea) to live out their fantasies of small-town life. Carmel has sandy beaches scattered with seaweed, a main street lined with boutiques and art galleries, and a carefully manufactured and maintained aura of quaintness. Local ordinances forbid address numbers, parking meters (though police chalk tires to keep careful track of how long cars have been parked), franchise stores, live music in bars, billboards, and, at one time, eating ice cream cones outside—all considered undesirable symbols of urbanization. All this effort to make Carmel absolutely *precious* ends up imparting a saccharine feeling. Though the waters off the coast are too cold for swimming, the white sand beaches of Carmel are beautiful, the mission is extraordinary, and your heart may race with the prospect of seeing resident and former mayor Clint Eastwood. Still, the town proper may simply be too snooty for some.

## ⚡ PRACTICAL INFORMATION

Carmel lies at the southern end of the Monterey Peninsula off **Highway 1 (the Pacific Coast Highway; PCH),** 126 mi. south of San Francisco. The town's main street, **Ocean Avenue,** cuts west from the freeway to (surprise) the ocean. All other east-west avenues are numbered, ascending toward the south. **Junípero Avenue** crosses Ocean Ave. downtown and leads south to the mission at **Rio Road.** Free town maps are available at most hotels and the Visitors Center. A public lot on the corner of Junípero Ave. and 3rd St. has **free all-day parking.**

**Public Transportation: Monterey-Salinas Transit** or **MST** (☎899-2555, TDD 393-8111). Buses #4, 5, and 24 go through Carmel. Bus #22 runs to Big Sur (2 daily). Schedules available at the Monterey info and transit centers. Fare per zone $1.75; seniors, disabled, and ages 5-18 85¢; same-zone transfers free up to 2hr.

**Bike Rental: Bay Bikes** (☎646-9090), based in Monterey, delivers for free to Carmel on 24hr. notice. Bikes $22 per day. Includes helmet and lock. Open daily 9am-7pm.

**Visitor Information: Carmel-by-the-Sea Business Association** (☎624-2522), on San Carlos St. between 5th and 6th St., on the 2nd fl. of the Eastwood Bldg. Free city maps available here. Open M-F 9am-5pm; plaza kiosk open Su and W-Sa 11am-4pm.

**Internet Access: Mail Mart** (☎624-4900), at Dolores Ave. and 5th St. $6 per 30min., $10 per hr. Open M-F 8:30am-6pm, Sa 9am-4pm.

**Post Office:** 5th St. between San Carlos St. and Dolores Ave. (☎624-3630). Open M-F 9am-4:30pm, Sa 10am-2pm. **Postal Code:** 93921.

## ⛑ ACCOMMODATIONS

The inns and lodges (no motels) in Carmel usually offer only double-occupancy rooms (that fall below $90 only in mid-week or in winter) and usually include full breakfasts. A 15min. bus ride to Monterey will yield lower rates at places with less charm. Camping is illegal within city limits, and no state parks are nearby. There is, however, a private campground 4½ mi. east at **Saddle Mountain Ranch ❷,** 27625 Schulte Rd. The 50 sites have showers and swimming pool access. (☎624-1617. Reserve in advance. $25.) Sampled below are Carmel's posh and pricey inns.

**Wayfarer Inn,** 4th and Mission St. (☎624-2711 or 800-533-2711). Nestled in Carmel Village, the Wayfarer has immaculate, simple English-country styled rooms with TV, VCR, phone, refrigerator, and private bath. Some have fireplaces. Buffet breakfast for guests in the morning, snacks in the afternoon. Welcoming staff. Rooms June 21-Sept. 30 M-F $109-189, Sa-Su $129-229; Oct. 1-June 20 $89-139/$109-159. Special events weekends are summer rates plus $50. ❺

**Coachman's Inn,** San Carlos at 7th St. (☎624-6421 or 800-336-6421). Many rooms have fireplaces. Outdoor patio, hot tub, and sauna available for all guests. English country rooms $99-250 depending on size. Check Visitors Center for mid-week deals. AAA, AARP, and senior 10% discounts. ❺

**The Green Lantern Inn,** 7th and Casanova St. (☎ 624-4292 or 888-414-4392). Each room is modeled after a country cottage and includes TV, phone, refrigerator, private bath, and private entrance. Continental breakfast buffet and afternoon wine and cheese. No pets or smoking. Street parking. Rooms $129-229; in winter $85-189. ❺

## 🍴 FOOD

**Em Le's,** Dolores Ave. (☎ 625-0563), between 5th and 6th St. This cafe is known for its fabulous breakfasts. Omelettes with potatoes or cottage cheese and toast $8-12; unique French toast $8.50, $6.50 for a half-order. Many lunch options $5-9. Dinner features a variety of meats for $14-20. Soda fountain. Breakfast served daily 7am-3pm. Dinner served daily 4:30pm-10pm. ❸

**The Tuck Box,** Dolores Ave. (☎ 624-6365), between Ocean and 7th. Built in 1927, this historic building is now home to the Tuck Box English Tea Room, famous for scones, preserves, and a fairytale facade. Salads ($4.50-9.50), omelettes ($6.50-8), and scones ($4). Open daily 7:30am-2:50pm for breakfast, lunch, and tea. ❷

**Jack London's,** Dolores Ave. (☎ 624-2336), between 5th and 6th St. Salads ($4.50-9.50), fish or fowl ($7-9), burgers (from $8), and sandwiches (from $7). Get a shrimp fajita or teriyaki chicken breast for $12 as an Early Bird special 4:30-6:30pm. Sit in the courtyard or near the action-packed bar. The only night-owl menu in town is served 10pm-midnight. Open daily 11:30am-12:30am. ❷

## 👁 🌀 SIGHTS & BEACHES

**▧ POINT LOBOS RESERVE.** This extraordinary 550-acre, state-run wildlife sanctuary is popular with skindivers and day hikers. Otters, sea lions, seals, brown pelicans, and gulls are visible from paths along the cliffs (bring binoculars). Point Lobos has tidepools, scuba access, and marvelous vantage points for watching the winter whale migration. No dogs are allowed. *(On Hwy. 1, 3 mi. south of Carmel. Park on Hwy. 1 before the tollbooth and walk or bike in for free. Accessible by MST bus #22. ☎ 624-4909. Open daily Apr.-Oct. 9am-7pm; Nov.-Mar. 9am-5pm. $4 per car, seniors $3; map included. Day-use free for campers registered with one of the state parks. Free daily nature tours; call for times. Divers must call ☎ 624-8413 or email ptlobos@mbay.net for reservations. Dive fee $7.)*

## THE LOCAL STORY

### HANGING 10 AND OTHER SURFER FAUX PAS

*Brian, a 19-year-old surfer dude from San Jose, was spotted with his long-board and wet-suit at Carmel City Beach.*

**Q:** How long have you been surfing?
**A:** 'Bout 12 years.

**Q:** And exactly how long did it take you to actually stand up on the board and "catch a wave"—is that the proper terminology nowadays?
**A:** No that's fine, some people still say that....And it took me a good year until I could really ride a wave.

**Q:** But how long did it take you to even stand up on the board? [It took our researcher 2hr.]
**A:** I think just about anyone could do it in a day with some instruction.

**Q:** [Feeling validated—he said *day*] What are the big rules of surfing?
**A:** The biggest one is that up-wave surfers have the right of way. So, like, if someone is on a wave before you then it is his and you can't get in his way.

**Q:** Now getting back to the issue of jargon or slang, you said that some people will say "catch a wave." What are some other examples of contemporary surfing parlance?
**A:** Um, like what do you mean?

**Q:** I mean, what words would you use to describe a fantastic surfing expedition? "Gnarly," "rad," "wicked"? And does anyone say "hang ten"?

**A:** [Pensive] I guess I say "killer" a lot and call going out to surf a "sesh" [short for session]. "Hang ten" is not something I hear.

**MISSION BASILICA SAN CARLOS BORROMEO DEL RÍO CARMELO.** It may be a mouthful to say, but it is a marvel to see. Established at its present site in 1771 by Father Junípero Serra, "the great conquistador of the cross," the mission converted 4000 Native Americans before it was abandoned in 1836. Fastidiously restored in 1931, the mission's marvels continue to astound. Complete with a stone courtyard, Mudéjar bell tower, lavish gardens, and a daily mass, the mission is one of the most extensive in the system today. Buried here are Father Serra and over 2300 Native Americans. The three museums display the original silver altar furnishings, handsome vestments, and a library. *(3080 Rio Rd. and Lausen Dr., off Hwy. 1. ☎624-1271. Open daily 9am-5pm; in winter 9am-4:30pm. $4, ages 5-17 $1, under 5 free.)*

**CENTER FOR PHOTOGRAPHIC ART.** The Center is housed in the Sunset Cultural Center, which was once occupied by Friends Photography, run by two of California's most famous photographers, Edward Weston and Ansel Adams. The Center's exhibits top-notch work by local and international artists, as well as celebrities. Recent exhibitors include Dennis Hopper and Rodney Smith. *(San Carlos St. between 8th and 9th St. ☎625-5181; www.photography.org. Open Su and Tu-Sa 1-5pm. Free.)*

**BEACHES.** The northern Big Sur coast begins at the end of Ocean Ave., at Carmel City Beach, a white, sandy crescent framing a cove of chilly waters. The beach ends abruptly at the base of red cliffs, which make a fine grandstand for sunsets. Carmel River State Beach, just south of City Beach, is windier and colder than Carmel City Beach, but it is blessed with better surf and parking, public restrooms, and smaller crowds. Bring a jacket or sweater, even in summer. *(Walk about 1 mi. along Scenic Rd., or drive to the end of Carmelo St. off Santa Lucía. Parking lot closes at dusk.)*

# BIG SUR                                                                    ☎831

Host to a handful of expensive restaurants and campsites booked up months in advance, Big Sur's huge appeal lies in its outdoor offerings—an array of terrain including redwood forests with freshwater rivers and rocky shores with surf crashing on golden beaches. As Big Sur is more of a region than a precise destination, a fair amount of driving is required to get around; no signs alert you to the fact that you are actually in Big Sur. You'll know you're there, though, because it's the first time you'll see any signs of civilization for miles in either direction.

## ▣ ORIENTATION

Monterey's Spanish settlers simply called the entire region below their town *El Sur Grande*—the Large South. Today, Big Sur is a more explicitly defined coastal region bordered on the south by San Simeon and on the north by Carmel. The coast is thinly inhabited, dotted with a few gas stations and exorbitant "getaway" hotels. Almost everything—fuel, food, beer, toiletries—costs more in Big Sur. Last-chance stops for the thrifty are at **The Crossroads,** the supermarket complex on Rio Rd. in Carmel to the north, and the market in Morro Bay to the south.

Despite its isolation, Big Sur can be reached by public transit in the summer (see below), though once you arrive, you'll want a car. Hwy. 1 from Carmel to Big Sur is simply amazing but curvy and crowded, so go slowly and find a time (early mornings recommended) when traffic won't impede your enjoyment of the seaside splendor. Spring is the optimal time to visit Big Sur, when delicate **wildflowers** bloom. No matter what the season, warm and cold weather clothing is essential—mornings are typically cool and foggy, afternoons sunny, and evenings chilly.

CENTRAL COAST

## 🔼 PRACTICAL INFORMATION

In general, it's best to plan a trip to Big Sur ahead of time and bring all necessary supplies along. In town, there is a Shell **gas station** and an **ATM** (near the post office), but visitors are better off taking care of such matters in Carmel to the north or Cambria to the south before going to Big Sur. As places in Big Sur do not have street addresses, general directions are provided.

**Public Transportation: Monterey-Salinas Transit (MST)** (☎899-2555). Bus #22 through Big Sur leaves from the Monterey Conference Center and runs as far as Nepenthe, 29 mi. south of Carmel, stopping at various points en route. Limited space for bikes; call ahead. 2 per day May-Oct. Fare per zone $1.75, seniors and under 18 85¢.

**Visitor Information: Big Sur Chamber of Commerce,** mailing address P.O. Box 87, Big Sur, CA 93920 (☎667-2100; www.bigsurcalifornia.org). Open M, W, F 9am-1pm. Leave a message any time to have a Big Sur travel brochure sent to you. **Big Sur Station** (☎667-2315), half a mile south of Pfeiffer Big Sur entrance on Hwy. 1. Multi-agency station includes the State Park Office, the US Forest Service (USFS) Office, and the Cal-Trans Office. Provides permits, maps, and info on hikes and campfires. Open daily June-Sept. 8am-6pm; Oct.-May 8am-4:30pm.

**Road Conditions:** ☎800-427-7623. **Highway Patrol:** ☎805-549-3261.

**Ranger Dispatch:** ☎649-2810.

**Post Office:** 47500 Hwy. 1 (☎667-2305), next to the Center Deli in Big Sur Center. Open M-F 8:30am-5pm. **Postal Code:** 93920.

## 🔼 CAMPING

Camping in Big Sur is heavenly, but neglecting to bring equipment is a big mistake; what little equipment is available is expensive. Site availability reflects the high demand for camping in the area, so reserve well in advance by calling ReserveAmerica. (☎800-444-7275. $7.50 non-refundable fee.) If all sites below are booked, check with the **US Forest Service.** Camping is free in the Ventana Wilderness, a backpack-only site at the northern end of Los Padres National Forest (permits at Big Sur Station). Detailed trail maps are necessary for this kind of backcountry camping; ask Big Sur rangers for essential information on current conditions.

🏕 **Ventana Big Sur** (☎667-2712), on Hwy. 1, 30 mi. south of Carmel. 80 shady sites in a gorgeous redwood canyon with picnic tables, fire rings, and water faucets. Hot showers. Sites for 2 people and 2 vehicles Su-Th $25, F-Sa $35; each additional person $4. 5-person max. ❷

**Andrew Molera State Park** (☎667-2315), on Hwy. 1, 5 mi. north of Pfeiffer Big Sur next to a horse ranch. A level three-quarter-mile trail leads to hike-in, tent-only campgrounds. 18 first-come, first-served sites. Beach, ornithology center, and pit toilets. No showers. 3-night max. stay. Sites $2. Day use $2 when entrance booth attended. ❶

**Big Sur Campground and Cabins** (☎667-2322), on Hwy. 1, 26 mi. south of Carmel on the Big Sur River. Hot showers and laundry. Reservations recommended. Sites for 2 people $27, 4 people with RV $27, each additional person or dogs $4. 5-person max. $4 extra for hookup. Day use (off-season only) $10. Tent cabins for 2 people $55, third person or dogs $12. Cabins $118-258. ❷

**Riverside Camp** (☎667-2414), right next door to the Big Sur Campground, has slightly more dusty sites for similar prices. Reservations fee $4. 2 people and 1 vehicle $28, each additional person (ages 5 and older) or dog $3. Additional untowed vehicle $6. Electricity and water hookup $4. 2 cabins ($105) and 5 rooms ($60-115) are also available, but no pets allowed. ❷

**Fernwood Resort and Campground** (☎667-2422), on Hwy. 1, 2 mi. north of the post office, downhill from the Fernwood Bar and Grill (see p. 346). Small but well-situated 63 campsites and 2 swimming holes in a redwood forest on the Big Sur River. Several state park trails start from the campground. Hot showers. On-site bar. Campground office open 8am-9pm. Reservation fee $4. Sites for up to 6 people $24, 2 people and 1 vehicle with hookup $27, each additional person $4. Vehicles $5. Dogs $3. ❷

**Pfeiffer Big Sur State Park** (☎667-2315), on Hwy. 1, 26 mi. south of Carmel, just south of Fernwood Park campgrounds. The diverse wildlife and terrain, the beautiful Big Sur River, and several hiking trails ensure that all 218 bustling campsites are always filled. No hookups. Firepits, picnic tables, softball field and hot showers. Trail maps available ($1). Park open sunrise-sunset. Sites $16, seniors $14, disabled $6. Bike-ins $2. Day use $5. Second vehicle $4. Dogs $2. ❶

## 🗲 FOOD

Grocery stores are at Big Sur Lodge (in Pfeiffer Big Sur State Park), Pacific Valley, and Gorda, and some packaged food is sold in Lucia and at Ragged Point, but it's better to arrive prepared because prices in Big Sur are generally high.

🍴 **Big Sur Restaurant and Bakery** (restaurant ☎667-0520, bakery 667-0524), just south of the post office, by the Shell gas station and the Garden Gallery. Serves 12" woodfire pizzas ($10-16) and entrees using free range meats and fresh local vegetables ($16-19) in a garden setting. The bakery specializes in organic breads and pastries. Beer and wine available. Open daily 8am-8pm, until 9pm if busy. ❸

🍴 **The Roadhouse** (☎667-2264), off Hwy. 1, north of mi. 48 marker. A relatively new dining venue with a lively, intimate atmosphere and flavorful food. Small, selective menu changes frequently. Patio seating available. Soups and salads $6-7. Entrees $11-15. Desserts $5-6. Beer and wine. Open M and W-Su 5:30-9pm. ❸

**Fernwood Bar and Grill** (☎667-2422), on Hwy. 1, 2 mi. north of the post office. Highly popular outdoor patio under redwood canopy. Chicken breasts, veggie burritos, and hamburgers (from $6.50). BBQ specials, often with live music ($8-10). Also has full bar and small grocery store. Open daily 11am-10pm. Bar open Su-Th 11am-12:30am, F-Sa 11am-2am. Grocery store open daily 8am-10pm. ❷

**Center Deli and General Store** (☎667-2225), 1 mi. south of Big Sur Station, beside the post office. This is where you will find the most reasonably priced goods in the area. $3.25-5 sandwiches include veggie options like avocado and egg salad. Pasta salads $5 per lb. Open daily 7:30am-8pm. ❶

**Ceilo** (☎667-4240), off Hwy. 1, 30 mi. south of Carmel, just south of Big Sur Station. It's one of the most chic and costly restaurants in the area, but unlike many other establishments, Ceilo offers more than a great view for your money; the food and atmosphere are first-rate as well. If dinner entrees ($25-34) are above your budget, try a smaller plate ($8-12). Lunches feature salads ($9-15), sandwiches ($11-12), and main courses like oak-grilled flatiron steak ($15-17). Open daily 11:30am-9pm. ❺

## 🗲 🟥 SIGHTS & OUTDOOR ACTIVITIES

Big Sur's state parks and **Los Padres National Forest** beckon outdoor enthusiasts of all types. Their **hiking** trails penetrate redwood forests and cross low chaparral, offering even grander views of Big Sur than those available from Hwy. 1. The northern end of Los Padres National Forest, accessible from Pfeiffer Big Sur, has been designated the **Ventana Wilderness** and contains the popular **Pine Ridge Trail,** which runs 12 mi. through primitive sites and the Sikes Hot Springs. The Forest Service ranger station supplies maps and permits for the wilderness area (see **Practical Information,** p. 345).

Within **Pfeiffer Big Sur State Park** are eight trails of varying lengths ($1 map available at park entrance). **Pfeiffer Falls** (1½ mi. round-trip) and **Valley View** (2 mi. round-trip) are short, easy hikes. Pfeiffer Falls is a scenic hike through redwoods along Pfeiffer Big Sur Creek to a 60 ft. waterfall. The Valley View Trail, from Pfeiffer Falls, offers views of Pt. Sur and Big Sur Valley. **Oak Grove Trail** is a bit more challenging, at 3 mi. round-trip from the Big Sur Lodge, and intersects with the Pfeiffer Falls trail. It features redwood groves, oak woodlands and dry chaparral. The strenuous **Mt. Manuel Trail** (8 mi. round-trip) begins at the Oak Grove Trail and is a steep, dry climb to the 3379 ft. Manuel Peak. **Buzzard's Roost Trail** is a rugged 2hr. hike up torturous switchbacks, but at its peak, hikers are rewarded with panoramic views of the Santa Lucia Mountains, Big Sur Valley, and the Pacific Ocean.

Big Sur's most jealously guarded treasure is the USFS-operated **Pfeiffer Beach** (day use $5). Travel 1 mi. south of Pfeiffer Burns State Park and roughly 10½ mi. north of Julia Pfeiffer Burns State Park. Turn off Hwy. 1 at the stop sign just past the bridge by Loma Vista. Follow the road 2 mi. to the parking area, where a path leads to the beach. An offshore rock formation protects sea caves and seagulls from the pounding ocean waves. Other beaches can be found at **Andrew Molera State Park** (5 mi. north of Big Sur station; day use $2), **Sand Dollar Beach** (33 mi. south of the Big Sur station near Kirk and Plaskett Creek campsites; day use $5), and **Jade Cove** (36 mi. south of Big Sur station; free). Roughly at the midpoint of the Big Sur coast lies **Julia Pfeiffer Burns State Park,** where picnickers find refuge in the redwood forest and sea otters in McWay Cove. (Backcountry camping permits at Big Sur Station. No dogs. Day use free.) At the point where McWay Creek flows into the ocean is a spectacular 80 ft. waterfall, visible from a semi-paved path a quarter-mile from the park entrance. **Ewoldsen Trail** (4½ mi. round-trip) starts in redwoods at McWay Creek, follows McWay Canyon, and climbs upwards, sometimes steeply, to reveal coastal views. **Tan Bark Trail** starts east of Hwy. 1 at Partington Cove. The 5½ mi. round-trip hike traverses oaks and redwoods to the Tin House and has excellent coastal views. To shorten the trip, take the road at the end of the trail. It leads back to Hwy. 1, one mile south of the trailhead.

Many state park trails are usually crowded, but solitude seekers can avoid the crowds by following highway turn-offs that lead to secluded inlets with terrific rock formations and crashing waves. One can also spend some time learning about one of the area's most celebrated former residents—Henry Miller. The **Henry Miller Memorial Library,** just south of Nepenthe and Cafe Kevah, displays books and artwork by the famous author. Miller's casual reminiscences and prophetic ecstasies introduced his readers to Big Sur. Many readers of his more explicit works came to Big Sur seeking a nonexistent sex cult that he purportedly led. While the sex cult is no longer a tourism draw, the cult of history suffices nicely. (☎667-2574; www.henrymiller.org. Open Su and W-Sa 11am-6pm and by special arrangement.) The library sells books and hosts concerts like the **Big Sur Jazz Festival** and readings such as the **West Coast Championship Poetry Slam.** There is also an interesting sculpture garden featuring a computer-and-wire crucifix and mammoth cocoon.

# CAMBRIA & SAN SIMEON ☎805

The original Anglo-Saxon settlers of the southern end of the Big Sur coast were awestruck by the stunning pastoral views and rugged shoreline, reminiscent of the eastern coast of England. In homage to the natural beauty of their homeland, they named this equally impressive New World area Cambria, the ancient Roman name for Wales. Today Cambria is a quaint country town offering travelers a pleasant place to enjoy food, shopping, and timeless views.

Ten miles north of Cambria, neighboring New San Simeon is a strip town along Hwy. 1 with few roads and many motels near spectacular beaches. It's the last stop for travelers heading north to Big Sur or those making the pilgrimage to Hearst Castle. Old San Simeon is north of New San Simeon and consists only of a 150-year-old store, **Sebastian Store,** and the homes of Hearst Corporation ranchers. Newspaper tycoon William Randolph Hearst built **Hearst Castle,** an extravagant hilltop villa that puts Disney to shame, over the course of 29 years (1919-1948) and invited the rich and famous (and his mistress Marion Davies) to visit him there.

## ⌐⌐▋ TRANSPORTATION & PRACTICAL INFORMATION

**Public Transportation: Central Coast Area Transit (CCAT)** (☎781-4472 or 541-2228). Bus #8 runs from San Luis Obispo to Morro Bay ($1-1.50). Connect to #12 for Cambria ($1-1.50) and San Simeon ($1-1.75); you may have to flag buses to get them to stop. Carry exact change. There is no service on Sundays. (Ask #8 driver for transfer; additional 75¢ fee.) **Cambria Village Transit** (☎927-0468) is a free trolley service through Cambria that runs every 30min. (July-Sept. 15 M and Th-Su 9am-6pm; Sept. 16-June 30 M and F-Su 9am-6pm). There is currently no public transportation to Hearst Castle.

**Visitor Information: Cambria Chamber of Commerce,** 767 Main St. (☎927-3624), provides maps of the area. Open daily 9am-5pm. **San Simeon Chamber of Commerce,** 250 San Simeon Dr. (☎927-3500 or 800-342-5613), on the west side of Hwy. 1; look for tourist info signs. Open Apr.-Oct. M-Sa 9am-5pm; Nov.-Mar. M-F 10am-2pm.

**24hr. ATM: Bank of America,** 2258 Main St., in Cambria.

**Sheriff:** ☎800-834-3346.

**Library and Internet Access:** Cambria Branch Library, 900 Main St. (☎927-4336), in Cambria. Open Tu-F 11am-5pm, Sa noon-4pm.

**Post Offices: Cambria,** 4100 Bridge St. (☎927-8610). Open M-F 9am-5pm. **San Simeon** (☎927-4156), on Hwy. 1, in the back of Sebastian's General Store (which also has gas pumps). To get there, take the road opposite the entrance to Hearst Castle. Open M-F 8:30am-noon and 1-5pm. **Postal Code:** 93428 (Cambria), 93452 (San Simeon).

## ▐▜ ACCOMMODATIONS & CAMPING

Cambria has lovely but pricey B&Bs. Budget travelers will have better luck in San Simeon. The arrival of the national chain Motel 6 set off a pricing war that has led to wildly fluctuating rates, so it is always a good idea to call ahead. Beware of skyrocketing prices in summer, when tourists storm the castle.

▧ **San Simeon State Beach Campground** (☎927-2053), just north of Cambria on Hwy. 1. San Simeon Creek has showers at its 134 developed sites near the beach. Neighboring Washburn sits on a breezy hill overlooking the ocean and has primitive camping, pit toilets, and cold running water. For reservations, call ReserveAmerica (☎800-444-7275). Sites $16, seniors $10. Day use (8am-sunset) $3. Hike/bike $2. ❶

▧ **Bridge Street Inn,** 4314 Bridge St. (☎927-7653), in Cambria. Originally built in the 1890s for the preacher of the church next door, this newly renovated house includes sunny and sparklingly clean rooms with sturdy bunks. White picket fence encloses a yard for volleyball and croquet. Pleasant living room with fireplace. Continental breakfast and linen included. Reception 5-9pm. Dorms $20; private rooms $40-70. ❷

**Creekside Inn,** 2618 Main St. (☎927-4021 or 800-269-5212), in Cambria. Look for a yellow cottage-like building. Some rooms have balconies overlooking the creek, and all have TVs and VCRs. In summer, rooms with a single queen bed M-F $89, Sa-Su $109; king bed with balcony $99/$129; double beds with balcony $109/$139. In winter, rooms are $40 less. Prices fluctuate with room availability. ❺

CENTRAL COAST

**Sands by the Sea,** 9355 Hearst Dr. (☎927-3243 or 800-444-0779), in San Simeon, west of Hwy. 1 near the beach. All rooms have cable TV and coffee makers. Some have VCRs and fridges. Coffee, muffins, and juice served in the morning. Indoor heated pool. Standard room with one king bed July-Aug. M-F $65-80, Sa-Su $85-143; May-July and Aug.-Oct. $65-80; Oct.-Apr. $35-65. Additional person $5. ❹

**Motel 6,** 9070 Castillo Dr. (☎927-8691), in San Simeon off Hwy. 1. The benefits of chain consistency and economies of scale are manifest in these big, new, clean, and comfy rooms with cable TV. Singles May-Sept. Su-Th $65, F-Sa $80; Oct.-Apr. $45-55. Each additional person (up to 4) $6 each. ❹

## ▐▌ FOOD

Food is more plentiful in Cambria than in San Simeon. Though most places have pre-established opening and closing times, they may close early if business is slow, so plan ahead, especially if you want to dine after 8:30pm. Groceries are available at **Soto's Market,** 2244 Main St., Cambria. (☎927-4411. Open M-Th 7am-8pm, F-Sa 7am-9pm, Su 8am-6pm.) Buy fresh local produce at the Cambria **farmer's market,** every Friday afternoon on Main St. next to the Veteran's Hall (open 2:30-5:30pm). All the establishments below are located in or closer to Cambria.

▨**Robin's,** 4095 Burton Dr. (☎927-5007). Many San Luis Obispo residents consider this the only reason to drive the 30 mi. to Cambria. Eclectic international cuisine in a crafts-man-style bungalow with outdoor gardens. Entrees $10-19. Sandwiches $7-9. Veggie options like Thai curry tofu $12. Extensive wine list. Reservations recommended for eve-nings. Open daily 11am-9pm or later. ❸

**Bistro Sole,** 1980 Main St. (☎927-0887). Offers an intimate, welcoming dining atmo-sphere and specializes in creative dishes, all made from scratch and changing season-ally. Su brunch features live music. Entrees $15-24 but early birds (5-6:30pm) pay less. Open daily 11:30am-2:30pm and 4:30pm-9pm. ❹

**Creekside Gardens Cafe,** 2114 Main St. (☎927-8646), at the Redwood Shopping Cen-ter. Locals frequent this petite eatery for hearty "California country cookin'." Indoor or patio dining. Pancakes $5-6.50. Desserts ($2-3) made fresh daily. Open daily 11:30am-2:30pm and 5-9pm. Su brunch 10am-2:30pm. No credit cards. ❶

**Main St. Grill,** 603 Main St. (☎927-3194). Extremely popular eatery serves fast, cheap, quality grill food in a spacious, sports-themed restaurant. The patio seating is pleasant on a sunny day. Burger $3.50, baby-back ribs $9. Vegetarians might go hungry. Beer available. Open M-F 11am-10pm, Sa-Su 11am-11pm. No credit cards. ❷

**The Hamlet at Moonstone Gardens,** (☎927-3535), off Hwy. 1, approximately 4 mi. north of Cambria at Moonstone Gardens. Don't judge from the driftwood exterior. A spectacular ocean view and lovely outdoor seating for lunch and an evening bar. Soft, live music often plays for a more mature dinner crowd. Summertime "Sunset Jazz" series Th 8-11pm ($7). Luncheon specials, like quiche lorraine ($7.50) or calamari and chips ($9.50). Bowls of chowder $6. Main entrees $14-30. Lunch served 11:30am-4pm. Dinner served 4pm-8:30pm, sometimes later. Bar usually open until 11pm. ❹

**French Corner Cafe and Bakery,** 2214 Main St. (☎927-8227). A cute little corner cafe and bakery modeled after Parisian cafes and boulangeries. Seeded baguette $3. Cream puffs $2. Fruit tartlettes $2.50. Cafe au lait $2.50. Open daily 7am-6pm. ❶

## ⬢ HEARST CASTLE

*On Hwy. 1, 3 mi. north of San Simeon and 9 mi. north of Cambria. Info ☎927-2020, reserva-tions through DESTINET 800-444-4445, international reservations 916-638-5883, wheelchair accessible reservations 927-2020. **Tours:** Call in advance, as tours often sell out. 4 different* *types of daytime tours leave frequently. 1¾hr. Tour 1, the "Experience Tour," $18, ages 6-12 $9, under 6 free. Tours 2, 3, and 4 $12 each; ages 6-12 $7; under 6 free. Tour 5 is available on most weekend evenings during the spring and fall, featuring costumed docents acting out the castle's legendary Hollywood history (2hr.; $24, ages 6-12 $12, under 6 free). Each tour involves climbing 150-370 staircase steps. **Theater:** ☎927-6811. Films show daily every hour 9:30am-5:30pm; the feature film is 40min. Tickets $7, under 12 $5. A film ticket is included with the purchase of a Tour 1 pass.*

Newspaper magnate and multi-millionaire owner William Randolph Hearst casually referred to it as "the ranch," or in his more romantic moments, "La Cuesta Encantada" (Spanish for the Enchanted Hill); locals and tourists today call it Hearst Castle. The hilltop estate is an indescribably decadent dreamland of limestone castle, shaded cottages, pools almost too exquisite to swim in, fragrant gardens, and Mediterranean *esprit*. The castle rests high on grassy hills sloping down to the Pacific. Officially referred to as the Hearst San Simeon State Historic Monument, it does indeed stand as a monument to Hearst's unfathomable wealth and Julia Morgan's architectural genius.

While traveling in Europe with his mother, young Hearst caught a bad case of art collecting fever at age 10. He spent the rest of his life gathering Renaissance sculpture, tapestries, and ceilings, and telling his architect to incorporate them into his castle's design. Julia Morgan, the first woman to receive a certificate in architecture from the Ecole des Beaux-Arts in Paris, orchestrated this artistic confusion into a coherent triumph of the Mediterranean Revival style, blending elements of ancient Greece, Spanish cathedrals, and red-tiled villas. Scores of celebrities and luminaries such as Greta Garbo, Charlie Chaplin, Charles Lindbergh, and Winston Churchill drove to the castle (by invitation only) to bask in Hearst's legendary hospitality. While countless memorable cast parties were held on these grounds, the only things ever filmed here were 30 seconds of *Spartacus* and the end of a Kodak Funsaver commercial. Hearst Castle is also famous for what was not filmed here—Orson Welles' *Citizen Kane*, one of the greatest American films of all time, which bears more than a passing resemblance to Hearst's life (Hearst reportedly tried to prevent the film from ever seeing the light of a film projector).

Before going to see the castle, your experience will be enhanced by stopping by the **Visitors Center** at the base of the hill, which features a surprisingly frank portrait of Hearst's failed days at Harvard University, his central role in yellow journalism, and the scandals of his life. At one point, Hearst's mistress, Marion Davies, had to sell her jewels so that construction of her indebted lover's mansion could continue without interruption. Five different tours are run by the State Parks Department and are a strictly hands-off experience. Tour 1 is recommended for first-time visitors, and includes a viewing of a National Geographic documentary on the architectural wonder. The banisters or staircases are the only things you may touch in the castle, but there's plenty to occupy your eyes.

## ◪♖ BEACHES & OUTDOOR ACTIVITIES

Big Sur's dramatic coastline comes to a stunning end in San Simeon. Sea otters, once near extinction, now live in the kelp beds of **Moonstone Beach,** on Moonstone Dr. off Hwy. 1 toward San Simeon. Along this stretch of coast, surfers are occasionally nudged off their boards by playful seals (and, far more rarely, by not-so-playful great white sharks, who thrive in these waters; see **Sharks Will Chew on You,** p. 44). Scenic **Leffingwell's Landing** offers the best spot for **whale-watching.** (Open Apr.-Dec. daily 8am-sunset.) Call **Virg's Landing** for info. (☎927-4676.) In addition to providing the best swimming for miles, **San Simeon** and **Hearst State Beaches,** just across from Hearst Castle, are ideal for cliff climbing and beachcombing.

# SAN LUIS OBISPO ☎805

Amid sprawling green hills and close to the rocky coast, San Luis Obispo (pop. 42,300; san-LEW-is oh-BIS-boh; frequently condensed to SLO) is a town that lives up to its nickname but by no means stands still. This area became a full-fledged town only after the Southern Pacific Railroad laid tracks here in 1894. Ranchers and oil refinery employees make up a large percentage of today's population, and California Polytechnic State University (Cal Poly) students add a young, energetic component to the mix. Along the main roads in downtown, hip, laid-back students mingle with locals in outdoor eateries, trendy shops, and music-filled bars, and top off all their drinks and meals with nutritious doses of wheatgrass and bee pollen.

## ⌐ TRANSPORTATION

**Trains: Amtrak,** 1011 Railroad Ave. (☎541-0505 or 800-USA-RAIL/872-7245), at the foot of Santa Rosa Ave., 7 blocks south of Higuera St. To: **LA** ($31); **San Francisco** ($36); **Santa Barbara** ($18-20). It's cheapest to reserve at least a week in advance. Open daily 5:45am-8:30pm. Ask for special rates for frequent riders.

**Buses: Greyhound,** 150 South St. (☎543-2121 or 800-231-2222), a half-mile from downtown. To get to downtown from the station, walk west on South St., then north on Higuera St. To **LA** (5-6hr.; 5 per day; M-Th $27.50, round-trip $55; F-Su $29.50/59) and **San Francisco** (6-7hr.; 5 per day; M-Th $41, round-trip $82; F-Su $44/88). Luggage storage $2 per day. Open daily 7:30am-9:30pm.

**Public Transportation:** The **Central Coast Area Transit** or **CCAT** (☎541-2228) links SLO to: **Morro Bay** (#8, #12; $1.50); **Los Osos** (#11, #12; 75¢-$1); **Pismo Beach** (#10, $1); **Paso Robles** (#9, $1.75). Unlimited use day pass $3. Buses depart from City Hall at Osos and Palm St. On Sa, only buses #10 (south to Santa Maria) and #12 (north to San Simeon) operate. **SLO Transit** (☎541-2877) runs buses throughout the city; they're faster than the acronym would suggest. Fare 75¢, seniors 35¢; free transfers. Buses run M-F 6am-11pm, Sa-Su 8am-6pm. Sa-Su only buses #3 and 5 operate. SLO Transit's **free downtown trolley** runs Su-W and F-Sa noon-5pm, Th noon-9:30pm. Additional service to hotels along Monterey St. **Ride-On** (☎459-3616) offers safe rides for $4 as well as many other shuttle services. Safe rides run F and Sa 9pm-3am.

**Car Rental: Thrifty,** 2750 Broad St. (☎544-3777). Cars start at $39 per day with unlimited mileage within California. Must be 21+; $5 per day under 25 surcharge. Open M-F 7am-9pm, Sa 8am-5pm, Su 9am-9pm.

## ✴❷ ORIENTATION & PRACTICAL INFORMATION

San Luis Obispo is the heart of the Central Coast. It sits inland on **US 101,** burrowed among ranch-laden mountains. This small town serves as a hub between the smaller towns of Morro Bay, 12 mi. north on Hwy. 1, and Avila Beach, Shell Beach, and Pismo Beach, all about 12 mi. south on Hwy. 1.

Downtown, **Monterey** and **Higuera Streets** (north-south) and **Broad** and **Garden Streets** (east-west), are the main drags. Walking here is easy and there is plenty of cheap parking. One-hour **free parking** is available on streets and in parking structures downtown at the Palm St. (at Morro St.) and Marsh St. (at Chorro St.) lots.

**Visitor Information: Visitors Center for the Chamber of Commerce,** 1039 Chorro St. (☎781-2777). Watch for signs on US 101. Staff and brochures. Open Su-M 10am-5pm, Tu-W 8am-5pm, Th-F 8am-8pm, Sa 10am-8pm. **State Parks Office,** 3220 S. Higuera St., #311 (☎549-3312). Open M-F 8am-5pm.

CENTRAL COAST

**San Luis Obispo**

**🏠 ACCOMMODATIONS**

Coachman's Inn Motel, **1**
Bill's Home Hostel, **4**
Peachtree Inn, **6**
San Luis Obispo Hostel, **7**
Sunbeam Hotel, **2**

**🍴 FOOD**

Big Sky Cafe, **11**
Grappolo's, **8**
House of Bread, **10**
Vieni Vai Trattoria, **9**
Woodstock's Pizza
   Parlour, **5**

**🌙 NIGHTLIFE**

Linnaea's Cafe, **14**
Mother's Tavern, **12**
SLO Brewing Company, **13**
Sycamore Springs, **3**

**Laundromat: California Coin Laundry,** 552 California Blvd. (☎544-8266). Wash $2, dry 25¢ per 8-10min. Open 24hr.

**Weather Conditions:** ☎541-6666. **Road Conditions:** ☎800-427-7623.

**Police:** 1042 Walnut St. (☎781-7317).

**Crisis Line:** (☎800-549-8989). Counseling and referrals 24hr.

**Hospital: SLO General Hospital,** 2180 Johnson Ave. (☎781-4871).

**Library and Internet Access: San Luis Obispo Branch Library,** 995 Palm St. (☎781-5989), on the 2nd fl. Open M-W 10am-8pm, Th-Sa 10am-5pm. **SLO Perk,** 1028 Chorro St. (☎541-4616). $1.50 per 15min., $5 per hr. Open daily 7am-6pm.

**Post Office:** 893 Marsh St. (☎543-3062). Open M-F 8:30am-5:30pm, Sa 9am-5pm. **Postal Code:** 93405.

# 🏨 ACCOMMODATIONS

Hotel rates in San Luis Obispo fluctuate daily, depending on the weather, the season, the number of travelers that day, and even the position of the moon. There is less fluctuation in nearby **Pismo Beach** and **Morro Bay,** but the average prices are the same. It is often cheapest to stay in hotels down-town during the week and hostels during the week-ends. However, make a reservation well in advance during summer weekends and events. (Cal Poly com-mencement is in mid-June.)

**San Luis Obispo (HI-AYH),** 1617 Santa Rosa St. (☎544-4678; www.hostelobispo.com). Convenient location just 1 block from the Amtrak station (exit to your right) and 3 blocks from downtown. Tight-knit atmosphere. The relaxing common room is great for conversations with fellow travelers. Free homemade sourdough pancakes daily 7:30am. Linen provided, towel 50¢. Laundry $2. Reception 7:30-10am and 4:30-10pm. Lockout 10am-4:30pm. Dorms $18, non-members $20; private family room for 2-4 adults $50-80 (children half-price); F-Sa in summer add $5 for private room. No credit cards. ❷

**Peach Tree Inn,** 2001 Monterey St. (☎543-3170 or 800-227-6396). Cozy, creekside country-style inn, located on the edge of town. Rooms with TV and tele-phone. Singles May-Sept. Su-Th $59-89, F-Sa $79-150. Nov.-Mar Su-Th $49-79, F-Sa $69-140. 10% discounts for seniors, AAA and AARP members, and off-times. ❹

**Bill's Home Hostel,** 1040 Cielo Ln. (☎929-3647), in Nipomo, 30 mi. south of SLO. Exit US 101 S on Tefft St., turn right on Tefft, left on Orchard, and a right on Primavera. Cielo Ln. is on the left. Travelers fleeing the city will find a base camp near the Pismo Dunes here at Bill's cluttered retreat. Those without cars need to walk into town for public transport. Check-in by 9pm. Donation of $12 can be replaced with farm work. ❶

**Sunbeam Hotel,** 1656 Monterey St. (☎543-8141). Looks like an apartment complex. Rooms have cable TV, A/C, fridges, phones, coffee makers. May-Sept. M-Th rooms $39-$59, F-Sa $49-109; Oct.-Apr. .$36-59. ❹

**Coachman Inn Motel,** 1001 Olive St. (☎544-0400). A few blocks from downtown, near the Hwy. 101 S. Exit. Sizable, immaculate rooms have cable TV and fridges. Pets OK. Singles and doubles May-Sept. $36-89 on weekdays, $110-198 on weekends; Oct.-Apr. singles $25-30, doubles $32-35. ❸

## CAMPING

All state park sites can be reserved through **ReserveAmerica** (☎800-444-7275) up to seven months in advance. For a list of more campsites in the area, contact State Parks Information (see **Practical Information,** p. 352). In summer, you need reservations at beach parks; especially crowded parks require reservations year-round.

## THE BIG SPLURGE

### VERGIN' ON TACKY

The **Madonna Inn,** in south SLO, is probably the only hotel in the world that sells postcards of each room. Alex S. Madonna, the contractor behind the construction of much of US 101 and I-5, decided in 1958 to build a Queen Anne-style hotel of 12 rooms fit for the most discerning material girl. He put his wife, Phyllis, in charge of the design. By 1962, the vision had grown into a hot-pink behe-moth of 101 rooms on 2200 acres of land. The men's room is truly a work of art, featuring a giant laser-operated waterfall that doubles as a urinal.

Every room has its own theme. Take a holiday in the Caveman Room, or express yourself in the Daisy Mae Room. One room even has a working waterwheel serving as a headboard. Even non-guests can cherish coffee and a bun from the Madonna's own oven or dine on steak in bubble-gum pink booths surrounding a giant gold caste tree, illuminated with flower shaped electric bulbs. You can also check out the photo album of the rooms in the reception area. At night, there's swing music from 7-11pm in the lounge to keep things hoppin'. (100 Madonna Rd., off US 101, take the Madonna Rd. Exit. ☎543-3000. Rooms from $127-320.)

**Montaña de Oro State Park** (☎528-0513), on Pecho Rd., 4 mi. south of Los Osos, 12 mi. from SLO via Los Osos Valley Rd. 50 primitive sites in a gorgeous, secluded park. Outhouses and cold running water (but bring your own drinking water). Reserve weeks in advance for sites May 31-Sept. 6. Sites $10. ❶

**Morro Bay State Park** (☎772-7434), 12 mi. west of SLO on Hwy. 1. Popular park between the ocean and forest with 135 developed sites (30 with hookups). Hot showers and running water. Sanitary disposal station. Reserve year-round. Sites $16; with hookup $20. ❶

**Morro Strand State Beach** (☎772-2560), off Hwy. 1, at the northern edge of Morro Bay. 81 contiguous sites along a beautiful stretch of sandy beach. Toilets and water but no hot showers. 24 ft. vehicle length limit. Your receipt allows you to use the showers at Morro Bay State Park without paying another entrance fee. Sites $18, seniors $14. ❷

**Pismo Beach State Park** (☎489-1869), on Hwy. 1, just south of scenic Pismo Beach. A huge campground split into two areas. **North Beach** has 103 tent sites with water, showers, and restrooms. Sanitary disposal. **Oceano** has 40 tent sites and 42 RV hookups. Water, flush toilets, showers. North Beach sites are larger and closer to the beach. Call for reservations. Sites $16; RV sites $20. ❶

## 🍴 FOOD

**Higuera Street** and its cross streets are lined with restaurants and cafes. One can find cheap, greasy-spoon fare as well as many healthy, organic choices. The area south of the mission along the creek is popular with lunchtime crowds. A **farmer's market** takes over Higuera St. every Thursday 6:30-9pm.

▧ **Big Sky Cafe,** 1121 Broad St. (☎545-5401). Voted "Best Restaurant in SLO" in a recent magazine poll and winner of many local awards, Big Sky delivers with vegetarian-friendly food. Sandwiches $6.50-10. Choice local wines $4-6 per glass. Margaritas $3.50. Open M-Sa 7am-10pm, Su 8am-9pm. Call for reservations for 6 or more between 4:30-6pm. ❷

▧ **House of Bread,** 858 Higuera St. (☎542-0255). Enticing smells will lure you into this warm bakery, which uses chemical-free Montana wheat in its delicious bread products. Free samples provide ample opportunity for choosing favorites. Raspberry pinwheel or huge cinnamon roll $2. Open M-W and F-Sa 7am-7pm, Th 7am-9pm, Su 9am-5pm. ❶

**Grappolo's,** 1040 Broad St. (☎788-0260). This new, Art Deco Italian restaurant and bar sits beside San Luis Obispo Creek. Dishes range $8-17 and the wine list is one of the most extensive in town. After dinner, head downstairs to the dimly lit basement bar. Kitchen open Su-Th 11:30am-9pm, F-Sa 11:30am-11pm; bar open until 2am. ❸

**Woodstock's Pizza Parlour,** 1000 Higuera St. (☎541-4420). This hangout invariably sweeps annual best pizza awards. Young crowds keep it lively into the night. Lunch specials like all-you-can-eat pizza and bottomless soda $6.50. Single slices $1.75, whole pies $5.25-20. Toppings 50¢-$1.50. Happy Hour M-W 8-11pm with pitchers of beer $4-8, slices $1.25. Open Su-Th 11am-midnight, F-Sa 11am-1am. ❷

**Vieni Vai Trattoria,** 690 Higuera St. (☎544-5282). Homemade organic pasta and ravioli with lots of vegetarian sauces ($8-12). Half-order portions are plenty for mid-sized appetites. Also serves dishes with seafood, chicken, and veal ($12-17) and pizza ($9-12). Full bar. Open daily 11am-11pm. ❸

## 👁 SIGHTS

**MISSION SAN LUIS OBISPO DE TOLOSA.** San Luis Obispo grew around the Mission San Luis Obispo de Tolosa, and the city continues to hold celebrations and general lunchtime socializing around its front steps. Founded in 1772, the mission was once covered in white clapboards and crowned with a steeple in the New England style. In the late 1800s, however, the town began reviving the mission's Spanish origins; by the 1930s it was fully restored. It still serves as the Catholic parish church for SLO. The mission also houses a small museum, which displays objects from the early days of the mission and a small collection of Chumash artifacts. (☎543-6850. Open daily early Apr. to late Oct. 9am-5pm; late Oct. to early Apr. 9am-4pm. $2 donation requested.) The mission faces beautiful Mission Plaza, where Father Serra held the area's first mass. At the edge of the plaza sits the **SLO Art Center,** 1010 Broad St., with lectures, art classes, poetry readings, and exhibits by regional artists. (☎543-8562. Open Su and Tu-Sa 11am-5pm. Free, but donations are appreciated.)

**APPLE FARM MILL.** A gurgling 14 ft. waterwheel and shady deck await visitors of 2015 Monterey St. Alternately churning ice cream and flour, the mill provides free samples of cider from a local farm and complimentary tea, popcorn, and chocolates on the deck. Also home to a restaurant, bakery, gift shop, and inn, the mill is a great way to spend a pleasant afternoon. (☎544-2040, gift shop 541-0369, dining reservations 544-6100. Gift shop and bakery open Su-Th 7am-9pm, F-Sa 7am-10pm.)

**OTHER SIGHTS.** The nearby **Jack House,** 536 Marsh St., is a restored Victorian residence with the original 19th-century furnishing inside and a gazebo and garden outside. (☎781-7308, tour info 781-7300. Open Feb.-Nov. only on the 1st Su of the month 1-4pm; June-Aug. also open Th 2-5pm. 45min. tours $2.) Kids might enjoy the **SLO Children's Museum,** 1010 Nipomo St. (☎544-5437. Open Su noon-4pm, Tu-Sa 11am-5pm. $5, under 2 free.) One million dollars of city money have transformed the old public library, 696 Monterey St., into the **SLO Historical Society Museum.** Dioramas and interactive displays depict eras of San Luis Obispo's history, catering to younger audiences. The museum gives special emphasis to local Native American civilization. (☎543-0638. Open Su and W-Sa 10am-4pm.)

# 🎵 🎭 ENTERTAINMENT & NIGHTLIFE

Half of SLO's population is under the age of 24, so the town can't help but party. It gets particularly wild along Higuera St. between Nipomo and Osos St. after the Thursday night **farmer's market,** which often resembles a raging block party more than a produce bazaar. **San Luis Little Theater,** 888 Morro St., has performances by local thespians. (☎786-2440. Shows Su 2pm, Th-Sa 8pm. $14, students and seniors $12; Th night $10.) The **Palm Theater,** 817 Palm St., screens artsy and revival films at odd times; call for schedule. (☎541-5161. $6.50, seniors and children $4, matinees $4; M night $4.) Standard Hollywood flicks often run at the grand **Art Deco Freemont Theatre,** 1035 Monterey St., designed in 1942 by the preeminent Southern Californian architect Charles Lee. The main theater maintains the original murals. ($7.50, seniors and children $4.75; matinees before 5:30pm $4.75.) Weekdays in SLO slow down a bit as the students attempt to salvage their grades. Consult the free weekly *New Times* regarding other local happenings; nightlife options range from disco dancing to live big bands, and from pool clubs to gallery openings.

🏠 **Mother's Tavern,** 725 Higuera St. (☎541-8733). This Yukon-inspired bar and restaurant with mounted animal heads draws mostly Cal Poly students who pile in for the W night disco (cover $3 after 10pm). Also offers 80s nights ($3) and karaoke (free). Happy Hour M-F 3-6pm. Live music Th-Sa usually draws more mature crowds. 21+ after 9pm. Live music cover $3-7. Open daily 11:30am-1:30am; kitchen closes 9pm.

**SLO Brewing Company,** 1119 Garden St. (☎543-1843). Winner of the World Beer Cup 2000 for its Amber Ale, the Brewing Co. also features amazingly good porter ("Cole Porter"; $3.75 per pint). Happy Hour M-F 4-5:30pm (half-price drafts). Live funk, reggae, and rock Th-Sa at 9:30pm (cover varies). Strict dress code. Seven billiard tables upstairs: $6 per hr., but $3 per hr. Su-W and before 6pm Th-Sa. Downstairs open M-W 11:30am-10pm, Th-Sa 11:30am-1:30am, Su 11:30am-9pm. Upstairs open M-W 4pm-midnight, Th-F 4pm-1:30am, Sa noon-1:30am, Su noon-midnight.

**Linnaea's Cafe,** 1112 Garden St. (☎541-5888). Evening hangout for the artsy set. Displays local artists' works on the walls and features music nightly at 8:30pm; jazz Su and F-Sa during the school year. No cover, but a hat is passed around after each performance. Open M-Sa 7am-midnight, Su 7am-3pm and 7pm-midnight. No credit cards.

**Sycamore Springs,** 1215 Avila Beach Dr. (☎595-7365), 1 mi. south of Avila Beach. Cal Poly students and vacationers alike unwind here. Private outdoor redwood hot tubs with sulfurous mineral water operate 24hr. a day for around-the-clock relaxation. Reservations recommended between 8pm-3am, especially on weekends. M-F between 4-6pm (non-holidays) $10 per person per hr., children $6; all other times $12.50/$7.50.

## ◪ BEACHES SOUTH OF SAN LUIS OBISPO

Two beaches just southwest of San Luis Obispo do not have signs marking their existence but are frequented by distinctly different crowds. Swimsuit-optional **Pirate's Cove** has unusually warm water, fortunately for the nude bathers' pleasure and pride. Take US 101 S from San Luis Obispo to the Avila Rd. Exit. Follow signs for Avila Beach, but turn left on Cave Landing Rd. Park in the dirt lot and take a path (500 yd.) to the cove. The rocky shore of **Shell Beach,** 1 mi. down US 101 south of Avila Beach and Pirate's Cove, is the launching point for many kayaks. Take the Shell Beach Exit from US 101 S and turn left on Shell Beach Rd. A right on Cliff Ave. will lead to Ocean Blvd. Park at the gazebo.

**Avila** and **Pismo Beaches** are both more developed and crowded than Shell Beach. Avila is known for its gaggle of fishermen. The adjoining city streets seem determined to mimic the boardwalk atmosphere of Pismo. Avila Beach is on the left after Cave Landing Rd. Pismo Beach, 1½ mi. south of Shell Beach, is the most developed and congested beach in the area; the lines for the public restrooms are practically social events. This booming spring break party spot is accessible by **Central Coast Area Transit** (☎541-2228) and **Greyhound** (☎800-231-2222). **Beach Cycle Rentals,** 150 Hinds Ave., rents all kinds of beach equipment next to the pier. (☎773-5518. Open daily 9am-dusk.) When the sun sets behind the hills that jut into the sea, Pismo Beach lights up with a gorgeous sand-on-fire effect.

**Pismo Dunes** (☎473-7223), south of Pismo Beach on Grover Beach, is a State Vehicular Recreation Area, where for a $4 day use (6am-11pm) fee, you can take your car or all-terrain vehicle (ATV) down onto the dunes. Rent ATV equipment from **BJ's ATV,** 197 Grand Ave. (☎481-5411. Open daily 8am-5pm. M-F $75-125 for 2hr., Sa-Su $40-75 per hr.) Keep your speed down to 15 mph or pay a $900 fine. At the south end of the park is **Oso Flaco Lake ❶,** accessible by hiking. Camping here is an option only for the most serious budget traveler; on weekends, prepare for revving engines and squealing tires. (☎473-7223. Sites $6, seniors $4, walk-ins $1.)

## ◪ SEASONAL EVENTS

Believe it or not, SLO hosts the most rollicking **Mardi Gras** this side of the Mississippi, celebrated the Saturday before Ash Wednesday. Thousands flock in for the debauchery. (Info ☎541-2183.) The **Mozart Festival,** in late July and early August, is also a favorite. Concerts are held at the Cal Poly theater, the Cohan Center, the mission, local wineries, and local churches. (For info, call ☎781-

3008 or write 1160 Marsh Street #310, San Luis Obispo, CA 93401. Tickets
☎756-2787 or 888-233-2787. $15-30, student rush tickets 30min. before show
$7.50.) The acclaimed **Central Coast Shakespeare Festival** runs two Shakespeare
plays for six weeks at the SLO City Playhouse. (☎546-4224. Starting the first or
second week in July, Su and Th-Sa. $14, students and seniors $12. No credit
cards.) The four-day **International Film Festival** features independent films, documentaries, and seminars. (☎546-3456; www.slofilmfest.org. First week of
Nov. $5 per screening.)

# NEAR SAN LUIS OBISPO ☎805

Gray whales, seals, otters, dolphins, and the occasional orca (killer whale) frequent **Montana de Oro State Park** (☎528-0513), 30min. west of SLO on Los Osos
Valley Rd. The 8000 acres and seven miles of shoreline remain relatively
secluded. **Spooner's Cove,** three-quarters of a mile north of Coralina Cove, has
tidepools and whale-watching spots from the bluffs above at the Bluff's Trail
trailhead. Get more info about hikes at the **Ranger Office** in the old ranch house.
(☎772-7434. Open in summer daily 8:30am-9:30pm; in winter M-Th 8:30am-
3:30pm, F-Su noon-4pm.)

The **wineries** around SLO are well-respected. **Paso Robles,** 25 mi. north of SLO
on US 101, is vintner central. The SLO Chamber of Commerce (see **Practical Information,** p. 352) and the **Paso Robles Chamber of Commerce,** 1225 Park St., have a
list of wineries, including visiting hours, tours, and tastings. (☎238-0506. Open
M-F 8:30am-5pm, Sa 10am-4pm.) Wild Horse, Justin Winery, Edna Valley, and
Steven Ross are some renowned labels. To taste in San Luis Obispo proper, try
**Central Coast Wineries** at 712 Higuera St. (☎544-8761. Local winemakers host tastings Th 6-9pm for $4. Open Su-W 11am-6pm, Th 11am-9pm, F-Sa 11am-8am.)

**Mission San Miguel Archangel** is 43 mi. north of San Luis Obispo in San Miguel,
just off US 101; take the San Miguel Exit. The 1818 complex has colorful frescoes,
painted in 1821 by Monterey's Esteban Munras and a team of Native American artists. (☎467-3256. Open daily 9:30am-4:30pm. $1 donation requested.)

## MORRO BAY ☎805

**CCAT bus** #8 and #12 serves Morro Bay from SLO. (Info ☎541-2228. Runs M-F. $1.)
Motels here are often cheaper here than in SLO. **Morro Bay Chamber of Commerce,**
880 Main St., has maps and listings. (☎772-4467 or 800-231-0592. Open M-F 8:30am-
5pm, Sa 10am-3pm.) For campground info, see **SLO: Camping,** p. 354.

The **Seven Sisters,** a chain of small ex-volcanoes, are remnants of a time when
SLO County was a hotbed of volcanic activity. The lava that once flowed here
formed the dramatic shorelines along Hwy. 1 from Morro Rock to SLO. The
northernmost sister, Morro Rock, and three large smokestacks from an electric
company shadow the tiny burg of Morro Bay, just north of its namesake park.

**Morro Bay State Park,** is home to coastal cypresses that are visited by Monarch butterflies from November to early February. The park's **Museum of Natural History** flexes its curatorial might on the aquatic environment and wildlife of
the coastal headlands. A bulletin board near the entrance lists free nature
walks led by park docents. (☎772-2694. Open daily 10am-5pm. $2, under 17
free). South Bay Blvd., which links the town and the park, winds through the
new **Morro Bay National Estuary,** a sanctuary for great blue herons, egrets, and
sea otters. Either take the trail or rent a kayak or canoe to roam through the
estuary. (☎772-8796. Open 9am-5pm. Kayaks $8 per hr; canoes $12.) Pack a
basket and paddle out to the sand dunes for a picnic lunch. Check for tides to
avoid (or take advantage of) numerous sandbars.

**CENTRAL COAST**

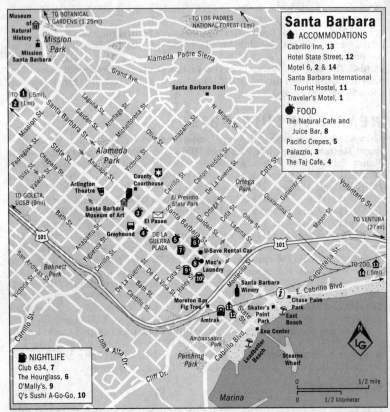

**Santa Barbara**

⚑ **ACCOMMODATIONS**
Cabrillo Inn, **13**
Hotel State Street, **12**
Motel 6, **2** & **14**
Santa Barbara International
 Tourist Hostel, **11**
Traveler's Motel, **1**

🍎 **FOOD**
The Natural Cafe and
 Juice Bar, **8**
Pacific Crepes, **5**
Palazzio, **3**
The Taj Cafe, **4**

🎵 **NIGHTLIFE**
Club 634, **7**
The Hourglass, **6**
O'Mally's, **9**
Q's Sushi A-Go-Go, **10**

Along the beach, the **Embarcadero** is the locus of Morro Bay activity and fish 'n' chips bargains. The **Morro Bay Aquarium,** 595 Embarcadero, is a rehabilitation center for distressed marine animals and has over 100 ocean critters and a seal-feeding station. (☎772-7647. Open daily 9am-6:30pm; in winter daily 9:30am-5:30pm. $2, ages 5-11 $1, under 5 free.) Morro Bay's pride and joy is the **Giant Chessboard,** in Centennial Park on Embarcadero across from Southern Port Traders. The board is 256 sq. ft., with 18 to 20 lb. carved redwood pieces. (Call the Morro Bay Recreation office at ☎772-6278 to set up a game. $17 per game for non-residents.)

# SANTA BARBARA                    ☎805

Santa Barbara (pop. 92,500) epitomizes worry-free living. The town is an enclave of wealth and privilege, true to its soap opera image, but in a significantly less aggressive and flashy way than its SoCal counterparts. Spanish Revival architecture decorates the hills that rise over a lively pedestrian district. State Street, Santa Barbara's main drag, is a sanitized, palm-lined promenade of inexpensive cafes, thrift stores, and glamorous boutiques and galleries. Santa Barbara's golden beaches, museums, historic missions, and scenic drives make it a frequent weekend escape for the rich and famous, and an attractive destination for surfers, artists, and backpackers alike.

CENTRAL COAST

# ⌐ TRANSPORTATION

Driving in Santa Barbara can be bewildering, as dead-ends, one-way streets, and congested traffic abound. Beware of intersections on State St. that surprise motorists with quick red lights. Many downtown lots and streets offer 1¼hr. of **free parking**, including two underground lots at Pasco Nuevo, accessible by the 700 block of Chapala St. All parking is free on Sundays. **Biking** is a nice alternative; most streets have special lanes. The **Cabrillo Bikeway** runs east-west along the beach from the Bird Refuge to the City College campus. MTD buses run throughout the city.

**Flights: Santa Barbara Municipal Airport** (☎683-4011; www.flysba.com), in Goleta. Offers intrastate and limited national service.

**Trains: Amtrak,** 209 State St. (☎963-1015; schedule and fares 800-USA-RAIL/872-7245). **Be careful around the station after dark.** To **LA** (5-6hr., 2 per day, $20-25) and **San Francisco** (7hr., 3 per day, $48-68). Reserve in advance. Open daily 6:30am-9pm. Tickets sold until 8pm.

**Buses: Greyhound,** 34 W. Carrillo St. (☎965-7551), at Chapala St. To **LA** (2-3hr., 9 per day, $12) and **San Francisco** (9-10hr., 7 per day, $34). Open M-Sa 5:30am-8pm and 11pm-midnight, Su 7am-8pm and 11pm-midnight. **Santa Barbara Metropolitan Transit District (MTD),** 1020 Chapala St. (☎683-3702), at Cabrillo Blvd. behind the Greyhound station, is a transit and visitors center that provides bus schedules and serves as the transfer point for most routes. Open M-F 6am-7pm, Sa 8am-6pm, Su 9am-6pm. $1, seniors and disabled 50¢, under 5 free; transfers free. The MTD runs a purple electric **crosstown shuttle** from Franklin Center on Montecito St. to Mountain and Valerio, running through the transit center on Chapala St. Runs M-F 7am-6:30pm. $1. The **downtown-waterfront shuttle** along State St. and Cabrillo Blvd. runs every 10min. Su-Th 10:15am-6pm, F-Sa 10:15am-8pm. Stops designated by circular blue signs. 25¢.

**Taxis: Yellow Cab Company** (☎965-5111). Open 24hr.

**Car Rental: U-Save,** 510 Anacapa St. (☎963-3499). Cars start at $22 per day with 150 free mi., $134 per week with 1050 free mi.; each additional mi. 20¢. Must be 21+ with major credit card. Open M-F 8am-6pm, Sa 8am-2pm.

**Bike Rental: Beach Rentals,** 22 State St. (☎966-6733). Surreys, choppers, slingshots, regular mountain bikes, and beach cruisers ($10-28 for 2hr.), as well as boogie boards, scooters, and in-line skates ($5-15). Rentals include safety gear. Open daily 8am-8pm.

# ✳ 🛈 ORIENTATION & PRACTICAL INFORMATION

Santa Barbara is 92 mi. northwest of Los Angeles and 27 mi. from Ventura on **US 101** (Ventura Fwy.). Since the town is built along an east-west traverse of shoreline, its street grid is slightly skewed. The beach lies at the south end of the city, and **State Street,** the main drag, runs northwest from the waterfront. All streets are designated east and west from State St. The major east-west arteries are US 101 and **Cabrillo Boulevard;** US 101, normally north-south, runs east-west between Castillo St. and Hot Springs Rd.

**Visitor Information: Tourist Office,** 1 Garden St. (☎965-3021), at Cabrillo Blvd. across from the beach. Hordes of folks clamor for maps and brochures. First 15min. free parking in summer and on weekends, then $1.50 per hr. Open July-Aug. M-Sa 9am-6pm, Su 10am-6pm; Sept.-Nov. and Feb.-June M-Sa 9am-5pm, Su 10am-5pm; Dec.-Jan. M-Sa 9am-4pm, Su 10am-4pm. Outdoor 24hr. computer kiosk. **Hotspots,** 36 State St. (☎564-1637 or 800-793-7666), is an espresso bar with free tourist info, hotel reservation service, and an **ATM.** Cafe open 24hr.; tourist info M-Sa 9am-9pm, Su 9am-4pm.

**Bi-Gay-Lesbian Organization: The Pride Foundation's Gay and Lesbian Resource Center,** 126 E. Haley St. #A-11 (☎963-3636). Counseling for alcohol and drug abuse. AIDS hotline, testing, and social services. Open M-F 9am-5pm.

**Laundromat: Mac's Laundry,** 501 Anacapa St. (☎966-6716). Pink-and-purple wonder-wash features ever-entertaining Spanish TV. Wash $1.25, dry 25¢ per 15min. Open daily 6am-midnight. Last load 10:30pm.

**Police:** 215 E. Figueroa St. (☎897-2300).

**Hospital: St. Francis Medical Center,** 601 E. Micheltorena St. (☎962-7661), 6 blocks east of State St.

**Library and Internet Access: Santa Barbara Public Library,** 40 E. Anapamu St. (☎962-7653). Open M-Th 10am-9pm, F-Sa 10am-5:30pm, Su 1-5pm.

**Post Office:** 836 Anacapa St. (☎800-275-8777), 1 block east of State St. Open M-F 8am-6pm, Sa 9am-5pm. **Postal Code:** 93102.

# ⌐ ACCOMMODATIONS

A 10min. drive north or south on US 101 will reward you with cheaper lodging than that in Santa Barbara proper. Trusty **Motel 6 ❹** is always an option. In fact, Santa Barbara is where this glorious chain of budget-friendly motels originated. There are two locations: at the beach at 443 Corona del Mar Dr. (☎564-1392), and north of the main drag at 3505 State St. (☎687-5400). Prices are more expensive by the beach ($76-86, based on 2-person occupancy). The State St. location starts at $68-80 in the summer and $55 in the winter. All Santa Barbara accommodations are more expensive on the weekends (peaking in July and August and on holidays).

▧ **Hotel State Street,** 121 State St. (☎966-6586), on the main strip one block from the beach and next to the train station. Welcoming, comfortable, and meticulously clean, this European-style inn offers a good and relatively cheap night's sleep. Common bathrooms are pristine. Rooms have sinks and cable TV; a few have skylights. Reservations recommended. Rooms $50-70; $5-10 higher July-Aug. ❹

**Santa Barbara International Tourist Hostel,** 134 Chapala St. (☎963-0154; reservations sbres@bananabungalow.com). Great location near the train station, the beach, and bustling State St. Bike and surfboard rentals. Laundry. Internet $1 per 20min. Ask about 2- to 3-day camping trips to surrounding areas. Dorm rooms sleep 6-8 people; private rooms have 1 double bed. Dorms $18-20; private rooms $45-55. Under construction at press time; call ahead to ensure you're not sleeping in a pile of plaster. ❷

**Traveler's Motel,** 3222 State St. (☎687-6009). Take bus #6 or 11 from downtown. Although it's a bit far from the downtown spread, this motel is clean and spacious, and has pastel floral bedspreads to soften the atmosphere and sweeten your stay in the gosh-darn prettiest place on State St. Cable TV, A/C, direct-dial phones, microwaves, and fridges. Complimentary fruit and coffee 7:30am-10am. Singles June-Sept. Su-Th $55-70, F-Sa $129-149; Oct.-May Su-Th $40, F-Sa $69-99. Palatial rooms with full kitchenettes $10-$15 more; each additional person (up to 4) $5. ❺

**Cabrillo Inn,** 931 E. Cabrillo Blvd. (☎966-1641 or 800-648-6708). Directly across from East Beach, 1 mi. east of Stearns Wharf at State St. The best oceanfront value in town. 2 swimming pools and oceanview lounge where continental breakfast is served. 2-night min. stay on weekends. Rooms May-Sept. Su-Th from $109, F-Sa $139; Oct.-Apr. $89/$109. Rooms with full ocean view, add $30; suites, add $60. Vacation home rentals by the week and month are also available. ❺

# ⚑ CAMPING

State campsites can be reserved through ReserveAmerica (☎800-444-7275) up to seven months in advance. To reach Carpinteria Beach State Park ❶, 12 mi. south of Santa Barbara, follow signs from US 101 (entrance is at the end of Palm Ave.) or take bus #20 or #21 express to Carpinteria. It has 261 developed sites with hot showers. (☎684-2811. Sites $12; with hookup $18; day use $2.) There are two other state beaches within 30 mi. of Santa Barbara, but these are not served by buses. All three are scrunched between the railroad tracks and US 101. El Capitán ❶, north of Santa Barbara off US 101, has 142 well-kept sites, some with views of the Channel Islands. However, it usually fills up months in advance. (☎968-1033. Sites $16.) Refugio ❶ has 84 crowded, wheel-chair-accessible sites just steps from the beach. (☎968-1033. Sites $15.) Gaviota ❶, off Hwy. 101 at 10 Rugio Beach Rd., is first-come, first-served and offers 43 sites. Though it's in a parking lot environment, it's near the beach and has a marsh. (☎968-1033. Sites $12. Cash only.)

# 🍴 FOOD

Santa Barbara may well have more restaurants per capita than anywhere else in America, so finding a place to eat is not exactly a problem. State and Milpas St. are especially diner-friendly; State St. is hipper while Milpas St. is cheaper. Ice cream lovers flock to award-winning **McConnel's ❶**, 201 W. Mission St. (☎569-2323. Scoops $2.50. Open daily 10am-midnight.) There's an open-air **farmer's market** packed with bargains on the 500 and 600 blocks of State St. (Tu in summer 4-7:30pm; in winter 3pm-6:30pm), and another on Santa Barbara St. at Cota St. (Sa 8:30am-12:30pm). **Tri-County Produce,** 335 S. Milpas St., sells both fresh produce and prepared foods. (☎965-4558. Open M-Sa 9am-7:30pm, Su 9am-6pm.)

▨ **Palazzio,** 1026 State St. (☎564-1985). Their reproduction of the Sistine Chapel ceiling is nearly as impressive as the enormous pasta dishes ($17-18, $12-14 for half-portion), amazing garlic rolls, and the serve-yourself wine bar. Open Su-Th 11:30am-3pm and 5:30-11pm, F-Sa 11:30am-3pm and 5:30pm-midnight. ❸

**Pacific Crepes,** 705 Anacapa St. (☎882-1123). This comfortable, classy French cafe is not only filled with the delicious smells of crepe creations, but is *authentique*—owned and run by a French couple who speak French only. Luckily, non-Francophiles can rely on the English menu. The heavenly "Brittany" is topped with fresh strawberries and blueberries, fruit sauce, and ice cream—the perfect dessert ($6.25). Lunch and dinner special $15. Beer, wine, and champagne available. Open Su-Tu and Th-Sa 9am-9pm. ❷

**The Taj Cafe,** 905 State St. (☎564-8280). Enjoy traditional village-style Indian cooking with all natural ingredients. Taj has tasty items like tandoori chicken in a sweet, tangy mango sauce ($10). Lunch specials $5.50-7.50. Many vegetarian entrees ($6.50-8). Open M-Th 11:30am-3pm and 5-10pm, F-Sa 11:30am-3pm and 5-11pm. ❷

**The Natural Cafe and Juice Bar,** 508 State St. (☎962-9494). Casual dining with a sophisticated, health-bent appeal. A variety of fresh salads, sandwiches, and hot entrees ($5-8). Smoothies with supplements like protein powder or bee pollen will keep you charged all day (from $2.75). Open Su-Th 11am-9:30pm, F-Sa 11am-10pm. ❷

# 🔆 SIGHTS

Santa Barbara is best explored in three sections—the beach and coast, swingin' State St., and the Missionary Mountains. Essential to discovering local events and goings-on is the *Independent*, published every Thursday and available at city newsstands. The downtown-waterfront **shuttle** (25¢) runs from the beach up State St. The **Visitors Center,** 1 Garden St., at Cabrillo Blvd., has a map and peppy, pamphlet-bearing employees. Pick up *Santa Barbara's Red Tile Tour,* a walking tour guide (free at the Visitors Center; 25¢ inside the courthouse).

## COASTAL SANTA BARBARA

Recently revamped, Santa Barbara's supreme coastal drive is along Cabrillo Blvd., the first leg of the city's "Scenic Drive." Follow the green signs as they lead you on a loop into the mountains and around the city, winding through the hillside bordering the town along Alameda Padre Serra. This part of town is known as the American Riviera for its elegance and high concentration of wealthy residents.

**SANTA BARBARA ZOO.** The delightfully leafy habitat has such an open feel that the animals seem kept in captivity only by sheer lethargy. A mini-train provides a park tour. There's also a miniaturized African plain where giraffes stroll lazily, silhouetted against the Pacific. *(500 Niños Dr., off Cabrillo Blvd. from US 101. Take bus #14 or the downtown-waterfront shuttle. ☎962-5339. Open daily 10am-5pm. $8, seniors and ages 2-12 $6, under 2 free. Train $1.50, children $1. Parking $2.)*

**SEA CENTER.** Stearns Wharf, at the foot of State St., is the oldest working pier on the West Coast, housing the newly renovated Sea Center and some restaurants and shops. The center is now a working lab with hands-on exhibits for visitors. *(At State St. and Cabrillo Blvd. ☎962-0885. Sea Center open daily 10am-5pm. Touch tank open daily noon-5pm. $4, seniors and ages 13-17 $3, ages 3-12 $2. First 1½hr. parking free on wharf.)*

**BEACHES & ACTIVITIES.** Santa Barbara's beaches are breathtaking, lined on one side by flourishing palm trees and on the other by countless sailboats around the local harbor. **East** and **Leadbetter beaches** flank the wharf on either side. **Skater's Point Park,** along the waterfront on Cabrillo Blvd., south of Stearns Wharf, is a free park for skateboarders. Helmets and gear are required. **Beach Rentals** will rent beachgoers a **retro surrey:** a covered, Flintstone-esque bicycle. You and up to eight friends can cruise the beach paths in this stylish buggy. *(22 State St. ☎966-6733. Open daily 8am-8pm. Surreys $15-28 per 2hr., depending on number of riders. Also see **Practical Information,** p. 359.)* **Beach House,** 10 State St., rents surfboards and body boards plus all the necessary equipment. *(☎963-1281. Surfboards $7-35; body boards $4-16; wet suits $3-16. Credit card required.)* **Paddle Sports,** 100 State St., offers kayak rentals and lessons. *(☎899-4925. Open in summer daily 7am-6pm; in winter Su and Sa 10am-5pm, Tu-F noon-6pm. Rentals $20-40 per 2hr., $40-60 per day.)* Across the street from the Visitors Center is idyllic **Chase Palm Park,** a beautiful public parkland complete with a vintage 1916 Spillman carousel. *(Carousel operates 10am-6pm. $2.)*

**BEST SUNSET.** For the best sunset view around, have a drink (soda $3.75-4.50, beer and wine $5.50-12) at the bar at the Four Seasons Biltmore Hotel. Appetizers run $9-100 (Beluga caviar costs $100). This five-star lodging is off-limits to most traveler's budgets, but the view of the Pacific is priceless. Free evening live music is also often featured. *(Take Hwy. 101 S to Channel Dr. Exit. 1260 Channel Dr., Montecito. ☎969-2261. Park across the street; valet parking runs to $50 including tip.)*

## STATE STREET

State St., Santa Barbara's monument to city planning, runs a straight, tree-lined two miles through the center of the city. Among the countless shops and restaurants are some cultural and historical landmarks that should not be missed. Everything that doesn't move—malls, mailboxes, telephones, the restrooms at the public library—has been slathered in Spanish tile.

**SANTA BARBARA COUNTY COURTHOUSE.** To take in the city's architectural homogeneity and a killer view of the ocean, go up the elevator in the courthouse to the observation deck. Compared to the more prosaic Mission Revival buildings found elsewhere in California, the courthouse is a work of genius with its sculpted fountain, sunken gardens, historic murals, wrought-iron chandeliers, and hand-painted vaulted Gothic ceilings. *(1100 Anacapa St. ☎ 962-6464. Open daily 10am-5pm; tower closes 4:45pm. Tours M-Tu and F 10:30am and 2-m, W-Th and -Sa 2pm. Free.)*

**SANTA BARBARA MUSEUM OF ART.** An impressive collection of classical Greek, Asian, and European works spans 3000 years. The 20th-century and Hindu collections are especially worthwhile. Over 90% of the permanent collection consists of gifts from Santa Barbara's wealthy residents. *(1130 State St. ☎ 963-4364. Open Su noon-5pm, Tu-Th and Sa 11am-5pm, F 11am-9pm. Tours Su and Tu-Sa noon and 2pm. $7, seniors $5, students ages 6-17 $4, under 6 free. Free Th and 1st Su of each month.)*

**ARLINGTON CENTER FOR PERFORMING ARTS.** This combination live performance space and movie theater comfortably seats 2018 people. The murals over the entrance of the Spanish-Moorish building depict scenes from California's Hispano-Mexican era. Its tower is one of the few structures in this low stucco town that rival the palm trees in height. The actual theater space resembles a Mexican village. Call the box office for info on upcoming events. *(1317 State St. ☎ 963-4408. Movie tickets $8, seniors and ages 2-12 $5; 1pm matinee and twilight show before 6pm $5.)*

**OTHER SIGHTS.** At the corner of Montecito Ave. and Chapala St. stands the notable **Moreton Bay Fig Tree.** Brought from Australia by a sailor in 1877, the tree's gnarled branches now span 160 ft.; it can provide shade for more than 1000 people at once. If you'd rather drink than stand in the shade with 999 other people, sample award-winning wine at the **Santa Barbara Winery.** *(202 Anacapa St. ☎ 963-3646. Open daily 10am-5pm. Tours daily 11:30am and 3:30pm. Tastings $4 for 6 wines.)*

## MOUNTAINS AROUND SANTA BARBARA

Up in the northern part of town, things get considerably more pastoral. In addition to awe-inspiring, rugged mountain terrain, multi-million dollar homes populate the land, adding well-manicured lawns and shrubbery to the landscape.

**MISSION SANTA BARBARA.** Praised as the "Queen of Missions" when built in 1786, the mission was restored after the 1812 earthquake and assumed its present incarnation in 1820. Towers containing splayed Moorish windows stand around a Greco-Roman temple and facade and a Moorish fountain bubbles outside. The museum contains items from the mission archives. The main chapel is colorful and solemn; visitors are welcome to (respectfully) attend mass. Today the Mission is not only a museum and parish, but also an infirmary and Franciscan friary. For more on missions, see **Suggested Itineraries: Mission Accomplished,** p. 7. *(At the end of Las Olivas St. Take bus #22. ☎ 682-4149. Open daily 9am-5pm. Self-guided museum tour starts at the gift shop. $4, under 12 free. Mass M-F 7:30am, Sa 4pm, Su 7:30, 9, 10:30am, noon.)*

**SANTA BARBARA MUSEUM OF NATURAL HISTORY.** Unlike the typical indoor museum, the only way to get from one exhibit to the next in this museum is by going outside. The founder's wishes to establish a museum of comparative oology (no, not zoology) were overturned by a Board of Trustees who thought that devoting the space to the study of eggs was silly. So they hatched the current exhibitions, which include the largest collection of Chumash artifacts in the West, a

CENTRAL COAST

natural history gallery, and a planetarium. *(2559 Puesta del Sol Rd. Follow signs to parking lot or take bus #22. Museum: ☎682-4711, astronomy hotline ext. 405. Open daily 10am-5pm. $6, seniors and ages 13-17 $6, under 12 $4, under 2 free. Planetarium shows in summer daily 1, 2, 3pm; in winter W 3pm, Sa-Su 1, 2, 3pm. $2 extra over admission.)*

**SANTA BARBARA BOTANICAL GARDEN.** Far from town but close to Mission Santa Barbara and the Museum of Natural History, the botanical garden offers an amazing array of non-native vegetation along easy, meandering paths. Five miles of hiking trails wind through 65 acres of native Californian trees, **wildflowers,** and cacti. The garden's water system was built by the Chumash and is now one of the last vestiges of the region's native heritage. *(1212 Mission Canyon Rd. ☎682-4726. Open Mar.-Oct. M-F 9am-5pm, Sa-Su 9am-6pm; Nov.-Feb. M-F 9am-4pm, Sa-Su 9am-5pm. Tours M-Th 10:30am and 2pm, Sa 2pm, Su 10:30am; special demonstrations Su and F at 2pm, Sa at 10:30am. $5; students, seniors, and ages 13-19 $3; ages 5-12 $1; under 5 free.)*

**HIKING.** Very popular **Inspiration Point** is a 3½ mi. round-trip hike and climbs 800 ft. Half of the hike is an easy walk on a paved road. The other half is a series of mountainside switchbacks. The reward on a clear day is an extensive view of the city, the ocean, and the Channel Islands. Following the creek upstream will lead to **Seven Falls.** *(From Santa Barbara Mission, drive toward the mountains and turn right onto Foothill Rd. Turn left onto Mission Canyon Rd. and continue 1 mi. Bear left onto Tunnel Rd. and drive 1¼ mi. to its end.)* **Rattlesnake Canyon Trail** is a moderate 3½ mi. round-trip hike to Tunnel Trail junction with a 1000 ft. gain. It passes many waterfalls, pools, and secluded spots, but is a highly popular trail—expect company. *(From Santa Barbara Mission, drive toward the mountains and turn right onto Foothill Rd. Turn left onto Mission Canyon Rd. and continue for a half-mile. Make a sharp right onto Las Conas Rd. and travel 1¼ mi. Look for a large sign on the left side of the road.)* The trek from the **Cold Springs Trail** to **Montecito Peak** (7¼ mi. round-trip, 2462 ft. elevation gain) or to **Camino Cielo** (9 mi. round-trip, 2675 ft. elevation gain) are considerably more strenuous but offer great views. *(From US 101 S, take Hot Springs Rd. Exit and turn left. Travel 2½ mi. to Mountain Dr. Turn left, drive 1¼ mi., and stop by the creek crossing.)* For a more extensive listing of trails, try the Botanical Garden gift shop or the Visitors Center in town. Another option is to join the local **Sierra Club** on their group hikes. *(For more information, call ☎564-7892. Social hike at Santa Barbara Mission 6:15pm. Strenuous hike at Hope Ave. by the Bank of America Sa-Su 9am. Led by expert hikers. Free.)*

**UNIVERSITY OF CALIFORNIA AT SANTA BARBARA (UCSB).** This beautiful outpost of the UC system is stuck in Goleta, a shapeless mass of suburbs, gas stations, and coffee shops, but the beachside dorms and gorgeous student body more than make up for the town. The excellent **art museum** is worth visiting. It houses the Sedgwick Collection of 15th- to 17th-century European paintings. *(Museum off US 101. Take bus #11. ☎893-2951. Open Su 1-5pm, Tu-Sa 10am-4pm. Free.)*

**OTHER NEARBY SIGHTS.** The beach at **Summerland** is east of Montecito and accessible by bus #20. Its biggest food attraction is **The Big Yellow House,** a Victorian-estate-turned-restaurant. It is reported to be inhabited by two ghosts: Hector haunts the wine cellars, while his mistress dwells in the women's bathroom upstairs. Ask to eat in the bedroom with the secret door. *(108 Pierpoint Ave. ☎969-4140. Open Su-Th 8am-9pm, F-Sa 8am-10pm.)* **Rincon Beach,** 3 mi. southeast of Carpinteria, has some of the county's best surfing. **Gaviota State Beach,** 29 mi. northwest of Santa Barbara, also has good surf. You can **whale-watch** from late November to early April, when the Pacific gray whales migrate.

## 🔘 SEASONAL EVENTS

One of the most special events in Santa Barbara is not organized by human hand. Starting in October, and assembling most densely from November to February, hordes of **monarch butterflies** cling to the eucalyptus trees in Ellwood Grove, just west of UCSB, and at the end of Coronado St., off Hollister Ave.; take the Glen Annie/Storke Rd. Exit off US 101. Other events include:

**Hang Gliding Festival** (☎965-3733; www.flyaboveall.com), Mesa Flight Park, early Jan.

**Santa Barbara International Film Festival** (☎963-0023; www.sbfilmfestival.com), late Feb. to early Mar. Sponsored by the Arlington Center, among others (see p. 363). Premieres US indies and foreign films and boasts celebrity patronage. Passes can be purchased online or by phone.

**Gay Pride Parade** (☎884-2974), on a Sa in mid-July. The 1-day festival held on Leadbetter Beach celebrates the local gay community.

**I Madonnari Italian Street Painting Festival** (☎569-3873), Memorial Day weekend. Professional and amateur chalk paintings decorate the Old Mission Courtyard. An Italian tradition since the 16th century.

**Summer Solstice Parade and Fair** (☎965-3396), on June 21, 2004. Pre-Bacchanalian, colorful fun precedes down State St. at noon. No words (on posters), no vehicles, no religious faith symbols, and no animals allowed.

**Old Spanish Days Fiesta** (☎962-8101), early Aug. Spirited fiesta, celebrated for the last 75 years, with rodeos, carnivals, parades, dancing, live flamenco guitar everywhere, and plenty of margaritas and sangria.

**Music Academy of the West,** 1070 Fairway Rd. (☎897-0300; www.musicacademy.org), holds a series of inexpensive concerts throughout the summer. Stop by for a brochure.

**Santa Barbara International Jazz Festival** (☎966-3000), early Sept. Big names in jazz.

## 🔲 SHOPPING

**State Street** is a shopping mecca with two miles of mildly trendy shops and the upscale **Paseo Nuevo Mall,** between Cañon Perdido St. and Ortega St. Local craftspeople line Cabrillo Blvd. for the **Arts and Crafts Show,** where they sell their handcrafted wares every fair-weathered Sunday from 10am to dusk.

**Scavenge,** 418 State St. (☎564-2000). Half clothing store, half garage sale, this bargain shopper's dream carries everything from framed Monet prints to screwdriver sets. Find that perfect Chinese lantern or a new pink tutu. Also sells retail clothing and shoes. Prices range $1-100. Open Su-Th 11am-10pm, F 11am-midnight, Sa 10am-midnight.

**2000 Degrees,** 1206 State St. (☎882-1817). Feeling left out of the California art scene? Experience the Santa Barbara ceramics circuit at this paint-your-own studio. Pay a $7 workshop fee and paint as many pieces of bisqueware as you can buy. Prices range from $2-60; a decent send-home-to-Mom mug is $6.50 (they'll even ship it home for you). Open M-F 11am-8pm, Sa 10am-9pm, Su noon-6pm.

## 🎵🎭 ENTERTAINMENT & NIGHTLIFE

Every night of the week, the clubs on **State Street,** mostly between Haley St. and Canon Perdido St., are packed. This town is full of those who love to eat, drink, and be drunk. Consult the *Independent* to see who's playing on any given night. Bars on State St. charge $4 for beer fairly uniformly; search for specials.

CENTRAL COAST

**The Hourglass,** 213 W. Cota Street (☎963-1436). Soak in an intimate indoor bath or watch the stars from a private outdoor tub; there are 9 spas total that you can choose from. No alcohol allowed. Towels $1. Two people $25 per hr.; each additional person $7. $2 student discount; children free with parent. Open Su and Th-Sa 5pm-midnight.

**Q's Sushi A-Go-Go,** 409 State St. (☎966-9177). A tri-level bar, 8 pool tables, and dancing. Chew on some sushi ($3.50-13.50) and accompany with *sake* for $3.50. Happy Hour M-Sa 4-7pm includes 20% off sushi plates and half-priced drinks and appetizers. M Brazilian night. W karaoke. Cover F-Sa after 9pm $5. Open daily 4pm-2am.

**Club 634,** 634 State St. (☎564-1069). Cocktails, dancing, and 2 large patios. Live bands and DJs. Su and W karaoke, Th Red Bull and vodkas $3, F 5-8pm select beers $1.50. Occasional cover. Open M-F 2pm-2am, Sa-Su noon-2am.

**O'Mally's,** 525 State St. (☎564-8904). An Irish pub and sports bar. DJs and dancing. Cover charged only 5 times a year during major local events. Open daily 1pm-1:30am.

# NEAR SANTA BARBARA     ☎805

## LOS PADRES NATIONAL FOREST

Once the land of the Chumash Indians and California condors, the vast **Los Padres National Forest** (district office ☎968-6640) stretches north of Santa Barbara into San Luis Obispo County and beyond. Los Padres is a leader in wildlife recovery programs, reintroducing many endangered plants and birds such as the bald eagle. The **San Rafael Wilderness** contains 125 mi. of trails and a sanctuary for the nearly extinct California condor. **Cachuma Lake,** 15 mi. from US 101 on Rte. 154, is a gorgeous, dark emerald-colored water source for the area, as well as a **campsite ❶** and recreational area (day use $5). Ask for trail information at the entrance. The nearby **Chumash painted cave** is 20min. north of Santa Barbara. Take US 101 to Rte. 154 to Painted Cave Rd. Go past the village and down into the oak glen. The cave is up on the right; parking is scarce. The impressive red ochre handiwork of native shamans dates to 1677. There are many outdoor opportunities in the area (see **Santa Barbara: Camping,** p. 361). The **Adventure Pass,** needed in all recreation areas in the forest, is available at the **Santa Barbara Ranger Office,** 3505 Paradise Rd. Take Rte. 154 for 10 mi. to Paradise Rd. and turn right; the office is 5 mi. ahead. (☎967-3481. Open M-Sa 8am-4:30pm. Pass $5 per day, $30 per year.)

## SANTA YNEZ VALLEY

To the northwest of Santa Barbara along Rte. 154 lies the lovely **Santa Ynez Valley,** home to thousands of acres of vineyards, hundreds of ostriches, and Michael Jackson's **Wonderland Ranch,** named after Lewis Carroll's fantasy world. The free *Santa Barbara County Wineries Touring Map,* available at the Santa Barbara Visitors Center, gives comprehensive listings. One of the prettiest vineyards is **Gainey Vineyard,** 3950 E. Rte. 246, at Rte. 154. (☎688-0558. Open daily 10am-5pm. Tours daily 11am, 1, 2, 3pm. Tastings fee of $5 includes 9 tastes and logo glass.)

At the intersection of Rte. 246 and US 101 is the town of **Buellton,** home of **Pea Soup Andersen's ❶,** where the split pea soup has been thick, hot, and fresh since 1924. (☎688-5581. Soup $3.50. All-you-can-eat soup plus a thick milkshake $7. Open daily 7am-10pm.) Four miles east on Rte. 246, thatched roofs cluster in **Solvang Village,** a supremely quaint Danish haven. Crammed with northern European gift shops, restaurants, and *conditoris* (bakeries), this overpriced, Disney-esque town is a tribute to its Danish ancestors and a peculiar tourist attraction. The **Solvang Bakery,** 460 Alisal Rd., claims to be "Solvang's favorite coffeehouse." (☎688-4939. Open daily 7am-6pm; in summer F-Sa until 8pm.) Next door is the graceful **Mission Santa Inés,** 1760 Mission Dr. Look for the footprint of a Chumash child in the Chapel of the Madonnas and pay respects to the graves of 1700 Chumash people. (☎688-4815. Open daily 9am-7pm; in winter 9am-5pm. $3, under 16 free.)

Farther to the northwest, at the juncture of Hwy. 1 and Rte. 246, is the city of **Lompoc,** home of the nation's largest producer of flower seed. The acres upon acres of blooms, which peak near the end of June, are both a visual and olfactory explosion. Lompoc holds a **flower festival** at the season's peak, usually the last weekend in June (info ☎735-8511). **La Purisma Mission State Park,** 2295 Purisma Rd., has the most fully restored of Father Serra's missions and 12 mi. of maintained trails. Follow Rte. 246; the entrance is off Mission Rd. (☎733-7781. Open daily 9am-5pm. Parking $5.)

# OJAI                                            ☎805

Lying only 80 miles north of LA, Ojai (OH-hi) is a pleasant retreat from the city. Its wooded valleys and mountain vistas have long been known to make mystics out of passersby. The town has capitalized on age-old traditions and made them New Age; Ojai is now home to chi-chi health spas, organic farms, and spiritual centers.

## ORIENTATION & PRACTICAL INFORMATION

The Ojai valley sits 15 mi. north of Ventura, just east of the Santa Ynez Mountains and south of Los Padres National Forest. To reach Ojai from LA, take US 101 N toward Santa Barbara, heading north off the Rte. 33 Exit. Fifteen miles of tree-lined roads lead to Ojai, where Rte. 33 becomes **Ojai Ave.,** the town's east-west spine. If you want to give your car a rest, the city of Ojai runs a **trolley** along Ojai Ave. (Runs M-F 6:58am-5:40pm, Sa-Su 8:58-5:04pm. 25¢.) The **Ojai Valley Chamber of Commerce,** 150 W. Ojai Ave., has maps and info on Ojai's art galleries, antique shops, campgrounds, and spa services. (☎626-8126; www.the-ojai.org. Open M-F 9:30am-4:30pm, Sa-Su 10am-5pm.)

**ACCOMMODATIONS.** Nestled in a beautiful valley, the **⛺Ojai Farm Hostel ❶** epitomizes the town's earthy aura—any fruit in the organic orchard is yours for the pickin'. The owner is extremely knowledgeable about the area and is often willing to help out with transportation. Free pick-up from the Ventura Greyhound bus station (with prior reservation) is offered, along with two TV rooms for movie watching (complete with video library), and free use of bikes. There are two lodges with a total of 12 beds; one is for couples and women, the other for men. (P.O. Box 723, Ojai 93024. ☎646-0311; www.hostelhandbook.com/farmhostel. Reservations are required; the hostel location will not be disclosed to anyone not staying at the hostel. $15 per person. Proof of international travel such as a recent plane ticket required.) The **Capri Motel ❸,** 1180 E. Ojai Ave., is situated in a perfect locale. Tall palms frame the pool and jacuzzi. (☎877-589-5860. Rooms with cable TV, A/C, fridge, microwave, and balconies. Standard rooms $80-110, with balcony $100-120. Weekly discounts available.) The **Rose Garden Inn ❺,** 615 W. Ojai Ave., has well-furnished and spacious rooms surrounding a heated pool, jacuzzi, sauna, and well-kept rose garden with hammocks. (☎646-1434 or 800-799-1881; www.rosegardeninnofojai.com. Singles $80-110; doubles $100-125. AAA discounts.) Budget travelers can also stay at pleasant camp sites shaded by oaks, which are plentiful in the surrounding areas (see **Santa Barbara: Camping,** p. 361).

**SIGHTS & HIKES.** Ojai was once the playpen of the Hollywood elite who came to romp in the spas and natural hot springs. But when Eastern philosophy luminary Jiddu Krishnamurti had a spiritual awakening under an Ojai tree (see **The Anti-Guru,** p. 368), the town added a glow of enlightenment to the sheen of glamour. Today, many visitors forego body wraps, masks, and scrubs ($55-200) at Ojai spas and come to free their minds for free. The **International Krotona Institute of Theosophy,** 46 Krotona Hill, operates a quiet library with classes on theosophy and comparative religion. (From downtown Ojai, drive west on Rte. 33 and turn right on Krotona Rd. ☎646-1139; www.theosophical.org/centers/krotona. Open Su 1-5pm, Tu-Sa 10am-5pm.) Other spiritual centers are the **Krishnamurti Library,** 1070 McAndrew Rd. (☎646-4948; open Su and W-Sa 1-5pm; head east on Rte. 33, turn left on Reeves Rd., and left on McAndrew Rd.) and the **Meditation Mount,** at the end of Reeves Rd. The Mount has a meditation room, a garden, and amazing views that soothe the soul (☎646-5508; open daily 10am-dusk; free).

**THE ANTI-GURU** **Jiddu Krishnamurti** may not have had Deepak Chopra's knack for self-promotion, nor was he ever able to whittle his spiritual teachings down to seven bite-sized laws, but there's no doubting Krishnamurti's influence in spreading Eastern philosophy worldwide. It all started on a beach in Madras (now Chennai), India, where the charismatic Englishwoman and theosophist **Annie Besant** (known for her friendship with Gandhi) picked out the 14-year-old Krishnamurti from the crowd and proclaimed him the coming World Teacher—the vehicle for the reincarnation of Christ in the West and Buddha in the East. Annie Besant adopted the boy and raised him in Britain in the tradition of the **theosophists,** who melded Eastern and Western religious thought into a belief both in the direct and often mystical experience of God and in the underlying unity of the universe. In 1922, when Krishnamurti came to the Ojai Valley, he had an awakening that eventually led him to repudiate his status as World Teacher—much to the dismay of his ardent throng of followers. He felt that man could not arrive at truth through any organized religion, nor through any guru or priest. This conviction became the core of his teaching: "The truth is a pathless land." Until his death in 1986, Krishnamurti traveled the world speaking to large audiences. His home and headquarters was in Ojai, but Krishnamurti established foundations in India, Europe, and elsewhere in the US. The Krishnamurti Foundation of America in Ojai continues to publish all of Krishnamurti's writings and talks.

For a scant $3, trace the history of the area, Chumash to New Age, at the **Ojai Valley Museum,** 130 W. Ojai Ave. (☎646-1390. Open Su and Sa 10am-4pm, W-F 1-4pm.) The **Ojai Center for the Arts,** 113 S. Montgomery St., has art, dance, poetry readings, workshops, and theater. (☎646-0117. Galleries open Su and Tu-Sa noon-4pm.) **Bart's Books,** on the corner of Canada and Matilija St., could only exist in Ojai. This open-air fortress of books has bookshelves outside the gates on the street where after-hour browsers can pay for their selections by dropping coins into a box. The books are cheap and plentiful, but the selection is better inside. (☎646-3755. Open Su and Tu-Sa 10am-5:30pm.)

A 10min. drive south of town on Rte. 33 leads to the **Old Creek Ranch Winery,** 10024 Old Creek Rd. Built in 1981 on the site of an 1880s historic winery—the oldest in Ventura County—this winery offers handmade premium wines. Buy a bottle and enjoy the quiet of the valley. (☎649-4132. Tastings Su and Sa 11am-5pm.)

Ojai is also the southernmost gateway to **Los Padres National Forest** (see p. 366). Get maps, camping info, and an Adventure Pass ($5 per day, $30 per year) at the **Los Padres Ojai Ranger Office,** 1190 E. Ojai Ave. Ask about trails to the **Punchbowls,** small water holes that sit like pools on the mountain near local waterfalls and large sandstone boulders called "moon rocks" for their bright nighttime gleam. (☎ 646-4348. Open M-F 8am-4:30pm.)

# LOS ANGELES

Greater LA (pop. 16.6 million; 4753 sq. mi.) is the epicenter of the "California Dream." This huge area covers LA, Orange, San Bernardino, Riverside, and Ventura counties, and stretches from Antelope Valley in the north to Catalina Island in the south, encompassing a desert basin center, two mountain ranges, and 76 mi. of dazzling coastline. Some see in its sweeping beaches and year-round sunshine a semi-paradise, a land of opportunity where the most opulent dreams can be realized. Others point to its congestion, smog, and crime, and declare LA a sham—a modern wasteland where media-numbed masses go to wither in the parching sun.

California's largest city has been plagued with crises: race riots, earthquakes, floods, wildfires, smoggy air the color of leather, drought, and homelessness. What could explain the Angeleno's loyalty to the sprawling metropolis in the face of so many difficulties? Perhaps it's the persistence of LA's mystique, the veneer of a city whose most celebrated industry is the production and dissemination of images. The glitter of the studios, the mammoth billboards on Sunset Strip, and the glamour of Rodeo Drive all attest to the reality of the LA illusion.

In a city where nothing seems to be more than 30 years old, the latest trends curry more respect than the venerable. Many come to this historical vacuum to make (or re-make) themselves. And what better place? Without the tiresome duty of bowing to the gods of an established high culture, Angelenos are free to indulge in a culture of their own—and the resulting atmosphere is delicious with potential. Some savor LA's image-bound culture, while others may be appalled by its narcissism and excess. Either way, it's one hell of a show.

## ✈ INTERCITY TRANSPORTATION

**BY PLANE. Los Angeles International Airport (LAX)** is in **Westchester,** about 15 mi. southwest of Downtown and 10 mi. south of Santa Monica. LAX can be a confusing airport, but there are electronic information kiosks everywhere in English, Chinese, French, German, Japanese, Korean, and Spanish. **LAX information** (☎310-646-5252) will help Spanish and English speakers. **Airport police** (☎310-646-7911) are there 24hr. a day. **Traveler's Aid,** a service for airport info, transportation and accommodation suggestions, and major transit emergencies, is in all terminals. (☎310-646-2270. Open M-F 8:30am-noon and 1-5pm.) There is also a **First Aid Station.** (☎310-215-6000. Open daily 7am-11pm.) Currency exchange is available at **International Currency Exchange (ICE) Currency Services** in all terminals. Local American Express offices, however, generally offer more attractive exchange rates (see **Currency Exchange,** p. 382).

Besides renting a car, there are several other **transit** options from the airport. Check with your place of lodging before hopping into any of the vehicles below; many accommodations offer deals on transportation from the airport.

**Metro Rail Subway:** The **Metropolitan Transit Authority (MTA)** oversees subway and bus transportation, including the local DASH buses. Call ☎800-COMMUTE/266-6883 or visit www.mta.net. Take the **Green Line Metro Rail shuttle,** which leaves every 10-15min. from any terminal to the Green Line Metro Rail Aviation station. (Open daily 4:30am-11:30pm.) From **Aviation** to: **Long Beach,** take the Green Line rail to the Rosa Parks station at Imperial and Wilmington, and switch to the Blue Line rail heading south to Long Beach; **Redondo Beach,** take the Green Line west to the end of the line; **Downtown,** go east to Rosa Parks, change to the Blue Line and head north until it meets the Red Line's 7th/Metro Center. From there, head northwest toward Hollywood.

## HIGHLIGHTS OF LOS ANGELES

**TINSELTOWN.** Hollywood (p. 405) was the cradle of the American film industry. Here, the Hollywood sign presides above historic theaters and bars frequented by stars and the anonymous beautiful hopefuls.

**BEACH LIFE.** An extensive beach culture thrives in **Santa Monica** (p. 407) and **Venice** (p. 376), where surfing, in-line skating, and beach volleyball mesh with wild cultural oddities in a non-stop circus sideshow.

**STUDIOS.** Television studios cluster in the smog-filled **San Fernando Valley** (p. 424), along with the world-famous **Universal Studios** theme park.

**MUSEUMS.** LA's museums are among the nation's finest, from the **Museum of Tolerance** (p. 411) to the **Getty** (p. 414) to the **Norton Simon Museum of Art** (p. 425) to the **Los Angeles County Museum of Art** (p. 415). In Santa Monica, the **Bergamot Station Art Center** (p. 408) is a conglomeration of galleries that include the Santa Monica Museum of Art and the Gallery of Functional Art.

**PAR-TAY.** **West Hollywood** (p. 417) is the heart of LA's thriving gay community and home to the **Sunset Strip,** center of the hippest **nightlife** (p. 439).

**THE CITYSCAPE.** The greatest view of the Hollywood sign and the city sprawl can be had by driving–or walking, God forbid–to the top of **Griffith Park** (p. 421), which is also home to a **planetarium** and the **LA Zoo.**

**TASTE.** Arguably tasteful **shopping** (p. 431) and **dining** (p. 393) culture flourishes along Melrose Ave. in West Hollywood and along the Third Street Promenade in Santa Monica. If you'd rather eat than taste, jump into LA's rockin' **diner** scene. Among the best are Duke's Coffee Shop (p. 395) and Canter's (p. 439).

**DOWNTOWN EXISTS!** Downtown (p. 417) is home to LA's *El Pueblo* historic center, the bustling **Grand Central Public Market** (p. 393), the **Museum of Contemporary Art** (p. 419), and many gleaming monoliths.

**MTA Buses:** Orange signs highlight the traffic island where airport shuttle "C" transports bus-bound passengers to the transfer terminal at Vicksburg Ave. and 96th St. To go to: **Westwood/UCLA,** take #561 (M-F 6am-midnight, Sa-Su 8am-midnight); **Downtown,** #42 (M-Sa 5am-7pm, Sa 5am-7pm, Su 7am-7pm; after hours, bus #40 picks up this route and runs all night) or the #439 express (every 40min.; M-F 5am-10pm, Sa-Su 6am-10pm); **Long Beach,** #232 (M-F 5:15am-11pm, Sa-Su 6am-11pm); **West Hollywood** and **Beverly Hills,** #220 (hourly; M-F 6:30am-7:30pm, Sa-Su 7:30am-7:30pm); **Hollywood,** from West Hollywood, #217 along Hollywood Blvd. (every 10-20min.; daily); #2 or #3 along Sunset Blvd. (every 10-30min.; M-F 5am-2am, Sa 6am-2am, Su 6:30am-2am), or #4 along Santa Monica Blvd. (every 15-20min.; daily).

**Taxis:** Follow yellow signs. Cabs are costly. Fare from airport to Hollywood $40; to Santa Monica $25. (For more info, see p. 379.)

**BY TRAIN. Amtrak** rolls into **Union Station,** 800 N. Alameda St. (☎213-683-6729 or 800-USA-RAIL/872-7245), at the northeastern edge of Downtown. When it opened in 1939, Union Station brought together the Santa Fe, Union Pacific, and Southern Pacific railroads. It was later featured many films, including *Bugsy* and *The Way We Were.* From the station, take MTA bus #33 (1½hr., every 15min., $1.35) or Santa Monica Big Blue Bus #10 (every 30min., $1.75) to **Santa Monica.**

**BY BUS.** If coming by **Greyhound** bus (☎800-231-2222 or 213-629-8401), consider bypassing its Downtown station, 1716 E. 7th St. at Alameda St. (☎213-629-8536), which is in an extremely rough neighborhood. If you must get off in Downtown, be very careful near 7th and Alameda St., one block southwest of the station, where

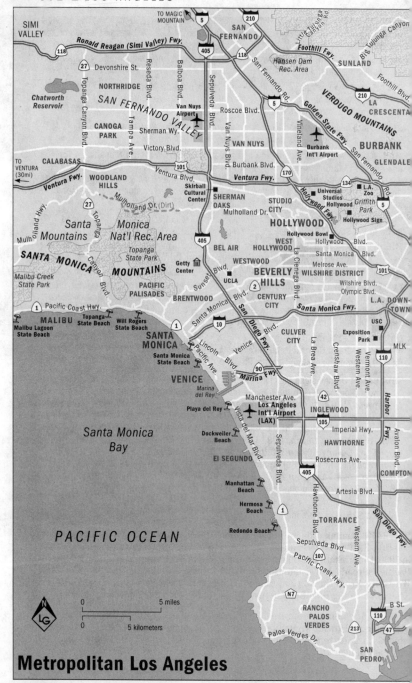

# Metropolitan Los Angeles

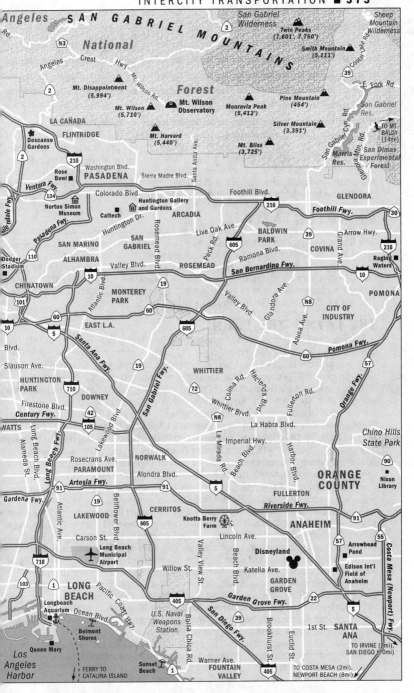

you can catch MTA bus #60 traveling north to the Gateway Transit Plaza at Union Station. The new terminal in Hollywood, 1715 N. Cahuenga Blvd. (☎323-466-1249), is at a great location close to many hotels, restaurants, and sights. There are several other Greyhound terminals in LA; the prices below are for Union Station.

> **Greyhound Routes: Santa Barbara** (7 per day; $12, round-trip $21); **San Diego** (every hr.; $15, round-trip $25); **San Francisco** (17 per day; $42, round-trip $82); **Las Vegas** (17 per day; $38, round-trip $71); **Tijuana** (4hr.; $17, round-trip $27). Route maps $3.

**BY CAR.** Despite LA's reputation for existing in a permanent celluloid vacation from reality, three major freeways connect California's vainest city to the rest of the state. **I-5** (Golden State Freeway), which travels the length of California, bisects LA on a north-south axis; it heads north to Sacramento and south to San Diego. **US 101** links LA to other coastal cities, heading west out of LA before turning north towards San Francisco and paralleling I-5. **I-10** comes in from the east, providing access from Las Vegas and Arizona.

# ⚡ ORIENTATION

The **City of Angels,** 420 mi. south of San Francisco and 130 mi. north of San Diego, spreads its wings across the flatland basin between the coast of Southern California (SoCal) and the inland San Gabriel Mountains. You can still consider yourself "in" LA even if you're 50 mi. from Downtown; in fact, the metropolis encompasses a vast conglomeration of over 80 cities and 'burbs, including those in Orange, Riverside, San Bernardino, and Ventura Counties.

## THE LAY OF THE L.A.ND

A busy web of crisscrossing interstate and state highways ensnares nearly ten million vehicles in the LA basin on a daily basis. Unless you are "in the know" with inside knowledge of local surface streets in the city, plan to spend intimate, quality time with your car while driving (and braking) in LA. The dozen major freeways, along with their offshoots and extensions, can seriously confuse even the savviest map-readers. Stick to the main six freeways, however, and it's smooth sailing (in bumper to bumper traffic, of course). **I-5 (Santa Ana Freeway, Golden State Freeway, and San Diego Freeway), I-405 (San Diego Freeway), I-110 (Harbor Freeway), US 101 (Hollywood Freeway),** and **Pacific Coast Highway (PCH or Highway 1)** all run north-south. **I-10 (Santa Monica Freeway)** is the most popular freeway for east-west drivers. I-5 intersects I-10 just east of Downtown and serves as one of the two major north-south thruways. I-405, which goes from Orange County in the South all the way through LA, parallels I-5 on a route closer to the coast, and separates Santa Monica and Malibu from the LA Westside.

A legitimate **Downtown** Los Angeles exists, but it won't help orient you to the rest of the city. Numbered streets (1st, 2nd, etc.) run east-west Downtown, forming a labyrinth of one-way roads. The heart of Downtown, full of towering skyscrapers, is relatively safe on weekdays, but **avoid walking there after dark and on weekends.**

The predominantly Latino section of the city is found east of Downtown in **Boyle Heights, East LA,** and **Montebello. Monterey Park** is one of the few cities in the US with a predominantly Asian-American population. Not surprisingly, Asian restaurants and stores line Atlantic Blvd. and Garfield Ave., the two main drags.

The **University of Southern California (USC), Exposition Park,** and the mostly African-American districts of **Inglewood, Watts, Huntington Park,** and **Compton** stretch south of Downtown. **South Central,** the name of this area, suffered the brunt of the 1992 riots. South Central is notorious for rampant crime and attracts few tourists. If you're hell-bent on visiting, go during daylight and take valuables out of the car.

**Hollywood** lies northwest of Downtown. Its main east-west drags (from north to south) are Hollywood Blvd., Sunset Blvd., Santa Monica Blvd., Melrose Ave., and Beverly Blvd. **Melrose Avenue** links a chain of self-consciously trendy cafes and boutiques. **Sunset Boulevard,** which runs from the ocean to Downtown, presents a cross-section of virtually everything LA has to offer: beach communities, lavish displays of wealth, famous nightclubs, and sleazy motels. The **Sunset Strip,** hot seat of LA's best nightlife, is the West Hollywood section of Sunset Blvd. closest to Beverly Hills. **Hollywood Boulevard,** home of the Walk of Fame and many tourist sights, runs just beneath the celebrity-ridden **Hollywood Hills.**

The region known as **Westside** encompasses prestigious **West Hollywood, Westwood** and **Westwood Village, Century City, Culver City, Bel Air, Brentwood,** and **Beverly Hills.** A good portion of the city's gay community resides in West Hollywood, while Beverly Hills is home to many celebrities and some of the highest tax brackets in the state. Aside from the fancy plastic surgeons and residential estates, Westside's attractions include the **University of California at Los Angeles (UCLA)** in Westwood and fashionable Melrose Ave. hangouts in West Hollywood. The name **West LA** is a municipal distinction that refers to Westwood and the no-man's land inland of **Santa Monica** that includes Century City (the corporate and shopping district on what used to be the 20th Century Fox backlot). The area west of Downtown and south of West Hollywood is known as the **Wilshire District,** named after its main boulevard. **Hancock Park,** an affluent residential area, covers the northeast portion of the district and intersects with Fairfax, a large Jewish community.

The **San Fernando Valley** sprawls north of the Hollywood Hills and the Santa Monica Mountains. For most people, the **San Fernando Valley** is, *like*, the Valley, where almost two million people wander among malls, cookie-cutter pools, and TV studios. The Valley is also home to **Burbank** and **Studio City,** which include the lion's share of today's movie studios. The basin is bounded to the north and west by the Santa Susana Mountains and Rte. 118 (Ronald Reagan Fwy.), to the south by Rte. 134 (Ventura Blvd.), and to the east by I-5 (Golden State Fwy.). The **San Bernardino Valley,** also home to about two million, stretches eastward from LA south of the San Gabriel Mountains. This valley is largely industrialized and heavily plagued by the county's notorious smog. In between these two valleys lie the affluent foothills of **Pasadena** and its famed Rose Parade.

Eighty miles of beaches line LA's **coastal region. Zuma,** the inspiration for the 1975 Neil Young album of the same name, is northernmost, followed by **Malibu,** which lies 15 mi. up the coast from **Santa Monica.** Farther south is the distended beach-side freak show known as **Venice.** The beach towns south of Venice include **Manhattan, Hermosa,** and **Redondo Beaches** (see p. 427). South across the Palos Verdes Peninsula is **Long Beach** (see p. 446), a port city of half a million people with a large gay population. Farthest south are the **Orange County** (see p. 456) beach cities: Seal Beach, Sunset Beach, Huntington Beach, Newport Beach, and Laguna Beach.

# LA COMMUNITIES

**HOLLYWOOD.** Nowhere is the myth/reality divide more dramatic in Los Angeles than in the sharp contrast between the movieland glamour associated with Hollywood and the unromantic squalor of its existence. In truth, Hollywood has long since ceased to be the home of the American movie industry. All the major studios (except Paramount, see p. 435) moved over the Hollywood Hills in the 1930s to the roomier locale and lower taxes of the San Fernando Valley. What remains are a few fragments of the silver screen industry: the Academy Awards, the star-studded Walk of Fame, a handful of historic theaters that host a few premieres, and an aura of decayed nostalgia that brings in visitors by the busload despite the relatively high proportion of pimps, panhandlers, and porn shops. For a brief history of Hollywood, see **The Boob Tube and the Silver Screen**, p. 18.

**SANTA MONICA.** The most striking characteristic of Santa Monica (pop. 87,000) is its efficiency. It is safe, clean, and unpretentious—and you can usually find a parking spot. Santa Monica is also easily navigable on foot or by bus. Its residential areas, once heavily populated by screen superstars, are just blocks away from its main districts. The **Third Street Promenade** is the city's most popular spot to shop by day and schmooze by night, and the nearby beaches are always packed. Many find that a drive down Ocean Ave. leaves them with the eerie feeling of being on a set. In fact, Santa Monica issues almost 1000 permits yearly to production companies who want to capture the Gold Coast on film. *(From Downtown LA, it takes about 30min. without traffic to reach Santa Monica on MTA #33 or 333 or on I-10 (Santa Monica Fwy.). Santa Monica's efficient **Big Blue Bus (BBBus)** system connects to other LA bus routes.)*

**VENICE.** Venice is a carnivalesque beach town where guitar-toting, wild-eyed, tie-dyed residents sculpt masterpieces in sand or compose them in graffiti, all before heading to the beach. Grab a corn dog and head to Ocean Front Walk; a stroll through in-line skating, bikini-flaunting, tattooed Venice is truly memorable. *(From Downtown, take MTA #33 or 333, during rush hr. #436. From Santa Monica, take Santa Monica BBBus #1 or 2. Avoid meters by parking in the $5-per-day lot at Pacific Ave. and Venice Blvd.)*

**MARINA DEL REY.** Venice's neighbor to the immediate south is older, more expensive, and considerably more sedate. While Marina del Rey does have a swimming beach, it spurns sunbathing in favor of boating. Once a duck-hunting ground, the area was used as an oil field in the late 1930s and was reincarnated in 1965 as a yacht harbor. Marina del Rey is now the largest manmade marina in the world, with 6000 pleasure boats and 3000 boats in dry storage.

**MALIBU.** Malibu makes its southern neighbor Santa Monica look like a carnival: Malibu is *the beach*. It has no amusement parks and no boardwalk—just sand, mountains, and surf. Although Tom Cruise, Bob Dylan, Martin Sheen, Diana Ross, Sting, and Cher are just a few of Malibu's better-known residents, it is not a see-and-be-seen type of town. The quiet shores and the 27 mi. of beautiful beaches that run along the 20,000 and 30,000 blocks of the **Pacific Coast Highway** (**PCH**; Hwy. 1 north from Santa Monica) will soothe the sunburnt soul.

**BEVERLY HILLS.** The very name Beverly Hills evokes images of palm-lined boulevards, tanned and taut skin, and million-dollar homes with pools shaped like vital organs. Beverly Hills glows in the televised mystique of expensive hotels, ritzy boutiques, and movie stars galore. These perceptions are not far from the truth. Although many silver screen starlets no longer call 90210 their postal code, Beverly Hills is still a spectacle of opulence and class. You can live it up on a budget here simply by being as showy as the town. Throw on your Sunday best, slip on the shades, and make clerks work for the money they think you have.

**WESTWOOD & UCLA.** Wedged between the exclusive neighborhoods of Brentwood and Beverly Hills, Westwood is a mecca for young and fun-loving travelers, mostly because it is home to the University of California at Los Angeles (UCLA) and its many thousands of students. Westwood Village (on, around, and between Gayley, Westwood, and Kinross Ave.) hosts myriad movie theaters, boutiques, outdoor cafes, and coffeehouses. Most cater to college kids, though some are rather upscale. Overall, Westwood is very clean, safe, and hip.

**BEL AIR, BRENTWOOD, & PACIFIC PALISADES.** Home to many celebrities, these three residential communities don't offer much to the economizing traveler in terms of accommodations or food, but the **Getty Museum** and a scenic drive along **Sunset Boulevard** are two free ways to experience the best the area has to offer. Veer off Sunset Blvd. onto any public (non-gated) road to see tree-lined rows of well-spaced six-bedroom homes—living here is as costly as in Beverly Hills.

**WILSHIRE DISTRICT.** LA's culture vultures drive south from Hollywood to peruse the Wilshire District's museums, which glorify everything from tar to Model Ts. **Museum Row** is on the Miracle Mile (Wilshire Blvd. from Fairfax to La Brea Ave.). Developed in the 1920s, the city's first shopping district was designed for those arriving in those new-fangled gizmos called automobiles.

**WEST HOLLYWOOD.** Once considered a no-man's land between Beverly Hills and Hollywood, West Hollywood is now a city unto itself, as well as the proud abode of Los Angeles's gay community—the city was one of the country's first to be governed by openly gay officials. Though spanning only 2 sq. mi., the area is packed with more restaurants, galleries, boutiques, theaters, and clubs than most cities. The section of Santa Monica Blvd. around San Vicente Blvd. is its oldest gay district. It is home of the legendary 1½ mi. stretch of Sunset Blvd. known as the **Sunset Strip,** which lies between Doheny Dr. and Crescent Heights Ave. Following its heyday in the 1940s and 50s, the Strip was a den of LA's rock 'n' roll scene in the 60s and a haven for burnouts in the 70s. Today it is the epitome of diversity, as the opulent from the Westside mix with the quaint from the east, creating the ultimate LA nightlife (see **Nightlife,** p. 439). To experience it all, park along the street or in a pay lot and walk or take the **CityLine,** which runs at night along Santa Monica Blvd. (☎800-447-2189. Su-F 25¢, Sa 50¢.)

**DOWNTOWN.** Say "downtown" to Angelenos and they'll wince—either because they don't know what you're referring to, they know but don't go there, or they work there and are none too happy about it. It is LA's netherland—the place over there. Mayor James Hahn and City Hall strive valiantly to project Downtown as a paradigm of LA's culture and diversity, but the Westside powers have a solid grip on the culture, and the neighborhoods in LA County are sharply defined by homogeneity of race and class. Downtown, an uneasy truce prevails between the bustling financiers and the street population, but visitors should be cautious—the area is especially unsafe after business hours and on weekends.

**GRIFFITH PARK & GLENDALE.** Five times larger than New York's Central Park, Griffith Park is an expansive 4107 acres and the site of many outdoor diversions ranging from golf and tennis to hiking. The LA Zoo, the Griffith Observatory and Planetarium, Travel Town, a bird sanctuary, and 52 mi. of trails brighten the dry hills. The park stretches from above North Hollywood to the intersection of Rte. 134 (Ventura Fwy.) and I-5 (Golden State Fwy.). Several of the mountain roads through the park (especially the Vista Del Valle Dr.) offer panoramic views of downtown LA, Hollywood, and the Westside. Sadly, heavy rains have made them unsafe for cars, but foot traffic is allowed on most (open daily 5am-10pm).

**SAN FERNANDO VALLEY.** All the San Fernando Valley wants is a little respect. Yet it can't seem to shake the infamy it gained for breeding the Valley Girl, who started a worldwide trend in the 1980s with her huge hair, and, like, ohmigod, totally far-out diction. The Valley has been disparaged by *Clueless* and *Beverly Hills 90210*, and is often overlooked in City Hall's affairs. It might not be the Westside, but it is more than just a satellite of LA; after all, most movies and television shows are produced here, not in Hollywood. With its cookie-cutter houses and strip malls, the Valley marks the suburban ritual elevated to its highest form.

**PASADENA.** Every New Year's Day in the US, masses of hung-over, snowbound TV viewers jealously watch the blessed few who march through sunny Pasadena for the **Tournament of Roses Parade** and **Rose Bowl** football game. For the nation, Pasadena is the home of the Rose Bowl; for Californians, it is a serene, ritzy suburb. With classy museums, graceful architecture, a lively shopping district, and idyllic weather, Pasadena lacks only a coastline. **Old Town,** the Promenade of Pasadena, combines intriguing historic sights with a lively entertainment scene.

**SOUTH BAY.** Head to LA County's more casual and less congested southern communities for the most precious of Southern Californian souvenirs: a tan. **Manhattan Beach** is one of the best-maintained of LA beaches, filled with yuppie married couples and uncommited singles enjoying the affluent good life. Immediately to the south lies **Hermosa Beach,** whose sweet waves, popular boardwalk, and swimsuit competitions attract high concentrations of surfers, volleyball players, and partiers. **Redondo Beach** is smaller and more commercial, known more for its marina and pier than its beach. Ritzy **Rancho Palos Verdes** is a different breed of coastal town, but down below the haughty cliffs are sandboxes overrun by gaggles of eager skaters, volleyball players, surfers, and sunbathers. The drive on **PCH** along the splendid cliffs of Palos Verdes will coax out your romantic side. **San Pedro** is home to Worldport LA, the nation's busiest harbor, which somehow supports huge ships and marine life at the same time.

# ☰ LOCAL TRANSPORTATION

Nowhere is the god Automobile more revered than in LA, home of so many lowriders and the most devoted and extravagant owners of cars. LA boasts the greatest density of Mercedes-Benzes outside Europe, and there's no shortage of vehicles sporting BMW, Audi, and Lexus logos either. Driving, along with simultaneous cell phone use, takes up a major chunk of any self-respecting Angeleno's day.

Sometimes it seems like all 16 million residents of Greater LA are flooding I-405 and I-101 all at once, transforming the City of Angels into Transportation Hell and leaving little room for clean air, patience, and sanity. The roadways are disgustingly jammed and overwhelmed, but commuters still refuse to surrender their independence by carpooling. New freeway construction projects, including those that may eventually alleviate the infamous congestion, are vociferously protested by LA residents who fear relocation and are tired of construction.

As a consequence of LA's obsession with individual driving, public transportation systems are limited and inconvenient. Though renting a car is expensive, especially if you are under 25, your own set of wheels is the best way to navigate the monstrous Southland counties. If you must forego the rental, use the subway and the bus to get around LA. See the **Practical Information** sections for **Hollywood,** p. 384, and **Santa Monica,** p. 384, for info on getting around in those areas of the city.

## PUBLIC TRANSPORTATION

In the 1930s and 40s, General Motors (GM), Firestone, and Standard Oil bought up LA streetcar companies and intentionally ran them out of business. After the rails were torn up by these companies, LA as a city grew increasingly reliant on buses and later on cars. In 1949, GM was convicted in federal court of criminal conspiracy—but by then the trolleys were becoming obsolete.

Six **Metropolitan Transit Authority (MTA) Metro Customer Centers** are available to point mass transit users in the right direction. They have MTA schedules and route maps, as well as a friendly staff to help plan your trip. **Downtown:** Arco Plaza, 515 S. Flower St., Level "C" (open M-F 7:30am-3:30pm); Gateway Transit Center, Union Station E. Portal (open M-F 6am-6:30pm). **East LA:** 4501-B Whittier Blvd. (open Tu-Sa 10am-6pm). **San Fernando Valley:** 14435 Sherman Way, Van Nuys (open M-F 10am-6pm). Centers are also located in Baldwin Hills and Wilshire.

For travelers who know where they want to go, MTA provides informative telephone and online assistance. (☎800-COMMUTE/266-6883; www.mta.net. Open M-F 6am-8:30pm, Sa-Su 8am-6pm.) MTA's hotline covers the metro rail subway and bus routes, as well as DASH connections. LA County's commuter rail, **Metrolink,** is under separate management (see below).

**BY DASH.** The local **DASH shuttle** (25¢), designed for short distance neighborhood hops, serves major tourist destinations in many communities, including Downtown, Hollywood (along Sunset Blvd.), Fairfax, Midtown, Crenshaw, and Van Nuys/Studio City, as well as Venice in the summer. (☎213-808-2273; www.ladot-transit.com. Open M-F 9am-5pm, Sa 10am-2pm.)

**BY MTA BUS.** No Angeleno will suggest moving about LA in anything but a car, but LA's buses are not altogether useless. The MTA used to be known as the RTD (Rapid Transit District), and some of its older buses may still be labeled as such. The name change was apt—most LA buses are not rapid in any sense of the word. Given the over 200 routes and several independent municipal transit systems that connect to the MTA, it's no easy task to study the timetables. Ninety percent of MTA routes have wheelchair-accessible buses. Appropriate bus stops are marked with the international symbol for disabled access.

Using the MTA to sightsee in LA can be frustrating because attractions tend to be spread out. Those determined to see *everything* should get in a car. If this is not possible, base yourself in Hollywood (where there are plenty of sights and bus connections), make daytrips, and keep plenty of change for the bus. Bus service is dismal in the outer reaches of the city and 2hr. journeys are not rare. Transfers often involve waits of an hour or more, and traffic congestion hinders everyone.

MTA's basic fare is $1.35 (transfer 25¢), seniors and disabled 45¢ (transfer 10¢); exact change is required. Weekly passes ($11) are available at customer service centers and local grocery stores. Transfers can be made between MTA lines or to other transit authorities. **Unless otherwise noted, all route numbers are MTA;** BBBus stands for **Big Blue Bus** and indicates Santa Monica buses (p. 384).

**BY SUBWAY.** LA's system of light-rail connections is spreading its tendrils, although it is still far from complete. Where rails do exist, they can often save commuters time otherwise wasted in traffic snarls. Several stations have park-and-ride lots available. The **Blue Line** runs from Downtown to the southern LA communities and Long Beach. The **Green Line** goes along I-105 from Norwalk to Redondo Beach, with shuttle service to LAX at Aviation/I-105. The **Red Line** runs from Downtown through Hollywood to the San Fernando Valley; other lines go west to Wilshire and east to Union Station. A one-way trip costs $1.35, with transfers to bus and rail $1.60; seniors and disabled are 45¢, with transfers 55¢. All lines run daily 5am-11pm (☎800-266-6883/COMMUTE; www.mta.net). The new **Beige Line** (Pasadena line) runs from Union Station to Sierra Madre Villa in Pasadena.

**BY METROLINK TRAIN.** Metrolink trains run out of the city from Union Station to Ventura and Orange Counties (M-F), and to Riverside via San Bernardino, Santa Clarita, and Antelope Valley (M-Sa). One-way fares are $4.25-10.75, depending on the destination. You can only buy them from machines in the station within 3hr. of your departure time. Discounts are available if traveling Saturday or during off-peak hours (8:30am-3:30pm and after 7pm). Beware—trains come and go up to 5min. ahead of schedule. For more info, call ☎800-371-5465.

**BY TAXI.** If you need a cab, it's best to call **Independent** (☎213-385-8294 or 800-521-8294), **LA Taxi/Yellow Cab Co.** (☎800-711-8294 or 800-200-1085), or **Bell Cab** (☎888-235-5222). Be prepared to wait at least 15min. Fare is about $2 per mi. anywhere in the city and approximately $30-35 from the airport to Downtown.

## NON-PUBLIC TRANSPORTATION

**✍ BY CAR.** LA may be the most difficult city in the US to navigate without a car. It may also be the most difficult city in which to **rent** a car for younger travelers. Most places will not rent to people under 21, and the ones that do will likely impose a surcharge that only the children of movie stars can afford to pay (nearly double the standard rate). Drivers between 21 and 25 incur a lower surcharge.

National rental agencies are reputed to have more dependable cars, but the high demand for rental cars assures that even small local companies can survive, and many have much lower rates than the big guys. They are worth looking into, but be forewarned: although you may be planning a budget trip, car rental is not the thing to be thrifty with. National agencies will replace a broken-down car hassle-free; if you want to use a local place, make sure they will do the same. Local rental companies might quote a very low daily rate and then add extra fees when you return the car. The prices quoted below are intended to give a very rough idea of what to expect; ask about airline-related and other discounts. National companies also offer free transportation services to and from LAX.

**Avon,** 7080 Santa Monica Blvd. (☎323-850-0826; www.avonrents.com), at La Brea Blvd. Cars $29 per day with 150 mi. free, $179 per week with 750 mi. free, or $550-600 per month with 3325 mi. free. Collision Damage Waiver (CDW) $9 per day. No under-25 surcharge. Open M-F 6am-7pm, Sa-Su 7am-5pm.

**Avis,** 11901 Santa Monica Blvd. (☎310-914-7700; www.avis.com), between Barrington Ave. and Bundy St. Economy cars $34 per day or $149 per week with unlimited mileage. CDW $9 per day. Will not rent if under 25. Pick-up available nearby. Open M-F 8am-6pm, Sa 8am-2pm, Su 9am-2pm.

**Thrifty** (☎310-645-1880 or 800-367-2277; www.thrifty.com), at LAX. Prices vary daily, but drop as low as $25 per day with unlimited mileage in CA, NV, and AZ. CDW $9 per day. Under-25 surcharge $25 per day. Open daily 6am-midnight.

**Alamo** (☎310-649-2242 or 800-327-9633; www.alamo.com), at LAX. Prices vary with availability; generally $27-35 per day or $110-155 per week, both with unlimited mileage. CDW $9 per day. Under-25 surcharge $25 per day. Open 24hr.

**Enterprise** (☎310-649-5400 or 800-RENT-A-CAR; www.enterprise.com), at LAX. Economy cars $23-40 per day or $169 per week, both with unlimited mileage. CDW $9 per day. Under-25 surcharge $10 per day. Open daily 6am-10pm.

**Lucky,** 8620 Airport Blvd. (☎310-641-2323 or 800-400-4736). Economy cars $20-30 per day with 150 mi. free or $109-169 per week with 1050 mi. free. CDW $9 per day. Under-25 surcharge $5-15 per day. Open M-Sa 8am-6pm, Su 8am-1pm.

**Universal Rent A Car,** 920 S. La Brea Ave. (☎323-954-1186). Cars from $20 per day with 150 mi. free, $140 per week with 1050 mi. free. No under-25 surcharge. Open M-F 8am-6pm, Sa-Su 9am-5pm.

There are many paid lots in LA (about $8 per day) and most accommodations offer free parking. Metered parking is on every major street, but authorized hours vary so be sure to read all the signs over and over and over. A quarter buys you anywhere from 7½-30min. The **Automobile Club of Southern California,** 2601 S. Figueroa St., at Adams Blvd., has additional driving info and maps. Club privileges are free for AAA members and cost $2-3 for nonmembers. Their *Westways* magazine is a good source for daytrip or vacation planning. (☎213-741-3686, emergency assistance 800-400-4222. Open M-F 9am-5pm. Other offices in greater LA.)

**FREEWAYS.** The freeway is perhaps the most enduring image of LA. No matter what may separate Angelenos—race, creed, or class—the one thing that unites them all is the freeway system, a maze of 10- and 12-lane concrete roadways.

"Caught in traffic" is the all-purpose excuse for tardiness, guaranteed to elicit knowing nods and consoling smiles. In planning your route, note that heavy traffic moves toward Downtown from 7 to 10am on weekdays and streams outbound from 4 to 7pm. However, since LA has a huge population that doesn't work 9-to-5, traffic can be almost as bad at 1pm as it is at 6pm. No matter how crowded the freeway is, though, it's almost always quicker and safer than taking surface streets to your destination, unless traveling under the guidance of a seasoned local (many of whom know tried-and-true shortcuts).

Uncongested freeways offer the ultimate in speed and convenience; the trip from Downtown to Santa Monica on a wide-open I-10 can take as little as 15min. A nighttime cruise on I-110 (Harbor Fwy.) beneath the tangle of interchanges and iconic LA skyscrapers can be exhilarating. For freeway info, call **CalTrans** (☎213-897-3693), listen religiously to the frequent traffic reports on KFWB (980 AM), and refer to the **LA Overview map** (p. 372).

**BICYCLES.** Unless you have legs and lungs of steel, a bicycle in LA is useful only for recreational purposes. Air quality is poor, distances are long, and drivers are very overprotective of their road space. Always wear a helmet; it's illegal and unsafe to bike on the road without one. For those who really want to explore on two wheels, **LA Bike Tours,** 6731 Hollywood Blvd. (☎323-466-5890 or 888-775-2453; www.labiketours.com), offers great advice as well as tours of Hollywood, Beverly Hills, and Venice Beach that range from 3hr. to an entire day ($50-94). They offer a daily bike tour to the Hollywood sign at 2pm; just show up. Advanced rides to the Hollywood Sign, the Getty, and a two-day coastal adventure to Santa Barbara are all available by request. Prices include bike rental and snack.

If you are not in a group, it's best to rent a bike from LA Bike Tours ($20 per day or $60 per week) and stick to one of many designated bike paths. The most popular route for the casual rider is the **South Bay Bicycle Path,** which runs from Santa Monica to Torrance (19 mi.), winding over the sandy beaches of the South Bay past sunbathers and spandex-clad in-line skaters. The path continues to San Diego. The new **LA River Bike Path** runs from Long Beach to Dodger Stadium. The **Nichols Canyon** to **Mulholland Drive Path** attracts many local riders. It also gives a mini-tour of celebrities' homes. Other bike paths include: **San Gabriel River Trail,** a 37 mi. pedal along the river with views of the San Gabriel Valley; **Upper Rio Hondo** (9 mi.) and **Lario Trails** (22 mi.), which are free of traffic; and **Kenneth Newell Bikeway,** a 10 mi. glide through residential Pasadena. For the more serious rider, the **Donut Ride** in **Palos Verdes,** South Bay, provides hill after hill after hill.

**BY WALKING AND HITCHHIKING.** LA pedestrians are a hapless breed. Unless you're running in the LA Marathon, moving from one part of the city to another on foot is a ludicrous idea—distances are just too great. And worse, it's just uncool. Nevertheless, some colorful areas such as Melrose, Westwood, Third Street Promenade in Santa Monica, Hollywood, and Old Town Pasadena are best explored by foot. Just remember that outside these sanctuaries, Californians will stare (and possibly run) you down, and cops may ticket you for setting foot in a crosswalk without a "Walk" signal. For coastal culture lovers, Venice Beach is one of the most enjoyable (and popular) places to walk, with nearby sights and shopping areas. *LA Now*, the publication of the Convention and Visitor Bureau, has an excellent list of walking tours (see **Practical Information: Publications,** p. 383). Since some of the best tour companies are one-person operations, schedules and prices are not written in stone. Look for theme tours (e.g., Graveyard) of celebrity homes geared toward your obsessions. The **Los Angeles Conservancy** (☎213-623-2489; www.laconservancy.org) offers 2½hr. tours of the Downtown area every Saturday at 10am. Tours cost $8; advance reservations are required (no strollers or young children). Call **Tree People** (☎818-753-4600) for info about the Full Moon Sunday walking tours in Coldwater Canyon Park, which occur once a month on the Sunday closest to the full moon.

Once the sun sets, those on **foot**, especially outside West LA and off well-lit main drags, should exercise caution, particularly when alone. Plan your pedestrian routes very carefully—it is worth a detour to avoid passing through heavily crime-ridden areas. **If you hitchhike, you will probably die.** It is exceptionally dangerous, not to mention illegal. There are many other options. Don't even consider it.

# ⚡ PRACTICAL INFORMATION

## TOURIST & FINANCIAL SERVICES

### Visitor Information:

**LA Convention and Visitor Bureau,** 685 S. Figueroa St. (☎213-689-8822; www.visitl-anow.com), between Wilshire Blvd. and 7th St. in the Financial District. Staff speaks English, French, German, and Japanese. Detailed bus map of LA available. California road map $3. Distributes *LA Now,* a free booklet with tourist and lodging info. Open M-F 8am-5:30pm.

**National Park Service,** 401 W. Hillcrest Dr. (☎818-597-9192), in Thousand Oaks, in the Conejo Valley. Info on the Santa Monica Mountains (including outdoor activities and special events) in *Outdoors,* a quarterly events calendar. Open daily 9am-5pm.

**Sierra Club,** 3435 Wilshire Blvd. #320 (☎213-387-4287), between Normandy and Vermont St. Hiking, biking, skiing, and backpacking info. Stores throughout LA. Sells 4-month event schedules for $10; call for locations. Open M-F 10am-6pm.

**Budget Travel: STA Travel,** 7280 Melrose Ave. (☎323-934-8722 or 800-777-0112 for 24hr. tele-booking), has services for travelers but no gear. Open M-Sa 10am-6pm. **Los Angeles/Santa Monica HI-AYH,** 1434 2nd St. (☎310-393-3413), in Santa Monica next door to the hostel. Info and supplies for travelers. Guidebooks, backpacks, money belts, rail passes, and ISICs. Open M-F 9:30am-5pm, Sa 9am-5pm.

**Consulates: Australia,** 2049 Century Park East, 19th fl. (☎310-229-4800). Open M-F 9am-5pm; visa desk open M-F 9am-1pm. **South Africa,** 6300 Wilshire Blvd. #600 (☎323-651-0902). Consulate and visa desk open M-F 9am-noon. **UK,** 11766 Wilshire Blvd. #1200 (☎310-481-0031). Open M-F 8:30-11:30am for visas, 8:30am-noon and 2-4pm for consular services, 8:30am-5pm for all other business.

**Currency Exchange:** At most airport terminals (see **Intercity Transportation,** p. 370), but rates are exorbitant. **American Express** offices have better rates, but charge a $5 fee to change currency and a 1% fee on traveler's checks if you are not a card holder. AmEx **Beverly Hills,** 327 N. Beverly Hills Dr. (☎310-274-8277). Open M-F 10am-6pm, Sa 10am-3pm. Also in **Pasadena,** 269 S. Lake Ave. (☎626-449-2281). Open M-F 9am-6pm, Sa 10am-2pm. Other locations in **Torrance** and **Costa Mesa. Banknotes Exchange,** 520 S. Grand Ave. L 100 (☎213-627-5404), has no fee for changing currency, but charges a 3% fee for traveler's checks. Open M-F 9am-5pm, Sa 9am-1pm.

## LOCAL SERVICES

**Central Public Library,** 630 W. 5th St. (☎213-612-3200, events line 213-228-7040), Downtown, between Grand Ave. and Flower St. Present ID with current local address to get a library card; reading room open to all card holders. Library houses foreign-language books, weekly exhibits, and activities including readings, films, and workshops. Tours M-F 12:30pm, Sa 11am and 2pm, Su 2pm. Open M-Th 10am-8pm, F-Sa 10am-6pm, Su 1-5pm. Validated parking available at 524 S. Flower St. with LA library card.

**Ticket Agency: Ticketmaster** (☎213-480-3232), charges high per-ticket fees. A better bet is to contact the box office directly.

**Surf Conditions:** Recorded info on Malibu, Santa Monica, and South Bay (☎310-457-9701). Most FM radio stations have a surf report at noon.

**Weather Conditions:** Detailed region-by-region report (☎213-554-1212).

**Highway Conditions:** Recorded info may help you prevent an afternoon on the freeway (☎800-427-7623). KFWB 980 AM and KNX 1070 AM give reports every 10min.

## LOCAL MEDIA

**Television Stations: ABC** (Channel 7); **CBS** (Channel 2); **Fox** (Channel 11); **NBC** (Channel 4); **KTLA/WB** (Channel 5); **UPN** (Channel 13).

**National Public Radio:** 91.5 FM for all things considered.

**Other Radio Stations: Old School/R&B** "Hot" 92.3 FM; **Country** KZLA 93.9; **Smooth Jazz** "The Wave" 94.7 FM; **Spanish** "El Sol" 96.3; **Pop/Rock/Top 40** "Star" 98.7 FM; **Oldies** KRTH 101.1 FM; **Pop/Top 40** KIIS 102.7 FM; **Adult Contemporary** KBIG 104.3 FM; **Classical** KKGO 10.51 FM; **Hip Hop** "Power 106" 105.9; **Rock** KROQ 106.7 FM.

## EMERGENCY & COMMUNICATIONS

**Rape Crisis:** ☎310-392-8381.

**24hr. Pharmacy: Sav-On,** 3010 S. Sepulveda Blvd. (☎310-478-9821), in West LA. For other 24hr. locations, call ☎800-627-2866.

**Hospitals: Cedars-Sinai Medical Center,** 8700 Beverly Blvd. (☎310-423-3277, emergency 423-8644). **Good Samaritan Hospital,** 616 S. Witmer St. (☎213-977-2121, emergency 977-2420). **UCLA Medical Center,** 10833 Le Conte Ave. (☎310-825-9111, emergency 825-2111).

**AREA CODES.** LA is big. Real big. There are many area codes:
**213** Downtown.
**323** Hollywood, Vernon, Huntington Park, Montebello, and West Hollywood.
**310** Santa Monica, Malibu, and Westside.
**562** Long Beach and southern LA county.
**626** San Gabriel Valley and Pasadena.
**818** Burbank, Glendale, San Fernando Valley.
**909** San Bernardino and Riverside.

**Planned Parenthood** (☎323-226-0800). Various locations in the city; call for the nearest one. Birth control, prenatal care, STD treatment, abortions, pregnancy testing, HIV testing, and counseling. Call 1 week in advance for appointments. Hours and fees vary.

**Free Clinics: Hollywood-Sunset Free Clinic,** 2815 Sunset Blvd. (☎213-989-1780). Provides general medicine, family planning, and psychiatric care for people without an insurance policy or HMO. No mandatory fees. Appointments only; call M, W, or F 10am-noon to schedule. **Valley Free Clinic,** 6801 Coldwater Canyon (☎818-763-8836), in North Hollywood. Women's health, birth control, medical counseling, drug addiction services, and free HIV testing. Appointments only; call weeks in advance M-F 10am-4pm.

**Post Office:** Central branch at 7101 S. Central Ave. (☎800-275-8777). Open M-F 7am-7pm, Sa 7am-3pm. **Postal Code:** 90001.

## PUBLICATIONS

The *Los Angeles Times* (newsstand 25¢, Su $1.50) defeats all rival papers west of the Rockies. The *Times* "Calendar" section has the scoop on the current LA scene. The free *LA Weekly*, which comes out on Thursdays, is the definitive source of entertainment listings, and is available at shops, restaurants, and newsstands. LA has a number of "industry" (i.e. movie) papers; the best-known are *Variety* and *The Hollywood Reporter*. *The Los Angeles Sentinel* is LA's largest **African-American** paper. UCLA's **student** paper, *The Daily Bruin*, comes out during the school year. Four of the most popular **gay and lesbian** entertainment magazines are *Fab!*, *Vibe*, *The Frontiers*, and *Edge*. LA also has numerous foreign-language publications. The **Spanish** *La Opinión* is the largest, but two **Korean** papers (*The Korean Central Daily* and *The Korea Times*) each have circulations approaching 75,000. The *International Daily News* and the *Chinese Daily News* serve the **Chinese**-speaking community. LA's gargantuan newsstands offer many of these foreign-language publications, in addition to the usual and proliferant muscle, car, sports, fashion, and skin mags. **World Wide,** 1101 Westwood Blvd., at Kinross Ave., is a fine example of one such stand. (Open daily 7am-midnight.)

## HOLLYWOOD PRACTICAL INFORMATION

**Public Transit:** Important buses: **#2** and **#3** run along Sunset Blvd., **#4** along Santa Monica Blvd., **#10** and **#11** along Melrose Ave. Fare $1.35, transfers 25¢. Weekly pass $11, monthly $42.

**Parking:** Ample metered parking on the street. 30min. for 25¢. Many public lots, charging from $1.50 per hr. to $10 per night. Public lot north of Hollywood Blvd. at Cherokee St. offers 2hr. free with each additional hr. $1 for up to 3 more hours.

**Currency Exchange: Cash It Here,** 6565 Hollywood Blvd. (☎323-464-2718), at Whitley St. 1% commission. Open 24hr. M-F, Su 8am-6pm; Sa hours vary.

**Police:** 1358 N. Wilcox Ave. (☎213-485-4302).

**24hr. Pharmacy: Rite-Aid,** 7900 W. Sunset Blvd. (☎323-876-4466), in Hollywood, at the intersection of W. Sunset and N. Fairfax Ave.

**Hospital: Queen of Angels Hollywood Presbyterian Medical Center,** 1300 N. Vermont Ave. (☎213-413-3000). 24hr. emergency room.

**Internet Access:** Many coffeehouses have **CaféNet** computers, which have Internet access but no text-based email. These Hollywood locations have both: **Cyber Java,** 7080 Hollywood Blvd. (☎323-466-5600). $2.50 per 15min., $9 per hr. or $45 for a 10hr. card. Open M-F 7am-11:30pm, Sa-Su 8am-11:30pm. **@coffee,** 7200 Melrose Ave. (☎323-938-9985). Happy Hour before 11am $5 per hr.; after 11am $2 per 10min., $5 per 30min., $7 per hr. includes a coffee. Open M-Sa 8am-8pm, Su 9am-7pm. **C&C Internet Cafe,** 7070 W. Sunset Blvd. (☎323-462-8100). $2 per 23min., $4 per hr., $10 per 3hr. Open 24hr. **Badlanz,** 1602 N. Cahuenga Blvd. (☎323-464-5269). $3 per hr. Open daily noon-4am. **Kinko's,** 7630 W. Sunset Blvd. (☎323-845-4501). 20¢ per min. Open M-Th 7am-11pm, F 7am-8pm, Sa 8am-6pm, Su 9am-10pm.

**Post Office:** 1615 Wilcox Ave. (☎323-464-2355). Open M-F 8:30am-5:30pm, Sa 8:30am- 3:30pm. **Postal Code:** 90028.

## SANTA MONICA PRACTICAL INFORMATION

**Visitors Information: Santa Monica Visitors Center,** 395 Santa Monica Pl. (☎310-393-7593), 2nd floor of the shopping center on the south end of Third St. Promenade. Open daily 10am-6pm. A smaller center is at 1400 Ocean Ave. Open daily 10am-5pm.

**Public Transit: Santa Monica Municipal Bus Lines** (☎310-451-5444; www.bigbluebus.com). With over 1000 stops in Santa Monica, LA, and Culver City, the "Big Blue Bus" (**BBBus,** as featured in *Speed;* see p. 23) is faster and cheaper than the MTA. Fare for most routes 50¢; transfer tickets for MTA buses 25¢; transfers to other BBBuses free. Important routes: **#1** and **2** connect Santa Monica and Venice to West LA via Santa Monica Blvd. and Wilshire Blvd., respectively; **#3** goes to LAX; **#10** provides express service from downtown Santa Monica (at 7th St. and Grand Ave.) to Downtown

LA. The **Tide Shuttle** runs from Broadway, south along Ocean Ave. to Marine St., and north along Main St. back to Broadway (25¢). Signs with route info litter downtown Santa Monica. Runs every 15min. M-Th noon-8pm, F-Sa noon-10pm.

**Equipment Rentals: Perry's Beach Rentals,** Ocean Front Walk (☎310-458-3975; www.actionsportsrentals.com), in the blue buildings north and south of the pier and just before Venice Beach. Four locations: 2400 and 2600 Ocean Front Walk, 930 and 1200 PCH. In-line skates and bikes $6 per hr., $20 per day; tandem bikes $11/$35; boogie boards $5/$12. Student discounts. Free beverage with rental. On-site **cafe ❶.** Open daily 9am-dark. **Skate City,** 111 Broadway (☎310-319-9272), rents in-line skates for $5 per hr., $10 per day. Open M-W 11am-7pm, Th 11am-9pm, F-Su 11am-8pm. **Blazing Saddles Bike Rentals,** 320 Santa Monica Pier (☎310-393-9778), is a bike rental bonanza ($6-11 per hr., $18-30 per day). Tandems and baby seats also available. Helmets, locks, and racks included. Open M-F 9:30am-7:30pm, Sa-Su 8:30am-7:30pm.

**Parking:** Six lots flank Third St. Promenade. Three are accessible from 4th St., and three from 2nd St. First 2hr. free, each additional 30min. $1. Santa Monica Place Mall has free parking for up to 3hr. ($3 flat fee after 5pm); others are metered (50¢ per hr.). Downtown streets have meters as well (50¢ per hr.). All-day beachside parking $6-10.

**Currency Exchange: Western Union,** 1454 4th St. (☎310-394-7211), at Broadway. Open M-F 9am-6pm, Sa 9am-3pm.

**Library: LA Public Library,** Santa Monica branch, 1234 4th St. (☎310-458-8600), at Santa Monica Blvd. Temporary location while the main branch undergoes construction from 2003-2005. Open M-Th 10am-9pm, F-Sa 10am-5:30pm, Su 1-5pm.

**Medical Services: Santa Monica/UCLA Medical Center,** 1250 16th St. (☎310-319-4765). Emergency room open 24hr.

**Police:** 1685 Main St. (☎310-395-9931).

**Post Office:** 1248 5th St. (☎310-576-6786), at Arizona Blvd. Open M-F 9am-6pm, Sa 9am-3pm. **Postal Code:** 90401.

# ⌐ ACCOMMODATIONS

Cheap accommodations in Los Angeles are often unsafe. It can be difficult to gauge quality from the exterior, so ask to see a room before committing. For those willing to share a room and a bathroom, hostels are a saving grace, although Americans should be aware that some only accept international travelers. These hostels require an international passport, but well-traveled Americans with proof of travel (passports, out-of-state identification, or plane tickets often do the trick) may be permitted to stay. It never hurts to ask for off-season or student discounts, and occasionally managers will lower prices to snare a hesitant customer.

In choosing where to stay, the first consideration should be location. If you don't have wheels, decide which element of LA appeals to you the most. Those visiting for beach culture should choose lodgings in Venice or Santa Monica. Avid sightseers will be better off in Hollywood or the more expensive (but cleaner and nicer) Westside. Downtown has public transportation connections, but is unsafe after dark. Even those with cars should choose lodgings close to their interests to keep car-bound time to a minimum. **Listed prices do not include LA's 14% hotel tax.**

## HOLLYWOOD

Staying in Hollywood puts you smack in the middle of it all, which is a blessing for some and a curse for others. Though the area crawls with people by day, avoid the streets late at night. Always exercise caution while scouting out the budget hostels on or around Hollywood Blvd., especially east of the main strips. Overall, the accommodations are a much better value than most others in LA.

🏠 **Hollywood Bungalows International Youth Hostel,** 2775 W. Cahuenga Blvd. (☎888-259-9990; www.hollywoodbungalows.com), just north of the Hollywood Bowl in the Hollywood Hills. This newly renovated hostel cultivates a wacky summer camp atmosphere. Spacious rooms and nightly jam sessions. Outdoor pool, billiards, weight room, big screen TV, and mini-diner. Cable in some rooms. Internet access $2 per 10min. Breakfast $3.50, dinner $10. Lockers 25¢. Linen and parking included. Laundry ($1.25 wash; 75¢ dry). On-site Universal Rent-a-Car (see p. 380). Check-in 24hr. 6- to 10-bed co-ed dorms with bathroom $15-19; private doubles for up to 4 $59. ❷

🏠 **USAHostels Hollywood,** 1624 Schrader Blvd. (☎323-462-3777 or 800-524-6783; www.usahostels.com), south of Hollywood Blvd., west of Cahuenga Blvd. Crawling with young travelers, this lime-green and blue-dotted chain hostel is filled with energy and organized fun. Special events nightly, with free comedy W and Su. Stay for 5+ days and get free pick-up from airport, bus, and train stations (3+ nights, half-price pick-up). Free beach shuttles run Su, T, and Th. To use lockers, bring your own lock or buy one for 50¢. Linen and all-you-can-eat pancakes included. Free street parking or parking lot is $4.50 per day. Dinner $4. Dorms (6-8 beds) with private bath $15-21; private rooms for 2-4 people $39-52. Prices $1-2 less in winter. **Passport or proof of travel required.** ❷

## ACCOMMODATIONS BY PRICE

| UNDER $18 (❶) | |
|---|---|
| Hostel California (388) | VN |

| $18-34 (❷) | |
|---|---|
| Cadillac Hotel (388) | VN |
| 🏠 Hollywood Bungalows Hostel (386) | HW |
| Hollywood International Hostel (387) | HW |
| 🏠 LA Surf City Hostel (392) | SB |
| 🏠 LA/Santa Monica HI-AYH (388) | SM |
| LA South Bay HI-AYH (392) | SB |
| 🏠 Orbit Hotel and Hostel (390) | WS |
| Student Inn International Hostel (387) | HW |
| 🏠 USAHostels Hollywood | HW |
| Venice Beach Cotel (388) | VN |
| Venice Beach Hostel (388) | VN |

| $35-54 (❸) | |
|---|---|
| Flamingo Hotel (386) | HW |

| $35-54 (❸; *CONT.*) | |
|---|---|
| Hotel Claremont (390) | WS |
| Jolly Roger Hotel (390) | VN |
| Liberty Hotel (387) | HW |
| The Little Inn (390) | WS |
| Orange Drive Manor (386) | HW |

| $55-79 (❹) | |
|---|---|
| The Beverly Hills Reeves Hotel (390) | BH |
| Bevonshire Lodge Motel (390) | WS |
| 🏠 Days Inn Metro Plaza Hotel (392) | DT |
| Hotel Stillwell (392) | DT |
| Inntowne Hotel (392) | DT |
| Milner Hotel (392) | DT |
| Moon Lite Inn (392) | SB |

| OVER $80 (❺) | |
|---|---|
| Hotel California (390) | VN |

**HW** Hollywood **WS** Westside **SM** Santa Monica **VN** Venice **DT** Downtown **SB** South Bay

**Flamingo Hotel,** 1921 N. Highland Ave. (☎323-876-6544), just north of Hollywood Blvd. An 8-story maze of rooms offering peace, quiet, and quick access to sights. Private rooms well-furnished and large. Use a common kitchen or ask for a room with its own kitchen. Lounge with free billiards, TV, and video games. Internet access $1 per 10min. Laundry ($1 wash; 75¢ dry). 4-bed dorms $15-19. Private rooms $40-80. ❸

**Orange Drive Manor,** 1764 N. Orange Dr. (☎323-850-0350). This pleasant, converted mini-mansion in a residential neighborhood is the perfect retreat. Don't be confused by the lack of a sign—this house is your hostel. Cable TV lounge, limited kitchen. Spacious, clean rooms with antique furniture. Internet access $1 per 10min. Lockers 75¢. Parking $5. Reservations recommended. 4- to 6-bed dorms, some with private baths, $19-23; private rooms $39-48. Minimal discount with ISIC card. No credit cards. ❸

**Liberty Hotel,** 1770 Orchid Ave. (☎323-962-1788), south of Franklin Ave. This small hotel, located on a quiet residential street only 1 block north of Hollywood Blvd., has very large, clean rooms that more than compensate for the bare walls. Some rooms connected to a full kitchen. Free coffee and parking, laundry ($1 wash, 50¢ dry), Internet access ($1 for 10min.), A/C. Reception 8am-1am. Check-out 11am. Singles $63, with kitchen $68; doubles $68/$72. ❸

**Student Inn International Hostel,** 7038½ Hollywood Blvd. (☎323-469-6781 or 323-462-9269 or 800-557-7038; www.studentinn.com), on the Walk of Fame. Hands down the most economical choice around. Free pick-up from airport, bus, and train stations with 3 night stay. 24hr. reception. Small kitchen, cable TV lounge. Discounted theme park tickets. Internet access ($2 for 30min.) and a free scanner, printer, and xerox machine. Continental breakfast, linen and lockers included. Work at reception in exchange for a night's stay. Only 13 rooms so call far in advance for reservations. Dorms $15 per night; rooms with 2 double beds and private bath $48 per night. ❷

**Hollywood International Hostel,** 6820 Hollywood Blvd. (☎323-463-0797 or 800-750-6561; www.hollywoodhostels.com). Front-row seats overlooking the Walk of Fame and the new Kodak Theatre. With 44 rooms that play host to starlets and aspiring screenwriters, as well as young and old visitors alike, this hostel is hopping. Discounted tours and car rentals, small kitchen, toast and tea breakfast, and a lounge with TV, billiards, and old arcade games. Lockers 25¢. Laundry ($1 wash; 50¢ dry). Internet access $1 for 10min. Reception open 24hr. Reserve ahead. Discounted pick-up shuttle from plane, train, and bus. Linens included. Single-sex and coed 4- to 6-bed dorms with shared bath $19; private rooms $40. Weekly dorms $119. ❷

**Hostel,** 6820 Hollywood Blvd. (☎323-463-0797 or 800-750-6561; www.hollywoodhostels.com). Front-row seats overlooking the Walk of Fame and the new Kodak Theatre. With 44 rooms that play host to starlets and aspiring screenwriters, as well as young and old visitors alike, this hostel is hopping. Discounted tours and car rentals, small kitchen, toast and tea breakfast, and a lounge with TV, billiards, and old arcade games. Lockers 25¢. Laundry ($1 wash; 50¢ dry). Internet access $1 for 10min. Reception open 24hr. Reserve ahead. Discounted pick-up shuttle from plane, train, and bus. Linens included. Single-sex and coed 4- to 6-bed dorms with shared bath $19; private rooms $40. Weekly dorms $119. ❷

# THE HIDDEN DEAL

## PRICELESS POOLS

Scattered throughout LA are some of the country's most exclusive hotels—catering to successful businessmen, celebrities, and anyone with a platinum card who hardly notices the $300 per night prices and $20 valet tips. For most budget travelers, these hotels are off-limits and the hope of hobnobbing with the rich and famous on their turf is a pipe dream.

But a little known secret that locals try to keep hush-hush is that within these big-name luxury hotels, the beautiful heated outdoor pools are free to the public by day for the minimal cost of an LA sunburn. So don't be shy; strut right into these swanky hotels, rip off your shirt like you don't need it, and claim a beach chair along the edge of the pool. Take a dip in the pool, order up a martini (with a twist!), lie back, and smile. You're wallowing in luxury without wallowing in bankruptcy.

**Hollywood Standard,** 8300 Sunset Blvd. (☎323-650-9090), in Hollywood, has an incredible view of the Los Angeles basin.

**The Standard,** 550 S. Flower St. (☎213-892-8080), at 6th St. in Downtown, has a rooftop pool and bar.

**W. Los Angeles Hotel,** 930 Hilgard Ave. (☎310-208-8765), in Westwood, has two pools.

**Avalon Hotel of Beverly Hills,** 9400 W. Olympic Blvd. (☎310-277-5221), in Beverly Hills.

## SANTA MONICA & VENICE

Accommodations in Santa Monica and Venice range from cheap oceanfront hostels to expensive oceanfront hotels. In general, however, the closer you stay to the beach, the more you dish out. **Depending on the hostel/hotel, the tax on your room may be 8.5% or 14%.** Everything fills quickly in summer; book early. Drivers should look for accommodations that include parking or consider staying farther from the beach since overnight parking near the beach is very limited. For those venturing into LA proper, the MTA or Santa Monica's Big Blue Bus (**BBBus,** see p. 384) connects Santa Monica to many other areas in the LA region.

Much of Santa Monica and Venice is best seen by foot or bike, so plan on parking in one of the main lots near Third St. Promenade in Santa Monica or near the intersection of Windward Ave. and Pacific Ave. in Venice before hitting the turf.

**⬛ Los Angeles/Santa Monica (HI-AYH),** 1436 2nd St. (☎310-393-9913; http://hostel-web.com/losangeles), Santa Monica. From Santa Monica Blvd., turn south onto 2nd St.; the hostel is a half-block away. Or take MTA #33 from Union Station to 2nd St. and Broadway or BBBus #3 from LAX to 4th St. and Broadway. Next door to the associated **SaMo Travelers Center.** 1 block from the promenade and 2 blocks from the beach. Welcoming travelers of all backgrounds and ages, this popular hostel is centered around a courtyard and fountain with small but well-attended rooms and common spaces. Regularly organizes discounted tours, outings, comedy shows, open mic, and movie nights. Dining room, newly renovated kitchen, game room, TV room, pool table, Internet access, linens, and library. No-alcohol policy and strict 10pm-8am quiet hours are enforced. Swipe keys enhance security. Breakfast 7:30-10:30am ($2-4). Safe deposits and lockers. Laundry $1 wash, 75¢ dry. 24hr. security and check-in. 10-day max. stay. In summer, reserve by phone or online. 4- to 10-bed dorms $28, non-members $31; private doubles $70/$75. Group packages available for 8 or more. ❷

**Venice Beach Hostel,** 1515 Pacific Ave. (☎310-452-3052; www.caprica.com/venice-beach-hostel), just north of Windward Ave in Venice. Its central location, friendly staff, and lively atmosphere make this a popular hostel for backpackers. A full kitchen, two enormous lounges, and 10 super-comfy couches encourage mingling. Lockers, storage rooms, and linen included. Internet access $1 per 10min. Laundry $1 wash, 75¢ dry. $25-100 security deposit at check-in. 4- to 10-bed dorms $19-22; private rooms for 1 or 2 people $55. Weekly discounts available. ❷

**Venice Beach Cotel,** 25 Windward Ave., (☎310-399-7649; www.venicebeachco-tel.com), above St. Mark's Restaurant in Venice. From LAX, take BBBus #3, transfer to #2 at California Ave., get off #2 at the post office and walk 1 block toward shore. International staff and guests make the cramped quarters lively. Aqua Lounge features big-screen satellite TV and a BYOB bar where guests chill at night (8pm-midnight). Free tea and coffee. Tennis rackets, table tennis, and boogie boards ($20 deposit). Lockers and linen included. No laundry. $5 key deposit. Reception and security 24hr. Reservations always recommended. 3-, 4-, and 6-bed dorms with ocean view and bath $15-18; doubles $36-50; triples with bath and view $60. **Passport required.** ❷

**Cadillac Hotel,** 8 Dudley Ave. (☎310-399-8876; www.thecadillachotel.com), in Venice off Ocean Front Walk. $10 airport shuttle ($5 each extra person). Discounted car rental. Free pick-up. Sauna, rooftop deck with great views, and well-equipped gym. Rooms have TVs, lockers, and private baths. Lounge with cable TV, juke box, and Internet. Laundry 75¢ wash, 50¢ dry. Free parking. Reserve ahead. 4-person dorms $25. Rooms $99; family rooms $110. Work in exchange for night's stay. **Passport required.** ❷

**Hostel California,** 2221 Lincoln Blvd. (☎310-305-0250; kschmahle@aol.com), in Venice. Park free in lot off Lucille Ave., 1 block north of Venice Blvd. Free airport pick-up. One mile from beach. Bikes $8. Spacious lounge with couches, pool table, and big-screen TV. Kitchen, lockers, linen, laundry included. Key deposit $5. Quiet hours from

TO PACIFIC PALISADES (2mi), MALIBU (8mi)

TO (1blk)

Lincoln Park

TO MONTANA AVE. (3blk)

California Ave.

Douglas Park

Wilshire Blvd.

Santa Monica State Beach

Ocean Ave.

Palisades Beach Rd.

3rd St. Promenade

2nd St.

Ocean Ave.

4th St.

5th St.

6th St.

Lincoln Blvd.

7th St.

9th St.

10th St.

11th St.

Euclid St.

12th St.

14th St.

15th St.

16th St.

17th St.

18th St.

19th St.

20th St.

Arizona Ave.

Santa Monica Blvd.

26th St.

Broadway

Colorado Ave.

Greyhound

Santa Monica Place

Big Blue Bus

Santa Monica Pier Aquarium

Santa Monica Pier & Pacific Park

Int'l. Chess Park

Main St.

SANTA MONICA

Memorial Park

Olympic Blvd.

Michigan Ave.

Delaware Ave.

Santa Monica Fwy.

10

Santa Monica Fwy.

TO 405, THE WESTSIDE

Bergamot Station Arts Center

Cloverfield St.

Santa Monica Bay

Perry's Beach Rentals

Bicknell Ave.

Pacific St.

Strand St.

Ocean Front Walk

Ocean Ave.

Main St.

2nd St.

3rd St.

4th St.

5th St.

6th St.

7th St.

11th St.

Euclid St.

14th St.

Pico Blvd.

Bay St.

Grant St.

Pacific St.

Pearl St.

Ocean Park Blvd.

Oak St.

Hill St.

Ashland Ave.

California Heritage Museum

OCEAN PARK

Boardwalk

Speedway

Neilson Way

Main St.

Barnard Way

Marine St.

Dewey St.

5th St.

6th St.

7th St.

Rose Ave.

Flower Ave.

Penmar Golf Course

Ocean Front Walk

Hampton Dr.

Sunset Ave.

Vernon Ave.

Indiana Ave.

Brooks Ave.

Broadway Ave.

Westminster Ave.

VENICE

Venice Canals

Electric Ave.

Grand Blvd.

Pacific Ave.

N Venice Blvd.

Abbot Kinney Blvd.

Shell Ave.

Oakwood Ave.

Linden Ave.

Lincoln Blvd.

California Ave.

Palms Blvd.

Vienna Wy.

Carlton Wy.

Victoria Ave.

Lucille Ave.

Venice Blvd.

Mildred Ave.

Washington Blvd.

Venice Fishing Pier

Venice Beach

Boardwalk

Via Dolce

Via Marina

Marquesas Wy.

MARINA DEL REY

Panay Wy.

Palawan Wy.

Burton Chase Park

Marina Boat Rentals

Fisherman's Village

Oxford Dr.

Marr St.

Thatcher Ave.

Yale Ave.

Admiralty Way

Stafford Ave.

Princeton Dr.

Penmar Ave.

Washington Blvd.

Del Rey Ave.

Maxella Ave.

Glencoe Ave.

Marina Expwy.

Ball Wy.

Mindanao Wy.

Fiji Wy.

see inset

Indiana Ave.

Brooks Ave.

Ocean Front Walk

Pacific Ave.

Main St.

Speedway

Abbot Kinney Blvd.

Riviera Ave.

Electric Ct.

Abbot Kinney Blvd.

Cabrillo Blvd.

Westminster Ave.

Market St.

Windward Ave.

Grand Blvd.

Venice Way

WINWARD PLAZA

Muscle Beach

17th Ave.

18th Ave.

19th Ave.

20th Ave.

21st Ave.

22nd Ave.

23rd Ave.

24th Ave.

25th Ave.

26th Ave.

27th Ave.

28th Ave.

29th Ave.

N. Venice Blvd.

S. Venice Blvd.

Venice Beach

Dell Ave.

Venice Canals

Ocean Ave.

28th Ave.

0    1/2 mi

0    1/2 km

## Santa Monica and Venice

### 🛏 ACCOMMODATIONS

Cadillac Hotel, 16
Hostel California, 17
Hotel California, 9
Jolly Roger Hotel, 18
LA/Santa Monica HI-AYH, 3
Venice Beach Cotel, 13
Venice Beach Hostel, 14

### 🍎 FOOD

Aunt Kizzy's Back Porch, 20
Big Daddy's, 12
Big Dean's "Muscle-In" Cafe, 7
Chez Jay, 8
Fritto Misto, 6
Healthy 4-U Cafe, 5
Lilly's, 10
Mariasol, 4
Reel Inn, 2
Rose Cafe and Market, 15
Sidewalk Cafe, 11
Tony P's Dockside Grill, 19
Toppers Restaurant and Cantina, 1

LOS ANGELES

midnight. Check-in until midnight. Co-ed and single-sex dorms. Military-style, 30-bunk barracks $12-14; small, dark, 6-bed dorms $16-18; doubles $34-46. 1 day free for week-long stay. **Passport** with proof of travel or **out-of-state driver's license** required. ❶

**Jolly Roger Hotel,** 2904 Washington Blvd. (☎310-822-2904 or 800-822-2904; www.jollyrgr.com), near Abbot Kinney Blvd., in Marina del Rey. Hotel and motel in same complex. Though located on a busy street, the hotel is a great mid-range option, especially for stays over a week. Pleasant rooms with A/C and satellite TV. Outdoor hot tub and pool, continental breakfast, and free parking. Hotel rooms $70. Cheaper (and, paradoxically, nicer) motel rooms drop to $40. Prices lower in winter. ❸

**Hotel California,** 1670 Ocean Ave. (☎310-393-2363 or 866-571-0000; www.hotelca.com), between Pico Blvd. and Colorado Blvd. Steps from the ocean with private beach access. Newly renovated. Well worth the steep price for its beachfront location and well-furnished rooms. Rooms include satellite TV and mini-fridge. Suites with kitchenette, dining table, pull-out bed, stereo, and balcony available. Room with queen or two doubles $169 in the high season. 20% off for stays over a week. ❺

# THE WESTSIDE: BEVERLY HILLS & WESTWOOD

The snazzy and safe Westside has excellent public transportation to the beaches. The area's affluence, however, means less bang for your buck. Those planning to stay at least one month in summer or six months during the school year (Sept.-June) can contact the **UCLA Off-Campus Housing Office,** 350 De Neve Dr. (☎310-825-4491; www.cho.ucla.edu), where an online roommate bulletin board lists students with spare rooms, as well as sublets and rentals. UCLA's student paper, the *Daily Bruin,* lists even more info (around campus or at www.dailybruin.ucla.edu).

**Orbit Hotel and Hostel,** 7950 Melrose Ave. (☎323-655-1510 or 877-672-4887; www.orbithotel.com), a block west of Fairfax Ave. in West Hollywood. Opened by 2 young LA locals 3 years ago, Orbit is setting new standards for swank budget living. Fashion-conscious furniture. Spacious retro kitchen, big-screen TV lounge, small courtyard, and late-night party room. Centrally located. Free breakfast. Free TV show tickets. Free lockers. Internet access. Car rental $20 per day. 6-bed dorms $20. Private rooms for up to 4 from $55. Dorms only accept international students with **passport** proof. ❷

**Hotel Claremont,** 1044 Tiverton Ave. (☎310-208-5957 or 800-266-5957), in Westwood Village near UCLA. Pleasant and inexpensive. Still owned by the same family that built it 60 years ago. Clean rooms, ceiling fans, and private baths. Fridge and microwave next to a pleasant Victorian-style TV lounge. Daily maid service. Reservations recommended, especially in June. Singles $50; doubles $56; 2 beds for up to 4 $65. ❸

**The Beverly Hills Reeves Hotel,** 120 S. Reeves Dr. (☎310-271-3006; www.bhreeves.com). Cheap stays are hard to come by in Beverly Hills, but this recently renovated mansion near Rodeo Dr. offers both budget and beauty. Rooms with A/C, TV, microwave, and fridge. Continental breakfast included. Rooms with shared bathrooms $50 per night, $250 per week. With private bathroom $69/$349. Parking $6. ❹

**Bevonshire Lodge Motel,** 7575 Beverly Blvd. (☎323-936-6154). Seconds from CBS Studios, the staff welcomes *The Price is Right* contestant hopefuls. A/C, mini-fridge, cable TV, daily maid service, outdoor pool, and parking. Singles and doubles $55-65; 5-person suites $70-80. King bed with kitchen for 2 $61-71. 10% ISIC discount. ❹

**The Little Inn,** 10604 Little Santa Monica Blvd. (☎310-475-4422). Right out of the movies, this classic motel offers well-furnished, color-coordinated rooms. A/C, cable TV, and fridges. Parking included. Check-out 11am. 1 bed (for up to 2) $50; 2 beds $55. $5 per extra person. During high season, expect prices to rise $5-10. Ask for weekly discounts. *Let's Go* readers get special rates Sept. 20-July 1 (excluding major holidays). ❸

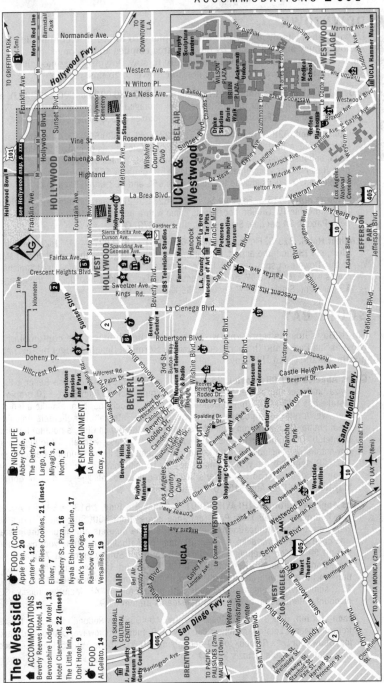

# The Westside

## ▲ ACCOMMODATIONS
Beverly Reeves Hotel, **15**
Bevonshire Lodge Motel, **13**
Hotel Claremont, **22 (Inset)**
The Little Inn, **18**
Orbit Hotel, **9**

## ● FOOD
Al Gelato, **14**
Apple Pan, **20**
Canter's, **12**
Diddie Riese Cookies, **21 (inset)**
Elixer, **7**
Mulberry St. Pizza, **16**
Nyala Ethiopian Cuisine, **17**
Pink's Hot Dogs, **10**
Rainbow Grill, **3**
Versailles, **19**

## ♪ NIGHTLIFE
Abbey Cafe, **6**
The Derby, **1**
Largo, **11**
Miyagi's, **2**
North, **5**

## ★ ENTERTAINMENT
LA Improv, **8**
Roxy, **4**

# DOWNTOWN

Downtown LA is probably not the best place to look for accommodations. Although busy and fairly safe by day, the area empties and becomes less safe at night. If you have an overwhelming desire to stay Downtown, some relatively affordable lodgings can be found. If possible, travel in groups.

**Days Inn Metro Plaza Hotel,** 711 N. Main St. (☎213-680-0200 or 800-223-2223), at Cesar Chavez Ave. near Union Station. Well managed with big, spotless rooms, TVs, fridges, and safes. Parking free. Singles $69; doubles $85. $10 per extra person. ❹

**Hotel Stillwell,** 838 S. Grand Ave. (☎213-627-1151 or 800-553-4774). Bustling and informal with a hostel feel, the Stillwell accommodates a lots of budget travelers. Low rates, in-house Indian and Mexican restaurants, and Hank's Bar. A/C. Parking $4 per day. Reservations recommended. Singles $56; doubles $67. Weekly singles $285; doubles $370. Prices include tax. Rooms are $51 and $63 with ISIC card. ❹

**Inntowne Hotel,** 913 S. Figueroa St. (☎213-628-2222). Clean and large rooms. Offers A/C and cable TV. Ground floor rooms come with a patio that opens onto an outdoor pool. Parking $4 per day. Singles $69; doubles $79. ❹

**Milner Hotel,** 813 S. Flower St. (☎213-627-6981 or 800-827-0411). Take the Prime Shuttle ($13) from the airport, bus, or train station, and get reimbursed when you stay at this Downtown spot near the Pantry restaurant (see p. 400). Small, well-furnished rooms with A/C, cable TV, and continental breakfast. Parking next door in the garage, $5 per night. Singles $60-70; doubles $80. ❹

# SOUTH BAY

South Bay's hostels represent two extremes in beach living: the contemplative roost at San Pedro and the party-going pad at Hermosa Beach. Budget motels pepper the Pacific Coast Highway.

**Los Angeles Surf City Hostel,** 26 Pier Ave. (☎798-2323), in Hermosa Beach's Pier Plaza, in the center of the local scene. Free airport pick-up 8am-8pm, $10 drop-off. Or take bus #439 to 11th and Hermosa St., walk 2 blocks north, and make a left on Pier Ave. A relaxed atmosphere with young, mostly international clientele enjoying the nightlife. On the bottom floor of the building is the Beach Club, a popular bar and nightclub. Discount car rentals, showers, Internet access, kitchen, TV lounge, and downstairs bar. Includes boogie boards, breakfast, and linen. Laundry. Key deposit $10. 28-night max. stay; 3-day max. stay for US citizens. No parking. Reservations recommended. Passport or driver's license required for all guests. 4-bunk dorms May-Nov. $19; Dec.-Apr. $15.50. Private rooms $48. ❷

**Los Angeles South Bay (HI-AYH),** 3601 S. Gaffey St., Bldg. #613 (☎831-8109), in San Pedro's in Angels Gate Park (entrance across from 36th St.). The 180-degree view from the hilltop location is unbeatable, but the quarters are simple; the hostel was once an army barracks. Kitchen, TV room, basketball court. Bring your own linen or rent for $2 (no sleeping bags allowed). Laundry. Strictly enforced 7-night max. stay. Parking included. Reception 7:30-11:30am and 1:30pm-midnight. Reservations in advance with credit card. 5-bed dorms for men, 16-bed dorms for women $21; semi-private rooms with 2-3 beds $23; private rooms $45. Members receive $3 discount. International or out-of-state residents preferred. ❷

**Moon Lite Inn,** 625 S. Pacific Coast Hwy. (☎540-4058), in Redondo Beach, 2 blocks from the ocean. Lots of amenities: cable TV, A/C, fridge, microwave, phone, and parking. Show your *Let's Go* book for a 1-bed rate of $50-65. 2 beds $65-85; king-sized bed with beautiful marble jacuzzis $95. ❹

# CAMPING

LA has no campgrounds convenient to public transportation. Even drivers face at least a 45min. commute from Downtown. One nearby LA County campground, **Leo Carrillo State Beach ❶** (☎805-488-5223), lies on Hwy. 1 (PCH), 20 mi. north of Malibu. It has 135 developed sites with flush toilets and showers ($13). Nearby **Point Mugu** has 57 sites at **Sycamore Canyon ❶** with flush toilets and showers ($13) and 75 primitive sites at the **Thornhill Broome ❶** area with chemical toilets and cold showers ($13). **Malibu Creek State Park ❶** (☎818-880-0367 for info), off Las Virgenes Rd., 6 mi. north of Hwy. 1, has over 50 sites with flush toilets and showers ($15).

# FOOD

Eating in Los Angeles, the city of the health-conscious, is more than just *eating*. Thin figures and fat wallets are a powerful combination—LA luxuriates in the most heavenly and healthy recipes. There are restaurants where the main objective is to be seen and the food is just a prop, and those where the food seems too beautiful to be eaten. And then there are those where the food just seems too *odd* to be called anything but California (con)Fusion. And though few are struck by the beauty of a wrapped burger, LA elevates fast food and chain restaurants to heights unknown. For the supreme burger-and-fries experience, try ▣In-N-Out Burger, a beloved chain symbolized by a '57 Chevy. **Mel's Diner** and **Johnny Rocket's** revive the never-really-lost era of the American diner; their milkshakes are a heady experience. All **Fatburgers** come with frank witticisms, free of charge. The current craze is lard- and cholesterol-free "healthy Mexican"—▣**Baja Fresh** leads the pack. Californians crave barbecue chicken pizza at **California Pizza Kitchen. Quizno's** reheats its fresh baked bread for sub lovers. Surfer meets Mexican at Hawaiian-born ▣**Wahoo's Fish Tacos** and **Rubio's Fresh Mexican Grill,** which flavors its fish tacos with a Baja California twist. Any Californian—North or South—will tell you that any time is a good time for a thick, cold fruit smoothie from ▣**Jamba Juice.** If you're looking to cook, ▣**Trader Joe's** specializes in budget gourmet food. They save by doing their own packaging and, as a result, amazing deals like $2.99 bottles of choice Napa wines abound. There are 74 locations in SoCal; call ☎800-SHOP-TJS/746-7857 to find the nearest one. (Most open daily 9am-9pm.)

Of course, food in LA isn't just about chain restaurants or California Cuisine. The expansive range of culinary options is a direct result of the city's ethnic diversity. Jewish and Eastern European food is most prevalent in Fairfax; Mexican in East LA; Japanese, Chinese, Korean, Vietnamese, and Thai around Little Tokyo, Chinatown, Koreatown, and Monterey Park; and seafood along the coast. Listings of **late-night** restaurants and cafes are on p. 439.

**MARKETS.** LA boasts enormous public markets which supply a variety of local foodstuffs and crafts. ▣**Farmer's Market,** 6333 W. 3rd St. at Fairfax Ave., attracts about 3 million people every year and has over 160 produce stalls, as well as international food booths, handicraft shops, souvenir stores, and a phenomenal juice bar. There's delectable produce, but bargains are becoming increasingly rare. You can also take lunch upstairs to the **Beverly Hills Art League Gallery** and munch among the paintings of local amateur artists. (☎323-933-9211; www.farmersmarketla.com. Open M-F 9am-9pm, Sat 9am-8pm, sun 10am-7pm.) A less touristy and less expensive source of produce is the **Grand Central Public Market,** 317 S. Broadway, a large building between 3rd and 4th St. in Downtown. Entrances are on both Broadway and Hill St. between 3rd and 4th St. Grand Central has more than 50 stands selling produce, clothing, housewares, costume jewelry, vitamins, and fast food. If you are around during Thanksgiving, be sure to vie for a frozen gobbler in the turkey giveaway. (☎213-624-2378. Open daily 9am-6pm.) Several smaller municipalities such as Santa Monica also have farmer's markets (see Santa Monica food section, p. 396).

# FOOD BY TYPE

**AFRICAN**
Nyala Ethiopian Cuisine (400) — WS ❷

**AMERICAN/GRILLS**
☒ Aunt Kizzy's Back Porch (398) — VN ❸
☒ The Bungalow Club (395) — HW ❷
Chez Jay (396) — SM ❹
Duke's Malibu (398) — MB ❸
Hennessy's Tavern (403) — SB ❸
Holly Street Bar and Grill (402) — PS ❹
Tony P's Dockside Grill (398) — VN ❹

**ARGENTINE**
Carlitos Gardel (395) — HW ❷

**BREAKFAST**
Bread and Porridge (396) — SM ❷
☒ Duke's Coffee Shop (395) — HW ❷
☒ The Griddle Cafe (395) — HW ❷
Roscoe's Chicken & Waffles (395) — HW ❷

**BURGERS, ETC.**
The Apple Pan (400) — WS ❷
Big Daddy's (398) — VN ❶
Big Dean's "Muscle-In" Cafe (396) — SM ❶
☒ Fair Oaks Pharmacy (402) — PS ❷
Pink's Hot Dog Stand (395) — HW ❶

**CHINESE**
Chin Chin (395) — BH ❷
Xi'an (399) — BH ❷

**CONTINENTAL/EUROPEAN**
Gypsy Cafe (400) — WS ❷
Lilly's (398) — VN ❹
Pita! Pita! (402) — PS ❷

**CUBAN**
Versailles (400) — WS ❸

**DELIS AND SANDWICHES**
Cafe Dolcini (401) — DT ❶
Healthy 4-U (396) — SM ❶
Malibu Chicken (398) — MB ❷
Nate 'n Al Delicatessen (399) — BH ❸

☒ Rose Cafe and Market (398) — SM ❷
Sandbag's Sandwiches (399) — WS ❷
The Sandwich Joint (403) — SB ❷

**DINER**
Johnny Rocket's (393) — WS ❷
☒ The Pantry (400) — DT ❷
Philippe, The Original (400) — DT ❶

**ITALIAN**
☒ Al Gelato (399) — BH ❶
☒ Fritto Misto (396) — SM ❷
Miceli's (402) — BU ❸
Mulberry Street Pizzeria (399) — BH ❶
Zucca Ristorante (401) — DT ❹

**LATE-NIGHT**
Barney's Beanery (439) — HW
Bob's Big Boy (439) — BU
☒ Canter's (439) — WS
☒ Fred 62 (439) — HW
Jerry's Famous Deli (439) — WH
The Kettle (440) — SB
Mel's Drive In (439) — WH
☒ The Rainbow Bar and Grill (439) — WH

**MEXICAN**
☒ Baja Fresh (393) — WS ❶
La Luz Del Dia (401) — DT ❷
Rubio's Mexican Grill (393) — WS ❶
Topper's Restaurant/Cantina (396) — SM ❸
☒ Wahoo's Fish Tacos (402) — SB ❷

**SEAFOOD**
Mariasol (396) — SM ❸
Neptune's Net Seafood (398) — MB ❷
Reel Inn (396) — SM ❸

**SWEETS**
☒ Diddie Riese Cookies (399) — WS ❶

**VEGETARIAN**
Native Foods (400) — WS ❷
The Spot (403) — SB ❷
Sprout (395) — WH ❷

**BH** Beverly Hills **BU** Burbank **DT** Downtown **HW** Hollywood **MB** Malibu **PS** Pasadena **SB** South Bay **SM** Santa Monica **VN** Venice **WH** West Hollywood **WS** Westside

# HOLLYWOOD

Screenwriters and starlets still looking for their big break constitute much of Hollywood's population. Most are single, hungry, and nearly broke. As a result, Hollywood offers the best budget dining in LA. As an added bonus, if you're in the right place at the right time, you may see celebrities chowing on the same lunch special as yours. **Hollywood** and **Sunset Boulevards** have excellent international cuisine, while **Fairfax Avenue** hosts Mediterranean-style restaurants and kosher delis. **Melrose Avenue** is full of chic cafes, many with outdoor people-watching patios. As Hollywood is the heart of LA's pounding nightlife, many of its best restaurants are open around the clock (see **Late-Night Restaurants,** p. 439).

■ **The Griddle Cafe,** 7916 Sunset Blvd. (☎323-874-0377), in West Hollywood. One of the most popular brunch spots on the strip, the Griddle prides itself on its breakfast food creativity. Especially popular are the "Apple Cobbler French Toast" ($6.95) and "Black Magic" (Oreo crumb-filled flapjacks; $6.95). Consider sharing the enormous portions. A 45min. wait is not uncommon on weekends. Open M-F 7am-3pm, Sa-Su 8am-3pm. ❷

■ **Duke's Coffee Shop,** 8909 Sunset Blvd. (☎310-652-3100), in West Hollywood. Legendary Duke's is the best place to see hungry, hungover rockers slumped over in the communal, canteen-style tables. The walls are plastered with autographed album covers. Try "Sandy's Favorite" (green peppers, potatoes, and scrambled eggs) for $7.25. Entrees $5-11. Attendant parking $1. Open M-F 7:30am-8:30pm, Sa-Su 8am-3:30pm. ❷

■ **The Bungalow Club,** 7174 Melrose Ave. (☎323-964-9494; www.thebungalowclubla.com), 1block west of La Brea Ave. Two waterfalls and a candlelit tropical dining room offer a romantic oasis. The large dining patio features 6 private bungalows; pull down the sheets and lock yourself in. Free live jazz in summer (M 8pm). Free, live comedy shows featuring comedians from Letterman, Leno, BET, and Comedy Central entertain customers in the upstairs ballroom throughout the year. Appetizers $5-9; entrees $7-13. Open 11am-11pm daily. Dinner reservations recommended. ❷

**Roscoe's House of Chicken and Waffles,** 1514 Gower St. (☎323-466-7453), at the corner of Gower and Sunset Blvd. The down-home feel and all-day menu make this a popular spot for regular folk and celebs alike. Try "1 succulent chicken breast and 1 delicious waffle" ($6.90). Be prepared to wait (30-60min.) on weekends. Open Su-Th 8:30am-midnight, F-Sa 8:30am-4am. Other location at 5006 W. Pico Blvd, LA. ❷

**Pink's Hot Dog Stand,** 709 N. La Brea Ave. (☎323-931-4223; www.pinksholly-wood.com), at Melrose. A hot dog stand institution since 1939, Pink's serves up chili-slathered happiness in a bun. The aroma of meaty chili and freshly-cooked dogs draws crowds far into the night. Rumor has it that Pink's played host to Sean Penn's marriage proposal to Madonna. Try the special "Ozzy Osbourne Spicy Dog" for $5. Chili dogs $2.40; chili fries $2.20. Open Su-Th 9:30am-2am, F-Sa 9:30am-3am. Cash only. ❶

**Chin Chin,** 8618 Sunset Blvd. (☎310-652-1818; www.chinchin.com), in West Hollywood. Other locations in Brentwood, Beverly Hills, Universal City Walk, Marina del Rey, and Encino. Sunglassed celebrities lounge on the patio. Extremely popular with lunchtime crowds for its handmade "dim sum and then sum" ($11.75). Chinese chicken salad ($9) is the sort of Chinese-Californian cuisine befitting a restaurant whose name means "to your health." Open daily 11am-11pm. ❷

**Sprout,** 8410 Sunset Blvd. (☎323-848-2195), in West Hollywood. Centrally located, this trendy vegetarian and vegan cafe is extremely popular during lunchtime and regularly attracts celebrities. At night, customers are often dressed to the nines, having come from the nightclubs. Try the filling Down South Meatless Loaf ($10) or the Flawless Falafel Burger ($8). Open Su-F 10am-11pm, Sa 10am-2am. ❷

**Carlitos Gardel,** 7963 Melrose Ave. (☎323-655-0891; www.carlitosgardel.com), 1½ blocks west of Fairfax Ave. Argentine restaurant with Italian flair. Its bread is accompanied with a chimichurri sauce so addictive, you'll want to hunt down the packaged bottles at the market. Try the signature "Papas Fritas Provenzal" ($6) or "Ojo de Costilla a la Criolla," a ribeye steak marinated in the chimichurri ($28). Open M-F 11:30am-2:30pm and 6-11pm, Sa 6-11pm, Su 5-10pm. Dinner reservations recommended. ❸

## SANTA MONICA

Giant, colorful table umbrellas sprouting from sidewalk patios along Third St.
Promenade and Ocean Ave. punctuate Santa Monica's upscale eating scene. Most
side streets have equally good food. Menus give a nod to (deep-pocketed) health
buffs by offering organic and vegetarian choices.

**Fritto Misto,** 601 Colorado Ave. (☎310-458-2829), at 6th St. "Neighborhood Italian
Cafe" with cheery waitstaff lets you create your own pasta ($6+). Vegetarian entrees
$8-12. Daily hot pasta specials $8. Weekend lunch special of all-you-can-eat calamari
and salad $12. Omelettes Su 11:30am-4pm ($7-8). Open M-Th 11:30am-10pm, F-Sa
11:30am-10:30pm, Su 11:30am-9:30pm. ❷

**Healthy 4-U Cafe,** 130 Colorado Ave. (☎310-394-2189), between Ocean Ave. and
Main St. This small, family-owned cafe serves only the freshest lunch foods. Sandwiches $6, freshly squeezed juices $2, smoothies $4. Ask Rosanna, the owner, about
the book of poetry she is completing. Open M-Sa 10am-5pm. ❶

**Big Dean's "Muscle-In" Cafe,** 1615 Ocean Front Walk (☎310-393-2666). When on the
beach or pier and craving a beach burger, don't go far for the management-proclaimed
"burger that made Santa Monica famous" ($5.75). Veggie burgers $4.75. Happy Hour
M-F 4-8pm with $2 domestic beers. Open M-F 10am-dark, Sa-Su 10:30am-dark, or until
the everybody-knows-your-name regulars empty out. ❶

**Toppers Restaurant and Cantina,** 1111 2nd St. (☎310-393-8080), sits 23 stories high
atop the landmark Radisson Huntley Hotel. Ride the glass elevator just inside the 2nd
St. entrance up to "R" (for Restaurant) for one of the best views of the ocean and Santa
Monica foothills. Happy Hour at the bar daily 4:30-7:30pm, with $6 margaritas and $2
appetizers. Mostly Mexican entrees $12-17. Open M-Th 6:30am-11:30pm, F-Su
6:30am-12:30am. Kitchen closes 1hr. before restaurant. ❸

**Mariasol,** 401 Santa Monica Pier (☎310-917-5050). Prime sunset views from the westward tip of the Santa Monica Pier accompany your meal in the glass-enclosed dining
room. Locals recommend the "campechana," a combination of shrimp, octopus
calamari, and ceviche ($12). Appetizers $6-10, entrees $9-15. Open Su-Th 10am-
10pm, F-Sa 10am-11pm. Reservations recommended for 2nd floor dining room. ❸

**Reel Inn,** 1220 Third St. Promenade (☎310-395-5538). Right on the popular tourist
strip, the Inn reels in fresh fish from all over the world, including Hawaii, New Zealand,
and the Pacific Northwest. Long, communal tables and outdoor seating. Tasmanian
salmon and Chilean swordfish are specialties ($10-14). Beer $3-4. Open Su-Th
11:30am-9:30pm, F-Sa 11:30am-10:30pm. ❸

**Bread & Porridge,** 2315 Wilshire Blvd. (☎310-453-4941). This all-day breakfast and lunch (after 11am) spot prides itself on an egalitarian division of
labor—dishwashers, busboys, servers, cashiers, and cooks all rotate jobs and
share in the daily tips. Exceptional service and pancakes—banana, strawberry,
chocolate chip, blueberry, pecan, and mixed 4-stack pancakes ($5.55-6.55).
Omelettes $9. Sandwiches and entrees $7-12. Oatmeal $4.55. Open M-F 7am-
2pm, Sa-Su 7am-3pm. ❷

**Chez Jay,** 1657 Ocean Ave. (☎310-395-1741), in Santa Monica. This 43-year-old establishment is a "celebrity hideaway" serving classic but pricey dishes. Jay, the owner,
mugs for the camera on his old-school movie posters. Steak and seafood $17-21. Open
M-F noon-1am, Sa-Su 9am-1am. Reservations recommended. ❹

## VENICE & MARINA DEL REY

Venetian cuisine runs the gamut from greasy to ultra-healthy, as befits its beachy-
hippie crowd. The boardwalk has cheap snacks in the fast food vein. Hit up boardwalk cafes and restaurants during Happy Hour for specials on food and drink.

## Where the famous stars boozed, binged, and blacked out.

3ogart. Sinatra. Hepburn. Gable. Monroe. The greatest livers of a generation were destroyed here. Those who say L.A. has no sense of history need look no further than bottom of their cocktail glass at these ven-ble (and still standing) Old Hollywood bars. e's looking at you, kid!

**ney's Beanery,** 8447 Santa Monica Blvd. 323-654-2287), in West Hollywood. Some it hot—especially Marilyn Monroe. While aing the picture of the same name, she'd o in for chili. Odd, because this rough-and-ble Rte. 66 roadhouse is more suited to is Joplin, who partied here the night she d. Expect an excellent jukebox, 50-cent l, and several hundred kinds of beer. py hour M-F 4-7pm. Open daily 11am-2am.

**z Jay,** 1657 Ocean Ave. (☎310-395-1741), in ta Monica. A tiny, crusty beachside dive :ooned with Christmas lights, red check ecloths, and pictures of Sinatra. Why not? Blue Eyes dented the red vinyl here regu-y in his day. Now, slip into the crowd of tstside types too "real" to go to a martini bar order up some Jack Daniels—the Chair-a's favorite. Open M-F 6pm-2am, Sa-Su pm-2am.

**ch & Horses Pub,** 7617 W. Sunset Blvd. 323-876-6900), in Hollywood. A dark, tiny ye e hole in the wall where Richard Burton d to start his benders. If you feel like fol-ing suit, start early on a weekday. On F and ights the hipsters invade, armed with apple tinis and leather pants. Open M-Sa 11am-, Su 5pm-2am.

**Gallery Bar at the Biltmore Hotel,** 506 S. nd Ave. (☎213-612-1532), in Downtown . Glide into wood-paneled elegance, sip a tini, and wonder what really happened to Black Dahlia. This was, after all, the last :e aspiring starlet Beth Short (nicknamed her pin-up quality black dresses) was seen e. Back in 1947, a doorman tipped his cap er and five days later, her severed body

made her the most famous victim of an unsolved murder case in city history. Open daily 4:30pm-1:45am.

**Formosa Cafe,** 7156 Santa Monica Blvd. (☎323-850-9050), in Hollywood. This Suzy Wong boite is equal parts black lacquer and 8"x10" glossies. The more than 250 star headshots plastering the walls are rumored to have been dropped off in person. Cozy up in a booth like Lana Turner used to (*L.A. Confidential* wasn't kidding—she really did hang out here) and drink all you want, but avoid the greasy "Chinese" food at all costs. Open M-F 4pm-2am, Sa-Su 6pm-2am.

**Musso & Frank Grill,** 6667 Hollywood Blvd. (☎323-467-7788), in Hollywood. Where Bogie boozed, Sinatra swilled and Bukowski blew his cash in later, more affluent years. The drinks ain't cheap, but oh, what ambience! Honeyed light, high-backed booths and curmudgeonly red-jacketed waiters. The martini is hands-down the city's best, but if you want something different, try a gimlet. Bar denizen Raymond Chandler immor-talized Musso's gin and lime juice concoctions in "The Long Goodbye." Open Tu-Sa 11am-10:45pm.

**The Polo Lounge at the Beverly Hills Hotel,** 9641 Sunset Blvd. (☎310-276-2251), in Beverly Hills. Where the loudest thing is the pink paint on the walls. Ask to be seated in the patio section, order up a Singapore Sling, and dream about the days when Kate Hepburn and Marlene Dietrich held court here. Come F mornings and see why this place coined the term "power breakfast"—tables on the outer edge of the ter-race are a classic place for movie deals to be struck. Open daily 7am-1am.

**Trader Vic's at the Beverly Hilton Hotel,** 9876 Wilshire Blvd. (☎310-274-7777), in Beverly Hills. A dim, linen tablecloth tiki bar that George Hamilton allegedly singled out as a great place for celebrity affairs owing to its two entrances, or rather, two exits. The house cocktails' $10 price tags are more than made up for in presentation—the pina colada is served in a whole pineapple; a floating gardenia graces the gin-laced scorpion bowl. Open Su-Th 5pm-2am, F-Sa 5pm-1am.

hanie L. Smith was a researcher-writer for *Let's Go: California 1997* and *New Zealand 1998*. She worked freelancer for CitySearch Los Angeles, reviewing restaurants, bars, and attractions, and is now working in Hollywood as the features editor/writer for the online division of Channel One News.

■ **Rose Cafe and Market,** 220 Rose Ave. (☎310-399-0711), at Main St. Gigantic walls painted with roses, local art, industrial architecture, and a gift shop might make you think this is a museum, but the colorful cuisine is the main display. Healthy deli specials, including sandwiches ($6-8) and salads ($6-8) available from 11:30am. Limited menu after 3pm. Open M-F 7am-5:30pm, Sa 8am-6pm, Su 8am-5pm. ❷

■ **Aunt Kizzy's Back Porch,** 4325 Glencoe Ave. (☎310-578-1005), in a huge strip mall at Glencoe Ave. and Mindanao Way in Marina Del Rey. A little slice of Southern heaven, offering specialties like Cousin Willie Mae's smothered pork chops with cornbread and veggies. Save room for sweet potato pie ($3). Dinner $12-13. All-you-can-eat brunch buffet $13 (Su 11am-3pm). Open Su-Th 11am-9pm, F-Sa 11am-11pm. ❸

**Sidewalk Cafe,** 1401 Ocean Front Walk (☎310-399-5547), just north of Windward St. A

---

# TOURING THE BURGER KINGDOM

Los Angeles has spawned many tasteless trends, but few realize that it's also the birthplace of perhaps the world's farthest-sweeping trend, one guaranteed to leave a curious taste in your mouth: good ol' American fast food. Unlikely as it sounds, this obsessively health-conscious city spawned some of the nation's greasiest, most cholesterol-packed grub. An international synonym for fast food, **McDonald's** was founded by Angeleno brothers Richard and Maurice McDonald in 1937 (serving, incidentally, hot dogs only). The oldest standing golden arches still glow proudly at 10807 Lakewood Blvd. in Downey, with walk-up rather than drive-thru service. A small museum pays tribute to the oldest operating franchise in the world. (The brothers granted Ray Kroc exclusive US franchising rights.) Home to the original double-decker hamburger, the oldest **Bob's Big Boy,** 4211 Riverside Dr. (☎818-843-9334), in Burbank, still looks as sleek and streamlined as the day it opened in 1949. Check out the car-hop service (Sa-Su 5-10pm). **Carl's Jr.** started off as a Downtown hot dog stand at Florence and Central Ave. in 1941. **Denny's** and doughnut joint **Winchell's** also got their start in the fast-food fertile LA Basin.

---

large capacity and prominent Boardwalk location attracts crowds. Regulars recommend the Timothy Leary (mushroom and avocado cheeseburger; $8.50). Big social bar. Happy Hour $2 pints, $3 appetizers. Open Su-Th 8am-midnight, F-Sa 8am-1am. ❷

**Lilly's,** 1031 Abbot Kinney Blvd. (☎310-314-0004). Classy French cafe and bar with beautiful outdoor garden. Walls decorated with Pollock-esque local art. $10 lunch and Su brunch specials. Have creme brulee for dessert ($6). Entrees $16-22. Lunch M-Sa noon-2:30pm, Su brunch 11am-2:30pm. Dinner M-Th 6-10pm, F-Sa 6-10:30pm. ❹

**Big Daddy's,** 1425 Ocean Front Walk (☎310-396-4146), across Market Ave. Surfboard tables and Beach Boys tunes make this the ultimate beach food shack. The grillmasters serve up everything the heart desires but knows it shouldn't. $1 menu includes hot dogs, pizza, vanilla ice cream, fries, and more. Burgers from $4. Fried everything (zucchini $4; calamari $4). Churros from an authentic Mexican machine with chocolate, strawberry, or caramel sauce center ($4). Open M-F 11am-dark, Sa-Su 9am-dark. ❶

**Tony P's Dockside Grill,** 4445 Admiralty Way (☎310-823-4534), in Marina del Rey. Pleasant marina views enhance the steak and seafood fare. Tavern walls are covered with framed and signed sports paraphernalia, TVs turned to the day's sport games, and over 400 beer taps. Lunch entrees $7-9, dinner entrees $10-22. Martinis shaken at your table ($7). Open M-Th 11:30am-10pm, F 11:30am-11pm, Sa 9am-11pm, Su 9am-10pm. Reservations recommended. ❹

# MALIBU

Cheap eats are hard to come by at Malibu's shoreside restaurants, which charge as much for their view as for their food. **Malibu Chicken ❷,** 22935 PCH, downstairs from Malibu Ocean Sports (see p. 410), has sandwiches named after old beach-movie idols, like "Gidget" (grilled chicken breast; $8) and "Big Kahuna" (chicken breast, eggplant, and feta; $8). The "Dora" (2 chickens, 4 large sides, salad, and bread; $29) could feed a family. (☎310-456-0365. Open daily 11:30am-9pm.) **Duke's Malibu ❸**, 21150 PCH, at Las Flores Canyon Rd., has walls that tell the history of surfing and serves reasonably priced fare in its "Barefoot Bar," where you can sit with your feet in the sand and watch the Pacific pound the cliffs. You can't go wrong with the parmesan and herb-crusted fish ($12). Entrees ($8-20) are half-price during Happy Hour M-F 4-7pm. (☎310-317-0777; www.hulapie.com. No food served 3-5pm. Barefoot bar open M-Th 11:30am-9:30pm, F-Sa 11:30am-10:30pm, Su 10am-9:30pm.) If you don't mind driving a few minutes north, make your way to **Neptune's Net Seafood ❷**, 42505 PCH, a friendly, lively restaurant known for some of the best seafood in Malibu for cheap ($8-10). It's biker heaven on weekends. (☎310-457-3095. Open M-Th 10:30am-8pm, F 10:30am-9pm, Sa-Su 10am-8:30pm.)

## BEVERLY HILLS

Yes, there is budget dining in Beverly Hills—it just takes a little looking to find it. An important tip: do not eat on Rodeo Dr. and stay south of Wilshire Blvd.

**Al Gelato,** 806 S. Robertson Blvd. (☎310-659-8069), between Wilshire and Olympic St. Popular among the theater crowd, this homemade gelato spot also does large portions of pasta with a delicious basil tomato sauce. Giant meatball ($4.75) and rigatoni ($11). For desert, stick to the famous gelato ($3.75-5.75) and made-to-order cannoli ($4.50). Open Su, Tu, Th 10am-midnight, F-Sa 10am-1am. No credit cards. ❶

**Nate 'n Al Delicatessen,** 414 N. Beverly Dr. (☎310-274-0101; www.natenal.com), near Little Santa Monica Blvd. For 55 years, this delicatessen has been serving up hand-pressed latkes (potato pancakes; $8.75), blintzes ($9), and Reuben sandwiches ($11.50). The waitresses wear pink pinstripes and there's a bottle of Hebrew National Deli Mustard on every table. Open daily 7am-9pm. ❸

**Mulberry Street Pizzeria,** 240 S. Beverly Dr. (☎310-247-8100) and 347 N. Canon Dr. in Beverly Hills. Great pizza by the slice is hard to come by in LA, which makes this pizzeria all the more exceptional; the wide, flat pizza is among the best anywhere. Everything from veggie to tomato and eggplant. Slice $2.50-4, whole pies $15-26. Open Su-W 11am-11pm, Th-Sa 11am-12pm. ❶

**Xi'an,** 362 N. Canon Dr. (☎310-275-3345), north of Wilshire Blvd. Affordable but top-notch contemporary Chinese cuisine in the heart of LA's ritziest shopping district. Entrees $9-13, but prices drop significantly for the lunch special. Open M-F 11:30am-10pm, Sa 11:30am-11pm, Su 5-10pm. ❷

## WESTWOOD & UCLA

Westwood Village, the triangular area just south of the University of California at Los Angeles (UCLA) and bordered by Weyburn, Glendon, and Broxton, caters to the tens of thousands of students who live in the area. Westwood overflows with good buys and beer. If you're down to your last few bucks, head to **Jose Bernstein's ❶**, 935 Broxton Ave., for $4 burritos. (Open Su-Th 11am-1am, F-Sa 10am-2:30am.)

**Sandbag's Gourmet Sandwiches,** 1134 Westwood Blvd. (☎310-208-1133), in Westwood. Other locations at 11640 San Vicente Blvd. (☎310-207-4888), in Brentwood, and 9497 Santa Monica Blvd. (☎310-786-7878), in Beverly Hills. A healthy, cheap lunch comes with a complimentary chocolate cookie. Try the "Sundowner" (turkey, herb stuffing, lettuce, and cranberries). Sandwiches $5.75. Open daily 9am-4pm. ❷

**Diddie Riese Cookies,** 926 Broxton Ave. (☎310-208-0448). Cookies baked from scratch every day. Popular late-night spot. Well worth the wait for a $1 ice cream and cookie sandwich. $1 also buys you 2 cookies and milk, juice, or coffee. Open M-Th 10am-midnight, F 10am-1am, Sa noon-1am, Su noon-midnight. ❶

**Gypsy Cafe,** 940 Broxton Ave. (☎310-824-2119), next to Diddie Riese. Modeled after a sister spot in Paris, this cafe's fare is more Italian than French (penne cacciatore $8.25), and its mood is more Turkish than Italian (hookahs for rent, $10 per hr.). Don't expect quick service unless you order takeout at the counter—the elegant atmosphere encourages customers to linger. The buffet is bountiful, but the hookah smoke might not appeal to some. Mediterranean kabobs $9. The tomato soup ($5) is famous throughout Westwood. Beer $3.50-4.50, wine $4.50. Open Su-Th 7am-2am, F-Sa 7am-3am. ❷

**Native Foods,** 1110½ Gayley Ave. (☎310-209-1055; www.nativefoods.com). A vegan eatery in Westwood. Order at the counter and fight for a seat. Locals love the "jerk burger with guacomole" ($7) and the "moby dick" ($7). Open daily 11am-10pm. ❷

# WILSHIRE DISTRICT

The Wilshire District's eateries are sadly out of step with its world-class museums. Inexpensive (and often kosher) restaurants dot Fairfax Ave. and Pico Blvd., but health nuts should stay away—there's no keeping cholesterol down in these parts.

**Nyala Ethiopian Cuisine,** 1076 S. Fairfax Ave. (☎323-936-5918), two blocks south of Olympic Blvd. The Fairfax area is known for its kosher delis, but it's also the backbone of LA's Ethiopian community. Nyala combines traditional African influences with LA's hip atmosphere, but as far as the food goes, there's no fusion—just large plates of spongy crepe *(injera)* topped with spicy stews (lunch $7.50, dinner $10.50). The vegetarian lunch buffet (M-F 11:30am-3pm) is a steal at $5.35. Open M-Th 11:30am-11pm, F 11:30am-2am, Sa noon-2am, Su noon-midnight. ❷

**Versailles,** 1415 S. La Cienega Blvd. (☎310-289-0302). Another location at 10319 Venice Blvd. Hidden in a mass of stores, this is Cuban food at its best. Family-oriented and always crowded. Appetizers $3; entrees $8-15; lunch specials (M-F 11am-3pm) $4-7. Open Su-Th 11am-10pm, F-Sa 11am-11pm. ❸

**The Apple Pan,** 10801 W. Pico Blvd. (☎310-475-3585), 1 block east of Westwood Blvd. across from the Westside Pavilion. Suburban legend has it that *Beverly Hills 90210*'s Peach Pit was modeled after The Apple Pan, so lean on the white counter and make like the 90210 crew. Famous original apple pies $4, hickory-smoked burgers $5-6, fries $2. Open Su and Tu-Th 11am-midnight, F-Sa 11am-1am. No credit cards. ❷

# DOWNTOWN

Financial District eateries vie for the businessperson's coveted lunchtime dollar. Their secret weapon is the lunch special, but finding a reasonably priced dinner can be a challenge. (It may not be a good idea to stick around that late, anyway.)

⚑ **Philippe, The Original,** 1001 N. Alameda St. (☎213-628-3781; www.philippes.com), 2 blocks north of Union Station. A long-time fixture of Downtown, Philippe's is one of the most popular lunch eateries. The invention of the French Dip sandwich occurred in 1918 when Philippe allegedly dropped a sliced French roll into a roasting pan filled with juice still hot from the oven. The policeman Philippe served loved the dipped sandwich so much, he showed up the next day with a dozen cop buddies requesting the same. Choose from pork, beef, ham, turkey ($4.40), or lamb ($4.70). Top it off with pie ($2.65) and coffee (9¢—no, that's not a typo). Free parking. Open daily 6am-10pm. ❶

⚑ **The Pantry,** 877 S. Figueroa St. (☎213-972-9279). Since 1924, it hasn't closed once—not for the earthquakes, not for the '92 riots (when it served as a National Guard outpost), and not even when a taxicab punched through the front wall. There aren't even locks on the doors. Owned by former LA mayor Richard Riordan. Diner-like atmosphere. Known for its large portions, free cole slaw, and fresh sourdough bread. Giant breakfast specials $6. Lunch sandwiches $8. Open 24hr. No credit cards. ❷

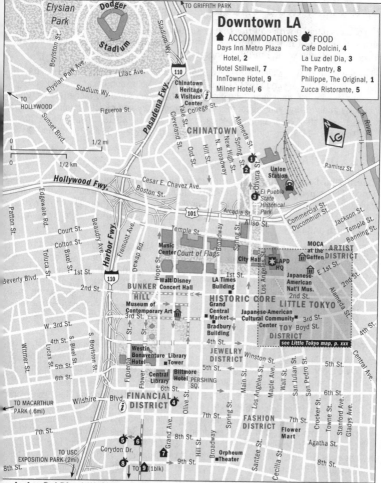

## Downtown LA

**⌂ ACCOMMODATIONS**

Days Inn Metro Plaza Hotel, **2**
Hotel Stillwell, **7**
InnTowne Hotel, **9**
Milner Hotel, **6**

**🍴 FOOD**

Cafe Dolcini, **4**
La Luz del Dia, **3**
The Pantry, **8**
Philippe, The Original, **1**
Zucca Ristorante, **5**

**La Luz Del Dia,** 1 W. Olvera St. (☎213-628-7495), tucked inside El Pueblo Historic Park along the circular walking path, this family-run Mexican restaurant provides an authentic eating experience. The park's trees and performance artists are a nice complement to the great food. Though most customers are Spanish-speaking, the owners are friendly and bilingual. Specialties are the homemade tortillas, tacos, and rice and beans ($5-6). Open Tu-Th 11am-9pm, F 11am-10pm, Sa 10am-10pm, Su 8:30am-10pm. ❷

**Zucca Ristorante,** 801 S. Figueroa St. (☎213-614-7800), in the Financial District. This classy and upscale restaurant is very popular among the downtown business set. Anti-pasti $9-13. Pasta $15-18. Fish $18-20. Open Su-Th 5pm-9pm, F-Sa 5pm-10pm. ❹

**Cafe Dolcini,** 619 S. Grand Ave. (☎213-624-4007), at the corner of Grand and Wilshire. A friendly sandwich joint with a selection of dirt-cheap lunch eats (turkey, ham and cheese, veggie, or roast beef $4). Best to place sandwich orders by phone during lunch hours. Wash it all down with a smoothie ($3). Open daily 7am-5:30pm. ❶

## SAN FERNANDO VALLEY

Burbank is packed with eateries that are in turn often packed with stars and celebrities in search of lunch. The rules of star-gazing dictate that you can stare and envy them all you want, but don't bother them or ask for autographs.

**Miceli's,** 3655 W. Cahuenga Blvd. (☎323-851-3344), in Universal City, and 1646 N. Las Palmas in Hollywood (☎323-466-3438). From Hollywood Blvd., go north on Highland Ave., which turns into Cahuenga. Would-be actors serenade dinner guests. Don't worry about losing your appetite during the Broadway and cabaret numbers—waiters must pass strict vocal auditions. Pizza, pizza, or lasagna $8-15. Open M-Th 11:30am-11pm, F-Sa 11:30am-midnight, Su 3-11pm. Lunch served M-Sa 11:30am-3pm. ❸

## PASADENA

Eateries line **Colorado Boulevard** from Los Robles Ave. to Orange Grove Blvd. in Old Town. The concentration of restaurants and sights around Colorado Blvd. make it Pasadena's answer to Santa Monica's Third St. Promenade. From Downtown, take I-110 north (Pasadena Fwy). In Pasadena, I-110 turns into the Arroyo Pkwy. Continue north and take a right onto Colorado Blvd.

**◪ Fair Oaks Pharmacy and Soda Fountain,** 1516 Mission St. (☎626-799-1414), at Fair Oaks Ave. in South Pasadena. From Colorado Blvd., go south 1 mi. on Fair Oaks Ave. to Mission St. This old-fashioned drug store, with soda fountain and lunch counter, has been serving travelers on Rte. 66 since 1915; now, a bit of Pasadena's upscale boutique flavor has crept in. Hand-dipped shakes and malts $4.25. Deli sandwiches $5.50. Patty melts $6. Soda fountain open M-F 9am-9pm, Sa 9am-10pm, Su 11am-8pm; lunch counter open M-F 11am-9pm, Sa 11am-10pm, Su 11am-8pm. ❷

**Pita! Pita!,** 927 E. Colorado Blvd. (☎626-356-0106), one block east of Lake Ave. Never has the pita deserved so many exclamation points. Free appetizers of green olives, yellow pepper, and tasty toasted pita. Spicy chicken pita $6. Lamb kebab $6. Open Su-Th 11am-9pm, F-Sa 11am-10pm. Street parking. ❷

**Holly Street Bar & Grill,** 175 E. Holly St. (☎626-440-1421), between Marengo St. and Arroyo Pkwy. From Colorado Blvd., go two blocks north on Marengo. Contemporary eatery with choice of seating in the peaceful garden or leopard-printed indoors. Live jazz complements the elegant dining experience on F and Sa nights (7pm), and live classical guitar at Su brunch (10:30am). Salads $9. Entrees $8-22. Full bar. Beer $3.50-4, cocktails $6. Open M 11am-2pm, Tu-Th 11am-2pm and 4:30-9:30pm, F-Sa 11am-2pm and 4:30-10pm, Su 10am-2:30pm and 4:30-9pm. Bar may stay open later. ❹

## SOUTH BAY

Each South Bay community offers more quality restaurants than you will have time to taste-test. Restaurants on the water may offer good views of both beach and beachgoers, but many popular food joints also lie a block or two inland.

**◪ Wahoo's Fish Tacos,** 1129 Manhattan Ave. (☎796-1044), in Manhattan Beach. Opened in 1988 by 2 Hawaiian surfers, the Wahoo family now comprises 28 stores stretching out to Colorado. Each funky shack pays homage to surfing with a non-stop surfing video, decal stickers, and surfing posters plastered over its counters and plywood walls. Famous for cheap, flavorful Mexican grub. 2 tacos or enchiladas (fish, chicken, steak, or vegetarian) with a large plate of beans and rice for only $5. Many swear by the teriyaki steak Maui Bowl ($7). Mug of Ono Ale for $2. Twenty-five locations in Southern California. Open M-Sa 11am-10pm, Su 11am-9pm. ❷

**Pasadena**

🍎 FOOD
Fair Oaks Pharmacy &
  Soda Fountain, **6**
Holly St. Bar & Grill, **1**
Pita! Pita!, **3**

🍸 NIGHTLIFE
Q's Billiard Club, **4**
Twin Palms, **5**

⭐ ENTERTAINMENT
The Ice House, **2**

**Hennessy's Tavern**, 8 Pier Ave, (☎372-5759), in Hermosa Beach. Located just where the concrete meets the sand, this restaurant and bar offers the best sunset views in South Bay, especially from the 2nd floor deck. 3 full bars all day. Sandwiches $6-9, entrees $10-18. Fantastic and unique specials include 2-for-1 Tuesdays and Luck of the Irish on Wednesdays (flip an Irish coin; if you call it correctly, any Irish meal is free). Saturdays after 5pm, dinner comes with a free martini. Happy Hour M-F 4-7pm with $3 beers. Open daily 7am-2am. Kitchen closes at 12:30am. ❸

**The Spot**, 110 2nd St. (☎376-2355; www.worldfamousspot.com), in Hermosa Beach. Opened in 1977, this is one of the oldest vegetarian restaurants in the LA area, and still a favorite with the resident New Age population. Turn a blind eye to the vinyl floral tablecloths and concentrate on the fat-free, non-dairy-based menu and outdoor garden. Tempeh, tofu, and tahini entrees hit the spot. Homemade bread and desserts $3.50. "Inflation buster" combos $5-7. Open daily 11am-10pm. ❷

**The Sandwich Joint**, 936 Hermosa Ave. (☎372-9276), in Hermosa Beach, three blocks south of the Pier. Superb sandwiches served on foot-long baguettes. Choose from turkey, ham, roast beef, salami, brie, and veggies ($4.50-6). Don't be surprised by the line during lunch hours. Open M-Th 11am-8pm, F-Sa 11am-7pm, Su 11am-6pm. ❶

**LOS ANGELES**

## Hollywood

**⌂ ACCOMMODATIONS**
Flamingo Hotel, **8**
Hollywood Bungalows
　Int'l Youth Hostel, **9**
Hollywood Int'l Hostel, **3**
Liberty Hotel, **2**
Orange Drive Manor, **1**
Student Inn Int'l Hostel, **7**
USAHostels Hollywood, **10**

**🍴 FOOD**
Chin Chin, **4**
Duke's Coffee Shop, **5**
Pink's Hot Dogs, **6**
Roscoe's House of Chicken
　and Waffles, **15**

**🍸 NIGHTLIFE**
3 of Clubs, **13**
Beauty Bar, **12**
Bourgeois Pig, **16**
Daddy's, **14**
The Room, **11**

## ⊙ SIGHTS

## HOLLYWOOD

Exploring the Hollywood area takes a pair of sunglasses, a camera, some cash, and a whole lot of attitude. It is best to drive through the famous Hollywood Hills of beautiful views and houses, and then park and explore **Hollywood Boulevard** on foot. Running east-west at the foot of the Hollywood Hills, this strip is the center of LA's tourist madness. The boulevard itself, home to the Walk of Fame, famous theaters, souvenir shops, and museums, is busy day and night, especially around the intersection of Highland St. and Hollywood Blvd. and then west down Hollywood Blvd. Recent efforts to revitalize the storied area and attract tourists along the lines of New York's clean-up of Times Square have so far been fairly successful.

**HOLLYWOOD SIGN.** Those 50 ft. high, 30 ft. wide, slightly erratic letters perched on Mt. Lee in Griffith Park stand as a universally recognized symbol of the city. The original 1923 sign read HOLLYWOODLAND and was an advertisement for a new subdivision in the Hollywood Hills. The sign was taken over by the Chamber of Commerce in 1949 and three decades later was replaced by a steel replica unveiled for Hollywood's 75th anniversary. The sign has been a target of many college pranks, which have made it read everything from "Hollyweird" to "Ollywood" (after the infamous Lt. Col. Oliver North). A fence keeps you at a distance of 40 ft. (*To get as close to the sign as possible requires a strenuous 2½ mi. hike. Take the Bronson Canyon entrance to Griffith Park and follow Canyon Dr. to its end, where parking is free. The Brush Canyon Trail starts where Canyon Dr. becomes unpaved. At the top of the hill, follow the road to your left; gaze at Hollywood on one side and the Valley on the other; the sign looms just below. For those satisfied with driving, go north on Vine St., take a right on Franklin Ave. and a left on Beachwood, and drive up until you are forced to drive down.*)

**GRAUMAN'S CHINESE THEATRE.** Formerly Mann's Chinese Theatre, this 75-year-old theater is back to its original name because of local efforts to establish historical culture. Loosely modeled on a Chinese temple, the theater is a hot spot for movie premieres. The exterior columns known as "Heaven Dogs" were imported from China, where they once supported a Ming Dynasty temple and were believed to ward off evil spirits. Setting foot in the theater means stepping into the footprints of more than 200 celebrities. Whoopi Goldberg's dreadlocks, R2D2's wheels, and George Burns' cigar are also here. (*6925 Hollywood Blvd., between Highland and Orange St. ☎ 323-461-3331. Tours 4-5 times a day; call ahead. $7.50, under 6 free.*)

**KODAK THEATRE AND HOLLYWOOD & HIGHLAND MALL.** For most, the ritzy brand name stores in the huge complex of Hollywood & Highland are best enjoyed by window shopping before a movie, or sitting down with a cold brewski in the Babylonian courtyard to watch other tourists drop loads of cash. A **visitors center** on the 2nd level can help with accommodations, reservations, sightseeing, and directions. (☎ 323-960-2331. M-Sa 10am-10pm, Su 10am-7pm.) The centerpiece of the complex is **Kodak Theatre,** a huge $94 million theater built specifically to be the new home of the Academy Awards. Designed to achieve the utmost intimacy between performers and spectators, the theater has a seating capacity that ranges from 2200 for live theater to 3500 for concerts and award shows. (*6801 Hollywood Blvd. Box office ☎ 323-308-6363. Non-show days 10am-6pm, show days 10am-9pm. Tours every ½hr., daily 10:30am-2:30pm. Adults $15, seniors and children under 12 $10.*)

# THE LOCAL STORY

## BATMAN BY DAY, CLOONEY BY NIGHT

*Max was spotted in costume as Batman outside of Grauman's Chinese Theatre on Hollywood Blvd.*

**Q:** So Batman, how long have you been working outside Mann's Chinese theatre?
**A:** About a year now. I'm actually George Clooney's stand in, I'll show you a script from the movie we are doing (pulls out script). It's called Celaris, you gotta see this, you like psychological thrillers?
**Q:** I love them. How did you land that job?
**A:** Well, 'cause I look exactly like him.
**Q:** You obviously have the experience as Batman
**A:** Obviously [laughs]. Technically speaking, I have actually fought crime. I've caught two purse snatchers and had five fights in this suit.
**Q:** WOW!
**A:** I have been on the news and everything else. I'm about as close to Batman as you can get.
**Q:** How do you feel about the success of Spiderman?
**A:** I like that.
**Q:** It must be good for the superhero world?
**A:** Yes it is.
**Q:** Do you have aspirations for leaving the Bat wings and getting into acting full time?
**A:** Well it's kind of hard. I'm having a real hard time due to the fact that I look so much like Clooney, it's hard to get an agent to take me seriously. So I double for him.

**WALK OF FAME.** Pedestrian traffic along Hollywood Blvd. mimics LA freeways as tourists stop midstride to gawk at the sidewalk's over 2000 bronze-inlaid stars, which are inscribed with the names of the famous, the infamous, and the downright obscure. Stars are awarded for achievements in one of five categories—movies, radio, TV, recording, and live performance; only Gene Autry has all five stars. The stars have no particular order, so don't try to find a method to the madness. Recent inductees include Muhammad Ali (in front of Kodak Theatre). The celebs to receive their stars in 2004 include Halle Berry and Kevin Costner. To catch today's (or yesterday's) stars in person, call the Chamber of Commerce for info on star-unveiling ceremonies. (☎323-469-8311; www.hollywoodchamber.net. Free.)

**HOLLYWOOD BOWL & MUSEUM.** The hillside Hollywood Bowl is synonymous with picnic dining and classy summer entertainment. All are welcome to listen to the LA Philharmonic at rehearsals on Mondays, Tuesdays, Thursdays, and Fridays. The Bowl also hosts a summer jazz concert series. The small but cozy museum tells the history of the Hollywood Bowl through a collection of photographs, recordings, archival films, programs, and artifacts, including several listening stations where you can swoon to recordings of Jimi, the Beatles, Dylan, and BB King. (2301 N. Highland Ave. ☎323-850-2058, concert line 850-2000; www.hollywoodbowl.org. Open July-Sept. Tu-Sa 10am-8pm; Sept.-June Tu-Sa 10am-4:30pm. Free.)

**HOLLYWOOD HERITAGE MUSEUM.** This museum provides a glimpse into early Hollywood filmmaking history. In 1913, famed director Cecil B. DeMille rented this former barn as studio space for Hollywood's first feature film, *The Squaw Man*. Antique cameras, costumes worn by Douglas Fairbanks and Rudolph Valentino, props, vintage film clips, and other memorabilia fill the museum. The surrounding hills provide an ideal picnic area. (2100 N. Highland Ave, across from the Hollywood Bowl. ☎323-874-2276; www.hollywoodheritage.org. Open Sa-Su 11am-3:45pm; call ahead. $3, ages 3-12 $1, under 3 free. Ample free parking, except during Bowl events.)

**HOLLYWOOD ENTERTAINMENT MUSEUM.** This landmark offers a behind-the-scenes look at the four arts of entertainment—radio, television, film, and recording. A Goddess of Entertainment statue welcomes visitors into the authentic set designs, costumes, and props. The original sets from *Star Trek* and *Cheers* deserve ooh- and aah-ing. The *Cheers* bar serves up drinks for Monday Night Football and Super Bowl Sunday. See where the stars carved their initials in the bar during the final episode. (7021 Hollywood Blvd., one block east of La Brea at Sycamore Ave. ☎323-465-7900. Museum open June-Aug. daily 10am-6pm; Sept.-May Su-Tu and Th-Sa 11am-6pm. Tours every 30min., last tour begins at 5:25pm. $8.75, students $4.50, seniors $5.50, ages 5-12 $4, under 5 free. Parking $2 off Sycamore Ave. Cheers cover $5.)

**ALTERNA-MUSEUMS.** The hit-and-miss accuracy of the **Hollywood Wax Museum's** over 200 life-sized pop icon figures has visitors droning, "That looks nothing/just like...." Choose your own object of distraction, from Legends to Super Heroes and Blockbusters to Chart Toppers. Don't miss the Hall of Presidents and the Horror Chamber. (6767 Hollywood Blvd., ☎323-462-5991. Open daily 10am-midnight. $11, seniors $8.50, ages 6-12 $7, under 6 free.) **Guinness World of Records Museum** displays the tallest, shortest, heaviest, most tattooed, and other curious superlatives, all on display. (6764 Hollywood Blvd. ☎323-463-6433. Open daily 10am-midnight.-$11, seniors $8.50, ages 6-12 $7, under 6 free; combined admission with wax museum: $16, children $9.) **Ripley's Believe It or Not!** "odditorium" aims to prove that Ripley was not "the world's biggest liar." Displays include a section of the Berlin Wall and the world's largest tire. (6780 Hollywood Blvd. ☎323-466-6335. Open Su-W 10am-11pm, Th-Sa 10am-midnight. $11; military, seniors, and students $9; ages 6-12 $8; under 6 free. With AAA membership $8.75; military, seniors, and children $7.) **Frederick's of Hollywood,** a lingerie store and mini-museum, gives a free peek at celebrity-worn corsets and bras, including those that gave Madonna, Marilyn Monroe, and Pamela Anderson their crucial push-up to pin-up stardom. Look hard enough and you will find Forrest Gump's boxers. *(6608 Hollywood Blvd. ☎ 323-957-5953. Open M-Sa 10am-9pm, Su 11am-6pm.)*

**CAPITOL RECORDS TOWER.** The tower is the pre-eminent monument of the modern recording industry, and has appeared in many LA films. The cylindrical building, constructed in 1954, was designed to look like a stack of records, with fins sticking out at each floor (the "records") and a needle on top, which blinks H-O-L-L-Y-W-O-O-D in Morse code. *(1750 Vine St., just north of Hollywood Blvd.)*

**EL CAPITÁN THEATRE.** "Hollywood's First Home of Spoken Drama," this cinema house hosted the 1941 world premiere of *Citizen Kane*. Restored by Walt Disney Co. in 1991, it is now a first-run theater for Walt Disney Pictures. Movies are not shown every day; call in advance for showtimes, and be sure to ask whether the movie opens with a live stage show. *(6838 Hollywood Blvd., just west of Highland Ave. ☎ 323-467-9545 or 800-347-6396; www.elcapitantickets.com. Tickets with live stage show $13-22, seniors and children 3-11 $11-20. Without show $11, children and seniors $8.)*

# SANTA MONICA

Given the cleaner waters and better waves at beaches to the north and south, Santa Monica is known more for its shoreside scene than its shore. Indeed, locals hop in the car and head away from the pier for swim and surf, since garbage from the pier and sewage runoff inevitably foul the water. Filled with gawkers and hawkers, the area on and around the carnival pier is the hub of local tourist activity. The fun fair spills over into the pedestrian-only **Third Street Promenade,** where street performers and a farmer's market make for cinematic "crowd" scenes. Farther inland, along Main St. and beyond, a smattering of galleries, design shops, and museums reveal the city's love for art and design.

**THIRD STREET PROMENADE.** Angelenos always claim that nobody walks in LA, but the rules change on this ultra-popular three-block stretch of mosaic art tiles, fashionable stores, movie theaters, and lively restaurants. Cars are prohibited so that everyone can shop, people-watch, and dine in peace. The Promenade truly heats up when the sun sets, the ocean breeze kicks in, and the ivy-lined mesh dinosaur sculptures that guard both ends of the avenue light up. Street artists strum guitars, breakdance, and sketch oddly flattering caricatures; families and couples window-shop and eat ice cream; young adults with clipboards sign people up for free movie passes. After all, this is the film screening capital of the world. The trendy shopping runs from overpriced bikini stores to some of LA's best book and art stores left over from the Promenade's artsier days. On Wednesday and Saturday mornings, the area transforms into a popular **farmer's market** selling fresh California-grown flowers and produce, with Saturdays featuring exclusively organic products. On the first Saturday of the month, renowned local chef Enrico Glaudo gives cooking demonstrations. *(Between Broadway and Wilshire in downtown Santa Monica. Exit off 4th St. from I-10. See p. 385 for parking details.)*

**SANTA MONICA PIER & PACIFIC PARK.** The famed pier is the heart of Santa Monica Beach and home to the carnivalesque family funspot, Pacific Park. Roller coaster lovers and ferris wheel fanatics over 4 ft. tall can twist and turn on the five-story West Coaster or soar 100 ft. above the ocean in the first solar-powered Ferris wheel. Along the pier, amidst pizza joints and souvenir shops, look for free TV show tickets (the variety and late-night kinds) near the north entrance. Buy temporary hipness at booths along the strip in the form of a painless henna tattoo for $5-20 or pose for a portrait from one of many talented artists for $20. *(Off PCH on the way to Venice Beach from Santa Monica Beach. ☎ 310-458-8900; http://santamonicapier.org.*

*Pier open 24hr. Park open in summer S-Th 11am-11pm, F-Su 11am-12:30am; in winter hours vary, so call ahead. Ticket window closes 30min. before the park closes. Tickets $2 each, most rides 2-3 tickets; day passes $20, children under 42 in. $11. Free Twilight Dance Series June-Aug. Th 7:30pm; for info, call ☎310-458-8900; www.twilightdance.org. Parking off PCH $5-8 per day.)*

**MAIN STREET.** Beginning at Colorado Ave. and heading south to Venice, Main St. mixes old-fashioned charm with designer knick-knack shops. Sporting numerous art galleries, it's much artsier and more urbane (but no more pretentious) than Third St. Promenade, with its open-air coffeeshops and restaurants. The historic Victorian-style Roy Jones House that contains the **California Heritage Museum** contrasts with the design-happy Main St. architecture. The museum has restored rooms and hosts temporary exhibits. *(2612 Main St., half a mile south of Pico. ☎310-392-8537. Open Su and W-Sa 11am-4pm. $3, students and seniors $2, under 12 free. Parking free.)*

**MONTANA AVENUE.** Just south of Santa Monica's exclusive residential district, the avenue's art galleries, vintage stores, high-end boutiques, delicious bakeries and dozens of restaurants can make for a delightful afternoon. A local favorite is the **Culture Shop Gallery,** with its funky furniture and jewelry. *(1511-A Montana Ave., between 15th and 16th St. ☎310-656-2656. Open M-F 11am-6pm, Sa 10am-6pm, Su 12-5pm.)*

**BERGAMOT STATION ARTS CENTER.** Once a train depot, these converted warehouses are now helping to move contemporary LA area artists—painters, sculptors, mixed-media designers, and photographers—to higher ground. While the art is pricey, the viewing is free and fabulous. The **Gallery of Functional Art** sells inspired art object creations such as bowls made by hand from fresh fruit and vegetables that have been dried, pressed, and aged ($32). The **Santa Monica Museum of Art,** in building G-1, exhibits the work of emerging artists. Featured art rotates regularly. Bergamot Station also houses a reasonably priced Gallery Cafe ❶ (sandwiches $6), as well as a **Colleagues Gallery** with more affordable works. *(2525 Michigan Ave., near the intersection of Olympic and Cloverfield Blvd. ☎310-586-6467. Gallery of Functional Art open M 9am-4pm, Tu-F 9am-5pm, Sa 10am-5pm. Free. Santa Monica Museum of Art open Tu-Sa 11am-6pm; call ahead, because it often closes for installation changes. Suggested donation $3, students and seniors $2.)*

**MUSEUM OF FLYING.** In the process of relocating to a larger hangar on the North side of Santa Monica Airport, this museum features WWI single-seat fighters, a tribute to the Apollo missions, and an aircraft simulator. The Air Traffic Control station allows you to listen to real-time transmissions from local towers. The museum's new location will provide access to a viewing area on the airport's active runway. *(2772 Donald Douglas Loop N. Take I-10 to either the Bundy S. or Centinela Exits. Go 2 blocks south and take a right onto Ocean Park Blvd. and a left at 28th St. The museum is at the end of the street. ☎310-392-8822; www.museumofflying.com. Open Sa-Su 10am-5pm. Group tours Su and W-Sa with advance reservations. Closed for special events; call ahead. Wheelchair accessible. $8, students and seniors $6, ages 3-17 $4. Virtual reality simulator $2.)*

**OTHER SIGHTS.** The paved beach path is a mini-freeway of cyclists, skaters, and runners, stretching 20¼ mi. between Santa Monica and Torrance Beaches. Under the Santa Monica Pier lies the newest attraction, the **Santa Monica Pier Aquarium,** a high-tech interactive aquarium where the kiddies can watch ocean movies and get their fingers fishy in the "touch tank." *(☎310-393-6149. Open July 1-Sept. 6 M-F 2-6pm, Sa-Su 12:30-6:30pm, but hours subject to change; hours limited in winter; call ahead. Suggested donation $5, children under 12 $3.)* At the Santa Monica Senior Recreation Center is the **Camera Obscura,** which uses convex lenses to project a 360-degree bird's-eye view of the beach onto a screen in a dark room—well worth the brief visit. *(1450 Ocean Ave. Open M 9am-2pm, Tu-F 9am-4pm, Sa-Su 11am-4pm. Free.)* Immediately south of the pier on Ocean Front

Walk, skilled players match wits at the public chess tables at the **International Chess Park.** Opposite the chess masters is the original location of **Muscle Beach** (now in Venice Beach), where bodybuilders and athletes used to show off chiseled, physical perfection in the 1930s, 40s, and 50s.

# VENICE

At the turn of the 20th century, legendary real-estate developer Abbot Kinney envisioned a re-creation of Italy's Venice on the California coast—a touch of Old World charm, with mustachioed gondoliers plying the canals and the social elite strolling on an elegant oceanside promenade. Instead, Kinney ended up with a massive dose of New World neuroses. **Ocean Front Walk,** Venice's main beachfront drag, is a seaside three-ring circus of fringe culture. Street people converge on shaded clusters of benches, evangelists drown out off-color comedians, and bodybuilders of both sexes pump iron in skimpy spandex outfits at **Muscle Beach,** 1800 Ocean Front Walk, closest to 18th St. and Pacific Ave. Fire-juggling cyclists, master sand sculptors, bards in Birkenstocks, and **"skateboard grandmas"** define the bohemian spirit of this playground population. Vendors of jewelry, henna body art, snacks, and beach paraphernalia overwhelm the boardwalk.

To untangle your wits after gaudy Venice, you can people-watch from the cafes or juice bars. **Boardwalk Skates,** 201½ Ocean Front Walk, rents bikes and skates. (☎310-450-6634. Bikes $5 per hr., $15 per day; skates $5/$12 for *Let's Go* readers; tandem bikes $7/$20. Open M-F 10am-7pm, Sa-Su 9am-8pm.) Or cross the bike path to **Venice One-Stop Beach Rental,** located in the bright yellow boxcar, and receive a free map and drink voucher. (Bikes or skates $5 per hr., $8 per 2hr., $12 per day.) Those who got game can play ball at the popular **basketball court** at 18th St. and Ocean Front Walk, which was featured in the movie *White Men Can't Jump,* but be warned: the competition is fierce and the trashtalking even fiercer.

Toward Culver City is the **Museum of Jurassic Technology,** 9341 Venice Blvd., four blocks west of Robertson Blvd. The museum is not really accessible by foot from the beach. By car, take I-10 to Robertson Blvd. South; turn right onto Venice Blvd. from Robertson Blvd. at the intersection of Venice and Bagley Ave. The museum is about four blocks down Venice Blvd. The museum walks a fine line between an elaborate practical joke and a profound statement on the ultimate inaccessibility of history. It is the only museum of its kind, with an unapologetic and unexplained juxtaposition of exhibits as incongruous as mole rat skeletons, fake gems, and trailer park art. Despite the professional displays, intoned audio narration, and deadpan introductory slide show, you might wonder how serious the museum actually is. (☎310-836-6131; www.mjt.org. Open Su and F-Sa noon-6pm, Th 2-8pm. Requested donation $4, students and seniors $2.50, active military $1.50.)

# MARINA DEL REY

For a low-key slice of seaside life in LA, take a walk along the marina or drive down to **Fisherman's Village** (at the eastern end of Fiji Way off Lincoln Blvd.). The small but pleasant wharf-meets-strip-mall area is home to a handful of restaurants, gift shops, and boating stores. The Village does not warrant a full daytrip, but can make a relaxing weekend afternoon in a boat rented from **Marina Boat Rentals,** 13719 Fiji Way (☎310-574-2822). Four-person powerboats and sailboats ($35-90 per hr. depending on size), 8-person electric boats ($65 per hr.), single and double kayaks ($12 and $20 per hr.), and 3-person pedal boats ($15 per hr.) are available. No experience is necessary for most rentals, but reservations are recommended. Relax afterward on the central patio, where locals gather to hear live music on weekend nights and some weekend afternoons.

# MALIBU

North of Santa Monica along PCH, the cityscape gives way to appealing stretches of sandy, sewage-free shoreline. Stop along the coast and you may see dolphin pods swimming close to shore, or at least pods of surfers trying to catch a wave. Malibu's beaches are clean and relatively uncrowded, easily the best in LA County for surfers, sunbathers, and swimmers alike. You can jet through the wave tubes at **Surfrider Beach,** a section of Malibu Lagoon State Beach north of the pier at 23000 PCH. Walk there via the Zonker Harris Access Way (named after the beach-obsessed Doonesbury character) at 22700 PCH. **Malibu Ocean Sports,** 22935½ PCH, across from the pier, rents surfboards ($10 per hr., $25 per day), kayaks (single $15/$35; double $20/$50), boogie boards ($12 per day), and wetsuits ($10 per day). The store also offers surfing lessons ($100 for 2hr. lesson and full-day gear rental) and tours. (☎310-456-6302. Open M-F 10am-6pm, Sa-Su 9am-6pm.)

To see one of the country's prettiest university locations, stop by the 830-acre campus of **Pepperdine University,** 24255 PCH, at the intersection of Las Virgenes and PCH. Wide lawns and sand-colored buildings rest on a Malibu hillside over the Pacific. Contact admissions (☎310-506-4000; www.pepperdine.edu) for tours.

**Corral State Beach,** a tiny windsurfing and swimming haven off the side of the road, lies on the 26000 block of PCH. The larger and generally uncrowded **Point Dume State Beach** (main entrance near 29000 PCH; look for signs) is just north of Corral State Beach, offering better currents for scuba-diving. Along the 30000 block of PCH stretches **Zuma Beach,** LA County's northernmost, largest, happiest sandbox. The location makes sections #5-7 a big draw for swarms of local kids, while distance from the only entrance makes sections #9-11 less crowded. Swimmers should stay as close as possible to lifeguard stations; because of the strong **riptide,** rescue counts are high. **The Zuma Cafe ❶,** 30066 PCH, with breakfast ($2.50-6), burgers ($3.50), and hot dogs ($2.50), refuels surfers and swimmers. (☎310-457-3143. Open daily 7:30am-6pm.) A trailer directly in front of the Cafe rents boogie boards ($5 per hr.), kayaks ($15), and bikes ($10). Free parking along PCH is coveted, so expect to use the beach lot ($6, after 6pm $2). Although it's disguised as a deli, **Malibu Ranch Market,** 29575 PCH, in the Zuma Beach Plaza at Busch Rd., rents boogie boards ($40 deposit; small $7 per day, large $9) and sells deli sandwiches, snacks, and alcohol. (☎301-457-0171. Open daily 8:30am-10:30pm.)

# BEVERLY HILLS

Conspicuous displays of wealth can border on the vulgar in this storied center of extravagance and privilege. Residential ritz reaches its peak along the mansions of Beverly Dr. The heart of the city, known for its flashy clothing boutiques and jewelry shops, is in the **Golden Triangle,** a wedge formed by Beverly Dr., Wilshire Blvd., and Santa Monica Blvd., centered on **Rodeo Drive.** Built like an old English manor house, Polo Ralph Lauren (444 N. Rodeo Dr.) stands out from the white marble of the other stores. The divine triple-whammy of Cartier (370 N. Rodeo Dr.), Gucci (347 N. Rodeo Dr.), and Chanel (400 N. Rodeo Dr.) sits on some of the area's prime real estate, where rents approach $40,000 per month.

At the south end of Rodeo Dr. (the end closest to Wilshire Blvd.) is the all-pedestrian shopping complex of **2 Rodeo Drive,** a.k.a. **Via Rodeo,** which contains Dior, Tiffany, and numerous salons frequented by the stars. Although it strives for authentic European antiquity, the promenade was constructed in the last decade—cobblestone street, lampposts, and all. Across the way is the venerable **Beverly Wilshire Hotel,** 9500 Wilshire Blvd. (☎310-275-5200), where Julia Roberts went from Hollywood hooker to Richard Gere's queen in *Pretty Woman.* A peek at the lobby will give you a good idea of just how extravagant the rooms might be.

Just north of the Golden Triangle is Santa Monica Blvd., which is lined with a series of small but pleasant parks. One such park, between N. Camden and N. Bedford Dr. on Santa Monica Blvd., contains the most varieties of **cacti** in one place in the world, an interesting, dusty sight amidst the opulence.

**MUSEUM OF TELEVISION & RADIO.** Complete with a radio broadcast studio and two theaters, this museum's biggest highlight is its library, which holds 117,000 television, radio, and commercial programs. You can request your favorite tube hits, and five minutes later the library staff will have the full-length episodes ready and waiting for your viewing pleasure at your own private screening station. Caricatures of television stars decorate the walls, and there is always someone watching *I Love Lucy*. *(465 N. Beverly Dr., corner of Santa Monica Blvd and Beverly Dr. ☎ 310-786-1000. Open Su and W-Sa noon-5pm. Suggested donation $10, students and seniors $8, under 14 $5. 2hr. free parking in the museum's lot off Little Santa Monica Blvd.)*

**CIVIC CENTER.** Just outside of the main area is the **Beverly Hills City Hall,** 455 N. Rexford Dr., right below Santa Monica Blvd. This Spanish Renaissance building was erected during the Great Depression, and is now engulfed by Beverly Hills's new white phoenix of a Civic Center, which took nine years to build at a cost of $120 million. The Civic Center houses what might be the country's most extravagant police and fire headquarters, as well as the **Beverly Hills Public Library,** 444 N. Rexford Dr., with its Thai marble interior but only average collection of books. *(City Hall ☎ 310-285-1000. Library ☎ 310-288-2222; www.bhpl.org.)*

**BEVERLY HILLS HIGH.** It may only be a local public high school, but it is still a mild marvel. The indoor swimming pool is open in the summer and has a sliding floor cover that converts the pool into a basketball court. That very floor is where Jimmy Stewart and Donna Reed danced the aquatic Charleston in *It's a Wonderful Life*. The school is still a popular filming location. *(241 Moreno, between Olympic Blvd. and Spalding. ☎ 310-551-5100. Pool open in summer M-F noon-9pm.)*

**BEVERLY HILLS HOTEL.** A pink, palm-treed array of 182 rooms and suites and 21 bungalows, hidden among 12 acres of tropical gardens and pools, this ludicrously extravagant hotel is as famous as the starlets who romanced here. Marilyn Monroe reportedly had trysts with both JFK and RFK in the bungalows. The hotel is home to the **Polo Lounge,** where countless industry deals have been negotiated. Owned by the Dorchester Group, rooms run $380-410, bungalows $430-4590, and suites $820-5000. *(9641 Sunset Blvd. ☎ 310-276-2251.)*

**MUSEUM OF TOLERANCE.** Just south of Beverly Hills is the sobering Museum of Tolerance. This hands-on, high-tech museum has interactive exhibits on the Holocaust, the Croatian genocide, the LA riots, the US civil rights movement, and the recent global refugee problem. In front of the entrance, required orientation sessions that run every 10-12min. The displays on the main floor of the museum take about 2hr. to get through—patience is encouraged. Visit the Point of View Diner, a re-creation of a 50s diner that serves a menu of controversial topics on video jukeboxes. Pick up a "passport" of a child from Nazi-occupied territory and plug it into a computer kiosk that provides the biography (read: awful fate) of your cardholder. Objects from concentration camps and original letters by Anne Frank are in the 2nd floor Multimedia Learning Center. The Museum has hosted speeches by many influential world figures, including President George W. Bush and the Dalai Lama. Holocaust survivors speak of their experiences M-W at 1pm and 2pm, and Su every hour 1-4pm. Diagonally across the street is the **Simon Wiesenthal Center** for Holocaust research. *(9786 W. Pico Blvd., at Roxbury St. Museum ☎ 310-553-9036; www.wiesenthal.com. Open Apr.-Oct. M-Th*

*11:30am-6:30pm, F 11:30am-5pm, Su 11:30am-7:30pm; Nov.-Mar. M-Th 11:30am-6:30pm, F 11:30am-3pm, Su 11;30am-7:30pm. Last entry 1½-2½hr. before closing. $10, seniors $8, students $7, ages 3-10 $6. Free parking.)*

## BEVERLY HILLS CELEBRITY TOUR

The reason why all the maps to stars' homes only seem to show dead stars is that while the A-list may still *shop* here, most no longer *live* here. The exquisite area still houses plenty of multi-millionaires and lives up to visitors' expectations, but the real fame and money has moved away from the hype to areas that afford privacy (see **Bel Air, Brentwood, and Pacific Palisades,** p. 414 and **Seeing Stars,** p. 414).

A conspicuous way to tour the city is in the 1914 trolley car replica operated by the Beverly Hills Chamber of Commerce (☎310-248-1000). The 40min. **tour of the city and stars' homes** costs $5 and leaves from the corner of Rodeo Dr. and Dayton (every hr. June-Sept. Tu-Sa 1-5pm). For a cooler approach, go solo with a star map ($8), sold along Sunset Blvd. but not within Beverly Hills, or take the following *Let's Go* abbreviated tour (consult the LA Westside map for reference).

From Hollywood, drive down Sunset Blvd. west towards the coast. Right after you pass Hillcrest Ave. on your left, keep your eye out for 9401 Sunset Blvd., home to rockstar **Phil Collins.** At the next intersection, take a left onto Palm Dr. and look for **Faye Dunaway's** residence on your left at 714 Palm Dr. Return to Sunset Blvd. and continue another four blocks. Turn right onto Lexington Dr. and then a quick right onto Coldwater Canyon Dr. The NRA's renowned **Charlton Heston,** whose residence featured prominently in Michael Moore's recent *Bowling for Columbine,* can be found at 2859 Coldwater Canyon Dr. Head back, but before you reach Lexington Dr., turn left onto Rexford Dr. and look for **Meg Ryan's** home at 805 Rexford Dr. Head north on Rexford Dr. back to Sunset Blvd. and turn left. Take your next right on Beverly Dr. and listen to **Meat Loaf's** new record while coasting by his house at 908 N. Beverly Dr. Continue on Beverly Dr. to laconic action hero **Sylvester Stallone's** home at 1121 Beverly Dr. Take Beverly Dr. south across Sunset Blvd. and pick up Canon Dr. south (one block south of Sunset). You will find **Kirk Douglas** at 707 Canon Dr. Another few blocks west on Sunset Blvd., turn left onto Roxbury Dr. and hope to glimpse material girl **Madonna** (1015 Roxbury Dr.). If you're into old school actors, return to Sunset Blvd. and head west another block. Turn right onto Whittier Blvd. and look for **Paul Newman** at 907 Whittier Blvd. As you continue down Sunset Blvd. another block, look for a small street off to the left called Copley Dr. Another long-time star, **Gene Hackman,** resides at 9901 Copley Dr. At this point, pop in the "oldies but goodies" tunes and relive the **Elvis** era. **Elvis** had two homes in LA. He purchased the first at 1174 Hillcrest Dr. shortly after his marriage to **Priscilla** in 1967, but quickly relocated to 144 Monovale Dr. because it offered more privacy. (Hillcrest Dr. is further east on Sunset Blvd., one block east of Palm Dr. where Faye Dunaway lives—see it on the return trip). A couple blocks west of Gene Hackman's place on Copley Dr., turn right onto Carolwood Dr. and then a quick right onto Monovale Dr. Today, **Priscilla** still lives near those old memories at 1167 Summit Dr. From Monovale Dr., go straight and take a left onto Lexington Dr., a left onto Benedict Canyon Dr., and then a right onto Summit Dr. **Bruce Springsteen** and **Eddie Murphy** are close by—turn around and take a right onto Benedict Canyon. "The Boss" is at 1224 Benedict Canyon and the famous comedian and actor is at 2727 Benedict Canyon. Return to Summit Dr. and take a right. At the fork, turn onto Ridgedale Dr. The world's most beautiful couple, **Brad Pitt and Jennifer Aniston,** beautify 1026 Ridgedale Dr. For those who love saccharine songs, look for a small road called Hanover Dr. and take it to Carolwood Dr. Hook a left and look for **Barbra Streisand's** old home at 301 Carolwood Dr. and **Walt Disney's** former residence at 355 Carolwood Dr.

# WESTWOOD & UCLA

## UNIVERSITY OF CALIFORNIA AT LOS ANGELES (UCLA)

*Directly north of Westwood Village and west of Beverly Hills. To drive to the campus, take I-405 (San Diego Fwy.) to the Wilshire Blvd./Westwood Exit and head east into Westwood. Take Westwood Blvd. north off Wilshire Blvd., and go through Westwood Village and directly into the campus. By bus, take MTA #2 along Sunset Blvd., #21 along Wilshire Blvd., #720 from Santa Monica, #761 from the San Fernando Valley, or Santa Monica BBBus #1, 2, 3, 8, or 12. Parking pass ($6) is valid all day at 14 different parking structures. Maps free.*

Get a feel for mass academia UC-style at this 400-acre campus in the foothills of the Santa Monica Mountains. A prototypical California university, UCLA sports an abundance of grassy open spaces, dazzling sunshine, massive buildings, and deeply-tanned bodies. Once voted the #1 jock school in the country by *Sports Illustrated*, UCLA also boasts an illustrious film school whose graduates include James Dean, Jim Morrison, Oliver Stone, Francis Ford Coppola, and Tim Robbins.

UCLA and Westwood are navigable on foot, so pay for a parking pass from campus information stands at any entrance, then park and walk. UCLA parking cops live to ticket unsuspecting visitors. **Tours** are offered by the Alumni Center, which is directly north of Westwood Plaza and parking structures #6 and 8. (☎310-825-8764. Tour times vary seasonally.) Outdoor highlights include the **Murphy Sculpture Garden** (in the northeast corner of campus), which contains over 70 pieces by major artists such as Auguste Rodin and Henri Matisse, and the UCLA **Botanical Gardens** (in the eastern part of campus, at the intersection of Le Conte and Hilgard Ave.), which contains approximately 5000 plant species from all over the world.

**UCLA HAMMER MUSEUM OF ART.** The UCLA Hammer Museum houses the world's largest collection of works by 19th-century French satirist Honoré Daumier and the collection of late oil tycoon Armand Hammer, with works by Rembrandt, Monet, and Pissarro. The museum's true gem is Vincent Van Gogh's *Hospital at Saint Rémy*. Hammer purportedly wanted to donate his collection to the LA County Museum of Art, but demanded that the works be shown together in a separate wing. The museum refused, telling Hammer to build his own place— which he did. The center hosts traveling exhibitions throughout the year, as well as free summer jazz concerts and seasonal cultural programs. *(10899 Wilshire Blvd., at the corner of Westwood and Wilshire Blvd. ☎310-443-7000; www.hammer.ucla.edu. Open Su, Tu, Sa noon-7pm, W-F noon-9pm. Summer jazz concerts F 6:30-8pm. $5, seniors $3, under 17 free, Th free. Free tours of permanent collection Su 2pm, of traveling exhibits Th 6pm, Sa-Su 1pm. 3hr. parking $2.75, $1.50 each additional 20min.)*

**FOWLER MUSEUM OF CULTURAL HISTORY.** The Fowler displays artifacts from contemporary, historic, and prehistoric cultures. The fact that it preserves Native American remains for their archaeological value (there are laws protecting Native Americans' rights to sacred burial) is controversial. *(In Haines Hall. ☎310-825-4361; www.fmch.ucla.edu. Open Su, W, F-Sa noon-5pm, Th noon-8pm. Free.)*

**ACKERMAN UNION.** With all their practical needs met by Ackerman Union services (which includes a campus credit union and post office), students never need to leave campus. Visitors can enjoy the **Food Court's** grill, pizza place, and smoothie bar ($2-3). A ride-share board on the first floor posts information on drivers and riders going everywhere from Vegas to Miami. There is free Internet access on Floor A (one floor up from the ground floor). The huge **UCLA Store** swallows up most of the ground floor with UCLA paraphernalia, a newsstand, a grocery store, and the always-essential Clinique counter. *(308 Westwood Plaza, downhill from the quadrangle on Bruin Walk. ☎310-206-0833. Store open M-F 9am-6pm, Sa 10am-5pm, Su noon-5pm. Union open mid-June to late Sept. daily 10am-11pm; late Sept. to mid-June 8am-11pm.)*

**TICKETS.** The **UCLA Central Ticket Office** sells tickets for on-campus arts events (including concerts and dance recitals), UCLA sporting events, and discounted tickets to local movie theaters and water parks (discounts not limited to UCLA affiliates). It also has a Ticketmaster outlet. (☎310-825-2101; www.cto.ucla.edu.) The renowned School of Film and Television Archive sponsors various film festivals, often with foreign films and profiles on groundbreaking filmmakers. (☎310-206-3456; www.cinema.ucla.edu. Double features $7, students $5; select films free.)

# BEL AIR, BRENTWOOD, & PACIFIC PALISADES

These three residential communities don't offer much to the budget traveler in terms of accommodations or food, but a stop at the Getty Museum or a scenic drive along Sunset Blvd. are two free ways to experience the best the area has to offer. Veer off Sunset onto any public (non-gated) road to see tree-lined rows of well-spaced six-bedroom homes that make living here as costly as Beverly Hills.

## J. PAUL GETTY CENTER & MUSEUM

*1200 Getty Center Dr. Take I-405 (San Diego Fwy.) to the Getty Center Dr. Exit. Public transportation is strongly recommended: take either Santa Monica BBBus #14 (for info call ☎310-451-4444) or MTA #761 (for info call ☎800-266-6883) to the Getty Center. ☎310-440-7300; www.getty.edu. Free; headset audio guides $3. Open Su and Tu-Th 10am-6pm, F-Sa 10am-9pm. Parking reservations required Tu-F before 4pm ($5 per car); no reservations necessary for college students or on weekends. A "panorami-tram" takes visitors up the hill to the museum. Off-site parking, also serviced by shuttle (10min.), is free.*

Above Bel Air and Brentwood in the Santa Monica Mountains shines a modern Coliseum, "The Getty." Indeed, the 16,000 tons of gleaming travertine marble used to build this museum came from the same quarry as that of the Roman Coliseum. Wedding classical materials to modern designs, renowned architect Richard Meier designed the stunning $1 billion complex, which opened to the public in 1997. The museum consists of five pavilions overlooking the Robert Irwin-designed Central Garden, a living work of art that changes with the seasons. The pavilions contain the permanent Getty collection (including Vincent Van Gogh's *Irises*), Impressionist paintings, Renaissance drawings, and a fantastic Rembrandt collection. Equally impressive is the sweeping, panoramic view of the Los Angeles Basin from the Getty's numerous balconies. The Getty also hosts gallery talks by local artists, lectures, films, and a concert series. The "Friday Nights at the Getty" program features plays, films, and readings.

## OTHER SIGHTS

**SKIRBALL CULTURAL CENTER.** Dedicated to the preservation of Jewish culture, this dynamic cultural institution explores the connection between 4000 years of Jewish heritage and American democratic ideals. It contains one of the world's largest collections of Judaica, a children's Discovery Center, and interactive exhibits. Tours (1hr.) daily at noon, 1, and 2:45pm, at the museum's entrance. *(2701 N. Sepulveda Blvd., just a few minutes north of the Getty. ☎310-440-4500; www.skirball.org. Open Su 11am-5pm, Tu-Sa noon-5pm.)*

# BEL AIR CELEBS

**SEEING STARS.** Many of today's stars live in Bel Air, Brentwood, and Pacific Palisades. The best way to see their cottages and compounds is to pick up a star map, available at the Santa Monica Pier, local newsstands, or from vendors along Sunset Blvd. However, you'll probably only see the stars themselves on screen. Lurking around their neighborhoods might get you a peek at their landscaping or a picture of their mailbox, but it's doubtful you'll ever see them taking out the trash.

North of UCLA is **Bel Air,** home to many a star. From UCLA northeastern corner, head north on Copa de Oro Rd., where **Nicholas Cage** lives at 363 Copa de Oro Rd. Return to Sunset and head west a few blocks to Bel Air Rd. Turn right and look for the **Beverly Hillbillies** mansion at 750 Bel Air Rd., **Judy Garland's** home at 924 Bel Air Rd., and **Alfred Hitchcock's** at 10957 Bel Air Rd. Head back to Sunset but take a left onto St. Cloud Rd. to find one of America's recent presidents, **Ronald Reagan,** at 668 St. Cloud Rd. Violet-eyed **Elizabeth Taylor** is close by at 700 Nimes Rd. If you still haven't had enough, continue straight on St. Cloud Rd., turn right onto Nimes Rd., left towards St. Pierre Rd., and then right onto St. Pierre Rd. Make your way to Beverly Glen Blvd. and turn left. **Steve Martin** is at 1005 Beverly Glen Blvd. Turn around and head south on Beverly Glen to 111 N. Beverly Glen where you can see **Tom Cruise's** former residence before he moved in with Nicole Kidman.

East of UCLA, take a right (if you're heading east on Sunset) onto Mapleton Dr., in the tony Holmby Hills area. **Lauren Bacall** and **Humphrey Bogart** resided at 232 Mapleton Dr. Producer **Aaron Spelling's** mansion, 594 N. Mapleton, is larger than the Taj Mahal. Wife Candy Spelling's closets reportedly take up an entire wing. To glimpse the home of infamous, invite-only, racy parties, turn around and head towards Sunset until you hit Charing Cross Rd. Turn right. The estate at 10236 Charing Cross Rd. is the **Playboy Mansion.**

Further west on Sunset Blvd., on the other side of I-405, is **Brentwood,** home to many a national scandal-starter. Take a left onto Bundy Dr. and another left onto Darlington Ave. The owner of America's greatest blue dress, former White House intern **Monica Lewinsky,** resides in southern Brentwood at 12224 Darlington Ave. A one-time Oval Office darling herself, **Marilyn Monroe,** was found dead at her home at 12305 Fifth Helena Dr. in 1962. To get there, return to Sunset, head west, and take a right onto Helena Dr. Further west and a right off Sunset brings you to famous accusé **O.J. Simpson's** old estate at 360 Rockingham Ave., which was repossessed and auctioned off for a meager $2.63 million. Celeb-studded Brentwood also includes the homes of **Michelle Pfeiffer, Harrison Ford,** and **Meryl Streep.**

The considerably more secluded and hilly **Pacific Palisades,** above the gorgeous westernmost stretch of Sunset Blvd., brings the stars closer to the ocean and farther from the *paparazzi.* **Andre Agassi** and **Brooke Shields** can be found at San Remo Dr., a right off of Sunset. Continue west on Sunset to Capri Dr. and turn right for **Kurt Russell** and live-in love **Goldie Hawn's** residence at 1422 Capri Dr. **Whoopi Goldberg** is in town at 1461 Amalfi Dr. (continue west on Sunset and take a right onto Amalfi Dr.), just down the road from **Steven Spielberg,** who lives in the house at 1513-1515 Amalfi Dr. that belonged to David O. Selznick while he was producing *Gone with the Wind.* The man with the master plan, bodybuilder, laconic movie star, social climber (married a Kennedy), and 2003 recall election front-runner **Arnold Schwarzenegger** and his wife **Maria Shriver,** who loved their lot so much they bought out their neighbor's for $5.4 million, practice family fitness at 14205, 14209, and 14215 Sunset Blvd.

## WILSHIRE DISTRICT

**HANCOCK PARK.** A good, green place to start in the crowded Wilshire District is the well-manicured **Hancock Park,** in the Miracle Mile stretch of Wilshire Blvd. between Fairfax and La Brea Ave. The park contains two famous museums and is near the Petersen Automotive museum. The CBS studios are slightly north of the park. Picnickers should be wary of the odorous tar pits, which may conflict with your otherwise sweet-smelling lunch. *(Park open daily 6am-10pm. Free.)*

**LOS ANGELES COUNTY MUSEUM OF ART (LACMA).** At the southwestern end of Hancock Park, LACMA's renowned collection contains "more than 110,000 works from around the world, spanning the history of art from ancient times to the present." Opened in 1965, LACMA is the largest museum on the West Coast, with six main buildings around the **Times-Mirror Central Court.** The **Steve Martin Gallery,** in the Anderson Building, holds the famed comedian's collection of Dada and Surrealist works, including R. Magritte's *Treachery of Images.* (This explains how Steve was able to roller skate through LACMA's halls in the film *LA Story;* see p. 23.) The latest additions are **LACMA West** and its **Children's Gallery.** The museum sponsors free jazz, chamber music, film classics and documentaries, and a variety of free daily tours. *(5905 Wilshire Blvd. General info ☎ 323-857-6000, Docent Council 857-6108; www.lacma.org. Open M-Tu and Th noon-8pm, F noon-9pm, Sa-Su 11am-8pm. $9, students and seniors $5, under 18 free; free 2nd Tu of each month. Free jazz F 5:30-8:30pm, chamber music Su 6-7pm. Film tickets $8, seniors and students $6. Parking $5, after 7pm free.)*

**PETERSEN AUTOMOTIVE MUSEUM (PAM).** This slice of Americana showcases one of LA's most recognizable symbols—the automobile. At 300,000 sq. ft., PAM is the world's largest car museum, showcasing over 150 race cars, classic cars, hot rods, motorcycles, and movie and celebrity cars. The museum also features a 1920s service station, a 1950s body shop, and a 1960s suburban garage. Call to set up a guided tour. *(6060 Wilshire Blvd., at Fairfax. ☎ 323-930-2277; www.petersen.org. Open Su and Tu-Sa 10am-6pm; Discovery Center closes at 5pm. $7, students and seniors $5, ages 5-12 $3, under 5 free. Full-day parking $6.)*

**GEORGE C. PAGE MUSEUM OF LA BREA DISCOVERIES.** The smelly **La Brea Tar Pits** fills the area with an acrid petroleum stench and provides bones for this natural history museum. Thirsty mammals of bygone geological ages drank from these pools of water, only to find themselves stuck in the tar that oozed below. Most of the three million specimens pulled from the pits are on display here, along with reconstructed Ice Agers and murals of prehistoric LA. The only human unearthed in the pits stands out in holographic horror—discovered in 1914, the La Brea woman, standing no more than 4 ft. and 8 in., was presumably thrown into the tar 9000 years ago after having holes drilled into her skull (not on display). A viewing station exists at Pit 91 where archaeologists continue to dig. *(5801 Wilshire Blvd., at Curson Ave. Buses stop in front of the museum. ☎ 323-934-7243. Open M-F 9:30am-5pm, Sa-Su 10am-5pm. Tours of grounds Su and Tu-Sa 1pm, museum tours Su and Tu-Sa 2:15pm. $7, students and seniors $4.50, ages 5-12 $2; 1st Tu of each month free. Parking $6 with validation.)*

**CRAFT AND FOLK ART MUSEUM.** Originally a small gallery in a local restaurant whose art began to win Angeleno hearts, the CAFAM now has its own space and features traveling exhibits from around the world. In October, the museum sponsors an "International Festival of Masks," a full-day street festival where children and adults alike can create their own masks while live musicians and dancers entertain. Call ahead to ask about the frequent lectures and seminars. *(5814 Wilshire Blvd., 3 blocks west of La Brea. ☎ 323-937-4230; www.cafam.org. Open Su and W-Sa 11am-5pm. $3.50, seniors and students $2.50, under 12 free. Street parking.)*

# WEST HOLLYWOOD

Bring your walking shoes and spend a day on the 3 mi. strip of **Melrose Avenue** from Highland Ave. west to the intersection of Doheny Dr. and Santa Monica Blvd. This strip began to develop its funky flair in the late 1980s when art galleries, designer stores, lounge-like coffee shops, used clothing and music stores, and restaurants began to take over. Now it is home to the hip, with the choicest stretch lying between La Brea and Fairfax Ave. While much sold here is used ("vintage"), none of it is really cheap (see **Shopping,** p. 431). Find outlandish vintage outfits at **Aardvark's** (p. 433), grab an enhanced smoothie at **Hollywood Smoothy's,** 7275 Melrose Blvd. (☎ 323-933-4803; open daily 11am-7pm), and rest your feet after a long march at ⚑**Elixer** (p. 440), as you rejuvenate in its peaceful Zen gardens with a herbal-rich tonic. North of the **Beverly Center** is the **Pacific Design Center**, 8687 Melrose Ave. (☎310-657-0800; www.pacificdesign-center.com), a sea-green glass complex nicknamed the Blue Whale and constructed in the shape of a rippin' wave. In addition to 172 design showrooms, which mostly showcase home and furnishing projects, this rich man's Home Depot has a public plaza and a 388-seat amphitheater called the Silver Screen, which stages free summer concerts and art exhibits. (Call for schedules. Open M-F 8:30am-5:30pm.)

# DOWNTOWN

Downtown is spotted with people but lacks any overpowering energy. Pick up the detailed **Angels Walk** brochure (available at the Visitors Center, central library, and museums), which plots out a worthwhile 15-point walking tour around El Pueblo, the Civic Center, the Financial District, and Little Tokyo. Each guide has a map and helpful MTA information. The **Los Angeles Conservancy** (www.laconservancy.org) also offers free, printable self-guided walking tours geared toward architectural landmarks on its website as well as a variety of docent-led Saturday tours featuring Downtown's historic buildings. (☎213-623-2489. Make reservations at least 1 week in advance. No strollers or young children. Tours $8.)

The **DASH Shuttle** runs six lines Downtown that cover most of the major tourist destinations. (25¢, see p. 378. References to DASH shuttles in the listings below are for M-F travel.) If driving, park in a secure lot, rather than on the street. Due to expensive short-term lot parking ($3 per 20min.) and exorbitant meter prices (25¢ per 10min.), it's best to park in a public lot ($5-10 per day) and hit the pavement on foot. The **LA Visitors Center**, 685 S. Figueroa St., should have answers to your travel queries and pamphlets for every place you could possibly want to visit. (Open M-F 8am-4pm, Sa 8:30am-5pm. See p. 382.)

**EL PUEBLO HISTORIC PARK.** The historic birthplace of LA is now known as **El Pueblo de Los Angeles Historical Monument**, bordered by Cesar Chavez Ave., Alameda St., Hollywood Fwy., and Spring St. (DASH B). In 1781, 44 settlers established a pueblo and farming community here; today, 27 buildings from the eras of Spanish and Mexican rule are preserved.

Established in 1825, the **Plaza**, with its Moreton Bay fig trees and huge kiosk, is the center of El Pueblo. It is the site of several festivals including the Mexican Independence celebration (Sept. 16), *Dia de los Muertos* celebrations (Nov. 1-2), and *Cinco de Mayo* (May 5). (See **Seasonal Events,** p. 429. Dates of festivals are subject to change so call ahead to confirm.) Treat yourself to the cheapest churros around (2 for $1). Walk down **Olvera Street,** which resembles a colorful Mexican marketplace, and bargain at *puestos* (vendor stalls) selling everything from Mexican handicrafts and food to personalized t-shirts. The **Avila Adobe** (c. 1818), 10 E. Olvera St., is the "oldest" house in the city. Following the earthquake of 1971 which damaged the house severely, it was restored as an example of LA life in the 1810s (open daily 9am-3pm). On the first floor of the **Sepulveda House** (1887) is the **Visitors Center,** where you can request to view *Pueblo* of Promise, an 18min. history of LA. (622 N. Main Street. ☎213-628-1274. Open M-Sa 10am-3pm. Walking tour maps 50¢. Free walking tours offered Tu-Sa at 10am, 11am, and noon beginning at the Hellman-Quon Building, off Los Angeles St. near the Firehouse Museum. Reservations required for groups of 10 or more.)

**CHINATOWN.** Today's **Chinatown** (DASH B), roughly bordered by Yale, Spring, Ord, and Bernard St., is home to less than five percent of the city's Chinese population. With its pagoda-like gates, pedestrian lanes, restaurants, *dim sum*, and

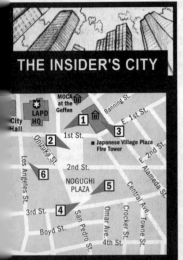

# THE INSIDER'S CITY

## LITTLE TOKYO

Angelenos of Japanese ancestry live elsewhere—suburban Gardena for example—but Little Tokyo is still an active cultural center, as well as home to fantastic and unique architecture.

**1** **Little Tokyo Visitor Center,** 307 E. 1st St. (☎213-613-1911) has maps and info.

**2** **Japanese Village Plaza,** 300 block E. 2nd St., is a florid fusion of shopping-mall Americana and Japanese design.

**3** **Japanese American National Museum,** 369 E. 1st St., is housed in a Buddhist temple and an accompanying building designed by Roy Obata.

**4** **Japanese American Cultural & Community Center,** 244 S. San Pedro St., is a showcase of community art. (see p. 418)

**5** **Japan America Theatre,** opens its handwoven silk *doncho* (curtain) to cultural events like Kabuki theater.

**6** **A Thousand Cranes,** 120 S. Los Angeles St. (☎213-629-1200), overlooks Japanese gardens and serves shabu-shabu tempura.

kitsch vendors, Chinatown is lively and vibrant. For a very different experience of Chinese-American culture, visit Monterey Park, 6 mi. to the east.

**CIVIC CENTER.** The **Civic Center** (DASH B and D) is a solid wall of bureaucratic edifices most notable for its remarkably uninteresting architecture. It sits south of El Pueblo Park, bounded by US 101, Grand Ave., 1st St., and San Pedro St. Unless you have a hearing for that parking ticket you got by Staples Center, there isn't much reason to go inside. One of the best-known buildings in the Southland, **City Hall,** 200 N. Spring St., "has starred in more movies than most actors."

**MUSIC CENTER.** Reminiscent of Lincoln Center in New York, the Music Center is an enormous, beautiful complex that includes **The Dorothy Chandler Pavilion,** home of the LA Opera (☎213-972-8001; www.laopera.org), former site of the Academy Awards, and until very recently, home of the world-renowned LA Philharmonic and the LA Master Chorale. Across the street rise the radical silver slices of the Frank Gehry-designed **Walt Disney Concert Hall,** the Music Center's fourth and newest performance venue. This gleaming 2265-seat structure is the brand new home of the LA Phil and the LA Master Chorale, and will also host theatrical productions, touring shows, and other popular cultural performances. (151 S. Grand Ave. ☎213-972-7211; www.disneyhall.org.) Also part of the Music Center are the **Mark Taper Forum,** honored for its development of new plays (many theatrical award winning plays that end up on Broadway had their start here), and the **Ahmanson Theatre,** best known for its world-class dramas, musicals, comedies, and classical revivals. (☎213-628-2772; www.taperahmanson.com. Tours of the three-theatre complex offered weekdays at 11:30am, 12:30, and 1:30pm as performance schedules permit. Go to the outdoor information booth in the large outdoor courtyard between the theatres.)

**LITTLE TOKYO & THE ARTS DISTRICT.** Southeast of the Civic Center, east of 2nd and San Pedro St., lies **Little Tokyo** (DASH A). Founded with the opening of a Japanese restaurant in 1886, Little Tokyo served as the spiritual, cultural, and commercial center for Japanese immigrants and their descendants until deportation during WWII. After returning from internment camps, many Japanese-Americans moved to the suburbs, but successful efforts to rejuvenate the area have led it to regain its traditional status as a community center (see **The Insider's City,** at left).

The **Japanese American Cultural and Community Center** is the largest Asian-American cultural center in the country. It is home to a plaza designed by the internationally renowned Japanese-American artist, Isamu Noguchi, a Japanese-American Veterans Memorial that honors Japanese-American soldiers who died in America's wars, and the Doizaki Gallery, an art gallery that presents work from local and international artists as well as special exhibitions on calligraphy, *ikebana* (flowers), and other traditional art forms. Make sure to visit the serene **James Irvine Garden**, better known as *Seiryu-en* or "Garden of the Pure Stream." *(244 S. San Pedro St. ☎213-628-2725. www.jaccc.org. Gallery open Tu-F noon-5pm, Sa-Su 11am-4pm. Small donation may be requested.)* The **Japanese-American National Museum** has a Resource Center with interactive computers and access to WWII relocation camp records. *(369 E. 1st St. ☎213-625-0414; www.janm.org. Open Su, Tu-W, and F-Sa 10am-5pm, Th 10am-8pm. Resource Center closes at 5pm. $6, seniors $5, students and ages 6-17 $3, under 5 free; Th after 5pm and third Th of each month free.)*

The Frank Gehry-renovated **MOCA at The Geffen Contemporary,** 152 N. Central Ave., was once the garage for the LAPD fleet. The "Temporary Contemporary" eventually became permanent to the delight of its adoring public, and is now leased for $1 per year. The museum closely resembles a warehouse and presents highly-acclaimed installation art exhibitions. *(☎213-626-6222; www.moca.org. Open Tu-W and F-Su 11am-5pm, Th 11am-9pm. Art talks led by artists, authors, critics, and curators—call ahead for schedule. $8, students and seniors $5, under 12 free; Th 5-8pm free. Admission good for both Downtown MOCA locations. Shuttle transportation between the 2 locations offered.)*

**OTHER SIGHTS.** LA's history is etched in stone on the sides of the respected **LA Times** building between 1st and 2nd St. and on the corner of Spring St. Free tours are offered; call the public relations department (☎800-LA-TIMES/528-4637) and set up an appointment. Bargain hounds can haggle to their hearts' delight in the **Fashion District,** which is bordered by 6th and 9th St. along Los Angeles St. On Saturdays, these small, open-front wholesale stores sell their flimsy brandname knockoffs (e.g. "DNKY") individually. Get sequin tube tops, push-up bras, colored contacts (non-prescription), or packs of socks for cheap cheap cheap. The equally well-stocked **Grand Central Public Market** (see **Food,** p. 393) has its own stars embedded in the sidewalk out front, each bearing the name of a Chicano celebrity—a *rambla de fama* to complement Hollywood's. An LA fixture, the market is one of the best spots to taste some local flavor.

**SOUTHERN DISTRICTS.** The **Financial District** (DASH B and C) is a fusion of glass and steel, where gigantic high-rises soar up from the flat LA basin, clustering in an area bounded roughly by 3rd, 9th, Figueroa, and Olive St. The **Library Tower,** 633 W. 5th St., has a distinctive glass crown and is the tallest building between Chicago and Hong Kong at 1017 ft. The **Westin Bonaventure Hotel,** 404 S. Figueroa St., is composed of five squat but somehow sleek cylinders sheathed in black glass, and has appeared in *Rain Man, In the Line of Fire,* and *Heat.* The easily amused can spend hours in the high-speed, glass-walled elevators. Don't scoff; the view from the 32nd floor is better than the view from most helicopters. Slightly southeast of the Bonaventure is the historic **Biltmore Hotel,** 506 S. Grand Ave., a $10 million, 683-room hotel designed by Schultze and Weaver (best known for New York's Waldorf-Astoria). It was a filming location for *Dave, Independence Day, Ghostbusters,* and *The Sting,* which featured scenes in the Crystal Ballroom.

Before **Bunker Hill** sprouted skyscrapers, it was a residential area with expensive Victorian homes. The one remaining relic from this era is **Angel's Flight,** "the shortest railway in the world." Unfortunately, the railway is closed indefinitely since an accident in February 2001. On the southwest side of the hill along 5th St. are the Bunker Hill Steps—a fantastic, florid maze of escalators, stairs, and landings modeled after the Spanish Steps in Rome.

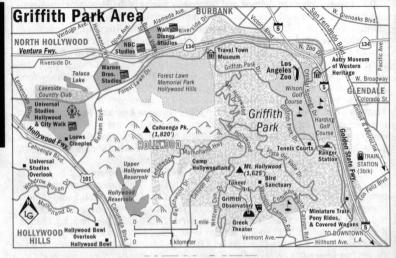

**Griffith Park Area**

**MUSEUM OF CONTEMPORARY ART (MOCA).** The Museum of Contemporary Art (MOCA) in the California Plaza is a celebrated piece of modern architecture. Arata Isozaki found inspiration for the facade's curve in LA's favorite daughter, Marilyn Monroe. The most compelling collection of Western modern visual art ever curated is now on permanent display at MOCA. *(250 S. Grand Ave. ☎ 213-626-6222; www.moca.org. Open Su, Tu-W, and F-Sa 11am-5pm, Th 11am-8pm. Art talks led by artists, authors, critics, and curators—call ahead for schedule. Free with admission. $8, students and seniors $5, under 12 free; Th 5-8pm free.)*

# NEAR DOWNTOWN

## EXPOSITION PARK

*Southwest of Downtown, off the I-110 Exposition Blvd. Exit, bounded by Exposition Blvd., Vermont Ave., Figueroa St., and Martin Luther King Jr. Blvd. From Downtown, take DASH shuttle F or MTA #81 or 442. From Hollywood, take MTA #204 or 754 down Vermont Ave. From Santa Monica, take MTA #20, 22, or 720 on Wilshire Blvd., and transfer to #204 at Vermont Ave. Parking at Figueroa St. and Exposition Blvd., $6.*

Once an open-air agricultural market and upscale suburb, Exposition Park began to decline in the early 1890s as wealthier citizens moved west. This population vacuum was filled by immigrants, who were barred from the Westside by home-owners' associations. The resulting low-cost, high-density housing further depressed the neighborhood. The deterioration was counteracted when the Olympic Games came to town in 1932, and the neighborhood was revitalized again for the 2nd Olympic Games at the park in 1984. Today, the area is much better off, with its museums generally safe and well visited, but **visitors should exercise caution outside the park, especially at night.**

**CALIFORNIA SCIENCE CENTER (CSC).** Dedicated to the sciences of California, the interactive exhibits in this spiffy new building educate kids and adults alike about West Coast issues: earthquakes, smog, traffic, and studio production. Eleven human embryos and fetuses are preserved in the World of Life gallery, and the display on California's fault line jarringly recreates an earthquake. You can even design your own earthquake-proof buildings. *(700 State Dr. ☎ 323-SCIENCE/724-3623; www.casciencectr.org or www.californiasciencecenter.org. Open daily 10am-5pm. Free.)* The seven-story, 91 ft. wide **IMAX Theater** shows critically acclaimed, often stunning 45min. films on nature, space, and special effects. *(☎ 213-744-7400. Shows every hr. M-F 10am-5pm, Sa-Su 10am-6pm. Evening shows often sell out; call ☎ 213-365-3500 to reserve tickets; $2 surcharge. $7.50, students and seniors $5.50, children ages 4-12 $4.50. Discounts for purchasing more than 1 ticket.)* The CSC's formal **rose garden** is the last remnant of the blessed days when the park was a horticultural exposition. The beautiful garden has over 19,000 specimens of 165 varieties of roses that maze through seven acres of lawn to surround gazebos and a large fountain. When the roses bloom (usually in late spring or early summer), the brilliant fragrance and colors are incredible. *(Open daily 8:30am-sunset. Free.)*

**OTHER MUSEUMS.** The **California African-American Museum** showcases the history of African Americans and their experience in California via rotating exhibits. *(600 State Dr. ☎ 213-744-7432; www.caam.ca.gov. Open W-Sa 10am-4pm. Free.)* The **Natural History Museum** is best known for its "habitat halls" where North American and African mammal specimens appear in lifelike poses. The museum also features some of the nation's best collections of Native American and Latin American artifacts. The hands-on **Discovery Center** is a must for children, who get to dig for dinosaur fossils and meet Jay and Cecil, the 12 ft. Burmese python and the 6 ft. iguana. *(900 Exposition Blvd. ☎ 213-743-DINO/3466. Open M-F 9:30am-5pm, Sa-Su 10am-5pm. Discovery Center animal presentations M-F 3pm, Sa-Su 11am and 3pm. $8, seniors and ages 13-18 $5.50, ages 5-12 $2, under 5 free; free 1st Tu of each month.)* The cavernous, Frank Gehry-designed **Aerospace Museum** has a blue and white F-104 Starfighter bolted to its south face, and a host of intriguing exhibits and displays inside. Design and launch your own model planes, pretend to pilot an LA Police Department chopper, or strap on a pair of wings and feel the wrath of a wind tunnel. *(700 State Dr. Open M-F 10am-1pm, Sa-Su 11am-4pm.)*

**UNIVERSITY OF SOUTHERN CALIFORNIA (USC).** North of Exposition Park, USC's 30,000 students bring a youthful character to the streets of Downtown. The alma mater of world-famous celebrities including Neil Armstrong, the school has had a gold-medal winning athlete in every summer Olympics since 1912. While it has kept busy churning out incredible athletes, USC's band has become the only US marching band to earn a platinum record—and then it earned one more. LA college sports fans salivate when the burnished USC Trojans clash with the blue-and-gold UCLA Bruins in annual football and basketball classics. *(University Park Campus. From downtown, take Figueroa St. south and turn right into campus on 35th street, or exit I-110 on Exposition Blvd. ☎ 213-740-2311; www.usc.edu. Campus tours offered M-F on the hour from 10am-3pm.)*

### GRIFFITH PARK & GLENDALE
*Nestled in the hills between US 101, I-5, and Rte. 134. Traveling by bus is not recommended because it affords little flexibility within the park; that said, if coming from Downtown, take bus #96 which goes north through the park along Crystal Springs Dr. From Hollywood, take bus #180 or 181 to intersection of Los Feliz Blvd. and Riverside. Transfer to #96 north.*

For a breath of fresh air and a respite from city life, take to the rugged, dry slopes of Griffith Park, the nation's largest municipal park, nestled in the hills between US 101, I-5, and Rte. 134. A stark contrast to the concrete heights of Downtown and the star-studded streets of Hollywood, the park is a refuge from the city and the site of many outdoor diversions. Fifty-two miles of hiking and horseback trails, three golf courses, tennis courts, a planetarium, an enormous zoo, several museums, an outdoor 6000-person amphitheater, and dozens of restaurants are con-

## ROM THE ROAD

### LENO'S LINES

I'm a night owl and I always watch the late-night talk shows, so couldn't pass up the chance to see Jay Leno tape The Tonight Show in the flesh.

I woke up at 5:30am. At 6:30am was standing in line behind 78 people, and at 8am, after the line had grown steadily, I was finally given two tickets and informed that seats weren't guaranteed—I had to be back in line no later than 3:30pm for the 4:30pm first-come, first served seating. After all this, seats weren't guaranteed! I was beside myself, but decided to play it safe. I returned at 2:30pm.

Nearly 100 people were already lined up. More surprising was the effort they had put into their appearances. Everyone was primping hair and adjusting clothing. I had shown up in a sweaty t-shirt and shorts held together by safety pins, having forgotten about our fleeting moment of glory: we clap and whistle as the camera sweeps over us and Jay walks onto the stage.

As the minutes passed, the line wrapped around the block. No wonder seating isn't guaranteed—in order to ensure a full house, the show distributes three times as many tickets as there are seats. As I stood there, about 100 people from the front, a quick calculation assured me I would get in. Wrong again. I learned about the guest list—friends and entourages of stars who want to attend a taping. Depending on the show, the guest list can swell to 200. After all my efforts and a day practically

tained within its rolling 4107 acres. Several mountain roads through the park (especially Vista Del Valle Dr.) afford panoramic views of the LA basin from Downtown to Century City. The 5 mi. hike to the top of Mt. Hollywood, the highest peak in the park, is quite popular. Keep a lookout for deer, opossum, squirrels, and the solitary cougar.

For info on trails, golf, tennis, biking, and horse rides, stop by the **Visitors Center and Ranger Headquarters,** 4730 Crystal Spring Dr. (☎323-913-4688, emergency 323-913-7390. Park open daily 5am-10pm.) The park has numerous equestrian trails and places to saddle up, such as **J.P. Stables.** No experience is necessary, and guides are provided. (1914 Mariposa St., Burbank. First come, first served. ☎818-843-9890. Open daily 8am-6pm. $18 1hr., $12 each additional hr. Cash only.)

**PLANETARIUM & OBSERVATORY.** The world-famous white stucco and copper domes of the castle-like mountaintop observatory would be visible from nearly any point in the LA basin, were it not for the smog. The observatory parking lot affords a terrific view of the Hollywood sign and the flat wastes of LA. You may remember the planetarium from the James Dean film *Rebel Without A Cause,* or most recently in the kitsch-on-speed *Charlie's Angels: Full Throttle.* Unfortunately, the observatory and planetarium are closed until 2005, when they will re-open with an additional 35,000 sq. ft. The grounds remain open. (Drive to the top of Mt. Hollywood on Vermont Ave. or Hillhurst St. from Los Feliz Blvd., or take MTA #180 or 181 from Hollywood Blvd. ☎323-664-1181, recording 323-664-1191; www.griffithobs.org. Grounds open in summer daily 12:30-10pm; in winter Tu-F 2-10pm, Sa-Su 12:30-10pm.)

**LA ZOO.** The park's northern end furnishes habitats for rare animals from around the world. The recently added Komodo dragon and Red Ape Rain Forest exhibits, along with the elephants and the chimps, are among the most popular spots in the zoo's well-kept 113 acres. The Children's Zoo offers a petting zoo, an interactive adventure theater, and a story-time area. Watch the sea lion training in the Aqautics Section, 11:30am and 2:30pm daily. During summer, the heat is often too much for the animals, especially the poor penguins, so viewing all your favorites is certainly not guaranteed. Be on the lookout for the completion of a new, spectacular home for the sea lions near the zoo's entrance, slated to finish in the summer of 2004. (5333 Zoo Dr. From Los Feliz Blvd, take Crystal Springs Dr. into the park; the Zoo will be on your left. ☎323-644-4200; www.lazoo.org. Open Sept.-June daily 10am-5pm; July-Aug. daily 10am-6pm. $8.25, seniors $5.25, ages 2-12 $3.25.)

**AUTRY MUSEUM OF WESTERN HERITAGE.** The Autry Museum draws the line between Old West fact and fiction in its exhibits on pioneer life, outlaws, and movies. City slickers and lone rangers may discover that the American West is not what they thought—the museum insists that the real should not be confused with the reel. Still, costumes worn by Robert Redford and Clint Eastwood are as much artifacts as the authentic saddles and spurs of California's first cowboys, the *vaqueros*. Check out "The Shoot-Out at OK Corral," a simulation of the legendary 1881 10-person gunfight waged by renowned desert lawman Wyatt Earp (who died in LA), his brother Virgil, and their sweet-shooting comrade, Doc Holliday. The Holdout Arm Cheating Device for concealing cards and the extensive Colt firearms collection in the Community Gallery are also worthwhile. During July and August, the museum sponsors live swing music in its outdoor atrium; call for times. *(4700 Western Heritage Way. From Downtown, take MTA bus #96 up Crystal Springs Dr. If driving, from Los Feliz Blvd., take Crystal Springs Dr. into the park; Museum will be on your right.* ☎ *323-667-2000. Open Tu-W and F-Su 10am-5pm, Th 10am-8pm. $7.50, students and seniors $5, ages 2-12 $3; Th after 4pm free.)*

**FOREST LAWN CEMETERY.** A rather twisted sense of celebrity sightseeing may lead some travelers to Glendale, where they can gaze upon stars who can't run away when asked for an autograph. Among the illustrious dead are Clark Gable, George Burns, and Jimmy Stewart. The cemetery has a 30 ft. by 15 ft. reproduction of Leonardo da Vinci's *The Last Supper* (every ½hr., 9:30am-4pm). A 20min. narrated show unveils the "largest religious painting on earth," the 195 ft. by 45 ft. *Crucifixion*, which is so large it had to be transported from Europe in sections wrapped around telephone poles (every hr., 10am-4pm). If you're still obsessed with oversized art, swing by the Forest Lawn in Hollywood Hills (only a 10min. drive) to see "Birth of Liberty," America's largest historical mosaic—a 160 ft. by 30 ft. masterpiece composed of 10 million pieces of Venetian glass. *(1712 S. Glendale Ave. From Downtown, take MTA #90 or 91 and get off just after the bus leaves San Fernando Rd. to turn onto Glendale Ave. From I-5, take Los Feliz Blvd. east and take a right onto Glendale Ave.; from the Glendale Fwy. (Rte. 134), take San Fernando Rd North and a right onto Glendale Ave.* ☎ *800-204-3131. Open daily 8am-6pm. Mausoleum open 9am-4:30pm.)*

**TRAVEL TOWN MUSEUM.** At the very northern tip of the park, this museum is the resting place of several antique train sections, given by the railroad companies to the children of LA. Locomotives pull-

wasted, I still might be shut out! Finally the moment of truth arrived. We were let in slowly, each person going through tight security. I was 28 people away when the line stopped. A Leno representative walked down the line, counting. He pointed to me, whispered 28, stopped, and recounted. After a 3rd and 4th count, he walked toward me with a plastic bin, saying, "Hold this—you're going to be the last one."

Several financial offers later, I was whisked inside and seated with throngs of excited people. Only when I saw the half-dozen cameras and countless workers did I realize that the show doesn't exist as it appears on TV.

The guests were spectacular. Chef Rocco, the star of the reality show *Restaurant*, gave Jay a cooking lesson, preparing spaghetti and meatballs from scratch. Next was the beautiful Daryl Hannah of *Northfork*. Finally, world-renowned blues artist Buddy Guy put on a stunning show.

As expected, Jay spent much of the time cracking jokes and chatting. What I wasn't prepared for were the frantic commercial breaks when Jay's personal preeners pounced on him to smooth his hair and touch up his makeup. I walked away from the experience unsure if I preferred the live or TV version. Seeing stars up close is certainly exciting, but the off-screen action did away with some of the magic. Though I have a good story to tell, watching *The Tonight Show* on TV will never be quite the same. If you're determined to see a taping, though, remember the one and only rule—arrive early.

*-Aaron Rudenstine, 2004*

ing freight cars, passenger cars, and cabooses are scuffed by kiddie shoes daily as pint-size visitors are invited to climb aboard. Although most of the historic automobiles and fire engines were donated to other museums, a few are still on display. Children will demand to take the train ride. If you are around on a weekend, be sure to check out the complex miniature model of LA, replete with dozens of model trains zipping through the city. *(5200 Zoo Dr. ☎323-662-5874. Open Apr.-Oct. M-F 10am-5pm, Sa-Su 10am-6pm; Oct.-Apr. M-F 10am-4pm, Sa-Su 10am-5pm. Model of LA open daily in summer 10am-5pm; in winter 10am-4pm. Free. Train ride $2, seniors $1.50, children 3 and older $2; free on the 1st weekend of the month.)*

## SAN FERNANDO VALLEY

TV and movie studios redeem the Valley (somewhat) from its bland warehouses, blond Valley Girls, and faceless strip malls. Passing Burbank on Rte. 134, you might catch glimpses of the Valley's most lucrative trademark studios: **Universal, Warner Bros., NBC,** and **Disney.** To best experience the industry, attend a **free TV show taping** or take one of the tours offered by most studios.

**▨ UNIVERSAL STUDIOS.** A movie and television studio that happens to have the world's first and largest movie-themed amusement park attached, Universal Studios Hollywood is the most popular tourist spot in Tinseltown. Located north of Hollywood in its own municipality of Universal City (complete with police and fire station), the park began as a public tour of the studios in 1964. It has since become a full-fledged amusement park with rides, attractions, and live shows based on some of Universal's classic films. The signature Studio Tour tram brings riders face-to-face with King Kong and Jaws, rattles through a massive earthquake, and wanders past blockbuster sets from America's movie tradition, including *Apollo 13, Jurassic Park,* and the infamous Bates Motel from *Psycho.* For some, though, the tour plays second fiddle to the park's interactive adventures. The movie itself may have bombed, but the live stunts and pyrotechnics at the *Waterworld* spectacular are impressive. Careen through time on Doc Brown's Delorean in **Back to the Future: The Ride,** take a magical bike trip with **E.T.** across the galaxies, or brave the blazing inferno in **Backdraft.** Don't miss **Animal Planet Live!** and the **Special Effects Stages.** *(Take US 101 to the Universal Center Dr. or Landershim Blvd. Exits. By MTA rail: exit North Hollywood Red Line at Universal Station. ☎800-UNIVERSAL; www.universalstudios.com. Open July-Aug. M-F 9am-8pm, Sa-Su 9am-9pm; Sept.-June M-F 10am-6pm, Sa-Su 10am-7pm. Last tram leaves M-F 5:15pm, Sa-Su 6:15pm; in off-season 4:15pm. Tours in Spanish daily. $47, under 48 inches $37, under 3 free. Parking $8.)*

**UNIVERSAL CITY WALK.** This neon-heavy, open-air strip of shopping, dining, movie theaters, and nightlife is the Valley's more colorful but less charming answer to Santa Monica's Third St. Promenade. The mammoth green guitar outside the Hard Rock Cafe, a lurid King Kong sign, and the towering IMAX screen at the Cineplex Odeon cinemas set the tone for the vivid, larger-than-life complex. *(☎818-622-4455; www.citywalkhollywood.com. City Walk parking $8. Full parking refund with purchase of two movie tickets before 6pm, $2 refund after 6pm.)*

**MISSION SAN FERNANDO REY DE ESPAÑA.** Founded by Father Fermin Lasuen in 1797, the San Fernando Mission is rich with history and is the largest adobe structure in California. The building that stands today is an amazing re-creation of the original destroyed by the 1971 Sylmar earthquake. The grounds, with museum and gift shop, are beautifully kept and definitely worth a visit. *(15101 San Fernando Mission Blvd. ☎818-361-0186. Mass M-Tu and Th-Sa 7:25am, Su 9 and 10:30am. Open daily 9am-4:30pm. $4, seniors and ages 7-15 $3, under 7 free.)*

**SIX FLAGS THEME PARKS.** At the opposite end of the Valley, 40min. north of LA in Valencia, is thrill-ride heaven **Magic Mountain.** Not for novices, Magic Mountain contains the most roller coasters in the world. Its newest addition, **Scream!,** is Southern California's first floorless mega-coaster where your feet dangle in the air as you scream through 4000 ft. of twists, dives, plunges, and loops. **X** flips, spins, and rotates riders 360 degrees, creating a sensation of flying. **Goliath** hits 85 mph and hurtles through an underground tunnel. Other highlights of the park include: **Revolution,** one of the earliest coasters to do a full loop; **Colossus,** California's largest wooden roller coaster; **Viper,** the world's largest looping roller coaster; **Tidal Wave** (stand on the bridge for a soaking); **Deja Vu,** a coaster with a "boomerang" track; the suspended **Batman;** and the 100 mph **Superman** (6½ seconds of weightlessness). Temperatures here frequently soar above 100°F in the summer, so bring a hat, sunblock, and plenty of bottled water. Next door, Six Flags' waterpark **Hurricane Harbor** features the world's tallest enclosed speed slide. *(Take US 101 N to Rte. 170 N to I-5 N to Magic Mountain Pkwy. ☎661-255-4100. Open daily Apr.-Sept. 6; hours vary. Sept.-Mar. open weekends and holidays. $45, seniors and under 48 inches tall $30, under 2 years free. Parking $7. Hurricane Harbor: ☎661-255-4527. Open May-Sept.; hours vary. $22, seniors and under 48 inches tall $15, under 2 years free. Combo admission to both parks that can be used on the same day, consecutive days, or for a return visit $55.)*

# PASADENA

The splendid **Convention and Visitors Bureau,** 171 S. Los Robles Ave., is a useful first stop in Pasadena, with numerous promotional materials and guides to regional events. (☎626-795-9311; www.pasadenacal.com. Open M-F 8am-5pm, Sa 10am-4pm.) The city-run **Art Buses** shuttle the loop between Old Town and the Downtown area around Lake Ave. approximately every 15min. (50¢). Each of the twelve buses has a theme (i.e., performing arts, Arroyo Seco desert, multiculturalism) reflected in its decor. (☎626-744-4055. Shuttles run downtown M-Th 11am-7pm, F 11am-10pm, Sa-Su noon-8pm; uptown M-F 7am-6pm, Sa-Su noon-5pm.)

■ **NORTON SIMON MUSEUM OF ART.** Rivaling the much larger Getty Museum in quality, this world-class private collection chronicles Western art from Italian Gothic to 20th-century abstract. The museum features paintings by Raphael, Van Gogh, Monet, and Picasso, as well as rare print etchings by Rembrandt and Goya. The Impressionist and Post-Impressionist hall, the Southeast Asian sculptures, and the 79,000 sq. ft. sculpture garden, by California landscape artist Nancy Goslee Power, are particularly impressive. *(411 W. Colorado Blvd., at Orange Grove Blvd. From I-110 N, exit at Orange Grove Blvd. and take a left onto Orange Grove Blvd. Continue 2 mi. and turn right on Colorado Blvd. Take MTA bus #180 or 181 west on Colorado Blvd. between Lake and N. Orange St. ☎626-449-6840; www.nortonsimon.org. Open M, W-Th, and Sa-Su noon-6pm, F noon-9pm. $6, seniors $3, students with ID and children under 18 free. Free parking.)*

**ROSE BOWL.** In the gorge that forms the city's western boundary stands Pasadena's most famous landmark. The sand-colored, 90,000-seat stadium is home to "the granddaddy of them all," the annual college football clash on Jan. 1 between the champions of the Big Ten and Pac 10 conferences. The Bowl Championship Series comes every four years, and the UCLA Bruins play regular-season home games here as well. *(1001 Rose Bowl Dr. ☎626-577-3100; www.rosebowlstadium.com. Bruins info: ☎310-825-29469; www.cto.ucla.edu.)* The bowl also hosts an enormous monthly flea market that attracts upwards of 2000 vendors, selling nearly one million items. *(☎323-560-7469. Held the 2nd Su of each month 9am-4:30pm. Admission 5-7am $20, 7-8am $15, 8-9am $10, 9am-3pm $7.)*

**FENYES ESTATE.** Built in 1905, the estate sits on the same grounds as the **Pasadena Museum of History** and the Pasadena city archives. It houses an impressive collection of Renaissance furniture, Egyptian sculpture, and local art amassed by Eva Scott Fenyes of the Scott Paper Company. Two galleries on the grounds have regularly rotating exhibitions. *(470 W. Walnut St., off Orange Grove Blvd. ☎626-577-1660. Museum tours Su and W-Sa 1:30 and 3pm. Tours $3, seniors and students $2. Gallery admission $5, seniors and students $4, under 12 free. Combined admission $7.)*

**PASADENA MUSEUM OF CALIFORNIA ART.** The only museum in Southern California committed solely to the art of California. Regularly rotating exhibits are dedicated to California art, architecture, and design from 1850 to the present. *(490 E. Union St. ☎626-568-3665. Open W-Th and Sa-Su 10am-5pm, F 10am-8pm. $6, seniors and students $4, under 12 free. First F of each month 5-8pm free.)*

**ARTS...** The **Pasadena Playhouse** nurtured the careers of William Holden, Dustin Hoffman, and Gene Hackman, among others. Founded in 1917 and restored in 1986, it now offers some of LA's finest theater. *(39 S. El Molino Ave., between Colorado Blvd. and Green St. ☎626-356-7529. For more info, see **Theater,** p.437.)* Housed in the concrete labyrinth of the Pasadena Center, the **Pasadena Civic Auditorium** is the centerpiece of the city's Spanish-influenced architecture. The Auditorium hosted television's **Emmy Awards** each year until 1998, when the ceremonies moved to Los Angeles. Since it is a rented venue, events are forever changing, but this 3000-seater usually hosts the Pasadena Symphony and the Distinguished Speaker Series, which hosts guests from Sharon Peres to Bob Woodward to Rudy Giuliani. *(300 E. Green St., at Marengo St. ☎626-449-7360, Distinguished Speaker Series tickets ☎800-508-9301. Box office open M-Sa 10am-5pm.)* If you're sick of the arts, work off your intermission snacks at the **Pasadena Ice Skating Center,** which holds public skate sessions every evening Wednesday through Saturday. *(310 E. Green St., in the Pasadena Center. ☎626-578-0801. Open M-Tu noon-4pm, W-Th noon-5pm, F noon-5pm and 8-10:30pm, Sa 8-10:30pm, Su 9:30-11:30am and 1-3:30pm. $7.)*

**...AND SCIENCES.** Some of the world's greatest scientific minds do their work at the **California Institute of Technology (Caltech).** Founded in 1891, Caltech has amassed a faculty that includes several Nobel laureates and a student body that prides itself both on its staggering collective intellect and its loony practical jokes. These jokes have ranged from simple frat-house pranks like unscrewing all the chairs in a lecture hall and bolting them in backwards to the nationally televised message that students added to the Rose Bowl scoreboard during the Jan. 1 game. *(1201 E. California Blvd., about 2½ mi. southeast of Old Town. ☎626-395-6327. Tours M-F 2pm. Take I-110 N until it becomes the Arroyo Pkwy. Turn right on California Blvd. and go 1¼ mi. Turn left on Hill Ave., left on San Pasqual St., and right on Holliston Ave. Proceed to 370 S. Holliston Ave. to register your car.)* **NASA's Jet Propulsion Laboratory,** about 5 mi. north of Old Town, executed the journey of the Mars Pathfinder. Ask to see pictures of the face of Mars. *(4800 Oak Grove Dr. ☎818-354-9314. Free tours by appointment.)*

**OTHER SIGHTS.** Besides spectator sports, Pasadena's main draw is **Old Town Pasadena,** bound approximately by Walnut St. and Del Mar Ave., between Pasadena Ave. and Arroyo Pkwy. This vibrant shopping and dining mecca, which proudly calls itself "trendy," is located in more than 200 buildings dating back to the 1880s and 1890s. The **Plaza Pasadena** contains a 14-screen movie cineplex, shopping mall, and gourmet supermarket just east on Colorado Blvd. On the north side of Plaza Pasadena is the beautiful **City Hall,** 100 N. Garfield Ave., with an open courtyard, lush gardens, and a fountain. *(☎626-744-4228.)*

# NEAR PASADENA

**HUNTINGTON LIBRARY, ART GALLERY, AND BOTANICAL GARDENS.** This institute that commemorates Henry Huntington, a wealthy Californian railroad and real estate developer, was founded in 1919 and opened to the public in 1928. Its stunning 150 acres of gardens are broken into thematic areas including the Rose Garden, the Shakespeare and herb gardens, and a Japanese Garden. (Picnicking and sunbathing among the greens is strictly forbidden.) The library holds one of the world's most important collections of rare books and British and American manuscripts, including a Gutenberg Bible, Benjamin Franklin's handwritten autobiography, a 1410 manuscript of Chaucer's *Canterbury Tales*, and a number of Shakespeare's first folios. The art gallery is known for its 18th- and 19th-century British paintings, but also boasts Rogier Van Der Weyden's *Madonna and Child* (1460), and a strong collection of American art, including Edward Hopper's *The Long Leg* (1935). The Arabella Huntington Memorial Collection displays Renaissance paintings and 18th-century French decorative art, and tea is served in the Rose Garden Tea Room. *(1151 Oxford Rd., between Huntington Dr. and California Blvd. in San Marino, south of Pasadena, about 2 mi. south of the I-210 Allen Ave. Exit. From Downtown LA, take MTA bus #79 and 379 out of Union Station to San Marino Ave. and walk 1½ mi. (45min. trip).* ☎ *626-405-2100; www.huntington.org. Open Memorial Day to Labor Day Su and Tu-Sa 10:30am-4:30pm; in winter Tu-F noon-4:30pm, Sa-Su 10:30am-4:30pm. $12.50, seniors $10, students $8.50, ages 5-11 $5, under 5 free; 1st Th of each month free.)*

**DESCANSO GARDENS.** The 165-acre garden includes one of the world's largest camellia forests, a historic rose collection, and manmade waterfalls. Events ($7-10) include tutorials on home gardening, bug displays, and cool night walks. Blooming peaks in early spring. *(1418 Descanso Dr., by the intersection of Rte. 2 and 210.* ☎ *818-949-4290. Open daily 9am-5pm. $6, students and seniors $4, ages 5-12 $1.50.)*

**SOUTHWEST MUSEUM.** Recent remodeling and innovative exhibits give this Highland Park museum the attention it deserves. The palatial Spanish-Moorish building has Native American cultural artifacts, including an 18 ft. Cheyenne Tipi. *(234 Museum Dr. Take MTA bus #83 along Broadway to Museum Dr. By car, take the I-110 (Pasadena Fwy.) to Ave. 43 and follow the signs.* ☎ *323-221-2164. www.southwestmuseum.org. Call for tours. Open Su and Tu-Sa 10am-5pm. Library open by appointment. $6, students and seniors $4, ages 7-18 $3, under 6 free.)*

**RAGING WATERS.** California's largest water park overflows with 50 acres of slides, pools, whitewater rafts, inner tubes, fake waves, and even a fake island (this is LA, after all). Hurl yourself over the seven-story waterslide **Drop Out** or rush down **Speed Slide**. *(111 Raging Waters Dr. in San Dimas. Just north of the I-10, I-210, and 57 interchange. Exit I-210/57 at Raging Waters Dr.* ☎ *909-802-2200; www.ragingwaters.com. Hours vary; call ahead or check website. $28, seniors $18, under 48 inches $17, under 2 years free; after 4pm $20, under 48 inches $12. Parking $7.)*

# SOUTH BAY

**MANHATTAN, HERMOSA, & REDONDO BEACHES.** About 20 mi. southwest of downtown LA, **Pacific Coast Highway** (Hwy. 1) swings by the sand at Manhattan Beach, Hermosa Beach, and Redondo Beach, collectively known as LA's beach communities. **Manhattan Beach** is favored for surfing but draws large crowds of families and school trips as well; **Hermosa Beach,** the most popular urban beach in LA County, is also one of the cleanest. Its culture is an upscale version of Venice. Most visit **Redondo Beach** for its harbor, pier, and seafood-rich boardwalk; locals who want the surf and sand head north to either Manhattan or Hermosa. To reach this strip of beaches, take I-405 (San Diego Fwy.) and follow signs to your destination or hop on Hwy. 1 S from Los Angeles. The communities are a few miles apart along the Pacific Coast Highway. Manhattan Beach, Hermosa Beach, and Redondo Beach pop up one after another as you head straight down the coast from LA. Rancho Palos Verdes and San Pedro are slightly farther apart, around the bend that separates the Santa Monica Bay from the San Pedro Bay.

The **International Surf and Health Festival** is one of the more established annual festivals of the beach cities. Each year at the end of July or beginning of August, hundreds participate in the two-day festival of competitions, food, music, dance, drink, and tans. Competitions include surfing, beach volleyball, bodysurfing, swimming, sand castle building, fishing, and running. Registration is open to all, but must be done at least a month in advance. Contact the Manhattan Chamber of Commerce or print out registration forms at www.surffestival.org.

Manhattan Beach's main drag, **Manhattan Avenue,** is lined with popular cafes and shops and slopes down to the Manhattan Beach Pier. The small **Roundhouse Marine Studies Lab & Aquarium,** at the end of the pier, displays Santa Monica Bay marine life and includes a shark aquarium. (☎379-8117. Open M-F 3pm-dusk, Sa-Su 10am-dusk. $2 donation requested.) Casual players can bump volleyballs on the courts by the pier; further north at the corner of Marin and Highland Ave., games are often more skilled and competitive. Dubbed the Wimbledon of beach volleyball, the **Manhattan Beach Open** draws crowds to the pier in high summer to watch some of the best pro players in the world serve, set, and spike from morning to night (☎426-8000; www.avp.com). **Manhattan Beach Concerts in the Park** is a summer-long series of free concerts in Polliwog Park. *(1601 Manhattan Beach Blvd. ☎802-5417; www.citymb.info. Late June to Sept. 6 5-7pm.)*

**In Hermosa Beach,** the core of the beach scene is at **Pier Plaza,** at the end of Pier Ave. between Hermosa Ave. and the beach. South Bay's best bars, cafes, and surf boutiques sit in a small, car-free promenade. **The Strand** is the bike path that runs along Manhattan Ave. from Hermosa to Marina del Rey until it hits the bike/skate path along Ocean Front Walk, which stretches north to Santa Monica. The **Hermosa Beach Open,** on the same pro tour as the Manhattan Beach Open, awards more prize money than any other beach volleyball tournament. Call the Hermosa Beach Community Center (☎318-0280) for info. **Surfing lessons** are offered at **Pier Surf,** 25 Pier Ave. (☎372-2012. $100 per 1½hr.; includes board.) **Gallery C** is the largest art gallery in the South Bay dedicated to contemporary painting, sculpture, and installation by California artists. *(1225 Hermosa Ave. ☎798-0102. Open Su noon-5pm, Tu-W and F-Sa 11am-6pm, Th 11am-8pm.)*

**Redondo Beach** is a little farther south and a little less upscale than its northern neighbors. Main attractions are the pier, boardwalk, and marina complex. Beginning in July, the city sponsors free concerts on the pier every Tuesday and Friday night that range from rock to jazz to Latin to country. Adjacent **King Harbor** shelters thousands of pleasure boats and hosts some excellent sport fishing. The **Monstad Pier** supports many restaurants, bars, clubs, and the local fishing community.

**RANCHO PALOS VERDES.** Spanish haciendas and ranch houses dot the stunning cliffs and tan hills of this lovely wealthy peninsula. For a dose of Southern California's floral profusion, head to **South Coast Botanic Gardens,** 26300 Crenshaw Blvd., off Hwy. 1 in Rancho Palos Verdes. This former county landfill has been redeemed by an 87-acre garden, where over three quarters of the plants are drought-resistant. *(☎544-6815. Open daily 9am-5pm. $6, students and seniors $4, ages 5-12 $1.50; free 3rd Tu of each month.)* The all-glass **Wayfarer's Chapel** sits on the south side of the hills. Known as the "glass church," the chapel was designed by Frank Lloyd Wright's son, **Lloyd Wright.** Like his father, Wright incorporates his architecture with its natural surroundings. *(5755 S. Palos Verdes Dr. ☎377-1650. Open daily 7am-5pm but closes for weddings and services. Free.)*

**SAN PEDRO.** Farther south and east, at the end of Rte. 213, still water, tidepools, and a nearby harbor draw families to **Cabrillo Beach** (beach parking $6.50; free parking in surrounding neighborhood). The **Cabrillo Marine Aquarium** presents touch tanks, marine history exhibits, and a rather disturbing look at pickled squid and whale skeletons. *(3720 Stephen White Dr. From Rte. 110, exit at Harbor Blvd. in San Pedro. Take a right onto Harbor Blvd, turn right onto 22nd St., and take a left onto Pacific Ave. Take a left onto 36th St. and Stephen White Dr.* ☎548-7562. *Open Su and Sa 10am-5pm, Tu-F noon-5pm. Suggested donation $5, children and seniors $1.)*Cafes and antique shops line **6th Street.** The **Fort MacArthur Military Museum,** inside the 64-acre **Angel's Gate Park,** is a nearly intact coastal fortification. *(3601 Gaffey St.* ☎548-2631. *Open Su, Tu, Th, Sa noon-5pm. Free.)* Right down the hill from the museum is the **Korean Friendship Bell,** a popular daytime recreation spot with amazing views of the ocean, but not a safe place for solitary musings by night. The bell was featured in *The Usual Suspects.*

# ■ SEASONAL EVENTS

**Tournament of Roses Parade and Rose Bowl** (☎626-449-7673), in Pasadena. New Year's Day, Jan. 1, is always a perfect day in Southern California. Some of the wildest New Year's Eve parties happen along Colorado Blvd., the parade route. If you miss the parade, which runs from 8-10am, you can still see the floats on display that afternoon and on Jan. 2 on Sierra Madre Blvd. between Washington Blvd. and Sierra Madre Villa Ave. ($6). The champs of the Pac 10 and Big 10 conferences meet on the afternoon of Jan. 1 for the Rose Bowl, and every 4 years, the championship game of the NCAA Football's **Bowl Championship Series (BCS)** is held here. Only a few end-zone tickets are available to the public; call ☎626-449-4100 after Nov. 1.

**Chinese New Year Parade** (☎213-617-0396), in Chinatown, along Broadway Ave. Saturday, Jan. 24, 2004. Fireworks and dragons usher in this Chinese celebration.

**UCLA Mardi Gras** (☎310-825-6564), at the athletic field. Billed as the world's largest collegiate activity. Festivities 7pm-2am on Fat Tuesday in mid-May. Proceeds to charity.

**Playboy Jazz Festival** (☎310-449-4070), at the Hollywood Bowl. A weekend of entertainment by top-name jazz musicians of all varieties, from traditional to fusion. Sorry, no bunnies. The 2004 festival will take place on June 19-20. Call Ticketmaster (☎213-381-2000) for prices. See the No Work, All Play: Playboy Jazz Festival, p. xxx.

**Gay Pride Celebration** (☎323-969-8302), funded by the Christopher Street West Association. The last or second-to-last weekend in June. LA's lesbian and gay communities celebrate in West Hollywood. Art, politics, dances, and a huge parade. Tickets $12.

**Shakespeare Festival/LA** (☎213-481-2273), in Downtown and Palos Verdes. June-July This theater company aims to make Shakespeare more accessible. Youth program performs Shakespeare adaptations in early Aug. Downtown shows begin at 8pm in Pershing Sq. between 5th and 6th St. and Hill and Olive Ave. Canned food donation accepted in lieu of admission at Downtown performances; Palos Verdes admission $15.

**Día de los Muertos,** along Olvera St., Downtown. Nov. 1. Rousing Mexican cultural celebration for the spirits of dead ancestors revisiting the world of the living. Food, vendors, costumes, and Halloween accoutrements.

**Los Posados** (☎213-485-9777), along Olvera St., Downtown. Held in Dec. This celebration includes a candlelit procession and the whacking of a piñata.

**Whale-watching** is best Dec.-Mar., when the Pacific grays migrate south. 90% of the world's blue whale population summers off the Channel Islands (see p. 484); catch sight of them June-Sept. Boats depart from Ventura, Santa Barbara, Long Beach, and San Pedro. From Ventura, contact Island Packers (☎805-642-1393); for Santa Barbara, Truth Aquatics (☎805-882-0088); from Long Beach, Pier Point Landing Charters (☎562-983-9300); from San Pedro, Spirit Cruises (☎310-548-8080).

**LOS ANGELES**

# ▓ LA BY REGION

So you've dropped your bags off, grabbed a bite to eat, and maybe even seen some sights. Now the real fun begins. From basketball to bookstores, cafes to clubs, LA's got something for you. Below are a few handy charts of LA's best options. There's shopping—including music (p. 432), books (p. 431), clothes (p. 433), and novelties (p. 433); entertainment—including cinemas (p. 435) and live theaters (p. 437); and nightlife—including late-night restaurants (p. 439), coffeehouses (p. 440), bars (p. 441), clubs (p. 443), and LGB nightlife (p. 444). They're grouped by region, so if you find yourself looking for a movie in Hollywood or craving a late-night snack in the Valley, you'll know where to go.

## HOLLYWOOD (& AROUND)

| SHOPPING | |
|---|---|
| ▓ Amoeba Music (p. 432) | Music |
| Aron's (p. 432) | Music |
| Counterpoint Records (p. 432) | Music |
| Hollywood & Highland (p. 434) | Malls |
| Larry Edmunds Bookshop (p. 432) | Books |
| ▓ Samuel French (p. 432) | Books |
| Skeletons in the Closet (p. 433) | Novelties |
| Studio Wardrobe Dept. (p. 433) | Clothes |

| ENTERTAINMENT | |
|---|---|
| ▓ Arclight Cinerama Dome (p. 436) | Cinema |
| Egyptian Theatre (p. 437) | Cinema |
| El Capitan Theatre (p. 436) | Cinema |
| ▓ Grauman's Chinese (p. 436) | Cinema |
| Pantages (p. 437) | Theater |
| Vine Theatre (p. 437) | Cinema |

| NIGHTLIFE | |
|---|---|
| ▓ 3 of Clubs (p. 442) | Bar |
| Arena (p. 444) | Club |
| Barney's Beanery (p. 439) | Late-Nite |
| ▓ Beauty Bar (p. 442) | Bar |
| Bourgeois Pig (p. 440) | Coffee |
| The Coach and Horses (p. 443) | Bar |
| Daddy's (p. 442) | Bar |
| ▓ The Derby (p. 444) | Club |
| ▓ Elixer (p. 440) | Coffee |
| ▓ Fred 62 (p. 439) | Late-Nite |
| G.A.L.A.X.Y. Gallery (p. 440) | Coffee |
| Groundling Theater (p. 441) | Comedy |
| The Lava Lounge (p. 443) | Bar |
| Lucky Strike (p. 443) | Bar |
| ▓ The Room (p. 442) | Bar |
| The Shelter (p. 444) | Club |
| Standard Lounge (p. 442) | Bar |
| Stir Crazy (p. 440) | Coffee |

## THE WESTSIDE: WEST LA & SOUTH BAY

| SHOPPING | |
|---|---|
| Beverly Center (p. 434) | Mall |
| Century City Complex (p. 434) | Mall |
| City Rags (p. 433) | Clothes |
| Necromance (p. 433) | Novelties |
| Rhino Records (p. 433) | Music |
| Westside Pavilion (p. 434) | Mall |

| ENTERTAINMENT | |
|---|---|
| Geffen Playhouse (p. 437) | Theater |
| LACMA's Bing Theater (p. 437) | Cinema |
| Mann's Village Theatre (p. 437) | Cinema |
| Nuart Theatre (p. 437) | Cinema |

| NIGHTLIFE | |
|---|---|
| 14 Below (p. 443) | Bar |
| Cafe Boogaloo | Bar |
| Catalina Coffee Co. | Coffee |
| Comedy & Magic Club | Comedy |
| Cow's End (p. 440) | Coffee |
| Lighthouse Cafe | Club |
| Maloney's (p. 443) | Bar |
| Rusty's Surf Ranch (p. 443) | Bar |
| The Kettle (p. 440) | Late-Nite |
| UnUrban Coffeehouse (p. 440) | Coffee |

## WEST HOLLYWOOD, FAIRFAX & SUNSET STRIP

| SHOPPING | |
| --- | --- |
| A Different Light (p. 432) | Books |
| A Touch of Romance (p. 434) | Novelties |
| Aardvark's (p. 433) | Clothes |
| Baby Jane of Hollywood (p. 434) | Novelties |
| ◙ Book Soup (p. 431) | Books |
| ◙ Dudley Doo-Right (p. 433) | Novelties |
| Hollywood Toys & Costumes (p. 434) | Novelties |
| Mr. Musichead (p. 432) | Music |

| NIGHTLIFE (CONT.) | |
| --- | --- |
| Key Club (p. 444) | Club |
| ◙ LA Improv (p. 441) | Comedy |
| Mel's Drive In (p. 439) | Late-Nite |
| Micky's (p. 445 | LGB |
| ◙ Miyagi's (p. 442) | Bar |
| ◙ North (p. 441) | Bar |
| The Palms (p. 445) | LGB |

| SHOPPING | |
| --- | --- |
| Out of the Closet (p. 433) | Novelties |
| Retail Slut (p. 433) | Clothes |
| Vinyl Fetish (p. 432) | Music |

| NIGHTLIFE | |
| --- | --- |
| ◙ Abbey Cafe (p. 445) | LGB |
| ◙ Canter's (p. 439) | Late-Nite |
| Comedy Store (p. 441) | Comedy |
| Here (p. 445) | LGB |

| NIGHTLIFE (CONT.) | |
| --- | --- |
| Rage (p. 445) | LGB |
| ◙ Largo (p. 444) | Club |
| Laugh Factory (p. 441) | Comedy |
| ◙ Rainbow Grill (p. 439) | Late-Nite |
| Roxy (p. 444) | Club |
| 7969 Peanuts (p. 445) | LGB |
| Whisky A Go-Go (p. 444) | Club |

## THE SAN FERNANDO VALLEY

| SHOPPING | |
| --- | --- |
| ◙ Samuel French (p. 432) | Books |

| ENTERTAINMENT | |
| --- | --- |
| ◙ Loews Cineplex (p. 436) | Cinema |
| Pasadena Playhouse (p. 437) | Theater |

| NIGHTLIFE | |
| --- | --- |
| Bob's Big Boy (p. 439) | Late-Nite |
| Jerry's Famous Deli (p. 439) | Late-Nite |
| The Ice House (p. 441) | Comedy |
| Q's Billiard Club (p. 443) | Bar |
| Twin Palms (p. 442) | Bar |

# ⌐ SHOPPING

In LA, shopping isn't just a practical necessity; it's a way of life. Popular shopping areas like Santa Monica's Third Street Promenade, Pasadena's Old Town, the Westside Pavilion, and the Century City Shopping Center are lined with chain boutiques and the latest cookie-cutter fashion of the moment. Nevertheless, a number of cool specialty shops with more one-of-a-kind items are tucked away from the shuffle. Remember, dahling: when the going gets tough, Angelenos go shopping.

## BOOKS

LA might not seem like the most literary of cities. After all, while subway commuters in other cities immerse themselves in the newspaper, Angelenos caught in an early-morning traffic jam listen to news or talk radio. The front shelves of LA bookstores are lined with more Hollywood bios and guides to becoming stars than most visitors have ever seen in their lifetime. But fear not, word-hungry literati, you don't have to resort to the ubiquitous Barnes and Noble megastores just yet.

◙ **Book Soup,** 8818 Sunset Blvd. (☎310-659-3110; www.booksoup.com), in **West Hollywood.** A maze of new books in every category imaginable, with especially strong film, architecture, poetry, and travel sections. The comprehensive newsstand that wraps around the building includes industry mags and international newspapers. **The Adden-**

**dum** next door is a gem for bargain-shopping book lovers, featuring major discounts (up to 50%) on hardcover art, photo, and design books, as well as fiction and non-fiction. Main store open daily 9am-11pm. Addendum open daily noon-8pm.

**Samuel French Bookshop,** 7623 Sunset Blvd. (☎323-876-0570), 5 blocks east of Fairfax, in **Hollywood,** and 11963 Ventura Blvd. (☎818-762-0535), in **Studio City.** Get prepped for your audition at this haven for entertainment industry wisdom: acting directories, TV and film reference books, trade papers, and a vast selection of plays and screenplays. Lists local theaters that are currently casting. Occasional script signings by local playwrights. Hollywood location open M-F 10am-6pm, Sa 10am-5pm. Studio City location open M-F 10am-9pm, Sa 10am-6pm, Su noon-5pm.

**A Different Light,** 8853 Santa Monica Blvd. (☎310-854-6601; www.adlbooks.com), at San Vicente Ave. in **West Hollywood.** The nation's largest gay and lesbian bookseller has an incredibly diverse selection: gay fiction and classics, biography and autobiography, self-help, travel, law, and queer theory. The shop also has videos, magazines, music, gift items, readings, and book signings. Open daily 11am-10pm.

**Larry Edmunds Bookshop, Inc.,** 6644 Hollywood Blvd. (☎323-463-3273), in **Hollywood.** One of the world's largest collections of books and memorabilia on cinema and theater. With 6000 movie posters that date back to 1932 and hundreds of biographies on big names and no-names in the entertainment world, this is the place to search for a book on, or full-length poster of, your obscure favorite actor. Open M-Sa 10am-6pm.

# MUSIC

Used music stores are a dime a dozen, especially in **Westwood** and along **Melrose Ave.** Many of the stores buy old CDs and tapes, which makes for good selections of "rejections." Below are some diamonds in the rough.

**Amoeba Music,** 6400 Sunset Blvd. (☎323-245-6400; www.amoebamusic.com), in **Hollywood.** Billed as the largest independent record store, Amoeba carries all genres and titles, including an extensive collection of underground music. Take advantage of the huge daily $1 clearance sales in each musical category. Live music 2-3 times per week; call ahead for times. Open M-Sa 10:30am-11pm, Su 11am-9pm.

**Counterpoint Records and Books,** 5911 Franklin Ave. (☎323-957-7965; www.counterpointrecordsandbooks.com), corner of Bronson Ave. in **Hollywood.** One of LA's best vinyl collections (from 50¢). A smaller collection of used CDs (from $1), videos, and tapes. Everything from blues to punk. Doubles as a used bookstore crammed with both popular and obscure titles. Open M-Th 11am-11pm, F-Sa 11am-midnight, Su 1-8pm.

**Vinyl Fetish,** 7305 Melrose Ave. (☎323-935-1300; www.vinylfetishrecords.com), in **West Hollywood.** The LP collection you wish you owned. Rock, funk, industrial, ska, punk, new wave, and disco. Records $1-20, depending on condition and rarity. CDs, tapes, books, t-shirts, stickers, pins, and other accessories. Open daily 11am-10pm.

**Aron's,** 1150 N. Highland Ave. (☎323-469-4700), in **Hollywood,** between Santa Monica and Sunset Blvd. Loved for its massive new and used CD collection, which ranges from ska to showtunes, and its large LP collection that features an extensive classical music section. Buys, sells, and trades. Open Su-Th 10am-10pm, F-Sa 10am-midnight.

**Mr. Musichead,** 709 N. Sierra Bonita (☎323-658-7625), at Melrose St. in **West Hollywood.** Although Mr. Musichead has a collection of 60s and 70s rock and jazz, it's better known for its posters and collectibles from the same era. Open daily 11am-7pm.

**Rhino Records,** 2028 Westwood Blvd. (☎310-474-8685; www.rhinowestwood.com), two blocks north of Olympic Ave., in **West LA.** Specializes in the obscure, the alternative, and those never-played promotional albums. Strong blues, jazz, exotica, and dance sections. Open M-Sa 10:30am-9:30pm, Su noon-7:30pm.

# CLOTHING

It's a fashion war out there, and you've got to look your best. Fashion in the City of Angels is one-half glitz and one-half retro, with both halves acutely aware that this is *not* New York—black just doesn't cut it. Your mission is to look like heaven at one hell of a low price. Unfortunately, with so many overpriced boutiques in LA, that's not always easy. Check out some of the great spots below.

**Aardvark's,** 7579 Melrose Ave. (☎323-655-6769), corner of Curson, in **West Hollywood,** and 85 Market St. (☎310-392-2996), in **Venice.** Used gear galore from practical used Levi's ($20-25) to fabulously funky wigs ($20). Lots of hats, leather jackets, and dresses from any decade. Open M-Th noon-8pm, F-Sa 11am-9pm, Su noon-7pm.

**Retail Slut,** 7308 Melrose Ave. (☎323-934-1339; www.retailslut.com), in **West Hollywood,** is a mecca for all manner of punks and goths. The place to find fetish gear or just browse the huge selection of earrings and body rings. Open daily noon-8pm.

**City Rags,** 10967 Weyburn Ave. (☎310-209-0889), in **Westwood Village.** This small but well-stocked 70s retro-wear-house has a friendly staff and great bargains on vintage stuff that's actually wearable. If they don't have what you need, they can hunt it down. Shirts $12-16; pants $18-30. Open Su-Th 11:30am-8pm, F-Sa 11:30am-10pm.

**The Studio Wardrobe Department,** 1357 N. Highland Ave. (☎323-467-9455), in **Hollywood.** Everything (including the register) is vintage in this brick warehouse of denims, furs, and polyesters. Known for its unscheduled but regular 50-items-for-$1 and 25-pairs-of-jeans-for-$5 sales. No refunds. Open M-Sa 10am-10pm, Su 10am-8pm.

# NOVELTIES

LA has its share of eccentrics, and after all, they shop *some*where. Some of these stores are a little morbid and some may be a little explicit, but none make apologies for what they sell or how they sell it.

▓ **Dudley Doo-Right Emporium,** 8200 Sunset Blvd. (☎323-656-6550), in **West Hollywood.** Cartoonist Jay Ward's old production office is now cluttered with memorabilia based on his characters, *Rocky and Bullwinkle, George of the Jungle,* and *Dudley Doo-Right.* T-shirts $16-20, stuffed animals from $10, show scripts $8.50, storyboards $16. Open Tu, Th, and Sa 11am-5 pm. No credit cards.

**Out of the Closet,** 8224 Santa Monica Blvd. (☎323-848-9760), in **West Hollywood.** With 17 stores in the LA area, this is the daddy of resale retail. You can find anything you need in at least one of their stores. Profits are donated to AIDS Healthcare Foundation. Look for OOC's trademark neon storefronts or call for other locations. Most stores open daily 10am-7pm. This store is open 10am-8pm because it offers free HIV testing.

**Necromance,** 7220 Melrose Ave. (☎323-934-8684; www.necromance.com), in **West LA.** In the front window of this store that specializes in death is a rug made from dog's hair with the dog's head still intact and cute as ever. Inside, you can buy genuine human temporal bones ($10) or real human skulls ($125-600). Open M-Sa noon-7pm, Su 2-6pm.

**Skeletons in the Closet,** 1104 Mission Rd. (☎323-343-0760, http://lacs-tores.co.la.ca.us/coroner), in **Downtown.** Actually the LA Coroner's gift shop and as tasteless as it sounds. Sells personalized toe tags, beach towels with body outlines, and other memorabilia. Profits go to drunk driving programs. Open M-F 8am-4:30pm.

**Baby Jane of Hollywood,** 7985 Santa Monica Blvd. (☎323-848-7080; www.babyjaneof-hollywood.com), at Laurel St. in the French Market restaurant in **West Hollywood.** Carries more than your typical array of posters, records, tabloids, and autographed glossies ($25-75). It also has a huge collection of *Pez*, "Penises on Parade" Mardi Gras videos, film industry collectibles, and shots of celebs in revealing poses. Open daily noon-8pm.

**A Touch of Romance,** 6650 Hollywood Blvd. (☎323-962-4776; www.atouchofro-mance.com), at Cherokee Ave. in **West Hollywood.** An all-you-can-imagine racy adult shop featuring an extensive collection of lubricants, fetish outfits, videos, and toys. Helpful and professional staff. Open M-Sa 10am-9pm, Su 11am-6pm.

**Hollywood Toys & Costumes,** 6600 Hollywood Blvd. (☎323-464-4444 or 800-554-3444; www.hollywoodtoys.com), in **West Hollywood.** Enormous warehouse of makeup and accessories. The largest wig store in Hollywood, selling wigs of all colors, styles, and fashions ($25-700). Open M-F 9:30am-7pm, Sa 10am-7pm, Su 10:30am-7pm.

# MALLS

Mall-shopping in LA is not just for the Valley Girl, and your retail-going experience need not be as unpleasant as, say, a trip to the Valley. Going to the mall can (and should) be a full-day activity, as you will need a few hours to see and be seen. Many Southland shopping complexes are open-air, which makes for a nice stroll down a sunny tree-lined walkway. The hub of the shop-'til-you-drop spots is West LA, with the following malls at the head of the pack.

**Century City Shopping Complex,** 10250 Santa Monica Blvd. (☎310-277-3898), in **West LA,** southwest of Beverly Hills. Exit I-405 at Santa Monica Blvd. and go east. Offers 140 stores, boutiques, and cafes, but few come just for the shops. Its well-manicured, arched walkways are a good place to spot celebrities. It also features an incredibly popular 14-screen **AMC Century Theater** (☎310-289-4262).

**Westside Pavilion,** 10800 W. Pico Blvd. (☎310-474-6255; www.westsidepavil-ion.com), corner of Westwood Blvd. in **West LA,** has 150 shops and restaurants including mall standards like Banana Republic, Barnes & Noble, and Nordstrom. And what would an LA mall be without a movie theater? This one features **Westside Pavilion Cinemas.** Open M-F 10am-9pm, Sa 10am-8pm, Su 11am-6pm; individual stores may vary.

**Beverly Center,** 8500 Beverly Blvd. (☎310-854-0070; www.beverlycenter.com), at La Cienega Blvd. in **Beverly Hills.** The prime example of bigger and better. A monstrous neon megalith smack-dab in the middle of the city, complete with voyeuristic escalators snaking up the building's glass siding. The display windows are quite showy. Attached to the Beverly Center is the nation's first (and the world's second) **Hard Rock Cafe** (☎310-276-7605; open Su-Th 11:30am-11pm, F-Sa 11:30am-midnight).

**Hollywood & Highland,** 6801 Hollywood Blvd. (☎323-960-2331), in **Hollywood.** 4 levels of over 70 specialty stores, fancy restaurants, a nightclub, and a multi-screen cinema surround the Babylon Court, a 64,000 sq. ft. complex that serves as an outdoor gathering place and event venue. Stand in the center of the Court and see the Hollywood sign perfectly framed by the Court's large arch. Its main attraction is the **Kodak Theatre,** the new home of the Academy Awards Ceremonies (see p. 405).

# 🎵 ENTERTAINMENT

There are many ways to get a taste of the silver screen glitz created and peddled by the entertainment capital of the world. **Shopping** (see p. 431) is a major pastime in the LA area, crafted by its devotees into performance art. For after-hours fun, LA features some of the trendiest, celeb-frenzied **nightlife** (p. 439) imaginable. For amusement parks, see the listings for giants like **Disneyland** (p. 460), **Knott's Berry Farm** (p. 462), **Magic Mountain** (p. 425), and **Universal Studios** (p. 424).

## FILM & TELEVISION STUDIOS

A visit to the world's entertainment capital isn't complete without some exposure to the actual business of making a movie or TV show. Fortunately, most production companies oblige. **Paramount** (☎323-956-5000), **NBC** (☎818-840-3537), and **Warner Bros.** (☎818-954-1744) offer 2hr. guided tours that take you onto sets and through backlots. The best way to get a feel for the industry is to land yourself tickets to a taping. Tickets are free but studios tend to overbook, so holding a ticket does not always guarantee you'll get in. Show up early. **NBC,** 3000 W. Alameda Ave., at W. Olive Ave. in Burbank, is your best bet. Show up at the ticket office on a weekday at 8am for passes to Jay Leno's **Tonight Show,** filmed at 5pm the same evening (2 tickets per person, must be 16+). Studio tours run on the hour. (☎818-840-3537. M-F 9am-3pm. $7.50, ages 5-12 $4.) Many of NBC's "Must-See TV" shows are taped at **Warner Bros.,** 4000 Warner Blvd. (☎818-954-6000), in Burbank. Sitcoms such as the *Drew Carey Show* and *Everybody Loves Raymond* are taped from August to May—call the studio at least five business days in advance to secure tickets. Network TV's most popular sitcom, NBC's *Friends,* no longer films in front of a public audience. Call for information about the VIP tour.

A **CBS box office,** 7800 Beverly Blvd. (☎323-575-2458; open M-F 9am-5pm), next to the Farmer's Market (see p. 393) in West Hollywood, hands out free tickets to Bob Barker's game-show masterpiece *The Price is Right* (taped M-Th) up to one week in advance. Audience members must be over 18. You can request up to 10 tickets on a specific date by sending a self-addressed, stamped envelope to *The Price is Right* Tickets, 7800 Beverly Blvd., Los Angeles, CA 90036, about four to six weeks in advance. If all else fails, **Audiences Unlimited, Inc.,** 100 Universal City Plaza, Building 4250, Universal City, CA 91608 (☎818-506-0067; www.tvtickets.com), is a great resource. To find out which shows are available during your visit, send in a self-addressed, stamped envelope or check the website.

## MOVIES

LA's movie palaces show films the way they were meant to be seen: on a big screen, in plush seats, and with top-quality sound and air-conditioning. It would be a cinematic crime not to partake of the city's incredible moviegoing experiences.

The gargantuan theaters at **Universal City,** as well as those in **Westwood Village** near UCLA, are incredibly popular, especially on weekends. Lines at all the best theaters are very long, especially for new releases. In **Santa Monica,** there are 22 screens within the three blocks between Santa Monica Pl. and Wilshire Blvd. along Third Street Promenade.

To ogle the stars as they walk the red carpet into the theater for a **premiere,** call the four premiere hounds: **Grauman's Chinese** (about 2 per month); **El Capitan** (Disney films only); **Mann's Village** and **Bruin,** in Westwood. For info on what's playing in LA, call ☎323-777-3456 or read the daily Calendar section of the *LA Times.*

## SO, YOU WANNA BE IN PICTURES? Honey! Baby!

Sweetheart! You don't have to be beautiful and proportionally perfect to grace cellu-loid—just look at Tom Arnold or Lili Tomlin. The quickest way to get noticed is to land yourself a job as an extra—no experience necessary. One day's work will land $40-130 in your pocket and two meals in your tummy. Step One is to stop calling yourself an extra—you're an "atmosphere actor" (it's better for both your ego and your resume). Step Two is to contact a reputable casting service. **Cenex Central Casting,** 220 S. Flower St., Burbank 91506 (☎818-562-2755), is the biggest, and a good place to start. You must be at least 18 and a US citizen or have a Resident Alien/ Employment Authorization card. Step Three is to show up on time; you'll need the clout of DeNiro before you can waltz in after call. Don't forget to bring $20 in cash to cover the "photo fee." Step Four is to dress the part: don't wear red or white, which bleed on film and render you unusable. Finally, after you collect three **SAG** (Screen Actors Guild; 5757 Wilshire Blvd., Los Angeles, CA 90036; ☎323-937-3441) vouchers, you'll be eligible to pay the $1272 to join showbiz society. See you in the movies!

Devotees of second-run, foreign-language, and experimental films are rewarded by the Santa Monica theaters away from the Promenade. Foreign films play consistently at the eight **Laemmle Theaters** in Beverly Hills (☎310-274-6869), West Hollywood (☎323-848-3500), Santa Monica (☎310-394-9741), Pasadena (☎626-844-6500), and Downtown (☎213-617-0268).

LA's giant movie industry does not, surprisingly, include world-class film festivals like Cannes or Sundance. On the other hand, the city hosts a number of smaller, less expensive, and more accessible film showings, including **Outfest,** an LA gay and lesbian film festival in July (☎213-480-7065; www.outfest.org; each film $7-12), and the **Asian Pacific Film and Video Festival** (☎213-680-4462, ext. 68; each film $8, seniors and students $5), in May. The largest film festival is the pricey **AFI LA International Film Festival,** late-October to early November, which shows 150 shorts, documentaries, and features from around the world. (☎323-856-7707; www.afifest.com. $50 for full-week matinee pass; $250 for the entire festival.)

## MOVIE THEATERS

▨ **Arclight Cinerama Dome,** 6360 Sunset Blvd. (☎323-466-3401), in **Hollywood,** near Vine St. The ultimate cineplex for the serious moviegoer. 14 movie screens surround a gigantic dome that seats 820 people and displays a screen that expands from 80 to 180 ft. A spectacular, rumbling sound system. Recent movies only. Don't be late—doors close 7min. after movies begin. Tickets range from $7.75 to $14.

▨ **Loews Cineplex** (☎818-508-0588), in **Universal City,** atop the hill at Universal City Walk. Opened in 1987 as the world's largest cinema complex, its 18 wide-screen theaters and Parisienne-style cafe put all competition to absolute shame. Tickets $9, seniors and under 13 $6; before 4pm $6.75. Full refund on parking with purchase of 2 regular admission tickets before 6pm M-F; $2 parking rebate on all other shows.

▨ **Grauman's Chinese Theatre,** 6925 Hollywood Blvd. (☎323-464-8111), between Highland and La Brea Ave. in **Hollywood.** Hype to the hilt. For details, see **Hollywood Sights,** p. 404. Tickets $10, ages 3-12 and over 65 $7; first show of the day $7.50.

**El Capitan,** 6838 Hollywood Blvd. (☎323-467-7674 or 800-347-6396), in **Hollywood,** across from Grauman's. A spectacle straight out of *Fantasia.* Disney movies and live Disney stage shows and exhibitions. Tickets with live stage shows $13-22, seniors and children (ages 3-11) $11-20; without live stage show $11/$8.

**Mann's Village Theatre,** 961 Broxton Ave. (☎310-208-0018), in **Westwood.** One huge auditorium, one big screen, one great THX sound system, a balcony, and Art Deco design. Watch the back rows and balcony for late-arriving celebrities. Tickets $10, students $7.50, seniors $7, under 12 $6.50. Weekday shows before 6pm $7.

**Vine Theatre,** 6321 Hollywood Blvd. (☎323-463-6819), just west of Vine St. in **West Hollywood.** Though selection is limited, you can't beat prices. 1 theater plays 2 recent movies back-to-back starting around 2pm. See 1 ($7) and get the 2nd movie free.

## REVIVAL THEATERS

🎦 **Nuart Theatre,** 11272 Santa Monica Blvd. (☎310-478-6379), in **West LA,** just west of I-405 (the San Diego Fwy.), at Sawtelle Ave. Perhaps the best-known revival house. The playbill changes nightly. Classics, documentaries, animation festivals, and foreign and modern films. *The Rocky Horror Picture Show* screens Sa night at midnight with a live cast. Tickets $9.25, seniors and under 12 $6. Discount card (5 movie tickets for $34).

**LACMA's Bing Theater,** 5905 Wilshire Blvd. (☎323-857-6010; www.lacma.org), at the LA County Museum of Art in the **Wilshire District.** Classic films on the big screen, sometimes for less than a video rental. Shows Tu 1pm and F-Sa 7:30pm only. Tickets Tu $2, seniors $1; F-Sa $8; students, seniors, and museum members $6.

**Egyptian Theatre,** 6712 Hollywood Blvd. (☎323-466-3456; www.egyptiantheatre.com), one block west of Las Palmas St. in **Hollywood.** For each old or new film it shows, the theater brings in the main actor, director, or producer to talk with the audience about the filming process. George Clooney recently spoke about his *Confessions of a Dangerous Mind.* Films change regularly. Open M-Sa. Tickets $9, seniors and students $8.

# LIVE THEATER

LA's live theater scene does not hold the weight of New York's Broadway, but its 115 "equity waiver theaters" (under 100 seats) offer dizzying, eclectic choices for theatergoers, who can also view small productions in art galleries, universities, parks, and even garages. Browse listings in the *LA Weekly* to find out what's hot.

**Geffen Playhouse,** 10886 LeConte Ave. (☎310-208-5454), in **Westwood.** Off-Broadway and Tony award-winning shows in a cozy space. Tickets range $34-46; student rush tickets ($10) available 1hr. before each show.

**Pasadena Playhouse,** 39 S. El Molino Ave. (☎626-356-7529 or 800-233-3123; www.pasadenaplayhouse.org), in **Pasadena.** California's premier theater and historical landmark has spawned Broadway careers and productions. Tickets $35-60. Call for rush tickets. Shows Su 2 and 7pm, Tu-F 8pm, Sa 5 and 9pm.

**Pantages,** 6231 Hollywood Blvd. (☎213-365-3500), across from the Metro red line's Hollywood/Vine station in **Hollywood.** Hosted the premieres of *Cleopatra* and *Spartacus.* A hot spot for big Broadway performances and cabaret acts. Tickets from $12.

# LIVE MUSIC

LA's music venues range from small clubs to massive amphitheaters. The **Wiltern Theater** (☎213-380-5005) shows alterna-rock/folk acts. The **Hollywood Palladium** (☎323-962-7600) is of comparable size with 3500 seats. Mid-sized acts head for the **Universal Amphitheater** (☎818-777-3931). Huge indoor sports arenas, such as the **Great Western Forum** (☎310-330-7300) and the newer **Staples Center** (☎213-742-7100), double as concert halls for big acts. Few dare to play at the 100,000-seat **Los Angeles Memorial Coliseum and Sports Arena;** only U2, Depeche Mode, Guns 'n' Roses, and the Warped Tour have filled the stands in recent years. Call Ticketmaster (☎213-480-3232) to purchase tickets for any of these venues.

■ **Hollywood Bowl,** 2301 N. Highland Ave. (☎323-850-2000), in **Hollywood.** The premier outdoor music venue in LA, the Bowl hosts a summer music festival from early July to mid-Sept. Although sitting in the back of this outdoor, 18,000-seat amphitheater makes the LA Philharmonic sound like it's on a transistor radio, bargain tickets and a panoramic view of the Hollywood Hills make it worthwhile. Free open house rehearsals by the Philharmonic and visiting performers usually Tu and Th at 10:30am, but the schedule is sometimes irregular. Parking at the Bowl is limited and pricey at $11. It's better to park at one of the lots away from the Bowl and take a shuttle (parking $5, shuttle $2.50; departs every 10-20min. starting 1½hr. before showtime). There are also lots at 10601 and 10801 Ventura Blvd., near Universal City; at the Kodak Theatre at 6801 Hollywood Blvd.; and at the LA Zoo, 5333 Zoo Dr. in Griffith Park. MTA bus #163 runs from Burbank and Hollywood and bus #156 goes west from Downtown or east from the Valley. Call Ticketmaster (☎213-480-3232) to purchase tickets.

**Music Center,** 135 N. Grand Ave. (☎213-972-7211), in **Downtown,** at the corner of 1st St. in the heart of the city. Includes the Mark Taper Forum, the Dorothy Chandler Pavilion, and the Ahmanson Theatre, and the spanking new Gehry-designed Walt Disney Concert Hall. Performance spaces host the LA Opera, Broadway and experimental theater, and dance. Parking $7 after 6pm, but you pay less at the many lots nearby.

**The Greek Theatre,** 2700 N. Vermont Ave. (☎323-665-5857; www.greektheatrela.com), nestled in the hills of Griffith Park. From I-10 or US 101, take the Vermont Ave. Exit north. Winner of the Best Small Outdoor Venue of the Year award for the last 3 years, this theatre is a 6000-seat venue that has played host to some of the biggest names in music entertainment. A constant line-up of pop, classical, reggae, rock, and more; call ahead or check the website to find out the schedule. Parking $10.

## SPORTS

**Exposition Park** and the often dangerous city of **Inglewood,** southwest of the park, are home to many sports teams. The **USC Trojans** play football at the **LA Memorial Coliseum,** 3911 S. Figueroa St. (tickets ☎213-740-4672), which seats over 100,000 spectators. It is the only stadium in the world to have the honor of hosting the Olympic Games twice. The torch that held the Olympic flame still towers atop the Coliseum's roof. Basketball's doormat, the **LA Clippers** (☎213-742-7500), and the dazzling, star-studded 2002 NBA Champion **LA Lakers** (☎310-426-6000) play at the new **Staples Center,** 1111 S. Figueroa St. (☎213-742-7100; box office 213-742-7340), along with the **LA Kings** hockey team (☎888-546-4752) and the city's women's basketball team, the **LA Sparks** (☎310-330-3939). Lakers tickets start at $23, Kings at $24.50, and Sparks at $7.50. Call Ticketmaster (☎213-480-3232) for tickets.

**Elysian Park,** about 3 mi. northeast of Downtown, curves around the northern portion of Chavez Ravine, home of **Dodger Stadium** and the popular **LA Dodgers** baseball team. Single-game tickets ($6-21) are a hot commodity during the April-October season, especially if the Dodgers are playing well (though recently they haven't). Call ☎323-224-1448 for info and advance tickets.

If you crave the rush of adrenaline that only comes from athletic participation, hop in your car and drive east to **Perris Valley Skydiving,** 2091 Goetz Rd. (☎909-657-1664 or 800-832-8818), in **Perris Valley,** near Riverside, a good two-hour drive. Not the most budget-savvy activity, but this is the place to fulfill that urge to leap 12,500 ft. The jumps accommodate both experienced jumpers and first-timers, who jump with a skydiving instructor strapped (tightly!) to their backs. After a 1min. free-fall, enjoy a 7min. canopy descent. Dives $199 cash, $209 with credit card; extra charge for people over 200 lbs. Group discounts and lessons available.

Both surfers and beach bums should make it a point to check out the annual **surfing competitions** held on Huntington Beach in Orange County, just south of LA (end of July. see p. 465). The multi-day festival features surfing and extreme sports such as skateboarding and BMX, as well as drunken revelry and sun-tanned bodies. For more information, call ☎310-473-0411 or visit www.fusion.philips.com.

# NIGHTLIFE

## LATE-NIGHT RESTAURANTS

Given the extremely short shelf-life and unpredictability of the LA club scene, late-night restaurants have become reliable hangouts. The reliable fall-back option of LA nightlife, they're the place where underage club kids and celebs come trolling.

**Canter's,** 419 N. Fairfax Ave. (☎323-651-2030), in **Fairfax,** north of Beverly Blvd. An LA institution and the heart and soul of historically Jewish Fairfax since 1931. Grapefruit-sized matzoh ball in chicken broth $4.50. Giant sandwiches $8-9. Visit the Kibbitz Room for nightly free rock, blues, jazz, and cabaret-pop (from 10pm). Lenny Kravitz is known to make appearances in the audience. Cheap beer ($2.50). Open 24hr.

**Fred 62,** 1850 N. Vermont Ave. (☎323-667-0062), in **Los Feliz.** "Eat now, dine later." Look for a booth with headrests. Hip, edgy East LA crowd's jukebox selections rock the house. The apple waffles ($4.62—all prices end in .62 and .97) are divine. Open 24hr.

**The Rainbow Bar and Grill,** 9015 Sunset Blvd. (☎310-278-4232; http://rainbowbarandgrill.com), in **West Hollywood,** next to the Roxy. Dark red vinyl booths, dim lighting, loud music, and colorful characters set the scene. Marilyn Monroe met Joe DiMaggio on a blind (and apparently, rather silent) date here. Brooklyn-quality pizza $6; calamari $8; grandma's chicken soup $3.50. Open M-F 11am-2am, Sa-Su 5pm-2am.

**Barney's Beanery,** 8447 Santa Monica Blvd. (☎323-654-2287), in **Hollywood.** Since 1920, Barney's has been serving over 600 items, 125 bottled beers, and 28 draft beers, all published on a newspaper instead of a menu. Over 50 omelette choices ($8.50-12), 75 burger options ($6-10), 25 Mexican dishes ($5-7), and 23 pizza flavors ($5-7). Not the place for the indecisive. Janis Joplin and Jim Morrison were regulars. Pool, ping-pong, air hockey, and video games. Experience the loud, riotous karaoke nights Su-M and W 10pm-2am. Happy Hour M-F 4-7pm (drafts $2; well drinks and house wines $2.50; appetizers $3). Valet parking $4. Open daily 11am-2am.

**Mel's Drive In,** 8585 Sunset Blvd. (☎310-854-7200; www.melsdrive-in.com), right on the strip in **West Hollywood.** Also at 1660 North Highland Ave. (☎323-456-2111), in **Hollywood,** and 14846 Ventura Blvd. (☎818-940-6357), in **Sherman Oaks,** with more limited hours. The 50s-style diner is a picture-perfect re-creation of the era. The original Mel's (in Modesto of northern California) was in the movie *American Graffiti,* and this is as artfully constructed as a Hollywood set. Play your part by ordering a cheeseburger, fries, and a vanilla milkshake—all for under $12. Free valet parking. Open 24hr.

**Bob's Big Boy,** 4211 Riverside Dr. (☎818-843-9334), in **Burbank.** Don't miss this classic 1940s spot, where a sculpture of Bob welcomes you. The oldest remaining establishment of the once-large chain was declared a State Point of Historical Interest in 1993. Daily specials $7-9. Burgers $6-7. F 6-10pm is Classic Car Night; Sa-Su 5-10pm offers a car hop service. Open 24hr.

**Jerry's Famous Deli** has multiple locations, including 8701 Beverly Blvd. (☎310-289-1811), corner of San Vicente Ave. in **West Hollywood,** 10925 Weyburn Ave. (☎310-208-3354), in **Westwood,** and 12655 Ventura Blvd. (☎818-980-4245), in **Studio City.** An LA deli with sleek red leather and sky-high prices. Note the menu's height—Jerry is rumored to have wanted "the longest menu possible while still maintaining structural integrity." Something on it is bound to be perfect for your 4am snack. Known for its jumbo triple deckers ($8-13) and salads served in a pizza crust ($13-15). Open 24hr.

**The Kettle,** 1138 N. Highland Ave. (☎545-8511), at the corner of Manhattan Beach Blvd. in **Manhattan Beach.** A rare late-night place, The Kettle steams with heaping platefuls of home-style cooking. Come nightfall, surfers invade. The menu is only a guide—creativity is encouraged. Salads and sandwiches $7-9. "Hangover" omelette $7. Beer and wine served until midnight. Open 24hr.

# COFFEEHOUSES

In a city where no one eats very much for fear of rounding out that mannequin figure, espresso, coffee, and air are vital dining options. Here you'll find the hip younger crowd that doesn't earn enough to hit the restaurants. Bring a book and hide behind it while scoping out everyone else.

▧ **Elixer,** 8612 Melrose Ave. (☎310-657-9300), just east of San Vicente Blvd. in **Holly-wood.** Drink your herbal tonic or tea in the outdoor garden that imitates a tranquil tropical paradise or sit among the trees that offer extraordinary privacy. An enormous collection of tonics ($4-5) based on Chinese herbal traditions and teas from all over the world. Free live music Tu night; chess, checkers, chinese checkers, and other board games are distributed W night. Licensed herbalists are on duty daily 11am-6pm for spontaneous consultations (call ahead for a comprehensive one-on-one session). Open M-Sa 9am-10pm, Su 10am-8pm; summer hours M-F 9am-11pm.

**UnUrban Coffeehouse,** 3301 Pico Blvd. (☎310-315-0056), in **Santa Monica.** 3 separate rooms of funky old furniture, campy voodoo candles, Mexican wrestling masks, musty books, and leopard-print couches. Iced mocha blends $3.50; Italian sodas $2. Open mic poetry W 8pm; open mic comedy Th 7:30pm; open mic songwriters F 8pm; music showcase Sa 7pm. Sign up for open mic a half-hour before the show. No cover. Open M-Th 7am-midnight, F 7am-1am, Sa 8am-1am, Su 8am-7pm.

**Bourgeois Pig,** 5931 Franklin Ave. (☎818-464-6008; www.bourgeoispig.com), in **Holly-wood.** Screenwriters tap away at their laptops and confer with their agents as they sip coffee ($1.75-4.25) and scarf down light turkey sandwiches ($5). At night, locals head to "The Pig" to play pool and lounge in the intimate, dimly lit Moroccan back room. Open Su-Th 8am-2pm, F-Sa 8am-2:30am. No credit cards.

**Cow's End,** 34 Washington Blvd. (☎310-574-1080), in **Venice.** With its asymmetrical whole-pane windows, uneven brick floor, two floors, pool table, and scantily clad beach patrons, the Cow's End is riotously popular. Sandwiches from $6.25. Smoothies from $3.75. Open daily 6am-midnight.

**Stir Crazy,** 6917 Melrose Ave. (☎323-934-4656), between Highland and La Brea Blvd. in **Hollywood.** By day, students read quietly. By night, the loud social scene takes over. Cappuccinos ($2.50) served to the sounds of Glenn Miller. Original sandwiches $5.50. Open daily 9am-9pm. No credit cards.

**G.A.L.A.X.Y. Gallery,** 7224 Melrose Ave. (☎323-938-6500), three blocks west of La Brea Blvd. in **Hollywood.** Much more than just a coffee shop, this spacious tobacco store has art on display, a collection of African djembe drums, and an enormous bong and hookah display for your tobacco needs and then some. Acid jazz jams on some weekend nights. Hemp coffee $1.75. 18+. Cover varies. Open M-Sa 11am-10pm, Su noon-9pm.

**Catalina Coffee Company,** 126 N. Catalina Ave. (☎318-2499; www.catalinacoffee.com), in **Redondo Beach.** Every beach town has its Bohemian coffeehouse with writers pondering the blank screens of their laptops, but this one stands out for its class. Plush couches, antique chess sets, working fireplace, Internet access, mystery library, and smooth jazz. Coffee beans roasted on site ($1.50-4), teas ($2.25), gourmet sandwiches ($6), and baked goods ($1-4). Open daily 7:30am-10pm.

# COMEDY CLUBS

The talent may be imported from New York, but it doesn't change the fact that LA's comedy clubs are the best in the world. Although prices are steep, it's worth the setback to catch the newest and wackiest comedians, watch skilled veterans hone new material, and preside over the latest trends in stand-up comedy.

■ **LA Improv,** 8162 Melrose Ave. (☎323-651-2583), in **West Hollywood.** LA's best, including Robin Williams and Jerry Seinfeld, have fished for laughs here. Drew Carey and Ryan Stiles often join the show. Dinner at the restaurant (entrees $6-14) includes priority seating for the show. 18+. Cover $10-15. 2-drink min. Shows Su-Th 8pm, F-Sa 8:30 and 10:30pm. Bar open daily until 1:30am. Reservations recommended.

■ **Groundling Theater,** 7307 Melrose Ave. (☎323-934-4747; www.groundlings.com), in **Hollywood.** One of the most popular improv and comedy clubs in town. The Groundling's alums include Pee Wee Herman and many current and former *Saturday Night Live* regulars like Will Farrell, Julia Sweeney, and Chris Kattan. Don't be surprised to see *SNL* producer Lorne Michaels sitting in the back. Lisa Kudrow of *Friends* also got her start here. Polished skits. Cover $7-18.50. Shows Su 7:30pm, W-Th 8pm, F-Sa 8 and 10pm.

**Comedy Store,** 8433 Sunset Blvd. (☎323-650-6268), in **West Hollywood.** The shopping mall of comedy clubs: 3 rooms each feature a different type of comedy. Main Room has big names and prices ($15-20). Original Room features mid-range comics ($15). Belly Room has grab-bag material (no cover). 21+. 2-drink min., drinks from $4.50. Show-times vary; call a week ahead to reserve tickets. Open daily until 2am.

**The Laugh Factory,** 8001 Sunset Blvd. (☎323-656-1336), in **West Hollywood.** Young talent here—you can say you saw them first. Audiences have been graced with the likes of Richard Pryor, Jerry Seinfeld, Damon Wayans, and Arsenio Hall. With nightly themed showcases, M is Latino night, Tu is open mic night for the first 15 people in line at 5pm. 18+. Cover M and F-Su $12, Tu-Th $10. 2-drink min. Shows M 8pm; Tu 5pm; W 8pm; Th-F 8pm; Sa 8pm, 10pm, and midnight; Su 8pm and 10pm.

**The Ice House,** 24 N. Mentor Ave. (☎626-577-1894; www.icehousecomedy.com), in **Pasadena.** The 30-year-old granddaddy of clubs, its alums pop in occasionally. The Annex has stand-up comedy F-Sa 8 and 9:45pm ($12). 21+. Cover $8.50-12.50; 2-drink min. Reservations recommended.

**The Comedy and Magic Club**, 1018 Hermosa Ave. (☎372-1193; www.comedy-clubandmagicclub.com), just south of the Pier in **Hermosa Beach.** This premier comedy club usually brings in 3 comedians, 1 magician, and 1 experimental performance (like juggling) nightly. Recent performances by Jerry Seinfeld, Jay Leno, Howie Mandel. Tickets $12-30. 2-drink min. Shows M-F 8pm, Sa 7pm and 9:15pm, Su 7pm.

# BARS

The 1996 film *Swingers* has had a homogenizing effect on LA's hipsters. Grab your retro-70s polyester shirts, sunglasses, goatees, and throwback Cadillac convertibles, 'cause if you can't beat them, you have to swing with them, daddy-o. **Unless otherwise specified, bars in California are 21+.**

■ **North,** 8029 Sunset Blvd. (☎323-654-1313), between Laurel Ave. and Crescent Heights Ave. in **West Hollywood.** A classic LA undercover bar where the entrance is hard to find and you need to be "in the know" to know about it. Small, upscale bar

## HE LOCAL STORY

### BENICIO AT THE BAR

Steve is manager and bartender at The Coach and Horses in Hollywood and until recently was the lead guitarist for the punk band Ten Foot Pole.

**On Ten Foot Pole:** The name of the album we just put out was called Bad Mother Trucker and we recorded that last summer. Right before the album came out, the singer and I got in a little tiff. I ended up leaving the band and let him continue with the name.

**On women:** Of course you have your "groupies," the people that hang out with the band. But I didn't do it for the women. I did it more because I enjoyed playing. And the women.

**On celebs visiting the bar:** A lot of famous people have sat in these seats here. Kiefer Sutherland, Edward Norton, various guys in the Foo Fighters, Dave Matthews. Whenever they're in town, they stop by here. It's just a cozy, comfortable bar that doesn't have that pretentious vibe.

**On Benicio Del Toro:** He came to the bar one time and it was right before traffic came out. He was with a really attractive young lady, and well, she looked very young. Obviously he didn't. When they opened the door, I said], "Hey, can I see your IDs?" and then I realized it was him. It was too late to take it back, and he gave me his look and started pulling it out. I think he was kinda tiffed about it.

**On carding Benicio Del Toro:** Yeah, I wanted to see where he lives. I'm just joking. He was really polite about it, and he's a nice guy...It was an awkward moment.

where good-looking people buy good-looking drinks and dance until the morning. Drinks $6. DJ spins hip-hop and house Th-Sa nights. Open daily 6pm-1am.

■ **Miyagi's,** 8225 Sunset Blvd. (☎323-650-3524), on **Sunset Strip.** With 3 levels, 7 sushi bars ($5-7), 6 liquor bars, and indoor waterfalls and streams, this Japanese-themed restaurant, bar, lounge, and hip-hop dance club is a Strip hot spot. "Sake bomb, sake bomb, sake bomb" $4.50. Open daily 5:30pm-2am.

■ **3 of Clubs,** 1123 N. Vine St. (☎323-462-6441), at the corner of Santa Monica Blvd. in **Hollywood.** In a small strip mall beneath a "Bargain Clown Mart" sign, this simple, classy, and spacious hardwood bar is famous for appearing in Swingers. Live bands Th, DJ F-Sa. Open daily 7pm-2am.

■ **Beauty Bar,** 1638 Cahuenga Blvd. (☎323-464-7676), in **Hollywood.** Where else can you get a manicure and henna tattoo while sipping a cocktail and schmoozing? It's like getting ready for the prom again, except that the drinking starts before rather than after. Drinks like "Perm" are $8. DJ nightly 10pm. Open Su-W 9pm-2am, Th-Sa 6pm-2am.

■ **The Room,** 1626 N. Cahuenga St. (☎323-462-7196), in **Hollywood.** This dimly lit bar and dance floor is a must for any serious hip-hop fan. Bumping hip-hop Su and Tu-Sa; Reggae on M. No advertising, no sign on the door. Another location in **Santa Monica** at 14th St. and Santa Monica Blvd. Open daily 9pm-2am.

**Twin Palms,** 101 W. Green St. (☎626-577-2567), in **Pasadena.** From Colorado Blvd., take De Lacy Ave. south one block. Inside it's hoppin', but outside, beneath the spacious tent and beside the stage, it's even bigger. Formerly owned by Kevin Costner. Regular live music and dancing; call ahead for schedule. Cover F-Sa after 10pm $10. Drinks $6. Happy Hour M-Th 4-7pm, F 4-6pm, Sa-Su 3-5pm.

**Standard Lounge,** 8300 Sunset Blvd. (☎323-822-3111), in **Hollywood,** in the Standard Hotel. Exclusively for the connected, well-heeled, and the gorgeous. Drinks $9. Reservations highly recommended. Open daily 10pm-2am.

**Daddy's,** 1610 N. Vine St. (☎323-463-7777), in **Hollywood,** between Hollywood and Sunset Blvd. Large, New York-style lounge. Low-to-the-ground booths, candle lighting, and the cheapest jukebox in town. Sip $5 drinks and $4 beers to the mellow stylings of Al Green. Open M-F 7pm-2am, Sa 8pm-2am, Su 9pm-2am.

**The Coach and Horses,** 7617 Sunset Blvd. (☎323-876-6900), in **Hollywood.** Former speakeasy-turned-pub. The bartenders know all the local legends. Aspiring stars retreat here to drown post-audition sorrows. Alfred Hitchcock was a regular. Beer $4-5. Open M-Sa 11am-2pm, Su 5pm-2am. See **Hollywood Canteens,** p. 397

**14 Below,** 1348 14th St. (☎310-451-5040), in **Santa Monica.** 3 pool tables and live music almost every night draws a young crowd that dances in the back. In the same unit, the sports bar **Over Under** (☎310-899-0076) serves a mean Philly cheesesteak. Happy Hour M-F 5-7pm (half-price appetizers and drinks). Cover Tu-Th $5-6, F-Sa $8-10. Open M-Th 11am-11pm, F 11am-1am, Sa noon-1am, Su noon-11pm.

**Q's Billiard Club,** 99 Colorado Blvd., just west of Arroyo Pkwy., in **Pasadena.** Play pool, sip cocktails, or dance the night away to a bumping mix of hip-hop, techno, and house. Happy Hour M 4-8pm, T-F 4-7pm. Open M-W 4pm-2am, Th-Su 11:30am-2am.

**Rusty's Surf Ranch,** 256 Santa Monica Pier, (☎310-393-7437), in **Santa Monica.** Known for its year-around pool tournaments, M night karaoke, and Th night dance parties. Locals love it. Dancing Su and Th-Sa. No cover. Open daily noon-midnight.

**Maloney's,** 1000 Gayley Ave. (☎310-208-1942), in **Westwood Village.** This *Cheers*-style hangout is a favorite of thirsty UCLA Bruins. No college town prices (drinks $3-9), but students still flock. On weekend nights, clips of famous movies are shown every 30min. Full menu. Su 2-for-1 draft beers after 9pm. Open daily 11:30am-2am.

**Lucky Strike,** 6801 Hollywood Blvd. (☎323-467-7776). Entrance is on Highland Ave., just north of the Highland and Hollywood Blvd. intersection in **Hollywood.** Reminiscent of 1940s bowling clubs; Lucky Strike is capitalizing on bowling's comeback. 12 bowling lanes blend with an upscale bar and lounge with pool table. Prices aren't cheap, but the good times are had. 21+ after 7pm. Drinks $6. $5-8 per person per game; shoe rental $4. Prices increase gradually the later it gets at night. Open daily 11am-2am.

**The Lava Lounge,** 1533 N. La Brea Ave. (☎323-876-6612), in **Hollywood.** Fun bar with outdoor motif—surf rock and Pacific Island sounds. Sip a Blue Hawaiian ($7) under a twinkling star ceiling. Entertainment from 10pm. Cover up to $5. Open daily 9pm-2am.

**Cafe Boogaloo,** 1238 Hermosa Ave. (☎318-2324), in **Hermosa Beach.** Top-notch blues, beautiful people, killer shrimp appetizers, and addictive cocktails ($7) with a dash of Louisiana soul. Full bar with 27 microbrews on tap ($3). Put your coaster over your glass when you go outside for a smoke to indicate you're still drinking. Nightly shows begin 8pm, weekends 9pm. Cover F-Sa $5-10. Dinner from $10. Happy Hour M-F 5-7pm. Open M-Th 5pm-midnight, F 5pm-2am, Sa 3pm-2am, Su 3pm-midnight.

# CLUBS

With the highest number of bands per capita in the world and more streaming in every day, LA is famous for its club scene. Most clubs are able to book top-notch acts and pack 'em in night after night. The distinction between music and dance clubs is murky in LA—most music clubs have DJs a few times a week, many dance clubs have occasional live music, and, after all, music makes people dance. Club events that promoters design for specific venues are prevalent and popular. These events give a venue its temporary character. When promoters move their events to different clubs, they often create a caravan effect among die-hard fans. Thus, club venues may host completely different crowds on different nights.

LA clubs are often expensive but many are still feasible for budgeteers. Coupons in *LA Weekly* (see **Publications,** p. 383) and those handed out by the bushel inside the clubs can save you a bundle. To enter the club scene, it's best to be at least 21 (although it also helps to be a beautiful woman). Nevertheless, if you're over 18, you can still find a space to dance, though it may mean a hefty cover charge in a less desirable venue. **All clubs are 21+ unless otherwise noted.**

▨ **The Derby,** 4500 Los Feliz Blvd. (☎323-663-8979; www.the-derby.com), corner of Hillhurst Ave. in **Los Feliz.** Still jumpin' and jivin' with the kings of swing. Ladies, grab your snoods; many dress the 40s part. Choice Italian fare from Louise's Trattoria next door. Full bar. Free swing lessons Sa 8pm and 9pm. Cover $5-12. Open daily 7:30-2am.

▨ **Largo,** 432 N. Fairfax Ave. (☎323-852-1073), between Melrose Ave. and Beverly Blvd. in **West Hollywood.** Intimate sit-down (or, if you get there late, lean-back) club. Original rock, pop, and folk, and comedy acts. Cover $2-12. Open M-Sa 8:30pm-2am.

**The Shelter,** 8117 Sunset Blvd., (☎323-654-3200), just west of Crescent Heights Ave. in **Hollywood.** The newest and hottest addition to the Sunset Strip club scene, this lounge and dance club spins different beats in each of its 7 rooms. Hip-hop spins in the main dancing room. Open F-Sa 10pm-2am.

**The Larchmont,** 5657 Melrose Ave. (☎323-467-4068), in **Hollywood.** Each night is a different, random theme. DJ promos bring a good mix of trance, house, and hip-hop. Limited seating makes for non-stop dancing on both floors and the outdoor patio. Cover $5-20. Open M and W-Su 9pm-2am, Tu 10pm-4am.

**Key Club,** 9039 Sunset Blvd. (☎310-274-5800), on **Sunset Strip.** A colossal, crowded multimedia experience complete with black lights, neon, and a frenetic dance floor. Live acts and DJ productions, depending on the night. 4 full bars. Cover $10-55. Open on club nights 10pm-2am, live music nights 7pm-2am.

**Roxy,** 9009 Sunset Blvd. (☎310-278-9457), on **Sunset Strip.** Known as the "Sizzling Showcase," it's one of the best-known Sunset Strip clubs. Bruce Springsteen got his start here. Live rock, blues, alternative, and occasional hip-hop. Many big tour acts. All ages. Cover varies. Opens at 8pm.

**Whisky A Go-Go,** 8901 Sunset Blvd. (☎310-652-4205), in **West Hollywood.** Historically, this is the great prophet of LA's music scene. It hosted progressive bands in the late 70s and early 80s and was big in the punk explosion. The Doors, Janis Joplin, and Led Zeppelin played here. All ages welcome. Cover M-Th $10, F-Su $13. Shows begin 8pm.

**Arena,** 6655 Santa Monica Blvd. (☎323-462-0714), in **Hollywood.** Paired with sister club **Circus,** this club lends itself to frenzied techno and Latin beats. Gay nights W and Sa at Arena, Tu and F at Circus; drag shows start at midnight on those nights. Cover $10-15. Open Su-Th 9pm-2am, F-Sa 9pm-4am.

**Lighthouse Cafe,** 30 Pier Ave. (☎372-6911; www.thelighthousecafe.net), in **Hermosa Beach's Pier Plaza.** Frequented by bronzed volleyball players, this cool dance club features nightly music ranging from reggae to 80s. Munchies $7. Th-Sa nights $5 cover. Su jazz brunch 11am-3pm. Open M-Th 6pm-2am, F 4pm-2am, Sa-Su 11am-2am.

## GAY & LESBIAN NIGHTLIFE

While the Sunset Strip features all the nightlife any Jack and Jill could desire, gay men and lesbians may find life more interesting a short tumble down the hill on **Santa Monica Boulevard.** Still, many ostensibly straight clubs have gay nights; check *LA Weekly* or contact the Gay and Lesbian Community Services Center. Free weekly magazine *fab!* lists happenings in the gay and lesbian community. **Motherload,** 8499 Santa Monica Blvd. (☎310-659-9700), and **Trunks,** 8809 Santa Monica Blvd. (☎310-652-1015), are two of the friendliest and most popular bars. Neither has a cover and both are open until 2am. **All clubs are 21+ unless otherwise noted.**

■ **Abbey Cafe,** 692 N. Robertson Blvd. (☎310-289-8410), at Santa Monica Blvd. in **West Hollywood.** 6 candlelit rooms, 2 huge bars, a large outdoor patio, and a hall of private booths make this beautiful lounge and dance club the best place around. The comfy couches cry out for some lovin'. Open daily 8am-2am.

**Micky's,** 8857 Santa Monica Blvd. (☎310-657-1176), in **West Hollywood.** Huge dance floor filled with delectable men. On a weekend night when other bars close, head to Micky's for another 2hr. of grooving. Music is mostly electronic dance. M night drag shows. Happy Hour M-F 5-9pm. Cover $3-5. Open Su-Th noon-2am, F-Sa noon-4am.

**Here,** 696 N. Robertson St. (☎310-360-8455), corner of Santa Monica Blvd. in **West Hollywood.** Known for Su nights when the bartenders dress up, this sleek bar and dance club caters to the well-dressed and trendy. DJ's Spin a mix of house and hip-hop. Thurs is lesbian night. Don't miss the frozen cosmopolitans ($8). Happy Hour daily 4-8pm ($2-3 off). Open daily 4pm-2am.

**Rage,** 8911 Santa Monica Blvd. (☎310-652-7055), in **West Hollywood.** Its glory days have passed, but this institution rages on with nightly DJs that spin house 'til you drop. W is Latin night. Mostly gay men; some lesbians during the day. A rowdier scene than Micky's. Full lunch and dinner menu served daily noon-9pm. Happy Hour (half-price drinks) daily noon-9pm. Th 18+. Open daily noon-2am.

**7969 Peanuts,** 7969 Santa Monica Blvd. (☎323-654-0280), just west of Fairfax in **West Hollywood.** Sometimes a strip club, sometimes a drag show, sometimes a go-go dance party—not for the faint of heart. Call for the crazy schedule. Most nights feature a mixed gay and lesbian crowd. Many nights 18+. Cover varies. Open daily 10pm-2am.

**The Palms,** 8572 Santa Monica Blvd. (☎310-652-6188), in **West Hollywood.** Pool room and full bar with lots of drink specials like Tu $3 frozen drinks. DJ Th-Sa; music ranges from house to disco to salsa. Men are welcome but may feel very alone. Don't hesitate to hop in the 2-person dance cage. W 9pm-midnight $1 drinks. Su Beer Bust 50¢ drafts and free buffet. Open daily 4pm-2am.

# AROUND LA

AROUND LA

Once you leave the city limits of Los Angeles (or, some might argue, even the Westside), the glam factor drops considerably. The cities and neighborhoods in southern LA and Orange County are a little hotter and a lot less cool. Unlike LA proper, where you would be hard-pressed to find a native Angeleno, the towns and cities in LA's outer orbit are populated by genuine natives. What these neighboring cities lack in glitz, they more than compensate for with natural beauty. Santa Monica National Recreation Area, just north of Malibu, is a stunning park even by Californian standards, and some of the world's most renowned beaches are an hour's drive south from LA in Orange County. Catalina Island, 22 miles west of Long Beach, offers a peaceful retreat from the manic mainland with beautiful coves perfect for snorkeling. And if all this doesn't cause you to burst out in song, the choreographed merriment of Disneyland just might do the trick.

## HIGHLIGHTS OF LA & ORANGE COUNTIES

**BEACH LIFE.** The beach communities of Orange County (p. 463) have legendary surfing and a fun sand scene, primarily at **Huntington Beach** and **San Clemente.**

**CATALINA ISLAND.** 22 mi. offshore rests beautiful, rugged Catalina (p. 456). Great hiking, camping, and snorkeling are a brief ferry ride from the mainland.

**AMUSEMENT.** Anaheim hosts such family fun centers as **Disneyland** (p. 460) and **Knott's Berry Farm** (p. 462).

**MISSION SAN JUAN CAPISTRANO.** The crumbling religious abode (p. 468) is among the most beautiful missions in California, as well as a famous roost for swallows.

**WILDERNESS. Big Bear** (p. 476), **Idyllwild** (p. 481), and the **San Gorgonio Wilderness** (p. 476) are tracts of mountainous terrain with excellent hiking above the LA smog. Ski resorts operate at Big Bear in winter, and the sailing is excellent in summer; Idyllwild attracts rock climbers to Tahquitz and Suicide Rock; and San Gorgonio has miles of untouched backcountry.

## SOUTHERN LA COUNTY

The sandy campsites on and the snorkeling spots off Catalina Island are the closest SoCal gets to an tropical island paradise. Directly east across the San Pedro Channel, Long Beach fosters a growing nightlife and shopping scene.

## LONG BEACH                                   ☎ 562

Its Chamber of Commerce proudly proclaims that Long Beach (pop. 430,000) is "the number one container shipping port in the world," and nothing could be more evident to the first-time visitor. The thriving entertainment district helps make up for the 10-story loading cranes, neon-lighted oil refineries, and container barges that puncture the views of the skyline.

## ✦ ☝ ORIENTATION & PRACTICAL INFORMATION

Long Beach is 24 mi. south of downtown LA and down the coast from South Bay. By **public transit,** take the Metro Blue Line from LAX, the Green Line from downtown transferring to the Blue Line at Imperial, or Bus #232 ($1.35). By **car,** take I-405 (San Diego Fwy.) and switch to I-710 S (Long Beach Fwy.), which runs right by the shipping ports into downtown Long Beach.

Long Beach's main tourist attractions lie by the bay. Pine Ave., the backbone of downtown, runs north from the bay and Ocean Blvd. runs west to the boutiques of Belmont Shores. Just south of Ocean Blvd. and east of the Convention and Entertainment Center is an enormous mural of life-sized whales, cited by locals as the largest in the world. **Be cautious** in the inland areas of industrial Long Beach.

**Buses: Greyhound,** 1498 Long Beach Blvd. (☎218-3011). Buses run to: **LA** ($9.50); **San Diego** ($15); **San Francisco** ($43). Open daily 5:30am-9:15pm.

**Public Transportation: Long Beach Transit (LBT),** 1963 E. Anaheim St. (☎591-2301), is the nation's safest transit agency. Most buses stop downtown at the newly renovated **Transit Mall,** on 1st St. between Pacific Ave. and Long Beach Blvd. High-tech bus shelters have route maps and video screens with bus info. 90¢, students 75¢, seniors 45¢, transfers 10-35¢. **Long Beach Passport,** 1963 E. Anaheim St. (☎591-2301), a separate division of the LBT, offers free service along Ocean Blvd. and Pine Ave. as well as to the Queen Mary (every 15min.). One route runs from downtown to Belmont Shores (90¢). Most routes operate daily 6am-midnight.

**Car Rental: Budget,** 249 E. Ocean Blvd. (☎495-0407), and at Long Beach Airport (☎421-0143). Cars with unlimited mileage $28 per day. Must be 21 with major credit card. Under-25 surcharge $20 per day. Open M-F 8am-5pm, Sa-Su 8am-4pm.

**Bike Rental: Bikestation** (☎436-2453), at 1st St. and the Promenade downtown rents bikes for $5-7 per hr., $20-28 per day. Open daily 7am-6pm.

**Auto Repair: AAA Road Service,** 4800 Airport Plaza Dr. (☎496-4130, emergency help 800-400-4222). Open M-F 9am-5pm.

**Visitor Information: Long Beach Convention and Visitors Bureau,** 1 World Trade Ctr., #300 (☎436-3645 or 800-452-7829), at Ocean Blvd. and I-710 (Long Beach Fwy.). Tons of help and free brochures. Open M-F 8am-5pm.

**Laundromat: Super Suds,** 250 Alamitos Ave. (☎436-1859). Practically Disneyland with its video games and jungle gym. Wash $1.25 per lb., dry 50¢. Open daily 7am-9pm.

**Police:** 100 Long Beach Blvd. (☎435-6711).

**Post Office:** 300 N. Long Beach Blvd. (☎628-1303). Open M-F 8:30am-5pm, Sa 9am-2pm. **Postal Code:** 90802.

## ⌂ ACCOMMODATIONS

Daytrips to Long Beach from LA are easy, something to keep in mind when considering an overnight trip in a place where good budget accommodations are scarce. Nevertheless, there are a few reasonably priced surf motels along Ocean Blvd. between Belmont Shores and downtown.

**Beach Plaza Hotel,** 2010 E. Ocean Blvd. (☎437-0771), at Cherry Ave. Bright turquoise exterior matches the ocean. Spacious, clean rooms have A/C, cable TV, fridges, and large windows to let in the light. Pool and private beach access. Doubles $80-130, with ocean view and kitchenette $150-180. Prices include parking. Reserve ahead. ❹

**AROUND L.A.**

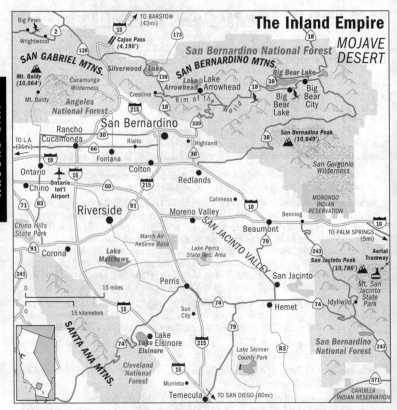

The Inland Empire

**Beach Inn Motel**, 823 E. 3rd St. (☎437-3464). Right off the water. Basic rooms come with fridge, satellite TV, and A/C. Doubles $50, with jacuzzi $70. Includes parking. ❸

# FOOD & NIGHTLIFE

The panoply of eateries lining Pine Ave. between 1st and 3rd St. aren't all as expensive as the valets along the sidewalk might lead you to believe. There are equally budget-smart eateries in Belmont Shores. Buy cheap produce at the **open air market** on Promenade St. (Open F 10am-4pm.) Long Beach supports a vibrant blues and jazz scene; try the **Blue Cafe,** 210 Promenade St. (☎983-7111), on any night, or **Captain's Quarters,** 5205 E. Pacific Coast Hwy. (☎498-2461), on Friday and Saturday nights. Most **gay and lesbian** night spots are around East Broadway and Falcon Ave. The 16-screen **AMC Theatres** (☎435-4262) is centrally located at 245 Pine Sq.

**The Shorehouse Cafe,** 5271 E. 2nd St. (☎433-2266), in Belmont Shores. Wicker beach furniture and wooden ceiling fans add to a comfy diner setting where you can order "anything at any time." The menu is vast and reasonably vegetarian-friendly. Great for lunch or late-night meals. Omelettes made with your choice of tasty fillings (from $4.25). Huge burgers $7-8. Pasta $12-14. Open 24hr. ❷

**The Omelette Inn,** 108 W. 3rd. St. (☎437-5625). "Good food prepared with your health in mind," brags the menu's organic-egg-in-sunglasses logo. For the health-conscious, there are egg white omelettes, brown rice, and veggie bacon strips. There's real hickory-smoked bacon, too. Create-your-own-omelettes $5.50-8; sandwiches and burgers $5-7. Early bird specials ($4.50) served until 9am. Open daily 7am-2:30pm. ❷

**The Library,** 3418 E. Broadway (☎433-2393). This gay-friendly library in the middle of Long Beach's gay neighborhood has attitude and coffee. Books line the walls (Danielle Steel to Bertolt Brecht; $1-10) and studious types settle into plush antique seats. Cup of gourmet coffee $1.50. Italian sodas $2.25. The great assortment of cakes wins many loyal fans. Live music Su and F-Sa 9pm. Su and Sa breakfast omelette bar 7am-1pm. **The Gift Horse** annex sells local art and other items. Open M-Th 6am-midnight, F 6am-1am, Sa 7am-1am, Su 7am-midnight. ❶

**Alegría,** 115 Pine Ave. (☎436-3388; www.alegriacocina-latina.com). Latin cooking and dancing in an excruciatingly hip Miró-inspired interior. Menu a bit pricey for the pennywise, but tapas are $2.25-7 and the musical entertainment attracts friendly and dance-happy crowds. M-W Latin jazz 7pm, Th tango 7pm, F-Su flamenco shows 7pm. At 10:30pm, live salsa bands bring the beat. Happy Hour daily 3:30-6pm (drinks $2, tapas $1). Must be 21+ after 9:30pm. After 10:30pm, 2-drink min. Open M 11:30am-11pm, Tu-Th 11:30am-midnight, F 11:30am-2am, Sa noon-2am, Su noon-midnight. ❹

**Shannon's Bayshore,** 5335 E. 2nd St. (☎433-5901), Belmont Shores. With California State Long Beach University right up the road, this neighborhood bar by day (the longest bar in the US, with long lines at the door to match) becomes one of the liveliest of 2nd St.'s many night spots. For decades, drunk Long Beach couples have carved their names into the bar. As you carve, swig Shoot-the-Root, a shot of root beer schnapps in a cup of beer ($3.50). Pool table 50¢. Happy Hour daily 11am-7pm with $2.75 drafts and well drinks. Free food M-F 4-7pm. Open M-F 11am-2am, Sa-Su 9am-2am. ❶

## 👁 🏴 SIGHTS & SEASONAL EVENTS

Shipping is the central occupation of Long Beach; tourism is clearly an afterthought. Beach life is, well, not a thought at all. Waves and beachgoers here are minimal due to the breakwater of the busy port. The shipping center does have some attractions, though. To get a hold on the city's cargo, cross the majestic **Vincent Thomas Bridge** to central San Pedro (50¢; free from the other direction).

## IN RECENT NEWS

### GRIDLOCK ON THE GRIDIRON

On fall Sundays, while football fans in 32 US cities organize tailgates, spill beer, and run around in the stands, forlorn Angelenos are stuck at home. LA has lacked a professional football team since the Rams (now in St. Louis) and Raiders (now in Oakland) departed because of poor ticket sales. In pro football, if a team doesn't sell out 48 hours before kickoff, local television networks can't air the game. The practice is called a blackout and aims to get hometown fans out of their recliners and into the stadium. Because its teams share television revenues and ticket sales equally, the National Football League (NFL) needs to ensure its teams are located in cities with sizable, loyal fan bases.

Now, after eight years, negotiations to bring an NFL team back are in the works. Officials from both LA and the NFL are hopeful that a team will relocate as early as 2006. The Indianapolis Colts and New Orleans Saints are free to relocate in 2006 and 2007, and are likely candidates. Proposals to either build a new stadium on a 157-acre landfill in Carson or undergo a 500-million-dollar renovation of the historic Pasadena Rose Bowl are also being hashed out.

Until the NFL returns to LA, football fans can get their fix by rooting for (or against) the UCLA and USC football teams, and budget travelers can take comfort by remembering that college football costs a whole lot less than the NFL.

**QUEEN MARY.** The legendary 1934 Cunard luxury liner has been transformed into a swanky hotel with art exhibits, historical displays, and upscale bars. There are still remnants of the days when she was a troop ship called "The Grey Ghost" during WWII when she held the honor of carrying the greatest number of passengers of any floating vessel: 15,740 troops and 943 crew. The Grey Ghost was so crucial to the Allied war effort that Hitler offered the highest honors to anyone who sank her. A tour of the ship is worthwhile; you won't be able to see more than the engine room, deck, and gift shops otherwise. *(At the end of Queen's Way Dr. ☎ 435-3511; www.queenmary.com. Open daily 10am-6pm. $25, seniors and military $23, children $13. Self-guided tour maps are included with admission. Guided tours are an extra $5, ages 5-11 $3.)* A Cold War-era Russian submarine code-named *Scorpion* is moored right next to the Queen Mary. *(From Rte. 710 S, take a right onto Queen's Way and follow the signs. Combo tickets $30, seniors and military $28, ages 5-11 $18.)*

**LONG BEACH AQUARIUM OF THE PACIFIC.** A $117 million, 156,735 sq. ft. celebration of the world's largest and most diverse body of water, the aquarium is situated atop one of the world's busiest and most polluted harbors. Meet the dazzling creatures of the deep that struggle to coexist with Long Beach's flotsam, jetsam, and effluvium. Among the most striking of the 12,000 displaced inhabitants are the unborn sharks floating about in semi-transparent embryos. The seals, sea lions, otters, sharks, and jellyfish are also sure to please. Regular feedings and performances by the seals and sea lions. Shark feedings at 11am and 2pm. *(100 Aquarium Way. ☎ 590-3100; www.aquariumofpacific.org. Follow Rte. 710 S into downtown, take a right on Queen's Way, and follow the signs. Open daily 9am-6pm. $19, seniors $15, children 3-11 $10. Behind the Scenes tour $11; boat tour $19. 13min. Animal Vision 3-D Movie every half-hour.)*

**MUSEUM OF LATIN AMERICAN ART.** The MoLAA is making critics say "ooh-la-la" for showing work by artists who are well known in their own countries but not in the US. Do not be put off by the drab exterior; superb contemporary art and brilliant colors awaits inside. Renovations are currently under way. *(628 Alamitos Ave. From Downtown, take 3rd St. east and make a left on Alamitos Ave. ☎ 437-1689; www.molaa.com. Open Su 11am-6pm, Tu-F 11:30am-7pm, Sa 11am-7pm. $5, seniors and students $3, under 12 free. Family art workshops Su noon-4pm. $7.50, students $5.)*

**LONG BEACH MUSEUM OF ART.** The original museum, built at the turn of the 20th century by famed Pasadena architects Greene and Greene, is now augmented by a new building built in the style of the original. The museum hosts a small permanent collection of impressionistic paintings by Jean Mannheim, Maurice Braun, and George Henry Melcher, but most of the museum is devoted to rotating exhibits and videos by its grant recipients. Seaside Jazz concerts are hosted in the summer. *(2300 Ocean Blvd., on the waterfront. From LA, take Rte. 710 S to Shoreline Dr. Continue on Shoreline and make a right on Ocean Blvd. ☎ 439-2119. Open Su and Tu-Sa 11am-5pm. $5, students $4; free first F of the month. Summer garden concerts Th 7-10pm. $27.75.)*

**NAPLES ISLAND.** Waterside cottages, curvy and narrow streets, peaceful canals, and footbridges. Sound like Venice? Almost. Arthur Parson, an American real estate developer, began creating this picture-perfect Italian community (with the obvious omission of Italians) in the early 20th century. An ideal place for a dusk stroll or a romantic gondola ride. *(Take 2nd St. east from downtown. For moonlight cruises, call ☎ 433-9595; www.gondolagetawayinc.com. 1hr. Bread-and-Cheese Cruise for 2 $65.)* It also harbors **Alamitos Bay,** from where the *S.S. Minnow* set sail on its infamous 3hr. tour (according to the opening sequence of *Gilligan's Island*).

**BEACHES.** In Long Beach's upscale, uptown neighborhood, the family-oriented beach of **Belmont Shores** is reputed to be the city's best. Park at meters near the intersection of Ocean Blvd. and La Verne St. (25¢ for 15min.; 10hr. max.)

**SEASONAL EVENTS.** The Parade of a Thousand Lights features a display of decorated boats along the harbor in mid-December. The Toyota Grand Prix of Long Beach (☎436-9953) revs along downtown streets in early April. Summer sounds jazz up downtown at Jazz Fest (☎424-0013; www.longbeach-jazzfestival.com) in mid-August and Long Beach KKJZ Blues Festival (☎985-1686; www.kkjz.org) in late August or early September. Pro basketball players train during the NBA summer basketball league at the Long Beach Pyramid in July (☎985-4949). For more on seasonal events, contact the Convention and Visitors Council (see p. 447).

# CATALINA ISLAND ☎310

Only 22 mi. off the coast of Southern California rises the idyllic island retreat of Catalina. Hills, rugged canyons and gorges, secluded beaches, unbeatable snorkeling and diving, and wild bison combine with crystal-clear air and water to create a splendid escape from the mainland's hustle and bustle. The island finds no need for traffic lights as cars are rare and people defer to golf carts, bikes, and pedestrians. Avalon, the island's largest town (1 sq. mi.; pop. 3500), is home to a casino without gambling, a memorial without a dead body, and a 3rd Street without a 1st or 2nd, as well as the majority of the island's restaurants and hotels. But to truly experience Catalina's beautiful and unspoiled land, head inland with any of the various tour companies or purchase a bike permit and set out on your own (hiking passes are free). The island's natural beauty is preserved mostly by the efforts of the Catalina Island Conservancy, a nonprofit group that owns 88% of the island and strives to ensure the survival of the island's rare and endangered species.

## ▐ TRANSPORTATION

**Ferries:** Without a yacht, the way to get to Catalina is via the **Catalina Express.** Shuttles depart from San Pedro (1hr.); Long Beach (1hr.); Dana Point (1½hr.) to Avalon, or San Pedro (1½hr.) to Two Harbors. Though there are over 30 departures each day, reservations should be made in advance. (☎800-618-5533; www.catalinaexpress.com. Round-trip $40-45,

# THE BIG SPLURGE

## WRIGLEY'S WONDER

In 1921 William Wrigley, the Chicago Cubs owner and bubble gum magnate, built his home on Catalina Island, on a mountain he named after his wife. In his abode atop Mt. Ada, he entertained the Prince of Wales, as well as Presidents Calvin Coolidge and Warren Harding.

Wrigley's gorgeous, white and green-roofed Georgian colonial home has been converted to the **Inn on Mt. Ada,** so now everyone can drink in the delicious views previously reserved for politicians and members of the upper-crust. On clear days, one can see across the 85-mile San Pedro Channel to Long Beach.

Most rooms have ocean views and fireplaces (one also has a private deck), and run from $300-640. Along with a room and a view, you also get breakfast, lunch, fresh fruit, champagne, and freshly baked cookies. Guests are given golf carts to make the three-minute drive into Avalon, and to zoom around. (398 Wrigley Rd. No children under 14. 2-night min. required on weekends and holidays. ☎510-2030.)

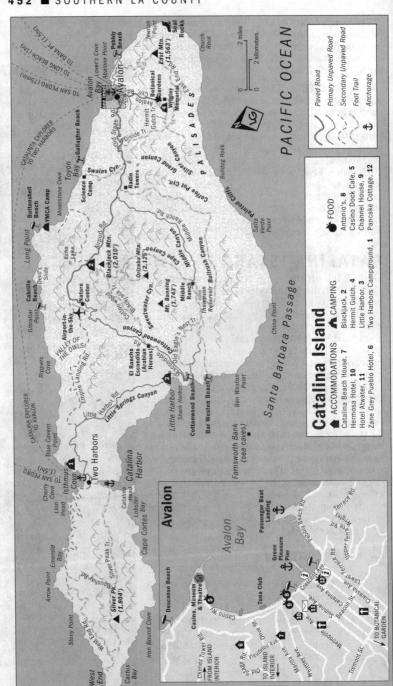

PACIFIC OCEAN

Paved Road
Primary Unpaved Road
Secondary Unpaved Road
Foot Trail
Anchorage

2 miles
2 kilometers

## Catalina Island

### ▲ ACCOMMODATIONS
Catalina Beach House, 7
Hermosa Hotel, 10
Hotel Atwater, 11
Zane Grey Pueblo Hotel, 6

### ▲ CAMPING
Blackjack, 2
Hermit Gulch, 4
Little Harbor, 3
Two Harbors Campground, 1

### ♦ FOOD
Antonio's, 8
Casino Dock Cafe, 5
Channel House, 9
Pancake Cottage, 12

### Avalon

seniors $37-41, ages 2-11 $31-35, under 2 $3.) **Catalina Explorer,** 34671 Puerto Pl., goes from Dana Point to Avalon and Two Harbors. (☎877-432-6276; www.catalinaexplorerco.com. 1½hr.; departs daily 9am, returns 5pm. $41, seniors $37.50, ages 3-11 $31, under 2 $5.) **Catalina Passenger Service,** 400 Main St., in Balboa, ferries vacationers once a day on the *Catalina Flyer* catamaran from Newport Beach to Avalon. (☎800-830-7744; www.catalinainfo.com. 1¼hr.; daily 9am, return 4:30pm; round-trip $42, seniors $39, ages 3-12 $25, under 2 $3.)

**Public Transportation: Santa Catalina Island Company** runs a bus between **Avalon** and **Two Harbors,** stopping at a few campgrounds en route (2hr.; daily 10:30am, return 4pm; $20). Call the Visitor Bureau (☎510-1520) for more info. **The Island Hopper,** a tram that leaves from Catalina Ave between 3rd and Beacon St., will take you to the Botanical Gardens or the Casino ($1.50).

**Bike and Golf Cart Rentals: Brown's Bikes,** 107 Pebbly Beach Rd. (☎510-0986), 360 ft. from the boat dock. Single-speed bikes $5 per hr., $12 per day; 21-speed mountain bikes $9/$20; 6-speed tandems $12/$30. Open daily in summer 9am-6pm; in winter 9am-5pm. **Island Rentals,** 125 Pebbly Beach Rd. (☎510-1456), rents **golf carts** ($30 per hr. with $30 deposit); must be 21+ to drive. Open daily in summer 8am-6pm; in winter 8am-5pm.

 ## ORIENTATION & PRACTICAL INFORMATION

**Visitor Information: Chamber of Commerce and Visitor Bureau,** P.O. Box 217, Avalon 90704 (☎510-1520; www.catalina.com), on the left side of Avalon's Pleasure Pier. Open in summer daily 8am-5pm; off-season M-Sa 8am-5pm, Su 9am-3pm. **Catalina Island Conservancy,** 125 Claressa Ave., P.O. Box 2739, Avalon 90704 (☎510-2595). This non-profit group owns 88% of Catalina. Hiking permits (free), maps (25¢), and trail advice available here. Open daily 8:30am-5pm. **Biking permits** ($50, families $75) are required outside of Avalon. They can be obtained at the Conservancy, as well as the Catalina airport and the Two Harbors Visitors Center (☎510-2880).

**Tours: Santa Catalina Island Company (SCIC)** is ubiquitous on the island, and runs major sightseeing tours, as well as campgrounds, hotels, and restaurants. On the island, tram tours run $10-80, boat trips $25-100.

**ATM: US Bank,** 303 Crescent Ave. **SCI Information Center** ATM across from Green Pier on Catalina St.

**Laundromat: Catalina Coin Wash,** in the Metropole Market Place next to Vons. Wash $1.50, dry 25¢ per 15min. Open 7am-10pm.

**Showers:** Public facilities on Casino Way across from the Tuna Club. Entrance $1, each 5min. $1. Assorted preening implements $0.25-$3 each; bring a towel. Open Su-Th 7am-7pm, F-Sa 7am-8pm; off-season daily 7-11am and 3-5pm.

**Emergency: Police** ☎510-0174; **fire** ☎510-0203; **hospital** ☎510-0700.

**Post Office:** (☎310-510-0084). Arcade Bldg., between Metropole and Sumner St. **Postal Code:** 90704.

> **PHONE CODES.** All seven-digit phone numbers on Catalina begin with **510.** Locals may often give phone numbers with only four digits (1234), requiring confused mainlanders to supply the missing ones (☎510-1234).

**AROUND L.A.**

# ACCOMMODATIONS

Hoteliers on the island know they have a captive audience and tons of demand; in summer, accommodation prices skyrocket way out of budget range, even in mediocre Avalon digs. Summer is peak season, and on most weekends, and some weekdays, there are no accommodations available on the island at all. **Call as far in advance as possible**—a month is recommended—to make sure you won't have to bed down with the bison and wild boar.

**Hermosa Hotel,** 131 Metropole Ave. (☎510-1000), whose motto is "sleep cheap," is an exception to Avalon prices. Offers clean, inexpensive rooms, some with ocean views, in a relaxed atmosphere maintained by the friendly management. 2-night min. stay on weekends. 18+. Double occupancy $25-65 with shared bath, $35-85 with private bath, $45-100 with kitchen. Rates depend on day and season. ❸

**Hotel Atwater,** 125 Sumner Ave. (☎800-851-0217), is likely the 2nd cheapest lodging option on the island. Located half a block from the ocean, the rooms are small but clean, with cable TV and fans. Rooms in summer from $72; off-season from $43. ❹

**Catalina Beach House,** 200 Marilla Ave. (☎510-1078 or 800-97-HOTEL/46835). One of the island's oldest hotels, dating back to 1912 when Captain Joseph McAfee established the Captain's Beach House. The rooms are tucked into the countryside on a hill a couple blocks above the ocean. Rooms with TV, VCR, kitchenette, fan. Some with whirlpool tubs. Free, fairly extensive video library. Doubles in summer from $60; in winter from $45. Special rates of $65 for summer weekdays, $35 for winter weekdays. ❹

**Zane Grey Pueblo Hotel,** 199 Chimes Tower Rd. (☎510-0966 or 510-1520). The Hopi Indian-style Pueblo that Grey built in 1926 is now a delightful B&B. Perched on a hillside, the ocean views are spectacular, as are the grounds which include a pool. Living room has a fireplace. 16 rooms have fan, wicker furniture, and private baths; some with balconies. Rooms in Apr.-Oct. $135-150; Nov.-Mar. $80-95. ❺

# CAMPING

While no wilderness camping is permitted, the five campgrounds on Catalina each offer distinct camping experiences. You must check in at Two Harbor Visitors Center at the foot of the pier (Two Harbors is 14 mi. west of Avalon). Required reservations at any of the five campgrounds can be made at www.catalina.com/camping. A two-night minimum stay applies at Hermit Gulch and Little Harbor from July-Aug. and on holiday weekends. Unless otherwise noted, the camping charge is $12 per adult and $6 per child; discounts may be available from November to March. Hermit Gulch is closest to Avalon, but you can get closer to nature at the other four campgrounds, all run by Two Harbors Management (☎510-2800). To get to any of these sites from Avalon, take the shuttle bus; you may have to hike 1½ mi. from the nearest stop.

**Little Harbor,** southeast of Two Harbors, on the western side of the island. 16 incredible beach sites offer a secluded cove, potable water, cold showers, picnic tables, and chemical toilets. ❶

**Hermit Gulch** (☎510-2000), a 1½ mi. walk inland from the Avalon boat landing, is populated by carousing campers. Hot showers, flush toilets, a coin microwave, BBQs, a vending machine, and a limited number of stoves and lanterns ($5). No gear, no problem—they also rent teepees ($30), tents ($10-16), and sleeping bags ($11). ❶

**Blackjack** is comprised of 10 large, secluded pine forest sites near the island's highest elevation. The camp has cold showers, running water, and fire rings, but prepare for large herds of buffalo ambling by. Accessible by Airport Shuttle, Safari bus, or by a 9 mi. hike from Avalon. ❶

**Two Harbors campground,** ¼ mi. east of Two Harbors, has the most popular beach camping, with 45 campsites, cold showers, chemical toilets, and rental gear. Tents $10-25; sleeping bags $11. Nov.-May 2- and 4-bunk "Catalina Cabins" $30. ❶

# ⚑ FOOD

**Avalon,** centered on **Crescent Avenue,** is Catalina's largest town and is the island's main restaurant and recreation scene. Crescent Ave. curves along Catalina harbor, arcing from the pier where cross-channel boats arrive at the iconic Avalon Casino. Eateries and bars line the street (paved with tile and off-limits to cars and golf carts), affording patrons spots to eyeball the sand and bottle-blue water. **Green Pleasure Pier** intersects Crescent Ave. and bustles with fish 'n' chips joints and cotton-candy vendors. Many of the larger restaurants host live music and karaoke nightly, and basic, cheap food is easy to find. For groceries, visit **Vons,** 121 Metropole Ave. (☎510-0280. Open daily 7am-10pm.)

▨ **Antonio's,** 230 Crescent Ave. (☎510-0008), is the seaside home of the island's best pizza. Walls are adorned with colorfully defaced one-dollar bills and floors are strewn with peanut shells. Outside seating on the deck. Huge pizzas $12-17. Open Su-Th 8am-10:30pm, F-Sa 8am-11:30pm. ❷

**Casino Dock Cafe,** 2 Casino Way (☎510-2755), at the end of the Via Casino, lying in the shadow of the Casino and overlooking the placid harbor, has one of the best views in Avalon. Burgers $4-6. Swordfish sandwich $7. Beer $3-4. Live music in summer Sa-Su 3-6pm. Open M-F 8am-5pm, Sa-Su 8:30am-6:30pm. ❶

**Pancake Cottage,** 118 Catalina Ave. (☎510-0726). The Breakfast Special (2 pancakes, 2 eggs, 3 strips of bacon; $6) puts the breakfast grills on Crescent Ave. to shame. Sandwiches $6-8. Open M-F 6:30am-1:30pm, Sa-Su 6am-1:30pm. No credit cards. ❷

**Channel House,** 205 Crescent Ave. (☎510-1617), serves Continental cuisine in its elegant dining hall and secluded patio overlooking the sea. Lunch $8-16. Dinners $15-25. Full bar. Early bird specials M-Th 4:30-6pm. Open M-Th 11am-3pm and 4:30-9pm, F 11am-3pm and 5-9:30pm, Sa-Su 10am-3pm and 5-9:30pm. ❹

# ◉ ⚑ SIGHTS & ACTIVITIES

The **Santa Catalina Island Company** runs a slew of tours. The **Skyline Tour** or the more complete **Inland Motor Tour** are your best bets; go to the Discovery Tours Center at Catalina Ave. and Crescent Ave. (Skyline Tour $26, seniors $23.50, children $13. Inland Motor Tour $44.50/$40/$22.50.) The best way to see underwater life is to snorkel. Before going down below, gather dive gear at **Catalina Diver's Supply** (☎510-0330 or 800-353-0330), on the left-hand side of Pleasure Pier (mask, snorkel, and fin package $7 for 2hr., $12 per day; wetsuit $11 for 2hr., $15 per day). Just east of Avalon, **Lover's Cove** is the most convenient snorkeling spot and best for novices and those who wish to avoid strong sea currents. It is also an excellent place to pick up on the tips shouted out by guided tours. You might get to swim among tiger sharks. Rent near the cove from **Catalina Snorkeling Adventures.** (☎510-8558. Open Apr.-Oct. Mask, snorkel, and fins $2.50 per hr., $5 per day; wetsuits $5/$10; deposit required.) The best place to snorkel among the bright orange garibaldi in the kelp forests off **Casino Point.** For a slightly less crowded beach and fewer boats, walk past the Casino to **Descanso Beach** (day use $1-2), run by the Descanso Beach Club. You can rent equipment just before the beach at **Descanso Beach Ocean Sports.** (☎510-1226. Mask and snorkel $3.50 per hr., $6 per day; fins $3.50/$6; wetsuits $6.50/$12; single kayak $12/$46.) Alternatives to snorkeling include **Glass Bottom Boat Trips** (30min.; $9.50-12, seniors $8.50-11, ages 2-11 $5-6) or the fantastic submarine **Undersea Tour** (45min.; $26-30, seniors $23.50-27, ages 2-11 $13-15).

The **Casino Building,** at the end of Crescent Ave., was never a gambling den; chewing gum magnate and former owner of the island William Wrigley, Jr. built it the $2 million dance hall in 1929 (*casino* means "gathering place" in Italian). The architectural tour of the building is well worth it. (☎510-7400. Tours $9.75, seniors $8.50, children $5.) You can also sneak a peek at the building's elegant Art Deco murals by catching a film in the 1000-seat **Avalon Theater;** F-Sa showings include a free concert on the antique page organ. (☎510-2414. Film showings M-Th 7pm, F-Su 7 and 9:45pm. $7.50, seniors and ages 3-11 $5.) The casino hosts occasional **jazz concerts** and a **New Year's Eve bash** that re-creates the Catalina of the 30s and 40s, when it was a palace for the sultans of swing. Ask about the **Silent Film Festival** (June; for tickets, call ☎510-2414) and the **Halloween Costume Ball** (☎888-330-5252). Beneath the casino is the **Catalina Island Museum,** with exhibitions on island history, Native American inhabitants, and author/filmmaker Zane Grey. (☎510-2414. Open daily 10am-4pm. $2.50, seniors $2, ages 6-15 $1, under 6 free.) Zane Grey's **Avalon pueblo** is now a hotel overlooking the Casino from the high bluffs above.

At the end of Avalon Canyon Rd. (2 mi. outside Avalon), you can pick up the hilly **Hermit Gulch Trail,** a 3½ mi. loop past canyons, secluded coast, and the monolithic **Wrigley Memorial.** The memorial no longer holds his dead body, which was removed from the island in the 1940s to LA's Forest Lawn Cemetery. Past the memorial is the 38-acre **Botanical Gardens.** (☎510-2288. Open daily 8am-5pm. $3 donation.) The Botanical Gardens grows eight plant species native to Catalina as well as a vast, needle-filled cactus garden with sweeping views across the blue Pacific, extending all the way to the mainland on a clear day. The Memorial and Gardens are accessible by walking straight up Avalon Canyon Rd. or by taking the **Island Hopper** (p. 453) from Avalon. **Bison and wild boars** inhabit the area along the 4 mi. **Blackjack-Cape Reservoir Loop.** The two or three hundred buffalo here are the descendants of the 25 originally ferried over for the filming of Zane Grey's 1924 film *The Vanishing American.* The rigorous 8 mi. **Blackjack Trail** leads to Little Harbor. Pick up either of the last two trails at the Blackjack Junction, accessible by the **airport shuttle** ($14.50, round-trip).

# ORANGE COUNTY

Directly south of LA County lies Orange County (pop. 2.9 million). Composed of 34 cities, it is a microcosm of Southern California: dazzling sandy shoreline, bronzed beach bums, oversized shopping malls, homogenized suburban neighborhoods, and frustrating traffic snarls. One of California's staunchest Republican enclaves, Orange County supports big business, and its economy (along with its multi-million-dollar hillside mansions oozing luxury cars and disaffected teens) shows it. It is also one of the safest areas in the country.

Disneyland, the stronghold of the late Walt Disney's ever-expanding cultural empire, is the premier inland attraction, home to dancing cartoon characters in the midst of the suburban sprawl. The self-proclaimed "Happiest Place On Earth" is now even happier as a result of the construction of California Adven-

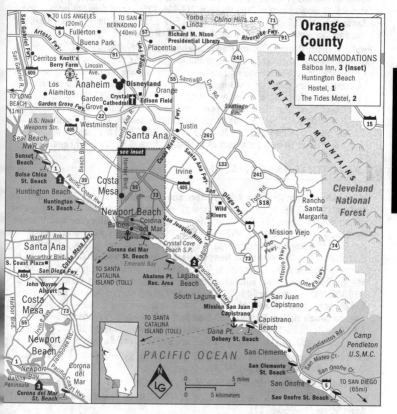

**Orange County**

⌂ ACCOMMODATIONS
Balboa Inn, **3 (Inset)**
Huntington Beach
Hostel, **1**
The Tides Motel, **2**

ture and Downtown Disney. Orange County's aesthetic appeal increases as one moves closer to the shore. A drive down the Pacific Coast Highway (PCH to locals) from Huntington Beach to Laguna Beach is well worth it. The coast runs the gamut from the budget- and party-friendly surf burg of Huntington Beach to the opulent excess of Newport Beach and the artistic vibe of Laguna. A little farther south lies the quiet mission of San Juan Capistrano, set amid rolling hills that spill onto the laid-back beaches of Dana Point and San Clemente.

# ▐ TRANSPORTATION

**Airport: John Wayne Airport,** 18601 Airport Way, Santa Ana (☎949-252-5006), 20min. from Anaheim. Newer, cleaner, and easier to get around than the LA Airport; domestic flights only.

**Trains: Amtrak** (☎800-USA-RAIL/872-7245; www.amtrakcalifornia.com) stations, from north to south: **Fullerton,** 120 E. Santa Fe Ave. (☎714-992-0530); **Santa Ana,** 1000 E. Santa Ana Blvd. (☎714-547-8389); **Irvine,** 15215 Barranca Pkwy. (☎949-753-9713); **San Juan Capistrano,** 26701 Verdugo St. (☎949-240-2972).

**Buses: Greyhound** (☎800-231-2222) has 3 stations in the area: **Anaheim,** 100 W. Winston Rd., 3 blocks south of Disneyland (☎714-999-1256; open daily 6:30am-9:15pm); **Santa Ana,** 1000 E. Santa Ana Blvd. (☎714-542-2215; open daily 6:15am-8:30pm); and **San Clemente,** 2421 S. El Camino Real. (☎949-366-2646. Open daily 7am-9pm.)

**Public Transit: Orange County Transportation Authority (OCTA),** 550 S. Main St., Orange County. Thorough service is useful for getting from Santa Ana and Fullerton Amtrak stations to Disneyland and for beach-hopping along the coast. Long Beach, in LA County, serves as the terminus for several OCTA lines. Bus #1 travels the coast from Long Beach to San Clemente (every hr. until 8pm). Buses #25, 33, and 35 travel from Fullerton to Huntington Beach; #91 goes from Laguna Hills to Dana Point. (☎714-636-7433; www.octa.net. Fare $1, day pass $2.50.) **Info center** open M-F 6am-8pm, Sa-Su 8am-5pm. **MTA Info** (☎213-626-4455 or 800-266-6883) available by phone daily 5am-10:45pm. MTA buses run from LA to Disneyland and Knott's Berry Farm.

# ▶ PRACTICAL INFORMATION

**Visitor Information: Anaheim Area Visitors and Convention Bureau,** 800 W. Katella Ave. (☎714-765-8888; www.anaheimoc.org), in Anaheim Convention Ctr. Lodging and dining guides. Open M-F 8am-5pm. **Huntington Beach Conference and Visitors Bureau,** 417 Main St. (☎714-969-3492 or 800-729-6232; www.hbvisit.com). If the helpful staff doesn't know something, they'll find someone who does. Good maps and brochures. Open M-F 9am-5pm. **Newport Harbor Area Chamber of Commerce,** 1470 Jamboree Rd. (☎949-729-4400), in Newport Beach. Offers free maps and info. Open M-F 8:30am-5pm; 24hr. automated answering service. **Newport Visitors Bureau,** 3300 West Coast Hwy. (☎949-722-1611 or 800-942-6278), in Newport Beach. Eager-to-help staff, maps of area attractions, and events brochures. Open M-F 8am-5pm. **Laguna Beach Visitors Bureau,** 252 Broadway (949-497-9229). Open M-F 9am-5pm, Sa 10am-4pm, Su 12pm-4pm. **San Clemente Visitors Center,** 1100 N. El Camino Real (☎949-492-1131). Open M-F 9am-5pm, Sa 9am-2pm, Su 9am-1pm.

**Gay-Lesbian Community Center:** 12832 Garden Grove Blvd., Suite A (☎714-534-0862), in Garden Grove. Open M-F 9am-10pm.

**Surf and Weather Conditions:** ☎213-554-1212.

**Police: Anaheim,** 425 S. Harbor Blvd. (☎714-765-1900). **Huntington Beach,** 2000 Main St. (☎714-960-8811).

**Crisis Lines: Sexual Assault Hotline** (☎714-957-2737). **Orange County Referral Hotline** (☎714-894-4242).

**Medical Services: St. Jude Medical Center,** 101 E. Valencia Mesa Dr. (☎714-871-3280), Fullerton. **Lestonnac Free Clinic,** 1215 E. Chapman Ave. (☎714-633-4600). Hours vary; call for an appointment.

**Post Office:** 701 N. Loara St. (☎714-520-2639 or 800-275-8777), 1 block north of Anaheim Plaza, Anaheim. Open M-F 8:30am-5pm, Sa 9am-3pm. **Postal Code:** 92803.

 **ORANGE COUNTY AREA CODES. 714** in Anaheim, Fullerton, Fountain Valley, Santa Ana, Orange, Garden Grove; **949** in Newport, Laguna, Irvine, Mission Viejo, San Juan Capistrano, and surrounding areas; **310** in Seal Beach.

# ANAHEIM ☎714

In the late 1950s, Anaheim (pop. 300,000) was considered the city of the future. Californians flocked to Orange County's capital city, where booming industry and Uncle Walt's dream machine created jobs and revenue galore. Today, people still pour into the city, but the tourists flowing in far outnumber the residents, and the ever-expanding Disney empire has made Anaheim a slave to the tourist dollar. Still, the city is a true hub of fun and entertainment, and though most roads in Anaheim do lead to Disneyland, a few other (mostly Disney-related) venues pull their weight. The Mighty Ducks play hockey at Arrowhead Pond and the Angels play baseball at Edison Field. The new House of Blues and The Grove attract the best in music. Disney recently built a new theme park adjacent to Disneyland, called "California Adventure," which, combined with the new "Downtown Disney," provide an enclave of restaurants, shops, and shows, and at times as if everything bears the stamp of Walt's manic influence; what lies underneath this massive framework of rides, costumes, frozen smiles, and overpriced food? Without Mickey, Anaheim comes dangerously close to resembling Middle America.

# ACCOMMODATIONS

The Magic Kingdom is the sun around which the Anaheim solar system revolves, so countless budget chain motels and garden-variety "clean, comfortable rooms" flank it on all sides. Keep watch for family and group rates posted on marquees, and seek out establishments offering the 3-for-2 passport (3 days of Disney for the price of 2). The good news about the California Adventure construction that went on two years ago is that it inspired hotel owners to revamp their establishments; the bad news is that hotel prices have gone up as a result.

**Fullerton Hostel (HI-AYH),** 1700 N. Harbor Blvd. (☎738-3721), in Fullerton, 10min. north of Disneyland. Shuttle from LA Airport $21. OCTA bus #43 runs along Harbor Blvd. to Disneyland. In the woods and away from the thematic craziness of nearby Anaheim, this hostel has an international feel. Enthusiastic, resourceful staff invites questions but forbids drinking. Offers services, including ISICs. Kitchen, relaxing living room, communal bathrooms. Linen $2. Laundry (wash 75¢; dry 75¢). 7-night max. stay. Check-in 8-11am and 2-11pm. No curfew. Reservations encouraged. Open June 1-Sept. 30. Single-sex and co-ed dorms $17.50, non-members $20.50 (including taxes). ❷

**Econolodge,** 1126 W. Katella Ave. (☎533-4505; www.econolodge.com), in Anaheim at the southwest corner of Disneyland. One of what seems like a trillion chain motels, this Econolodge has clean, newly revamped rooms with HBO, phones, and A/C. Balconies offer a good view of Disney's nightly fireworks. Small pool, many kids. Reservations recommended; 10% discount with Internet reservations. Rooms range $45-95. ❹

# FOOD

Anaheim is more mini-mall than city. Resist the siren call of the countless fast places and try one of the inexpensive ethnic restaurants in the strip malls that line Anaheim's streets. Many specialize in takeout or will deliver to your motel room.

**Rutabegorz,** 211 N. Pomona Blvd. (☎738-9339; www.rutabegorz.com), in Fullerton. Other locations at 264 N. Glassell St. (☎633-3260) in Orange and 158 W. Main St. (☎731-9807) in Tustin. With a name derived from the unloved rutabaga, this hippie-cum-hipster joint supplies a 20-page menu (on recycled newsprint, of course). Crepes, curries, quesadillas, and club sandwiches are all fresh and veggie-heavy. Heaping salads with homemade dressings $4-9. Mexican casserole $7. Smoothies, veggie juices, and coffee drinks $1.50-4. Open M-Th 11am-10pm, F-Sa 11am-11pm, Su 4-9pm. ❷

**Angelo & Vinci's Cafe Ristorante,** 550 N. Harbor Blvd. (☎879-4022), in Fullerton. Padded red chairs, iron-rod table lamps, and indoor awnings are all part of the cluttered Sicilian motif. The food is unmistakably the stuff of family recipes (Cannelloni Vinci $10.75), with more than enough to feed the family at the lunch buffet ($6). Su champagne brunch ($10) 11am-3pm. Open Su-Th 11am-10pm, F-Sa 11am-midnight. ❸

**Inka Anaheim,** 400 S. Euclid Blvd. (☎772-2263), in Anaheim. Locals congregate under a back-lit mural of the mountain Machu Picchu while devouring great Peruvian food. The *arroz con pollo* (rice with chicken; $8) is delicious, and the *mazzomorra morada* (purple corn pudding; $2.50) makes an excellent dessert. Live Andean music F-Sa 7:30-10pm. Open M-Th 11:30am-9pm, F 11:30am-11pm, Sa noon-11pm, Su noon-9pm. ❷

**Watson Drugs and Soda Fountain,** 116 E. Chapman (☎663-1050; www.watson-drug.com), in Orange. Established in 1899, the oldest drugstore in Orange County has been the set for a number of movies, including Tom Hank's *That Thing You Do.* Located in Old Towne Orange, the soda fountain and surrounding streets are a trip back in time. That thing they do is serve great burgers ($6-8) and sweet treats like milkshakes and ice cream sodas ($3-4). Open M-Sa 6:30am-9pm, Su 8am-6pm. ❷

# 👁 🎵 SIGHTS & ENTERTAINMENT

## DISNEYLAND

*Main entrance on Harbor Blvd., and a smaller one on Katella Ave. By car, take I-5 to Katella Ave. From LA, MTA bus #460 travels from 4th and Flower St. (about 1hr.) to the Disneyland Hotel (service to the hotel begins at 4:53am; service back to LA runs until 1:20am). Free shuttles link the hotel to Disneyland's portals, as does the Disneyland monorail. The park is also served by Airport Service, OCTA, Long Beach Transit, and the Gray Line (see **Practical Information,** p. 458). Parking $8. ☎781-4565; www.disney-land.com. Disneyland open Su-Th 8am-11pm. F-Sa 8am-midnight; hours may vary; call ahead. California Adventure open Su-Th 9am-10pm, F-Sa 9am-10:30pm. Disneyland passport $43, ages 3-9 $33, under 3 free; allows repeated single-day entrance. 2- and 3-day passes also available. California Adventure passports $43, ages 3-9 $33, under 3 free. Combination tickets available. Lockers are located west of the ticket booths and at the lost and found facility on Main Street, USA.*

Disneyland calls itself the "Happiest Place on Earth," and a part of everyone agrees. After a full day there, your precious wallet, of course, may not. Even though the admission (and anything else sold within the park) is steep, this is probably the best place in Southern California to spend your money. Weekday and off-season visitors will undoubtedly be the happiest, but the clever can wait for parades to distract children from the epic lines. Walt's innovative Disney team has finally arrived at the line-busting solution they have been looking for: the **FastPass** program. Available at most major rides, FastPass lets you pick up a reservation ticket when you insert your parking ticket into a computer terminal. The ticket specifies a time window during which you can walk right on and ride, cruising past the bulk of the lines. If you are willing to ride without your friends, **Single-Rider** tickets allow you to skip almost the entire line. The Guide to the Magic Kingdom has parade and show times, as well as important shopping information.

**MAIN STREET, USA.** This is a children's-book walk through the golden age of small-town America. Disney and his designers skewed the perspective on Main Street so that the street seemed longer upon entering and shorter upon exiting, thereby creating visitor anticipation and making the walk to the car less daunt-

AROUND L.A.

ing after a long day. Main Street's shops stay open an hour after the park itself closes, but don't be fooled into thinking you'll get your souvenirs on the way out—everyone else has the same idea.

**FANTASYLAND.** The geographical and spiritual center of the park, Fantasyland contains the trademark castle as well as the scintillating **Matterhorn Bobsleds,** and numerous kiddie rides like the trippy **It's A Small World,** which will fiendishly engrave its happy, happy song into your brain. This area is best enjoyed when the rides light up at night, the kiddies go home, and you have twenty bucks to blow on the addictive $2.50 ⬛churros (cinnamon-sugary sticks of fried dough).

**ADVENTURELAND.** To the left of Main Street is the home of **Tarzan's Treehouse,** a walk-through attraction that replaced the Swiss Family Robinson Treehouse. The **Indiana Jones Adventure** is just next door. Pass the time in line by decoding the inscriptions inside the Temple of Maya (hint: the ride is sponsored by AT&T). Indiana Jones fans' palms will sweat when an animatronic Harrison Ford suggestively says, "You were good in there...very good." The **Jungle Cruise** next door has a new landing with a swing band to entertain the poor souls languishing in the hot sun. For lunch, the **Bengal Barbecue** offers chicken and beef skewers ($3), tasty breadsticks ($2), and cold grilled bananas ($4).

**NEW ORLEANS SQUARE.** In the west corner of the park are the best shops and dining in Disneyland. Find New Orleans cuisine at the **French Market** (dinner $7) or the much more expensive **Blue Bayou,** where there seems to be a surcharge for atmosphere. The low-key but entertaining rides are evocative of lazy evenings on the humid Southern bayous. Try the creepy, campy **Haunted Mansion,** or the ever-popular, if now politically correct, **Pirates of the Caribbean.**

**FRONTIERLAND.** Wild West fetishists will find amusement galore here, especially on the speedy **Big Thunder Mountain Railroad.** Grab a bite at the **River Belle Terrace,** famous for its Mickey Mouse-shaped pancakes. The **Mark Twain riverboat** tours around Tom Sawyer's Island, which looks suspiciously like a clever way to isolate harmful children on an island away from smart adults (see **Alcatraz,** p. 116).

**CRITTER COUNTRY.** Most of the park's cuter things lurk in this section, where the main attraction is **Splash Mountain,** a soaking log ride past singing rodents and down a thrilling vertical drop. Its host, **Brer Rabbit,** originated in the humorous "Uncle Remus" stories of the Reconstruction-era South. You might enjoy the snapshot they take of your horror-frozen face on the way down.

**MICKEY'S TOONTOWN.** At the rear of the park, this cartoon playland provides the key source of fun for the 10-and-under crowd. Mickey and Co. can often be found strolling about, followed by a stampede of kids in hot pursuit. Disney seems to be phasing out Mickey's old-school compadres like Donald, Goofy, and Chip 'n' Dale, in favor of newer, sexier favorites Ariel, Simba, Aladdin, and Belle.

**TOMORROWLAND.** To the right of Main Street is this futuristic portion of the park, recently remodeled after Disney executives realized that its supposed imagination of the future was gloriously stuck in the 1950s. Though the **Astro-Orbiter**—rockets that circle around moving planets—will thrill young children, the overwhelming favorite of the rush-seeking set is still **Space Mountain,** a darkened roller coaster that banks and swoops beneath a mountain of sheer exhilaration. **Star Tours** promises a routine shuttle to Endor, but delivers an exciting simulation ride.

**CALIFORNIA ADVENTURE.** Just recently, Disneyland introduced its new kid brother, "California Adventure," to the Southern California theme park family. The park features ambitious attractions divided into four districts. **Sunshine**

**Plaza,** the gateway to the park, is anchored by a 50-foot-tall sun enlivened by a wealth of red, orange, and yellow lights at night. Built as a shrine to the greatest state of them all, **Golden State** offers an eight-acre mini-wilderness, a citrus grove, a winery, and even a replica of San Francisco. **Paradise Pier** is dedicated to the so-called "Golden Age" of amusement park—with rides such as **California Screamin'** and **Mulholland Madness.** Finally, the **Hollywood Pictures Backlot** realizes your aspirations to stardom without those embarrassing before-you-were-famous nude photos hanging over your head. Admission to California Adventure is not included in admission to Disneyland, but combined passes are available (see p. 460).

## (K)NOT(T) DISNEYLAND

Back in 1932, Walter Knott combined a red raspberry, a blackberry, and a loganberry to make a flavorful superberry he called the boysenberry. The future site of **Knott's Berry Farm,** his popular roadside stand quickly grew into a restaurant. When he imported the Old Trails Hotel (from Prescott, AZ) and the last narrow gauge railroad in the country to form "Ghost Town," the precursor to the first theme park in America was born. After the opening of Disneyland in Anaheim in 1955, Knott's Farm added more rides and other theme park sections such as Fiesta Village. Knott's is a local favorite and aims at being "the friendliest place in the West"—it has long since given up on being the happiest place on Earth. The park's highlights include roller coasters like **Montezooma's Revenge, Boomerang,** and **Ghostrider,** the largest wooden roller coasters in the West. The latest addition is **Xcelerator,** bringing you from 0 to 80 mph in three seconds. If you are brave enough, try **Supreme Scream,** the tallest thrill ride of its kind, where you will fall 30 stories in three seconds. The Doolittle-ish **Birdcage Theater** is where comedian Steve Martin got his start, and now showcases special seasonal entertainment. At Halloween, the park is rechristened and redecorated into Knott's Scary Farm, and at Christmas, Knott's Merry Farm. While the rides at Knott's might one-up Disney's, the Wild West atmosphere pales in comparison; after all, you're pitting a hybrid fruit against a charismatic mouse. The best deal for food is **Mrs. Knott's Chicken Dinner Restaurant ❸** (☎714-220-5080), outside the park. The Mrs. offers soup, salad, corn, biscuits, chicken, and dessert (the specialty is—surprise—boysenberry pie) for only $13. Prepare to line up; this is a popular place for a hearty meal. *(8039 Beach Blvd. at La Palma Ave., 5 mi. northeast of Disneyland. From downtown LA, take MTA bus #460 from 4th and Flower St.; 1¼hr. If driving from LA, take I-5 south to Beach Blvd., turn right at the end of the exit ramp and proceed south 2 mi. Recorded info ☎220-5200. Open Su-Th 9am-10pm, F-Sa 9am-midnight; hours may vary, so call ahead. $43, seniors and ages 3-11 $33, under 3 free; after 4pm all tickets half price. Summer discounts available. Parking under 3hr. free, each additional hr. $2.)*

**SOAK CITY USA.** This 13-acre water park marks Knott's latest effort to make a splash in the already drenched local theme park scene. Its 21 water rides and attractions are fashioned after the longboards, surf woodies, and waves of the 1950s Southern Californian coast. *(Next to Knott's Berry Farm. ☎220-5200. Open Su-Th 10am-6pm, F-Sa 10am-8pm; hours may vary, so call ahead. $24, ages 3-11 $17, under 3 free.)*

**RICHARD NIXON LIBRARY & BIRTHPLACE.** Further inland in Yorba Linda is this highly uncritical, privately funded monument to Tricky Dick. The first and only native Californian to become president was born in this house, which has now become an extensive museum. Rotating exhibits cover such fashionable topics as "Barbie as First Lady," with the presidents' wives all dolled up, and

"Secret Treaties" from Westphalia to Spy Paraphernalia. Skeptics can investigate the Watergate Room and listen to the tapes themselves. Throughout the museum are letters from "small Republicans" to their big GOP idol, who was laid to rest here alongside his wife. Museum curators consistently portray Nixon as a victim of circumstance, plotting enemies, and his own immutable honor—an interpretation of history that admittedly has a certain charm. *(18001 Yorba Linda Blvd. ☎993-5075. Open M-Sa 10am-5pm, Su 11am-5pm. $6, seniors $4, ages 8-11 $2, under 8 free.)*

**CRYSTAL CATHEDRAL.** Seating 3000 faithful in Garden Grove, the cathedral is where televangelist Dr. Robert H. Schuller's weekly TV show *Hour of Power* is taped. The 40-acre "campus" on which it sits is a non-denominational Protestant mecca with impressive and modern glass towers. The Crystal Cathedral's own Ministry of Traffic provides the opportunity for In-Car Worship at a huge outdoor television. *(12141 Lewis St. ☎971-4000; www.crystalcathedral.com. 45min.-1hr. tours M-Sa 9am-3:30pm. English services Su 9:30 and 11am; Spanish service 12:45pm. Free. Broadcast on UPN, channel 13 in Orange County, and on the Discovery Channel.)*

**HSI LAI TEMPLE (INTERNATIONAL BUDDHIST PROGRESS SOCIETY).** Notorious for its involvement in a 1996 Clinton-Gore fundraising scandal, Hsi Lai's recent political abstinence has hardly extinguished "Buddha's Light" from its halls. The Bodhisattva Hall up the stairs from the main gate anticipates the main shrine with miniature bodhisattva sculptures lining the walls. For a dollar, you can get your fortune-cookie readings or *dharma* (translated as "religion" or "duty"). In the main shrine are three huge enamel Buddhas, each holding a different symbolic object. Toss pennies at a bell in the Statue Garden; hit it one, two, or three times and receive increasing levels of health, intelligence, and prosperity. Informative signboards along the pathways and in front of shrines make the largest Chinese Buddhist temple outside China as much a museum as a place of worship. Don't forget that it is the latter, though—no shorts or tank tops may be worn in the main shrine. *(3456 S. Glenmark Dr., Hacienda Heights. From Anaheim, take Rte. 57 north to Rte. 60 west; Exit Hacienda Blvd. and go south to Glenmark Dr. ☎626-961-9697. Vegetarian lunch buffet ($5) M-F 11:30am-1:30pm, Sa-Su 11:30am-2:30pm. Services Sa 1:30pm, Su 10:30am.)*

**SOUTH COAST PLAZA.** 3333 Bristol St. (☎714-435-2000), in Costa Mesa, off the Fairview Exit on I-405. True shopaholics head to this mother of all malls, one of the largest, most profitable, and popular malls in the United States. The 300 stores and a 1.6-acre garden path in the mall are impressive, and the novice LA shopper will appreciate the free maps. *(Open M-F 10am-9pm, Sa 10am-7pm, Su 11am-6:30pm.)*

**SPORTS.** For more evidence of Disney's world domination, catch a game by one of the teams they own: The major league **Anaheim Angels** play baseball from early April to October at **Edison Field.** *(☎940-2000 or 800-626-4357. General tickets $6-25.)* To check out some NHL action, catch a **Mighty Ducks** hockey game at **Arrowhead Pond.**

# ORANGE COUNTY BEACH COMMUNITIES

Orange County's various beach communities have cleaner sand, better surf, and less madness than their LA County counterparts. Other than the ocean view, sights are scarce along the 35 mi. stretch of the Pacific Coast Highway (PCH) between Huntington Beach and San Clemente, with the exception of the graceful Mission San Juan Capistrano. LA residents seek refuge among Orange County's natural wonders—its surf, coastal cliffs, and wooded canyons.

AROUND L.A.

AROUND L.A.

## ACCOMMODATIONS

Orange County's prime coastline and pricey real estate result in a dearth of bargain rates. Those without multi-million-dollar summer homes in the area can try their luck along PCH or Newport Blvd. in Newport Beach.

**Huntington Beach Colonial Inn Youth Hostel,** 421 8th St. (☎714-536-3315), in Huntington Beach, 4 blocks inland at Pecan Ave. Take OCTA #29 (which also goes to Knott's Berry Farm) or #50. From PCH, turn onto 8th St. This large, early 20th-century yellow and blue house was once a brothel but things have quieted down since (quiet hours after 10pm). Common bath, large kitchen, reading/TV room, coin-op laundry, Internet access, deck, and shed with surfboards, boogie boards, and bikes. Linen and breakfast included. Key deposit $5. Check-in 8am-10pm. No lockout. Reserve 2 days in advance for summer weekends. 3-4 person dorms $18; doubles $48. Any and all travelers welcome. ❷

**Balboa Inn,** 105 Main St. (☎949-675-3412; www.balboainn.com), on the sand at Newport. From PCH, follow signs to Balboa Peninsula and turn onto Main St. This recently renovated historical landmark offers rooms with ocean or bay views and is close to area attractions. Relax in the pool or jacuzzi. Continental breakfast and room service offered. Fans, cable TV, and fridge. Room rates start at $119. Overnight parking $7. ❺

**The Tides Motel,** 460 N. Coast Hwy. (949-494-2494; www.tideslaguna.com), in **Laguna Beach.** 1 block from the beach and four blocks from downtown. Small collection of relatively inexpensive, basic rooms surrounding a nice pool. Fans, cable TV, and free parking. Doubles $80 in summer; $70 in winter. Senior and AAA discounts. ❺

## CAMPING

Orange County's state beaches have campgrounds, but they are somewhat cramped and crowded. Reservations are required for all sites (reservation fee $7). Reserve through ReserveAmerica (☎800-444-7275) a maximum of seven months in advance and as soon as possible in the summer. Beachside camping outside official campgrounds is both illegal and unsafe.

**Doheny,** 25300 Dana Point Harbor Dr. (☎714-496-6171), in Dana Point, along Hwy. 1. The most popular Orange County campground. Fire rings, grills, showers, volleyball nets, bike and in-line skate rental. The Doheny Blues Music Festival arrives in mid-May with loud music, big crowds, and late nights. Beachfront sites $13-16. ❶

**San Clemente,** 3030 Del Presidente (☎949-492-3156), in San Clemente. From I-5 North, exit at Christianitos and turn right onto Del Presidente and then left onto Calafia after three-quarters of a mile; from I-5 South, exit at Calafia. Ocean bluffs, nature trail, and coin-operated hot showers draw all kinds of folks. Hookups at 72 sites. Sites $13-16, with hookup $18-22. ❶

## FOOD & NIGHTLIFE

Orange County's restaurants tend toward California Cuisine of the light and seafood-oriented variety.

**Laguna Village Market and Cafe,** 577 S. Coast Hwy. (☎949-494-6344), 5 blocks south of Broadway in **Laguna Beach.** Located on top of a cliff, the restaurant is housed in an open-air gazebo selling art and jewelry by local artists and designers. Its oceanfront terrace is the main draw. Lap up the view, along with some seafood or the house specialty, Village Huevos ($9.50). Calamari plate $9. Open daily 8:30am-dark. ❷

**Ruby's** (☎714-969-7829), at the end of the **Huntington Beach** Pier. A 5-7min. trek down the pier. Enclosed by windows on all walls, this flashy white and neon red 50s-style diner has great burgers ($6) and a fabulous ocean view. ❷

**Cafe Zoolu,** 860 Glenneyre (☎949-494-6825), in **Laguna Beach.** This small evening restaurant offers an opportunity to dine on the freshest fish possible in a bustling atmosphere, undoubtedly enhanced by zebra-striped chairs and red-stone walls. It's best to pick from the seafood specials like the scallop salad. Nothing prepares you for Alaskan halibut ($26) like ahi tar-tar ($15). Open Su and Tu-Sa 5pm-late. ❺

**The Dutch Bakery,** 32341 Camino Capistrano (☎949-489-2180), in **San Juan Capistrano.** Located in the Vons Center plaza down the street from the Mission, this bakery provides excellent chicken, turkey, ham, salami, and roast beef sandwiches, all on fresh-baked ciabatta bread. The chicken paisano (with havarti cheese, tomato, lettuce, and paisano mayo; $6) is unbeatable. Wash it down with a strawberry banana smoothie ($3). Open Tu-F 6am-4pm, Sa 7am-3pm. ❷

**Taco Mesa,** 211 Broadway, (949-497-4341), at PCH, in **Laguna Beach.** Quality Mexican fast-food restaurant where you can fill your stomach with just a fistful of dollars. Chicken, fish, calamari, and shrimp tacos $2-3. Open daily 8am-sunset. ❶

**The Cottage,** 308 N. Coast Hwy. (☎949-494-3023), at Cliff Dr., across from the Laguna Art Museum, in **Laguna Beach.** In a turn-of-the-century "board and batten" beach home, The Cottage is a Laguna landmark. Overflowing portions of home-style cooking (surfer's breakfast $9.25) and omelettes galore ensure that guests are fed like family. Prices go up for dinner. Breakfast served daily until 3pm. Open daily 7am-3pm and 5-9:30pm. ❸

**Streetlight Espresso Café,** 201D Main St. (☎714-969-7336), 2 blocks inland from the Pier, entrance is right off Main St. on Walnut St., in **Huntington Beach.** Streetlight is as bohemian as staid Huntington Beach gets. This non-denominational cafe hosts Christian rock bands F-Sa nights. Its board games get regular play. Super-sweet white chocolate mocha ($3-3.50) is a godsend. Sandwiches $4.50; cup of soup $4.50. Open M-F 8am-midnight, Sa 7am-1am, Su noon-midnight. ❶

**The Boom-Boom Room,** 1401 S. Coast Hwy. (☎949-494-7588; www.boomboom-room.com), at Mountain St., in **Laguna Beach.** Lively gay hangout has international reputation, pool tables, live DJs spinning everything from house to hip-hop, and a "surfing, muscle-bound, cruising, tanned" clientele. Boom-Boom specials include "Beer Busts" (Tu-Th and Sa-Su 4-8pm) with $2.50 beers and free appetizers. "Go-go Boyz" on Sunday night. Cover begins at 9pm. Open Tu-F 11:30am-2am, Sa-Su 9:30am-2am.

**Joe's Crabshack,** 2607 Pacific Coast Hwy. (949-650-1818; www.joescrab-shack.com), in **Newport Beach.** Brightly colored chairs, neon beer lights on the walls, a fantastic view of the harbor, and a balloon person who comes to the tables to make animal balloons set the festive, family-friendly mood. Locals applaud the Dungeness Crabs ($23). Appetizers from $6, entrees from $10. Open M-F 11am-10pm, Sa-Su 11am-11pm. ❸

## 🔆 ⑤ BEACHES & SIGHTS

Apart from pre-fabricated amusement park joy, fun in the sun Orange County-style lies along the Pacific Coast Highway (PCH). On average, the beaches are cleaner, less crowded, visited by younger, toned beachgoers, and more elegant than those in LA County. Nevertheless, visitors should not be lulled off-guard by the swishing coastal waters. As in any city, pedestrians should take care after dusk.

### ▸HUNTINGTON BEACH

*From LA, take the I-405 south to Hwy. 39 (Beach Blvd.). Follow Hwy. 39 south to PCH, then turn right (north). The pier is on the left at intersection of the PCH and Main St.*

The prototypical Surf City, USA, the city is a beach bum playground. This town has surf lore galore, and the proof is on the **Surfing Walk of Fame** (the sidewalk along PCH at Main St.) and in the **International Surfing Museum,** 411 Olive St.

*(☎714-960-3483. Open daily noon-5pm; call for details. $2, students $1.)* You can join the wave-riding for about $40 per hour for an instructor, board, and wet-suit. Inquire at any of the local surf shops or make an appointment with the lifeguard-staffed **Huntington Beach Surfing Instruction** *(☎714-962-3515).* The pier is the best place to watch the cavalcade of official surfing contests. By night, H.B.'s bars become a beach party brouhaha. **Duke's Barefoot Bar** *(☎714-374-6446),* at the foot of the pier, is a major beach landmark, and **Perq's,** 117 Main St. *(☎714-960-9996),* is Orange County's oldest rock & blues house. **Main St.,** Huntington Beach's central lane, is a surf shop superstore. Locals lament the loss of familiar establishments. Malls and shiny new bars have replaced the rustic charm of Huntington's surfing subculture.

## NEWPORT BEACH & BALBOA PENINSULA

*From LA, take I-405 or the I-5 (San Diego Fwy.) south to Hwy. 55 (Costa Mesa Fwy.) and head west. Hwy. 55 turns into Newport Blvd., the main drag leading to the peninsula.*

Multi-million dollar summer homes, the world's largest leisure-craft harbor, and Balboa Peninsula are all packed closely enough on the Newport Beach oceanfront to make even New Yorkers feel claustrophic. The young, scantily clad hedonistst partying on the sand are a solid mix of locals and out-of-town-ers. Surfing and beach volleyball are popular, as is strolling on the residential streets of Balboa Peninsula. The Newport Pier is an extension of 22nd St. at West Balboa Blvd.

**BALBOA PENINSULA.** The sands of Newport Beach run south onto the Balboa Peninsula, separated from the mainland by Newport Bay. The peninsula is only two to four blocks wide and can be reached via PCH. Ocean Front Walk, which extends the length of the peninsula and lined with neat rows of expensive cot-tages, is the best place to stroll. The Balboa Pier, flanked by beautiful sands, is at Main St. and East Balboa Blvd. Basketball games can be found at the ocean-side courts at 13th St. At the farthest tip of the peninsula, **The Wedge** is a body-surfing mecca where the ocean depth changes suddenly and waves that appear safe suddenly rise to over 20 ft. near the shore.

On the opposite side of the peninsula, at the end of Main St., is the ornate **Balboa Pavilion.** Once a sounding ground for big band great Benny Goodman, it is now a hub for harbor tours and whale watching. The double-deck *Pavilion Paddy* offers 45min. *($7, ages 5-12 $3)* and 90min. *($10, ages 5-12 $3)* cruises. The *Catalina Flyer* leaves for Catalina Island at 9am and departs Catalina Island that same afternoon at 4:30pm between March and November. *(Both ships ☎949-673-5245. Call for reservations and for Dec.-Feb. schedule.* Catalina Flyer *round-trip $42, seniors $39, ages 3-12 $25, under 3 $3.)* A harborside mêlée, **Fun-zone** stretches its Ferris wheel and bumper cars west of the pavilion. *(Open daily 10am-10pm.)*

Most of the crowds navigate Newport Beach and the Balboa Peninsula by bicycle, 5-person bicycle surrey, or in-line skates. Stands everywhere rent all necessary gear. *(Bikes $5-7 per hr., $15 per day; skates $3-6 per hr., $15 per day; boogie boards $5-6 per day.)* Bikers should pick up *Bikeways,* a map of trails in Newport Beach, at the Visitors Center (see p. 458).

**BALBOA ISLAND.** Across the harbor from the pavilion where Errol Flynn, Shir-ley Temple, Humphrey Bogart, and many another celeb once docked a yacht is Balboa Island, a haven for ice cream shops (locally famous for Balboa bars and frozen bananas), artsy gift boutiques, and bikini stores. It was once just a sand-spit, but the area was dredged and filled right before WWI. A vintage **ferryboat** travels there from the peninsula. *(☎673-1070. Ferry runs daily every 5min., but* *expect a delay at rush hour. Car and driver $1.50, each additional passenger 60¢, children 30¢; bikes 40-75¢.)* The island is also accessible from PCH via the Jamboree Rd. bridge. The island's outermost sidewalk, which traces the shore, is a popular place for morning walks and runs (no biking or skating permitted).

**OTHER SIGHTS.** Newport's **Harbor Nautical Museum**, aboard the 190 ft. *Pride of Newport*, 151 E. Pacific Coast Hwy., displays Newport maritime history and extraordinary model ships. *(☎ 949-675-8915: www.nhnm.org. Open Su and Tu-Sa 10am-5pm. Free.)* A few miles east, in what was formerly Corona del Mar, is the **Sherman Library and Gardens**, 2647 E. Pacific Coast Hwy., a museum of living plants where pristine botanical collections range from desert cacti and succulents to tropical blooms. *(☎ 949-673-2261; www.slgardens.org. Gardens open daily 10:30am-4pm. Library open Tu-Th 9am-4:30pm. $3, ages 12-16 $1, under 12 free. From 405, take MacArthur turn-off South to PCH. Turn left on PCH and then right onto Dahlia.)*

Just inland, above the PCH and between MacArthur Blvd. and Jamboree Rd., sits **Fashion Island.** Divided into seven courts, this outdoor mall has all the amenities of a regular mall and allows you to get a tan while shopping.

## LAGUNA BEACH

*From LA, take I-405 south to Hwy. 133 (Laguna Canyon Rd.); follow it to Laguna Beach.*

Punctuated by rocky cliffs, coves, and lush hillside vegetation, this lovely beach town's character is decidedly Mediterranean and artsy. **Ocean Avenue,** at the Pacific Coast Hwy., and **Main Beach** are the prime parading areas. **Westry Beach,** which spreads south of Laguna just below Aliso Beach Park, and **Camel Point,** between Westry and Aliso, form the hub of the local gay community. For beach access, park on residential streets to the east and look for "Public Access" signs between private properties. If you can find a spot, there is a good parking lot half a block inland from Beach St. between Ocean and Forest Ave. *($1 per hr.)*

From the turn of the century, Laguna has been an artists' colony. The latest incarnation of the original 1914 Laguna Beach art association is the **Laguna Art Museum,** 307 Cliff Dr. The collection showcases local and state art, including some excellent early 20th-century Impressionist works. Pick up the museum's guide to local art, which lists information on over 100 **art galleries** in the immediate Laguna Beach area. *(☎494-8971;*

## NO WORK, ALL PLAY

### PAGEANT OF MASTERS

For years, artists around the world have sought to imitate life by immortalizing it upon canvas. The Pageant of the Masters in Laguna Beach does the opposite: it uses life to immortalize some of the finest and most famous works of art in a 2hr. extravaganza. Volunteers from around the world create living replicas of famous works from Rockwell's *Saturday Evening Post* covers to Da Vinci's *Last Supper* (the perennial finale). The actors, heavily made up and costumed, step into a painted background as the piece is framed in front of the audience. The lights dim, and when the picture is revealed, the actors have disappeared into a 2-D canvas. In addition to paintings, the Pageant also replicates statues and sculptures, brilliantly imitating marble, stone, gold, and countless other mediums. In all, more than 30 works are recreated each year, encompassing everything from Renaissance to contemporary art, and each Pageant has a different theme.

The real genius of the Pageant lies in its execution. Developed over 70 years and enhanced by lighting techniques, the Pageant's ability to eliminate a dimension from the human perspective is truly awesome. With the musical accompaniment and the anticipation of the crowd, the extravaganza is extremely unique. The Pageant of Masters has a home as beautiful as the works found on its stage: the outdoor amphitheater in Laguna Beach. For more info, see **Seasonal Events,** p. 469.

*www.lagunaartmuseum.org. Tours daily 2pm. Open daily 11am-5pm. $7, students and seniors $5, children under 12 free. free first Th of each month.)* Art festivals abound in the summertime; ask for the *What's On Laguna Beach Arts* brochure at the Visitors Center.

## SAN JUAN CAPISTRANO

*From LA, take I-5 S to the Ortega Hwy., make a right, and follow it downtown. ☎ 949-248-2048; www.missionsjc.com. Besides English, self-guided tours available in Italian, Spanish, and German; call ahead. Open daily 8:30am-5pm. $6, seniors $5, ages 3-12 $4.*

The **Mission San Juan Capistrano,** 30min. south of Anaheim on I-5, was founded in the same year as the United States of America, 1776, and is the birthplace of Orange County. It is full of romance and beauty and stands as a monument to Native American, Mexican, and European cultures. Established by Father Junípero Serra, this is considered the "jewel of the missions." Although most of the original structure collapsed in an 1812 earthquake, this is the only standing site where Serra himself is known to have given mass, and the oldest building still in use in California. The crumbling walls of the beautiful **Serra Chapel** are warmed by a 17th-century Spanish altar and Native American designs. Gregorian chants evoke the spiritualism that Serra once envisioned. On March 19 of each year, the city of San Juan Capistrano gathers in the Mission to celebrate the famous "miracle of the Swallows," a celebration of the migrating birds that always return to the Mission.

The **Swallows Inn,** 31786 Camino Capistrano (☎949-493-3188), has been a local hub in San Juan for over 50 years. It is home to the largest chili cook-off in the country and is the best place to catch the **Swallows Day Parade** in March.

San Juan Capistrano's village core offers abundant evidence that the West still lives. Lovers of John Wayne and the Western era must take an afternoon and stroll the few square blocks and absorb the history of western small towns.

## DANA POINT & SAN CLEMENTE

*To get to Dana Point from LA, take the I-5 (San Diego Fwy.) south to PCH. Follow PCH toward Dana Point Harbor. To San Clemente from LA, take the I-5 south to El Camino. Exit in San Clemente. Don't miss your exit; there are no exits for 30min. through Camp Pendleton.*

Dana Point's spectacular bluffs were popularized in namesake Richard Henry Dana's 1841 account of Southern California's sailing culture, *Two Years Before the Mast.* The harbor holds 2500 yachts and also serves as a point of departure for Catalina Island. Dana Point's **swimming beach** lies at Salt Creek and the Strands.

Neighboring **San Clemente,** a "small Spanish village by the sea," has the powerful waves of Huntington and Newport minus the beach party noise and antics. Its downtown is now known as "Antique Mecca," where unrivaled antique stores and the buildings themselves are reminiscent of the Revolutionary days. In stark contrast, the US Marine Corps flexes its modern military might at Camp Pendleton, located along the coast. Farther south is **San Onofre State Beach** and its "Trestles" area, a break point and thus a prime surfing zone for experienced thrill-seekers.

## WILD RIVERS WATERPARK

If you haven't had enough amusement park action, make a splash in the over 40 waterslide rides and two wave pools at **Wild Rivers Waterpark,** 8770 Irvine Center Dr., in Irvine, off I-405. (☎949-788-0808; www.wildrivers.com. Open daily 10am-8pm. $26, ages 65+ free, under 48 inches $18. Parking $6. From 405, exit Irvine Ctr. Dr., turn south one block to Lion Country Rd., and turn left into the park.)

## SEASONAL EVENTS

**Strawberry Festival** (☎ 714-638-0981; www.strawberryfestival.org), in downtown Garden Grove on the village green. Late May. Garden Grove is the US's leading producer of strawberries, and the festival includes some arduous strawberry pie-eating contests.

**Festival of Arts** and **The Pageant of the Masters,** 650 Laguna Canyon Rd. (info ☎ 949-494-1145, tickets 800-487-3378; www.foapom.com), in Laguna Beach, take place together in the Irvine Bowl July-Aug. Life literally imitates art in the Pageant as actors recreate famous paintings. Festival grounds open daily 10am-11:30pm; $5, seniors $3. Pageant shows nightly 8:30pm; tickets $15-80. Box office opens Dec. 1 for the following summer, and tickets sell out quickly. For reservations, contact the Festival of Arts, P.O. Box 1659, Laguna Beach, 92652. See **No Work, All Play,** p. 467.

**Sawdust Festival,** 935 Laguna Canyon Rd. (☎ 949-494-3030; www.sawdustfestival.org), across the street from The Pageant of the Masters, July-Aug. Lots of local art. Festival grounds open daily 10am-10pm. Tickets $6.50, ages 6-12 $2, under 6 free.

**Christmas Boat Parade of Lights** (☎ 949-729-4400), the week before Christmas, in Newport Harbor. Over 200 boats and innumerable lights create a dazzling display.

# EAST OF LA

LA's huddled masses who yearn to breathe free often pack up their kids, cell phones, and cares and head for the hills. Granite mountains, scenic hiking trails, campgrounds, and scented pine forests await a mere 45min. drive above and beyond the inversion layer (the altitude at which the smog ends).

In the mountains, outdoor activities abound at all times of the year, but winter is undeniably the high season. While the Sierra Nevada resorts around Lake Tahoe (p. 237) and Mammoth Lakes (p. 303) are the destinations of choice for serious California skiers, daytrips to the smaller resorts of the San Bernardino mountains have become increasingly popular. Temperatures typically allow ski resorts to operate from November through April, but always call ahead to check conditions. Even when the snow melts, the coastal mountains are an ideal getaway. The Angeles and San Bernardino National Forests sprawl across majestic mountains and have many campgrounds, hiking trails, and mountain villages.

# ANGELES NATIONAL FOREST                  ☎ 626

National forests cover about one quarter of LA County north of Pasadena and east of Valencia. Cradling the northern edge of the LA Basin and the San Gabriel Valley are the San Gabriel Mountains, whose highest peak, Mt. San Antonio ("Mt. Baldy"), tops out at 10,064 ft. This area is popular year-round, attracting mountain bikers, anglers, bird watchers, and hikers. Harsh weather and frequent brush fires often rearrange the place, so rangers can give helpful directions. Skiers will probably find Big Bear more worthwhile than the closer resorts at Mt. Baldy (☎ 909-982-0800) and Mt. High East and West (☎ 760-249-5808).

## PRACTICAL INFORMATION

The national forest is divided into three ranger districts: Los Angeles River, San Gabriel River, and Santa Clara. Each houses a district office, a visitors center, a work center, and an information station, each with info specific to the district. For general forest information, call ☎ 626-574-5200 or visit the Forest Headquarters (see below). In an **emergency,** contact the Angeles National Forest Dispatcher (☎818-447-8999 in the Arcadia area, 661-723-7619 in the Lancaster area). All ranger stations listed below are open Monday through Friday 8am to 4:30pm.

**Angeles National Forest Headquarters,** Supervisor's Office, 701 N. Santa Anita Ave. (☎626-574-1613), in Arcadia. Comprehensive forest maps ($6-8).

**Los Angeles River Ranger District,** 12371 N. Little Tujunga Canyon Rd. (☎818-899-1900), in San Fernando. **Chilao Visitors Center** lies on Rte. 2 (Angeles Crest Hwy.), 26 mi. from La Cañada (☎626-796-5541). Open M and F-Su 8am-4:30pm. Rte. 2 leads into the south-central area of the forest, north of Pasadena. 27 campgrounds in this district; many are high country camps. The **Tujunga Work Center,** 12371 N. Little Tujunga Canyon Rd. (☎818-899-1900), in San Fernando, covers the west end of the San Gabriel Mountains. Hiking, horseback riding, and 5 campgrounds.

**San Gabriel River Ranger District,** 110 N. Wabash Ave. (☎626-335-1251), in Glendora. **Mount Baldy Visitors Center,** on Mt. Baldy Rd. north of Ontario. Open daily 8am-4:30pm. The southeastern district of the forest has 8000 ft. peaks, hiking trails, the San Antonio Falls, and scenic Glendora Ridge Rd. Four developed campgrounds.

**Santa Clara Ranger District,** 30800 Bouquet Canyon Rd. (☎661-296-9710), in Saugus, northwest of the main forest. Two Visitors Centers: **Big Pines,** on the east end of Rte. 2 (Angeles Crest Hwy.) near the turn-off for Valyermo (☎760-249-3504; open M and F-Su 8am-3:30pm), and **Grassy Hollow,** also on Rte. 2, 6 mi. west of Wrightwood (☎626-821-6737; open Sa-Su 10am-4pm). Pyramid, Elizabeth, and Castaic Lakes have boating and fishing. A few of the 22 campgrounds have been vandalized. **Mojave River Work Center,** P.O. Box 15, 29835 Valyermo Rd. in Valyermo, is in the northeastern part of the San Gabriel Mountains (☎661-944-2187; open M-F 8:30am-5pm).

## 🏕 CAMPING

The US Forest Service maintains 557 mi. of well-groomed hiking trails and camping facilities. Many of the trails cross, so maps are vital. Most campsites run by the Forestry Service are free, though parked vehicles must display an **Adventure Pass** ($5, available at ranger stations, visitor centers, and various local retailers; see p. 472). Campsites run by concessionaires are $10-15 per night. Sites are first-come, first-camp (14-night max. stay), and many are closed in the winter. There are many campgrounds along Big Pines Hwy. that are convenient and free, but they offer little seclusion. A site beyond the front country affords more privacy and security, though probably no drinking water or bathrooms.

**Chilao Recreation Area** (☎818-790-1151), 5300 ft., off Rte. 2, 26 mi. northeast of La Cañada. Visitors Center, 1 mi. north of the campground and south of Three Points and Devil's Canyon trailheads, offers walks, talks, and children's activities. The 111 sites have fire rings, tables, water, and toilets. No hookups. Sites $12. ❶

**Buckhorn,** 6300 ft., on Rte. 2, 26 mi. southwest of Wrightwood and 36 mi. northeast of La Cañada, has 38 sites surrounded by lush ferns and redwoods. Near Burkhart Trailhead. Fire rings, tables, water, and toilets. No hookups. Open June-Nov. Sites $12. ❶

**Spunky,** 3300 ft., on Spunky Canyon Rd. From I-5 in Valencia, take Magic Mtn. Pkwy. Exit, drive east to Valencia Blvd., continue 2 mi., turn left to Bouqet Canyon Rd., and drive 14 mi. to Spunky Canyon Rd. Near the Pacific Coast Trail, this campsite has easy access to the backcountry, picnic tables, fire pits, and vault toilets. No piped water. ❶

**Glenn Trail Camp,** 2000 ft., off Rte. 39 North. The end of the West Fork National Bike Trail (16 mi. round-trip). Walk or bike in from a gate. The physically challenged can get a driving permit; contact the San Gabriel Ranger Station (☎626-335-1251). 10 free sites with vault toilets. Stream water only; treat before drinking. Free. ❶

## 👁 🏔 SIGHTS & OUTDOOR ACTIVITIES

**HIKING.** Just outside the national forest in a county park, the **Devil's Punchbowl** entices hikers and climbers with its spooky sandstone formations. (Take Longview Rd. from Hwy. 138 to Devil's Punchbowl Rd., where a right turn will take you into the park.) For a moderately easy and scenic morning or afternoon hike, try **Charlton Flat to Vetter Mountain** (3 mi.). The trail climbs past pine, oak, and a wide variety of birds and flowers from near the Charlton Flat picnic area (off Rte. 2) to an old fire lookout point on Vetter Mountain, providing fine views. A different trailhead from Charlton Flat leads to **Devil Peak,** another short and enjoyable hike. A popular, moderate full-day hike leads from **Vincent Gap to Mt. Baden-Powell** (8 mi.), climbing 2800 ft. through ancient pines and peaking at 9400 ft. with spectacular views of the San Gabriel range, including Old Baldy and, on clear days, the looming desert. The trailhead is located in the Vincent Gap parking lot, off Rte. 2, 52 mi. from La Cañada. The **Blue Ridge Trail** to **Mt. Baldy** (12 mi.), the highest peak in the San Gabriel range at 10,064 ft., is a challenging, high-elevation hike that should only be attempted by the fit. Those who summit, however, will be rewarded with unsurpassed views of the alpine country. To reach the trailhead, drive 1½ mi. west of Big Pines on Rte. 2 to Blue Ridge Rd. From there, it is three miles to the Blue Ridge campground and the trailhead.

The three- to five-day **Gabrielino Trail** (53 mi. round-trip) connects Oak Grove Park and the north end of Windsor Ave., in La Cañada Flintridge. The five-day **Silver Moccasin Trail** (53 mi. one-way), once a rite of passage for adventurous Boy Scouts, is now a popular backcountry route. The trail connects Chantry Flats with Vincent Gap, crossing forest, stream, mountain, and canyon. Long hikes such as these necessitate **trail camping.** Fortunately, it is free and legal, but fire permits (available at ranger stations) are strictly required for anything with a flame, including cigarettes, and camping is not allowed within 200 ft. of any stream. There are also numerous opportunities to hike a portion of the renowned **Pacific Crest Trail** (see **From Crest to Crest: The Trail of the West,** p. 235). Trailheads are scattered along the length of the **Hwy. 2** (Angeles Crest Hwy.).

**WALKING AND SITTING.** Visitors in search of a more contemplative experience may care to stop at the Benedictine **St. Andrews Abbey** in the village of **Valyermo.** Three-day weekend retreats, including room and board, begin at $130, and focus on diverse theological themes like spirituality in modern cinema and the writings of C.S. Lewis. A ceramic craftworks helps to support the abbey. Visitors are welcome at mass. **Rooms ❹** with A/C are also available on a regular basis for $60 per person per night. (Retreat office ☎661-944-2178; www.valyermo.com. Take Valyermo Rd. from Hwy. 138. Open daily 9am-5pm; mass daily noon-1:30pm.)

# SAN BERNARDINO NATIONAL FOREST

The San Bernardino National Forest makes up over 700,000 acres of pristine, mountainous public lands on the outer northeastern edge of Southern California's urban expanse. Five federally designated wilderness areas—Cucamonga, San Gorgonio, Bighorn Mountain, San Jacinto, and Santa Rosa—host largely undisturbed snow-capped peaks, desert transition zones, deep canyons, green meadows, and dark blue lakes. Outside the wilderness areas are more developed attractions like Big Bear and Arrowhead Lakes. For detailed info on exploring, pick up a Visitor Guide at the Big Bear Discovery Center (see p. 472).

## AT A GLANCE

**AREA:** 723,161 acres.

**CLIMATE:** Temperate forest.

**FEATURES:** Big Bear, San Gorgonio Wilderness Area, Arrowhead Lakes.

**HIGHLIGHTS:** Ski in Big Bear Lake by summer, ski down Big Bear Mountain by winter, hike the forest all year long.

**GATEWAYS:** San Bernardino (p. 477), Big Bear (below), Los Angeles (p. 370).

**CAMPING:** Camping is permitted at US Forest Service sites throughout the area. Also allowed at more remote sites with free visitors permit available at Ranger Station.

**FEES & RESERVATIONS:** Recreational use of national forest land requires an Adventure Pass (p. 472).

# BIG BEAR                    ☎909

Big Bear Lake serves as a gateway to the San Bernardino National Forest and a destination unto itself. In the summer, the central lake provides ample opportunities for fishing, sailing, and watersports, while the nearby mountains and forest offer enjoyable hikes and well-preserved campgrounds. The village surrounding the lake is a quiet slice of civilization in the woods, with accommodations of snow chalets and mountain cabins mainly geared toward the skiing set, which arrives en masse from LA and elsewhere around December.

## ■ ▐ ORIENTATION AND PRACTICAL INFORMATION

To reach Big Bear, take **I-10** to **Route 30** in San Bernardino. Take Rte. 30 north to **Route 330** (Mountain Rd.),which turns into **Route 18,** a winding 30-45min. ascent. Rte. 18 hits the west end of Big Bear Lake and forks into a continuing Rte. 18 branch along the south shore, where it is called Big Bear Blvd., and Rte. 38 along the north shore. A less congested, longer route approaches from the east via I-10 to Redlands and then **Route 38** to Big Bear Lake. Driving time from LA is about 2½hr., barring serious weekend traffic or road closures. The loneliest route to Big Bear Lake curls in from the north, across the high desert along Rte. 18 through the Lucerne Valley, from **I-15** in Victorville. Weekend day skiers should wait until after 6pm to head home in order to avoid the 4pm rush. Driving to Big Bear should not be attempted during the winter without checking road conditions with **CalTrans.** (☎427-7623; www.dot.ca.gov.) **Mountain Area Regional Transit Authority (MARTA)** runs two **buses** per day from the Greyhound station in San Bernardino to Big Bear. (☎584-1111. $5, seniors and disabled $3.75.) Buses also run the length of Big Bear Blvd. (End-to-end trip 1hr.; $1, students 75¢, seniors and disabled 50¢.) MARTA also operates **Dial-A-Ride.** ($2, students $1.50, seniors and disabled $1.)

The **Big Bear Chamber of Commerce,** 630 Bartlett Rd., in Big Bear Village, dispenses glossy brochures and info on lodging, local events, and skiing and road conditions. (☎866-4608, fax 866-5412; www.bigbearchamber.com. Open M-F 8am-5pm, Sa-Su 9am-5pm.) Located directly above the Chamber of Commerce, the **Big Bear Lake Resort Association** arranges lodging and ski packages. (☎866-

7000 or 800-424-4232; www.bigbearinfo.com. Open M-F 8am-6pm, Sa-Su 9am-5pm.) **Big Bear Discovery Center** or **BBDC**, on Rte. 38 four miles east of Fawnskin and 1¼ mi. west of the Stanfield Cutoff, is a ranger station that sells the **National Forest Adventure Pass** (day $5, year $30), which is required for vehicles at camping sites that charge no additional fee. (☎866-3437. Open daily Apr.-Sept. 8am-6pm; Oct.-Mar. 9am-5pm.) The National Forest Adventure Pass can be purchased at ranger and information stations throughout the state, through a number of private vendors, or at www.fsadventurepass.org. In **emergencies,** call ☎383-5651 to reach a ranger station. **Internet access** is available at Big Bear Public Library, 41930 Garstin Dr. (☎866-5571. Open M-Tu noon-8pm, W-F 10am-6pm, Sa 9am-5pm.) The **post office,** 472 Pine Knot Blvd., is off Big Bear Blvd. (☎866-7481. Open M-F 8:30am-5pm, Sa 10am-noon.) **Postal Code:** 92315.

# ACCOMMODATIONS

In the winter, budget accommodations are next to impossible to find, but in the summer bargains abound. Even then, though, rooms below $50 a night are often found only in San Bernardino (see p. 477), down the mountain. Big Bear Blvd. is lined with lodging possibilities, and groups can find the best deals by sharing a cabin. Solo travelers and couples may have better luck at chain motels. **Mountain Lodging Unlimited** arranges lodging and lift packages. (☎866-5500. Packages from $100 per couple. Open in ski season 7am-midnight; off-season 9am-midnight.)

**Robinhood Inn,** 40797 Lakeview Dr. (☎866-4643 or 800-990-9956). Unlike its namesake, this chalet-style motel won't rob from the rich or poor. Courtyard complete with spa and barbecue. Fireplaces, kitchenettes, and coffeemakers in many rooms. John Wayne once stayed here. Singles and doubles begin at $64 in summer and $79 in winter; suites accommodating up to 6 under $100. ❹

**Hillcrest Lodge,** 40241 Big Bear Blvd. (☎866-7330, reservations 800-843-4449; www.hillcrestlodge.com). Pine paneling and skylights give these cozy rooms a stylish feel. Jacuzzi, cable TV, and free local calls. In winter, small rooms $48-119; 4-person units and suites $79-159. In summer, small rooms $48-70; 4-person units with kitchen $90-140; 2-bedroom suites with hearth and kitchen $100-150. ❸

**The Vintage Resort,** 41060-41082 Big Bear Blvd. (☎866-4978). Friendly hosts, an unbeatable location on Big Bear Lake, and a surf & turf restaurant are great perks. Kitchenettes in some units. Singles and doubles $70-80 on weekdays, $90-100 on weekends; 2-room units with kitchenette $90-110. ❹

**Embers Lodge,** 40229 Big Bear Blvd. (☎866-2371; www.embberslodge.com). Simple studios, some with kitchens, fireplaces, and TVs for 2-8 people. Dec.-Mar. Su-Th $65, F-Sa $95-120; Apr.-Nov. Su-Th $25, F-Sa $50-60. ❸

# CAMPING

Camping is permitted at many surrounding US Forest Service sites. Several of these sites accept reservations through the National Recreation Reservation Service (☎877-444-6777; www.reserveusa.com) or the US Forest Service (☎800-280-2267). Most are open from May to Nov. Campers can tent on US Forest Service land if they stay 200 ft. from water and roads and a quarter-mile from developed areas. The entire north shore of Big Bear Lake is national forest and contains many campsites. The Big Bear Discovery Center (see **Practical Info,** p. 472) offers free visitors permits and info about Remote Camping Areas and Yellow Post Sites.

**Pineknot,** 7000 ft., on Summit Blvd., south of Big Bear. Amid thick woods, these 48 sites are secluded and cool. At the base of steep Snow Summit, mountain bikers rule the single-track. Flush toilets and water. Wheelchair-accessible. Sites $18. ❷

**Hanna Flats,** 7000 ft., on Forest Rd. 3N14, 2½ mi. northwest of Fawnskin. Lush vegetation surrounds 88 roomy sites. Hiking, water, pit and flush toilets. Sites $17. ❷

**Holcomb Valley,** 7400 ft., 4 mi. north on Polique Canyon Rd. 2N09, then east for ¾ mi. on Forest Rd. 3N16. 19 sites. Pit toilets; no water. Near the PCT. Sites $10. ❶

**Serrano,** 40650 North Shore Ln. (☎866-8021, reservations 877-444-6777), 6500 ft., right off Hwy. 38 in Fawnskin. The most popular campground in Big Bear, with the highest occupancy of national forest campgrounds in the nation. Only a few hundred feet from the lake. All 132 sites (including 28 RV) have showers and flush toilets. Many sites are reserved up to 8 months in advance, so make reservations early. Sites $23. ❷

## ◨ FOOD

Food can get pricey, so those with kitchens should forage at **Stater Bros.,** 42171 Big Bear Blvd. (☎866-5211. Open daily 7am-11pm.) Many of the cutesy village eateries offer all-you-can-eat specials.

**Virginia Lee's,** 41003 Big Bear Blvd. (☎866-3151). A motley collection of hot dogs, tamales, ice cream, fancy hot chocolate, and potato and pasta salads make the menu in this tasty little roadside shack. Everything $2-4. Open Su and W-Sa 10am-4pm. ❶

**Grizzly Manor,** 41268 Big Bear Blvd. (☎866-6226). A local favorite for breakfast. Get some combination of the breakfast staples of eggs, pork, and potatoes for $4-7 or just say t'hell with it and get "The Mess" ($7). Open Su and Sa 6am-2pm, W-F 7am-2pm. ❷

**La Paws,** 1128 W. Big Bear Blvd. (☎585-9115), in Big Bear City. A fun little family-run spot serving authentic and inexpensive Mexican specialties (burritos $4-6) and American favorites. Open daily 7am-8pm. ❶

**Boo Bear's Den,** 572 Pine Knot Ave. (☎866-2162). A relaxing outdoor patio in the heart of downtown Big Bear, this local den is your best bet for casual dining near the lake and village shops. The "Boo Burgers" ($5-7) are a good choice. Sandwiches $6-9; entrees $11-15. Open M-F 8am-9pm, Sa-Su 7am-10pm. ❸

## ⚑ OUTDOOR ACTIVITIES

### SUMMER RECREATION

The **National Forest Adventure Pass** (p. 472) is required for parking at trailheads, though not at picnic areas.

**HIKING.** Although hiking often takes a back seat to higher velocity recreation in Big Bear, the trails in the surrounding mountains are a superb way of exploring the San Bernardino wilderness. Maps, trail descriptions, and the *Visitor's Guide to the San Bernardino National Forest* are available at the Big Bear Discovery Center. Perfect for an afternoon stroll, the 3½ mi. **Alpine Pedal Path** runs its gentle, paved course from the Stanfield Cutoff on the lake's north shore to the Big Bear Discovery Center. The moderately difficult 2½ mi. **Castle Rock Trail,** starting one mile. east of the dam on Hwy. 18, is a short but steep haul, finishing atop a colossal granite blob (the final rock scramble can be a tad risky). The views of Big Bear Lake and the surrounding area are stupendous. A more challenging day hike, **Cougar Crest Trail** (5 mi.) starts a half-mile west of the Discovery Center on Rte. 38 and ascends to meet the Pacific Coast Trail. Continuing east to the summit of Bertha Peak (8502 ft.), it affords unobstructed views of desert. Serious hikers may want to catch a longer piece of the **Pacific Crest Trail (PCT)**, which extends 2638 mi. from Mexico to Canada, and is moderately difficult in this area. (For more info, see **From Crest to Crest: the Trail of the West**, p. 235.) The trail runs parallel to the lake on the north shore and then continues to the east of the lake; the Big Bear Discovery Center can direct hikers to any of the multiple entry points in the area.

**BIKING.** When the snow melts, **mountain biking** takes over the Big Bear slopes. In the San Bernardino National Forest, mountain biking is allowed on all public trails except the PCT and within designated wilderness areas. Grab a *Ride and Trail Guide* at the Discovery Center or at **Snow Summit**, 1 mi. west of Big Bear Lake, which runs lifts in summer so armored adrenaline monsters can grind serious downhill terrain. (☎866-4621. $10 per ride, day pass $20; ages 7-12 $5/$10. Helmet required. Open M-F 9am-4pm, Sa 8am-5pm, Su 9am-4pm.) **Team Big Bear,** 476 Concklin Rd., operating out of the **Mountain Bike Shop** at the base of Snow Summit, rents bikes and sponsors organized bike races each summer. (☎866-4565. $9 per hr., $27 for 4hr., $50 per day; helmet included. For more race info, call daily Apr.-Oct. 9am-5pm, or write Team Big Bear, Box 2932, Big Bear Lake, CA 92315.) **Big Bear Bikes,** 41810 Big Bear Blvd., rents and sells the best bikes on the mountain. (☎866-2224. Front suspension $7 per hr., $35 per day; full suspension $10/$50. Open daily 10am-5pm, extended F-Sa hours if it's busy.)

**FISHING.** Stocked during fishing season with a mighty supply of rainbow trout and catfish, Big Bear Lake is a major angling attraction in the summer. State **fishing** licenses are available at area sporting goods stores (day $10, season $28). Any part of the lake will afford good fishing, but only the north shore is accessible to all; the south shore is mostly private property. The dam at the west end of the lake has the deepest water, making it the best fishing area on the lake. For weekly updates on stocking info, call ☎562-590-5020. **Boats** can be rented at any one of Big Bear's marinas, including **Holloway's Marina and RV Park,** 398 Edgemor Rd., on the south shore. (☎866-5706 or 800-448-5335; www.bigbearboating.com. Full day $50-175.)

**OTHER ADVENTURES.** If you don't have the patience to scout for wildlife in the national forest, head over to **Moonridge Animal Park,** south of Big Bear Blvd. at the end of Moonridge Rd. (☎584-1171. Open daily May-Oct. 10am-5pm; Nov.-Apr. 10am-4pm. $4, seniors and children ages 3-10 $3.) This zoo and care center for wounded or abandoned animals has the only big bears in Big Bear; **Grizzlies** Harley and Hucklebeary (a 3-legged bear) are the featured attractions. **Magic Mountain Recreation Area,** 800 Wild Rose Ln., west of Big Bear Lake Village, operates an **alpine slide** (☎866-4626; open M-F 10am-6pm, Sa 10am-9pm; 1 ride $4, 5 rides $18), a **waterslide park** (1 ride $1, 10 rides $7, unlimited rides $12), a **snowplay hill** in the winter for all sorts of sledding (day pass $18), and a **miniature golf** course with go-karts for summer visitors (open daily 10am-9pm; $4 per round, under 13 $3; single kart $3.50, double $5.50). Human wildlife can be observed in its natural habitat at the **Bowling Barn,** 40625 Lakeview Dr. (☎878-2695; $4.25 per game, children $3.25; shoes $2.75), and mating rituals proceed next door at **Alley Oops** in the form of karaoke and dancing. (Both open daily Su-Th 10am-11pm, F-Sa 10am-1am.)

For those more interested in adventures on water, **Big Bear Parasail,** 439 Pine Knot Landing, drags everything from parachutes to waterskis to inner tubes behind high-speed watercraft. Yamaha Wave Runners are also available for rent. (☎866-IFLY/4359. Parasailing $45 per hr., tandem $80; waterskiing and tubing $95 per hr.; 2-person Wave Runner $75 per hr., 3-person $95 per hr.)

AROUND L.A.

AROUND L.A.

## WINTER RECREATION

When snow conditions are favorable, ski areas run out of lift tickets quickly. **Tickets** for the resorts listed below may be purchased through Ticketmaster (☎714-740-2000). The crowded mountain roads can challenge both vehicle and driver. Gas stations are scarce on the way up the mountain, and signs notify drivers of tire chain requirements. Call CalTrans (☎800-427-7623) for info on road conditions.

**Cross-country skiing** along Big Bear's many trails is a popular way to enjoy the mountain's wintertime scenery. The **Rim Nordic Ski Area,** across the highway from Snow Valley, is an undulating network of cross-country ski trails. An Adventure Pass ($5) is required (see p. 472). Open in winter when snow conditions permit.

For those renting ski and snowboard equipment, hitting the ski stores along Big Bear Blvd. can save you up to half the price of renting at the mountains. The following resorts cater to **downhill skiing and snowboarding:**

**Big Bear Mountain Resorts** (www.bigbearmountainresorts.com) runs two separate mountain resorts, **Bear Mountain,** 43101 Goldmine Dr. (☎585-2519, activities report 800-BEAR-MTN/232-7686; www.bearmtn.com), 1½ mi. southeast of downtown Big Bear Lake, and **Snow Summit,** 880 Summit Blvd. (☎866-5766, activities report 888-SUMMIT-1/786-6481; www.snowsummit.com), 1 mi. east of Big Bear Lake. With 195 acres of terrain, including huge vertical drops, expert runs, and undeveloped land for adventure skiing, Bear Mountain is geared toward freestyle skiing and snowboarding. Snow Summit is a more family-oriented resort with a well-rounded assortment of beginner runs, snowmaking, and night skiing capacities. Between the two resorts, there are 23 lifts and over 55 runs; lift tickets are interchangeable, and a shuttle runs between the two parks. Lift tickets $43, ages 13-19 $35, ages 7-12 $14; holidays $50/$50/$21. Skis $25, snowboards $30; deposit required. Beginner packages available.

**Snow Valley** (☎867-2751, snow report 867-5151), near Running Springs. 12 lifts, 800-5000 ft. runs, snowmaking, night skiing, and a skate park in the summer. The most family-oriented resort in Big Bear, with a children's obstacle course and beginner trails. Lift ticket $37, ages 6-13 $23. Ski rental $17, snowboard $30.

## SAN GORGONIO WILDERNESS AREA                    ☎909

The rugged 60,000-acre San Gorgonio Wilderness Area is set aside from the rest of the San Bernardino National Forest and protected from development. Wheeled vehicles, anything mechanized, and fires of any sort are prohibited. Almost 100 mi. of trails converge on remarkable summits, the highest of which is **Mt. San Gorgonio** (dubbed "Old Grayback" for its barren summit), at 11,500 ft. the tallest in California outside the Sierras. On a clear day, the panoramic summit view includes the southern Sierras, Mexico, the Pacific Ocean, and the Mojave Desert. There are no campgrounds within the Wilderness Area, but backcountry camping is allowed.

To forge into the backcountry, you must have a **wilderness permit.** Obtain these for free up to three months in advance from the **Mill Creek Ranger Station,** near Mentone, about 40 mi. west of Big Bear on Rte. 38 (☎909-794-1123; open M-F 8am-4:30pm, Sa-Su 6:30am-3pm; in winter daily 8am-4:30pm), or at the **Barton Flats Visitor Information Center,** on Rte. 38 about 25 mi. from Big Bear (☎909-794-4861; open June-Oct. Su and W-Sa 8am-4:30pm). An easier way to access the wilderness from LA is to take I-10 to Redlands, take any exit to Rte. 38, and head east.

All but the toughest trekkers will need two days to traverse Mt. San Gorgonio (typical routes are 15-22 mi. round-trip). Consult rangers at Barton Flats or Mill Creek for indispensable local info and excellent topographical maps ($6). The **South Fork Trail,** a challenging 22 mi. haul, is one way to reach the summit, though the **Fish Creek Trail** will start you off higher and get you to the top faster.

The **Vivian Creek Trail** is the shortest and steepest path to the top, and is used as a training spot for those preparing to climb Mt. Whitney. While backcountry camping is free, parking isn't. Anyone who uses a trail needs an **Adventure Pass** for each day of parking (see p. 472). The dry, thin air quickly dehydrates hikers, so bring ample water.

If you prefer seeing San Gorgonio from the road, there are a handful of campgrounds along a 5 mi. stretch of Rte. 38 near Barton Flats Visitor Center. San Gorgonio and **Barton Flats Campgrounds ❶**, near the Visitor Center, are the most expensive ($20) and have showers; **Heart Bar ❶**, toward Big Bear, is the cheapest ($15). Sites fill up quickly on summer weekends, and reservations (☎800-280-2267) are recommended for the more developed campgrounds.

# SAN BERNARDINO ☎909

San Bernardino (pop. 181,718), the seat of America's largest county, is a generic southern Californian smog-bowl, despite its self-billing as the hub of the Inland Empire. The only real empires in this sulfurous city are the rampant corporate franchises—the side benefit being the inexpensive food and lodging available for those en route to a more palatable destination.

**🔏 PRACTICAL INFORMATION.** MARTA **buses** (☎338-1113) run to Big Bear via Arrowhead (3hr., 2 per day, $5). For a **taxi**, call YellowCab (☎884-1111). The Metrolink **trains**, 1204 W. 3rd St., connect LA and San Bernardino with 15 trains running daily on weekdays and 8 on weekends. (☎800-371-5465. Call M-F 4:30am-10:30pm, Sa-Su 9am-9pm. $6-8 one-way; $11-15 round-trip.) The **San Bernardino Convention and Visitors Bureau,** 201 North E. St. #103, at the 2nd St. Exit off Rte. 215 N or the 3rd St. Exit off Rte. 215 S, distributes a thin selection of visitor guides and maps. (☎889-3980. Open M-Th 7:30am-5:30pm, F 7:30am-4:30pm.) Other services include **police** (☎384-5742) and **San Bernardino Community Hospital,** 1805 Medical Ctr. Dr. (☎887-6333), with 24hr. emergency care. **Internet access** is available at San Bernardino Public Library, 555 W. 6th St. (☎381-8201. Open M-W 10am-8pm, Th-Sa 10am-6pm.) The **post office** is at 390 W. 5th St., downtown. (☎800-275-8777. Open M-F 8am-5pm.) **Postal Code:** 92401.

**🔏 ACCOMMODATIONS, FOOD & THE FIRST MCDONALD'S.** The   area along Mt. Vernon Ave. (old Rte. 66) is not so safe, so out-of-towners should stick to either the north end of town or Hospitality Ln., which crosses Waterman Ave. just north of I-10. All lodgings prices **do not include the 10% accommodations tax.** At the **Guesthouse Inn ❹**, 1280 S. E St., the rooms have fridges and breakfast is included. (☎888-0271. Singles $50; doubles $65.) **Motel 6 ❸**, 1960 Ostrems Way, at the University Pkwy. Exit off Rte. 215, is near Cal State University Bernandino. (☎887-8191. Singles M-F $38, Sa-Su $47; doubles $44/$53.) The three-star **Hilton San Bernardino ❺**, 285 E. Hospitality Ln., is reasonably priced (for a Hilton) and offers all the amenities of an upscale hotel. (☎889-0133. Singles and doubles $100-$130.) In 1936, the **Stater Bros. Markets** chain was founded in nearby Yucaipa, and now there are 46 of the stores in the county. Several local branches can supply provisions for the long drive ahead: 1085 W. Highland Ave. (☎886-1517; open daily 7am-11pm), 648 W. 4th St. (☎888-0048; open daily 7am-10pm), and 277 E. 40th St. (☎866-4517; open daily 7am-10pm). For relief from the greasy clutches of fast food chains, **Rosa Maria's ❶**, 4202 N. Sierra Way, serves up quick and delicious Mexican food. Dispose of the house favorite "Garbage Burrito" for $4. (☎881-1731. Open M-F 11am-7pm, Sa 11am-6pm.) **Hogi Yogi ❶**, 4594 University Pkwy., serves tasty sandwiches (regular "hogi" $3-4), and frozen yogurt (small "yogi" $2.15) with your choice of mix-in. (☎887-7812. Open M-Sa 10:30am-9pm, Su noon-4pm.) The original **McDonald's** once stood at 1398 N. E St., but don't expect 15-cent burgers anymore. The only thing offered at this half-hearted historic site is a growing display of Golden Arches memorabilia and Happy Meal toys.

# IDYLLWILD & SAN JACINTO MOUNTAINS ☎909

Unlike the teeming resort hubs of Palm Springs and Big Bear, Idyllwild refuses to become a tacky tourist town in spite of its many attractions and natural beauty. Amid the scrub and stocky pines of the San Jacinto mountain range, Idyllwild offers outdoor enthusiasts many steep and dusty challenges. Hundreds of miles of well-maintained hiking trails, including routes to the nearly 11,000 ft. summit of Mt. San Jacinto, surround the town. Full-service and wild backcountry campgrounds abound, as well as chalet-style accommodations for the less rugged. The monstrous granite of Tahquitz Rock and Suicide Rock tests rock climbers of all abilities. A bustling local art scene nicely complements all the hikers scaling the mountain backdrop. Nestled in the mountains more than 6000 ft. above the desert, this Californian version of an alpine village not only escapes the incinerating heat that besieges Palm Springs, but also enjoys snowy, blustery winters.

## ✳ ⁊ ORIENTATION & PRACTICAL INFORMATION

From LA to the west or Palm Springs to the east, the swiftest approach to Idyllwild is via **I-10** and **Highway 243** south from Banning. The scenic **Palms-to-Pines** Hwy. 243 climbs 6000 ft. from the desert to temperate alpine climate. The **Palm Springs Aerial Tramway** (see p. 570) offers the only **public transportation** to Mt. San Jacinto. There is a network of trails leading from the tram into Idyllwild— buy a map to the San Jacinto National Forest while in Palm Springs. For more info on the tramway, see **Practical Information**, p. 478, or **Palm Springs: Sights and Activities**, p. 570.

**Idyllwild Chamber of Commerce,** 54295 Village Center Dr. (☎659-3259; www.idyllwild-chamber.com), downstairs in the *Town Crier* (the local paper) building across from the Idyllwild Inn. Info and restaurant coupons. Open M-F 9am-1pm.

**San Jacinto Ranger Station (US Forest Service),** 54720 Pine Crest Ave. (☎659-2117). Maps of hiking trails and campgrounds $1-6. Free mandatory wilderness permits for day hiking and overnight backpacking in the San Jacinto National Forest. Buy an Adventure Pass ($5) if you plan to park your car on US Forest Service property, which includes all picnic sites and trailheads. The Pass covers access to all the area national forests. Open daily 8am-4:30pm.

**Mt. San Jacinto State Park and Wilderness Headquarters,** 25905 Rte. 243 (☎659-2607). Free mandatory wilderness permits. Maps $1-8. Open daily 8am-4:30pm.

**Aerial Tram Info** (☎888-515-8726/TRAM), on Tramway Rd. off North Palm Canyon Dr. in **Palm Springs.** Tram from Palm Springs to Mt. San Jacinto runs every 30min. Round-trip $19, seniors $17, children 5-12 $12.50. Open M-F 10am-8pm, Sa-Su 8am-8pm.

**Gear: Nomad Ventures,** 54414 N. Circle Dr. (☎659-4853), sells a vast array of hiking, camping, and climbing gear. Rock climbing shoe rentals $7.50 per day. Open M-F 9am-5pm, Sa 8am-6pm, Su 9am-5pm; in winter closed Tu-W.

**Emergency: Riverside Mountain Rescue Unit, Inc.** (☎659-2900). Search-and-rescue missions for injured or lost hikers in the San Jacinto mountains.

**Police: Riverside County Sheriff Department** (☎800-950-2444). Open 24hr.

**Library and Internet Access: Idyllwild Public Library,** 54185 Lower Pinecrest (☎659-2300). Open M and F 10am-6pm, W 11am-7pm, Sa 10am-4pm.

**Post Office:** 54391 Village Center Dr. (☎659-1969), in the Strawberry Creek shopping center. Open M-F 9am-5pm. **Postal Code:** 92549.

# ⌂ ⌂ ACCOMMODATIONS & CAMPING

Hiking and camping enthusiasts could stay here for weeks on a pittance. **Idyllwild Lodging Information** (☎659-5520) gives a rundown of options. For Forest Service campsite reservations, call ☎800-280-CAMP/2267. For State Park campsites at Idyllwild or Stone Creek, call ☎800-444-PARK/7275, or go to www.reserveamerica.com. Sites fill up quickly in summer; make reservations or plan on arriving early. Check with the rangers for other camping options.

**Atipahato Lodge,** 25525 Scenic Highway 243 (☎888-400-0071; www.atipahato.com). Cozy and romantic, each of the rooms at this immaculate alpine chalet has antique and outdoor-themed furniture, a kitchenette, and a private balcony. Rooms look out on a wooded ravine and waterfall. The lodge owns 5 acres of private land for quiet, moonlit strolls; the land backs into miles of Idyllwild's hiking trails. Rooms with one queen bed M-F $59, Sa-Su $69. Two beautiful cabins, complete with jacuzzi baths, fireplaces, and full kitchens available for $135-159 a night. ❹

**Knotty Pine Cabins,** 54340 Pine Crest Dr. (☎659-2933), off Rte. 243 north of Idyllwild. Eight different cabins are available, each with kitchens or kitchenettes, dishes and utensils, linens, BBQ, TV and VCR. Cabins with one queen bed $56-79. $8 discount with a 2-night stay midweek. ❹

**Dark Canyon Campground,** 5800 ft., located 6 mi. north of Idyllwild on Rte. 243. This Forest Service Campsite is tucked away amid tall pines and large rocks. RVs up to 22 ft. in length are welcome. All 22 sites have water, fire pits, vault toilets, and access to hiking trails. Nearby sites at **Fern Basin** (6300 ft., 22 sites) and **Marion Mountain** (6400 ft., 22 sites) are just as lovely. Both are accessible to RVs up to 15 ft. All sites $12. ❶

**Idyllwild Campground,** 5400 ft., located off Rte. 234 just south of Idyllwild. This State Park campsite offers a few more amenities, but less seclusion and natural pine scent than Dark Canyon. Nonetheless, most of the 90 sites are quiet and pretty. Water, restrooms, coin-operated showers, and fire rings. Sites $15. ❶

# ⌂ FOOD

Restaurant bills rise with the altitude, making the supermarket an attractive option. **Fairway Supermarket,** 5411 Village Center Dr., in the Strawberry Creek shopping center, has reasonable prices. (☎659-2737. Open spring-fall M-Sa 9am-9pm, Su 9am-7pm; in winter M-Sa 9am-8pm, Su 9am-7pm.) If cooking doesn't sound appealing, the pricier options below serve up wonderful meals.

**The Bread Basket,** 54710 N. Circle Dr. (☎659-3506; www.thebreadbasket.net). This European-style bakery is one of Idyllwild's most beloved eateries. Hearty breakfast omelettes ($6-10), specialty sandwiches ($8-10), and a wide variety of dinner entrees ($11-14) are made with fresh, quality ingredients. The apple loaf is popular. Plenty of vegetarian options. Monthly wildflower teas. Open Su-Th 8am-8pm, F-Sa 8am-9pm. ❷

**Cafe Aroma,** 54750 N. Circle Dr. (☎ 659-5212; www.cafearoma.org). A funky combination bistro, gallery, and salon. In this casual but classy restaurant, art is on the walls, and artists are on the waitstaff. Live music acts include an opera-belting waiter and a tap-dancing bus boy. Fine Italian fare (entrees $7-15) with full wine list. Open M 7am-4pm, Tu-Th and Su 7am-9pm, F-Sa 7am-10pm. Reservations recommended. ❸

**Restaurant Gastrognome,** 54381 Ridgeview Dr. (☎ 659-5055). "The Gnome," as locals fondly refer to it, serves up an excellent array of steaks, seafood (lobster tacos $23), and pasta in a sit-down dinnerhouse with dimmed lights. Dinner entrees $12-18. Open Su-Th 11:30am-2:30pm for lunch, daily 5-9:30pm for dinner. ❹

**Idyllwild Pizza Company,** 54391 Village Center Dr. (☎ 659-5900), next to the post office. Relaxed, family-style atmosphere. Pizzas $8-20. All-you-can-eat lunch M-F $6. Open spring-fall Su-Th 11:30am-8:30pm, F-Sa 11:30am-9pm; in winter open daily 11:30am-8pm. ❸

**Squirrel's Nest,** 25980 Rte. 243 (☎ 659-5274). This small joint offers fresh Californian and Mexican grill specialties. Take-out popular. Open Su-Tu and Th-Sa 11am-7pm. ❶

## 👁 🔲 SIGHTS & SEASONAL EVENTS

Visitors come to this largely undiscovered, uncommercialized town to explore the rough alpine terrain of the San Jacinto range. Hundreds of miles of established trails snake through the boulder-strewn slopes, and the glacier-polished granite of Tahquitz and Suicide Rock teem with wiry rock climbers. The comparatively high altitude keeps the temperature reasonable even when Palm Springs swelters in hellish torment a vertical mile below. Winters often dump glorious powder on the San Jacinto range, blessing cross-country skiers with ample cause to frolic here.

The **Palms-to-Pines Highway,** the section of Rte. 243 that connects Rte. 74 with I-10, rises from the low Colorado Desert into the sky. The highway offers spectacular views and a fascinating opportunity to drive-by study the ecological transition from the desert's tumbleweeds to a temperate, lush alpine forest. Though Idyllwild is only 26 mi. from I-10, plan to spend some time navigating the steep and curvy road, as well as stopping for pictures and views from the many scenic pull-offs.

The **Ernie Maxwell Scenic Trail** (2½ mi.), great for day hikes, is a scenic, downhill path through the forest. This is one of the few trails that does not require a wilderness permit. The trail will take you back to the town center. More serious backpackers can travel a section of the 2600 mi. **Pacific Crest Trail** (55 mi. lie in the San Jacinto District; for more info, see **From Crest to Crest: the Trail of the West,** p. 235). The trail picks up at Rte. 74 1 mi. east of Rte. 371 or at Black Mountain's scenic **Fuller Ridge Trail,** which is a strenuous hike (14 mi. round-trip) to the 10,834 ft. summit of Mt. San Jacinto. Alternately, reach the top of Mt. San Jacinto from **Devil's Slide Trail** (16 mi. round-trip); its lower portion provides dramatic views out to Tahquitz Peak and the desert below. On summer weekends, the limited number of permits for this area run out very quickly, so get to the ranger station early (see **Practical Information,** p. 478). Those who want great views with only a moderately strenuous hike should try the **Deer Spring Trail** out to Suicide Rock (3.3 mi. one-way), which continues out to Strawberry Junction Campground.

**Idyllwild ARTS,** 52500 Temecula Dr. (☎ 659-2171), at the end of Toll Gate Rd. off Rte. 243, gives free dance, drama, and music performances, as well as exhibitions and workshops. The **Jazz in the Pines** festival is every August. (☎ 659-4885. Tickets $40-45.) Sophisticates can imbibe culture and bubbly during the fall's **Art Walk and Wine Tasting,** a walking tour of Idyllwild's art galleries with wine glass in hand. Contact the **Idyllwild Gallery of Fine Art** for details. (☎659-1948 or 888-882-5264.) The **Incredible Edible Art Tour** in June is a chance to sample house specialities from over a dozen popular Idyllwild restaurants. (☎866-IDYLART/439-5278. Tickets $20.)

# NORTH AND WEST OF LA

Government legislation ensures a prime hiking and camping in the vast expanse of park land north of Los Angeles. Unspoiled coastline, chaparral, and rolling hills stretch from the Santa Monica Mountains to the end of the Central Coast.

## SANTA MONICA MOUNTAINS NATIONAL RECREATION AREA ☎805

Extending 46 mi. west from the Hollywood Bowl to Point Mugu in Ventura County, these 150,050 acres of oaks, dry brush, low mountains, and arroyos comprise the world's largest urban national park. Two indigenous groups, the Chumash and the Gabrielleno-Tongva, have made their home there. The highest peaks in the park border the ocean, creating spectacular ocean-side landscapes as you drive along PCH. The best place for info is the **National Park Service Visitors Center,** 401 W. Hillcrest Dr., Thousand Oaks, off US 101 at the Lynn Rd. Exit. (☎370-2301. Open daily 9am-5pm.) Call to request *Outdoors*, the recreation area's quarterly calendar of events and programs. Reserve state-run campsites through ReserveAmerica (☎800-444-7275). **Leo Carrillo ❶, Point Mugu ❶,** and **Malibu Creek ❶** all cost $12. **Topanga State Park** has backcountry camping on a first-come, first-served basis.

**HIKING TRAILS.** These hills are braided with more than 570 mi. of hiking trails of widely varying difficulty, so ask a ranger for advice before heading out. *Hike Los Angeles, Vol. 1 and Vol. 2* ($10 each, sold at the Visitors Center), feature the most popular walks in the park, with relevant info about the area's ecology and history. If **Malibu Creek** reminds you vaguely of the set of *M\*A\*S\*H*, that's because it was. Much of the set was dismantled after the television show's shooting ended in 1982, and more of it was destroyed in subsequent fires, but an easy 1½ mi. hike from the Crags Rd. trailhead leads to the remaining jeep and ambulance. The flat area above the bank was the helipad. Die-hard outdoor enthusiasts might want to taste the pain of the **Backbone Trail,** a 70 mi., three- to five-day journey from Point Mugu to Sunset Blvd. in Pacific Palisades. Consult a ranger before going.

**WILD, WILD WEST.** The National Park Service administers the **Paramount Ranch Site,** which was used as a location for several Paramount films between 1927 and 1953. Director Cecil B. DeMille and actors Gary Cooper and Mae West all worked here. The versatile ranch served as colonial Massachusetts in *The Maid of Salem* (1937), ancient China in *The Adventures of Marco Polo* (1938), and early San Francisco in *Wells Fargo* (1937). After purchasing the property in 1980, the US Park Service revitalized the old movie set, and it is now open to visitors. Rangers conduct regular tours. In summer, Paramount Ranch screens silent movies from the 1920s with live musical accompaniment; call for dates. *(To reach the ranch, take US 101 to Kanan Rd. Exit (in Agoura Hills). Continue for half a mile and turn left onto Cornell Way, veer right onto Cornell Rd., and continue 2½ mi. to the entrance on the right.)*

**SATWIWA.** On the western edge of the recreation area lies Rancho Sierra Vista/ Satwiwa. At one time, a nearby Chumash village had the name Satwiwa, which means "the bluffs." Park rangers or special Native American guests host "fire circles" as part of the fascinating twilight program at the **Native American Indian Culture Center.** The 8 mi. hike from this site down through Big Sycamore Canyon to the sea is one of the park's most rewarding. *(Culture Center ☎ 375-1930; www.satwiwa.org. Open Sa-Su 9am-5pm. Fire circles Sept. 1-May 31 Su 6:30-8pm; June 1-Aug. 31 Sa 6:30-8pm.)*

# VENTURA  ☎ 805

The Central Coast's southernmost city, Ventura (pop. 102,000), is blessed with great weather and easygoing charm. Visitors to "California's Rising Star" flock to the recently revitalized downtown, now home to numerous restaurants, shops, museums, galleries, and an abundance of thrift stores. A cultural district for performers of all genres is emerging, though most of the culture goes inside after dark. Ventura Harbor, a bustling center of activity with over 30 restaurants and shops, concerts, and festivals, lies 10min. from downtown by car. A **farmer's market** descends on the center on Saturdays. To best locate all that Ventura has to offer, pick up the historic walking tour map from the Visitors Bureau.

■ ◪ **ORIENTATION & PRACTICAL INFORMATION.** Ventura lies 30 mi. south of Santa Barbara and 70 mi. north of LA off US 101. **Main Street** runs east-west in the historic downtown area on the east side of town, intersecting with **California Street,** which runs down to the pier. **Ventura Harbor** lies south along the coast; from downtown, take Harbor Blvd. to **Spinnaker Drive.**

Pick up maps and helpful information at the **Ventura Visitors Bureau,** 89 S. California St. (☎ 648-2075 or 800-333-2989; www.ventura-usa.com. From 101 N, exit at California St. Open M-F 8:30am-5pm, Sa 9am-5pm, Su 10am-4pm.) Those interested in visiting the **Channel Islands National Park** (see p. 484) should seek out the **National Park Visitors Center,** 1901 Spinnaker Dr. (☎ 658-5730. Tidepool talk given Sa-Su at 11am, and a movie on the Channel Islands is shown every hr. Open daily 8:30am-5pm.) **Ventura Bike Depot,** 239 W. Main St., rents bikes. (☎ 652-1114. $21 per half-day, $30 per day. Open Sa-Su 9am-5pm, M-F by appointment only.) Other services include **police,** 1425 Dowell Dr. (☎ 339-4400); **County Hospital,** 3291 Loma Vista Rd. (☎ 800-746-8885); and the **post office,** 675 E. Santa Clara St. **Postal Code:** 93001.

◪ ◪ **ACCOMMODATIONS & CAMPING.** Prior to its rejuvenation, Ventura was treated exclusively as a stopover point along the coastal routes. As a result, the city has a number of budget motels, particularly along East Thompson Ave., though many are decades old and in desperate need of renovation. A good bet is the **Mission Bell Motel ❹,** 3237 E. Main St, near Pacific View Mall. (☎ 805-642-6831. Queen-size bed or double beds $55.) For something fancier, try the **Clocktower Inn ❺,** 181 E. Santa Clara St. Once a firehouse, the inn is located minutes away from the heart of the city, and offers an outdoor jacuzzi. (☎ 805-652-0141. From Main St., go south 1 block on California St. right on Santa Clara. Some rooms have balconies and fireplaces. Singles and doubles $73-160 in high season, $69-120 in low season.)

Beach camping is in no short supply around Ventura, but conditions lean toward the primitive. Reservations can be made through ReserveAmerica (☎ 800-444-7275) and should be made months in advance. **McGrath State Beach Campground ❷,** just south of town in Oxnard, is a popular spot with 174 campsites ($22).

**◨☐ FOOD & ENTERTAINMENT.** Cheap food in Ventura clusters along **Main Street,** in the heart of historic downtown. **Franky's ❷,** 456 E. Main St. between California and Oak St., is a Ventura institution, showcasing local art on the walls and offering healthy, delectable pita pockets ($7.50) and turkey burgers ($6.35) to wash down with jam jars of soda. (☎648-6282; www.frankys-place.com. Open daily 7am-3pm.) **Top Hat ❶,** 299 E. Main St., at Palm St., is a roadside burger shack serving chili cheeseburgers ($2.15), hot dogs ($1), and fries ($1) to a never-ending local crowd. (☎643-9696. Open Tu-Sa 10am-6pm.) **Jonathan's at Peirano's ❹,** 204 E. Main St., is a popular Mediterranean spot. Its beautiful patio, adjacent to a well-manicured park and large fountain, make for a pleasant dining experience. (☎648-4853; www.jonathansatpeiranos.com. Lunch entrees $9-15. Dinner entrees $12-25. Open Su 5:30-9pm, Tu-Th 11:30am-2:30pm and 5:30-9:30pm, F-Sa 11:30am-2:30pm and 5:30-10pm.) If the desire for pasta strikes, try **Capriccio Restaurant ❷,** 298 Main St., at the corner of Main and Palm St. This quiet, warm Italian restaurant is popular among both the lunch and dinner crowd. Some patio seating is available. (☎643-7115. Lunch entrees $7-10. Dinner entrees $8-15. Open M-Th 11:30am-8:45pm, F-Sa 11:30am-10pm, Su noon-8:45pm.) One of the few late-night establishments, **Nicholby's Night Club ❷,** 404 E. Main St., offers drinking and dancing on Th, F, and Sa nights. Come before 10pm and get in free; buy one drink and get the 2nd for 25¢. (☎653-2320. After 10pm, cover $6-10. Open Th-Sa 8:30pm-1:30am.) In Ventura Harbor, head to **Hornblowers Restaurant and Comedy Club ❸,** 1559 Spinnaker Dr., which offers superb seafood ($12-15) and terrific comedy on Friday and Saturday nights. (☎805-658-2202. 21+ Cover $12. Restaurant open Su-Th 11am-9pm, F-Sa 11am-10pm. Shows F 8pm, Sa 8pm and 10pm.) **The Greek at the Harbor ❹,** 1583 Spinnaker Dr., features belly dancing (☎805-650-5350; www.greekventuraharbor.com. Greek specialties $15-20. Shows Su and Tu-Th 7:30pm, F-Sa 7:15pm and 9pm).

**◨☐ SIGHTS & BEACHES.** Billed as California's "Gold Coast," the clean beaches near Ventura roar with fantastic surf. **Emma Wood State Beach,** on Main St. (take State Beaches exit off US 101), and **Oxnard State Beach Park,** about 5 mi. south of Ventura, are quiet and peaceful except on weekends. On the other hand, **San Buenaventura State Park,** at the end of San Pedro St., entertains families and casual beach-goers with its volleyball courts and nearby restaurants. **Surfer's Point,** at the end of Figueroa St., has the best waves around, but novices should start at **McGrath State Beach,** about 1 mi. south of Ventura down Harbor Blvd. Be forewarned that the surfers tend to be territorial. Pick up insider surfing tips and Patagonia outlet gear at **Real Cheap Sports,** 36 W. Santa Clara St. (☎650-1213. From Main St., go 1 block south on Ventura Ave. and turn right onto Santa Clara St. Open M-Sa 10am-6pm, Su 10am-5pm. For info on surf sessions, call ☎648-2662 or check out www.surfclass.com.)

Inland from Ventura Harbor and next to Olivas Park Golf Course, on Olivas Park Dr., is the **Olivas Adobe.** The restored 1847 home sits on almost 5000 acres of land that the Mexican army gave to Raymundo Olivas for services rendered. The house is decorated in period furnishings and is a tribute to the early rancho period of Ventura's history. Olivias was not only one of the richest ranchers in California, but also an early host to the budget traveler. Next to the visitors' beds, Raymundo placed bowls of coins from which guests could draw some pocket change. (☎644-4346. From US 101, take the Telephone Ave. Exit south to Olivas Park Ave. and turn right. Look for signs. Open Sa-Su noon-4pm. Tours during open hours. Free.)

**Mission San Buenaventura,** 211 E. Main St., still functions as a parish church, although it also houses a tiny museum of treasures from Father Junípero Serra's order. (☎ 643-4318. Open M-F 10am-5pm, Sa 9am-5pm, Su 10am-4pm. $1 donation requested.) Across the street is the **Museum of History and Art,** 100 E. Main St., which has one permanent and two rotating exhibits. Among the stellar works are over 200 George Stuart Historical Figures, together an internationally acclaimed collection of small-scale sculptures of people from world history that George Stuart, a historian, created to accompany his lectures. He occasionally gives presentations at the museum. (☎ 653-0323; www.vcmha.org. Open Su and Tu-Sa 10am-5pm. $4, seniors and AAA members $3, ages 5-17 $1, under 5 free.)

# CHANNEL ISLANDS NATIONAL PARK                                    ☎ 805

Ventura and Santa Barbara are the only two points of departure to the wind-swept, desolate Channel Islands, which are home to ancient Chumash sites, historic ranches, underwater kelp forests, seals, and **wildflowers.** The **Channel Islands National Park Visitors Center,** 1901 Spinnaker Dr., has info, in addition to an observation tower that looks out on the islands, an indoor tidepool, a native plant garden, and other exhibits. (☎ 658-5730. Open May-Sept. M-F 8am-5pm, Sa-Su 8am-5:30pm; Oct.-Apr. M-F 8:30am-4:30pm, Sa-Su 8am-5pm.)

The park consists of five islands. **Anacapa** (time to the island 1-1½hr.) is composed of three islets and is home to the largest brown pelican rookery on the Pacific Coast. The largest island, **Santa Cruz** (1-1½hr.), is said to be a miniature of what Southern California looked like more than 100 years ago. It is renowned for pristine beaches, lonely canyons, and one of the world's largest sea caves, Painted Cave. The Chumash called **Santa Rosa** (3-3½hr.) *Wima,* or "driftwood," because currents washed ashore logs from which they built canoes. It has deep canyons, a coastal lagoon, and sand dunes that house flightless geese, giant mice, and island fox. **San Miguel** (4-5hr.) is the western-most island with severe weather that makes landings difficult. If you are able to land through the surf, however, you will be greeted by no less than 30,000 seals and sea lions. Though tiny **Santa Barbara** is only one sq. mi. and farthest away from the mainland, it boasts magnificent views of steep volcanic rock cliffs rising above rocky shores. It is also home to a rare plant called live-for-ever, which is only found on this island, and the giant Northern elephant seal (3hr.). Because of the island geography, it is usually faster to sail out of Santa Barbara when visiting Santa Cruz, Santa Rosa, or San Miguel Islands. Ventura is preferable for Anacapa or Santa Barbara.

Unless you happen to have brought your own boat with you, you'll have to ride with one of the park's "official concessionaires" to the islands. The concessionaires offer various diversions on each island, such as camping, hiking, kayaking, and tours. **Island Packers,** 1691 Spinnaker Dr. in Ventura Harbor, has a virtual monopoly on island transport from Ventura. (Recorded info ☎ 642-7688. Reserve well in advance at ☎ 642-1393. Daytrips and overnight camping excursions depart around 8am. Anacapa daytrip $37, overnight $48; Santa Cruz $42-48/$54-60; Santa Rosa $62/$80; Santa Barbara $49/$75; San Miguel over-night only, $90. Island Cruise with no landing $24.) **Truth Aquatics** also runs regular boats to the islands out of Santa Barbara. (☎ 805-962-1127 or 805-963-3564; www.imall.com/stores/taqua.)

All recreational gear must be rented in advance. Full-day guided kayaking tours, a safe and enjoyable way to see wildlife and island formations, are run by **Channel Islands Kayak Center,** 3600 S. Harbor Blvd., in Oxnard. (☎ 805-984-5995; www.cikayak.com. Transportation to either Santa Cruz or Anacapa, kay-aking gear, a kayaking lesson, and a guided tour through the sea caves, reefs, and beaches included. Tours $170.) For snorkel and dive gear, try **Pacific Scuba Center,** 480 S. Victoria Ave., in Oxnard. (☎805-984-2566; www.pacific-scuba.com. Scuba package $40 first day, $20 each additional day. Snorkel package with mask, snorkel, fins, boots, wetsuits, and gloves $40/$15.) **Camping ❶** at the islands requires your own gear, food, and water. (Reservations ☎800-365-2267; www.reservations.nps.gov. Sites $10.)

The best part of a Channel Islands trip can be the **boat ride,** on which you may spot flying fish, sea lions, whales, and pods of common dolphins playing in the boat wake. Those averse to long hours on a swaying, rolling boat can consider flying like the birds to Santa Rosa Island. Contact **Channel Islands Aviation,** 305 Durley Ave. in Camarillo. (☎805-987-1301; www.flycia.com. $106 daytrip, $162 camping.)

# SAN DIEGO

San Diegans are fond of referring to their near-perfect seaside hometown as "America's Finest City." The claim is difficult to dispute—San Diego (pop. 1,130,000) has all the virtues of other California cities without the frequently cited drawbacks. No smog fills this city's air, and no sewage spoils its silver shores. Its zoo is the nation's best, and the temperate year-round climate is unbeatable.

The city was founded when the seafaring Spanish extended an onshore leave in 1769 and began the first permanent European settlement on the western coast of the United States. San Diego remained a nondescript town until it became the headquarters of the US Pacific Fleet following the 1941 attack on Pearl Harbor. Over a dozen naval and marine installations exist in and around the city, and the military presence shapes both the economy and the somewhat conservative local culture. Indeed, much of the skyline is formed by the super-structures of colossal aircraft carriers. Today, high-tech industries have fueled an impressive renaissance, as well as an explosion in ethnic and economic diversity. It is the country's sixth- and California's second-largest city, and one of the fastest-growing.

## HIGHLIGHTS OF SAN DIEGO

**ZOOS.** The **San Diego Zoo** (p. 499) and **San Diego Wild Animal Park** (p. 513) are some of the best places in the world to view animals in captivity.

**BEACHES. Coronado Island** (p. 502), **Mission** and **Pacific Beaches** (p. 503), and **La Jolla Shores** (p. 505) are fabulous oceanside spots.

**CULTURE.** History buffs go to **Old Town** for museums, historic buildings (some reputedly haunted), and the **Mission Basilica San Diego de Alcalá** (p. 505), while museum lovers head to **Balboa Park** and the **El Prado Museums** (p. 500).

**AREA CODE** For most of San Diego, including downtown, Coronado, and Ocean Beach: **619.** Northern San Diego area codes (including Del Mar, La Jolla, parts of North County, and Pacific Beach): **858** and **760. Unless otherwise specified, the area code for the San Diego area is 619.**

## ▣ INTERCITY TRANSPORTATION

San Diego rests in the extreme southwest corner of California, 127 mi. south of Los Angeles and 15 mi. north of the Mexican border. Three freeways link the city to its regional neighbors: **I-5** runs south from LA through the North County cities of Oceanside and Carlsbad and skirts the eastern edge of downtown on its way to the Mexican border; **I-15** runs northeast through the desert to Las Vegas; and **I-8** runs east-west along downtown's northern boundary, connecting the desert with Ocean Beach. The downtown core is laid out in a grid, making it easy to navigate. In **North County,** the **Pacific Coast Highway** runs parallel to I-5, and is known as Old Hwy. 101, 1st St., or Carlsbad Blvd., depending on location.

**Airport: San Diego International (Lindbergh Field),** at the northwest edge of downtown. Call the Travelers Aid Society (☎231-7361) for info. Society open daily 8am-11pm. Bus #2 goes downtown ($2), as do cabs ($8).

**Trains: Amtrak,** 1050 Kettner Blvd. (☎800-872-7245), just north of Broadway in the historic Santa Fe Depot. To **LA** (11 trains daily; 6am-8:30pm; $25, in summer $28). Station has info on bus, trolley, car, and boat transportation. Ticket office open daily 5:15am-10pm.

**Buses: Greyhound,** 120 W. Broadway (☎239-8082 or 800-231-2222), at 1st St. To **LA** (30 per day; 5am-11:35pm; $15, round-trip $25) and **Tijuana** (16 per day; 5am-11:35pm; $5, round-trip $8). Ticket office open 24hr.

# ORIENTATION

The epicenter of San Diego tourism is historic **Balboa Park.** It is home to the world-famous **San Diego Zoo** and a cluster of diverse museums and cultural attractions. Northwest of the park is the stylish **Hillcrest** neighborhood, the city's gay enclave with great shopping and restaurants. The reinvigorated **Gaslamp Quarter** sits in the southern section of downtown between 4th and 6th St. and contains many of San Diego's signature theaters and nightclubs, as well as fine restaurants. Just north of downtown in the southeast corner of the I-5 and I-8 junction lies a little slice of old Mexico known as **Old Town.** Discriminating travelers may find Old Town's touristy kitsch a bit contrived, but the fantastic Mexican food and lively scene make this place worth a visit. Downtown San Diego is surprisingly safe, but nevertheless, always exercise reasonable caution and avoid the somewhat run-down, eastern section of downtown that abuts I-5, as well as the district south of the Gaslamp.

San Diego Bay opens up south of downtown and is bounded by glorious **Coronado Island.** While often exasperatingly touristy and too pricey for most budget travelers, Coronado offers sunny outdoor fun like surfing and cycling. Northwest of town sits the collection of shiny beaches and man-made inlets known as **Mission Bay.** The beaches west of the bay, and those north and south, are some of the finest urban beaches in America. Don't forget to get splashed by flopping, spurting water creatures at the original **Sea World.** A jaunt up the coast leads to the swanky tourist haven of **La Jolla** (p. 505), where the profusion of upscale shops and Euro-designer brand names might distract tourists from the real reasons to visit: the excellent snorkeling at **La Jolla Cove,** the sparkling beaches at **La Jolla Shores,** and the relaxing grounds of the surrounding parkland. Up the coast beyond La Jolla are the laid-back and sun-soaked beach communities of the **North County** (p. 508).

# LOCAL TRANSPORTATION

**PUBLIC TRANSPORTATION.** The city of San Diego provides fairly extensive public transportation through the **San Diego Metropolitan Transit System (MTS).** MTS's automated 24hr. information line, **Info Express** (☎685-4900), has info on San Diego's buses, trains, and trolleys. To talk to live people, visit the **Transit Store** at 1st Ave. and Broadway, which has timetables, a free pamphlet with tips for riding, and bus, trolley, and ferry tickets. Be sure to pick up a one- to four-day **Day Trippers Pass** if you plan to use public transit of any kind more than once. (Open M-F 8:30am-5:30pm, Sa-Su noon-4pm. One-day pass $5, two-day $9, three-day $12, four-day $15.) The **Regional Transit Information Center** is also a good source, although it can be difficult to get through. (☎233-3004. Open M-F 5:30am-8:30pm, Sa-Su 8am-5pm.) **Bus** fares range from $1 to $3.50 depending on the route. Bus transfers are good for 1½hr. after they are issued. They require exact fare, but accept dollar bills. All buses are wheelchair-accessible. If getting to a

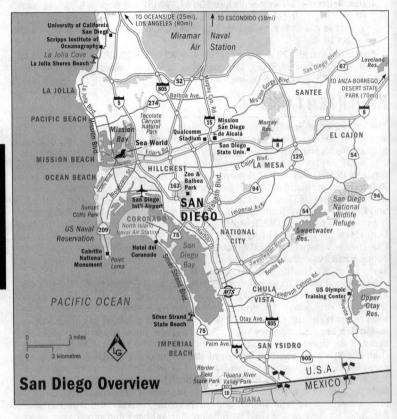

San Diego Overview

bus stop is a problem, call the door-to-bus-stop service **DART**. (☎887-841-DART/ 3278. $2.25. Operates M-F 5:30am-8pm.) The **COASTER** sends trains daily between San Diego (downtown and Old Town) and the coastal communities of Solana Beach, Encinitas, Carlsbad, and Oceanside. (☎800-COASTER/262-7837; www.sdcommute.com. $3.50-4.75 one-way; 10-trip passes $29-43.)

The bright-red **San Diego Trolley** consists of two lines leaving from downtown for El Cajon, San Ysidro, and points in between. The El Cajon line leaves from 12th Ave. and Imperial St.; the San Ysidro line leaves from the Old Town Transit Center (at Taylor St. and San Diego Ave.) and continues to the Mexican border. Although there are no turnstiles, the inspector does indeed check for tickets, and the fine for sneaking on is definitely not within reach of the budget traveler. (☎231-8549; www.sdcommute.com. Trolleys run daily 5am-1am. $1.25-3.)

**BY CAR.** Southern California is the land of the automobile; renting a car will make your life easier and your trip more enjoyable. Most places will not rent to drivers under 21, but a letter from your insurer stating that you are covered for rental car crashes may go a long way toward getting you a set of wheels.

**Bargain Auto,** 3860 Rosecrans St. (☎299-0009). Used cars available to renters 18+. Cars from $19 per day with 150 mi. free, $105 per week with 500 mi. free. Ages 18-25 pay $6 per day surcharge, $35 per week. $39 per day for insurance if driving to Mexico. Credit card required. Open M-F 8am-6pm, Sa-Su 8am-4pm.

**Dollar,** 2499 Pacific Hwy. (☎234-3388; www.dollar.com), at the airport. Cars $28-54 per day with unlimited mileage. Must be 21+ with credit card; ages 21-25 pay $20 per day surcharge. Travel to Mexico $25 per day surcharge. Open daily 5:30am-midnight.

**BICYCLES.** San Diego has an extensive system of **bike routes.** Some are separate from the road, while some are specially marked outer lanes. The flat, paved route along Mission and Pacific Beaches toward La Jolla affords ocean views and soothing sea breezes. Bikers beware: pedestrian traffic along the beaches rivals that of the automobiles on the boulevards. Buses with bike racks make it possible to cart bikes almost anywhere in the city (call ☎233-3004 for info). For more bike info, contact the **City Bicycle Coordinator** (☎533-3110) or **CalTrans** (☎231-2453).

**RENTALS: BIKES, BOARDS & BLADES.** Gear is available throughout San Diego and the surrounding communities. Most rental stores are cheap enough for the budget traveler and bolster San Diego's reputation as an outdoor sports haven.

**Action Sports,** 4000 Coronado Bay Rd. (☎424-4466), at the Marina Dock of the Loews Coronado Bay Resort on **Coronado Island.** Beach cruisers and mountain bikes $10 per hr., $30 per 4hr. Open M-F 9am-6pm, Sa-Su 8:30am-6:30pm.

**Bike Tours,** 509 5th Ave. (☎238-2444), in the **Gaslamp.** Well maintained mountain bikes $18 per day, $50 per week. Lock, protective gear, maps, and roadside assistance are included. Open daily 8am-7pm.

**Little Sam's,** 1343 Orange Ave. (☎435-4058), near the Hotel Del Coronado on **Coronado Island.** Beach cruisers $6 per hr., half-day $14, full-day $20. Roller blades $5/$14/$20. Surfboards $15 per hr., full-day $25. All gear comes with safety equipment, locks, maps, and advice. Open daily 8am-6pm.

**Bikes and Beyond** (☎435-7180), at the ferry landing on 1st St., on **Coronado Island.** Mountain bikes $6 per hr., $18 per 4hr.; in-line skates $5/$15; 4-peddler surrey $15 per 30min., $25 per hr. Locks, protective gear, and maps included. Open 8:30am-dusk.

**South Coast Longboards,** 5037 Newport Ave. (☎223-8808) in **Ocean Beach.** Soft surfboards $5 per hr., full-day $25; glass boards for the more experienced $10/$50. Credit card or cash deposit of $250 for soft boards, $350 for glass boards. Open June-Aug. M-Sa 9am-7:30pm, Su 10am-6:30pm; Sept.-May daily 9am-6pm.

**Cheap Rentals,** 3221 Mission Blvd. (☎858-486-5533 or 800-941-7761. www.cheap-rentals.com) in **Mission Beach.** Beach cruisers $6 per hr., full-day $15; skateboards $6/$15. Open daily 8am-6pm.

**Star Surfing Co.,** 4652 Mission Blvd. (☎858-273-7827) in **Pacific Beach.** Surfboards $5 per hr., full-day $2; bodyboards $3/$12. Driver's license or credit card for deposit. Open daily 10am-6pm.

**Dana Landing Boat Rentals,** 1710 W. Mission Bay Dr. (☎226-2929) on **Mission Bay.** Fourteen foot Capri sailboats $20 per hr. Other water-sports equipment, such as jetskis and power boats, are also available. Open daily 6am-10pm.

**Windsport,** 844 W. Mission Bay Dr. (☎858-488-4642; www.windsport.net) in **Mission Beach.** Kayaks $15 per hr., full-day $75. 2½hr. kayak tours including equipment rental $60 per person. Open M-F 10am-6pm, Sa-Su 9am-6pm.

**WALKING.** Downtown, Balboa Park, and Old Town can easily be covered on foot, but beaches are less accessible because of the wide distances between them. **Walkabout International,** 4639 30th St. Suite C, sponsors about 100 free walks each month, from downtown architectural strolls to 20 mi. La Jolla treks. (☎231-7463. Open M-F 10am-2pm.) Because jaywalking is actively prosecuted in San Diego, pedestrians almost always heed the walk signals.

# 🚆 PRACTICAL INFORMATION

## TOURIST & FINANCIAL SERVICES

**Visitor Information:**

**International Visitor Information Center,** 11 Horton Plaza (☎236-1212), downtown at 1st Ave. and F St. Helpful, multilingual staff dispenses publications, brochures, and discount coupons. 3hr. parking validation for lots with entrances on G St. and 4th Ave. Open daily 9am-5pm.

**San Diego Convention and Visitors Bureau,** 401 B St., #1400, Dept. 700, San Diego 92101 (☎236-1212; www.sandiego.org), also provides info.

**Old Town and State Park Info,** 4002 Wallace Ave. (☎220-5422), in Old Town Sq. Take the Taylor St. Exit off I-8 or bus #5. Free walking tours daily 11am and 2pm. Open daily 10am-5pm.

**Just Call** (☎615-6111) is an information line operated by the city of San Diego.

**Budget Travel: San Diego Council of American Youth Hostels,** 521 Market St., San Diego, CA 92101 (☎525-1531; www.sandiegohostels.org), in the Metropolitan Hostel at 5th St. Offers budget guides and info. Open daily 6:30am-midnight.

**American Express,** 7610 Hazard Center Dr. (☎297-8101). Open M-F 9:30am-6pm, Sa 10am-3pm. Call for other locations throughout the area.

## LOCAL SERVICES

**Library: San Diego Public Library,** 820 E St. (☎236-5800), offers **Internet access,** foreign newspapers, borrowing privileges for visitors, a California information room, and an ongoing concert, film, and lecture series. Centrally located with an ultra-friendly staff. Open M-Th 10am-9pm, F-Sa 9:30am-5:30pm, Su 1-5pm.

**Senior Citizens Services,** 202 C St. (☎236-6905), in the City Hall Bldg. Provides senior ID cards (W 9am-12:30pm) and plans daytrips. Open M-F 8am-5pm.

**The Access Center,** 1295 University Ave., #10 (☎293-3500, TDD 293-7757), in Hillcrest. Attendant referral, wheelchair repair and sales, emergency housing, motel/hotel accessibility referral. Open M-F 9am-5pm. **Accessible San Diego,** 1010 2nd Ave. (☎858-279-0704), also has info. Open M-F 9am-5pm.

**The Center for Community Solutions,** 4508 Mission Bay Dr. (☎233-8984, 24hr. hotline 272-1767), at Bunker Hill St. in Pacific Beach. Offers rape and domestic violence counseling, as well as legal services. Open M-F 8am-4:30pm.

**Bi-Gay-Lesbian Organizations: Lesbian and Gay Men's Center,** 3909 Centre St. (☎692-2077), provides counseling and info. Open M-Sa 9am-10pm. The **Gay Youth Alliance** (☎233-9309) is a support and social group for people under 24. For a listing of queer events and establishments, check *Update* (☎299-0500), available at virtually all queer businesses, bookstores, and bars. The *Gay and Lesbian Times,* published every Th, provides event, bar, and club listings.

**Ticket Agencies: Ticketmaster** (☎220-TIXS/8497, concert info 581-1000). Beware of the high service charge. Get half-price tickets from **Times Arts Tix** (☎497-5000), at the corner of 3rd and Broadway. Open Su 10am-5pm, Tu-Th 11am-6pm, F-Sa 10am-6pm.

**Laundromat: Metro Wash and Dry,** 724 4th Ave. (☎544-1284), between F and G St. Wash $2, dry 25¢ per 8min. Open daily 6am-7:30pm.

Weather Conditions: Weather Report (☎221-8824). Updated daily—as if the weather ever changes. The average daily temperature is 70°F, with nighttime lows around 60°F.

# EMERGENCY & COMMUNICATIONS

Police: ☎531-2000.

Auto Repairs: AAA Emergency Road Service (☎800-400-4222).

Hospitals: Kaiser Foundation, 4647 Zion Ave. (☎528-5000); Columbia Mission Bay, 3030 Bunker Hill St. (☎858-274-7721), in Mission Bay.

24hr. Crisis Lines: Lesbian and Gay Men's Center Crisis Line (☎800-479-3339). Women's Center Rape Hotline (☎233-3088).

24hr. Pharmacy: Rite Aid, 535 Robinson Ave. (☎291-3705), in Hillcrest.

Radio: News/talk on KSDO (1130 AM), National Public Radio on KPBS (89.5 FM), popular top-40 on 103.5 FM.

Post Offices: 2535 Midway Dr. (☎800-275-8777); take bus #6, 9, or 35; open M 7am-5pm, Tu-F 8am-5pm, Sa 8am-4pm. 2150 Comstock St; open M-F 8am-5pm, Sa 8am-4:30pm. Postal Codes: 92186 (Midway Dr.), 92111 (Comstock St.).

# ⛁ ACCOMMODATIONS

Rates predictably rise on weekends and during the summer season. Reservations are recommended for all of the places listed below, particularly if you intend to stay during the busy summer. Beyond the hostel and residential hotel scene, San Diego is littered with generic chain motels, which are generally safe and clean, though a little more expensive. There is a popular cluster known as Hotel Circle (2-3 mi. east of I-5 along I-8), where summer prices begin at $60 for a single and $70 for a double during the week ($70 and $80, respectively, on weekends). If you choose to stay in a motel, be sure to pick up one of the traveler discount coupon books at a visitors center. Several beaches in North County, as well as one on Coronado, are state parks and allow camping.

## DOWNTOWN

USA Hostels San Diego, 726 5th Ave. (☎232-3100 or 800-GET-TO-CA/438-8622; www.usahostels.com), between F and G St. in the Gaslamp. This colorful Euro-style fun house fits in well with the rocking atmosphere of the Gaslamp district. Hosts frequent parties and organizes Tijuana tours ($10.50) and Gaslamp pub crawls ($4). Pancake breakfast included. Dinner available for $4. Free linen and lockers. Coin-op laundry with free detergent. Rooms are clean, and common areas are festive. International passport or student ID required. Dorms $19-21. The three private rooms are often booked, and go for $46-50 a night. $1 off for ISIC VIP and BUNAC cardholders. $3 off with brochures available at other USA hostels. ❷

San Diego Downtown Hostel (HI-AYH), 521 Market St. (☎525-1531 or 800-909-4776, ext. 156; www.sandiegohostels.org), at 5th Ave., in the heart of the Gaslamp, 5 blocks from the Convention Center. In contrast to USA Hostels and the vibrant nightlife outside, this hostel is clean and quiet almost to the point of being sterile. Caters well to the traveler seeking calm. Airy common room, kitchen, and communal bathrooms. Smoking and drinking are not allowed. Free pancake breakfast. No curfew. Lockers (bring a lock) and laundry. Reception 7am-midnight. IBN reservations available. Groups welcome. 4- to 6-bed dorms $18-25, non-members add $3; doubles $45-60. ❷

**J Street Inn,** 222 J St. (☎696-6922), near the convention center and ritzy waterfront. All 221 fabulous studio rooms have cable TV, microwave, fridge, and bath. Gym and reading room. Enclosed parking $8 per day, $26 per week. Singles and doubles $80 per night or, with a 3-week min. stay, $199 per week. ❹

**La Pension Hotel,** 606 W. Date St. (☎236-8000 or 800-232-4683), in the heart of Little Italy. Euro-style hotel with small, comfortable rooms and modern furnishings. Covered parking available. Singles and doubles $75. Look for specials at down times. ❹

**Horton Grand Hotel,** 311 Island Ave. (☎544-1886 or 800-542-1886) in the Gaslamp. Lavish period furnishings and gas fireplaces complete the Victorian time warp in this classy historic hotel. All of the standard amenities, plus many extras. Rooms $169-289; may drop as low as $129 with advance booking or during off-peak times. ❺

## HILLCREST & OLD TOWN

**Old Town Inn,** 4444 Pacific Hwy. (☎260-8024 or 800-643-3025; www.old-towninn.com), near I-5 and I-8. Clean rooms with standard amenities are a 10min. walk from Old Town. Some rooms have kitchenettes. Pool. Large continental breakfast included. Rooms can go as low as $60, but prices vary depending on the season. ❹

**Heritage Park Bed and Breakfast Inn,** 2470 Heritage Park Row (☎299-6832; www.heritageparkinn.com). This old Victorian mansion in Heritage Park now functions as a cozy B&B tucked away in a quiet enclave near Old Town. Each of the 12 guest rooms is unique, and includes afternoon teas and nightly showings of vintage films. Rooms $135-250. Reserve at least 1 month in advance. ❺

**The Hillcrest Inn,** 3754 5th Ave. (☎293-7078 or 800-258-2280; www.bryx.com/hillcrestinn). 44 tastefully decorated rooms with a fridge and microwave. Sunning patio and jacuzzi. Very popular with gay visitors (though not exclusively catering to a gay clientele). Singles only; $59-79 in all seasons. 2-night min. stay on weekends. ❹

**Studio 819,** 819 University Ave. (☎542-0819; www.studio819.com). Tidy and compact studios with a range of amenities, including kitchenettes usually rented on a weekly or monthly basis, but also available for nightly rates. Underground parking ($5 per day) and laundry. Rooms for 1-2 people $55-63, slightly higher on weekends and holidays; weekly $345-400; monthly $690-770. ❹

## COASTAL SAN DIEGO

▨ **International House at the 2nd Floor,** 4502 Cass St. (☎858-274-4325) in Pacific Beach, and 3204 Mission Bay Dr. (☎858-539-0043) in Mission Beach. To reach PB via bus from downtown, take the #34 from Broadway to Mission and Garnet. Turn right onto Garnet and walk two blocks to Cass St. To reach MB via bus from downtown, take the #34 from Broadway to Mission Blvd. and Mission Bay Dr. These two new sister hostels offer excellent service, clean and airy rooms, comfortable beds, Internet access, breakfast, free surf and boogie board use, and great beach locations. 28-day max. stay. Out-of-state ID or international passport required. Dorm rooms $20, students with ID $18; $110 per week. ❷

▨ **Ocean Beach International (OBI),** 4961 Newport Ave. (☎223-7873 or 800-339-7263; www.oceanbeach.com/hostel), in **Ocean Beach.** Look for international flags. Free transport to and from airport, train, and bus terminals. If driving, take I-8 toward the beach until it becomes Sunset Cliffs Blvd. Take a right on Newport Ave. The OBI features clean rooms, cable TV, and a kitchen near the beach. Beach gear rental, laundry. Free breakfast, BBQ Tu and F night, and pasta Tu in winter. 29-day max. stay. **Proof of international travel in the last or next 6 months required** (stamped passports or plane tickets). 4- to 6-bed dorms $18-20; doubles (some with bath) $40-43. ❷

**HI-Point Loma,** 3790 Udall St. (☎223-4778), 1½ mi. inland (east) from **Ocean Beach.** Take bus #35 from downtown to the 1st stop on Voltaire St. If driving, head west on Sea World Dr. from I-5 and bear right on Sunset Cliff Blvd. Take a left on Voltaire St., then a right on Worden St. Udall St. is 1 block away. Large kitchen, patio with ping pong, and common room with TV. Pancake breakfast and laundry. Reception 8am-10pm. 14-night max. stay. Reserve at least 2 days in advance. Dorms $16; private rooms $38; triples $54. Nonmembers pay $3 more. ❷

**Shell Beach,** 981 Coast Blvd. (☎858-459-4306 or 888-525-6552; www.lajolla-cove.com), in **La Jolla.** Considering its beachfront location, this is one of the most reasonably priced accommodations in the area. This otherwise expensive oceanfront property has a few tiny studios that make staying here possible even for budget travelers. Comfy, older rooms are mere steps from the beach. Non-oceanfront studio with queen-sized bed $65; lower Sept.-May. ❹

**Inn at Mission Bay,** 4545 Mission Bay Dr. (☎858-483-4222; www.innatmission-bay.com), near **Mission Bay.** Standard rooms and amenities including kitchenettes. Singles and doubles $89-99 in summer; in winter from $54. 10% AAA discount. ❺

**Tradewinds Motel,** 4305 Mission Bay Dr. (☎858-273-4616) near **Mission Bay.** This pink and avocado green motel not only looks like a flash from times past, but its prices have come straight from the 50s. Clean, older rooms $40; on weekends $50. ❸

**Silver Strand State Beach Campground** (☎435-5184), along the 7 mi. strip connecting Coronado Island to the mainland. An endless ribbon of sand and rhythmic waves. Excellent surfing. The small and undeveloped camping areas set aside for RVs are first-come, first-camp. Sites $13. ❶

# ▣ FOOD

With its large Hispanic population and proximity to Mexico, San Diego is renowned for its exemplary Mexican cuisine. **Old Town** serves some of the best authentic Mexican food in the state. Beyond this, San Diego also offers a spectacular assortment of ethnic and more traditional eateries, highly concentrated in both the **Hillcrest** neighborhood and the historic **Gaslamp Quarter.**

## DOWNTOWN

True budget food in the downtown area can be harder to come by than in nearby beach communities. However, for a few extra dollars, excellent eating is abundant, particularly in the **Gaslamp Quarter.** For super-quick bargain basement chow, try the food court at the **Horton Plaza,** a large shopping center between 1st and 4th Ave., and E and G St. It's cheap, but it still aspires to be more than fast food. Buy your own groceries downtown at **Ralph's,** 101 G St. (☎595-1581. Open 24hr.)

**Kansas City Barbecue,** 610 W. Market St. (☎231-9680), near **Seaport Village.** The location of *Top Gun*'s Great Balls of Fire bar scene. While the wooden piano remains, all that's left of Goose, Maverick, and sexy Charlie is an abundance of autographed posters and neon signs. Vegetarians will find themselves in the Danger Zone in this BBQ-slathered meatfest. Entrees $9-16. Open daily 11am-2am; kitchen closes at 1am. ❷

**The Fish Market,** 750 N. Harbor Dr. (☎232-3474), within walking distance of **Seaport Village.** This local landmark serves up an amazing array of the freshest seafood; the menu is updated twice a day based on the catch. Ask for a patio table and enjoy your meal with an incomparable view of the bay. Entrees $12-28. Open daily 11am-10pm. The **Top of the Market** is the swankier version located directly upstairs. While the catch is the same, the added linens, view, ambience, and gourmet names will cost an extra $10 per plate. Open M-Sa 11am-10pm, Su 10am-10pm (brunch 10am-2pm). ❹

**Trattoria Fantastica,** 1735 India St. (☎234-1735; http://trattoriafantas.signonsand-iego.com). In the heart of **Little Italy,** this family-owned restaurant serves heaping portions of scrumptious Italian food. Outdoor seating available. Entrees from $10; try the popular calamari parmigiana ($14). Open daily 11:30am-3pm and 5-10pm. ❸

**Gaslamp Strip Club,** 340 5th Ave. (☎231-3140). Don't be fooled by the name, the 21+ age requirement, or the red lights and red leather; the only meat on display here are the fine 8-20 oz. steaks and kabobs ($10-20). This retro grill-your-own-steak lounge allows you to order a raw steak on a slab of wood, throw it on one of many grills, and cook and season it to your own taste. Open Su and Tu-Sa 5pm-late. ❸

## BALBOA PARK, HILLCREST & UNIVERSITY HEIGHTS

The best food near Balboa Park is in nearby **Hillcrest** and **University Heights.** These trendy, youth-oriented, gay-friendly neighborhoods are home to a diverse array of inexpensive restaurants. Health nuts will find many low-fat and vegetarian options. Shop for organic groceries in Hillcrest at **Whole Foods Market,** 711 University Ave. (☎294-2800. Open daily 8am-10pm.)

▨ **The Corvette Diner,** 3946 5th Ave. (☎542-1001), in Hillcrest. The ultimate flashback to the days of nickel milkshakes, this 50s-style diner has more chrome than Detroit and more neon than Las Vegas. Serves extraordinary greasy-spoon classics and a number of unique creations like the house favorite, the Rory Burger (peanut butter and bacon burger; $7). A live DJ spins oldies every night (6-9pm) while costumed waitresses give as much lip as service. Open Su-Th 11am-10pm, F-Sa 11am-midnight. ❷

**Extraordinary Desserts,** 2929 5th Ave. (☎294-7001; www.extraordinarydes-serts.com). Decadent mounds of chocolate, cake, fruits, and other delectables can be savored at this desserts-only restaurant. The Asian-influenced decor and rich chocolate may lull you into a state of bliss. Whole cakes also available for carry-out ($35-42). Open Su-Th 8:30am-11pm, F 8:30am-midnight, Sa 11am-midnight. ❸

**The Prado,** 1549 El Prado (☎557-9441; www.pradobalboa.com), in the heart of **Balboa Park.** Since this Latin-Italian fusion restaurant opened three years ago, it's had nothing but rave reviews. The patio seating is beautiful any time of the year, and the calamari appetizer is big enough to be a meal ($10). Dinner entrees from $19. Open M-Sa 11am-9:30pm, Su 11am-8pm. ❺

## OLD TOWN

Frequented by both locals and visitors, Old Town has the best Mexican food in San Diego, which is saying a lot. Don't be intimidated by the gigantic lines; Old Town's colorful and authentic restaurants have perfected the art of "move 'em in, move 'em out" without compromising quality. Many Old Town eats are in the **Bazaar del Mundo,** a cluster of restaurants and stores near Calhoun St. accessible only by foot.

▨ **Casa de Bandini,** 2754 Calhoun St. (☎297-8211). An Old Town institution, repeatedly voted best Mexican restaurant in San Diego. Set in a Spanish-style architectural landmark (built in 1829), Bandini dishes out superb food and boisterous Mariachi music. The colossal combo plates ($5-8) are fantastic, but it's the heavyweight margarita ($4-7) that's responsible for Bandini's legendary status and flowery decor. Indoor tables are far outnumbered by outdoor tables on a beautiful tiled patio with fountain. Open M-Th 11am-9:30pm, F-Sa 11am-10pm, Su 10am-9:30pm. ❷

**Casa de Pico** (☎296-3267), just off Calhoun St. in the Bazaar. Similar in menu, atmosphere, and house specialty (margaritas) to Casa de Bandini, this strictly outdoor eatery serves gigantic plates overflowing with gooey cheese enchiladas ($8). Soup-bowl-sized margaritas are terrific ($5-7). Open M-F 10am-9pm, Sa-Su 10am-10pm. ❷

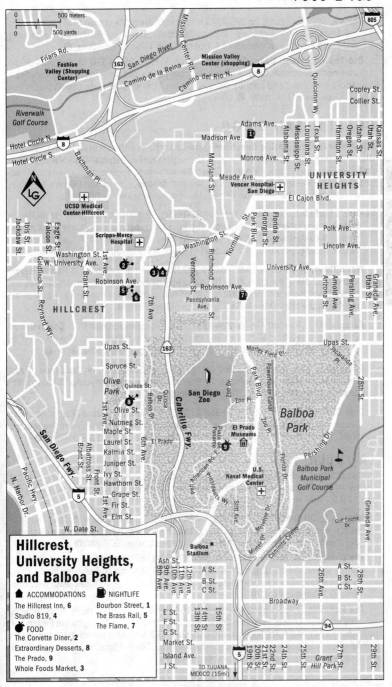

**Hillcrest, University Heights, and Balboa Park**

🏠 ACCOMMODATIONS
The Hillcrest Inn, **6**
Studio 819, **4**

🍎 FOOD
The Corvette Diner, **2**
Extraordinary Desserts, **8**
The Prado, **9**
Whole Foods Market, **3**

🍸 NIGHTLIFE
Bourbon Street, **1**
The Brass Rail, **5**
The Flame, **7**

**Berta's,** 3928 Twiggs St. (☎295-2343). You may have to buy a copy of ■ *Let's Go: Central America* to make your way through this menu. Dozens of Guatemalan, Honduran, and Costa Rican specialities $9-14. Open Su and Tu-Sa 11am-10pm. ❸

**Old Town Mexican Cafe,** 2489 San Diego Ave. (☎297-4330 or 888-234-9836; www.oldtownmexcafe.com). A slightly cheaper but no less tasty option. 115 varieties of tequila are served and tortillas are made in the front window. Huge combo plates from $7. Open 7am-11pm daily. ❷

## COASTAL SAN DIEGO

**Mission Beach** and **Pacific Beach** are crowded with youth-oriented bars and surfer dives. To bag your own meal, head to the supermarket **Ralph's,** 4315 Mission Blvd. (☎273-0778. Open 24hr.) Most of **Ocean Beach's** inexpensive restaurants and bars are along the westernmost stretch of **Newport Avenue,** one of San Diego's trendiest drags and where shots for the movie *Almost Famous* were filmed.

■ **Kono's Surf Club,** 704 Garnet Ave. (☎483-1669), across from the Crystal Pier in **Pacific Beach.** Identifiable by the line stretching for a block out the door, Kono's is a surfer's shrine. Breakfast served all day ($3-4). Try the huge Egg Burrito #3, which includes bacon, cheese, potatoes, and sauce ($4). Open M-F 7am-3pm, Sa-Su 7am-4pm. ❶

**World Curry,** 1433 Garnet Ave. (☎689-2222; www.worldcurry.com), in **Pacific Beach,** farther east along the main drag. The amazingly quick service delivers delicious curries from all over the world for $7. Mango, green tea, and Thai tea frappes ($3) provide zen relief from the heat. Open M-Sa 11am-10pm, Su 4-9pm. ❷

**Eatopia,** 5001 Newport Ave. (☎224-3237; www.eatopiaexpress.com), in **Ocean Beach.** Earthy vegan fast-food with refreshing smoothies and excellent wraps. The popular Cosmic California wrap is especially delicious ($4.75). Open daily 10am-8pm. ❶

**Rhinoceros Cafe and Grill,** 1166 Orange Ave. (☎435-2121), on **Coronado Island.** Fresh pasta, salads, and seafoods. Try their specialty: penne a la vodka ($9 lunch, $14 dinner). Open daily 11am-2:30pm and 5-9pm. ❸

**Cafe Crema,** 1001 Garnet Ave. (☎858-273-3558), in **Pacific Beach.** Euro-style coffeehouse with pastries and sandwiches ($5-6). **Internet** ($1 per 10min.) and live music at night (Th-Sa). Open Su 8am-1am, M-Th 7am-1am, F 7am-2am, Sa 8am-2am. ❶

## LA JOLLA

**Prospect Street,** the main drag in La Jolla, is crammed with upscale shops and galleries, but tucked among these are a number of excellent places to eat. **Girard Avenue** and its side streets also hold their own.

**Rimel's,** 1030 Torrey Pines Rd. (☎858-454-6045). Savory smells waft down the street from the spits right behind the counter of this tiny restaurant and rotisserie. Half-chicken $9, salads and sandwiches from $6. Open daily 11:30am-9:30pm. ❷

**The Living Room,** 1010 Prospect St. (☎858-489-1187). Home to mismatched sets of comfy chairs and amazingly large sandwiches ($6.50), this coffeehouse in the village is a local fave. The cauldron-sized hot chocolate ($4) is good for at least two. Open daily 6:30am-midnight. ❷

**The Pannikin,** 7467 Girard Ave. (☎858-454-5453). This artsy, funky eatery specializes in coffee concoctions like the famous and delicious white chocolate Frozen Iced Whitey ($4) and spicy Mexican hot chocolate ($2.50). Also serves great breakfasts, lunches, and homemade desserts. Open M-Th 5:30am-10pm, F 5:30am-11pm, Sa 6:30am-11pm, Su 6:30am-10pm. ❷

# ⊙ SIGHTS

San Diego's world-famous attractions are extremely varied, offering more than enough to keep any traveler engaged. Community events take place regularly, especially during the summer. Pick up a free copy of the weekly *Reader* at most stores for local event listings. The **San Diego 3-for-1 Pass** offers unlimited admission for five consecutive days at a discounted price to three of the city's premier sights—Sea World, the San Diego Zoo, and the San Diego Wild Animal Park. (Visit www.sandiegozoo.org or the websites of the other two parks for information and online ticketing. $89, children 3-9 $63.)

## DOWNTOWN

San Diego's downtown attractions are concentrated in the corridor that includes its business, Gaslamp, and waterfront districts—all testaments to San Diego's continuing renaissance. Within this center of commerce and entertainment are the city's skyscrapers, its modern convention center, and its newest nightlife nexus. Farther to the north and near the water, Little Italy is its own tiny international epicenter of food and entertainment. Travelers should be careful outside these areas; in particular, the neighborhood to the southeast of the corridor is not as safe as the rest of San Diego.

**GASLAMP QUARTER.** The Gaslamp houses antique shops, Victorian buildings, trendy restaurants, and many nightclubs, but recent development has seen far more of the last, making the Gaslamp a hot, hot place to be at night. Formerly the city's Red Light District and now home to Hustler, a three-story adult store, the area has new bars and bistros that are growing popular with upscale revelers (see **Nightlife**, p. 507). By day, the area's charm lies in its fading history. The **Gaslamp Quarter Foundation** offers guided walking tours as well as a small museum. *(William Heath Davis House, 410 Island Ave. ☎233-4692; www.gaslamp-quarter.org. Museum open Su and Tu-Sa 11am-3pm. $3 donation suggested. 2hr. guided walking tours Sa at 11am. $8; students, seniors, and military $6; under 12 free. Self-guided tour maps are available for $2.)* The **Horton Grand Hotel**, like most old buildings in San Diego, is supposedly haunted. Believers may catch a glimpse of Wild West lawman Wyatt Earp or even Babe Ruth. *(311 Island Ave. ☎544-1886. Tours W at 3pm. Free. See **Accommodations**, p. 492.)*

**SAN DIEGO MUSEUM OF CONTEMPORARY ART.** This steel-and-glass structure encases 20th-century works of art from the museum's permanent collection and visiting works on a rotational basis. Artists represented in the permanent collection include Andy Warhol, John Baldessari, Philip Guston; works include a wall that looks as though it breathes. This is a smaller, but worthy, branch of the main museum (see p. 504) in La Jolla. *(1001 Kettner Blvd. ☎234-1001. Open Su-Tu and Th-Sa 11am-5pm. Free.)*

**SAN DIEGO MARITIME MUSEUM.** Housed within some of San Diego's oldest ships, this museum showcases San Diego's rich maritime history and maintains five ships. These include the magnificently restored 1863 sailing vessel *Star of India* (the world's oldest active merchant ship), the ferryboat *Berkeley*, and the steam yacht *Medea*. During the summer, there are movie screenings (F and Sa nights) on the *Star of India* and sleepovers aboard the ships. *(1492 N. Harbor Dr. ☎234-9153; www.sdmaritime.org. Open daily 9am-8pm. $7; seniors, military, and ages 13-17 $5; ages 6-12 $4. Movies $12, ages 12 and under $7. Sleepovers $65.)*

# Downtown San Diego

**🏠 ACCOMMODATIONS**
Downtown HI-AYH, **7**
USA Hostels San Diego, **6**

**🍎 FOOD**
El Prado, **2**
The Fish Market, **3**
Kansas City Barbeque, **4**

**🍷 NIGHTLIFE**
The Casbah, **1**
Croce's, **5**

**EMBARCADERO.** Spanish for "dock," the Embarcadero has boardwalk shops and museums that face moored windjammers, cruise ships, and the occasional naval destroyer. Military and merchant marine vessels are anchored here, as well as the distantly visible North Island Naval Air Station, the Point Loma Submarine Base, and the South Bay's mothballed fleet; they serve as reminders of the US Navy's prominent presence in San Diego. *(Most afternoon tours of naval craft free.)*

**OTHER SIGHTS.** The jewel of San Diego's redevelopment efforts is **Horton Plaza**, at Broadway and 4th. This pastel-hued urban creation is an open-air, multi-level shopping center covering seven blocks. Three blocks west, **Santa Fe Amtrak Depot,** 1050 Kettner Blvd., is a masterpiece of Mission Revival architecture. Its gorgeous arches welcomed visitors to the 1915 Panama California Exposition. The kitschy **Seaport Village** houses over 75 shingled boutiques, ice cream shops, and a century-old carousel. *(649 W. Harbor Dr. ☎ 235-4014. Village open daily 10am-10pm; off-season 10am-9pm. Carousel rides $1. Free 2hr. parking, $1 per additional 30min.)*

# BALBOA PARK & THE SAN DIEGO ZOO

Balboa Park was created from the baked dirt of an abandoned pueblo tract when pioneering horticulturists planted its first redwood seedlings in 1889. Today, the park nurtures these spectacular trees and a veritable profusion of flora. The centerpiece of the park is the world-famous San Diego Zoo, which houses a diverse array of animals in authentic and humane habitats. South of the zoo is a Spanish-style promenade lined with museums and other cultural attractions. You can reach the park by bus #7, and parking is free. Most museums offer free admission at least one Tuesday a month.

## SAN DIEGO ZOO

SAN DIEGO

*2920 Zoo Dr., Balboa Park. From the north or south, take I-5 or I-15 to Rte. 163, get off at the Zoo/Museums Exit (Richmond St.), and follow signs. From the east, take I-8 to Rte. 163 south. Exit at Park Blvd. and turn left; zoo entrance is off Park Blvd. at Zoo Pl. ☎ 234-3153, Giant Panda viewing info 888-MY-PANDA/697-2632; www.sandiegozoo.org. Open daily late June to early Sept. 9am-10pm; early Sept. to late June 9am-dusk. Most of zoo is wheelchair-accessible and wheelchairs can be rented, but assistance may be necessary on the zoo's steep hills. $19.50 ($32 with 35min. bus tour and 2 tickets for the aerial tramway), ages 3-11 $11.75 ($19.75 with 35min. bus tour and aerial tramway; free in Oct.). Military in uniform free. Group rates available. Free on Founder's Day, the 1st M in Oct.*

With over 100 acres of exquisite habitats, this zoo well deserves its reputation as one of the finest in the world. Its unique "bioclimatic" exhibits group animals and plants together by habitat. The Polar Bear Plunge is one of the most elaborate habitats, housing Siberian reindeer, arctic foxes, fish, and of course, the polar bears themselves. Visitors watch the bears underwater through a gigantic glass-walled pool. The legendary **panda** exhibit is the most timeless feature of the park, and the zoo invests over one million dollars a year on panda habitat preservation in China.

The most thorough way to tour the zoo is on foot. During the summer, while sweaty tourists wander about in the sun, the wily animals often snooze in shade hidden from the guests. The best time to visit is early morning or late afternoon, when the sun isn't at its peak. Instead of walking, visitors can also board the educational 40min. **double-decker bus tour** that covers about 75% of the zoo. Although the popular choice (bringing lines twice as long) is for seats on the upper deck, the trees can obstruct views and the seats are in the sun; the lower deck is a better choice. Afterwards, the non-narrated express bus will take you to any of five stops throughout the park anytime during the day. *($8.50, ages 3-11 $6.50.)* The **Skyfari Aerial Tramway** rises 170 ft. above the park and lasts about two minutes but can save on walking time. Don't except to see anything but a pleasant view of the tops of trees and the skyline. *(One-way $2.)* If the bus and tramway appeal to you, purchase your tickets in advance when you buy your zoo admission.

## BALBOA PARK & THE EL PRADO MUSEUMS

Most of the museums reside within the resplendent Spanish colonial-style buildings that line **El Prado Street,** which runs west-to-east through the Park's central **Plaza de Panama.** These ornate structures—designed for the Panama California

Exposition of 1915-16 and for the International Expositions of 1935-36—were originally intended to last two years. Since many of the buildings are now going on 80, they are being renovated, this time with more permanence in mind.

**BALBOA PARK VISITORS CENTER.** The Visitors Center is in the House of Hospitality on El Prado St. at the Plaza de Panama. It sells park maps (50¢) and the Passport to Balboa Park ($30), which allows admission into 13 of the park's museums. Passports are also available at participating museums. The center also sells cold beverages, which are scarce within Balboa Park. *(1549 El Prado.* ☎ *239-0512. www.balboapark.org. Open in summer daily 9am-4:30pm; in winter 9am-4pm.)*

**MUSEUM OF MAN.** Creationists beware: this museum dedicates an entire floor to the 98.4% of DNA we share with chimpanzees. Exhibits trace human evolution from primates to man, with life-sized mannequins and staged civilizations. The real treat, however, is on the outside and doesn't require admission. Formerly a state building, the museum's much-photographed tower and dome gleam with beautiful Spanish mosaic tiles. *(On the west end of the park.* ☎ *239-2001; www.museumofman.org. Open daily 10am-4:30pm. $6, seniors $5, ages 6-17 $3; free 3rd Tu of each month. Special exhibits require an additional ticket, usually $8.)*

**NATURAL HISTORY MUSEUM.** At the east end of Balboa Park, this museum was entirely redone in 2002. It presents rotating exhibits that are hit or miss. The new IMAX theater, however, is a consistent winner; all shows are free with admission. *(Near the intersection of Park Blvd. and Village Pl. at the east end of Balboa Park.* ☎ *232-3821; www.sdnhm.org. Open daily Memorial Day-Labor Day 9:30am-5:30pm; Labor Day-Memorial Day 9:30am-4:30pm. $7, seniors $6, children ages 6-17 $5; free 1st Tu of each month.)*

**AEROSPACE MUSEUM.** The museum displays 24 full-scale replicas and 44 original planes, as well as aviation exhibits in the drum-shaped Ford Pavilion that walk through the history of man's quest to soar. The museum is one of 62 Star Station One sites nationwide that provide information on the International Space Station project. *(2001 Pan American Plaza.* ☎ *234-8291; www.aerospacemuseum.org. Open daily 10am-4:30pm. Extended summer hours. $8, seniors $6, ages 6-17 $3, under 6 and military in uniform free; free 4th Tu of each month.)*

**REUBEN H. FLEET SPACE THEATER AND SCIENCE CENTER.** The Fleet houses the world's very first Omnimax theater, complete with 153 speakers and a hemispheric planetarium. The science center has interactive exhibits which change several times per year. *(1875 El Prado Way.* ☎ *238-1233; www.rhfleet.org. Open daily 9:30am-8pm. Exhibit entrance $6.75, with one Omnimax show $11.50; seniors over 65 $6/ $8.50; children ages 3-12 $5.50/$9.50. Exhibit entrance free 1st Tu of each month.)*

**CASA DE BALBOA MUSEUMS.** The small, ultra-modern **Museum of Photographic Arts (MOPA)** features contemporary photography in 8 to 10 exhibits per year. Its film program ranges from cult classic film festivals to technical and thematic examination of more serious cinematic works. *(*☎*238-7559; www.mopa.org. Open M-W and F-Su 10am-5pm, Th 10am-9pm. $6, students $4; free 2nd Tu of each month. Theater admission $5, students $4.50.)* The **San Diego Hall of Champions,** a slick sports museum complete with Astroturf carpeting, chronicles the San Diego sports scene and immortalizes local heroes like Carlsbad native and skater legend Tony Hawk. Only an odor-proof glass pane separates you from jerseys and shoes worn by Ted Williams and Bill Walton. *(*☎*234-2544. Open daily 10am-4:30pm. $6, seniors and military $4, ages 6-17 $3; free last Tu of each month.)* The recently renovated 1915 Electricity Building houses the **Museum of San Diego History.** *(*☎*232-6203. Open M-W and F-Su 10am-5pm, Th 10am-8pm. $6, seniors and military $5, children 5-12 $2; free 2nd Tu of each month.)* Also in the building are the **Research Archives.** *(Open W-Sa 10am-5pm. $6.)* Downstairs, hobbyists can drool in the **San Diego Model Railroad Museum.** *(☎696-0199. Open Su and Sa 11am-5pm, Tu-F 11am-4pm. $5; seniors and students $4; military $2.50; free 1st Tu of each month.)*

**ART IN THE PLAZA DE PANAMA.** The **San Diego Museum of Art** has a collection ranging from ancient Asian to contemporary Californian works. At the adjoining outdoor **Sculpture Garden Court,** a sensuous Henry Moore piece presides over other large abstract blocks. *(Museum ☎232-7931; www.sdmart.org. Open Su and Tu-Sa 10am-6pm, Th 10am-9pm. $8, seniors and students with college ID $6, ages 6-17 $3; special exhibits $2-20 more.)* **Mingei International Museum,** one of the more interesting museums in Balboa Park, emphasizes unusual media and art from outside the US and Europe. *(Across from the Visitors Center. ☎239-0003; www.mingei.org. Open Su and Tu-Sa 10am-4pm. $5, students and ages 6-17 $2. Free 3rd Tu of each month.)* Across the Plaza, the **Timken Art Gallery** houses a newly restored portrait by Rembrandt and a collection of Russian church icons. *(1500 El Prado Way. ☎239-5548; www.timkenmuseum.org. Open Oct.-Aug. Su 1:30-6pm, Tu-Sa 10am-4:30pm. Free.)* **Spanish Village** is a colony of 300 artists at work in 36 studios. *(At the end of El Prado Way, which is closed to cars, take a left onto Village Pl. ☎233-9050. Open daily 11am-4pm. Free.)*

**BALBOA PARK GARDENS.** The fragrant **Botanical Building** looks like a giant, wooden birdcage, but it's filled with plants. The orchid collection is particularly striking among the murmuring fountains. The **Desert Garden** and **Rose Garden** offer a striking contrast of flora. The Desert Garden is in full bloom from January to March, while the roses are best admired between April and December. Free ranger-led tours of the central part of Balboa Park leave Tuesday and Sunday at 1pm. Free volunteer-led tours meet on Saturdays at 10am; each Saturday tour covers a different set of sights within the park. *(2200 Park Blvd. ☎235-1100, tour info 235-1121. Botanical Building open M-W and F-Su 10am-4pm. Free.)*

**PERFORMANCE SPACES.** Constructed in 1937, the **Old Globe Theater** is the oldest professional theater in California. Classical and contemporary plays are performed at the adjoining Lowell Davies Outdoor Theatre and the Cassius Carter Center Stage. Tickets for all three stages can be purchased at the box office. *(☎239-2255; www.theoldglobe.org. Call for listings, show times, and ticket prices.)* At the Pan American Plaza, actors in the **Starlight Musical Theater** occasionally freeze mid-soliloquy and wait for the roar of passing aircraft to subside before resuming. *(☎544-7827.)* Screaming turbines scarcely affect the action down the road at the **Spreckels Organ Pavilion,** as the racket created by the world's largest outdoor musical instrument can be heard for miles around. Local and visiting organists perform here throughout the week; call for times. *(☎226-0819. Free performance Su 2pm.)*

# OLD TOWN

In 1769, Father Serra, supported by a brigade of Spanish infantry, established the first of 21 missions that would eventually line the California coast in the area now known as Old Town. The remnants of this early settlement have become one of San Diego's tourist mainstays. At the center of Old Town is the State Park, where nine original buildings are home to a number of museums. The rest of Old Town spawns from this center in a somewhat contrived set-up of shops in reconstructed adobe huts. But while Old Town is certainly a tourist trap, it does offer visitors a genuine glimpse into California history while stuffing them silly with the best Mexican food around (see **Food,** p. 494).

# 502 ■ SAN DIEGO

**OLD TOWN STATE PARK.** The most popular of the area's attractions, the park's early-19th-century buildings contain museums, shops, and restaurants. **Seely Stable** houses a huge museum of 19th-century transportation, namely of the horse and carriage. (☎ 220-5427. *Open daily 10am-5pm. Tours every hr. 11am-2pm.*) Take a tour of the **Whaley House,** which stands on the site of San Diego's first gallows. It is one of two **official haunted houses** recognized by the State of California (the other is Winchester Mystery House in San Jose; see p. 153). It houses the *Gone With the Wind* piano and has witnessed some inexplicable phenomena. (*2482 San Diego Ave.* ☎ *298-2482, Old Town Historical Society tours 293-0117. Open daily 10am-4:30pm; entrance closes at 4pm. $5, seniors $4, ages 3-12 $2.*) Across the street is **Heritage Park,** a group of seven 150-year-old Victorian buildings (six houses and a temple) collected from around the city. Four are open to the public, one of which you can stay in (see p. 492).

**SERRA MUSEUM.** Its stout adobe walls were raised at the site of the original fort and mission in 1929, and now beautiful Presidio Park surrounds what remains. While the small exhibits documenting the settlement leave something to be desired, the grounds are spectacular, worth a stroll and a wander up to the top of the hill where a truly huge flagpole marks the former location of **Fort Stockton.** (*In Presidio Park.* ☎ *279-3258. Open in summer Su and Tu-Sa 10am-4:30pm; Sept.-May Su and F-Sa 10am-4:30pm. $5; seniors, students, and military $4, ages 6-17 $2.*)

# COASTAL SAN DIEGO

While cultural and business centers downtown make San Diego a world-class city, it is the sandy coast that brings the city near perfection. Steady winds blow in off the ocean, guaranteeing reliable surf and the year-round temperate climate for which San Diego is renowned.

## CORONADO ISLAND

Lovely Coronado Island is now actually a peninsula. A slender 7 mi. strip of hauled sand known as the "Silver Strand" tethers it to the mainland down near Imperial Beach. Famous for its elegant colonial Hotel Del Coronado, the island is perfect for strolling and browsing through the quaint downtown area. Water babies love the frothy waves that break along the southern shore, and outdoor enthusiasts jog, roller-skate, and bike along over 7 mi. of paved trails. Coronado has a huge military presence, and its entire northern chunk comprises the **North Island Naval Air Station,** the birthplace of American naval aviation. In fact, it was a group of diligent navy men in 1947 who carted wheelbarrows full of sand to connect the island to the rest of Coronado. Among the island's many naval enterprises is the training area of the elite Navy SEAL (sea, air, and land) special forces teams.

Built in 1969, the graceful **Coronado Bridge** guides cars to Coronado from downtown San Diego along I-5. Bus #901 follows the same route, carrying passengers from the Hotel Del Coronado to San Diego and back ($2.25). Those who would rather skim the ocean can take the **Bay Ferry.** (Leaves for Coronado every hr. 9am-9pm, returns every hr. 9:30am-9:30pm. Tickets $2, bikes 50¢ extra. Tickets available at San Diego Harbor Excursion, 1050 N. Harbor Dr., ☎ 234-4111, and at the Ferry Landing Marketplace on the Coronado side.) Once across, the **#904 Shuttle** carries passengers from the landing to the Hotel Del Coronado and back. (Leaves every hr. 10:30am-6:30pm. $1.) Another scenic route is I-5 S to the Palm Ave. Exit. Follow the signs to Silver Strand Blvd., which goes north into Coronado.

**HOTEL DEL CORONADO.** Coronado's most famed sight is its Victorian-style Hotel Del Coronado, one of America's largest wooden buildings. The long white verandas and the vermilion spires of the "Del" were built in 1888. It has since become one of the world's great hotels (rooms start at $270 per night), hosting 10 presidents and one blonde bombshell—Marilyn Monroe's 1959 classic *Some Like it Hot* was filmed here. *Wizard of Oz* author L. Frank Baum wrote a number of his books from the porch. *(1500 Orange Ave. ☎435-6611.)* **Coronado Touring** offers easy 1½hr. walking tours of the area around the hotel. *(Departs from the lobby of the Glorietta Bay Inn, 1630 Glorietta Bay Blvd. ☎435-5993. Tours Tu, Th, Sa 11am. $8 per person.)*

## POINT LOMA

Although the US government owns the outer two-thirds of this peninsula, most of it remains open to citizens and visitors. The **Cabrillo National Monument,** at the tip of Point Loma, is dedicated to the Portuguese explorer Juan Rodríguez Cabrillo, the first European to land in California, but is best known for its views of San Diego and migrating whales. The Visitors Center offers hourly videos or slide presentations as well as information about the monument. (☎557-5450; www.nps.gov/cabr/. Visitors Center open daily 9am-5:15pm, 7-day pass $5 per vehicle, $3 per person on foot or bike; Golden Eagle Passport accepted. **Whale-watching** season is mid-December to February. The **Bayside Trail** (2 mi.) has stations that explain native vegetation and historic military installations and offer magnificent views of the bay and Coronado Island. Point Loma's oceanfront is rife with **tidepools;** turn right off Rte. 209 onto Cabrillo Rd. and drive down to the parking lot at the bottom of the hill. At the highest point of the peninsula sits the interesting museum at **Old Point Loma Lighthouse.** (Open daily 9am-5:15pm.)

## OCEAN, MISSION & PACIFIC BEACHES

Much of San Diego's younger population is drawn to these communities by the surf and hopping nightlife; noisy bars and grills crowd these shores (see **Food,** p. 496, and **Nightlife,** p. 507). The three beaches line up consecutively, but each has its own flavor. It is said that **Ocean Beach (O.B.)** is what the world would be like if the hippies had lasted past the 70s. With a home-grown, earthy atmosphere and gentle surf, O.B. is the most laid-back of the beaches and the best place to learn the art of wave-riding. Anglers can try their luck on the Western Hemisphere's longest fishing pier. **O.B. Pier Cafe and Baitshop,** on the pier itself, rents fishing poles and a bucket of bait. No license is required as long as you use no more than one pole. (☎226-3474. Open Su-Th 8am-9pm, F-Sa 8am-10pm. $14 per day.) From atop the majestic **Sunset Cliffs Park,** romantics can smooch in the ocean breeze while watching the sun set over the surfers and the area's best waves. (Gates open 4am-11pm; quiet hours after 7pm. No camping.) Ocean Beach also hosts an awesome **farmer's market** that lasts throughout the year. (Open W 3-9pm.)

Further north, **Mission Beach,** at the corner of W. Mission Bay Dr. and Mission Blvd., is a people-watcher's paradise. **Belmont Park,** a combination amusement park and shopping center, draws a youthful crowd. Take advantage of the rare free parking and rattle your brains on the bumpy **Giant Dipper** roller coaster ($4).

**Pacific Beach** and its boisterous Garnet Ave. is the most lively of the three beaches, and home to the best nightlife. The **Ocean Front Walk** is always packed with joggers, walkers, cyclists, and the usual beachfront shops. Although all the beaches accommodate those who limit their physical activity to shifting on their towels, beachside sports are very popular. Swimmers and boogie boarders should avoid prime surfing areas.

**SEA WORLD.** Take Disneyland, subtract most of the rides, add a whole lot of fish and marine life, and you've got Sea World. Though critics have long condemned the practice of training highly intelligent marine mammals to perform unnatural circus acts,

**Scripps Park**
San Diego-La Jolla Underwater Park
**Shell Beach**
**The Children's Pool**
**La Valencia Hotel**
La Jolla Cove
La Jolla Caves
Coast Blvd. Park
**Museum of Contemporary Art**
Silverado St.
TO UCSD, AQUARIUM
**Wipeout Beach**
Kline St.
Virginia Wy.
Torrey Pines Rd.
Herschel Ave.
Prospect St.
**Marine St. Beach**
Pearl St.
**LA JOLLA**
Marine St.
Genter St.
La Jolla Country Club
Fay Ave.
Westbourne St.
Nautilus St.
Draper Ave.
**Windansea Beach**
Nautilus Wy.
Bonair Wy.
Neptune Pl.
Electric Ave.
W. Muirlands Ave.
**Strand Park**
Beaumont Ave.
Camino de la Costa
La Jolla Blvd.
**THE MUIRLANDS**
**Hermosa Park**
TO LA JOLLA SCENIC DRIVE
**Bird Rock**
Forward St.
La Jolla Mesa Dr.
Midway St.
Chelsea Ave.
Colima St.
0   400 yards
**Calumet Park**
0   400 meters
Van Nuys St.
Archer St.
Agate St.
Turquoise St.
**Tourmaline Surfing Park**
Tourmaline St.
Opal St.
Loring St.
**PACIFIC OCEAN**
Wilbur St.
Bayard St.
Cass St.
Dawes St.
Everts St.
Mission Blvd.

## La Jolla, Pacific Beach & Mission Beach

▲ ACCOMMODATIONS

Inn at Mission Bay, **11**
International House at the 2nd Floor:
  Mission Beach, **13**
  Pacific Beach, **8**
Shell Beach, **1**

🍴 FOOD

Café Crema, **10**
Kono's Surf Club, **6**
The Living Room, **2**
The Pannikin, **4**
Rimel's, **3**
World Curry, **9**

🌙 NIGHTLIFE

Canes Bar and Grill, **12**
The Comedy Store, **5**
Pacific Beach Bar and Grill and Club Tremors, **7**

**PACIFIC BEACH**
Felspar St.
**Pacific Beach Park**
Garnet Ave.
TO 🚗
**Crystal Pier**
Grand Ave.
TO MISSION BAY DR., **11** (2.25mi.)
Pacific Beach Dr.
Palisades Park
Ocean Blvd.

**Sail Bay**
**Santa Clara Recreation Center**
**MISSION BEACH**
San Juan Cove
**Mission Bay**
Santa Barbara Cove
**Cheap Rentals**
**Windsport**
Mission Beach Park
**Mission Bay Yacht Club**
W. Mission Bay Dr.
**Mission Bay Park**
**Belmont Park**
TO OCEAN BEACH (2mi.)

---

the goofy shows are surprisingly charming. The A-list star and poster-whale is the killer whale **Shamu,** whose signature move is a cannon-ball splash that soaks anyone in the first 20 rows (the original Shamu died long ago, but each of his successors has proudly borne the moniker). The best show in the park, however, is **Fools with Tools,** a delightful takeoff on Tool Time from Home Improvement. Tim Allen gets pushed aside as precocious sea lions and otters take the stage. The nearby dolphin show is also a favorite. In addition to the performances, there are habitats for sharks, penguins, and other water-dwellers such as the endangered manatee, as well as shows featuring watersports and daredevil jet-ski riders. Visitors receive a map and schedule upon entering the parking lot; even the most popular events occur only a few times daily, so take a quick look at the schedule. One of the newest attractions is the **4-D movie theater** in the back of the park. If Shamu's splash wasn't wet enough, head towards **Shipwreck Rapids,** Sea World's first adventure ride. While a dousing is almost guaranteed, the gurgling voyage is less than thrilling. Those looking to cool down sans Shamu's tail and a face full of saltwa-ter should head to the free **Bud-weiser's Beer School** and brewery. The 30min. class, free beer, and general merriment come courtesy of Anheuser-Busch, the proud owners of Sea World. (☎ 226-3900; www.sea-world.com. Open daily in summer 9am-11pm. The park opens at 10am in winter, but closing hours vary. $45, ages 3-9 $35. Parking $7, RVs $9.)

**MUSEUMS.** The 🐚**Birch Aquarium at the Scripps Institute of Oceanogra-phy** in La Jolla has great educa-tional exhibits including a tank with a portly octopus, half a dozen different types of oozing jellyfish, a large collection of seahorses, and a 70,000-gallon kelp and shark tank. (2300 Expedition Way. ☎ 858-534-

*3474; http://aquarium.ucsd.edu. Open daily 9am-5pm. $9.50, students with ID $6.50, seniors $8, ages 3-17 $6. Parking $3.)* The **San Diego Museum of Contemporary Art** houses a rotating exhibition of pop, minimalist, and conceptualist art beginning in the 1950s. It shares its collection with the downtown branch (see p. 497). The museum is as visually stunning as the art it contains, with gorgeous ocean views, high ceilings, and light-filled spaces. There are daily guided tours at various hours in both English and Spanish. *(700 Prospect St. ☎858-454-3541; www.mcasd.org. Open M-Tu and F-Su 11am-5pm, Th 11am-7pm. $6; students, seniors, military, and ages 12-18 $2. Free 3rd Tu and 1st Su of every month.)*

**OTHER SIGHTS.** The somewhat isolated **University of California at San Diego (UCSD)** sits above La Jolla. Buses #30 and 34 take you to campus, but cars or bikes are invaluable for getting to the campus's many residential and academic colleges. Be sure to check out the terraces and buttresses of **Geisel Library,** a space-age structure endowed by La Jolla resident Theodore Geisel, better known by his middle name as the late and beloved children's books author, Dr. Seuss. Kiosks on Gilman and Northview Dr. dispense maps and give information about campus tours. *(☎858-534-2208. Open M-F 7am-9pm, Sa-Su 7am-5:30pm.)* At the foot of Girard Ave. in **La Jolla Village** is **Scripps Park,** where great waves shake the rocky shore, sending up plumes of silver sea spray. Ocean lovers, or lovers of any kind, can stroll here in the evenings and linger on the carefully manicured lawns.

# LA JOLLA

The Spanish named the area *La Jolla* ("The Jewel") for its physical beauty. Later the hilly promontory developed as an exclusive hideaway for wealthy Easterners, and today it remains true to its tony roots. The gaudy pink hues of opulent **La Valencia Hotel,** 1132 Prospect St., testify to an age of seaside luxury. While La Jolla is still an upscale enclave, it has evolved into a more inclusive area. With brand-name shopping districts and the rugged beauty of La Jolla Cove, this eclectic community is a must-see. Take the Ardath Exit west from I-5 or bus #30 or 34 from downtown.

**BEACHES.** La Jolla claims some of the finest beaches in the city. The **La Jolla Cove** is popular with scuba divers, snorkelers, and brilliantly colored Garibaldi goldfish. Wander south along the cliffs to a striking semi-circular inlet known as **The Children's Pool.** Established in 1931 by local philanthropist Ellen Browning Scripps as a wildlife preserve, the pool's inhabitants are a famously thriving community of sea lions who frolic and cavort in the sun. Don't feed the animals, and confine yourself to the established viewing areas lest you disrupt the fragile ecological enclave. Some of the best breaks in the county can be found in La Jolla at **Tourmaline Beach** and **Wind 'n Sea Beach.** However, these are notoriously territorial spots, so outsiders might be advised to surf elsewhere. **La Jolla Shores,** next to Scripps and UCSD, has gentle swells ideal for new surfers, boogie boarders, and swimmers. **Black's Beach** is not officially a nude beach, but that doesn't seem to stop sunbathers from spurning clothing. The north end generally attracts gay patrons. **Torrey Pines Glider Port** is where hang gliders leap into the breeze for unadulterated views of the beaches below. To reach the Glider Port, take I-5 to Genesee Ave., go west, and turn left on N. Torrey Pines Rd. The beach is accessible by a steep staircase just south of the glider port and can be very popular with surfers.

# ELSEWHERE IN SAN DIEGO

**MISSION BASILICA SAN DIEGO DE ALCALÁ.** Father Serra's brigade of soldiers were apparently a rough and unholy bunch; in 1774 the padre moved his mission some 6 mi. away from their settlement to its current location. The mission is still an active parish church and contains gardens, a small museum, and a reconstruction of Serra's living quarters. *(Take bus #43 or I-8 East to the Mission Gorge Rd. Exit. Go north. Turn left on Twain Ave. The mission will be 2 blocks ahead on the right side.* ☎281-8449. *Visitors Center open daily 9am-4:45pm. $3, students and seniors $2, under 12 $1, 45min. tote-a-tape guided tours $2. Mass held daily at 7am and 5:30pm; visitors welcome.)*

**QUALCOMM STADIUM.** Home to a number of Super Bowls (including the 2003 drubbing of the Oakland Raiders at the hands of the Tampa Bay Buccaneers) and the **San Diego Chargers** (the city's pro football team), the "Q" begins its term in 2004 as a football-only venue. The **San Diego Padres** (pro baseball) have moved to greener pastures downtown at Petco Field. *(West of the Mission near the junction of I-8 and I-15. Chargers tickets* ☎280-2121. *Padres tickets* ☎1-877-FRIAR-TIX/374-2784.)

**IN THE NAVY NOW.** Freedom lovers can take a free tour of the gigantic **USS Constellation** (the vessel with the number "64" on its super-structure, visible from San Diego's downtown waterfront) and other aircraft carriers. *(Reservations* ☎545-2427. *Daily tours at 10am, 1, and 3pm. Reserve at least 48hr. in advance for weekend tours.)*

# ◘ SEASONAL EVENTS

Gorgeous weather and strong community spirit make the San Diego area an ideal place for local festivals. The following is by no means a comprehensive list, so check the beach community weeklies for further festival information.

**Penguin Day Ski Fest,** De Anza Cove (☎858-270-0840), in Mission Bay. Jan. 1, 2004. This festival requires participants to water-ski in the Pacific and lie on ice without a wet suit. Those who do get a "penguin patch"; those who fail get a "chicken patch."

**Ocean Beach Kite Festival,** 4726 Santa Monica Ave. (☎531-1527), in Ocean Beach. 1st Sa in Mar. Kite-construction and kite-flying competitions.

**San Diego Crew Classic,** Crown Pt. Shores (☎858-488-0700), in Mission Bay. 1st weekend in Apr. Crews from around the world compete at the only major collegiate rowing regatta on the West Coast. $5.

**San Diego Earthfair 2004,** in Balboa Park (☎858-496-6666; www.earthdayweb.org). One day in mid-Apr.; 10am-5pm. World's largest environmental festival with free admission. Kids' activities, booths, exhibits, and dancing.

**Summer Stargazing,** at San Diego State University's Mt. Laguna Observatory (☎594-1415). May 31-Sept. 6 F 2-6pm, Sa 9am-6pm. Open to the public with free tickets available through the US Forest Service.

**Summer Pops 2004** (☎235-0804), performed all summer by the San Diego Symphony. Late June-Sept. 2 on a stage in the harbor. Tickets begin at $15.

**Ocean Beach Street Fair and Chili Cook-Off** (☎226-1936). Last weekend in June. Newport St. is lined with arts booths during this 2-day festival.

**Taste of Pacific Beach and Restaurant Walk** (☎858-273-3303). One in early May and one in mid-Sept. Reduced-fare eats from more than 20 Pacific Beach restaurants.

**Beachfest** (☎858-273-3303), in Pacific Beach on the Boardwalk. Mid-Oct. Live entertainment, arts and crafts, food, and family fun.

**Hillcrest Cityfest Street Fair** (☎299-3330), on 5th Ave. between Ivy Ln. and University Ave., in the heart of San Diego's gay community. 2nd Su in Aug. Arts, crafts, food, live entertainment, and beer garden.

**US Open Sand Castle Competition** (☎424-6663), Imperial Beach pier. 3rd weekend in July. Sand-sculpturing demigods exercise their craft in this largest and longest-running of American sand castle events. Parades, fireworks, and a children's castle contest.

**SummerFest La Jolla Chamber Music Festival** (☎858-459-3724), La Jolla Museum of Contemporary Art. First three weeks of Aug. Be prepared to shell out money for this high-brow event. Concert tickets can exceed $50.

**La Jolla Rough Water Swim** (☎858-456-2100), early Sept. Start and finish at the La Jolla Cove. Largest annual rough water competition in the US.

# 📷 📄 NIGHTLIFE & ENTERTAINMENT

Nightlife in San Diego isn't centered around any one strip, but scattered in several distinct pockets of action. Upscale locals and party-seeking tourists flock to the **Gaslamp Quarter,** where numerous restaurants and bars feature live music nightly. The **Hillcrest** area, next to Balboa Park, draws a young, largely gay crowd to its clubs and dining spots. Away from downtown, the **beach areas** (especially Garnet Ave. in Pacific Beach) are loaded with clubs, bars, and cheap eateries that attract college-age revelers. The city's definitive source of entertainment info is the free *Reader,* found in shops, coffeehouses, and visitors centers. Listings can also be found in the *San Diego Union-Tribune's* Thursday "Night and Day" section.

If cruisin' and boozin' isn't your idea of nightlife, you can spend a more sedate evening at one of San Diego's excellent theaters, such as the **Balboa Theatre,** 225 Broadway Ave. (☎544-1000), and the **Horton Grand Theatre,** 444 4th Ave. (☎234-9583), both downtown. Call for show information; ticket prices vary according to the show. The **La Jolla Playhouse,** 2910 La Jolla Village Dr., presents shows at the Mandell Weiss Theatre on the UC San Diego campus in La Jolla. To get there, turn onto Expedition from N. Torrey Pines Rd. (☎858-550-1010; www.lajollaplayhouse.com.) On Coronado Island, sophisticates can take in a performance at the **Lamb's Players Theatre,** 1142 Orange Ave., San Diego's only year-round professional theater. (☎437-0600; www.lambsplayer.org.)

## LATE-NIGHT RESTAURANTS

Although the restaurants below offer complete meals, they are better known as night spots, be they bars, music clubs, or dance clubs.

**Pacific Beach Bar and Grill** and **Club Tremors,** 860 Garnet Ave. (☎858-483-9227), one of the only dance clubs in **Pacific Beach.** Live DJ packs the 2-level dance floor with a young and slinky crowd. The Bar and Grill has respectable food, more than 20 beers on tap, and live music on Sundays. Cover $5 if you enter through Club Tremors, but the same club is accessible through the Grill for free, so start there. Club open Tu-Sa 9pm-1:30am; bar open 11am-1:30am; kitchen closes at midnight.

**Canes Bar and Grill,** 3105 Oceanfront Walk (☎858-488-1780 or 858-488-9690), in Mission Beach. One of the best live music venues in the city, this beachside bar has unbeatable sunset views from the 2nd story terrace, and a DJ and dancing every night until 2am. Directly on the water. Canes features standard Mexican fare, and the Tacos Supremas ($9-10) are a favorite. Open daily 11am-2am.

**Dick's Last Resort,** 345 4th Ave. (☎858-231-9100), in the **Gaslamp.** Buckets of Southern grub attract a wildly hedonistic bunch. Dick's stocks beers from around the globe, from Africa to Trinidad, on top of native brews like the Dixieland Blackened Voodoo Lager. No cover for the nightly rock or blues, but you'd better be buyin'. The snobby staff purposefully gives guests a hard time. Lunch burgers under $6-7, dinner entrees $10-18. Open daily 11am-1:30am.

**Cafe Lu Lu,** 419 F. St. (☎238-0114), in the **Gaslamp.** Coffeehouse designed by local artists. See and be seen as you sip a raspberry mocha ($3.75), or consider this a low-key alternative to the aggressive bar scene. Standing room only after midnight on weekends. Open Su-Th 9am-1am, F-Sa 9am-3am.

## CLUBS & BARS

**Croce's Top Hat Bar and Grille** and **Croce's Jazz Bar,** 802 5th Ave. (☎233-4355), at F St. in the **Gaslamp.** Ingrid Croce, widow of singer Jim Croce, created this rock/blues bar and classy jazz bar side-by-side on the 1st floor of the historic Keating building. Live music nightly. Cover $5-10, includes 2 live shows. Top Hat open F-Sa 7pm-1:30am. Jazz bar open daily 5:30pm-12:30am with shows starting at 8:30pm.

**The Casbah,** 2501 Kettner Blvd. (☎232-4355). Eddie Vedder of the alternative rock legend Pearl Jam owns this intimate nightspot, one of the best live music venue in the city. Cover varies, but it is always 21+. Call ahead for a schedule, as sometimes tickets sell out. Hours vary, usually 5pm-2am.

**The Bitter End,** 770 5th Ave. (☎338-9300), in the **Gaslamp.** This upscale, 3-level dance club is always packed with people dressed to impress, so leave the torn Levi's and sandals at home. DJs spin everything from hip hop to Top 40 to trance on the upper floors, while live music pounds below. Happy Hour on Th and F (3-7pm) features a free buffet. 21+. $5-10 cover after 9pm. Open daily 5pm-2am.

**The Comedy Store,** 916 Pearl St. (☎858-454-9176), in **La Jolla.** Sister to the landmark Hollywood club. Go for your big break on open mic Su nights. No cover, but a 2-drink minimum. 21+. Drinks $3. Shows W-Sa 8 and 10:30pm. W-Th $5-10, F $15, Sa $20.

**Cafe Sevilla,** 555 4th Ave. (☎233-5979; www.cafesevilla.com), in the **Gaslamp.** Downstairs, live bands gets patrons' hips swaying to Latin dances from salsa to flamenco every night. The Friday night flamenco dinner show includes a 3-course meal, the show, and admission to the club afterwards for $40. Dress to impress. 21+ downstairs. Open daily 5pm-1:30am.

## GAY & LESBIAN NIGHTLIFE

Lesbian and gay clubs cluster in **University Heights** and **Hillcrest. The Flame,** 3780 Park Blvd., in Hillcrest, is one of the most popular lesbian dance clubs in the nation. (☎295-4163. 21+. Open daily 5pm-2am.) **Bourbon Street,** 4612 Park Blvd., in University Heights, is a neighborhood bar with a gay following. (☎291-0173. 21+. Open M-F 2pm-2am, Sa-Su 11am-2pm.) **The Brass Rail,** 3796 5th Ave., in Hillcrest, was the first gay bar in San Diego. It features dancing on weekends. (☎298-2233. 21+. Cover F-Sa after 9pm $4-7. Open daily noon-2am.)

# SAN DIEGO'S NORTH COUNTY

San Diego's North County is a nearly unbroken beachland that stretches north from La Jolla toward Los Angeles. Sun and surf lovers alike come to enjoy this ocean playground. Several resort communities have emerged along the sand and crumbling cliffs. Large-scale attractions have also found their homes here; San Diego's Wild Animal Park and Legoland each provide a day's worth of entertainment. North County towns are easily accessible along I-5 and US 101 (the Pacific Coast Hwy.) by car, bike, or bus. Take North County Transit District bus #301 from La Jolla's University Towne Centre as far as Oceanside. (Daily every 30min. 5am-10pm; $1.50; free transfers.) The Coaster, a high-speed commuter train, also provides transportation from North County into downtown San Diego. (☎800-COASTER/262-7837; www.gonctd.com. 11 trains daily. 5am-7pm. Fares $3.50-4.75 depending on distance.) For more North County Transit info, call ☎800-266-6883.

Opportunities to sportfish off a pier or to book passage on a **deep-sea fishing** charter abound up and down the coast (see p. 512). The waters off the coast all the way down to Baja California teem with monstrous yellowfin tuna, giant grouper, and the ultimate trophy fish—the marlin.

# DEL MAR                                                    ☎ 858

North of La Jolla is the affluent suburb of Del Mar (pop. 5100), home to thoroughbred racehorses and famous fairgrounds. Many small boutiques and good eats line Camino Del Mar. During June and early July, Del Mar hosts the **San Diego County Fair,** one of the largest fairs in California. Solana Beach to the north boasts the Cedros Design District, full of warehouses converted to artist studios.

**▓ PRACTICAL INFORMATION.** The **Del Mar Chamber of Commerce and Visitor Center,** 1104 Camino Del Mar #214, has brochures and handouts. (☎ 755-4844; www.delmarchamber.org. Open Tu-Th 10am-4pm.) The **Amtrak** station, 105 Cedros Ave. (☎ 800-USA-RAIL/872-7245), in Solana Beach, is not only architecturally interesting, but also sends 11 **trains** per day to LA ($22 one-way). **Internet access** is available at the **Del Mar Public Library,** 1309 Camino Del Mar. Call ahead to reserve a one-hour block of time, or drop in to use one of the computers for 15min. (☎ 755-1666. Open Su 1-5pm, Tu 10am-6pm, W-Th 10am-8pm, F-Sa 10am-5pm.)

**▓▓ FOOD & NIGHTLIFE.** Surf-weathered locals favor **Board and Brew ❶,** 1212 Camino Del Mar, for its cheap beer ($2-2.50) and delicious sandwiches such as the California Delight ($4.50), full of turkey, cream cheese, and sunflower seeds. (☎ 481-1021. Open daily 10am-7pm.) One block away, a little taste of Europe can be found at **Le Cafe Bleu ❷,** 1140 Camino Del Mar, which specializes in delicious French pastries and $5 gourmet lunch specials such as quiches or crepes. (☎ 350-1432. Open M-Sa 6am-6pm, Su 7am-6pm.) **Tony's Jacal ❶,** 621 Valley Ave., is a family-run establishment serving up zesty burritos for $4. (☎ 755-2274. Open M and W-Th 11am-2pm and 5-9:30pm, Tu 11am-2pm, F-Sa 11am-2pm and 5-10pm.) For some awesome deep-dish pizza and "grog," **Pizza Port ❷,** 135 N. Hwy 101 in Solana Beach, is your place. Expect a wait; the place is usually packed. (☎ 481-7332; www.pizzaport.com. Pizzas from $6. Pints from $3. Open daily 11am-11pm.) The **Belly Up Tavern,** 143 S. Cedros Ave., off Lomas Santa Fe Dr. in Solana Beach, was once a warehouse near the train tracks, but now hosts blues, rock, reggae, and jazz. Keep your eyes peeled for some well-known acts. Charge tickets in advance (☎ 481-8140 or 220-TIXS/8497; www.bellyup.com), or at the door. (☎ 481-9022. 21+. Cover varies with artist; expect $5-40. Open daily noon-2am; live music nightly.)

**▓▓ SIGHTS & BEACHES.** The celebrity-studded **Del Mar Thoroughbred Club,** at the corner of Via de la Valle and Jimmy Durante Blvd., fills with racing fans from late July to the week after Labor Day. Founded in 1937 by Bing Crosby and Pat O'Brien, the racetrack is one of the most beautiful in the world. (☎ 755-1141 or 795-5533; www.delmarracing.com. 8 races per day M and W-F, 10 on Sa, 9 on Su. Post Time 2pm. Gates open M and W-F noon, Sa-Su 11:30am. $5 general admission, $8 clubhouse.) **Torrey Pines State Reserve and Beach,** along the coast just south of Del Mar, is one of only two native torrey pine groves on earth. (The other is on Santa Rosa Island in Channel Islands National Park; see p. 484.) Look for the entrance at 12600 off N. Torrey Pines Rd. about ½ mi. south of Del Mar Village. (☎ 755-2063; www.torreypine.org. Park open 8am-sunset. $4 per vehicle, pedestrians and bicyclists free.) The **Torrey Pines Lodge,** at the top of the hill on the entrance road, provides info on activities and hiking trails, as well as an exhibit on why the torrey pines are so unique. (Open daily 9am-5:30.) The park trails are wonderful for runners, cyclists, hikers, and those who enjoy rules—there is no camping, no picnicking, no food, no smoking, no dogs (even if kept in cars), and no straying off the established trails. Try the beach trail down to flat rock for amazing views (1½ mi., round-trip). The 6 mi. of rocky beach are popular with hang gliders.

SAN DIEGO

# ENCINITAS, LEUCADIA & CARLSBAD ☎760

North of Del Mar along the Pacific Coast Highway lie the towns of Encinitas and Leucadia, which betray traces of their hippie-mecca past through their hallucinogenic beauty and tie-dyed inhabitants. Farther up the coast is the charming lagoon hideaway of Carlsbad, where US 101, known here as Carlsbad Blvd., winds past silky sands and shingled homes adorned with wild rosebushes.

**⁊ PRACTICAL INFORMATION.** Orient yourself at the **Carlsbad Convention and Visitors Center,** 400 Carlsbad Village Dr. (☎434-6093; www.carlsbadca.org. Open M-F 9am-5pm, Sa 10am-4pm, Su 10am-3pm.) **Internet access** is available at the **Georgina Cole Library,** 1250 Carlsbad Village Dr., near downtown (☎434-2870; open M-Th 9am-9pm, F-Sa 9am-5pm), or the **Carlsbad City Library,** 1775 Dove Ln. (☎602-2039. Open M-Th 9am-9pm, F-Sa 9am-5pm.)

**⌂⌂ ACCOMMODATIONS & FOOD.** Inexpensive lodging is difficult to find in these resort communities. **Surf Motel ❺,** 3136 Carlsbad Blvd., is a decent value with large, comfy rooms located across the street from the beach and a block from Carlsbad Village. (☎729-7961. Rooms $109-149; in winter $55-69.) A cheaper and more reliable alternative is **Motel 6 ❸,** 1006 Carlsbad Village Dr., just east of Carlsbad Village. (☎434-7135. Singles $50; doubles $56. Rates $6-8 higher on weekends.) Other locations are at 6117 Paseo del Norte, off I-5 at the Palomar Airport Rd. Exit (☎438-1242), and farther south on Raintree Dr. (☎431-0745). The **Portofino Beach Inn ❺,** 186. N. Hwy. 101, in Encinitas, has nice rooms and a jacuzzi near the beach. (☎944-0301. Singles $109-169; doubles $139-169.)

Camping near the beach is allowed at **South Carlsbad State Park ❶** or at **San Elijo State Park ❶.** Both campgrounds are situated atop cliffs and don't offer much in terms of privacy. However, the beaches below are beautiful. (South Carlsbad ☎438-3143. San Elijo ☎753-5091. Water, restrooms, showers, general stores, picnic tables, BBQ stands, and fire pits are all available. Reservations for both campgrounds can be made up to 7 months in advance by calling ☎800-444-7275 or via www.reserveamerica.com. Reservations essential in summer. Oceanside sites $20, inland $16. Call for availability of RV sites.)

There is a variety of great beachfront restaurants along Old US 101 (Pacific Coast Hwy.). Locals and tourists cram into the small and intimate dining area at ▨**Trattoria I Trulli ❸,** 830 S. Coast Hwy. 101, for good reason: the food is simply delicious. (☎943-6800. Dinner entrees from $10. Open Su-Th 11:30am-2:30pm and 5-10pm, F-Sa 11:30am-2:30pm and 5-10:30pm.) If the wait is too much, head one block away to **Rosanna's Italian Trattoria ❸,** 806 S. Coast Hwy. 101. Though the decor might not be as elegant, the food is just as excellent. (☎942-0738. Dinner entrees from $10. Open daily 10am-4pm and 5-10pm.) Life is sweet at **Honey's Bistro and Bakery ❶,** 632 S. Coast Hwy., in Encinitas, where they serve up large, fresh salads ($6), sandwiches ($5), and soups ($4), as well as mouth-watering baked goods. (☎942-5433. Open daily 5:30am-3:30pm.) At the **Miracles Cafe ❷,** 1953 San Elijo Ave., in Encinitas, six dollars will get you banana Belgian waffles or a Supreme Scream sandwich. (☎943-7924. Open M-Th 6am-10pm, F-Sa 6am-11pm, Su 7am-9pm.) Find the artsy **Village Buzz ❶,** 519 Grand Ave., in downtown Carlsbad. Owner and waverider Scott serves an electrifying organic espresso and coffee collection ($1.50-3.50) and delicious pastries for $2-4. (☎729-2495. Open M-W 6:30am-6pm, Th-F 6:30am-8pm, Sa 7am-8pm, Su 7am-6pm.)

**◐▣ SIGHTS & SEASONAL EVENTS.** In Encinitas, truth-seekers can partake in restorative contemplation at the New Age ▨**Self-Realization Fellowship,** 215 K St. The lush and immaculate gardens ensure meditative serenity, especially when lit by a set-

SAN DIEGO

**San Diego North County**

ting sun. (☎ 753-1811. Retreats available; call for reservations. Gardens open Su 11am-5pm, Tu-Sa 9am-5pm. Free.) To counter the asceticism of the Self-Realization Fellowship, you can indulge your materialistic appetites at the weekly **Seaside Bazaar,** which peddles trinkets, jewelry, crafts, foods, and other odds and ends, along US 101 at the north end of town. (☎ 753-1611. Sa-Su 9am-4:30pm.) For floral fun, stroll through the **Quail Botanical Gardens,** 230 Quail Gardens Dr., where you will find one of the world's most diverse plant collections. Be sure to check out the huge bamboo groves and the beautiful waterfall. (☎ 436-3036; www.qbgardens.com. Open daily 9am-5pm. Free tours with admission Sa at 10am. $8, seniors $5, ages 5-12 $3.) **Legoland** is a fun, goofball tribute to the interlocking kiddie blocks that have inspired countless junior architects. Exit I-5 in Carlsbad at Cannon Rd. and continue to One Legoland Dr. (☎ 918-LEGO/5346. Open in spring Su-M and Th 10am-5pm, F-Sa 10am-6pm; in summer daily 10am-8pm; in fall M and Th-Su 10am-5pm. $40, ages 3-16 $34. Parking $7.) Shake, rattle, and roll at the extensive **Museum of Making Music,** 5790 Armada Dr., where over 450 vintage musical instruments illustrate a survey of 20th-century American music. (☎ 438-5996 or 877-551-9976; www.museumofmakingmusic.org. Open Su and Tu-Sa 10am-5pm. $5; seniors, students, military, and ages 4-18 $3.)

On the first Sunday in May and November, the famous biannual **Carlsbad Village Street Faire,** the largest one-day fair in California, attracts over 900 vendors and 80,000 people. From early March to late April, the kaleidoscopic **Flower Fields** bloom with diverse wildflowers. The flowers cover a mile of hillside along I-5 north of Palomar Airport Rd. Take the Palomar Airport Exit off I-5, head east along Palomar Airport Rd. to the light at Paseo del Norte, and turn left. (☎ 431-0352. $4, ages 3-12 $2.) You can't pick the flowers, but there's always fruit. **U-Pick Strawberries,** north of Cannon Rd. at Paseo del Norte, opens its farms up to the public for harvesting. (Open May to mid-July daily 8:30am-6:30pm. Small bucket $4, large $8.)

◪ **BEACHES.** The California state park system maintains a number of beautiful beaches in the area. **Carlsbad State Beach** is long and attractive, marred slightly by the mammoth power plant which occupies the coast to the south. **Offshore Surf Shop,** 3179 Carlsbad Blvd., rents boogie boards and 6-8 ft. "soft" surfboards. (☎ 729-4934. Open daily 9am-7:30pm. Boogie boards $3 per hr., $10 per day. Surfboards $5/$25. Use a credit card for rentals; otherwise, a deposit of $50 for boogie board and $300 for surfboard is required.) The **Encinitas City Beach** has multiple access points. Try the **Stonesteps** at the end of South El Portal St. to reach over 3 mi. of public sands. Surfing neophytes can score a board at **Leucadia Surfboards,** 1354 N. Highway 101. Woody, the chill manager, is always happy to help. (☎ 632-9700. Open M-F 10am-5pm, Sa-Su 9am-5pm. Boards $5 per hr., $20 per day.) Cardiff-by-the-Sea is near **San Elijo Beach State Park** (☎ 753-5091) and **Cardiff State Beach.** If you have a car, these beautiful beaches are worth the drive.

# OCEANSIDE                                                                       ☎ 760

Oceanside (pop. 146,230) is the largest and probably the least glamorous of San Diego's coastal resort towns. Home to Camp Pendleton, a Marine Corps base as well as one of the world's greatest surfing beaches at Oceanside Harbor, Oceanside has a split personality. The pier at Pierview Way attracts serious surfers year-round. Lifeguards patrol the beaches, and surfers stick to designated areas. Free parking in the lots off Mission Ave. is quickly filled, but metered spots are nearby.

▨ **PRACTICAL INFORMATION.** The **Oceanside Transit Center,** 195 S. Tremont St., houses the local **Amtrak** (☎ 800-USA-RAIL/872-7245 or 722-4622) and **Greyhound** (☎ 722-1587) stations. The newly-renovated **California Welcome Center,** 928 N. Coast Hwy., has info about goings-on and a toll-free hotel reservation line. (☎ 721-1101 or 800-350-7873. Open daily 9am-5pm; closed holidays.) Thirty-minute blocks of **Internet access** are available at the **Oceanside Public Library,** 330 N. Coast Hwy. in the Civic Center. (☎ 435-5600. Open M-W 10am-8pm, Th-Sa 10am-5:30pm.) **Internet access** is also available at the **Oceanside Public Library Community Computer Center,** 321 North Nevada St. (☎ 435-5660. Open M-Th 10am-9pm, F-Sa 10am-5pm, Su noon-5pm. Call to reserve a computer.)

▐▐ **ACCOMMODATIONS & FOOD.** Unlike its ritzier neighbors, Oceanside offers many inexpensive lodgings. Budget motels line Hwy. 101 through the town, though not all are reputable. Power up before hitting the waves at **The Longboarder ❶,** 228 N. Coast Hwy., which serves burgers ($5-6) and heaping omelettes ($6) to its surfer crowd. (☎ 721-6776. Open M-F 7am-2pm, Sa-Su 7am-3pm.)

▣▧ **SIGHTS & ACTIVITIES.** The pier gets crowded during the **World Body Surfing Championships** in mid-August. Call the Oceanside Special Events Office (☎ 435-5540) for more info. With so much surfing history made along its shores, Oceanside is the perfect place for the ▨**California Surf Museum,** 223 N. Coast Hwy. (☎ 721-6876. Open M and Th-Su 10am-4pm. Free.) You can catch your dinner by renting gear at **Helgren's Sportfishing Trips,** 315 Harbor Dr. S. (☎ 722-2133. One-day license $7.25. Surface fishing rod $10, deep fishing rod $12. Half-day trips on the fishing boat $29, full-day

$55. Non-fishing harbor cruise daily $10, ages 5-12 $5. Times vary with the seasons.)
If you prefer good old-fashioned American mayhem, squeeze off a few rounds at **Iron Sights Public Indoor Shooting Range,** 618 Airport Rd. (☎721-4388. Shotguns, rifles, and handguns available. Prices vary but basic packages including ammo begin at $25. Open daily 10am-10pm.) **Mission San Luis Rey de Francia,** 4050 Mission Ave., was founded in 1798, but the only original building still standing is the church built in 1807. Follow Mission Ave. east from N. Coast Hwy. for 4 mi. or take NCTD bus #303 at Rte. 21 and Mission Ave. (☎757-3651. Museum open daily 10am-4:30pm. $4, students and seniors $3, ages 8-14 $1. Cemetery free.)

# ESCONDIDO ☎760

Escondido (pop. 125,000) lies thirty miles north of San Diego, amid rolling, semi-arid hills that blossom with wildflowers in the spring. The **San Diego North Convention and Visitors Bureau,** 360 N. Escondido Blvd., gives info on Escondido, the surrounding countryside, and the beach cities to the west. (☎745-4741, 24hr. hotline 800-848-3336. Open M-F 8:30am-5pm.) **Greyhound** (☎745-6522) stops at 700 W. Valley Pkwy. and sends seven buses per day to San Diego ($9) and 12 to LA ($13).

Off Rte. 78, budget motels and fast food chains sprout like weeds, even by Southern Californian standards. Exit at Center City Pkwy.; turn right on Mission Ave. **The Mt. Vernon ❷,** 501 W. Mission Ave., just before Washington on Center City Pkwy., offers unusually large, well-worn rooms with pool, jacuzzi, and a tennis court. (☎745-6100. Singles $40; doubles $44. $5 higher on weekends.)

A look at the free-roaming endangered species of the 2100-acre **San Diego Wild Animal Park** is an essential part of any trip to San Diego. From I-15, take the Via Rancho Pkwy. Exit (County Rte. S78) and follow the signs. While some of the exhibits are similar to any other zoo, the highlight of the park is the large enclosures where many species roam freely. African safari creatures like rhinos, giraffes, gazelles, and tigers can be found on the park plains. Watching a baby rhino teetering around will warm all hearts. The best way to see these enclosures is via the open-air **Wgasa Bush Line Railway,** a one-hour monorail safari included in park admission that travels through four created habitat areas. The park has typical shops, restaurants, and animal shows, but for adventure, try the 1 mi. Heart of Africa hike, meant to simulate a real African safari. For those willing to shell out more money, the open-air **Photo Caravan** offers up-close and personal views of many animals. (☎619-718-3050. 1¾hr. safari $99, 3½hr. safari $145. Reservations required.) Another option is falling asleep to the sounds of elephant snores at the **Roar and Snore overnight camping safari.** (☎619-718-3050. Apr.-Oct. Su and F-Sa nights $126. Includes park admission, all meals, camping equipment, and special tours and programs.) Most of the park, including the monorail, is wheelchair- accessible, but steep hills may require detours. (☎747-8702; www.wildanimalpark.org. Rail tours June-Aug. 9:30am-9pm; Sept.-May 9:30am-4pm; sit on the right if possible, unless you didn't get enough of the California chaparral on the drive in. Park open daily 9am, closing times vary with the season. $26.50, ages 3-11 $19.50. Parking $6. Discounts are often available at tourist bureaus and hotels.)

## NORTH OF ESCONDIDO

Although the Hale telescope at Palomar Mountain's **Palomar Observatory** is over 40 years old, it remains one of the world's largest and greatest astronomical instruments. The observatory is accessible via S6. Diehard science buffs will find the sparse museum fascinating. (☎742-2119. Open daily 9am-4pm. Free.)

**Cleveland National Forest** contains the observatory and several excellent campgrounds, all of which are closed in the winter. S6 passes the wooded **Fry Creek ❶** and more airy and open **Observatory campgrounds ❶,** both of which provide water, toilets, and access to hiking trails (sites $12). A left onto S7 at the mountaintop

SAN DIEGO

store will bring you to **Palomar Mountain State Park ❶.** The park offers camping, showers, hiking trails, and fishing, but swimming is not allowed. (☎800-444-PARK/7275; www.parks.ca.gov. Advance reservations necessary on summer weekend. Sites $12; hiker/biker sites $3; vehicles $2.) All of these campgrounds are above 5000 ft., so warm clothing even in summer is a necessity.

One of California's still-operating missions is west of Mt. Palomar, on Rte. 76, 6 mi. east of I-15. The **Mission San Antonio de Pala,** on the Pala Indian Reservation, was an outpost of Oceanside's Mission San Luis Rey in 1816; it has since converted thousands of Native Americans. (☎742-3317. Open Su and W-Sa 10am-4pm. $2.)

**Find** (Our Student Airfares are cheap, flexible & exclusive)
great Student Airfares everywhere
at StudentUniverse.com and **Get lost.**

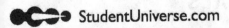 StudentUniverse.com

**Student Airfares everywhere**

# BAJA
# CALIFORNIA

Cradled by the warm, tranquil Sea of Cortés on the east and the chilly Pacific Ocean on the west, the peninsula of Baja California claims one of the most spectacular and diverse landscapes in the world. Sparse deserts surround barren mountains jutting into cloudless sky. High-altitude pine forests fill with winter snow. Unbelievably blue-green water laps at thousands of miles of white sandy beaches. Called *"el otro México"* (the other Mexico), Baja ("under" or "lower" in Spanish) California is neither here nor there, not at all California, yet nothing like mainland Mexico. A solid stream of tourists flows from the state of California across the border to surf, shop, and drink to their heart's content. To explore Baja south of Ensenada, pick up a trusty copy of ▧*Let's Go: Mexico*.

Baja is a popular vacation spot, but be prepared for rugged driving conditions—potholes in the pavement, livestock milling around on the asphalt, and a general lack of guardrails. Driving in Baja can be reasonably secure if you stay slow, never drive at night, and keep your tank full. If you need roadside assistance, the *Ángeles Verdes* (Green Angels) pass along **Mex. 1 (The Transpeninsular Highway)** twice per day. Unleaded gas may be lacking along this highway, so don't pass a **PEMEX station** without filling up. If you are driving in from the US, obtain a **vehicle permit**, which is required south of San Felipe on the Sea of Cortés side and Ensenada on the Pacific side. Those visiting Baja for longer than three days should get an US$18 tourist card and a free permit (show the vehicle's title and proof of registration) at a border station. It is a good idea to pick up additional **car insurance** (about US$9.50 per day) at a drive-through insurance store in San Ysidro (the southernmost California town, just before the Mexican border), or through AAA.

If your travels in Mexico will be limited to the border and Ensenada, you will probably not need to exchange your dollars for pesos; the vast majority of shops and restaurants near the US are happy to take greenbacks. Any travel farther south will require exchanging currency (as a rough guide, US$1 was equivalent to 10.7 Mexican pesos in Aug. 2003). **For emergency help in Baja California, dial ☎060.**

## HIGHLIGHTS OF BAJA CALIFORNIA

**CERVEZA (BEER).** The drinking age in Mexico is 18.

**THE BORDER.** The border town of Tijuana (p. 518) thrives on transition—on those who cross the border from the California side to indulge in the benefits of less stringent Mexican laws and those who await immigration into the US.

# BAJA ESSENTIALS

## FOOD- AND WATER-BORNE DISEASES

**Traveler's diarrhea**, or *turista*, is one of the less charming experiences encountered by many visitors to Mexico. Symptoms include cramps, nausea, vomiting, chills, and fever, and generally last two to three days. Scientifically speaking, *turista* is a temporary reaction to new bacteria in food ingredients. In plain speak, *turista* will blow your bowels inside out. **Impure water and poorly cooked food** are the major culprits. Never drink unbottled water (don't even brush your teeth or rinse your toothbrush with tap water) and avoid ice cubes. **Drink only purified, bottled water** *(agua embotellada)*. If you must purify your own water, bring it to a rolling boil (simmering isn't enough) for about 30min. or treat it with **iodine drops or tablets.** You may want to follow the golden rule in Mexico: don't drink the water, drink beer (did we mention that the drinking age is 18?)

If you have the common misfortune of developing *turista*, eat things like tortillas and salted crackers to keep your energy up. The most dangerous side effect of *turista* is dehydration; drink lots of water (pure this time) with ½ tsp. of sugar or honey and a pinch of salt, uncaffeinated soft drinks, and bottled juices. If you develop a high fever or your symptoms don't go away after four to five days, consult a doctor; it might be more than just *turista*.

---

**ALL THE SPANISH YOU WILL EVER NEED.**
**agua purificada; refrescos:** purified water; soft drinks
**avenida; calle; centro:** avenue; street; city center or downtown
**barato/a; caro/a, gratis:** cheap; expensive; free (the -a ending is feminine)
**borracho/a:** drunk
**Dónde está el baño?** (pronounced BAN-yo): Where is the bathroom?
**cara de cholita:** slutface
**casa de cambio:** currency exchange house
**chupacabra:** demon that sucks goat blood
**comida; desayuno; almuerzo; cena:** food; breakfast; lunch; dinner
**dinero:** money
**extranjero; gringo; turista:** foreigner; American (slang); tourist or diarrhea
**hotel; posada:** hotel; posada

---

# TELEPHONES

**CALLING MEXICO FROM HOME.** Dial the international access code of your home country, then 052 (Mexico's country code), and then the Mexico city code (see the city's **Practical Information** section).

**CALLING ABROAD FROM MEXICO.** The **LADATEL phones** that have popped up all over the country have revolutionized the way Mexico calls. To operate one, obtain a colorful **pre-paid phone card,** available at most *papelerías* (stationery stores) or *tiendas de abarrotes* (general stores)—look for the posted "De venta aquí LADATEL" signs. Cards come in 30-, 50-, and 100-peso increments. To call directly home, insert your LADATEL card and dial 00 (to get an international line), the country code of the place you are calling, the area code, and the phone number. Making direct international calls can get very expensive, so you might want to talk quickly. At 5 pesos per minute, calling the US is only somewhat pricey. Dial ☎**87 on a LADATEL phone for toll-free assistance or go online at http://www.telmex.com.mx/internos/deviaje/tladatel.htm for calling costs information.

To call from Mexico with a calling card, contact the operator for your service provider by dialing the appropriate toll-free Mexico access number: **AT&T:** ☎01 800 288 2872 (using LADATEL phones) or 001 800 462 4240; **Sprint:** ☎001 800 877 8000; and **MCI WorldPhone Direct:** ☎001 800 674 7000. If your provider does not have a Mexico access code, inquire beforehand as to the correct dialing procedures.

If you speak Spanish and can't reach the international operator, dial 07 to make a collect call to the national operator *(llamada por cobrar)*, who will connect you. Calling from hotels is usually faster, but beware of exorbitant surcharges. There can be a fee of 1-5 pesos for collect calls that are not accepted.

> **BORDER TRAFFIC.** At the world's largest border crossing, northbound lanes often have backups of more than 150 cars. To minimize the wait, cross during a weekday morning, generally the slowest time. The southbound ride tends to be smoother, but weekends can be rough in both directions. If you're crossing into Tijuana for a day or so, it's easier to leave your car in a lot on the US side and join the crowds walking across the border. You will still meet long lines returning to the US. If you're in a hurry, rent a bike in Mexico, pass through the remarkably shorter bike line, and return it once across the border. Remember that you need a **tourist card** (US$18) if you plan to travel farther south than Ensenada or San Felipe. Regardless of which way you are crossing, bring proper ID—ideally a driver's license or passport—and leave your bushels of fruit, truckloads of livestock, stashes of drugs, and armory of weapons behind.

# TIJUANA ☎ 664

In the shadow of sulfur-spewing factories and the fences of the US-Mexican border lies the most notorious specimen of border subculture: Tijuana (pop. 2 million; often referred to as "TJ"). The city's cheap booze, haggling vendors, and kitschy, unapologetic hedonism attracts 30 million US visitors each year. *Revolución*, the city's main strip, reverberates with *mariachi* bands, thumping dance beats from the packed nightclubs, and the sounds of eager tourists unloading wads of cash on everything from *jai alai* gambling to slimy strip shows. In recent years, the city's officials have made a conscious effort to clean the place up, virtually eliminating sex shops and prostitution from the town center. This is not to say Tijuana has lost its sleazy luster; TJ is one of the largest ports of entry for illegal drugs and undocumented migrants into the US. As an introduction to Mexican culture, flashy, shady TJ is about as unrepresentative and unrepentant as they come.

## ⬛ TRANSPORTATION

### INTERCITY TRANSPORTATION

**From San Ysidro:** Take the red Mexicoach bus (☎619-428-9517 in the US) from its terminal at Border Station Parking. It stops right in the middle of all the Revolución madness. (Every 20-30min., 9am-9pm, US$2.) Alternatively, just follow the signs to the *centro* on foot from the pedestrian footbridge; head for the tall slender arch at the top of Revolución (15min. walk). Either of these methods is preferable to a taxi (US$5).

**From San Diego:** Grab a trolley on the blue line and take the 25min. ride down to the border (approx. US$2.50). From there, follow the instructions for San Ysidro above.

**From Rosarito:** Head north until the intersection with Agua Caliente and turn left to reach the *centro*. From 1D, drive in on Calle 2A, which continues east to Revolución.

**Buses:** Tijuana has 2 main bus stations. **Downtown Station** is conveniently located just a block away from the top of Revolución. **Greyhound** (☎688 1979) runs to **LA** (3hr., every hr. 6am-1am, US$20). **Subrubaja** (☎688 0082) sends buses to **Ensenada** (3¾hr., every 3hr.). The **Central Camionera**, however, is right near the airport, and accessible only by overpriced taxi (US$12-15) or local bus (30min., 5½ pesos). To get from Central Camionera to Tijuana's center, leave the main exit, turn left, walk to the end of the building, and take the "Centro/Buena Vista" buses. These will let you off on Calle 3 and Constitución, 1 block west of Revolución. At Calle 1 and Constitución, you can catch the bus back to the Central. **Autotransportes de Baja California** (☎621 2424 ext. 1214) runs from the Central to **Ensenada** (1½hr., 32 per day 6am-midnight, 80-89 pesos). There is a separate **Mexicoach station** on Revolución between Calles 6 and 7 that sends buses to the **San Ysidro border crossing** (30min., every 20-30 min. 8am-9pm, US$2) and **Rosarito** (1hr., every 2hr. 9am-7pm, US$5; *colectivos*—see below—are much cheaper).

## LOCAL TRANSPORTATION

Traditional **yellow cabs** prey almost exclusively on tourists and charge absurd rates; set a price before getting in. White and orange **taxis libres** are likely to offer slightly better value. Much cheaper *colectivos* **(route taxis)** are a popular option with locals, running designated routes painted above the rear tires and on the windshield for 10-20 pesos. Most originate on or around Madero or Constitución between Calle 1 and Calle 5. These colorful station wagons go to: **Parque Morelos** (5 pesos, orange and gray); **Rosarito** (10 pesos, yellow and white); and **El Toreo** (5 pesos, red), among other destinations. **Tipping** cabdrivers is not a common practice in Mexico, but drivers will often refuse to make change. While crowded during the day, even the Zona Centro can be unsettling at night; it's advisable to take a cab if you need to cross this area. **Exercise caution when walking at night.** Officials recommend avoiding the notorious **Zona Norte,** downhill from Calle 1a, which is filled with prostitution and drugs at all times—**not a safe place for tourists to explore.**

## ✦ ❓ ORIENTATION AND PRACTICAL INFORMATION

For the vast majority of visitors, Tijuana simply *is* **Avenida Revolución,** in the middle of **Zona Centro,** the tourist hot spot. *Calles* run east-west and are named and numbered; *avenidas* run parallel to Revolución and perpendicular to the *calles.*

**Tourist Office:** (☎685 2210), in the small free-standing booth on the corner of Revolución and Calle 3. English-speaking staff offer good maps and advice. Open M-Th 10am-4pm, F-Su 10am-7pm. They also have branches inside the Mexicoach station (next to the ticket office) and at the border crossing. **Customs Office:** (☎683 1390) at the border on the Mexican side, after crossing the San Ysidro bridge. Open 24hr.

**Consulates: Canada,** Gérman Gedovius 10411-101 (☎684 0461 or 800 706 2900 for after hrs. emergency assistance), in the Zona Río. Open M-F 9am-1pm. **UK,** Salinas 1500 (☎681 8402 or 681 5320 for after-hours emergency assistance), in Col. Aviación, La Mesa. Open M-F 9am-5pm. **US,** Tapachula Sur 96 (☎622 7400 or 681 8016), in Col. Hipódromo, adjacent to the racetrack southeast of town. In an **emergency,** call the San Diego office (☎619-692-2154) and leave a message and phone number; an officer will respond. Open M-F 8am-4pm.

**Currency Exchange:** Banks along Constitución exchange money and traveler's checks at the same rates. **Banamex,** Constitución at Calle 4, has shorter lines (☎688 0021; open M-F 8:30am-4:30pm) than more central **Bital,** Revolución 129 at Calle 2. (☎688 1914. Open M-F 8am-7pm, Sa 8am-3pm.) Both have 24hr. **ATMs.** *Casas de cambio* offer better rates but may charge commission and refuse to exchange travelers' checks.

**Car Rental: @West Rent a Car,** 3045 Rosecrans St. #215, just north of downtown San Diego, rents to drivers age 18-25 and charges decent rates. (☎619-223-2343; www.atwestrentacar.com. Open daily 8am-8pm.) **Budget,** Paseo de los Héroes 77, next to the Hotel Camino Real (☎634 3303; open M-F 8am-7pm, Sa 8am-4pm), and **Hertz,** Av. Centenario (☎607 3949; open M-Sa 8am-6pm), offer similar rates.

**Police:** (☎685 6557), Constitución at Calle 8. English spoken. Specialized tourist assistance (☎688 0555).

**Red Cross:** (☎621 7787; emergency 066) Gamboa at Silvestre. Some English spoken.

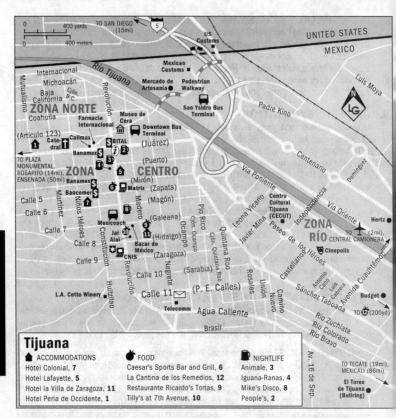

**Tijuana**

| ♠ ACCOMMODATIONS | 🍴 FOOD | 🍺 NIGHTLIFE |
|---|---|---|
| Hotel Colonial, **7** | Caesar's Sports Bar and Grill, **6** | Animale, **3** |
| Hotel Lafayette, **5** | La Cantina de los Remedios, **12** | Iguana-Ranas, **4** |
| Hotel la Villa de Zaragoza, **11** | Restaurante Ricardo's Tortas, **9** | Mike's Disco, **8** |
| Hotel Perla de Occidente, **1** | Tilly's at 7th Avenue, **10** | People's, **2** |

**Pharmacy: Farmacia Internacional** (☎685 2790), at Constitución and Calle 2.

**Hospital: Hospital General,** Centenario 10851 (☎684 0237 or 684 0922), in the Zona Río. **IMSS** (☎629 6342), Agua Caliente and Francisco Zarabia. Both have 24hr. emergency service.

**Internet Access: Matrix Internet Place,** Revolución and Calle 5 (☎688 2273; open 8am-1:30am; 10 pesos per 30min., 15 pesos per hr.) and **CNIS** at Revolución between Calles 8 and 9 (☎688 3840; open 24hr.; 15 pesos per hr.)

**Post Office:** (☎684 7950), on Negrete at Calle 11 (Elías Calles). Open M-F 8am-5pm, Sa 9am-1pm. **Postal Code:** 22000.

# 🏠 ACCOMMODATIONS

As a general rule, hotels in Tijuana become less reputable the farther north you go. Avoid any in the area downhill from Calle 1 (the Zona Norte). Rooms at some motels may not fit the standards of cleanliness expected by US travelers.

**Hotel Colonial,** Calle 6a 1812 (☎688 1620), between Constitución and Niños Héroes, in a quieter, residential neighborhood away from Revolución. Large, very clean, comfortable rooms have A/C and private baths. Singles and doubles 260 pesos. ❷

**Hotel Perla de Occidente,** Mutualismo 758 (☎685 1358), between Calles 1a and 2a, 4 blocks from Revolución. Private baths. Singles 150 pesos; doubles 300 pesos. ❶

**Hotel Lafayette,** Revolución 325 (☎685 3940 or 685 3339), between Calles 3a and 4a. Quiet considering its location in the middle of Revolución's chaos. Large rooms have color TV, phone, fans, and private baths. Singles 220 pesos; doubles 290 pesos. ❸

**Hotel La Villa de Zaragoza,** Madero 1120 (☎685 1832), between Calles 7a and 8a. Semi-affordable luxury for those too squeamish for Tijuana's truly budget offerings. Spacious rooms come with TV, phone, king-sized beds, and many clean towels. Laundry, room service, and 24hr. security to keep you and your car very safe. Singles from 393 pesos; doubles 474 pesos (excluding tax). Credit card reservations accepted. ❸

## 🍴 FOOD

Like with most things in Tijuana, loud, in-your-face promoters try to herd tourists into the overpriced restaurants lining **Revolución.** For ultra-cheap food, **taco stands** ❶ all over the *centro* sell several tacos or a *torta* for 10 pesos. The supermarket **Calimax** is at Calle 2 at Constitución. (☎633 7988. Open 6am-midnight.)

**🏴 La Cantina de los Remedios,** Diego Rivera 19 (☎634 3065), in the Zona Río. Local memorabilia, competing *mariachis,* a huge range of *tequilas,* and a big crowd. Authentic Mexican cuisine extending well beyond the usual options (from 75 pesos). Open M-Th 1pm-midnight, F-Sa 1pm-2am, Su 1pm-10pm. ❷

**Restaurante Ricardo's Tortas** (☎685 4031), at Madero and Calle 7. Popular among both locals and *gringos;* serves the best *tortas* in town (25-40 pesos). Try the *super especial,* with ham, *carne asada,* cheese, avocado, tomato, and mayo. Open 24hr. ❶

**Tilly's 7th Avenue,** on Revolución and Calle 7. Airy atmosphere and uncommonly good Mexican dishes (US$7.50). Tecate beer on tap. Happy Hour 4-7pm (beer US$1). ❷

**Caesar's Sports Bar and Grill,** Revolución between Calles 4 and 5. This place claims to be the home of the Caesar salad. Have the genuine article lovingly made for you at your table (US$6.50)—it might just be the best you ever taste. Open 9am-late. ❸

## 📷 SIGHTS

Many of the most entertaining sights in town are, of course, right on Revolución. While the so-called "attractions" of the main tourist drag have a tendency to mind-numbing predictability, such as zebra-painted donkeys and gaudily-dressed costumes, Tijuana's cultural assets and parks counter its one-dimensional image. Pay them a visit and you'll go home with a less impressive collection of straw hats but also with a more balanced sense of the city's present-day life.

**🏴 CENTRO CULTURAL TIJUANA (CECUT).** The most visually striking feature of Paseo de los Héroes is probably the huge sphere and plaza of Tijuana's cultural center (☎687 9633). The main attraction for visitors is the superb **Museo de las Californias,** which traces the history of the peninsula from its earliest inhabitants through the Spanish conquest to the Mexican-American war and the 20th century. It's attractively presented and (unlike the city outside) makes for the best possible introduction to the peninsula's cultural heritage. CECUT also hosts science and art exhibitions and showcases Tijuana's cultural vitality with dance performances, concerts, and opera in the **Sala de Espectáculos.** Panoramic films are shown on a vast 180-degree screen every hour in the afternoon in the spherical building **Cine Omnimax.** There's also the charming **Jardín Caracol,** a garden with reproductions of pre-Columbian sculptures. *(Museum open daily 10am-7pm. 20 pesos, students and children 12 pesos. Cine Omnimax tickets 40 pesos, students and children 20 pesos.)*

**MUSEO DE CERA.** Eighty-six life-size figures await you in this wax museum, one of three in Mexico. Memorable combinations (and there are several) include President Vicente Fox and Fidel Castro towering over Mother Theresa and Mahatma Gandhi. *(Calle 1 and Madero. ☎688 2478. Open daily 10am-7pm. 15 pesos.)*

**PARQUE MORELOS.** This sprawling state-run park offers pleasant walks, rides, an open-air theater, and a small zoo. *(Blvd. de los Insurgentes 26000. Take an orange and grey communal cab (5 pesos) on Calle 4 and Madero. ☎625 2470. Open Su and Tu-Sa 9am-5pm. Adults 5 pesos, children 2 pesos; parking 10 pesos.)*

**L.A. CETTO WINERY.** Established in 1926 by Italian immigrants, the family-run winery maintains its vineyards in the Valle de Guadalupe, northeast of Ensenada. Underwhelming tours are offered, preceded by a video presentation on the vineyards' resources, traditions, and exports; the real draw is the chance to sample and purchase the products. *(Cañón Johnson 2108. Follow Constitución away from the party district to Calle 10a and turn right; the winery is on the left. ☎685 3031. Tours M-F 10am-6:30pm, Sa 10am-5pm; avoid coming during lunch hour around 1-2pm. US$2 includes tasting.)*

# 🎭 ENTERTAINMENT

## SPORTS

If you're in town on the right Sunday, you can watch the graceful and savage battle of *toreador* versus bull in one of Tijuana's two bullrings. **El Toreo de Tijuana,** southeast of town just off of Agua Caliente, hosts the first round of fights (Catch a bus on Calle 2a west of Revolución. Alternate Su, May-July). The seaside **Plaza Monumental** hosts the second round (Aug.-Oct.). Mexicoach sends buses (US$4 roundtrip) to Plaza Monumental on fight days. Alternatively, take the blue-and-white local buses (5 pesos) on Calle 3a at Constitución all the way down Calle 2a. Tickets to both rings go on sale at the gate (☎685 1510 or 685 1219) or at the Mexicoach office (☎685 1470) on Revolución between Calles 6A and 7a the Wednesday before a fight (tickets 95-400 pesos).

## 🛍 SHOPPING

As soon as tourists cross the footbridge from the US, they're bombarded with vendors peddling everything a *gringo* could possibly desire. The gaudy shopping scene continues most of the way up Revolución, as far as the intersection with Calle 7a. Other spots for assorted tourist-oriented wares are the **Mercado de Artesanía,** on Calle 1a under the pedestrian footbridge and the vendors on **Plaza Santa Cecilia,** near the arches on Revolución, and the **Bazar de México** on Revolución at Calle 7a. **Bargaining** is a must, as quoted prices can be over twice the bottom line.

## 🍸 NIGHTLIFE

In the 1920s, Prohibition drove US citizens south of the border to revel in the forbidden nectars of cacti, grapes, and hops. The flow of North Americans thirsty for booze remains unquenched, with many taking advantage of Mexico's drinking age (18) to circumvent US prohibitions. Stroll down Revolución after dusk and you'll be bombarded with thumping music, neon lights, and abrasive club promoters hawking "two-for-one" margaritas at the not-so-low price of US$5. Those who prefer laid-back nights of bar chat are in the wrong place. Clubs catering to gays and lesbians cluster in the southern part of the *centro* around Calle 6a and 7a or down the hill to the north of Calle 1a.

   **Animale,** Revolución at Calle 4a. The biggest, glitziest, and loudest hedonistic haven of them all. 2 drinks for US$5. Watch out—the similarly named Animale Continental next door is an altogether more "adult" experience. Open daily 10am-4am.

**Iguanas-Ranas** (☎685 1422), Revolución at Calle 3a. A sublimely wacky, tacky world of life-sized plaster clowns, balloons, and kitschy US paraphernalia. Pound beers (US$3) in an authentic yellow school bus high above Revolución. Slogans and beer jokes are painted over the walls. Packed on weekends. Open M-Th 10am-2am, F-Su 10am-5am.

**People's** (☎688 2706), Revolución and Calle 2a. Fluorescent constellations and crudely painted sportsmen decorate the purple arches of the open-air terrace, where revelers guzzle 10 beers for US$15. Open M-Th 10am-2am, F-Su 10am-4am.

**Mike's Disco** (☎685 3534), Revolución south of Calle 6a. A wild bunch, mostly men, gets down on the dance floor, cheering on the drag queens who perform every weekend. Straight by day, but gay Su-Tu, Th-Sa 10pm-5am.

# ROSARITO ☎661

Baja's youngest city, Rosarito (pop. 120,000), has transformed recently from elite hideaway to all-out *gringo*-magnet where the two most widely accepted languages are English and the American dollar. Just 15 mi. from the border, Rosarito remains a popular Hollywood filming site while expanding at breakneck pace. You probably won't find the "real Baja" here, but if weekend hordes of SUV-driving visitors don't bother you, the placid beaches and throbbing clubs are yours to enjoy.

**☰ TRANSPORTATION.** To get to Rosarito from **Tijuana,** grab a yellow-and-white *taxi de ruta* (30min., 9 pesos) from Madero near Calle 3. In Rosarito, taxis congregate in front of the Rosarito Beach Hotel and can be flagged down anywhere along northbound Juárez to take you back to TJ or elsewhere in the city. **Mexicoach** runs to **Tijuana** (US$5) from the Rosarito Beach Hotel and also serves **Foxploration** (see p. 524) on request. Just behind where the taxis wait is the **ABC bus terminal** (☎613 1151). Buses run to **Ensenada** (1¼hr., 4 per day, 53 pesos); you can also ask the station to call Tijuana to ask their next hourly Ensenada service to pick you up.

**▓▞ ORIENTATION AND PRACTICAL INFORMATION. Mex. 1** runs straight through Rosarito, becoming the city's main drag, **Juárez,** before continuing south. Most of the town's businesses are concentrated at the southern end of Juárez, between the PEMEX at the corner of Avenida Cipres and the Rosarito Beach Hotel. Police recommend staying in this area of town, and warn that the area around Col. Constitución and Co. Lucio Blanco is particularly unsafe.

The **SECTUR tourist office** recently relocated, inconveniently, to the very southern end of town. (☎612 0200. Open M-F 8am-8pm, Sa-Su 9am-1pm). **Banamex,** on Juárez at Ortiz Rubio, exchanges cash and checks and has a 24hr. **ATM,** but most get by with dollars. (☎612 1556. Open M-F 9am-4pm, Sa 10am-2pm.) In an **emergency,** call ☎060, or contact the **police** (☎613 0612 or 613 3411), at Juárez and Acacias next to the post office, or **Red Cross** (☎613 1120, emergency 066), on Juárez at Ortiz Rubio, around the corner from the police; some English spoken at both. Other services include: **laundry** at **Lavamática,** on Juárez near Acacias (open daily 9am-9pm; 40 pesos for wash and dry); **Internet access** at **El Tunel.com,** Juárez 208 near Cárdenas, in the yellow building with the arcade (☎612 5061; 20 pesos per hr.; open M-F 9am-10pm, Sa-Su 10am-10pm); the pharmacy **Farmacia Roma,** set back from Juárez at Roble (☎612 3500; open 24hr); and the **post office** on Juárez, near Acacias (☎612 1355; open M-F 8am-3pm, Sa 8am-noon). **Postal Code:** 22710.

**▐▟ ACCOMMODATIONS AND FOOD.** Most budget hotels in Rosarito are cramped or situated on the outskirts of town. Prices soar during spring break, holidays, and summer weekends. One cheery "budget" option is **Hotel el Portal de Rosarito ❷**, at Juárez and Via de las Olas, with TVs, A/C, large rooms and parking spaces. (☎612 0050. Singles US$27; doubles US$33.) **Hotel Palmas Quintero ❷** is a well-kept secret, tucked away on Privada Guadalupe Victoria 26. To find it, drive up Cárdenas until it turns into a dirt road, continue for one block, and turn left; the hotel is ahead and to the right. Large rooms have cable TV and clean baths. (☎612 1359. Su-Th singles US$20; doubles US$40. F-Sa US$25/US$50.)

Although Rosarito's culinary scene caters mostly to tourists who consider US$10 cheap, careful searching yields quality budget eateries. ▓**La Flor de Micho-acán ❷**, Juárez 291, at the north end of town, is a pig lover's paradise that serves huge *órdenes de carnitas* (60 pesos) with either "solid" or "mixed" pork (mixed includes tongues, stomachs, and all sorts of good stuff). Football players or those with lots of friends can order by the kilogram. (☎612 1858. 240 pesos per kg. Open Su-Tu, Th-Sa 9am-10pm. Also a branch on Juárez at Encinas.) Enjoy the best tacos in town at **Macho Taco ❶**, Juárez 60, across from Hotel Festival Plaza. The special combo, two tacos, rice, beans, and a soda (US$3), can't be beat. (Attached to the nightclub of the same name. ☎613 0630. Open daily 10am-2am.)

▓▓ **SIGHTS AND ENTERTAINMENT.** Rosarito entices with fancy resorts, beautiful shores, and wild nightlife. Spanning the coast two blocks west of Juárez, **Rosarito Beach** has soft sand and gently rolling surf. Rosarito's long relationship with Hollywood (many stars vacationed here in years past) continues in the form of the **Foxploration** tourist park, 1 mi. south of Rosarito. Fox's blockbuster *Titanic* was filmed here, and the park houses props from the movie, a showcase of special effects, and a observation deck to observe current film shoots, but no ship. (☎614 9444; www.foxploration.com. Open Su-M and Th-Sa 9am-5pm.)

Rosarito's nightlife revolves around the mega-clubs packed with drunken revel-ers on the streets behind the Hotel Festival Plaza. **Iggy's** is a behemoth of a night-spot with its own pool, foam party, ATVs on the beach, and even bungee jumps from an onsite crane. The three bars offer all-you-can-drink cocktails. (☎612 0537. Cover approx. US$10. Open 8pm-3am, later on weekends.) **Papas and Beer** is a mul-tilevel party palace which can accommodate up to 7,000 guests, plus a mechanical bull. (☎612 0444. Drinks US$1.50-7. Open Su-Th 11am-3am, F-Sa to 4am.) **Tequila Safari,** on Juárez between Roble and Encino, is a good place for cheap drinks, with Happy Hour from 5-7pm (all drinks half price), and buckets of 6 beers available for US$10 all day. (☎612 0202. M-Th noon-10pm, F-Su noon-2am.)

# ENSENADA
☎ **646**

Nestled in the beautiful Bahía de Todos Santos (Bay of All Saints), Ensenada (pop. 370,000) still retains some of the salty atmosphere of a fishing harbor, but the big-gest catch these days is likely to be the tourist crowd visiting from cruise ships.

▐ **TRANSPORTATION.** Ensenada is 50 mi. south of Tijuana on **Mex. 1D** (a *cuota* or toll road; cars 21 pesos). The last 20min. stretch of the 1½hr. drive is especially breathtaking. The less scenic, poorly maintained **Mex. 1** parallels the *cuota* inland. Drive only during the day, since there are no streetlights. Follow signs to down-town Ensenada or "Centro"; these lead you to **Costero,** which runs by the harbor, one block south of Mateos. Local *urbanos* (☎178 2594) leave from Juárez at Calle 6 and from Calle 2 at Macheros (5½ pesos for most destinations in the city). **Buses** from TJ arrive at the **Central de Autobuses,** at Calle 11 and Riveroll. To get to the *centro*, turn right as you come out of the station, walk south 10 blocks, and you'll be at Calle Mateos (also called Primera). **Autotransportes de Baja California** (☎178 6680) runs buses to **Tijuana** (1½hr., every 30min. 5am-11pm, 90 pesos). **Transportes Brisas** (☎178 3888), Calle 4 771, near Macheros, runs buses to small towns nearby.

**BAJA CALIFORNIA**

**⊞🔁 ORIENTATION AND PRACTICAL INFORMATION. Mateos,** the main tourist drag, is also called **Primera** (Calle 1). *Calles*, including **Juárez** (Calle 5), run east-west, parallel to Mateos. Alphabetized *avenidas* run north-south, starting with Alvarado and moving east. Street signs are nonexistent more than one block from Mateos. After sundown, **exercise caution** near the shore and in the region bounded by Miramar, Macheros, Mateos, and Calle 4.

The English-speaking staff at the **tourist office,** Costero 540, at Azueta Friendly, doles out maps and pamphlets. (☎172 3022; fax 172 3081. Open M-F 8am-8pm, Sa-Su 9am-1pm). The closest bank to the main tourist area is **Santander Serfin,** at Ruíz and Calle 3. (☎174 0009. Open M-F 9am-5pm, Sa 10am-3pm.) The **police,** Calle 9 at Espinoza, speak some English (☎176 4343). The **Policía Federal Preventativa,** Mateos 1360 near the post office, may help with information on roads in the surrounding countryside (☎176 1311.) Other services include: **Hospital General,** on M-1 km 111 (☎176 7800); **San Martín** pharmacy at Ruíz and Calle 8 (☎178 3530; open 24hr); **Internet access** at **Café Internet MaxiComm,** on Mateos between Miramar and Macheros, upstairs from the souvenir stalls (☎175 7011; 15 pesos per 30min., 20 pesos per hr.; open M-F 9am-9pm, Sa-Su 9am-8pm); and the **post office,** on Mateos at Espinoza. (☎176 1088. Open M-F 8am-6pm, Sa 9am-1pm.) **Postal Code:** 22800.

**🔃🔆 ACCOMMODATIONS AND FOOD.** In Ensenada, budget motels cluster at the eastern end of Mateos. **Motel América ❷,** at Mateos at Espinoza has huge rooms with overhead fans, baths, and cable TV; some have kitchens. (☎176 1333. Singles US$24; doubles US$32-36.) **Motel Caribe ❷,** Mateos 627/8 is in the lively center of town. The main building's rooms are spacious and carpeted, with cable TV, fans, and baths, while those in the building across the street are more modest and cheaper. (☎178 3481. Singles US$15-20; doubles US$25. Weekends US$5 higher.) One block off Mateos, on Alvarado at Calle 2, **Hotel Hacienda ❷** rents large rooms with phone, cable TV, and tiny showers. (☎178 2344. Singles Su-Th 180 pesos, F-Sa 210 pesos; doubles 300/340 pesos; jacuzzi suite 350/430 pesos.)

At the waterfront fish market, **loncherías ❶** sells savory fish tacos for under US$1 apiece. **Calimax** sells groceries at Gastelum and Calle 3. Open daily 7am-11pm. **Mariscos Playa Azul ❶,** on Rivveroll between Mateos and Calle 2. serves seafood cheap as water. (☎174 0622. Entrees 50-60 pesos. Open daily 10am-10pm.) Tasty breakfasts are cooked up in a homey setting at **La Holandesa ❶,** at Mateos and Rayón. (☎177 1965. Shrimp omelettes 50 pesos. Open Su 8am-5pm, M-F 7am-10pm, Sa 8am-10pm. **Los Farroles Villa Mexicana ❶,** at Riveroll and Calle 2, has quick, yummy *tortas* (25 pesos) at its outdoor counter. (Open daily 7am-4pm.)

**🔳🔂 SIGHTS AND ENTERTAINMENT.** A cosmopolitan dream by North Baja standards, Ensenada has enough museums and other cultural attractions to fill a few pleasant days. The lovely Moorish buildings and perfectly maintained gardens of the huge **Riviera del Pacífico,** on Costero one block from the tourist office, once housed a world-famous casino but today welcomes kids and adults alike into its elegant interior. Stop for a drink at the original **Andaluz Bar** or the **coffee shop.** The museum also houses temporary exhibitions in the **Galería de Arte de la Ciudad.** (☎176 4310; www.ensenadahoy.com/riviera. Open daily 8am-8pm. Free. Bar open Su-Tu and Th-F 4pm-midnight, W and Sa 9am-midnight. Coffee shop open daily 9am-9pm. Galeria open M-F 8am-7pm, Sa 10am-4pm.) The permanent display **Museo de Historia,** in the Riviera, charts the history of the region in a cavern-shaped gallery. (☎177 0594. Open M-F 9am-

BAJA CALIFORNIA

5pm, Sa-Su 10am-5pm. 7 pesos, children under 12 5 pesos.) Originally built in 1886 as a barracks, the **Museo Histórico Regional,** on Gastelum between Uribe and Mateos, houses an eclectic range of exhibits on the Spanish conquest and the history and lifestyle of indigenous tribes. (☎178 3692. Open daily 10am-5pm. 22 pesos.) The highlight of the geology and natural history exhibits at **Museo de Ciéncias,** Obregón 1463, at Calle 14 near Mateos, is the Noah's Ark boat outside that has photographs and info on Baja's endangered species. (☎178 7192. Open M-F 9am-5pm, Sa 10am-3pm. 16 pesos, children 14 pesos.)

The mild, dry climate of Baja's northern coast is perfect for growing grapes, and the **Bodegas de Santo Tomás,** Miramar 666, at Calle 7, has been distilling those grapes into wine since 1888. Tours conclude with a tasting with breads and cheeses. (☎178 3333. Tours daily 10, 11am, noon, 1, and 3pm. Tours US$5 with tasting of 5 wines, US$10 with a wider selection.) At the top of Calle 2, the **Chapultepec Hills** offer a stunning view of the bay and the city.

No trip to Ensenada would be complete without a pilgrimage to █**Hussong's Cantina,** Ruiz 113, possibly the most famous watering hole in all of Mexico, in business since 1892. (☎178 3210. Beer 20 pesos, margaritas 7 pesos. Open daily 10am-1am.) Cross the street to the modern, rowdy bar/dance scene at **Papas and Beer** with, finally, no *mariachi.* (☎174 0145. 40-peso margaritas. Open M-W noon-midnight, Th-Su noon-3am. Live music F-Sa, DJ Su-Th. Cover F-Sa US$5.)

🢒 **DAYTRIPS FROM ENSENADA.** A car, ideally with 4WD, is needed to reach many of the sights near Ensenada. Tijuana and San Diego are the best bets for rental (see **Tijuana: Car Rental,** p. 519). Ensenada's shoreline is devoted to shipping rather than sunbathing, so daytrippers stream southwest along the Punta Banda Peninsula to a series of beautiful beaches and ocean views in **Bahía de Todos Santos.** On the northern side of the bay, **Playa Estero** is packed with volleyball courts, banana boats, and *norteamericanos.* Sea lions come ashore during low tide. Access the bay through the Estero Beach Resort. (Take a right at the "Estero Beach" sign on Mex. 1 heading south. Free parking in the first hotel lot. Or catch a bus marked "Aeropuerto," "Zorrillo," "Maneadero," or "Chapultepec" from Pl. Cívica.) 5 mi. south of Ensenada, **Playa El Faro** is similarly crowded but has slightly better sand and allows **beach camping ❶.** Signs warn swimmers about strong offshore currents. Horse rentals are often available at nearby **Playa Santa María.** (☎177 4620. Camp space, parking, and bathroom privileges US$7 per car. Full RV hookup US$12.) Undeterred by the rocky beach, surfers flock to **Playa San Miguel,** to the north. (Campsite ☎174 7948. Drive west on Calle 10, which joins Mex 1D; continue to the toll gate, make a U-turn, then turn right onto the cobbled road. 24hr. parking. **Camping ❶** facilities include hookup and hot baths for US$10. All-day surfing until 8pm US$6. Prices drop with stays of several days.)

**Punta Banda,** the peninsula at the southern end of the bay, boasts beautiful solitary trails and more secluded beaches than the north. Heading south on **Mex.1,** take a right on Mex. 23 at "La Bufadora.") **Baja Beach's** clean, soft sands are buffeted by small waves that provide some of the best swimming in the area. A number of remote hiking trails start from **Cerro de la Punta,** under the radio tower on the road to La Bufadora near the end of the peninsula. The ascent to the top provides sweeping views of the surrounding area. You can also descend to secluded rocky coves along the shoreline. Most of the trails are unmarked footpaths, but be sure to stick to them; trailblazing damages the flora. **La Bufadora,** the Pacific coast's largest geyser, is one of Ensenada's biggest attractions. Once you've reached the end of the curving road and peninsula, there's no missing the trinket stalls and churro stands on the way to the blow hole. (Parking US$1-2.)

Situated 1650m above sea level, the thick mountain pine forest of the **Parque Nacional Constitución de 1857** is unlike the rest of Baja. A long desert drive winds its way high up into an enchanting landscape of deep greens, excellent trails, and isolated ranches. The focal point of the park is **Laguna Hanson,** a small lake with small campsites along its perimeter (US$7 for a tent spot). Bring warm clothes and a good sleeping bag—temperatures drop dramatically at night.

BAJA CALIFORNIA

# THE DESERT

California's desert can be one of the most beautiful places in the world; it can also be the loneliest. Roads cut through endless expanses of barren earth and landscapes that seem untouched by human existence. Only a few hours from the complicated hustle of LA lies the wide open space of the Mojave. Exploration turns up elusive treasures: diverse flora and fauna, staggering topographical variation, and scattered relics of the American frontier. Through the year, the desert transforms from a pleasantly warm refuge to an unbearable wasteland, and back again.

## ⚐ ORIENTATION

California's desert divides roughly into the Low and High Deserts, names that indicate differences in both altitude and latitude. The **Sonoran,** or **Low Desert** (see p. 566), occupies southeastern California from the Mexican border north to Needles and west to Anza-Borrego. The **Mojave** and **Colorado** comprise the **High Desert** (see p. 529), which averages elevations of 2000 ft. and spans the southern central part of the state, bounded by the Sonoran Desert to the south, San Bernardino to the west, the Sierra Nevada to the north, and Death Valley to the east. Four major east-west highways cross the desert. In the Low Desert, **I-8** hugs the California-Mexico border, while **I-10** passes Joshua Tree and Palm Springs. Cutting through the heart of the Mojave is **I-15.** From Barstow, the Mojave's central pit stop, I-15 continues on to Las Vegas, while **I-40** runs east through Needles to Arizona's deep red desert.

All of the destinations in this chapter are on or near the major highways listed above. The High Desert follows destinations along I-15; the Low Desert follows destinations along I-8 and I-10; **Route 66** follows the old highway along I-40 through the Mojave Desert, continuing into Arizona as far as the Grand Canyon.

## 🛈 DESERT SURVIVAL

Here, **water** is life. The body loses at least a gallon of liquid per day in the desert (two gallons during strenuous activity), so *keep drinking.* Consuming huge quantities of water to quench your thirst after physical exertion is not as effective as drinking water before and during activity, even if you're just driving. Whatever you're doing, tote **two gallons of water per person per day.** Designate at least one container as an emergency supply. In the car, keep backup containers in a cooler. Drink the water you have. Avoid alcohol and caffeine, which cause dehydration. Keep your strength up for long stays with a high-quality beverage that contains potassium compounds and glucose, such as **ERG** (an industrial-strength Gatorade).

Most people need a few days to adjust to the heat, especially before difficult hikes. Sunglasses with 100% UV protection, sunscreen, and a wide-brim hat are essential **sun protection,** but proper clothing is the most effective shield. Light-colored clothing helps reflect the sun's rays. Although it may be uncomfortable to wear a sweaty shirt, it prevents dehydration more effectively than going shirtless.

Heat is not the desert's only climatic extreme. At high elevations, temperatures during winter nights can drop well below freezing (a sweater is often necessary even in summer). Fall and spring **flash floods** can cause water to rush down from rain-drenched higher elevations and wreak biblical devastation upon lands below, turning dry gulches into raging rivers. Don't walk in washes you can't scramble out of, beware of thunderstorms on the horizon, and never camp in washes or gullies. For more advice, consult the excellent *Desert Survival Handbook* (Primer; $8).

**DRIVING IN THE DESERT.** Conditions in the desert are as grueling on cars as they are on bodies; only recently serviced cars in good condition can take the heat. Bring at least five gallons of radiator water, extra coolant, a spare tire, proper tools for minor repairs, and a few quarts of oil (car manuals recommend appropriate oil weights for varying temperatures). Avoid running out of gas by keeping your tank more than half-full; gas can be hard to find in the desert. Beware of gravel roads that turn to sand. A board and shovel may also be useful for stuck cars.

Although towns are sometimes sparse, major roads usually have enough traffic to ensure that breakdowns are noticed. Still, isolated areas of the parks pose a threat, especially in summer when few tourists visit. **Stay with your vehicle if it breaks down;** it is easier to spot than a person and provides crucial shade. Turn off **air-conditioning** immediately if the car's temperature gauge starts to climb. Air from open windows should be sufficiently comfortable at highway speeds. If your car overheats, pull off the road and turn the heater on full force. If radiator fluid is steaming or bubbling, turn off the car for 30min. If not, run the car in neutral at about 1500 RPM for a few minutes, allowing the coolant to circulate. Never pour water over the engine or try to lift a hot hood. **Desert water bags** ($5-10) are available at hardware or auto stores. When strapped onto the front of the car and filled with water, these prevent overheating by speeding up evaporation. Pick up a manual with more specific desert driving tactics if you plan to be traveling extensively in the Mojave. The above-mentioned *Desert Survival Handbook* is a good choice.

# THE HIGH DESERT

The High Desert is the picture of desolation. Atop a plateau, the desert unfolds at heights around 5000 ft. The Mojave conceals unlikely treasures for those patient and hardy enough to explore it. Genuine summer attractions are rare, but temperate winters allow one to trudge across drifting dunes and creep through ghost towns. At Joshua Tree, some of the best bouldering in the US awaits climbers.

## JOSHUA TREE NATIONAL PARK ☎760

When devout Mormon pioneers crossed this faith-testing desert in the 19th century, they named the enigmatic tree they encountered after the Biblical prophet Joshua. The tree's crooked limbs resembled the Hebrew general, and, with arms upraised, seemed to beckon these Latter-Day pioneers to the Promised Land. Even today, Joshua Tree National Park inspires reverent awe in those who happen upon it. Its piles of wind-sculpted boulders, guarded by the legions of eerie Joshua Trees, continue to evoke the devastation of the walls of Jericho. The park's five oases appear lushly Edenic against the desolate desert backdrop.

Now climbers, campers, and daytrippers from Southern California add to the mosaic. The boulder formations strewn across the desert badlands have nearly limitless potential. "Josh," as outdoor enthusiasts call it, has become a world-renowned mecca for both casual and elite climbers. History buffs will appreciate the vestiges of human occupation: ancient rock petroglyphs, 19th-century dams built to catch the meager rainfall for livestock, and gold mine ruins. But the most attractive aspect of Joshua Tree is its remoteness and freedom from the commercial mayhem of many national parks. Its natural beauty is interrupted only by a few paved roads and signs, with vast tracts left almost untouched since the days when miners coaxed precious metals out of the scarred terrain.

At the north entrance to the park lies Twentynine Palms, settled after World War I by veterans looking for a hot, dry climate to soothe their battle-weary bodies. Today the town also hosts the world's largest US Marine Corps base, as well as murals depicting people and events from the town's past.

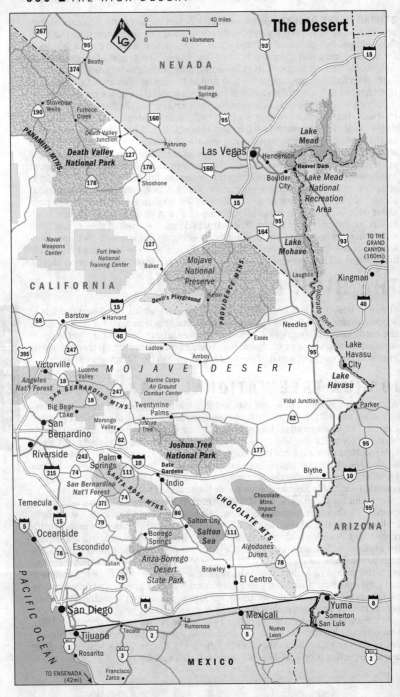

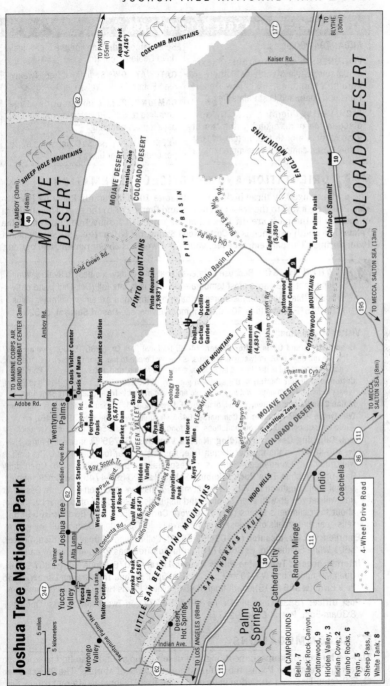

# Joshua Tree National Park

TO PARKER (55mi)

Aqua Peak (4,416')

COXCOMB MOUNTAINS

177

TO BLYTHE (30mi)

Kaiser Rd.

62

COLORADO DESERT

TO AMBOY (30mi)

SHEEP HOLE MOUNTAINS

40

TO AMBOY (48mi)

MOJAVE DESERT

MOJAVE DESERT Transition Zone

COLORADO DESERT

EAGLE MOUNTAINS

10

Chiriaco Summit

Gold Crown Rd.

PINTO BASIN

Black Eagle Mine Rd.

Old Dale Rd.

Eagle Mtn. (5,350')

Lost Palms Oasis

TO MARINE CORPS AIR GROUND COMBAT CENTER (3mi)

Amboy Rd.

PINTO MOUNTAINS

Pinto Mountain (3,983')

Pinto Basin Rd.

9

Cottonwood Visitor Center

195

TO MECCA, SALTON SEA (13mi)

Adobe Rd.

Oasis Visitor Center
Oasis of Mara
North Entrance Station

Cholla Cactus Garden

Ocotillo Patch

COTTONWOOD MOUNTAINS

Pinkham Canyon Rd.

Monument Mtn. (4,834')

HEXIE MOUNTAINS

Thermal Cyn.

MOJAVE DESERT Transition Zone

COLORADO DESERT

TO MECCA, SALTON SEA (8mi)

Twentynine Palms

Indian Cove Rd.

Canyon Rd.
Fortynine Palms Oasis

7   8

Queen Mtn. (5,677')
Barker Dam
Skull Rock
6

Geology Tour Road

PLEASANT VALLEY

Pinto Basin Rd.

Berdoo Canyon

Dillon Rd.

INDIO HILLS

111

TO MECCA, SALTON SEA

Entrance Station

Boy Scout Tr.

2

3

West Entrance Station
Wonderland of Rocks
Quail Mtn. (5,814')

La Contenta Rd.

Hidden Valley

Lost Horse Mine

Ryan Mtn.

5

Keys View

Inspiration Peak

California Riding and Hiking Trail

LITTLE SAN BERNARDINO MOUNTAINS

SAN ANDREAS FAULT

86

Indio

Coachella

111

Joshua Tree

62

Palmer Ave.

Alta Loma Dr.

Eureka Peak (5,516')

1

Yucca Trail
Yucca Valley Visitor Center
Joshua Lane

247

Twentynine Palms Hwy.

Morongo Valley

TO LOS ANGELES (98mi)

Desert Hot Springs

Indian Ave.

62

Rancho Mirage

111

10

Cathedral City

Palm Springs

0   5 miles
0   5 kilometers

▲ CAMPGROUNDS
Belle, 7
Black Rock Canyon, 1
Cottonwood, 9
Hidden Valley, 3
Indian Cove, 2
Jumbo Rocks, 6
Ryan, 5
Sheep Pass, 4
White Tank, 8

-- 4-Wheel Drive Road

## AT A GLANCE: JOSHUA TREE NATIONAL PARK

**AREA:** 794,000 acres.

**FEATURES:** Pinto Mountains, Hexie Mountains, Eagle Mountains, Little Bernardino Mountains, High/Low Desert Transition Zone, and Lost Palms Oasis.

**HIGHLIGHTS:** Climbing virtually anyplace in the park, hiking to the top of Ryan Mountain or to the bottom of Lost Palms Oasis, camping at the more remote

Belle Campground, driving the four-wheel-drive Geology Tour Rd.

**GATEWAY TOWNS:** Joshua Tree, Twentynine Palms, Yucca Valley.

**CAMPING:** Park campgrounds range from free to $35. Registration required for backcountry camping.

**FEES:** Weekly pass $10 per vehicle, $5 per pedestrian or bike.

## ORIENTATION AND PRACTICAL INFORMATION

The park is ringed by three highways: **Interstate 10** to the south, **Route 62 (Twentynine Palms Highway)** to the west and north, and **Route 177** to the east. The northern entrances to the park are off Rte. 62 at the towns of **Joshua Tree** and **Twentynine Palms.** The south entrance is at **Cottonwood Spring,** off I-10 at Rte. 195, southeast of Palm Springs. The **park entrance fee,** valid for a week, is $5 per person, $10 per car.

**WHEN TO GO.** Because of intense heat and aridity, it's best to avoid visiting June-Sept. The park's most temperate weather is in late fall (Oct.-Dec.) and early spring (Mar.-Apr.); temperatures in other months span extremes (summer highs 95-115°F, winter lows 30-40°). For more advice, see **Desert Survival,** p. 528.

**Visitor Information:**

**Headquarters and Oasis Visitor Center,** 74485 National Park Dr. (☎367-5500; www.nps.gov/jotr), ¼ mi. off Rte. 62 in Twentynine Palms, is the best place to familiarize yourself with the park. Friendly rangers, plus displays, guidebooks, maps, restrooms, and water. Open daily 8am-5pm.

**Cottonwood Visitor Center,** at the southern gateway of the park, 7 mi. north of I-10 and 25 mi. east of Indio. Information, water, and picnic areas are available here. Open daily 8am-4pm.

**Indian Cove Ranger Station,** 7295 Indian Cove Rd. (☎362-4367). Open Oct.-May daily 8am-4pm.

**Twentynine Palms Chamber of Commerce,** 6455 Mesquite Ave., Ste. A (☎367-3445), provides info on transportation, accommodations, and food. Open M-F 9am-5pm; may close for lunch.

**Rock Climbing Gear and Guiding: Nomad Ventures,** 61795 Twentynine Palms Hwy. (☎366-4684), in the town of Joshua Tree, has lots of gear for sale or rent. The staff is well qualified; experienced climbers will especially appreciate their help. Open daily 9am-6pm. **Joshua Tree Rock Climbing School** (☎800-890-4745; www.rockclimbingschool.com), south on Hillview off Twentynine Palms Hwy. and then right onto Desert Air Rd., will set you up with gear, guiding, and instruction, regardless of experience. Inquire about their climber's cabins ($125). **Coyote Corner,** 6535 Park Blvd. (☎366-9683), sells gear that smells of incense. Showers available. Open daily 9am-6pm.

**Emergency: 24hr. dispatch** (☎909-383-5651). Call collect. **Hi-Desert Medical Center,** 6601 White Feather Rd. (☎366-3711), in Joshua Tree, has 24hr. emergency care.

**Internet Access: Twentynine Palms Branch Library,** 6078 Adobe Rd. (☎367-9519). Open M-T noon-8pm, W-F 10am-6pm, Sa 7am-5pm. **Joshua Tree Branch Library,** 6465 Park Blvd. (☎366-8615), north from the Twentynine Palms Hwy. Open M-F 10am-6pm.

**Post Office:** 73839 Gorgonio Dr. (☎800-275-8777), in Twentynine Palms. Open M-F 8:30am-5pm. **Postal Code:** 92277.

## ACCOMMODATIONS

Those who cannot stomach the thought of desert campgrounds can find inexpensive motels in Twentynine Palms, the self-proclaimed "Oasis of Murals." The **29 Palms Inn ❹,** 73950 Inn Dr., is an attraction in its own right. Its 19 distinctly different rooms face the Mara Oasis, which has supported life for over 20,000 years. More recently, the life here has been of the celebrity genus, with guests like Michelle Pfeiffer, Nicholas Cage, and Robert Plant, who composed his post-Zeppelin hit "29 Palms" here. Check out the garden and enjoy its produce in the restaurant. (☎367-3505; www.29palmsinn.com. Reservations required Feb.-Apr. Doubles June-Sept. Su-Th $50-75, F-Sa $75-115; Oct.-May $10-20 extra. Cottages for 4-8 people also available.) Clean, reliable **Motel 6 ❸**, 72562 Twentynine Palms Hwy., has a pool and laundry. (☎367-2833; www.motel6.com. Singles $40-44; doubles $46-50. Each additional adult $3. Make reservations online to save $3-4.) While creating the album *Joshua Tree* in 1987, U2 stayed in one of the 10 units here at **Harmony Motel ❹**, 71161 Twentynine Palms Hwy. Rooms were recently refurbished and have A/C and access to a communal kitchen. (☎367-3351; www.harmonymotel.com. Singles and doubles $60-70; negotiable in the summer low season.)

# CAMPING

Camping is an enjoyable and inexpensive way to experience the beauty of the park, except in the scorching heat of summer. But even then, when the sun goes down, the temperatures may drop to comfortable levels. Pre-noon arrivals are the best way to guarantee a site, since most campgrounds in the park operate on a first-come, first-camp basis and do not accept reservations (campgrounds that require separate fees do take reservations). Spring weekends and holidays are the busiest times. Reservations can be made for group sites at Cottonwood, Sheep Pass, Indian Cove, and Black Rock Canyon, via the Internet at www.nps.gov/jotr. Well-prepared and experienced campers can register for a backcountry permit at the Visitors Center or at self-service backcountry boards located throughout the park. Regulations require camping at least 1 mi. from roads and 500 ft. from trails; rangers can provide maps of designated wilderness areas. All established campsites have tables, firepits, and pit toilets, but no hookups. Only campgrounds that take reservations offer water or flush toilets; visitors who plan a longer stay should pack their own supplies. (14-day max. stay Oct.-May; 30-day limit per year.)

**Indian Cove,** 3200 ft., on the north edge of Wonderland of Rocks. Enter at the north entrance on Indian Cove Rd. off Twentynine Palms Hwy. Popular spot for rock climbers. 101 sites, including 13 for groups. Sites $10; group sites $20-35. ❶

**Jumbo Rocks,** 4400 ft., near Skull Rock Trail on the eastern edge of Queen Valley. Take Quail Springs Rd. 15 mi. south of Visitors Center. The highest and coolest campground. Front spots have shade and protection. Wheelchair accessible. 125 sites. Free. ❶

**White Tank,** 3800 ft. Few people, but watch for coyotes that may try to keep you company as you gaze at the Pinto Mountains. Cowboys built up White Tank as a reliable watering hole for cattle. 15 sites amid huge boulder towers. Free. ❶

**Hidden Valley,** 4200 ft., in the center of Queen Valley off Quail Springs Rd. Secluded alcoves are perfect for pitching tents and enormous shade-providing boulders serve as perches for viewing the sun at dawn and dusk. Its proximity to numerous popular climbing boulders makes it a rock climber's heaven. The 39 sites fill up quickly. Free. ❶

**Sheep Pass,** 4500 ft., on the trail to Ryan Mountain. Huge boulders and lots of Joshua trees make this site fairly cool and secluded. Only 6 group spots, which can be reserved up to 3 months in advance. $20-35. ❷

**Belle,** 3800 ft., is an ideal place to stare at the starry heavens. Hold out for one of the sites on the road's second loop. 18 sites tucked in the crevices of big boulders. Free. ❶

**Ryan,** 4300 ft., has fewer rocks, less privacy, and less shade. The 3 mi. round-trip trail ascends to Ryan Mtn., which served as headquarters and water storage for the Lost Horse mine. The sunrise is spectacular from Key's View (see p. 534). 31 sites. Free. ❶

**Black Rock Canyon,** 4000 ft., at the end of Joshua Ln. off Rte. 62 near Yucca Valley. Good for those who haven't camped before; close to Yucca Valley, water, and a ranger station. A great place to spot animals, with various hiking trails nearby. Flush toilets. Wheelchair accessible. 100 sites. Reservations accepted. Sites $10. ❶

Cottonwood, 3000 ft., is the easiest place to see the Colorado Desert and its famous spring **wildflowers.** Flush toilets and running water. Wheelchair accessible. 62 sites, 30 in summer; 3 are for groups. Sites $10; group sites for 10-70 people $25. ❶

## ☐ FOOD

Although there are no food facilities within the park, Twentynine Palms offers both groceries and grub. If you are willing to cook, the **Stater Brothers** supermarket, 71727 Twentynine Palms Hwy., has a good selection and saves you a bundle. (☎367-6535. Open Su-Th 6am-10pm, F-Sa 6am-11pm.)

**Wonder Garden Cafe,** 73511 Twentynine Palms Hwy. (☎367-2429). Locals recommend this spot—an organic juice pub, fresh sandwich deli, and smoothie joint in one. Adjoins a natural foods market. Open M-F 6:30am-6pm, Sa 8am-5pm, Su 8am-4pm. ❷

**Rocky's New York Style Pizza,** 73737 Twentynine Palms Hwy. (☎367-9525). No surprises here. Satisfy your cravings. Pizzas and subs $7-15. Open M-Sa 11am-10pm. ❸

**Edchada's,** 73502 Twentynine Palms Hwy. (☎367-2131). Good for margaritas or meals, its airy layout offers respite from heat. Lunch $5-9, dinner $9-11. Open 11am-9pm. ❷

**Andrea's Charbroiled Burgers,** 73780 Twentynine Palms Hwy. (☎367-2008). Wise old men and others in the know dine here for hearty eggs, pancakes, and burgers of varying types ($2-7). Open daily 6am-9pm. ❶

**Desert Ranch Market,** 73544 Twentynine Palms Hwy. (☎367-7216). Deli and bakery offer potato salads, cold cuts, and sandwiches. Open daily 7am-10pm. ❷

**The Beatnik Cafe,** 61597 Twentynine Palms Hwy. (☎366-2090). Serves hot coffee, but soothe your heat-addled brain with beer or ice cream as you search the Internet for heat stroke treatments. Check door for live music schedule. **Internet** access $2 per 15min., $3.50 per 30min., $6 per hr. Open Su-Th 7am-midnight, F-Sa 7am-2am. ❶

## ☐☒ SIGHTS AND OUTDOOR ACTIVITIES

Over 80% of Joshua Tree is designated wilderness, safeguarding it against development and thus paved roads, toilets, and campfires. The park offers truly remote territory for backcountry desert hiking and camping. Hikers eager to reap the rewards of this primitive territory should pack plenty of water and keep alert for flash floods and changing weather conditions. Be sensitive to the extreme fragility of the desert and refrain from venturing off established trails. Do not enter abandoned mine shafts, as they are unstable and often filled with poisonous gases.

The tenacious **wildflowers** that struggle into colorful bloom each spring (mid-Mar. to mid-May) attract thousands of visitors. To avoid the social stigma accompanying floral ignorance, get updates via the **Wildflower Hotline** (☎367-5500); the menu at this number is also useful for weather and tour information. The trees and reeds of the oases host golden eagles and bighorn sheep. Kangaroo rats, lizards, and stinkbugs scamper about by day, while wily coyotes, bobcats, and the occasional rattlesnake stalk their prey (including your unleashed pet) after dusk.

**BY CAR.** The craggy mountains and boulders of Joshua Tree acquire fresh poignancy at sunrise and sunset. A self-paced **driving tour** is an easy way to explore the park and linger until **sunset.** All roads are well marked, and signs labeled "Exhibit Ahead" point the way to unique floral and geological formations. One of these tours, a 34 mi. stretch winding through the park from Twentynine Palms to the town of Joshua Tree, provides access to the park's most outstanding sights and hikes. An especially spectacular leg of the road is **Keys View** (5185 ft.), 6 mi. off the park road and just west of Ryan Campground. On a clear day, you can see to Palm Springs and the Salton Sea. The sunrise from here is renowned. The longer drive through the park from Twentynine Palms to I-10 traverses both High and Low Desert landscapes, and the Pinto Basin with its impressive views. The **Cholla Cactus Garden,** a grove of spiny succulents, lies just off the road.

Those with **four-wheel-drive** vehicles have even more options, including the 18 mi. **Geology Tour Road,** which climbs through striking rock formations and ends in the Little San Bernardino Mountains. Though dry years leave the roads sandy and difficult to navigate for cars without high clearance and 4WD, in the spring and fall of wetter years, even **bikers** can enjoy these roads, especially the unpaved and relatively unpopulated 4WD-only roads through **Pinkham Canyon** and past the **Black Eagle Mines,** both beginning at the Cottonwood Visitors Center. Bikers should check with rangers for info regarding the opening of bike trails.

**BY FOOT.** Despite the plethora of driving routes, hiking is perhaps the best way to experience Joshua Tree. The desert often appears monotonous through a car window, and it is only by walking slowly that one begins to appreciate the subtler beauties of the park. On foot, visitors can tread through sand, scramble over boulders, eye the occasional historical artifact, and walk among the park's namesakes.

Anticipate slow progress even on short walks; the oppressive heat and the scarcity of shade can force even the hardiest of hikers to feel the strain. Drinking a liter of water an hour is not unreasonable on desert hikes. Although the 1 mi. **Barker Dam Trail,** next to Hidden Valley, is often packed with tourists, its petroglyphs (though sadly vandalized) and eerie tranquility make it a worthwhile stroll, especially at twilight. **Lost Horse Mine/Mountain** (4-8¼ mi. round-trip), near Key's View, rests at the end of a 2 mi. trail, commemorating the region's gold prospecting days with rusted machinery and abandoned mine shafts. If you don't want to return yet, keep following the trail up to the saddle of Lost Horse Mountain and beyond; the trail loops around back to the trailhead. From the top of **Ryan Mountain** (3 mi. round-trip), the boulders in the encircling valley share an uncanny resemblance to enormous beasts of burden toiling toward a distant destination. Bring lots of water for the strenuous, unshaded climb to the summit. Or head to the northern edge of the park and hike the 1½ mi. moderately strenuous climb to the pristine **49 Palms Oasis.** The Visitors Center has info on the park's other hikes, which range from a 15min. stroll to the **Oasis of Mara** to a three-day trek along the 35 mi. **California Riding and Hiking Trail.** The ranger-led **Desert Queen Ranch Walking Tour** covers the restored ranch of resourceful homesteader Bill Keys ($5; call for reservations).

**ROCK CLIMBING.** The crack-split granite of Joshua provides some of the best rock climbing and bouldering on the planet for experts and novices alike. The world-renowned boulders at **Wonderland of Rocks** and **Hidden Valley** are always swarming with hard-bodied climbers, making Joshua Tree the most climbed area in America. Adventurous novices will find thrills at the **Skull Rock Interpretive Walk,** which runs between Jumbo Rocks and Skull Rock. The walk offers not only info on local plants and animals, but also exciting yet non-technical scrambles to the tops of monstrous boulders. The area's potential for climbing is limitless; see the listings in **Practical Information,** p. 532, for guides and instructors.

# DEATH VALLEY NATIONAL PARK ☎ 760

The devil owns a lot of real estate in Death Valley. Not only does he grow crops (at Devil's Cornfield) and hit the links (at Devil's Golf Course), but the park is also home to Hell's Gate itself. The area's extreme heat and surreal landscape support just about anyone's idea of the Inferno. Visitors can stare into the abyss from Dante's View, one of several panoramic points approaching 6000 ft. in elevation, or gaze wistfully into the distant, cool heavens from Badwater, the lowest point (282 ft. below sea level) in the western hemisphere. Winter temperatures dip well below freezing in the mountains and summer readings in the Valley average 115°F. The second-highest temperature ever recorded in the world (134°F in shade) was measured at the Valley's Furnace Creek Ranch on July 10, 1913.

Fortunately, the fatal threshold of 130°F is rarely crossed, and the region sustains a motley crew of rugged plants and animals. Many threatened and endangered species, including the desert tortoise and the desert bighorn sheep, inhabit

Death Valley. If you see something unusual, go to a visitors center and fill out a wildlife sighting card. Though much of the land seems desolate and barren, over 500 different species of plants grow in Death Valley.

Human inhabitants have a long history inside the Valley as well. The Shoshone Indians lived in the lower elevations during winters and retreated into the cooler peaks during summers. In the Gold Rush era, travelers came here searching for a shortcut across the Sierras. They were unsuccessful, and skedaddled as soon as they could find a way out, but not before lives were lost. Looking back at their scene of misery, someone said, "Goodbye, Death Valley!," and the name stuck. Later, miners looking for gold found borax instead and boom towns grew around the mines. Once the borax was depleted, the prospectors took off and left behind a medley of skeletal towns like Skidoo and Rhoylite. These ghost towns now lend Death Valley a deserted, post-apocalyptic atmosphere that suits the stark landscape. The desolate beauty gave rise to the tourism industry; in 1933 the US government set aside over 3 million acres as a national park. The park entrance fee ($10 per vehicle, $5 for non-vehicles) is collected at Furnace Creek Visitors Center, Grapevine, Stovepipe Wells, and the ranger station in Beatty.

---

## AT A GLANCE

**AREA:** 3.3 million acres.

**CLIMATE:** Very arid and dry.

**FEATURES:** Badwater, Mosaic Canyons, Telescope Peak, Scotty's Castle.

**HIGHLIGHTS:** Take Dante's View, drive to the bottom of Ubehebe Crater, photograph the Death Valley Sand Dunes.

**GATEWAYS:** Beatty, NV (p. 543), Lone Pine (p. 298), Shoshone (p. 544).

**CAMPING:** 30-day max. stay, 14-day max. stay in Furnace Creek. Backcountry camping is free.

**FEES & RESERVATIONS:** $10 entrance fee per vehicle, $5 for non-vehicles.

---

## ■ ORIENTATION

Death Valley is on the eastern edge of the state, next to Nevada and south of Inyo National Forest. Rte. 190 cuts east-west across the Valley. Many sites fall along Rte. 178, which runs north-south through the lower part of the park. Most of Death Valley is below sea level. Wildflowers, snow-capped peaks, and some of the hottest, driest land in the world can all be found in Death Valley. It rains very infrequently in the park, but when it does, traffic is often impeded because the hard, compacted ground is prone to flash floods. In this harsh and overheated corner of California, even the topography runs into the extremes.

## ■ TRANSPORTATION

**BY CAR.** Cars are virtually the only way to get to and around Death Valley (3½hr. from Las Vegas; 5hr. from LA; 7hr. from Tahoe City; 10½hr. from San Francisco). If you are sharing gas costs, renting a car can be cheaper and more flexible than any bus tour. The nearest agencies are in Las Vegas (p. 555), Barstow, and Bishop.

Conditions in Death Valley are notoriously hard on cars. **Radiator water** (*not* for drinking) is available at critical points on Rte. 178 and 190 and Nevada Rte. 374. There are only four **gas stations** in the park (see Gas Stations, p. 538), and though prices are as much as 50¢ more per gallon than outside the Valley, be sure to keep the tank at least half full at all times. Check ahead with park rangers for road closings and do not drive on wet and slippery backcountry roads.

Although **four-wheel-drive vehicles** and high-clearance trucks can be driven on narrow roads that lead to some of Death Valley's most spectacular scenery, these roads are intended for drivers with backcountry experience, and are dangerous no matter what you're driving. Always travel with 2 gallons of water per person per day. In the case of a breakdown, stay in the shade of your vehicle. (For more tips, see **Driving in the Desert**, p. 529.)

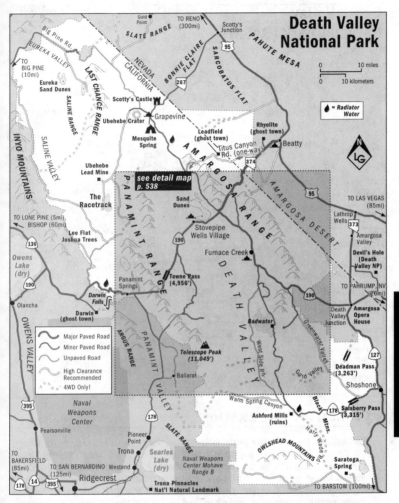

Of the seven **park entrances,** most visitors choose Rte. 190 from the east. Although this is the steepest entrance, the road is well-maintained and the visitors center is relatively close. Since most of the major sights adjoin the north-south road, though, the day-tripper can see more of the park by entering from the southeast (Rte. 178 W from Rte. 127 at Shoshone) or the north (direct to Scotty's Castle via Nevada Rte. 267). Unskilled mountain drivers in passenger cars should not attempt to enter on the smaller Titus Canyon or Emigrant Canyon Dr.

**BY OTHER FORMS OF TRANSPORTATION.** No regularly scheduled public transportation runs in the Valley. **Guaranteed Tours,** at the World Trade Center on Desert Inn Rd. between Swensen and Maryland Pkwy. in Las Vegas, runs bus tours from Las Vegas to Death Valley. (☎702-795-7177. Open for reservations daily 6am-10:45pm. 9½hr. tours depart Tu, Th, Sa 8am. $130. Includes lunch.) Those who **hitchhike** walk through the Valley of the Shadow of Death. You shouldn't.

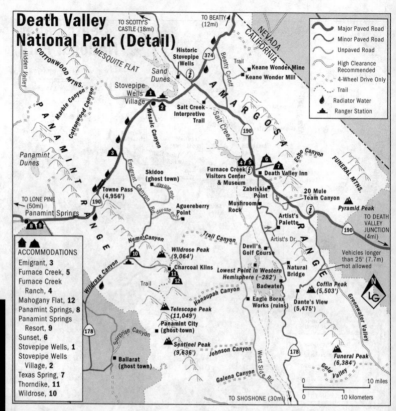

**Death Valley National Park (Detail)**

ACCOMMODATIONS
Emigrant, **3**
Furnace Creek, **5**
Furnace Creek
 Ranch, **4**
Mahogany Flat, **12**
Panamint Springs, **8**
Panamint Springs
 Resort, **9**
Sunset, **6**
Stovepipe Wells, **1**
Stovepipe Wells
 Village, **2**
Texas Spring, **7**
Thorndike, **11**
Wildrose, **10**

THE DESERT

## 🛈 PRACTICAL INFORMATION

**Gas Stations:** Fill up outside Death Valley at Lone Pine, Olancha, Shoshone, or Beatty, NV. Once in Death Valley, pay 15-50¢ more per gallon to maintain a high gas level. Don't play macho with the fuel gauge; fill up often. For gas in the Valley: Furnace Creek Visitors Center (open 7am-7pm), Stovepipe Wells Village (open 7am-9pm), Panamint Springs (open 24hr.), or Scotty's Castle (open 9am-5:30pm). **AAA towing service, minor repairs, propane gas,** and **diesel fuel** available at the Furnace Creek Chevron.

**Furnace Creek Visitors Center** (☎ 786-3244; www.nps.gov/deva), on Rte. 190 in the Valley's east-central section. For info, write: Superintendent, Death Valley National Park, Death Valley, CA 92328. Guides and hiking maps ($4-8), schedules of activities, and weather forecasts. Park entrance fee can be paid here. Open daily 8am-6pm.

**Contact Stations:** Weather reports, small book selection, and park info at each station. Emergency help provided. **Grapevine** (☎ 786-2313), at Rte. 190 and 267 near Scotty's Castle; **Stovepipe Wells** (☎ 786-2342), on Rte. 190; **Shoshone** (☎ 832-4308), at Rte. 127 and 178 outside the Valley's southeast border; **Beatty, NV** (☎ 702-553-2200), on Nevada Rte. 374. All are technically open daily 8am-5pm but are staffed sporadically.

**Hiking Information:** The private website **www.deathvalley.com** has general information on Death Valley, as well as message boards and detailed hiking resources.

**Laundromat:** (☎ 786-2345) On Roadrunner Ave. at Furnace Creek Ranch. Wash and dry each $1. Open 24hr.

**Showers: Stovepipe Wells Village** (☎786-2387). Non-guests $2. Open daily 8am-midnight. **Furnace Creek Ranch** (☎786-2345) also $2. Open daily 7am-11pm.

**24hr. Ranger Dispatch and Police:** ☎911 or 786-2330.

**Post Office:** Furnace Creek Ranch (☎786-2223). Open Oct. to mid-May M-F 8:30am-5pm; mid-May to Sept. M, W, F 8:30am-3pm, Tu and Th 8:30am-5pm. **Postal Code:** 92328.

**WHEN TO GO.** Although the average high in July is 115°F and the nighttime low 88°F, summer visits can be enjoyable with wise planning. The Furnace Creek Visitors Center distributes the free pamphlet *Hot Weather Hints.*

Some summer days are simply too hot to hike, even with abundant water. Severe heat exhaustion strikes even the fittest; don't overestimate your tolerance. (See **Desert Survival,** p. 528.) You can drive through and admire the beauty of the Valley in July and August, but to enjoy the hiking and camping options, visit between November and April. Winter is the coolest time (temperatures average 39-65°F in the Valley, with freezing temperatures and snow in the mountains) and also the wettest, with infrequent but violent rainstorms that can flood canyons and obliterate roads, trails, and ill-placed tract housing. Call ahead to find out which areas, if any, are washed out before exploring the park. Desert wildflowers bloom everywhere in March and April, but the season is accompanied by tempestuous winds that whip sand and dust into a blinding frenzy for hours or even days. Over holidays and three-day weekends, congested trails and campsites, traffic jams, hour-long lines for gas plague the area.

## ACCOMMODATIONS & FOOD

In Death Valley, affordable beds and inexpensive meals can be as elusive as the desert bighorn sheep. Motel rooms in surrounding towns are cheaper than those in Death Valley, but are over an hour away from top sights. Never assume that rooms will be available, but your chances (and the prices) will be better in the summer. In the winter, camping with a stock of groceries saves money and driving time, but camping in the summer, especially at lower elevations, can be uncomfortable, to say the least. (For more affordable accommodations outside the Valley, see **Life After Death Valley,** p. 543.) For groceries, **Furnace Creek Ranch Store** is well-stocked but expensive. (☎786-2381. Open daily 7am-9pm.) **Stovepipe Wells Village Store** is smaller and also expensive. (☎786-2578. **ATM** inside. Open daily 7am-9pm.) Both stores sell charcoal, firewood, and ice.

**Stovepipe Wells Village** (☎786-2387), 30 mi. northwest of Furnace Creek Visitors Center on Rte. 190, is at sea level, though nothing seems more remote than the ocean. When it's too hot to camp, the village offers comfortable rooms and a mineral water swimming pool. The rooms lack TVs and phones, but who cares—they're well air-conditioned. The **dining room** ❸ offers plenty of food at stiff prices (breakfast buffet 7-10am, $8; dinner buffet 6-9pm, $17). Rooms for up to 2 people $50-92; each additional person $11. RV sites available. Full hookups $22. ❸

**Panamint Springs Resort** (☎775-482-7680; www.deathvalley.com), 23 mi. east of the park's western border on Rte. 190, is remote but comfortable at a higher elevation than other lodging options. The complex includes 18 rooms, RV hookups, campsites, a restaurant and bar, and gas. None of the rooms include TV or phones, but a pay phone is available for public use. The only other tie to civilization here is the overhead roar of naval fighters jets on maneuvers from China Lake Naval Weapons Station. Doubles from $65; RV sites $10-25; campsites $12. ❹

**Furnace Creek Ranch** (☎786-2345; www.furnacecreekresort.com), in Furnace Creek. A central location (a cafe, bar, restaurant, laundromat, and grocery store are all in the same complex) makes this place supremely convenient, though it is more pricey than other options. Singles and doubles from $85 in the summer and $105 in the winter. ❺

THE DESERT

## ▨ CAMPING

The National Park Service maintains nine campgrounds in Death Valley, all of which can provide an inexpensive and comfortable way of seeing the park as long as time of year is taken into consideration. Some of the hottest sites are closed during the summer (Sunset, Texas Spring, and Stovepipe Wells) and Thorndike and Mahogany Flat are closed due to snow and ice in the winter. Pay attention to elevation: the higher up you are, the more comfortable your visit will be when the temperature climbs into the triple digits. Unfortunately, the higher campsites tend to be further from the park's main sights. The Visitors Center (see **Practical Information,** p. 538) keeps records about site availability; be prepared to battle for a space if you come during peak periods (see **When to Visit,** p. 536). All campsites have toilets, but none have showers. All provide water except for Thorndike and Mahogany Flat, and the Visitors Center has unlimited free water (as warm as bath water), but never depend heavily upon any source of water except what you carry with you. Collecting wood is forbidden, so pack your own firewood. Since fires are prohibited outside of firepits, a camping stove may prove extremely useful. Roadside camping is not permitted, but **backcountry camping** is free and legal, provided you check in at the Visitors Center and pitch tents at least 2 mi. from your car and any road and a quarter-mile from any backcountry water source. All sites limit stays to 30 days except Furnace Creek, which has a 14-day limit.

**Furnace Creek** (☎ 800-365-2267), 196 ft. below sea level, north of the Visitors Center. Furnace Creek is particularly uncomfortable in summer, even though many of the 136 sites are shaded. Fills up the first in winter, especially with RVs. Near Furnace Creek Ranch's facilities ($2 shower access; laundry). 14-day limit. Reservations Oct.-Apr. Beginning on the fifth of each month, reservations can be made five months in advance. Sites $16 in winter; $10 in summer. ❶

**Sunset,** 196 ft. below sea level, and **Texas Springs,** at sea level, in the hills above the Furnace Creek Ranch Complex. These two sites are the best place for tents near Furnace Creek activities. Over 1000 sites available, some with shade. For wind protection, stick close to the base of the hills. Generators prohibited. Water, some firepits, and some tables. Flush toilets and dump station. Open Oct.-Apr. Sites $10-12. ❶

**Stovepipe Wells,** at sea level, near the airstrip, 4WD trails, and sand dunes. Reminiscent of a drive-in movie lot. Tents compete with RVs for 190 gravel sites. Spots near the trees offer better protection from sandstorms. Hotel and general store nearby. A few tables and fireplaces. Easy to confuse it with the trailer park. Open Oct.-Apr. Sites $10. ❶

**Mesquite Spring,** 1800 ft., near Scotty's Castle, 2 mi. south of Grapevine Ranger Station. Located in a small valley among dry brush, some of the 30 gravel sites offer shade and protection from wind. Listen for the howls and hoots of coyote and owls. Picnic tables, firepits, water, and flush toilets. Sites $10. ❶

**Emigrant,** 2100 ft., off Rte. 190, 9 mi. west of Stovepipe Wells Village across from the ranger station, on the way down from Towne Pass through Panamint Range. This is a tent-only site. Gorgeous view of Stovepipe Wells and the Valley's sand dunes, though sites are located directly next to Rte. 190. The 10 sites can be relatively comfortable even in the summer. Flush toilets and water. No fires. Free. ❶

**Wildrose,** 4100 ft., on the road to the Charcoal Kilns in Wildrose Canyon, at the end of Emigrant Canyon Rd. An old summer residence of the Shoshone Indians, this 23-site campground is nestled between two hillsides and is a comfortable summer option that is well-protected from the sandstorms. Convenient base for trips to Skidoo, Aguereberry Point, and Telescope Peak. Water, firepits and pit toilets. 30 sites. Free. ❶

## ▨ SIGHTS & OUTDOOR ACTIVITIES

Plan your approach to Death Valley (see **Transportation,** p. 536, for a discussion of the various entrances). If exploring the Valley in one day, adopt a north-south or south-north route. You'll be able to see a lot of the park without backtracking. If you're going for a few days, get your bearings first at the Furnace Creek Visitors Center on Rte. 190 (which connects east-west). Camera-toters should keep in mind that the best photo opportunities are at sunrise and sunset.

**TOURS.** Rangers can provide the distances and times of recommended hikes. Ranger-led programs are generally unavailable in summer, but a number of guided hikes may take place when the rangers feel like arranging them. Astronomy buffs should speak to one of the rangers, since they often set up telescopes at Zabriskie Point and offer freelance stargazing commentary during meteor showers.

**DANTE'S VIEW.** From this 5475 ft. summit, one can truly appreciate the astonishing and primeval landscape of the Valley's floor. A palette of light hues washes over a 100 mi. stretch. Temperatures at the summit are around 20 degrees cooler than in the Valley and the area is perfect for a breakfast picnic when the rising sun fills the valley with golden light. *(From the Visitors Center, drive 14 mi. east along Rte. 190. Turn right at the Dante's View turn-off. The 13 mi. climb is especially steep at the top.)*

**ZABRISKIE POINT.** There is a reason Zabriskie Point crawls with shutterbugs, both tourists and professional photographers: it provides beautiful views of Death Valley's corrugated badlands, especially when the first or last rays of the sun soften the colors. For an intimate view of the Valley, take the short detour along **20-Mule-Team Rd.** The well-maintained dirt road is named for the gigantic mule trains that used to haul borax 130 mi. south to the rail depot at Mojave. The view of the dry lakebeds and undulating yellow rock formations is particularly stunning late in the day. Before the sunset ends, scamper 2 mi. down Gower Gulch to see the glittering cliffs of **Golden Canyon.** *(3 mi. south of Furnace Creek by car. Take the turn-off from Rte. 190, 1 mi. east of the museum.)*

**BADWATER.** A briny pool four times saltier than the ocean, this body of water is huge in the winter, but withers into a salt-crusted pond by summer. The surrounding flat is the lowest point (282 ft. below sea level) in the Western Hemisphere. The pools shelter extremely threatened Badwater snails, many of which are crushed by oblivious waders. The boardwalk provides a closer look at the strange orange floor, but getting in the water is prohibited. *(18 mi. south of the Visitors Center.)*

**DEVIL'S GOLF COURSE.** Lucifer himself probably couldn't stay below 100 strokes on this "golf course," actually a vast expanse of gnarled salt pillars formed by cyclical flooding and evaporation. This is Death Valley at its most surreal; the jagged crystalline deposits, some quite delicate and beautiful, stretch as far as the eye can see. In the summer you can occasionally hear tinkling sounds as hollow structures expand and shatter. *(15 mi. south of the Visitors Center.)*

**ARTIST'S DRIVE.** This one-way loop contorts its way through brightly colored rock formations. The loop's early ochres and burnt siennas give way at **Artist's Palette** to sea green, lemon yellow, periwinkle blue, and salmon pink mineral deposits in the hillside. The scene is most dramatic in the late afternoon, when the setting sun causes rapid color changes in the deposits. The dizzying and intense 9 mi. drive turns back on itself again and again, ending up on the main road only 4 mi. north of the drive's entrance. *(On Rte. 178, 10 mi. south of the Visitors Center.)*

**DEATH VALLEY'S SAND DUNES.** Two miles from Stovepipe Wells, these large dunes made of extremely fine quartz sand may seem out of place in the Valley, but make for a great day hike that feels good between the toes. But be warned that perceived distances can be misleading; peaks that appear close may really be a 2hr. arduous climb. If you want to try your hand at making like Ansel Adams and snapping some memorable pictures, ask at the Visitors Center for the handout on photographing in the setting or rising sun. *(22 mi. north of the Visitors Center.)*

**MOSAIC CANYON.** A half-mile-long corridor of eroded marble walls, this site stands out as a true natural wonder. A simple and relatively flat 2 mi. trail leads from the parking lot around the canyon to some awesome vistas. Occasional big-

## ROM BADWATER TO WORSE

In 1977, Al Arnold inaugurated one of the world's most painful endurance races when he ran from Badwater, the lowest point in the western hemisphere, to the top of Mt. Whitney, the highest peak in the contiguous US. It took him 84 hours and he shed 17 pounds. Now this brutal run is the Badwater Ultramarathon.

Each year, in Death Valley's blazing July heat, 70-80 runners embark on this grueling 135-mile run to halfway up Mt. Whitney. There's no prize money; there's no relief. But there are scorching temperatures that reach 130°F, 13,000 feet in cumulative elevation change, and 4700 feet of joint-rattling descents. IVs are prohibited and there are no official aid stations. Members of runners' support crews have passed out from the heat as they sat in their cars. To the Associated Press, two-time finisher Greg Minter reported hallucinating: "I saw a dinosaur around mile 108." Runners get a belt buckle if they finish.

Pam Reed, a 42-year-old mother from Arizona, has won the past two years, finishing in just under 28 hours. She never ate or slept, sustaining herself on an all-liquid diet, including eight Red Bull energy drinks. Her support crew of four people in two vans raced to spray her down with water every quarter-mile.

"People I meet there don't brag about it, they just do it," Al Arnold, now 75, told the *Contra-Costa Times*. He addresses the runners every year. When he's done, he shouts "BANG!" at 6am sharp, and they're off.

horn sheep sightings are a bonus. *(Take the turn-off from Rte. 190, 1 mi. west of Stovepipe Wells, to the 2½ mi. alluvial fan, accessible by foot, horse, or car.)*

**EMIGRANT CANYON ROAD.** This winding road leads from the Emigrant Campground to Wildrose Canyon Dr. In between, there is a turn-off for the 4WD skedaddle to the ruins of **Skidoo,** a ghost town 5700 ft. up in the Panamint Range. Skidoo was the backdrop for the only full-length movie ever shot in Death Valley (Erich von Stroheim's *Greed*, 1923). A few miles down Emigrant Canyon Rd. is the turn-off for the dirt road to **Aguereberry Point** (may require 4WD), known for its fine sunset views. A left turn at Wildrose Canyon Dr. followed by a 10 mi. drive (last 2 mi. unpaved gravel) brings you to the 10 beehive-shaped furnaces known as the **Charcoal Kilns,** huge ovens built in 1876 that once fired 45 cords of wood at a time to process silver and lead ore. It boggles the mind to imagine these ovens operating full-blast in Death Valley, in a time before air-conditioning existed

**TELESCOPE PEAK.** This trail (7 mi. one-way) through the **Panamint Mountains** leads to the summit of the park's highest peak (11,049 ft.). The strenuous hike begins at Mahogany Flat campground and winds 3000 ft. up past charcoal kilns and bristlecone pines, providing unique views of Badwater and Mt. Whitney. It helps to buy topographical maps at a ranger station. The trek becomes a technical mountain climb in winter, requiring axes and crampons, but is usually snow-free by June. Let a ranger know when you'll be climbing and when you'll return.

**TITUS CANYON ROAD.** This 27 mi. one-way road off Rte. 374 winds through rugged and colorful mountains and passes Indian petroglyphs and the Leadfield ghost town. A high-clearance vehicle is needed to drive through the canyon. Those without such vehicles can hike in via either end. *(The entrance to the canyon is off Rte. 374, 21 mi. east of the junction with Rte. 190.)*

**SCOTTY'S CASTLE.** Remarkably out of place in the desert, this castle's imaginative exterior rises from the sands, complete with minaret and Arabian-style colored tile. The saga of the Castle's construction began with the friendship between Chicago insurance millionaire Albert Johnson and infamous local con-man Walter Scott (a.k.a. "Death Valley Scotty"). Scott had conned wealthy Easterners (including Johnson) into investing in his non-existent gold mine. After Scott and Johnson became friends and then partners in crime, Johnson built this ridiculous vacation home and told people it was built on the gold fortune. The museum and "living" tour guides provide more details of the bizarre story. *(From Rte. 190, look for sign near mile marker 93 and take road junction to Park*

*Rte. 5; follow Rte. 5 for 33 mi. to castle. ☎ 786-2392. Open daily 9am-5pm. Tours every hr. May-Sept.; more frequently Oct.-Apr. $8, seniors $6, ages 6-15 $4. Tickets can be purchased until 1hr. before closing, but there are often lines.)*

**UBEHEBE CRATER.** This blackened volcanic blast site is nearly 1 mi. wide and 600 ft. deep. It can be seen by car but take the gravel trail leading to the floor of the crater to truly appreciate the hole's dimensions. The climb back out is grueling. A 4WD unpaved road continues 23 mi. south of the crater to the vast **Racetrack Playa,** a dried-up lake basin with access to Hidden Valley and White Top Mountain. See the trails left by mysterious **moving rocks** on this basin. For an outstanding view of the Racetrack, follow **Ubehebe Peak Trail** (6 mi. round-trip) from the Grandstand parking area along a steep, twisting pathway. *(8 mi. west of Scotty's Castle.)*

---

# HOMETOWN OF THE LIVING DEAD

Authentic California ghost towns are hard to find. Darwin, which housed 5000 at its peak and allegedly produced 50% of the lead used by the US in WWII, is probably the closest thing you'll find to a genuine, decaying-yet-walkable ghost town. Its mines and mills closed in the 1970s, leaving a population of 35-40 artists, writers, artisans, and retirees, plus a multitude of buried dead. The graveyard boasts poorly buried corpses, wooden markers, and the ostentatious tomb of Nancy Williams, Darwin's brothel keeper from better, lustier times. The only place in town where you're liable to find living people is the post office, which doubles as the business headquarters for "suspension eyewear," worn by the astronauts and Arctic explorers whose photos cover the walls. "The only thing you can buy in Darwin," they'll tell you, "is stamps." Take a look around anyway. If the abandoned tract housing, ramshackle homes, and RVs don't freak you out, the graveyard outside of town probably will. Spoooky.

---

# LIFE AFTER DEATH VALLEY

## NORTHEAST OF DEATH VALLEY: BEATTY ☎ 775

The small town of Beatty, Nevada, concentrates on its handful of casinos and is a convenient and comfortable place to stay while visiting Death Valley. Situated 90 mi. northwest of Las Vegas on Rte. 95, Beatty offers weary travelers gaming, great accommodations, and that all-important A/C. Compared to those in Reno and Las Vegas, Beatty's casinos are very relaxed. Wager as little as $1 at blackjack and jaw with the dealers, folks who seem genuinely sorry to take your money. All casinos are theoretically open 24hr., but by 2am the dealers start eyeing the clock.

Info can be found at **Beatty Visitor Information Center,** 119 E. Main St. (☎553-2424. Open M-F 10am-3pm.) There is public **Internet access** for a nominal fee at the **Beatty Public Library.** (☎553-2257. Open M, W, Th 9am-3pm, Tu noon-7pm, Sa 9am-noon.) The **Beatty Ranger Station** is well stocked with books, maps, and safety info for desert-bound drivers. (☎553-2200. Open Tu-Sa 8am-4pm, though the hours aren't strictly observed.) The comfortable **Happy Burro Hostel ❶**, 100 Main St., located in a former brothel, offers free breakfast and kitchen use to guests. (☎553-9130. Reception 8am-10pm daily. 3-bed dorms $15.) Sleep in peace at the **Stagecoach Hotel ❸**, on Rte. 95, half a mile north of town. Amenities include a pool, jacuzzi, casino, and bar. The **restaurant ❷** serves up diner favorites 24hr., with dinners ranging from $6-10. (☎533-2419. Singles from $35; doubles from $40.) Slightly cheaper rooms can be found at the **El Portal Motel ❷**, on Rte. 374, one block from the junction with Rte. 95. (☎553-2912. Singles $30; doubles $33.) For a cold beer, check out the **Sourdough Saloon,** 106 Main St. This is the favorite bar of auto industry engineers who test top-secret prototype cars in the Valley. Every year, each test team leaves a memento. Get a friend to check out the brilliantly engineered BMW birdhouse to the left of the door. (☎553-2266. Open daily 12pm-12am.) Don't neglect to grab water and cheap Nevada gas before leaving town.

## WEST OF DEATH VALLEY

Ghost towns like **Darwin** and a few slightly more populated communities are the only developments that remain on Rte. 190 west of the park. In **Olancha,** the **Ranch Motel ❸** on US 395 provides clean, homey rooms in cottage-like buildings. (☎764-2387. Singles $49; doubles $59; cabins for 4-8 $130. Rates may vary with the Lone Pine Film Festival or on other holiday weekends.) Further north along US 395 at the junction with Rte. 136 is the town of **Lone Pine.** Sitting at the base of Mt. Whitney, the area has elevation and trees on its side; it stays pleasantly cool compared to the desert. (See **Lone Pine,** p. 298.)

## SOUTHEAST OF DEATH VALLEY

In **Death Valley Junction,** at Rte. 127 and 190, 29 mi. from Furnace Creek, lives mime and ballet dancer Marta Becket, whose **Amargosa Opera House** is the sole outpost of high culture in the desert. Becket incorporates parts of classical ballet, modern dance, and pantomime into a one-woman show with 47 different characters that draws packed houses. (Show and hotel info ☎852-4441. Performances Oct., Dec.-Jan., May Sa; Nov. and Feb.-Apr. M and Sa. Shows begin at 8:15pm. $15.) The town of **Shoshone,** at Rte. 127 and 178, 56 mi. southeast of Furnace Creek, serves as a gateway to Death Valley and a base for outdoor adventures. The **Charles Brown General Store and Service Station** is a good place to stock up and fill up. (☎852-4242. Open daily 7am-8:30pm.) Next door is the brown **Shoshone Inn ❹,** which offers clean (but slightly tacky) rooms, a swimming pool, and cable TV. (☎760-852-4335. Singles $53; doubles $62.) The nearby **Shoshone Trailer Park ❶** has RV hookups, showers, a pool, and even some shade. (☎760-852-4569. Sites $10; hookups $15.) Stop by **Cafe C'est Si Bon ❷,** a relaxing and funky outpost of French cuisine in the middle of the desert. Crepes, coffee, and **Internet access** come at fair prices. (☎760-852-4307. Crepes $5-7. Internet $1 per 5min. Open M and W-Su 7am-5pm.)

South of Shoshone is the small town of **Tecopa,** which offers hot springs and a hostel for outdoor adventurers. Follow the signs to **Desertaire Hostel HI-AYH ❷,** 2000 Old Spanish Trail Hwy., for cheap sheets. The hostel also has a full kitchen and sells groceries. (☎852-4580. Check-in 5-9pm. Open July-May. Dorms $20.)

# LAS VEGAS                                    ☎702

Rising out of the Nevada desert, Las Vegas is a shimmering tribute to excess. It is the actualization of a mirage, an oasis of vice and greed, and one very, very good time for those who embrace it. This playground town was founded on gambling, whoring, and mob muscle, and though the mob has slunk away, the gambling and whoring remain. Nowhere else do so many shed inhibitions and indulge with such abandon. For every high roller slinging dice at the Bellagio, there are dozens of soccer moms slinging fanny-packs and hitting the slots at Holiday Inn, and dozens of seniors cashing in their social security checks at Slappy's House of Blackjack. Vegas is about money and sex—but mostly money. Know thy tax bracket; walk in knowing what you want to spend and get the hell out when you've spent it. In Las Vegas, there's a busted wallet and a broken heart for every garish neon light.

The main draw of Las Vegas lies south of downtown on the fabled Strip, the glittering concentration of casinos along Las Vegas Blvd. Here, corporations fall over themselves to one-up the competition and attract tourist dollars with progressively more extravagant and over-the-top attractions. Promoters have ransacked and stereotyped every culture from Ancient Egypt to King Arthur's England in attempts to heighten the kitschy splendor of their giant hotels, casinos, mini-malls, and amusement parks. Drawn by the lavishness, people flock to this flashing, buzzing corner of the American dream to get married, celebrate anniversaries, and then to introduce their kids to the lure of Las Vegas.

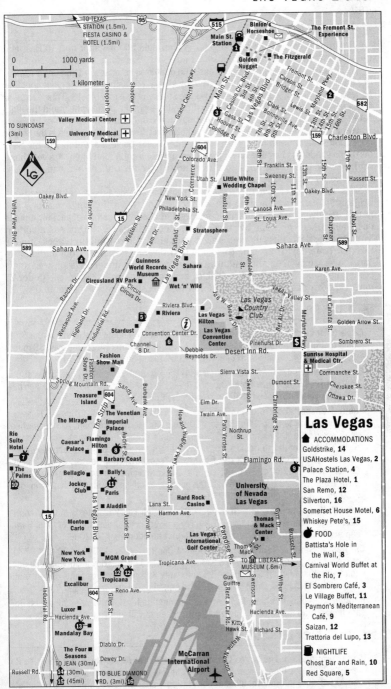

## ■ ORIENTATION

Driving to Las Vegas from Los Angeles is a straight 300 mi. shot on I-10 East and then I-15 North (4-5hr.). From Arizona, take I-40 to Kingman, then US 93 North.

Las Vegas has two major casino areas. The **downtown** area, around 2nd and Fremont St., has been converted into a pedestrian promenade. Casinos cluster close together beneath a shimmering space-frame structure spanning five city blocks. This area is far less spectacular than the Strip, but can offer relief from the burning heat and the high-roller lifestyle. However, the surrounding area can be unsafe—if you're not sure whether you belong somewhere, you probably don't. The other main area is **the Strip,** a collection of mammoth hotel-casinos along **Las Vegas Boulevard.** Parallel to the Strip and in its shadow is **Paradise Road,** also strewn with casinos. Both areas are very busy; traffic can be frustrating. For faster travel north or south, use one of the major roads further east, such as Maryland Pkwy.

As in any large city, many areas of Las Vegas can be unsafe. Always stay on brightly lit pathways, and do not wander too far from the major casinos and hotels. **The neighborhoods just north and west of downtown can be especially dangerous.** Despite (or perhaps because of) its debauchery Las Vegas has a **curfew.** Those under 18 aren't allowed unaccompanied in most public places Sunday through Thursday from 10pm to 5am and Friday and Saturday from midnight to 5am. Laws are even harsher on the Strip, where no one under 18 is allowed unaccompanied 9pm-5am, ever. **The drinking and gambling age is 21.** People under 21 may walk through the casinos, but loitering on casino floors is prohibited.

## ■ TRANSPORTATION

**Airport: McCarran International** (☎261-5743), at the southwestern end of the Strip. Main terminal on Paradise Rd. Shuttle buses run to the Strip ($4.25 one-way, $8 round-trip) and to downtown ($5.50 one-way, $10.50 round-trip); taxis $13-14.

**Buses: Greyhound,** 200 S. Main St. (☎384-9561 or 800-231-2222), downtown at Carson Ave., near the Plaza Hotel/Casino. Tickets sold 24hr. to **LA** (5-7hr., 22 per day, $38) and **San Francisco** (13-16hr., 6 per day, $65).

**Public Transportation: Citizens Area Transit** or **CAT** (☎228-7433). Bus #301 serves downtown and the Strip 24hr. Buses #108 and 109 serve the airport. All buses wheelchair accessible. Buses run daily 5:30am-1:30am (24hr. on the Strip). Routes on the Strip $2, residential routes $1.25, seniors and ages 6-17 60¢. For schedules and maps, try the tourist office or the **Downtown Transportation Center,** 300 N. Casino Center Blvd. (☎228-7433), complete with poker machines and a cashier. **Las Vegas Strip Trolleys** (☎382-1404) are not strip joints; they cruise the Strip every 20min. daily 9:30am-1:30am. Trolley fare $1.65 in exact change.

**Taxis: Yellow, Checker,** and **Star** (☎873-2000). All Las Vegas taxis initially charge $2.70, with each additional mile $1.80. For pick-up, call 30min. ahead of time. Handicap accessible cabs available. McCarran Airport an additional $1.20 fee.

**Car Rental: Sav-Mor Rent-A-Car,** 5101 Rent-A-Car Rd. (☎736-1234 or 800-634-6779), at the airport. From $30 per day, $130 per week; 150 mi. per day included, each additional mi. 20¢. Must be 21+, under-25 surcharge $12 per day. Discounts can be found in tourist publications. Open daily 5:30am-1am; airport window opens at 7am.

**Parking:** Free parking abounds. Major casinos offer both valet and self-park areas. Both are free, but tip the valet. At some lots you'll need to validate your parking stub.

## ■ PRACTICAL INFORMATION

**Visitor Information: Las Vegas Convention and Visitor Authority,** 3150 Paradise Rd. (☎892-0711), 4 blocks from the Strip in the big pink convention center by the Hilton. Up-to-date info on headliners, conventions, shows, hotel bargains, and buffets.

THE DESERT

Open M-F 8am-5pm. To make reservations for tours, hotels, shows, or travel packages, try the **Las Vegas Tourist Bureau,** 5191 S. Las Vegas Blvd. (☎739-1482; www.lvtb.com). Open daily 7am-11pm.

**Tours: Coach USA,** 795 E. Tropicana Ave. (☎384-1234 or 800-634-6579). City tours (3½hr., 1 per day, $39). Bus tours from Las Vegas to **Hoover Dam/Lake Mead** (4hr., 2 per day, $39) and the **Grand Canyon's South Rim** (full-day, $149). Discounts for children ages 3-11 and with coupons from tourist publications. Reserve in advance.

**Bank: Bank of America,** 1140 E. Desert Inn Rd. (☎654-1000), at the corner of Maryland Pkwy. Open M-Th 9am-5pm, F 9am-6pm. Phone assistance 24hr.

**ATMs:** Plentiful in all major casinos, but there is at least a $2 charge for each use. Those at gas stations or banks often charge lower fees.

**Laundry: Cora's Coin Laundry,** 1099 E. Tropicana Ave. (☎736-6181). Wash $1, dry 25¢ per 10min. Open daily 8am-8pm. Video poker (or Miss PacMan for the underaged) is available while you wait for your socks to dry.

**Gaming Lessons:** Free at some major casinos in blackjack, roulette, craps, pai gow, Caribbean stud poker, and baccarat. Call **Aladdin** (☎785-5555) for session times, or walk up to Kim Rusch's table at the **Stardust** (☎800-634-6757) every M-F 10am-6pm.

**Library and Internet Access:** Free Internet access is available at **Clark County Library,** 1401 E. Flamingo Rd. (☎507-3400), but expect a wait. Open M-Th 9am-9pm, F-Su 10am-6pm. A better bet may be **Kinko's,** 4440 Maryland Pkwy. (☎735-4402). 20¢ per min. Open 24hr.

**Marriage: Marriage License Bureau,** 200 S. 3rd St. (☎455-4416), in the courthouse. 18+ or at least 16 with parental consent. Licenses $55; cash only. No waiting period or blood test required. Open Su-Th 8am-midnight, F-Sa 24hr.

**Divorce:** Must be a Nevada resident for at least 6 weeks. $150 service fee. Permits available at the courthouse M-F 8am-5pm.

**Road Conditions:** ☎877-687-6237. **Weather Conditions:** ☎263-9744.

**24-Hour Crisis Lines: Compulsive Gamblers Hotline** (☎800-LOST-BET/567-8238). **Gamblers Anonymous** (☎385-7732). **Rape Crisis Center Hotline** (☎366-1640). **Suicide Prevention** (☎731-2990 or 800-885-4673).

**Police:** Corner of Russell Rd. and S. Las Vegas Blvd. ☎229-3111.

**Post Offices:** 301 E. Stewart Ave. (☎385-8944), downtown station. Open M-F 8:30am-5pm. Closer to the Strip: 4975 Swenson St. (☎736-7649). Open M-F 8:30am-5pm. **Postal Codes:** 89101 (Stewart Ave.), 89119 (Swenson St.).

# ⌐ ACCOMMODATIONS

Though Las Vegas has over 100,000 rooms, most hotels fill up on weekend nights. Room rates fluctuate greatly, and a room that costs $30 during a slow period can cost hundreds during a convention weekend. The prices below are only a general guide. Also check local, free, readily available publications such as *What's On In Las Vegas, Today in Las Vegas, 24/7, Vegas Visitor, Casino Player, Tour Guide Magazine, Best Read Guide,* and *Insider Viewpoint of Las Vegas* for discounts, coupons, general info, and schedules of events. If you get stuck, call the **Room Reservations Hotline** (☎800-332-5333), or go to one of the tourist offices.

**Strip hotels** are at the center of the action and within walking distance of each other, but their inexpensive rooms sell out quickly. More hotels cluster around Sahara Rd. and S. Las Vegas Blvd. Motels also line **Fremont Street,** though this area is a little rougher; it is best to stay in one of the casinos in the **Fremont Street Experience** (see **Casinos,** p. 550) itself. There is another concentration of inexpensive motels along the southern stretch of the Strip, across from the ritzy **Mandalay Bay.** In the room rates listed below, **the 9% state hotel tax is not included.**

■ **San Remo,** 115 E. Tropicana Ave. (☎800-522-7366). Just off the Strip, this is a smaller, friendlier version of the major player casinos, without the gimmicks, crowds, and high prices. Live entertainment every night, featuring the "Showgirls of Magic" ($39). Rooms may go as low as $32 during slow periods, but are usually Su-Th $42, F-Sa $70. ❹

■ **Silverton,** 3333 Blue Diamond Rd. (800-588-7711; www.silverton-casino.com). Cheaper because it's off the Strip, this mining town-themed gambling den has clean, new rooms. Free Las Vegas Blvd. shuttle until 10pm. Singles Su-Th $35, F-Sa $69. Beyond 2 adults, additional person $10. RV hook-ups $24-28. ❸

■ **Whiskey Pete's** (☎800-367-7383), in Primm Valley, NV, 45min. south of Vegas on I-15, just before the CA state line. The cheapest of 3 Western-themed casinos in the middle of the desert. Cheap as fool's gold and across the street from the wildest coaster in Nevada ($6). Must be 21+ to rent. Su-Th $19, F-Sa $50; prices vary with availability. ❷

**USAHostels Las Vegas,** 1322 Fremont St. (☎800-550-8958 or 385-1150; www.usahos-tels.com). A funky, fun place to stay, though far from the Strip and in an unattractive neighborhood. Rooms sparse but clean. Friendly staff that caters to students and interna-tional travelers. Private and dorm rooms available. Pool, jacuzzi, laundry, kitchen, and bil-liard room. Shared bathrooms. Offers free pick-up from Greyhound station 10am-10pm. Su-Th dorms $14-19; suites $40-42. F-Sa dorms $17-23; suites $49-51. **Must have international passport, proof of international travel, or student ID.** ❷

**Goldstrike,** 1 Main St. (☎800-634-1359), in Jean, NV, 20min. from the Strip on I-15. Restaurants (prime rib $7, buffet $7.50), loose slots, and low-limit tables. Reservations may get cheaper prices. Rooms Su-Th $20-30, F $40, Sa $50. Additional person $3. ❸

**Somerset House Motel,** 294 Convention Center Dr. (☎888-336-4280; www.somerset-house.com). A no-frills establishment within walking distance of the Strip. Many of the large and impeccably clean rooms feature kitchens. Dishes and cooking utensils pro-vided upon request. Unbeatable weekend rates. Singles Su-Th $35, F-Sa $44; doubles Su-Th $44, F-Sa $55. Additional person $5. Senior discount available. ❸

**Palace Station,** 2411 W. Sahara Ave. (☎800-634-3101). All the features of a Strip hotel plus a railroad theme. Free shuttles run to Las Vegas Blvd. 9am-midnight. Airport shuttle available. Daily charge for utilities $3, phone $1. Rooms Su-Th $40-80, F-Sa $100-130. Additional person $10. ❺

**Plaza Hotel/Casino,** 1 Main St. (☎800-634-6575; www.plazahotelcasino.com), in the heart of downtown across from Fremont St.'s casinos. Includes tennis courts, barber-shop, salon, and pool. Singles Su-Th $32, F-Sa $79. ❸

## CAMPING

**Lake Mead National Recreation Area** (☎293-8906), 25 mi. south of town on Rte. 93/95. A huge artificial lake on the Nevada-Arizona border fed by the Colorado River. Watersports rentals and numerous campsites throughout. Las Vegas Bay is closest to the city. Showers only at Calville and Overton Beach. Sites with flush toilets $10. ❶

**Valley of Fire State Park** (☎397-2088), 50 mi. northeast of Las Vegas. Take I-15 north to Rte. 169, a fun, solitary drive through desert foothills. Named for its diabolical rock formations that seem to bleed in the sun. Splendid campground near the ancient petro-glyph site of Atlas Rock. No electricity or hookups. Sites $13. ❶

**Circusland RV Park,** 500 Circus Circus Dr. (☎734-0410). Pool, jacuzzi, convenience store, showers, laundry. Open 5am-midnight. Hookups Su-Th $18-28, F-Sa $2 extra. ❷

## FOOD

Everyone comes to gorge themselves at Vegas's gigantic buffets. For the really, really hungry, there's no better value than these caloric cornucopias. The trick to buffet bliss is to find places that are more than glorified cafeterias; unfortunately, this sometimes proves difficult. Beyond buffets, Vegas has some of the best restau-rants in the world, though few have prices palatable to the true budget adventurer.

**Le Village Buffet,** 3655 Las Vegas Blvd. (☎946-7000). French cooking without French portions. In a recreated French Alps village, this buffet, crammed with crab, salmon, prime rib, veal, and crepes, is worth its higher price. Restrain yourself; the dessert will reward. Breakfast $13, lunch $17, dinner $22. Open daily 7am-10pm. ❺

**Carnival World Buffet at the Rio,** 3700 W. Flamingo Rd. (☎252-7777). One of the great Vegas feasts. Perhaps the most well-known and highly-rated buffet in Vegas, the Rio boasts 12 uniquely themed food stations, from sushi to Mexican. Breakfast $10, lunch $12, dinner $17. Open daily 7am-10pm. ❹

**El Sombrero Cafe,** 807 S. Main St. (☎382-9234), is where the locals go for authentic Mexican food. The portions are huge and the staff is friendly. Their combination plates offer a lot of food for a little money ($8-11). Lunch $7. Open M-Sa 11am-10pm. ❷

**Benihana Village at the Las Vegas Hilton,** 3000 Paradise Rd. (☎732-5755). Koi pond, rain, bonsais, and multi-level area. Charismatic hibachi chefs slice, sear, and serve your 5-course meal. Filling entrees are worth the $16-30. Open daily 5:30-10:30pm. ❹

**Paymon's Mediterranean Cafe,** 4147 S. Maryland Pkwy. (☎731-6030), serves fresh, delicious Greek and Mediterranean specialties. Try the delicious combo plate with couscous, tabouli, and stuffed grape leaves ($10) or a big falafel and hummus pita bread sandwich ($6). Attached to **The Hookah Lounge** (see Nightlife, p. 553). Open M-Th 11am-1am, F-Sa 11am-3am, Su 11am-4pm. ❷

**Battista's Hole in the Wall,** 4041 Audrie Ave. (☎732-1424), behind the Flamingo. 33 years' worth of celebrity photos and novelties from area brothels, as well as the head of "Moosolini" (the fascist moose), adorn the walls. Portions are generous. Dinner ($18-34) includes all-you-can-drink wine. Open Su-Th 4:30-10:30pm, F-Sa 4:30-11pm. ❺

**Saizan,** 115 E. Tropicana Ave. (☎739-9000), in San Remo behind the first floor slots. The best sushi bar near the Strip, offering only the freshest sushi and sashimi. Combo platters ($14-19) provide an excellent sampling. Open daily 5:30pm-midnight. ❹

**Trattoria del Lupo,** 3590 S. Las Vegas Blvd. (☎740-5522), in Mandalay Bay, beside a number of classy nightspots and dining options. Celebrity chef Wolfgang Puck's first Italian restaurant. The pizzas and salads ($11) are big and delicious. Open M-Th 5-10pm, F 5-11pm, Sa-Su 11:30am-4pm and 5-10pm. ❸

# ⓒ SIGHTS

Before the mega-casinos inject you full of glitz and suck you dry of greenbacks, you might explore some of the simpler oddities of the city.

**LIBERACE MUSEUM.** Fans of classical music and kitsch will be delighted by this museum devoted to the flamboyant "Mr. Showmanship." Liberace's extravagant tastes for fur, velvet, and rhinestone boggle the rational mind. (1775 E. Tropicana Ave. ☎ 798-5595. Open M-Sa 10am-5pm, Su 1-5pm. $8, students and seniors $5, under 12 free.)

**GUN STORE.** It's been said that God made men, and Sam Colt made 'em equal. Experience Coltish justice—$10 plus ammo lets you try out an impressive array of pistols, including the enormous Magnum 44. And for $30, Rambo, they'll even let you pop off on a real machine gun. Friendly, gun-nutty staff spout off Gatt knowledge. (2900 E. Tropicana Ave. ☎454-1110. Open daily 9am-6:30pm.)

**DESPERADO ROLLERCOASTER.** Way out in Primm Valley where no one can hear you scream, this is the tallest and fastest bad boy in the Las Vegas area. (Primm Valley, NV, along I-15 near the California border. ☎800-248-8453. Open M and Th noon-6pm, F 11am-midnight, Sa 10am-midnight, Su 10am-10pm. $6 per ride.)

**GUINNESS WORLD RECORDS MUSEUM.** This relatively small display showcases intriguing and repulsive human oddities, as well as other bests and greatests. A compendium of the wacky. (2780 S. Las Vegas Blvd. ☎792-3766. Open daily June-Aug. 9am-6pm; Sept.-May 9am-5pm. Adults $6.50, students and seniors $5.50, ages 5-12 $4.50.)

## ON THE MENU

### BOUNTIFUL BUFFET

Want to save some of that money for gambling? Haven't yet struck it rich at the black jack table? Though most buffets in Las Vegas are good deals, the **Circus Buffet,** at Circus Circus, is perhaps the best, and definitely the cheapest, buffet on the Strip.

Inside Circus Circus casino, which also holds a roller coaster, slot machines, card tables, a carnival mid-way, and seven other restaurants, Circus Buffet offers the most bang for your buck. Circus Buffet was recently renovated and upgraded; its blue booths and warm wood interior give it a homey appeal. Likewise, the sparkling service line and friendly chefs do little to dissuade your appetite.

But the best thing of all is that, unlike at other obesity-inducing Las Vegas buffets, you won't have to stuff yourself to feel like you got your money's worth. With breakfast at a reasonable $5.50 and dinner at a mere $8, Circus Buffet is by far the easiest way to keep yourself fueled for those future hot streaks, and comforted after those devastating losses. (2880 S. Las Vegas Blvd. ☎ 734-0410. Open daily 7am-1pm and 4:30-10pm.)

**LITTLE WHITE WEDDING CHAPEL.** From 3min. drive-through whirlwinds to elaborate fantasy-themed extravaganzas, this Vegas wedding chapel is legend among the city's matrimonial traditions. Vegas luminaries like Frank Sinatra and Liberace as well as more recent celebrities Michael Jordan and Rikki Lake have been hitched here (not to each other). Basic drive-through packages begin at a friendly $40 and end at the limits of imagination. All wedding necessities are provided, including photographer, tux and gown, flowers, and for honeymooners on the go, a lollipop-pink Caddy. Be sure to pick up your marriage license first; see **Practical Information,** p. 547. *(1301 Las Vegas Blvd. ☎ 382-5943; www.alittlewhitechapel.com. No reservations required for the drive-through services. Open 24hr.)*

## 🏛 CASINOS

Casinos spend millions of dollars attracting tourists dollars, and they do this by fooling guests into thinking they are somewhere else. As if Las Vegas wasn't escapist enough already, spittin' images of Venice, New York, Monte Carlo, Paris (complete with the Eiffel Tower), and ancient Egypt (complete with the Pyramids) thrive on the Strip. Efforts to bring families to Sin City are evident with arcades and thrill rides around every corner. Still, Vegas is no Disney World. With the plethora of steamy nightclubs and topless revues, not to mention the scantily clad waitresses serving up free liquor, it's clear that casinos' priorities center on profits.

**Casinos, bars, and some wedding chapels are open 24hr.,** so whatever your itch, Vegas can usually scratch it. Look for casino "funbooks" that feature deals on chips and entertainment. Cash goes in a blink when you're gambling, so it pays to have a budget. Gambling is illegal for those under 21. There are far more casinos harboring far more attractions than can be listed here; use the following as a compendium of the best, but explore Las Vegas for yourself.

### THE STRIP

The undisputed locus of Vegas's surging regeneration, The Strip is a fantasyland of neon, teeming with people, casinos, and restaurants. The nation's 10 largest hotels line the legendary 3½ mi. stretch of Las Vegas Blvd., named an "All-American Road" and "National Scenic Byway." Despite the sparkling facade, porn is still peddled in the shadow of family fun centers and night denizens still sport open alcohol containers wander from casino to casino in search of elusive jackpots.

**Mandalay Bay,** 3950 S. Las Vegas Blvd. (☎ 632-7777; www.mandalaybay.com). Undoubtedly Vegas's hippest, Mandalay Bay tries to convince New York and LA fashionistas they haven't left home. With all the swank restaurants and chi-chi clubs, gambling seems an afterthought. Shark Reef features 100 aquatic species from all over the globe, including 15 shark species, and House of Blues is one of the best music venues.

**Bellagio,** 3600 S. Las Vegas Blvd. (☎ 693-7444; www.bellagio.com). The world's largest 5-star hotel. Houses a gallery of fine art and carefully maintained botanical gardens that change with the seasons. The Via Bellagio Shops, home to Prada and Tiffany's, offer Vegas's finest shopping. Muscle your way up for a view of the spectacular fountains, where water is propelled several stories into the air during daily free water ballet shows.

**Venetian,** 3355 S. Las Vegas Blvd. (☎ 414-1000; www.venetian.com). This palatial casino features the upscale Grand Canal Shoppes, named for the 3 ft. deep chlorinated "canal" that runs through it. Singing gondoliers push tourists along in small boats. The Guggenheim Hermitage Museum presents the apotheosis of the new Vegas with artwork from Russian, Austrian, and Guggenheim Foundation collections. Elaborate architectural replicas of Venetian plazas, bridges, and towers adorn the Strip-side exterior.

**Caesar's Palace,** 3570 S. Las Vegas Blvd. (☎ 731-7110; www.caesars.com). At Caesar's, busts abound: some are plaster, while others are barely concealed by the low-cut get-ups of cocktail waitresses. None are real. The pricey Forum Shops led the high-end shopping craze at Strip casinos. With constant construction and ever-changing attractions, Caesars continues to set the standard for class and excitement on The Strip.

**Monte Carlo,** 3770 S. Las Vegas Blvd. (☎ 730-7000; www.monte-carlo.com). One of the most elegant casinos, Monte Carlo takes after its namesake by providing a sophisticated gaming experience where players bet enormous amounts of money in style.

**Luxor,** 3900 S. Las Vegas Blvd. (☎ 262-4000; www.luxor.com). This iconoclastic casino and architectural marvel recreates the majestic pyramids of ancient Egypt in opaque glass and steel. Luxor has all sorts of diversions when gambling loses its appeal; there's an IMAX Theater and a full-scale replica of King Tut's Tomb.

**Paris,** 3655 S. Las Vegas Blvd. (☎ 946-7000; www.parislasvegas.com). The smallest of the "theme" casinos, with mimes, tasty crêpes, a near-scale Arc de Triomphe, and a half-scale Eiffel Tower that houses a restaurant and a summit view of The Strip.

**The Mirage,** 3400 S. Las Vegas Blvd. (☎ 791-7111; www.mirage.com). Arguably the casino that began Vegas's reincarnation in the early 90s. It shelters 8 bottlenose dolphins and Siegfried and Roy's white tigers and lions. A volcano erupts fire every 15min.

**MGM Grand,** 3799 S. Las Vegas Blvd. (☎ 891-1111; www.mgmgrand.com). A huge bronze lion guards Las Vegas's largest hotel and casino and a few live

# THE LOCAL STORY

## KATHLEEN, SHOWGIRL OF MAGIC

Kathleen, originally from the Seattle area, works with the Showgirls of Magic at the Hotel San Remo.

**LG:** So what brought you to Vegas?

**A:** I wanted to dance. I grew up in dance class, went to school in Seattle, and told my parents I was moving to Vegas to be a dancer. They weren't too stoked about it. But now they support me 180%.

**LG:** What was your first gig in Vegas?

**A:** I worked at Caesar's Palace as a belly dancer.

**LG:** Were you ever interested in magic as a kid, or did [Showgirls of Magic] just pop up?

**A:** No, in fact, I wasn't, to be quite honest, but now I think it's really fun. There's a certain power to it because nobody really knows how it's done.

**LG:** Part of your show is an element of topless distraction. Is it hard to go up there and be confident?

**A:** The topless part? There's so much else to think about that we really forget that—you get comfortable with everything, then you start noticing what other people are wearing, or that person looks like my sister, and then you're like, oh, they're staring at my boobs.

**LG:** In your travels, what's the coolest thing you've seen, the most unusual thing that's happened?

**A:** We were captured in Lebanon and escorted out by the American embassy in a bullet-proof suburban.

**LG:** Geez, what were you guys up to?

**A:** It was a good show, but it was on the Muslim side of town.

felines dwell inside at the Lion Habitat. In addition to more than 5000 rooms, the MGM hosts world-class sporting events and concerts, packing the essence of Sin City under one roof.

**New York, New York,** 3790 S. Las Vegas Blvd. (☎ 740-6969; www.nynyhotelcasino). Towers mimic the Manhattan skyline and re-create the Big Apple. Walk under a replica of Brooklyn Bridge or check out Coyote Ugly, where bartenders strut their stuff on counters. Manhattan Express, the wildest ride on the Strip, is open daily 11am-11pm ($12).

**Treasure Island,** 3300 S. Las Vegas Blvd. (☎ 894-7111; www.treasureisland.com). Newly refurbished and fully embracing the recent wave of pirate chic, this once-tired casino is trying to reinvent itself as an "in" spot for young crowds. The Buccaneer Bay Sea Battle, deemed one of the best free shows in Vegas, will debut in the fall of 2003.

**Circus Circus,** 2880 S. Las Vegas Blvd. (☎ 734-0410; www.circuscircus.com). While parents run to card tables and slot machines downstairs, children spend their quarters upstairs on the souped-up carnival midway and in the titanic video game arcade. Adventuredome, inside the hotel complex, is the world's largest indoor theme park. The Canyon Blaster ($5), a double-loop, double-screw roller coaster, is among the rides.

## DOWNTOWN AND OFF-STRIP

The tourist frenzy that grips The Strip is less noticeable in "old" Downtown Vegas. Glitter Gulch offers smaller hotels, cheaper alcohol and food, and some serious gambling. The family atmosphere that the Strip tries to cultivate is substantially lacking here; the feel is grittier. Years of decline were reversed with Las Vegas's city-wide rebound and the 1995 opening of the Fremont Street Experience. A canopy of neon has arisen. The construction of a pedestrian promenade furthered the area's renaissance. **Despite the renewal, don't stray far from Fremont Street at night.**

**Golden Nugget,** 129 Fremont St. (☎ 385-7111; www.goldennugget.com). A vein of Strip-like class downtown, this perennial four-star hotel charms with marble floors, elegant chandeliers, and high-end gambling. Without the distractions of rollercoasters and replicas, the Golden Nugget stands for what Vegas used to be.

**Binion's Horseshoe Hotel and Casino,** 128 Fremont St. (☎ 382-1600). The Binion family brought their love of high-stakes gaming from Texas. A place to learn the tricks of the trade by watching rather than playing, this casino is the site of the World Series of Poker—a serious gambler's paradise. High craps odds, single-deck blackjack, and a willingness to honor almost any bet are Horseshoe hallmarks.

**The Plaza,** 1 Main St. (☎ 386-2110). Grandiosely standing guard at the western end of the Fremont Street Experience, the Plaza has 1-2¢ slots that make it pretty tough to go broke. The Center Stage Restaurant furnishes a great view of the nightly light shows.

**The Palms,** 4321 W. Flamingo Rd. (☎ 942-7777; www.palms.com). This trendy spot melds local casino and tourist destination, shaking up the city's gambling establishment. Known especially for its wild clubs and lounges, the Palms is the place to be if you're young, single, and in Las Vegas. Just ask Britney Spears.

**Las Vegas Hilton,** 3000 Paradise Rd. (☎ 732-5111). You won't miss this casino thanks to the enormous sign. Inside, the $70 million Star Trek: The Experience immerses you in the Trekkie universe, complete with slot machines on "the bridge." Entrance to The Experience includes admission to the Star Trek Museum, which presents this kooky cultural phenomenon with astonishing intricacy.

## 🎭 ENTERTAINMENT

Vegas entertainment revolves around the casino axis. Big bucks will buy you a seat at a made-in-the-USA phenomenon: the **Vegas spectacular.** These stunning, casino-sponsored productions feature marvels such as waterfalls, explosions, fireworks, and casts of hundreds (including animals). You can also see Broadway plays and musicals, ice revues, and individual entertainers in concert. All hotels have city-wide ticket booths in their lobbies. Check out some of the ubiquitous free show guides—*Showbiz, Today in Las Vegas, What's On*—for summaries of shows, times, and prices. For a more opinionated perspective, check out one of the independent weeklies—*Las Vegas Mercury*, *City Life*, *Las Vegas Weekly*, or *Neon*, the *Las Vegas Review-Journal's* weekly entertainment supplement. Some "production shows" are topless, veering into tastelessness, but there are a few exceptions. The ⬛**Cirque du Soleil's** creative shows—*O*, *Mystere*, and the brand new, racy *Zumanity*—are bank-busting ($88-150) yet awe-inspiring displays of human agility and physical strength channeled as artistic expression at the Bellagio, Treasure Island, and New York, New York, respectively. "Limited view" tickets are discounted, and the view isn't that limited. Another show worth seeing is **Blue Man Group** at the Luxor, a production that pushes the limits of stage entertainment with unique percussion and audience participation ($79-90). For a show by one of the musical stars who haunt the city, e.g. **Celine Dion** (Caesar's Palace), **Gladys Knight** (Flamingo), or **Wayne Newton** (Stardust), you'll have to fork over at least $50 and often considerably more. "Magicians of the Century" **Siegfried and Roy** go for a fabulous $105.50 at the Mirage. Incredible impersonator/singer/dancer **Danny Gans** also entertains at The Mirage, and tickets run $100. The tricks of **Lance Burton** (a mainstay at the Monte Carlo) are a display of good old magic ($55-60), while **Penn and Teller** at the Río are far darker. With some of everything, former street performer **The Amazing Jonathan** stages one of Vegas's edgiest productions ($47-58). The best deals by far, however, are the free shows at the major casinos.

## 🅖 NIGHTLIFE

Nightlife in Vegas starts at midnight and runs until everyone drops—or runs out of money. In a city that never sleeps, inebriated clubhoppers bounce from one happening joint to the next, and the cabs languish in line, waiting to take them there.

**Ghost Bar** and **Rain,** 4231 W. Flamingo Rd. (☎938-BOOO/2666 or 940-RAIN/7246), at the Palms, indisputably the hottest Vegas nightspot. You may have to wait in line for hours, but once you're in, be ready to groove with the hottest bodies in Vegas while DJs throw down. Ghost Bar is on the hotel's 55th floor, with a deck and 360° view of Vegas. Open M-Sa 8pm-"late." Rain features over 25,000 sq. ft. of dance floor and intense displays of fire, fog, and (surprise!) rain. Cover $10-20. Open Th-Sa 11pm-5am.

**Red Square,** 2950 Las Vegas Blvd. (☎632-7407), in Mandalay Bay. This Miami Beach import pulls off post-Communist chic with ease. Serving amazing martinis and frozen vodkas, Red Square is the trendiest possible way to enjoy the fall of the Soviet Union. Cocktails $9.50. Open Su-Th 5pm-1am, F-Sa 5pm-5:30am.

**Baby's,** 4455 Paradise Rd. (☎693-5555), in the Hard Rock Hotel. With multiple levels and bars—including one that floats in a pool—this eye-catching club offers as chill a scene as you'll find in Las Vegas. World-class DJs spin house, trance, and hip-hop. Perfect for a night on the town. Cover $10-20. Open W-Sa 11pm.

**V Bar,** 3355 Las Vegas Blvd. (☎414-3200). This elegant bar in the Venetian deftly recreates the New York lounge scene. A minimalist design and mellow beats make V Bar equally suitable for dancing and hanging low. Open daily 6pm-4am.

**Gipsy,** 4605 Paradise Rd. (☎731-1919). This enormous LGBT club heats up every night with drag queens (M), go-go dancers (W), lip sync contests (Th), cabaret shows (Su), and wild dance parties to create one of the town's most swinging scenes. Happy Hour daily 9pm-2am with $2 mixed drinks. Cover $5-7. Open daily 9pm.

**Hookah Lounge,** 4147 S. Maryland Pkwy. (☎732-3203). Features nearly 20 flavored tobaccos (no opium, though) and a funky, intimate vibe that attracts pre-club crowds. Full bar and flavored teas. Open M-Th 5pm-1am, F-Sa 5pm-3am.

**Ra,** 3900 S. Las Vegas Blvd. (☎262-4949). Egyptian-themed nightclub at the Luxor where famous DJs spin a variety of sounds with trance/break beats (W), hip-hop and R&B (Th, Sa), and house (F). Vegas's trendiest club with a dress code (not casual) that's strictly enforced. Cover men $20, women $10. Open W-Sa 10pm.

**Club Paradise,** 4416 Paradise Rd. (☎ 734-7990), across from Hard Rock Casino. Repeatedly voted best gentlemen's cabaret (read: strip joint) in America. It's safe and the g-strings stay on. About as sophisticated as a topless bar gets. Beer $6, cocktails $6-8. Cover $10 before 9pm, $20 after. Open M-F 4pm-6am, Sa-Su 6pm-6am. ■

# LEAVING LAS VEGAS

Away from Vegas, the mountains and lakes offer opportunities for outdoor excitement. Roadtrippers stop to gawk at the monumental engineering of the Hoover Dam, boaters enjoy the waters of Lake Mead, and hikers and climbers test the canyons and crags of Red Rocks. While Las Vegas swelters in heat and sin, the higher elevations around it are cooler and more pristine; there's even skiing in the winter.

## RED ROCKS

Less than 20 mi. west of The Strip, the Red Rock Canyon National Conservation Area escarpment is an astounding network of crimson sandstone bluffs and washes. From Las Vegas, take Hwy. 159 (Charleston Blvd.) west. You can stick to the 13 mi. **scenic auto route,** hike into the desert, or take advantage of the fact that Red Rocks is a premier **rock climbing** destination. An excellent **visitors center** (☎ 363-1921) introduces the wonders of the flourishing desert ecosystem. The **campground ❶** sits off Hwy. 159, 2 mi. east of the visitors center, with picnic tables, grills, water, and toilets ($10). For group reservations, call ☎ 515-5352. Backcountry camping and overnight climbing require free permits (☎ 515-5050). The most popular **hikes** are those through the washes of **Calico Hills** and **Calico Tanks,** accessible from the first few pullouts along the scenic road. If you're looking to cool off, **Ice Box Canyon** lives up to its name; the shady trail climbs 300 ft. over a little more than a mile to pools and waterfalls when there's been rain.

## HOOVER DAM

*Take I-15, Hwy. 93/95, south 26 mi. from Las Vegas to Boulder City. From Boulder City, head east 5 mi. on Hwy. 93. ☎ 291-8687. Open daily 9am-5pm. Tours, including an elevator trip down to the generators, every 15min. daily 9:30am-4:30pm. Parking on Nevada side $5; free on Arizona side. $10, seniors $8, ages 7-16 $4, 6 and under free.*

Built to subdue the flood-prone Colorado River and provide vital water and energy to the southwest, this looming ivory monolith, also known (by Democrats) as the Boulder Dam, took 5000 men five years of seven-day weeks to construct. By the time the dam was completed in 1935, 96 men had died. Their labor rendered a 726.4 ft. colossus that now shelters precious agricultural land, pumps more than 4 billion kilowatt-hours of power to Las Vegas and LA, and furnishes the liquid playground of Lake Mead amid the sagebrush. Though the dam has altered the local environment, it is a spectacular engineering feat, weighing 6,600,000 tons and measuring 660 ft. thick at its base and 1244 ft. across the canyon at its crest. It is a lasting tribute to America's "think-big" era. Tours and an interpretive center explore the dam's history and future.

## LAKE MEAD

*There are a few of ways in to access the lake. Take Lake Mead Blvd./Hwy. 147 off I-15 east 16 mi. to Northshore Rd., which provides access to the lake all the way up to Overton at the north end and reaches south toward Las Vegas Bay. Alternatively, Lakeshore Dr. departs Hwy. 93, 4 mi. east of Boulder City, and 30 mi. south of Vegas, at the Visitors Center and follows the southeast shore of the lake. $5 fee to enter the recreation area. Visitors Center: ☎ 293-8990; www.nps.gov/lame. Open daily 8:30am-4:30pm.*

When the rushing waters of the Colorado River met the stolid concrete of Hoover Dam, Lake Mead was formed. This 100 mi. long behemoth is the largest reservoir in the US and the country's first national recreation area. First-time visitors to the lake will benefit from a trip to the **Alan Bible Visitors Center,** 4 mi. east of Boulder City, which is home to a helpful staff as well as informative brochures and maps. Pick up the *Desert Lake View* at one of several ranger stations dotting the shores. **Backcountry hiking** and camping is permitted in most areas. **Hunters** can target deer and bighorn sheep in season, and Lake Mead offers some of the best sport **fishing** in the country, with prevalent largemouth and striped bass. Contact the **Nevada Division of Wildlife** *(NDOW;* ☎ *486-5127)* for info on obtaining licences and hunting and fishing restrictions. Despite these other diversions, Lake Mead seems to be the overwhelming domain of armies of weekend adventurers driving white pick-up trucks with **jet skis** in tow. For those who come unprepared, boats and other watercraft can be rented at the various concessionaires along the shores. **Boulder Beach,** the most popular beach on Lake Mead and the departure point for many water-based activities, is accessible from Lakeshore Dr. at the south end of the lake, about 2 mi. north of the visitors center. *(☎800-752-9669 or 293-3484. Jet skis $55 per hr., $285 per day; fishing boats $60 per 4hr., $110 per day. Hefty security deposits required on all vessels.)* Alongside the Park Service **campsites ❶** *($10),* concessionaires often operate marinas, restaurants, the occasional motel, and RV parks, most of which have become mobile home villages.

# ROUTE 66 & INTERSTATE 40

Route 66 was designated as such in November 1926, replacing the National Old Trails Road as the principal road for commerce and migration between the Mississippi Valley and Southern California. Running from Chicago to Los Angeles and spanning seven states, the road was taken by Okies fleeing the Dust Bowl (see p. 12), by wide-eyed Easterners seeking to partake in the post-war boom, and now by tourists headed for the Grand Canyon and Disneyland.

If the Smithsonian Museum is America's attic, Rte. 66 is its junk drawer. Scattered along the heat-buckled asphalt are the remnants of an earlier tourist culture. Greasy-spoons, gaudy motels, and odd little towns—now stripped of their former luster for most tourists, save the most romantic—testify to the American urge to embellish even the harshest of places. The shift over the last generation toward the super-interstate, with its generic restaurants and chain motels, suggests a fundamental transformation in the lifestyle of Middle America.

Much of Rte. 66 has been swallowed up by the interstate or left to languish in the form of gravel or forlorn dirt. In other places, it forges on as a patchwork of state and county roads (businesses along it sell $4 maps tracing its modern-day route). A good portion of Rte. 66 is not worth traveling, particularly through the vast desert stretches, where the interstate is invariably faster and more convenient.

# BARSTOW ☎760

Sitting midway between LA and Las Vegas on I-15, Barstow (pop. 23,056) is replete with cheap eats and sheets, not to mention the beauty of the California desert for those willing to explore the hot, desolate area.

**◪ PRACTICAL INFORMATION.** The Amtrak **train** station, 685 N. 1st St. (☎800-USA-RAIL/872-7245), lacks ticket counters, so buy tickets by phone. One northbound and one southbound train leave the station per day. One train per day departs for LA (4am, $26). Greyhound **buses,** 681 N. 1st St. (☎256-8757 or 800-231-2222; open M-Sa 9am-2pm, 3:30-6pm), go to LA (6 per day, $23) and Las Vegas (7 per day, $25). The **Barstow Chamber of Commerce,** 409 E. Fredricks St., off Barstow Rd., has info on hotels, restaurants, and attractions. (☎256-8617. Open M-F 10am-4pm.) Other services include: **police,** 220 E. Mountain View Rd. (☎256-2211); **Barstow Community Hospital,** 555 S. 7th St. (☎256-1761); and the **post office,** 425 S. 2nd Ave. (☎256-9304. Open M-F 9am-5pm, Sa 10am-1pm.) **Postal Code:** 92311.

**█▐ ACCOMMODATIONS & FOOD.** East Main St. offers an endless line of motels. Prices fluctuate depending on the season, day of the week, and whether Vegas accommodations are full. One of the best values is the **Best Motel ❸**, 1281 E. Main St., which is fairly clean and quite friendly, with all the usual motel amenities. (☎256-6836. Singles $34; doubles $38. Weekly rates available.) Eight miles north of Barstow, the adventurous can set up tents at the **Owl Canyon Campground ❶** while visiting the arid beauty of the **Rainbow Basin Natural Area.** To get there, head north on N. 1st St. away from Main St. in Barstow. Take a left onto Fort Irwin Rd. Continue for 7 mi., then turn left onto Fossil Bed Rd. Follow this dirt/gravel road for 3 mi. until you see signs to the campground and scenic loop. Hikers can investigate the colorful canyon, search for the desert tortoise, and gaze at a night sky unpolluted by city lights. The 31 camping sites are equipped with fire rings, drinking water, and pit toilets. (☎256-8313; www.ca.blm.gov/barsow.basin.html. Sites $6.) For more information and maps, contact the **California Desert Information Center,** 831 Barstow Rd. (☎255-8760; www.caohwy.com/c/caldesic. Open daily 9am-5pm.)

Every restaurant chain imaginable has a branch on Main St., but Barstow's local food may be more promising. The aroma of tasty dishes fills the festive dining room of **Rosita's Mexican American Food ❷**, 540 W. Main St. (☎256-9218. Lunch specials Tu-F under $5. Dinners $6-11. Open Tu-Sa 11am-9pm, Su 11am-8pm.) For some good, hearty Italian food, head to **DiNapoli's Firehouse Italian Eatery ❸**, 1358 E. Main St. Traditional pizzeria fare is served in a recreated old-fashioned firehouse, complete with the front of a fire engine and a fire pole. (☎256-1094. Dinner entrees $8-15. Open Su-Th 11am-9pm, F-Sa 11am-10pm.)

# EASTERN MOJAVE DESERT                                    ☎760

The land between I-15 and I-40 is among the most isolated in California. There are few towns and one can never assume that services will be available between Barstow and Baker along I-15 or Barstow and Needles along I-40. But travelers who only use these towns as pit stops miss out on the Mojave's stunning natural features. Many of the region's attractions exist within the confines of the **Mojave National Preserve,** whose 1.6 million acres of federally stewarded desert boast dry lake beds, volcanic cinder cones, sweeping sand dunes, and the occasional splash of water. Dramatic geological formations rise from the seemingly infinite landscape and resilient creatures crawl along the scorched terrain. Most drivers press onward, praying that their cars up to the task (see **Desert Driving,** p. 528).

**Hunting** and **fishing** are allowed in the preserve, but finding water may be an angler's toughest challenge. For those with the required California hunting license, deer and quail are popular targets in season. Watch out for protected desert tortoises sunning themselves on desert roads and avoid disturbing them in the desert, their last natural stronghold. **Afton Canyon Natural Area** (Barstow BLM, ☎252-6000) lies 36 mi. northeast of Barstow en route to Las Vegas. Follow I-15 to Afton Rd. and follow the dirt road east. The flowing water in this "Grand Canyon of the Mojave" is no mirage; it's a rare above-ground appearance of the Mojave River. Canyon walls tower above the rushing water and willow-lined shores. Golden eagles, bighorn sheep, and tortoises reside here. **Hikers** with flashlights may explore the side canyons along unmarked trails. Camping is available at the 22 developed sites with water, fire pits, shaded picnic tables, and restrooms ($6 per person).

The **Kelso Dunes** blanket a spectacular, barren landscape within the Mojave National Preserve. Stretching 4 mi. and reaching heights of 700 ft., the dunes offer a 2-3hr., one-way hike from the trailhead. Keep in mind that the formation acts like a giant oven in the summer—don't get baked. From the top you can hear the dunes sing on a windy day; the cascading sand groans like bending metal. The dunes are about 30 mi. southeast of Baker via Kelbaker Rd. from Barstow; either take I-40 to Kelbaker Rd. Exit (80 mi. to the east) or I-15 to

Baker. Kelbaker Rd. itself offers phenomenal views of every conceivable desert formation from the Kelso Dunes and crusty lava flows to glacier-hewn granite heaps. **Dune buggies** and **jeeps** are still permitted at Dumont Dunes, just off Rte. 127 about 33 mi. north of Baker. Look for the 3½ mi. road turning off Rte. 127 just after Harry Wade Rd. There is no sign; keep your eyes peeled. The dunes are strewn with man-made striations—those from WWII training exercises are still visible in parts of the Mojave. Tracks remain in the sand for decades; don't leave a legacy.

**Providence Mountains State Recreation Area** is a popular, high-altitude (4000-5000 ft.) region with six **primitive campsites** (☎928-2586; sites $10) and a **Visitors Center,** both on Essex Rd., 17 mi. north of I-40. View the spectacular **Mitchell Caverns** on an informative 1½ mi. tour through the stalactite-cluttered limestone chambers. (1½hr. Sept.-May M-F 1:30pm, Sa-Su 10am, 1:30, 3pm. June-Aug. Su and Sa 1:30pm. $4, 16 and under free. Tour reservations ☎928-2586; $2 surcharge.) There are 61 primitive but beautiful sites surrounded by piñon and juniper trees at the unseasonably cool **Mid Hill ❶** (5600 ft.) and **Hole-in-Wall ❶** (4200 ft.) in the East Mojave National Scenic Area. (Both $12; limited water, pit toilets, no hookups.) The road into Mid Hill is neither paved nor recommended for RVs. From Essex Rd., follow Black Canyon Rd. to Mid Hill or Wild Horse Canyon Rd. to Hole-in-Wall.

# ARIZONA

Home to a little rut in the ground known as the Grand Canyon, the northwest Arizona region draws adventurers and tourists who come to scramble along the edge of its awesome ravine. It is also home to small, dusty towns, and often seems like the land of an endless desert highway. To enter the state, cross the Colorado River on I-40 and head east toward the Grand Canyon (most often accessed from the base town of Flagstaff, AZ), or jet down Highway 95 South to the resort town of Lake Havasu City. Route 66 splits off from Highway 95 in Golden Shores—bear right off the highway. The road meanders through undulating deserts before starting its climb through the Black Mountains. A sunset drive will silence anyone who's ever had snooty words for western sunset paintings. Be careful after dark, however; the road can be treacherous once it enters the rugged hills. For more on Arizona, see ▧ *Let's Go: Southwest USA 2004* or ▧ *Let's Go: USA 2004.*

# GRAND CANYON ☎928

Long before its designation as a national park in 1919, the Grand Canyon captured the imagination of those who strolled up to its edge and beheld its inconceivable span. The biggest attraction in the southwest, the Canyon welcomes millions of visitors from across the globe who want to validate the breathtaking images they've seen on postcards and calendars. The Canyon never fails to elicit individual thought and reflection, sometimes as deep or wide as the huge chasm itself.

The Grand Canyon extends from Lee's Ferry, AZ all the way to Lake Mead, NV. In the north, the Glen Canyon Dam backs up the Colorado River into mammoth Lake Powell, a water sports paradise. To the west, the Hoover Dam traps the remaining outflow from Glen Canyon to form Lake Mead, another haven for water enthusiasts. Grand Canyon National Park proper divides neatly into three sections: the most frequently visited South Rim, the more remote North Rim, and, of course, the forbidding canyon gorge.

THE DESERT

## AT A GLANCE: GRAND CANYON NATIONAL PARK

**AREA:** 1,218,376 acres.

**FEATURES:** The Canyon, Colorado River, North Rim, South Rim, West Rim, Kaibab Plateau, Tonto Platform.

**HIGHLIGHTS:** Taking a mule ride to Phantom Ranch, rafting in luxury down the Canyon, backpacking from Rim to Rim on the South and North Kaibab Trails, standing in awe at the edge of either rim.

**GATEWAY TOWNS:** Flagstaff, Williams.

**CAMPING:** Mather Campground on the South Rim and North Rim Campground require reservations. Backcountry camping requires permit ($10 per permit, plus $5 per person per night, $10 per group).

**FEES:** Weekly pass $20 per car, $10 for other modes of transportation; covers both South and North Rim.

# SOUTH RIM ☎928

During the summer, everything on two legs or four wheels converges on this side of the Grand Canyon. If you plan to visit at this time, make reservations well in advance for lodging, campsites, and/or mules, and prepare to battle the crowds. Still, it's better than Disney World. A friendly Park Service staff, well-run facilities, and beautiful scenery ease crowd anxiety. Fewer tourists brave the canyon's winter weather; many hotels and facilities close during the off-season. Leading up to the park entrance, Rte. 64 is surrounded by Kaibab National Forest.

## ▌ TRANSPORTATION

There are two park entrances: the main **south entrance** is 58 mi. north of I-40; the eastern **Desert View entrance** is 27 mi. away off Hwy. 89. Both are accessed via Rte. 64. From Las Vegas, the fastest route to the South Rim is US 93 S to I-40 E, then Rte. 64 N at Williams. From Flagstaff, head north on US 180 to Rte. 64. If the haul is too much for your car, **Grand Canyon Garage** (☎638-2631) will take a look.

The **Grand Canyon Railway** (☎800-843-8724) runs an authentically restored train from Williams, AZ to Grand Canyon (2¼hr.; leaves 10am, returns 3:30pm; $68, children $27). **North Arizona Shuttle and Tours** (☎866-870-8687) departs its Flagstaff depot, 1300 S. Milton St., for the Grand Canyon daily (2hr.; leaves 7:30am, 2:30pm, returns 10am, 4:30pm.) Fares don't include the $6 entrance fee. **Free shuttle buses** run the West Rim Loop (daily 1hr. before sunrise to sunset) and the Village Loop (daily 1hr. before sunrise to 11pm) every 10-30min. A free **hiker's shuttle** runs every 30min. between the info center and the South Kaibab Trailhead, on the East Rim near Yaki Point. For **taxi** service, call ☎638-2822.

## ❖ ORIENTATION

Maps and signs in the park make it easy to orient yourself, though the size of the park can be overwhelming. Lodges and services concentrate in **Grand Canyon Village,** at the end of Park Entrance Rd. The east half of the village contains the Visitors Center and the general store, while most of the rim lodges and the challenging **Bright Angel Trail** lie in the west section. The shorter but more difficult **South Kaibab Trail** is off **East Rim Drive,** east of the village. Free shuttle buses to eight rim overlooks run along **West Rim Drive** (closed to private vehicles during the summer). Avoid walking on the drive; the rim trails are safer and more scenic. For most services in the park, call the **main switchboard** (☎638-2631).

**WHEN TO GO.** The South Rim, open year-round, is jam-packed in the spring, summer, and fall, and only the winter offers some measure of solitude, though services are closed and temperatures are chilly (lows in the 10s and 20s, highs in the 30s and 40s). Colder and less visited than its southern counterpart, the North Rim is open for day use only from October 15 to December 1, and from December 1 to May 15, the Rim closes entirely due to snow and ice. Summer temperatures rise with visitation figures but are highly variable from rim to rim—average summer highs are about 85°F on the South Rim, 75°F on the North Rim (due to higher elevation), and 110°F in the Inner Canyon.

## PRACTICAL INFORMATION

**Visitor Information:** The new **Canyon View Information Plaza,** across from Mather Point and just after the park entrance, is the one-stop center for info. The Plaza houses the **Visitors Center** (open daily 8am-6pm), a bookstore, restrooms, and kiosks. The Center stocks copies of *The Guide* (also given at the park entrance) and pamphlets with info on reservations, handicapped access, backcountry secrets, and ranger projects. Park at Mather Point and hoof it for a half-mile to the plaza. For

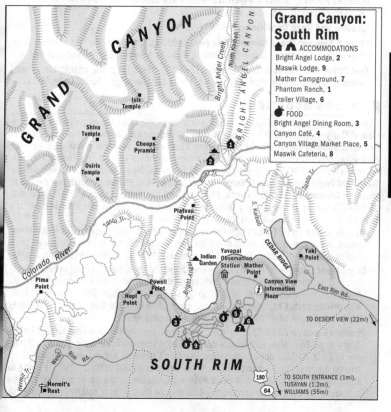

**Grand Canyon: South Rim**

♠ ♠ ACCOMMODATIONS
Bright Angel Lodge, **2**
Maswik Lodge, **9**
Mather Campground, **7**
Phantom Ranch, **1**
Trailer Village, **6**

🍴 FOOD
Bright Angel Dining Room, **3**
Canyon Café, **4**
Canyon Village Market Place, **5**
Maswik Cafeteria, **8**

THE DESERT

those looking for pre-trip info, the Park Service sells a variety of books and packets (☎800-858-2808; www.grandcanyon.com). **Transportation info desks** in **Bright Angel Lodge** and **Maswik Lodge** (☎638-2631) handle reservations for mule rides, bus tours, plane tours, Phantom Ranch, taxis, and more. Open daily 6am-8pm.

**Bank: Bank One** (☎638-2437), in Market Plaza. Full-service branch with **ATM. Currency exchange** on traveler's checks, but not cash. Open M-Th 10am-3pm, F 10am-5pm.

**Luggage Storage: Bright Angel Lodge** (see p. 560). Open 6:30am-9pm.

**Equipment Rental:** In general store (below). Hiking boots ($8 1st day, $5 per additional day); sleeping bags ($9 1st day, $5 per extra day); tents ($15 1st day for a 2-person, $16 1st day for 4-person, $9 per extra day); packs (large $6, small $4); and other gear (stoves $5). Deposit required; major credit cards accepted. Open daily 7am-8:30pm.

**Groceries: Canyon Village Marketplace** (☎638-2262), a general store at Yavapai Lodge. Offers 1hr. photo processing. Open daily in summer 7am-9pm. Near the east entrance, **Desert View General Store** also stocks food. Open daily 7am-8:30pm.

**Showers and Laundry:** Available at concession-run **Camper Services,** adjacent to Mather Campground in Canyon Village. Showers $1 per 5min. Showers daily 6am-11pm. Laundry daily 6am-9:45pm.

**Internet Access: Grand Canyon National Park Library** (☎638-7768). Open M-Th 8:30am-noon and 1pm-4pm, except holidays.

**Weather and Road Conditions:** ☎638-7888.

**Medical Services: Grand Canyon Clinic** (☎638-2551). Go left at the first stoplight after the South Rim entrance. Open M-F 7am-7pm, Sa 10am-4pm. 24hr. emergency first aid.

**Post Office:** 100 Mather Business Ctr. (☎638-2512), in market plaza, next to the general store at Yavapai Lodge. Open M-F 9am-4:30pm, Sa 10am-5pm. **Postal Code:** 86023.

# ACCOMMODATIONS

Compared to the six million years it took the Colorado River to carve out the Grand Canyon, the year it will take you to get indoor lodging near the South Rim is nothing. **Summer rooms should be reserved 11 months in advance.** Even so, there are cancellations every day; you can check for vacancies or call the Grand Canyon operator (☎638-2631) and ask to be connected with the proper lodge. Reservations for **Bright Angel Lodge, Maswik Lodge, Trailer Village,** and **Phantom Ranch** can be made through **Xanterra Parks and Resorts,** 14001 E. Iliff, Ste. 600, Aurora, CO 80014 (☎303-297-2757). Yavapai Lodge may have remaining rooms when all other lodges are full. Most accommodations on the South Rim are very pricey.

**Maswik Lodge** (☎638-2631), in Grand Canyon Village near the rim and restaurants. Small, clean cabins with showers but no heat are $66. Motel rooms with queen beds and ceiling fans available. Singles $79; doubles $121. $7-9 per additional person. ❹

**Bright Angel Lodge** (☎638-2631), in Grand Canyon Village. The cheapest indoor lodging in the park, located in a historic building right on the rim. Very convenient to Bright Angel Trail and shuttle buses. "Rustic" lodge singles and doubles with shared bath $53, with private bath $71. "Historic" cabins, some of which have fireplaces, are available for 1 or 2 people $84-107. $7 per additional person. ❸

**Phantom Ranch** (☎638-2631), on the canyon floor, a day's hike down the Kaibab Trail or Bright Angel Trail. Male and female dorms $28; seldom-available cabins for 1 or 2 people $71.50; $10.50 per additional person. Don't show up without reservations, which can be made up to 23 months in advance. Expensive meal options. If you're dying to sleep on the canyon floor but don't have a reservation, show up at the Bright Angel transportation desk at 6am on the day prior to your planned stay and try the wait-list. ❷

THE DESERT

## CAMPING

The campsites listed here usually fill up early in the day. In the **Kaibab National Forest,** along the south border of the park, you can pull off a dirt road and camp for free. No camping is allowed within a quarter-mile of US 64. **Dispersed camping** sits conveniently along the oft-traveled N. Long Jim Loop Rd.—turn right about one mile south of the south entrance station. For quieter and more remote sites, follow signs for the Arizona Trail into the national forest between miles 252 and 253 on US 64. Sleeping in cars is not permitted within the park, but it is allowed in the Kaibab Forest. For more info, contact the **Tusayan Ranger Station,** Kaibab National Forest, P.O. Box 3088, Tusayan, AZ 86023 (☎638-2443). Reservations for some campgrounds can be made through **SPHERICS** (☎800-365-2267).

**Mather Campground** (call SPHERICS, ☎800-365-2267) in Grand Canyon Village, 1 mi. south of the Canyon Village Marketplace; follow signs from Yavapai Lodge. 320 shady, relatively isolated sites with no hookups. Check at the office even if the sign says the campground is full. 7-night max. stay. For Mar.-Nov., reserve up to 3 months in advance; Dec.-Feb. first-come, first-served. Sept.-May $12; June-Aug. $15. ❶

**Ten-X Campground** (☎638-2443), in Kaibab National Forest, 10 mi. south of Grand Canyon Village off Rte. 64. Offers shady sites removed from the highway and surrounded by pine trees. Toilets and water. No hookups or showers. Open May-Sept. First-come, first-served; sites $10. ❶

**Desert View Campground** (☎638-7888), 25 mi. east of Grand Canyon Village. Short on shade and far from the hub of the South Rim, but a perfect place to avoid the crowd. 50 sites with phone and rest room access, but no hookups or campfires. Open mid-May to Oct. No reservations; usually full by early afternoon. Sites $10. ❶

**Camper Village** (☎638-2887), in Tusayan, 1 mi. south of the park entrance behind the general store. Showers and flush toilets. Two-person hookups and tent sites $18-26; $2 per additional adult. First-come, first-served tent sites; reservations required for RVs. ❷

**Trailer Village** (☎638-2631), next to Mather Campground. 84 sites designed for the RV. Showers, laundry, and groceries nearby. Office open daily 8am-noon and 1-5pm. 2-person hookups $24; $2 additional person. Reserve 6-9 months in advance. ❷

## FOOD

Fast food has yet to sink its greasy talons into the South Rim (the closest McDonald's is 7 mi. south in Tusayan), but you can find meals at fast-food prices and get a slightly better return for your money. The **Canyon Village Market Place ❶,** at the Market Plaza 1 mi. west of Mather Point on the main road, has a deli counter with the cheapest eats in the park, a wide selection of groceries, a camping supplies department, and enough Grand Canyon apparel to clothe each member of your extended family. (☎638-2262. Open daily in summer 7am-8:30pm; deli open 7am-6pm. Sandwiches $2-4.) The well-stocked **Canyon Cafe ❶,** across from the general store at Yavapai Lodge, offers a wider variety of food than the deli. (Open daily 6:30am-9pm. Hamburgers $3, pizza $3.50-5, dinners $5-7.) **Maswik Cafeteria ❶,** in Maswik Lodge, serves a variety of grilled food, country favorites, and Mexican specialties (including veggie options and healthy alternatives) in a wood-paneled cafeteria atmosphere. (Open daily 6am-10pm. Hot entrees $6-7, sandwiches $3-5.) **Bright Angel Dining Room ❷,** in Bright Angel Lodge, serves hot sandwiches for $7-9. Breakfasts run $6-7 and pricey dinner entrees range $10-15. (☎638-2631. Open daily 6:30am-10pm.) Just out the door of the dining room, the **Soda Fountain ❶** at Bright Angel Lodge keeps eight flavors of ice cream chilled and stocks a variety of snack-bar sandwiches. (Open daily 8am-8pm. 1 scoop $2.)

THE DESERT

From your first glimpse of the canyon, you may feel a compelling desire to see it from the inside—an enterprise harder than it looks. Even the young at heart and in body should remember that an easy downhill hike can become a nightmarish 50° incline on the return journey: plan on taking twice as long to ascend as you took descending. Also keep in mind that the lower you go, the hotter it gets; when it's 85°F on the rim, it's around 100°F at Indian Gardens and around 115°F at Phantom Ranch. Heat stroke, the greatest threat to any hiker, is signaled by a monstrous headache and red, sweatless skin. For a day hike, **you must take at least a gallon of water per person; drink at least a liter per hr. hiking upwards under the hot sun.** Wearing a cotton t-shirt that is soaking wet is a good way to hike in extreme temperatures. Apply sunscreen regularly. Hiking boots or sneakers with excellent tread are a must—the trails are steep, and every year several careless hikers take what locals morbidly call "the 12-second tour." Poor preparation and over-exertion greatly magnify the risks of canyon hiking. Check *The Guide* for safety tips and speak with a ranger before embarking on a hike. Hiking down to the river and back to the rim in the same day is discouraged by rangers, though it seems these discouragements are often ineffective; most Helivac rescues are the result of these attempts. Resting at a campground is recommended. Parents should think twice before bringing children more than 1 mi. down any trail.

## ◢ HIKING AND BACKPACKING

Although the Grand Canyon experience for the majority of park visitors involves stepping out of the air-conditioned tour bus, walking eagerly to the rim with camera in hand, and then retreating to the bus before beads of sweat begin to form, there are many more invigorating ways to enjoy the Canyon's grandeur. Outdoor recreation in the park focuses mainly on hiking and backpacking, though commercial outfits provide services like mule rides, rafting, and "flightseeing."

In choosing a day hike, remember that the Canyon does not have any loops; be prepared to retrace every single footstep uphill. For longer day hikes, begin before 7am. Because walking and climbing in the summer heat requires exceptional effort, the Park Service recommends not hiking between the hours of 10am and 4pm. Rangers present a variety of free informative **talks** and **guided hikes;** details are listed in *The Guide*. Rangers will also gladly offer advice regarding trail guides and maps; the *Official Guide to Hiking the Grand Canyon*, published by the Grand Canyon Association, is the preferred choice. The so-called corridor trails, which include the **Rim, Bright Angel, South Kaibab,** and **River Trails,** are the only South Rim trails regularly maintained and patrolled by the Park Service.

Stifling heat, scarce water, and drastic elevation changes, all under the weight of a heavy pack, make **backpacking** around the Grand Canyon a grueling experience. Still, applications for **backcountry permits** far outnumber availability, especially during the summer. If you get there late in the day, you can forget about getting a permit and start planning to arrive earlier the next day. The most popular backpacking routes connect the rim-to-river trails listed below and demand little in the way of navigational skills. Camping along these corridor routes is limited to **designated areas.** The Park Service divides the park into use areas, each with restrictions on camping and recreation. Much of the park remains inaccessible to trekkers because of cliffs and other impassable terrain. The footbridge spanning the Colorado River near Phantom Ranch is the only **river crossing,** making the ranch a necessary stop when traveling rim to rim. **Through-hiking** from the South to the North Rim generally connects either the Bright Angel or South Kaibab Trail with the North Kaibab Trail, covering 21-23 mi. and 10,000 ft. of elevation change.

All overnight trips require a **backcountry permit** ($10 fee, plus $5 per person per day, $10 per group), obtainable at the Backcountry Information Center next to the Maswik Lodge (P.O. Box 129, Grand Canyon, AZ 86023; www.nps.gov/grca). Permits are available on the 1st of the month, four months before the proposed hike (e.g., July permits available March 1). Requests should include the proposed route, campsites, license plate numbers, group size, and contact info.

**Rim Trail** (12 mi. one-way, 4-6hr.). With only a mild elevation change (about 200 ft.) and the constant security of the nearby shuttle, this trail is great for hikers seeking a tame way to see the Canyon. The handicapped-accessible trail follows shuttle bus routes along Hermit Rd. past the Grand Canyon Village to Mather Point. The Rim Trail covers both paved and unpaved ground, with 8 viewpoints along Hermit Rd. and 3 east of it. Near Grand Canyon Village the trail gets crowded, but toward the eastern and western ends, hikers have more elbow room. Hopi Point has panoramic canyon views perfect for watching sunsets. Bring lots of water, as little is available along the trail.

**Bright Angel Trail** (up to 18 mi. round-trip, 1-2 days). Bright Angel's frequent switchbacks and refreshing water stations make it the into-the-canyon choice of moderate hikers. The trail can be a day or overnight hike. It departs from Rim Trail near the western edge of Grand Canyon Village, and the first 1-2 mi. of the trail attract droves of day hikers eager for a taste of canyon descent. Rest houses are strategically stationed 1½ and 3 mi. from the rim, each with water between May and Sept. **Indian Gardens,** 4½ mi. down, offers restrooms, picnic tables, 15 backcountry sites open year-round, and blessed shade. From rim to river, the trail drops 4420 ft. Although spread over only 9 mi., the round-trip is too strenuous for a day hike. With a permit, overnighters can camp at Indian Gardens or on the canyon floor at Bright Angel Campground, while day hikers are advised to go no farther than Plateau Point (12¼ mi. round-trip) or Indian Gardens (9¼ mi. round-trip). Yield and wave enviously to tourists descending by mule train. The **River Trail** (1½ mi.) runs along the river, linking the Bright Angel with South Kaibab.

**South Kaibab Trail** (7 mi. one-way to Phantom Ranch, 4-5 hr. descent). Beginning at Yaki Pt. (7260 ft.), Kaibab is trickier, steeper, and lacks shade or water, but it rewards the intrepid with a better view of the canyon. Unlike most canyon-descending trails, the South Kaibab avoids the safety and obstructed views of a side-canyon route and instead winds directly down the ridge, offering panoramic views across the expanse of the canyon. Day hikes to Cedar Ridge (3 mi. round-trip; toilet facilities available) and Skeleton Point (6 mi. round-trip) are reasonable only for experienced, well-conditioned hikers. Many hikers believe that the best route is to descend the South Kaibab Trail (4-5hr.) and come back up the Bright Angel (7-8hr.) the following day, though this is very strenuous. The elevation change from trailhead to river is 4880 ft.

**Grandview Trail** (6½ mi. round-trip to the Mesa). The costs of hauling ore up to Grandview Point (7400 ft.) from Horseshoe Mesa (4800 ft.) along this Hopi Indian-built trail proved too great for turn-of-the-century miners. Eventually, they gave up on mining and started hauling tourists up and down the harrowing hike. Grandview requires route-finding and delicate footing, so hiking boots are a must. Backpackers can continue a steep 1¾ mi. to the Tonto Trail junction and follow Tonto to canyon-floor destinations like Bright Angel Campground. Expect a full day of hiking to Horseshoe Mesa and back.

**Hermit Trail** (9¼ mi. one-way to the river). Embarking from the Hermit Trailhead at Hermit's Rest (6640 ft.), this strenuous route descends the Supai cliffs, switching back and forth on loose rocks. The Hermit Trail offers panoramic views of the West Rim, less frequently seen than the rim surrounding the Grand Canyon Village because during the summer it's accessible only by the red shuttle line. The trail ends near the Hermit Creek rapids, where water must be treated before drinking. Following the trail all the way to Colorado River covers 9¼ mi. Hikers should allow at least 7hr. to reach the first overnight camping area,

THE DESERT

Hermit Creek (7¾ mi.), because of the steep, rocky paths. Occasional rock slides and floods may obscure the trail, making route-finding skills vital. Day hikers should go beyond Santa Maria Springs, 2½ mi. down the trail (5-6hr. each way).

**Tonto Trail** (up to 95 mi.). Threading its way along the entire length of the Tonto Platform, the solid sandstone Tonto Trail travels 95 mi. and connects all of the other routes traveling from rim to river. The Tonto Platform, a jutting esplanade that appears table-flat from the rim, actually contains washes and gullies. The trail itself is a rugged wilderness path and requires route-finding skills. Most hikers use the trail to connect other popular routes. There are 4½ mi. of the trail between the Bright Angel and South Kaibab Trails, 21¼ mi between S. Kaibab and Grandview Trails, and 12 mi. between Hermit Trail and Indian Gardens on the Bright Angel Trail. West past Hermit Trail, Tonto becomes less trafficked. Creeks cutting through the platform provide year-round water.

## ■ OTHER OUTDOOR ACTIVITIES

Beyond using your feet, there are other ways to conquer the canyon. **Mule trips** from the South Rim are expensive and booked up to one year in advance, although some reservations do get canceled. (☎303-297-2757. Daytrip to Plateau Point 6 mi. down the Bright Angel Trail $127, overnight including lodging at Phantom Ranch and all meals $343.) Mule trips from the North Rim (☎435-679-8665) are cheaper and more readily available. An 8hr. day trip to Roaring Springs waterfall is $95. Looking up at the Grand Canyon from a **whitewater raft** is both popular and pricey. Trips into the Grand Canyon proper vary in length from a week to 18 days and are booked far in advance. The *Trip Planner* (available by request at the info center) lists several commercial guides licensed to offer trips in the canyon; check the park website for info before you visit. The only company permitted to guide one-day trips on the Colorado, **Wilderness River Adventures** (p. 564), operates out of Page, AZ. If the views from the rim fail to dazzle and astound you, try the higher vantages provided by one of the park's many **flightseeing** companies, all located at the **Grand Canyon Airport** outside of Tuyasan. **Grand Canyon Airlines** flies 45min. canyon tours hourly during the summer. (☎866-235-9422. $75, children $45. Reservations recommended, but walk-ins generally available. Discount for lunchtime tours 11am-2pm.) Flying smaller planes on a wider range of trips, **Air Grand Canyon** offers 30-90min. flights. (☎800-247-4726. $74-174.) Both airlines team up with Wilderness River Adventures to offer one-day combination flightseeing/rafting tours. For a rapid vertical thrill, check out the popular helicopter flights from **Papillon Grand Canyon Helicopters.** Tours of the Canyon depart as frequently as every 30min. between 8am and 5pm. (☎800-528-2418. Tours 30min.; $105, children $95. $175 per 50min., children $155.) Both **Scenic Airlines** (☎800-634-6801) and **Air Vegas Airlines** (☎800-255-7474) offer flight/hotel/canyon tour packages out of Las Vegas's northern airport. For a list of flight companies in the park, write the Grand Canyon Chamber of Commerce, Box 3007, Grand Canyon, AZ 86023.

# LAKE HAVASU CITY                    ☎928

Created by the damming of the Colorado River in 1938, Lake Havasu embodies a new West, fueled by tourist dollars and an urge to kick back. Entrepreneur Robert McCulloch willed the city (now 50,000-strong) to life in 1963 as a place to test boat engines. He drew up a community plan, brought the London Bridge from England, and people arrived with boats in tow. Motorboats and jet skis ceaselessly churn the green waters into a roiling froth. When not thundering along, the boats float down the channel with well-oiled, bikini-clad gals reclining languidly on the bow. Spring break is prime time in this party town, while high temperatures keep the adrenaline to a minimum in the summer.

**🔣🔢 ORIENTATION AND PRACTICAL INFORMATION.** The lake is located on the California and Arizona borders, and the city lies on Arizona's Rte. 95, 21 mi. south of I-40. The tiny town of Parker lies 40 mi. to the south, and the gambling halls of Laughlin are a tempting 70 mi. north. **Route 95** runs north-south through the city, intersected downtown by the east-west thoroughfare of **McCulloch Boulevard.** Just east of Rte. 95 is **Lake Havasu Avenue,** which hosts stucco installations of familiar fast-food spots. McCulloch runs west over a channel, spanned by the actual London Bridge, and connects to The Island, where beach resorts flourish.

The **Visitors Center** is in English Village, a mock British square with a brewery and food stands at the corner of Rte. 95 and London Bridge Rd. (☎855-4115. Open daily 9am-4pm.) **City Transit Services** is on call with curb-to-curb shuttle services throughout Lake Havasu City. (☎453-7600. Operates M-F 6am-9pm, Sa-Su 6am-6pm. $3, under 10 $2, under 5 free.) Bike rental is available at **MBK Bikes,** 151 Swanson Ave. (☎453-7474. Open M-F 9am-6pm, Sa 10am-5pm, Su 11am-4pm. Mountain bikes $20 per day, cruisers $13.) For those not interested in motorboats (a decided minority here), **Crawdaddy's Kayak Rental and Tours** rents kayaks ($24 per day) and other small watercraft and provides maps of the waterways. Services include: **police,** 2360 McCulloch Blvd. (☎855-1171); **emergency** (☎911); **laundry** at Sundance Country, 121 N. Lake Havasu Ave. (☎855-2700); **Havasu Regional Medical Center,** 101 Civic Center Ln. (☎855-8185); and the **post office,** 1750 McCulloch Blvd. (☎855-2361. Open M 7:45am-5pm, Tu-F 8:30am-5pm, Sa 10am-1pm.) **Postal code:** 86403.

**🔣 ACCOMMODATIONS.** There is an abundance of affordable motels along London Bridge Rd., though rates tend to be higher on summer weekends. The shiny **Windsor Inn ❷,** 451 London Bridge Rd., offers inexpensive rooms and all the desert amenities. Since you pay by the bed, two people can get the single price if they're willing to share a bed or one crashes on the couch. (☎855-4135, 800-245-4135. Singles Su-Th $36, F-Sa $49; doubles $42/$59.) The budget chain **Super 8 Motel ❸,** 305 London Bridge Rd., offers predictable accommodations at predictable prices. (☎855-8844. Singles Su-Th $41, F-Sa $51; doubles $45/$56.) Campers should visit **Lake Havasu State Park ❶,** west off Rte. 95 on Industrial Rd., where there's a main campground (☎855-2784; 43 sites; showers, toilets, boat-launch; $14 per site) and **Cattail Cove ❶** (61 sites; showers, toilets, RV hookups; $19), with a beach and boat docks.

**🔣🔣 FOOD AND NIGHTLIFE.** In addition to Lake Havasu Ave., there is also a tremendous concentration of fast food along Rte. 95, particularly where it intersects London Bridge Rd. For a less generic taste, try the Irish-inspired **Slainee's ❷,** 1519 Queens Bay Rd., which has hearty entrees ($7 and up, with soup/salad), a slew of pool tables, and live tunes on weekends. (☎505-8900. Open daily 10am-1am.) At the **Barley Brothers Brewery and Grill ❷,** 1425 McCulloch Blvd. on The Island, knowledgeable bartenders serve inventive local brews (pint $4) as well as more refined cuisine. (☎505-7837. Open Su-Th 11am-10pm, F-Sa 11am-11pm. Sandwiches $8.) A short but dark walk over London Bridge from the Brewery, the colossal **Kokomo's on the Channel,** 1477 Queens Bay Rd., is the London Bridge Resort's open-air super-club where you can shake your sun-burned tailfeathers. Expect the action to pick up after 11pm. (☎855-0888. Weekend cover $5-15. Mixed drinks $4, DJ-announced specials $1. Open daily 11am-1am.)

**🔣🔣 SIGHTS AND ACTIVITIES.** Lake Havasu's most unusual claim to fame is the **London Bridge.** Originally built in London, England in 1824, it was painstakingly dismantled and reconstructed under the sponsorship of Robert McCulloch. The reconstructed bridge was dedicated in October 1971. See the

THE DESERT

## FROM THE ROAD

### THE LONE CAMPER

When I approached Borrego Springs at night, I hadn't seen another car for an hour, and the only life in sight was the ghostly desert underbrush silhouetted by the full moon. I compared myself (in my rusty red Cherokee) to the Lone Ranger, riding Trigger under the stars, but as darkness settled in, camping alone in the sand seemed somehow less appealing. I drove to the first motel I could find, but the cheapest room was $60. I did the math—that was 55 Slurpees, 12 GI Joes, or 240 chances at a Vegas quarter slot—and headed back to my car. After finding the nearest campground in Anza Borrego, I circled a site in my car for 20 minutes. When I finally decided the site was secure, without apparent wild animal or tarantula infestations, I moved in for the kill; I set up my tent 12 feet from a well-lit shower station.

As it turned out, the night was perfect for desert camping. A full moon hung overhead among stars, lighting up the desert so well I had no use for my flashlight. A desert breeze kept the temperature around 80°F, which felt like a cold front. I stayed up late, enjoying the night. I drifted off at around 2am to the sounds of a soft breeze and the howl of a distant coyote. Hours later I woke up groggy and sweating bullets in my starkly illuminated tent. It was 7am. The sun was blazing; the desert heat was unbearable. Here I learned the most important lesson of desert camping: enjoy the cool dark while you can by shutting your fool eyes and going to sleep.

-Jay Gierak, 2004

bridge and associated tourist "attractions" at the intersection of Rte. 95 and London Bridge Rd. Without a doubt, the place to be in Lake Havasu is on the water. Any number of tourist publications can direct you to a reputable boat rental. Loungers should try **Windsor Beach,** west on Industrial Rd. from Rte. 95, in Lake Havasu State Park (day-use $8). Free beaches line the eastern shore of The Island, but swimmers can avoid boat traffic by sticking to the southern end. Take Smoketree from Rte. 95 to get to **Rotary Beach,** where sand, volleyball, and picnic areas await.

# THE LOW DESERT

The Low Desert, home of Anza-Borrego Desert State Park and the Salton Sea, is at first glance flat and barren, with few easily observed signs of life beyond the artificial tourist oases of Palm Springs and the date groves of Coachella Valley. Only a few resilient species like the hardy Joshua Tree have learned to flourish amid the dust and broken rocks, but there remains a simple and striking beauty to the mountain vistas and the simultaneous toughness and fragility of life in the desert.

## ANZA-BORREGO DESERT STATE PARK ☎760

The largest state park in California, Anza-Borrego is layered with both natural and human history. A short drive from San Diego or Palm Springs, this harsh desert sprouts over 1000 different plant species, many of which are found nowhere else in California. Barbed cholla cacti, bruise-blossomed indigo bush, and thirsty tamarisk flourish in the withering heat. The scrub sprawls over a diverse landscape of dunes, badlands, mountains, oases, and active faults. Hidden among these natural wonders are the abandoned dwellings of Native Americans, Spanish settlers, and oil pioneers. Over 56 species of reptiles or amphibians and 30 species of mammals, including the endangered Bighorn Sheep, live within the park's borders. Though Anza-Borrego is just as beautiful as Death Valley or Joshua Tree, it remains less popular than the national parks because the state park lacks the funding to adequately maintain and develop roads, campgrounds, and facilities. In addition, the park is far from major highways and difficult to access. The beauty of Anza-Borrego can only be found by a true desert adventurer. Visit in the winter or early spring when temperatures are more manageable; high summer temperatures can make daytime activity in the desert dangerous.

**⊞ 🖼 ORIENTATION & PRACTICAL INFORMATION.** To reach the park from the west, take **State Route 78** east from I-15 in Escondido. From the south, take **State Route 79** northbound from I-8 to Rte. 78. From the east, take **County Route S22** west from Rte. 86, which connects to I-10 in Indio. Once in the park, head to **Borrego Springs,** its only town, via **County Route S3** for info, lodging, and food. No roads approach Anza-Borrego from the north.

The **Northeast Rural Bus System** serves the region. (☎767-4287. Info line open daily 7am-noon and 2-5pm.) **AAA Emergency Road Service** (☎800-222-4357) can refer troubled motorists to a towing company. For visitor information, stop by the **Anza-Borrego Desert State Park Visitors Center,** 200 Palm Canyon Dr., Borrego Springs. They have topographical maps, books, exhibits, and slideshows. Rangers offer backcountry and safety info; stop here before hiking or camping. (☎767-4205. Open Oct.-May daily 9am-5pm; June-Sept. Sa-Su 9am-5pm.) For info in summer months, call the **Anza-Borrego State Park Headquarters** (☎767-5311; open M-F 8am-5pm) or stop by the **Borrego Springs Chamber of Commerce and Visitor Center,** 786 Palm Canyon Dr. (☎767-5555, weather conditions 289-1212; open M-F 10am-4pm). The **Borrego Medical Center,** 4343 Yaqui Pass Rd., Borrego Springs, on Rams Hill, provides medical help. (☎767-5051. Open June-Sept. M-Tu and Th-F 9am-1pm, W 1-6pm; Oct.-May M-F 9am-5pm, Sa 9am-1pm.)

**🖼 🖼 🖾 ACCOMMODATIONS, CAMPING & FOOD.** The small community of Borrego Springs provides adequate accommodations for park visitors, from basic motels to resorts of the Palm Springs variety, though bargains are hard to find. **Hacienda del Sol ❹,** 610 Palm Canyon Dr., offers comfy, old rooms. (☎767-5442. Singles and doubles $60. Additional persons $15.) Prices at **Stanlunds ❹,** 2771 Borrego Springs Rd., are just as low. (☎767-5501. Breakfast included on weekends. Pets welcome. In summer singles $55; doubles $65. In winter $75/$85.) The western-themed **Palm Canyon Resort ❺,** 221 Palm Canyon Dr., offers more niceties—two pools, fitness center, restaurant, saloon, and laundry are all available. (☎800-242-0044. In summer singles and doubles $70-85; in winter $95-130.)

Anza-Borrego is one of the few places left in the United States that still allows **open camping.** Since lodging prices in Borrego Springs tend towards the high side, the park is a great opportunity to practice your tent-pitching skills. Sites must be 100 ft. away from water and any road, and fires are not permitted unless they're in your own metal container. The $4 daily park fee must be paid prior to camping; park entrance is free if you are not camping. Besides backcountry camping, Anza-Borrego hosts four developed campgrounds, as well as ten primitive campgrounds. **Borrego Palm Canyon ❶** has 123 developed sites for tents, RVs, and groups. (Flush toilets, water, showers, sun shades, fire rings, and picnic tables. Sites $10-19.) **Tamarisk Grove ❶** has 27 developed sites for tents and RVs. (Flush toilets, water, showers, sun shades, fire rings, and picnic tables. Sites $10.) For those who wander in without the aid of machines, **Horse Camp ❶** has 10 developed sites for horses and people only. (Flush toilets, water, showers, fire rings, and picnic tables. Sites $14-17.) **Bow Willow ❶** has 16 sites for tents or RVs. (Vault toilets, water, picnic tables, sunshades, and fire rings. No showers. Sites $7.) Make reservations with **ReserveAmerica** (☎800-444-7275; www.reserveamerica.com). Call ahead to check if all camps are open in the summer, as some may be closed due to inadequate funding. The primitive campgrounds all have vault toilets (except Yaqui Pass, Dos Cabezas, and Sheep Canyon), but no distinct sites or other amenities.

THE DESERT

**Center Market,** 590 Palm Canyon, Borrego Springs, sells groceries and supplies. (☎767-3311. Open M-Sa 8:30am-6:30pm, Su 8:30am-5pm.) Across the street is the local favorite, **Kendall's Cafe ❷**, 528 Palm Canyon Dr. Entrees ($6-10) include ½ lb. buffalo burgers. (☎767-3491. Open daily 6am-8pm.) Those thirsty for a cold one can follow the locals into the one nightspot option in town, **Carlee's Bar and Grill ❷**, 660 Palm Canyon Dr. (☎767-3262. Entrees $7-15. Open 11am-2am daily.)

**◎ ⚑ SIGHTS & HIKES.** Hiking and desert exploration abound in Anza-Borrego for those willing. The 3 mi. round-trip **Palm Canyon Creek Trail** leads up to a huge fan palm oasis, where desert bighorn sheep come to water in the summer months. The trailhead is located in the back of the **Borrego Palm Campground.** Another short but rewarding hike can be found at **Slot Canyon.** Exit Rte. 78 east of Borrego Springs on a small dirt road labeled "Buttes Pass Rd." At the first fork, bear left. About 1 mi. down the road is a small parking area; Slot Canyon is below. The **Southern Emigrant Trail,** a 26 mi. self-guided auto-tour, follows a wagon trail used by Mormon settlers. Along the trail is a sod stage station built in 1852. **Font's Point,** accessible with a 4WD vehicle, looks down on the spectacular Borrego Badlands—bare knuckles of pink-hued rocks and gullies. Those without 4WD can view the badlands from S22 east of Borrego Springs. Continue east on S22 to reach the huge, salty **Salton Sea.** The park's chief attraction is **wildflower** season, which transfigures barren wastelands into blossoming wonderlands in spring after just the right amount of rain has fallen. Some years, no flowers bloom at all due to inadequate rainfall. Call the **Wildflower Hotline** (☎767-4684) in the spring to learn if the unpredictable blooming has occurred. Rangers also offer special guided activities.

# PALM SPRINGS                                    ☎760

From its first known inhabitants, the Cahuilla Indians, to today's geriatric fun-lovers, the restorative oasis of Palm Springs (pop. 43,520) has attracted many. The medicinal waters of the city's natural hot springs ensure not only the vitality of its wealthy residents, but also its longevity as a resort town. With warm winter temperatures, celebrity residents, and more pink than a Miami Vice episode, this city is a sunny break from everyday life. But beach lovers beware: while the warmth, desert sand, and sparkling blue pools may put you in the mood for the surf and sand, the only waves rolling in are composed of dry summer heat.

# ⌐ TRANSPORTATION

**Airport: Palm Springs Regional,** 3400 E. Tahquitz-Canyon Rd. (☎318-3800). Only has state and limited national service.

**Buses: Greyhound,** 311 N. Indian Canyon Dr. (☎325-2053 or 800-231-2222), near downtown. Open daily 8am-6pm. To: **LA** (7 per day, $19.50-21, round-trip $32-36); **San Diego** (7 per day, $23.50); **Las Vegas** (6 per day, weekdays $53, weekends $59).

**Public Transportation: SunBus** (☎343-3451). Local bus connecting all Coachella Valley cities (Info office open daily 5am-10pm). Lines #23, 24, and 111 cover downtown and surrounding locales. The *SunBus Book,* available at info centers and in most hotel lobbies, includes schedules and a system map. Fare 75¢, transfers 25¢.

**Taxis: Yellow Cab** (☎345-8398) and **Ace Taxi** (☎321-6008).

**Trains: Amtrak,** at the corner of N. Indian Canyon Rd. and Train Station Dr., a few blocks south of I-10 (☎800-872-7245).

**Car Rental:** Starting at about $35 per day (excluding insurance); higher in winter. **Rent-A-Wreck,** 67555 Palm Canyon Dr. #A102, Cathedral City (☎324-1766 or 800-535-1391; www.rentawreck.com). Usually only rents to those 21 and older. $10 surcharge for those under 25. **Budget** (☎327-1404 or 800-221-1203), at Palm Springs Regional Airport. Must be 21 with major credit card; under 25 surcharge $20 per day.

**Bike Rental: Bighorn Bicycles,** 302 N. Palm Canyon Dr. (☎325-3367). Mountain bikes $8 per hr., $22 for 4hr., $29 per day. Tours available. Open Sept.-June Su-Tu and Th-Sa 8am-4pm. **Tri-A-Bike,** 44841 San Pablo Ave. (☎340-2840), in Palm Desert. Mountain bikes $7 per hr., $19 per day, $65 per wk. Open M-Sa 10am-6pm, Su noon-5pm.

# ☀ 🔢 ORIENTATION & PRACTICAL INFORMATION

Palm Springs is a 2-3hr. drive from LA along **I-10.** Exit I-10 at Indian Ave., which becomes **Indian Canyon Drive,** the major north-south road through Palm Springs. Indian Canyon Dr. and the north-south stretch of **Palm Canyon Drive,** the city's two main drags, connect to I-10. East Palm Canyon Dr. (Rte. 111) borders the southern edge of the city. The two major east-west boulevards are **Tahquitz-Canyon Road** runs east to the airport, while **Ramon Road,** four blocks south, provides access to I-10.

**Visitor Information: Visitors Center,** 2781 N. Palm Canyon Dr. (☎778-8415 or 800-347-7746; www.palm-springs.org), 1 block beyond Tramway Rd. Free hotel reservations and friendly advice. Pick up *The Official Visitor's Guide* or *Weekender* for attractions and entertainment. Open daily 9am-5pm. At the **Chamber of Commerce,** 190 W. Amado Rd. (☎325-1577; www.pschamber.org), grab the seasonal *Palm Springs Visitors Guide,* buy a map ($1), or make hotel reservations. Open M-F 8:30am-4:30pm.

**Laundromat: Arenas Coin-Op,** 220 E. Arenas Rd. (☎322-7717), half a block east of Indian Canyon Dr. Wash $2, dry 10min. 25¢. Open daily 7am-9pm. Last wash at 8pm.

**Road Conditions:** ☎800-427-7623. **Weather Conditions:** ☎345-3711.

**Police:** 200 S. Civic Dr. (☎323-8116).

**Rape Crisis Hotline:** ☎568-9071.

**Medical Services: Desert Regional Medical Center,** 1150 N. Indian Canyon Dr. (☎323-6511).

**Library and Internet Access: Palm Springs Public Library,** 300 S. Sunrise Way (☎322-7323). Free access available in 30min. slots. Open M-Tu 9am-8pm, W-Th and Sa 9am-5:30pm, F 10am-5:30pm.

THE DESERT

**Post Office:** 333 E. Amado Rd. (☎800-275-8777). Open M-F 9am-5pm, Sa 9am-1pm.
**Postal Code:** 92262; General Delivery 92263.

# ▐ ACCOMMODATIONS

Like most famous resort communities, Palm Springs caters mainly to those seeking a tax shelter, not a night's shelter. Nonetheless, affordable lodgings are fairly abundant. Motels cut prices 20-40% in the summer. Many offer discounts through the Visitors Center, and promotional publications often have terrific coupon deals, offering rooms for as little as $25. Reservations may be necessary in the winter. Prices listed don't include the county's **11.5% accommodation tax.**

**Orchid Tree Inn,** 251 S. Belardo Rd. (☎325-2791 or 800-733-3435). Large rooms with tasteful Spanish ambience overlook a courtyard with lush gardens and pool. Tucked behind the main downtown strip and near good shopping. 1- or 2-person rooms start at $79 in July and Aug., but increase to $110-175 during the winter. Weekend rates $15-20 more. Studios, suites, and bungalows also available. ❺

**Miracle Springs Resort and Spa,** 10625 Palm Dr. (☎251-6000 or 800-400-4414; www.miraclesprings.com), in Desert Hot Springs. The newer, classier, and more luxurious of the 2 hotels atop the famed hot springs. 110 spacious units with bedrooms and living areas, some of which overlook the 8 pools of "miracle" water. Spa, restaurants, and banquet facilities. Standard rooms from $99 in off-season; from $139 in winter. ❺

**Cambridge Inn,** 1277 S. Palm Canyon Dr. (☎325-5574 or 800-829-8099). Large rooms with refrigerators and phones. Laundry, continental breakfast, pool and jacuzzi. Rooms July-Aug. Su-Th from $44, F-Sa from $60; Sept.-June $69-$125. ❹

**Motel 6,** 660 S. Palm Canyon Dr. (☎327-4200 or 800-466-8356), south of the city center. Other locations at 595 E. Palm Canyon Dr. (☎325-6129) and 63950 20th Ave. (☎251-1425), near the I-10 off-ramp. Pool and A/C. Sept.-June singles Su-Th $40, F-Sa $46; doubles Su-Th $46, F-Sa $52. July-Aug. $5 less. Additional person $3. ❸

**Palm Court Inn,** 1983 N. Palm Canyon Dr. (☎416-2333 or 800-667-7918), between I-10 and downtown. Inside the melon-colored walls are 107 rooms as well as pool and jacuzzi. Oct.-May singles $69; doubles $79. June-Sept. singles $59; doubles $69. All prices slightly higher on weekends. Look for discount coupons in visitor guides. ❹

# ▐ FOOD

Palm Springs offers a kaleidoscope of great food, from the classic greasy-spoon to ultra-trendy fusions. Prices, however, can get high. To cook for yourself, head to **Ralph's,** 451 S. Sunrise Way, for groceries. (☎323-9799. Open daily 6am-1am.)

▨ **Thai Smile,** 651 N. Palm Canyon Dr. (☎320-5503). Just as friendly as the name implies, Thai Smile serves authentic and inexpensive Thai cuisine. Classy wood-heavy decor and a fashionable wine rack. Vegetarian options (tofu pad thai $8). Don't miss the $5 lunch specials. Open daily 11:30am-10pm. ❷

**Banducci's Bit of Italy,** 1260 S. Palm Canyon Dr. (☎325-2537). The promise of delicious Italian food draws an older crowd to this Palm Springs staple every night of the week. The rich fettucine alfredo comes with antipasto, minestrone soup, and buttery garlic bread ($13). Entrees $8-15. Open daily 5-10pm. ❸

**Las Casuelas—The Original,** 368 N. Palm Canyon Dr. (☎325-3213). Its success made chainhood inevitable, but locals insist The Original lives up to its name. Authentic Mexican dishes ($7-13), tight eating quarters, and colorful decor. Open Su-Th 10am-10pm, F-Sa 10am-11pm. Trendier, expanded, and with live music, try **Las Casuelas Terraza,** 222 S. Palm Canyon Dr. (☎325-2794). Open M-F 11am-11pm, Sa-Su 10am-11pm. ❷

**THE DESERT**

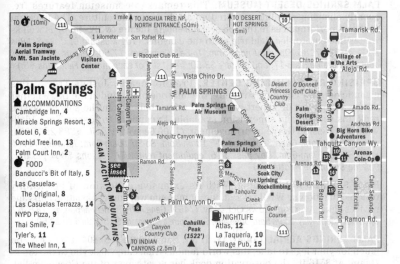

TO 🚋 (10mi) (111)

0 ——— 1 mile
0 ——— 1 kilometer

TO JOSHUA TREE NP,
NORTH ENTRANCE (50mi)

TO DESERT
HOT SPRINGS
(5mi)

Palm Springs
Aerial Tramway
to Mt. San Jacinto

Tramway Rd.

San Rafael Rd.

Whitewater River Storm Channel

Tamarisk Rd.

Visitors
Center

E. Racquet Club Rd.

Chino Dr.

Village of
■ the Arts

Avenida Caballeros

N. Sunrise Wy.

(111)

Vista Chino Dr.

Alejo Rd.

**Palm Springs**

N. Palm Canyon Dr.

Indian Canyon Dr.

PALM SPRINGS (111)

Desert
Princess
Country
Club

O'Donnell
Golf Club

Belardo Rd.

Palm Canyon Dr.

▲ ACCOMMODATIONS
Cambridge Inn, 4
Miracle Springs Resort, 3
Motel 6, 6
Orchid Tree Inn, 13
Palm Court Inn, 2

🍴 FOOD
Banducci's Bit of Italy, 5
Las Casuelas-
    The Original, 8
Las Casuelas Terrazza, 14
NYPD Pizza, 9
Thai Smile, 7
Tyler's, 11
The Wheel Inn, 1

see
inset

Tamarisk Rd.

Palm Springs
Air Museum

Alejo Rd.

Tahquitz Canyon Wy.

Palm Springs
Regional Airport

Ramon Rd.

S. Sunrise Wy.

Farrell Dr.

El Cielo Rd.

Palm
Springs
Desert
Museum

Amado Rd.

Andreas Rd.

Big Horn Bike
Adventures

Tahquitz Canyon Wy.

Arenas
Coin-Op

Arenas Rd.

Knott's
Soak City/
Uprising
Rockclimbing

Baristo Rd.

Indian Canyon Dr.

Belardo Rd.

Calle Encilia

Calle Segundo

SAN JACINTO MOUNTAINS

S. Palm Canyon Dr.

La Verne Wy.

Canyon
Country Club

E. Palm Canyon Dr.

Mesquite Ave.

Tahquitz
Creek

Golf
Course

Ramon Rd.

Cahuilla
Peak
(1522')

TO INDIAN
CANYONS (2.5mi)

🎵 NIGHTLIFE
Atlas, 12
La Taquería, 10
Village Pub, 15

(111)

**Tyler's,** 149 S. Indian Canyon Dr. (☎325-2990). If Starbucks were a burger shack, it'd probably resemble this trendy lunch spot in the middle of La Plaza. Classic American fare—tasty burgers, malts, and root-beer floats. Don't let the unremarkable prices fool you; everything is a la carte, so it adds up. Burgers $4-6. Soda-fountain drinks $2.50-4. Open M-F 11am-4pm, Sa 11am-5pm; in summer Tu-Sa 11am-4pm. ❷

**NYPD—New York Pizza Delivery,** 260 N. Palm Canyon Dr. (☎778-NYPD/6973). An alternative to the high prices and suffocating trendiness of Palm Springs. Slices of pizza pie ($2) and other filling pizza joint fare. Open M-F 11am-9pm, Sa-Su 11am-10pm. ❶

**The Wheel Inn,** 50900 Seminole Dr. (☎909-849-7012), in Cabazon, directly off I-10 west of Palm Springs. The legendary joint guarded by life-sized brontosaurus and T-Rex sculptures. Where Pee-Wee Herman met Simone. Check out the dinosaur gift shop in the bronto's belly. Daily specials ($6-7). Pies ($2.50-3.75). Open 24hr. ❷

## 📷 🏔 SIGHTS & ACTIVITIES

Most people come to Palm Springs' balmy winter climate to drink, party, golf, lounge poolside, and schmooze with celebs, but the city also has its share of sights. **Mt. San Jacinto State Park,** Palm Springs's primary landmark, offers a variety of outdoor recreation. Hiking trails in the park are accessible year-round via the aerial tram, and cross-country skiing is available in winter at higher elevations, though access is easier and cheaper from nearby Idyllwild. Despite its benign appearance in the crowded winter season, the desert surrounding Palm Springs is a summertime furnace, with highs consistently into the hundreds.

**DESERT HOT SPRINGS SPA.** A trip to Palm Springs would not be complete without a visit to the town's namesake. This spa features eight naturally heated mineral pools of different temperatures, as well as saunas, massages, and body wraps. *(10805 Palm Dr. in Desert Hot Springs. ☎800-808-7727. Open daily 8am-10pm. M and W $5; Tu $3; Th men $3, women $5; F men $5, women $3; Sa-Su $6. After 3pm weekdays $3, weekends $4, holidays $7. Rates include admission to pools, dry sauna, and locker rooms.)*

**PALM SPRINGS DESERT MUSEUM.** This remarkable museum features frequently changing exhibits centered on art, history, and culture. The museum sponsors performances in the 438-seat **Annenberg Theatre** (☎ 325-4490) as well as wintertime curator-led field trips into the canyons. *(101 Museum Dr. Take SunBus #111. ☎ 325-7186. Open Su noon-5pm, Tu-Sa 10am-5pm. $7.50; seniors $6.50; students, children ages 6-17, and military $3.50; free 1st F of each month. Field trips $5.)*

**UPRISING ROCKCLIMBING CENTER.** Prep for nearby Joshua Tree at this gigantic outdoor climbing structure, the only one of its kind in the US. Whether you're a beginner or expert, you'll find a fun challenge in the shaded plastic rock. Instruction and supervision available. Excursions to Joshua Tree, Idyllwild, and Mission Gorge by arrangement. *(1500 Gene Autry Trail. ☎ 888-254-6266; www.uprising.com. Open Sept.-June M-F 10am-8pm, Sa-Su 10am-6pm; July-Aug. Tu-F 4-8pm, Sa-Su 10am-6pm. Day pass $15, equipment rental $7, lessons $45+ per day. Parking $6, in the Knotts lot.)*

**PALM SPRINGS AIR MUSEUM.** With its extensive collection of beautifully restored functioning WWII aircraft, the air museum will impress aviation buffs and novices alike. Aviation shows Oct.-May. *(745 N. Gene Autry Tr., near airport. ☎ 778-6262. Open daily Sept.-May 10am-5pm; June-Aug. 9am-3pm. $8, seniors $6.50, children $3.50.)*

**PALM SPRINGS AERIAL TRAMWAY.** If Mt. San Jacinto's 10,804 ft. peak is too much for your legs to take, this world-famous tram can whisk you to the top in 10min. At 8516 ft., the observation deck has great views of the Coachella Valley. Travelers planning to take one of the beautiful hikes from the upper tram station should note that temperatures are invariably 20-30 degrees cooler than the desert floor. *(On Tramway Rd. off N. Palm Canyon Drive. ☎ 325-1449 or 888-515-8726; www.pstramway.com. Trams run at least every 30min. Last tram down at 9:45pm. M-F 10am-8pm, Sa-Su 8am-8pm. Round-trip $21, seniors $19, ages 3-12 $14, ages 2 and under free.)*

**INDIAN CANYONS.** These four canyons hold the city's only naturally cool water, as well as remnants of the Cahuilla Indian communities. Ranger-led tours demonstrate how the Cahuilla people once utilized the area's flora and fauna, including the world's densest patch of naturally occurring palm trees. In the cooler months, these canyons are beautiful places to hike, picnic, or horseback ride. *(Three of the canyons are located 5 mi. south of town at the end of S. Palm Canyon Dr. ☎ 325-3400 or 800-790-3398. Open daily 8am-5pm. Tours M-Th 10am-1pm, F-Su 9am-3pm. Admission $6; students, seniors, and military $4.50; ages 6-12 $2; 5 and under free. Tours $6; children $2. Tahquitz Canyon is located at the west end of Mesquite Rd. ☎ 416-7044. It has a separate visitors center, as well as a spectacular 60 ft. waterfall during the winter. Tours $12.50, children $6.)*

**TENNIS & GOLF.** Palm Springs has several public tennis and golf facilities. There are 8 courts at **Ruth Hardy Park.** *(700 Tamarisk Dr., at Avenida Caballeros. Open dawn-dusk.)* **Tahquitz Creek Golf Resort,** managed by Arnold Palmer, says it is one of the nation's top municipal golf courses. *(1885 Golf Club Dr. ☎ 328-1005. 18 holes in winter M-F $60-90, Sa-Su $70-95; in summer M-F $29, Sa-Su $35. Discounts after 2pm. Fees include carts.)*

**KNOTT'S SOAK CITY WATER PARK.** Nothing spells Palm Springs frivolity better than splashing around in thousands of gallons of the desert's most precious resource. Slip, slide, and soak in the wave pool, inner tube river, and on 18 different waterslides and attractions. *(Off I-10 S at Gene Autry Trail between Ramon and E. Palm Canyon Dr. ☎ 327-0499. Open Mar.-Aug. daily 11am-6pm; Sept.-Oct. Su and Sa 11am-6pm. $24, children under 5 ft. and seniors $14, ages 2 and under free. $14 after 3pm. Parking $6.)*

**CELEBRITY TOURS.** Find further evidence that celebrities are wealthier and more glamorous than you—just don't expect to see an actual celebrity. Your closest brush with fame might be seeing a gardener weeding on the estate of dead celebrities like Frank Sinatra and Bob Hope. The 1hr. narrated tour drives past 30-40 celebrity homes. *(4751 E. Palm Canyon Dr., Ste. D. ☎770-2700. In winter open daily 8am-5pm; summer Tu-Sa 7:30am-2:30pm. Guided tours $17, seniors $15, under 17 $8.)*

**WIND FARM TOURS.** The unusual topography and outrageous temperatures of the Palm Springs region generate some of the world's strongest sustained winds. On the wind farm, about 3500 high-tech windmills harness this energy. Even if you forgo the tours by **Windmill Tours, Inc.,** a drive down I-10 will take you past this oddly spectacular forest of whirling blades. Drive with **caution,** as the high winds may shift your car around on the highway. *(Located 1¼ mi. west of Indian Canyon Drive on 20th Ave., just across I-10. ☎251-1997. Tours M-Sa 9, 11am, 1, 3pm. Reservations required. $23, seniors $20, students $15, children ages 6-13 $10, under 6 free.)*

## ▨ NIGHTLIFE

The glitz of Palm Springs doesn't disappear with the setting sun; this city's nightlife is almost as heralded as its golf courses. Although a night of total indulgence here might cost a small fortune, several bars provide drink specials and lively people-watching. Relive college glory days at the popular **Village Pub,** 266 S. Palm Canyon Dr. Tourists and locals alike swap jokes, swill beer, and groove to the folksy live rock. The crowd is usually 25+, but it gets younger on the weekends. Under 21 restricted to the front eating area after 9pm. (☎323-3265. Open daily 11am-2am.) Those more interested in glow sticks, tight bodies, and techno beats can head to **Atlas,** 210 S. Palm Canyon Dr. This hip, ultra-modern **restaurant ❷** and dance club is in the heart of downtown. Its fusion specialties are as modern as its music. (☎325-8839. Entrees $15-25. Local DJs nightly. 21+ for dancing. Open daily 11am-2am.) **La Taquería,** 125 E. Tahquitz Way (☎778-5391), specializes in ultra-fresh and healthy Mexican cuisine; the mist-enshrouded tile patio is great for Moonlight Margaritas ($8.50) and some tipsy swaying in the conga lines.

Palm Springs is a major destination for gay and lesbian travelers. The gay scene sparkles with bars, spas, and clothing-optional resorts. The *Gay Guide to Palm Springs,* available at the Visitors Center, provides a wealth of pertinent info.

## ▨ SEASONAL EVENTS

Downtown, **Village Fest** (☎320-3781) takes over Palm Canyon Dr. every Thursday night from 6-10pm (in summer 7-10pm). Vendors market food, jewelry, and arts and crafts wares, while people of all ages sample the booths and enjoy live entertainment and cool evening air. This weekly event is a great time to bring the kids.

Attempting to fulfill his campaign promise to heighten Palm Springs's glamour quotient, former mayor Sonny Bono instituted the annual **Nortel Networks Palm Springs International Film Festival** (☎778-8979; Jan. 8-19 in 2004). The **58th Annual National Date Festival,** Rte. 111 in Indio (☎863-8247; Feb. 13-22 in 2004), is not a hook-up scene but a bash for dried fruit lovers. Palm Springs is also famous for its tennis tournaments and its professional golf tournaments, like the **45th Annual Bob Hope Chrysler Classic** (☎346-8184; Jan. 21-25 in 2004) and the LPGA's **33rd Annual Kraft Nabisco Championship** (☎324-4546; Mar. 22-28 in 2004).

# NEAR PALM SPRINGS

Since the **Coachella Valley** is the self-proclaimed "Date Capital of the World," slick back your hair, suck down a breath mint, and head to the **Shields Date Gardens,** 80225 Rte. 111, in nearby Indio. This palm grove sets itself apart with its amusing free film *The Romance and Sex Life of the Date*. A date crystal milkshake ($3) shows how sweet a good date can be. (☎347-0996 or 800-414-2555. Open Sept.-May daily 8am-6pm; June-Aug. daily 9am-5pm.) Zoo-lovers can enjoy the rugged **Big Morongo Canyon Preserve,** off Rte. 62 on East Dr., a wildlife sanctuary. (☎363-7190. Open daily 7:30am-dusk. Free.) Northeast of Palm Springs in Thousand Palms, the **Coachella Valley Preserve's** Visitors Center can help you plan a hike through mesas, bluffs, or the **Thousand Palms Oasis,** a grove of palm trees which is home to the protected fringe-toed lizard. (☎343-2733 or 343-4031. Open Sept.-June sunrise-sunset.)

**Living Desert Wildlife and Botanical Park,** 47900 Portola Ave., Palm Desert, 1½ mi. south of Rte. 111, has Arabian oryx, camels, meerkats, and more. Wear sunscreen and bring water; there isn't much shade, though hand-held misters are available. (☎346-5694; www.livingdesert.org. Open Sept.-June daily 9am-5pm, last admission at 4pm; July-Aug. daily 8am-1:30pm, last admission at 1pm. Sept.-June $8.50, seniors and military $7.50, ages 3-12 $4.50; July-Aug. $6.50, ages 3-12 $3.50.)

# ABOUT LET'S GO

## FORTY-THREE YEARS OF WISDOM

For over four decades, travelers have relied on *Let's Go* for inside information on undiscovered backstreet cafes, secluded beaches, and the best routes from border to border. All that is still in there, but this year is different: we've revamped the series to bring you not only the hard facts you need to get around, but also the information you need to make sense of the place you're in. With new features focused on current events, culture, and politics, this year's *Let's Go* series provides depth you won't find in any other guidebook. For the last 20 years, our rugged researchers have stretched the frontiers of backpacking and expanded our series into Australia, Asia, Africa, and the Americas. This year we've beefed up our coverage of Latin America with *Let's Go: Costa Rica* and *Let's Go: Chile*. On the other side of the globe we've added *Let's Go: Thailand* and *Let's Go: Hawaii*. Some say you can't go to Hawaii without breaking the bank, but we beg to differ.

It all started in 1960 when a handful of well-traveled students at Harvard University handed out a 20-page mimeographed pamphlet offering a collection of their tips on budget travel to passengers on student charter flights to Europe. The following year, in response to the popularity of the first volume, students researched the first full-fledged edition of *Let's Go: Europe*. Throughout the 60s and 70s, our guides reflected the times—in 1969, for example, we taught you how to get from Paris to Prague on "no dollars a day" by singing in the street. In the 90s we focused on producing guides that showed how to get off the beaten path and experience destinations without hordes of tourists in the way. Now in its 43rd edition and translated into seven languages, *Let's Go: Europe* reigns as the world's bestselling travel guide. Our new guides bring the total number of titles to 61, each infused with the spirit of adventure that travelers around the world have come to count on. But some things never change: our guides are still researched, written, and produced entirely by students who know first-hand how to see the world on the cheap.

## WHY WE DO IT

We don't think of budget travel as the last recourse of the destitute; we believe that it's the only way to travel. Our books will ease your anxieties and answer your questions about the basics, so you can get off the beaten track and explore. Once you learn the ropes, we encourage you to put *Let's Go* down and strike out on your own. You know as well as we that the best discoveries are often those you make yourself. When you find something worth sharing, please drop us a line. We're Let's Go Publications, 67 Mount Auburn St., Cambridge, MA 02138, USA (feedback@letsgo.com). For more information visit our new website, feauring our full text, online at www.letsgo.com.

## HOW WE DO IT

Every spring, we recruit over 300 well-traveled students to overhaul the series. After several months of training, researcher-writers hit the road for seven weeks of exploration, from Anchorage to Adelaide, Iceland to Indonesia. Hired for their rare combination of travel savvy, writing ability, stamina, and courage, these adventurous travelers know that train strikes, stolen luggage, food poisoning, and marriage proposals are all part of a day's work. Back at our offices, the editors work from spring to fall, massaging copy written on Himalayan bus rides into witty, informative prose. A student staff of typesetters, cartographers, publicists, and managers keeps our lively team together. In September, the collected efforts of the summer are delivered to our printer, turned into books in record time, and delivered to stores so you have the most up-to-date information available for your trip. Even as you read this, work on next year's editions is well underway.

# INDEX

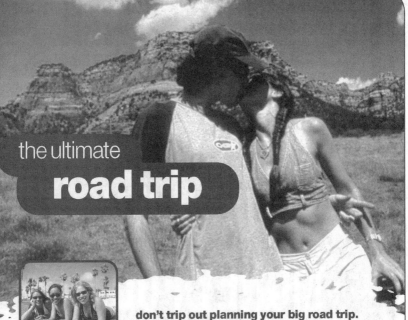

## the ultimate
# road trip

**don't trip out planning your big road trip.**
put contiki in the driver's seat with a hassle-free vacations designed for 18 to 35 year olds. make new friends, enjoy your free time and explore the sights in a convenient vacation that gives you more bang for your buck... **from only $70/day** including accommodations, sightseeing, many meals and transportation. with contiki leading the way, you can leave the road map at home!

> 7 days **eastern discovery**
  new york, washington d.c., us naval academy, kennedy space center

> 10 days **canada & the rockies**
  vancouver, calgary, banff national park

> 13 days **wild western**
  san francisco, grand canyon, las vegas, yosemite national park

*prices subject to change, land only.

for more info on our trips...
**see** your travel agent
**call** 1-888-CONTIKI
**visit** www.contiki.com

# contiki
VACATIONS for 18-35 year olds

> europe   > australia   > new zealand   > america   > canada

©2003 Orbitz, LLC. CST# 2065530-50 *Savings based on comparison with published rack rates.

pictures - reports - friends - discounts

# GLOBOsapiens.net
## travel community

"*My passion in life is travel.
Thank you for giving me and others
like me a resource from which to learn
and a podium from which we can share
our pictures, experiences and stories.*"

member feedback

**Are YOU a GLOBOsapiens as well?**

**Get your free member page at**
**www.GLOBOsapiens.net**

# MAP INDEX

## MAP LEGEND

| | | | | | |
|---|---|---|---|---|---|
| | **Boat Ramp** | | **Library** | | **Ranger Station** |
| ■ **Site/Point of Interest** | **Border Crossing** | ‡ | **Mission** | | **Ski Resort** |
| ● **Service** | **Botanical Garden** | ▲▲▲ | **Mountain** | | **State Park/Grove** |
| **Hotel/Hostel** | **Bus Station** | | **Mountain Pass** | **[bɑ](M)** | **SUBWAY STATION** |
| **Camping** | **Castle/Fort** | | **Movie Studio** | | **Theater** |
| **Food** | **Cave** | 🏛 | **Museum** | (i) | **Tourist Office** |
| **Nightlife** | **Church** | | **Observatory** | † | **Trailhead** |
| ★ **Entertainment** | ⚓ **Ferry Landing** | P | **Parking** | | **Train Station** |
| **Airport** | **Gate or Entrance** | | **Pedestrian Zone** | | **Waterfall** |
| **Amusement Park** | **Golf Course** | | **Picnic Ground** | | **Winery** |
| $ **Bank** | ⊞ **Hospital** | | **Police** | | **Zoo** |
| **Beach** | **Internet Café** | ✉ | **Post Office** | | |